HANDBOOK OF

MUSICAL
IDENTITIES

HANDBOOK OF

MUSICAL
IDENTITIES

Edited by

RAYMOND MACDONALD

DAVID J. HARGREAVES

and

DOROTHY MIELL

OXFORD

UNIVERSITY PRESS

OXFORD
UNIVERSITY PRESS

Great Clarendon Street, Oxford, OX2 6DP,
United Kingdom

Oxford University Press is a department of the University of Oxford.
It furthers the University's objective of excellence in research, scholarship,
and education by publishing worldwide. Oxford is a registered trade mark of
Oxford University Press in the UK and in certain other countries

Published in the United States of America by Oxford University Press
198 Madison Avenue, New York, NY 10016, United States of America

British Library Cataloguing in Publication Data
Data available

Library of Congress Control Number: 2016931926

ISBN 978–0–19–967948–5

Printed and bound by
CPI Group (UK) Ltd, Croydon, CR0 4YY

PREFACE

....

THE Disney Pixar film *Inside Out,* a huge global success in 2015, has issues of identity at its core. Alongside the psychodynamic concepts and trait theories of personality, which manifest as central characters, plot lines, and exotic surreal locations, music has an important part to play. The function of music is not just in the soundtrack but music is a thematic device that helps to convey the film's conceptions of personality. In an important repeating theme the main character, Riley, has a recurring daydream where an imaginary space rocket is fuelled by songs. The more passionate the singing, the more fuel is there for the rocket. Here the metaphor is clear and unambiguous; the power of music is such that it can propel rockets into space. Ultimately, it is the power of music that fuels the rocket to make its most important journey, leaving Riley's imaginary friend Bing Bong behind in the "memory dump" and propelling Joy (one of Riley's traits) back to "Headquarters".

A memory that involuntarily returns consistently in Riley's life, sometimes at inopportune moments, is a song from a TV advert. This type of continually repeating and involuntary occurring musical memory is commonly called an "earworm". The film pairs the earworm with a chewing gum advert and every time the catchy tune is heard, we see a short clip of the chewing gum advert. It's probably no coincidence that some research suggests that chewing gum may be a "cure" for earworms. In another repeating scene, Bing Bong is vividly portrayed as being part of Riley's imaginary pop band. The message here is also clear; being in a pop band with your imaginary friend who plays tunes on his nose while you play pots and pans is the epitome of good fun. The overarching point is that in a blockbuster family film, produced for a mass global audience, whose main focus is upon the fundamental aspects of people's identities, music plays an important role in the delineation of some central ideas about the nature of human personality.

The use of music as a plot device in a globally marketed film serves to highlight several of its key features. Music is a separate and distinct channel of communication; music provides a unique and social context for collaboration and discussion; musical activities can be accessed by everyone, regardless of age, location, socio-economic status, or state of health. Furthermore, music is ambiguous, and no matter how composers or performers wish to imbue their music with particular intentions, listeners will construct their own meanings for the music: these meanings will never be wrong and will always be unique, regardless of their earth-shattering importance or superficial banality. Thus, all music making, all music listening, all music talking, all musicking is essentially an identity project. Music provides a forum in which we construct and negotiate our constantly evolving sense of who we are, and our place in the world.

Although this idea of music as an "identity project" may sound abstract and vague, musical identities can be conceptualized in a very straightforward way. Firstly, our musical tastes help define us: for example, Sue is a Beatles fan. Her liking for the Beatles will merge with other aspects of her life to help shape how she views herself and relates to the world. Secondly, our sense of musicality also helps define us: for example, Bob loves to sing. This aspect of Bob's personality will also merge with other features to influence his life in many ways. However, the universal presence and importance of music means that the implications of these two simple features (our musical tastes and our musical practice) are profound and far-reaching. Therefore, music is inextricably and fundamentally linked to our sense of self. This assertion necessitates psychological investigations about the importance and nature of music within contemporary life that also link to theorizing about current conceptualizations of identity. This was a primary motivation for our first edited text, *Musical Identities*, which appeared in 2002 and whose impact has been a driving force for producing this much-enlarged and completely rewritten volume.

When we produced *Musical Identities* we were emphatic that the idea of musical identities was timely and relevant, and in the intervening 15 years, the topic has blossomed: writing and interest in this area now includes research from across the full spectrum of academia. Over this period there has also been a huge growth in the number and variety of books on issues related to music psychology. We therefore felt that it was timely to return to the topic of musical identities, and attempt to draw together a comprehensive set of chapters highlighting current multidisciplinary approaches to the topic. We were clear with the first text that we did not strive to be complete in our coverage and, while it is impossible to cover every facet of the many fields of study which might include aspects of musical identities, we have tried this time to be more comprehensive in presenting the myriad ways in which musical identities can be conceptualized.

This is our fourth co-edited text for Oxford University Press, and throughout those four books we have worked consistently with Martin Baum, senior commissioning editor at OUP. We would like to thank Martin for his support, encouragement, and friendship, which have been crucial to our happy and productive working relationship with OUP. We have also been lucky to work with a number of other colleagues at OUP who have been vital in helping us develop our work, in particular, Charlotte Green and Matthias Butler were both instrumental in helping us. We would also like to thank Tracy Ibbotson, Maria MacDonald, Eva MacDonald, and Nadia MacDonald, and Linda, Jon, and Tom Hargreaves for all their support and encouragement, and to welcome Alice Miell into a world full of music. Pulling together a project of this size is a big task and we would like to thank all the authors for their time, dedication, and collegiality in working with us to produce this text. It has been an immense pleasure, and we hope you enjoy the results.

Raymond MacDonald
David J. Hargreaves
Dorothy Miell
December 2016

Contents

SECTION 1 EDITORS' INTRODUCTION

SECTION 2 SOCIOLOGICAL, DISCURSIVE, AND NARRATIVE APPROACHES

SECTION 5   MUSICAL INSTITUTIONS AND PRACTITIONERS

SECTION 6   EDUCATION

SECTION 7   HEALTH AND WELL-BEING

SECTION 8   CASE STUDIES

LIST OF ABBREVIATIONS

ASD	autistic spectrum disorder
BBM–C-NC	body–brain–mind–conscious–non-conscious
BDM	Bund Deutscher Mädel
BFI	Big Five Inventory
BRIGHT	Borough Centre for Rehabilitation, Interaction, Group Activity, Hospitality, and Training
C-NC	conscious–non-conscious
CR	commercially released
GI	Getty Images
GIO	Glasgow Improvisers Orchestra
Gold-MSI	Goldsmiths Musical Sophistication Index
HJ	Hitlerjugend
ICC	intraclass correlations
IIM	identities in music
IMP	intrinsic motive pulse
IRCAM	Institut de Recherche et Coordination Acoustique/Musique
IRI	Interpersonal Reactivity Index
ISI	Identity Style Inventory
MADRS	Montgomery Åsberg Depression Rating Scale
MELP	music early learning program
MEQ	Music Experience Questionnaire
MII	music in identities
MMR	Music in Mood Regulation
MMOG	Massive Multiplayer Online Game
MSCEIT	Mayer-Salovey-Caruso Emotional Intelligence Test
MUSE	Music Use Questionnaire
NA	negative affect
OM-EIS	Objective Measure of Ego Identity Status

PA	positive affect
PD	Parkinson's disease
PIML	personal inner musical library
PMLD	profound and multiple learning difficulties
QCAE	Questionnaire of Cognitive and Affective Empathy
SAQ	Self-Attributes Questionnaire
SDT	self-determination theory
SEM	strong experiences with music
SFTB	Singing for the Brain
SIT	social identity theory
SLD	severe learning difficulties
SNRI	selective norepinephrine reuptake inhibitor
STS	science and technology studies
TIPI	Ten-Item Personality Inventory
ToM	Theory of Mind
UTM	University of Toronto Mississauga
VAMS	Visual Analogue Mood Scale
WWU	Western Washington University

LIST OF CONTRIBUTORS

Myung-Sook Auh
School of Education
University of New England
Armidale, NSW
Australia

Felicity A. Baker
Melbourne Conservatorium of Music
University of Melbourne
Melbourne
Australia

Margaret S. Barrett
School of Music
University of Queensland
Brisbane, QLD
Australia

Olivier Brabant
Department of Music, Art and
Culture Studies
University of Jyväskylä
Finland

Gianna G. Cassidy
Department of Computer,
Communications & Interactive Systems
Glasgow Caledonian University
Glasgow, UK

TanChyuan Chin
Melbourne Graduate School of Education
University of Melbourne
Carlton
Australia

Martin Cloonan
Music, University of Glasgow
Glasgow, UK

Robert Colls
International Centre for Sports History
and Culture
De Montfort University
Leicester, UK

Nicholas Cook
Faculty of Music
University of Cambridge
Cambridge, UK

Jane W. Davidson
Melbourne Conservatorium of Music
University of Melbourne
Melbourne
Australia

Tia DeNora
Department of Sociology
University of Exeter
Exeter, UK

Byron Dueck
Department of Music
The Open University
UK

Sebastian P. Dys
Department of Psychology
University of Toronto Mississauga
Mississauga, Ontario
Canada

David J. Elliott
Department of Music and Performing
Arts Professions
New York University
New York, USA

Jaakko Erkkilä
Department of Music, Art and
Culture Studies
University of Jyväskylä
Finland

Paul Evans
School of Education
University of New South Wales
Sydney
Australia

Jörg Fachner
Department of Music and Performing Arts
Jerome Booth Music Therapy Centre
Anglia Ruskin University
Cambridge, UK

Paul Flowers
Psychology
Glasgow Caledonian University
Glasgow, UK

Göran Folkestad
Malmö Academy of Music
Lund University
Sweden

David M. Greenberg
Department of Psychology
University of Cambridge
Cambridge, UK

Susan Hallam
Institute of Education
University College London
London, UK

David J. Hargreaves
Applied Music Research Centre
University of Roehampton
London, UK

Jonathan James Hargreaves
School of Music and Fine Art
University of Kent
Chatham, UK

Katie Palmer Heathman
School of Arts
University of Leicester
Leicester, UK

Cherry Hense
Music Therapy
Faculty of VCA & MCM
University of Melbourne
Melbourne
Australia

Richard Holloway
Chair of Sistema Scotland
Raploch
Stirling, UK

Beatriz Ilari
Department of Music Teaching and
Learning
Thornton School of Music
University of Southern California
Los Angeles, USA

Julie Joseph
Faculty of Arts and Sciences
Department of Performing Arts
Edge Hill University
Ormskirk, UK

Kathryn Jourdan
Board member of Sistema Scotland
Raploch
Stirling, UK

Alan Karass
New England Conservatory
Boston, MA, USA

Vicky Karkou
Department of Performing Arts and
Department of Applied Health and
Social Care
Edge Hill University
Ormskirk, UK

Sidsel Karlsen
Department of Fine Arts and Computer
Science
Hedmark University of Applied Sciences
Hamar
Norway

Alexandra Lamont
School of Psychology
Keele University
Keele, UK

Adam Linson
Institute for Advanced Studies
in the Humanities
University of Edinburgh
Edinburgh, UK

Marion Long
Rhythm for Reading
www.rhythmforreading.com
UK

Raymond MacDonald
School of Music
University of Edinburgh
Edinburgh, UK

Wendy L. Magee
Music Therapy Program
Boyer College of Music and Dance
Temple University
Philadelphia, USA

Stephen Malloch
Director, HeartMind
Executive Coaching, Workshop Design
and Facilitation, Psychotherapy
Sydney, Australia
and Westmead Psychotherapy Program
University of Sydney
Sydney
Australia

Katrina Skewes McFerran
Melbourne Conservatorium of Music
University of Melbourne
Melbourne
Australia

Andy McKinlay
School of Philosophy, Psychology and
Language Sciences
University of Edinburgh
Edinburgh, UK

Kate C. McLean
Department of Psychology
Western Washington University
Bellingham, WA, USA

Gary E. McPherson
Melbourne Conservatorium of Music
University of Melbourne
Melbourne
Australia

Chris McVittie
Centre for Applied Social Sciences
Queen Margaret University
Edinburgh, UK

Dorothy Miell
College of Arts, Humanities and
Social Sciences
University of Edinburgh
Edinburgh, UK

Susan A. O'Neill
Faculty of Education
Simon Fraser University
Vancouver
Canada

Jane Oakland
Performing Arts Medicine
University College London
London, UK

Adam Ockelford
Applied Music Research Centre
Queens Building, Southlands College
University of Roehampton
London, UK

Nigel Osborne
University of Edinburgh
Edinburgh, UK

Anna M.J.M. Paisley
School of Engineering & Built
Environment
Glasgow Caledonian University
Glasgow, UK

Heidi Partti
Department of Music Education, Jazz
and Folk Music
Sibelius Academy
University of the Arts Helsinki
Helsinki
Finland

Peter J. Rentfrow
Department of Psychology
University of Cambridge
Cambridge, UK

Nikki S. Rickard
School of Psychological Sciences
Monash University
Clayton
Australia

John Rink
Faculty of Music
University of Cambridge
Cambridge, UK

Even Ruud
Department of Musicology
University of Oslo
Oslo
Norway

Suvi Saarikallio
Department of Music
University of Jyväskylä
Jyväskylä
Finland

E. Glenn Schellenberg
Department of Psychology
University of Toronto Mississauga
Mississauga, Ontario
Canada
and Faculty of Music
University of Toronto
Toronto, Ontario
Canada

Emery Schubert
Empirical Musicology Laboratory
School of the Arts and Media
University of New South Wales
Sydney
Australia

Marissa Silverman
John J. Cali School of Music
Montclair State University
Montclair, NJ, USA

Maria B. Spychiger
University of Music and Performing Arts
Department of Teacher Education,
Research, and Composition
Frankfurt (Main)
Germany

Jennifer E. Symonds
School of Education
University College Dublin
Ireland

Johannella Tafuri
Professor of Methodology of Music
Education and Developmental Psychology
of Music
Conservatorio di musica "G.B. Martini"
Bologna
Italy

Colwyn Trevarthen
School of Philosophy, Psychology
and Language Sciences
University of Edinburgh
Edinburgh, UK

John Vorhaus
Institute of Education
University College London
London, UK

Robert Walker
School of Education
University of New England
Armidale, NSW
Australia

Graham F. Welch
International Music Education Research
Centre (iMerc)
Institute of Education
University College London
London, UK

Heidi Westerlund
Department of Music Education, Jazz and
Folk Music
Sibelius Academy
University of the Arts Helsinki
Helsinki
Finland

Graeme B. Wilson
Reid School of Music
Edinburgh College of Art
University of Edinburgh
Edinburgh, UK

Gloria P. Zapata Restrepo
School of Education
Fundación Universitaria
Juan N Corpas.
Bogotá
Colombia

SECTION 1

....

EDITORS' INTRODUCTION

....

CHAPTER 1

....

THE CHANGING IDENTITY
OF MUSICAL IDENTITIES

....

DAVID J. HARGREAVES,
RAYMOND MACDONALD, AND DOROTHY MIELL

WE published an edited collection of essays on "Musical identities" over a decade ago (MacDonald, Hargreaves, & Miell, 2002), which was based on the contributions made to a small invited conference that we organized at the Open University, UK. While the topic of identity had been discussed and theorized in several other disciplines, notably in philosophy and sociology, our conference was designed to deal specifically with identities in relation to music, and also to delineate the main dimensions of the *psychological* study of musical identity. Since then, different writers' uses of the concept of musical identity have broadened substantially, many empirical studies of musical identities have been conducted, and the field as a whole has become increasingly multidisciplinary in character.

Indeed, it has grown so quickly that we felt it was appropriate to follow up our first collection, well over 10 years later, with this much larger scale Handbook, which is intended to reflect more fully the contemporary multidisciplinary character of this field of study, including examples from at least some of the wide range of empirical research approaches that are now used to investigate the different dimensions of musical identities. In this introductory chapter we will try to reflect the breadth and depth of current scholarship and research in this rapidly growing field: to look at the changing identity of musical identities, and at some of the main ways in which they are being studied.

A great deal of this chapter is based on the rich body of scholarship that we have drawn together in the current volume, and the chapter falls into seven main sections. In the first of these, we summarize three main features of the current psychological approaches to the study of musical identity, namely the diversity of *definitions* and conceptions that have been proposed, the different views of their *development*, and the question of *individual differences* in musical identity. Each of the four remaining sections of this chapter reviews one of the four main contexts in which musical identities have been investigated, namely in *music and musical institutions* themselves, including subsections on the specific role of developments in music technology in its different guises; specific geographical communities; in education; and in the area of health and well-being, which incorporates different clinical and therapeutic contexts. In doing this, we will encounter a range of theoretical approaches that go well beyond psychology, including in particular, sociological, sociocultural, ethnomusicological, musicological, philosophical, and educational approaches.

1.1 PSYCHOLOGICAL APPROACHES TO MUSICAL IDENTITY

1.1.1 Definitions

The definition of musical identity has developed and widened over the last decade or so, and the issue of definition is one of the three main topics within current psychological approaches, along with the development of individual differences within musical identities. In 2002, we made a distinction between what we called identities in music (IIM) and music in identities (MII). We proposed that IIM deals with those aspects of musical identity that are defined by established cultural roles and categories, such as "musician," "composer," "performer," "improviser," "music teacher," or "critic." These categories are reinforced by musical institutions such as schools and conservatories and form an important part of the self-concepts of professional musicians or, indeed, anybody involved in musical activities. An important aspect of this suggestion is that these types of musical identities are universal. We all have a sense of our musicality, whether that is "I only sing in the bath," "I'm the Beatles' greatest fan," or "I play first violin in the Berlin Philharmonic Orchestra." Identity constructs such as "I can play a few chords on the guitar," "music is my life," "my family are not really musical," or even "I am tone deaf" all represent different types of IIM. A key point is that these identities may not be linked to technical skill or proficiency on an instrument, but rather to social influences such as family dynamics and educational contexts. MII, on the other hand, refers to how we use music within our overall self-identities—to the extent to which music is important in our self-definitions as masculine–feminine, old–young, able–disabled, extravert–introvert, and so on.

Although this two-way distinction has proved to be useful, it can only get us so far, and another important aspect of the definition of musical identities has come to the fore in the meantime. This is the idea that musical identities are performative and social—they represent something that we *do*, rather than something that we *have*, namely, the ways in which we jointly engage with music in everyday life. In Chapter 2, "Identities and musics: reclaiming personhood," Elliott and Silverman develop this argument, suggesting that if "musics are conceived, carried out, taught, and learned as musical *praxes*, then music-making and listening are capable of providing exceptionally rich means of and contexts for nurturing, forming, and informing the positive and ethical growth of people's self-identity, self-other identities, and musical identities."[1] This brings in the Aristotelian concept of praxis—in essence, the ways in which people engage *practically* with music together. In Elliott and Silverman's view, music-making provides important social, inter-active, and intersubjective contexts in which people can co-construct each other's musi-cal, social, and personal identities (p. 29). This involves empathy and mutual respect, such that an ethical dimension is built into their conception of identity construction. Aristotle saw praxis as guided by a moral disposition to act rightly, and as including concern for human well-being. This dimension, which includes healthiness, joy, and an "ethic of care" for oneself and others, was summarized in Aristotle's concept of *eudaimonia*.

When a baby first starts to develop her musical self by means of what Colwyn Trevarthen has described as "communicative musicality" with her caregivers, their ini-tial communications are fairly basic and might not even be described as "musical" by conventional musical standards. The fact that parents and other adults around the child treat these utterances with respect, however, and reciprocate in a way that enables the infant's musical self to develop and grow also reflects this notion of a relational dimen-sion in the development of identity. These interactions are driven by emotion and a social concern for others just as much as by the cognitive need for learning in the child.

This latter example leads on to another aspect of the definition of musical identity—what constitutes music, and what constitutes a musician? The example of a baby's sing-ing in interaction with adults makes it very clear that "musicianship" in this sense is by no means restricted to individuals who have high levels of conventional instrumental performance ability, which is one of the more traditional views of what constitutes musi-cianship. In Chapter 16, "Defining the musical identity of 'non-musicians'," Rickard and Chin have gone further in arguing that it is equally possible to define musicianship in terms of listening and engagement with music as it is in terms of high levels of per-formance skill. In particular, these examples provide evidence for the universality of human musicality, and this implies that the widespread use of the term "non-musician" should occur far less often than it currently does.

1.1.2 Development

This is the second main topic within the psychological approach to the study of musical identities, and although there has been a great deal of discussion about whether or not

---

[1] Editors' note: All references to "Author (Chapter XX)" in this chapter refer to that chapter in this Handbook.

developmental stages can be identified in musical learning and development, the development of musical identities poses more rarefied questions (see Hargreaves & Lamont, 2017). There seem to be four main points across the life span that represent distinct transition points for musical identity, namely:

- In infancy, when children are developing their physical and motor skills, and engaging in interactions with their caregivers through play, stories, and singing.
- In early childhood, they start to engage with the music of the culture around them, including pop songs and other music from the media, nursery rhymes and songs that they learn in playgroups and nursery schools. Interaction between these and their own musical ideas and creations provides a fascinating arena for development.
- In adolescence, it has been clearly established in many research studies that musical preferences are a key indicator of personal identity, and that musical taste forms a "badge of identity" at this stage. Furthermore, these "badges" are used to discriminate between the characteristics, preferences, and lifestyles of other members of the "in-group," and to contrast them with those of members of other "out-groups" (see, e.g., Tarrant, North, & Hargreaves, 2002).
- Finally, in old age, people become increasingly aware of their limitations and declining powers, and develop a more contemplative relationship to music, in many cases using it also as a powerful source of well-being and continued skill development. It is quite notable in describing these results of studies of life-span developmental progression that there has been relatively little research on musical identities in adult life between the ages of 25 and 60 or so.

In Chapter 12, "Processes of musical identity consolidation during adolescence," Evans and McPherson apply Ryan and Deci's (2000) self-determination theory to explain the ways in which musical identities develop, drawing in particular on Marcia's (1980) development of Erikson's (1950, 1968) well-known model of psychosocial development, which characterizes different identity processes that go on in people with differing levels of commitment to music. In Chapter 10, "Musical identity, interest, and involvement," Alexandra Lamont takes a life-span approach to the development of musical identity, focusing on the key contexts that affect its growth at different points of the life span, including the home, school, peer group, and family at different stages.

1.1.3 Individual differences

This is the third main topic within the psychological approach: whether it is possible to identify and assess individual variation in musical identity, and whether or not clear group differences exist with respect to factors such as age, gender, level of musical expertise, and social environment. Several empirical researchers have investigated this topic from the psychological/psychometric point of view. For example, in Chapter 15, "From musical experience to musical identity: musical self-concept as a mediating psychological structure," Maria Spychiger puts the musical self-concept at the center of her account of musical identity and describes some of her own empirical research from which eight distinct factor analytic dimensions of musical identity emerged, namely "technique and information," "social," "musical ability," "emotional," "physical," "spiritual," "ideal," and "adaptive." She was able to show some group differences in people's scores on these eight dimensions, for example, between participants with different levels of musical expertise.

A similar general conclusion was reached in Chapter 14, "Musical identities, music preferences, and individual differences," by Dys, Schellenberg, and McLean, who also carried out a large-scale factor analytic study, in this case of 330 undergraduate students, who were given various measures of personality and ego identity, as well as questions about musical preferences and identity. These authors noted that the concept of musical identity has largely been equated, in the research literature to date, with musical preferences—and suggested that

> although music preferences tell us much about individuals ... other psychological factors, such as the degree to which one is invested in particular music preferences, may provide important additional information to consider in relation to identity formation ... Whereas music preferences are concerned with how much someone likes specific genres of music, musical identity—based on psychological theories of identity development in general—reflects the degree to which someone is *committed* to liking *any* specific genre or genres, shifting the focus away from the actual genres.
>
> (p.248)

Their own empirical results suggested that over and above preferences, these determinants of musical identity included group processes and cultural factors, such as ethnicity and geographical location.

A study by Greenberg and Rentfrow (Chapter 17, "The social psychological underpinnings of musical identities: a study on how personality stereotypes are formed from musical cues") also looked at "manifestations of musical identities" not only in terms of musical preferences, but also in terms of the normative beliefs that people hold about the characteristics of fans of particular styles, and about their personality characteristics. The results showed that some common stereotypes were indeed held by the participants in the study and also by members of the general public about fans of different styles of music. These were formed not only in terms of characteristics such as clothing styles, leisure interests, friendship groups, and so on but also about perceptions of their personalities and attitudes.

There is little doubt that psychological theory and research on musical identities is proliferating, not only as the range and diversity of musical activities available to all is increasing, but also as the breadth and depth of music psychology continues to expand. In the remainder of this chapter we look at four of the main domains, or contexts, in which musical identities have been investigated, drawing on a number of different theoretical perspectives in doing so.

1.2 IDENTITIES IN MUSIC
AND MUSICAL INSTITUTIONS

We saw in Section 1.1 how the increasing diversification and democratization of roles within and between musical institutions, and the widening of the traditional concept of a "musician" has meant that a much wider range of musical domains and phenomena now need to be covered within the study of musical identity. In this section, we review some of those which appear within this Handbook, with a specific focus on the identity of musicians themselves.

In Chapter 8, " 'Will the real Slim Shady please stand up?' identity in popular music," McKinlay and McVittie, for example, investigate the negotiation of identities in popular music by using discursive psychology. They see social interaction and *talk about* pop music as providing an important forum for discourse between individuals, especially teenagers and young adults, which can serve to develop their attitudes, preferences, and prejudices, and thereby to enable their decision-making about issues such as career choices. They refer to Carlisle's (2007) study of 18–22-year-olds' talk about the consumption of online music, which identified three broad types of discourse. These were a "romantic" discourse, which emphasized musicians' expertise and skill, and their corresponding right to gain financial rewards from this; a "consumer" discourse, which saw financial reward as the main purpose of making music; and a "multicultural" discourse, which emphasized the diversity of online music and, therefore, its potential to appeal to many different groups across cultural barriers.

These different discourses or "repertoires," as Carlisle calls them, may well form the basis for some aspects of musical identities, and McKinlay and McVittie look further at how this relates to the issue of in- and out-groups in relation to musical preferences. They suggest that it is possible to construct identities within the music itself, and in particular in the lyrics, such as the ways in which rap music lyrics may express sexist or homophobic attitudes, or how different rappers from different ethnic groups may use their lyrics to compete with one another. This kind of dynamic interaction demonstrates how identities are constantly in flux, are continually being negotiated by talk in and about music, and this is an essential characteristic of a social constructionist approach to the explanation of identities.

When considering how musical identities are negotiated and maintained, it is important to view talking about music as an important aspect of the musical communication process (MacDonald, Wilson, & Miell, 2012). Talking about music is a type of musical praxis in itself. It is not an attempt to describe an objective reality in terms of, for example, a memory of a concert, but it represents the reality of the experience directly. In Chapter 6, "The ear of the beholder: improvisation, ambiguity, and social contexts in the constructions of musical identities," Wilson and MacDonald studied the verbal accounts of groups of free improvisers from varied musical backgrounds who were collaborating on different activities. These authors have previously published studies of the talk and interaction between jazz musicians in relation to their identities (e.g., Wilson & MacDonald, 2012), although the level of melodic, rhythmic, harmonic, structural, and other aspects of freedom allowed to free improvisers is far greater than in most other forms and genres of music. Wilson and MacDonald's view is that musicians' accounts of their activities are strongly influenced by the contexts within which the music takes place, as well as by the personalities, experiences, and expectations of the musicians themselves, and they go on to suggest that all interpretations of music can be viewed as "identity projects," not only for the musicians in discussing their own practices, but also for listeners giving their interpretation of musical events.

Their chapter is based on comparisons between transcripts from two distinct types of interview with improvising musicians, namely, those carried out for research purposes, in which the participants might be expected to speak with more candor about their mistakes, problems, disagreements, and so on, than in those carried out for the purposes of publicity, media, and marketing, in which musicians would be much more likely to express positive and uncritical views. This technique enables the comparison of identity statements made in the different interview contexts, thereby gaining insight into the nature of these musicians' identities, in particular into the ways in which they see themselves as free improvisers. Wilson and MacDonald (Chapter 6) suggest that:

> The talk of improvisers examined here suggests that, in the public eye, improvisers will champion their music against potential dislike or criticism by emphasizing quality, challenge, and power of their practice, and constructing heroic identities for themselves and colleagues in doing so. In the confidential context of a research interview, a range of evaluations may be made of group improvisation by those taking part, and as such the identities they construct for fellow improvisers may position them positively or negatively.
>
> (p.118)

Like McKinlay & McVittie (Chapter 8), Wilson & MacDonald put a social constructionist interpretation upon their interview data, in the last paragraph of their chapter, for example:

> Exploring the accounts of a range of musicians, concentrating on their experiences when improvising together, therefore, is vital to increasing the understanding of a unique psychological process, but so too is highlighting the processes by which identity is constructed in those accounts. Analysis of other sources of data, such as autobiographies or recordings of talk at rehearsal, or recordings of improvised music, may further enhance understanding of the remarkable phenomenon whereby improvisers construct each other and their collaboratively created music.
>
> (p.119)

To these we would add those approaches that use the music produced as the primary source of data in investigating musical communication and identity. For example, Ockelford (2013) has made a convincing case for the importance of this approach by applying his own zygonic theory to the musical *content* of improvisations and other interactions.

Another example of the way in which specific contexts and personal circumstances can exert a powerful effect on musicians' identities is in Oakland, MacDonald and Flowers' (Chapter 23, "Who am I? The process of identity renegotiation for opera choristers following redundancy") study of eight professional opera choristers who were forced to deal with a certain loss of identity when financial cuts led to their redundancy. They look in particular at the fragility of an identity in music that is work dependent. A critical factor in these singers' transition to new roles and identities was found to be the close relationship between the voice and self, which had to be rethought when these musicians were forced to contemplate alternative careers.

1.2.1 The role of music technology

Rapid recent developments in the musical applications of digital technology have had many widespread effects (see Hargreaves & Lamont, 2017). One of the most important of these is what we have called a "democratization" of musical styles and genres, in that the previous association of certain styles with "seriousness" and others with "popularity" no longer exists to anything like the same extent. Furthermore, the traditional divisions between musical roles such as composer, performer, producer, improviser, and arranger are now far less clear-cut than heretofore. Three of the chapters in this volume look specifically at how these technological changes have affected musical identities.

In Chapter 22, "Patterns of sociohistorical interaction between musical identity and technology," Linson adopts what he calls a socio-historical viewpoint on this matter, investigating three significant developments in the history of musical instruments, and the playing techniques associated with them, which have affected the ways in which musicians have seen themselves. These phenomena all need to be seen in the context of the prevailing musical and social conventions of specific times and places. The first development is the bowing of string instruments, which developed in order to achieve the aesthetic ideal of matching the human voice, as well as of producing continuous sound (without gaps caused by the need to breathe); the second was the development of the pianoforte, in which technical improvements in the hammer mechanisms enabled performers to play much more quickly and loudly. Both of these important developments were imposed by the demands of larger audiences and the emergence of new musical tastes and imaginations. These, in turn, placed greater demands on the performer, and eventually led to the phenomenon of the virtuoso or "star" performer, of which two prominent examples, from quite different genres, were Franz Liszt and Art Tatum.

Linson's third technological development is the very rapid recent growth of electronic and digital instruments, recording technology, and the associated use of the internet.

This can probably be traced back to Karlheinz Stockhausen's experimentation in the 1960s with non-acoustic technologies, such as pulse generators, amplifiers, oscillators, and bandpass filters, some of which were adopted early on by rock musicians such as Jimi Hendrix and Pink Floyd. There is little doubt that there are strong associations between these technologies, the social conditions within which they were developed, and the musical aspirations of the performers who adopted them, even though it is often quite difficult to work out the causal directions between these influences. Another recent development is that of music-based computer games, which have become very popular (see Cassidy and Paisley, Chapter 31, "Music games and musical identities"), and which may well be exerting an influence on people's personal and social identities.

More important still may be the phenomenon of the widespread use of social media as a primary means of communication and sharing not only of information, but also of music, video, and photographs amongst many people spread all over the world. In Chapter 43, "Musical identities in Australia and South Korea and new identities emerging through social media and digital technology," Auh and Walker have undertaken a fascinating comparison between musical identities in Australia and South Korea, looking specifically at the new musical identities which have emerged through the use of social media and digital technology. These use social identity theory (e.g., Tajfel, Flament, Billig, & Bundy, 1971) in order to explain ways in which "fandom" emerges as an important part of the identities of young people. They trace the development of the main musical traditions in both Australia and in South Korea, which have very different origins (in the original colonization of Australia by the British, and by strong influences from China and colonization by Japan in 1910–45 in South Korea).

In South Korea the development of K-pop, which marked a sharp turn away from the Korean pop music of the 1970s and 1980s, emerged soon after South Korea and Japan jointly hosted the 2002 World Cup. K-pop is Korean music that reflects contemporary South Korea, as well as the external influences upon it, including those from Anglo-American pop music, such as rapping and hip-hop, and from China. In essence, it reflects the globalization of South Korean culture. As a result, the South Korean government has promoted K-pop as a national cultural product.

Auh and Walker (Chapter 43) comment that "The emergence of new and more powerful digital technology over the last two decades has gradually changed the whole field of music perception and reception, especially in the popular music field," and that "Instead of local peer groups or localized interest groups generating identities through shared allegiances to certain types of music, the new technology has allowed individuals from anywhere in the world to become linked through interest, similar allegiances, and shared musical tastes" (p. 803). Perhaps the best-known South Korean example of this is "Gangnam style," a song by the artist Psy, which was posted on YouTube on July 15, 2012, and which had been viewed by 170 million people 2 months later, and by over 2000 million in 2012 as a whole, representing an unprecedented global phenomenon.

It seems inevitable that musical identities will develop, change, and diversify still further and more rapidly as this technology develops further, and as its latest features become the main province of younger and younger members of society.

1.3 MUSICAL IDENTITIES IN SPECIFIC GEOGRAPHICAL COMMUNITIES

The field of ethnomusicology deals with ways in which people in different parts of the world invent, use, compose, listen to, and engage with music. This involves considering the social, environmental, cultural, and material conditions in the musical communities in which they grow up, as well as the properties of the sounds themselves. People's musical identities are clearly shaped by these external conditions, and looking at social communities on a broader scale also brings in the approaches of sociology and sociocultural psychology, amongst others. In Chapter 3, "Music-ecology and everyday action: creating, changing, and contesting identities," DeNora develops this view further by identifying five main themes about identities that emerge from this kind of analysis.

In summary, she sees identities as resources that have status: one's identity can be raised ("promoted") or lowered ("demoted") in relation to those of others. This gives rise to identities being exchangeable, tradable and stealable. Social interaction involves negotiation, which means that one partner may take on some of the characteristics of the other, on a temporary or permanent basis. Furthermore, identities are plastic and malleable—they can be changed at any time and this malleability of identities can involve *hybridization*; different aspects of different identities can be combined to form new ones. Hybridization indicates how identities are created relationally, i.e., by reference to social and environmental artifacts, and conditions that are external to the individuals. These could be other people or inanimate objects, such as landscapes, buildings, furnishings, or technologies.

This analysis is very helpful in explaining the development of musical identities in relation to specific geographical communities. For example, Ilari (Chapter 29, "Children's ethnic identities, cultural diversity, and music education") looks at the phenomenon of ethnic identity, which can be defined in terms of the cultural values and traditions of the society into which one is born, which in itself is dependent on the level of cultural diversity in that particular society, and which correspondingly overlaps with cultural identity to a considerable extent. Ilari was particularly interested in this question in relation to the perceptions and interactions of minority groups living among other ethnic groups, and the corresponding development of their perceptions of their own ethnic identity. There are many examples of such minority groups, such as Mexicans in the USA, South-Eastern Asians and (most recently) Eastern Europeans in the UK, and immigrant and refugee communities, facing particular challenges in this respect.

Ilari argues that an important aspect of the ability to deal with the immigrant and refugee experience is to be able to negotiate multiple identities, the basic mechanisms for which have been specified in DeNora's analysis; and one valuable forum in which this can be accomplished is by means of music. Indeed, Ilari argues that music education can be used as a powerful means of resolving differences between perceived in- and out-groups in societies, as in the famous case of Daniel Barenboim's Western–Eastern Divan Orchestra, which includes musicians from Egyptian, Iranian, Israeli, Jordanian, Lebanese, Palestinian, Syrian, and Spanish backgrounds.

Similarly, in Chapter 40, "Musical identities, resilience, and wellbeing: the effects of music on displaced children in Colombia," Zapata Restrepo and Hargreaves write about the effects of musical participation upon displaced families in Colombia, which is important because it reveals the potential *power* of musical identity for those forced to live in the big cities of South America. These authors consider the origins of the current violence in Colombia, which involve a complex of factors, including drug dealing, the weakness of the social and judicial systems, the presence of the paramilitary and of guerillas in the rural areas, and many years of armed conflict. This violence is the cause of the displacement of many people from the country to the big cities, like Bogotá in Colombia, and these become the ultimate destination for the majority of those who have been displaced.

One of the effects of these consequences of violence is the adverse effect on personal identity. Children suffer its impact in many different ways, in particular in their loss of a sense of ownership of their relationship to the town or area in which they grew up—they cease to be part of that community. Some of DeNora's themes about identity, mentioned previously, are useful here, in particular the idea that identities can confer status, such that these children are, in effect, "demoted". DeNora's notion of hybridization is used in explaining how displaced people from different cultural backgrounds mix over centuries to produce a rich hybrid cultural environment. This provides a strength that can be deployed against the conditions of deprivation—hybrid identities can provide a wider family in which people feel welcome and fully human.

One of the main ways in which this can happen is through music. Cultural musical heritage is one thing that cannot be taken away from children as a result of external circumstances. Zapata Restrepo's research involved the development of a program of musical activities for 6- to 8-year-old displaced children in Colombia and assessed its effects on self-esteem and other aspects of psychosocial development in relation to a control group. She was able to show that musical activities helped not only the children, but also their families to cope with the problems of displacement, and this was partly achieved by maintaining their cultural musical traditions.

Another such region has been studied by Osborne (Chapter 39, "The identities of Sevda: from Graeco-Arabic medicine to music therapy"), who looks specifically at Sevda—a traditional music from Bosnia and Herzegovina, which has related forms throughout the Balkan region and is "a historical synthesis of many diverse social and cultural identities, embracing both Slav and Turkish social traditions, four religions, and a diversity of wide-ranging musical cultures," including that in the Western classical tradition. Because of these intercultural features, it "expresses a collective cultural identity with profound implications for the 'common life' of Bosnia and Herzegovina, for the region, and indeed perhaps for Europe as a whole" (p. 722).

Osborne describes the nature and development of Sevda, looking at its musical structures, the history of its development, and in particular the historical and political context
within which it was formed. There is a strong emphasis on political and social developments in this region of Europe, and in particular on the devastating effects of the war and
of "ethnic cleansing" in the region in the 1990s. Sevda was under pressure as a result of
these developments but seems to have survived. Osborne describes his own work in the
Balkan region, working with his community music students from Edinburgh University
on projects including the Sarajevo Experimental Schools Project. He proposes that
the use of Sevda music is valuable because its obvious intercultural characteristics can
serve to foster mutual understanding and reconciliation and has the potential to bring
together what might otherwise have been very disparate cultural groups. This provides
yet another example of how music and musical identity can be used in the mediation of
conflict and the reconciliation between different cultural groups.

Colls and Heathman's (Chapter 41, "Music of Englishness: national identity and
the first folk revival") historical account of the social and cultural background of the
"first folk revival" in England serves as a means of investigating the musical identity of
England and its role in "Englishness." Their perspective is very different from that taken
by many of the other chapters in the Handbook in that the phenomena in question are
extremely culturally specific, focusing on activities in England and the nature of English
identity as expressed through music. There is no attempt to generalize to other nations
or cultural groups, as might be the case in social science.

Colls and Heathman explain the motivations behind and origins of the first folk
revival, with a focus on the role of key figures such as Ralph Vaughan Williams and Cecil
Sharp, both of whom had a powerful influence on music education, as well as on musical
thought. They feel that these figures, as well as others in the middle class cultural establishment of the UK in the early part of the 20th century, were proposing an idealized and
probably mythical conception of Englishness as a pure expression of the characteristics
of the "common people", but that in fact, this was an artificial view. It is more likely to
have been the case that the authentic music of the people was represented by other genres and styles, such as in marching songs, bar room ballads, and so on, and that the "folk
revival" view of Englishness may have had no basis in reality. The folk tunes collected
by Vaughan Williams and others may not in fact have been representative of the people,
and they were subsequently edited and "refined" by the collectors for their own uses in
any case.

This contrast between this very culture-specific historical approach to a musical movement and the tendency of social scientists to generalize from specific cases makes Colls
and Heathman's chapter a very valuable contribution, representing a distinctive and complementary approach to the study of musical identity. The issues that they raise are more
nuanced and subtle than those that can be investigated by research methods in psychology or sociology, but they are correspondingly much more difficult to test empirically.
A comprehensive understanding of musical identities in different geographical areas
almost certainly needs to adopt both approaches, and no doubt others besides.

1.4 MUSICAL IDENTITIES IN EDUCATION

Educational institutions, and schools in particular, exert a powerful influence on the developing musical identities of children (see e.g., Hargreaves & Marshall, 2003; Hargreaves, Purves, Welch, & Marshall, 2007; North & Hargreaves, 2008; see also Lamont, 2002; and Chapter 10, "Musical identity, interest, and involvement"). Hallam (Chapter 26, "Musical identity, learning, and teaching") argues, as we have done elsewhere, that musical identities constantly change and develop throughout the life span in response to interactions with others. She adds that music can be a central part of an individual's identity, even though that person is not a professional performer, and this is congruent with our earlier argument for a broadening of the definition of "music" and of "the musician."

Hallam and her colleagues have conducted large-scale studies of people's conceptions of musical ability, including musicians, non-music educators, adults in other occupations, and others, and they come to the general conclusion that musical ability is associated by most people with being able to read music, to play an instrument, or to sing. She has also conducted studies of large samples of instrumental music students of different ages (Hallam, 2013; Hallam, in preparation) in which she was interested in their motivation for musical involvement, and in identifying the factors that might predict three different kinds of musical aspiration, namely, wanting to be involved in music, music being useful to a future career, and aspiring to be a musician. She found that valuing music, enjoyment, and practising strategies were the best predictors of aspiring to be a musician and that support from others and self-belief were important in wanting to be involved in music, and of seeing music as useful to a future career. Many individuals maintain an interest in music at some level throughout their lives, and some return to it fairly intensively in later life, which is not true to the same extent of many other subjects studied at school. This confirms the role of music as an important means of identity development throughout the life span.

Symonds, Hargreaves, and Long (Chapter 28, "Music in identity in adolescence across school transition") focus on the effects of the transition from primary to secondary school on young people's musical identities. Since music plays such a key role in the lives of adolescents, it is hardly surprising that school transition can have a powerful influence. This chapter is based on the *Changing Key project*, in which pupils were interviewed about "myself and music" in each of four school terms, spanning the final term of primary and the first year of secondary school. In these, they were asked to discuss their musical experiences and identity in eight different contexts—namely, family, friendships, teachers, resources, curriculum, assessment, extracurricular activities, and instrumental lessons. The results led the researchers to conclude that the extent to which musical activities are *embedded* in these other areas of life seems to determine whether their musical identities flourish and develop, or whether they decline if the appropriate support networks are not present. The important point here is that music is seen as a general forum for identity development across all of the contexts of everyday existence, rather than as being specific to education.

O'Neill (Chapter 5, "Young people's musical lives: learning ecologies, identities and connectedness") makes a valuable attempt to chart different pathways through these complexities by looking at young people's "learning ecologies." The theoretical basis of her chapter is based on two main approaches—Habermas' notion of life worlds, which is rooted in phenomenology, and ecological systems theory. The notion of "life worlds" places emphasis on "connectedness," in that young people may be seen as creating shared musical identities with others, which may exist for varying periods of time. Ecological systems theory is represented, amongst others, by the approaches of Bronfenbrenner, Vygotsky, and Engeström's cultural-historical activity theory—a basic idea running through all of these is that young people display *agency* in creating their own identities by drawing on what they see as the most important influences that they find in their social and cultural environments.

O'Neill describes "Mapping young people's musical lives," her interview study of 10- to 19-year-olds, which used a *music engagement map* to identify all the musical activities in which they were involved inside and outside school. The overall pattern of results was explained in terms of three musical life styles, which differed in terms of their level of *connectedness*. First, *segmented* musical life styles have different episodes that are not necessarily linked to one another. O'Neill links this with Giddens' (1991) notion of "segmentation" in 20th century life. Secondly, *situated* musical life styles center on the places or spaces in which interaction occurs, rather than on the musical activities themselves. Thirdly, *agentive* styles are those in which all of these aspects are clearly connected, such that musical activity provides a transformative space and place for identity work.

The notion of agency is also central to Westerlund, Partti, & Karlsen's (Chapter 27, "Identity formation and agency in the diverse music classroom") account of children's developing musical identities in the context of multicultural classroom cultures. Agency is seen as a key aspect of identity formation—it "refers to aspects related to one's perceived and actual ability to act in the world, and hence concerns matters such as self-esteem, experienced purpose of life, ego strength, internal locus of control" (p. 495). Westerlund et al. prioritize everyday interactions and the relational networks that exist within classrooms over a simple transmission model in which the teacher passes on knowledge to pupils. They draw attention in particular to the hegemony of western classical music in most music education contexts and also raise the issues of the relationship between music education and nationalism, the challenges posed by using popular music in classrooms, and some issues concerning gender.

In essence, agency is seen as enabling individuals to reach beyond their current identities and to look forward to what they might like to become in the future. This involves taking a sense of responsibility for their own life courses and developing the confidence to overcome obstacles that might occur. Music provides an important arena in which this might be made possible, and so we might summarize this section by saying that all children have musical identities in one sense or another, but that soon after school transition, in many cases, they have to make important decisions about their future activities and careers, which in some cases turn out to be in musical professions. Educational institutions play a key role in guiding these decisions.

1.5 MUSICAL IDENTITIES IN HEALTH AND WELL-BEING

A substantial literature has built up in recent years on the relationship between music, health, and well-being, and this field has been comprehensively reviewed by MacDonald, Kreutz and Mitchell (2012). Saarikallio (Chapter 33, "Musical identity in fostering emotional health") examines the close relationship between musical experience and emotional health and places a great deal of emphasis on the importance of emotional expression, emotional intelligence, emotion regulation, and the self-reflective awareness of one's own emotional states in health and well-being. Västfjäll, Juslin, and Hartig (2012) also placed everyday emotions at the heart of the relationship between music and subjective well-being and proposed a number of different mechanisms that mediate this relationship. Saarikallio sees the ability to perceive and recognize emotional states in the self and in others as one of the most fundamental aspects of healthy emotional behavior, and therefore as a key aspect of well-being. She also sees music as having the capacity to promote core aspects of emotional health and well-being in a way that is possible in very few other domains. Musical experience can contribute to the recognition and regulation of a very wide range and variety of emotional nuances of varying intensity.

This has a lot in common with Ruud's (Chapter 32, "Music, identity, and health") view that a strong sense of identity derived from music can contribute to certain specific aspects of health, and he identifies four of these. These are:

- A *sense of vitality* (of being alive, and of being competent to take part in different activities).
- A *sense of agency* (empowerment, internal locus of control), which emerged as a key concept in our discussion of musical identities in education, above.
- A *sense of belonging*, which is linked with the notion that our personal identities are created in interactions with others, such that we might be able to conceive of "community identities" in relation to those of individuals.
- A *sense of coherence and meaning* (of flow, or transcendence).

Ruud's conception of health goes beyond a strictly biomedical model, and includes our quality of life, and our everyday experience of our health. He proposes that music can act as what he calls a *cultural immunogen*—"a self-technology that protects, promotes, and maintains our health and quality of life" (p. 589).

Saarikallio also discusses the question of the negative emotion, and how it can be regulated. We adopt various strategies in order to deal with environmental stresses and negative states, such as in the experience of pain, or in depression. Research has clearly shown that engagement with music can enable children and adults to manage pain (see e.g., Mitchell, MacDonald, & Brodie, 2006; Longhi, Pickett, & Hargreaves, 2013). Mitchell et al. suggest that the use of music in pain management involves the experiences of distraction and relaxation and that music can transform negative into positive emotions. Enjoyment, mood improvement, and positive emotional experiences are part of many people's motivation for music listening, and several studies have shown these effects. Juslin and Laukka (2004), for example, reported that the three most common emotions in response to music in daily life were feeling happy, relaxed, and calm.

One very practical application of the study of musical identity in relation to health and well-being is in therapeutic contexts, and Magee (Chapter 34, "Music-making in therapeutic contexts: reframing identity following disruptions to health") discusses the ways in which people re-work their self-concept and identity in response to traumatic events that lead to disability or disfigurement, such as facial disfiguration from burns or the sudden loss of mobility through loss of limbs. Music has been found to provide a powerful means of dealing with the psychological effects of these events and can offer positive experiences that can empower individuals and begin to challenge the sense of a damaged or "spoiled identity" by increasing feelings of mastery and agency.

Magee discusses some of her own therapeutic work with people with complex physical disabilities stemming from multiple sclerosis: they were wheelchair users, and supported by others in everyday activities, such as washing, eating, and dressing (see e.g., Magee, 1999: Magee & Davidson, 2004). She started by establishing a repertoire of favorite songs with each individual, and the early stages of the work tended to focus on the negotiation of physical boundaries. She explains how the gradual improvement over time in the physical skills involved in playing an instrument gave rise to what she calls "performance validation," which gradually developed as a result of working with the therapist. The next stage was that "performance validation" could enable individuals to "sound out" their emotional selves, such that the emotional qualities of the therapeutic work gradually emerged and that agency could eventually return. The re-establishment of musical identities that can occur in this way provides a key to clients regaining control over their own lives, which involves overcoming emotional responses to their earlier feelings of lack of control.

This is quite similar to Baker and MacDonald's (Chapter 24, "Re-authoring the self: therapeutic songwriting in identity work") description of therapeutic songwriting, a therapeutic intervention designed to deal with the emotional communicative, psychological, or social needs of individuals, using the creative and storytelling features of songs (see e.g., Baker & MacDonald, 2013). A variety of different techniques can be used, some of which emphasize the creation of lyrics, some of which emphasize the music, and others which emphasize both. The therapist's role is not only to help to develop both of these aspects, but also positively influence the identity of the songwriter. As in Magee's study (Chapter 34, "Music-making in therapeutic contexts: reframing identity following disruptions to health,") Baker and MacDonald raise the issue of the effects of the sudden acquisition of a permanent disability on the self and identity of the person, which can challenge a person's previously established sense of self. The aim of therapeutic songwriting is to try to compensate for this by building a new identity, in that songs can embody and express extremely personal feelings and tell the songwriter's story, they have the potential to develop and maintain a positive sense of self.

McFerran and Hense (Chapter 36, "'I would die without out my music': relying on musical identities to cope with difficult times") discuss how adolescents use music and their musical identities to cope with the various difficulties that they experience in their lives. They discuss the use of music therapy in dealing with the identities of young people who are struggling with mental illness, comparing these with the identities of others not dealing with these challenges. It is clear that there is no simple equation between music and the positive benefits in that music can be a negative, as well as a positive, resource for young people. McFerran and Hense caution that people use music for the expression of identity in different ways, such that therapists and researchers need to avoid making simplistic assumptions about its effects. Having said that, there is little doubt that music can have enormous power in relation to self-reflection about one's emotions and the control of them, and Saarikallio (Chapter 33) sees these two features as key mediators of the relationship between musical identity and emotional health.

This chapter has set the scene for what is to follow in the rest of the Handbook and describes some of the main features of the theorizing and research that has been devoted to musical identities since our first book appeared in 2002. We have looked at some of the ways in which the definitions of musical identity have had to be expanded, sketched out the main features of the psychological approach to this topic, and then provided an overview of the four main domains, or contexts, in which musical identities have been investigated. This has meant drawing on a number of different theoretical perspectives which go well beyond psychology, as well as using a variety of different research methods.

1.6 STRUCTURE AND CONTENTS OF THE HANDBOOK

This conceptual framework has also established a rationale for the structure of the Handbook as a whole, which is divided into seven main sections, Sections 2–8, following the Editors' Introduction (Section 1). The first of these, "Sociological, discursive, and narrative approaches," includes general theoretical accounts of musical identities from this perspective by Elliott and Silverman, DeNora, and Barrett. O'Neill, Wilson and MacDonald, Folkestad, and McKinlay and McVittie also use this approach to investigate specific aspects of musical identities, namely, "learning ecologies" in young people, the identity constructions of free improvisers working together, the use of intertextuality in the definition of post-national identities in music, and identities in popular music, respectively.

The second and third main sections deal in depth with two of the three topics described in the present chapter as the central foundations of the psychological approach to musical identities, namely *development* and *individual differences*. The "Development" section includes chapters by Trevarthen and Malloch, and Lamont, both of which take a broad-ranging view of the development of musical identities across the life span: and those by Tafuri, Evans and McPherson, and Karkou and Joseph deal more specifically with development in early infancy and in adolescence respectively. The third main section on "Individual differences" incorporates three chapters that investigate musical identities empirically from a psychometric point of view. Dys, Schellenberg, and McLean, Spychiger, and Greenberg and Rentfrow are interested in the psychometric structures of different measures of musical identity, and in their relationships with other dimensions of individual differences, such as musical preferences, musical self-concepts, and personality factors. Rickard and Chin's chapter "Defining the musical identity of 'non-musicians'" presents some controversial ideas that extend the definition of the musician well beyond that which many musicians might accept, and Schubert proposes that susceptibility to emotional contagion and one's perspective-taking abilities are also individual difference factors that contribute to musical identity.

The fourth, fifth, and sixth main sections also follow the conceptual framework of the present chapter by using three of the main contexts within which musical identities are observed as their basis. The fourth section, "Musical institutions and practitioners," includes chapters by Rink and by Davidson, which look at the nature of musical identity in performance, and the chapters by Dueck and Cloonan examine some of the ways in which musicians from different genres and those in music-related professions align the activities of musicians with their potential publics and audiences. Linson's chapter looks at the role of music technology, considered from a socio-historical point of view, in shaping the identities of performers and in the corresponding audience reactions to them, and the chapters by Oakland, MacDonald, and Flowers, and by Baker and MacDonald consider different aspects of the regeneration of musical identities following redundancy in opera choristers, and in therapeutic songwriting respectively.

In the fifth main section, "Education," the chapters by Hallam and by Westerlund, Partti, and Karlsen are broad-ranging accounts which adopt psychological and sociological approaches respectively. Hallam describes her own investigations of the motivational factors underlying different types of musical aspiration, noting that it is possible for music to be a central element of a person's identity even when that person would not conventionally be described as a "musician" in the sense of playing an instrument professionally. Westerlund et al. base their account of identity on the notion of agency in the music classroom. The four other chapters in this section deal with more specific aspects of musical identities in education. Symonds, Hargreaves, and Long consider the effects of the transition from primary to secondary school, concluding that music should be seen as a general forum for identity development across all of the contexts of everyday existence, rather than as being specific to education. Ilari focuses on ethnic identity and cultural diversity in music education, considering the musical experiences of ethnic minority groups, immigrants, and refugees. Welch looks specifically at the developing identities of singers in relation to their educational environments, while Cassidy and Paisley investigate what it means to be "musical" in the digital age by assessing the extent to which musical participation is influenced by computer music games.

The sixth section of the Handbook, "Health and well-being," contains two chapters that take a broad-ranging view of musical identity in relation to the promotion of health and well-being. Ruud's chapter on "Music, identity, and health" adopts a view of health that goes beyond physical well-being to include one's quality of life and everyday experience of one's health: and Saarikallio takes this further by proposing that the emotions, and their recognition and regulation, form a key constituent of health and well-being. Three of the other chapters in this section focus on the role of musical identities in relation to therapy. Magee considers the role of music making in therapeutic contexts, looking at the ways in which this enables people to reframe their identities following its disruption as a result of disability or disfigurement following traumatic accidents. Fachner, Erkkilä, and Brabant explore the interactions between social pharmacology, i.e., the nature and timing of medical drug-taking, lifestyle, and personal identity. Treating depressed clients with individual psychodynamic music therapy worked well with those also taking anti-depressants but also initiated a process in which the need for medication started to decrease. McFerran and Hense focus on music therapy with adolescents, investigating how they use musical identities to cope with difficult times, and Ockelford and Vorhaus investigate the development of identity in people with severe or profound and multiple learning difficulties, using the distinction between the "minimal self" and the "narrative self" to assess the effects of musical engagements on people's "inner, subjective lives" compared with those on their "enduring selves."

We have seen that some of the chapters in each section have chosen to give broad-ranging accounts of the main themes of those sections, whereas others have focused on one or more specific topics within that theme. Other authors of the book have chosen to specialize still further by looking at particular musical identities in specific times, places, or contexts, and using these detailed analyses to formulate more general ideas and principles. We have collected these chapters together in the seventh and final main section of the Handbook, which we have described as "Case studies." Four of these represent musical identities in specific geographical areas, and we have already looked at these in the third section of this chapter. Zapata Restrepo and Hargreaves, Auh and Walker, Osborne, and Colls and Heathman, in their very different ways, have written about musical identities in Australia and South Korea, Colombia, the Balkan region of Europe, and in England respectively, and these rich and insightful accounts of specific musical identities provide a valuable complement to the more general theoretical accounts. Nicholas Cook's chapter, "The imaginary African: race, identity, and Samuel Coleridge-Taylor" provides a fascinating insight into the racial aspects of musical identity by considering the case of Samuel Coleridge-Taylor, the son of a black medical student from Sierra Leone and a white Englishwoman who brought him up in Croydon, and who was seen as the outstanding member of a group of students at the Royal College of Music that included Holst and Vaughan Williams. Jourdan and Holloway describe the adaptation of the South American "Sistema" approach to the development of musical learning and identity in Scotland, showing that some of the same principles can be applied across cultural boundaries, while Karass, in the final chapter, looks at the role of music and festivals in the articulation of national, political, religious, and ethnic identities, in this case in southern Tunisia.

This proliferation of different kinds of case study of musical identity and the substantial number of chapters in each of our six other main sections, confirm the view that formed our starting point for this Handbook, namely, that the study of musical identity has proliferated, and become increasingly multidisciplinary, since our first book in 2002. The increasingly rapid changes that are taking place in music, in technology and its uses, and indeed in society as a whole, more or less guarantee that the study of musical identity is likely to develop much further, even more quickly, and could well assume even greater importance in the years to come.

References

Baker, F.A., & MacDonald, R.A.R. (2013). Flow, identity, achievement, satisfaction and ownership during therapeutic songwriting experiences with university students and retirees. *Musicae Scientiae*, 17, 129–44.

Carlisle, J. (2007). Digital music and generation Y: discourse analysis of the online music information behaviour talk of five young Australians. *Information Research*, 12: Article number:n colis25.

Erikson, E.H. (1950). *Childhood and society.* New York: Norton.

Erikson, E. (1968). *Identity: youth and crisis.* New York: Norton.

Giddens, A. (1991). *Modernity and self-identity: self and society in the late modern age.* Cambridge, MA: Polity Press.

Hallam, S. (2013). What predicts level of expertise attained, quality of performance, and future musical aspirations in young instrumental players? *Psychology of Music*, 41(3), 265–89.

Hallam, S. (in preparation) Changes in motivation as musical expertise develops. *Psychology of Music.*

Hargreaves, D.J., & Lamont, A. (2017). *The psychology of musical development.* Cambridge: Cambridge University Press.

Hargreaves, D.J., & Marshall, N.A. (2003). Developing identities in music education. *Music Education Research*, 5(3), 263–73.

Hargreaves, D.J., Purves, R.M., Welch, G.F., & Marshall, N.A. (2007). Developing identities and attitudes in musicians and music teachers. *British Journal of Educational Psychology*, 77(3), 665–82.

Juslin, P.N., & Laukka, P. (2004). Expression, perception, and induction of musical emotions: a review and a questionnaire study of everyday listening. *Journal of New Music Research*, 33, 217–38.

Lamont, A.M. (2002). Musical identities and the school environment. In: R.A.R. MacDonald, D.J. Hargreaves, & D.E. Miell (Eds.) *Musical identities*, pp. 41–59. Oxford: Oxford University Press.

Longhi, E., Pickett, N., & Hargreaves, D.J. (2015). Wellbeing and hospitalized children: can music help? *Psychology of Music*, 43, 188–96.

MacDonald, R.A.R., Hargreaves, D.J., & Miell, D.E. (Eds.) (2002). *Musical identities.* Oxford: Oxford University Press.

MacDonald, R.A.R., Kreutz, G., & Mitchell, L. (Eds.) (2012). *Music, health, and wellbeing.* Oxford: Oxford University Press.

MacDonald, R.A., Wilson G.B., & Miell D. (2012). Improvisation as a creative process within contemporary music. In: D. J. Hargreaves, D. Miell, & R.A.R. MacDonald (Eds.) *Musical imaginations: multidisciplinary perspectives on creativity, performance and perception*, pp. 242–55. Oxford: Oxford University Press.

Magee, W. (1999). 'Singing my life, playing myself': music therapy in the treatment of chronic neurological illness. In: T. Wigram & J. De Backer (Eds.) *Clinical applications of music therapy in developmental disability, pediatrics and neurology*, pp. 201–23. London: Jessica Kingsley.

Magee, W.L., & Davidson, J.W. (2004). Singing in therapy: monitoring disease process in chronic degenerative illness. *British Journal of Music Therapy*, 18(2), 65–77.

Marcia, J.E. (1980). Identity in adolescence. In: J. Adelson (Ed.), *Handbook of adolescent psychology*, pp. 159–87. New York: Wiley.

Mitchell, L.A., MacDonald, R.A.R., & Brodie, E.E. (2006). A comparison of the effects of preferred music, arithmetic, and humour on cold pressor pain. *European Journal of Pain*, 10, 343–51.

North, A.C., & Hargreaves, D.J. (2008). *The social and applied psychology of music.* Oxford: Oxford University Press.

Ockelford, A. (2013). *Applied musicology: using zygonic theory to inform music education, therapy, and psychology research.* Oxford: Oxford University Press.

Ryan, R.M., & Deci, E.L. (2000). Self-determination theory and the facilitation of intrinsic motivation, social development, and well-being. *American Psychologist*, 55, 68–78.

Tarrant, M., North, A.C., & Hargreaves, D.J. (2002). Youth identity and music. In: R.A.R. MacDonald, D.J. Hargreaves, & D.E. Miell (Eds.) *Musical identities*, pp. 134–50. Oxford: Oxford University Press.

Tajfel, H., Flament, C., Billig, M.G., & Bundy, R.P. (1971). Social categorization and intergroup behaviour. *European Journal of Social Psychology*, 1, 149–78.

Västfjäll, D., Juslin P.N., & Hartig, T. (2012). Music, subjective wellbeing, and health: the role of everyday emotions. In: R.A.R. MacDonald, G. Kreutz, & L. Mitchell (Eds.) *Music, health and wellbeing*, pp. 405–23. Oxford: Oxford University Press.

Wilson, G.B., & MacDonald, R.A.R. (2012). The sign of silence: negotiating musical identities in an improvising ensemble. *Psychology of Music*, 40(5), 558–73.

SECTION 2

SOCIOLOGICAL, DISCURSIVE, AND NARRATIVE APPROACHES

CHAPTER 2

....

IDENTITIES AND MUSICS
Reclaiming Personhood

....

DAVID J. ELLIOTT AND MARISSA SILVERMAN

> To be nobody-but-myself—in a world which is doing its best, night and day, to make
> you everybody else—means to fight the hardest battle which any human being can
> fight, and never stop fighting.
>
> e. e. cummings

PSYCHOLOGICAL, sociological, and philosophical discussions of the relationships
between musics and identities provide a wide range of more or less plausible alternatives. Less plausible alternatives tend to skip the logically prior issue of what personhood is and/or assume that identity is the same as personhood.

In this chapter we suggest that the search for a plausible explanation of why and how
music-making and listening are especially pertinent to individual and group identity
formation should begin with the nature of personhood. In other words, we posit that
human identities—including musical, social, cultural, gendered, and other identities,
e.g., selfhood, spirituality, and "person-ality"—arise from the nature of personhood and
intersubjective relationships. From this viewpoint, selfhood and identities are not identical to personhood; they are primary dimensions of it (Carr, 2002).

Our discussion unfolds in three parts. Part one discusses major dimensions of our
embodied-enactive concept of personhood (Elliott & Silverman, 2015). To foreshadow
key themes in part one, we argue that personhood depends on and emerges from a vast
network of embodied, integrated, fluid, and enactive processes that enable and power
each person's conscious awareness of his/her*self*, his/her multiple identities, and the
world(s) in which he/she lives. Framed in musical terms, we propose that personhood
is analogous to a huge jazz ensemble whose many millions of players—i.e., your embodied-enactive "personhood processes"—are so expert at improvising collaboratively with
the dynamic circumstances of your human and natural ecosystems that the "beautiful
music that is *you*"—which includes your conscious subjective life experiences, selfhood,

self-efficacy, and spirituality—flow seamlessly and continuously from moment to moment. The "players" in your ensemble create *your experience of you* as the arranger and performer of your life's music "in all its complexity, emotional nuance, crescendo and diminuendo—*the ballad that is the you-ness of you*" (Blakeslee & Blakeslee, 2007, pp. 207–8).

Part two supports and expands the preceding themes with philosophical concepts that explain the roles of empathy, ethical idealization, and ethical communities in the co-construction of personhood and identities.

Part three knits parts one and two together toward an explanation of the links between identities-as-narratives and the concept of music-making, music listening, and musical "praxes" as "affordances"—as sonic-artistic "technologies" for identity creation and expression. Foreshadowing the concept of identities-as-narratives, Lieblich and Josselson (2013) propose that "first-person narratives are an effective means for capturing the elusive concept of identity" (p. 206) because their significance is multidimensional. That is, the values of a first-person account of an individual's personhood, identities, and history are not limited to the factual and/or fictional content of his or her narration because first-person narratives are also "performatives."

Austin (1962) introduced the concept of a performative to challenge the narrow, commonplace assumption that sentences (declarations and utterances) function primarily to communicate facts, concepts, arguments, and so forth. Austin argued that words do not simply say things—*words do things*. For example, when a person says "I do" in the context of a marriage ceremony, his or her words not only make a statement, they construct or *perform* the act of marriage because a couple's mutual declaration of "I do" creates and enacts a commitment. Likewise, when a person says, "I love Jay-Z," he is not simply making a statement. He is affiliating himself with a specific community of music makers and listeners, and arguably, "performing" his self-narrative. In doing so, he also affiliates himself with the musical praxis that Jay-Z represents and "performs," literally and in terms of performatives. From this perspective, the performative nature of a person's self-narrative and accompanying gestures enrich his or her verbal narrative.

Giroux (2006) provides (below) a vivid example of the role of performatives in his youthful identity formation, which occurred in a racially divided community in Providence, Rhode Island. Specifically, Giroux explains how the words "race" and "class" were not just nouns to him, but verbs or performatives. He also stresses that music was an important cultural medium (of "resistance") that enabled him to negotiate his everyday life and develop an awareness of himself as a white male.

> In my working-class neighborhood, race and class were performative categories defined in terms of the events, actions, and outcomes of our struggles as we engaged with kids whose histories, languages, and racial identities appeared foreign and hostile to us. Race and class were not merely nouns we used to narrate ourselves; they were verbs that governed who we interacted with and performed in the midst of "others," whether they were white middle-class or black youths.

Most of the interactions we had with "others" were violent, fraught with anger and hatred ... My own sense of what it meant to be a white male emerged *performatively* through my interactions with peers, the media, and the broader culture ... Popular culture provided the medium through which we learned how to negotiate our everyday lives, especially when it brought together elements of resistance found in Hollywood youth films ... or the rock n' roll music of Bill Haley and the Comets, Elvis Presley, and other artists.

Giroux, 2006, p. 5.

Given the above, we argue that first-person "performances," and everyday "presentational" and "participatory" (Turino, 2008) musical performances (e.g., professional and amateur music-making, listening, and dancing of different kinds), are themselves constructive acts. They serve as tools, technologies, or "affordances" by means of which individuals create their social–cultural gendered communities, and form and inform their identities. This leads to the obvious conclusion that identity is "an ever-evolving, dynamic (rather than a substantive, stable, static) entity" (Lieblich & Josselson, 2013, p. 207).

Clearly, people have always expressed, "performed," and "composed" their first-person narratives through songs and the texts of choral music. The same applies to instrumental musics that are open to a vast range of emotional–personal interpretations. This interpretive openness allows listeners to feel and embody themselves in the sounds, spaces, performers, and relationships of instrumental musics that, in turn, mirror, portray, validate, invalidate, and otherwise express their first-person narratives.

In the last section of this chapter we weave these themes together to argue that if musics are conceived, carried out, taught, and learned as musical *praxes*, then music-making and music listening are capable of providing exceptionally rich means of and contexts for nurturing, forming, and informing the positive and ethical growth of people's self-identity, self-other identities, and musical identities.

The term "praxes" is meant to spotlight a key distinction that discussions of musics and identities frequently omit. That is, if musics are conceived and carried out simplistically, as musical "practices"—in the commonplace sense of musical styles and/or sets of skills and understandings alone—then acts of music-making and music listening are vulnerable to unethical and self-destructive identity formation. Examples of the latter include numerous youth and adult musics that people deliberately create to promulgate racist, homophobic, and antidemocratic beliefs and activities. Reiterated as a question: can musics play a *positive* and unique role in the development and communication of various forms of identity? It depends fundamentally on whether or not informal, non-formal, and/or formal music learning processes and contexts are *ethical* or not.

We argue that musics—conceived and carried out ethically as social praxes—provide powerful intersubjective contexts in which people of all ages and abilities can positively co-construct each other's musical–social–personal identities and narratives and, more deeply, co-construct empathetically each other as persons. In doing so, music makers and listeners acquire the musical means they need to build "a certain way of life"—a meaningful life of fellowship, happiness, healthfulness, joy, respect for others, an "ethic of care" for oneself and others, and many other dimensions of human flourishing that Aristotle summarized in the word *eudaimonia*.

At this point we need to elaborate and substantiate our proposals by examining more closely what a holistic, embodied-enactive concept of personhood entails.

2.1 PERSONHOOD: TOWARD A HOLISTIC EMBODIED-ENACTIVE CONCEPT

What is personhood? We do not pretend to provide a full answer in this chapter. Instead, we outline a concept of personhood explained in much greater detail elsewhere (Elliott & Silverman, 2015). Our concept owes a large debt to past and present scholars across several fields of inquiry, including the philosophy of mind (e.g., Dewey, 1929; Thompson, 2007; Noë, 2009; Chappell, 2011; Prinz, 2012), neuroscience (e.g., Varela et al., 1992; Damasio, 1994; LeDoux, 1996), evolutionary biology (e.g., Oyama, 2000), and cognitive science (e.g., Johnson, 2007; Di Paolo et al., 2010). What unites these scholars is their commitment to *holistic* concepts of the nature of personhood (Martin & Bickhard, 2013), which we endorse.

Holistic concepts of personhood oppose dualistic concepts that depend on different versions of Descartes' false belief that a person is a binary organism—an invisible, immaterial thing (i.e., a mind, spirit, or soul) and an observable, physical thing. Most cognition-centered theories of mind and personhood are little more than sophisticated variations on Descartes' dualism. Powered by robust research in neuroscience, brain imaging, and other innovations, today's dualists want to claim that you = your brain. These scholars assume that everything we need to know about human experiences can and will be explained when scientists locate the neural correlates of consciousness, including the neural correlates of each person's subjective experiences of (say) red, green, love, *The Rite of Spring*, Sky Ferreira's "Night Time, My Time," and everything else people hear, see, feel, think, and do.

The obvious counterpoint, however, is that scientists' current knowledge of the human brain is extremely incomplete. For example, says Marcus (2013), "brains—even small ones—are dauntingly complex" (p. 1). He elaborates:

> Information flows in parallel through many different circuits at once; different components of a single functional circuit may be distributed across many brain structures and be spatially intermixed with the components of other circuits; feedback signals from higher levels constantly modulate the activity within any given circuit; and neuromodulatory chemicals can rapidly alter the effective wiring of any circuit. (p. 1)

Thus, says a cautious commentator,

> the entire history of brain science has been characterized by every new discovery being hopelessly mis/over-interpreted. This is perfectly natural because any new knowledge is always understood within the current context. But in brain science our

level of understanding is so [primitive that] we can be very confident any context is going to be wrong, and possibly in a serious way.

Aporic, 2013.

It seems safe to say, then, that neither scientists nor philosophers of mind will ever understand completely why or how one person's conscious experiences of romantic love, Mahler's First Symphony, or Lady Gaga's "Applause" come about, or why one person's experience of human actions differs from another. The same holds for the nature, formation, and sustainability of personal identities.

In contrast to dualistic and other reductionist views, we argue that a person is an embodied, enactive, social-cultural being that becomes him- or herself in or through the processes of continuously constructing and co-constructing her sociocultural contexts and communities, which include her ethical community. To say that persons are *embodied* beings means that each person's body–brain–mind–conscious–non-conscious processes (BBM–C-NC processes, for short) are completely fused and always interacting dynamically with each other and with his or her world(s). All aspects of a person's perceiving, thinking, and doing (and much more) are seamless because personhood is enabled and powered by thousands of interconnected layers and levels of conscious–non-conscious (C-NC) processes. Thus, as Damasio (1999) and Schulkin (2004) argue, our multiple cognitive systems are embedded in our multiple emotion systems, which are embedded in our multiple memory systems, which are embodied in our somatic-sensory systems, which are embedded in our social worlds, and so forth, ad infinitim. So the question is not whether sensory systems, bodily operations, emotional experiences (and so on) are cognitive or emotional, or whatever, but to what degree (Schulkin, 2004, p. 35). In the absence of one or more human dimensions discussed above, personhood will be compromised in one or more ways.

Moreover, just as the body–brain–mind is unified and embodied, a person's powers and processes of attention, perception, cognition, emotion, memory, volition, and C-NC processes are *socially situated* and co-constructed through her continuous engagements with complex webs of social, cultural, physical, moral, and hundreds of other environmental aspects of her world. Johnson (2007) explains that personhood includes a brain operating *in and for* "a living, purposive body, in continual engagement with complex environments that are not just physical but social and cultural as well" (p. 175). Importantly, the brain is only one part of personhood, albeit an exceptionally important part. Personhood includes and combines a human brain "in a living human body, interacting with complex physical, social, and cultural environments, in an ongoing flow of experiences" (Johnson, 2006, p. 279). A person is not two ontologically different kinds of things joined together. The human mind is not only *em*bodied; it emerges from and co-evolves with the body *in situ*. "No body, never mind" (Johnson, 2006, p. 47).

Van der Schyff (2013) summarizes some musical implications of an embodied concept of personhood:

> music cognition has been dominated by a largely disembodied conception of the mind. This so-called "cognitivist" perspective treats mental activity in terms of abstract information-processing—where the world is represented in the mind via

the computation of "sub-personal" symbols; and where the mind–brain relationship is explained in terms of a collection of cognitive modules shaped by natural selection. Recent decades have seen an ecological-embodied paradigm emerge in cognitive science, as well as more plastic and interactive conceptions of the mind-brain and organism-environment relationships. These new perspectives offer a much broader understanding of meaning making and the mind and are becoming increasingly influential in music cognition studies. (p. 3)

What does the enactive component of personhood involve?

2.2 ENACTION

Recent theorizing in the philosophy of mind, experimental philosophy, and neuroscience argues that we are *enactive* beings, which is to say that each person generates, maintains, *brings forth*, and effectually creates his/her*self* by interacting with other persons and all aspects of his or her contexts. From an enactive point of view, "perceiving is a way of acting. Perception is *not* something that happens to us, or in us. *It is something we do*" (Noë, 2009, p. 2). More broadly, "brain, body, and world form a process of *dynamic* interaction. *That is where we find ourselves*" (p. 95). Thompson (2007) agrees: "Like two partners in a dance who bring forth each other's movements, organism and environment enact each other through their structural coupling" (pp. 204–5).

These concepts represent a major paradigm shift in consciousness studies and scholars' thinking about the nature of mind and personhood. That is—and however counterintuitive it may seem at first—human consciousness is *not* isolated or closed off "in one's head"; consciousness is not sequestered in the skull. Rather, consciousness is simultaneously embodied and embedded in the world. This leads to another crucial realization: since all dimensions of personhood are socially situated, each person's conscious awareness of her*self* and her self-other embeddedness "presupposes a certain empathetic understanding of self and other" (Thompson, 2007, p. 383). Indeed, *empathy* is a cornerstone of human consciousness and the formation and maintenance of self-identity. Why and how people conceive themselves and identify with certain actions, values, and social praxes (e.g., specific ways of making music, gathering together to listen to music, using music as an affordance for emotional regulation, etc.) depends on how they enact their social worlds. Enaction pivots on and is motivated by the intersubjective "response-abilities" persons feel toward other persons.

It follows from this that each person's sense of musical identity—and other identities—is *not* isolated or fixed; it is contingent, fluid, and ever-changing, albeit imperceptibly at times. Our musical and personal identities change in relation to our musical and personal interactions, contexts, and the affordances that musical experiences provide. Turino (2008) puts it another way: identity is how we "represent ourselves to ourselves and others" (p. 101). For example, people often present themselves one way in one set of circumstances and another way in a completely different set of circumstances. This does not mean a person is being untrue to herself. It only means that her identity shifts depending on her engagements with her worlds. As Lieblich and Josselson argue, the term identity also "evokes a list of characteristics and attributes, values, and motives" (p. 205) that change in relation to circumstances based on "a past that foreshadows the present and a planned-for-future" (p. 205).

Thus, holistic theorists view a person and her identity formation as a "joint project." Each person emerges from, lives in, and develops because of his or her dynamic, reciprocal, co-constructive relationships with others and her ecological interactions. Each person *enacts* herself and others, her identities, and her world(s). Without other people, we would not and could not *be*. An "I" becomes an "I" because there is also a "you," a "me," a "we," an "us," and ethical communities in which self and others live. A baby's "I-ness" develops in and through her intersubjective and embodied collaborations between herself and her caregivers, her extended family and playmates and, eventually, a web of more or less significant others. As Bruner (2009) argues, personhood "is not just a product of inner processes but it expresses the outcome of real or imagined exchanges with Others" (p. vii). Martin and Bickhard (2013) add that, within and because of the numerous personhood-processes we have explained above, persons possess many integrated sets of social-psychological capacities. These include "the use of language, the creation of culture, self-consciousness and self-understanding, an agency that includes intentionality and two-way volitional control (to act or refrain from acting)," various intelligences, ethical concerns, the capacity to consider competing viewpoints, and the disposition and ability to interweave past, present, and future narratives of the self and self-identities (p. 2).

Philosophical perspectives on personhood and identity, which are frequently omitted in past psychological research, help to deepen the proposals we have made so far.

2.3 ENTER PHILOSOPHY

Let us now pinpoint key philosophical aspects of the development of personhood and identity by drawing from the work of philosopher Timothy Chappell (2011), who contrasts two diametrically opposed views—criterialism and humanism.

Various philosophers have conceived identity in relation to the conditions of change under which something can be said to remain the same, or in reference to a sense of self and identity, and external relations that are contingent. Aristotle (1941) and Plato (1993) explored identity in terms of change. They asked, "How can something which goes through either mutation or growth be considered the same thing?" In different ways, both concluded that human beings have an inner substance or soul that remains constant throughout physical change. Hegel (2010), on the other hand, viewed identity in terms of social activity. He believed that our self-awareness and self-identity arise from our interactions with others. For Hegel, the social foundations of identity include issues of race, nationality, class, and culture. James (1983) related identity to the spiritual self and to a person's inner or subjective being, both of which emerge from one's stream of consciousness. To us, this small sample of ideas illustrates what thinkers overlook when they fail to recognize the embodied and enactive nature of persons.

To explain what we mean in contemporary terms, let us begin with criterialist philosophers, who typically argue that a set of necessary and sufficient conditions must be in place before it is possible to grant that this-or-that being counts as a person, which is the logically prior condition for any form of identity. As Chappell (2011) notes, criterialists tend to argue that to qualify as a person a being must exhibit all or most of six "markers" of personhood—rationality, sentience, emotionality, self-awareness, moral agency, and the ability to communicate (p. 3). Some criterialists add self-identity, moral identity, and other forms of identity. At first glance, criterialism may seem plausible because the necessary and sufficient conditions that these theories spell out *seem* to apply to most human beings. However, says Chappell, the fatal flaw in criterialism is that if (say) rationality, self-awareness, and a sense of self-identity are necessary conditions for counting something as a person, then a severely mentally disabled child and a newborn baby fail to count as persons. If the capacity to communicate is a necessary condition for personhood, then many stroke victims fail to count as persons. Clearly, criterialism makes it difficult, if not impossible, for many human beings to qualify as persons. Moreover, criterialism is implausible because it does not match what happens in typical human interactions. That is, we don't stop to decide whether "an-other" of some kind counts as a person by evaluating "its" behaviors according to a list of predetermined criteria. Moreover, and even more seriously, criterialism is morally abhorrent because it automatically omits any and all human beings who are, somehow, less than "perfect specimens" of so-called human normality. As Chappell (2011) says:

> to treat someone as a person is *not* to tick a box by her name to show that she has passed some kind of inspection or met some standard of rationality or self-awareness or emotionality or whatever. Indeed, it seems no less arbitrarily discriminating to say, "Sorry, you are not rational or self-aware or linguistically capable … enough to count as a person" than to say "Sorry, you are not white enough to count as a person." (p. 12)

Humanistic philosophers take an entirely different view. They argue that when a person consciously or non-consciously interprets an-other as a person—rather than a rock, a refrigerator, a rose, a rat, or a roast beef sandwich—he or she understands consciously and/or non-consciously that, as a person him/herself, he/she is a member of a moral community of persons and, therefore, that he/she has (or he/she feels) an ethical responsibility to treat the other with some degree of respect, consideration, and *empathy*. In return, when he/she acknowledges the other as a person, it is reasonable to expect a certain degree of consideration in return, which would not be expected from non-persons, such as rocks or rats (Chappell, 2011).

So, contrary to using checklists to "test" for the so-called personhood markers of an unfamiliar other, we begin at the *end*: we treat the unfamiliar other as a person (Chappell, 2011). Once we do, we expect to communicate with him or her, experience his rationality, and more. Why and how does this happen? Consider the example of parenting. Chappell explains that while parents are fully aware that their infant does not possess the same levels of rationality and communication skills as adults, their attitudes toward their child are always what Wittgenstein eloquently describes as "an attitude towards a soul" (Chappell, 2011, p. 7). Put another way, a parent

> … treats her child from the very beginning—and from before … it is literally and actually true—as a creature that can reason, respond, reflect, feel, laugh, think about itself as a person, think about others as persons too, and do everything else that persons characteristically do. (p. 8)

A parent *empathetically* conceives and interacts with her baby or toddler as a person in the process of developing her personhood as much as possible, which of course includes developing her many identities and her "person-ality." This leads to a closely allied concept—an ethical father, mother, or other caregiver treats his/her child in relation to an "ideal of personhood" (Chappell, 2011, p. 9). Singing to, playing with, or asking the baby questions, even though it is obvious to anyone that the baby cannot participate fully or answer with adult rationality, all these actions are instances of a parent's *ethical idealization of the child* as a being that possess personhood, self-identity, and all other attributes that will develop over time, as long as the baby is raised with care and empathy in morally, socially, and culturally humanistic contexts.

This leads to another crucial concept. By conceiving and interacting with one's child as a person endowed with the fundamental attributes and potentials of personhood and identity, a parent—and other members of the child's moral community—enacts or "performs" something deeply profound: he or she "*makes it true*" that the child is a person— she enacts the personhood and potential identities of her child (Chappell, 2011, p. 9). The process of becoming persons (and communities of persons) and developing a range of identities is one in which we "*constitute* each other as persons … by *treating* each other as persons"—we enact each other's selfhood, self-identity, and group identities. Deeply embedded in our empathetic, emotional, conscious, non-conscious, and somatic dispositions, actions, and interactions with others *as* persons is what Davidson (1980) calls the "principle of charity" (cited in Chappell, 2011, p. 178). That is, says Chappell, "by charitably … interpreting the other as a person, I *make* him a person" (p. 10). I construct, embody, and enact him or her as an individual person, and I identify him as one-with-me in the social group to which I belong, or not.

Thompson (2007) supports these themes when he emphasizes that "my body is lived by me in the first person, but it also appears to you in the third person (or second person), and in empathetically grasping that experience of yours, I experience myself as an other to you" (p. 400). If not, "if the 'I' were to appear only in a first-person singular format, then it would not be possible to have any non-egocentric understanding of the 'I' as a bodily individual in a public intentional world that transcends the self" (p. 400).

In musical terms, to approach a new music maker in one's classroom or community music group with a charitable stance is an act of ethical idealization. The hidden assumption in such an "en-actment" includes (or should include) the belief that this unfamiliar music maker's aspirations, and your aspirations for him or her (as your fellow music maker), deserve your respect and that they are achievable simply because he/she is a person. To treat others—school music students, community music makers, other teachers, professional and amateur musicians, etc.—with charity empowers them to flourish as individuals and as productive members of their communities, however small or large these may be. Teaching and learning music for its transformative values requires that we rise above simplistic aims defined in terms of observable behaviors and empirical measures of student performance. These paralyzing terms and notions have nothing to do with education as a praxis—as a process of empowering people to achieve their musical and educational "life goals" through critically reflective and ethical doing and making toward human flourishing.

MacIntyre (1999) agrees and calls attention to another crucial component of personhood and personal and social identity—*unconditional care.*

> The kind of care that was needed to make us what we have in fact become … had to be, if it was to be effective, unconditional care for the human being as such … And this is the kind of care that we in turn now owe or will owe. Of the brain-damaged, of those almost incapable of movement, of the autistic, of all such we have to say: "This could have been us."
>
> Cited in Chappell, 2011, p. 100.

Chappell's discussion ends with this ancient wisdom: "Charity bears all things, believes all things, hopes all things, endures all things."

2.4 MUSICAL IDENTITIES AND MUSICAL AFFORDANCES

Music is not simply a body of pieces, objects, or "works": music is something people do. As several authors (e.g., Elliott, 1995; Small, 1998; Elliott & Silverman, 2015) argue, "doing" music includes all possible forms of music-making, listening, and musical praxes. In and through musical "particip-*actions*," people make meanings and construct identities according to how and why they experience different forms of music-making, listening, and musical contexts as "good for" various purposes in various contexts. Of course, this perspective is not completely satisfactory. Why? Because it omits concepts that may provide deeper understandings of how music-making, listening, and musical praxes provide us with opportunities and mechanisms, or musical "technologies," that empower us to construct identities, regulate our emotions, communicate with others, and much more. One way to search for and develop the explanations we need is to combine the embodied-enactive concept of personhood with the concept of affordances.

What is an affordance? Gibson (1979) was one of the first to conceptualize affordances:

> The *affordances* of the environment are what it *offers* the animal, what it *provides* or *furnishes*, either for good or ill. The verb to *afford* is found in the dictionary, but the noun *affordance* is not. I have made it up. I mean by it something that refers to both the environment and the animal in a way that no existing term does. It implies the complementarity of the animal and the environment. (p. 127)

For instance, a flat or curved surface that matches a person's height affords a place to sit; the handle of a hammer affords grasping, hitting, and the possibility of constructing; a door knob affords pushing and pulling (Kosa, 2012). The naturally occurring or deliberate design of visual and physical objects (e.g., visual displays, spears, knives, buttons, dials, drums, trumpets), sound patterns, and different kinds of places and spaces afford all sorts of human uses and creative possibilities, depending on the contexts in which they exist and a person's BBM-C-NC abilities to develop background knowledge, whether acquired non-formally, informally, or formally. As Sanders (1997) explains: "affordances are opportunities for action in the environment of an organism, the opportunities in question include everything the organism can do, and the environment includes the entire realm of potential activity for that organism" (p. 108).

For example, whereas a hungry person may perceive a long, narrow piece of wood as affording the opportunity to spear a fish or make a fishing rod, a sparrow might perceive a long, narrow piece of wood as a place to sit. Windsor and de Bezenac (2012) provide examples:

> we might perceive that a stone affords throwing because it is liftable and throwable: the information for these affordances would be provided by a combination of visual information and touch. A pen will be a shape that fits the hand, exudes a coloured liquid, which can mark a surface: to discover these properties would require exploration, a key element of ecological psychology. (p. 104)

These examples remind us of a basic principle of embodiment and enaction:

> Think of a blind person tap-tapping his or her way around a cluttered space, perceiving that space by touch, not all at once, but through time, by skillful probing and movement. This is, or at least ought to be, our paradigm of what perceiving is. The world makes itself available to the perceiver through physical movement and interaction ... Perceptual experience acquires content thanks to our possession of bodily skills.
>
> Noë, 2004, pp. 1–2.

A blind person's cane (an affordance in itself) allows that person to navigate her places and spaces by means of perceiving, enacting, and interacting with her environment.

Windsor and de Bezenac (2012) argue that the enactive approach to affordances is significant because it insists on the importance of interrelationships in perception and action. In doing so, this approach reveals the richness of environmental features that allow humans and animals to act constructively. Affordances prioritize "the concrete over the abstract" in human perception (p. 103) and highlight the mutuality of perception and action in relation to the human and non-human dimensions of our worlds. Implicit in the latter is the necessity of empathy. Altogether, the concept of affordances involves an acquired capacity to perceive, understand, or imagine how something might be used and co-constructed empathetically.

Implicit in the above is another consequence of affordances. Humans have a tendency to elaborate all aspects—all affordances—of ordinary life. For example, it's easy to understand why people run or jump to escape danger. Many people, however, run and jump for the sake of running and jumping, or as part of kicking goals in football, or scoring points in basketball. Similarly, although eating and drinking are necessities, the creation of gourmet restaurants and extraordinary menus are not. In all these examples, so-called necessary activities spawn identifiable pursuits. Ordinary activities like running, dining, and driving become pursuits in and of themselves (or aspects of games and sports) with specific aims, rules, standards, traditions, heroes, legends, lore, and competitions. Because people have the capacities to perceive and imagine the affordances of necessary activities, they create new affordances and social praxes that revolve around these affordances.

It would be most unusual if the same thing did not occur in relation to one of our most basic human necessities: the need to listen-*for* sounds. Musics—by which we mean the instruments of musicing (vocal and instrumental), simultaneous music-listening, listening to/with others, and musical praxes—are multidimensional affordances that emerge from our embodied-enactive interactions with our world(s). As Krueger (2011) says, "from birth, music is directly perceived as an affordance-laden structure ... music ought to be thought of as a tool that we appropriate and use to construct different forms of self-experience and social relatedness" (p. 2), identity construction, musical and otherwise.

> Music making ... provides players with many affordances, each player taking the meaning that is specified at any particular point in the performance as a means for further specifying what is afforded both by the part before him and the mutually constituted musical product of the joint activity of all the players.
>
> Davidson & Good, 2002, p. 200.

For example, a mother's everyday voice provides a rich range of affordances that are crucial to the development of her infant. By consciously and/or non-consciously altering the pitch, timbre, dynamics, and other qualities of her everyday voice, she creates motherese, which she uses to comfort and soothe her baby, regulate her infant's emotions, and create an "acoustic-musical womb" of safety—all of which generate "emotional affordances" that facilitate mother-infant social bonding. Schutz (1976) refers to this kind of mutuality as a "mutual tuning-in relationship ... a relationship in which the 'I' and the 'Thou' are experienced by both participants as a 'We' in vivid presence" (p. 161). Krueger (2011) links the latter to Small's (1998) premise: "[t]he act of musicing establishes in the place where it is happening a set of relationships, and it is in those rela-tionships that the meaning of the act lies" (p. 13).

Motherese, and all other forms of music-making and listening, are (among many other things) musical affordances. They allow us to experience and create the "social affordances" and "emotional affordances" (Krueger, 2011, p. 15) that infuse and underpin our musical identities and contribute to the development of all other forms of identity. Affordance-laden musical actions, musical-emotional listening, and musical praxes are the "technologies" we use to experience and create "social affordances" and "emotional affordances" that play crucial roles in non-conscious and conscious musical memory formation and, therefore, the formation of all types of identity.

Regarding social affordances, small or large groups of music makers usually coor-dinate and/or synchronize their actions and perceptions to achieve mutually valued goals—musical, personal, emotional, and ethical. The active context they share and value is shaped partly by the affordances of their voices, instruments, and bodies, and partly by the actions of other music makers (Windsor & de Bezenac, 2012, p. 111). Citing Gibson (1979), Windsor & de Bezenac (2012) emphasize that "the richest and most elaborate affor-dances of the environment are provided by … other people" (p. 110); they "afford, above all, a rich and complex set of interactions … and communicating," which comprise "the whole realm of social significance" (Gibson, p. 128, cited in Windsor & de Bezenac, 2012).

One example must suffice to illustrate how a particular musical style-community or praxis can function as an affordance to facilitate and reinforce personal and musical identity formation. Drawing from the research of Wolfe, Loy, & Chidester (2009), cited below, we posit that recordings of popular songs are affordances that:

> … can influence the on-going process of listener identity construction, because these texts present characters that rhetorically invite listener identification. The more a song character's values invite the listener to think they accord with the listener's val-ues, the more likely the listener will identify with that character—and with the iden-tity or cultural identification that the listener is invited to assign to that character. If the listener does identify with a character inscribed in a musical text, then that text may be said to have helped construct, reinforce, modify, or in some other way shape the identity of the listener. (p. 74)

Of course, numerous details of any song's musical structure, its performance, and the personalities of the performers are directly and/or indirectly communicated and felt determinants (or modifiers) of a listener's conscious and non-conscious dispositions to:

- Identify with the piece or style of the recorded song.
- Embody and enact the song to maintain his or her personal, musical, and other identities.
- Maintain or modify attributes of the song to make it "fit" his or her personal and musical memories.

Turino (1999) agrees: "musical [texts] signify our personal and collective experiences in a particularly direct manner. They are 'really' attached to events and aspects of our lives, and hence are experienced as real; they are signs of our lives, not signs about them" (p. 236). He continues: "Music can help construct or maintain identity, because it is experienced as *truth*" (p. 238).

Let us propose another way people may construct (non-consciously) their musical, personal, social, cultural, gendered, and other identities. That is, and following from our philosophical view of personhood, it may be that specific persons and/or groups of people perceive and feel "their musics" as opportunities for identity development because they—or we—do something close to what we do when we *constitute others as persons*, when we invest others with personhood. It may be that during the processes of responding to (and/or making) specific kinds of vocal and instrumental music—and responding to music makers who sing and play music that moves us emotionally—we are engaging in something like an *ethical idealization of the other*: the piece and/or performance becomes an-other because *we make it so*. We may be interpreting the music holistically and humanistically—with *a principle of charity* that makes the music feel like a person who is similar to ourselves, or who is, in fact, our *self*. Put another way, it may be that we *make it true* that a specific piece or musical-social event possesses the musical equivalent of personhood, in which case we, henceforth, embody and make that music part of our autobiographical personal-musical identities and selfhood.

A person's accumulation of lifetime memories—including their musical memories— contributes profoundly to the development of her autobiographical self. Our autobiographical selves underpin our identities: "life without memory is no life at all … our memory is our coherence, our reason, our feeling, even our action. Without it, we are nothing" (LeDoux, 2002, p. 133). Affordances are among the various tools we use to form memories and construct our autobiographical selves and identities, including our musical identities. By means of memories, we identify our*selves* with specific pieces, styles, instruments, and voices, and important personal–social landmarks in our lives. Memories, including significant musical memories, are the glue that holds together our individual and collective identities. However, the personal and musical identities we are consciously aware of are not the entirety of what "identity" refers to. There is something deeper at work—our embodied non-conscious life. LeDoux (2002) agrees: recent research in social psychology indicates that many important aspects of identity formation, "social behavior, including decision-making as well as the way we react to members of racial and ethnic groups," are mediated non-consciously (p. 134).

2.5 CONCLUSION: MUSICAL IDENTITIES AND MUSICAL PRAXES

Discussions of musical identities and music in/for musical identity formation range across a broad spectrum of topics, including, for example:

- The origins of musical identities in infancy.
- Students' perceptions of themselves as musical or non-musical.
- Differences between/among adolescents' perceptions of their in-school and out-of-school musical identities.
- Musical identity construction associated with singing, playing specific instruments, composing, and/or new music technologies.
- The role of musical preferences in the formation of non-musical identities (e.g., gender identity).
- Differences among local, regional, national, and global musics and musical identities.

Notwithstanding the richness of the current and ever-growing research literatures on musical identity, it seems fair to suggest that the majority of scholarship tends to assume that "music is a good thing," and, therefore, that musical identity construction—in and of itself—is always or usually positive and ethical. However, are all instances of music-making, music listening, and musical identity formation "good things"? Probably not. If so, then researchers have a major role to play in theorizing and operationalizing what we might call "the ethics of musical identity construction." The latter would include examining the "hidden ethics," and lack thereof, in different kinds of musics and in the actions of different music makers, listeners, contexts, affordances, teachers, and community musicians. Before offering some concluding remarks on "a foundation for ethical musical identity formation," let us consider examples of the opposite, which serve to remind us how easily musics and musical identity construction can be corrupted.

Bohlman (2003) asserts that:

the twentieth century witnessed unprecedented levels of human destruction and death, and music, too, was present in unprecedented ways at moments of massive violence and death. Music ... was a participant in the cultural work of persecution and genocide ... Music mobilized the fascism and racism of the Nazis. (p. 53)

Indeed, school and community music education programs played a central role in the indoctrination and dehumanization of children and adolescents in the "Hitlerjugend" (HJ, or Hitler Youth) and the "Bund Deutscher Mädel" (BDM, or League of German Girls). Nazi songbooks, choirs, and choral singing were tools of social and emotional bonding and pride among the HJ and the BDM. From this perspective, the "products" of Nazi music "education"—meaning musical–personal–social identity formation developed in or through Nazi music-making, music listening, and musical–social bonding—were cornerstones of the Nazi war machine, the atrocities of the SS, and the Holocaust (see http://holocaustmusic.ort.org/politics-and-propaganda/third-reich/music-hitler-youth/). Similarly, says Bohlman, "'Skinhead music' and 'Oi' thrived in the subculture of the radical right during the 1990s" (p. 54) and played a key role in fomenting violence against minorities.

True, these are horrific examples of musical identity construction, but we must not overlook the fact that other instances and types of "musical identity abuse" still exist. Indeed, musical identity formation is open to corruptions of all kinds, and whether these corrupting forces continue depends on many variables, which are often beyond our control. Considering what we have just said about why and how the Nazis deliberately, directly, and "successfully" abused music and young people's musical identity formation for evil purposes, it is clear that the responsibility for ensuring *positive* and *ethical* musical identity formation rests on the shoulders of people who have the most frequent and direct access to music makers and listeners of all ages, abilities, and preferences: *ethical music makers, school music teachers, and community musicians of all kinds*.

How might we facilitate the construction of ethical musical identities? Where do we begin? We posit that the first step involves thinking deeply and critically about the values of musics and musical processes toward developing a philosophy or philosophies of musical identity formation, music education, and community music. Beginning with philosophical perspectives may be objectionable to some psychologists who study musical identity. Our response to such objections is that there are "philosophies of" all scholarly and practical pursuits: philosophy of mind, medicine, law, education, science, and so forth, ad infinitim. Why should it be any different for studies of musical identity? Logically prior to all forms of investigation in our domain(s) are careful probes of one's fundamental assumptions about and basic concepts of music(s), music education (in the broadest sense), and "identity."

With this in mind, we propose that a praxial philosophy of music education (e.g., Elliott & Silverman, 2015) has the potential to provide logical foundations and pragmatic principles for ensuring that the facilitation of people's musical and personal identity development is ethical and beneficial in many ways. For example, a praxial philosophy argues that people should not simply learn to sing, play, conduct, listen, compose, and so forth—after all, many Nazis could carry out one or more of these musical actions very well (e.g., Herbert von Karajan). Rather, implicit in being ethical musical mentors is our responsibility to make sure that people's involvements in any form of music-making and/or listening include *critically reflective thinking-and-doing for the positive transformation of people's everyday lives and situations*. A praxial orientation focuses on:

- The why–what–how–where–when of effective, democratic, and ethical informal and/or formal education in, about, and through all forms of music-making—including performing, improvising, composing, arranging, conducting/leading, music and dancing, musical therapeutic participations, etc.
- Empowering people to make and listen to music with an "ethic of care"—care for individuals and their communities.

As we explain in detail elsewhere (Elliott & Silverman, 2015), a praxial philosophy is guided by musical mentors' informed and ethical dispositions to "act truly and rightly," with continuous concern for protecting and advancing human well-being.

From this viewpoint, musical mentors who are *only* concerned with teaching music-making techniques, or organizing community music groups, or teaching information about music (and so forth) are not engaged in praxis and praxial musical identity formation. To promote socially constructive and ethical musical and personal identity formation, musical mentors of all kinds must harness musical affordances with a conscious commitment to an *"ethic of care"* and care-guided actions.

A central humanistic purpose of musical involvements is to pursue what Aristotle and many other philosophers consider the highest human values: a "good" life of flourishing, well-being, fellowship, virtue, and happiness for the benefit of oneself *and* others. All these values can be summarized by one word: *eudaimonia*. Providing that we conceptualize and engage with musics as musical *praxes*—a "move" that emphasizes the critically reflective and ethical dimensions of music-making and listening—all forms of music-making offer numerous opportunities for pursuing *eudaimonia*. In addition, if researchers and mentors examine and guide musicing and musical identity formation in relation to praxial concepts and *eudaimonia*, it is more likely that musical and personal identity construction will become central aims of informal and formal school and community music programs.

References

Aporic. (2013). Online forum comment on Marcus, G. 2013. A map for the future of neuroscience. *The New Yorker*, 17 September. Available at: http://www.newyorker.com/online/blogs/elements/2013/09/mapping-the-future-of-neuroscience.html (accessed February 2, 2016).

Aristotle. (1941). *Basic works of Aristotle*. Richard McKeon (Ed.). New York: Random House.

Austin, J. L. (1962). *How to do things with words: The William James lectures delivered at Harvard University in 1955*. J. O. Urmson *(Ed.)*. Oxford: Clarendon.

Blakeslee, S., & Blakeslee, M. (2007). *The body has a mind of its own*. New York: Random House.

Bohlman, P. (2003). Music and culture: historiographies of disjuncture. In: M. Clayton, T. Herbert, & R. Middleton (Eds.), *The cultural study of music*, pp. 45–56. New York: Routledge.

Bruner, J. (2009). Foreword. In: P. Rochat (Ed.) *Others in mind: self origins of self-consciousness*, p. vii. Cambridge: Cambridge University Press.

Carr, D. (2002). Personal and moral selfhood. In: A. Musschenga, W. van Haaften, & B. Spiecker (Eds.) *Personal and moral identity*, pp. 99–121. London: Kluwer.

Chappell, T. (2011). On the very idea of criteria for personhood. *Southern Journal of Philosophy*, 49(1), 1–27.

Damasio, A. (1994). *Descartes' error: emotion, reason and the human brain*. New York: Putnam.

Damasio, A. (1999). *The feeling of what happens: body and emotion in the making of consciousness*. New York: Harcourt, Brace.

Davidson, D. (1980). *Inquiries into truth and interpretation*. Oxford: Clarendon.

Davidson, J., & Good, J. (2002). Social and musical coordination between members of a string quartet: an exploratory study. *Psychology of Music*, 30, 186–201.

Dewey, J. (1929). *Experience and nature*. New York: Norton.

Di Paolo, E., Rohde, M., & De Jaegher, H. (2010). Horizons for the enactive mind: values, social interaction, and play. In: J. Stewart, O. Gapenne, & E. Di Paolo (Eds.), *Enaction: towards a new paradigm for cognitive science*, pp. 33–87. Cambridge, MA: MIT Press.

Elliott, D.J. (1995). *Music matters: a new philosophy of music education*. New York: Oxford University Press.

Elliott, D.J., & Silverman, M. (2015). *Music matters: a philosophy of music education*, 2nd edn. New York: Oxford University Press.

Gibson, J. J. (1979). *The ecological approach to visual perception.* Boston: Houghton Mifflin.

Giroux, H. (2006). Personal essay from channel surfing: racialized memories and class identities. Available at: http://www.henryagiroux.com/bio.html (accessed February 2, 2016).

Hegel, G.W.F. (2010). *The science of logic.* Cambridge: Cambridge University Press.

James, W. (1983). *The principles of psychology.* Cambridge, MA: Harvard University Press.

Johnson, M. (2006). Mind incarnate: from Dewey to Damasio. *Daedalus,* 135(3), 46–54.

Johnson, M. (2007). *The meaning of the body: aesthetics of human understanding.* Chicago: University of Chicago Press.

Kosa, R. (2012). Affordances. Eagereyes: visual and visual communication, 2, December. Available at: http://eagereyes.org/techniques/affordances (accessed February 2, 2016).

Krueger, J. (2011). Doing things with music. *Phenomenology and the Cognitive Sciences,* 10(1), 1–22.

LeDoux, J. (1996). *The emotional brain.* New York: Simon & Schuster.

LeDoux, J. (2002). *Synaptic self: how our brains become who we are.* New York: Viking.

Lieblich, A., & Josselson, R. (2013). Identity and narrative as root metaphors of personhood. In: J. Martin & M. Bickhard (Eds.), *The psychology of personhood: philosophical, historical, social-developmental, and narrative perspectives,* pp. 203–22. Cambridge: Cambridge University Press.

MacIntyre, A. (1999). *Dependent rational animals: why human beings need the virtues.* Chicago: Open Court.

Marcus, G. (2013). A map for the future of neuroscience. *The New Yorker,* 17 September 17. Available at: http://www.newyorker.com/online/blogs/elements/2013/09/mapping-the-future-of-neuro science (accessed December 10, 2013).

Martin, J., & Bickhard, M. (2013). Introducing persons and the psychology of personhood. In: J. Martin & M. Bickhard (Eds.), *The psychology of personhood: philosophical, historical, social-developmental, and narrative perspectives,* pp. 1–16. Cambridge: Cambridge University Press.

Noë, A. (2004). *Action in perception.* Cambridge, MA: MIT Press.

Noë, A. (2009). *Out of our heads.* New York: Hill and Wang.

Slack, G. (2009). You are not your brain. *Salon,* 25 March 25. Available at: http://www.salon.com/env/atoms_eden/2009/03/25/alva_noe/ (accessed on 2 February 2, 2016).

Oyama, S. (2000). *Evolution's eye: a systems view of the biology-culture divide.* Durham: Duke University Press.

Plato. (1993). *Phaedo,* transl. D. Gallop. New York: Oxford University Press.

Prinz, J. (2012). *The conscious brain.* New York: Oxford University Press.

Sanders, J.T. (1997). An ontology of affordances. *Ecological Psychology,* 9, 97–112.

Schulkin, J. (2004). *Bodily sensibility: intelligent action.* New York: Oxford University Press.

Schutz, A. (1976). Making music together: a study in social relationship. In: A. Broderson (Ed.) *Collected papers* Vol. 2, pp. 159–78. The Hague: Martinus Nijhoff.

Small, C. (1998). *Musicking.* Middletown: Wesleyan University Press.

Thompson, E. (2007). *Mind in life: biology, phenomenology, and the sciences of mind.* Cambridge, MA: Harvard University Press.

Turino, T. (1999). Signs of imagination, identity and experience: A Peircian semiotic theory for music. *Ethnomusicology,* 43(2), 221–55.

Turino, T. (2008). *Music and social life: the politics of participation.* Chicago: University of Chicago Press.

Van der Schyff, D. (2013). Music, meaning and the embodied mind: towards an enactive approach to music cognition. MA thesis, University of Sheffield.

Varela, F., Thompson, E., & Rosch, E. (1992). *The embodied mind, cognitive science and human experience.* Cambridge, MA: MIT Press.

Windsor, L., & de Bezenac, C. (2012). Music and affordances. *Musicae Scientiae,* 16(1), 102–20.

Wolfe, A., Loy, M., & Chidester, P. (2009). Mass communication and identity construction: theory and a case study of song-recordings by a popular musician. *Journalism and Communication,* 11(1), 67–113.

CHAPTER 3

···

MUSIC-ECOLOGY AND
EVERYDAY ACTION
Creating, Changing, and Contesting Identities

···

TIA DENORA

… Ah me, Agnello, how you change! Just see,
   you are already neither two nor one!

Dante, 1995, p. 167.

LET'S go to Hell, with Dante Alighieri as our guide. There, in the seventh pouch of the Eighth of Hell's nine circles, Dante describes the astonishing metamorphoses of the Florentine thieves. Three of the thieves have just realized that a fourth, their colleague Cianfa, is missing. What they do not yet realize is that Cianfa has been changed into a serpent.[1] Then one of the thieves, Agnello, is attacked by Cianfa (in his new guise as a serpent). Held in Cianfa's claws, the two are transformed into a "perverse image," simultaneously man and snake:

> Then just as if their substance were warm wax,
>   They stuck together and they mixed their colors,
>   So neither seemed what he had been before …

When Agnello and Cianfa finally part, their identities have been exchanged. The serpent (Cianfa) resumes his human identity, and the thief Agnello has transformed into a serpent. Meanwhile, a fifth thief, Cavalcanti, also in the guise of a serpent, attacks one of the other thieves, Buoso. Dante describes that second metamorphosis, once again in lurid anatomical detail. As with the first transformation, this one too culminates in an identity exchange:

---

[1] By which is meant lizard; see the reference referring to running on "all fours."

The soul that had become an animal,
  Now hissing, hurried off along the valley;
  The other one, behind him, speaks and spits.
  And then he turned aside his new-made shoulders
  And told the third soul: "I'd have Buoso run
  On all fours down this road, as I have done"

Dante, 1995, p. 169.

3.1 AFFORDANCES, APPROPRIATIONS, AND ENACTED IDENTITIES

The passages from this canto of *The Divine Comedy* that I have just quoted help to set out five key themes to be addressed in this chapter:

1. *Identities as exchangeable, tradable and stealable*: in the situation described by Dante, the identities of Agnello and Cianfa are exchanged against Agnello's will (identity theft). In this case, the thief recognized potentially valuable resources associated with the other (in this case Agnello's bodily property). He then misappropriated those resources often involving, as in this case, violence and harm.

2. *Identities are both resources and statuses*: from the point of view of the thieves and the narrator, we see how the exchange of identities involves *promotion, demotion*,[2] *and changed capabilities.* (Cavalcanti, upon recovering his original identity, stands up proudly and turns his shoulders, while Buoso scurries down the road, now on all fours.) In this regard, the theft that Dante describes highlights identities as sites of struggle and contestation. This is to say that identities imply forms of entitlement, capacity, opportunity for action, and vulnerability. In the example of Agnello and Cianfa, these things cycle and recycle as circumstances shift, as serpent bites man to become man, and as man becomes vulnerable to serpent's bite.

3. *Identities are plastic, malleable*: to say that identities are plastic is to say that they are matters in process (at which moment, precisely, did Buoso "become" the serpent?).

4. *The malleability of identities involves hybridization*: Dante shows us how parts are added and exchanged, as man becomes beast, and beast becomes man, and as both are temporarily fused into one monstrous entity.

5. *This hybridization highlights the ways that identities take shape **relationally**, produced through reference to things outside individuals*: these things outside include other people (the mutual give and take described in point 3, above),[3] but also

---

[2] I do not necessarily endorse the view that there is anything intrinsically "lesser" about serpents.

[3] In Dante, these are the victims of the body snatching. Their person and physical being offers a resource to the identity thieves. Note the parallel here to Garcin's remark in *No Exit*, "There's no need for red-hot pokers. HELL IS—OTHER PEOPLE!" (Sartre, 1944).

materials such as technologies, furnishings, and aesthetic media (e.g., one needs a road if one is to be the kind of creature who can run down a road on two feet or "upon all fours").

These five themes, in turn, help to underscore the ways in which identities can be understood to be produced, distributed, and consumed over time and space, how the plasticity of identities arises as people make and move through situations, social relations, and circumstances, as they become attached and detached from aspects of their material and symbolic environments. Drawing upon a scheme that I have used before (DeNora, 2003, 2013a), we can imagine this fusion in terms of a tripartite process:

- *Before, Time 1, identity a, b, c*: Cianfa is a serpent; he is attached or fused to certain things (bodily features).
- *During, Time 2, identity understood as: a, b, c, d, e, f*: Cianfa fuses with ("appropriates") Agnello (they make a man/serpent entity).
- *After, Time 3, identity d, e, f*: Cianfa is a man (having acquired "things" from Agnello and also become detached from other things).

If this seems too "literary" an example, too detached from "real life," consider the following version.

- *Before, Time 1, identity a, b, c*: John is flabby; he is attached or fused to certain things (bodily features and, say, doughnuts at breakfast). Near him is a rowing machine. It hurts him (makes his muscles ache) any time that attempts to use (appropriate) it.
- *During, Time 2, identity understood as: a, b, c, d, e, f*: John fuses with (appropriates) the rowing machine (he and it make a man/machine entity, repeatedly every morning from 7.15 to 7.45 am from January 1 to July 1) and stops eating doughnuts.
- *After, Time 3, identity d, e, f*: John is a muscular man (having acquired "things" from the rowing machine and also become detached from earlier practices [such as doughnut eating]). Meanwhile, the rowing machine, like Agnello, has also been transformed now, unless it is adjusted, it is no longer challenging to John, (though that might change if the machine is adjusted) and in fact its joints are often loosened in response to so much use.

In both these examples, appropriation of affordances, attachment, and detachment lead to identity change. Through these processes, identities may change in big ways ("Wow John! Look at you now! You sure have changed!"), but they may also change in ways that for all practical purposes may be imperceptible (e.g., 1 month into the rowing program, "there's something subtly different about John, but what is it?").

This perspective on identities, with its focus on attachment, plasticity, hybridity, ecology, and change offers a rich seam for the socio-musical study of identity. Theoretically, it is presaged by work within sociology, especially work in the area of science and technology studies (Gomart & Hennion, 1998; Law & Mol, 2001; Mol, 2003; Latour, 2005; Pickering, 2010). Methodologically, and taking a cue from Dante's meticulous description of Agnello described above, this perspective implies detailed, ethnographic investigations of musically-afforded metamorphoses from within the frame of their real time occurrence, in short, an "in action" perspective (DeNora, 2011) and the tripartite diagram just discussed ("before, during, after") was used to highlight the ways that change "in action" is always change "somewhere" and "in time."

To explore this seam, and after a brief discussion of sociological perspectives on musical identity, I will consider examples of liminal identities or, as Victor Turner calls them (2008[1969], p. 81), "liminal personae" or "threshold people." These are people with identities such as Agnello's, neither one thing nor the other, but are rather, disorientated, incoherent, and uncomfortably poised between, or prone to, conflicting identity statuses. While I will later describe how all identities are potentially liminal (coherent identity is, in other words, an artifact of "fit" within a cultural ecology or ecological niche), for purposes of theory development I will consider liminal identities in relation to well-being, specifically, in relation to mental dis/ability (psychosis and mental illness, dementia, cognitive impairment). I will describe how this five-part understanding of identity not only undermines the notion that identity (via the case of dis/ability) is an objective condition and thus that "how" questions of identities (i.e., a focus on processes of achievement, attribution, perception of identities (see DeNora, 2014) are, simultaneously, questions about the provenance of enablement/disablement.

How identities are resolved, then, is a traceable matter. How musical identities are enacted in real time and place is also an empirical matter, one that promises to shed quite a lot of additional light on the question of how music "helps" or can be seen to be of benefit to health and well-being. For at least two reasons, music studies is especially well equipped to address the ways in which identities are flexible and situationally performed. First, as various scholars have observed, musical tastes and practices serve as proxies for social standing, status, and lifestyle stances (Bourdieu, 1984, p. 119; Bryson, 1996; Savage, 2006). Second, scholars have described the more dynamic ways in which music is not merely a badge of social affiliation but also performs its consumer, re-mediating that consumer and her/his music simultaneously (Hennion And, 2014; 2007). In this regard, music is used by individuals (Bull, 2000, 2007; DeNora, 2000) and by organizations (DeNora, 2000, 2003; Korczsynski, 2011) to *do things* such as organize, appropriate, and generally configure identity and subjectivity in relation to situational and pragmatic circumstances, requirements, and aspirations. It is this latter perspective that I wish to explore as music can be seen to push and pull identification processes—people, selves, roles, relationships, and social situations of health and illness, capacity and incapacity.

3.2 MENTAL DIS/ABILITIES, THRESHOLD IDENTITIES

If mental capacities, and their associated identities can be seen to emerge from background practices in the social environment, then it is possible to rethink many forms of illness identity and, through this rethinking, to rethink the ontological status of illness itself. If those identities can be seen to undergo transformation, to shift, from Time B, into hybrid states and, at Time B are differently resolved, then it is possible to rethink identity as a byproduct of social situation. That re-conception simultaneously highlights the question of how environments are designed. I now present four case studies to illustrate the processes by which liminal identities form and reform, and take shape in relation to things outside of individuals and in ways that query their status as fixed property or "given" features incapable of change.

3.3   CASE STUDY 1: SINGING FOR THE BRAIN, OR SINGING TO BE TOGETHER?

This question is pursued in ethnographic research conducted by Mariko Hara (2011a,b), which examined socio-musical interaction in and around a singing group for people living with dementia, their loved ones, carers, and volunteers. Hara's work illustrates how music not only triggers people's self-conceptions, but how a situation can be musically crafted in ways that enhance togetherness and diminish the significant differences between participants that might otherwise provide the basis for the identification of cognitive impairment ("a person with dementia").

Taking a person-centered approach, Hara describes how participants (Laura and later Arnold) can be seen to undergo a kind of metamorphosis in real time:

> ... the SFTB sessions enable Laura to be a very a different person from the Laura I met outside the sessions. In the sessions she is always very confident and cheerful when interacting with others, she is alert and accurate about the words she sings and easily follows the facilitator's instructions when it comes to challenging activities such as singing in parts. It seems that SFTB sessions allow her to reconnect to the enjoyment of being with others and the joy of taking the initiative. Out of this context, she is not as cheerful or confident as in the sessions.
>
> Hara, 2011a.

Laura "becomes" a more extrovert, joyful person within the temporal and spatial, highly-crafted context of a Singing for the Brain (SFTB) session. Within that context she finds sources of enjoyment, confidence, and skill that, in other environments, elude her. It is worth noting that this point is by no means germane only to personal and cultural management of dementia. To the contrary, crafting musical environments has been shown by a growing body of researchers to be part of the care of self (DeNora, 2000) and an important part of salutogenics (Batt-Rawden, 2006; Ruud, 2008). In Laura's case, this sense of what kind of person she is or can be is emergent—it takes shape in situ—it is achieved in relation to the social, cultural, and material environment. Laura's "disability" then is also more plastic then might otherwise seem: it takes shape in relation to cues, materials, and the "somewhere" of interactive occasions where capacities are fostered or suppressed.

After her transformation, Laura no longer stands out as a "person with dementia." Instead, she becomes a "joyful person." At the same time, as Hara describes, it becomes more difficult to perceive within this group identities such as "carer" or "volunteer," and to see them as doing anything markedly different from what people like Laura are doing. In other words, the boundaries between different types of identities are broken down and are subsumed into a different type of ordering principle, singing together:

> Inside the musical community of SFTB , which encompasses a variety of ways of participating, the differences between people with and without dementia are reduced. Within this community there are a number of different relationships; care-receiver to carer, carers to carers, carers to volunteers, volunteers to volunteers, student volunteers to experienced volunteers, carers to facilitator, care-receivers to care-receivers, care-receivers to facilitator and care-receivers to volunteers. These relationships and the "whole ecology of relationship; to each other, to their context, to their culture" (Stige et al., 2010, p. 37), emerge through the shared responsibility of this very simple action: singing together.
>
> Hara, 2011b.

These occasions are not governed cultural codes, categories, rules, or images. Rather they are achieved through situated, artful practices. So, for example, Laura does not emerge as her former and more active, coherent self *simply* because she is sitting in a circle at a SFTB session, or even because she is taking part in the singing of a particular song. Rather, her renewal is achieved through something much more complicated, more "hand-crafted" by Laura and her peers:

> The way that a music therapeutic environment can affect one to become "someone else" has also been discussed in community music therapy (Ansdell, 2002). Aasgaard (2001) has talked about how song creation in a paediatric oncology ward shifted one client's role from "patient" to "song maker" or "creative person." He defines this process as an "ecological music therapy practice." This practice, in Bruscia's words, equates healthcare with the health of the social environment, "helping an individual to become healthier is not viewed as a separate enterprise from improving the health of the ecological context within which the individual lives" (Bruscia, 1998, p. 229). The SFTB sessions are planned and carried out taking the limitations and the capacities of the members with dementia into consideration; however, the sessions do not target individual behavioral or emotional problems. Rather, Jessica and around 10 volunteers attempt to craft an inclusive structure, enlivened by group singing and the various relationships between all the participants, the so-called "ecological context", which allowed Laura and Arnold to be "uninhibited" and feel confident about themselves. In other words, this carefully crafted "ecological context" offers them an opportunity to shift roles from "people with dementia" to "cheerful singers and dancers."
>
> Hara, 2011a.

Carefully crafting social situations of musical action can, in other words, offer new grounds for relating and action, new ways of perceiving people. Like the magic trick, attention is diverted from what (some) people cannot do (remember the date, the name of the Prime Minister [DeNora, 2013a]) to, through participatory activity, what they can do and are doing, which in turn is constructed in ways that give pleasure, and are enabling, to all.

While not just any music would work for this purpose (no point in attempting, for example, to learn the Mozart *Requiem*, a previous favorite of one group member who used to sing in a high-level amateur choir) and while some aesthetic negotiation is undergone to find what will suit the purpose, it is important to note that it is not the presence of music per se, but what is done with it in situ, emergently in time and in relation to other developments as they happen. This crafting, the joining together of repertoire, situated practices of introducing music, the order of play, style, and associated physical positioning/movement activities together achieve something akin to magic, a set of circumstances that—for a time—transfigure participants (all of them, not just the ones who are "living with dementia")—for a time and, in so doing enable relationships to be rekindled and enjoyed. As one participant put it, "this is when I meet 'old mum'. (…) Those moments are very important for me" (Hara, 2011, no. page number).

Hara's work allows us to see that the area of (dis)ability studies is one of the best natural laboratories for examining how, potentially always multiple, identities come to be resolved, and how this resolution also distributes forms of ability between people within social settings. More specifically, in relation to the five themes with which I began this discussion, Hara's work shows us how:

1. *Identities as exchangeable, tradable, and stealable*: the difference between people with dementia (care-receivers) and their carers (care-givers) is "reduced" during the musical event, the balance of difference is evened out such that each takes some of what, prior to engagement with music, the other "had."
2. *Identities are both resources and statuses*: now everyone has a more equal chance to be "joyful" and to be a (music-making) participant.
3. *Identities are plastic, malleable*: all participants show they are capable of change, but it is not possible to identify precise moments at which transformations occurred.
4. *The malleability of identities involves hybridization*: the participants become people-fused-with-music and music's associated activities.
5. *This hybridization highlights the ways that identities take shape **relationally**, produced through reference to things outside individuals*: these things outside include other people (others at the event and in ways that illustrate the opposite of Beckett's "hell is other people"), but also materials such as a piano, lyric sheets, material cultural features of the event (such as chairs arranged in a circle), and various socio-cultural practices (the "craft" that Hara describes in detail).

3.4 CASE STUDY 2: ANSDELL ET AL.
ON SONGS WITHOUT WORDS

Now let us consider that these five features of identity can be seen in yet another music-transformative setting, this time in the context of a one-on-one music therapy session.

> Pam hits the xylophone hard with the beaters and throws them towards the piano, which they hit, causing the piano strings to vibrate. She shouts "This fucking life!" and becomes very upset. (The therapist [Gary Ansdell] later finds out that the outburst was caused by her seeing the letter names on the xylophone spelling out abusive messages to her from an internal voice). Immediately after the blow-up the therapist encourages Pam to come to the piano, to sit beside him, and encourages her back into musical engagement again. She begins playing a few notes on the top of the piano, which leads into a short piano duet and then into shared singing with the therapist. Pam takes over the singing herself after a short time (accompanied by the therapist on the piano), becoming involved and expressive. The music seems to take her somewhere else. After the music cadences she sighs and says "That's better!" The entire episode has lasted just over four minutes.

> Ansdell, Davidson, Magee, Meehan, & Procter, 2010.

> Text extract from Ansdell et al, From "this f***ing life" to "that's better"…in four minutes: An interdisciplinary study of music therapy's "present moments" and their potential for affect modulation, Nordic Journal of Music Therapy, copyright © The Grieg Academy Music Therapy Research Centre, reprinted by permission of Taylor & Francis Ltd, www.tandfonline.com on behalf of The Grieg Academy Music Therapy Research Centre.

In this example of "live" musical participation, music can be seen as a way of being together. Here, music is a great deal more than the producing and sharing of organized sound. It involves *collaborative, interactive, literally concerted drawing together* of postures, mutual orientation, para-musical action (talk, movement, gesture, and ancillary activities, such as sitting together in Beethoven's lodgings or in a music therapy studio). It also involves materials and objects—pianos, xylophones, beaters—which may themselves be imbued with connotations, personal or historical and cultural (for example, the piano may be understood as "the instrument my father played" or as a "posh" instrument, the xylophone is associated in popular and classical musical culture with skeletons and the musical macabre). It is artful practice and it re-makes the sense of what transpires between these participants, Pam and Gary, and how each of them is involved in deploying and displaying a knack for this musical production which is the contact between them. (In this way we see how musical communicative action offers what Procter calls "proto-social capital," or a means by which people can become connected, and a foundation upon which other forms of connection can accumulate [Procter, 2011].) It could have been otherwise and that otherwise could have led to very different outcomes, short and longer term.

Through this artful practice—in this case beyond words albeit culminating in words ("that's better")— relationships are established, quickly and for a time such that all is "well" in the sense that the different aspects of this scene (talk, movement, gesture, ancillary activities, objects, and participants) are perceived as complementing, facilitating, and therefore validating each other. The little "cap" or "coda" of narrative offered by Pam is both enabled and supported by this mutual complementarity *and* enhances that complementary as it enacts a sense of "better-ness." In this sense, we can see how complex, and how minute is the artfulness of making "what happened" *in and as it is being made*, and also in this sense we can see how the sense of reality as it is made and remade is consequential. In this example, a lot happened in, seemingly, a very short time, although during this short time again we see:

1. *Identities as exchangeable, tradable, and stealable*: the marked difference between "the therapist" and "the client" is diminished and exchanged for a more egalitarian form of coupled identity—participants in a musical duet.
2. *Identities are both resources and statuses*: the identity of client is associated with "this fucking life" whereas the role of therapist is associated with an attempt to manage this identity. The activity of musicking dispenses with these trappings and effects the exchange as described in point 1.
3. *Identities are plastic and malleable*: during the activity of musicking, change occurred, but when? It is marked at the point when the client says, "That's better."
4. *The malleability of identities involves hybridization*: the participants become people-fused-with-music and music's associated activities. More specifically, on this occasion, as I have described elsewhere (DeNora, 2013c), the material/symbolic identity of person-xylophone player affords outbursts and exclamations of dissatisfaction and unease; the identity of person-piano player affords cooperation and companionship.
5. *This hybridization highlights the ways that identities take shape relationally, produced through reference to things outside individuals*: in this case through attachments to instruments, musical parameters and each other.

3.5 CASE STUDY 3: BRIGHT MUSIC

From 2006 to 2011 I was involved in a collaborative, interdisciplinary, longitudinal study of music and mental health in and around a community center for mental health known as Borough Centre for Rehabilitation, Interaction, Group Activity, Hospitality and Training (BRIGHT; Ansdell & DeNora, 2012; DeNora, 2013b; Ansdell, 2014). Designed by Gary Ansdell as a Community Music Therapy project (Pavlicevic & Ansdell, 2004), the study followed music therapy clients in weekly and twice-weekly group music sessions. (The sessions were a mixture of solo performances, group singing, and group improvisation, coupled with a tea break and informal conversation.)

We have found that making music with others provides an important resource for the paving of pathways away from the places, embodied and social situations, and identities associated with being mentally ill. At its most basic, this musicking offers distraction from care, entertainment, and occupation, but making music together, in Schutz's resonant phrase, is associated with much more than this. It affords transferrable skills of many kinds for example, taking a musical stance in a solo performance allows for identity stances to be crafted and rehearsed (DeNora, 2013b). Musicking requires coordination and self-control. It is also a hobby that adds to identity and one may point to oneself as "a musician" in ways that deliver confidence. As quasi-therapy and/or problem-solving, music offers a "safe" medium in which to explore difficult and sensitive issues ("it was only a song"). Perhaps most importantly, making music is simultaneously about making situations and remaking relations between participants. At BRIGHT, for example, Gary is as much musician as he is "therapist" and, indeed, there are musical logics that drive interaction and thus that cut across social roles and differences in ways that are capable of fostering new relations and new identities, which in turn feed back, recursively, at time B. Music, in short, changes things between people and what music does happens at a *social* level.

3.5.1   In the middle of music: resounding situation, role, and place

Among its musical activities, BRIGHT offers its members the opportunity to sing in a choir, The Bright Singers who, in the spring of 2008, gave a concert (as it happened, their first semi-professional gig) in the atrium of a large metropolitan hospital. When the concert ended, the Singers toured the hospital's wards, accompanied by the Hospital's Arts and Culture Officer.

In one of these wards were two men, one of whom was very elderly and extremely thin, seemingly very close to death. Despite his physical condition, he was attentive to the music, smiling and applauding. When the second piece ended and the Singers were preparing to move on, he made a request—did the group know and would they please sing "Swing Low, Sweet Chariot"? The group, unphased at this impromptu request (and luckily enough being familiar with the song), began to sing. The man and his ward-mate joined in with gusto:

> *Swing low, sweet chariot*
> *Coming for to carry me home,*
> *Swing low, sweet chariot,*
> *Coming for to carry me home.*
> If you get there before I do
> Tell all my friends I'm coming too …
> *Swing low, sweet chariot …*
> If I get there before you do,

I'll cut a hole and pull you through
Comin' for to carry me home.

The song has many, indeed, contradictory, connotations. Thought to have been composed in or before 1862, it is known primarily as an African-American spiritual. Its author
(Wallis Willis) was reputedly inspired by the Red River (which divides Oklahoma from
Texas), which, the story goes, reminded him of the biblical account of the River Jordan
and Elijah's transportation to Heaven in a Chariot of Fire (2 Kings 2:11). For these reasons,
it is often used at funerals and memorial services today. More generally, though, the song's
lyrics speak of passing over or moving to another side, across, as it were, a Great Divide
and, as such, "Swing Low" has been associated with other topics, in the 19th century, in
coded terms as a reference to the Underground Railroad in antebellum America. In addition, since the 1990s in the UK, it has been known as the rugby anthem for England. In
that context, the lyrics make reference to "swinging it wide to the winger" and also, more
crudely (according to the various rugby fan sites where gestures clarify ribald meanings
line-by-line), to low-swinging testicles, i.e., that the team has "large balls" [sic]. There
were, in other words, multiple meanings and registers that this song could sound, and
it could do so simultaneously. What, then, did this music do, at this time and for whom?
I suggest that, like the contradictions associated with the song's meaning, singing in the
ward was itself associated with "productive" forms of contradictions.

One of the first of these contradictions was the way it transformed the physical space
of the hospital ward. Hospitals are often replete with sound, and not always or even usually desired sound from the patient perspective (Rice, 2013), but they are less often places
where live musical sounds are heard, despite increasing evidence that music in hospitals is considered by patients, carers, and their families to be beneficial (Batt-Rawden,
Trythall, & DeNora, 2007). Singing reclaimed the ward space as a multi-purpose space; it
reappropriated that space as one for making music, and the sheer incongruity of making
music there was in itself a pleasure. The ward, suddenly noisy, indeed, boisterous, was resounded. There was obvious pleasure all around associated with the surprising new use
of the ward and the sounds of life normally excluded from medical settings. Music's presence in the ward contradicted the work-a-day connotations of the ward as a type of space.

A second contradiction was more musically specific. This was not just "any" music.
Here, the music's topic, its setting, its style (call and response format), and its performers
were refracted through each other and in ways that musically underscored an intense
and seemingly contradictory cluster of topics and emotions—a "great divide," being
swept up into the other world and "carried home," or even just "going home" as in being
discharged from the hospital, team spirit, and mutual aid, ("I'll cut a hole and pull you
through"), robust and ribald, boisterous singing (of a rugby tune), bittersweet reflections on death and dying, playful musical collaboration, sacred communion through the
sharing of this music in this place. Like play therapy or techniques used with children
in difficult courtroom testimony, music can offer a "safe" medium in which to explore
difficult issues. Unlike the plastic arts, and certainly unlike literature, however, music's
semiotic content is slippery: even with lyrics, as in the case of "Swing Low," music

affords different and sometimes contradictory stances to its performers/listeners. And because a song can, at any time, be set aside as "just something being played at," it is easy to get out of "trouble" if things become fraught, easier, for example, than having to talk oneself out of "going too far."

A third contradiction, linked to the specific dynamic between "audience" and "performer" on this occasion, was social. The Singers, of course, are people living with and recovering from acute and enduring mental health problems, and not, for the most part, trained musicians. On this occasion, their first semi-professional performance, concert performance was new and involved taking risks. Their main performance in the atrium had been successful and the irony had not been lost on them when, mingling with the audience afterward, someone happened to ask if they were doctors and nurses from the hospital. So it was with renewed confidence that they went out on to the wards and it was perhaps for this reason that they so ably rose to the occasion of offering a "request," perhaps even one of the last requests that this man in the bed would make. As such, their own identities were transfigured. They were not a "mental health choir," and they were more than a "choir": they were ministering to the needs and requests of others. They were musical carers and their position was yet sweeter due to these dual or multiple identities, and multiple forms of vulnerability, both revealed and concealed.

Conversely, the men in the ward were no longer patients per se; they became audience members and then, with "Swing Low," members of the choir. Via music, in other words, they were enrolled into a new activity, and thus at least temporarily diverted from where they "were" a moment earlier. They were active in a way that literally allowed their voices to be heard. Watching from the side lines (holding the coats, cameras, and tape recorder), I chatted afterward with some of the nursing aids and hospital orderlies. While all concerts of live music in the wards were lovely, they said, and welcomed as much by the staff as by the patients. Indeed, they said that the concerts facilitated communication between patients and staff, and equally importantly according to one nurse, between nurses and doctors, providing an occasion for bonding. This concert, the nurse told me (who did not know the history of the Bright Singers), was if anything extra special because the choir was more homely and personal, less professionally distant in its performing role (and thus more "accessible"—not all musicians were asked to sing "requests" and not all audiences/patients were drawn in to the musical event in the role of co-performer).

Brought together in mutual performance, this was no longer a situation "about" some mental health clients and their concertizing success any more than it was about some men in a ward for the terminally ill. Both of those "stories" (narratives) were yesterday's news. In the new *now*, the story was about what these people were now doing together and the meanings, actions and transformations rendered through their joint activity. As Simon Procter (2011) has put it, music-making generates a kind of proto-social, expressly musical form of capital and here, in this ward, these participants were arguably binding themselves together, at least for a time, in ways that were musically mediated and musically articulated. However, within this musical frame, simultaneously, was the possibility to bridge and bond around other things, whether shared human condition, mutual support, or perhaps even, for some, a love of English rugby.

In short, here, in the middle of music, there are a lot of good things that music can do, a lot of potential affordances for well-being and sociability, and in this sense what music does in relation to health and well-being is not dissimilar to what music does in relation to forms of social agency and consciousness/perception in other life realms, where it has been documented as getting into action. It is also from within this middle that it is possible to propose an emergent ontology for *both* music and mental health. In this situation, simultaneously, both the music and the relational identities of the musickers were performed and transformed—who, where, and what both music and these people were at Time 1 was resounded at Time 2 (the time in the middle) through musical activity, and in ways that, at Time 3, i.e., after the music stopped, after we left the ward, reconfigured both music and its agents. It is the complexity and potential flexibility of both music and illness/wellness that is the health resource and that resourcefulness of music is produced, literally, in concert. Music is not a stimulus, health is not a static state, and health/illness, dis/ability identities can be seen to be plastic or malleable according to the contextualizing conditions to which they are attached.

3.6 CASE STUDY 4: LIFE AT END OF LIFE

Conditions associated with illness can, in short, be linked to varying identities and music can be used as an ecological resource for identity transformation. I have so far presented three case studies, each of which highlights the emergent features of identity and their connection to musical arrangements. Each of these cases dealt with a form of identity that was initially "problematic" (i.e., linked to statuses that are hailed as in need of repair, help, or disability) and each illustrated how identities can be transformed, or perhaps more accurately, transcended, through joint musical activity. I will now present a fourth and final case, an end of life identity. I will also describe how considering this question helps to develop an ontology of music as, itself, an emergent and temporally situated object, figured in and through use, and thus an understanding of the realities of both music and identity as created through artful practice (DeNora, 2014).

To speak of health states as con/fused identities is to say that they are, ontologically, no different from seemingly more "ordinary," everyday "healthy" identities insofar as, and depending upon how they are coupled with other things, they are also subject to change. Even the seemingly most definite of health/illness identities—being gravely ill—is subject to re-fusion, at least in some respects. That is, the "facts" associated with end of life—its meaning, the definition of the situation, the sense—potentially—of being well despite being in the process of dying, are, in other words, negotiable. Their statuses depend upon, as in the examples above, the interrelations between people, practices and things. For example:

2005: S was, when young, a graceful and exuberant dancer and an athlete (skating, swimming). She is now suffering from a degenerative physical disease and has started to shy away from social interaction outside the family circle [S was at this time roughly 1 year away from her death]. She recently discovered the music of André Rieu, after a television broadcast of one of Rieu's concerts [Rieu was all the rage in the USA at this time and the programs continue to be broadcast on the American Public Television Network]. S has always adored "classical music," ballet, and ice dancing (Swan Lake, Debussy, Skater's Waltz, Scheherazade). S is thrilled and energised even by talking about Rieu's renditions of her favorite music, describing how "wonderful" the music was, how warm, personal and enthusiastic Rieu seemed as a violinist/conductor and particularly how "the audience was dancing in the aisles." A new programme of Rieu's concerts is aired on public television. S and S's family watch it together. As the music plays, S smiles and taps the arm of a chair in rhythm, and speaks about reliving embodied memories of "good times"—in this case the joy of moving to music. (In earlier days, S would have jumped up and waltzed around the room, probably drawing in her daughter as a partner to the dance.) Following a forty year feature of family culture (rubbing her mother's feet while watching TV), S's daughter is squeezing S's feet which, half-jokingly, she starts to do in time with the music (ONE two three, ONE two three …) and they discuss how the music makes you just want to jump up and dance to it.

DeNora, 2012.

I have described elsewhere (DeNora, 2012) how, in this example it is possible to see how music makes social connection sustainable. As an aesthetic practice, music-making together (in this case through synchronized activity in front of the televised concert) can recall and reclaim old identities (S as a dancer, S and her daughter's shared history). Also here, as with the examples from Hara and the Bright singers, music evens out the playing field of action, and identity in and through the ways it is received—sitting down, finger tapping, foot squeezing. Between these two participants lay nearly 40 years and yet in this moment of socio-musical activity they were equal and they met as equals and together remembered S in the old days. Music and the ways it enlisted the body (movements and actions), and in this case embodied memory, did things that verbal reminiscence alone probably could not have done. Once again we see the five features of identity (exchangeable, status linked, plastic, hybridized, relational) in the process of this transformation.

3.7 CONCLUSION: MUSICAL FUSIONS

The four examples considered in this chapter highlight how identities are emergent statuses and how they depend upon five key features:

1. Identities are exchangeable, tradable, and stealable.
2. Identities are both resources and statuses.

3. Identities are plastic and malleable.
4. The malleability of identities involves hybridization.
5. This hybridization highlights the ways that identities take shape *relationally*, produced through reference to things outside individuals.

We have also seen some of the ways that music can be invaluable for identity transformation, in particular for creating a level playing field for interaction, in supporting identities of ability and apparent agency, and in dispelling potentially threatening identities associated with illness, disability, isolation, anxiety, and grave illness. We have also seen how musical forms of interaction highlight the moral economy of identity assignment and thus the ethical character of musical, and aesthetic action more widely. Finally, we have seen, through the prism of musical interactions, some of the ways that identities emerge and are altered in action, in real time and place. While I have specifically chosen to focus on so-called threshold identities, or cases where identity is precarious and associated with difficult matters (illness, stigma, distress) it should be clear that the lessons taken from these liminal identities apply to identity formation writ large—and to music's role in that process. In extremis, as in everyday life, we use music, and cleave to music, to effect transformation, to suffuse and infuse identities, and to refuse and confuse unwanted or uncomfortable identities. Music is, in short, a valuable ecological affordance when used with, and for, care.

References

Aasgaard, T. (2001). Song creations with children who have cancer: process and meaning. PhD thesis, Aalbord University. Available at: http://vbn.aau.dk/files/195251818/trygve_aasgaard_thesis_150909.pdf (accessed August 31, 2013).

Ansdell, G. (2014). *How music helps: In music therapy and everyday life.* Farnham: Ashgate Publishing.

Ansdell, G., Davidson, J., Magee, W., Meehan, J., & Procter, S. (2010). From "this f***ing life" to "that's better"... in four minutes: An interdisciplinary study of music therapy's "present moments" and their potential for affect modulation. *Nordic Journal of Music Therapy*, 19, 3–28.

Ansdell, G., & DeNora T. (2012). Musical flourishing: community music therapy, controversy, and the cultivation of wellbeing. In: R. MacDonald, G. Kreutz, & L. Mitchell (Eds.) *Music, health and wellbeing*, pp. 97–112. Oxford: Oxford University Press.

Batt-Rawden, K. (2006). Music: A strategy to promote health in rehabilitation? An evaluation of participation in a 'Music and Health Promotion Project'. *International Journal of Rehabilitation Research*, 29(2), 171–3.

Batt-Rawden, K., Trythall, S., & DeNora, T. (2007). Health musicking as cultural inclusion. In: J. Edwards (Ed.), *Music: promoting health and creating community in healthcare*, pp. 64–83. Cambridge: Scholars Press.

Bourdieu, P. (1984). *Distinction: social critique of the judgement of taste.* Cambridge, MA: Harvard University Press.

Bryson, B. (1996). Anything but heavy metal: symbolic exclusion and musical dislikes. *American Sociological Review*, 61, 884–99.

Bull, M. (2000). *Sounding out the city*. London: Bergh.

Bull, M. (2007). *Sound moves: iPod culture and urban experience*. London: Routledge.

Dante, A. (1995). *The Divine Comedy*, transl. A. Mandelbaum. London: Everyman's Library, Knopf.

DeNora, T. (2000). *Music in everyday life*. Cambridge: Cambridge University Press.

DeNora, T. (2003). *After Adorno: Rethinking music sociology*. Cambridge: Cambridge University Press.

DeNora, T. (2011). *Music in action: Selected essays in sonic ecology*. Farnham: Ashgate Publishing.

DeNora, T. (2012). Resounding the Great Divide: music in everyday life at the end of life. *Mortality*, 17(2), 92–105.

DeNora, T. (2013a). Time after time: a quali-t method for assessing music's impact on well-being. *International Journal of Qualitative Studies of Health and Well-being*, 8, 20611.

DeNora, T. (2013b). *Music asylums: wellbeing through music in everyday life*. Farnham: Ashgate Publishing.

DeNora, T. (2013c). Music and talk in tandem. The production of micro-narratives in real time. In: E. Ruud, L. O. Bonde, M. Strand Skånland, & G. Trondalen (Eds), *Musical life stories. Narratives on health musicking*, pp. 165–80. Trondheim: Akademika forlag.

DeNora, T. (2014). *Making sense of reality: Culture and perception in everyday life*. London: Sage.

Gomart, E., & Hennion, A. (1998). A sociology of attachment: music amateurs, drug users. In: J. Hassard & J. Law (Eds.) *ANT and after*, Sociological Review Monograph, pp. 220–47. Oxford: Blackwell.

Hara, M. (2011a). Expanding a care network for people with dementia and their carers through musicking: participant observation with "Singing for the Brain." *Voices: A World Forum for Music Therapy*, 11(2). Available at: https://normt.uib.no/index.php/voices/rt/printerFriendly/570/459 (accessed February 2013).

Hara, M. (2011b). Music in dementia care: increased understanding through mixed research. *Music and Arts in Action*, 3(2), 34–58.

Hennion, A. (2014). *The passion for music: A sociology of meditation*. Farnham: Ashgate Publishing.

Korczsynski, M. (2011). Stayin' alive on the factory floor: an ethnography of the dialectics of music use in the routinized workplace. *Poetics*, 39, 87–106.

Latour, B. (2005). *Re-assembling the social: An introduction to actor network theory*. Oxford: Oxford University Press.

Law, J., & Mol, A. (2001). Situating technoscience: an inquiry into spatialities. *Society and Space*, 19, 609–21.

Mol, A. (2003). *The body multiple: Ontology in medical practice*. Durham: Duke University Press.

Pavlicevic, M., & Ansdell, G. (2004). *Community music therapy*. London: Jessica Kingsley.

Pickering, A. (2010). *The cybernetic brain: Sketches of another future*. Chicago: University of Chicago Press.

Procter, S. (2011). Reparative musicing: thinking on the usefulness of social capital theory within music therapy. *Nordic Journal of Music Therapy*, 20(3), 242–62.

Rice, T. (2013). *Hearing and the hospital: Sound, listening, knowledge and experience*. Hertford: Sean Kingston Publishing.

Ruud, E. (2008). Music in therapy: increasing possibilities for action. *Music and Arts in Action*, 1(1), 46–60.

Sartre, J.P. (1944). No exit. Available at: http://archive.org/stream/NoExit/NoExit_djvu.txt (accessed February 2, 2016).

Savage, M. (2006). The musical field. *Cultural Trends*, 2–3, 159–74.

Turner, V. (1969/2008). *The ritual process: Structure and anti-structure*. New Brunswick NJ: Aldine Transaction.

CHAPTER 4

···

FROM SMALL STORIES

Laying the Foundations for Narrative Identities
In and Through Music

···

MARGARET S. BARRETT

4.1 INTRODUCTION

THE last decade has witnessed a burgeoning of interest and research activity in the theoretical and practical applications of identity theory to music and music education. Researchers have explored topics as diverse as:

- The delineation between Identities in Music (IIM) and Music in Identities (MII) (Hargreaves, Miell, & MacDonald, 2002; Hargreaves, MacDonald, & Miell, 2012; MacDonald, Hargreaves, & Miell, 2015).
- The distinctions between professional identities and motivations for musician/ performers, musician/music teachers, and musician/therapists (Hargreaves et. al., 2007; Pellegrino, 2009; Juuti & Littleton, 2010; Baker & MacDonald, 2013; Preti & Welch, 2013;).
- The emergence of music teacher identities (Ballantyne et al., 2012; Draves, 2014).
- Musical identities in infants (Barrett, 2011), school-aged children (Borthwick & Davidson, 2002; Lamont, 2002; Pitts, 2014) and adolescents, in and beyond the school setting (Campbell, Connell & Beegle, 2007; Baker, 2012; Gardikiotis & Baltzis, 2012; Cleaver & Riddle, 2014).
- The roles of music in cultural (O'Hagin & Harnish, 2006; Karlsen, 2013) and national (Folkestad, 2002; Winston & Witherspoon, 2015) identities.

Amidst this plethora of research less is known about the *beginnings* of musical identities. This may be attributed in part to the apparent difficulties of undertaking research with infants and young children due to language constraints, issues of access, and prevailing perceptions concerning children's capacity to communicate thoughts and feelings. Research work in identity theory has been intimately connected to language as researchers have sought to elicit and analyze verbal accounts of how individuals and groups describe their beliefs, perceptions, and practices in and through music. Clearly, such an approach with infants and young children is problematic. However, when consideration is given to the notion that identities are performed as well as told, that narration of self may be enacted as well as spoken (Wortham, 2001), the investigative possibilities are expanded. Specifically, through the investigation and analysis of the ways in which infants and young children act and interact musically with self and others we may begin to understand the ways in which they develop musical identities and draw on music as a resource for self and world-making.

Research indicates that young children evidence a cultural understanding well before the age of 5 (Rogoff, 2003; Trevarthen, 2002; Trevarthen & Malloch, Chapter 9, "The musical self: affections for life in a community of sound"). These understandings emerge through the rich interplay between the developing child and the home and community environments (at micro-, meso-, exo-, and macro-levels) in which children live (Rogoff, 2003). Any cultural understanding necessarily involves an understanding of the self, and the relationships that hold between the self and the multiple factors of people, places, objects, environments, and events the young child encounters. For example, the family plays a major role in shaping early identity work through:

- The roles that are assigned to the child in relationship with parents, carers, siblings, and the extended environments of family and friends.
- The rituals of communication and interaction that are afforded in these relationships.
- The shared stories and codes of conduct that are constructed with the child.

Beyond the family unit, encounters with the environments of the church, childcare center, playground, and early learning programs, including music early learning programs (MELPs) constitute further shaping forces in identity work. Music is often an ubiquitous presence in the relationships, rituals, and environments outlined above; paradoxically, its role as a resource or technology of self (DeNora, 2000) for the young child is often ignored or misunderstood.

The chapter will examine the ways in which children draw on music to establish themselves in the socio-cultural spheres of home, extended family and friends, and other socio-cultural settings (such as religious observance, playgroups, festivals, and events). Children's identities in these settings are multiple and flexible (the youngest child in playgroup, the oldest sibling in the family) and music is often employed as both a process in which identity/ies are constructed and a vehicle by which these are told to self and others. Specifically, the chapter will explore the ways in which young children draw on music as a means of narrating identities both in and through music.

In what follows I shall first examine views of narrative as a means of both constructing identity and "telling" identity to self and others. This discussion presents the theoretical perspectives of "big" and "small" stories, and considers the ways in which these perspectives might inform our understandings of the ways in which young children construct and "tell" identity in and through music. Subsequently, I shall examine the ways in which young children's early song and music-making may be viewed as "small" stories, which young children use as both a means of constructing and "telling" identity to self and others.

4.2 Narrative and identity work

Narrative research draws on the stories individuals and groups tell about themselves and others as a means to understand the complex phenomena that comprise human experience. Bruner's work as a narrative theorist and psychologist has been particularly influential in developing an understanding of the role of narrative in human thought and action (1986, 1987, 1990, 1996, 2002, 2006, 2008). Bruner suggests that to narrate a life story is more than the direct expression of an internal state, rather, it is a cognitive and interpretive feat. Such a view emphasizes the role of memory, the selective nature of recollection, and the ways in which narratives are subject to "cultural, interpersonal, and linguistic influences" (Bruner, 1987, p. 14). Crucially, Bruner suggests here that stories are both *lived* and told, that "... narrative imitates life, life imitates narrative" (1987, p. 13); in short, that we may enact the narratives we tell about ourselves as a means to trial different ways of being (see also Wortham, 2001).[1]

Historically, narrative data are autobiographical, recount past events, and tend to be episodic in nature. In research, the narrative interview seeks to elicit rich accounts of individuals' life stories and provide a means for individuals to fashion a version of themselves and their life experiences. Through the lenses of how, what, when, where, and to whom individuals tell accounts of themselves and their life experiences, narrative researchers strive to understand the nature and uses of identity work. As Bamberg & Georgakopoulou assert,

> The guiding assumption here is that stories are privileged forms/structures/systems for making sense of self by bringing the coordinates of time, space, and personhood into a unitary frame so that the sources "behind" these representations (such as "author", "teller", and "narrator") can be made empirically visible for further analytical scrutiny in the form of "identity" analysis.
>
> 2008, p. 378.

The assumption that narratives provided as face-to-face interactions ensure privileged access to "an interior authentic self" has been challenged on a number of grounds (Atkinson & Delamont, 2006, p. 166). Atkinson and Delamont remind us that:

- There are many narrative forms beyond the face-to-face interview.
- Narratives are performative and are used to establish status and authority amongst other functions.

[1] Sandra Stauffer (2014) provides an overview of the ways in which music education researchers have drawn on the work of Bruner and others in designing narrative inquiry in the field.

- Narratives can *"create* the realities they purport to describe" (Atkinson & Delamont, 2006, p. 167).

These authors urge researchers to practice some methodological skepticism to ensure that the social context, action, and interaction are recognized as shaping forces in the narrative work. It should be noted that despite their reservations, Atkinson and Delamont affirm the potential for narrative research to provide insight into issues of identity. Their observations concerning narrative research are pertinent to this discussion as they open up for consideration narrative forms beyond those of the face-to-face interview. Specifically, they recommend consideration of narratives afforded through new technologies and performative narrative forms such as "ballet, opera, and serious literature" (Atkinson, 2006). In this chapter I present the view that young children's generative/performative musical practice, specifically that of invented song-making (Barrett, 2006, 2011) may be considered a narrative form in which they undertake identity work.

4.3 BIG AND SMALL STORIES
IN NARRATIVE DATA

Increasingly, distinction is being made between "big" and "small" stories in narrative research (Bamberg, 2004; Freeman, 2006; Georgakopoulou, 2006; Bamberg & Georgakopoulou, 2008). Big stories in narrative research are those "prototypical narrative(s)" that include "… personal, past experience stories of non-shared events" (Georgakopoulou, 2006, p. 123). These narratives include "… life stories, autobiographies, short-range stories of landmark events" (Bamberg & Georgakopoulou, 2008) and tend to feature character, place, time, and event with a clear beginning, middle, and end structure (Ochs & Capps, 2001). They are told with a particular audience in mind (e.g., the self, researcher, and consumers of research texts), and in a context (the research interview) that shapes particular ways of telling, and re-telling. For Freeman, through narrative reflection, big stories provide a "distance" from the "now" that enables us to move "beyond the confines of the moment" (2006, p. 136). He asserts that neither small nor big stories

> … have privileged access to the "truth". Rather they tell about different regions of experience, one that involves the quotidian workaday world of incidents and exchanges, of routine talk about this or that, and another that involves a kind of holiday, in which one takes time to consider what it is that's been going on.
>
> Georgakopoulou, 2006, p. 137.
> Text extract from Alexandra Georgakopoulou, Thinking big with small stories in narrative and identity analysis in Narrative Inquiry (16.1), Copyright © 2006 John Benjamins Publishing Company with permission from John Benjamins Publishing Company.

In this way he seeks to demonstrate the need for both big and small stories in narrative research.

Small stories by contrast to big stories are described as

> … tellings of on-going events, … allusions to tellings, deferrals of tellings, and refus-
> als to tell. These tellings are typically small …

2006, p. 123.

Small stories tend to be located in the present or near future, and, in the case of the latter, may

> … become rehearsals for later action more than reconstructions of the past; they are
> more about imagining the future than about remembering the past.

Georgakopoulou, 2006, p. 127.
Text extract from Alexandra Georgakopoulou, Thinking big
with small stories in narrative and identity analysis in Narrative Inquiry (16.1),
Copyright © 2006 John Benjamins Publishing Company with
permission from John Benjamins Publishing Company.

To elaborate:

> Small stories can be about very recent ("this morning," "last night") or still unfolding
> events, thus immediately reworking slices of experience and arising out of a need to
> share what has just happened or seemingly uninteresting tidbits. They can be about
> small incidents that may (or may not) have actually happened, mentioned to back up
> or elaborate on an argumentative point occurring in on-going conversation. Small
> stories can even be about—colloquially speaking—"nothing;" as such, they indi-
> rectly reflect something about the interactional engagement between the interact-
> ants, while for outsiders, the interaction is literally "about nothing."

Bamberg & Georgakopoulou, 2008, pp. 381–2.

Significantly, small stories emerge from an interactional context of the present in which the researcher is largely an on-looker or eaves-dropper in the process, rather than an active participant. As such, small stories are a product of a social practice (including mediational tools such as text-messaging, emails; Georgakopoulou, 2006), rather than a formal research interview. As a consequence, the orginators of the concept of "small stories," Bamberg and Georgakopoulou, focus on "stories in interaction," rather than facilitated monologues to interrogate identity issues for the individual (Bamberg, 2011).

4.4 THE USES OF SMALL STORIES
IN IDENTITY WORK

Researchers who focus on small stories are interested in the function and uses of these phenomena (as a psychological tool for exploring identity) in identity work as much as what these stories tell about the individual's representations of self and their worlds (as a singular representation of identity). Specifically, the focus on small stories as "narratives-in-interaction," rather than singular big stories, provides opportunity to explore the function of small stories as "… sites of engagement where identities are continuously practiced and tested out" (Bamberg & Georgakopoulou, 2008, p. 379). For example, in an analysis of talk between a group of adolescent boys (aged 10–15) Bamberg and Georgakopoulou demonstrate how the telling of a "small story" about another (third person) provides an opportunity for the teller to undertake "rhetorical work through story-telling" in a process that involves putting forth arguments, challenging views, and constantly attuning the story as it unfolds (p. 383). Consequently, small stories can be told through second (interactional) and third person (stories of others) narratives, through which individuals shape and re-shape the perspectives presented (Bamberg, 2011) and negotiate aspects of identity. This establishment of a "referential (third person) world" in concert with "remembering, thinking, introspecting, and at times … of reflecting" becomes a narrative space in which ideas, beliefs, values, etc., can be trialed and reviewed. Such uses of small stories in identity work provide a further contrast with the generation and presentation of big stories in identity work in their focus on future possibilities for thought and action, as well as the re-viewing and re-negotiation of past experience.

4.5 MUSICAL IDENTITIES

In the first major collection of studies on the topic of musical identities the editors, MacDonald, Hargreaves, & Miell (2002) proposed a "conceptual distinction" between *identities in music* (IIM) and *music in identities* (MII). The former, IIM, is concerned with defined musical roles, such as performer, composer, and critic; in short, how one is described as or describes oneself as a musician. The latter is concerned with how we use music as a resource for self-making, and the ways in which music is drawn on by individuals, groups, and institutions (loosely termed) as a marker of forms of identity (e.g., national identity). In later work, these authors argue that musical identities are fundamental to music development as they mediate the ways in which individuals and groups engage with and through music (Hargreaves, MacDonald, & Miell, 2012). The theory of identity that informs this work has its roots in social and developmental psychology, and recognizes that identity is not fixed or monolithic, rather that it evolves over time, and may be shaped differently by place, culture, relationships, and social setting. Importantly, there is recognition that identities are multiple, in that individuals develop and perform multiple identities dependent on the social and cultural settings in which they find themselves and the socio-cultural categories available to them including "… gender, age, race, occupation, gangs, socio-economic status, ethnicity, class, nation states or regional territory" (Bamberg, 2010, p. 4). Whilst such a view would seem to anchor us in an entirely relativist view of identity there is recognition that within these shifting notions of self a "core" identity emerges through an autobiographical narrative that is unfolded, told, and retold throughout the life course (Bruner, 1986, 1990, 1996).

This recognition of the role of narrative in shaping and presenting identity is evident in the emergence of the field of Narrative Psychology, and the use of narrative as a means of identity construction and identity analysis (Freeman, 2006; MacAdams, Josselson, & Lieblich, 2006; Bamberg, 2010).

Rather than provide a comprehensive survey of the ways in which the notion of musical identities (IIM and MII) has been taken up within and across the disciplines of music, my concern here is to focus on the foundations of music identity, that is, in examining what is understood about young children's (0–5) early identity work in and through music. Accordingly, in what follows, I shall focus on what is known of early music identity work.

4.6 Developing musical identities

Writing in 2002, Colwyn Trevarthen sets out an argument that the origins of musical identity lie in infants' early musico-linguistic interactions with parents and caregivers. He draws on a range of research (e.g., Papoucek & Papoucek, 1981; Fernald, 1992) to argue that the characteristic features of "motherese" or "parentese" are primarily musical in nature and mutually responsive between infant and carer. Significantly, such interactions are more than imitations by the infant of the adult music-making; rather, they are creative dialogues of shared music-making constructed from improvisatory, spontaneous musical gestures (Trevarthen, 2012). Drawing on earlier work undertaken in conjunction with Stephen Malloch that lead to the formulation of the theory of *communicative musicality* (Malloch, 1999; Trevarthen, 1999), Trevarthen points to the role music plays in building memories, marking individuals and events, declaring allegiances, and strengthening social and emotional bonds. In outlining *how* music engagement achieves these outcomes Trevarthen suggests that we possess a "fundamental intrinsic motive pulse (IMP)" comprised of

> (1) a rhythmic time sense (that detects syllables, the beat, phrases and longer elements); (2) sensitivity for "sentic forms" (Clynes, 1973) or temporal variation in intensity, pitch and timbre of voices and in instrumental sounds that mimic the human voice; and (3) a perception of "narrative" in the emotional development of the melodic line, which supports anticipation of repeating harmonies, phrases and emotional forms in a vocal or musical performance.
>
> Trevarthen, 2002, p. 25.

Recognition of the IMP as the mechanism by which infants attune themselves to and interact with the music-making and vocal-gestural play of others suggests that they are far more conscious of their environment than previously thought. Indeed, psychologist Alison Gopnik suggests that "It's plausible that babies are actually aware of much more, much more intensely, than we are … less of their experience is familiar, expert, and automatic, and so they have fewer habitual, unconscious behaviors ... They are more conscious than we are" (Gopnik, 2009, p. 120).

Trevarthen reflects on the role of music in socio-dramatic play as a means to addressing infants' needs for human companionship, and building repertoires of rituals and emotions that are culturally appropriate. He suggests the "origin and function of a sense of 'musical identity' (lies) in the 'mass intimacy' of an adult 'public,' where recognition of pieces and genre of music can be harnessed to powerful emotions of sympathy or antipathy" (Trevarthen, 2002, p. 32). Most recently, Trevarthen and Malloch (Chapter 9) assert that the "innately musical infant" has a "strong motivation to express stories before speech" (Chapter 1). They arrive at the "radical conclusion" that infants are born with the capacity to "make or detect the *aesthetic* value of melodic stories, and *moral* feelings ... sustained with a respectful and sympathetic other in expressive body movements and song" (Chapter 3). This conclusion rests in a recognition of the narrative character of "melodic stories" and their role in identity work and relationship. I suggest that "melodic stories" constructed and performed in interaction, *and* subsequent independent song and music-making undertaken by young children may be viewed as a form of "small story" narrative practice. Furthermore, I suggest that this melodic "small story" narrative practice underpins the developing child's identity work in and through music. I shall explore these notions further in what follows.

4.7 CHILDREN'S INVENTED SONG-MAKING

In other work (Barrett, 2003, 2006, 2011) I have suggested that infants' early generative musical activity, evidenced in the babblings and cooings that underpin "motherese" or "parentese" are the basis of invented song-making and children's early identity work and world-making.[2] Invented song-making as independent musical action is evident in the pitch and rhythm patterns of children's musical babbling at the age of 6–7 months (Moog, 1976; Tafuri & Villa, 2002) developing around 18 months of age into more extended melodic patterns (Moog, 1976) and song forms (Barrett, 2011). This period marks the emergence of "pot-pourri" songs (Moog, 1976), songs that are constructed from fragments of known songs (words, rhythms and melodies) that the child has encountered in her culture, and original material.

The years between 18 months and 6 years appear to be the most productive for invented song-making as children draw on the repertoires of music available to them in the cultural systems (Rogoff, 2003) of the home and family (micro-), the school and local community, including church and cultural group affiliations (meso-), and the media (exo-). This latter may include music *for* children (works targeted specifically at a child audience such as those written and performed by early childhood performance groups such as

---

[2] See Saint-George et al. (2013) for a comprehensive review of research in the cognitive and emotive functions of Infant Directed Speech or "motherese."

"The Wiggles", and/or those intended to be sung by young children), and music by and for adults. Increasingly, during this period, young children's invented song-making demonstrates greater adaptation and novel re-working of known song and independent, original music-making (Barrett, 2012a, b). Children's invented song-making has been observed across a range of cultures, including Norway (Bjørkvold, 1989), Sweden (Sundin, 1998), the UK (Davies, 1986; Young, 2004), Italy (Tafuri and Villa, 2002; Tafuri, 2008), the USA (Moorhead & Pond 1941/1978; Dowling, 1984; Campbell, 2010), Germany (Moog, 1976), and Australia (Barrett, 2006, 2009; Whiteman, 2009; Barrett, , 2011, 2012a, b;).

4.8 Singing, music-making, identity, and "small stories"

The focus on invented song-making provides a window into multiple intersecting worlds of identity—those of the self and the ways in which the young child is coming to understand her worlds and her place/s in that world (accessed through analysis that foregrounds text against music); and the child's musical identity (accessed through analysis that foregrounds music against text). Beyond the analysis of the musical and textual content of children's invented songs, the identification of the uses to which children put these songs, extrapolated through analysis of the times, spaces, audiences, and occasions on which the young child sings, provides us with further insights into the functions of invented songs as a means of "performing" or "enacting" identity. For example, in an investigation of the "everyday" musical engagement of a young child (Barrett, 2009) we see the ways in which music is used within the family as a means of identifying and reinforcing relationships, feelings, and familial bonds. The song below (see Fig. 4.1, "Lucy's song") was sung by Lucy, a 4-year-old girl, to her younger brother (aged 2 years) and infant sister as they were waiting in the back seat of the family car. In this song Lucy sings about herself as a "special girl," of her infant sister as "my special girl too" (Bars 10–15), and of her brother as a "special little boy" (Bars 15 – 17). Having identified herself, her sister and brother as "special" she goes on to sing "oh beautiful you are." Here, we see Lucy drawing on song as a mechanism to affirm her relationships with her brother and sister, and their "specialness" in her world. As a form of "small story" Lucy is singing of current relationships and emotions that hold between herself and her siblings, and the vital part these play in their individual and collective identities as family members.

Children's invented song-making may also tell "small stories" that focus on the events in their lives that hold significance for them in that moment, and the people and places that are important to them. In a study of a young boy's (aged 3 years) singing and invented song-making (Barrett, 2012a) there are numerous examples of songs that are prompted by his location (in the kitchen), the immediate events in his life (baby crying), or common events (telephone ringing). In relation to this latter (see Fig. 4.2—the telephone ringing) Jay sings about the event of the phone ringing and his response

Lucy's Song

FIG. 4.1 "Lucy's Song."

"and I say hello" (see bars 3–4). This song was captured on video and the analysis of the footage shows Jay acting out the process of answering the phone by holding a length of tinsel (hung from the family Christmas tree) to his ear, alternating from left to right ear in time to the pulse of the song and directing his performance to the appreciative audience of his baby brother who is strapped into a high chair nearby. Jay is enacting the processes that attend to a telephone ringing, those of lifting the receiver to his ear and saying "hello". The song is performed with a "swung" rhythm, reflecting Jay's interest in syncopation and jazz rhythms and his musical preferences. His song-making reveals a strong understanding of song structure and musical phrase, and the capacity to abstract the characteristic features from a musical style to construct his own original music. His performance evidences a strong identity in music (IIM) as performer and song-maker. As a "small story," the song provides a means to reflect on and practice the social norms ("and I say hello") of answering the phone.

Telephone Ringing

Jay

FIG. 4.2 "Telephone Ringing."

The examples provided in Figs 4.1 and 4.2 refer to people, places, and events in the children's actual worlds (Bruner, 1986). Invented song-making may also be employed by young children as a tool to explore possible worlds through fictional narratives. For example, a study of a 4-year-old girl's song-making over approximately 1 year revealed the ways in which she drew on a

> … fantasy world of fairies to explore the consequences of actions. Throughout these songs, missing meals and being late are attributed to the fairies, who are then admonished. Charli uses the processes of invented song making as a means to find and make meaning of actions, to reflect on these and consider the ways in which these might be viewed by others.
>
> Barrett, 2005, p. 214.

In a further study of a 2-year-old girl's (Cara) invented song and music-making, music was employed as a means to reflect on activity, accompany activity, comment on and elaborate on activity, mark affiliation with others, and establish a dialogue of shared concerns with others (Barrett, 2016). For example, Cara creates a pot-pourri song "Stars" as she rests on the couch in preparation for bedtime. The song is sung in a contemplative and quiet manner, reminiscent of a lullaby, and draws on the texts of a song from the Peter Pan movie, "Second star to the right" and "Twinkle, twinkle little star". The song appears to function as a "small story" situated in the present in which she prepares herself in a form of embodied story-telling for sleep.

Such examples of children's song-making for a range of purposes are evident in the invented songs collected by others including Patricia Shehan Campbell (2010), Lori Custodero (2006), Coral Davies (1986, 1992), and Susan Young (2006). When considered as a form of melodic "small story" narrative practice, the powerful function of such song and music-making in young children's identity work is evident.

4.9 MUSIC IN IDENTITY AND IDENTITY IN MUSIC

In the previous section I have provided an overview of studies that have investigated young children's invented song-making and considered these through the lens of "small story" narrative activity. Through their invented song-making young children engage in "Music in Identity" work as they use song and song-making as a means to establish and affirm relationships (Lucy), locate themselves in the world (Jay), articulate their preferences and current fantasies (Charli), trial various identity claims and social norms (Jay), self-manage (Cara), and use the medium of song as a means to explore the consequences of action (Charli). When viewed as a form of "small story" narrative activity, children's invented song-making may be viewed as a means to explore, perform, and enact multiple aspects of identity. The songs and musical forms the children draw on in their music-making are revealing of their musical preferences (for example, Jay's love of swing and syncopated rhythms), and the musical repertoires with which they engage and to which they are exposed. In a complementary manner these children are also laying the foundations for their emerging identity in music. Here, we see them working as composers, song-makers, and singers.

The degree to which these identities in music are sustained as the child grows depends to a large extent on the responses given to their music-making by those significant others (parents, siblings, caregivers, teachers) in their environment. Too often, young children's invented music-making (be it vocal, instrumental, or employing found sounds such as those afforded by household utensils) is regarded as "noise-making" that *needs to* be discouraged. To make full use of music as a resource in young children's musical identity work we need to recognize and celebrate this music-making and extend it through musical interactions with others, exposure to and engagement with other forms of music-making, and opportunities to present.

4.10 CONCLUSION

In this chapter I have outlined the ways in which musical identity work originates in the early babblings and cooings of "motherese" or "parentese" and develops through increasingly independent music-making as singers and song-makers. I have examined young children's song-making through the lens of melodic "small story" narratives to demonstrate the ways in which such musical activity may be viewed as a means of both constructing and telling narrative identity to self and others. I have also located such work as essential in both the development of "Music in Identity" and "Identity in Music". From these small beginnings much might be effected, if only we stop to listen.

References

Atkinson, P.A. (2006). *Everyday arias*. Lanham, MD: AltaMira.

Atkinson, P.A., & Delamont, S. (2006). Rescuing narrative from qualitative research. *Narrative Inquiry*, 16(1), 164–72.

Baker, F., & MacDonald, R. (2013). Flow, identity achievement, satisfaction and ownership during therapeutic song-writing experiences with university students and retirees. *Musicae Scientiae*, 17(2), 131–46.

Baker, J. (2012). Learning in a teen garage band: a relation inquiry. In: M. S. Barrett & S. L. Stauffer (Eds.), *Narrative soundings: an anthology of narrative inquiry in music education*, pp. 61–78. Dordrecht: Springer.

Ballantyne, J., Kerchner, J.L., & Aróstegui, J.L. (2012). Developing music teacher identities: an international multi-site study. *International Journal of Music Education*, 30(3), 211–26.

Bamberg, M. (2004). Talk, small stories, and adolescent identities. *Human Development*, 47, 331–355.

Bamberg, M. (2010). Who am I? Narration and its contribution to self and identity. *Theory and Psychology*, 2(1), 1–22.

Bamberg, M. (2011). Who am I? Big or small—shallow or deep? *Theory and Psychology*, 21(1), 1–8.

Bamberg, M., & Georgakopoulou, A. (2008). Small stories as a new perspective in narrative and identity analysis. *Text and Talk*, 3, 377–96.

Barrett, M.S. (2003). Meme engineers: children as producer of musical culture. *International Journal of Early Years Education*, 11(3), 195–212.

Barrett, M.S. (2006). Inventing songs, inventing worlds: the 'genesis' of creative thought and activity in young children's lives. *International Journal of Early Years Education*, 14(3), 201–20.

Barrett, M.S. (2009). Sounding lives in and through music: a narrative inquiry of the 'everyday' musical engagement of a young child. *Journal of Early Childhood Research*, 7(2), 115–34.

Barrett, M.S. (2011). Musical narratives: a study of a young child's identity work in and through music-making. *Psychology of Music*, 39(4), 403–23.

Barrett, M.S. (2012a). Mutuality, belonging and meaning-making: pathways to developing young boys' competence and creativity in singing and song-making. In: S. Harrison, G. F. Welch, & A. Adler (Eds.), *Perspectives on males and singing*, pp. 167–87. Dordrecht: Springer.

Barrett, M.S. (2012b). Preparing the mind for musical creativity: Early music learning and engagement. In: O. Odena (Ed.), *Musical creativity: insights from music education research*, pp. 51–71. Farnham: Ashgate.

Barrett, M.S. (2016). Attending to "culture in the small": a narrative analysis of the role of play, thought, and music in young children's world-making. *Research Studies in Music Education*, 38: 41–54.

Bjørkvold, J. (1989). *The muse within: creativity and communications, song and play from childhood through maturity*, transl. W. H. Haverson. New York: Harper Collins.

Borthwick, S.J., & Daivdson, J.W. (2002). Developing a child's identity as a musician: a family 'script' perspective. In: R.A.R. MacDonald, D.J. Hargreaves, & D. Miell (Eds) *Musical Identities*, pp. 60–78. Oxford: Oxford University Press.

Bruner, J. (1986). *Actual minds, possible worlds.* Cambridge, MA: Harvard University Press.

Bruner, J. (1987). Life as narrative. *Social Research,* 54(1), 11–32.

Bruner, J. (1990). *Acts of meaning.* Cambridge, MA: Harvard University Press

Bruner, J. (1996). *The culture of education.* Cambridge, MA: Harvard University Press.

Bruner, J. (2002). *Making stories: law, literature, life.* New York: Farrar, Straus, and Giroux.

Bruner, J. (2006). A narrative model of self-construction. *Annals of the New York Academy of Sciences,* 818(1), 145–61.

Bruner, J. (2008). Culture and mind: Their fruitful incommensurability. *Ethos,* 36(1), 29–45.

Campbell, P.S. (2010). *Songs in their heads: music and its meaning in children's lives,* 2nd edn. New York: Oxford University Press.

Campbell, P.S., Connell, S.C., & Beegle, A. (2007). Adolescents' expressed meanings of music in and out of school. *Journal of Research in Music Education,* 55(3), 220–36.

Cleaver, D., & Riddle, S. (2014). Music as engaging, educational matrix: exploring the case of marginalized students attending an "alternative" music industry school. *Research Studies in Music Education,* 36(2), 241–56.

Custodero, L. (2006). Singing practices of ten families with young children. *Journal of Research in Music Education,* 54(1), 37–56.

Davies, C. (1986). Say it til a song comes: reflections on songs invented by children 3–13. *British Journal of Music Education,* 3(3), 279–93.

Davies, C. (1992). Listen to my song. *British Journal of Music Education,* 9(10), 19–48.

DeNora, T. (2000). *Music in everyday life.* Cambridge: Cambridge University Press.

Dowling, W.J. (1984). Development of musical schemata in children's spontaneous singing. In: W.R. Crozier & A.J. Chapment (Eds) *Cognitive processes in the perception of arts,* pp. 145–63. Amsterdam: North-Holland.

Draves, T. (2014). Under construction: undergraduates perceptions of their music teacher role-identities. *Research Studies in Music Education,* 36(2), 199–214.

Fernald, A. (1992). Meaningful melodies in mothers' speech to infants. In: H. Papoucek, U. Jürgens, & M. Papoucek (Eds.) *Nonverbal vocal communication: comparative and developmental aspects,* pp. 262–82. Cambridge: Cambridge University Press.

Folkestad, G. (2002). National identity and music. In: R. MacDonald, D.J. Hargreaves, & D. Miell (Eds.) *Musical identities,* pp. 161–2. Oxford: Oxford University Press.

Freeman, M. (2006). Life "on holiday"?: in defense of big stories. *Narrative Inquiry,* 16(1), 131–8.

Gardikiotis, A., & Baltzis, A. (2012). 'Rock music for myself and justice to the world!': Musical identity, values, and music preferences. *Psychology of Music,* 40(2), 143–63.

Georgakapoulou, A. (2006). Thinking big with small stories in narrative and identity analysis. *Narrative Inquiry,* 16(1), 122–30.

Gopnik, A. (2009). *The philosophical baby: what children's minds tell us about truth, love, and the meaning of life.* Picador: New York.

Hargreaves, D.J., Macdonald, R., & Miell, D. (2012). Musical identities mediate musical development. In: G.E. McPherson & G.F. Welch (Eds.) *The Oxford Handbook of Music Education,* pp 125–42. Oxford: Oxford University Press.

Hargreaves, D.J., Miell, D., & R.A.R. MacDonald (2002). What are musical identities and why are they important? In: R.A.R. MacDonald, D.J. Hargreaves, & D. Miell (Eds), *Musical identities,* pp. 1–20. Oxford: Oxford University Press.

Hargreaves, D.J., Purves, R.M., Welch, G.F., & Marshall, N.A. (2007). Developing identities and attitudes in musicians and classroom music teachers. *British Journal of Educational Psychology*, 77(3), 665–82.

Juuti, S., & Littleton, K. (2010). Musical identities in transition: solo piano students' accounts of entering the academy. *Psychology of Music*, 38(4), 481–97.

Karlsen, S. (2013). Immigrant students and the "homeland music": meanings, negotiations and implications. *Research Studies in Music Education*, 35(2), 161–77.

Lamont, A. (2002). Musical identities and the school environment. In: R. MacDonald, D.J. Hargreaves, & D. Miell (Eds.) *Musical identities*, pp. 41–59. Oxford: Oxford University Press.

MacDonald, R., Hargreaves, D. J., & Miell, D. (2015). Musical identities. In: G. E. McPherson (Ed.) *The child as musician: a handbook of musical development*, 2nd edn, pp. 97–116. New York: Oxford University Press.

MacAdams, D., Jossellson, R., & Lieblich, A. (2006). *Identity and self: creating self in narrative*. Washington, DC: American Psychological Association.

Moog, H. (1976). *The musical experience of the pre-school child*, transl. C. Clarke. London: Schott.

Moorhead, G.E., & Pond, D. (1941/1978). *Music of young children*. Santa Barbara: Pillsbury Foundation for Advancement of Music Education. (Reprinted from works published in 1941, 1942, 1944, and 1951.)

Ochs, E., & Capps, L. (2001). *Living narrative*. Cambridge, MA: Harvard University Press.

O'Hagin, I.B., & Harnish, D. (2006). Music as a cultural identity: a case study of Latino musicians negotiating tradition and innovation in northwest Ohio. *International Journal of Music Education*, 24, 56–70.

Papoucek, M., & Papoucek, H. (1981). Musical elements in the infant's vocalisations: their significance for communication, cognition and creativity, In: L.P. Lipsitt (Ed.), *Advances in Infancy Research*, pp. 163–224. Norwood: Ablex Pub Co.

Pellegrino, K. (2009). Connections between performer and teacher identities in music teachers: Setting an agenda for research. *Journal of Music Teacher Education*, 19(1), 39–55.

Pitts, S.E. (2014). Exploring musical expectations: Understanding the impact of a year-long primary school music project in the context of school, home and prior learning. *Research Studies in Music Education*, 36(2), 129–46.

Preti, C., & Welch, G.F. (2013). Professional identities and motivations of musicians playing in healthcare settings: cross-cultural evidence from UK and Italy. *Musicae Scientiae*, 17(4), 359–75.

Rogoff, B. (2003). *The cultural nature of human development*. New York: Oxford University Press.

Saint-George, C., Chetouani, M., Cassel, R., et al. (2013). Motherese in interaction: at the crossroad of emotion and cognition? A systematic review. *PLOS ONE*, 8, E78103.

Stauffer, S. (2014). Narrative inquiry and the uses of narrative in music education research. In: *American music education*, pp. 163–185. New York: Oxford University Press.

Sundin, B. (1997). Musical creativity in childhood: a research project in retrospect. *Research Studies in Music Education*, 9(1), 48–57.

Sundin, B. (1998). Musical creativity in the first six years. In: B. Sundin, G.E. McPherson, & G. Folkestad (Eds.), *Children composing*, pp. 35–56. Malmö: Malmö Academy of Music, Lund University.

Tafuri, J. (2008). *Infant musicality: new research for educators and parents*. Farnham: Ashgate.

Tafuri, J., & Villa, D. (2002). Musical elements in the vocalisations of infants aged 2–8 months. *British Journal of Music Education*, 19(1), 73–88.

Trevarthen, C. (1999). Musicality and the intrinsic motive pulse: evidence from human psy-chobiology and infant communication. *Musicae Scientiae*, 3, 157–213.

Trevarthen, C. (2002). Origins of identity: Evidence from infancy for musical social awareness. In: R. MacDonald, D.J. Hargreaves, & D. Miell (Eds.), *Musical identities*, pp. 21–38 Oxford: Oxford University Press.

Trevarthen C. (2012). Communicative musicality: the human impulse to create and share music. In: D.J. Hargreaves, R. A. R. MacDonald, & D. E. Miell (Eds.) *Musical imaginations*, pp. 259–84. Oxford: Oxford University Press.

Whiteman, P. (2009). *Type, function and musical features of preschool children's spontaneous songs*. Charlotte: Information Age.

Winston, N., & Witherspoon, K. (2015). 'It's all about our great Queen': the British National Anthem and national identity in 8–10 year old children. *Psychology of Music*, 44 (2), 263–77.

Wortham, S. (2001). *Narratives in action: a strategy for research and analysis*. New York: Teachers College Press.

Young, S. (2004). Young children's spontaneous vocalizing: insights to play and pathways to singing. *International Journal of Early Childhood*, 36(2), 59–74.

CHAPTER 5

......

YOUNG PEOPLE'S MUSICAL LIVES
Learning Ecologies, Identities, and Connectedness

......

SUSAN A. O'NEILL

5.1 INTRODUCTION

DURING a speech at a recent event sponsored by Youth Music UK, Jen Long was referred to as a youth music entrepreneur and a "young, fresh music talent from outside of the normal channels" (Long, 2013). By the age of 22 years, Jen had already presented her first radio show for the BBC, and was writing about, promoting, recording, and managing new bands—mostly young unsigned, undiscovered, and under the radar musicians. In her speech "Music careers in the 21st century," Jen reiterated a common assumption that researchers have been advancing for several decades—music is important in the lives of young people, it shapes their identities, and for many it is a "passion." She went on to describe how she wanted to "play in a band," but didn't think it was something "you could learn;" rather, she thought it needed to happen "organically and through practice." She also didn't think being able to play an instrument or sing was the only way young people could express themselves musically. Her only memory of music at school was playing the recorder, which was in stark contrast to the rich musical life she was discovering outside of school across different life spaces. In her speech, she advocates a "do it yourself" ethos to *making* a career in music and suggests that music education should provide more young people with opportunities to develop skills in music technologies and "hands-on" experience through music apprenticeships and internships. She also advocates the need for more to be done to encourage girls because music is "a very male dominated industry."

Through Jen's description of her musical life, it is possible to recognize how she both shapes (through agentic, individual distinctiveness, and autonomy) and is shaped by (through structural, culturally bounded, but not closed, networks of people who come to share the meaning of specific ideas, material objects, and practices through inter-action) the construction and promotion of a particular kind of music learning self-identity. Jen sees herself as a learner who believes in her ability to learn within specific musical contexts, and she seeks out and engages in life experiences that are sustained and nurtured through relationships within those contexts. Her music learning identity has developed over time within particular learning ecologies consisting of social struc-tures and power relations that address, represent, and act upon her as a certain kind of learner who is able "to become involved in music in many different ways." Her learn-ing identity is infused with modern notions of independent authority and autonomous expertise that "reshape" the way her actions are interpreted and understood as emerging from her own initiative to discover, create, record, write about, and share music. She also learns and works within her own peer group and youth culture, either in person physi-cally or online. She engages in self-directed and collaborative music activities using technological advances, information sharing, and social media, which tend to promote the experiential expertise of many different "lay experts" who mediate the expertise of professional musicians in ways that may or may not reflect accurately their experiences. Jen's engagement in music-related activities permeates deeply into her everyday life but also mediates her sense of connectedness in particular ways. These complex social processes and relationships contribute to Jen's notion of "making" of her own musical career, which is indicative of an imaginative act that is woven into the textures of her everyday life, personal aspirations, and sense of self.

This chapter considers and reflects critically on how these ideas are echoed in young people's descriptions of their experiences of engaging in music activities as part of their everyday lives. I begin by drawing on a nexus of theoretical approaches that place the meaning-making experiences of young people as central and capable of revealing criti-cal understandings of their musical life worlds and learning identities. My aim is to gain insights into the unique configurations of music learning ecologies that young people inhabit and to highlight the usefulness of documenting personal learning environ-ments, and exploring their affordances and constraints on what young people perceive as desirable and possible music activity horizons and learning identities. Ecological per-spectives provide an interface between activity, materiality, networks, human agency, and the construction of identities within the contexts that render young people's expe-riences meaningful (Barron, 2006; Barnett, 2012). As such, music learning ecologies include young people's engagement in their own music learning ventures, as well as interconnected layers of their reflection and action on social, cultural, and educational practices that take place within their life worlds.

In the second part of the chapter, I draw on an ecological theoretical framework to explore three portraits of young people's musical lives that were derived from mapping the music learning ecologies of 93 young people aged 11–18 years in Canada (O'Neill, 2015). These portraits demonstrate a common patterning of music learning ecologies, which I refer to as *segmented*, *situated*, and *agentive*. Although these learning ecolo-gies may overlap in complex ways, they are separated here to emphasize how each one creates and promotes distinctive forms of identities and connectedness to provide an illustration of the theoretical trajectories of young people's engagement in music-related activities. The intent is not to produce a straightforward empirical account of music learning identities; rather, as Loveless and Williamson (2013) set out to do in their work, my aim is more modest and focused on considering how particular kinds of music learners have been "assembled," "made plausible," and "intelligible" (p. 24) through music learning ecologies that emphasize different aspects of what it means to be a young musician. Music-related identity development is a dynamic, fluid, and complex process and yet the implications stemming from this discussion might provide insights for both researchers and educators with interests in re-envisioning pedagogical approaches to music learning. In highlighting the need to view music learning ecologies as ensembles of different forms of authority, expertise, materials, ideas, and people involved in ongoing contests and alliances, we are better able to identify affordances and constraints on the possible spaces where young people might encounter a sense of connectedness, and more expansive and creative alternatives for remaking and reimagining their musical selves.

5.2 Musical worlds and identities

Mans (2009) takes up the concept of *musical worlds* as "culturally informed systems of musical thinking and creating" (p. 10). She maintains that a person's musical world can be understood as one paradigm of a person's entire social world, which is "conceptualized, understood, inhabited, its rules played out, and its customs, knowledge, and aesthetics transmitted, through formal and informal education" (p. 11). Mans draws on a phenomenological approach and the notion that identity is central to the development of a sense of self-in-relationship with people, ideas, and objects. She argues that musical identity is situated and adapts to the "nature of the lived space of past and present" (p. 100). She gives an example of how a group of young people might "seek music together," thereby creating "a common, possibly short-lived, musical identity" (p. 100) whereas, at other times, "a young person might seek isolation in a room, interacting with 'his'/'her' music on a purely personal level" (p. 100). In other words, musical worlds are fluid and transitory. Furthermore, Mans points out that people are also able to cross cultural and musical boundaries and have identities "in-between" and "lodged with activities" (p. 102). This draws attention to the ontological entanglement of musical worlds and identities. For Mans, young people's musical identities are located in the world "where they know, accept, and understand the inherent value systems" (p. 102). Yet, as Mans suggests, many young people growing up in urban, contemporary societies are experiencing "increasing tensions between different identities" in ways that foster an "uncertainty about where they belong" (p. 102).

In a series of essays first published in the *Journal of Aesthetics and Art Criticism*, Walton (1998) describes musical worlds as "radically indeterminate with respect to the identity and individuation of agents" (p. 52). Walton immediately draws our attention away from the notion that musical worlds are (at least not completely) culturally determined and focuses instead on the indeterminacy of relations between music (non-human) and human agents. According to Walton, "what the music does is to supply us with experiences [...] and we use these experiences as props [...] that generate fictional truths" (p. 60). These "fictional truths" become historical, social, and cultural phenomena that recruit, allocate, and apportion people in relation to different musical landscapes. They become "cultural models" or what Gee (1996) describes as "simplified worlds in which prototypical events unfold" (p. 78). These "worlds" that individuals participate in are intimately tied to identity work and how people come to understand or "figure" out "who they are" (Urrieta, 2007).

In the seminal book *Identity and Agency in Cultural Worlds,* Holland and colleagues (1998) conceptualize *figured worlds*, which are "socially and culturally constructed realm(s) of interpretation" (p. 52) that "take shape within and grant shape to the coproduction of activities, discourses, performances, and artifacts" (p. 51). According to Urrieta (2007), "figured worlds are encountered in day-to-day social activity and lived through practices and activities. Identities are thus formed in the processes of participating in activities organized by figured worlds" (p. 109). Through this sociocultural lens, musical "figured" worlds might be described as an intricate web of contexts, formal and informal structures and practices, and a nexus of relationships whereby individuals "come to conceptually (cognitively) and materially/procedurally produce (perform) new self-understandings (identities)" (p. 108). Young people's identities provide a navigational system and a means of reference and orientation within their perceptual (space-time) and cultural (place-time) life worlds, which include the music activities, material resources, relationships, and interactions that emerge across the physical and virtual life spaces and places of home, school, local and online communities, and (mostly through the Internet) the wider world. Life worlds, according to Habermas (1984, 1987) who adapted the concept from Alfred Schutz, can be thought of as the shared understandings, values, and common sense beliefs that young people develop through their interactions with various people and social groups over time. Life worlds can also be thought of as ecological systems where music encounters and learning take place on two main levels: within the young person and between the young person and his or her environment.

5.3 MUSIC LEARNING ECOLOGIES

At any given time, young people's musical lives are embedded within particular figured worlds and interconnected systems of learning ecologies. These learning ecologies are located within wider societal, cultural, and global systems and although it is impossible to disentangle these systems and the sociocultural structures and practices that initiate and sustain them, it is possible to gain deeper insights into the multiple settings and relationships that comprise young people's music learning ecologies. A focus on learning ecologies is also likely to reveal new directions that will advance both our theoretical and empirical future research.

The notion of a learning ecology has been described as a thick concept (Williams, 1985/2008, as cited in Barnett, 2012), which means it is a multifaceted and multidimensional *description* of a system and at the same time a value-laden *explanation* for how a system came to be the way it is. The people embedded within particular systems maintain the well-being of those systems. This conceptualization captures both the *embeddedness* and sense of *connectedness* of young people themselves within learning systems that they are ultimately (at least in part) responsible for. These learning systems are fragile; they contain elements of agency, responsibility, meaning, and creativity that are interconnected and yet fluid and changeable. Although we might aspire for interconnectedness as a way for people to "intermesh with each other" (Barnett, 2012, p. 15) to combat this inherent fragility, there is also a "counter story of separateness" that is maintained by people who lack "the resources for mutual comprehension" (p. 15) and who may maintain a separate identity through essentialism and its double bind that "ambiguously simultaneously demands and rejects translation" (Edgerton, 1996, p. 49), for example, "this is who I am" (try to understand me) and at the same time "don't label me" (you can't understand me).

Learning ecologies have their origins in Bronfenbrenner's early theorizing when he referred to changes in person-environment relations as *ecological transitions*, which were thought to be both motivators and consequences of development (Bronfenbrenner, 1979; Spencer, Dupree, & Hartmann, 1997). Building on ecological systems theory, Spencer and her colleagues (1997) developed an integrated perspective that combined phenomenology in an attempt to capture *intersubjectivity* and "afford a more dynamic, culturally responsive, context-sensitive perspective for interpreting the individual's own meaning making process" (p. 828). More recent work by Overton (1998, 2007) and Lerner (1991) has been influential in conceptualizing within developmental psychology a relational, organism-context as the main unit of analysis within a developmental systems theory that consists of mutually influential relations among integrated and interactive processes. Other related work can be found in sociocultural and activity theory (Vygotsky, 1978; Engeström, 1987; Stetsenko, 2012) and situated learning theory (Lave & Wenger, 1991; Cole, 1996; Rogoff, 2003).

Within a learning ecological framework, we might examine how changes in technology and the creation of new "tools" "can create shifts in interaction that play out in individual lives" (Barron, 2006, p. 200). Learning ecologies help us to recognize that "boundaries are often more permeable" as young people "draw on multiple cultural forms" (p. 200). Thus, learning can be "intertwined with processes of identity authoring" and this can influence the emergence of "secondary developmental processes" from "more distal learning events" (p. 200). Indeed, for young people, the boundaries around their particular musical worlds may not be perceived as bounded at all but rather surrounded by a zone of entangled or interwoven pathways. Consider, for example, that when children begin to go to school, they might perceive the music classroom as *surrounded* and therefore connected in multiple and diverse ways to their lives outside school. This might be in contrast to how they later come to see the music classroom as *bounded* and therefore disconnected from their lives outside the music classroom. This is an example of how learning ecologies offer a dynamic, culturally responsive, and context-sensitive approach to conceptualizing and interpreting young peoples' own meaning making processes in relation to the music learning opportunities that are an integral part of their musical lives.

The interrelatedness of the diverse social, contextual, and material circumstances of young people's music learning ecologies entails a consideration of their *funds of knowledge* (e.g., personal semiotic resources; González, Moll, & Amanti, 2005) that shape and privilege certain modes of action, activity, and states of being. At the same time, *networks of actors* (e.g., objects, subjects, human beings, machines; Law, 2009) provide a "family of material-semiotic tools" that continuously "produce and reshuffle all kinds of actors" within the "webs of relations" in which they are located (p. 141). We might consider these complex constructions as similar to Foucault's (1980) notion of "heterogeneous ensembles" (p. 194), or spaces where musical identities might be reimagined and reconfigured. This view of music learning ecologies also helps us move beyond seeing them as mere contexts and instead draws attention to their affordances and constraints for constructing and promoting identities, which in turn provides insights into young people's perspectives and orientations. We might bring these ideas together by drawing on Deleuze & Guattari's (1987) notion of the social world as an *assemblage* of complex configurations that are heterogeneous, transitory, and fluid. For young people to navigate and negotiate the multiple assemblages and the "changing and contested interpretations of the world" (Barnett, 2012, p. 11), they need the kinds of dispositions and qualities that will "take them through an ever-present turbulence" (p. 11). For Deleuze & Guattari, this "ever-present turbulence" of multiple assemblages is created through *movement* between relations involving the making and unmaking of a particular territory (a place system), technology (a pragmatic system), and language or representation (a semiotic system) (Stivale, 2011). In relating these systems to the notion of music learning ecologies, we might provide a conceptual foundation for future research to examine how these three systems (place, pragmatic, semiotic) within young people's musical lives create a consistency and coherence for young people to develop "identity tools" for cultivating resilient and growth-producing music learning identities.

5.4 MUSICAL SELVES AND LEARNING IDENTITIES

I refer to the concept of musical selves, rather than musical identities, to reassert the "person" into explanations of young musicians as encultured, embodied, moral, and aesthetic beings, and this is also in accord with concepts such as multiple selves, selfhood, or personhood (O'Neill, 2012a). Harré (1998) describes personhood as expressions of our sense of personal *distinctiveness, continuity,* and *autonomy,* and Taylor (1989) argues that personhood can only be defined in *relation to others.* These ideas emphasize the interconnected nature of the life world (Husserl, 1936/1970; Schultz & Luckmann, 1973; Habermas, 1987), or the phenomenology of connectedness (or lack thereof) in our everyday life. In conceptualizing "selves," Martin & McLellan (2013) refer to "agentic personhood and communal agents" (p. 183) after Mead's (1938) perspectival approach to communal agency within social psychology as "a co-constructive, reciprocal interrelation between selves and their societies" that enable "integrative theorizing across personal, interpersonal, social, and cultural levels of human experience" (p. 183).

Musical selves derive in part from our attempts to figure out who we are and our place in the world as active agents in making sense of our own lives in relation to the lives of others (O'Neill, 2012a). When young musicians reflect critically on their values and make conscious efforts to plan and implement actions that bring about new ways of viewing themselves, others, and their world in relation to music activities, they are actively constructing their musical selves. This notion of musical selves can also be conceptualized according to Benson's (2001) concept of selves as a locative, navigational system, "simultaneously containing its world and being contained by it" (p. 239). As such, young people's musical selves might also be viewed as "pathways" through their musical lives, which are sometimes found, sometimes forged, and sometimes forced, while still appearing to act in the name of individual autonomy and agency. When young people are interested in music, they will pursue learning opportunities across different activities and resources, with different companions, and in different places and spaces over time. However, the fact remains that constraining influences, such as embodiment, materiality, and power, are still deeply enmeshed in their sense of musical selves no matter how much their musical activities may appear to transcend, subvert, or construct a reality that falls outside of traditional notions of music learning. In today's digital age, young people's selves are "intricately connected to their ongoing learning" (Loveless & Williamson, 2013, p. 10) where "learning is now being 'made up' and imagined as being distributed via networked media into the textures of everyday life" (p. 11). Young people's musical selves are aligned and woven into their experiential worlds and their personal aspirations as they go about "making up" their musical selves within the unique configuration of the music learning ecologies they inhabit.

Over a decade has passed since I explored what it means to be a young musician in *Musical Identities* (O'Neill, 2002). At that time, we saw few young people transcending traditional and dominant discourses about what it means to be a musician. Rather, young people seemed to accept notions of identities that were dictated by social structures and roles considered appropriate within those structures. This ideological component of identity construction acted (and continues to act) as a constraining influence, restricting images, self-narratives, and connections that generate or transform identity options. However, in the intervening years of the past decade, the complexity and turbulence of today's world and fast-paced technological advances have encouraged young people to "understand themselves anew and to find a new relationship with the world" (Barnett, 2012, p. 9). As we have come to witness increased fragmentation, mobility, and uncertainty in the world, these have been reflected in the developmental challenges that young people face in what Larson (2011) refers to as "coming of age in a disorderly world" (p. 330)—a world marked by dissolving boundaries and rapid change (Barnett, 2012). Bauman (2000) describes it as a "liquid world" that signals a "fluid modernity," which requires us to rethink old concepts that bind systemic structures and envision in their place new possibilities—including new possibilities for "making up" musical selves.

5.5 SENSE OF CONNECTEDNESS

In seeking to understand music learning identities, we might begin by considering how young people navigate and negotiate their musical lives in ways that initiate and sustain a sense of *connectedness*. Connectedness encompasses many aspects of relatedness, such as belonging (Wenger, 1998), affinity groups or spaces (Gee, 2004; Gee & Hayes, 2010), and social inclusion (Crisp, 2010). Although the term connectedness is used in different ways, an overarching focus is on the psychological state of *belonging*—a sense of feeling "cared for, acknowledged, trusted, and empowered within a given context" (Guerra & Bradshaw, 2008, p. 12). Having a sense of connectedness is also tied to values that are relational in that they need to work in both directions: young people need to feel valued and cared for *and* they need to care about their own social environment and feel that they make a valuable contribution (Stetsenko, 2012). This idea of *relationality* has been extended beyond the sense of connectedness that is created through social interaction alone to recognize various ways young people engage with non-human, multimodal, and technological objects and the significance of these in their everyday lives within particular landscapes—including musical landscapes in today's digital age.

One of the most prominent discourses associated with 21st century learning is *connectivity or connected learning*. The OECD (2012) report, *Connected minds*, defines connectedness as "the capacity to benefit from connectivity for personal, social, work or economic purposes" and goes on to say that this concept is "having an impact on all spheres of human activity" (p. 15). When combined with digital technology, connectedness is seen as a dual state (despite the obvious limitations to this conceptualization) whereby "people, institutions, firms or governments are either connected (on) or not (off)" (p. 17). The argument is that technology creates connectivity, which is "promoted by a 'Web 2.0' emphasis on learning through networked communities and interest-driven affiliations" (Loveless & Williamson, 2013, p. 26), but that this does not necessarily translate into actual connectedness. What is needed is a better understanding of how young people's attachment to digital media "can be used to promote connectedness" (p. 19). The report concludes with a quotation from Dede's (2007) call for research to observe how young people are using technology in other aspects of their lives to sift out "the dross of behaviors adopted just because they are novel and stylish from the ore of transformational approaches to creating, sharing, and mastering knowledge" (p. 4).

For a growing number of young people today, their artistry or creative expression, which is intimately tied to digital media technologies, is an integral part of constructing their own meaningful life project as an artist or musician—a sense of self-identity that is *assumed, packaged,* and *shared,* rather than achieved or bestowed as it was in past generations (Kress, 2010). We see young people crossing boundaries and producing new modes of creative expression by braiding, blending, and blurring old and new ways of "doing music" (O'Neill, 2012b). Young people are beginning to view music as *multimodal*—often describing their musical encounters and creative collaborations as a form of *seeing or sensing music* through visual images, digital media, mobile devices, and movement (Gauntlett, 2007; Rowsell, 2013). We might adopt Ingold's (2007) notion of *meshwork* or "entanglement of lines" (Ingold, 2007, p. 81) to describe the way young people's musical experiences increasingly involve blurred and fluid boundaries between physical and virtual life spaces (O'Neill, 2016a). As young people are increasingly being positioned as *youth-as-musical resources*, there is an increased need to understand how they navigate and negotiate their music lives in relation to their sense of musical potential or *achievable aspirations* (O'Neill, 2016b). Knowing what youth are interested in and actively involved in, as well as how they think and feel about their involvement, seems an important basis for furthering our understanding of how young people negotiate and find a *sense of place* within the unique configurations, contexts, and situations that constitute their musical selves.

We have seen increased accessibility, mobility, and affordability of digital media technologies, and an unprecedented amount of autonomy as young people shape themselves "in ways that are their own" (Gardner & Davis, 2013, p. 197). Identity and agency have become more intertwined (Holland, Lachicotte, Skinner, & Cain, 1998) and learning environments more participatory in "youth-only" spaces (Goldman, Booker, & McDermott, 2008). Discourses associated with technological change and enterprise education encourage young people to think of themselves and their aspirations anew. Young people have come to be identified collectively as the "digital generation" immersed in social networks and participatory media cultures. They are encouraged to act and aspire to "connected learning," "peer-based learning," and "do it yourself learning," and to identify themselves, think, act and aspire to the future in terms of new technologies and media (Loveless & Williamson, 2013, p. 12). Their learning identities are increasingly "being-assembled-together" (Rose, 1996, p. 171) and "shaped around a constellation of web-like terms and concepts" (Loveless & Williamson, 2013, p. 22). They are being "addressed, represented and acted upon" as if they are a "particular type" (Rose, 1996, p. 169), with identities "assumed to be technologically reticulated and extended through social networks" (Loveless & Williamson, 2013, p. 23). Particular visions of the arts as a catalyst for the creative economy (Howkins, 2001) or the "ultimate economic resource" (Florida, 2002), have "re-thought, reimagined and reshaped" (Loveless & Williamson, 2013, p. 11) young people's learning identities as distinct and disconnected from historical and structural practices, as well as the material, physical, and biological conditions of their lives. These critical insights into how learning identities have been assembled "by certain authorities for certain ends" (p. 24) remind us that we must not take the simplistic view that these transformations in young people's learning identities have developed naturally in response to technological change or are the mere result of socialization processes. Rather, these learning identities are "constructed by authorities and promoted" in education and elsewhere "to deal with cultural, economic, and technological change" in the hope that they will "bring new economic and cultural configurations and stabilities in the future" (p. 24). Of particular interest here, is that technologies, as well as young people's digital learning identities have opened up new musical opportunities that position young people as *youth-as-musical resources*, which also entails discovering and 'making up' new musical selves.

5.6 Mapping young people's music learning ecologies

Mapping, according to organizational theorists and psychologists, is viewed as way of describing key characteristics within particular contexts to provide a useful reference and guide to understanding the changes and processes that bring about transformations in a given landscape. Within educational contexts, mapping the structure of learning networks is used to discern a pattern of learning episodes (Bailey & Barley, 2011). I was interested in adapting this approach to the study of young people's musical selves. Specifically, I wanted to map music learning ecologies within particular contexts that render young people's musical experiences meaningful within their life spaces and places of home, school, local, and online communities, and through the Internet, the wider world. To achieve this aim, I drew on ecological theoretical perspectives that provided an interface between music activity, human agency, and the construction of identities (Barron, 2006; Barnett, 2012). These perspectives enabled me to explore the learning ecologies of 93 young people aged 11–18 years in Canada (O'Neill, 2015a). A phenomenological approach to the life world was used as an overarching framework, as well as temporal, spatial, and relational lenses for thinking about the complex layering, structures, and processes that make up young people's music learning ecologies. According to Spinelli (1989), phenomenological approaches give psychologists a way of clarifying the "variables and invariants" (p. 180) of the world as it appears to those we seek to understand better. Throughout the analysis process, an attempt was made to include the participants' voices and as much of the context as possible.

The data source for the mapping procedure was based on individual, one-to-one interviews with young people about their music engagement in everyday life. The interview protocol involved the use of a *music engagement map* as a visual guide and young people were asked to begin by identifying all the music activities they were involved in at school and outside school. Respondents were then asked a series of follow-up questions about each activity to gain a rich description of each type of activity—where it took place, who was usually present, how long they had been doing the activity, how often they usually engaged in the activity, and how they felt about engaging in the activity. Then, each respondent was asked to choose his or her two favorite music activities: "Which activities are the most meaningful to you—that you do the most or like the most or are the most interested in?" Follow-up questions were then asked about each favorite music activity in relation to:

Initiators: "What got you started doing the activity?"
Sustainers: "What keeps you involved in the activity?"
Outcomes: "What do you get out of being involved in the activity and what impact does it have on your life?"

Respondents were told that impacts could be positive things, such as benefits, or negative things, such as consequences or things you have to give up to be able to do the activity. For each response (initiators, sustainers, outcomes), respondents were also asked whether their answer had more to do with reasons that were *personal* "who you are as a person" (your own values, temperament, attitudes, motivations, time, abilities), *social* "who is around you at the time" (family members, friends, teachers, role models), or *systemic* "something to do with the place you were in at the time" (school, church, community, group, organization), drawing on youth involvement research by Rose-Krasnor (2009).

In the section that follows, the results of mapping the interview accounts are summarized into three illustrative portraits of young people's music learning ecologies, which I refer to as *segmented, situated,* and *agentive.*

5.7 SEGMENTED MUSIC LEARNING ECOLOGIES

Segmented music learning ecologies, using the mapping procedure described above, revealed little or no sense of connectedness in young people's descriptions of their different music activities. The main significance and focus of segmented ecologies focused on recurring events or *episodes*, such as formal music instruction (usually, but not always, involving individual or one-to-one teaching), the amount of practicing that is done to prepare for music lessons, or the pursuit of other relatively isolated goals, such as passing graded music examinations, playing in recitals, and competing in music festivals. Harré and Secord (1972) define episodes, following on from the work of Goffman (1968) and Garfinkel (1967) as "any sequence of happenings in which human beings engage which has some principle of unity" (Harré and Secord, 1972, p. 10). Episodes include visible behaviors, as well as the thoughts, feelings, intentions, and plans of the people involved. Participants define episodes, while at the same time episodes also shape participants' actions (Harré & van Langenhove, 1999). Furthermore, explicit rules determine the sequence of actions within episodes. A music lesson is a good example of a formal or well-structured episode, with rules that govern how both teacher and student should behave. The structures of these episodes are described "like melodies in that they come into existence sequentially" (p. 5), with three main features:

The "rights and duties" of participants to say certain things and behave in certain ways.
The historical sequence of things that have already been said and done and that reinforce existing structures and practices.
The immediate conversations and behaviors, and "their power to shape certain aspects of the social world" (p. 6).

In segmented musical selves, episodes tended to unfold sequentially and independently, with each activity description related to its own chain of particular events, characteristics, people, places, and times.

Relationships were not the main significance in segmented music learning ecologies, although when they were mentioned, the focus was placed on relatively formal and deferential relationships. Some solidarity or bonding was described, such as liking a music teacher, having a supportive parent, and/or like-minded friends that were involved in the same or similar forms of music instruction. Furthermore, digital media, such as listening to music with iPods, were often interwoven into other music activities, but these were rarely described as an important or necessary component of other music activities. There was almost no mention of music creation or collaboration, either with or without digital media technology.

Giddens (1991) describes the segmented nature of modern social life, with both public and private lives becoming increasingly "attached to, and expressive of, specific milieux of action" (p. 83). He draws on Berger, Berger, & Kellner's (1974) notion of the "pluralisation of life-worlds" that emphasizes how much more diverse and segmented social settings are today compared with pre-modern cultures that were much more closely connected with each other and reinforced by the dominance of the local community. Today, decisions to become more immersed in different "lifestyles" are often made at the expense of alternative options. According to Giddens, some choices and activities in one context may be at odds with those adopted in other contexts. Giddens refers to these segments as "lifestyle sectors"—"a time-space 'slice' of an individual's overall activities, within which a reasonably consistent and ordered set of practices is adopted and enacted" (p. 83). There is a compartmentalization happening that may be deliberate or that the individual may be unaware of. In the case of segmented music learning ecologies, it was as if two or more parallel music learning systems coexisted independently from each other. For many individuals, this segmentation appeared to be unproblematic as activities often occurred only inside or only outside school hours, with different people, or during different times of the week. These distinctive attributes gave each music activity a sense of internal coherence, each with a sense of self-identity that was used to negotiate each activity in a context-dependent, but isolated way. This resembles the so-called silo effect in music education, where one music-learning activity appears incapable of reciprocal interaction and sense of connectedness with another music-learning activity.

5.7.1 Amy's segmented music learning ecology

Amy is a 13-year-old girl who has been playing the piano for 4 years, and the violin for 8 years. Her descriptions of her music activities take place outside of school only. For Amy, the significance of her music activities is in relation to particular recurring events or *episodes*, specifically the "music lessons" she has with "piano every Tuesday and violin lessons every Sunday." Both her music lessons and her piano and violin activities are described as segmented and sequential, with no sense of connectedness between them or any other music activities. Even her musical goals of completing graded music examinations (which she undertakes on both instruments), playing in recitals, or music competitions are described as highly specialized task-orientated activities that she engages in with the main purpose of completing them: "I personally don't like to quit when I start 'cause like, I like to keep on going until I'm done." Amy's sense of music activity as formal episodes further serves to reinforce her segmented musical life. This is evident in her description of her music lessons (which take place at her home), where "the teacher comes to your house and then you play for like an hour and then she like teaches you how to play stuff." She also describes how she practices at home every day "two hours for piano and then thirty minutes every day for violin." When mapping Amy's description of her music engagement within a learning ecological framework, there were few connections described and she did not elaborate on the function or benefits she derived from her music activities—even when prompted to do so. At most she responded, "you practice by yourself, but then during recitals, it's like you get to relate with each other the experiences. But it's most often alone." Amy illustrates how young people might experience segmented music learning ecologies as isolated and isolating, lacking in a sense of connectedness and agency, replete with mundane routines, and driven by mostly external goals that offer possible rewards and recognition, rather than a sense of contribution—all of which act as constraining influences on their developing sense of musical selves.

5.8 SITUATED MUSIC LEARNING ECOLOGIES

Using the mapping procedure, the main significance of situated music learning ecologies was associated with places or spaces of social cohesion. The music activities themselves were not the focus; rather, it was the *situatedness* of the activities within particular places and relationships that rendered the music activities meaningful. It could be argued that the same is true for segmented music learning ecologies—that meaningfulness was also derived through aspects of situated learning. However, what was distinctive about situated ecologies was that young people described them as holistic and *transformational experiences.* In other words, engaging in music activities within situated music learning ecologies appeared to change a young person's perspective in some significant way, often influencing or being influenced by other aspects of his or her non-musical life. Transformative experiences enabled young people to use *actively* concepts and/or relationships in one context to enable them see and experience a different context in new and meaningful ways. Transformative experience has been described as a form of deep engagement that features an intensity and emotional involvement in the activity (Fredricks, Blumenfeld, & Paris, 2004). According to Pugh (2004), transformative experience has three interrelated and interdependent qualities:

> Motivated use that refers to the application of learning from one context to another.
> Expansion of perception that refers to seeing and understanding aspects of the world in a different way.
> Experiential value that refers to the intrinsic and utility aspects of task values (Eccles, O'Neill, Wigfield, 2005), and the feeling of actualized personal interest (Schiefele, 2001).

I have written extensively elsewhere about the conceptual features of transformative music engagement (O'Neill, 2012c, 2014) and the impact on youth empowerment (O'Neill, 20116b) and musical flourishing (O'Neill, 20116a).

Within situated music learning ecologies, there was a strong focus on collaborative music-making; transformative music experiences occurred through social interactions. Situated ecologies tended to be found among secondary school-aged youth and may therefore be tied to developmental (maturational), as well as environmental influences that afford opportunities for greater independence and autonomy as young people progress through secondary school. There was a sense of connectedness and contribution within situated music learning ecologies, but not necessarily a strong sense of *empowerment* (which was a key feature of agentive music learning ecologies). Relationships were the main significance, particularly when they involved collaborative music-making, such as playing in a band or singing in a choir, where there was a high level of solidarity and shared purpose among a group of young musicians. Peers tended to be the dominant focus of relationships, although strong family relationships were also found. Digital media, such as listening to music with iPods, were often interwoven into other music activities, but these were rarely described as important or a necessary component of other music-related activities. There was almost no mention of music creation or composition, either with or without digital technology.

Benson (2001) reminds us that both place and time are a condition of existence: "'who' and 'what' you are is a function of 'where' you are" (p. ix). According to Casey (1993), "to be in the world, to be situated at all, is to be in place" (p. xv). Place-time is inextricably linked to self-identity through the embodied connections we make during moments of experiential time. Casey describes experiential time as "paces of ebb and flow that don't map onto the rigid regularity with which clock time is arranged to pass" (p. xv). For many young people, music activities in their daily lives were described in relation to the particular "communities of practice" in which they were embedded. Lave and Wenger (1991) refer to this as *situated learning*, which "promotes a view of knowing as activity by specific people in specific circumstances" (p. 52). Situated musical selves were also at times segmented and sequential, with a chain of functions, purposes, and events attached to one or more music activity that was not necessarily connected with another cluster of music activity. However, a key difference was that situated musical selves were related to explicit notions of music-making occurring in places and spaces involving social cohesion. This is similar to situated learning, which evolves from a form of membership or a "system of relations" whereby "learning thus implies becoming a different person with respect to the possibilities enabled by these systems of relations" (p. 53). Within situated learning, "identity, knowing and social membership entail one another" (p. 53).

Benson further elaborates this notion of situated identities, drawing on Harré (1998) and Bruner (1990), whereby selves are conceived "as situated perspectives functioning as reference points (ways of being centered), as agents or originators of action accompanied by narrative powers which produce versions of autobiography appropriate to the demands of particular times and circumstances" (pp. 209–10). Situated musical selves were also relational or dialogical in that they were always constructed and maintained in relation to other music activities, to other non-music activities, and to other people who may or may not have been considered part of a person's musical world. Further, as Bakhtin (1986) points out, it is also possible to reflect on oneself as an object of focus, which reflects a "sociocentric" self (Holland & Kipnis, 1994) that seeks out the collaboration of like-minded others and expressions of solidarity through collective action. This was apparent within situated music learning ecologies but was far less apparent in both segmented and agentive ecologies.

5.8.1 Jason's situated music learning ecology

Jason is an 18-year-old male and has been playing the drums for 5 years. He is involved in many different musical groups, including a youth-led band with friends (that rehearses in a garage), a band that plays at his church, and school music groups that include playing in band class, a jazz band, and a jazz combo. For Jason, the significance of his music activities is in the situatedness of particular people in particular circumstances. He describes learning to play the drums as resulting from the environment he grew up in, specifically the church, "cuz my dad's a pastor, so I guess it's sorta natural for me to like to do [music] because I started the drums at church." His family's involvement in his church community influenced his music activity, both initially and over the longer term. He describes how his family moved many times to different places, and that being part of a church band provided a sense of stability and continuity in his life, "I move around a lot so [...] we go to church and I get involved [...] music is sort of my obligation [...] the church, like God, you know, that's how I express myself." He further adds, "we are a religious family I guess, and we listen to a lot of Christian music, and that really affects what I play and why I am involved."

Jason describes his musical goals in relation to playing music with others, "cuz when you play with different musicians you have to push yourself to play better the next time [...] you're in that kind of environment where you play with people and you just get more ideas and you know, you get them off of each other." Jason also describes the challenges of finding like-minded friends outside of the church to play in a band with him, "it was kinda hard finding people who actually wanted to start a band. Because a lot of people play wind instruments and they aren't really into...like rock or anything." The transformative experiences that Jason describes are situated within collaborative music-making activities with others that challenge his own musical perspective,

> [playing in a band] doesn't let me go into my own world of my own music, but like I can explore something else and get something out of it [...] I have to listen to their [music] and they want to listen to that kind of music I guess. I can kinda identify myself with it.

Jason ended his interview by adding the following about what it means to him to be involved in music, "it opens up your world into [...] its not just hearing or listening to the music, but you understand how you make the music and you realize that music is not just on paper—it's in emotion and feeling as well." Jason offers us an insight into young people's ability to establish a sense of connectedness by tapping in effectively to social networks with the goal of being part of and accepted by a larger community where they feel valued and that their musical contributions matter.

5.9 AGENTIVE MUSIC LEARNING ECOLOGIES

The main significance of agentive music learning ecologies is an intense sense of *connectedness*. Connectedness within agentive ecologies often related to a sense of positive relationships and experiences with others, and more specifically, "relationships and experiences from which youth garner esteem and competence" (Karcher, Holcomb, & Zambrano, 2006, p. 655). In addition, connectedness tended to promote "a sense of comfort, well-being and anxiety reduction" (Hagerty, Lynch-Sauer, Patusky, & Bouwsema, 1993, p. 293). In thinking about connectedness as the capacity to benefit from connectivity across personal, social, educational, and musical domains, it is likely that a lack of connectedness would contribute to a sense of social isolation. Over time, a lack of connectedness within agentive music learning ecologies may result in decreased motivation to learn music and engage in music activities (O'Neill, 2012c, 2014, 2016a).

Another prominent aspect of agentive music learning ecologies was the *engaged agency* that permeated young people's descriptions of their music-related activities. I refer to the concept of agency here as "the capacity of individuals to act independently and to make their own decisions based on an awareness of their situa-tion and the range of responses open to them" (Hammond & Wellington, 2013, p. 7). Garfinkel (1963) argues that most people are complacent and view the world without questioning taken-for-granted meanings and predictable behaviors, provided that they lead to sought after or satisfactory outcomes. By creating awareness and "chang-ing the 'rules of the game' other possibilities for action open up" (p. 8). Rather than focus on agency directed towards musical activities that reproduced existing struc-tures and practices (such as playing in a band), agentive music learning ecologies were focused intentionally and intensely on the process of musical creation, experi-mentation, and innovation that "opened up" possibilities for obtaining personally meaningful musical goals.

For Bandura (2001), an agentic perspective on human agency includes "the tem-poral extension of agency through intentionality and forethought, self-regulation by self-reactive influence, and self-reflexiveness about one's capability, quality of function-ing, and the meaning and purpose of one's life pursuits" (p. 1). According to Bandura, intentional acts are a form of agency that can be used to produce different outcomes. These outcomes are the consequences of agentive acts. Although intentional acts involve advance plans of action, these plans "are rarely specified in full detail at the outset" (p. 6). Larson (2011) reminds us that this is particularly the case in our modern world, where young people need to navigate outcomes that are increasingly "destandardized, com-plex, and disorderly" (p. 318). As Larson states, "in real-life situations the pathway to a goal is not always clear, you may have to deal with the challenges and obstacles in the way. You need to navigate disorderly ecological systems—and the people who compose them" (p. 318). He argues that a key challenge for young people's agency is the develop-ment of "ecological reasoning" to navigate the "heterogeneity and complexity of the real world" (p. 319). An agentive form or construction of young people's musical selves also appears to take as its starting point a sense of agency and this was apparent when young people within agentive music learning ecologies reflected on their music engagement. In other words, a sense of agency was infused in their accounts of what, where, when, why, and how they related to music.

Within agentive music learning ecologies, music activity was described by young people as more than a transformative experience (as was found in situated music learn-ing ecologies)—it was a *transformative journey*, shaping their decision-making in their musical lives, including how they engaged in challenging processes aimed at expanding their knowledge and skills. This journey was particularly evident among older youth, and when digital technology was involved it was almost exclusively evident in males', rather than females', descriptions of music engagement. This relates to wider notions of gender differences in digital technology use. For example, Ito et al. (2010) differenti-ated between friendship-driven activities (which are more common among girls) and interest-driven "specialized" activities where "interest or niche identity" moves engage-ment beyond "merely socializing with local peers" (p. 192). Buckingham (2007) argues that this results in "a much deeper and more sophisticated engagement with new media" by males compared with females and also brings males into more contact with people

of diverse ages and backgrounds. According to Ito et al. (2010), "interest-driven practices are what youth describe as the domain of the geeks, freaks, musicians, artists, and
dorks, the kids who are identified as smart, different, or creative, who generally exist at
the margins of teen social worlds" (p. 16). Two forms of interest-driven participation
have been identified as the first stage of *messing around* or "tinkering, exploring, and
extending their understanding" (Ito et al., 2008, p. 20), and the more advanced stage of
geeking out or showing an "intense commitment to or engagement with media or technology" and "learning to navigate esoteric domains of knowledge and practice and participating in communities that traffic in these forms of expertise" (p. 28). This is not to
suggest that agentive music learning ecologies are not possible for females; rather, the
deep level of engagement in musical activities that aligned with young people's interests and appeared to foster a sense of agency, connectedness, and empowerment was
something we only saw happening among some of the males we interviewed who were
engaged in music *and* technology and who articulated a kind of digital learning identity. These young males also expressed what Rose (1996) refers to as an *enterprising self*.
Improvisation, experimentation, and innovation were key activities that gave focus and
direction to their music activities. This is illustrated in the complex music and technol-
ogy-related activities described by one male aged 18 years:

> I did a piece a while ago that I had grabbed my sister's iPod and mine, I don't have any
> recording programs or anything so I recorded different tracks through her, both of
> our iPods and then I lined them up together and did vocals. I don't have a drum set
> so I had to grab my um Rock Band sets, like the video game, and um, I had to play
> this free-style drum thing in there and make a drum track through that, and played
> through some strings and piano, and put a little solo in it too.

TapScott (1998) argues that for many young people using digital media is "as natural
as breathing" and is the means of their empowerment; particularly if they voluntarily
engage in music activities or *user created content* within online affinity groups (Gee,
2000) and participatory cultures (Jenkins, 2009). Although technology is not an essential feature in agentive music learning ecologies, it did feature prominently. It may be
that for today's young people, agentive learning ecologies are an outcome of the digital
age and are therefore revealed in ways that we have not seen in previous generations.
Loveless and Williamson (2013) argue that emerging digital learning identities are an
assemblage "formed out of complex contests and alliances" that are "being acted out
by the multitude of new authorities and experts on learning in the digital age" (p. 23).
While this might be particularly the case within educational policy and the practice
of "schooling" there is an element of *prospective identities* that ground identities in the
future, which stand in contrast to *retrospective identities* "promoted by traditional curriculum of canonical texts, official knowledge, cultural heritage and so forth" (p. 23). In
a similar way, agentive music learning ecologies appear to be concerned with the promotion of prospective identities "construed as active, creative, autonomous and self-
responsible" (p. 23). However, the reality may be that agentive musical selves are merely

reflecting a "mode of life" that is "shaping young people's self-understandings and self-techniques" and "making up" or assembling them into a particular kind of music learner whose "experiential worlds and personal aspirations" align with, rather than drive, the dominant discourses of innovation and a sense of connectedness found in today's digital age.

For young people operating within agentive music learning ecologies, their identities and subjectivities were enacted through the musical creations and expressions that comprised their musical lives. There was a sense of individualization or *personalization* as a musician that both reinforced a construction of what it means to be a musician (musical, creative, innovative) and secured the young person's sense of identity as a musician in the process. For the most part, the musical creations and expressions within agentive ecologies were rarely identical or unified over time; rather, they tended to be improvisational, innovative, and increasingly multimodal when they involved digital media technology. They also tended to involve the creation of, or participation in, zones of interaction or *contact zones* where musical creation could be mutually developed and/or shared. Contact zones were replete with multifaceted opportunities for transformative engagement, self-organization, and creative innovation. They also offered the potential for meaningful social and musical interactions to take place.

5.9.1 David's agentive music learning ecology

David is an 18-year-old male who describes his first music activity as composing music, followed by his participation in a school musical, playing the guitar and drums, and playing in a youth-led band outside of school. David describes music as something he has "always been into," stating "I've always been inclined to do music. So when [my mom] brought home the instrument, that was kind of like a stepping-stone, I could really apply it." He views music as "a creative outlet" saying, "it enriches my life [...] no matter what, [music] is really important to me." For David, the significance of his music activity is in the sense of connectedness and engaged agency that infuse his descriptions of musical activities that are both intentional and meaningful. He describes learning to play the guitar as "a way to express myself [...] it's fun to get up there and play in front of people." His sense of connectedness to other people is in relation to his music-making, "because if I'm doing music, other musicians are going to be around me [...] I'm around musicians all day, so I guess that helps me grow." He also describes how music provides a medium for him to express part of his identity, "Um I have a quiet side to myself, and I have this other side to me, where I like to really get out there and express myself. So ... maybe that's my outlet for that."

David describes his main musical goal as "I would like to compose" and that a key challenge that would prevent him in achieving his goal is "if I didn't have access to information. So, I guess the Internet is a big help." He also states that he gets his inspiration to compose music from watching films, "sometimes if I watch something emotional, like a film or something, it will give me inspiration to write [music]." He talks about his use of digital media technology as both a tool ("I write most of my music on a computer program [...] I transcribe it into the program [...] I usually improvise and something will come"), a resource ("If I'm watching a commercial, I'll hear the music and dissect it"), and a form of expression for his music activity by playing the music video game *Guitar Hero* and recording and sharing his music compositions. He describes composing as "always in the foreground of my mind" and says that although he is around other young people with similar interests, he does not believe that this impacts on his relationships with other people in general because, "I wouldn't be there if it wasn't for the music." Young people, such as David, are increasingly using the affordances of digital technology and social media networks for creative and often collaborative forms of music-making and sharing. The Internet also affords "space and place" for complex identity work (Stern, 2008), and the fluidity of online identities that enable young people to construct and try on identities that might bear little resemblance to their offline sense of self (Turkle, 1995). Males similar to David tended to describe an evolving and transformative *engaged agency* or active engagement through their use of the Internet and other forms of digital media technology. David and other young people enmeshed within agentive music learning ecologies, tended to demonstrate a sense of empowerment and connectedness that appeared to align in a reciprocal relationship with their musical selves to create a sense of agency from which they were able to navigate and negotiate new music learning opportunities. Yet, we are left wondering to what extent young people within agentive music learning ecologies are "being positioned to adopt the identities required to create and maintain particular visions of the future" (Loveless & Williamson, 2013, p. 27)—visions that reject or ignore many cultural and historical music traditions, thereby reducing rather than expanding young people's "choices" and constraining their horizons of music-related activities.

5.10 CONCLUSION

Young people's music learning identities are aligned and woven into their experiential worlds and their personal aspirations as they go about "making up" their musical selves within the unique configuration of the music learning ecologies they inhabit. Young people's musical selves might be conceived of as *navigational systems* or "pathways" through their music learning ecologies that encompass complex self and social structures and interrelationships that inform and shape a sense of "who I am is what I care about and am able to do, which is also related to where I am and how I feel about it." Three portraits of music learning ecologies—segmented, situated, agentive—were presented as mere representations of what can only be understood fully through a detailed knowledge of how each young person engages in music activities in relation to the contexts and learning ecologies within which their music engagement takes place. These portraits, therefore, offer only a modest contribution with the aim of troubling some assumptions and providing a catalyst for future research. Such knowledge can provide new insights into the dynamic, interconnected, fluid, and multifaceted nature of music learning identities among young people growing up in today's digital age. Smith-Lovin (2003) claims that we can gain a more subtle view of these complex interrelationships and a more complex notion of self through an ecological perspective as learning ecologies provide "a necessary condition for multiple identities to be enacted in a given situation" (p. 172). Although it is not possible to disentangle the complex meshwork and pathways of musical selves, and the sociocultural structures and practices that initiate and sustain them, efforts to understand young people's music engagement processes better by gaining deeper insights into the multiple settings and relationships that comprise their music learning ecologies is likely to help advance our understanding.

A key concern raised in this chapter is the extent to which young people's music learning ecologies are becoming intertwined within digital learning identities that are assumed, assembled, shared, and promoted. Young people today are lifewide learners (Barnett, 2012, p. 12), and their music learning takes place in contact zones across physical and virtual life spaces, and places of home, school, local, and online communities, and (mostly through the Internet) the wider world. There is a sense that today's young people are being positioned as youth-as-musical resources or music entrepreneurs who are being shaped "through a dense, heterogeneous web of practical developments, political objectives, conceptual and theoretical advances related to the deployment, in various ways and through various programs advanced by various authorities, of technologies in education" (Loveless & Williamson, 2013, p. 29). Yet, for young people, this description is at odds with their sense of agency and autonomy, which they do not perceive as "fabricated"; rather, they perceive their music learning opportunities as happening *organically* as they discover and "make" music in ways that differ from past generations. To what extent are these "fictional truths" tied to technological change and enterprise education? Are young people being "addressed, represented and acted upon" as if they are a "particular type" (Rose, 1996, p. 169) in the realm of music? What are the affordances and constraints of musical selves that are embedded in segmented, situated, and agentive music learning ecologies? How are young people recruited, allocated, and apportioned in relation to different music learning landscapes? These are questions I hope future research will help us to understand.

A sense of connectedness appears to play an integral role within both situated and agentive music learning ecologies, and yet it was largely absent within segmented ecologies, where young people often reported experiencing a sense of isolation or a lack of connectedness. For situated ecologies, there was a strong focus on collaborative music-making and social interactions within particular communities and contexts. As such, there was a sense of connectedness and contribution within situated ecologies but not necessarily a strong sense of empowerment. This is in contrast to agentive music ecologies, where young people tended to navigate in ways that mattered to them, indicating both a strong sense of connectedness and empowerment. The increasing presence of technology within agentive ecologies was accompanied by increased motivation and aspirations, as well as potential anxieties to "act out" the dominant discourses of connectedness in today's digital age. Furthermore, young people's accompanying agency also appeared to be "made up" and fully integrated within their musical selves, which were infused with a sense of autonomy and self-actualization. Young people within agentive ecologies appeared to be "remaking" and developing their own unique and multifaceted roles and personal musical meanings with increasingly fluid interconnections. Their music learning ecologies were no longer a bounded place; rather, they became contact zones in which they navigated several pathways that were thoroughly entangled. According to Ingold (2007), in a zone of entanglement, "there are no insides or outsides, only openings and ways through" (p. 103).

References

Bailey, D.E., & Barley, S.R. (2011). Teaching-learning ecologies: mapping the environment to structure through action. *Organization Science*, 22(1), 262–85.
Bakhtin, M.M. (1986). *Speech genres and other late essays.* Austin: University of Texas Press.
Bandura, A. (2001). Social cognitive theory: an agentic perspective. *Annual Review of Psychology*, 52, 1–26.
Barnett, R. (2012). The coming of the ecological learner. In: P. Tynjälä, M.-L. Stenström, & M. Saarnivaara (Eds.) *Transitions and transformations in learning and education*, pp. 9–20. New York: Springer.
Barron, B. (2006). Interest and self-sustained learning as catalysts for development: a learning ecology perspective. *Human Development*, 49, 193–224.
Bauman, Z. (2000). *Liquid modernity.* Cambridge, MA: Polity Press.
Benson, C. (2001). *The cultural psychology of self: place, morality and art in human worlds.* New York: Routledge.
Berger, P.L., Berger, B., & Kellner, H. (1974). *The homeless mind: modernization and consciousness.* New York: Vintage Books.
Bronfenbrenner, U. (1979). *The ecology of human development: experiments by nature and design.* Cambridge, MA: Harvard University Press.
Bruner, J. (1990). *Acts of meaning.* Cambridge, MA: Harvard University Press.
Buckingham, D. (2007). *Beyond technology: children's learning in the age of digital culture.* Cambridge, MA: Polity Press.
Casey, E.S. (1993). *Getting back into place: toward a renewed understanding of the place-world.* Bloomington, IN: Indiana University Press.
Cole, M. (1996). *Cultural psychology: a once and future discipline.* Cambridge, MA: Harvard University Press.
Crisp, B.R. (2010). Belonging, connectedness and social exclusion. *Journal of Social Inclusion*, 1(2), 123–32.
Dede, C. (2007). Foreword. In: G. Salaway, J. B. Caruso, & M.R. Nelson (Eds.) *The ECAR study of undergraduate students and information technology*, Vol. 6, pp. 5–9. Boulder, CO: Educause.
Deleuze, G., & Guattari, F. (1987). *What is philosophy?* London: Verso.
Eccles, J.S., O'Neill, S.A., & Wigfield, A. (2005). Ability self-perceptions and subject task values in adolescents and children. In: K. A. Moore & L. H. Lippman (Eds.) *What do children need to flourish? Conceptualizing and measuring indicators of positive development*, pp. 237–49. New York, NY: Springer.
Edgerton, S.H. (1996). *Translating the curriculum: multiculturalism into cultural studies.* New York: Routledge.

Engeström, Y. (1987). *Learning by expanding: an activity-theoretical approach to developmental research*. Helsinki: Orienta-Konsultit Oy.

Florida, R. (2002). *The rise of the creative class. And how it's transforming work, leisure and everyday life*. New York: Basic Books.

Foucault, M. (1980). The confession of the flesh. In: C. Gordon (Ed.) *Power/knowledge: selected interviews and other writings*, pp. 194–228. New York: Pantheon.

Fredricks, J.A., Blumenfeld, P.C., & Paris, A. (2004). School engagement: potential of the concept, state of the evidence. *Review of Educational Research, 74, 59–109*.

González, N., Moll, L., & Amanti, C. (2005). *Funds of knowledge: theorizing practices in households, communities, and classrooms*. New York: Erlbaum.

Gardner, H., & Davis, K. (2013). The app generation: How today's youth navigate identity, intimacy, and imagination in a digital world. New Haven, CT: Yale University Press.

Garfinkel, H. (1963). A conception of, and experiments with, "trust" as a condition of stable concerted actions. In: O.J. Harvey (Ed.) *Motivation and social interaction: cognitive approaches*, pp. 187–238. New York: Ronald Press.

Garfinkel, H. (1967). *Ethnomethodology*. Cambridge, MA: Polity Press.

Gauntlett, D. (2007). *Creative explorations: new approaches to identities and audiences*. Abingdon, Oxon: Routledge.

Gee, J.P. (2000). Identity as an analytic lens for research in education. *Review of Research in Education*, 25(1), 99–125.

Gee, J. P. (1996). *Social linguistics and literacies: Ideology in discourses*, 2nd edn. London: Taylor and Francis.

Gee, J.P. (2004). *Situated language and learning: a critique of traditional schooling*. London: Routledge.

Gee, J.P., & Hayes, E.R. (2010). *Women as gamers: the Sims and 21st century learning*. New York: Palgrave.

Giddens, A. (1991). *Modernity and self-identity: self and society in the late modern age*. Cambridge, MA: Polity Press.

Goffman, E. (1968). *Stigma: notes on the management of spoiled identity*. London: Pelican.

Goldman, S., Booker, S., & McDermott, M. (2008). Mixing the digital, social, and cultural: Learning, identity, and agency in youth participation. In: D. Buckingham (Ed.) *Youth, identity, and digital media*, pp. 185–206. Cambridge, MA: MIT Press.

Guerra, N.G., & Bradshaw, C.P. (2008). Linking the prevention of problem behaviors and positive youth development: core competencies for positive youth development and risk prevention. *New Directions for Child and Adolescent Development*, 122, 1–17.

Habermas, J. (1987). *The theory of communicative action*, Vol. 1. Boston: Beacon.

Habermas, J. (1987). *The theory of communicative action*, Vol. 2. Boston: Beacon.

Hagerty, B. M. K., Lynch-Sauer, J., Patusky, K. L., & Bouwsema, M. (1993). An emerging theory of human relatedness. *Image: The Journal of Nursing Scholarship*, 25(4), 291–6.

Hammond, M., & Wellington, J. (2013). *Research methods: the key concepts*. New York: Routledge.

Harré, R. (1998). *The singular self: an introduction to the psychology of personhood*. London: Sage.

Harré, R., & Secord, P.F. (1972). *The explanation of social behaviour*. Oxford: Blackwell.

Harré, R., & van Langenhove, L. (1999). *Positioning theory*. Oxford: Blackwell.

Holland, D. & Kipnis, A. (1994). Metaphors for embarrassment and stories of exposure: the not-so-egocentric self in American culture. *Ethos*, 22, 316–42.

Holland, D., Lachicotte, W., Skinner, D., & Cain, C. (1998). *Identity and agency in cultural worlds*. Cambridge, MA: Harvard University Press.

Howkins, J. (2001). *The creative economy: how people make money from ideas*. London: Allen Lane.

Husserl, E. (1936/1970). *The crises of the European sciences and transcendental phenomenology*, transl. D. Carr. Evanston, IL: Northwestern University Press.

Ingold, T. (2007). *Lines: a brief history*. New York: Routledge.

Ito, M., Horst, H., Bittanti, M., et al. (2008). Living and learning with new media: summary of findings from the Digital Youth Project. Chicago, IL: MacArthur Foundation. Available at: http://digitalyouth.ischool.berkeley.edu/files/report/digitalyouth-WhitePaper.pdf (accessed February 4, 2016).

Ito, M., Baumer, S., Bittanti, M., et al. (2010). *Hanging out, messing around, and geeking out: kids living and learning with new media*. Boston: MIT Press.

Jenkins, H. (2009). *Confronting the challenges of a participatory culture: media education for the 21st century*. Cambridge, MA: MIT Press.

Karcher, M.J., Holcomb, M.R., & Zambrano, E. (2006). Measuring and evaluating adolescent connectedness. In: H. L. K. Coleman & C. Yeh (Eds.) *Handbook of school counseling*, pp. 651–72. New York: Erlbaum .

Kress, G. (2010). *Multimodality: a social semiotic approach to contemporary communication*. London: Routledge.

Larson, R. W. (2011). Positive development in a disorderly world. *Journal of Research on Adolescence*, 21(2), 317–34.

Lave, J. & Wenger, E. (1991). *Situated learning: legitimate peripheral participation*. New York: Cambridge University Press.

Law, J. (2009). Actor-network theory and material semiotics. In: B. S. Turner (Ed.) *The new Blackwell companion to social theory*, 3rd edn, pp. 141–58. Oxford: Blackwell.

Lerner, R.M. (1991). Changing organism-context relations as the basic process of development: a developmental contextual perspective. *Developmental Psychology*, 27, 27–32.

Long, J. (2013). Fresh thinking for music education. Presentation to Youth Music UK. Available at: http://www.youtube.com/watch?v=FZA1Inn9gVI (accessed February 4, 2016).

Loveless, A. & Williamson, B. (2013). *Learning identities in a digital age: rethinking creativity, education and technology*. London: Routledge.

Mans, M. (2009). *Living in worlds of music: a view of education and values*. New York: Springer.

Martin, J. & McLellan, A.-M. (2013). *The education of selves: how psychology transformed students*. New York: Oxford University Press.

Mead, G.H. (1938). *The philosophy of the act*. Chicago: University of Chicago Press.

OECD. (2012). *Connected minds: technology and today's learners*. Educational Research and Innovation, OECD Publishing.

O'Neill, S.A. (2002). The self-identity of young musicians. In: R.A.R. MacDonald, D. J. Hargreaves, & D. Miell (Eds.) *Musical identities*, pp. 79–96. Oxford: Oxford University Press.

O'Neill, S.A. (2012a). Personhood and music learning: an introduction. In: S. A. O'Neill (Series & Vol. Ed.), *Research to Practice: Vol. 5. Personhood and music learning: connecting perspectives and narratives*, pp. 1–15. Waterloo, ON: Canadian Music Educators' Association.

O'Neill, S.A. (2012b). Blending, blurring and braiding the boundaries of digital media, artistic learning and youth culture. Keynote Address presented at the Futures in ICT-Collaboration Conference, Simon Fraser University, Faculty of Education, Surrey Campus, Canada.

O'Neill, S.A. (2012c). Becoming a music learner: towards a theory of transformative music engagement. In: G. E. McPherson & G. Welch (Eds.) *The Oxford handbook of music education*, Vol. 1, pp. 163–86. New York: Oxford University Press.

O'Neill, S.A. (2014). Mind the gap: transforming music engagement through learner-centred informal music learning. *The Recorder: Journal of the Ontario Music Educators' Association*, 56(2), 18–22.

O'Neill, S.A. (2015a). Youth music cultures and identities in a digital age: An interview study of young people's sense of connectedness. Paper presented at the Journal of Youth Studies Conference: Contemporary youth, contemporary risk. Copenhagen, Denmark.

O'Neill, S. A. (2016a). Transformative music engagement and musical flourishing. In: G. E. McPherson (Ed.) *The child as musician: a handbook of musical development*, 2nd edn, pp. 606–25. New York: Oxford University Press.

O'Neill, S. A. (2016b). Youth empowerment and transformative music engagement. In: C. Benedict, P. Schmidt, G. Spruce, & P. Woodward (Eds.) *Oxford handbook of music education and social justice* pp. 388–405. New York: Oxford University Press.

Overton, W.F. (2007). A coherent metatheory for dynamic systems: relational organicism-contextualism. *Human Development*, 50, 154–9.

Overton, W.F. (1998). Relational-developmental theory: A psychological perspective. In: D. Gorlitz, H. J. Harloff , G. Mey, & J. Valsiner (Eds.) *Children, cities, and psychological theories: developing relationships*, pp. 315–35. Berlin: Walter De Gruyter & Co.

Pugh, K.J. (2004). Newton's laws beyond the classroom walls. *Science Education*, 88, 182–96.

Rogoff, B. (2003). *The cultural nature of human development*. New York: Oxford University Press.

Rose, N. (1996). *Inventing ourselves: psychology, power and personhood*. Cambridge: Cambridge University Press.

Rose-Krasnor, L. (2009). Future directions in youth involvement research. *Social Development*, 18(2), 497–509.

Rowsell, J. (2013). *Working with multimodality: rethinking literacy in a digital age*. Abingdon: Routledge.

Schiefele, U. (2001). The role of interest in motivation and learning. In: J. Collis & S. Messick (Eds.), *Intelligence and personality: bridging the gap in theory and measurement*, pp. 163–194. Mahwah, NJ: Erlbaum.

Schutz, A. & Luckmann, T. (1973). *The structures of the life-world*, transl. R. M. Zaner and H. T. Engelhardt, Jr. Evanston, IL: Northwestern University Press.

Smith-Lovin, L. (2003). Self, identity, and interaction in an ecology of identities. In: P. J. Burke, T. J. Owens, R. T. Serpe, & P. A. Thoits (Eds.) *Advances in identity theory and research*, pp. 167–78. New York: Kluwer/Plenum.

Spencer, M.B., Dupree D., & Hartmann, T. (1997). A phenomenological variant of ecological systems theory (PVEST): a self-organization perspective in context. *Development and Psychopathology*, 9, 817–33.

Spinelli, E. (1989). *The interpreted world: an introduction to phenomenological psychology*. London: Sage.

Stern, S. (2008). Producing sites, exploring identities: youth online authorship. In: D. Buckingham (Ed.) *Youth, identity, and digital media*, pp. 95–118. Cambridge, MA: MIT Press.

Stetsenko, A. (2012). Personhood: An activist project of historical becoming through collaborative pursuits of social transformation. *New Ideas in Psychology*, 30, 144–53.

Stivale, C.J. (2011). *Gilles Deleuze: key concepts*, 2nd edn. New York: Routledge.

Tapscott, D. (1998). *Growing up digital: the rise of the net generation*. New York: McGraw-Hill.

Taylor, C. (1989). *Sources of the self: the making of the modern identity*. Cambridge, MA: Harvard University Press.

Turkle, S. (1995). *Life on the screen*. New York: Simon and Schuster.

Urrieta, L. Jr. (2007). Figured worlds and education: an introduction to the special issue. *Urban Review*, 39(2), 107–16.

Vygotsky, L.S. (1978). *Mind in society*. Cambridge, MA: Harvard University Press.

Walton, K. (1998). Listening with imagination: Is music representational? In: P. Alperson (Ed.) *Musical worlds: new directions in the philosophy of music*, pp. 47–62. University Park PA: Pennsylvania State University Press.

Wenger, E. (1998). *Communities of practice: learning, meaning and identity*. Cambridge: Cambridge University Press.

Williams, B. (1985/2008). *Ethics and the limits of philosophy*. Cambridge, MA: Harvard University Press.

CHAPTER 6

....

THE EAR OF THE BEHOLDER

Improvisation, Ambiguity, and Social Contexts
in the Constructions of Musical Identities

....

GRAEME B. WILSON AND RAYMOND MACDONALD

IN this chapter, we discuss how identity work among improvisers leads musical events to be constructed in context-specific ways. We compare accounts of musical free improvisation in interviews with two groups of improvisers from varied musical backgrounds, one interviewed for the purpose of media publicity and one group interviewed for the purpose of research. The comparison indicates that reports of this musical practice are shaped by the identities that can be constructed for the improvisers involved and that these are specific to the interview context. The fluidity of musical meaning that this suggests has significant implications for how we understand the practice of improvisation, and the music produced in this way.

6.1 IMPROVISERS AND IDENTITIES

....

Live renditions of free improvised music by groups of two or more individuals are a unique psychological phenomenon, whether taking place in a concert hall, a classroom, or the front room of a house (Nettl & Russell, 2008; Mazzola, Cherlin, Rissi, & Kennedy, 2009; MacDonald & Wilson, 2014). Yet our understanding of how individuals spontaneously and simultaneously create music together is limited compared with what is known about other aspects of musical performance (MacDonald, Wilson, & Miell, 2012). Some qualitative studies have followed Berliner (1994) in theorizing that the meaning or emotional content of individual contributions to an emerging group improvisation may be shared by those taking part, at least during optimal interaction (Seddon, 2005; Schober and Spiro, 2014). However, agreement as to content may only be achievable in broad terms; it is notable that experiments trying to quantify shared or objectively verifiable interpretations of musical improvisation have found sizeable levels of divergence in interpretation (Gilboa, Bodner, & Amir, 2006; Schober & Spiro, 2014). A series of qualitative studies suggests alternatively that musicians' accounts of improvising are characteristic of a discourse model of conversation, whereby musical meaning is constructed in context-specific ways by the improviser (MacDonald & Wilson, 2005; Wilson & MacDonald, 2005). For instance, an improviser's choice not to play during a performance could be constructed by another ensemble member in various ways (e.g., a rallying signal, an act of minimal creativity, a warning of individual or group problems with the music in play, a stop sign, an indication of inhibition, a lack of concern with the quality of the music, or an act of aggression) depending on the identities that the ensemble member perceives for each player (e.g., willful individualist, proactive collaborator, sensitive and wary contributor, disengaged malcontent, one careful to give ground). Improvisers' talk thus functions to position themselves and others in relation to culturally available discourses or means of expression, rather than paralleling a transfer-of-information model of language use (Monson, 1996; Sawyer, 2005). This suggests that in the course of performing this music, an individual improviser may make a contribution to the music with a particular intent, but both musical content and intent are flexible and will be shaped by the identities that that individual can construct for themself and others within the social and temporal context of performance (MacDonald, Miell & Hargreaves, 2002). That musical contribution may, in turn, be interpreted and responded to, in idiosyncratic and unpredictable ways by the other improvisers, depending on the meanings they assign to it in the context of what has gone before, and the identities they recognize for themselves and others in the group. This fluidity in meaning is particularly facilitated in engagement with non-verbal music, in that its essential ambiguity or "floating intentionality" (Cross, 2005; Bryan-Kinns & Hamilton, 2009) leaves it open to interpretation. Given the sheer range of possible musical contributions in some forms of improvisation, performers are likely to arrive at different understandings of musical events in which both take part, as Ferguson & Bell (2008) suggest:

> A performer on the receiving end may not realize that an emerging sound was unintentional, or that a gesture happened by accident, however, they will respond to it nonetheless.

pp. 4-5.

Identity work is likely to have considerable importance for individuals improvising together. In describing their practice, improvisers have attested that they are more focused on those they are playing with than on, audiences, for example (Wilson & MacDonald, 2005). Furthermore, improvisation in contemporary music has expanded to encompass a bewildering diversity of musical practices and choices and is now widely practiced by improvisers from different musical spheres or backgrounds coming together to create music (Lewis, 2007; Biasutti & Frezza, 2009; MacDonald, Wilson, & Miell, 2012). In particular, the growing numbers of post-idiomatic free improvisers seek to avoid any parameters on improvisation arising from genre expectations, allowing their music to unfold in any direction at any given moment in the interests of maximizing innovation (Bailey, 1993). Within such diversity, identities are likely to be vital in positioning self in relation to other improvisers on the spectrum of improvisatory practice. When, for example, members of a free improvising group from varied backgrounds referred in separate interviews to a particular musical event in which all had participated, their interpretations of a moment of silence within the piece were distinct and shaped particular identities for themselves and other musicians involved (Wilson and MacDonald, 2012).

However, previous work highlights methodological issues for research aiming to understand what happens when people improvise. Interviewing is, for better or worse, the modus operandum of qualitative investigation. Whatever interviewees try to tell researchers is filtered through their own identity work, the culture surrounding them and in particular, the expectations that a researcher's presence inevitably engenders in an interviewee (Wetherell, Taylor, & Yates, 2001). Qualitative theorists argue, against the positivist expectation of objectivity, that research findings are therefore more usefully understood as the product of their particular contexts and that analysis should embrace and explore any contextual influences. In music research, recruitment is often through professional or educational networks. Such familiarity with the target population, or "insider" status in the field of interest, can be invaluable in facilitating recruitment and boosting understanding or trust between interviewer and interviewed, but their wider relationship and networks are all the more important to consider as influences on the emergent discourse. Despite this, the context of data gathering and potential reflexive influences on the analysis are frequently given limited treatment in the analysis of qualitative work on improvisation (MacDonald & Wilson, 2006).

Furthermore, research interviews are greatly overrepresented in literature among possible sources of qualitative data. Recognizing this, discursive psychologists have repeatedly called for qualitative research to broaden its scope beyond transcripts of research interviews (Potter & Hepburn, 2005) and to analyze corpuses of publicly available discourse. Data other than research interviews that have been examined by researchers include transcriptions of the broadcast congressional hearings of US President Clinton (Locke & Edwards, 2003) and news interviews with public figures (Montgomery, 2008). Discourses around celebrity identity in the media have also been the focus of studies, highlighting for instance the delicate negotiation of identity in terms of relationships or motherhood in interviews with singer Britney Spears and actress Sarah Jessica Parker (Jermyn, 2008; Meyers, 2009). This is an approach with much to offer the investigation of improvisation, which is widely discussed in public forums and media. Talk gathered in interviews for the purposes of media coverage and mainstream publication must inevitably generate different expectations in the interviewee and thus lead to alternate constructions of self and improvising practice. Such data could allow the triangulation of views expressed in research interviews.

Qualitative research on improvisation, then, could reach novel and more robust findings by paying greater attention to the influences upon research interviews, particularly that of the researcher, and through analyzing data from sources other than research interviews. To illustrate this, we examine talk about musical practice in media interviews, publicly available on the Internet, with participants in a celebrated collaboration between prominent improvisers and talk in research interviews with a large improvising ensemble of musicians from different backgrounds. We highlight the aspects of improvising and of identity as improviser that are foregrounded by musicians in these two corpuses and compare their attributions of self and others to consider how musical identity work among cross-genre improvisers is distinct or similar across the contexts of interviewing for publicity and comparatively confidential research interviewing. The results inform new directions for research into contemporary improvisatory practice. In particular, they highlight the potential contribution of examining discourse about improvising in wider contexts and considering the influence of context on the accounts that emerge.

6.2 Methods

In a previous study (Wilson & MacDonald, 2012) participants for research interviews were recruited from the Glasgow Improvisers Orchestra (GIO), an ensemble rehearsing and performing together regularly (www.glasgowimprovisersorchestra.com) and dedicated to free improvisation. Its line-up includes more than 20 players from a wide range of musical backgrounds including jazz, classical, pop, and avant-garde. Individual in-depth interviews ($n = 10$, 2 female and 8 male) about improvising and playing in the ensemble were conducted by Wilson. A sample of 10 musicians diverse in gender and musical backgrounds was sought. Eleven ensemble members in all, including all female ensemble members, were invited to take part, with only one declining. Participants were assured of confidentiality and it was made clear that participation was voluntary at all times. Both authors have participated in and performed with GIO since its inception. This familiarity meant that requests for interview and the aims of the research were not associated by the potential recruits with an "outsider" but with someone whose musical and other values and knowledge they were acquainted with through previous association and likely to treat as aligned with their own. Interviews were tape recorded with consent at participants' convenience and lasted between 45 and 120 minutes. Interviewees were asked to describe their own experience of instances of group improvising within the ensemble. The interviews were transcribed anonymously, then analyzed by the authors, whose familiarity with the interviewees meant that they potentially shared some of the performing experiences discussed. However, since analysis aimed to appraise each account in the interviewee's terms, the interviewer accepted any accounts of shared events as they were described to him, and analysis did not seek to privilege any one account of events as having greater external veracity than any other.

To provide comparable publicly available data, an Internet search was carried out in December 2013 for interviews with participants in Spring Heel Jack's collaborations with Evan Parker, Han Benninck, and others. This series of performances and recordings over a number of years from 2001 onward involved cross-disciplinary interaction between musicians best known for producing rave or rock music, and prominent free improvisers on various instruments.[1] The high profiles of those involved means their views are sought by the media. An Internet search identified 12 reported interviews in English conducted with project participants in which Spring Heel Jack was mentioned (Miller, 1999; Edelstein, 2001; Eyles, 2003a, b; Fordham, 2003; Collins, 2004; Currin, 2008; Adler, 2010; Cooke, 2010; Freeman, 2010; Bath, 2013; Smith, 2013). These involved seven collaborators from the project: Ashley Wales and John Coxon of Spring Heel Jack (AW, JC), saxophonist Evan Parker (EP), drummer Mark Sanders (MSa), guitarist Jason Pierce (JP), pianist Matthew Shipp (MSh), and trumpeter Wadada Leo Smith (WLS). Text from these interviews was copied to a Word file for analysis.

All transcripts were coded through repeated reading. Any recurring features in the content of the interview talk were labelled as themes under appropriate headings. Emergent codes, and in particular themes relating to improvising together or musical identities, were compared across the two datasets and discussed by the authors, with coding definitions refined and redefined to account for any instances of divergence. Key themes identified in this way included:

- Intuitive improvising.
- Respect for the "greats."
- Importance of musicianship.
- Identity as improviser.
- Other genre identities.
- Commercial pressures and popularity.
- Truth to vision.
- Struggle.
- Eclectic tastes and knowledge.

In addition, instances of structural features of discourse identified in previous studies were noted, in particular any use of repertoire: "a lexicon or register of terms and metaphors drawn upon to characterize and evaluate actions and events" (Potter & Wetherell, 1994, p. 138). The coding strategy was thus refined to arrive at a consistent interpretation of the data (Potter, 2004).

The authors' status as active practitioners and proponents of free improvised music gives them a particular insight and orientation towards this field of musical practice, and a shared professional milieu with both groups of interviewees. In keeping with qualitative approaches, the authors did not claim an objective relationship to either dataset, but sought to account for any subjective influences on the gathering and analysis of either corpus.

---

[1] CDs from this collaboration, all released on Thirsty Ear, include "Masses" (2001) THI57103.2; "AMaSSED" (2003) THI57123.2; "Live" (2003) THI57130.2; "The Sweetness of the Water" (2004) THI57146.2; and "Songs and Themes" (2008) THI57183.2.

6.3 PUBLICLY AVAILABLE INTERVIEWS

The SHJ collaborators construct group improvisation as an activity dependent on an intuitive or unconscious grasp of a common musical purpose and approach. AW, for instance, perceives other musicians having an uncanny ability to recognize as one when a section should end:

> Although it was all improvised, you had the feeling that these people know what they are doing, know where they are going now … What I love is the way there are no nods, no signs, no conducting or conduction, or anything like that. They just seem to know when they have run out of steam and someone is going to take a break. And then the other two are going to get on with their scraping and scrabbling.
>
> AW.

JC points to an instinctive understanding of shared intent between EP and JP, and the drummer Han Benninck as a musician from whom music "pours forth." EP asserts that improvising requires "telepathic" intuitive understanding of musical signals and responses between group members, even at an unconscious level. This is consistent with what we have previously termed the "mystery" repertoire: improvisation described as operating through a process that players themselves are not fully aware of or able to account for. The mastery repertoire, accounting for improvisation as requiring the lengthy and demanding acquisition of skills and understanding, is less consistently apparent in these interviews. AW and JC nevertheless stress the extensive experience and technical abilities of the musicians they have invited to the project. Both describe the invited musicians as "consummate" and present with their own capacities as limited in contrast. For instance, AW sets out a deferential relationship to these others:

> They are consummate musicians. That is what they do … It is a little bit presumptuous to say, "Do you want to play on this electronic soundscape we've made in the studio?"
>
> AW.

Any hierarchy among participants might be interpreted as calling into question the equivalence of the contribution made by all. This discourse is, therefore, accompanied by an assertion that improvisation does not depend on what the interviewees construct as conventional "musicianship": the ability to read, learn and execute precomposed music. EP, for instance, positioned the memorizing or reading of music as interfering with the intuitive interaction necessary when improvising.

Instead, their ability to engage in interdisciplinary improvisation together is accounted for with reference to shared musical and other values, which together create a basis for trust vital to successful group improvisation. Thus, enthusiasm for, and knowledge of, an eclectic range of music is repeatedly claimed for all those involved. MSa, for instance, signals his breadth of understanding of different musical traditions by referring to his abilities and participation in diverse musical styles including dub reggae and contemporary classical music:

> I enjoy listening to and playing modern classical music and I hope the future brings more opportunity to be a part of it
>
> MSa.

Such other genres are nevertheless described as essentially limited, or "safe and structured;" AW for instance summarizes punk as "three chords blundering around." Constructing other music in these terms functions to distinguish it from improvisation, which is asserted as an unpredictable, powerful, and risky musical practice that is of greater interest than any other musical affiliations. Free improvisation is also underscored as a particularly personal vision of how music should be made, in the face of expectations of more commercial or popular music:

> … it [current project] is so refreshing that the idea is to make exactly what you want to make, exactly how you want to make it and fuck the consequences, whether one person buys your record or nobody buys it.
>
> JC.

Identities for musicians are constructed around these accounts. Where collaborators treat themselves or others as having been associated with a particular genre, they are positioned as having moved on from that identity in order to fulfil their musical potential, implying that the other identities are potentially incongruous with the free improvisation project. For instance, JC acknowledges previous identity for himself and AW as producers of club music, familiar with the basis of its popular or commercial appeal, before distancing the pair from this genre:

> We're not interested in getting accessible, understandable breakbeats and putting stuff with them. It is not interesting to us.
>
> JC.

MSh recalls his surprise that the pair did not fulfil his expectations of DJs, in that the music produced through their collaboration was not driven by danceable beats; and WLS suggested that AW and JC have moved beyond their previous identity to bring about their wider collaborations. AW and JC in turn position other musicians as having emerged from the jazz tradition but identify them as improvisers who have transcended constraints associated with that genre. For instance, one contributor's improvising was associated with jazz, but endorsed as "cool," rather than the more deprecating "goatee-beardy":

> It was cool, in a nice way, not in a goatee-beardy jazz way. He was in complete control. He knew what he was doing. Although it was all improvised …
>
> AW.

In support of the principle that successful group improvisation requires shared understanding, interviewees proposed certain attitudes and beliefs as common to the identities of this interdisciplinary group, particularly remaining true to a personal vision of what was valuable in music. JP, for instance, endorsed the "honesty" of the collaborators' approach that was "not about producing a record," and EP stated:

> He [HB] never takes a great deal of interest in what is supposed to be fixed and what is supposed to be free anyway, which is good because he knows his own temperament very well indeed.
>
> EP.

Collaborators accepted that this placed them "outside" musical traditions and identified with each other as being informed by democratic principles in their approach to music, seeking not to impose hierarchies or leadership on their interaction. They positioned themselves and others as not being bound by external criteria of musicianship; WLS and MSh, for instance, assert that they do not find that improvising together necessarily depends on objectively verifiable musical mastery:

> ... for me, I don't believe that musicians can be made. Don Cherry took a lot of amateurs and made great music from it. Background, maybe it's important in some contexts, but not always.
>
> WLS.

> To sit around and have an abstract concept about whether this guy is a musician or not because he's playing with records, there are obviously sensibilities you have to have to be good at it. To make up an abstract category in your mind that this is a musician and this is not, doesn't mean anything to me.
>
> MSh.

In summary, the identity constructed from these features is that of improvisers who appreciate, but see beyond various genres and conventional standards of musicianship, who must struggle to produce the music that fulfils them in an essentially collaborative way with others who share their values. Identifying these qualities as positive validates the group's ability to make high-quality music through improvising together in spite of their varied backgrounds.

6.4 RESEARCH INTERVIEWS

The accounts of improvising given in research interviews share some similarities with the features above. Members of GIO likewise described improvising within the large ensemble in terms of an unpredictable, unfathomable or risky undertaking: for instance as something "chaotic," involving "a frisson of danger" (GIO6). Improvising together involved concentration in order to feel "as one" with the group, or locked in with an "almost subconscious" connection between them that could not be readily accounted for:

> it's almost in unison and it, and shifting up more than, you know, up fourths and it's like how do you know, how does he know I'm going to play a fourth, how do I know he's going to play a fourth? [yeah] You just do. [it's …] Er and that's that's something that's um yeah, it's quite weird, I can't quite explain that.
>
> GIO3.

This playing relationship was seen to depend on a keen instinctive understanding among players, allowing them to "tune into" each other's musical intentions while improvising (GIO5). One interviewee recalled that when she had started improvising with the group it had been a surprise compared with her previous musical experience to find other musicians following what she had decided to play. Another interviewee noted that this state of unified purpose could be reached very quickly in a performance through "tuned in" and intuitive improvising, paying close attention to those around him:

> so I'm listening to [player X], hearing [player Y] and, and I'm hearing what I'm doing is, is antagonistic I think, so I'm actually going to try and follow you immediately, so immediately did a sort of little chromatic pattern to get me into the zone.
>
> GIO6.

Mutual trust and respect between group members were, as in the media interviews, held up as an important basis for this musical approach. For instance, fellow ensemble members were characterized as great musicians deserving of respect, and improvisers were characterized as holding beliefs in common:

> it's not [an] overtly musical kind of connection, it's more a philosophical connection again, this is the way we believe … and you'd then, you'd have a language and have a trust.
>
> GIO1.

As in the media interviews, interest in an eclectic range of musical genres was frequently emphasized. Being "open to other sounds" (GIO4) was held up as a key feature of their own or others' identity as improvisers, tied to a suggestion that other forms of music in which they had participated had been found limiting.

6.5 Contrasting features of media and research interviews

In both sets of data, then, cross-disciplinary free improvisation is orientated to as a collaborative, intuitive, and personally fulfilling practice among musicians who share an eclectic aesthetic and democratic outlook. This account may thus be read as an accessible and unproblematic discourse for musicians identifying with this approach across different contexts. However, there were also distinct and differing features of the interviews intended for research and those intended for publicity, consistent with their differing purposes and contexts. For instance, when conducting interviews for research, leading questions from the interviewer that might invite particular answers are strongly proscribed. In the transcribed research interviews, Wilson's questioning shows his attempts to avoid implying an expected response, for instance:

> What were you, what were you kind of finding yourself able to do, at that point in time, you know in terms of what you're contributing and or playing?
>
> GW.

However, media interviewers are not subject to the same constraints, and it can be seen that some questions to Spring Heel Jack collaborators overtly shape the response from the interviewee. For instance, a question from the interviewer Seth Cooke to MSa invites him to see his improvisation as taking place through shared intuitive understanding:

> … you and Butcher both seem to have an almost paradoxical sense of where the music is at any given time. How do you achieve this? By internalising structural devices from the different forms of music you've experienced, or by building yourself escape routes, ways of quickly exiting any patterns you've constructed?
>
> Cooke, 2010.

The media interviews were undertaken in the knowledge that what is said is likely to be widely read by potential audience members and fellow musicians as the views of the interviewee; two features of those musicians' accounts in suggest this as an influential factor. First, they treat the SHJ project as requiring explanation, and thus as a collaboration across disciplines that is unlikely or unexpected, and emphasis on the value of their music as interesting, challenging and rewarding coincides with anticipation of a potential negative reaction to the project. EP talks of improvised music as potentially unpopular due to a commitment to explore "dark corners"; JC predicts their collaboration as unlikely to appeal to fans of the DJs' earlier music, or to JP's band. AW, for example, asserts the beauty of free improvisation by his collaborators against possible detractors:

> You'd have to hate music per se, everything, not to be moved by that. I was playing Trombolenium by Paul Rutherford the other day, and there is nothing on it that is unpleasant, avant-garde, squeaky door, nothing. It is just great playing. He is playing beautiful notes there, notes you recognise, sequences you recognise. Some of it sounds like Vaughan Williams towards the end, where he is playing all those natural tunings. This is beautiful, fantastic.
>
> AW.

In this excerpt, anyone who might not see this improvised music as enjoyable, who might see it as "squeaky door" sounds, is positioned as a "hater" of music in general.

AW's invocation of Vaughan Williams is consistent with a pattern throughout the interviews of validating improvisation through comparison to classical music as a yardstick—for instance, MSa positions free improvisation as exciting in the same way as contemporary composed works by Fell or Ferneyhough.

Secondly, the frequent emphasis by the media interviewees on their high regard for other musicians, and endorsement of the success and value of the project, can be read as a reflection of the visibility of these opinions to other musicians. The possibility of peers "listening in" is indicated, for example, when EP refers to HB directly, even though the latter is not present at the interview:

> In fact, Han is a good deal quieter in the mix than he was in the studio. That is very often the case with drummers. It is one of the ways you can domesticate music so that people can play it at home. The last thing people really want is Han Benninck in their living room. You know that, Han! [Laughs.]
>
> EP.

HB is thus treated as a potential audience for EP's talk. He may become aware of this comment, which positions him as somehow not "domesticated," which could be interpreted as critical. By addressing him directly in an aside EP implies a close link between them, and signals with laughter that the comment should be interpreted as good-natured. Crucially, his account here is shaped by recognition that the purpose of this interview means that he may have to justify anything he says to fellow musicians. The interview was carried out specifically to be uploaded on a website readily accessible not just by HB but by fans of their music worldwide and acquaintances, any of whom may comment to either musician or on social media if one appears critical of the other. EP therefore has to feel able to justify anything he may say at a later date to avoid causing offense or appearing to do so.

This is a cardinal feature of the media interview, distinct from the anonymity afforded by a research interview. It is illustrated in an interview with collaborator MSh in which he is described, on the basis of previously published comments about venerated jazz musicians, in the following terms:

> Along with his stature as a pianist, Shipp has gained notoriety as a rhetorical bomb-thrower—venomous toward his critics, dismissive of icons as prominent as Herbie Hancock, grandiloquent in his view of himself.
>
> Adler, 2010.

MSh is challenged by Adler to respond to this characterization and seeks to repair any damage to his public identity by treating previous comments as a justifiable lapse given the struggle faced by musicians such as himself:

> Sometimes when I do interviews I'm sort of playing a character. I mean everything I say, but there's a slight schizophrenic element. People have to realize that being a jazz musician is very frustrating. On any given day, you end up saying stuff …
>
> MSh.

A string of criticisms and counter-criticisms posted as responses to the article amplify this argument. At one level, such attention functions to increase MSh's profile (there being no such thing as bad publicity). At another, it indicates the pressure that may be at stake for any media interviewee commenting on a fellow musician.

The research interviewer, in contrast, was a fellow ensemble member with the same stake in the value of the improvisation, who had specified that the interviewee would not be identified in any published material. Interviewees in this context, therefore, did not need to defend their practice to a potential audience. Although research interviewees, as noted, tended to praise the abilities of their fellow improvisers, they also frequently took a more critical stance towards fellow musicians and group improvising, something that was not apparent in the media interviews. They expressed frustration with how group improvisations unfolded at other times. They recognized moments during improvising together when the intention of other musicians appeared ambiguous or uncertain, or that two improvisers in a group may have had different understandings of what was taking place musically. One individual for example described moments where unrecognized clashes between contributions meant that group improvisations lost momentum or foundered through collective uncertainty:

> I guess there was a lot of people not making decisions, and so the few decisions that came on people either, it was just really odd it was like a kind of, a pan of water all just bubbling and not and just little ideas just dying and starting, and there wasn't a collective, there wasn't like "let's all go with that idea" and […] and that's when you kind of realise that "oh this is why bands have leaders."
>
> GIO8.

Other musicians' contributions are perceived by GIO8 in this quote as signaling indecisiveness, which he interprets negatively. Understanding a musical act to display a particular intention, in turn, shapes an identity for that player in the perceiver's account. Interviewees spoke of their difficulty in contributing to improvisation when they perceived tension and thus saw other players as irritated, or described feeling that other players' contributions were forcibly limiting their own scope to contribute:

> … if I'm sitting on stage with somebody and they they look like they're really pissed off with what's going on, if they're looking really hacked off and or and sometimes it can be just someone's natural expression, know that they're just kind of contemplating just not playing, but if I get it into my head that they don't like what's going on, then I'll like I'll deliberately start not do it anymore.
>
> GIO5

> Lots of mad sounds, people playing out of tune … because there's so many people you can't really hear what everyone's doing so, [aye] you don't really have an idea about the overall sound that's getting projected out towards the audience.
>
> GIO10.

The research interviews should not, however, be regarded as unmediated by context. The familiarity between interviewer and interviewee is apparent in that, while participants were prepared to voice criticism of other improvisers, they stopped short of naming them, avoiding any risk of appearing critical of common acquaintances.

6.6 Conclusions

In this chapter we have compared research and media interviews with cross-disciplinary improvising ensembles to consider how the identity work involved in improvisation may be shaped by the context or mode of interview. Some similarities confirm the generalizability of findings in our previous studies. In both sets of interviews, improvisers are constructed as individuals whose shared musical values and eclectic tastes are consistent with a shared understanding when improvising, a telepathic "intuitive" sense that all know where the music is going and what each other is doing. This allows them to generate music whose unpredictability and power lends it unique excitement and interest. Both ensembles are described by interviewees as forums where musicians associated with diverse musical scenes and with varied skills can transcend their associated genre-specific identities.

The importance of a shared awareness of known social practices when improvising has been highlighted in previous research, but specifically in relation to improvisation within the genre of jazz (Bastien & Hostager, 1988; Seddon, 2005; Seddon and Biasutti, 2009). We have previously observed that the non-ironic account of improvisation as an intuitive or instinctive phenomenon by cross-genre improvisers in GIO stands in contrast to the accounts of musicians within the specific genre of jazz, who privilege technical accomplishment over intuition when explaining improvisation (Wilson and MacDonald, 2012). It may be that once the agreed parameters or conventions of a particular genre are abandoned when improvising, instinct and intuition must be relied on to a greater extent. This account is sustained throughout the media interviews. The positive aspects of the music are emphasized by the media interviewees in relation to a perceived potential for it to be disliked or misunderstood by readers of the interview. A heroic identity is shaped for participants; they are frequently asserted as championing niche music in the face of adversity and commercial interests, through personal and musical struggle. Care is taken not to appear to be disparaging colleagues. In the research interviews, in contrast, a negative account of group improvisation is also apparent such that in performances, fellow improvisers may be identified as antagonistic or as interpreting musical exchanges in incompatible ways. Interviewees sometimes attribute these characteristics to specific individuals, though without naming them in the presence of the interviewer, a fellow ensemble member. These aspects of identity work are vital to consider in qualitative work examining musical interaction not only in free improvising, but also in any music-making in groups. For instance, even though symphonic music is highly scripted and the replication of composers' scores is highly prized, musicians and audiences in that sphere still make differing attributions of interpretative intent on the part of a performer to researchers and others. Rather than providing a definitive assessment of musical practice, our findings underline that these constructions will reflect contextual influences.

These two sets of interviews were necessarily gathered in different ways; they are not contemporaneous, and there are significant differences between the individuals and ensembles in each set of interviews. GIO performs and records as a considerably larger ensemble of 20 or more players; in a large ensemble, frustration may arise from the scale of the enterprise. Moreover, the media interviews may have been edited for presentation or publication, whereas the transcripts analyzed for research purposes were verbatim representations of the speech that took place. Demand characteristics, whereby individuals modify their accounts or behaviour when examined according to what they think is expected of them, may also have brought different influences to bear on these two sets of data (Orne, 1962). Thus, the media interviewers may have been perceived by interviewees as fans of the music wishing to hear a eulogistic account of it, while the research interviewer, as a fellow improviser in the ensemble, may have been viewed as valuing particular approaches to improvisation. While the interviewer's membership of GIO may have facilitated recruitment, this relationship cannot be taken as ensuring the interviewees' uncomplicated trust. They may, for instance, have viewed the improviser as having previously expressed critical views on some aspect of shared improvising that they felt obliged to acknowledge.

However, the differences in how improvisation is characterized between these datasets can also be seen to reflect the distinct parameters and function of their two contexts. Media interviews require that interviewee is identified, with the explicit intention that what is said will be disseminated to a core audience as their views; comments made may be persistently attached to them and cause controversy, as MSh recognized above. Research interviews specify anonymity and are not intended for publication where they might count as publicity; if people other than the researchers read content from these interviews they will not identify whose words they are reading. The talk of improvisers examined here suggests that, in the public eye, they will champion their music against potential dislike or criticism by emphasizing quality, challenge, and power of their practice, and constructing heroic identities for themselves and colleagues in doing so. In the confidential context of a research interview, a range of evaluations may be made of group improvisation by those who took part and, as such, the identities they construct for fellow improvisers may position them positively or negatively.

The authors acknowledge that they are practitioners and proponents of free improvisation themselves, acquainted with at least some of the interviewees considered here, and must therefore be understood as inclined to offer a sympathetic orientation towards these musicians and their practice. An analyst with antipathy towards free improvisation (and the media interviewees' accounts point to the existence of such individuals) might, for example, have understood appeals to intuition as evasive, or as glossing over a lack of insight among free improvisers, whereas we read this as an expression of the difficulty of explaining a rapid, complex, wordless, and startling process that we have experienced for ourselves. Our own familiarity with this field nevertheless enables us to offer a particular interpretation that may not be accessible by a more external researcher; for instance, our awareness or recognition of etiquette among musicians inclines us to take account of these niceties when musicians refer to each other in interviews. Our subjective stance is consistent with our aim to consider differences in how these musicians express themselves differently in different contexts, rather than to arrive at a generalizable objective definition of what takes place in free improvising. Further considerations of the words of improvisers by researchers with a more critical stance toward free improvisation would only serve to enrich our understanding in this area and would be an interesting direction for future research.

In researching improvisation through qualitative strategies dependent on self-report, examining musicians' talk beyond the research interview can highlight the influence of the ubiquitous research interview setting on how identities are constructed (Potter & Hepburn, 2005). This is not to suggest that one type of interview is necessarily a better source of data than another, and we have sought in this chapter to avoid suggesting that views emerging from one set of data are more "correct" than those emerging from the other. Nevertheless, accessing the voice of the improviser across multiple contexts can show how accounts may vary depending on who is asking about improvisation, as well as where, and for what purpose, and demonstrate the arguments of discursive theorists that richer perspectives can be gleaned through triangulating data sources. In particular, bringing together these two sets of data has allowed us to identify an anticipation of wider negative reactions towards free improvising that is not apparent when examining only views expressed in a research interview. This "embattled" attitude seems important to take into account when considering how improvisers perform and present their work. Exploring the accounts of a range of musicians, concentrating on their experiences when improvising together, therefore, is vital to increasing the understanding of a unique psychological process, but so, too, is highlighting the processes by which identity is constructed in those accounts. Analysis of other sources of data, such as autobiographies or recordings of talk at rehearsal, or recordings of improvised music, may further enhance understanding of the remarkable phenomenon whereby improvisers construct each other and their collaboratively created music.

References

Adler, D.R. (2010). Matthew Shipp: song of himself. *Jazz Times*. Available at: http://jazztimes.com/articles/25439-matthew-shipp-song-of-himself (accessed December 22, 2014).*

Bailey, D. (1993). *Improvisation: its nature and practice in music*. Boston, MA, Da Capo.

Bastien, D.T., & Hostager, T.J. (1988). Jazz as a process of organizational innovation. *Communication Research*, 15(5), 582–602.

Bath, T. (2013). Avoiding a career in music: about group talk improv. *The Quietus*. Available at: http://thequietus.com/articles/12649-about-group-interview (accessed December 22, 2014).*

Berliner, P. (1994). *Thinking in jazz: the infinite art of improvisation*. Chicago, IL: University of Chicago Press.

Biasutti, M., & L. Frezza. (2009). Dimensions of music improvisation. *Creativity Research Journal*, 21(2), 232–42.

Bryan-Kinns, N., & F. Hamilton. (2009). Identifying mutual engagement. *Behaviour & Information Technology*, 31(2), 101–25.

Collins, T. (2004). Interview with Matthew Shipp. *Junkmedia*. Available at http://www.junk-media.org/index.php?i=1276 (accessed February 9.2014).*

Cooke, S. (2010). An audience with Mark Sanders. *Bang the Bore*. Available at: http://www.bangthebore.org/archives/224 2014 (accessed December 22, 2014).*

Cross, I. (2005). Music and meaning, ambiguity and evolution. In: D. Miell, R. MacDonald, & D. J. Hargreaves (Eds.) *Musical communication*, pp. 27–43. Oxford: Oxford University Press.

Currin, G. (2008). Spiritualized. *Pitchfork Media*. Available at: http://pitchfork.com/features/interviews/6867-spiritualized (accessed December 22, 2014).*

Edelstein, P. (2001). Checking in with … Matthew Shipp. *Sounds of Timeless Jazz*. Available at: http://www.matthewshipp.com/press/51-sotj/sotj.html (accessed December 22, 2014).*

Eyles, J. (2003a). Evan Parker. *All About Jazz*. Available at: http://www.allaboutjazz.com/evan-parker-by-john-eyles.php - .UqzMRc1aH40 2014 (accessed December 22, 2014).*

Eyles, J. (2003b). Spring Heel Jack: John Coxon and Ashley Wales. *All About Jazz* Available at: http://www.allaboutjazz.com/spring-heel-jack-john-coxon-and-ashley-wales-spring-heel-jack-by-john-eyles.php(accessed December 22, 2014).*

Ferguson, J. & Bell, P. (2007). The role of ambiguity within musical creativity. *Leonardo Electronic Almanac*, 15 (11-12). Available at: http://www.leoalmanac.org/leonardo-electronic-almanac-volume-15-no-11-12-november-december-2007/ (accessed February 4, 2016).

Fordham, J. (2003). Interview with Ashley Wales. *The Guardian*, January 20, 2003.*

Freeman, P. (2010). Wadada Leo Smith Uncut. *The Wire*, p. 312.*

Gilboa, A., Bodner, E., & Amir, D. (2006). Emotional communicability in improvised music: the case of music therapists. *Journal of Music Therapy*, 43(3), 198–225.

Jermyn, D. (2008). Still something else besides a mother? Negotiating celebrity motherhood in Sarah Jessica Parker's star story. *Social Semiotics* 18(2), 163–76.

Lewis, G.E. (2007). Mobilitas animi: improvising technologies, intending chance. *Parallax*, 13(4), 108–22.

Locke, A., & D. Edwards (2003). Bill and Monica: memory, emotion and normativity in Clinton's Grand Jury testimony. *British Journal of Social Psychology*, 42(2), 239–56.

MacDonald, R.A., Hargreaves, D.J., & Miell, D. (2002). *Musical identities*. Oxford: Oxford University Press.

MacDonald, R.A., & Wilson, G. (2005). Musical identities of professional jazz musicians: a focus group investigation. *Psychology of Music*, 33(4), 395–417.

MacDonald, R.A., & Wilson, G.B. (2006). Constructions of jazz: how jazz musicians present their collaborative musical practice. *Musicae Scientiae*, 10(1), 59–83.

MacDonald, R.A., & Wilson, G.B. (2014). Billy Connolly, Daniel Barenboim, Willie Wonka, jazz bastards and the universality of improvisation. In: B. Piekut and G. Lewis (Eds.) *The Oxford handbook of critical improvisation studies* . Oxford: Oxford University Press.

MacDonald, R.A., Wilson, G.B., & Miell, D. (2012). Improvisation as a creative process within contemporary music. In: D.J. Hargreaves, D. Miell, & R.A.R. Macdonald (Eds.) *Musical imaginations: multidisciplinary perspectives on creativity, performance and perception*, pp. 242–55. Oxford, Oxford University Press.

Mazzola, G.B., Cherlin, P.B., Rissi, M., & Kennedy, N. (2009). *Flow, gesture, and spaces in free jazz: towards a theory of collaboration*. Berlin: Springer.

Meyers, E. (2009). "Can you handle my truth?": authenticity and the celebrity star image. *Journal of Popular Culture*, 42(5), 890–907.

Miller, B. (1999). Spring Heel Jack. *Highwire Daze*. Available at: http://bretthehitman.tripod.com/springheel.html (accessed December 22, 2014).*

Monson, I. (1996). *Saying something: jazz improvisation and interaction*. Chicago: University of Chicago Press.

Montgomery, M. (2008). The discourse of the broadcast news interview. *Journalism Studies*, 9, 260–77.

Nettl, B., & Russell, M. (Eds.) (2008). *In the course of performance: studies in the world of musical improvisation*. Chicago, IL: University of Chicago Press.

Orne, M. (1962). On the social psychology of the psychological experiment: with particular reference to demand characteristics and their implications. *American Psychologist*, 17(11), 776–83.

Potter, J. (2004). Discourse analysis and discourse psychology. In: P. Camic, J. Rhodes, & L. Yardley (Eds.) *Qualitative methods in psychology: expanding perspectives in methodology and design*, pp. 73–95. Washington DC: American Psychological Association.

Potter, J., & Hepburn, A. (2005). Qualitative interviews in psychology: problems and possibilities. *Qualitative Research in Psychology*, 2(4), 281–308.

Potter, J., & Wetherell, M. (1994). *Discourse and social psychology: beyond attitudes and behaviour*. London: Sage.

Sawyer, R. (2005). Music and conversation. In: D. Miell, R. MacDonald, & D. Hargreaves (Eds.), pp. 45–60. *Musical communication*. Oxford: Oxford University Press.

Schober, M.F., & Spiro, N. (2014). Jazz improvisers' shared understanding: a case study. *Frontiers in Psychology*, 5, 808.

Seddon, F., & Biasutti, M. (2009). A comparison of modes of communication between members of a string quartet and a jazz sextet. *Psychology of Music*, 37(4), 395–415.

Seddon, F.A. (2005). Modes of communication during jazz improvisation. *British Journal of Music Education*, 22(01), 47–61.

Smith, S. (2013). Complicated sublimity: Evan Parker interviewed. *The Quietus*. Available at: http://thequietus.com/articles/12819-evan-parker-interview (accessed December 22, 2014).*

Wetherell, M., Taylor, S., & Yates, S. (Eds.) (2001). *Discourse theory and practice: a reader*. London: Sage.

Wilson, G.B., & MacDonald, R.A. (2005). The meaning of the blues: musical identities in talk about jazz. *Qualitative Research in Psychology*, 2(4), 341–63.

Wilson, G.B., & MacDonald, R.A. (2012). The sign of silence: negotiating musical identities in an improvising ensemble. *Psychology of Music*, 40(5), 558–73.

*Media interviews used as data.

CHAPTER 7

....

POST-NATIONAL IDENTITIES IN MUSIC

Acting in a Global Intertextual Musical Arena

....

GÖRAN FOLKESTAD

7.1 INTRODUCTION

....

WHEN the Beatles play "The Marseillaise," the French national anthem, as the introduction to their song "All you need is love" (1967), to me it contextualizes the song to France and marks with the help of this musical intertextual reference to national identity that what is sung about is the French view of love, a stereotype of "real love" based on feelings and passion. Today, globally shared intertextual references have become very common, not least in popular culture. Musical imagination and creation thus involves acting in a global intertextual musical arena in which national or ethnic backgrounds are negotiated and reconfigured in new cultural surroundings.

This chapter takes as its point of departure my chapter in *Musical Identities* (Folkestad, 2002), and the distinction made there between national, ethnic and cultural identities, respectively, with the conclusion that "these concepts need to be defined explicitly in relation to the context in which they are used" (p. 154).

At a time when the idea of the national state is being eroded in favor of identifications that are simultaneously local and global, national identity in music in the traditional sense (meaning that the music itself carries basic inherent national values and ideas) mainly manifests itself in sport events, television music programs, such as the Eurovision Song Contest, and in top-down projects in school curricula "in which the 'official' definition of national identity is based on the different cultural and ethnic identities within the regions that are defined as a nation" (Folkestad, 2002, p. 153). However, the idea of national identity in music, meaning that the music itself carries basic inherent national values and ideas to which immigrants and new citizens should be assimilated, is today still emphasized by political groups, in opposition to the view of the formation of new national identities based on a multitude of ethnic and cultural identities.

Hall (1993) describes history, language, and literature as "the great supporting pillars of national identity and national culture" (p. 107). He warns of a backlash for multiculturalism if the attempt to restore a national canon is used in "the defence of ethnic absolutism, of cultural racism" (p. 107), as this might result in "aggressive resistance to difference" (p. 107).

On the other hand, in the informal musical interaction and learning that actually takes place, not least on the Internet, the individual's musical identity is formed in dialogue with many different cultural contexts. It is therefore important to recognize the many and varied ways in which people relate to their national, ethnic, and cultural backgrounds, and how they choose to put these into play in their cultural practices.

Hall (1993) argues that "popular culture has historically become the dominant form of global culture" (p. 108), and Folkestad (2002) describes cultural identity as a "bottom-up" concept and states that:

> Most cultural utterances, such as music, typically originate from popular forms developed either long before today's national boundaries were drawn, or among groups of people sharing the same musical preferences, for example, despite their national and/or ethnic affiliations. This means that cultural identity has a direct bearing on the music itself, and the musical context in which it exists. This also means that an individual can have more than one cultural identity, and it might be that the global multicultural person of today is characterized by having the possibility of and ability to choose and change between several cultural identities.
>
> p. 154.

This "bottom-upness" and socio-cultural situatedness of popular culture is described by Hall (1993) as follows:

> Popular culture always has its base in the experiences, the pleasures, the memories, the traditions of the people. It has connections with local hopes and local aspirations, local tragedies, and local scenarios that are the everyday practices and the everyday experiences of ordinary folks.
>
> pp. 107–8.

An event that illustrates the issue of national identity and music, and the role of contemporary popular music in the formation of new musical identities, is the memorial ceremony held in Oslo on August 21, 2011, in conciliation with survivors and those grieving, and in honor of the victims of the terror attacks on the government quarters and on the isle of Utøya in July 22, 2011. As Knudsen (2014) points out, "a national ceremony of this kind most often has a clearly expressed purpose defined by the organiser— in this case the Ministry of Culture and the Norwegian government—but additionally, through symbols and actions, it implies far more than what is explicitly expressed" (p. 49). Accordingly, on such occasions "the music is not primarily legitimized as entertainment, but as a tool for expressing, strengthening and elaborating moods and emotions of a particular historical situation of great importance to the nation" (p. 52).

The production of the memorial ceremony contained thoroughly considered combinations of pictures and sound, for example, the faces of a Rabbi and a Hindu priest were shown on the screen at the same time as an Imam read a text from the Koran. In their short speeches, Prime Minister Jens Stoltenberg put the weight on the importance of openness and tolerance, and King Harald emphasized democracy and multicultural understanding. Taken together, the program and the performances manifested the desired official Norwegian statement of a national identity of multiplicity and diversity (Knudsen, 2014).

One of the things clearly expressed at this ceremony was the ambition—not to say the mission—to manifest the identity of what Knudsen (2014) describes as "the post-national 'new Norway'" (p. 50). That is, a multicultural Norway of the 21st century, entering into the future as a modern society resting on modern human values and with an openness to, and inclusion of, all ethnic and cultural groups.

One musical performance that focused very clearly on cultural multiplicity and the meeting between the local and the global was Karpe Diem, a Norwegian hip-hop duo (Magdi and Chirag) with many fans among young people of different national backgrounds (Knudsen, 2014). Magdi introduced their performance in the following way:

> Dear Norway, I am a Muslim, Chirag here is a Hindu and our friends look like a box of M&M's. But we have never felt as Norwegian and as little different as after July 22. Something has changed, and it might be naïve, but I wish this change would last forever.
>
> p. 59.

In my 2002 chapter, I concluded that "global youth culture and its music, because it is the same regardless of the national, ethnic or cultural heritage of the context in which it operates, might have a non-segregating and uniting function" (Folkestad, 2002, p. 160). The descriptions above are good illustrations of the formation of new or post-national identities, and constitute an important foundation of musical identities in the musical activities of young people acting in a post-national global intertextual musical arena.

Knudsen (2011) argues that a post-national perspective might be helpful in understanding today's youth engagement in hybridized and globalized musical practices. He states that "it is important to recognize the many and varied ways in which people relate to their backgrounds and how they choose to put them into play in their cultural practices" (p. 80), and that "a common frame of reference in minority music research is how national or ethnic backgrounds are negotiated and reconfigured in new [cultural] surroundings" (p. 79). He continues by arguing that "a postnational perspective not only challenges the significance of national identity, but also questions the emphasis placed on identity in general" (p. 79).

From the examples given above, a fundamental question arises: what makes the processes of musical identification and the formation of musical identities possible when people meet and share musical experiences, and when new identities are formed, changed and negotiated on both individual and collective levels?

The aim of the rest of this chapter is to suggest a conceptual framework that should help in the analysis and understanding of issues regarding the formation of musical post-national identities. I will do this by presenting and discussing three concepts that I have found to be at the core of our understanding of how people are now acting in a global intertextual musical arena:

- Intertextuality.
- The personal inner musical library.
- Discourse in music.

In doing this, I will focus mainly on young people's collaborative musical creativity from both local and global perspectives and on the consequences of this for music education—the reader should bear in mind that *all* musical activities also involve the dialectic processes of "*identities in music* (IIM) and *music in identities* (MII)" (Hargreaves, Miell, & MacDonald, 2002, p. 2). On an individual level, the formation of or any change in one of these results in a change in the other, and vice versa.

I start by presenting and discussing *intertextuality*, the process of which is a general prerequisite for the connection or link between something already known and something new, a fundamental process in all musical activities, including in the formation of musical identity.

I continue by presenting the concept of the *personal inner musical library*, previously described in Folkestad (2012), which in short constitutes a person's individual archive and intrapersonal resources in the musical intertextual processes, and as such also constitutes the foundation of the personal musical identity.

Finally, I present and discuss *discourse in music*, a concept introduced by Folkestad (1996) and further developed in Folkestad (2012) in order to analyze and understand the interpersonal processes of interaction and negotiation in musical activities on collective levels, including the negotiation and formation of new musical identities.

7.2 INTERTEXTUALITY

Issues regarding the relationships between previous knowledge and experiences and the formation of new knowledge are at the core of all educational sciences, and music education is no exception. The same is true of all musical activities, including the creation of music, and in the formation of musical identities.

From this perspective, the theories of intertextuality, originating in writings on literature and linguistics, become particularly interesting not only in the analysis of the relationships between different texts—adopting a widened text concept, including all kinds of "texts," such as music, visual art, theatre, body movement, etc., but also in general in analyzing various phenomena of teaching, learning and identity.

Dyndahl (2013) references Barthes (1977) and Kristeva (1980), who state that intertextuality is everywhere and that all texts are related to each other. This new approach to the analysis of "texts" is described by Dyndahl (2013) as follows:

> Instead of analyzing the intrinsic meaning of a text, scholars would now examine its intertextual connections with other texts. In addition, texts would be considered as multiple plays of meaning, rather than as consistent messages. The individual text loses its individuality; texts are instead seen as manifestations of a text universe without clear boundaries between singular texts.
>
> p. 2.

Barthes (1986) argues that a text is "a multi-dimensional space in which a variety of writings, none of them original, blend and clash" (p. 146). He continues by suggesting that "the text is a tissue of quotations drawn from the innumerable centres of culture" (p. 146). Moreover, Barthes (1986) states that, traditionally, the explanation of a piece of art has been sought in the person who did it, whereas from the perspective of intertextuality "it is language which speaks, not the author" (p. 143). He continues by arguing that writing is "to reach that point where only language acts, 'performs'" (p. 143), and not the author. In contrast to the traditional view, "the author is never more than the instance writing ... [and] ... the modern scriptor is born simultaneously with the text" (p. 145).

Fiske (1987) states that "the theory of intertextuality proposes that any one text is necessarily read in relationship to others and that a range of textual knowledges is brought to bear upon it" (p. 108). He continues by arguing that "these relationships do not take the form of specific allusions from one text to another and there is no need for readers to be familiar with specific or the same texts to read intertextually" (p. 108). On the basis of this he concludes that "intertextuality exists rather in the space *between* texts" [italics in original] (p. 108).

Fiske (1987) distinguishes between intertextual relations on two dimensions:

- *Horizontal intertextuality*, defined as the relations "between primary texts that are more or less explicitly linked, usually along the axes of genre, character, or content" (p. 108).
- *Vertical intertextuality*, relations between a primary text, e.g., a television program, and "other texts of a different type that refer explicitly to it" (p. 108), e.g., secondary texts such as studio publicity, journalistic features, or criticism.

Middleton (2000) concludes that "the best umbrella term for the popular music practices ... is probably intertextuality" (p. 61). He takes his point of departure in a definition of intertextuality as "the idea that all texts make sense only through their relationships, explicit or implicit, with other texts" (p. 61). He also notes that "digital technology ... offered a radically new compositional setting, one that seemed to signal that works were now always works-in-progress, and that music was just material for reuse" (pp. 61–2). Today, this development has reached a point where "from here [the 're-mix culture'], it is a short step using recordings as raw material; through sampling, scratching, talkover and live mixing techniques the record becomes an instrument of performance" (p. 78).

From the definitions proposed above we might reach a definition of intertextuality in musical contexts as all kinds of relationships, implicit and explicit, between different "texts," including music, visual art, theatre, body movement, etc., in the process of creating, interpreting, performing, and listening to music, and in the formation of musical identities.

One example of intertextuality, today very common in the sampling culture described by Dyndahl (2005a, b), is to be found in Kanye West's "Through the Wire." Early in the morning on October 23, 2002, Kanye West was in a near-fatal car crash on his way home from the studio. As a result, his jaws were wired due to the medical treatment needed. In November, only 1 month after the crash and with his jaws still wired, he recorded "Through the Wire," released in September 2003 as the lead single of his debut album "College Dropout" (2004). The lyrics start with "They can't stop me from rapping can they? ... I spit it through the wire," and continue by describing how he feels about the situation of being in hospital, seriously injured with his jaws wired, which allowed him to consume only liquid food, still having so much on his mind that he wanted to communicate through his music.

The title "Through the Wire" is a good example of intertextuality as it obviously came not only from Kanye West's present situation after the car crash, but from David Foster's song "Through the Fire," written for and recorded by Chaka Khan in 1985. The original recording, including Chaka Khan's lead vocal, sampled and speeded up, is also the basis of Kanye West's composition and production, on top of which he performs his rap. Moreover, the connection between "wire" and "fire" is already made in the original chorus, ending with Chaka Kahn singing the lines "For a chance at loving you/I'd take it all the way/Right down to the wire/Even through the fire."

This is only one example of many hip-hop songs through which today's young listeners of hip-hop get to meet older songs and artists. In this way, I would argue, the samplings of older songs by hip-hop artists, which then serve as elements in their contemporary compositions, have brought not only older genres and styles into their music; this process has also implicitly contributed to the informal music education of young people of today. Through the sampling culture of hip-hop music they have been introduced to earlier music styles and artists—often described in curricula of formal school music as an important objective for music teachers to achieve—and then with the help of their extensive knowledge of how to use computers, the Internet, web sites, and products, such as iTunes and Spotify, they have been able to trace back the origins of the intertextual elements, thus finding their ways ahead to new musical experiences. In that sense, Kanye West's albums might be described as serving as a journey through the history of African American music.

In Folkestad (2008) I described this music teachers' task of bridging the already acquired knowledge of students with new musical experiences and knowledge as follows:

> Using the original meaning and function of the word *pedagogue* as a metaphor (in ancient Greece the *paidagōgos* was the slave who met the student at the doorstep of his house and followed and guarded him on his way to school), what we should do as

music educators is to meet the students where they stand, musically and elsewhere, but then not stop there, but take them by the hand and lead them on a journey of new musical endeavours and experiences.

p. 502.

As I see it, this task of music education is implicitly and unconsciously executed and performed by the sampling hip-hop artists in their creation of music in which intertextuality is at the core of both the processes of composition and listening. Their songs thus become intertextual resources for their students' further musical learning.

This educational component of hip-hop music and its artists is described by Söderman (2011) in terms of *folkbildning*, a Scandinavian movement established in 1912 "to provide voluntary education for the general population" (p. 211). *Folkbildning* is also used to describe "the process of learning in which self-education is an important dimension" (p. 211). Söderman argues that "in the same way as the Swedish working class once found a way out of their marginal position through *folkbildning*, today's immigrant youth, "new Swedes", access Swedish society by articulating their position through hip-hop" (p. 211). I would argue that the *folkbildning* approach to music might be described as a core element in the Swedish national identity of music education.

In the following section, I will present and discuss a concept that has been developed in order to understand and discuss the *intrapersonal resources* of intertextuality in musical activities, and in the formation of musical identities—*the personal inner musical library*.

7.3 THE PERSONAL INNER MUSICAL LIBRARY

As a tool for understanding and illustrating the relationship between previous musical experiences and musical activities, such as the compositional process or the formation of musical identities, Folkestad (2012) suggests the coining of a new concept—*the personal inner musical library* (PIML). In short, *personal* refers to Polanyi's (1958) thesis that all knowledge is personally acquired and unique. *Inner* indicates that the musical library is not an ordinary collection of recordings and musical scores, which by tradition is understood as a musical library, but comprises all the musical experiences of a person's mind and body. The word *library* points to how all musical experiences, just like all recordings, scores and books in an ordinary musical library, are present and accessible, even when they are not explicitly in focus. They may be brought to the forefront and referred to on demand, when the need or wish arises. The PIML thus illustrates that, while individual musical compositions and performances might draw on specific musical experiences, the full musical library still forms and functions as a backdrop of implicit references to the totality of musical experiences in the process of musical creation. This can be phrased in Gurwitsch's (1964) terms of intentionality. At the same time as the piece of music under creation and some specific musical experiences are in explicit intentional focus—the theme—so, implicitly, are all the other musical experiences of the full personal inner musical library—the thematic field. This refers to all the musical creations and performances of that individual, as a *tacit dimension* (Polanyi, 1967) of the musical and compositional process.

The concept of PIML originates from observations in empirical studies on composition and creative music making from Folkestad (1996) onwards, in which informants described their musical resources in the creative process in terms of general statements such as "all I've ever heard before" and more specific ones like "the really catchy children's songs one's been brainwashed with since early childhood."

At first sight, the description above of the PIML might appear to have similarities with descriptions made by other scholars, for example, Ruud (1997) and DeNora (2000), of the relationship between musical experiences and identity. Ruud (1997) investigates the meaning and function of music in the formation of identity. He does not base this on all the music the individual has experienced, but rather the music that the informants have defined themselves as significant in the formation of their identities. DeNora (2000) investigates the role of music in people's everyday lives with a special focus on its uses and powers in social life, arguing that music has a social identity. However, there is an important difference between these approaches and descriptions compared to that of the PIML: while Ruud and DeNora investigate and describe the relationships between music, and the formation of identity and music and everyday life respectively, that is, *the relation between music and phenomena outside the music*, I investigate and describe by PIML *the relation between music and music itself,* that is, between previously heard and experienced music, and new music being created.

In the process of musical creativity, the composer establishes a constant intertextual dialogue with his/her *PIML*, that is, as described above, with all previous musical experiences of that individual, all the music ever heard, collected, and stored in the mind and body of that person. Applying Barthes' (1986) ideas of intertextuality to composition, the only power of a composer is to mix elements from previous compositions knowing that "the inner 'thing' he thinks to 'translate' is itself a ready-formed dictionary, its words only explainable through other words, and so on indefinitely" (p. 146).

In that respect, in this interactive process of composition, the first receiver of the musical message, and the first to assess the composition, is the composer herself/himself. The composition process incorporates two basic phases:

- The creative, subjective-intuitive phase, or state of flow (Csikszentmihalyi, 1990), in which new musical material is produced.
- The evaluation of that material on the basis of knowledge and previous experiences, the context of the composition, with the parts always simultaneously related to the whole, and with the *PIML*, with its collective cultural and historical dimension, as the reference.

Similarly, in the process of musical creation and performance, *intertextuality* is manifested in two different ways:

- On an intrapersonal level in the ongoing creation of a new piece of music, in which the creative ideas of the new piece are constantly interacting with the personal inner musical library of the creator(s).
- When the piece of music is performed and is thus being recreated by the listener(s).

This also implies, in line with Vygotsky's (1930/2004) view that creativity increases with experience, that the more musical experiences—intertextual resources—that exist in the personal inner musical library, the more references and resources are available for creative musical actions:

> The creative activity of the imagination depends directly on the richness and variety of a person's previous experience because this experience provides the material from which products of fantasy are constructed. The richer a person's experience, the richer is the material his imagination has access to.
>
> pp. 14–15.

In summary, the PIML is the intrapersonal intertextual resource in musical activities, such as composition and music-making, in the processes of which intertextuality appears between new ideas and existing pieces of music by other composers, as well as previous music of one's own. It is also the resource and backdrop against which new musical identities are reconfigured and negotiated.

When individuals are interacting in collective musical activities, the personal inner musical libraries of the participating individuals constitute the resources or archives of musical experience and knowledge that meet and interact on the *interpersonal* activity level of *discourse in music*. In the following section, this concept will be presented and discussed.

7.4 DISCOURSE IN MUSIC

Folkestad (1996) introduced a new concept—*discourse in music*, which was further elaborated by Folkestad (2012). Its essence is the assumption that music itself might be regarded as a discourse—musical actions and activities, including the formation of musical identities, are seen as discursive practices and discursive activities.

The point of departure is *discourse,* "language in use," implying that for a conversation between people, an agreed meaning of the words is required. Wittgenstein (1967/1978) states that no words have any meaning in themselves, but are defined by the context in which they are uttered. The same applies to music, which like language, is connected to practice—literal, as well as musical expressions that are adequate and make sense in one practice might be incomprehensible in others, and discourse in music has developed differently within various musical practices. Thus, *discourse* marks a view of language and other forms of human utterances, and ways of communicating as what is used during an ongoing process rather than as a static code that can be analyzed separately from its social practice.

Although *discourse* is mainly associated with talk, the concept of discourse also includes non-verbal forms of dialogue such as music, body movement, gestures, etc. Thus, wider definitions of *discourse* emerge, which include all forms of human communication and negotiation in situations of practice.

The concept of *discourse in music* points to the fact that there is an intertextual level in music, in which people relate to and converse/interplay in dialogue with the personal inner musical library. Young people today, by listening and sometimes by playing, have built up knowledge and familiarity with different forms of musical expression, usually called styles or genres, and may thus be able to express themselves within these musical languages in various musical practices. One result of music being a historically and collectively defined object is that every composer, whether professional or novice, has a dialogue with his/her personal inner musical library in which the music also mediates the societal, traditional, national, cultural, and historical features of the *discourse in music*, the musical language in use.

One of the challenges in defining *discourse in music* is to describe its similarities and differences as compared with *genre*. Fiske (1987) states that the "the most influential and widely discussed form of horizontal intertextuality is that of genre" (p. 109) and points out that "genre works to promote and organize intertextual relations" (p. 114). He defines genre as "a cultural practice that attempts to structure some order into the wide range of texts and meanings that circulate in our culture for the convenience of both producers and audiences" (p. 109). He continues by arguing that "conventions are the structural elements of genre ... [and that] ... conventions are social and ideological" (p. 110). This statement has much in common with the descriptions of discourse, as has Fiske's statement that "genres are popular when their conventions bear a close relationship to the dominant ideology of the time" (p. 112), where "the dominant ideology" is presumably equivalent to the dominant discourse.

In the context of television culture, including cop shows, sitcoms, and soap operas, Fiske (1987) states that "a genre seen textually should be defined as a shifting provisional set of characteristics which is modified as each new example is produced" (p. 111). I would argue that this definition has its origin in the Ancient Greek dramas and has been transformed through history via *Commedia dell'Arte*, Shakespeare plays, and operas, to give a few examples. In music, the historically grounded genres and musical practices might be described as different discourses in music.

Hall (1993) describes the "black" discourse in black popular culture as follows:

> In its expressivity, its musicality, its orality, in its rich, deep, and varied attention to speech, in its inflections toward the vernacular and the local, in its rich production of counternarratives, and above all, in its metaphorical use of the musical vocabulary,

black popular culture has enabled the surfacing, inside the mixed and contradictory modes even of some mainstream popular culture, of elements of a discourse that is different—other forms of life, other traditions of representation.

p. 109.

Hall (1993) describes the origin of this black discourse, in which black people "have found the deep form, the deep structure of their cultural life in music" (p. 109) as "selective appropriation, incorporation, and rearticulation of European ideologies, cultures, and institutions, alongside an African heritage" (p. 109), which led to "linguistic innovations in rhetorical stylization of the body, forms of occupying an alien social space, heightened expressions, hairstyles, ways of walking, standing, and talking, and a means of constituting and sustaining camaraderie and community" (p. 109). He concludes by stating that "it is this mark of difference *inside* forms of popular culture ... that is carried by the signifier 'black' in the term 'black popular culture'" (p. 110, italics in original).

Similarly, other cultural discourses and identities, including specific discourses in music, have emerged and are constantly emerging when people encounter and interact with different cultural and musical traditions and expressions. However, the new music produced and performed must always be heard and understood "not simply as the recovery of a lost dialogue bearing clues for the production of new musics ... but as what they are—adaptations, molded to the mixed, contradictory, hybrid spaces" (Hall, 1993, p. 110). In other words, the new music being produced is *based on* a discourse in music, at the same time as it is *developing* that particular discourse in music.

As seen above, as compared with genre, tradition, and style, discourses create meaning and sense, are hierarchical, and have a normative and evaluative function. The discourse works on both macro- and micro-levels—simultaneously constituting and constituted—and also operates on both an individual and collective level in all kinds of musical discursive practices including music education (Nerland, 2003).

As an example, when the hippies in the musical and movie *Hair* meet in Central Park, NYC, celebrating the spiritual and lifestyle values of the hippie movement in singing "Let the Sunshine In," the harmonies of the choir arrangement, as well as the expression and singing style, are almost identical with the singing of the congregation in, for example, a black Baptist church—they sound "gospelish," thereby telling the audience that the hippie movement is the new religion and spiritual community. That is, the intertextual process enables the discourse in music and the singing in "gospelish" to be understood as "gospelish."

As described above, Kristeva (1980) argues, in line with Barthes (1977), that everything reveals intertextuality in the sense that all texts are related to previous texts. This statement has, in its character, very much in common with the statement that "everything is discourse" (Laclau & Mouffe, 1985, p. 110). On an overarching and simplified level it might also be argued that discourse presupposes intertextuality, and vice versa. However, even though intertextuality and discourse analysis have much in common, I perceive some essential differences. Intertextuality focuses on how the texts, as such, are related to each other. Instead of regarding the author as an independent freestanding individual or subject, and his/her text as a new original creative product (Barthes, 1986), intertextuality describes how no text is essentially new, but that all texts stand in a relation to earlier texts by being either a new combination of fragments and parts of previous texts and/or an answer and continuation of what has been presented and argued in previous texts (Bakhtin, 1981).

Accordingly, where intertextuality focuses on texts' relationship to each other, discourse focusses on the use of language in different situations, contexts, and practices, which includes a focus on the relationship between different discourses. Thus, core aspects of discourse which I have not found in the descriptions of intertextuality, are *power relations* and *the exertion of power functions*.

In conclusion, as seen above, there are many similarities between the ways in which intertextuality—with its origin in linguistics (the structure of language)—and discourse (language in use) are defined and explained. Discourse in music presupposes and rests on intertextuality, and the discussion above demonstrates how theories of intertextuality might be an important conceptual tool in developing the understanding of *discourse in music*. This occurs in particular as a tool for analyzing the relationship between different ideas, fragments, and elements in the process of composition and creative musicmaking, as well as in understanding the processes involved in the formation of musical identities.

7.5 CONCLUSIONS

All the levels of interactive and intertextual processes described above presuppose a common agreement of discourse in music, the musical language in use in a certain musical discursive practice. Moreover, these interactions imply the meeting of the personal inner musical libraries of the people involved.

As seen from the presentation above, intertextuality might be regarded as a core element in all learning and creational processes. From this perspective, the idea in some national music curricula of a collective cultural heritage forming a common national identity might be interpreted as an ambition to establish a common foundation of intertextual resources for all children in schools, regardless of their national, ethnical, and cultural background.

On an epistemological level, it might be argued that intertextuality is a prerequisite for all learning and formation of identity. If the construction of knowledge requires that the new is connected to something already learnt, acquired, and assimilated, this connection rests on intertextuality. This implies that intertextuality might be a powerful pedagogical tool—the already known and the introduction of new intertextual references become the point of departure for knowledge formation on the "journey of new musical endeavours and experiences" (Folkestad, 2008, p. 502).

Today, the sampling culture previously described in this chapter has spread to, and has been adopted/adapted by, almost every area of artistic and creative activity all over the world. This occurs increasingly without the original author, composer or artist being explicitly acknowledged or paid.

Returning to the national memorial ceremony in Oslo 2011, and the role of music in establishing and expressing national identity, it might be argued that the formation of a new national identity was accomplished by taking up a post-national approach. Interestingly, enough, in the official national memorial ceremony none of the most established official national symbols were present: the Norwegian flag was absent, and the national anthem was not sung. Instead, the ceremony was concluded with the song "To the Youth", the identity of which has gone through many phases since it was written in 1936; from originally being a socialist song supporting the ideas of the Stalinistic Soviet Union, it became an important part of the song canon of the Labour Party and was often sung at the summer camps at Utøya. After the memorial ceremony in 2011 it was suggested that this song might be included in the hymn book of the Norwegian church (Knudsen, 2014). However, at an informal occasion only 3 days after the terror attacks, when 200,000 people met spontaneously to bring roses in memory of the victims, the national anthem was spontaneously sung by the people present. This shows that at the same time as the national establishment had concerns about explicitly displaying the old established national symbols, the young people in the streets had no problems with using these symbols as a unifying element of identity in expressing their grief.

This also demonstrates how porous the concept of identity is, being constantly negotiated and reconfigured from situation to situation and from context to context. The symbols and music used as a means of developing and negotiating interpersonal relationships and identities might vary and change, on an individual as well as a national level, on a spectrum ranging from the most established and formal (e.g., a national anthem) to something antagonistic and informal (e.g., a revolutionary song with a new social identity).

It is not only national identities that are being eroded in favor of the establishment of more post-national identities. The theories of intertextuality and the "death of the author" (Barthes, 1986) imply that most traditional roles and identities of creative artists are under constant reconfiguration and negotiation. In the context of composition and music-making, this development has implications and consequences for the identities of being "a composer," "a producer," "a sound engineer," "a musician," etc. It has been argued, on the basis of the established values of authorship and distribution of royalties, that "copyright" does not mean the "right to copy." However, for the new generation of creators and receivers acting in a global intertextual musical arena, i.e., for the *homo sampliens* (Folkestad, 2013), for which "stealing" is regarded more as an acknowledgment of the original creator than as a theft, this distinction between "copyright" and "right to copy" might be decreasingly valid. From what we have seen so far, this change in attitude and approach might continue to the point where "copyright" is *replaced* by "right to copy," both in practice and by law. For that to happen would mean "the death of the composer". The whole idea of copyright, royalty and authorship, which has been regarded as the historic foundation on which future developments rest, turns out to be a historic parenthesis that survived for 300 years, starting at the beginning of the 18th century with the printing and selling of scores, and with its final death struggle in front of our eyes today. In other words, the dominant discourse of copyright and royalty might be replaced by a new discourse of open access. This development would also include the formation of new *discourses in music* and new musical identities.

In the case of music, this development implies that your PIML is now free to be used not only as a reference, but as an open-access archive from which any parts or elements might be retrieved and used as material in new original compositions. Whether this can be regarded as good news or bad news is beyond the scope of this chapter. However, I think we can all agree upon the fact that for all these new means of creative musical activity—in which we *copy-write* and *write to copy*—*intertextuality* is not only a prerequisite, but a fundamental and indispensable quality for the process of creation.

Acting in the global intertextual musical arena of today, a few examples of which have been presented and discussed in this chapter, implies the formation of new musical identities on both individual and collective levels: identities in which the national, ethnic and cultural identities blend into the *artistic identity* of the individuals involved in the musical activities as well as of the artistic product—the music itself.

REFERENCES

Bakhtin, M. (1981). *The dialogic imagination*. Austin: University of Texas Press.

Barthes, R. (1977). From work to text. In: R. Barthes (Ed.) *Image, music, text*, pp. 155–64. New York, NY: Hill & Wang.

Barthes, R. (1986). The death of the author. In: R. Barthes (Ed.) *The rustle of language*, pp. 142–8. New York, NY: Hill & Wang.

Csikszentmihalyi, M. (1990). *Flow. The psychology of optimal experience*. New York: Harper & Row.

DeNora, T. (2000). *Music in everyday life*. Cambridge: Cambridge University Press.

Dyndahl, P. (2005a). Hypertekst og musikalsk spatio-temporalitet [Hypertext and musical spatio-temporality]. In: S. Furuseth (Ed.) *Kunstens rytmer i tid og rum* [*Rhythms of art in time and space*], pp. 89–104. Trondheim: Tapir Akademisk Forlag.

Dyndahl, P. (2005b). Kulturens xerox-grad eller remixet autentisitet? Gjenbruk og originalitet i hiphop og samplingkultur [The Xerox-degree of culture, or, authenticity remixed? Re-use and originality in hip-hop and sampling culture]. In: P. Dyndahl & L.A. Kulbrandstad (Eds.) *High fidelity eller rein jalla? Purisme som problem i kultur, språk og estetikk* [*High fidelity or pure Yalla? Problems of purism in culture, language and aesthetics*], pp. 201–28. Vallset: Oplandske Bokforlag.

Dyndahl, P. (2013). Towards a cultural study of music in performance, education, and society? In: P. Dyndahl (Ed.) *Intersection and interplay. Contributions to the cultural study of music in performance, education, and society*, pp. 35–55. Malmö: Malmö Academy of Music, Lund University.

Fiske, J. (1987). Intertextuality. In: J. Fiske (Ed.) *Television culture*, pp. 108–27. London: Methuen.

Folkestad, G. (1996). *Computer based creative music making: Young people's music in the digital age*. Göteborg: Acta Universitatis Gothoburgensis.

Folkestad, G. (2002). National identity and music. In: R.A.R. MacDonald, D.J. Hargreaves, & D. Miell (Eds.) *Musical identities*, pp. 151–62. Oxford: Oxford University Press.

Folkestad, G. (2008). Review article: music, informal learning and the school: a new classroom pedagogy, by Lucy Green. *Music Education Research*, 10(4), 499–503.

Folkestad, G. (2012). Digital tools and discourse in music: the ecology of composition. In: D.J. Hargreaves, D. Miell, & R.A.R. MacDonald (Eds.) *Musical imaginations*, pp. 193–205. Oxford: Oxford University Press.

Folkestad, G. (2013). Intertextuality and creative music making. In: P. Dyndahl (Ed.) *Intersection and interplay. Contributions to the cultural study of music in performance, education, and society*, pp. 157–72. Malmö: Malmö Academy of Music, Lund University.

Gurwitsch, A. (1964). *The field of consciousness*. Pittsburgh, PA: Duquesne University Press.

Hall, S. (1993). What is the "black" in black popular culture? *Social Justice*, 20(1–2), 104–14.

Hargreaves, D. J., Miell, D., & MacDonald, R.A.R. (2002). What are musical identities, and why are they important? In: R.A.R. MacDonald, D.J. Hargreaves, & D. Miell (Eds.) *Musical identities*, pp. 1–20. Oxford: Oxford University Press.

Knudsen, J.S. (2011). Music of the multiethnic minority. A postnational perspective. *Music and Arts in Action*, 3(3), 77–91.

Knudsen, J.S. (2014). Den nasjonale minneseremonien etter 22. juli 2011 [The national memorial ceremony after July 22, 2011]. In: J.S. Knudsen, M.S. Skånland, & G. Trondalen (Eds.) *Musikk etter 22. Juli [Music after July 22]*, pp. 49–72. Oslo: Norwegian Academy of Music.

Kristeva, J. (1980). *Desire in language. A semiotic approach to literature and art*. Oxford: Blackwell.

Laclau, E., & Mouffe, C. (1985). *Hegemony and socialist strategy. Towards a radical democratic politics*. London: Verso.

Middleton, R. (2000). Work-in(g)-practice: configurations of the popular music intertext. In: M. Talbot (Ed.) *The musical work. Reality or invention?*, pp. 59–87. Liverpool: Liverpool University Press.

Nerland, M. (2003). *Instrumentalundervisning som kulturell praksis [Instrumental teaching as a cultural practice]*. Oslo: Norwegian State Academy of Music.

Polanyi, M. (1958). *Personal knowledge: towards a post-critical philosophy*. Chicago, IL: University of Chicago Press.

Polanyi, M. (1967). *The tacit dimension*. London: Routledge & Kegan Paul Ltd.

Ruud, E. (1997). *Musikk og identitet [Music and identity]*. Oslo: Universitetsforlaget.

Söderman, J. (2011). "Folkbildning" through hip-hop: how the ideals of three rappers parallel a Scandinavian educational tradition. *Music Education Research*, 13(2), 211–25.

Vygotsky, L.S. (1930/2004). Imagination and creativity in childhood. *Journal of Russian and East European Psychology*, 42(1), 7–97.

Wittgenstein, L. (1967/1978). *Filosofiska undersökningar [Philosophische Untersuchungen/ Philosphical investigations]*. Stockholm: Bonniers.

CHAPTER 8

"WILL THE REAL SLIM SHADY PLEASE STAND UP?"

Identity in Popular Music

ANDY MCKINLAY AND CHRIS MCVITTIE

Whoever likes my stuff, likes my stuff. But just know Slim Shady is hip-hop. I grew up on hip-hop, it's the music I love and it's the music I respect. I respect the culture ... that's me.

Eminem

8.1 INTRODUCTION

WHEN we talk about popular music, we have a certain sense of what that description might involve. The term popular music is often taken to refer to a genre of music that is contemporary, and that is "widely experienced and/or enjoyed" (Hesmondhalgh & Negus, 2002, p. 2). Yet the meaning of producing, listening to, and enjoying such music has long been debated across musicology and related disciplines. Such debates center primarily on what is taken to be the value (or lack of value) of different forms of music. As Frith (2007, p. 257) writes, music critics have often drawn a distinction between "serious" and "popular" music: "serious music matters because it transcends social forces; popular music is aesthetically worthless because it is determined by them (because it is 'useful' or 'utilitarian')." In contrast to such views, many writers have recently argued that distinctions of this sort say more about the person offering the distinction than about the value of different genres of music. On this view, "popular music" is a particularly loaded term that is commonly used to criticize forms of music that do not reflect the individual preferences of music commentators.

One especially relevant example is that of rap music, or hip-hop. Critics have argued that rap music reflects norms and values that are shared only by particular groups and, moreover, that these values are socially divisive in enacting prejudice (Lillian, 2007). On such grounds, it is argued that the socially excluding features of rap music rule out the possibility of it being considered to have any intrinsic value. By contrast, Caldwell (2010, p. 236) argues that the defining feature of musical value is "whether an artist's songs are widely consumed or not." Citing the example of the rap musician Kanye West, Caldwell points to the popularity of West's music as demonstrated by the volume of sales of his work and the music awards gained by West during his career. For Caldwell, the consumption and recognition of this work offers clear evidence of the worth of West's music as determined by a wide and diverse listening public.

Here, we do not propose to enter into debates as to what is to count as musical value. These debates, however, are of interest to social psychologists for other reasons. For, matters of whose interests are reflected and enacted in popular music, how popular music is taken up (or not) by a wide social audience, and how it relates to broader culture all go to the very heart of identities in a social world. These issues provide the focus for this chapter.

8.2 IDENTITIES AND DISCOURSE

In order to examine the relationships between popular music and identities, we draw upon the perspective of discursive psychology. From a discursive perspective, identities are not straightforward descriptions of who we *are* or of how we are located in patterns of social relations. Rather, identities are what we *do* as we live our lives in interactions with others, and within the social and cultural contexts that we inhabit. Thus, discursive psychologists point to how identities are continually in flux, negotiated in the moment-to-moment of interaction (McKinlay & McVittie, 2008, 2011). The negotiation of identity is accomplished in discourse. As people describe themselves or others in specific ways, so they are identifying themselves and those around them as particular individuals. The descriptions that are on offer, of course, are by no means final or fixed. Any description, whether a claim to identity or the ascription of identity to another, is available to others to accept, challenge, resist, or rework according to the requirements of the interactional context. From a discursive perspective, therefore, to understand identity we do not seek to work out who the person "really" is, but instead we examine how the person is identified in his or her social interactions with others. Thus, the discursive study of identities becomes the study of what identities are claimed, ascribed, resisted, or reworked, and how this is accomplished in discourse.

More than this, discursive psychology draws attention to the action orientation of discourse. Discourse never comprises "neutral" description; instead, it is always directed towards some social action outcome. People can always be described in a range of different possible ways—according to the oft-quoted example, one person's freedom-fighter is another person's terrorist. The version that is deployed is designed toward some end, whether justifying, praising, criticizing, or otherwise. Identity is no exception: the identities that we claim, resist, or rework are directed toward some outcome depending on the demands of the local context. In order to examine identity, therefore, we have to examine not just the identities that are available in any passage of discourse, but also the functions that these possibilities might serve in social terms (Potter & Wetherell, 1987).

This approach offers two particular advantages in the present case. First, it focuses attention on how people make sense of popular music in their everyday lives. We need not attempt to determine from an external perspective the relative merits of popular music, or the implications of any definition for people's sense of inclusion or exclusion from listening, enjoyment, or social participation. Instead, we can examine how individuals identify or do not identify with music—how in talk about music they accomplish identity work for themselves and for others. Secondly, by treating music as discourse, we can consider how popular music makes available identity possibilities. As with other forms of discourse, music lyrics draw upon, reproduce, and rework shared social understandings of people, actions, events, and so on. In doing so, music itself provides a site for the negotiation of identities. The identities that popular music offers up will inevitably resonate more with some listeners than others, but they do nonetheless construct and propose possibilities that might be understood in a broader system of social relations. Talk about popular music and music itself, then, both provide fertile ground for the discursive psychologist to study identities.

8.3 MUSIC TALK AND IDENTITIES

Here, a useful starting point is the question of how a listening public understands the music to which they listen. In a study of the perspectives of users of digital music, Carlisle (2007) explored how young people aged between 18 and 22 years talked about consumption of online music. As well as being listeners, the majority of participants were musicians or involved in the music industry and talked about both making music and listening to it.

What Carlisle found was that in describing digital music her participants used three broad forms of talk, or "repertoires." The first repertoire, which Carlisle terms the "romantic repertoire," emphasized the value of musicians' expertise and skill. This repertoire privileged musicians' knowledge of music over that of the average listener and was used to criticize listeners who freely distributed and illegally downloaded digital music for failing to recognize the value of musicians' efforts. Within the second repertoire, termed the "consumer culture" repertoire, online music was described as produced primarily for financial reward. Here, participants identified musicians in two highly contrasting ways: those who simply made music to make money, and "real musicians" who made music for the love of doing so and not for financial gain. Listeners, consequently, were identified as people who had to differentiate between music of value and music produced for money. Moreover, the participants described listeners as entitled to download music (illegally) for this purpose, in that "real musicians" would not object in that they are not motivated by financial reward. The third form of talk, the "multi-cultural repertoire," was less directed towards making music or downloading it than towards listeners and their judgments of music. Within this repertoire, all online music was treated as having value for someone and the range of different forms of music had potential to communicate across cultural barriers. The participants used this repertoire to distinguish between two types of listener—those who appreciated the broad potential of different forms of music and those who did not. The latter group were criticized for failing to recognize this potential and for attempting to impose unwarranted judgments of quality or tastes, that is, for being in effect musical "snobs."

From Carlisle's (2007) findings, there are three points of immediate relevance here. First, each of the three repertoires proposes specific music-related identities for musicians, for listeners, or both. Secondly, these identities are mutually inconsistent across the repertoires. For example, musicians cannot consistently be identified as people with specific knowledge and skills ("romantic repertoire") and as people who produce music merely for commercial gain ("consumer culture repertoire"). Similarly, it is difficult to describe listeners simultaneously as individuals who are entitled to download music in order to judge quality ("consumer culture repertoire") and as individuals who should refrain from imposing judgments of quality ("multi-cultural repertoire"). Finally, we can note that all these identities are bound up with specific action outcomes. For example, actions of justifying or criticizing downloading of digital music, and of justifying or criticizing judgments of musical quality, are inextricably interlinked with how musicians and listeners are identified in these passages of talk. This demonstrates how identities are negotiated in talk about music and used to accomplish outcomes in the immediate context.

8.3.1 Claiming identities through music talk

As noted above, identities of musician and listener can be constructed in very different ways. Let us now consider contexts in which people claim for themselves particular versions of these identities. One such instance comes from a study by Xanthapolou (2010) of interviews conducted on evangelical television programs. A main focus for these interviews was that of "defectiveness" in Xanthapolou's terms, with interviewees being invited to provide accounts for personal shortcomings or failings in not living up the standards required by allegiance to a higher entity (God). One interviewee, Jessie, describes how she ceased singing in the church choir in order to form a band and pursue a musical career. Elsewhere, the ability to write and perform songs, and choice of career based on this ability might be evaluated positively. In this instance, however, that is less likely to be the case, with withdrawal from the church choir in favor of pursuit of individual desires and reward potentially being treated as just the sort of failing that the program is discussing and Jessie being held accountable for her choices. Here, we see how Jessie accounts for her actions. (Transcription symbols used in the extracts in this chapter are shown in the footnote.[1])

Jessie: God really challenged me (.) >and I had wr↑itten< (.) a whole album worth of so:ngs (0.4) e:rm (.) ↑non Christian songs but just kinda like out of my own experience and they were just s↑itting in (0.2) in a- (.) a b:oo:k (0.4) a:nd ↑God really said to me J↑essie? you've been that wicked lazy ((pointing with hands)) servant (0.3) who: is just playing it safe ↓a:nd I'm: I'm not having it (.) ↑so I guess right then I had a dec↑ision (0.3) whether (0.2) to: (0.2) ↑stay c↑omfortable and keep singing in the church (0.2) and you know doing the ou and a:r (.) o:r (0.2) ↑push myself forward (.) as a singer song wri:ter (.) and get a band together and start rec[o:rding].
Host: [°mm::°]
Jessie: (0.4) a:nd (.) I di:d ((nodding))(0.2) ↓because (0.2) I felt the lord had challenged me.

Adapted from Xanthapolou, 2010, p. 686.

This extract forms part of an extended response following the interviewer's introduction of the topic of "playing it safe." In responding, Jessie takes up this topic in describing her previous action of singing in the church choir as an example of precisely that action. In doing so, she presents "playing it safe" as reprehensible in that it reflects a failure to make good use of a God-given talent. By characterizing her previous actions in this way, Jessie evaluates herself in highly negative terms as "a wicked lazy … servant." This evaluation becomes all the more emphasized through her attribution of the description to "God" himself, constructing her previous identity and actions as highly criticizable. The actions that she has taken to address these shortcomings by pursuing a musical career thereby become laudable rather than any indication of "defectiveness." Thus, Jessie presents her abandonment of the identity of choir singer, and the adoption of the identity of musician as matters of fulfilling a religious duty instead of merely personal choice.

Music talk, of course, is as available for the negotiation of collective identities as for individual identity. For example, ever-increasing use of the Internet, including social networking sites, and ease of access through rapidly developing information and communication technologies have led to a proliferation of online music forums where users can share and discuss musical preferences. Two points of particular note arise here for the study of identities. First, in using such sites members often identify themselves by selecting screen names that describe musical preferences. Members of hip-hop chat rooms, for example, often use screen names such as Snoop Dog, Slim_Shady, lil_kim, or screen names that are designed to identify with hip-hop culture generally (e.g.,

---

[1] Transcription symbols used in the extracts in this chapter are as follows: ((cough)), transcriber's descriptions of sounds appear in double parentheses; (.), a dot within parentheses indicates a brief pause between utterances; (2.5), numbers between parentheses indicate a pause between utterances measured in seconds; e::h , colons indicate that the immediately preceding sound has been prolonged; > text <, left and right carats indicate faster speech; °I know°, degree" signs indicate speech that is hearably quieter; ↑, an upward arrow indicates rising intonation; [ ], square brackets indicate start and end of overlapping speech; ^, upward carat indicates non-verbal reaction.

GaNgStA_BoY). Interestingly, even contributors to the chat room who do not share a like of hip-hop orientate to this expectation, using names such as never_hiphop, or RAVER1 (Rellstab, 2007). Second, a community that is organized around music preferences will often promote their collective identities and seek to exclude others who do not share these tastes. For example, in a study of an online community for fans of the rock band R.E.M., Bennett (2013) notes how fans construct the band as producing music for the "thinking" fan. Intruders who do not accept or who question this description will be targeted by members who do share the community's identification of R.E.M. Members of other music-based communities similarly seek to enforce their agreed boundaries of identities when faced with attempts to infiltrate their online activities for ideological reasons rather than expressions of musical preferences (Spracklen, 2013).

Even for groups or communities that are not primarily organized around musical preferences, music talk can provide central elements of collective identities. This becomes all the more relevant when the understanding of music provides a sense of a shared history and current identity. Clary-Lemon (2010) points to how Irish immigrants living in Canada draw upon appreciation of music in developing a shared Irish history and culture that can be celebrated in their chosen multicultural homeland. Constructing identity in this way can, however, bring its own problems. Sharing enjoyment of music with others makes for inclusion within a group or imagined group with similar tastes. At the same time that preference can mark out members of the group as being different from others in the broader community. Although such differences might be accepted and celebrated in some contexts, they can prove more problematic in others. Thus, for example, groups in north-east Brazil can draw upon imagined notions of folklore and commonality in constructing identities that reflect the essence and history of the region. As such representations become more popular, however, they can identify the groups as part of a romanticized past that differs from contemporary Brazilian life (Sharp, 2011). Thus, managing and popularizing inclusion can simultaneously give rise to exclusion in terms of the identities that result.

8.3.2 Ascribing identities to others

Just as talk about music is available for constructing identities for oneself, either individually or as a member of a social group, so too can it be used to ascribe identities to others to accomplish specific actions. One such example is seen in a study by Saghaye-Beria (2012) of the testimony given to a US Congressional Hearing held in 2011, "The Extent of Radicalization in the American Muslim Community and That Community's Response." This Hearing, as the name suggests, was set up in the aftermath of the attacks of the World Trade Center in New York on September 11, 2001, and continuing unease and misgivings of many Americans as to the presence and activities of Muslims in the United States. Much of the evidence given to the Hearing focussed on the issue of whether Muslim Americans were becoming radicalized, and the extent of any resulting threat to US security. Of particular interest here is how speakers constructed evidence of radicalization. For some, radicalization relied on a contrast between activities that reflected ordinary American values and activities that signaled a departure from these values. Thus, one witness at the Hearing Melvin Bledsoe, in providing testimony relating to the conversion of his son to Islam, described how his son changed from being "a normal American kid who 'loved swimming, and dancing, listening to music'" (2012, p. 518) to a practicing Muslim who ceased all these activities. In this context, the absence of enjoyment of music was claimed to demonstrate that Bledsoe's son had been "brainwashed" into becoming an entirely different person.

According to Bledsoe's testimony, then, listening to music should be understood as an ordinary part of everyday life. On other occasions, however, listening to music can be described as just the opposite: something so exceptional and unacceptable that it provides the legitimate basis for formulating a complaint about the person or people who do engage in it. For example, as Stokoe & Hepburn (2005) note, music (especially when described as loud) can readily be reformulated as noise, thereby removing particular qualities that might suggest it is enjoyable and presenting it as a breach of accepted norms of everyday behavior. Thus, "what one person counts as 'delightful music' may be defined as a 'hideous cacophony' by another" (Stokoe & Hepburn, 2005, p. 648). Defined in this way, music becomes a "complainable" (Edwards, 2005), indicating reprehensible and criticizable behavior on the part of the listener.

In a similar vein, Dixon & Durrheim (2004) point to how descriptions of music are interwoven with descriptions of place to identify others in a prejudicial fashion. They cite the example of Scottburgh, one particular coastal town in South Africa. In the apartheid era, the beachfront and environs of the town were classed as "whites only," whereas post-apartheid these areas are multiracial, allowing access to all. Changes such as this, however, have not been well received by white South Africans who holiday at Scottburgh. As Dixon & Durrheim note, the complaints made by white South Africans in response to these changes are not founded in race itself, but instead in the activities of those now allowed to use the beach. We see next one holiday-maker, Mary, describing what she would like to experience on the beach.

> Mary: I want to be in a natural situation. I don't wanna be with music blaring. And the wilder it is, the whole, generally all of us
>
> Peter: Want a bit of peace and quiet.
>
> Mary: Ja, we want to be in nature.
>
> Dixon & Durrheim, 2004, p. 467.

In this description, we see on offer a contrast between what white South Africans would wish from the beach and what happens there now. Here nature is linked to "peace and quiet" and contrasted with the activity of "music blaring." These activities are themselves bound up with the space in which they took place or now occur. Taken together, they make for identities associated with relaxation and tranquility that have given way to identities of victims of unreasonable and criticisable behavior by others. Far from being a pleasurable activity that is enjoyed by many, listening to music is here presented as associated with unwanted change and culpable behavior.

Similarly, in a study of white US college students, Foster (2009) points to how talk about music can provide a basis for racist talk. Instead of grounding complaints about fellow students in race itself, interviewees could seek to avoid being viewed as prejudiced by complaining about the activities of fellow students, listening to music included. Below we see one interviewee, Kaitlin, talking about her black roommate and the "weird" activities that she and her friends engaged in while in the room.

> R: like all the time ((laughs)) they're over there, and they just do stuff that (.) I don't do, like they move the table and like da:nce in the middle of our room
>
> I: Right.
>
> R: Which I would never do with my frie(h)nds
>
> I: Like listen to music?
>
> R: Yeah, like rap which doesn't bother me like listening to rap music but I just find it kind of weird 'cause I wouldn't have my friends over and like breakdance all over my living room like they do ((laughs))
>
> Adapted from Foster, 2009, p. 693. (I = interviewer, R = participant)

Above, Kaitlin develops a criticism of her roommate based upon the actions of that roommate and her friends in the house. These actions, invoking descriptions of listening to and dancing to music, need not in themselves be grounds for criticism. Kaitlin, however, contrasts them with what she and her friends do in the same situation: "I would never do with my frie(h)nds." This contrast, and the characterization of her roommate's and her friends' actions as "weird," presents these actions as exceptional. Foster notes that, in the course of the interviews, the students repeatedly complained about the actions of fellow (black) students who played loud (rap) music together and danced. These descriptions were offered as a basis for others being legitimately annoyed at such behavior. Their complaints, moreover, were always targeted at black students who were portrayed as the only students who did engage in such complainable music-related behaviors. As Foster points out, identifying black students in terms of music-related activities allowed students to present themselves as non-racist in that none of their complaints were grounded in issues of race itself. Nonetheless, the characterizations of black students' actions as annoying, and consequent identifications of black students as unreasonable people, allowed the white students to enact prejudice, defending their own actions and blaming black students for ongoing lack of racial integration.

8.4 IDENTITIES IN MUSIC

We have seen how people in talk about music claim identities for themselves and ascribe identities to others. We now turn to consider the arena of music itself.

Music can be used to construct a diverse range of social phenomena and events in particular ways. For example, Flowerdew (2004) analyses the case of a promotional video devised by the City of Hong Kong. This video was accompanied by a musical soundtrack that combined Chinese music and Western music, a combination that promoted the theme of Hong Kong as a multicultural city where "East meets West." On a similar note Edwards (2004), in an analysis of the music selected for use in the memorial service held after the 9/11 attacks on the World Trade Center, notes that organizers drew on a combination of musical choices to mark the occasion as reflecting both a sense of grief and a desire for vengeance against those responsible for the attacks.

Of greater interest to the discursive psychologist, however, are the identity possibilities offered up in music lyrics. As with other talk, music lyrics provide a realm for construction of identities for self, others, and social groups, and for the enactment of social processes that can be inclusive, exclusive, or prejudicial. Writing on the notion of "manipulation," van Dijk (2006) argues that music as part of discourse in a broad sense provides the same possibilities as any other discourse for "positive self-presentation and negative other presentation expressing ideological conflict ... enhancing the power, moral superiority and credibility of the speaker(s), and discrediting dissidents, while vilifying the others" (p. 380). Thus, music can act as a locus for establishing moral assessments of respect and disrespect (Buttny & Williams, 2000). As, however, van Dijk (2006) also points out, "discourse structures are not manipulative; they only have such functions or effects in specific communicative situations and the way in which these are interpreted by participants in their context models." What this means is that we cannot simply "read off" the meanings of music lyrics; rather we have to examine how individuals in specific settings relate to, take up, or challenge the identity formulations that are on offer.

8.4.1 Constructing identities in music

Perhaps the most obvious case of the construction of identities in music occurs where specific songs provide identities that individuals take up and enact in their own lives. Such an identity can be found in the work of the singer Avril Lavigne who in her song "Skater Girl" proposed a form of femininity that could be viewed as alternative to other prevailing forms. Kelly, Pomerantz, & Currie (2005) point to how schoolgirls in British Columbia (Canada) drew upon this "skater girl" identity in making sense of their own activities and experiences at school, contrasting their identities with those of their peers. As one student, Jessica, explained:

> pop stars sing mainly about "love and relationships," whereas alternative bands write songs that "have meaning" and are "worth hearing." The lyrics are "about them growing up or them having trouble with friends, not liking school or dropping out."
>
> Kelly et al., 2005, p. 138.

By identifying with music that had meaning for them, the skater girls constructed identities that rejected the notions of emphasized femininity commonly found among other schoolgirls. Below we see another student, Grenn, describe how the skater girls' identity work was received by other students.

> They ((the preps)) don't agree with the way I look. They don't agree with the way I act. They just don't agree with my music. They don't agree with like anything about me, right?
>
> Adapted from Kelly et al., 2005, p. 141.

The contrast between the skater girls and other students is clearly expressed in the description above. By identifying themselves as "skater girls," the girls were able to criticize and challenge prevailing (and unwanted) forms of femininity, while claiming identities of greater authenticity, grounded in the music to which they listened and the actions it described.

In other instances, the identity possibilities that music makes available are rather more contested. Brown (2011) cites the example of the phrase "no homo." This phrase originated in the lyrics of many hip-hop songs in the 1990s, especially those of The Diplomats, Juelz Santana, and Cam'ron. Since then, "no homo" has gained wider currency, appearing in contexts that include other hip-hop lyrics, discussions on Internet forums, and YouTube postings. It is also found in everyday conversations, as in the following instance of two (male) students making arrangements to meet up to study: "Are we meeting up tonight? No homo" (Brown, 2011, pp. 299–300). As in this example, the phrase is commonly found after a speaker has made an utterance that might be taken up as "inadvertently gay" and is used to ward off any inference of homosexuality. For such reasons, critics have argued that such uses of "no homo" amount to blatant homophobia that reflects the prejudiced culture of rap music (Catucci, 2009; Matson, 2009).

Brown (2011), by contrast, argues that such criticisms proceed upon a misunderstanding of how "no homo" is used in rap music. For Brown, "no homo" operates in the reverse way to that suggested, in allowing hip-hop musicians to introduce the possibility of homosexuality into their music and thereby to provide for masculine identities that differ from the homophobic versions that previously dominated. In doing so, the music offers, even if tentatively, wider opportunities for inclusion and diverse identities than before. Thus, the identity possibilities made available by rap music are not static but always fluid, changing over time to enable and to reflect more diverse and pluralistic versions of identity (Kunzler, 2011). In order to understand the effects of discourse such as "no homo," therefore, instead of adopting external perspectives, we have to examine how this discourse is used and treated by people in "specific communicative situations" as proposed by van Dijk (2006).

8.4.2 Contesting identities in music

Rap music differs from other forms of popular music in its emphasis on verbal rhymes. As Alim (2009) comments:

Rappin, one aspect of hip-hop culture, consists of the aesthetic placement of verbal rhymes over musical beats, and it is this element that has predominated in hip hop cultural activity in recent years. Thus, language is perhaps the most useful means with which to read the various cultural activities of the Hip Hop Nation.

Alim, 2009, p. 272.

It is no surprise therefore that the lyrics of rap music have attracted considerable attention. We noted above debates as to the extent to which rap music lyrics allow for or marginalize homosexual identities. Other critics have argued that rap music is divisive also in promoting a predominantly black male culture that is not only excluding of others, but indeed prejudicial towards them. Lillian (2007), for example, argues that the lyrics found in rap music are degrading to women if not outright sexist. She proposes that, although such lyrics fall under the right of the First Amendment of the US Constitution to free speech, these lyrics meet the linguistic criteria for what would otherwise be regarded as "hate speech."

Arguments such as this, however, point again to the need for close examination of the lyrics found in rap music and how individuals relate to and make sense of them in identity terms. Richardson (2007) examined the discussions of a group of young African American women relating to depictions of women in rap music videos. One particular video, performed by an African American male rap group called "Nelly featuring the St. Lunatics," depicted scantily-clad women simulating sexual acts watched by male viewers who threw money on their bodies, in a manner similar to a performance ritual used by strip dancers (a "Tip Drill"). The lyrics in this video gave rise to somewhat divergent understandings of female identity, as seen below:

BE: Why you say it's degrading?

ED: Because. Foreal. You just don't. You ain't got to say all that. Know what uhm saying? Like you said, Some women are and some women ain't. But, the way they was puttin it, was like, females. Point blank. Period. That's in that song, females. Generalizing just all the females like that. But, know what uhm sayin, you're right. It is some tip drills out here. It is. But then again, it ain't some.

BE: That's true.

ET: Well, a lot of the lyrics in the song is degrading to women. For instance, it said, "It must be yo ass cause it ain't yo face." He said, "It ain't no fun unless we all get some." You know what uhm saying, so. Basically, meaning we gone run a train on you.

Richardson, 2007, p. 796.

In the discussion of "Tip Drill" above, we see ED arguing that the lyrics are indeed degrading to women. She claims that, notwithstanding that women differ markedly in their willingness to engage in the sorts of performance that is being depicted, the lyrics portray all women as sexual objects who will take part in "tip drills." In taking up this point, ET voices some of the lyrics that she has heard that refer to anatomical features. She continues by referring to other lyrics suggesting that the inference is that, regardless of their own wishes, women are expected to provide sexual gratification for men ("we gone run a train on you"). Not all of the participants, however, share these interpretations. Following her minimal agreement in the extract above BE thereafter continues:

> BE: But that's not degrading if the girls is wit it. It's some girls who wit dat. I don't think it's degrading. It's girls who is like that and they down for the git down, just how the boys is. Know what uhm saying. I don't. I don't know.
>
> Richardson 2007, p. 799.

In this turn, we see BE disagreeing with ED's and ET's assessment that the video is degrading to women. She argues instead that the video and lyrics are referring only to "some girls" and not to all women. She also argues that "girls who is like that" would participate in such activities willingly and not due to pressure to do so ("they down for the git down"). Accordingly, the identities presented are left uncertain, as is the issue of whether or not the video and lyrics should be regarded as sexist in their portrayal of women.

Just as the lyrics of rap music offer up possibilities for construction and reworking of identities in the descriptions that they offer, so too do they open up such possibilities as the music itself unfolds. Mullins (2013) points to how the female rap artist Rah Digga in her work "Dirty Harriet" challenges the versions of female sexuality found within what is still predominantly a male-dominated realm. For example, Rah Digga takes up the description "bitch" often applied pejoratively in rap music to refer to women and applies it to herself, thereby neutralizing its offensive overtones. By delivering her lyrics in a manner similar to that of male rap artists and engaging in "battles" with other (male) rap artists on this album, Rah Digga stakes out her own power in this context and challenges male dominance in hip-hop culture.

We turn finally to examine how identities are negotiated in rap "battles." This example comes from a study by Alim, Lee, & Carris (2011) of rap "battles" as a site for the coproduction of black normativity. In these contexts, black emcees marginalize others in seeking to maintain rap as a black space. Non-black emcees both uphold and challenge this marginalization, as do non-black audience members. Black emcees monitor the audience reaction in looking to gain support for themselves and undermine support for their opponents. We see this in action in one extended rap battle involving a black emcee "Flawliss" and Lil Caesar, a Latino emcee. In the extract below, Lil Caesar challenges the skills of his opponent.

```
C:    look it
      this shit if funny as fuck,
      his mind is crooked.
      just like his fuckin f ^feet, ^((looks directly at F))
F:    ((looks down at his feet)) ← sequential action
A1:   ((looks down at Flawliss f feet, begins head bob))
      (.) mee:t defeat
      delete
F:    ((scans crowd to left))
A1:   ((stops head bob))
      (.) never heard what he said
```

^rhyming off the head ^((waves right pointer))
you should [go home and write instead.

A1: [((A1 shakes head from side to side with intensity,
begins to smile))
^put some [more [ti:me~under~the~pen

F: [((F glances at A1))

A1: [((A1 stops shaking head, continues bobbing))

(Adapted from Alim et al. 2011, p.431;
C = Lil Caesar, F = Flawliss, A1 = audience member)

Here, we see Lil Caesar attack Flawliss on two counts: first, on grounds of personal features that are described as "crooked" and, second, on the basis of his perceived (lack of) rapping skills. We can see also that one member of the watching crowd (*A1*) appears to respond favorably to this attack, with the crowd all the time being monitored by Flawliss for their reactions. In his turns, by contrast, Flawliss does not attack Lil Caesar on the basis of personal features or skills, but instead on other grounds:

F: how you gon me with her ((points to himself))
beef with her? ((taps on C's chest))
just go on dawg ((waves his hand away))
go on and break my sprin-ka-lers
go on rake ma lawn

C: [((C looks down, hand on chin, shaking his head while waving hand towards F))]
go on shake along

(Adapted from Alim et al., 2011, p. 430;
C = Lil Caesar, F = Flawliss)

Earlier in this turn, Flawliss had introduced race and ethnicity in referring to his opponent. Above he draws upon a popular stereotype of Latinos as people who commonly engage in work involving manual labor or landscaping. We see also his reference to "her," characterizing Lil Caesar as female and not a worthy opponent in rap terms. Flawliss therefore seeks to marginalize Lil Caesar from the groups predominantly associated with hip-hop in two ways, first in being Latino and not belonging to the dominant (black) racial group, and secondly, as being female instead of being part of macho hip-hop culture.

The "battle" between Flawliss and Lil Caesar does not reach any final conclusion, with issues as to whether hip-hop culture is to be treated as black, male, macho, or otherwise remaining to be contested another day. Thus, the identities on offer, the meanings of these for the immediate audience and for a broader public are continually available for individuals to take up, resist, or rework, in local discursive contexts to accomplish particular actions. As with other talk, rap music lyrics provide resources for the negotiation of identities even as they are being produced. It is for individuals who participate in producing this music, or who enjoy (or even do not enjoy) such music, to make sense of these identities in their everyday lives.

8.5 CONCLUSIONS

We have seen ways in which people understand popular music and how they do or do not identify with it. The examples considered here are necessarily drawn from particular discussions, from specific songs, and in many cases from the talk of certain age groups. Nonetheless, detailed examination of such instances highlights the diverse range of identity possibilities that popular music makes available. Talk about music allows speakers to claim specific identities, to identify others, and to mobilize concerns, such as complaints or prejudice. Music itself constructs and provides contrasting versions of identities, some more attractive than others to different musicians and listeners. Thus, discursive psychology shows how popular music is inextricably linked to identities in a broad range of ways. When we claim or resist identities for ourselves, or attribute identities to others, we are all the time engaged in accomplishing social actions. To return to the point at which we began, it is unhelpful (if not incorrect) to regard popular music as "determined" by social forces (Frith, 2007)—popular music, its meanings, and who we are in relation to it are central parts of our lives as we live them and negotiate our identities in doing so.

REFERENCES

Alim, H.S. (2009). Hip hop nation language. In: A. Duranti (Ed.) *Linguistic anthropology: a reader*, 2nd edn, pp. 272–89. Malden, MA: Wiley-Blackwell.

Alim, H.S., Lee, J., & Carris, L.M. (2011). Moving the crowd, "crowding" the emcee: the coproduction and contestation of black normativity in freestyle rap battles. *Discourse & Society*, 22, 422–39.

Bennett, L. (2013). Discourses of order and rationality: drooling REM fans as "matter out of place". *Continuum: Journal of Media & Cultural Studies*, 27, 214–27.

Brown, J.R. (2011). No homo. *Journal of Homosexuality*, 58, 299–314.

Buttny, R., & Williams, P.L. (2000). Demanding respect: the uses of reported speech in discursive constructions of interracial contact. *Discourse & Society*, 11, 109–33.

Caldwell, D. (2010). Making many meanings in popular rap music. In: A. Mahboob and N. Knight (Eds.) *Appliable Linguistics*, pp. 234–51a. London: Continuum.

Carlisle, J. (2007). Digital music and generation Y: discourse analysis of the online music information behaviour talk of five young Australians. *Information Research*, 12, Article number: colis25.

Catucci, N. (2009). "No homo": cause for hope in hip-hop? *Vulture* [Online], December 20, 2013. Available at: http://www.vulture.com/2009/08/no_homo_cause_for_hope_in_hip.html (accessed February 5, 2016).

Clary-Lemon, J. (2010). 'We're not ethnic, we're Irish!': oral histories and the discursive construction of immigrant identity. *Discourse & Society*, 21, 5–25.

van Dijk, T.A. (2006). Discourse and manipulation. *Discourse & Society*, 17, 359–83.

Dixon, J., & Durrheim, K. (2004). Dislocating identity: desegregation and the transformation of place. *Journal of Environmental Psychology*, 24, 455–73.

Edwards, D. (2005). Moaning, whinging and laughing: the subjective side of complaints. *Discourse & Society*, 7, 5–29.

Edwards, J. (2004). After the fall. *Discourse & Society*, 15, 155–84.

Flowerdew, J. (2004). The discursive construction of a world-class city. *Discourse & Society*, 15, 579–605.

Foster, J.D. (2009). Defending whiteness indirectly: a synthetic approach to race discourse analysis. *Discourse & Society*, 20, 685–703.

Frith, S. (2007). *Taking popular music seriously: Selected essays*. Aldershot: Ashgate.

Hesmondhalgh, D., & Negus K. (2002). *Popular music studies*. London: Arnold.

Kelly, D.M., Pomerantz, S., & Currie, D. (2005). Skater girlhood and emphasized femininity: "you can't land an ollie properly in heels". *Gender and Education*, 17, 229–48.

Kunzler, D. (2011). South African rap music, counter discourses, identity, and commodification beyond the prophets of da city. *Journal of Southern African Studies*, 37, 27–43.

Lillian, D.L. (2007). A thorn by any other name: sexist discourse as hate speech. *Discourse & Society*, 18, 719–40.

Matson, A. (2009). The continuing saga of KUBE morning host Eddie Francis and American English's current homophobic lexicography. *The Seattle Times* [Online], December 20, 2013. Available at: http://seattletimes.nwsource.com/html/matsononmusic/2009546491_the_continuing_saga_of_kube_mo.html (accessed February 5, 2016).

McKinlay, A., & McVittie, C. (2008). *Social psychology and discourse*. Oxford: Wiley-Blackwell.

McKinlay, A., & McVittie, C. (2011). *Identities in context: individuals and discourse in action*. Oxford: Wiley-Blackwell.

Mullins, K.L. (2013). Black female identity and challenges to masculine discourse in Rah Digga's Dirty Harriet. *Popular Music and Society*, 36, 425–43.

Potter, J., & Wetherell, M. (1987). Discourse and social psychology: beyond attitudes and behaviour. London: Sage.

Rellstab, D.H. (2007). Staging gender online: gender plays in Swiss internet relay chats. *Discourse & Society*, 18, 765–87.

Richardson, E. (2007). "She was workin like foreal": critical literacy and discourse practices of African American females in the age of hip hop. *Discourse & Society*, 18, 789–809.

Saghaye-Beria, H. (2012). American Muslims as radicals? A critical discourse analysis of the US congressional hearing on "The Extent of Radicalization in the American Muslim Community and That Community's Response." *Discourse & Society*, 23, 508–24.

Sharp, D. (2011). Performing the migrant, performing home: televised nostalgia in Northeast Brazil. *Latin American Music Review—Revista de Musica Latino Americana*, 32, 181–204.

Spracklen, K. (2013). Nazi punks folk off: leisure, nationalism, cultural identity and the consumption of metal and folk music. *Leisure Studies*, 32, 415–28.

Stokoe, E., & Hepburn, A. (2005). "You can hear a lot through the walls": noise formulations in neighbour complaints. *Discourse & Society*, 16, 647–73.

Xanthapolou, P. (2010). The production of 'defectiveness' as a linguistic resource in broadcast evangelical discourse: a discursive psychology approach. *Discourse & Society*, 21, 675–91.

SECTION 3

DEVELOPMENT

CHAPTER 9

··

THE MUSICAL SELF

Affections for Life in a Community of Sound

··

COLWYN TREVARTHEN AND STEPHEN MALLOCH

There are certain aspects of the so-called "inner life"—physical or mental—which have formal properties similar to those of music—patterns of motion and rest, of tension and release, of agreement and disagreement, preparation, fulfilment, excitation, sudden change, etc.

> Langer (1942, p. 228), quoted by Kühl (2007, p. 223).
> Ole Kühl, *Musical Semantics*, 2008

Now, how does it happen, that, while I am at work, my compositions assume a form or style which characterize Mozart and are not like anyone else's? Just as it happens that my nose is big and hooked, Mozart's nose is not another man's. I do not aim at originality and I should be much at a loss to describe my style. It is quite natural that people who really have something particular about them should be different from each other on the outside as well as on the inside.

> Wolfgang Amadeus Mozart*

9.1 INTRODUCTION

··

In this chapter we examine how an innately musical human infant, with a strong motivation to express stories before speech, being already skilled in moving in both voice

---

* From Mozart's letter to his father, on July 31, 1778, when he was aged 22, about his experience of composing music, as quoted by Hadamard, 1945, pp. 6–7. Republished with permission of Princeton University Press from The mathematician's mind: the psychology of invention in the mathematical field, Jacques Hadamard, 1945; permission conveyed through Copyright Clearance Center, Inc.

and body, seeks to become a particular person, an individual with a recognized place or status in society. We consider how the creative *personal identity* of a self-other-conscious infant performer learns to become a part of a consensual musical group, with its own *communal identity* guided by musical conventions. In the development of a musician, enjoyment of moving with rhythms, and feelings of the body becomes a "We-consciousness" of display and companionship in a tradition or "habitus" of artful invention. This consciousness may become strongly regulated by graphical signs and logic that represent elements and forms of music. Comprehension and use of this "artificial language" of musical technique and tradition depends on the sense of musicality we are born with.

We identify stages in the natural growth of a musical self in relationship, from the intimate imitative dialogues with newborns and proto-conversations with two-month-olds through toddlerhood in which the drama of invention and co-created narrative is negotiated playfully, with love and intuitive skill, and with the whole body. From early childhood, demonstrations of pride and shame in musical games, with passionate variations in their negotiation, underpin the lasting value of what may be achieved by training for live collective performance of music, or for private composition imagined for others' pleasure and approval. In adolescence, music is often a vital part of the language of belonging and differentiation, of the development and defense of self-confidence forming new attachments and discovering a new identity with peers. In old age, music becomes the messenger of remembrances of vitality shared with companions and of contemplation on the finiteness of the individual life within the continuing flow of the rhythm and melody of human culture and hopefulness.

The improvised regulations of emotion and precisely timed forms of action that play with and share attractive stories in sound with affectionate companions from birth remain of importance in the teaching and practice of conventions of musical skill at all levels. This is the natural growth of a life of music-making for friendship and self-expression that is expressed within the practice of fashion and technique.

Finally, we examine how music-making with the responsive company of a person or group which has learned how to encourage inherent musical feelings in movement can be an effective therapy. Music therapy can help an isolated and sad person escape from a debilitating confusion of identity and loss of affinity and meaning in relationships and groups, whether it has been caused by a disorder of development, such as autism, or by neglect and loneliness, or abuse and emotional trauma.

At the start, however, we have to confront a conceptual barrier: an "out-of-body" and "out-of-time" account of consciousness as a product of information taken in from the environment. This exclusively cognitive view of human intelligence and its growth neglects our natural powers of a mutual awareness gained by sharing an innate imagination for moving with feeling and prevents acceptance of a spontaneous way of being that leads to a sense of music alive in a community and that gives aesthetic and moral value to all our arts.

9.2 THE PHILOSOPHICAL PROBLEM
OF "OTHER"

9.2.1 How human identities share meaning from life's beginning

From Plato and Aristotle to Kant and Hegel, European philosophy and psychology has preferred to investigate and explain a reality that is referred to when we think and talk about experience. It defines the matter of *"what" and "why" we mean* in relation to facts of an outer time and space, not the primary subjective and intersubjective life processes of *"how" we mean*. It disregards the generative inner feelings of moving-in-time with its interpersonal affections, the "auto-poetic" regulations of a human life that will not be reduced to a universal, dispassionate physics (Maturana & Varela, 1992).

Some philosophers have addressed the problem of embodied cognition, and the sharing of phenomenal experience created in purposeful movement (Merleau-Ponty, 1968; Husserl, 1969; Goodrich, 2010; Stuart, 2010). Especially noteworthy is the work of the existential philosophers such as Martin Buber (1923/1970); and there is an emerging influence on Western philosophy and psychology of Eastern thought that places directly embodied personal experience at the center of psychological health (e.g., the work of Jon Kabat-Zinn [2006] on mindfulness).

Since the 1980s, there has been a revolutionary change of understanding in brain science. Neural events "mirroring" the intentions in movements of other individuals were demonstrated to have a specific and leading location in functional cerebral anatomy. Furthermore, new awareness of how much our emotional system resembles that by which animals generate and evaluate their awareness of objects, and how sensibility to each other's intentions motivates social cooperation, confirms Darwin's theory of the origin of human intelligence and the role of emotions and their signals for conceptions of how to move in the world and of how to communicate (Darwin, 1872; von Uexküll, 1957; Damasio, 1999; Panksepp, 2012).

Well-established evidence that an animal's brain is an organ evolved to regulate a totality of coordination of movements in time with prospective affective appraisal of risks and benefits of engagement with the world in relationship to others (Sherrington, 1906; Llinàs, 2001; Buzsaki, 2006) is commonly unattended by the cognitive sciences with their focus on how single heads process structures of information about the outside world, and how they make theories to explain, in words, the structures and systems they conceive. The essential and primary principles and powers of movement and emotions *within us* and *between us* have been persistently left out. This bias creates bewildering gaps in the literature between body and experience and between one mind and another.

It makes the power of metaphor in body movement and poetry and the messages of music utterly obscure (Lakoff & Johnson, 1980; Varela, Thompson, & Rosch, 1991; Clark, 1997; Gallese & Lakoff, 2005; Trevarthen, 2012a).

One strategy to correct the neglect of movement with emotion is to investigate how infants, who lack both experience of the world and symbols and explanations for representing what they might know and believe, communicate their intentions, awareness, and feelings so well with attentive partners, and with such confident invention (Trevarthen, 1977; Bullowa, 1979; Trevarthen, 1998; Stern, 2000; Reddy, 2008; Stern, 2010; Trevarthen, 2011, 2012b; Fig. 9.1).

Music makes powerful messages without words, and infants show complex musical sensibilities and willingness to share them. To study this we have measured the dynamics of how an infant can time and modulate their expressive movements and convey emotional signals for engagement with an adult. The sounds of vitality and feeling that an infant offers to a parent companion in shared "compositions" are felt by the adult to be narrations. The infant is "telling a story" (Trevarthen & Delafield-Butt, 2013). The product of this research is a model of the innate parameters of communicative musicality, presented as the foundation for human companionship in stories of meaning (Malloch, 1999; Malloch & Trevarthen, 2009).

Our radical conclusion is that an infant is born a humanly social creature, an artful person or Self, with a motor intelligence equipped with uniquely human talents to make or detect the *aesthetic* value of melodic stories, and *moral* feelings of the relationship, both of which may be sustained with a respectful and sympathetic Other in expressive body movements and song (Schögler & Trevarthen, 2007). Baby and caregiver are musically participating in what Martin Buber (1923/1970) distinguished as an I–Thou relationship, a recognizing of one another's humanity, not just receiving novel patterns of sound stimulation from a thing in motion.

Clappa, clappa handies

Mommy's at the **well**,

Daddy's away to Hamilton

To buy wee Emma a **bell**.

FIG. 9.1 Emma, six months old, loves sharing "Clappa, clappa handies" with her mother. She knows the tune and may vocalize with the rhyming vowels, and she is proud to perform her part in the action. Stressed and unstressed beats are indicated by ' and • respectively. Rhyming vowels are printed in **bold**.

Moreover, the sympathetic expressions of interest and delight with which the infant receives playful offers of response from the "Other" (Reddy & Trevarthen, 2004) are readily transformed into teasing games or jokes that trigger relationship-strengthening smiles and laughter. Joy is part of early musical play and how infants know other embodied minds and co-explore the love of second-person awareness (Reddy, 2008).

9.2.2 The infant as a musical self

To understand how musical companionship brings delight from birth and develops, we need a new psychology of motives for communication, one that recognizes the nature of the special imitative abilities we exhibit from infancy, which rely on our innate motor intelligence coupled with prospective self-awareness of moving in deliberately expressive ways to become connected emotionally and practically with the life of other persons (Trevarthen, 2001a, 2009a).

Before birth a human body and brain are not only formed with organs adapted by their form to take part in conversation that will lead to speaking and other forms of language (Trevarthen & Delafield-Butt, 2013). They also possess measures of body movement that are adapted for participation in rhythmic celebrations of dancing body actions and gestures, and of vocal narratives (Malloch & Trevarthen, 2009). They demonstrate the pulse and flow of vitality and affections, which resemble the musical "inner life" that Langer describes (see the quote at the start of the chapter).

In the last trimester the musical features of the mother's voice may be learned as a desirable experience of her individual self, in preparation for their postnatal cooperation (DeCasper & Spence, 1986). From birth their engagements are adapted to create rhythmic and affective habits. Research on the timing and emotions of neonatal imitations, which are so important in nurturing love between parents and the new family member, confirms that a primary musical intersubjectivity, mediated by rhythmic expressions of intention and feelings of vitality, is innate.

In the first hours after birth, even if the infant is premature, he or she can engage in time and in tune with skillful intention and feelings of another human being, intimately sharing movement. The way infants participate in the rituals of action songs with age-related changes as the body and brain grow, has made it clear that their play with someone they love is constructive of a cultural social awareness (Trevarthen, 2012b). It becomes behavior with a conventional form to be proud of, wanting appreciative attention from a partner (Fig. 9.1). Failure to gain this sympathetic appreciation causes the infant to express the withdrawal and distress of shame (Murray & Trevarthen, 1985; Trevarthen, 2005). This is the essential process of "attunement" by which affective relations or "attachments" are established and nurtured in living with emotions in musical time—a musical "companionship" of selves within which language and other cultural skills may be learned.

9.2.3 The meaning of play: emotions in well-timed movement

The social life of animals—development of selves in complex interrelationship—depends on play, the signaling of inner emotional states and testing of their regulation creatively in a shared experience of life in movement. Human cultural life explores its meanings in play with actions and ideas, and in their communication. The biology of play is the creativity of actions with emotional values of the body, generated from within, engaging with the objects of the world experimentally, and seeking social cooperation (Panksepp, 2012).

Play depends on innate rhythms and expressive codes. Vitality dynamics of movements (Stern, 2010) signal the balance of energetic resources of the body for "autopoesis" or self-creation of adaptive activity (Maturana & Varela, 1980). Social play regulates these resources in the creative "consensuality" of the group (Maturana, 1978), by connecting measures of prospective and remembered life times in different worlds with different companions, synchronizing biological clocks or a biochronology of life activities operating over a range of milliseconds to centuries (Trevarthen, 2008; Osborne, 2009a; Trevarthen, 2009b). Expressions of feeling become the inventive signals by which communities of ambitious human selves regulate their cooperations. Play is unreasonable. It is not a *cognitive*, outside-fact-driven activity. It is *conative* or willful and hopeful, and *emotional* or passionate. Its invention and self-related delights and fears benefit cognition and develop with it (Panksepp, 2012).

Musical play builds affection and enriches consciousness, both individual and collective. It is a powerful ally for both teaching of more practical skills, and for therapy. Music is, we believe, cultivated from a primary human motivation for creation of cultural meaning, with affective dynamics displayed as seductive messages from birth (Malloch, 1999; Malloch & Trevarthen, 2009; Trevarthen, 2012b). Song with dance contributes to both the autopoesis and the consensuality of linguistic skills, which while they become the most refined and precise medium for sharing knowledge and skills, never lose their syntactic dependence on whole body expressions of intentions and feelings in vocal sound (Maturana et al., 1995; Kühl, 2007). Languaging has its origins in evolution and development in communicative musicality of body movement in song and audible gesture (Brown, 2000; Dissanayake, 2009).

9.2.4 The maturation of musical vitality

There are four times in life when the human body is clearly transforming its powers, when new awareness of the rhythms of movement and of affect lead to greater pleasure in the communicative musicality of being human—in infancy, among children aged 3-11, in adolescence, and in old age. These four stages of transformation can be mapped to Erik Erikson's eight stages of psychosocial development (Erikson, 1950,

1968). Infants (Erikson's first stage of Trust vs. Mistrust) are discovering how to use all their movements, mostly in the expressive upper parts of the body, experiencing the intimate company of peers and family, and sharing creative stories in play with face, eyes, voice, and hands (Malloch & Trevarthen, 2009, chapters by Bradley, Eckerdal, and Merker, Gratier and Apter-Danon, Mazokopaki and Kugiumutzakis, Powers and Trevarthen, Rodrigues, Rodrigues, and Correia). Their movements are accompanied by and encouraged through play-songs and lullabies (Vlismas, Malloch, & Burnham, 2013).

Toddlers and those going through early childhood (Erikson's second, third, and fourth stages of Autonomy vs. Shame, Initiative vs. Guilt, and Industry vs. Inferiority, respectively) enjoy exploring new and exciting powers of whole body movement, jumping, running, dancing, singing, and talking enthusiastically with playmates of all ages in a familiar community (Custodero, 2009) (Fig. 9.2). They create in their play a "children's musical culture" full of audacious experiments in sound (Bjørkvold, 1992) and are "linguistic geniuses" (Chukovsky, 1963).

In adolescence (Erikson's fifth stage of Identity vs. Role Confusion) new vitality with emerging sexual feelings and a wish to explore new relationships and responsibilities away from the family gain pleasure and meaning from association with contemporary cultural fashions, often with group performances in song and dance. Everywhere music has cultural-developmental importance for adolescents who, as persons engaged with culture, show

FIG. 9.2 Ana Almeida, when a PhD student in the Institute for Music and Human Social Development (IMHSD), Edinburgh University, recorded how 4- and 5-year-old children move their bodies when they hear music. Each child was invited to move within a square while musical rhythms were played for them. They were told, "when you hear the music you move as you wish and when the music stops you freeze like a statue." These three children move with all their body, running, jumping, and arresting their movements, making eloquent gestures with their hands, translating the rhythmic patterns and moods. They show delight on their faces. The children create a variety of performances, responding to the beat and changes of tempo, each child expressing an individual repertoire of movements.

With permission of Ana Almeida. From Almeida, 2015

strong preferences and aversions that vary with social and ethnic groups (Miranda et al., 2015). Adulthood (Erikson's stages six and seven: Intimacy vs. Isolation, and Generativity vs Stagnation, respectively) is less about physical and psychological transformation and more about creating and consolidating achievements, building lasting relationships, creating a family, career, and settling into a sense of purpose in the world. Music is there as an activity for practice, study, or recreation. In old age (Erikson's eighth stage, Ego Integrity vs. Despair), with growing awareness of the infirmity of the body, its limitations of vitality, its weakness and pains, and a turning towards one's own mortality, a more contemplative relationship to music arises, with growing importance of time for reminiscence of companionable activities and stillness that is accompanied by remembrances of one's musical life.

It appears that a musical lifetime has changing needs that relate to changing physical and psychological dynamics and motivations, with phases of hopeful enjoyment, of feelings of competence and periods of satisfaction in mastery of skill, with infancy, 3–11, adolescence, and old age being times when the emotional richness in music is especially relevant. However, it is also evident that performing, creating, and appreciating music can bring a person of any age or stage back in touch with the playfulness of expression in movement and with the strong bonds of enjoyment these feelings bring with others. Learning satisfying, enjoyable skill in music requires that this hold on the pleasures of authentic musical play is alive and secure (Trevarthen & Malloch, 2012).

9.3 BEST PRACTICE OF MUSICAL EDUCATION

9.3.1 Supporting natural enjoyment of creativity and shared performance.

It is interesting that we "play" music, but we do not "play" talk or practical tasks. Music is an imitative art and a practice of celebratory ritual that must retain "the human seriousness of play" if it is to maintain its human aliveness (Turner, 1982). The spontaneous singing and dancing play of young children, and the most creative compositions and most loved performances by mature artists in music or dance, are rich in metaphorical invention expressive of the energetic ways motivated human bodies regulate movements, imagine, think, and communicate (Langer, 1953; Lakoff & Johnson, 1980; Varela et al., 1991; Clark, 1997; Gallese & Lakoff, 2005; Malloch & Trevarthen, 2009, chapters by Bond, Custodero, Fröhlich). Our bodies show forms of vitality that transmit passionate meanings immediately, enabling actors to perform together in creative ways (Stern, 2010). This is the expression of a musical "zest for learning", which Alfred North Whitehead said is the essential motivator for any culture of education (Whitehead, 1929) (Fig. 9.3).

The Norwegian musicologist Jon-Roar Bjørkvold (1992) studied the musical games of children in Oslo, Moscow, St Petersburg, and Los Angeles, where educational, cultural, social, and political practices are very different. He found that in all three countries

FIG. 9.3 In a 2010 project run by Robin Duckett of Sightlines Initiative in Newcastle upon Tyne (UK), two musician-educators, Catherine Reding and Zoe Bremner, worked in Trimdon Grange Infant and Nursery School, County Durham, with school staff Chris Ramsay and Melanie Clark. They chose eight 5-year-old girls who were good friends fond of inventing stories and worked with them over a 5-month period to record their expression in music and dance, with the aim of encouraging their educators to value creative music-making by the children. The girls decided to make a new version of "Sleeping Beauty," called "Awakening Beauty", the story of the princess who danced with good fairies and then was put to sleep by wicked fairies and rescued by a prince. They composed the story with songs, cleverly adapting tunes they knew. They were asked to talk about their feelings, making movements to show emotions, and drawing them. They were offered instruments with different tones, including drums and stringed and wind instruments, to "play" the full range of their feelings. The good fairies danced gracefully to the "happy" plucked string melodies. Then angry music was made on drums, with Polly, the energetic dancing leader of the musicians, using her whole body. She became Evil Bird, one of the wicked fairies who put the princess to sleep. In these pictures the girls experiment with the musical instruments and dancing, making their own creative projects, some inspired by well-known stories or the media.

With permission of Robin Duckett, http://www.sightlines-initiative.com/.

children showed spontaneous musicality, but in the nations of Russia and the US, where formal training in music was given greater value than it was in Norway, he found reduced spontaneous music-making. He insists, "It is critically important for children to master spontaneous singing, for it is part of the common code of child culture that gives them a special key to expression and human growth" (Bjørkvold, 1992, p. 63). A comparable inhibitory effect of conventions of schooling has been recorded on the spontaneous expression of religious feelings and spirituality in the early years (Hay & Nye, 1998). These innate sources of human imagining give value and meaning to the cultivation of advanced cultural ideas and skills.

Infants and young children use the voice with a singing kind of expression in progressively more "symbolic" ways. What Bjørkvold calls *Fluid/Amorphous songs* "evolve in a completely natural way from infants' babbling as part of their first playful experiments with voice and sound. This type of song, with its fanciful glissandi, micro-intervals, and free rhythms, is quite different from what we adults traditionally identify as song." (Bjørkvold, 1992, p. 65). *Song formulas*, such as teasing songs, are symbolic forms for communicating with other children and they flourish after the child begins to play with peers, typically at two or three years. Elements of musically more complex *Standard Songs* are picked up from play with adults and hearing them sing and soon are adapted to fit what the child is doing. This progressive "ritualization" of vocal creativity clarifies the adaptive motives for learning to sing, and how they express increasing narrative imagination for sharing ideas in culturally specific ways (Gratier & Trevarthen, 2008; Eckerdal & Merker, 2009). Its natural development parallels the way language is mastered (Chukovsky, 1963)

Teachers and students of music at all levels may learn how best to do their work by deliberately invoking such creative vitality (Flohr & Trevarthen, 2008). Infants and toddlers make imaginative play in affectionate friendships with parents or peers (Custodero, 2009); primary school children build relationships with the invention of stories in groups with free instrumental play and dance (Fröhlich, 2009); and an advanced music student is assisted to master their instrument through their teacher encouraging their playing to be like a dance representing a narrative rich in expressive feelings (Rodrigues, Rodrigues, & Correia, 2009) (Fig. 9.4).

As Bjørkvold points out, mastery of written music can distract from the feeling of enjoyment for the musical story:

FIG. 9.4 On the day of the performance of "Awakening Beauty" all the children were extremely excited. The whole school came to watch them, with their parents and other visitors. Here is shy Sleeping Beauty and her brave prince after the show; and the final bow.

With permission of Robin Duckett, http://www.sightlines-initiative.com/

A child who is asked to play a printed score must turn their attention from the primary experience of making music (spontaneous singing within the child culture, for example) to a kind of secondary music making in accordance with the notes on the page. For many children, the result is that their ability to make music in the primary sense withers and dies. … Their oral musical competence … can be irretrievably lost as a result of premature preoccupation with written music.

Bjørkvold, 1992, p. 188.

In all instances the motives of the learner, and how they may change with development of the body and experiences gained, are of crucial importance (Bannan & Woodward, 2009). As with all education, the success of teaching depends on recognition of how children's "zest for learning" (Whitehead, 1929) changes with age and the development of body and mind. Children belong to different places, where particular forms of music are cultivated for shared enjoyment in a living community of practices, myths, and values (Blacking, 1995; Cross & Morley, 2009). In short, the way for a young child to learn how to read musical scores and master an approved art tradition of singing or playing is easier and more sure if the teacher strives to be a companion in the enjoyment of moving with the subtleties of children's musical invention and celebration (Deliège & Sloboda, 1996, chapters by Hargreaves, Imberty, Papoušek, Sloboda, & Davidson; Trehub, 2003; Flohr & Trevarthen, 2008; Custodero, 2009).

9.4 A FIRST-HAND EXPERIENCE OF MUSICAL IDENTITIES

9.4.1 Creating enjoyable music in community

Amateur musical societies, people singing and playing with hopeful effort and a wish to create with others, exist across the world, providing opportunities for people who would otherwise not have the opportunity to create music in a community, often for public performance.

This is a short description of the second author's experience of being a conductor in one such amateur music group, the varied and changing musical identities he evolved as a result of both motivated inner expression and outer demands, and the various musical identities he encountered along the way of those involved in the creation of the show.

I was first involved in this music group, one devoted to the works of Gilbert and Sullivan, in my early twenties. It provided a place for me to exercise my emerging talent and love for conducting, and also my enjoyment of being at the center of things. It placed me in a pivotal role in an organizing committee, needing to co-ordinate auditions and make decisions who would be cast, to create a rehearsal schedule and to manage changes to this schedule as the rehearsal period unfolded. It necessitated my close interaction with the director and others charged with creative responsibility, making decisions around how the music would unfold, how much time was needed for rehearsing different facets of the production, and how the music would be interpreted so that it meshed with ideas on character interpretation. I found myself to be central to the running of this small "village" of around 40 people, being the center of attention. It took up a lot of time.

In addition, there was the social aspect, which for a somewhat introverted young man as I was then, was not always easy or wanted.

There were the rehearsals themselves, and the necessity to discover the right degree of diplomacy, charm, and forcefulness in order to cajole from the singers first the right notes and then a particular interpretation. Through all of this ran my visceral enjoyment of creating music with others, of hearing and seeing improvement over the course of rehearsals, and of being the leader of a co-created musical endeavor.

Roles of organizer, administrator, diplomat, counselor, and motivating leader were all called for. I loved the way the job of conductor, and its satellite responsibilities, held me in a defined role. When I was there I knew better who I was, and, importantly for this introverted young man, I knew better how to interact with others.

After conducting a number of shows I left the country. Years later I returned, and fate would have it I was asked to conduct this same music society—over twenty years after my first performances with them (Fig. 9.5).

Being now in my mid-forties I found my role was different to what it had been when I was in my early twenties. There was still the need for organizing, administrating, and leading, but I found I had less need to be a diplomat and counselor. I just

FIG. 9.5 The second author, Stephen (far left), conducting a performance of the Gilbert and Sullivan opera "Iolanthe" in 2013. The lords (right) discover that the Fairy Queen (center) and her accompanying fairy subjects (left) are a force to be reckoned with!

got on with it. If someone had a problem I was much more inclined to let them sort it out, rather than feeling I needed to intervene. I was more inclined to lose my temper when it felt necessary. I approached the role more as one with clear boundaries, rather than one where I felt I needed to search for its scope, and wait till I bumped into boundaries. My need to be liked was noticeably less. It was a job, and it occupied a much smaller part of my overall identity, and my time, than it had twenty years previously.

Because I approached it as a more narrowly defined "professional" role, I enjoyed it more, and I think I was more effective in the role. My attention was not as scattered. I was more focused on the job at hand. My identity was much more as "conductor whose role is to rehearse and conduct", rather than "conductor in search of an identity."

Many others in the music society were also in search of or had already created a "show identity", usually on a larger scale than the one they inhabited in their "outside" life. The show provided a ready-made set of identity templates for people to step in to and play with. Two nights a week during rehearsals, and during the run of performances, they could become a larger version of themselves, courtesy of the vehicle of the character. A young woman in her mid-twenties, experimenting with her power and sexuality, could become the Queen of the Fairies. An older man, sensing the waning of his vitality, could become King of the Pirates. A single man in middle age, in a job he doesn't like, could become the romantic tenor lead, heir to the throne of Japan. I was with people playing with their identities, trying out parts of themselves for which the dramatic narrative gave them a vehicle. They, and I, had a lot of fun. It filled a gap of human play and creative fantasy much needed in a world of adult, serious, un-embodied cognitive endeavor.

In the broadest sense, this is a type of music therapy. It allows people to relate playfully, imaginatively, using voice and body in story-telling ebullience. It creates pride in achievement and meaningful belonging.

9.5 Supporting the primary motives of personal identity with music therapy

Like music education, improvised music therapy is a *creative partnership*, one that progresses with sensitive guidance of a skilled musician who has been trained in responsive therapy. The aim of the therapist is to strengthen self-confidence in company and to explore and enable resolution of feelings that prevent both happiness and achievement. The anxious, confused, and self-absorbed client is given confidence and joy in company by carefully managed steps with the therapist, who is using imitation and creative extension within an unfolding predictable structure to build "playful" dialogues that lead to fuller participation in a flowing musical collaboration, with mutual affection (Nordoff & Robbins, 1977/2007; Bruscia, 1987; Wigram et al., 2002; Pavlicevic & Ansdell, 2004;

Wigram, 2004; Oldfield, 2006; Zeedyk, 2008; Bond, 2009; Osborne, 2009b; Robarts, 2009; Wigram & Elefant, 2009).

The principles resemble those in jazz improvization (Duranti & Burrell, 2004; Kühl, 2007; Schögler & Trevarthen, 2007), which is based on reference themes and rules of variation, where predictability is challenged with chance accidents and discoveries, which "play" with or "tease" a partner's anticipation (Ansdell, 1995; Gratier & Trevarthen, 2008). The creativity is the product of endless negotiation of a sensitive and sympathetic "contract" between therapist and client in intimate communication, generating a dialogue of imaginative identities (Meares, 2005; Wigram & Elefant, 2009).

Experimental and non-experimental case studies using methods developed for the analysis and interpretation of creative improvization confirm the therapeutic value of improvisational music therapy (Nordoff & Robbins, 1977/2007; Bruscia, 1987; Edgerton, 1994; Warwick, 1995; Wigram, Pedersen, & Bonde, 2002; Oldfield, 2006; Wigram & Gold, 2006; Mukherjee, 2009; Wigram & Elefant, 2009). Stages of the process of music therapy can be measured by detailed analysis of the cooperative music-making in recorded sessions, demonstrating the gain in confidence and shared experience for individuals who have in the past found communication and relationships difficult (Pavlicevic & Ansdell, 2004). Measures of responses to music therapy also serve in diagnosis (Raijmaekers, 1993; Wigram & Gold, 2006).

There is a strong psychobiological theory or "biopsychosocial paradigm" (Osborne, 2009b) for the creative and curative effects of intersubjective "art" therapies that employ the vitality effects of regulated movement in live engagement to encourage communication and cooperation (Stern, 1999, 2004, 2010). The temporal arts—dance, music, drama, and poetry—entrain the vital regulations within the body and excite emotional states within the brain (Trevarthen & Malloch, 2000; Sacks, 2007; Haas & Brandes, 2009; Osborne, 2009b; Trevarthen, 2009a; Wigram & Elefant, 2009). Interactive music therapy supports this autonomic/emotional regulatory system, modulating the impulses of a traumatized or avoidant psyche by way of sensitive hearing, coordinating heartbeat, respiration, and body movement, giving the Self emotional harmony and promoting companionship in a "psycho-biological loop" (Osborne, 2009b, p. 349).

Music therapy thus promotes well-being by sharing of creative activities and projects in relationships and in the community for which human beings have strong motivation and sensitive emotions (Trevarthen, 2001a, b; Porges, 2003; Pavlicevic & Ansdell, 2004; Panksepp & Trevarthen, 2009; Trevarthen, 2009a). As humans are active in relationships through all stages of development, from "dyadic regulation of psychobiological states" (Tronick, 2005) to participation in a meaningful culture, a sensitively supportive partner may transform a disturbed or traumatized Self, bringing vitality to weakened motives for sharing (Trevarthen et al., 2006). This enables human beings to find enthusiasm together for great and small actions both inventively and cooperatively (Csikszentmihalyi & Csikszentmihalyi, 1988). William James (1890) drew attention to the creative "flow" of consciousness that animates conversation for practical cooperation, which is the foundation of psychotherapies that aim to build companionable memories by fostering dialogue in imaginative and playful projects, helping build a conversation in which the patient feels the growth, or re-growth, of a secure personal identity in a present emotional relation (Ryle & Kerr, 2002; Stern, 2004; Meares, 2005).

9.6 CONCLUSIONS: COMMUNICATIVE MUSICALITY AS THE HUMAN WAY OF LIFE

The development of a musical individual born for sharing the creation of cultural life is a topic in natural science with a message for the humanities and philosophy. It has important implications for how individual lives and society can be better regulated or supported for well-being, and how the vitality of children's lives can be accompanied and tutored so children thrive in their creative spontaneity and their desire for cultural learning and building in affectionate companionship. There are implications for understanding the nature of musical art and how its practice and education may benefit a more alive and playful approach by parents, performers, teachers, and musicologists.

Human well-being and enjoyment of life, both individually and in company, depend upon a sense of the rhythm of movements and an appreciation of the risks and benefits that are generated with what Daniel Stern has called the "hidden realm" of vitality dynamics (Stern, 2010, Chapter 1). The inner resources are maintained by imagination and memory of the body in action, a sense of self in life that can be transmitted to others in what Stein Bråten (2009) calls "felt immediacy".

Music is an expression of the human need for synchrony and syntony or sympathy of self-expression with that of others. Our innate musical powers and sensibilities grow with the body and the company we keep. Within a few months a baby is an active and inventive musical companion and soon can learn to be a co-performer in ritual action games and songs, beating time with arms and banging sonorous objects. This musicality of performance needs the affectionate company of a person who feels happy with "belonging" in a musical community and remembering their own childish confidence in discovery. Baby and caregiver share a growing "proto-habitus" of celebrations in musicality (Gratier and Trevarthen, 2008)

By 1 year old, singing with words and artful repetition of phrases, and playing with prosody and rhyming vowels, our musicality flourishes along with the explosion of talk, enormously enriching companionship with friends of all ages. Five-year-olds can create dance and performance with song and musical instruments to make dramatic stories (see Figs 9.1–9.4). They can appreciate favorite melodies and poems, repeating the songs in often comical variations. Their innate musicality becomes recognized as art.

After this, activities performed for others' appreciation can become more conventional, intelligent, and serious. A child of five may be a willing and perhaps exceptionally gifted pupil in the technique and motor skill of song and instrumental performance. This is when an especially gifted child such as a Bach or Mozart in a family of musicians can be made a star in a musical world. But it is also a time when a cautious or impulsive child can be overcome with a feeling of inadequacy and judged amusical. Then the natural gift of rhythm and melody for sharing meaning is being betrayed.

When adolescence changes the feelings of a young person's self in relationships and they start to seek their own individual place in society, the sense of individuality is growing and being tested. Music is a way of belonging and differentiating, and musical skills can mature with expert help.

In old age, music becomes a way of remembering and reflecting on how one has spent one's time. It can be a source of solace, a companion in times of aloneness, and a way of celebrating remembered shared experiences.

Every step along the way the musical individual is in need of company who is willing to share the improvization of new stories of being.

References

Almeida, A. (2015). Embodied musical experiences in early childhood. Unpublished doctoral dissertation, University of Edinburgh.

Ansdell, G. (1995). *Music for life*. London: Jessica Kingsley.

Bannan, N., & Woodward, S. (2009). Spontaneity in the musicality and music learning of children. In: S. Malloch & C. Trevarthen (Eds.) *Communicative musicality: exploring the basis of human companionship*, pp. 465–94. Oxford: Oxford University Press.

Bjørkvold, J.-R. (1992). *The muse within: Creativity and communication, song and play from childhood through maturity*. New York: Harper Collins.

Blacking, J. (1995). *Music, culture and experience*. London: University of Chicago Press.

Bond, K. (2009). The human nature of dance: towards a theory of aesthetic community. In: S. Malloch & C. Trevarthen (Eds.) *Communicative musicality: Exploring the basis of human companionship*, pp. 401–22. Oxford: Oxford University Press.

Bråten, S. (2009). The intersubjective mirror in infant learning and evolution of speech. Amsterdam: John Benjamins Publishing Company

Brown, S. (2000). The "musilanguage" model of music evolution. In: N. Wallin, B. Merker, & S. Brown (Eds.) *The origins of music*, pp. 271–300. Cambridge, MA: MIT Press.

Bruscia, K.E. (1987). *Improvisational*. Springfield: Charles C. Thomas.

Buber, M. (1923/1970). *I and Thou*, transl. W. Kaufmann. Edinburgh: T. and T. Clark.

Bullowa, M. (Ed.) (1979). *Before speech: the beginning of human communication*. London, Cambridge University Press.

Buzsáki, G. (2006). *Rhythms of the brain*. Oxford: Oxford University Press

Chukovsky, K. (1963). *From two to five*, transl. K.M. Morton. Berkeley: University of California Press.

Clark, A. (1997). *Being there: Putting brain, body and world together again*. Cambridge, MA: MIT Press.

Cross, I., & Morley, I. (2009). The evolution of music: theories, definitions and the nature of the evidence. In: Malloch, S. & Trevarthen, C. (Eds.) *Communicative musicality: exploring the basis of human companionship*, pp. 61–81. Oxford: Oxford University Press.

Csikszentmihalyi, M., & Csikszentmihalyi, I.S. (Eds.) (1988). *Optimal experience: psychological studies of flow in consciousness*. New York: Cambridge University Press.

Custodero, L.A. (2009). Intimacy and reciprocity in improvisatory musical performance: pedagogical lessons from adult artists and young children. In: S. Malloch & C. Trevarthen

(Eds.) *Communicative musicality: exploring the basis of human companionship*, pp. 513–30. Oxford: Oxford University Press.

Damasio, A. (1999). *The feeling of what happens: Body, emotion and the making of consciousness.* London: Heinemann.

Darwin, C. (1872). *The expression of emotion in man and animals.* London: Methuen.

DeCasper, A.J., & Spence, M.J. (1986). Prenatal maternal speech influences newborns' perception of speech sounds. *Infant Behavior and Development, 9,* 133–50.

Deliège, I., & Sloboda, J. (Eds.) (1996). *Musical beginnings: origins and development of musical competence.* Oxford: Oxford University Press

Dissanayake, E. (2009). Root, leaf, blossom, or bole: concerning the origin and adaptive function of music. In: S. Malloch, and C. Trevarthen (Eds.) *Communicative musicality: exploring the basis of human companionship*, pp. 17–30. Oxford: Oxford University Press.

Duranti, A., & Burrell, K. (2004). Jazz improvisation: a search for hidden harmonies and a unique self. *Ricerche di Psicologia, 3,* 71–101.

Eckerdal, P., & Merker, B. (2009). 'Music' and the 'action song' in infant development: An interpretation. In: S. Malloch & C. Trevarthen (Eds.) *Communicative musicality: exploring the basis of human companionship*, pp. 241–62. Oxford: Oxford University Press.

Edgerton, C.L. (1994). The effect of improvisational music therapy on the communicative behaviours of autistic children. *Journal of Music Therapy, 31*(1), 31–62.

Erikson, E.H. (1950). *Childhood and society.* New York: Norton.

Erikson, E.H. (1968). *Identity: youth and crisis.* New York: Norton.

Flohr, J., & Trevarthen, C. (2008). Music learning in childhood: early developments of a musical brain and body. In: W. Gruhn and F. Rauscher (Eds.) *Neurosciences in music pedagogy*, pp. 53–100. New York: Nova Biomedical Books.

Fröhlich, C. (2009). Vitality in music and dance as basic existential experience: applications in teaching music. In: S. Malloch, and C. Trevarthen (Eds.) *Communicative musicality: exploring the basis of human companionship*, pp.495–512. Oxford: Oxford University Press.

Gallese, V.,& Lakoff, G. (2005). The brain's concepts: the role of the sensory–motor system in reason and language. *Cognitive Neuropsychology, 22,* 455–79.

Goodrich, B.G. (2010). We do, therefore we think: time, motility, and consciousness. *Reviews in the Neurosciences, 21*(5), 331–61.

Gratier, M., & Trevarthen, C. (2008). Musical narrative and motives for culture in mother-infant vocal interaction. *Journal of Consciousness Studies, 15,* 122–58.

Haas, R., & Brandes, V. (eds.) (2009). *Music that works: contributions of biology, neurophysiology, psychology, sociology, medicine and musicology.* Vienna: Springer.

Hadamard, J. (1945). *The psychology of invention in the mathematical field.* Princeton: Princeton University Press.

Hay, D., & Nye, R. (1998). *The spirit of the child.* London: Fount.

Husserl, E. (1969). *The phenomenology of internal time-consciousness (1893–1917)* [*Zur Phänomenologie des inneren Zeitbewusstseins (1893–1917)*], transl. R. Boehm. The Hague: Martinus Nijhoff.

Kabat-Zinn, J. (2006). *Coming to our senses: Healing ourselves and the world through mindfulness.* New York: Hyperion.

Kühl, O. (2007). *Musical semantics.* Bern: Peter Lang.

Lakoff, G., and Johnson, M. (1980). *Metaphors we live by.* Chicago: University of Chicago Press.

Langer, S. (1953). *Feeling and form: A theory of art developed from philosophy in a new key.* London: Routledge and Kegan Paul.

Llinàs, R.R. (2001). *I of the vortex: from neurons to self.* Cambridge, MA: MIT Press.

Malloch, S. (1999). Mother and infants and communicative musicality. *Musicae Scientiae*, 3, 29–57.

Malloch, S., & Trevarthen, C. (Eds.) (2009). *Communicative musicality: exploring the basis of human companionship*. Oxford: Oxford University Press.

Maturana, H., & Varela, F. (1992). *The tree of knowledge: The biological roots of human understanding*. Boston: Shambhala.

Maturana, H.R. (1978). Biology of language: the epistemology of reality. In: G.A. Miller and E. Lenneberg (Eds.) *Psychology and biology of language and thought: essays in honor of Eric Lenneberg*, pp. 27–63. New York: Academic Press.

Maturana, H., Mpodozis, J., & Letelier, J.C. (1995). Brain, language and the origin of human mental functions. *Biological Research*, 28, 15–26.

Meares, R. (2005). *The metaphor of play: origin and breakdown of personal being*. London: Routledge.

Merleau-Ponty, M. (1968). *The Visible and the Invisible*, transl. A. Lingis. Evanston: Northwestern University Press.

Miranda, D., Blais-Rochette, C., Vaugon, K., Osman, M., & Arias-Valenzuela, M. (2015). Towards a cultural-developmental psychology of music in adolescence. *Psychology of Music*, 43, 197–218.

Mukherjee, B.B. (2009). Nurturing musicality to enhance communication skills in children with autism: A study on musical interaction therapy. Presented at the World Association for Psychosocial Rehabilitation 10th World Congress, November 12–15, 2009, Bangalore, India.

Murray, L., & Trevarthen, C. (1985). Emotional regulation of interactions between two-month-olds and their mothers. In: T. Field & N. Fox (Eds.) *Social perception in infants*, pp. 177–97. Norwood: Ablex.

Nordoff, P., & Robbins, C. (2007). *Creative music therapy: a guide to fostering clinical musicianship*, rev. edn. New York: John Day.

Oldfield, A. (2006). *Interactive music therapy in child and family psychiatry*. London: Jessica Kingsley.

Osborne, N. (2009a). Towards a chronobiology of musical rhythm. In: S. Malloch & C. Trevarthen (Eds.) *Communicative musicality: exploring the basis of human companionship*, pp. 545–64. Oxford: Oxford University Press.

Osborne, N. (2009b). Music for children in zones of conflict and post-conflict: a psychobiological approach. In: S. Malloch & C. Trevarthen (Eds.) *Communicative musicality: exploring the basis of human companionship*, pp. 331–56. Oxford: Oxford University Press.

Panksepp, J., (2012). How primary-process emotional systems guide child development: ancestral regulators of human happiness, thriving and suffering. In: D. Narvaez, J. Panksepp, A. Schore, & T. Gleason (Eds.) *Evolution, early experience and human development: from research to practice and policy*, pp. 74–94. New York: Oxford University Press.

Panksepp, J., & Trevarthen, C. (2009). The neuroscience of emotion in music. In: S. Malloch & C. Trevarthen (Eds.) *Communicative musicality: exploring the basis of human companionship*, pp.105–46. Oxford: Oxford University Press.

Pavlicevic, M., & Ansdell, G. (2004). *Community music therapy*. London: Jessica Kingsley.

Porges, S.W. (2003). The Polyvagal Theory: phylogenetic contributions to social behavior. *Physiology and Behavior*, 79, 503–13.

Raijmaekers, J. (1993). Music therapy's role in the diagnosis of psycho-geriatric patients in the Hague. In: M. Heal & T. Wigram (Eds.) *Music therapy in health and education*, pp. 126–36. London: Jessica Kingsley.

Reddy, V. (2008). *How infants know minds*. Cambridge, MA: Harvard University Press.

Reddy, V., and Trevarthen, C. (2004) What we learn about babies from engaging with their emotions. *Zero to Three*, 24(3), 9–15.

Robarts, J.Z. (2009). Supporting the development of mindfulness and meaning: Clinical pathways in music therapy with a sexually abused child. In: S. Malloch & C. Trevarthen (Eds.) *Communicative musicality: exploring the basis of human companionship*, pp. 377–400. Oxford: Oxford University Press.

Rodrigues, H.M., Rodrigues, P.M., & Correia, J.S. (2009). Communicative musicality as creative participation: From early childhood to advanced performance. In: S. Malloch & C. Trevarthen (Eds.) *Communicative musicality: exploring the basis of human companionship*, pp. 585–610. Oxford: Oxford University Press.

Ryle, A., & Kerr, I.B. (2002). *Introducing cognitive analytic therapy: principles and practice.* Chichester: Wiley.

Sacks, O. (2007). *Musicophilia: tales of music and the brain.* New York: Random House.

Schögler, B., & Trevarthen, C. (2007). To sing and dance together: from infants to jazz. In S. Bråten (Ed.) *On being moved: from mirror neurons to empathy*, pp. 281–302. Amsterdam: John Benjamins.

Sherrington, C.S. (1906). *The integrative action of the nervous system.* New York: Charles Scribner's Sons.

Stern, D.N. (1999). Vitality contours: the temporal contour of feelings as a basic unit for constructing the infant's social experience. In: P. Rochat (Ed.) *Early social cognition: understanding others in the first months of life*, pp. 67–90. Mahwah: Erlbaum.

Stern, D.N. (2000). *The interpersonal world of the infant: a view from psychoanalysis and development psychology*, 2nd edn. New York: Basic Books.

Stern, D.N. (2004). *The present moment in psychotherapy and everyday life.* New York: Norton.

Stern, D.N. (2010). *Forms of vitality: exploring dynamic experience in psychology, the arts, psychotherapy and development.* Oxford: Oxford University Press.

Stuart, S. (2010). Enkinaesthetia, biosemiotics and the ethiosphere. In: S. J. Cowley, J. C. Major, S. V. Steffensen, & A. Dinis (Eds.) *Signifying bodies: biosemiosis, interaction and health*, pp. 305–30. Braga: Faculty of Philosophy, Braga Portuguese Catholic University.

Trehub, S.E. (2003). Musical predispositions in infancy: an update. In: I. Peretz & R. Zatorre (Eds.) *The cognitive neuroscience of music*, pp. 3–20. New York: Oxford University Press.

Trevarthen, C. (1977). Descriptive analyses of infant communication behavior. In: H.R. Schaffer (Ed.) *Studies in mother–infant interaction: the Loch Lomond Symposium*, pp. 227–70. London: Academic Press.

Trevarthen, C. (1998). The concept and foundations of infant intersubjectivity. In: S. Bråten (Ed.) *Intersubjective communication and emotion in early ontogeny*, pp. 15–46. Cambridge: Cambridge University Press.

Trevarthen, C. (2001a). Intrinsic motives for companionship in understanding: their origin, development and significance for infant mental health. *Infant Mental Health Journal*, 22, 95–131.

Trevarthen, C. (2001b). The neurobiology of early communication: intersubjective regulations in human brain development. In: A.F. Kalverboer & A. Gramsbergen (Eds.) *Handbook on brain and behavior in human development*, pp. 841–82. Dordrecht: Kluwer.

Trevarthen, C. (2005). Stepping away from the mirror: pride and shame in adventures of companionship. Reflections on the nature and emotional needs of infant intersubjectivity. In: C. S. Carter, L. Ahnert, et al. (Eds.) *Attachment and bonding: a new synthesis*, Dahlem Workshop Report 92, pp. 55–84. Cambridge, MA: MIT Press.

Trevarthen, C. (2008). The musical art of infant conversation: narrating in the time of sympathetic experience, without rational interpretation, before words. *Musicae Scientiae, 12* 15–46.

Trevarthen, C. (2009a). The functions of emotion in infancy: The regulation and communication of rhythm, sympathy, and meaning in human development. In: D. Fosha, D. J. Siegel, & M. F. Solomon (Eds.) *The healing power of emotion: affective neuroscience, development, and clinical practice*, pp. 55–85. New York: Norton.

Trevarthen, C. (2009b). Human biochronology: on the source and functions of "musicality." In: R. Haas & V. Brandes (Eds.) *Music that works: contributions of biology, neurophysiology, psychology, sociology, medicine and musicology*, pp. 221–65. Vienna: Springer.

Trevarthen, C. (2011). The generation of human meaning: how shared experience grows in infancy. In: A. Seemann (Ed.) *Joint attention: new developments in philosophy, psychology, and neuroscience*, pp. 73–113. Cambridge, MA: MIT Press.

Trevarthen, C. (2012a). Embodied human intersubjectivity: imaginative agency, to share meaning. *Cognitive Semiotics*, 4(1), 6–56.

Trevarthen, C. (2012b). Communicative musicality: the human impulse to create and share music. In: D. J. Hargreaves, D.E. Miell & R.A.R. MacDonald (Eds.) *Musical imaginations: multidisciplinary perspectives on creativity, performance, and perception*, pp. 259–84. Oxford: Oxford University Press.

Trevarthen, C., & Delafield-Butt, J. (2013). Biology of shared experience and language development: Regulations for the inter-subjective life of narratives. In: M. Legerstee, D. Haley, & M. Bornstein (Eds.) *The infant mind: origins of the social brain*, pp. 167–99. New York: Guilford Press.

Trevarthen, C., Aitken, K.J., Vandekerckhove, M., Delafield-Butt, J., & Nagy, E. (2006). Collaborative regulations of vitality in early childhood: Stress in intimate relationships and postnatal psychopathology. In: D. Cicchetti & Cohen (Eds.) *Developmental psychopathology*, 2nd edn, pp. 65–126. New York: Wiley.

Trevarthen, C., & Malloch, S. (2000). The dance of wellbeing: defining the musical therapeutic effect. *Nordic Journal of Music Therapy*, 9(2), 3–17.

Trevarthen, C., & Malloch, S. (2012). Musicality and musical culture: sharing narratives of sound from early childhood. In: G. McPherson & G. Welch (Eds.) *Oxford handbook of music education*, pp. 248–60. Oxford: Oxford University Press.

Tronick, E.Z. (2005). Why is connection with others so critical? The formation of dyadic states of consciousness: coherence governed selection and the co-creation of meaning out of messy meaning making. In: J. Nadel & D. Muir (Eds.) *Emotional development*, pp. 293–315. Oxford: Oxford University Press.

Turner, V.W. (1982). *From ritual to theatre: the human seriousness of play*. New York: PAJ Publications.

Varela, F., Thompson E., & Rosch, E. (1991). *The embodied mind*. Cambridge, MA: MIT Press.

Vlismas, W., Malloch, S., & Burnham, D. (2013). The effects of music and movement on mother–infant interactions. *Early Child Development and Care*, 183(11), 1669–88.

von Uexküll, J. (1957). A stroll through the worlds of animals and men: A picture book of invisible worlds. In: C.H. Schiller (Ed. and transl.) *Instinctive behavior: the development of a modern concept*, pp. 5–80. New York: International Universities Press.

Warwick, A. (1995). Music therapy in the education service: research with autistic children and their mothers. In: T. Wigram, B. Saperston, and R. West (Eds.) *The art and science of music therapy: a handbook*, pp. 209–25. London: Harwood Academic.

Whitehead, A.N. (1929). *The aims of education and other essays*. New York: Macmillan.

Wigram, T. (2004). *Improvisation: Methods and techniques for music therapy clinicians, educators and students.* London: Jessica Kingsley.

Wigram, T., & Elefant, C. (2009). Therapeutic dialogues in music: nurturing musicality of communication in children with autistic spectrum disorder and Rett syndrome. In: S. Malloch & C. Trevarthen (Eds.) *Communicative musicality: exploring the basis of human companionship,* pp. 423–45. Oxford: Oxford University Press.

Wigram, T., & Gold, C. (2006). Music therapy in the assessment and treatment of autistic spectrum disorder: clinical application and research evidence. *Child: Care, Health and Development,* 32(5), 535–42.

Wigram,T., Pedersen, I.N., & Bonde, L.O. (Eds.) (2002). *A comprehensive guide to music therapy: theory, clinical practice, research and training.* London: Jessica Kingsley.

Zeedyk, M.S. (Ed.) (2008). *Promoting social interaction for individuals with communication impairments.* London: Jessica Kingsley.

CHAPTER 10

MUSICAL IDENTITY, INTEREST, AND INVOLVEMENT

ALEXANDRA LAMONT

THIS chapter considers the role of musical identity in shaping lifelong involvement with music. I start by looking at identity in childhood, focusing on how people, contexts, and opportunities can shape children's musical identities and how children define the concept of being a musician through their own words and drawings. Negotiating transitions is a key element of theorizing in identity (e.g., Erikson, 1982) and I consider how children and adults manage the transitions through and from different types of educational settings and into the world of work and, later, retirement in relation to their involvement with music. I draw on data from studies with adults reflecting back on their childhood experiences and how important they are (e.g., Lamont, 2011a, b; Pitts, 2009, 2012) as well as on more fine-grained longitudinal work looking at musical involvement and engagement across transitions (Davidson & Burland, 2006; Marshall & Hargreaves, 2007; McPherson, Davidson & Faulkner, 2012). After reviewing empirical data on the prevalence of amateur music-making in adulthood, the chapter ends with a consideration of the role of music in later life, drawing on research with mainstream and marginalized populations (e.g., Bailey & Davidson, 2005; Clift, Hancox, Morrison, Hess & Kreutz, 2010; Dingle, Brander, Ballantyne & Baker, 2013; Lamont et al., in preparation). The chapter brings together mainstream developmental theory on the processes of identity achievement (Marcia, 2002) and on lifespan approaches to identity challenges (Erikson, 1982), contemporary approaches to theorizing identity as fragmented, multiple, and shifting (Oyserman, 2004; Weber, 2001), and work in positive psychology, which provides a context for understanding how and why identity matters in engaging people in music for well-being and flourishing (Lamont, 2011c, 2012).

10.1 Conceptions of Identity and Development

There are many different theoretical approaches to identity which can be useful in a musical setting. Models drawn from mainstream social psychology provide a structure for understanding some of the behaviors and particularly patterns of change that can be predicted and mapped across the lifespan. These view identity as a developing construct, but one which goes through relatively stable phases. From a developmental perspective, the first step is to differentiate the self from the other, forming the beginnings of Mead's (1934) distinction between the personal and social aspects of self. Self-knowledge and knowledge of others tends to develop in parallel, leading to identity shifts at various points. For example, at the same point that babies are able to recognize their own reflections consistently in a mirror (around 18 months), they also begin to recognize and remember other people in terms of their physical features (Lewis & Brooks-Gunn, 1979). Another major developmental shift occurs in identity around the age of 7, where children begin to compare their own achievements and attitudes with those of their peers and use these in their self-definitions (Festinger, 1954; Damon & Hart, 1988). Social identity theory (Tajfel & Turner, 1979) explains how interpersonal behavior (prioritizing individual characteristics, or personal identity) and intergroup behavior (prioritizing group membership, or social identity) interrelate in the processes of self-categorization, applicable particularly in the period of adolescence to explain in-group and out-group behavior. The process of identity "achievement" has been explored by Marcia (2002), outlining the twin concepts of exploration and commitment which together shape identity, and the broadest theory of identity across the lifespan is that of Erikson (1982), which outlines stages of identity crisis and resolution from early childhood through to older adulthood; both these theories are considered in more detail later in the chapter.

Conversely, an alternative view of identity presents it as more contested and subject to variation and change. Some of this thinking originates from the work of Dweck (2000) who highlighted that individuals could hold different self-theories. Some people believe in the fixed nature of competences, holding an entity self-belief, meaning that they do not strive to change or improve, while others believe competences and skills can be malleable, holding an incremental self-belief which supports them through learning and development. The growth mindset is held to be necessary to develop resiliency which can support future learning (Dweck, 2006). Another alternative approach championed by Kahneman (2011) argues that we can adopt different "selves" (he proposes the remembering self and the experiencing self) depending on our cognitive priorities. These ideas take attention away from fixed-stage or fixed-identity views, and fruitful approaches to the development of identity have developed from a sociocultural perspective. In this view the individual's sense of self and purpose is understood as being socially constructed and negotiated by and through relationships with others. Identity is thus viewed as a way of finding a place in the world, of comparing oneself to others, and of providing a source of internal motivation and strength. The sociocultural approach is also grounded in phenomenology, and this gives rise to the notion of multiple (and sometimes contested) identities. Goffman (1959) had explored the ways in which different roles are or can be adopted and promoted to present a particular version of the self to others, for particular purposes. According to this definition of identity, who we are in one setting at one point in time is only one, sometimes temporary, construction of our underlying self (Harter, Bresnick, Bouchey & Whitesell, 1997), and we put on different identities for different settings. I present myself very differently to my parents, my friends, and my students, adjusting my identity accordingly as daughter, friend and equal, or supervisor. The degree of detail (and honesty) with, which I might divulge information about the music I engage with and the settings where this takes place, for instance, would be mediated through those different identities. Identity, like knowledge, in this newer formulation is thus temporary, highly subject to social influence, and subject to reinterpretation at different points in life (Oyserman, 2004).

In the first edition of this volume, Hargreaves, Miell & MacDonald (2002) articulated a useful distinction between "identities in music" and "music in identities". The former refers to the specifically musical roles taken on (for instance, a singer, an orchestra leader, a bass guitarist), while the latter refers to the role that music plays in the overall construction of a person's more global identity. As with any categorization, however, when it comes to considering how people understand what it means to "be a musician" (the best easily understood terminology we have for interrogating the concept of musical identity) the very construction of the concept invokes both approaches. In this chapter I focus more on how music sits alongside other aspects of lifespan development, but evoking the concept raises a working definition of a particular type of musician (a performer, an instrumentalist, a teacher, etc.), and the ways children and adults generate their own definitions come with exclusions as well as inclusions, elaborated further below. For many, being a musician seems to demand *multiple* roles in music.

10.2 The beginnings of defining musical identity

Thinking about very early musical experiences, music is central to many caregiving routines around the world from early infancy. In a Western setting, mother-infant singing is something that the vast majority of mothers report doing. In a survey of a hundred mothers, Street, Young, Tafuri & Ilari (2003) found that all mothers sang to their infants at one time or another. They also identified one of the main purposes of singing as early communication: for example, one mother explained "I sing to my baby at home because … it makes him smile. … It's easier than finding things to say and I don't like to not communicate with him" (Street et al., 2003, p. 628). In the same research, however, 50%

of participants agreed with the statement that they did not have a singing voice. This issue of musical skill is central to the notion of musical identity and will be returned to throughout the chapter. However, the infant being sung to has no concept of musical identity in either themselves or their caregiver and simply engages, with increasing activity and agency as they get older, in musical interactions as part of learning to be human (Young, 2008). Early forms of musical interaction between caregiver and infant, or even between infants, such as coordinated rhythmic movements also take place in a highly intuitive way and seem to be connected to the powerful positive affect that joint interaction and attention affords (e.g., Bradley, 2009; Zentner & Eerola, 2010). As Bannan & Woodward (2009) point out, "children acquire musical culture as naturally as they learn to walk and talk" (p. 467).

Where might these definitions and distinctions begin, and the concept of being musical—and, importantly, the counter of *not* musical—originate? Many non-Western cultures do not draw any distinction between those with and without skill in relation to music (cf. Sloboda, Davidson & Howe, 1994), and many Western scholars have argued based on a growing knowledge base that almost everyone has the potential to develop musical skills of some kind (with the exception of those with specific kinds of neurological impairments) (e.g., Welch, 2001). Even at one of the most challenging periods in human development mothers use music as a way of interacting with their infants. Yet there is a commonplace concept amongst adults in Western society of the difference between a "musician" and "non-musician" firmly embedded in folk beliefs (Sloboda et al. 1994), mirrored in participants in relation to many different kinds of musical activity (Street et al., 2003; Ruddock & Leong, 2005; Lamont, 2011a), and embedded in the literature in music psychology. While there is some evidence that those with high levels of formal musical training may process music in different ways to those without (e.g., Gaser & Schlaug, 2003; Schaal et al., 2014), there is no evidence to support any innate predispositions or different brain physiology: the contribution of neuroscience to date has simply been to highlight the results of differing prior experiences on the way the brain develops. Similarly, reviewing a multitude of evidence, Howe, Davidson & Sloboda (1998) concluded that for music, there was no convincing weight of empirical evidence to support any talent argument. Rather, the evidence showed that practice and support from others (parents, teachers, and peers) explained most of the variation in individual achievement in music performance, and so-called talented individuals still required substantial training and support to reach high levels of achievement.

I will present data below that illustrates just how contested this distinction between "musicians" and "non-musicians" can be, particularly amongst those with complex and shifting patterns of actual involvement with musical activity. Adopting a sociocultural perspective, the challenge is to identify the personal and individual factors that shape our understanding of what it means to be a musician, however defined, and how this construction takes shape at different stages and under different circumstances.

10.3 EXTERNAL INFLUENCES
ON IDENTITY: THE SYSTEMS APPROACH

One very useful way of conceptualizing the influence of environment is the ecological systems theory of Bronfenbrenner (1979), which identifies different contextual influences on individual behavior and attitudes. This model begins with the microsystems within which the individual—in this case a child—directly participates and which shape children's behaviors and attitudes. Within each of these contexts (home, school, and local neighborhood being the primary ones) the individual child is engaged in social processes of construction and negotiation of meaning. At the mesosystem level, relationships between these microsystems are captured. There may be differences in the processes operating at home and at school, for instance, which could create conflicts in children's lives. The exosystem reflects a wider influence that children do not directly participate in but, which influences them, such as government policy and the media: views on whether music is part of formal education or the value of musicians in broader society will influence children's experiences indirectly. Finally, the broadest level of context, the macrosystem, reflects the dominant beliefs of a particular culture, such as the belief in the value of education for all children from a given age, which again influence the course of development for an individual child. This framework can be used to locate the different kinds of contexts that shape development and consequently identity.

From a Vygotskian sociocultural perspective, it is clear that children's development is shaped and guided by "more competent others", and much research has focused on the influence of parents and teachers on children's involvement in music (Sloboda, Davidson, Howe, et al., 1996; McPherson & Davidson, 2002, 2006; Creech, 2009). This has mainly been from the perspective of *access*. As Bronfenbrenner & Ceci (1994) outline, opportunity structures are vitally important to help capitalize on interest to engage in the acquisition of skills. The opportunities to make music during childhood often require support (practical, moral, and financial) from parents, so parents' own conceptions of their children's abilities and aptitudes are clearly important. Teachers are the gatekeepers to opportunities in many settings and can also have a powerful influence on access. Musical opportunities are far more widespread than even 20 years ago, perhaps due to the growth of research highlighting the many non-musical benefits to be gained through training as well as an increased recognition of the intrinsic value of music. To give one example, in England in the 1960s and 70s most children were only able to access extra-curricular music lessons if they showed particular "aptitude" as measured through standardized tests such as the Bentley tests. However, the 2001 Government Manifesto embodied the principle of providing opportunities for every child to learn an musical instrument (DfES/DCMS, 2004) and there have been many different government-funded schemes such as Wider Opportunities Whole Class Instrumental and Vocal Tuition, and Sing Up to promote music for school-aged children (Bamford & Glinkowski, 2010; Lamont, Daubney & Spruce, 2012), as well as many out-of-school schemes led by organizations such as Youth Music. School pupils often see their teachers

FIG. 10.1 Draw a musician.

Leighton & Lamont, submitted.

as powerful musical role models, as illustrated by a drawing from one Year 3 pupil at a school where all the children learned to play musical instruments (Fig. 10.1).

Little work has explicitly addressed the ways in which parents' and teachers' expectations shape children's musical identities. However, from the early work of Dolloff (1999), Hargreaves and colleagues (Hargreaves & Marshall, 2003; Hargreaves, Purves, Welch & Marshall, 2007) and Davidson and colleagues (Davidson & Burland, 2006; McPherson et al., 2012) there has been a focus over the past twenty years on how the educational environment has influenced both children's and teachers' constructions of their own musical identities. In my early work in identity and music (Lamont, 2002), framed by a very simple survey question, "Do you play a musical instrument" (Yes/No), I was able to trace out the influence of context on the way in which children aged 5–16 provided a definition of their own musical identity. All the 1,800 children in the studies were attending local education authority schools in England who were delivering the new National Curriculum, including a structured program of study and attainment targets in music alongside nine other core and foundation subjects. Playing a musical instrument of some kind was an integral part of the program (DfES/QCA, 1999). However, not all children responded positively to the question. I was able to disentangle some systemic features of the children's education that seemed to be responsible for some of the variation in responses. Looking only at primary school (children aged 5–11), I found striking differences which could be explained by the musical culture of the schools. In one school where around 40% of children were taking extra-curricular music tuition given by peripatetic teachers, more of the children *not* benefiting from this tuition positioned themselves negatively and said they did not play an instrument. However, in a different school where very few pupils were learning instruments at school, a very much larger proportion of the remaining children said they did play an instrument. The systemic explanation for this is that children are using a process of social comparison to decide whether their music-making counts in terms of identity: if there is a sizeable group of "other" children who visibly engage in a particular activity, those who do not reach more negative conclusions, but when the playing field is more level (i.e., fewer "others"), opinions about musical identity are much more positive.

Since school provides a highly influential context within which to shape musical identity, attitudes towards music at school seem particularly relevant when exploring how this identity develops. From a large-scale survey, Lamont, Hargreaves, Tarrant & Marshall (2003) established that, in general, pupils aged between 8 and 14 had more positive attitudes towards music at school than previous studies had suggested (with two-thirds reporting enjoying music at school) and that the desire to get involved with music-making was relatively strong (nearly half the pupils not having lessons saying that they would like to). However, this desire was somewhat fluid, as returning to conduct a series of follow-up focus groups we found that some children had changed their minds in the few months between the survey and our follow-up visit. The focus groups revealed more about children's understandings of what it meant to be a musician: they all firmly connected the concept with "playing a musical instrument" (Lamont, Hargreaves, Marshall & Tarrant, 2003). This is supported by recent findings looking at drawings of musicians amongst primary aged pupils (Leighton & Lamont, submitted), which revealed that 75% of drawings were of an instrumentalist or group of players (see Fig. 10.2).

FIG. 10.2 Drawing of a musician: instrumentalists.

Leighton & Lamont, submitted.

More subtle patterns were revealed in the focus group data, however, with the notion of "more" musical skills making the construct more robust, such as playing lots of different instruments, knowing every note on an instrument, or being able to carry out different musical activities such as teaching, singing, playing, and memorizing (Lamont et al. 2003). In subsequent investigation of children's musical identities at school (Lamont, Hargreaves, Marshall & Tarrant, in preparation) it has become clear that pupils themselves have very subtly nuanced views of what they think it means to be good at music, incorporating many diverse aspects such as instrumental mastery, the ability to play different instruments, skill at performing in front of others, teaching someone else to play, being able to read music, singing, concentrating in music, conducting, talking about music, being tolerant of other people's views about what is good in music, and passing examinations. This sets up the idea of a complex multi-faceted definition of musical identity: to be a musician, one has to fulfil multiple roles. However, pupils feel their teachers and their parents value different aspects of music: pupils think parents value public performances and demonstrations of skill, while teachers value examinations and formal achievements in music. Pupils themselves are very much aware of the provisional nature of what counts as success, and the fact that different stakeholders have different opinions of this, deepening the concept still further. These attitudes may influence their subsequent engagement in music. In England, music is seen as a school subject which increasingly demands a combination of specialist skills and knowledge as well as developing a "feel" for it in terms of expression (Lamont & Maton, 2008), unlike other subjects which are seen as emphasizing either "knowledge" or "knower" codes (maths and science depending more on knowledge, and English literature and history more on the knower). This could be related to the particularly low uptake of music at the point in English education where it becomes optional, as even pupils who have considerable skill recognize the complexity of the criteria for success and decide music is no longer "for" them (Lamont & Maton, 2010).

10.4 TRANSITIONS WITHIN EDUCATION

Much research has explored the reasons around why children choose to engage and disengage with musical activities at various points. As hinted at by our own data above, decisions are often rapidly made about involvement or lack of involvement. For instance, McPherson et al. (2012) discuss the case of Lily, a keen and accomplished clarinetist, who seemingly gave up the clarinet almost overnight when she left primary school, lost her school instrument, and was bought a computer. This story resonates with much evidence from longitudinal studies tracking children around the age of 11 making school transitions (see e.g., Sloboda, 2001; Marshall & Hargreaves, 2007), and following the logical implications of the influences of school context on pupil motivation outlined above, it could be presumed that changes in school environment (such as whether standards or opportunities increase or decrease) might be responsible for changes in individual students' motivations to continue with music and thus their musical identities. Certainly the changes in what is valued in music as exemplified by the assessment criteria embodied in the English National Curriculum and examination boards seem to influence their willingness to continue to be involved (Lamont & Maton, 2008, 2010), and recent studies have highlighted the importance of considering decisions about music as part of the wider matrix of choices that children have to make at different points in their school careers. Many dropouts from music arise due to changing circumstances, such as competing extra-curricular activities and academic work. For instance, as Mike (Year 3) reported, "I know it's hard to say that but like I, I got like more important things to do. Practice football, homework and all that, and then today they say practice your violin, and I got a football match" (Lamont, 2011a, pp. 376–7).

Do these patterns of involvement under pressure have anything to do with the robustness of children's musical identities? And if so, how might we understand this process? Marcia's (2002) social psychological theorizing is useful in providing a formulation of the optimal sequence leading to identity formation. Hinging on the key concepts of exploration and commitment, he outlines four different stages: identity diffusion (where there is no commitment to any kind of lifestyle or activity), foreclosure (commitment without exploration), moratorium (exploration without commitment), and finally identity achievement (commitment after exploration). Marcia suggests that out of crisis comes commitment. However, he also argues that the individual has to achieve their own identity achievement without unnecessary intervention for fear of "shattering" their rigid identities; individuals must seek their own paths rather than following those of others. The idea that people try out different identities or "provisional selves" before emerging as an expert is also found in Ibarra's work (1999). This moves away from the straightforward influence of others on developing identity. In other domains such as sports and exercise it has been demonstrated that specializing too early is not optimal for establishing extended commitment to a given activity and that early specialization is more likely to lead to dropout (Stambulova, Alfermann, Statler & Côté, 2009). In sport, Abbott & Collins (2004) propose an ideal progression through an extended sampling phase through to specialization, which is then followed by a stage of investment and eventually a maintenance stage, which echoes Marcia's notion of commitment and provides a useful sense of what might be necessary to maintain commitment once it has been achieved.

This sequence of sampling followed by specialization and subsequently investment has become an accepted view in the development of talent in sport (see also Côté, Baker & Abernethy, 2007) yet is far removed from thinking in musical development. Opportunities are provided for pupils to specialize from a fairly early stage, and specialization is encouraged. It may be that if this does not map onto children's own aspirations and intentions, dropout is more likely. Lamont, Leighton, Underhill & Hale (2009) found that at the end of one year of Wider Opportunities whole-class instrumental tuition on either strings or brass instruments, most children were enthusiastic about continuing with music but wanted to choose their own (different) instruments. Marshall & Hargreaves (2007) found that transitions in school environment were perceived as a major catalyst for opening up more musical opportunities, and contrary to the conventionally observed decline in instrumental tuition between primary and secondary school at age 11, pupils in their study were looking forward to having access to more interesting and relevant musical experiences (notably for boys playing drums and guitars). A systemic approach to fostering and supporting musical involvement across transitions might fruitfully capitalize on the sports model and provide multiple and varied opportunities.

10.5 INTERNAL INFLUENCES ON IDENTITY: AGENCY, CHOICE, AND MOTIVATION

In addition to the influence of external systems forces, it is also important to recognize the role of agency in the development of identity. Many of the ways in which children and adults express their musical identities come through personal choice and agency, and choice appears to be a central concept in sustaining a musical identity over time (cf. Pitts, 2012). The key mainstream framework which helps to explain how the individual develops and shapes his or her own identity is Erikson's lifespan model (1982). Erikson argued that the lifespan presents a series of ongoing identity "crises", posing challenges of adjustment, growth, and character development. He proposed eight different psychosocial tasks, resulting in eight stages of identity development (illustrated in Table 10.1). The model is not entirely based on the individual in isolation, as the outcomes of these identity struggles are held to be reflected in cultural terms (illustrated in the far right-hand column of Table 10.1). While a developmental trajectory is implied by the age-linked stages, each task can be revisited as necessary and as future tasks present themselves.

One of Erikson's major contributions when introduced to the concept of developing musical identities is the need to consider the whole lifespan, rather than just thinking about development during the school years. This mirrors arguments from music education (e.g., Myers, 2008) that its role is to lay foundations for lifelong involvement with and enthusiasm for music, which have importantly been taken on board recently by policy-makers in the UK. Erikson's positive characteristics at the early stages of identity crisis map neatly onto features that have been empirically demonstrated as required for success in musical development; there is an extensive literature on the importance of practice (e.g., Hallam, 1997; McPherson, 2001), relating to industry developing competence; McPherson's features of competence, autonomy, and relatedness are all encapsulated in this model, and Creech et al. (2007) have suggested that higher levels of autonomy, independence, and responsibility in music—a "resilient" musician with a fully-fledged robust musical identity—ought to result in sustained involvement and engagement with music (see also Green, 2002).

Considering how experiences in childhood shape later life, Davidson & Burland, (2006) asked adults to reflect on the period of adolescent transition that led some of them to a professional music career and others into different non-performance-related careers. The professionals showed clear motivation, the development and use of coping strategies, and

Table 10.1 Erikson's stages of identity

Age	Conflict between		Positive characteristics	Societal manifestation
0–1 years	Trust	Mistrust	Hope	Religion and faith
1–6 years	Autonomy	Shame and doubt	Will	Law and order
6–10 years	Initiative	Guilt	Purpose	Economics
10–14 years	Industry	Inferiority	Competence	Technology
Adolescence	Identity	Role confusion	Fidelity	Ideology
Young adulthood	Intimacy	Isolation	Love	Ethics
Middle age	Generativity	Stagnation	Care	Education, art and science
Older adulthood	Integrity	Despair	Wisdom	All major cultural institutions

Text extracts from Leonie Sugarman, Life-span Development: Frameworks, Accounts and Strategies, Second Edition, p.89, Copyright © 2001 Psychology Press, with permission from Psychology Press.

the ability to use music for personal expression in their construction of identity; non-professionals also demonstrated similar characteristics, but rather than focusing on music, they applied them to non-musical domains. In my own research (Lamont, 2011a, b), I have found much evidence of highly convoluted pathways through music across the lifespan (cf. Lonie & Sandbrook, 2011a, b; Pitts, 2012). Many older adults seem to find new enthusiasm for different forms of music-making which are not typically taught in formal education, such as folk bands or new styles like jazz, and, like the school children faced with Wider Opportunities in the UK, many of them go on to take up different instruments to the ones they devoted so many hours to as child learners. In a worldwide survey, adult beginners often talked about going through various life crises and wanting something more through music, such as impressing others or achieving something for themselves.

> My playing music is a classic middle age crisis phenomena, I started learning the bass when I was around 48 and was able to join a band and play a concert for my 50th birthday.
>
> Paul, 53, US; Lamont, 2011a.

Lamont, A. (2011a). The beat goes on: Music education, identity and lifelong learning. *Music Education Research*, 13(4), 369–88.
© Taylor & Francis Ltd http://www.tandfonline.com

These examples illustrate the potency of Erikson's approach in explaining lifelong patterns of musical participation. Many adults already have a working knowledge of the technical and musical features of instrumental playing. They often report being grateful for the opportunities they had as children even if they did not appreciate them at the time, since these allow them an easier passage back into music (cf. Pitts, 2012) and perhaps a quicker progression through the necessary stages.

> My piano playing was really a result of parental and teaching pressure but now I am very grateful for having learned the basics and the musical foundation it gave me.
>
> Frances, 42, UK, currently plays trombone; Lamont 2011a, p. 373.
>
> Lamont, A. (2011a). The beat goes on: Music education, identity and lifelong learning. *Music Education Research*, 13(4), 369–88.
> © Taylor & Francis Ltd http://www.tandfonline.com

This highlights the impact that competence has in enabling and supporting the development of identity. However, these concepts arise only half way through the lifespan model. Evidence can be also found for the influence of later stages in shaping involvement with music (cf. Davidson & Burland, 2006). For many middle-aged adults, involvement in music provides a way of exercising the need for generativity and care, ensuring that they have a lasting legacy that goes further than just their own personal involvement, and they may move beyond simply taking part to take on an organizing role within the music group.

> I don't just turn up and sing, you know, and go away again, there's stuff that goes on, and, um, planning happens. Especially over the auditions, and the hiring, and so on, it took so much of our time and effort to do. But even just printing out all of the audition music, the hassle, the absolute hassle … There's an awful lot of work that goes on. I mean, I keep saying this, but we won't necessarily be around for ever, you know, I'd quite like to leave it in good order, so that the next publicity person doesn't find it a complete shambles.
>
> Sarah, 45, UK; Lamont, 2011a, p. 382.
>
> Lamont, A. (2011a). The beat goes on: Music education, identity and lifelong learning. *Music Education Research*, 13(4), 369–88.
> © Taylor & Francis Ltd http://www.tandfonline.com

Many older adults seek new opportunities as part of what Erikson describes as the "end of life review" and their descriptions of their musical activities indicate that music is a way of achieving integrity (Lamont, 2011a). Through a combination of motivation, opportunity and social support older adults find a means of challenging despair in what Erikson describes as the last phase in life (which may last many years) and also share many characteristics of generativity in acting as powerful advocates for musical participation.

The task of developing and sustaining a robust musical identity is complex and long-lasting, according to this view. However, it is important to add in the concept of provisional selves to Erikson's somewhat structured formulation. In all the research looking at transition in music, the thorny issue of provisionality is involved, whether it is tackled explicitly or not. McPherson et al. (2012) have illustrated a range of provisional selves in music through a complex longitudinal study of a number of young instrumentalists studied from the age of 7 through to their early 20s, which has enabled a rich pattern of the complexities of transitions and pathways in and out of music to be painted. This highlights the rapidly changing nature of individual investment, which can either follow a linear path through the opportunities provided or sometimes take more twisting or disconnected routes. McPherson et al. highlight the contradictory ways in which their participants describe themselves as musicians or not at different times in their musical trajectories: Bryan, for instance, who had taken up the guitar after starting the clarinet, aged 22 simply says "Yeah, well I'm a musician" (p. 133), while Tristram, who spent most of his childhood and adolescence playing percussion, bassoon, and vibraphone, described being a musician as a former role (showing explicit awareness of provisional shifting selves). Bryan's confidence in his own musical identity is unusual even in McPherson et al.'s data, and many other studies find musically active or engaged adults self-defining as non-musicians or as lacking in musical confidence (Ruddock &Leong, 2005; Lamont, 2011a).

> I am not a musician in the accepted sense; I cannot read music, I do not play an instrument, and I would not know a Neapolitan Sixth if it bit my leg. On the other hand, personal relationships aside, music is the passion of my life.
>
> Robert; Pitts, 2012, p. 123.

Provisionality also relates to understanding oneself in different ways depending on the activity or the context. In the realm of singing, some adults self-define as "tone deaf" while also describing themselves as "musical" (Sloboda, Wise & Peretz, 2005), suggesting that a different identity can be constructed as a singer (the facet of identities in music to, which tone-deafness typically refers) and as someone who enjoys music. Both training and practicing music teachers also show awareness of a distinction between their own identities as musicians and as teachers (Hargreaves et al., 2007). These findings support the notion that musical identity is multifaceted and that certain aspects may be more developed than others. This matters because it affects decisions to engage or not: self-defined tone-deaf adults do not participate in singing (Sloboda et al., 2005), and adults who consider themselves to be unmusical performers stop being involved in active music-making (Ruddock & Leong, 2005).

Many adults seem to take lengthy breaks from music at various key points in life: leaving school, university, starting a new job, and having children are common points that lead to a re-evaluation of priorities and "extra-curricular" activities such as music and sport often get left behind. However, changing life conditions also provide opportunities to re-engage, such as learning alongside one's children or grandchildren or finding music a good way of filling time after retirement (Lamont, 2011a). McPherson et al.,

(2012) found Lily "suddenly" returning to music at university after a 5-year break; many adults take breaks of much longer and return to music when life and circumstances will permit. It could be predicted that many of the 22-year-olds in McPherson et al.'s study who had spent considerable time, effort, and energy on music in childhood and stopped playing by early adulthood would return at some point, having gained insights into how much music can bring to enrich their lives. This points the importance of dormant identity and the concept of finding, or rediscovering, your passion (Robinson & Aronica, 2009).

10.6 (RE)DISCOVERING
PASSION IN LATER LIFE

Research into passion demonstrates that having a core activity which provides "harmonious" passion (where, it is argued, the activity has become internalized into the person's identity) leads to higher levels of well-being (Philippe et al., 2009). This connects research on identity to principles from positive psychology, which can fruitfully be applied to musical engagement. Well-being is supposed to result from a combination of hedonistic elements (pleasure and the absence of negative affect) and eudaimonic elements (engagement in the activity through flow, relationships with others, meaning, and achievement) (Seligman, 2011), and a balance between these elements is desirable (Seligman, Parks & Steen, 2005). As well as the pleasure gained from being integrated into and generating a musical performance itself, playing a musical instrument sets considerable challenge so a skilled performer will be able to achieve a state of flow (Csikszentmihalyi, 2002). The social dimensions of playing music with and/or to other people provides many other means of achieving meaningful social connections (e.g., Dingle et al., 2013), and the sense of accomplishment which can be gained from music-making is often high. Active music-making thus seems to embody considerable potential to generate balanced well-being over longer timeframes (Lamont, 2012). This underlying sense of passion may explain some of the patterns of behavior observed over long timescales, such as Lily's re-engagement with music after a 5-year break (McPherson et al., 2012), or the case of many adults who return to music after much longer gaps.

> Ultimately, there is all of this music inside of me that really wants to come out. It is hard to find the time, but that is the core of it for me. It is my true passion in life but with many yet unfulfilled ambitions. What I gain from it is a strong sense of self-expression, intellectual stimulation, and freedom.
>
> Chad, 39, US; Lamont, 2011a, pp. 380–81 .
>
> Lamont, A. (2011a). The beat goes on: Music education,
> identity and lifelong learning. *Music Education Research*, 13(4), 369–88.
> © Taylor & Francis Ltd http://www.tandfonline.com

There has recently been a surge of interest in exploring the role of music in later life, with findings suggesting that older adults prefer more complex musical styles such as classical and jazz and that music can play an important role in supporting adults with age-related cognitive decline, in the early stages of dementia, and in cases of brain damage. Music-making can also provide a clear focus for adults around the stage of retirement, and this maps on to the final stage in Erikson's life transitions, where wisdom is the desired state. Singing in particular has been enthusiastically embraced by many older adults, with considerable investment being made in choirs and singing groups for older adults from mainstream funders more interested in other aspects of the ageing process (e.g., AgeUK, city councils). Research is beginning to explore the effects of singing on health and well-being in older participants, and what emerges from the little qualitative work with these groups is that the musical activity provides them with a powerful sense of personal and social identity, giving structure to their time and meaning to their life (Davidson, 2011; Dingle, Brander, Ballantyne & Baker, 2013; Lamont, Murray, Hale & Wright-Bevans, in preparation).

Qualitative studies have uncovered the substantial benefits that group singing can bring to individuals experiencing issues such as homelessness or mental and physical health problems (Bailey & Davidson, 2005; Dingle et al. 2013). Taking a still more inclusive and social dimension, theories of community music propose that music-making is a kind of musical activity which has the potential to transform and mobilize communities (Murray & Lamont, 2012), and research has begun to explore particular communities such as choirs for the homeless or in specific sociocultural niches (Bailey & Davidson, 2005; Faulkner & Davidson, 2006) and to describe this potential. I combine the systemic and the individual approaches to conclude this chapter.

Since music-making is an inherently social activity that individuals engage with, a framework that enables the combined and interactive perspectives of the individual and the group to be taken into account is essential. Our research into a community choir over a period of four years, using a combination of observation, interview, and World Café methodologies, has shown that initially participants engage enthusiastically with the choir as a new activity which widens their social circles, gives them opportunities to leave home and interact with others, and provides important boosts for mental, physical, and psychological health (Lamont, Murray, et al., in preparation). Many projects for older people have an explicit agenda of *social* change, with the concept of 'being musical' very much at the periphery (although often a highly musically experienced leader is directing the group; cf. Davidson, 2011). For example, there is a key emphasis on inclusion in the choir we have studied, as one of its participants, Charles (71), noted: "Even if you're in a wheelchair, if you're disabled, if you've got a voice, even if you can't sing, we can always find you something to do" (cited in Lamont, 2011a, p. 371). This resonates with the needs of the group, as many older adults have not engaged in music since their school years. It also chimes with evidence from other groups where members regularly define themselves as "not musical necessarily" (cf. Ruth, cited in Lamont, 2011a, p. 371). Many of these groups start with the concept of being musical very much at their periphery and welcome all comers, although they often have a very musically experienced leader (see also Davidson, 2011). We have previously identified a tension in community arts between the emphasis on the social (non-artistic) benefits and the artistic outcomes (Murray & Lamont, 2012), and others have argued that the art must be approached as something of value in itself, not just a tool for social change (Putland, 2008). What we have observed over the period of the choir's establishment and support in the last four years is that opinions and expectations of the musical standards of the choir from members have grown. As one participant noted in the World Café: "the singing was a lot more frustrating near the beginning because we were nowhere near as good as what we are now ... now we are a very very good choir". This development of higher artistic goals and higher desired standards shows how people can make the transition from music in identity to identity in music, and the collective identity is far more important than any sense of individuals within it (although each individual certainly plays their part). This is an illustration of how music can act as a unifier, fostering collective identity and creating meaning (Lowe, 2000). Over time, and through music, the choir had developed a very strong performance identity, and members both old and new felt part of this collective endeavor.

10.7 CONCLUSIONS

This chapter has given an overview of the flourishing field of research on musical identity in a range of educational and informal settings and has explored the development of the amateur musician identity—in the true sense, making music for the love of it—across the lifespan. The research highlights the power of identity as a flexible concept in explaining patterns of motivation and engagement, whether these be smooth or constantly changing direction, interrupted, and over short or long time spans. Musical identity is also seen to be a complex and broad concept, often requiring multiple musical roles, but through adopting and engaging with these musical roles, amateurs can develop their own individual and collective identity through music. Future research will need to try to disentangle the influences of these two aspects of musical identity and how they support each other to sustain interest, engagement, and involvement with music.

REFERENCES

Abbott, A., & Collins, D. (2004). Eliminating the dichotomy between theory and practice in talent identification and development: considering the role of psychology. *Journal of Sports Science*, 22(5), 395–408.

Bailey, B., & Davidson, J.W. (2005). Effects of group singing and performance for marginalized and middle-class singers. *Psychology of Music*, 33(3), 269–303.

Bamford, A., & Glinkowski, P. (2010). *"Wow, it's music next": Impact evaluation of Wider Opportunities Programme in Music at Key Stage Two*. Federation of Music Services. Available at: www.devon.gov.uk/dms-theimpactofwideropportunities-fullreport.pdf (accessed Feb 22, 2016).

Bannan, N.& Woodward, S. (2009). Spontaneity in the musicality and music learning of children. In: S. Malloch and C. Trevarthen (Eds.) *Communicative musicality: exploring the basis of human companionship*, pp. 465–94. Oxford: Oxford University Press.

Bradley, B.S. (2009). Early trios: patterns of sound and movement in the genesis of meaning between infants. In: S. Malloch and C. Trevarthen (Eds.), *Communicative musicality: exploring the basis of human companionship*, pp. 263–80. Oxford: Oxford University Press.

Bronfenbrenner, U. (1979). *The ecology of human development: experiments by nature and design*. Cambridge, MA: Harvard University Press.

Bronfenbrenner, U., & Ceci, S.J. (1994). Nature-nurture reconceptualized in developmental perspective: a bioecological model. *Psychological Review*, 101, 568–86.

Clift, S., Hancox, G., Morrison, I., Hess, B., & Kreutz, G. (2010). Choral singing and psychological wellbeing: quantitative and qualitative findings. *Journal of Applied Arts and Heath*, 1(1), 19–34.

Côté, J., Baker, J., & Abernethy, B. (2007). Practice and play in the development of sport expertise. In: G. Tenenbaum and R.C. Eklund (Eds.) *Handbook of sport psychology* 3rd edn, pp. 184–202. Hoboken: Wiley.

Creech, A. (2009). Teacher-parent-pupil trios: a typology of interpersonal interaction in the context of learning a musical instrument. *Musicae Scientiae*, 13, 163–82.

Creech, A., Papageorgi, I., Duffy, C., et al. (2007). *From undergraduate to professional musician: supporting critical transitions*. Paper presented at the Society for Research into Higher Education, Brighton, UK, September 2007.

Csikszentmihalyi, M. (2002). *Flow: the classic work on how to achieve happiness*. London: Rider.

Damon, W., & Hart, D. (1988). *Self-understanding in childhood and adolescence*. Cambridge: Cambridge University Press.

Davidson, J.W. (2011). Musical participation: expectations, experiences, and outcomes. In: I. Deliège & J. W. Davidson (Eds.) *Music and the mind: essays in honour of John Sloboda*, pp. 65–87. Oxford: Oxford University Press.

Davidson, J.W., & Burland, K. (2006). Musician identity formation. In: G. McPherson (Ed.) *The child as musician: a handbook of musical development*, pp. 475–90. Oxford: Oxford University Press.

Davidson, J.W., Howe, M.J.A., Moore, D.G., & Sloboda, J.A. (1996). The role of parental influences in the development of musical performance. *British Journal of Developmental Psychology*, 14, 399–412.

DfES/DCMS. (2004). *Music Manifesto Report No. 1*. London: Department for Education and Skills/Department for Culture, Media and Sport.

DfES/QCA. (1999). *The National Curriculum for England*. London: HMSO.

Dingle, G.A., Brander, C., Ballantyne, J., & Baker, F.A. (2013). 'To be heard': the social and mental health benefits of choir singing for disadvantaged adults. *Psychology of Music*, 41(4), 405–21.

Dolloff, L.A. (1999). Building professional identity: the role of personal story in music teacher education. *Canadian Journal of Research in Music Education*, 40(4), 35–7.

Dweck, C.S. (2000). *Self-theories: their role in motivation, personality and development*. Philadelphia: Psychology Press.

Dweck, C.S. (2006). *Mindset: the new psychology of success*. New York: Ballantine Books.

Erikson, E.H. (1982). *The life cycle completed: a review*. New York: Norton .

Faulkner, R., & Davidson, J. (2006). Men's vocal behavior and the construction of self. *Musicae Scientiae*, 8(2), 231–55.

Festinger, L. (1954). A theory of social comparison processes. *Human Relations*, 7, 117–40.

Gaser, C., & Schlaug, G. (2003). Brain structures differ between musicians and non-musicians. *Journal of Neuroscience*, 23(27), 9240–45.

Goffman, E. (1959). *The presentation of self in everyday life*. New York: Doubleday.

Green, L. (2002). *How popular musicians learn: a way ahead for music education*. Aldershot: Ashgate.

Hallam, S. (1997). Approaches to instrumental music practice of experts and novices: implications for education. In: H. Jørgensen & A.C. Lehmann (Eds.) *Does practice make perfect? Current theory and research on instrumental music practice*, pp. 179–231. Oslo: Norges Musikkhøgskole.

Hargreaves, D.J., & Marshall, N.A. (2003). Developing identities in music education. *Music Education Research*, 5(3), 263–74.

Hargreaves, D.J., Miell, D., & MacDonald, R.A.R. (2002). What are musical identities, and why are they important? In: R. A. R. MacDonald, D. J. Hargreaves, & D. Miell (Eds.) *Musical identities*, pp. 1–20. Oxford: Oxford University Press.

Hargreaves, D.J., Purves, R.M., Welch, G.F., & Marshall, N.A. (2007). Developing identities and attitudes in musicians and classroom music teachers. *British Journal of Educational Psychology*, 77(3), 665–82.

Harter, S., Bresnick, S., Bouchey, H.A., & Whitesell, N.R. (1997). The development of multiple role-related selves during adolescence. *Development and Psychopathology*, 9(4), 835–53.

Howe, M.J.A., Davidson, J.W., & Sloboda, J.A. (1998). Innate talents: reality or myth? *Behavioral and Brain Sciences*, 21, 399–443.

Ibarra, H. (1999). Provisional selves: experimenting with image and identity in professional adaptation. *Administrative Science Quarterly*, 44(4), 764–91.

Kahneman, D. (2011). *Thinking, fast and slow*. London: Allen Lane.

Lamont, A. (2002). Musical identities and the school environment. In: R.A.R. MacDonald, D. J. Hargreaves and D.E. Miell (Eds.) *Musical identities*, pp. 41–59. Oxford: Oxford University Press.

Lamont, A. (2011a). The beat goes on: music education, identity and lifelong learning. *Music Education Research*, 13(4), 369–88.

Lamont, A. (2011b). The path of true music never does run smooth. In: L. McCullough, C. Harrison, (Eds.) *Musical pathways*, pp. 16–24. Reston: National Association for Music Education.

Lamont, A. (2011c). University students' strong experiences of music: Pleasure, engagement and meaning. *Musicae Scientiae*, 15(2), 229–49.

Lamont, A. (2012). Emotion, engagement and meaning in strong experiences of music performance. *Psychology of Music*, 40(5), 574–94.

Lamont, A., Daubney, A., & Spruce, G.J. (2012). Singing in primary schools: Case studies of good practice in whole class vocal tuition. *British Journal of Music Education*, 29, 251–68.

Lamont, A., Hargreaves, D.J., Marshall, N.A., & Tarrant, M. (2003). Young people's music in and out of school. *British Journal of Music Education*, 20(3), 229–41.

Lamont, A., Hargreaves, D.J., Marshall, N.A., & Tarrant, M. (In preparation). Musical identities at school. *Psychology of Music.*

Lamont, A., Leighton, G., Underhill, J., & Hale, R. (2009). *The impact of whole-class instrumental tuition in primary schools: an evaluation of a wider opportunities initiative.* Paper presented at the Research In Music Education conference, University of Exeter, April.

Lamont, A., & Maton, K. (2008). Choosing music: exploratory studies into the low uptake of music GCSE. *British Journal of Music Education,* 25(3), 267–82.

Lamont, A., and Maton, K. (2010). Unpopular music: beliefs and behaviors towards music in education. In: R. Wright (Ed.), *Sociology and Music Education,* pp. 63–80. Farnham: Ashgate.

Lamont, A., Murray, M., Hale, R., & Wright-Bevans, K. (In preparation). Singing in later life: the anatomy of a community choir. *Arts and Health.*

Leighton, G.S., & Lamont, A. (Submitted). "A musician is …": windows into children's musical self-identity. *Music Education Research.*

Lewis, M., & Brooks-Gunn, J. (1979). *Social cognition and the acquisition of self.* New York: Plenum.

Lonie, D., & Sandbrook, B. (2011a). 'Ingredients' for encouraging the talent and potential of young musicians. In: M. Schwartz (Ed.) *Foundations for Excellence Conference Publication 2011,* pp. 66–70. Exeter: South West Music School.

Lonie, D., & Sandbrook, B. (2011b). *'Ingredients' for encouraging the talent and potential of young musicians.* Poster presented at the SEMPRE conference "Developing the Musician," Reading, March 2011.

Lowe, S.S. (2000). Creating community: art for community development. *Journal of Contemporary Ethnography,* 29(3), 357–86.

Marcia, J.E. (2002). Adolescence, identity, and the Bernardone family. *Identity,* 2(3), 199–209.

Marshall, N.A., & Hargreaves, D.J. (2007). Crossing the humpback bridge: primary–secondary school transition in music education. *Music Education Research,* 9(1), 65–80.

McPherson, G.E. (2001). Commitment and practice: key ingredients for achievement during the early stages of learning a musical instrument. *Bulletin of the Council for Research in Music Education,* 147, 122–27.

McPherson, G.E. (2009). The role of parents in children's musical development. *Psychology of Music,* 37(1), 91–110.

McPherson, G.E., & Davidson, J.W. (2002). Musical practice: mother and child interactions during the first year of learning an instrument. *Music Education Research,* 4, 143–58.

McPherson, G.E., & Davidson, J.W. (2006). Playing an instrument. In: G.E. McPherson (Ed.) *The child as musician: a handbook of musical development,* pp. 331–51. Oxford: Oxford University Press.

McPherson, G.E., Davidson, J.W., & Faulkner, R. (2012). *Music in our lives: rethinking musical ability, development and identity.* Oxford: Oxford University Press.

Mead, G.H. (1934). *Mind, self and society.* Chicago: University of Chicago Press.

Murray, M., & Lamont, A. (2012). Community music and social/health psychology: linking theoretical and practical concerns. In: R.A.R. MacDonald, G. Kreutz, & L. B. Mitchell (Eds.) *Music, health and wellbeing,* pp. 76–86. Oxford: Oxford University Press.

Myers, D. (2008). Lifespan engagement and the question of relevance: challenges for music education research in the twenty-first century. *Music Education Research,* 10(1), 1–14.

Oyserman, D. (2004). Self-concept and identity. In: M. B. Brewer & M. Hewstone (Eds.), *Self and social identity: perspectives on social psychology*, pp. 5–24. Malden: Blackwell Publishing.

Philippe, F.L., Vallerand, R.J., & Lavigne, G.L. (2009). Passion does make a difference in people's lives: a look at well-being in passionate and non-passionate individuals. *Applied Psychology: Health and Well-Being*, 1(1), 3–22.

Pitts, S.E. (2009). Roots and routes in adult musical participation: investigating the impact of home and school on lifelong musical interest and involvement. *British Journal of Music Education*, 26(3), 241–56.

Pitts, S.E. (2012). *Chances and choices: exploring the impact of music education*. Oxford: Oxford University Press.

Putland, C. (2008). Lost in translation: The question of evidence linking community-based arts and health promotion. *Journal of Health Psychology*, 13(2), 265–76.

Robinson, K., & Aronica, L. (2009). *The element: how finding your passion changes everything*. London: Allen Lane.

Ruddock, E., & Leong, S. (2005). "I am unmusical": the verdict of self-judgement. *International Journal of Music Education*, 23, 9–22.

Schaal, N.K., Krause, V., Lange, K., Banissy, M.J., Williamson, V.J., & Pollok, B. (2014). Pitch memory in nonmusicians and musicians: revealing functional differences using transcranial direct current stimulation. *Cerebral Cortex*, 25(9), 2774–82.

Seligman, M.E.P., Parks, A.C., & Steen, T. (2005). A balanced psychology and a full life. In: F.A. Huppert, N. Baylis, & B. Keverne (Eds.) *The science of well-being*, pp. 275–304. Oxford: Oxford University Press.

Seligman, M.E.P. (2011). *Flourish: a new understanding of happiness and well-being—and how to achieve them*. London: Nicholas Brealey Publishing.

Sloboda, J.A. (2001). Emotion, functionality and the everyday experience of music: where does music education fit? *Music Education Research*, 3(2), 243–53.

Sloboda, J.A., Davidson, J.W., & Howe, M.J.A. (1994). Is everyone musical? *The Psychologist*, 7, 349–54.

Sloboda, J.A., Davidson, J.W., Howe, M.J.A., & Moore, D.G. (1996). The role of practice in the development of performing musicians. *British Journal of Psychology*, 87, 287–309.

Sloboda, J.A., Wise, K., & Peretz, I. (2005). Quantifying tone deafness in the general population. *Annals of the New York Academy of Sciences*, 1060, 255–61.

Stambulova, N., Alfermann, D., Statler, T., & Côté, J. (2009). ISSP Position stand: career development and transitions of athletes. *International Journal of Sport and Exercise Psychology*, 7, 395–412.

Street, A., Young, S., Tafuri, J., & Ilari, B. (2003). Mothers' attitudes to singing to their infants. In: R. Kopiez, A.C. Lehmann, I. Wolther, & C. Wolf (Eds.) *Proceedings of the 5th Triennial ESCOM Conference*, pp. 628–31. Hanover: University of Music and Drama.

Sugarman, L. (2001). *Life-span development: frameworks, accounts, and strategies*. Hove: Psychology Press.

Tajfel, H., & Turner, J.C. (1979). An integrative theory of intergroup conflict. In: W.G. Austin & S. Worschel (Eds.) *The social psychology of intergroup relations*, pp. 33–47. Monterey: Brooks/Cole.

Weber, R. (2001). *The created self: reinventing body, persona, spirit*. New York: Norton.

Welch, G. (2001). *The misunderstanding of music*. London: University of London, Institute of Education.

Young, S. (2008). Lullaby light shows: everyday musical experience among under-two-year-olds. *International Journal of Music Education*, 26(1), 33–46.

Zentner, M., & Eerola, T. (2010). Rhythmic engagement with music in infancy. *Proceedings of the National Academy of Sciences of the United States of America*, 107(3), 5768–73.

CHAPTER 11

....

BUILDING MUSICAL SELF-IDENTITY IN EARLY INFANCY

....

JOHANNELLA TAFURI

11.1 INTRODUCTION

....

THE challenge of this chapter is to explore the construction, in infancy, of the first building blocks of musical identity.

According to Clarke (2008), experience of "the self" is not possible without having experience of "the others" and therefore the experience of "difference". The "others" are others because they are different, and the notion of difference leads to recognition, even intuitively, of the existence of "us" and "them", and therefore of the existence of possible relationships that mark the personal and social aspects of identity. In particular, Clarke stresses the "sense of emotion, passion, or motivation in the construction of self" (p. 511). The prominence of the role of the imagination and of emotions in this process reveals their importance in the first phases of life: infants experience their first emotions in their pre-natal life, and the imagination starts to work quite soon after birth (Stern, 1985; Imberty, 2002).

Trevarthen pointed out in 2002 that the origin of identity is to be found in communication, as this is a key feature of animal and human existence. Since music is a socio-cultural domain, it is clear that the pleasure experience (Schubert, 2009), and its communication function (Miell, Hargreaves & MacDonald, 2005) are fundamental in musical identity. Infants possess an innate motivation to communicate, beginning with their mother. During the early dialogues with their mother, infants experience, even intuitively, self-other awareness, and intense emotions of enjoyment and pleasure.

The aim of this chapter is to examine the characteristics of musical behaviors, which have been investigated in some recent research, and in particular in two longitudinal studies carried out in Italy with large numbers of infants: the *inCanto* project

(Tafuri, 2008) and the *Nido sonoro* project (Delalande, 2009), in order to identify the "signs" of musical identity.

After this brief Introduction, the second section of the chapter is dedicated to listening activities and their consequences on infants. Its three subsections deal with the pre-natal situation, with reactions after birth to the music heard, and with interactions with caregivers during listening. The third section deals with vocalization and singing: even though this separation between listening and vocal/singing activities may seem somewhat artificial in the sense that vocal sounds cannot be produced without "self-listening", the importance and development of infants' vocal/singing activity demand specific consideration. Its two subsections consider musical babbling, vocal-singing dialogues and interactions with singing words and songs. Finally, the fourth section deals with infants playing instruments and moving, so as to explore their interests and activities.

11.1.1 The social nature of listening

As we saw above, listening is the first musical experience of animals and humans. In this section we examine the different kinds of listening in which infants engage from the last trimester of pre-natal life until the first year after birth. During the first year, it is possible to identify reactions and interactions during listening. In this context, the term "reaction" is used to indicate those behaviors through which infants show their awareness that something happened, and the effects of that event on themselves: turning their head, staring, or turning their eyes, moving some part of the body, smiling, producing vocal sounds, etc. The term "interaction" is used to indicate those behaviors through which infants show their willingness to establish a relationship with the loved person (parents or other caregivers), and to continue "the game", smiling, chuckling or laughing, producing some movements and gestures, or some sounds, musical babbling, etc.

Infants become more and more emotionally connected and consequently wait for the "other" to intervene: they feel emotionally involved when they take turns, and their relationship with caregivers is more socially significant. The analysis of these behaviors, documented by several researchers (Malloch, 1999; Trehub & Nakata, 2001) highlights the appearance of the first building blocks of their identity and, in particular, of their musical identity. The following subsections will consider, in detail, some reactions and interactions that were observed during the pre-natal stage and in the first year of life.

11.1.2 In the mother's womb

Regarding pre-natal life, it has already been shown (Lecanuet, 1996; Parncutt, 2006) that the foetus hears and reacts to sounds present in his/her exterior environment (voices, music, and sounds of different quality) and in the maternal womb (intra-uterine sounds of various kinds, from the mother's heartbeat to the ripples made by his/her own movements). These reactions are manifested by variations in fetal heartbeat (acceleration/deceleration) and by movements of the eyelids, the head, the limbs, and the trunk, which can vary in their intensity. The quality and quantity of these reactions depend on the sound quality of the stimulus, on the behavioral state of the foetus (deep sleep, active sleep, quietly awake, or actively awake) and on their effects on the mother (relaxation, anxiety, shock, tension, etc.).

During the fetal stage it is possible that habitual reactions can develop in response to certain stimuli, such as the frequent singing by the mother or listening to the same song, or other kinds of repeated sounds: for example, the frequent noise of airplanes taking off if the expectant mother lives near an airport. This phenomenon shows not only the discriminatory ability of the foetus and his/her sound memory but also the possible effects on learning. In summary, all infants start to build their sound world and their own relationship with it before birth.

11.1.3 Diversity of reactions to sounds and music

If we look at the first reactions of newborn infants to ordinary sounds or to songs and music, we can glimpse different kinds of behavior. They react in different ways, and it is important to be aware of these different reactions and of their "relational" nature. In studies on musical development, attention has been paid to expressive vocal and bodily dialogues, in particular in the important studies of Trevarthen (2002), Malloch (1999), and Trevarthen & Malloch (2012).

By examining mothers' attitudes towards their infants and perceiving the relationship established through their singing, Street (2003) concludes that this relationship is generally grasped intuitively. When mothers observe infants' reactions, they can see that their own singing can calm the infants, entertain them, and make them laugh and play, so that mothers become aware of the emotional role that their voices play in the child's experience.

Some interesting results emerged from the *inCanto* project (Tafuri, 2008), a longitudinal research study carried out in Italy and lasting 6 years, which was carried out by the author with her colleague Donatella Villa; 119 pregnant mothers agreed to take part in the study, and they participated in the weekly meetings during pregnancy and after birth with their children (and some of them with their partners). They were invited to sing together and invent songs, to dance, to listen to music and to play percussion instruments with music. They were also invited to continue the musical activities at home as part of daily family life, to record any sung dialogues with their babies and to fill in a diary with several questions prepared by the researchers.

Some of the mothers took up the researchers' suggestion to choose a special song and to sing it daily, more frequently in the last month, so that this could form a kind of affectionate link with their child, representing the beginning of their musical relationship.

The aim was to invite mothers to verify if their newborns, even in the first week of life, could show signs of recognition of a song heard repeatedly before birth.

The results from 13 children who were video-recorded and observed show that all of the newborns reacted when they heard, after some minutes of silence, the pre-natal song; five of them stayed still and some of these opened their eyes wide, whilst others relaxed and half-closed their eyes; five opened their eyes wide and gazed attentively; four moved their eyes from side to side and some of these turned their head at the same time; others turned their head towards the source of the music located at their left side.

> When Tobia was two days old, [...] spent the second night wailing desperately all the time and I remember well that my mother, exhausted from walking back and forth along the hospital corridors at three in the morning, at a certain point she brought Tobia to me and told me to hold him for a while because she didn't know what else to do. I took him in my arms and started to whisper one of the lullabies learned in the prenatal course: "Fai la nanna bambin, fai la nanna bel bambin, fra le braccia della mamma, fai la ninna fai la nanna" [Sleep my little baby in your mummy's arms]. When Tobia heard the music he turned his head and fixed his misty newborn eyes on me, just as if he had recognized my voice and the song that I had sung so often during pregnancy. This is a precious memory that still continues to move me.
>
> Alessandra; Tafuri, 2008, p. 111.

Analysis of the answers of 53 of the mothers to questions about what happens if the infants are crying or restless, and the mothers then sang or played recorded music, show some interesting and statistically significant results. During the first month of life:

- The average number of infants who stop crying is very high if their mother sings (94.5%), and is lower when recorded music is played (78.4%).
- The average number of children who cease to be restless if their mother sings is a little lower than in the case of crying (89.4%), and the same difference occurs with recorded music (74.8%).

> It was lovely to see how Andrea changed expression when we sang the songs we had sung during the Project *inCanto* meetings. As soon as he was born and still in the incubator, he was a bewildered, disoriented, frightened little thing [...] but when I (the father) started to sing *L'occhio bello* (heard so often while he was still inside his mother), peace and tranquillity came over him like a warm covering.
>
> Matteo and Anna Rita; Tafuri, 2008, p. 43.

Analysis of data concerning the effects of listening in a quiet situation during the first three weeks of life showed that some infants fall asleep (43.2%), while others become more alert (41.5%), and that this difference increases if the mother plays recorded music, when the babies are more likely to be alert (44.9%).

The effect of putting them to sleep falls suddenly from the fourth week onward, both when the mother sings (from 43.2–15.1%) and when recorded music is played (from 36.4–16.1%). From the fifth and sixth weeks on, movement and smiling appear. As regards the first of these, the data revealed evidence of a motor reaction in the legs and arms that occurs in response both to singing and to recorded music, and a marked increase of leg movement in the period from 4–6 months. Smiling becomes more established at around 3–4 months and, as a reaction to the mother's singing, it maintains a steady level, but is a little less frequent with recorded music than with singing.

11.1.4 Diversity of ways of interacting

As documented in their diaries, toward the third to fourth month, mothers often entertain and amuse their newborns by singing songs with different gestures or movements (clapping hands, jumping, turning, dancing, and so on), with pauses at strategic points, getting faster and getting slower, inventing words for existing songs, or inventing new songs based on situations that the babies are experiencing: bath time, feeding time, etc. A sizeable proportion of the children (62.4%) began to play singing games, even producing a few little vocalizations by 2–4 months, and the number of these increased by 4–6 months (69.7%).

From 6 months to 1 year, the number of mothers that played singing games, with varying frequency during the six months, was very high (81.5%). It is easy to imagine that this was due to greater participation by the children and the corresponding increase in their possible interactions. The analyses of their reactions showed that children expressed enjoyment, laughed or smiled, became alert (eyes wide open, staring), and moved their legs and/or arms and that after 6 months they jumped, rocked, and "danced". The interaction with music through body movement is really very frequent and engaging: as well as moving their arms and legs when their mother sings or plays recorded music, they typically move their whole body, when rhythmic music is played, as soon as they can sit up.

> Giulia, 11 months old, is sitting on the mat with an instrument in her hands (castanets with a handle) like the other children around her. The parents start to sing a song with piano accompaniment. Immediately Giulia begins to rock back and forth. The rhythm changes for the refrain and Giulia begins to bounce up and down and shake the instrument. When we come back to the verse, Giulia goes back to rocking.
>
> Tafuri, 2008, p. 73.

From the age of 1 year onward, as children acquire autonomy of movement in space, they show a noticeable increase in their ability to move together with the music. As documented in the mothers' diaries, it is easy to see children at this age giving a motor response when the music starts, mainly when there is a clear rhythmic structure. Rocking, bouncing, clapping hands, dancing… babies make their own motor choice, have fun, and at the same time develop their motor coordination, emotional involvement, ability to structure time, and a personal motor style. The musical experience through bodily movement produces clear affective reactions and gives rise to certain behavioral patterns, which are also dependent on the musical structures that generated them.

Children manifest their musical preferences from about the second month of life. As the parents confirmed, after choosing a certain song or piece of music, their baby might manifest a certain degree of annoyance by whimpering or gurgling; but if they then changed the song or music, he/she would become quiet and stare with satisfaction. When the infants became a little older, they would smile, babble, and be amused; and when they were able to pronounce some words, they would frequently say "no, no" or "no like" to refuse some particular song or piece of music.

These preferences were first observed by the *inCanto* mothers during the babies' second month of life (24%,) and were then seen to increase markedly until 8 months old (66%). If they liked the song or piece, however, they asked to listen to it over and over again.

> When she was a year old and we were on our summer holidays, she pestered us in the car asking us to sing an English song that she loved called *Roxanne* (pronounced "ocken") and she joined in. What a joy it was for us! She already had definite tastes!
>
> Manila; Tafuri, 2008, p. 100.

At a basic level there was evidence for common preferences for music with specific musical structures: simple melodic contours, clear metrical structures, consonant intervals, conventional phrase endings (cf. Trehub, Schellenberg, & Hill, 1997). However, perhaps more interesting are individual children's preferences: their preferred music for sleeping, for bathing or eating, or to enjoy time with mother. These experiences involve memory, preferences, emotions, and feelings: the essence of their identities.

11.1.5 Summary

From the evidence, which has been documented and collated in the *inCanto* project, we can conclude that infants and young children, from pre-natal life onward, process sound/musical information in a multisensory fashion as they experience it through the body, in movement, and through the emotions that it arouses. These results provide us with important information about how "listening to music" can be experienced from the first days of life as a form of social interaction. Research evidence shows that children enjoy, are delighted, and affirm their presence when interacting with a caregiver by manifesting their pleasure, their willingness to continue, to repeat, or to change the experience. Listening to someone singing/playing (live or recorded), the neonate reacts and interacts, starting to build the basis for communicative musicality.

All of these experiences develop children's innate predisposition to music and hence the acquisition of musical abilities and the appropriation of different modalities in musical self-expression. The progressive assimilation of the rhythmic-melodic patterns belonging to their culture helps them build their own cultural patrimony and gives them the possibility of making different choices through which they manifest their own embryonic musical identities.

11.2 FROM MUSICAL BABBLING TO SINGING

From birth onwards, infants manifest their discomfort or satisfaction by using vocal sounds. After crying and screaming (to signal pain, hunger, anger), they soon discover different kinds of sounds such as wailing, whimpering, whining, gurgling etc., and produce them in a progressively richer and more varied ways. Very early on, newborns are sensitive to adults' reactions to their sounds: the "other" starts to be present to them and the foundations of the self-other relationship are laid. Infants begin to vocalize to attract adults' attention or when the adult talking to them stops. If this situation occurs again several times infants start to be involved in a "conversation" (deBoysson-Bardies, 1999, p. 76).

Key prosodic characteristics of speech (frequency, intensity, rhythm), which many researchers classify as "musical" qualities, or the "melodies of maternal language", are perceived by newborns very early. They prefer their mother's speech with a high-pitched voice and sing-song intonation (Fernald, 1992; Papoušek, 1996). Trehub & Nakata (2001) found that the melodic contours used by mothers in these interactions are unique in each case and that they seem to have beneficial effects on the newborn as a reinforcement of emotional ties.

Malloch (1999) analyzed the temporal characteristics and the pitch of the responses to mothers of some newborns (from 6 weeks of age), and identified a high level of attunement as a manifestation of a communicative interaction, which was described as both cooperative and codependent. On observing the role of the infants' body movements, Malloch underlined the emotional energy, the dynamic quality, and the narrative message stemming from them. On the basis of these results, he developed the notion of "communicative musicality".

The aim of Stadler Elmer (2000), in her study on singing development, was to look for developmental stages from the social and emotional points of view. She underlined that "the reciprocal vocal imitation in infant-parent dialogues reveals how parents intuitively facilitate a child's integration into sociocultural communication and customs" (p. 337). Joyful play and imitation are essential activities that lead, in the long run, towards "more conscious systems of actions and knowledge about one's own embodied cultural identity" (p. 338).

It is also worthwhile considering the role attributed by Imberty (2007) to the temporal structuring of events that infants start to experience after birth. The use in music of the repetition/variation structure, evidenced by Daniel Stern (1985), leads Imberty to emphasize the importance of the time control that infants start to acquire very early during vocal-musical dialogues, often accompanied by different kinds of movement.

Repetition allows the child to anticipate the event that follows and to exert some control over it, but this variation can cause some astonishment and uncertainty. The infant then starts to build his/her own unity through multiple experiences. On the temporal structuring of interactional behavior should be based, according to Imberty, an understanding of musical cognitive development and narrativity (p. 3).

The importance of temporal structures is also demonstrated in the research carried out by Addessi (2009) at the University of Bologna. This action research studied child-parent vocal-musical interaction during different daily routines considered as "cyclical repetition of daily events with variations and changes" (p. 748). The dialogues accompanying diaper changing happened at home, during two weeks with a 9-month-old child, in the dyadic mother-child and father-child and in the triadic mother-father-child interactions. Among several interesting results, Addessi found that excessive interventions by adults in turn-taking experiences can disrupt the child's vocalizations. During these dialogues, infants need time to "feel" the self-other relationship and to "respond".

The following sub-sections will consider the first communicative musical babblings in more detail, the discovery of emotions and attunement in the dialogues with adults, and the pleasure of singing to others in an expressive way.

11.2.1 First musical babblings and dialogues

The first days of life are characterized by spontaneous vocal reactions such as crying, babbling, and wailing, but after some weeks, infants begin to produce free sounds for the proprioceptive pleasure, which they feel through the vibrations of their own voice, or to attract attention so as to interact with caregivers. These are three behaviors through, which they become progressively aware of "the other" and therefore of "the self". Elicited by their mothers, infants imitate vocal intonation in an increasingly active way and learn to recognize and share emotions.

More evidence on the richness of babbling and dialogues between mother and infant can be found in the results of the research *inCanto* project (Tafuri, 2008). From the second to the third month onwards, infants start to discover new vocal expressions and to use their voices for richer communication. The analysis of the quantity and quality of sounds made by 39 babies in the *inCanto* project and aged aged 2, 4, 6, and 8 months, in sung dialogues with their mothers, which were recorded at home, showed that most of them produced several different sounds, little sequences, and melodic fragments.

> One afternoon while I was feeding her and the music playing in the background was one of the children's songs from the Project *inCanto*, Arianna stopped sucking, looked at me and repeated: "oh oh oh oh oh". I didn't think it was possible! She was singing! She was 10 months old! This episode was repeated on other occasions under the same conditions. (Manila; Tafuri 2008, p. 101)

The vocal productions of the children (about 4,000 in all) were classified into three categories: generic sounds ("ah," "eh," "boh," "hummm," "pa," etc.), glissandi, and intervals. The intervals (of which there were about 500) often had quite clear pitches, and other characteristics approximating the Western musical scale (CD attached to Tafuri, 2008).

From observing the wealth and variety of these babies' vocalizations, which became progressively more varied and longer with age (from a maximum duration of around 45 seconds at 2 months, to about 90 seconds between 6 and 8 months), and considering in particular the presence, after 6 months, of short melodic motifs that were rhythmically varied, we can say that these babies showed a particularly creative "communicative musicality" in their dialogues from the age of 2 months onward. It was clear in the majority of cases that there was enjoyment in "sliding", with the voice moving up and down along a continuum of pitch (glissando), as well as evident pleasure in "singing", that is of producing interval sequences, thereby manifesting creative and imitative behaviors. The dialogues were generally initiated by their parents, but sometimes the infants took the lead in this.

The infants' willingness to imitate and the development of their voice-ear coordination gave rise to the accurate repetition of some intervals, in particular major or minor thirds, and the invention of short melodies towards the age of 7–8 months. Repetition and variation processes appear soon after this in infants' singing: short and long sounds are easily combined in rhythmic structures, either spontaneously or by imitating their mothers' prompts, and these are accompanied by different movements that express energy and vitality.

11.2.2 From sung words to expressive singing

Towards the age of 1 year, the first words appear. Babies want to talk, to express themselves and communicate not only through musical but also through verbal interactions, as parents and other adults do. The analysis of the recordings collected during the *inCanto* project showed a wide variety of vocal productions, which were characterized by the appearance of sung syllables from the songs ("ju, ju, ju"; "qua, qua", "cuckoo"), and of sung words and phrases, often reproducing the same intervals as in the original song. Having grown up surrounded by musical experiences, at 18–24 months these babies liked to join in with their mother, take turns with her in singing short fragments of songs heard many times, or create their own short songs (Barrett & Tafuri, 2012).

In these situations, the emotional expressions are different from those in the earlier dialogues. Here the infants are pleased by the evocation of previous memories and emotions, and the impulse to participate has an added value for them in that the activity becomes something that "belongs to me": i.e., it is "part of myself". Children start to show a more explicit awareness of their identity, for example, by being willing to feel proud of themselves singing alone. When analyzing some of the recordings it was possible to hear a mother or father starting a song and the baby saying "no you, me!". The baby then started again. They enjoy singing to their toys, peers, and to their parents so as to entertain them, or to be listened to.

Ferrari & Addessi (2009) made an interesting contribution to research on singing to/among peers in a study that demonstrated the presence of musical elements in the vocal interactions of 15 young children aged between 12 and 15 months in two Italian (Bologna) nursery schools. The children were observed in groups of five during free play in a room in their nursery school and were found to interact with one or two peers at most, using different types of vocalizations such as babblings, glissandi, and proto-songs, which could be characterized by their distinctive musical features, expressed by rhythm, intensity, and pitch. Interacting among themselves, the children were listening with attention to each other, imitating and, more interestingly, taking turns. This mode of musical communication shows its essentially social nature.

A study with slightly older children was conducted by Tidoni (2011), who studied the spontaneous singing of 18 children aged 24–34 months in their nursery school in Trento (Italy). In groups of three, they were asked to sing to "Pico", a teddy bear containing a digital audio recording system inside its body. In each short session, the children interacted with the bear and jointly sang known songs, or more often fragments of songs, which they sometimes modified musically and/or verbally, all accompanied by movements and expressing feelings and emotions.

Some children sang alone to Pico, but in other cases, the children established communicative interaction. In some duets and trios the children sang together, and in others they took turns. Some special "cooperative" singing was observed in the sense that the reciprocal influence between the children produced genuine "attunement". In general they manifested the musical competence they had assimilated, and jointly continued to develop the construction of their own competence and musical identity.

Towards 2–3 years of age, children that have grown up in a musically stimulating family environment are able to sing many songs and, in particular, to sing them expressively (Tafuri, 2011), meaning that they are able to communicate emotions. Their ability to spontaneously manage musical features like dynamics, time variation, and timbral quality develops from their first intuitive assimilation of the principal codes of social communication in their own culture.

11.2.3 Summary

Infants express their developing identities by using vocal sounds, which become progressively more organized and varied, and which reflect aspects of the surrounding culture. Invention and imitation soon become entwined, in that children like to repeat the songs they have learnt, and are proud to sing to others in an expressive way (Tafuri, 2011). At the same time, they develop their singing skills, and mother-infant dialogues play an important part in this. These dialogues are characterized by frequent small changes in rhythmic-melodic contours, in the quality of the voice, in dynamics, tempo (*rallentando* and *accelerando*) and in the related physical movements: they produce sequences of events that are social and temporal in their essence and that convey emotional content. The alternation between tension and relaxation contributes to creating a structured exchange of emotions and feelings through time.

In these exchanges, mother and child "attune" to each other and produce what Stern (1985) calls an "affective attunement". Imberty (2007) emphasizes that musicality and affective attunement form an essential basis for genuine communicational interaction in the earliest stages of development. In a temporal exchange between mother and child there is a beginning, an end, and something happening in the middle. This "something" is the pattern of emotional change, which represents a line of "dramatic tension" that creates the "proto-narrative structure": this is theorized by Stern (1985), evidenced by Malloch (1999), applied to early musical experiences by Imberty (2007), and more recently emphasized by Nattiez (2013) in his study of musical narrativity.

11.3 Playing instruments: moving, expressing, and communicating

Infants are extraordinarily attentive to sound from birth onward. Their ears are their main windows on the world, as sounds bring them most of the information they receive about what is happening around them, especially when they are lying down in the cradle. The practice of hanging bells and other sounding toys on the cradle allows infants to have their first experience as "players". At first they may touch them by chance, and later on they intentionally try to repeat that experience of sound production by repeating the gesture (which Piaget called a "circular reaction"). Sound and movement appear to be closely related right from the beginning. From 3–4 months, babies intentionally start to bang objects or to hold in their hands things that produce sound if shaken or banged against another surface. They are attracted by an inner sensory (proprioceptive) satisfaction, brought about by the energy of the movement and by the "massage" of the body caused by the sound waves.

Research on infants making sounds with external objects and musical instruments is limited and, in general, is carried out with children aged 2–3 years onward (e.g., Mialaret, 1997; Addessi & Pachet, 2005). However, the *inCanto* project (Tafuri, 2008) and especially the longitudinal research project *Nido sonoro* (Delalande, 2009) make new contributions to this field and are discussed in the next section. It could perhaps be argued that the exploration of instruments manifests an individual pleasure rather than a communicative interaction. On the other hand, what is such exploration if it is not interaction between two "personages"—the human being and the "object"—like a "partner" that sometimes can resist playing the sounds intended by the composer/performer (i.e., is susceptible to soundmaking to a greater or lesser extent)? This is a strong concept, which forms the basis, for example, of the nine *Sequenza* composed by Luciano Berio, each for a different solo instrument. Berio (1981) declared that these are each intended to be a dramatic interaction, a challenge (almost a battle) between the performer and his/her instrument. The instrument is a "personage" for the children: it is a partner, like some toys, with which to engage in a relationship.

11.3.1 Exploring and interacting with instruments

In planning the *Nido sonoro* project, Delalande (2009) explored the musical dimensions of the first sounds produced by children through the exploration of objects/instruments, and on trying to establish whether this exploration and organization of sounds could be considered as an embryonic form of creative music-making.

The research was carried out in nursery schools in Lecco (Italy), with children aged between from 10 months to 3 years, with the main aim of studying the musical "*conduites*" (behaviors) of children, according to Delalande's (1993) theory on this subject. During the first year of the research, 104 sessions of about 20 minutes each were video-recorded, produced by 55 children from 10–37 months old. Each child was accompanied by an educator in a room of his/her own nursery school where there was an instrument—either a zither or (in another session) two big cymbals on a support stand. The educator was briefed to leave the room, on a pretext, and the child was therefore left alone. After about 10 minutes the educator came back, and if the child was still playing, the educator would wait in silence. All these sessions were recorded by two video cameras with sound recording.

Detailed analysis of the videos showed that during the first year of the research, in 46% of the sessions the children were quite active, whereas in 33% of the sessions the children did not explore the instruments at all. In 39% (of these 46%) sessions, the children played only after the educator left, and in 20% (of the 46%) they played only in the presence of the educator. In the second and third years of the research project, a smaller number of the same children were given different experiences. They explored more instruments (an amplified zither, a tympanum, tubular bells, and a *sanza*), and they did so in couples with either a peer or a teacher, or in a collective group with several children.

The first approach to the instruments was multisensory, that is, audio-visual-motor-tactile. Children produced several sounds by changing the way they played: banging the strings with a metal spoon that had been left at their disposal, rubbing them with their hands or with the spoon, or pulling them as in pizzicatos, etc.: these reactions are shown on a DVD attached to Delalande's book.

Each gesture produced a different sound and so provoked the attention and curiosity of the children. In most of the sessions the children showed their ability and interest in music-making: each child, after producing different sounds, was attracted by one or more of them and started to build an "event", or sequence, by repeating the same sound with gradual transformations, by combining it with another, and by repeating, varying, and transforming their sounds.

One of the features of the recordings analyzed by Delalande and his team members was the extent to which musical style could be identified in the ways the children were exploring each instrument and were playing and interacting with others through them. Pizzorno & Rosatti (2009), using the concept of musical style articulated by Baroni (1996) as "the symbolic representation of the identity", noted different strategies manifesting children's preferences for some specific gestures and for some organizations of sounds sequence. The children's choices were marked, along with the characteristics of the instruments, by their own tastes and culture and by their interaction with others.

In the results of the *inCanto* project regarding the use of instruments, the mothers' diary entries showed very clearly that the infants were attracted by the instruments. Parents bought some of these and continued to involve the babies at home by interacting with them using the instruments. From the age of 6 months, almost all of the children (97%) became very alert if an instrument was present; and if they saw their parents playing, they wanted to do the same. Instruments exerted a very strong expressive and social influence. Almost all of the children (94%) had also made sounds with objects in a fairly consistent way until the age of 2. They wanted to play an instrument whether or not there was music going on, and this confirms how instruments are a source of a global sensory-motor and interactional pleasure.

> He always showed an interest in the piano from the time he was small. At first, he banged all the keys of the keyboard with his hands, and then at about 12 months he pressed single keys with one finger and later (at about 18 months) he paused to listen to the sound produced by pressing down on each key, and he repeated this over and over.
>
> Roberta; Tafuri, 2008, p. 105.

After the first year, the parents were asked to record in the diaries if the children sang while playing at home. The answers brought a pleasant surprise: many did so at home, some of them "quite often" (26% of children), and others "sometimes" (43%). During the project meetings, as well as at home, the children liked to play an instrument while listening to music and, after 2 years of age, they enjoyed the game of "The Band". In this they played an instrument while moving in a circle ("ring-a-ring-o'roses") to the music of a march. The children were fascinated by the actions of shaking, banging, or rubbing objects of different forms and colors and by the sounds that came from them. These activities, and that of moving in a circle with their friends, were all part of a unique social communicative experience.

11.3.2 Summary

In conclusion, the opportunities offered to these children to produce and organize sounds and to play music together undoubtedly enriched their opportunities to express themselves and communicate musically, as well as to develop their metric-rhythmic skills. Sound and movement share the temporal dimension, and they are the first means by which infants express themselves and communicate. Vocal sound is certainly the first to appear (wailing and crying), but it does not involve movement in a substantial way, while instrumental playing does. Shaking and banging are movements that are "felt" by the body. Movement also allows children to interpret sound and to express and verify the perception of it, and this is seen in small children especially when the sounds clearly mark out a time structure, inducing them to rock, bounce, etc.

In the use of instruments, certain aspects of children's identity appear through the manifestation of their own preferences for certain instruments, qualities, and organization of sounds, and for certain gestures and movements while playfully interacting with others. It is easy to see, in these musically rich behaviors, how children have different ways of intentionally interacting through sounds, thus giving us hints of their musical identity.

11.4 CONCLUSIONS

In concluding this chapter it is useful to refer back to Clarke's (2008) affirmation, mentioned at the beginning, that the recognition, even intuitively, of the existence of "us" and "them", and therefore of the existence of possible relationships, marks the personal and social aspects of identity. Considering the features of the numerous musical manifestations of children described in this chapter, we can recognize the signs of musical identity in many kinds of behavior, as follows:

- The social, relational aspects of the interactions that are continuously present in musical activity.
- The positive emotions shown by infants and children during activities felt to be joyful, happy, and exciting, and their involvement in dialogues that demonstrate "affective attunement", and willingness to engage in these with caregivers and peers.
- The predominant presence of movement, through which they manifest vitality and energy, and the mastery of temporal structures that allow for narrativity.

This list could go on to include other aspects highlighted here, including the early appearance of preferences for certain songs, music, instruments, and movements, and the presence of a creative attitude in music-making, moving with music, and inventing motifs and short songs. Through all of these musical experiences, infants and children develop their own ways of being and thereby lay the first building blocks of their musical identities.

REFERENCES

Addessi, A. R., & Pachet, F. (2005). Experiments with a musical machine: musical style replication in 3 to 5 year old children. *British Journal of Music Education*, 22(1), 21–46.

Addessi, A. R. (2009). The musical dimension of daily routines with under-four children during diaper change, bedtime and free-play. *Early Child Development and Care*, 179(6), 747–68.

Baroni, M. (1996). Per una definizione del concetto di stile. In: J. Tafuri (Ed.) *La comprensione degli stili musicali. Quaderni della SIEM*, 10, 23–36.

Barrett, M. S. & Tafuri, J. (2012). Creative meaning-making in infant's and young children's musical cultures. In: G. E.McPherson & G.F. Welch (Eds.), *The Oxford handbook of music education* (pp. 296–313). Oxford: Oxford University Press.

Berio, L. (1981). *Intervista sulla musica*, a cura di R. Dalmonte. Roma-Bari: Laterza.

Clarke, S. (2008). Culture and identity. In: T. Bennett & J. Frow (Eds.), *The SAGE handbook of cultural analysis*, pp. 510–29. London: Sage.

de Boysson-Bardies B. (1999). *How language comes to children*. Cambridge, MA: The MIT Press.

Delalande, F. (1993). *Le condotte musicali*. Bologna: CLUEB.

Delalande, F. (Ed.) (2009). *La nascita della musica. Esplorazioni sonore nella prima infanzia*. Milano: Franco Angeli.

Fernald, A. (1992). Meaningful melodies in mothers' speech to infants. In: H. Papoušek, U. Jürgens, & M. Papoušek, *Nonverbal vocal communication*, pp. 262–82. Cambridge: Cambridge University Press.

Ferrari, L., & Addessi, A. R. (2009). I "gesti vocali" al nido: Interazioni fra pari. In: M. Baroni (Ed.), *L'insegnamento come scienza*, pp. 51–66. Lucca: LIM.

Imberty, M. (2007). Interazioni vocali adulto/bambino e sintonizzazione affettiva. In: A.R. Addessi, C. Pizzorno, & E. Seritti, *Musica 0-3. Proceedings of the National Conference of SIEM*, Torino: EDT (CDRom attached to *Musica Domani* n. 144).

Imberty, M. (2002). La musica e il bambino. In: J.J. Nattiez, *Enciclopedia della musica*, Vol. 2, pp. 477–95. Torino: Einaudi.

Lecanuet, J.-P. (1996). Prenatal auditory experience. In: I. Deliège & J.A. Sloboda (Eds.) *Musical beginnings*, pp. 3–34. Oxford: Oxford University Press.

Malloch, S. N. (1999). Mothers and infants and communicative musicality. *Musicae Scientiae*, 3, 29–54.

Mialaret, J. P. (1997). *Explorations musicales instrumentales chez le jeune enfant*. Paris: Presses Universitaires de France.

Miell, D., Hargreaves, D., & MacDonald, R. (Eds.) (2005). *Musical communication*. Oxford: Oxford University Press.

Nattiez, J.J. (2013). La narratività della musica: Narrazione o proto-narrazione? *Quaderni della SIEM*, 27, 9–31.

Papoušek, M. (1996). Intuitive parenting: a hidden source of musical stimulation in infancy. In I. Deliège & J. Sloboda (Eds.) *Musical beginnings*, pp. 88–112. Oxford: Oxford University Press.

Parncutt, R. (2006). Prenatal development. In: G.E. McPherson (Ed.) *The child as musician*, pp. 1–31. New York: Oxford University Press.

Pizzorno, C., & Rosatti, L. (2009). I bambini hanno uno stile? In: F. Delalande (Ed.), *La nascita della musica. Esplorazioni sonore nella prima infanzia*, pp. 97–119. Milano: Franco Angeli.

Schubert, E. (2009). The fundamental function of music. *Musicae Scientiae*, 13, 63–79.

Stadler Elmer, S. (2000). Stages in singing development. *Quaderni della SIEM*, 16, 336–43.

Stern, D. (1985). *The interpersonal world of the infant: A view from psychoanalysis and developmental psychology*. New York: Basic Books.

Street, A. (2003). Mothers attitude to singing to their infants. In: R. Kopiez, A.C. Lehmann, I. Wolther, & C. Wolf (Eds.), *Proceedings of the 5th Triennial ESCOM Conference*, pp. 628–9. Hanover: University of Music and Drama.

Tafuri, J. (2008). *Infant musicality: new research for educators and parents.* Farnham : Ashgate (or. ed. *Nascere musicali.* Torino: E.D.T., 2007).

Tafuri, J. (2011). Analysis of expressive singing in children 2–3 years old. In: *Euromac VII European Analysis Conference, Roma 29/9-2/10/2011, Abstracts Book,* p. 9. Roma: University of Roma-Tor Vergata.

Tidoni, F. (2011). Cantare spontaneamente: un'esperienza con bambini da due anni a due anni e dieci mesi. *Quaderni della SIEM, 25,* 66–81.

Trehub, S. E., & Nakata, T. (2001). Emotion and music in infancy. *Musicae Scientiae, 5,* 37–59.

Trehub, S., Schellenberg G., & Hill, D. (1997). The origins of music perception and cognition: A developmental perspective. In: I. Deliège & J. Sloboda (Eds.) *Perception and cognition of music,* pp. 103–28. Hove: Psychology Press.

Trevarthen, C. (2002). Origins of musical identity: evidence from infancy for musical social awareness. In: R. MacDonald, D. Hargreaves, & D. Miell, (Eds.) *Musical identities,* pp. 21–38. Oxford: Oxford University Press.

Trevarthen, C., & Malloch, S.N. (2012). Musicality and musical culture: Sharing narratives of sound from early childhood. In: G.E. McPherson & G.F. Welch (Eds.) *The Oxford handbook of music education,* pp. 248–60. Oxford: Oxford University Press.

CHAPTER 12

....

PROCESSES OF MUSICAL IDENTITY CONSOLIDATION DURING ADOLESCENCE

....

PAUL EVANS AND GARY E. MCPHERSON

ADOLESCENCE is a time of major change and development. At a biological level, hormonal and physiological changes cause a marked difference in physical appearance, while rapid cognitive development provides adolescents with the capacity to think about their worlds in increasingly sophisticated ways. Such changes mean that adolescents are constantly dealing with new ways of interacting with their social environments. An important part of the latter process is the formation of a personal sense of identity—defining one's sense of self in terms of values, strengths, abilities, and goals, and negotiating a place for that self in the social environment. It is well documented that music plays an important part of this identity formation process (see other chapters in this volume), particularly during adolescence (Hargreaves & Marshall, 2003; Hargreaves, MacDonald, & Miell, 2012; McPherson, Davidson, & Faulkner, 2012). Less well understood are the *processes* by which music and music learning become a part of adolescents' identities. How do individuals who persevere with music learning address the immense personal challenges it poses, mature into independent learners, and incorporate strategies for dealing with these challenges into their personal identity? How does all of this unfold in their lives as they think about and plan their musical futures?

Another concern is for those adolescents who exit their formal musical engagement and for whom being an actively engaged musician does not become a centrally important way of defining their identity. These adolescents still have a musical identity in the sense that they have ideas and values about their musical abilities and about musical abilities in general. This can even extend to holding highly developed opinions on the nature of their own and others' musical abilities, such as whether musicians are born or made. These identities are important because they come to play a role in the way people think about music. For example, when asked about music learning, most adults respond that they wish they had successfully learned to play a musical instrument (Davis, 1994; Nexus Research, 2007). They may not pursue music activities, even though they may be quite capable, and their self-exclusion from music can have negative effects on their sense of self (Ruddock & Leong, 2005; Knight, 2011). At the same time, they may believe that a quality music education is worthwhile only for the few that are gifted, and this may influence their support for music education for their own children or for music education in schools. Given the health and well-being benefits of music engagement (MacDonald, Kreutz, & Mitchell, 2012), it is important for researchers to understand what needs to be achieved to maximize the proportion of the population that is able to enjoy the benefits of music through active participation, as well as those who choose not to develop specialized skills in music performance.

In this chapter we draw on the Eriksonian view of identity formation as one of the critical tasks of adolescence (Erikson, 1968). Specifically, we look at the most prominent line of research emerging from this view, Marcia's (1980) implementation of Erikson's work, along with recent expansions, to frame our discussions. We begin with a theoretical overview of the Erikson-Marcia model of identity formation and its relationships with self-determination theory and then draw on our research with highly engaged adolescent musicians to describe the processes through which musical identity is consolidated during adolescence and to understand the significance of music learning to the self.

12.1 ADOLESCENT IDENTITY DEVELOPMENT

12.1.1 The Erikson–Marcia perspective on identity development

Erikson (1968) contended that one of the major tasks for adolescents is to reflect on their place within their social networks (peers, family, society), including the ways that others in their social networks view them, and to plan for a future to look forward to. It is also a time through which adolescents must, from a huge range of possible ways to continue their adult lives, select from an ever-narrower range of personal, occupational, and social paths. Erikson's theory generated decades of empirical work, the most fruitful line of which was based on the way Marcia (1980) operationalized his process of identity formation. Marcia used two activities, conceptualized as dimensions, which form several possibilities or statuses for the process of adolescent identity formation: *exploration* refers to the degree to which adolescents have considered or tried various different kinds of identity-related pursuits, while *commitment* defines the degree to which adolescents have made decisions regarding a personal identity that they will pursue in the future.

The degree to which these two activities are undertaken can be depicted in a 2 × 2 matrix, shown in Fig. 12.1, which represents four different possible outcomes. The first, characterized by the absence of either exploration or commitment, represents identity

FIG. 12.1 Identity outcomes based on the processes of exploration and commitment.

diffusion, typical of most children upon entering adolescence. Identity diffusion is an incomplete or incoherent sense of identity, in which the person has not consciously tried various identities, reflected on the way they are perceived by others, learned from those perceptions, or selected possible social roles to actively pursue. The second outcome is *moratorium*, where the person has explored various roles, activities, images, and behaviors, but not yet made firm commitments to any of these. Erikson posed this as an important part of adolescence, and evidence supports that this stage, possible only in societies that have the economic affordances to allow such a period of experimentation, results in adults who have explored a fuller range of potential commitments and thereby maximize their potential. The third outcome is *foreclosure*, where the person has prematurely committed to an identity without fully exploring and experimenting with the range of possible identities or activities. Finally, identity *achievement* occurs when the person has fully explored and experimented with a range of personal and social identities and arrived at a conscious and coherent identity that dictates a path for their future.

More recently, these dimensions have been extended to include qualitatively different types of exploration and commitment (Luyckx, Goossens, Soenens, & Beyers, 2006; Luyckx et al., 2008). Exploration was relabeled *exploration in breadth,* to refer to the search for different alternatives in relation to goals and values, while *exploration in depth* refers to talking with others and judging how well the exploration fits with personal goals, and *ruminative exploration* refers to indecisiveness and flawed decision-making. Commitment was also elaborated, with the dimension relabeled *commitment making* to refer to identity choices having been made, and the dimension *identification with commitment* added to refer to the degree to which adolescents identify with and feel certain about those choices.

Within this conception, adolescence involves a process of continually exploring various identities and making decisions and commitments to those in which one identifies. In music learning, this could involve an identity as broad as being a person who plays a musical instrument or a person who is knowledgeable about music. More specifically, it could include being a classical musician or someone who has a profession but plays music recreationally. A healthy process of identity seeking would involve adolescents exploring these various identities and reflecting on whether they align with their personal interests and values, eventually making a decision on an identity that they feel is aligned with their sense of self. There are also possible maladaptive outcomes. For example, an adolescent committing to playing a musical instrument for some time without considering whether it is really in his or her interests or long-term goals, or someone who commits to music learning as a long-term goal but does not understand the importance of the extensive practice that is necessary to achieve that goal.

In our work with children learning to play musical instruments, we uncovered the importance of identity processes before children even began formal learning on their instruments (Evans & McPherson, 2015). The children in our sample of 157 were asked, before they had begun formal instruction, how long do you think you will continue to play your instrument? Those who articulated a longer-term view (e.g., until I'm an adult, for the rest of my life) continued their active involvement in music activities for longer, on average, than those who articulated a short-term view (e.g., until the end of this year, until I'm in high school). This relationship only held up if they undertook commensurate amounts of practice (the relationship was not evident by examining practice alone). We interpret this result to suggest that it is important for children to have a sense of their future selves, and within that context, their music learning and practice would be more likely to be perceived as an active identity exploration process.

What are the drivers of healthy identity formation processes? Our next step is to consider what facilitates *exploration in depth* and *identification with commitment*, rather than only the shallower *exploration in breadth, ruminative exploration,* or poorly considered *commitment making.* Self-determination theory offers some explanation of how these forms of identity pursuit might lead to better alignment with the self.

12.1.2 Self-determination theory and identity development

Self-determination theory (SDT), which emanates from over 30 years of research led by Edward Deci and Richard Ryan, is based on the assumption that humans are inherently oriented towards growth and well-being, and that people thrive most when origins of their behavior are perceived as emanating from and regulated by the self rather than the external social environment (Ryan & Deci, 2000). Regulation is internalized through the fulfilment of three basic psychological needs (Deci & Ryan, 2000). *Competence* is the need for mastery and effectiveness in ones actions (White, 1959; Elliot, McGregor, & Thrash, 2002), *relatedness* is the need to feel a sense of belonging and acceptance in one's social environment (Baumeister & Leary, 1995), and *autonomy* is the need to feel as though one's actions are self-endorsed and volitional (deCharms, 1968; Reeve, 2002).

Activities that are undertaken for the inherent satisfaction and enjoyment derived from them are said to be *intrinsically motivated.* In SDT terms, children's play is the prototype of intrinsic motivation (Ryan & Deci, 2000). Intrinsically motivated activities are experienced as volitional and are undertaken for the joy of having an effect on one's environment; thus, they are closely linked to the needs for competence and autonomy. The need for relatedness is also critically important, because not only do significant others (e.g., parents, peers, teachers) provide the necessary tools in the social environment (such as instruments, lessons, a structured household in which music practice can take place), but they also provide encouragement, coaching, and involvement. If this is achieved with care and warmth, then positive outcomes are much more likely to ensue (Pomerantz, Moorman, & Litwack, 2007; Grolnick, 2009). Thus, an adolescent undertaking self-determined behaviors is naturally encouraged to pursue and explore multiple commitments and identity paths. The more that the psychological needs are fulfilled within activities, the more likely those activities are to be assimilated to the self (La Guardia, 2009; Luyckx, Vansteenkiste, Goossens, & Duriez, 2009).

Of course, not all behaviors can be intrinsically motivated. Many activities are not inherently intrinsically motivating, such as practicing scales, and not every music lesson can resemble the characteristics of "play" exemplified by the intrinsic motivation construct. In SDT, these extrinsically motivated activities can still be relatively self-determined, because the extrinsic–intrinsic distinction is less important than whether the activity or goal is perceived as emanating from or endorsed by the self versus being initiated or regulated by others. SDT distinguishes four types of extrinsicmotivation (see Fig. 12.2): those that are relatively external to the self (external and introjected regulation) and more autonomous, self-determined behaviors (identified and integrated regulation).

Thus, when a young adolescent's practice behavior is regulated by his or her parents using punishments or rewards, or simply by the feeling that he or she "ought" to practice, the regulation will not encourage the fulfilment of the basic psychological needs, and the adolescent is unlikely to come to identify with the activity as an important part of his or her identity (Faulkner, Davidson, & McPherson, 2010; Evans, McPherson, & Davidson, 2013). On the other hand, an adolescent's identity is more likely to be aligned with the self if

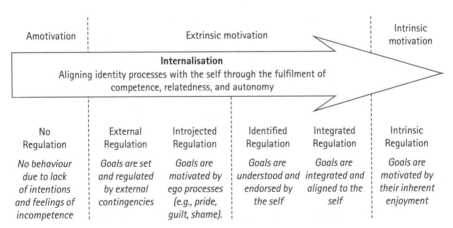

FIG. 12.2 Self-determination theory's organismic integration theory (adapted from Ryan & Deci, 2000).

Figure adapted from Deci and Ryan, *The "what" and "why" of goal pursuits: human needs and the self-determination of behavior, Psychological Inquiry,* © 2000 Taylor & Francis, reprinted by permission of the publisher (Taylor & Francis Ltd, http://www.tandfonline.com).

their parents help to regulate the practice behavior in an autonomy-supportive way and provide structure around the activity. With such support, the adolescent is more likely to understand the value of music practice and other music activities in helping to improve his or her abilities and thereby achieve personal goals.

12.1.3 Summary

Erikson's (1968) theory of identity development and its interpretation by Marcia (1980) proposes that adolescence is a time in which individuals' transition from a diffuse patchwork of possible identities to a process of exploring different identities and committing to some, the successful product of which is identity achievement. Self-determination theory explains why. Adolescents will value those identity explorations that are fulfilling of basic psychological needs. The more adolescents experience fulfilment of the basic psychological needs within their identity explorations, the more likely they will become to commit to them, value them, and regard them as being an integral part of their sense of self.

12.2 ADOLESCENT MUSICAL IDENTITY PROCESSES

What do the various exploration and commitment processes look like? In this section, we draw on interviews with adolescent music students to describe various manifestations of commitment and exploration as they discussed their career intentions, the role of music in their lives, and the degree to which they valued their music learning. The students, who were all aged between 15 and 18, were part of a sample of 30 students who we interviewed in and around a large city in the United States. Teachers and our colleagues helped to identify all of the students based on their exceptional music performance abilities and because they were all regarded as being highly involved in music. The classical musicians we studied, for example, were engaging in many hours of practice every week and were likely to be on track to compete for positions in outstanding university music schools. Given the level of their performance skills, some would be candidates for eventual employment as professional musicians in major orchestras. Likewise, some of the popular musicians were performing at functions such as weddings, recording jingles for radio stations, entering regional ensemble competitions, and devoting enormous resources and time to rehearsing, composing, listening, and experiencing music with similarly minded peers.

These students were part of a project examining the role of school and nonschool music activities in constructing meaning in people's lives. For this chapter, however, we chose several of our participants because in our conversations with these adolescents about the meanings that they derive from their music participation, illustrations naturally emerged of the identity formation processes described in the previous section. We found that these students had strong ideas about the role of music in their lives, beliefs about their musical abilities, and strong connections with social environments. In this section, we discuss examples of several of the possible combinations of identity processes described earlier in this chapter. (Identifying features and some details of the participants involved have been changed.)

12.2.1 Judy: exploration in depth of strengths versus passions

Our first student, Judy, was at a stage in her life where she was exploring several possible identities. As a junior in high school (aged 16), she was at a time where she could freely explore various identity pursuits without having to commit but also faced choices (e.g., for elective subjects in high school) that would have consequences for pursuing different career paths. In our conversation, she was weighing music, in which she was highly involved and passionate, with the goal of being a pharmacist. Judy made a distinction between strength or ability in an area, and passion. When asked about her strengths, she responded:

> *Judy*: Well, my strengths kind of lie in the maths and sciences, I guess. My voice teacher tells me that I try too hard to be like a student in choir, like a student more than a musician. So I'll either try too hard or want to be perfect all the time. I love musical theatre, and I love choir, but I just don't know if I have necessarily the strengths to major in music or to pursue it professionally. I've got the passion. The passion is there. But it's probably more the ability isn't very strong.
> *Researcher*: In an ideal world, what would you do? What would your heart tell you to do?
> *Judy*: Music education.

Judy appears to have discovered a fact about musical ability development that researchers have uncovered in recent decades. Although she may have exceptional ability, it is the values, resources, and orientations to the activity that lead to the self-regulatory abilities required to initiate and sustain longer-term commitment. Judy seemed aware, during her exploration of these various possible selves, that balancing ability with interest was important, as she did not want one to outweigh the other in her decision-making:

> I guess I'm trying to be, like, the realistic, like, "where do I see myself?" I want to start a family and have that flexible schedule, and then I just, with … I don't know. I guess I don't want to let my passion take over. You know, that kind of thing. So I guess it's just … again, I'm probably going to change because I toil over it all the time. Like, why am I not going into music when I love it so much?

Judy had not yet made a commitment, but as a junior in high school, it would be expected that she should explore various kinds of identity pursuits; thus, it is appropriate for her to be in identity moratorium. Judy is reflecting on the various influences in her life and considering her future self. In the above excerpt, she is weighing two factors—the perception of the need to be "mature" and balance things that she believes she wants for her future— such as starting a family—and whether that conflicts with her selecting a musical future for herself. She feels free to discuss the various options as future possible selves without any anxiety about extrinsic motivators, such as money or image. This thinking illustrates *exploration in depth*, exploring activities, considering their alignment with the sense of self, and reflecting on their benefits of the identity pursuit.

This autonomous exploration may have been facilitated by her own parents, who she suggested encouraged her to "do whatever I want—It's hard enough to wake up in the morning, let alone do something you don't want to do." Her extended family was a source of information, helping her to weigh her options as she talked to them about the kind of work involved. It appeared that Judy's family fulfilled the background need for relatedness for her to make her own autonomous decision about her future.

In Judy we therefore clearly see identity formation at work. In her thorough exploration of a potential musical identity, she is well aware of aligning her intrinsic interests with the activities she chooses to do (autonomy), has a well-developed sense of her ability (competence), along with a backdrop of family and peer support (relatedness).

12.2.2 Margaret: ruminative exploration and an uncertain future identity

Margaret was one of most exceptionally talented performers of our sample at the time of the interview, yet we believe she displayed *ruminative exploration*. This kind of exploration is maladaptive because while it involves exploring various identities, it is characterized by a lack of reflection about how those identities might fit into the current and future sense of self and thus produces anxiety, indecisiveness, and uncertainty (Luyckx et al., 2008). Although Margaret had reached an extraordinary level of ability, she showed considerable anxiety and indecisiveness about the role of music in her life and in her future self.

First, there is no doubt that at 17 years of age, Margaret possessed a high level of intrinsic interest in music:

> Music motivates me. It consoles me and excites me. It's an intangible means of improving my life; it gives my life more glory than it often deserves ... It's important to me because I enjoy it so much. I love the challenge. My entire weekends are eaten up by music. The kids I meet in the youth orchestra are amazing people. I love that companionship. To experience music with others is divine! It's the most special thing I have.

While Margaret demonstrated a significant level of involvement—devoting entire weekends to individual and various ensemble rehearsals—she admits to only beginning to seriously focus on music and to systematically practice from the age of 15. Prior to that, she had owned her instrument since she was 9 years old and had taken lessons but completed only minimal levels of practice. While this response should be interpreted carefully—she must have practiced extensively for at least a few years in order to have made it to the standard she was at when we interviewed her —it appears that music as an identity pursuit may only have been undertaken seriously in the most recent year or two. At the time of the interview, she practiced approximately 24 hours per week and frequently "rushes home from school" to unpack her instrument and practice. Margaret's lack of conscious exploration was evidenced in her talk about auditioning for and eventually becoming principal in a prominent youth orchestra and her major decisions about music in recent years:

> I auditioned for the orchestra, I think, three times. I don't really count the first one because I was 14, and I didn't actually know what I was auditioning for. My teacher told me that I had to go and play, and I was like, "okay." And it was awful. But I think sophomore year was really a transition year for me. Actually sophomore year, I actually tried to come to [the music academy] in the middle of the year, which was not a bad idea, but I really didn't know anything about it.

This process and others reflect a lack of conscious decision-making, perhaps leading to some of the anxiety she had about her choice of career. Margaret's auditions for the orchestra and for the music academy did not appear to have the volition and initiative of truly autonomous, self-determined motivation. Her process of selecting a university or deciding on her future was also characterized by procrastinated decision-making, portrayed to us with considerable negative affect, anxiety, and a sense of being overwhelmed:

> I'm not really good at making decisions. Ideally, I would double major and pursue two degrees. At some point, there would be some epiphany, and I would say, "oh, I got it. This is what I'm going to do." The end. Now, Margaret lives happily ever after. Even if I go to university and pursue two degrees, I'm thinking that at some point in time there'd be some kind of light bulb that will say, "this is what I want." And I will scratch the other one and go for it. But I have no idea. I want to do something interesting, whether it is music or otherwise. I wanted to be something that is new and interesting every day, and that is, it is not a static position. For a while, I wanted to be an architect, and then I wanted to be a journalist, and then I wanted to be a doctor, and then I realized that I would have to do math so I gave up on the doctor idea. I have no idea what I want. I think the problem is that I have no plan A. Without a plan A, there cannot be a plan B. And for a while, I wanted to be a book editor. I don't know. Now, I just tell people that I want to be a mermaid and get it over with.

When asked if she had consulted her parents for advice, there is no evidence of the reflection characterized by healthy exploration. Unlike others in our study, she had not sought information from her parents or teachers and considered the relative weight of that advice based on how much she trusts them and what she wanted for her future self. Rather, her parents—her mother in particular—seemed to influence her in a different way:

> I guess that I have been so busy I haven't asked them what they think. My mom is supportive but worried. I think she just wants me to be happy. She likes security. She's worried that I won't have a secure position, or my life will be sort of all over the place. She hates that. I'd love to play in a great orchestra. But there is an opening once every seven years, and thousands of people are trying for that one shot. You have to move somewhere. My mom made me promise that I won't leave this city. She left her parents, and she doesn't want me to do the same to her. I can always break my promise, but I would like to have options.

This quotation shows the considerable pressure placed on Margaret to abide by a promise she had made to her mother not to leave the city in which she was raised. In some cases, pressure of this kind may be indicative of a damaging parenting practice known as conditional regard, whereby parents apply unnecessary pressure, or withhold affection and autonomy support, in order to elicit certain behaviors from their children (Assor, Roth, & Deci, 2004). In this case, it is possible that Margaret's promise to her mother may act to apply undue pressure and is distracting from her ability to sensibly weigh her various exploratory identity pursuits and assimilate them into a future self that she feels comfortable with and is able to look forward to.

Margaret therefore provides an illustrative contrast with Judy. Both cases show a highly developed level of musical ability. Judy shows considered identity exploration, while talk of Margaret's possible future selves invokes considerable anxiety. Margaret appears indecisive about how to weigh various factors in her identity pursuits, anxious about the need to make a commitment, and unable to narrow the numerous possible future selves she has considered. She enjoys the solace of practicing and spends considerable amounts of time on it, but rather than being a means to achieving her identity commitments, it may simply be an activity that distracts her from making the difficult vocational decisions that she faces.

12.2.3 Derek: exploration in breadth and foreclosed commitment

Derek came from an affluent family with a father who was able to pick up any sort of instrument, and who possessed a strong interest in the music of his youth, such as the Beatles, the Rolling Stones, and Bob Dylan, which he remembers hearing in various family contexts from when he was very young.

As a 5-year-old, his parents "tricked" him into learning the violin—an instrument that "nobody else I liked played"—and then compelled him to stick with this instrument for another 9 years. His first violin teacher left the area after 1 year, so he transferred to a Suzuki teacher who he reports as "awful," in part because there were no opportunities to select pieces he wanted to play, with a curriculum that involved a set order of pieces, which he either did not like or did not know. The lack of autonomy contrasted dramatically with his guitar playing which commenced around the age of 12:

> I hated taking [violin] lessons so much that I refused to let my parents put me in [guitar] lessons because I thought it would be a lot worse for me ... When I started learning guitar I went online and found like three chords and just learned how to play them and practiced them for hours. I think I must have spent a good seven months just playing three chords. I got really good at those three chords! I found something I was really passionate about and finally I could play things that I loved. I started writing music immediately.

"I want the right way to be my way" were typical comments that displayed a strong sense of autonomy that had resulted from having taught himself to play the guitar and compose his own music. Unlike his sense of competence on the violin, where he reported being always behind the other students, Derek was in three rock bands for which he was writing most of the music and had multiple mastery experiences leading to a strong sense of competence as a musician. One of the most important of these experiences occurred when his band won a local music festival competition performing one of his songs:

> It was so nice when we won the competition. The next day we played again and I just remember looking out there. The entire front two rows were singing along to a song I wrote. I must have smiled for like a week and a half after that.

At the time of the interview, Derek, unlike the other members of the bands in which he played, had committed himself to becoming a professional rock musician. When he first spoke to his parents about this "they were horrified. They thought that I was losing valuable time," referring to the need to study and do well at school, but for Derek, music was

> the truest expression of my soul. The expression of my own feelings and stuff. Even if I don't make it and I'm stone-broke somewhere it will be OK. If I don't give it my all, it will haunt me for the rest of my life. That's what I need to do. It's not like I *want* to be a musician. I *need* to be a musician.

This quest for reaching his dreams, however, involved some direction from his parents, who wanted him to at least get a college education. Because of their influence to "get a degree" before following his dreams, Derek was intent on applying to a particular university with a prominent music school. While we had a sense that Derek was passionately involved in his guitar playing and songwriting, we sensed that when the conversation shifted to discussing what would happen in the coming years, Derek had not deeply considered a precise image of what kind of musician he would want to be as an adult and had only vague ideas about what steps were necessary in the coming years to achieve his goals. Strangely, the sketchy plans he had developed actually excluded any kind of further formal music learning:

> I'm not applying to the music program, but I want to get into the university. I think I might study environment studies there or something else. And then I plan on hopefully moving to the city, just getting a cheap job somewhere, somewhere close to the city … lowest apartment I can, just trying to make it for a couple of years. I mean, I know it's very unrealistic, but that's what I want to do with my life, you know? I want to go toward it … I guess I have a pathological fear of being taught music, so I guess I try to avoid going to a place where they're going to show me how to do it. I don't know why. I just hate it so much. I don't ever want to be told how to do it, you know. The way I learned guitar was just by watching people.

The decision to throw himself head first into attempting to succeed as a rock musician raises the question of how realistic this might be for any similar 16-year-old adolescent. This was something of which Derek was very aware, even though he had been participating in the choir and musicals at school and was heavily involved in drama as ways of developing his voice and his confidence to perform as a musician:

> Well, I think … the biggest thing that I'm worried about is just getting music out there with the competition that's out there today. I mean like, I know to say, "Oh, I'm going to be a musician" is a ridiculous claim in today's society. I don't expect most people to believe me when I say that. I don't have any, like, it took me a lot to believe it myself when I said, you know, I used to be like, "Oh, I'll just be a musician when I grow up." Like, now, it's become something serious.

Our impressions of Derek led us to conclude that while he may be exploring his musical identity, it is exploration in breadth. In other words, he may be enjoying the activity and be intrinsically motivated by it, but there is a lack of active reflection and information-seeking from others about exactly what this identity pursuit might mean in the future. He had committed to a musical future, but unlike others in our study, could not articulate a specific set of characteristics of his future musical self and, crucially, did not have an understanding of the requirements and costs of the path that might lead to his goal. Some of his comments were explicit in stating that his motivation to succeed drew from the control he experienced in being pressured to learn the violin as a child. Therefore, we suggest that Derek had made a *foreclosed commitment* to his future musical self.

12.2.4 Brian: resolved identity and commitment with identification

Brian was in his final year of high school and an accomplished pianist and clarinettist in both jazz and classical traditions. In responding to questions about his career, Brian's responses resemble those of identity achievement. He had not only experienced a number of different activities and identity pursuits but had committed to ideas about the nature of his education in the future and where it might lead him. When asked about his future beyond his final year in high school, Brian responded by describing not only the kinds of university majors and careers he wanted to choose, but the role and value of his interests:

> I'll be going to [an Ivy League university]. Right now, I'm considering music and philosophy as a double major. They don't actually have pre-law, so I would just have to go to law school. I read somewhere that music is the second most accepted major into law school. It's all about getting a good liberal arts education. I think the really top musicians—there's a certain creativity—and I think that overall they probably have good minds and they tend to think a little more abstractly and be very—obviously—hard workers. It's more of the qualities that will really carry them through, and I think that probably, in a sense, would help me to get into some more competitive colleges.

In this excerpt, Brian appeared to be bringing his strongly identified musical identity into the service of his long-term goals. When we asked him about why he had decided on law, his response further clarified this, and he articulates the ways in which all three of these interests come together in the service of his future self:

> I started to read more about philosophy, and I really like debating and talking about that stuff. Law has always been something that interests me. The little bit that we did studying the constitution, things like that already, has interested me. I like to debate, and I think a lot of that works with philosophy. I think really the only purely philosophical thing that I could do is to teach philosophy, and I wasn't exactly sure that I wanted to do that, but law is pretty close. In 10 or 20 years, if I go into law, I hope I would be working in a firm, working my way up. I would still be playing piano, even if it was something just for fun. I would always be playing the piano.

Brian had already thought about how he was going to live a life that was fulfilling of his need for achievement, where the work itself was aligned with his personal interests and which would enable him to continue pursuing the identity he was most passionate about. He had considered not only his interests—his various identity explorations—but also the role those explorations and identities would play in his future self. Sometimes, rejecting an identity is just as powerful as selecting one as a commitment for the future. During our conversations, Brian clearly rejected two identities—teacher and musician:

> If you want to be a performer, it's tough to find work some times. I talked to my band teacher who is really active in the job community here, things like that. His wife is an oboist in [a prominent city orchestra]. They tell me things, and it sounds like a really, really tough life, making it in these bigger orchestras and landing gigs and record deals. It's hard, and so I guess if you don't want to teach, then it's kind of a tough life. I'm not exactly sure if I'd want to teach at this point.

However, when we drilled down, he revealed that he would reconsider music teacher identity as a commitment if he found that, down the track, he no longer enjoyed law school. This is particularly important, because it means that Brian had not only made plans for his future but also made plans to actively and continually re-evaluate his commitments in relation to his sense of self. When asked about whether, if he found that university level law and philosophy did not satisfy his sense of self he would then consider switching to music, he responded, "Oh sure. If I was still in college, I would definitely feel comfortable switching."

Brian is an example of someone who explored various identity pursuits throughout high school—jazz music, classical music, debating, philosophy—and reflected deeply on how much he enjoyed each of these and their value in his life. Also, not only had he made a firm commitment, but the commitment had been informed by imagining his future self and considering the specific roles of his various identity pursuits. Debating and philosophy explorations led him to select law as a career ambition and he knows he will always have music, at least as a leisure activity that gives meaning and value to his life. If he does change his mind at university, his decision will be well backed by years of reflection and understanding about various identity pursuits that have given him the skills to examine the merits of his various options and make an informed decision.

12.2.5 Summary

The point we are making with these illustrative case studies is not that it is necessarily important for adolescents to have firm ideas about their futures and what they will do when they finish school and enter young adulthood. Rather, the ongoing dynamic processes involving exploration and commitment are part of healthy identity formations that should involve conscious reflections about the self and the future self. It is not simply enough to form the commitments by trying out different activities and identities before settling on one of them. Functional identity formations appeared to be supported by competence, relatedness, and particularly autonomy, and two of our illustrations, Margaret and Derek, showed the particularly negative effects of experiencing parental pressure and control in childhood.

In Fig. 12.3, we summarize our four examples of adolescents who started from a point of identity diffusion. Derek appears to have foreclosed on his identity, making an ambitious commitment without extensive exploration. In contrast, Judy, Margaret, and John explored their identities. Judy was still in a process of exploration and contemplating making a commitment as she approached the final years of high school. Margaret was ruminating anxiously on her exploration and, despite being in her final year of schooling, was indecisive about her commitment. Brian had thoroughly explored his musical identities and committed to his future self.

Healthy and adaptive identity formation involves consciously and continuously gathering information and reflecting on whether one's commitments are aligned with and fulfilling one's sense of self. In our illustrative examples throughout this section, we have

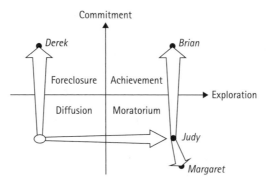

FIG. 12.3 Summary of identity exploration and commitment processes by Derek, Judy, Margaret, and Brian.

shown that these more healthy forms of identity pursuit and formation seem to occur in environments where the basic psychological needs of competence, relatedness, and autonomy are fulfilled.

12.3 Transitioning into adulthood

After the period of moratorium, where adolescents are, to varying extents, free to explore various identities without having to commit to them, young adulthood demands selection and commitment to a specific identity. The identity formation process is not final, and it is entirely healthy for people to continually reflect on various identity explorations and commit to them. Crucial decisions regarding tertiary education and entering the workforce, however, need to be made, which require significant identity commitments in order to be successful.

12.3.1 Investment and commitment versus exiting musical involvement

There has always been a strand in music education research that has attempted to understand why students "drop out" of active music learning activities (such as studio music lessons or elective music at school). Researchers have viewed this as a problem and attempted to investigate it by focussing on the reasons for ceasing instruction (Hallam, 1998; McEwan, 2012) or by examining socioeconomic indicators (Klinedinst, 1991; Corenblum & Marshall, 1998). The negative view of "dropping out" of music learning reflects the anxiety teachers often express about retaining student numbers in elective programs, or the need to maintain full instrumentation in a school ensemble. Too often, such discussions view students' choices to cease their musical participation as negative or inappropriate, rather than considering it in the context of the child's overall psychological well-being.

In this section, we describe the process of "dropping out" in terms of identity formation processes. Our preference is to articulate a view of ceasing music instruction, or "exiting" music involvement, that frames selecting or rejecting an identity as a musician more positively. We also describe why people who exit from music learning maintain a kind of musical identity into the future, and why this is important for music educators.

In the context of this chapter, dropping out of music activities represents the rejection of a kind of musical identity, such that a person might actively explore and reflect on his or her identity, for example, as a clarinet player, but decide that it is not an activity that aligns with a sense of self and reject it in favor of an alternative identity pursuit. A music teacher evaluating his or her program should be interested in whether the music learning environment was supportive of the student developing a positive musical identity—that is, whether the environment was supportive of the psychological needs of autonomy, competence, and relatedness. We believe this to be a helpful way to frame discussions with students around why they are considering ceasing their music learning. Indeed, our research has noted that students continuing in music learning when their psychological needs are being thwarted may experience negative effects on their overall well-being (Evans et al., 2013). There will always, of course, be students, no matter how supportive their learning environment is, who decide not to dedicate significant proportions of their lives to the extensive practice necessary to develop in an ongoing way as a musician, just as there will always be students who choose not to dedicate significant proportions of their lives to studying history, mathematics, or any other particular pursuit offered in schools or the community.

Teachers should be concerned about students who exit formal music learning, not because specialized music learning is for everyone but because even those who leave formal music learning continue to have a musical identity in that they have beliefs, tastes, preferences, and attitudes about music and music education (McPherson et al., 2012). If learners depart music education because of negative experiences of psychological needs thwarting, they should be a concern for teachers and researchers. These students are likely to develop negative beliefs about the nature of music and the benefits of music learning. Evans (2009), for example, found evidence to suggest that beliefs and values about music learning in young adulthood related strongly to the experience of psychological needs fulfilment in early music experiences, not later ones. This suggests that disaffected students—those who experienced thwarting of their needs for competence, relatedness, and autonomy in their early music learning—may be less able to appreciate and enjoy the emotional, affective, and well-being benefits that music confers. They are probably also less likely to support music education in schools and are less likely to dedicate the personal and economic resources to providing a quality music education to their own children.

Identity formation processes therefore have implications for educators. For all students, music learning environments should fulfil the basic psychological needs of competence, relatedness, and autonomy. With these experiences, those who continue to choose formal music learning as a key identity pursuit will be able to make healthy and balanced decisions about the development of their careers. Many students will inevitably depart formal music learning as an identity pursuit. For these students, their experiences should have led to the formation of positive beliefs about the nature of music learning and the relationship between practice and achievement, and some experience of the well-being and psychological health benefits that music learning confers.

12.4 CONCLUSIONS

Adolescence is a stage of life in which people undergo processes related to attaining autonomy and independence from parents, as well as negotiating a place and role in a complex social environment. Crucial to these processes is the formation of a personal identity: a detailed response to the question, "Who am I?" For all adolescents, music is an integral part of this identity formation process. For some, active music-making may not play an core part of their eventual adult identity, but these individuals will still hold values and beliefs about music. Others may commit to a life of specialized musical expertise. All adolescents should be provided the opportunity to actively explore and reflect on the role of music in their lives and commit to a musical identity that is fulfilling, that is aligned to their sense of self, and that allows them to enjoy the health and well-being benefits that music confers to everybody. The key to fruitful and enjoyable musical identity pursuits lies in the degree to which their experiences are fulfilling of the basic psychological needs of competence, relatedness, and autonomy.

REFERENCES

Assor, A., Roth, G., & Deci, E.L. (2004). The emotional costs of parents' conditional regard: a self-determination theory analysis. *Journal of Personality*, 72(1), 47–88.

Baumeister, R.F. & Leary, M.R. (1995). The need to belong: desire for interpersonal attachments as a fundamental human motivation. *Psychological Bulletin*, 117(3), 497.

Corenblum, B., & Marshall, E. (1998). The band played on: predicting students' intentions to continue studying music. *Journal of Research in Music Education*, 46, 128–40.

Davis, M. (1994). Folk music psychology. *The Psychologist*, 7, 537.

deCharms, R. (1968). *Personal causation: the internal affective determinants of behavior.* New York: Academic Press.

Deci, E.L., & Ryan, R.M. (2000). The "what" and "why" of goal pursuits: Human needs and the self-determination of behavior. *Psychological Inquiry*, 11, 227–68.

Elliot, A.J., McGregor, H.A., & Thrash, T.M. (2002). The need for competence. In: E.L. Deci & R.M. Ryan (Eds.) *Handbook of self-determination research*, pp. 361–87. Rochester, University of Rochester Press.

Erikson, E.H. (1968). *Identity, youth, and crisis*. New York, NY: Norton.

Evans, P. (2009). Psychological needs and social-cognitive influences on music learning. *Dissertation Abstracts International*, AAT 3362780.

Evans, P., & McPherson, G.E. (2015). Identity and practice:The motivational benefits of a long-term musical identity. *Psychology of Music*, 43, 407–22

Evans, P., McPherson, G.E., & Davidson, J.W. (2013). The role of psychological needs in ceasing music and music learning activities. *Psychology of Music*, 41(5), 600–19.

Faulkner, R., Davidson, J.W., & McPherson, G.E. (2010). The value of data mining in music education research and some findings from its application to a study of instrumental learning during childhood. *International Journal of Music Education*, 28(3), 212–30.

Grolnick, W.S. (2009). The role of parents in facilitating autonomous self-regulation for education. *Theory and Research in Education*, 7, 164–73.

Hallam, S. (1998). The predictors of achievement and dropout in instrumental tuition. *Psychology of Music*, 26, 116–32.

Hargreaves, D.J., Macdonald, R., & Miell, D. (2012). Musical identities mediate musical development. In: G.E. McPherson & G.F. Welch (Eds.) *The Oxford handbook of music education*, Vol. 1, pp. 125–42. New York: Oxford University Press.

Hargreaves, D.J., & Marshall, N.A. (2003). Developing identities in music education. *Music Education Research*, 5, 263–74.

Klinedinst, R.E. (1991). Predicting performance achievement and retention of fifth-grade instrumental students. *Journal of Research in Music Education*, 39, 225–38.

Knight, S. (2011). Adults identifying as "non-singers" in childhood: cultural, social, and pedagogical implications. In: A. Williamon, D. Edwards, & L. Bartel (Eds.) *Proceedings of the International Symposium on Performance Science*, pp. 117–22. Utrecht: European Association of Conservatoires.

La Guardia, J.G. (2009). Developing who I am: a self-determination theory approach to the establishment of healthy identities. *Educational Psychologist*, 44(2), 90–104.

Luyckx, K., Goossens, L., Soenens, B., & Beyers, W. (2006). Unpacking commitment and exploration: validation of an integrative model of adolescent identity formation. *Journal of Adolescence*, 29, 361–78.

Luyckx, K., Schwartz, S.J., Berzonsky, M.D., et al. (2008). Capturing ruminative exploration: extending the four-dimensional model of identity formation in late adolescence. *Journal of Research in Personality*, 42, 58–62.

Luyckx, K., Vansteenkiste, M., Goossens, L., & Duriez, B. (2009). Basic need satisfaction and identity formation: bridging self-determination theory and process-oriented identity research. *Journal of Counseling Psychology*, 56, 276–88.

MacDonald, R.A.R., Kreutz, G., & Mitchell, L. (2012). *Music, health, and wellbeing*. Oxford: Oxford University Press.

Marcia, J.E. (1980). Identity in adolescence. In: J. Adelson (Ed.) *Handbook of adolescent psychology*, pp. 159–87. New York: Wiley.

McEwan, R. (2012). Secondary student motivation to participate in a Year 9 Australian elective classroom music curriculum. *British Journal of Music Education*, 30(01), 103–24.

McPherson, G.E., Davidson, J.W., & Faulkner, R. (2012). *Music in our lives: rethinking musical ability, development, and identity*. Oxford: Oxford University Press.

Nexus Research. (2007). *Australians' attitudes to music: a market research report*. Richmond, Australia: Nexus Research.

Pomerantz, E.M., Moorman, E.A., & Litwack, S.D. (2007). The how, whom, and why of parents' involvement in children's academic lives: more is not always better. *Review of Educational Research*, 77, 373–410.

Reeve, J. (2002). Self-determination theory applied to educational settings. In E.L. Deci & R. M. Ryan (Eds.) *Handbook of self-determination research*. Rochester: University of Rochester Press.

Ruddock, E., & Leong, S. (2005). "I am unmusical!": the verdict of self-judgement. *International Journal of Music Education*, 23, 9–22.

Ryan, R.M., & Deci, E.L. (2000). Self-determination theory and the facilitation of intrinsic motivation, social development, and well-being. *American Psychologist*, 55, 68–78.

White, R.W. (1959). Motivation reconsidered: the concept of competence. *Psychological Review*, 66, 297–333.

CHAPTER 13

THE MOVING AND MOVEMENT IDENTITIES OF ADOLESCENTS

Lessons from Dance Movement Psychotherapy in a Mainstream Secondary School

VICKY KARKOU AND JULIE JOSEPH

13.1 INTRODUCTION

ADOLESCENCE is a stage in one's development where everything appears to be in flux. Changes in one's physical self from being a child to becoming an adult is inevitably linked with changes in the way young people experience themselves and the way others perceive them. As a consequence, the identity of adolescents can be seen as "moving" in a number of ways in the form of regressing to earlier times and to unresolved traumas, trying out new roles and new relationships, fluctuating between diffusion, confusion, and/or successful identity formation.

In this chapter we will argue that shifts and changes in identity are closely linked with shifts and changes in externalized movement. We will refer to external, physical manifestations of movement associated with self-definition as "movement identities." We will argue that movement identities are very similar to musical identities and draw parallels between these two concepts. Furthermore, we will argue that in order to achieve a movement forward and towards adulthood, adolescents often need to revisit the past and to re-organize inner perceptions. This can be done within the context of a movement-based therapeutic intervention, such as dance movement psychotherapy, where changes and shifts in movement and their connections with self-definition are often focused upon as a way of enabling the adolescent transition to adulthood (Karkou & Sanderson, 2006; Karkou, Fullarton, & Scarth, 2010). Drawing from a project in dance movement psychotherapy, we will present and discuss ways in which dance-based interventions can "speak" to adolescent needs, to their fluid and thus moving identities, and they can support young people to revisit their past, explore old, and experiment with new, identities, and thus enable an easier transition to adulthood.

13.1.2 Adolescent needs

Adolescence is a time in one's development of substantial change and transition that have impact on a number of different areas. Adolescents need to cope with complex and paradoxical physical, cognitive, moral, emotional, and social changes.

Physically, they have to deal with accelerated physical growth in terms of height and weight, and associated issues relating to body image and sexuality (Coleman, 2011). The skeletal and muscular development requires adolescents to readjust how they move, how they navigate or transition through their physical environment and how they hold themselves as physical beings in that space. According to Coleman (2011) these changes can be further complicated by physical growth taking place in spurts, rather than following a constant growth pattern, gross and fine motor skills altering hormonal changes linking to the physical development.

Such changes are not always in accordance to cultural perceptions of what is a beautiful body, affecting body image, creating fluctuations in self-esteem and heightening the potential for self-consciousness. In movement terms, they can be manifested as shyness where the adolescent may try to hide his/her new shape with rounded shoulders, dropped head or stooped appearance (Joseph, 2011a). In externalized movement, there often seems to be a lack of integration, or a separateness of parts, with adolescents often seeming uncoordinated or clumsy. According to Otis (2014), becoming comfortable and competent within this new physique can take time.

While adolescents are physically growing and changing, they are also in the process of growing cognitively. In particular, during this stage of development, adolescents develop abstract thinking. This is what Piaget referred to as the formal operational stage (Piaget, 1950; Inhelder & Piaget, 1958). According to Piaget's cognitive development model, high-order reasoning and skills in combining and classifying begins at around 11 years of age. Even if people like Byrnes (2003) argue that this is due to particular types of exposure, rather than an innate skill, adolescents are often perceived as being able to develop the capacity to understand ideas without having to rely on concrete references. A shift from concrete to abstract thinking is therefore often taking place during this stage, as is creative thinking and imagining potential outcomes from actions.

Ward & Overton (1990) argue that there is a difference between competence and performance. Some young people may be competent but less able to demonstrate this through performance, especially if they are not interested in the task. Either way, it becomes apparent that adolescent development involves considerable changes in cognitive aspects of their lives in major ways.

Psychotherapeutic literature suggests that, similar to physical and cognitive domains, emotional changes also take place with the identity of the adolescent being in constant flux, full of internal movement. Anna Freud (1958), for example, suggests that radical changes in body image give rise to feelings of depression. She also talks about this period as a movement back to older, unresolved issues. Similarly, Winnicott (1965) describes adolescence as a cry for help involving an unconscious movement towards old traumas. Blos (1962) discusses this as a time when internal perceptions are reorganized into new ways that allow for autonomy and independence. Erikson (1968) discusses this period as dealing with "ego-identity" versus "role confusion" and the time when one shifts from being a child to exploring new ways of becoming an adult. "Identity crisis" can be part of one's experience, again suggesting shifts and changes that can be closely linked with one's changing body and manifested in their actual physical movement. A synthesis of earlier stages of development is asked for, while one negotiates what they are to be and what society expects them to become. Because of these, often conflicting demands, "identity confusion" is part of adolescent experience, closely linked with a period of exploration and experimentation.

Marcia (1966) has expanded Erikson's ideas around this stage and describes four types of adolescent identity:

- *Identity diffusion*: the adolescent does not feel he/she has choices and thus does not appear willing to make a commitment to any one particular identity.
- *Identity foreclosure*: the young person commits early, before an identity crisis has been experienced and before sufficient exploration has taken place. It is often others (i.e., parents or another significant adult/s) who make a decision for him/her.
- *Identity moratorium*: this is a state in which there are a number of different options available, and the adolescent is willing and able to explore these choices, but he/she has not made a commitment to this as yet.
- *Identity achievement*: this is a state in which the adolescent, having gone through a crisis and through exploration, makes a commitment to a sense of identity.

All of these types of identity can be closely linked with movement and moving identities. They can be linked with arguments put forward by people like Damasio (1994), Schore (1994), and Panksepp (1998) that there is a direct connection between the body and emotions. With regard to identity in particular, Trevarthen & Malloch (Chapter 9, "The musical self: affections for life in a community of sound") discuss links to Erikson's stages of psychosocial development and argue that vitality is a concept closely connected with adolescent preferences in music and dance.

If there is a link between emotions, on the one hand, and music and dance, on the other, it is reasonable to expect connections between Marcia's (1966) four types of identity and their manifestations in the adolescent movement and body. It is possible, for example, to observe some adolescents being hooked in an undefined movement presentation if diffusion is the primary identity. Alternatively, if identity foreclosure is the main experience, they may appear prematurely old, "wearing" the movement of another, often an adult. They may change types of movement presentation regularly when identity moratorium is their main state, moving from presenting with a particular movement repertoire one day and with another the next. When this type of identity takes over, there is curiosity, experimentation and risk-taking; adolescents try out new ways of being while looking for a fit. Finally, they may present clarity and commitment to a particular way of moving if identity achievement is reached. In this case, unlike identity foreclosure, their commitment appears as coming from the inside out rather than as something artificially adopted from the environment.

Finally, this is often the time when adolescents develop their own moral framework and social capacity for empathy. Associations with peers groups and peer relationships become extremely important, especially as they separate from their familiar family ties (Wilson, 1991). Social identity theory discusses the importance of groups for adolescents, group identity, and the interpersonal benefits that may arise from a shared world view (Tajfel, 1978). This becomes particularly relevant amongst adolescents when they are experiencing major transitions and feel vulnerable in terms of their identity. The status of their group is important in terms of defending them from perceived threats from other groups or adults, and they will often denigrate other groups to help enhance their own status. Groups are also an ideal place to guide adolescents through the transition phase and to safely practice for democratic adult life, offering a space for experimentation (Linesch, 1988; Malekoff, 2004). Group work can, therefore, be an important tool for therapeutic work with adolescents. Another benefit of groups, rather than individual work, is that they help to combat the adolescent fear of being excluded and guard against self-consciousness (Payne, 1992). Therefore, group work within dance movement psychotherapy with this client group is common.

To summarize, with so much change to manage, adolescence is a complex phase even for those young people with healthy internal resources and sufficient support in their environments. For those with significant unresolved past issues, attachment issues or environmental adversity, it can become a time of real vulnerability, which threatens or prevents any healthy transitioning into adulthood. Either way, movement back and forth appears to be a characteristic of adolescent identity, while the adolescent prepares for a new future (adult) identity. The fluidity, and thus movement of identity from the past to the present and future, appears to be particularly relevant in this life stage.

13.2 Musical and movement identities

When it comes to musical identities, Hargreaves et al. (2002) define them as ways in which medium and longer-term taste patterns in music become part of the personal identity of the individual. Similar definition can be considered for a much less developed concept: "movement identities." These can be seen as ways in which patterns of moving associated with different contextual situations including dance genres, become part of the identity of the individual.

However as with musical identities (Hargreaves, Miell, & MacDonald, 2002), movement identities can be seen as being in a constant state of flux, subjected and shaped by ongoing interactions with others, new dance and other movement stimuli, and different movement expectations as determined by the contexts of operation. This is even truer for adolescents whose identity is a moving one as they let go of their childhood, negotiate a new adult self, and experience what Marcia (1966) calls "identity moratorium."

The changes in musical identities as children transition from middle childhood through adolescence are discussed by Lamont (2002). Whereas in middle childhood the focus is on peer group comparisons, in adolescence there is a shift towards a musical identity that is closely linked with feelings and attitudes. Within the context of defined musical styles, movement identities can be seen as becoming equally important. This is particularly apparent in the stereotyped movement of the "hip hopper," for example, where particular gestural movements are preferred (e.g. in "krumping") alongside bent knees, and forward hip movement (e.g. in "breaking"); fluid movements with sudden muscle tensions and stops giving the illusion of travelling in space (e.g. in "popping" and "locking"); or the "rocker," who may present him/herself with loose arms and concaved torso, and explosive, full-body, changes.

Multiple definitions of self are not only the result of growth. Context can also play a significant role. Referring to musical identities in particular, Lamont & Tarrant (2001) concluded that the school environment has a clear influence on children's self-descriptors as musicians, and whether they self-report they are non-musicians, playing musicians, or trained musicians. Similarly, the relationship with (and availability of) existing dance classes within the school may define the type of dance identity or identities one may hold. The way dance identities are defined in the body allows for a lot of variation across contexts. An adolescent sitting in a classroom will be expected to behave and hold themselves in a very different way than when the same adolescent "hangs out" in the school yard or when they attend a club. Different movement expectations in each of these places may be competing in shaping movement patterns that are longer lasting and deeper engrained.

The peer group adolescents may belong to will also influence their movement identity, especially when they feel under threat in this period of transitioning. As Tajfel (1978) argues, there are major interpersonal benefits for adolescents who have a shared world view. Tarrant, Hargreaves, and North (2001) discuss the links to music preferences in helping create positive social identity and self-esteem. They argue that successful identity development is associated with positive peer relationships. Furthermore, adolescents use musical behaviors as a means of demonstrating this identity and their associated relationships (Parkhurst & Asher, 1992).

However, instead of seeing the individual and the adolescent in particular as a passive recipient of external stimuli, similar to musical identities, we see movement identities as entering a "reciprocal feedback relationship" (Hargreaves et al., 2002, p. 12). During these significant interactions and exposures to particular movement styles may be negotiated and renegotiated in such a way that they enter longer-term taste patterns. Active engagement on the part of the adolescent is a key feature to this. Unlike simply being exposed to movement interactions and/or dance/movement styles, long-term taste patterns are created when adolescents choose (and practice) a particular genre, adopt a particular dress code, and listen to a particular type of music. Often, active engagement also involves adopting a particular movement repertoire that is in accordance with the particular subculture chosen.

At times and when this is done in a stereotyped manner, adopting a particular musical/movement identity may function as a protection against the fear of exploration and change. In this state, the peculiarities and uniqueness of the individual can be sacrificed for a particular movement style as it offers an easy solution to an otherwise scary and unchartered future. Similar to Marcia's (1966) description of "identity foreclosure," it offers the promise of acceptance from others, and often, in the case of fully adopting the style of a musical or movement subculture, it offers the promise of being accepted by peers. This is supported by the study completed by Brown & O'Leary (1971) who have found that adolescents used knowledge of music they liked and disliked to ensure acceptance of peers. Interestingly, the ratings they gave fluctuated depending on whether they were given in private or company of peers. It is possible that being "cool" and thus accepted, may also have a very particular movement manifestation that is adopted when with peers and is different from that adopted when one is in the privacy of their own space.

Furthermore, given the regressive nature of adolescent identity, movement identity consists not only of adopting a particular movement/dance style but often also of visiting and revisiting older developmental movement patterns. Assuming there is a direct link between motion and emotion, returning and renegotiating early object relations and developmental needs, as argued by psychotherapists such as Anna Freud (1958) and Winnicott (1965) referred to before, has a direct implication on the preferred movement patterns of the adolescent. Similarly, music has been identified as being appealing to adolescents in addressing developmental issues (Larson & Kubey, 1983).

The style of dance adolescents are drawn to can support revisiting earlier developmental movement patterns (Dell, 1977; Sherborne, 1990; Amighi et al., 1999). For example, the "downrock" movement in breakdance involves the feet and hands on the ground where the dancer demonstrates speed, coordination, and, importantly, transitions into more athletic moves. According to Petracovschi, Costas, & Voicu (2011), push, pull, and reach elements are very present in this movement. Links can be drawn between this movement and what in Kestenberg Movement Profile (Amighi et al., 1999) is termed the body-based rhythm of "strain/release," where assertiveness, strong will, and stubbornness are developed. It is possible that practicing the "downrock" movement supports one's exploration of these psychological traits, while others may find other types of movement more fitting to their developmental needs. Movement-based explorations that highlight the psychological aspects of one's movement choices constitute the main content of dance movement psychotherapy sessions.

13.3 DANCE MOVEMENT PSYCHOTHERAPY FOR ADOLESCENTS

Dance movement psychotherapy is one of the arts therapies that uses movement and dance as a form of psychotherapy.[1] When used with adolescents in schools, referrals to the discipline may be triggered from disruptions in class, unruly or withdrawn behavior, or concerns around the risk of developing or worsening existing mental health problems (Karkou et al., 2010).

A couple of meta-analyses that are looking at the effectiveness of dance movement psychotherapy with adolescents have concluded that adolescents do benefit from this type of intervention (Ritter & Low, 1996; Koch, Kunz, Lykou, & Cruz, 2014). However, the literature also recognizes the impact on findings of the limited number and low quality of quantitative studies, as did a study by Meekums, Karkou, & Nelson (2015).

Clinical papers in the wider arts therapies literature with adolescents (e.g., Linesch, 1988; Emunah, 1995; Riley, 1999) discuss the need to offer space for role experimentation, a key need for this client population raised in psychotherapeutic literature (e.g. Marcia, 1966; Erikson, 1968).

Van der Merwe (2010) discusses the use of dance movement psychotherapy for identity exploration and expression and suggests that it does have a role to play in identity formation. However, to date, there is no systematic analysis of the impact of this work on adolescents identity. Furthermore, adolescent movement patterns and their links to development, dance/movement preferences, and identity formation amongst adolescents remain areas that are insufficiently explored in the existing literature. Equally unexplored remains our understanding of the most popular (let alone the best) way of working with this client population. Karkou & Sanderson (2006) argue that psychoanalytic/psychodynamic thinking becomes particularly relevant to practitioners who find the work with certain client populations difficult. Working with adolescents can be notoriously difficult for a number of reasons, including the simple fact that being an adolescent can be an exceptionally difficult period in one's life.

An example of how dance movement psychotherapy can be used with this client population within a mainstream school follows. Particular references will be made to ways in which therapeutic action allowed for an exploration of movement preferences and enabled adolescents to shape and reshape these preferences into more adaptive movement identities.

---

[1] The discipline is also known as dance therapy, dance movement therapy, dance/movement therapy, dance–movement therapy, movement therapy, and movement psychotherapy.

13.3.1 Case study: working with adolescents in dance movement psychotherapy

This example is taken from a project completed by Joseph (2011a) that explored the use of movement in creating opportunities for the development of self and identity. The project involved a group of seven adolescent girls between the ages of 15 and 16 years. They were referred to the group by teachers who identified issues around poor school attendance, anti-social behavior, and academic under achievement. They agreed to participate because the group was the only available support and it did not involve the usual school professionals. The students themselves identified that they would work on self-esteem, confidence, and socializing skills. It seemed important to them that the group was kept confidential and outside the normal school monitoring processes.

Each session followed a similar routine. It began with a verbal check-in in a circle, then a movement activity and creative reflection, and closed with a verbal check-out back in the circle. In order to evaluate the work, data was generated from the art work produced by the group participants (see examples in Fig. 13.1). The verbal group discussion in the end of each session also formed part of the data collection. The therapist kept records of each session in the form of reflective notes and responded to the work through her own movement that was video recorded. Using principles from artistic inquiry

FIG. 13.1 Images created by adolescents in dance movement psychotherapy sessions.

(Wadsworth-Hervey, 2000), the last type of data was synthesized in a final movement piece that contributed to the creative evaluation of this work (Joseph, 2011b).

From the beginning of the group it was apparent that the adolescent fear of being "seen" that Payne (1992) talked about, hindered their willingness to overtly move. The most effective method appeared to be to introduce movement through play and music, where they could be less self-conscious.

The group began with clear sub-groups. One sub-group (sub-group A) tended to present themselves with an upright, confident manner, louder voices, a larger kinesphere, and bigger, more directional moves and gestures. They preferred rock music to pop music and chose to interrupt the flow of the sessions by distracting or cutting across others.

Sub-group B were more ball-like (i.e., their torso was shaped concavely, rounded shoulders, dipped head) with small gestures and movements, appearing much more vulnerable. They did not offer any music preferences, but when encouraged would acknowledge they preferred pop music, particularly popular boy bands. When they moved, their movement appeared influenced by hip-hop and pop movements. They would try to move like robots or create the illusion of moving through space, while actually hardly traveling. They did a lot of hip thrusting, and leg crossing and locking.

Finally, there were a couple of girls who moved between the two groups. They took on the identity of whichever group they were aligning themselves with at the time and mirrored their movements, gestures, and behaviors. When with sub-group A they "acted out"; when with sub-group B they became more gentle, considerate, and conciliatory. The notes from the reflective journal of the therapist stated:

> two groups, then three, no defined circle … doing their own thing, laughing, making fun of me.
>
> Notes from reflective journal, session 4.

Being in a group, and a sub-group in particular, appeared to be very important for this group of teenagers, supporting relevant references to this in the literature (Tajfel, 1978). It enabled them to deal with their identity crisis (Erikson, 1968) since, given that sufficient space was offered, it allowed for them to explore different identities. It is common for such groups to be linked with a particular music/movement preference, which, as Hargreaves et al. (2002) argue, if it is medium- to long-lasting can become part of one's identity. If, however, they prematurely and rigidly identified with the one musical/movement style, they were in danger of engaging in what Marcia (1966) referred to as "identity foreclosure." Nevertheless, at this stage and for this dance movement psychotherapy group, particular music preferences, and their associated movement patterns, enabled some participants to feel connected with other group participants. Interestingly, the two girls who did not seem to be clearly affiliated with one group appeared to explore what Marcia (1966) called "identity moratorium," i.e., explore different identities, without as yet committing to one.

However, over the weeks and for particular periods of time, gradually participants began to function as one group within the session, creating a new, context-specific culture. This tended to be when they all together were testing the therapist or when they felt particularly vulnerable (especially in the first five sessions), but also when the structure/activity engaged them.

With most of the girls clear movement patterns existed and some of the dominant features involved twisting of the upper torso towards the therapist when communicating with her. "Twisting" and its associated coyness is described by Kestenberg (Amighi et al., 1999) as an early developmental pattern that adolescents may have to revisit. At the same time, through twisting, participants were keeping as much of their body as possible away or shielded from sight, which is consistent with Payne's (1992) description of adolescent fear of being "seen." The therapist's overwhelming sense was of awkwardness and discomfort. It was possible that while participants were revisiting earlier developmental patterns, they were also faced with an "identity crisis" (Erikson, 1968) that generated awkwardness and discomfort in the way they held their bodies and moved in space. The therapist, responding to the sessions through somatic countertransference (Dosamantes-Beaudry, 2007), could feel these same feelings in her own body.

During session 5, participants were still requiring that the therapist took responsibility for the group. They were working and moving as one group and as sub-groups, self-conscious, reluctant to stand out or to separate from the others. They required music to be on in the room, not to move to, but to fill the space. All movement tended to be with props and accompanied by music. The music was often selected by the therapist to help support the activity, but the group would also request a particular music style, which they used in order to support themselves into movement.

When they arrived for session 5, they had very little energy, they sat sunk down in their chairs, bodies defended, and there was a distinct lack of sound or movement in the room. The therapist felt a rising anxiety, tension, and a sense of uncertainty. In her reflective journal she notes:

> No energy, no sound, no movement. Building anxiety, still in chairs, sunk down.
>
> Notes from reflective journal, session 5.

Her sense was to try and support them to relax and become more centered. For this she suggested that they blew bubbles as an opportunity for them to focus on their breath, connect with an early developmental stage (resembling the "oral" stage in Kestenberg terms), and explore shifting from breath and "oral rhythms" to different, more adult, rhythms. It also created an opportunity to play, which was important to them.

The immediate response was almost transformational. They began rhythmically blowing bubbles and the room had a calmness that had never been experienced before. Initially, the group; shared a common rhythm, but as time passed they started to become more intently focussed on their own process of blowing bubbles and were observed beginning to separate from each other and the group. They turned their bodies away from the group; the focus on breath seemed to have created a moment for them to arrive in their bodies and to become more centered, settled, emotionally available, and independent of others. For the first time they seem prepared to be seen as individuals. Hartley (2004) suggests that we create our sense of identity by awareness of what is self and not self through drawing of boundaries, with the primary boundary being skin. By using breath the girls arrived in their bodies, perhaps becoming more aware of their physical boundaries, ribs, chest cavity, and skin, with their perception extending to understanding physical boundaries between self and other.

It seemed as if they had moved some of the ambivalence and anxiety of the identity moratorium phase (Marcia, 1966); becoming inwardly focused and boundaried helped this. The need for subgroups became less important as they formed one single group.

Furthermore, in sharing one rhythm (in this case an "oral rhythm" in Kestenberg terms), enabled them to join together as one group with a clear sense of physical separateness, finding their own identity as individuals but still within the one group. It gradually started shaping into a much more mature and age-appropriate rhythm for them (i.e., a "swaying" rhythm in Kestenberg terms [Amighi et al., 1999]). From then onward and through several dyadic and group connections, more mature rhythms seemed to be commonly presented by the group members, especially fluctuating between an indulgent (swaying) and a fighting (surging/birthing) rhythm, in particular, a rhythmical exploration that was highly relevant to this group of young women as it is seen as linked with the psychosexual development of inner genitals. The fact that this rhythm persisted, a rhythm that was coming from the inside out, indicated that a degree of what Marcia (1966) called "identity achievement" was reached, one that was to be further explored and consolidated long after the end of the particular dance movement psychotherapy group.

13.4 CONCLUSIONS

It appears that since adolescence is largely an exploration of identity, a movement-based intervention, such as dance movement psychotherapy allows space and encourages explorations that may be particular beneficial in terms of forming new identities. However, it seems that the work on movement identities, an extension and link from the literature in music identities has only recently began. As such, this area of work is still highly underdeveloped within dance movement psychotherapy and related literature. However, it is an area that has a lot to offer to different client populations and certainly, as a movement-based intervention, has a lot to offer to this particular client population.

Further research in this area that explores the formation of adolescent identity would be of particular interest. The use of multiple types of data collected specifically on identity formation would allow for deeper and more solid understanding of how movement identity can be achieved and how adolescents struggling to enter adulthood, with or without mental health problems, can be best supported.

REFERENCES

Amighi, J.K., Loman, S., Lewis, P., & Sossin, K.M. (1999). *The meaning of movement: developmental and clinical perspectives of the Kestenberg movement profile.* London: Routledge.

Blos, P. (1962). *On adolescence.* New York: Free Press.

Brown, R.L., & O'Leary, M. (1971). Pop music in an English secondary school system. *American Behavioral Scientist,* 14, 400–13.

Byrnes, J. (2003). Cognitive development during adolescence. In: G. Adams & M. Berzonsky (Eds.) *Blackwell handbook of adolescence.* Oxford: Blackwell Publishing.

Coleman, J.C. (2011). *The nature of adolescence,* 4th edn. London: Routledge.

Damasio, A (1994). *Descartes' error: emotion, reason, and the human brain.* New York: Putnam Publishing.

Dell, C. (1977). *A primer for movement description. Using effort-shape and supplementary concepts.* New York, NY: Dance Notation Bureau Press.

Dosamantes-Beaudry, I. (2007). Somatic transference and countertransference in psychoanalytical intersubjective dance/movement therapy. *American Journal of Dance Therapy,* 29, 73–89.

Emanuh, R. (1995). From adolescent trauma to adolescent dramatherapy with emotionally disturbed youth. In: S. Jennings ed. *Dramatherapy with children and adolescents,* pp. 15–69. London: Routledge.

Erikson, E. (1968). *Identity, youth and crisis.* London: Norton .

Freud, A. (1958). Adolescence. *Psychoanalytic Study of the Child,* 13, 255–78.

Hargreaves, D.J., Miell, D., & MacDonald R.A.R. (2002). What are musical identities and why are they important? In: R. MacDonald, D. Hargreaves, & D. Miell (Eds.) *Musical identities,* pp. 1–20. Oxford: Oxford University Press.

Hartley, L. (2004). *Somatic psychology. Body, mind and meaning.* London: Whurr Publishers.

Inhelder, B., & Piaget, J. (1958). *The growth of logical thinking from childhood to adolescence.* London: Routledge.

Joseph,. J. (2011a). An artistic inquiry: how group dance movement psychotherapy facilitated moments of holding with adolescents in a main stream school. MSc dissertation, Queen Margaret University.

Joseph, J. (2011b). A sense of holding. Available at: https://youtu.be/hvq3W1GBpq4 (accessed February 11, 2016).

Karkou, V., & Sanderson, P. (2006). *Arts therapies: a research-based map of the field.* Edinburgh: Elsevier.

Karkou, V., Fullarton, A., & Scarth, S. (2010). Finding a way out of the labyrinth through dance movement psychotherapy: collaborative work in a mental health promotion programme in secondary schools. In: V. Karkou (Ed.) *Arts therapies in schools: research and practice,* pp. 59–84. London: Jessica Kingsley.

Koch, S., Kunz, T., Lykou, S., & Cruz, R. (2014). Effects of dance movement therapy and dance on health related psychological outcomes: a meta-analysis. *Arts in Psychotherapy,* 41(1), 46–64.

Lamont, A. (2002). Musical identities and the school environment. In: R. Macdonald, D. Hargreaves, & D. Miell (Eds.) *Musical identities,* pp. 41–59. Oxford: Oxford University Press.

Lamont, A., & Tarrant, M. (2001). Children's self-esteem, identification with and participation in music and sport. Paper presented at the Xth European Conference of Developmental Psychology, 2001, Uppsala, Sweden.

Larson, R., & Kubey, R.K. (1983). Television and music: contrasting media in adolescent life. *Youth and Society,* 15, 13–31.

Linesch, D.G. (1988). *Adolescent art therapy*. New York: Brunner.

Malekoff, A. (2004). *Group work with adolescents: principles and practice*, 2nd edn. New York: Guilford Press.

Marcia, J. (1966). Development and validation of ego-identity status. *Journal of Personality and Social Psychology*, 3, 551–8.

Meekums, B., Karkou, V., & Nelson, E.A. (2015). Dance movement therapy for depression. *Cochrane Database of Systematic Reviews*, Issue 2. Art. No.: CD009895.

Otis, C.L. (2014). Growth & development: coaching through the phases of growth and development. Available at: http://www.usta.com/Improve-Your-Game/Sport-Science/114686_Growth__Development_Coaching_Through_the_Phases_of_Growth_and_Development/ (accessed February 17, 2016).

Panksepp, J. (1998). *Affective neuroscience: the foundations of human and animal emotions*. New York: Oxford University Press.

Parkhurst, J.T., & Asher, S.R. (1992). Peer rejection in middle school: subgroup differences in behavior, loneliness and interpersonal concerns. *Developmental Psychology*, 28, 231–41.

Payne, H. (1992). Shut in, shut out. In: H. Payne (Ed.) *Dance movement therapy: theory and practice*, pp. 39–80. London: Routledge.

Petracovschi, S., Costas, C., & Voicu, S. (2011). Street dance: form of expressing identity in adolescents and youth. *Timisoara Physical Education and Rehabilitation Journal*, 3(6), 7.

Piaget, J. (1950). *The psychology of intelligence*. London: Routledge.

Ritter, M., & Low, K. (1996). Effects of dance/movement therapy: a meta analysis. *The Arts In Psychotherapy*, 23(3), 249–60.

Riley, S. (1999). *Contemporary art therapy with adolescents*. London: Jessica Kingsley.

Schore, A.N. (1994). *Affect regulation and the origin of the self*. Mahwah: Erlbaum.

Sherborne, V. (1990). *Developmental movement for children*. Cambridge: Cambridge University Press.

Tajfel, H. (1978). Social categorisation, social identity and social comparisons. In: Tajfel, H. (Ed.) *Differentiation between social groups*, pp. 61–76 London: Academic Press.

Tarrant, M., Hargreaves, D.J., & North, A.C. (2001). Social categorization, self-esteem and the estimated musical preferences of male adolescents. *Journal of Social Psychology*, 141, 565–81.

Van der Merwe, S. (2010). The effect of a dance movement intervention program on the perceived emotional well-being and self esteem of a clinical sample of adolescents. Unpublished study. University of Pretoria.

Wadsworth-Hervey, L. (2000). *Artistic inquiry in dance movement therapy*. Springfield: Charles C. Thomas.

Ward, S., & Overton, W. (1990). Semantic familiarity, relevance and the development of deductive reasoning. *Developmental Psychology*, 26 (3), 488–93.

Wilson, P. (1991). Psychotherapy with adolescents. In: J. Holmes (Ed.) *Text book of psychotherapy in psychiatric practice*, pp. 443–67 London: Churchill Livingstone Publications.

Winnicott, D.W. (1965). *The maturation process and the facilitating environment*. London: Hogarth Press.

SECTION 4

··

INDIVIDUAL

DIFFERENCES

··

CHAPTER 14

MUSICAL IDENTITIES, MUSIC PREFERENCES, AND INDIVIDUAL DIFFERENCES

SEBASTIAN P. DYS, E. GLENN SCHELLENBERG,
AND KATE C. MCLEAN

THE formation of a healthy identity is the central psychosocial challenge facing adolescents and emerging adults (Erikson, 1968). Identity development during this time capitalizes on cognitive advances, such as the ability to think abstractly so that one can engage in self-reflection and consider the possibilities of who one might become (Case, 1985; Harter, 2003). By engaging in self-reflection, individuals develop an increasingly coherent sense of self. Identity development is further shaped by emerging social relationships within cultural contexts (Erikson, 1968). At the macro level, sociocultural influences modulate the range of possible identities (Schwartz, Montgomery, & Briones, 2006). At the micro level, intimate relations with parents and friends create important contexts for identity exploration (e.g., Grotevant & Cooper, 1985; Youniss & Smollar, 1985; McLean & Thorne, 2003). For example, a sense of group cohesion with one's friends is important not only for adolescent adjustment, but also as a way of defining the self (e.g., Barber, Eccles, & Stone, 2001). Because friendships are usually formed based on common interests (e.g., Arnett, 1996; Rose, 2002), examination of these interests is important to further our understanding of the social aspects of identity formation.

Music provides a medium that allows for the expression of perspectives, emotions, and creativity. For many adolescents and emerging adults, listening to music is their most preferred leisure activity and a central topic of conversation (Fitzgerald, Joseph, Hayes, & O'Regan, 1995; Rentfrow & Gosling, 2006). In addition to satisfying their personal needs (e.g., regulating emotion; see Lonsdale & North, 2011), music can play a central role in self and identity formation. For the most part, however, musical identities have been considered in terms of music preferences. Music preferences help individuals explore and construct a meaningful social identity (Lonsdale & North, 2011), and enhance or preserve the identity of social groups through group differentiation (Tarrant, North, & Hargreaves, 2001, 2002). In fact, when young adults try to become acquainted with someone new, music is the most common topic of conversation (Rentfrow & Gosling, 2006). After listening to an unknown individual's favorite recordings and rating his/her personality, listeners' ratings correlate with those of the individual, particularly for openness-to-experience (Rentfrow & Gosling, 2006). In short, your music preferences reveal much about who you are.

Although music preferences tell us much about individuals (see also North & Hargreaves, 2007a, b, c), other psychological factors, such as the degree to which one is invested in particular music preferences, may provide important additional information to consider in relation to identity formation (e.g., Abrams, 2009). Whereas music preferences are concerned with how much someone likes specific genres of music, musical identity—based on psychological theories of identity development in general—reflects the degree to which someone is *committed* to liking *any* specific genre or genres, shifting the focus away from the actual genres.

To summarize, it is clear that music plays a meaningful role in adolescents' and emerging adults' efforts to negotiate an identity and to understand who they are. Nevertheless, the nature of this process remains unclear. To what extent are individuals' musical identities related to insights about themselves? Do these associations vary as a function of music preferences? What is the role of personal, cultural, and experiential factors? In the present chapter, we propose that more complete answers to these questions can be obtained by incorporating broader concepts of identity.

14.1 IDENTITY DEVELOPMENT IN ADOLESCENCE AND EMERGING ADULTHOOD

Erik Erikson is regarded as a central figure in the conceptualization of identity. His framework has been used across disciplines and as a starting point for many other prominent identity theorists (Schwartz, 2001; Côté & Levine, 2002; see also McLean & Syed, 2014). In the following paragraphs, we review Erikson's theory of identity development and discuss relevant expansions to his theory that have been proposed by prominent neo-Eriksonians.

To Erikson (1980), identity refers to a sense of self-consistency across time (i.e., past, present, and future) and context, including self-perceptions and how others perceive one's self. Erikson (1950, 1968) asserted that adolescence and emerging adulthood is the central time for identity development, a claim that has been supported by subsequent research showing increases in identity-related activity during this time of life (e.g., Habermas & de Silveira, 2008; Kroger, Martinussen, & Marcia, 2010). This life stage provides many opportunities for youth to explore various identities (Erikson, 1968). Failure to develop appropriately during this period, which Erikson referred to as identity confusion, impedes subsequent development and can be costly in terms of well-being (see Meeus, 2011 for a review). Although adolescence and emerging adulthood are considered to be crucial times for identity development, such development continues across the lifespan (e.g., Whitbourne, Sneed, & Skultety, 2002; Kroger, 2007; McLean, 2008). In short, the roots of one's identity are established in adolescence and emerging adulthood, but revised continually as new experiences and roles become important.

In addition to discussing the importance of cognitive mechanisms necessary for personal reflection in the development of identity, Erikson (1956, 1968) acknowledged three key processes centered on interactions with one's environment (which have received more attention elsewhere; see Blos, 1967; Grotevant & Cooper, 1985, 1986), commonly referred to as *identification, individuation*, and *integration*. Identification describes the process of relating to admired individuals, groups, or cultures and taking on some of their characteristics. As it relates to music, identification could involve using music in the same way as one's admired parent by, for example, listening to music in one's downtime to promote relaxation. As such, identification is responsible for a sense of belonging with others, particularly in one's salient social and cultural groups, what Erikson termed social identity. Through the processes of individuation, individuals also develop a sense of continuity across contexts, in terms of personal characteristics, such as beliefs and goals, as well as continuity across time. These aspects of personal continuity—personal and ego identity—allow individuals to find distinction and similarity with others, including family and close friends (Sabatelli & Mazor, 1985). For instance, an adolescent who shares an interest in pop music with her friends may also enjoy classical music on her own. Finally, integration refers to organizing the characteristics derived through identification and individuation into a framework that comprises a continuous sense of self across the levels of social, personal, and ego identity (Erikson, 1968). Together, these processes implicate the importance of environment and social relations, because an individual's identity is defined in relation or contrast to elements in their surroundings. As such, identity formation needs to be understood as situated in a specific cultural space and time (Erikson, 1968; see also Hammack, 2008; McLean, 2008).

One of the first empirical articulations of Erikson's theory was Marcia's (1980) model, in which he proposed two independent processes of identity development—*exploration* and *commitment*. Exploration refers to a process of examination and discovery while searching for a renewed sense of self; commitment reflects the degree to which one adheres to a set of beliefs or a course of action (Marcia, 1988). Exploring possible identities increases the probability that the identity to which one eventually commits will receive approval from society and satisfy the needs of the individual (Grotevant, 1987; Schwartz, Mullis, Waterman, & Dunham, 2000). In turn, commitment to an identity improves one's ability to navigate life's obstacles successfully (Bosma, 1992; Schwartz et al., 2000).

Marcia's (1980) framework provides four dimensions labeled identity *achievement, moratorium, foreclosure,* and *diffusion* (for reviews see Schwartz, 2001; Meeus, 2011; Schwartz, Luyckx, & Crocetti, 2014). A person who has committed to an identity after extensively exploring a variety of possibilities is said to have an "achieved" status. Achieved individuals are considered the most mature because they demonstrate balanced thinking, effective decision-making skills, and strong social relationships (Orlofsky, Marcia, & Lesser, 1973; Boyes & Chandler, 1992; Marcia, 1993). Those with achieved musical identities have likely considered a broad array of genres, but having adequately explored, settle on a smaller range of genres with which they identify more deeply. Someone who has *not* committed to an identity but is undergoing the exploration process is said to be in "moratorium." People with this status often experience heightened stress and uncertainty (Kidwell, Dunham, Bacho, Pastorino, & Portes, 1995), because they are still considering what is personally relevant and representative of the self, and therefore lack the protective factors afforded by a committed identity (Erikson, 1968). Erikson (1956) considered a stage of moratorium as a normative precursor to identity achievement (for a contemporary revision, see Luyckx et al., 2008). In the case of music, individuals in this stage are likely to expose themselves to a broad range of genres beyond those present in their immediate environments.

Individuals who have committed to an identity without having explored alternatives, typically due to close identification with parents or peers, are said to have a "foreclosed" status. Youth in this category tend to resist change and to be closed-minded (Marcia, 1967) and would simply model their music preferences based on their family's or friends' tastes. Lastly, an individual who has not committed to an identity, or even engaged in the exploration process, is considered to have a "diffused" identity. This category is related to apathy, disinterest, and a lack of agency (Marcia, 1980). Individuals with a diffused musical identity would not assign much importance to music in their lives, typically listening to music only when it is being played by someone else (e.g., in a store, at a friend's house). Compared with individuals in the foreclosed or diffused stages, those in the achieved and moratorium stages tend to process information from multiple sources and to generate judgments about which they feel confident (Read, Adams, & Dobson, 1984; Berzonsky, 1989). Although the four dimensions are often considered to represent mutually exclusive categories, they can vary independently, such that someone whose identity status is primarily achieved may also exhibit signs of a moratorium, foreclosure, or diffused status.

Berzonsky (1989, 1990) developed a model of identity development centered on individual differences in processing styles. He posited distinct cognitive orientations, or identity *styles*, that reflect individual differences in approaches to assessing, structuring, revising, and using self-relevant information. Individuals with an *informational* style tend to be more vigilant in decision-making and to show higher levels of self-esteem, conscientiousness, and openness-to-experience (Berzonsky, 1992; Berzonsky & Ferrari, 1996; Nurmi, Berzonsky, Tammi, & Kinney, 1997). This style is believed to form the foundation for achievement and moratorium statuses (Berzonsky, 1989). By contrast, a *normative* style is associated with conforming to the expectations of significant others, particularly close friends and family (Berzonsky, 2003). The normative style is characterized by structure, rigidity, and close-mindedness (Berzonsky & Sullivan, 1992) and is related to a foreclosed identity status (Berzonsky & Neimeyer, 1994; Schwartz et al., 2000). Finally, a *diffuse-avoidant* identity style is characterized by delaying, procrastinating, and avoiding identity conflicts as long as possible (Berzonsky, 2004). Consequently, self-relevant decisions and behavior become highly dependent on situational factors, which explains its link to the diffusion-identity status.

To review, Erikson's psychosocial model argues that adolescence and emerging adulthood are critical time periods for the development of one's identity, which is nevertheless a lifelong process. Erikson claimed that cognitive advances and an evolving social environment provide adolescents and emerging adults with an opportunity to explore and evaluate a variety of identities. Some of his notions of identity development were expanded by Marcia, who emphasized the components of exploration and commitment as key developmental mechanisms in identity formation. Berzonsky further developed these models by identifying more stable and unique social-cognitive processing styles that underlie the formation of each identity status and are related to broader personality characteristics. Considered jointly, these approaches provide valuable insight into the ways in which individuals arrive at a sense of identity, and how these changes are associated with environmental factors, social-cognitive mechanisms, and individual differences in personality.

14.2 MUSICAL IDENTITIES

The remaining goals of the present chapter are to determine:

- Whether musical identities parallel identity formation in general.
- Whether the concepts described in the preceding section, particularly identity statuses and processing styles, provide a useful framework for understanding the formation of musical identities.

As with identity statuses in general, musical identities can fit into one of Marcia's four statuses. To illustrate, musical identities can be achieved, such as when individuals have listened to a variety of music genres and know clearly which ones they like, such as, say, jazz and alternative. A moratorium musical identity refers to individuals who are still trying to figure out whether they like, say, pop or classical music, or both. Individuals with a foreclosed musical identity simply like the music that their parents or friends like. Finally, a diffused musical identity characterizes individuals who have thought little about what kind of music they like and who consider music to be relatively unimportant to their life and self-concept.

If identity statuses in the musical domain are a marker of identity formation in general, individual differences in Berzonsky's processing styles should correspond as they do in non-musical domains, with an information-orientation style predicting achievement and moratorium musical identities, a normative orientation predicting a foreclosed identity, and a diffuse orientation predicting a diffused identity. By contrast, if musical identities reflect statuses that are distinct from identity development in general, such associations should be weak or non-existent. Individual differences in music preferences and personality are also likely to play a role in musical identities.

We will now report results from an empirical study that was designed to determine whether musical identities are associated with preferences for different genres of music, and if so, whether the concept of musical identity adds valuable information beyond that provided by preferences. Because liking for some music genres (e.g., classical) is certain to be associated with liking for other genres (e.g., opera), we begin by asking about the dimensional structure of music preferences, whether the solution we find replicates those reported previously in the literature (Rentfrow, Goldberg, & Levitin, 2011), and whether music preferences in general vary as a function of the particular population that is sampled, and as a function of individual differences within samples. We also consider personality characteristics that have been linked previously to an information-processing style (Nurmi et al., 1997; Schwartz, 2001) and to music preferences (Rentfrow & Gosling, 2006). Finally, we examine the role that performing music plays in musical identities and music preferences. Musically trained individuals are likely to have increased exposure to different genres of music (e.g., exposure to classical music in formal lessons in addition to exposure to pop music in everyday life), which should enhance consideration of self-identifying with different genres and the maturation of musical identities (Marcia, 1980).

14.3 PRESENT STUDY

As a means to test the hypotheses described above, we recruited 330 first-year undergraduate students from two university campuses. One campus (University of Toronto Mississauga [UTM]; 189 students; 24% white) was located in an ethnically diverse suburb situated next to the largest city in Canada. The other campus (Western Washington University [WWU]; 141 students; 82% white) was located in a small, relatively homogenous American city that had many characteristics of a US college town. Students completed a measure of ego identity (Objective Measure of Ego Identity Status [OM-EIS]; Adams, Shea, & Fitch, 1979), which was adapted to quantify *musical* identity on four different scales (achieved, moratorium, foreclosed, and diffuse); a measure of processing styles related to *non-musical* identity (Identity Style Inventory [ISI3]; Berzonsky, 1992); a widely used measure of the big five dimensions of personality (Big Five Inventory [BFI]; John & Srivastava, 1999); a measure of self-concept clarity (Self-Concept Clarity Scale; Campbell, Trapnell, Heine, Katz, Lavallee, & Lehman, 1996); the Short Test of Music Preferences (Rentfrow & Gosling, 2003) in a revised format (STOMP-R) that included 22 genres instead of the original 14; and a background questionnaire that asked about demographic characteristics and formal music lessons.

14.3.1 Music preferences

We explored the dimensional structure of preferences for different genres of music, in order to reduce the number of genres to a manageable size for subsequent analysis and to determine whether the observed structure would be similar to those reported by Rentfrow and colleagues (Rentfrow & Gosling, 2003; Rentfrow et al., 2011; Rentfrow et al. , 2012). Although a five-dimensional model was identified from ratings of actual musical excerpts (Rentfrow et al., 2011, Bonneville-Roussy et al., 2013), the STOMP-R— with paper-and-pencil ratings of genre preferences—is not well suited to reproduce this solution. Accordingly, we conducted an exploratory principal component analysis. An orthogonal (varimax) rotation produced an interpretable seven-factor solution (based on eigenvalues >1), which accounted for 65.2% of the variance in the original 22 genres (see Table 14.1). We labeled our factors as *roots/retro* (bluegrass, blues, folk, funk, jazz, oldies), *rocker* (heavy metal, punk, rock), *rhythmic/urban* (rap/hip-hop, soul/R&B), *spiritual* (gospel, religious), *conservative* (classical, international/foreign, opera, soundtrack), *cool* (alternative, indie, dance/electronica), and *pop/country* (pop, country).

Although our seven-factor structure bears some similarities to the five-factor solution reported by Rentfrow et al. (2011), it also shows marked differences. Similarities include correspondences between the rocker and roots/retro factors and Rentfrow's *intense* (e.g., alternative, heavy metal) and *unpretentious* (e.g., bluegrass, country) factors, respectively. Notable differences include separate factors in the present solution for music that celebrates a belief in God (spiritual), for contemporary popular music that differs from conventional pop or rock forms (cool), and for rhythm-based music that is associated primarily with African American culture (rhythmic/urban). Jazz is also grouped with other traditional music genres instead of with the conservative genres, and pop and country music load onto the same factor, reflecting the blurred distinction between these genres that is exemplified in the music and chart-topping popularity of Taylor Swift.

Our interest in contextual influences motivated us to examine whether music preferences would be associated with campus and/or ethnicity, using dummy-coded variables (UTM = 0, WWU = 1; students of color = 0; white students = 1) as predictor variables and factor scores as outcome variables. Multiple regression analyses allowed us to determine whether there were differences between campuses that were independent of ethnicity, and conversely, whether there were ethnic differences that were independent of location. Results are summarized in Table 14.2. The unstandardized slopes represent differences between campuses or ethnicities in terms of *standard deviations* on the factor scores (with the other variable held constant). Ethnic and/or campus differences were evident for six of the seven factors. Preferences for roots/retro and rocker genres were higher for white students than for students of color, preferences for spiritual and conservative genres were higher for students of color than for white students, preferences for cool genres were higher for students at WWU than at UTM, and preferences for rhythmic/urban genres were higher for students of color *and* for students at UTM. Examination of interactions between predictors revealed only one significant

Table 14.1 Principal components analysis of music preferences

Genre	Factors						
	1	2	3	4	5	6	7
Bluegrass	**0.69**	0.17	-0.10	0.01	0.17	-0.09	0.11
Blues	**0.80**	0.11	0.04	0.09	0.08	0.01	-0.06
Folk	**0.69**	-0.02	-0.30	-0.01	0.00	0.15	0.14
Funk	**0.70**	0.21	0.20	0.11	0.03	0.15	-0.18
Jazz	**0.71**	-0.03	0.06	0.17	0.21	0.12	-0.16
Oldies	**0.58**	-0.02	-0.04	0.00	0.07	0.19	0.35
Heavy Metal	0.05	**0.75**	-0.16	0.10	0.02	-0.08	-0.33
Punk	0.11	**0.82**	0.08	-0.07	0.09	0.06	0.11
Rock	0.14	**0.74**	-0.10	-0.22	-0.04	0.23	0.09
Rap/Hip-Hop	-0.06	-0.01	**0.84**	-0.01	-0.12	0.00	0.03
Soul/R&B	0.03	-0.11	**0.79**	0.18	0.10	-0.04	0.07
Gospel	0.28	-0.05	0.09	**0.82**	0.05	0.00	0.06
Religious	0.00	-0.09	0.05	**0.88**	0.09	-0.02	0.15
Classical	0.40	0.14	-0.28	0.09	**0.49**	0.04	-0.25
Foreign/World	0.15	-0.11	0.15	0.27	**0.52**	0.34	-0.07
Opera	**0.43**	0.12	-0.06	0.18	**0.59**	-0.08	-0.07
Soundtrack	0.06	0.00	0.01	-0.06	**0.70**	0.04	0.25
Alternative	0.24	0.37	-0.34	-0.03	-0.08	**0.64**	0.12
Indie	0.35	0.32	-0.27	0.07	-0.07	**0.63**	-0.05
Dance/Electronica	-0.03	-0.08	0.28	-0.08	0.29	**0.66**	-0.10
Pop	-0.07	0.03	0.38	0.02	0.34	0.10	**0.63**
Country	0.04	-0.02	-0.05	0.20	-0.06	-0.13	**0.75**

Note. Factor loadings >0.40 are in bold type. Extraction method: Principal Component Analysis.
Rotation method: Varimax with Kaiser normalization. Factors were labeled (1) roots/retro, (2) rocker, (3) rhythmic/urban, (4) spiritual, (5) conservative, (6) cool, and (7) pop-country.

finding—preferences for rocker genres were particularly high among white students at UTM. Perhaps being part of a minority group (white) at the local (campus) level motivated increased identification with genres exemplified by all-white (and all-male) bands, such as Bon Jovi, Metallica, and Green Day. For pop-country genres, preferences did not differ as a function of campus or ethnicity. In any event, these findings document that

Table 14.2 Results from multiple regressions predicting preference factor scores from campus and ethnicity

	R	b	t	p
Roots/retro	0.23*			
Campus		0.23	10.72	0.087
Ethnicity		0.28*	20.13	0.034
Rocker	0.18*			
Campus		−0.10	−0.74	0.458
Ethnicity		0.40*	20.99	0.003
Rhythmic/urban	0.41*			
Campus		−0.34*	−20.72	0.007
Ethnicity		−0.59*	−40.71	< 0.000
Spiritual	0.19*			
Campus		−0.08	−0.63	0.532
Ethnicity		−0.33*	−20.42	0.016
Conservative	0.18*			
Campus		−0.09	−0.67	0.506
Ethnicity		−0.29*	−20.17	0.031
Cool	0.23*			
Campus		0.43*	30.18	0.002
Ethnicity		0.04	0.31	0.760
Pop/country	0.10			
Campus		0.14	10.03	0.302
Ethnicity		0.08	0.57	0.566

Note: * $p < 0.05$.
Campus (0 = UTM, 1 = WWU) and ethnicity (0 = students of color, 1 = white students).

preferences for different music genres vary depending on cultural environment and ethnic background, as a probable consequence of differential exposure to Western culture and music, and of different culture- and ethnic-based attitudes toward music.

Although the orthogonal solution guaranteed independence of the seven factors, factor scores could nevertheless correlate within campuses, and differently across campuses. Indeed, at WWU, but not at UTM, preferences for roots/retro genres were associated negatively with preferences for rocker ($r = -0.25$) and pop/country ($r = -0.21$) genres, and preferences for rocker genres were associated negatively with preferences for cool genres ($r = -0.23$). In other words, compared with students at UTM, students at WWU had more extreme opinions about their likes and dislikes, with *higher* liking for one factor predicting *lower* liking for other factors. In one case, correlations were actually reversed across campuses. At WWU, as preferences for roots/retro genres increased, preferences for spiritual genres decreased ($r = -0.21$). At UTM, preferences for roots/ retro and spiritual genres increased and decreased in tandem ($r = 0.20$). We speculate that the average student at the WWU campus tends to be fully embedded in popular Western culture, such that distinctions between different factors are particularly meaningful. By contrast, the high proportion of new Canadians at UTM probably means that these students tend to be less identified with Western culture in general, with less extreme views about different genres of Western music.

We also examined whether music preferences were associated with personality variables, as they have been in the past (e.g., Rentfrow & Gosling, 2003, 2006). Because there were five personality variables and seven factors (i.e., 35 correlations), we discuss only those associations that were highly significant ($p \leq .005$) after controlling for campus and ethnic differences. The strongest association revealed that as scores on openness-to-experience increased, so did preferences for roots/retro genres ($pr = 0.33$). Openness was also associated positively with preferences for cool genres ($pr = 0.16$). Higher levels of extraversion were accompanied by increases in preferences for rhythmic/urban genres ($pr = 0.21$), and higher levels of agreeableness were accompanied by increases in preferences for spiritual genres ($pr = 0.18$). Because these associations were evident after accounting for campus and ethnicity, they highlight the role of individuation in participants' lives and confirm that characteristics of their personalities (e.g., being open and adventurous) are related to their music preferences, even beyond what one would expect based on their cultural contexts and ethnic background. The findings also confirm that preferences are influenced not only by broad social structures but also by individual differences within those structures. As in previous research (Rentfrow & Gosling, 2003, 2006), openness to experience was the personality dimension most closely associated with music preferences.

To examine associations with performing music, we measured years of playing music regularly (square root transformed to correct skewness). This variable represents a combination of formal lessons, practice, and general engagement with music. Previous research confirmed that associations with music training tend to be maximized when measured in this manner (Schellenberg, 2006; Corrigall, Schellenberg, & Misura, 2013). Using the criteria above ($p \leq 0.005$ after controlling for campus and ethnic differences), we found that as duration of playing music increased, so did preferences for roots/retro genres ($pr = 0.24$). Although genre preferences were unrelated to self-concept clarity, we found associations with identity-processing styles (with other identity styles held constant in addition to campus and ethnicity). As information orientation increased, preferences for roots/retro (pr = 0.22) and spiritual (pr = 0.20) genres increased, but preferences for pop/country genres decreased (pr = −0.28). As normative orientation increased, preferences for spiritual genres increased (pr = 0.26), but preferences for roots/retro genres decreased (pr = −0.19). In short, five of the seven music-factor scores were associated with identity formation in non-musical domains as measured by processing styles.

Finally, we considered all of the significant associations with genre preferences simultaneously, using all-subsets regression. This approach allowed us to identify parsimonious models (with only significant predictor variables) for each preference factor. Preferences for roots/retro genres were best explained by white ethnicity, higher levels of openness-to-experience, and longer duration of playing music regularly. Preferences for rocker genres were greater among white students, particularly those at UTM. Preferences for rhythmic/urban genres were greater among participants of color, participants at UTM, and participants with higher extraversion scores. Preferences for spiritual genres were greater among participants of color, participants who were more agreeable, and participants who scored relatively high on information-orientation and normative-orientation processing styles. Preferences for conservative genres were higher among participants of color. Preferences for cool genres were higher among WWU than UTM students, and among students with higher levels of openness-to-experience. Finally, preferences for pop/country genres were negatively associated with scores on the information-orientation processing style.

14.3.2 Musical identities

Our measure of musical identities was formed by taking an established scale of identity statuses (Adams et al., 1979) and changing all items so that they pertained to music. For example, one item from the original scale that measured achieved identity—"It took me a while to figure it out, but now I really know what I want for a career"—was changed to "It took me a while to figure it out, but now I really know what types of music I like". Foreclosure items were reworded in two ways—in relation to friends and in relation to parents.

In general, scores were highest for achievement status, followed by moratorium, diffusion, and then foreclosure status, with significant differences between each successive pair of means. This pattern was identical across campuses and ethnicities. It was not unexpected, however, given the age of our participants (emerging adults). In contrast to music preferences, which showed notable campus and ethnic differences, the four main identity statuses did not differ as a function of campus or ethnicity. When foreclosure status was considered separately for friends and parents, however, students of color were slightly more likely than white students to conform their tastes to those of their friends, while students at WWU were slightly more likely than UTM students to conform their tastes to those of their parents. Both associations were very weak

Table 14.3   Results from multiple regressions predicting musical-identity status from music-preference factor scores

	R	b	t	p
Achieved	0.17			
Roots/retro		0.02	0.27	0.785
Rocker		0.06	10.08	0.282
Rhythmic/urban		−0.04	−0.74	0.458
Spiritual		0.01	0.12	0.903
Conservative		−0.11	−10.95	0.052
Cool		0.06	10.05	0.294
Pop/country		−0.10	−10.73	0.086
Moratorium	0.38*			
Roots/retro		0.18*	20.77	0.006
Rocker		0.08	10.21	0.228
Rhythmic/urban		0.23*	30.59	<0.001
Spiritual		−0.09	−10.35	0.177
Conservative		0.18*	20.80	0.005
Cool		0.09	10.44	0.150
Pop/country		0.28*	40.31	<0.001
Foreclosed (friends)	0.28*			
Roots/retro		−0.16*	−20.94	0.004
Rocker		−0.04	−0.72	0.473
Rhythmic/urban		0.20*	30.59	<0.001
Spiritual		−0.05	−0.83	0.407
Conservative		0.01	0.19	0.851
Cool		−0.09	−10.66	0.099
Pop/country		−0.01	−0.10	0.921
Foreclosed (adults)	0.31*			
Roots/retro		0.13*	20.67	0.008
Rocker		−0.13*	−20.75	0.006

Table 14.3 Continued

	R	b	t	p
Rhythmic/urban		−0.11*	−20.35	0.020
Spiritual		0.13*	20.82	0.005
Conservative		−0.01	−0.13	0.895
Cool		−0.08	−10.63	0.104
Pop/country		0.05	10.03	0.305
Diffused	0.38*			
Roots/retro		0.03	0.47	0.642
Rocker		0.02	0.28	0.778
Rhythmic/urban		0.32*	40.73	<0.001
Spiritual		0.03	0.44	0.658
Conservative		0.23*	30.26	0.001
Cool		−0.01	−0.18	0.855
Pop/country		0.30*	40.37	<0.001

($p = 0.05$), however, and not easily interpretable, so campus and ethnicity were not considered further in relation to musical-identity statuses.

In order to test whether participants' musical-identity statuses were associated with identity formation in other domains, we regressed each identity status on the three processing styles. An information orientation had a significant partial correlation with achievement status ($pr = 0.12$), and a normative orientation had a partial correlation with foreclosure status ($pr = 0.16$), whether it was measured in relation to parents or to friends. These results are consistent with theory and previous findings (Berzonsky & Adams, 1999; Schwartz et al., 2000). The different processing styles individuals use to deal with the challenges and opportunities of their environments are related to their musical identities, much in the same way as they are to their broader identities. Nevertheless, the associations were small in magnitude, which confirms that musical identities are not simply a reflection of identity formation in nonmusical domains.

Next, we sought to investigate how music preferences are related to musical identities. We ran multiple regression analyses, with all seven music-preference factor scores predicting each of the musical-identity statuses. Results are summarized in Table 14.3. The regression model was not significant for achievement status and none of the preference scores made a significant unique contribution to the model, although preferences for conservative genres came very close. Greater preferences for conservative genres were associated with slightly *lower* scores on achievement status for musical identities. For moratorium status, however, the model was highly significant and preferences for roots/retro, rhythmic/urban, conservative, and pop/country genres all had significant and positive partial associations with moratorium scores. In other words, individuals who preferred these genres were still in the process of exploring a musical identity.

Foreclosed status showed different patterns whether it was measured in relation to parents or to friends. In both cases, the model was significant. Foreclosure scores in relation to friends increased as preferences for rhythmic/urban genres increased and as preferences for roots/retro genres decreased. Scores in relation to parents tended to increase as preferences for roots/retro and spiritual genres increased, and as preferences for rocker and rhythmic/urban genres decreased. Considered jointly, preferences for roots/retro genres involved identifying with one's parents' musical tastes and distancing oneself from friends' preferences, but preferences for rhythmic/urban genres involved identifying with peers and distancing from parents.

Finally, the regression model had robust predictive power for diffusion-identity scores. Strong and positive partial associations were evident with preferences for rhythmic/urban, conservative, and pop/country genres. These results imply that many individuals who liked these genres did not seek to form a musical identity, and/or they did not consider music to be an important part of their self-concept.

The next analyses tested whether musical identities were associated with individual differences in personality, self-concept clarity, and music training. For personality, two associations emerged that appeared to be reliable. One indicated that as levels of agreeableness increased, so did scores on foreclosure status in relation to parents ($pr = 0.16$). The other indicated that as openness-to-experience increased, foreclosure status in relation to friends decreased ($pr = -0.20$). Both of these associations were calculated with the other four personality dimensions held constant. These findings indicate that those who were high in agreeableness were particularly *likely* to have musical identities that conformed to those of their parents, whereas those who were high in openness were particularly *unlikely* to have musical identities that conformed to those of their friends.

In order to gauge whether individuals' musical-identity statuses were associated with their self-understanding in general, we predicted scores for self-concept clarity from the four statuses using multiple regression. Clarity of self-concept tended to be relatively low among participants with higher scores on moratorium ($pr = -0.19$) and friend foreclosure ($pr = -0.12$) musical identities. Because participants who were high in moratorium had yet to commit to a musical identity, it is understandable that they lacked a clear understanding of themselves, as they were still actively exploring in the hopes of defining their identities. Those who identified with the same musical interests as their friends demonstrated a similar lack of self-understanding: individuals do not need a clear sense of self simply to like music that their friends like.

We also predicted active experience with music from the identity statuses using multiple regression. As duration of playing music regularly increased, foreclosed status in relation to friends decreased ($pr = -0.18$). In other words, participants with more experience playing music were less likely to have musical identities that conformed to the tastes of their friends.

The final analyses sought to determine which combination of variables best predicts musical identities, considering all of the associations identified above. As with music preferences, all-subsets regression was used to derive models that had only significant predictors. The results revealed that achieved musical identities increased as information-orientation processing style increased, and as preferences for conservative genres decreased. Moratorium identities were best explained as a combination of five variables. Specifically, higher moratorium identities were evident among participants with greater preferences for roots/retro, conservative, rhythmic/urban, and pop/country genres, and among participants with relatively unclear self-concepts. Foreclosed identities based on friends' tastes were higher among participants with greater preferences for rhythmic/urban genres of music and lower scores on openness-to-experience. Foreclosed identities based on parents' tastes were more likely to be evident among participants with higher normative-orientation processing styles, agreeable participants, participants who preferred roots/retro genres, and participants who did *not* like rhythmic-urban genres. Finally, diffuse musical identities tended to increase as preferences for conservative, rhythmic/urban, and pop/country genres increased.

14.4 Discussion and conclusions

We began by discussing the challenge of identity formation that faces adolescents and emerging adults, and how music is an important part of their identities. We also noted that to date, the concept of a musical identity has largely been equated with music preferences. By borrowing the notion of an ego-identity status from Marcia, we argued that considering one's identity status—a function of exploration and commitment to an identity—in the music domain may yield insight into identity formation beyond music preferences. Adopting this framework allowed us to better understand how individuals come to form music preferences through interactions with their surroundings. This approach integrated efforts to identify how musical identities function in relation to group processes (Tarrant et al., 2002) and individual differences (e.g., Rentfrow & Gosling, 2006). Moreover, we identified a complex association between individual differences (e.g., personality and processing styles), and cultural factors (e.g., ethnicity and geographical location) in the formation of music preferences and musical identities, and confirmed the importance of studying these individual- and group-level phenomena jointly.

Do psychological constructs related to personal commitment improve our understanding of musical identities above and beyond music preferences? Although a definitive answer remains unclear, the findings reported here clarify that liking certain genres is not the same thing as a personal commitment to some genres. For example, music preferences varied across campuses and ethnicity, but musical identities did not. The dimensional structure of music preferences also appears to vary based on the historical and cultural context (i.e., different in the present sample than in previous reports), but musical identities are unlikely to show similar patterns. Music preferences were also more closely associated with personality variables and, surprisingly, with identity-processing styles. In other words, identity formation in non-musical domains is more closely associated with preferences for different music genres than it is with a personal commitment and identification with any genre.

Associations between musical identities (especially moratorium and diffusion) and music preferences were particularly interesting. Although liking classical music is typically considered to be a marker of sophistication (Rentfrow & Gosling, 2003; Rentfrow et al., 2011), our results suggest otherwise. Specifically, preferences for conservative genres were indicative of a lack of interest in music, or at least of identifying closely with any music genres, and of searching but not yet formulating a musical identity. Preferences for pop/country and rhythmic/urban genres showed a similar association with diffused musical identities, with pop/country being additionally associated with decreases in an information-orientation processing style.

In the present samples, one could argue that the most sophisticated listeners were:

- Those who preferred cool genres and tended to score high on openness-to-experience.
- Individuals who preferred roots/retro music, who, in addition to scoring high on openness, exhibited high levels of an information-orientation processing style, a longer duration of playing music regularly, greater independence from their friends' musical tastes, but greater conformity with their parents' tastes.

To summarize, whether researchers choose to measure music preferences, musical identities, or both depends on the questions they have and the particular associations that are hypothesized to be evident.

In future research, we suggest that efforts be made to consider additional dimensions of musical identities, to build upon what we know from music preferences. We also encourage additional study of factors that promote identity formation. For instance, we have shown that music training promotes exploration among music genres, but what leads to identity commitment in light of exploration remains unclear. As such, it may be worthwhile to consider a broader array of psychological constructs (e.g., attachment) in conjunction with previous variables of interest (e.g., reasons for listening to music) in order to reach a more complete understanding of musical identities.

References

Abrams, D. (2009). Social identity on a national scale: Optimal distinctiveness and young people's self-expression through musical preference. *Group Processes & Intergroup Relations*, 12, 303–17.

Adams, G.R., Shea, J., & Fitch, S.A. (1979). Toward the development of an objective assessment of ego-identity status. *Journal of Youth and Adolescence*, 8, 223–37.

Arnett, J.J. (1996). Sensation seeking, aggressiveness, and adolescent reckless behavior. *Personality and Individual Differences*, 20, 693–702.

Barber, B.L., Eccles, J.S., & Stone, M.R. (2001). Whatever happened to the jock, the brain, and the princess? Young adult pathways linked to adolescent activity involvement and social identity. *Journal of Adolescent Research*, 16, 429–55.

Berzonsky, M.D. (1989). Identity style: Conceptualization and measurement. *Journal of Adolescent Research*, 4, 268–82.

Berzonsky, M.D. (1990). Self-construction over the lifespan: a process perspective on identity formation. In: G.J. Neimeyer & R.A. Neimeyer (Eds.) *Advances in personal construct theory*, Vol. 1, pp. 155–86. Greenwich: JAI Press.

Berzonsky, M.D. (1992). Identity Style Inventory (ISI3,) revised version. Unpublished manuscript.

Berzonsky, M.D. (2003). Identity style and well-being: does commitment matter? *Identity*, 3, 131–42.

Berzonsky, M.D. (2004). Identity style, parental authority, and identity commitment. *Journal of Youth and Adolescence*, 33, 213–20.

Berzonsky, M.D., & Adams, G.R. (1999). Reevaluating the identity status paradigm: still useful after 35 years. *Developmental Review*, 19, 557–90.

Berzonsky, M.D., & Ferrari, J.R. (1996). Identity orientation and decisional strategies. *Personality and Individual Differences*, 20, 597–606.

Berzonsky, M.D., & Neimeyer, G.J. (1994). Ego identity status and identity processing orientation: the moderating role of commitment. *Journal of Research in Personality*, 28, 425–435.

Berzonsky, M.D., & Sullivan, C. (1992). Social-cognitive aspects of identity style: need for cognition, experiential openness, and introspection. *Journal of Adolescent Research*, 7, 140–55.

Blos, P. (1967). The second individuation of adolescence. *The Psychoanalytic Study of the Child*, 22, 162–86.

Bonneville-Roussy, A., Rentfrow, P.J., Xu, M.K., & Potter, J. (2013). Music through the ages: Trends in musical attitudes and preferences from adolescence through middle adulthood. *Journal of Personality and Social Psychology*, 105, 703–17.

Bosma, H.A. (1992). Identity in adolescence: managing commitments. In: G.R. Adams, T. P. Gullotta, & R. Montenayor (Eds.) *Adolescent identity formation*, pp. 91–121. Newbury Park: Sage.

Boyes, M.C., & Chandler, M. (1992). Cognitive development, epistemic doubt, and identity formation in adolescence. *Journal of Youth and Adolescence*, 21, 277–304.

Campbell, J.D., Trapnell, P.D., Heine, S.J., Katz, I.M., Lavallee, L.F., & Lehman, D.R. (1996). Self-concept clarity: measurement, personality correlates, and cultural boundaries. *Journal of Personality and Social Psychology*, 70, 141–56.

Case, R. (1985). *Intellectual development: birth to adulthood*. New York: Academic Press.

Corrigall, K.A., Schellenberg, E.G., & Misura, N.M. (2013). Music training, cognition, and personality. *Frontiers in Psychology*, 4, 222.

Côté, J.E., & Levine, C.G. (2002). *Identity formation, agency, and culture: a social psychological synthesis*. Mahwah: Erlbaum.

Erikson, E.H. (1950). *Childhood and society*. New York: Norton.

Erikson, E.H. (1956). The problem of ego identity. *Journal of the American Psychoanalytic Association*, 4, 56–121.

Erikson, E.H. (1968). *Identity: Youth and crisis*. New York: Norton.

Erikson, E.H. (1980). *Identity and the life cycle: A reissue*. New York: Norton.

Fitzgerald, M., Joseph, A.P., Hayes, M., & O'Regan, M. (1995). Leisure activities of adolescent schoolchildren. *Journal of Adolescence*, 18, 349–58.

Grotevant. H.D. (1987). Toward a process model of identity formation. *Journal of Adolescent Research*, 2, 203–22.

Grotevant, H.D., & Cooper, C.R. (1985). Patterns of interaction in family relationships and the development of identity exploration in adolescence. *Child Development*, 56, 415–28.

Grotevant, H.D., & Cooper, C.R. (1986). Individuation in family relationships. *Human Development*, 29, 82–100.

Habermas, T., & de Silveira, C. (2008). The development of global coherence in life narratives across adolescence: temporal, causal, and thematic aspects. *Developmental Psychology*, 44, 707.

Hammack, P.L. (2008). Narrative and the cultural psychology of identity. *Personality and Social Psychology Review*, 12, 222–47.

Harter, S. (2003). The development of self-representations during childhood and adolescence. In J.P. Tagney & M.R. Leary (Eds.) *Handbook of self and identity*, pp. 610–42. New York: Guilford Press.

John, O.P., & Srivastava, S. (1999). The Big Five trait taxonomy: history, measurement, and theoretical perspectives. In: L. A. Pervin & O. P. John (Eds.) *Handbook of personality theory and research*, pp. 102–38. New York: Guilford Press.

Kidwell, J.S., Dunham, R.M., Bacho, R.A., Pastorino, E., & Portes, P.R. (1995). Adolescent identity exploration: A test of Erikson's theory of transitional crisis. *Adolescence*, 30, 785–93.

Kroger, J. (2007). Why is identity achievement so elusive? *Identity*, 7, 331–48.

Kroger, J., Martinussen, M., & Marcia, J.E. (2010). Identity status change during adolescence and young adulthood: a meta-analysis. *Journal of Adolescence*, 33, 683–98.

Lonsdale, A.J., & North, A.C. (2011). Why do we listen to music? A uses and gratifications analysis. *British Journal of Psychology*, 102, 108–34.

Luyckx, K., Schwartz, S.J., Berzonsky, M.D., Soenens, B., Vansteenkiste, M., Smits, I., & Goossens, L. (2008). Capturing ruminative exploration: extending the four-dimensional model of identity formation in late adolescence. *Journal of Research in Personality*, 42, 58–82.

Marcia, J.E. (1967). Ego identity status: relationship to change in self-esteem, "general maladjustment," and authoritarianism. *Journal of Personality*, 35, 118–33.

Marcia, J.E. (1980). Identity in adolescence. In: J. Adelson (Ed.) *Handbook of adolescent psychology*, pp. 159–87. New York: Wiley.

Marcia, J.E. (1988). Common processes underlying ego identity, cognitive/moral development, and individuation. In: D.K. Lapsley & F.C. Power (Eds.) *Self, ego, and identity: integrative approaches*, pp. 211–66. New York: Springer.

Marcia, J.E. (1993). The relational roots of identity. In: J. Kroger (Ed.) *Discussions on ego identity*, pp. 101–20. Hillsdale: Erlbaum.

McLean, K.C. (2008). The emergence of narrative identity. *Social and Personality Psychology Compass*, 2, 1685–702.

McLean, K.C., & Syed, M. (Eds.) (2014). *The Oxford handbook of identity development*. New York: Oxford University Press.

McLean, K.C., & Thorne, A. (2003). Late adolescents' self-defining memories about relationships. *Developmental Psychology*, 39, 635–45.

Meeus, W. (2011). The study of adolescent identity formation 2000–2010: a review of longitudinal research. *Journal of Research on Adolescence*, 21, 75–94.

North, A.C., & Hargreaves, D.J. (2007a). Lifestyle correlates of musical preference: 1. Relationships, living arrangements, beliefs, and crime. *Psychology of Music*, 35, 58–87.

North, A.C., & Hargreaves, D.J. (2007b). Lifestyle correlates of musical preference: 2. Media, leisure time and music. *Psychology of Music*, 35, 179–200.

North, A.C., & Hargreaves, D.J. (2007c). Lifestyle correlates of musical preference: 3. Travel, money, education, employment and health. *Psychology of Music*, 35, 473–97.

Nurmi, J., Berzonsky, M.D., Tammi, K., & Kinney, A. (1997). Identity processing orientation, cognitive and behavioural strategies and well-being. *International Journal of Behavioral Development*, 21, 555–70.

Orlofsky, J.L., Marcia, J.E., & Lesser, I.M. (1973). Ego identity status and the intimacy versus isolation crisis of young adulthood. *Journal of Personality and Social Psychology*, 27, 211–19.

Read, D., Adams, G.R., & Dobson, W.R. (1984). Ego-identity status, personality, and social influence style. *Journal of Personality and Social Psychology*, 46, 169–77.

Rentfrow, P.J., Goldberg, L.R., & Levitin, D.J. (2011). The structure of musical preferences: a five-factor model. *Journal of Personality and Social Psychology*, 100, 1139–57.

Rentfrow, P.J., Goldberg, L.R., Stillwell, D.J., Kosinski, M., Gosling, S.D., & Levitin, D.J. (2012). The song remains the same: a replication and extension of the MUSIC model. *Music Perception*, 30, 161–85.

Rentfrow, P.J., & Gosling, S.D. (2003). The do re mi's of everyday life: The structure and personality correlates of music preferences. *Journal of Personality and Social Psychology*, 84, 1236–56.

Rentfrow, P.J., & Gosling, S.D. (2006). Message in a ballad: the role of music preferences in interpersonal perception. *Psychological Science*, 17, 236–42.

Rose, A.J. (2002). Co-rumination in the friendships of girls and boys. *Child Development*, 73, 1830–43.

Sabatelli, R.M., & Mazor, A. (1985). Differentiation, individuation, and identity formation: The integration of family system and individual developmental perspectives. *Adolescence*, 20, 619–33.

Schellenberg, E.G. (2006). Long-term positive associations between music lessons and IQ. *Journal of Educational Psychology*, 98, 457–68.

Schwartz, S.J. (2001). The evolution of Eriksonian and neo-Eriksonian identity theory and research: A review and integration. *Identity*, 1, 7–58.

Schwartz, S.J., Luyckx, K., & Crocetti, E. (2014). What have we learned since Schwartz (2001)? A reappraisal of the field of identity development. In: K.C. McLean and M. Syed (Eds.) *The Oxford handbook of identity development*, pp. 539–61. New York: Oxford University Press.

Schwartz, S.J., Montgomery, M.J., & Briones, E. (2006). The role of identity in acculturation among immigrant people: theoretical propositions, empirical questions, and applied recommendations. *Human Development*, 49, 1–30.

Schwartz, S.J., Mullis, R.L., Waterman, A.S., & Dunham, R.M. (2000). Ego identity status, identity style, and personal expressiveness: an empirical investigation of three convergent constructs. *Journal of Adolescent Research*, 15, 504–21.

Tarrant, M., North, A.C., & Hargreaves, D.J. (2001). Social categorization, self-esteem, and the estimated musical preferences of male adolescents. *Journal of Social Psychology*, 141, 565–81.

Tarrant, M., North, A.C., & Hargreaves, D.J. (2002). Youth identity and music. In: R.A.R. MacDonald, D.J. Hargreaves, & D. Miell (Eds.) *Musical identities*, pp. 134–50. Oxford: Oxford University Press.

Whitbourne, S.K., Sneed, J.R., & Skultety, K.M. (2002). Identity processes in adulthood: theoretical and methodological challenges. *Identity*, 2, 29–45.

Youniss, J., & Smollar, J. (1985). *Adolescent relations with mothers, fathers, and friends*. Chicago: University of Chicago Press.

CHAPTER 15

FROM MUSICAL EXPERIENCE TO MUSICAL IDENTITY

Musical Self-Concept as a Mediating Psychological Structure

MARIA B. SPYCHIGER

15.1 IDENTITY, SELF, AND SELF-CONCEPT

THROUGHOUT the process of individualization in late modernity, human beings are more and more recognized as single persons, and individuals become more and more self-aware. Self-concepts are agents of consciousness, and powerful predictors of what people feel confident to do, and what they think about themselves. *Self-concept* is a prominent concept in the academic field of psychology, whereas *identity* is a much more widely recognized topic, which reaches into many disciplines, in particular philosophy and sociology, as well as into the life sciences and the arts, and which also has a secure presence in everyday life and language.

Identity has numerous contexts, and various meanings. Experts have drawn attention to the increasing ambiguity of the concept (Brubaker & Cooper, 2000). Identity, framing the whole of a person, is now understood as a fluid, evolving, adaptive entity. From an interdisciplinary point of view it is close to the *self*, which is the term widely used in psychology and which is closely related to the main topic of this contribution, i.e., the self-concept. "The self" goes back to beginnings of psychology with William James, who depicted it in his 1890 book as a *sense*, a "sense of self." Other influential psychologists in the field, including Erik Erikson (1959) in his life span approach to development, spoke of the "sense of identity" and had a rather similar psychological power in mind. One may roughly say that "self" is a 20th century psychological term (for an overview see Mischel & Morf, 2003). In comparison, "identity" is strongly rooted in philosophy and the social sciences. Sociologist Anthony Giddens (1991) uses the term "self-identity," perhaps in order to give the individual human being, who is the addressee and the carrier of it, even greater prominence.

15.1.1 Cognitive accessibility of the self-concept

In this chapter, the terms "identity" and "self" are applied more or less synonymously, according to their shared meaning. The differentiation is taken between identity/self and self-*concept*. As Ulrich Neisser (1993) in his seminal book on the *perceived self* puts it, self-concept is what comes to mind when one thinks of oneself. Other researchers who untangled the concepts of self, self-concept, and identity, have framed self-concept as a reflective system linked to cognitive style, emotional reaction, and as a moderator of thinking and behavior (Oyserman, Elmore, & Smith, 2012).

The self-concept is open to empirical investigation due to its cognitive accessibility. Numerous measurements of self-concept are available. Self-concept can be part of all kinds of investigations, be they theoretical, or empirical method- and research-related. After decades of psychological research, Herbert Marsh (2005, p. 119) describes it as "a hot variable that makes things happen," theorizing self-concept as being intertwined with the motivational system and linked with perception and action, and learning and development. However, it is important to keep in mind that an inner structure that impacts on affective states, and is likely to evoke behavior, is nevertheless not something like a steering, computational program. As neuroscientist John Searle (1993, p. 14) said, "there is no logical connection, no necessary connection, between inner, subjective, qualitative mental states and external, publicly observable behaviour (…), the behaviour that they cause has to be distinguished from the states themselves."

A person's self-concept embraces the areas of the self which can be reached by reflection, and elevated from the unconscious. To a certain extent, someone who thinks about his or her self remains separate from, or keeps some distance, from *that* self. To put it more strongly, the self is made an object, as Robert Kegan (1982) says in his deliberations on the "evolving self." In doing so, in building up a concept of oneself, one can relate to its contents.

15.1.2 Domain specificity: musical self-concept and musical identity

Musical self-concept summarizes a person's answers to his or her inquiries into "who-I-am" and "what-I-can-do" questions with regards to music. Investigations into the musical self-concepts of larger numbers of people should allow us to gain a better understanding of the nature of musical identity.

To start with domains of the self-concept, the seminal work of Shavelson, Hubner, & Stanton, in 1976, opened up the idea of segregating and structuring the self-concept. Their approach was new in that they found their model by empirical analysis of data. It presents hierarchically ordered layers of a person's self-concept, each layer with a number of parts. Layers, as well as their parts, are called *domains* of self-concept. While the domains within a layer are similar with regard to their formal value, they distinctively differ from one another with regard to their content. The first layer distinguishes between the *academic* and the *non-academic* self-concept, and the second between their sub-domains. There are subjects such as mathematics, language, or history within the academic section, whereas social, emotional, and physical self-concepts are sub-domains of the non-academic self-concept.

The major insight offered by this approach is that the sub-domains are related to life-domains. Furthermore, and more importantly for our discussion, they differ from one another within a single person. To know about a domain or sub-domain means to have a perspective on this person's motivation for action, feelings and concerns within this specific area of life. The domain-orientation within self-concept research and theory may relate to the postmodern fragmenting view of the person, observing and considering its various aspects, or "parts," with no fear of losing "wholeness." It also corresponds with Heiner Keupp's (2002) "patch-work identities."

Following Shavelson et al., the doors between the domains and sub-domains swing both ways, that is, we can look at the model from the top or from the bottom. Keeping this in mind, musical self-concept, and consequently musical identity, may be a *sub-domain*, being part of a person's general self-concept and identity. We may, however, recognize that the general psychological unit of identity is just as much set in place by its sub-units, of which musical identity is one.

15.1.3 Social constructivist views on identity, self, learning, and development

Self-concept is an outcome of an individual's accumulated experience and the corresponding structural formations in the brain created by neurobiological processes (Harter, 1999). Psychological research has paid increasing attention to self-processes in recent decades, in contrast to the focus on external stimuli in behaviorism during the first half of the 20th century. As Albert Bandura (1993) summarized, "the impact of most environmental influences on human motivation, affect, and action is heavily mediated through self-processes. They give meaning and valence to external events" (p. 118). According to contemporary constructivist and social-constructivist views, individuals experience their actions by interaction, as feedback from surroundings, which then become the source of learning and development. Taking this a step further, the advancement of "dialogical self-theory" is under way (Hermans & Gieser, 2012). The pioneers in this area, notably George Herbert Mead (1863–1931), foresaw this development, describing mechanisms later summarized as *symbolic interactionism*, and projecting the self to be a social product (Mead, 1934; Blumer, 1969).

For music in everyday life, this means that *context*, and within this a person's social relationships, play out crucial roles with regard to the nature and quality of musical experiences and related developmental processes. McPherson, Davidson, & Faulkner (2012) have carefully documented this and have used Arnold Sameroff's transactional approach to child development (Sameroff, 2009) as their theoretical framework. One can say that music itself impacts on the human emotional system, and furthermore, that it has access to the system of consciousness, and the power to alter it. All this starts and continues in social environments. With this in mind, we can now progressively address the musical self-concept and its multiple dimensions.

15.1.4 Self-concept, musical self-concept, and musical identity in relation to other terms

The most general definition of self-concept is "how one describes oneself" (Harter, 2003, p. 612). This reaches from perception to action, covering self-perceptions, self-representations, self-evaluations, and self-esteem, implying that these facets may stand for rather neutral self-descriptions on the one hand, and on the other as being valence-orientated.

Self-terminology has been inconsistent throughout recent decades. Some observers have concluded that this "plethora of terminology" has "rendered much of the literature uninterpretable" (Harter, 2003, p. 612, relating to Wylie's early work from 1979). However, a number of terms are used by many researchers and have developed a shared meaning. This is true also in the musical field; for example, *self-esteem* was found to be a variable that influences musical achievement (Schmitt, 1979). One of the latest derivatives is *musical self-efficacy* (Busch, 2013).[1]

Furthermore, musical identity has been subdivided by Hargreaves, Miell, & MacDonald (2002, p. 2) in that they distinguish between "music in identities" ("MII") and "identities in music" ("IIM"). From a formal point of view, musical self-concept may represent "IIM," as well as "MII." The two overlap and relate to identity in a non-hierarchical way. A statement of a participant in our study (Spychiger, 2010) may exemplify how interrelated the layers and the concepts of identity, self, and self-concept can be. The interviewee was a 45-year-old male participant who was asked questions about music in his life. He beautifully connected music and self by briefly stating: "My concept of myself is largely musical." In his professional life he is a carpenter, not a musician, but he loves music, sings and plays the guitar, shares his musical life with others, be it at church or in relaxing with friends at home. What he expresses with his statement is that there is so much music in his general identity that he projects music to be not just a genuine but a dominant part of it, which then accounts for his identity in music.

---

[1] For reviews of self-variables in music education, see Reynolds (1992); Katsochi (2008).

Attempts to measure aspects of the music-related self-system started a few decades ago. Early on, Edward Asmus (1986) created the "Music Attribution Orientation Scale" for musicians and music students in order to explore their perceived attributions for success and failure in their achievements. As for musical self-concept itself, the most detailed work has been carried out, and measurements provided so far, by Walter Vispoel (summarized in Vispoel, 2000). In comparison, approaches and procedures to measuring musicality and musical ability, or musical achievement, have a much longer history and last into the present.[2]

15.1.5 Multi-dimensionality

Hierarchical models of self-concept still adhere to the idea of a global self. Other models opt for dividing its domains non-hierarchically. In the latter case, the differentiation is not from global to specific, but from uni- to multi-dimensional. More recent research gives rise to this type of classification (e.g., Byrne, 1996; Harter, 1999), and so does our own (Spychiger, 2007, 2010). In the case of musical self-concept especially, a non-hierarchical view seems to be more successful in accommodating the diverse roles that music plays in people's lives. The styles and amounts of music that are widely available have multiplied in the past few decades, such that music is often used to express and articulate individuality, as well as to regulate moods and mental states.

The dimensions of musical self-concept, which emerged in our own extended investigations started with a heuristic model and resulted in an empirical study. The heuristic model embraced a small number of dimensions, three of which reflected the sub-domains of Shavelson, Hubner, & Stanton's 1976 model, namely, *social, emotional*, and *physical* as non-academic ("who-I-am") dimensions, and *ability* as an academic ("what-I-can do") dimension. The model has further dimensions, one of them labelled *cognitive* (since music can be a carrier of memories and can contain types of knowledge which are not musical ability-related), and another one labelled *spiritual* (since we assumed that music is related to religious experience in many people's lives). We would expect these dimensions of music-related self-representations to be found in almost everybody, but to differ between people with respect to their perceived importance.

At the turn of the millennium, Hargreaves et al. (2002, p. 18) suggested that "the nature of musical experience is changing rapidly in the globalized world." What are these changes, and how are they occurring? What does this mean in terms of musical identity, which they influence? We look next at the dimensions of musical self-concept

---

[2] A recently developed test is The Goldsmiths Musical Sophistication Index (Gold-MSI, see http://www.gold.ac.uk/music-mind-brain/gold-msi/). However, the long history of testing musicality is accompanied by a history of criticism concerning the objectivity and validity of such tests. Law & Zentner (2012, p. 1) even summarize this as "absence of objective measurement tools" and give this as a reason why researchers often use the method of self-reports in order to diagnose participants' musicality.

as they emerged in our extended empirical study (Spychiger, 2010).[3] Some of these confirmed the heuristic model, and others added to it. We keep in mind the idea that those dimensions represent conscious musical experiences and mediate these experiences in forming an aggregated musical identity.

15.2 EMPIRICALLY ACCESSING DIMENSIONS AND CONTENTS OF MUSICAL SELF-CONCEPT

The samples of participants in this study included all segments of the population regarding age, gender, professional occupation, and musical expertise, with a total of $n = 819$. Data were collected first by qualitative methods, interviewing about 70 participants of all social backgrounds, ages, and professional lives. Then, based on the results of content analyses, a questionnaire was gradually developed by quantitative methods. Throughout three waves of investigation, the number of items was reduced from 212 to 63 items, by reliability analyses, and factor analyses. The final questionnaire was named MUSCI, the Musical Self-Concept Inquiry. It comprises 12 scales, of which four scales are to be completed by musicians only.[4]

15.2.1 Technique and information—a new dimension of musical self-concept

Principal component analyses were performed on the data from the questionnaire study, and a new dimension emerged, which refers to technical and computer-related interest in music and which was found to explain 5.5% of variance from a total of 65.7% for all components. This dimension was labeled "technique and information," and was defined by four items that persisted throughout the three waves of analysis, namely:

- The technical options to produce music are fascinating to me.
- I pay a lot of attention to the technical quality of my music reproduction devices.

[3] The Swiss National Science Foundation supported this research with grant no. 100013-116208. The project was located at the University of Music and Performing Arts, Frankfurt (Main), Germany, in 2008–2010. We thank both institutions for the generous support of our research. A small team of researchers carried out the investigations throughout 30 months: Lucia Gruber, Franziska Olbertz, Dieter Ratz, Philipp Senft, Joy Stephens, Marco Schöni, and they were assisted by a number of student volunteers. Multiple thanks are dedicated to all of them, for their work and a great time with shared insights.

[4] Participants check each item on a four-point Likert scale, from 4, "fully agree," to 3, "rather agree," to 2, "rather disagree," to 1, "fully disagree." Very few items are worded negatively; those few are marked in the text with "(-)," and have to be reversed for calculation (1 = 4, 2 = 3, 3 = 2, 4 = 1).

- I am concerned with the question of how music is produced.
- I am interested in how musical instruments function.

The second item is well represented by an interviewee in the qualitative study, a 69-year-old opera lover, who said:

> What really matters is that the technical quality of equipment is excellent, that is, the music should not *squawk* out of the radio. My reproduction techniques have to be of as good quality as possible. Under this condition, music has much more impact on me than if I hear it through equipment of lesser quality.

It is quite interesting that item 4 belongs to the technology-dimension (having the strongest loadings on that component). This may make us aware that a technical component has always been present in musical experience and behavior, resulting in more and more sophisticated musical instruments throughout their history and evolution (see Alperson, 2008). Today, sources of sound production and rhythm exist that were hitherto unknown. It has often been observed that some people focus predominantly on musical instruments, not just in order to play them, but also because of the technical perfection of their production. Interest in how external sources are to be used in order to generate sound, indeed, seems to be part of people's thoughts about themselves, that is, of their musical self-concepts. With enhanced technology, computer-based applications, etc., changes in musical experience are to be expected in general, although this still differs from one person to another.

15.2.2 The social dimension: overestimated so far?

Music is a social phenomenon which connects and coordinates people. Music is performed mostly in groups and accounts for shared experiences, as well as a forming cultural, national or group identity. Investigating hundreds of participants, we initially thought that the social dimension would be one of the most prominent in our empirical findings. But a large set of items dwindled down to only four items which were representative of "community," explaining no more than 5.2% of the variance:

- The convivial facet in music means a lot to me.
- To me, music is an expression of community more than it is to others.
- I go to music happenings in order to meet people.
- I easily socialize by the means of music.

This narrowing of the social dimension is not predicted by a social-constructivist standpoint and may be unexpected altogether. In older studies, such as Alan Merriam's *Anthropology of Music*, five of the ten well-known functions of music are social—communication, enforcing conformity to social norms, validation of social institutions and religious rituals, contribution to the continuity and stability of culture, and contribution to the integration of society (Merriam, 1964, pp. 222–7; the remaining functions are emotional expression, aesthetic enjoyment, entertainment, symbolic representation, and physical response). Social functions of music are often hypothesized to be the origins of music, and folk tunes and songs are expressive of social bonds. Leo Kestenberg in Germany, as well as Zoltán Kodály in Hungary, had strong hopes and made great efforts to re-elevate national identity through music at times when the national self-esteem of their peoples had been damaged (Ehrenforth, 2005).

However, in the present day, the individual—and not a group, nation, gender, or class—should be prioritized with regards to identity. A recent empirical analysis (Schäfer, Sedlmeier, Städtler, & Huron, 2013) of a large literature-based collection of functions of music ($n = 129$) also emphasizes the functions for the individual, rather than its social functions. The three major factors these researchers extracted were "self-awareness," "social relatedness," and "arousal and mood-regulation," with social relatedness scoring significantly lower than the other two dimensions. What can these findings possibly mean? Music listening and music-making seems to influence the individual's self-awareness and emotional organization. This does not necessarily weaken the deeply social aspect of music, nor does it indicate that the human species has become less social. Rather, options for expressing social attitudes and behavior have multiplied in recent decades by radically increased mobility, technology, communication media, and digital information and processing. The thoroughly social orientation of the human species is prevalent in the musical life-domain as much as ever, and so is music's agency in social connection.

However, looking at the multitude of dimensions of the musical self-concept, we observe that they vary with regards to the extent of their interactional function. Other dimensions, most of all those which emerged from the factor analyses—the *spiritual*, *the ideal*, and *the adaptive musical self*—seem to refer more to communication *within* the person. The function of the musical self-concept is then part of self-related mental activities, in the sense of *intra*-action. We will elaborate on this in Section 15.4, after the empirically strongest factors are discussed, namely, "musical ability," "mood management," and "movement and dance."

15.2.3 Musical ability: the strongest dimension in music-related self-representations

Within the multi-dimensional musical self-concept, people are most sensitive to appraising their own musical abilities. This factor may emerge so strongly because this is what pupils remember first and have been told about most: how good they are in music, whether they are musical, sing beautifully, have a good sense of rhythm, and so forth—how "gifted" they are overall. Also, they may have a strong sense of whether or not they sing in tune, can hold their part securely in polyphonic singing, dance well, or can play on several musical instruments. This factor represents the "What-I-can-do" part of musical self-concept. The 10 items listed below, out of the many which addressed self-representations of musical competence (such as singing, rhythmical ability, listening, playing instruments, arranging, composing ability, etc.), retained strong statistical loadings in each wave of the analysis, explaining 13% of the total variance:

- My musical ability is above average.
- I have the ability to teach other people about music.
- I have no musical talent. (-)
- That I am musically competent means a lot to me.
- I easily hear harmonics and can sound out voices.
- I feel that I could have become a great musician.
- I can sing well.
- I am challenged to make the most of my musical ability.
- I am an expert as regards to certain musical styles.
- Learning to play an instrument is too laborious to me. (-)

Items with (-) are worded in negative terms with regards to the value of the dimension, which means that when calculating the numeric values have to be inverted (4 = 1, 3 = 2, 2 = 3, 1 = 4). The last item requires explanation. It comes from many interviewees telling us, often expressing regret, that they had given up playing an instrument in their teenage years. They attributed this to various causes. Limitation of talent was given as a major reason, but most of the interviewees also mentioned to lack of time for practicing and that other occupations were more important and more attractive. It is noteworthy that the attribution of lack of effort, or willingness to invest time, remained in the pool of items.

15.2.4 Emotional and physical dimensions

The second strongest component in our investigation of musical self-concept was *mood management*. It accounted for 8.4% of the total variance, and involves six items:

- Music helps me to cope with stress.
- I can relax with music.
- Music relieves me from daily routine.
- With music I can forget my sorrows.
- Music helps me to diminish anger.
- For me, music is a specific source of mood management.

"Mood management" fits well into the body of literature on music and emotion (Juslin & Sloboda, 2010; Liljeström, Juslin & Västfjäll, 2013). The relationship between music and emotion is the subject of increasing investigation and has an impact on many fields of modern life—health, sports, commerce, and so forth. This has become an identifiable academic field, with groups of scientists, conferences, journals, etc. Before conceiving of this as part of the musical self-concept, we initially held a much broader dimension of music and emotion, which was subsequently narrowed down to "mood management." This raises the question as to whether, as with the social dimension, the role of emotion in music is overestimated, or generalized, or oversimplified.

Our heuristic model of self-concept conceived of the physical dimension as being close to the emotional dimension, bearing in mind that music has much to do with movement, and that the physical expression of emotions is an important part of being for many people. This dimension was empirically represented by five items, which together explained a considerable proportion of the variance, namely 7.4%. These items were as follows:

- I passionately love to dance.
- I avoid dancing since I don't dance well. (-)
- I easily move to the rhythm of music.
- Dancing satisfies my need for physical movement.
- I respond to the rhythm of music with movement.

The component is labelled *movement and dance*, since all of the items are strongly movement-orientated. A statement like this one from a 36-year-old female theatre manager, reflecting upon her abilities with regard to energy and motivation, may suggest that this dimension is often forgotten when describing musical abilities:

> I think of singing to be unbelievably great. But I have difficulty even to keep a sound right and this is frustrating. If I put the same amount of energy and time into dance training I simply have a much better outcome. My body is more apt and obeys much better to this than to singing.

There may also be a strong link between this physical dimension and what we originally conceived as "emotional," other than mood management, and which did not emerge from the factor analysis. Interestingly, although not really surprisingly, the contents of "movement and dance"—the empirical remains of the heuristic model's "physical dimension"—are poorly represented in classical musicians but are well to the fore in the group of amateur musicians. Group differences will be addressed again in Section 15.3.

15.2.5 Further dimensions: spiritual, ideal, and adaptive musical self-concept

Further dimensions concern the individual self in a very private sense. As for the spiritual dimension, spirituality in the musical self-concept may fit well with Schäfer et al.'s (2013) "self-awareness" function of music. One can ask whether the evolutionary bond between music and religion still persists in today's secular world. A number of contemporary studies and theoretical reflections on music and religion suggest that it does (e.g., von Belzen, 2012). Many people reported on their music-related spiritual experiences in our investigations, and when it was then included into the questionnaire, the topic proved to be distinctive. Many participants ticked the "fully agree" or "agree" options, although a substantial number of them also rejected the idea of such a relationship in their life. The dimension was represented by the following four items, which accounted for 6.8% of the variance:

- Spirituality in music means more to me than to other people.
- I am not the type for spiritual experiences with music. (-)
- Music listening is a spiritual experience to me.
- By the means of music I can get in touch with God.

Many people think about themselves, about life itself, its meaning and its tasks, by listening to music. One more emerging component, *ideal musical self*, may relate to self-awareness as well. The items representing it were as follows:

- I regret that I am not more musically creative.
- I would like to have higher musicianship.
- I would like to have a greater understanding of music.
- I would like to know more about the characteristics of the different musical styles.
- I would like to have more knowledge of the technical features and options in music.

The fact that people hold, or even retain such thoughts about themselves, and wish for a musical life, is impressive in itself. This dimension overlaps with the concept of "possible selves," as formulated by Markus & Nurius (1986). Accounting for 6.5% of the variance, the component is not one of the strongest, and is less important than spirituality, but this result may nevertheless indicate that music does indeed play a role in identity ("MII"). People do think about who they are, and would like to be, with regard to music in their lives.

An additional component which emerged from the factor analysis shows that musical self-concept is not only represented as what it could or should be but can also show real change throughout one's life-course. Four items were grouped as what we identified as "adaptive musical self." This component addresses the changes, losses and gains in one's musical life, accounted for 5.5% of the variance and was represented by the following items:

- Today my emotional perception of music is different from earlier in my life.
- My physical reaction to music is different from what it was formerly.
- My intellectual understanding of music has changed during the years.
- With regards to spirituality in music, my current susceptibility is different from earlier in my life.

Having gained a *concept* of aspects of one's self may serve as a means to guide and lead individuals' actions towards autonomy. To be self-determining is a key part of some of the theories of motivation which emerged in the 1980s, starting with Deci & Ryan (1985). The capacity for adaptation of the self-concept may then be the real factor that improves self-management, since self-concepts are required to adapt to the specific demands of the culture and the times in which individuals live.

15.3 INDIVIDUAL DIFFERENCES

We now look into the differences in musical self-concept between groups, and individuals, including children. The variable of *age* was found to be a factor in explaining differences between participants on a number of components, and so was *gender* (see Spychiger, 2010), but the most obvious differentiating factor was the extent to which individuals deal actively with music.

15.3.1 Between-group differences

Recognizable levels of expertise were defined in our study by whether or not a person was musically active, whether the activity was more than merely listening to music, whether this was more than just in his or her leisure time, and whether the person identified him- or herself as a musician. In the latter case, a follow-up question was asked: whether he or she was an amateur musician or held a degree in music. The musical self-concepts of the following five groups with different levels of expertise proved to be statistically different from one another (*t*-test results: for more details, see Spychiger, et al., 2009, p. 503; Spychiger, 2010):

- *Group 1*: professional and employed (or retired) musicians, holding degrees from educational institutions[5]

---

[5] Additional items and scales were inserted into the inquiry for Groups 1 and 2, the identified musicians (M), with the following topics and contents ("M-scales"):
  (1) *Communication*: "I sense that the music I perform connects people."
     - I play music in order to communicate with other people.
     - I love the applause.
     - I easily become part of a musical ensemble.
     - I usually play music for my self-satisfaction. (-)
     - To perform on stage is easy for me.
  (2) *Ability and ambition*: "I strive toward high musical achievement."
     - I am musically ambitious.
     - I take advantage of any opportunity in order to advance my musical ability.
     - I am capable of achieving the musical goals that I have set.
     - I am proud of my musical aptitude.

- *Group 2*: amateur musicians, having professional identity, and being perceived as musicians, but not holding degrees from state institutions. Earning their living completely, or partly, from music. (Group 2 has additional MUSCI scales, as does Group 1).
- *Group 3*: leisure time musicians, i.e., individuals who make music as a hobby or casual activity, but who do not declare themselves to be musicians.
- *Group 4*: music workers, i.e., individuals who are professionally occupied with music, not as performers, but in providing, listening to or playing music (i.e., audio engineer, piano tuner, concert manager, etc.).
- *Group 5*: music listeners, i.e., individuals who engage with music more or less exclusively by listening to it, and do not produce it.

These groups differed from one another, unsurprisingly, on the component of *musical ability*. High expertise levels were associated with high scores. The opposite result was found on the component of *community*: high scores were achieved by Groups 2, 3, and 5, whereas members of Group 1 (professional musicians) had average scores. Interestingly, Group 1 was high on *technique and information* along with Group 5, the music listeners, while the leisure time musicians had significantly lower scores. The example of the opera listener reported in Section 15.2 may illustrate this general result. Another outcome was that *mood management* played a more important role in the group of the music listeners than in the music-making groups (significant difference between Groups 1 and 3). One of the most interesting and meaningful results with regard to understanding musical self-concept is that all music-making individuals scored higher not only on the ability dimension but also on *adaptive musical self*.

This in turn relates to a measure that we introduced to investigate individual differentiation between the dimensions, which we called *nearness-to-self*. We borrowed this construct from Kessels & Hannover (2004), who created and used it in order to assess students' preferences for school subjects. Nearness-to-self measurement allowed for estimates of the valence of each dimension (for the procedure and results, see Spychiger et al., 2009). It might also be a useful tool for investigating a person's inclination towards singing or playing an instrument, which deserves further attention.

- I consider myself proficient in my instrument/my voice.

(3) *Emotion*
- The music in which I am involved impacts on my emotions.
- When making music I have to be able to forget time and place.
- I make music for the sake of expressing my emotions.
- Musical activity can alter my mood.
- I enjoy experiencing strong emotions in making music.

(4) *Spirituality*
- For me, making music is a special kind of prayer.
- I make music in order to feel the divine.
- I like to make music which promotes spiritual experience.
- With my music I can elicit change in people.

15.3.2 The voice and musical instruments: two types of music-orientation?

One aspect of the rapid changes in musical experience addressed by Hargreaves et al. (2002) is that fewer children of the late modern age experience the intergenerational singing of folk and religious songs. All previous societies had this as a common cultural orientation and behavior. By emotional involvement in singing and dancing in the community, members of such societies build up their musical identities as a group identity, with cultural, and perhaps national or ethnic characteristics.

Many musicians, as well as lay musicians and leisure time musicians, use and have developed both their singing and instrumental playing skills, though usually these two musical domains turn out not to be equal. One major force—the primary identity— seems to be either in one or the other activity—the voice or the instrument. The latter perhaps relates to the "technique and information" dimension of musical identity. These two avenues are observed also in many educational institutions' music tuition: some teachers focus more on singing, and others more on teaching pupils to play musical instruments.

Songs, by their musical parameters, verbal content, social contexts, and aesthetic atmospheres, may elicit strong experiences. *Singing* has many more implications. It is first of all connected with the hormonal system and causes discharges of "happiness hormones" such as oxytocin, and dopamine (see Mlejnek, 2013). From this perspective, singing has an impact on the performer's affective responses and is able to change mental states such as anxiety, pain, loneliness, etc., which are known as negative emotions. The initial societal or ethnic context of singing has started to fade in modern society. These days, many singing activities take place—if at all—in small units, perhaps during family car-rides, or when a mother sings to her child. This individualizing process may account for the apparent reduction of prominence of the "social dimension" of the musical self-concept, as discussed in Section 15.2. Groups such as school classes, private singing ensembles and choirs, or musical bands may be able to encourage singing. This matters because the experience of voice and its impact on the human psyche can have a long-term influence on musical identity.

Singing is highly represented in most people´s musical self-concept. Individuals are conscious of whether they do or do not love to sing, and most of them relate this to their self-appraised singing skills. Many interviewees in our study remarked that they could not sing in tune, or "hold" a part by themselves. Children also are aware of their ability to sing in tune. For example, a 9-year-old child who participated in a program for the enhancement of singing skills reported excitedly about the experience he had had with his voice: "The best part is, I am now able to hit the notes at the right pitch."[6] Adult interviewees on musical self-concept also frequently mentioned their experiences with playing an instrument, often in critical ways, such as: "I did not have the patience,

---

[6] In original German: "Das Beste ist, ich treffe jetzt die Töne" (Spychiger & Aktas, 2011, p. 11).

nor the talent, to pursue long-term tuition." Another interviewee's transcript noted that "Learning to play an instrument is too laborious for me." It was noted by the researchers that many participants reported self-representations of singing that were more deeply felt than those for instrumental playing.

15.4 IMPLICATIONS, CONCLUSIONS, OPEN ENDS

The contents, examples, and theory discussed so far should now be drawn together. Doing this will reveal that our picture of musical self-concept is not complete and not geometrically even, elegantly logical, or aesthetically beautiful. To some degree, there are open ends, and relationships that have not been clarified. For example, discovering the importance of group identity as expressed by musical preference and expression does not help us to understand how it relates either to personal identification or to individual musical identity. Furthermore, the urgent questions of contemporary human sciences—what brings the brain to consciousness, and which neurobiological processes change its states—have been touched upon but are a long way from being answered.

15.4.1 Individualized experience—self-awareness— self-concept—individual identity

The activities of listening to and producing music may have contributed to the processes of self-awareness, acting as a means for people to focus on their feelings, think about themselves, and about life itself. Becoming conscious of topics that have not yet reached self-consciousness transcends the self. Such processes first of all are part of "MII," music's contribution to a person's identity. Enhanced self-awareness while listening to music will ultimately include an awareness of the music being listened to. By this process, musical preferences, attitudes, knowledge, skills, and emotional responses are built up and come into consciousness. This process leads to a self-*concept*. The self-aware person is capable of looking at him- or herself from an outside perspective, making him- or herself the object of reflection (as Robert Kegan put it; see Section 15.1). In doing so, individuals can conceive of ideas about who they are, and perceive a sense of continuity in this: the latter is defined as *identity* by many theorists (e.g., Erikson, 1959; Krappmann, 1971; Greve, Rothermund, & Wentura, 2005).

This line of thought brings us back to the hypothesis that musical experience builds up the musical self-concept and that musical identity takes its course from there. Consciousness is a late development in evolution, and *self*-awareness rarely appears within it. Self-awareness is most prominent in the human species (Donald, 2001). The German philosopher Hans Joas (1989, p. 104) calls this *self-reflective awareness*, which relates to one's own actions and which is different from the awareness of an object. To summarize, humans are *self*-conscious. In our present society, musical experience has become highly individualized and as such is reflected upon. Sometimes this reflection is connected to *strong experiences with music* ("SEM"), as investigated by Alf Gabrielsson over the past two decades (Gabrielsson, 2011). Such experiences emerge from the constant stream of experience, which project, for a given time-span, into the sphere of consciousness (Dewey, 1980/1934).

Other authors have dealt with the question of awareness and music, which has been referred to on more than one occasion throughout this chapter. For example, Björn Merker (1999/2000) drew attention to the phenomenon of *entrainment,* the capacity to raise awareness of and tune into an external beat, which humans started to do eons ago in synchronous chorusing. Merker thinks that the capacity to entrain is intertwined with the dramatic rise of social interaction in the species, and that this is at the core of cultural development. Of course, this question goes far beyond the discipline of music. John F. Searle (1993) wrote that answering the question of consciousness will be "the most important scientific discovery of the present era" (p. 3). Searle explains how consciousness is at first just one of many phenomena which belong to the evolution of the human species and is part of the material world, strictly biological—"such as digestion, growth, mitosis, and meiosis." It also has a characteristic that he labels as subjectivity, which is what distinguishes consciousness from these other biological processes. Consciousness is *private,* he says; others cannot enter or observe it (Searle, 1993, p. 4, italics by M.B.S.). Dealing with music, however, may lead us to speculations about the individualizing constraint of Searle´s views on consciousness.

15.4.2 Experiences in music and the role of recognition

We can easily find examples in the domain of musical action and experience which go beyond the privacy of consciousness: music, and especially singing, has some kind of special power to connect minds, and to synchronize consciousness. It coordinates the actions and movements of groups in that performing a song in a community can establish the awareness of a shared goal, for example, by marching in synchrony. It coordinates attention to specific tasks that have to be accomplished by a group. In earlier days, before machines took over the hard work which no individual could accomplish by himor herself, such as hunting an animal, or pulling a heavy load, it was music and rhythm that made such interpersonally coordinated activities possible (Spychiger, 2008).

Strong experiences leave traces in the memory. They become part of self-perception, self-reflection, self-evaluation, and, finally, self-description—in summary, of self-concept. This directly relates to social-constructivist theories of learning and development, and to dialogical self-theory, as briefly introduced in Section 15.1. Building an identity involves people in discovering themselves through their actions: they cause changes in the current environment. From reading those, and the reactions in the faces of others, the person derives identity-relevant information.

One can summarize with Paul Ricoeur (2006, p. 42) that what really matters in these processes is *to be recognized*. The course of recognition is built upon differentiating something from something else—on *identifying* something. The recognizing person may see and know more than the recognized one does about him- or herself at that time. The reader may allow at this point the recall of a personal childhood experience about "Schlafe, schlafe, holder süsser Knabe," the Schubert lullaby, which I sang spontaneously to my 1-year-old classmates. The teacher accompanied me on the piano. What I remember, as if it was yesterday, is the delight in the teacher´s eye at the end of the three verses, and the glorious and thankful feeling I encountered in return. My state of consciousness was elevated. That very moment I felt a strong experience of being recognized. I feel safe in saying that this musical experience was immediately transferred to my musical self-concept—mainly in its dimension of singing ability—and that this sense of "I can sing," and/or "I can lighten up a teacher's eye by singing a song" became part of my musical identity. Recognition is what fulfills friendships and partnerships and is what causes growth in developmental and pedagogical milieux. One can say that my musical self-concept was built up through this event with regard to singing, with a positive valence. However, the teacher´s gratification addressed not just something that had built up that very moment. It also shed a light onto something that was already there. He had discovered it, and it caused a positive reaction in him. In response, I became self-aware of my singing ability at that very moment—by means of a social interaction.

At this point, we may perhaps consider that constructivism reaches its limits in explaining the phenomenon, namely, the happy feeling of being recognized. Similarly, Brubaker & Cooper (2000) ask, with regard to identity: "If it is fluid, how can we understand the ways in which self-understanding may harden, congeal, and crystallize? If it is constructed, how can we understand the sometimes coercive force of external identifications?" (p. 1). I myself have expressed doubts about constructivism providing the best general explanatory paradigm for musical learning and development and have suggested an additional way to look at it, in the sense that the coordinating power of music can also be a learning and developmental agent (Spychiger, 2008).

15.4.3 Measuring musical self-concept: benefits and limitations

Returning now to the basic issue of this chapter, and concluding with it, the rationale for and benefits of measuring musical self-concept can be summarized with regard to musical identity. In short, measuring musical self-concept cannot define or untangle the psychological structure of self-concept. The construct keeps its mystery as a function of consciousness.

If musical behavior is a door to human consciousness, then individual differences in musical self-concepts may shed light on the extent to which and the ways in which one makes use of this door, and how important these can be to someone. The metaphor of the door may be misleading: it is perhaps more appropriate to think that the "different doors" are not distinct from one another, in terms of neural structures, perceptions, or actions, but rather that they are interrelated and combined in many ways, according to situational needs and possibilities.

A measuring tool measures a construct as understood by researchers *so far*. It is more or less valid, and reliable, according to the quality of the test construction. It provides diagnostic results, but it is also a research tool and, as such, may enhance the accuracy and extend the boundaries of knowledge about the construct and its meaning. It promotes further research in that it operationalizes theory, makes it accessible, brings outcomes which offer new insights into and developments of the construct, advances communication about it, and invites the criticism of other researchers and theorists.

15.4.4 Open-ended: musical identity as an ongoing construction in social and self-processes

Results from MUSCI, the musical self-concept inquiry, often show that people do *not* have a positive musical self-concept. Many participants indicate that they are not musical, not talented, did not have enough determination to learn an instrument, cannot sing at all, or at least not in tune. Looking at this more closely through qualitative data, it turns out that musical self-concepts are often closely associated with emotional, social or spiritual meanings, which are relevant to a person's identity as well. What does musical identity mean to a person's identity in general? What is the relationship between identity in music, and music in identity? The two approaches both look at human experience involving music, and this relationship concerns movements between them. We try to understand mental processes that are relevant to musical experience and are also part of a person's identity.

Self-concepts do not become relevant because we really understand what measuring tools are, and what they do. Nor do we know at what times the process as hypothesized in my title—that they mediate between experience and identity—takes place in individuals, and why this may not always occur. Measurements cannot explain the phenomenon but can make researchers think and give them orientation in many kinds of designs and investigations. Thankfully, musical identity remains open-ended to the influence of any future real-life experiences.

REFERENCES

Alperson, P. (2008). The instrumentality of music. *Journal of Aesthetics and Art Criticism*, 66(1), 37–51.

Asmus, E.P. (1986). Student beliefs about the causes of success and failure in music: a study of achievement motivation. *Journal of Research in Music Education*, 34(4), 262–78.

Bandura, A. (1993). Perceived self-efficacy in cognitive development and functioning. *Educational Psychologist*, 28(2), 117–48.

von Belzen, J.A. (Ed.) (2012). *Musik und Religion. Psychologische Zugänge.* Wiesbaden: Springer.

Blumer, H. (1969). *Symbolic interactionism: perspective and method.* Englewood Cliffs, NJ: Prentice-Hall.

Brubaker, R., & Cooper, F. (2000). Beyond "Identity." *Theory and Society, 29*, 1–47.

Busch, T. (2013). *"Was glaubst du, kannst du in Musik?" Musikalische Selbstwirksamkeitserwartungen und ihre Entwicklungen zu Beginn der Sekundarstufe I.* Berlin: LIT-Verlag.

Byrne, B.M. (1996). *Measuring self-concept across the life span: issues and instrumentation.* Washington, DC.: American Psychological Association.

Deci, E.L., & Ryan, R.M. (1985). *Intrinsic motivation and self-determination in human behavior.* New York, NY: Plenum Press.

Dewey, J. (1980 [1934]). *Art as experience.* New York, NY: Perigee Books.

Donald, M. (2001). *A mind so rare. the evolution of human consciousness.* New York: Norton & Co.

Ehrenforth, K.H. (2005). *Geschichte der musikalischen Bildung. Eine Kultur-, Sozial- und Ideengeschichte in 40 Stationen.* Mainz: Schott.

Erikson, E.H. (1959). *Identity and the life cycle.* New York, NY: International Universities Press.

Gabrielsson, A. (2011). *Strong experiences with music. Music is much more than just music.* Oxford: Oxford University Press.

Giddens, A. (1991). *Modernity and self-identity: self and society in the late Modern Age.* Cambridge, MA: Polity Press.

Greve, W., Rothermund, K., & Wentura, D. (Eds.) (2005). *The personal continuity and intentional self-development.* Cambridge: Hogrefe & Huber.

Hargreaves, D.J., Miell, D., & MacDonald, R.A.R. (2002). What are musical identities, and why are they important? In: R.A.R. MacDonald, D.J. Hargreaves, & D. Miell (Eds.) *Musical identities,* 2–20. Oxford: Oxford University Press.

Harter, S. (1999). *The construction of the self: a developmental perspective.* New York: Guilford Press.

Harter, S. (2003). The development of self-representations during childhood and adolescence. In: M. R. Leary and J. P. Tangney (Eds.) *Handbook of self and identity,* pp. 610–42. New York: Guilford Press.

Hermans, H.J.M., & Gieser, T. (2012). *Handbook of dialogical self theory.* Cambridge: University Press.

James, W. (1890). *The principles of psychology.* London: Macmillan.

Joas, H.(1980/1989). *Praktische Intersubjektivität. Die Entwicklung des Werkes von G.H. Mead.* Frankfurt: Suhrkamp.

Juslin, P.N., & Sloboda, J.A. (Eds.). (2010). *Handbook of music and emotion: theory, research, applications.* New York, NY: Oxford University Press.

Katsochi, C. (2008). Student's self-beliefs and music-instruction: a literature review. In: M.M. Marin, M. Knoche, & R. Parncutt (Eds.) *Proceedings of the First International Conference of Students of Systematic Musicology (SysMuso8),* Graz, Austria, 14–15 November 2008. Available at: http://uni-graz.at/richard.parncutt/homepage%20sysmuso8/index2-Dateien/Content/Proceedings_SysMuso8/SysMuso8_Katsochi_Charikleia.pdf (Accessed March 3, 2013).

Kegan, R. (1982). *The evolving self. Problem and process in human development.* Cambridge, MA: Harvard University Press.

Kessels, U., & Hannover, B. (2004). Empfundene "Selbstnähe" als Mediator zwischen Fähigkeitsselbstkonzept und Leistungskurswahlintentionen. *Zeitschrift für Entwicklungspsychologie und Pädagogische Psychologie, 36*(3), 130–8.

Keupp, H. (2002). *Identitätskonstruktionen. Das Patchwork der Identitäten in der Spätmoderne.* Reinbek b. Hamburg: Rowohlt.

Krappmann, L. (1971). *Strukturelle Bedingungen für die Teilnahme an Interaktionsprozessen.* Stuttgart: Klett.

Law, L.N.C., & Zentner, M. (2012). Assessing musical abilities objectively: construction and validation of the profile of music perception skills. *PLOS ONE, 7*(12), 1–15.

Liljeström, S., Juslin, P.N., & Västfjäll, D. (2013). Experimental evidence of the roles of music choice, social context, and listener personality in emotional reactions to music. *Psychology of Music, 41*(5), 579–99.

Markus, H., & Nurius, P.S. (1986). Possible selves. *American Psychologist, 41,* 954–69.

Marsh, H.W. (2005). Gasteditorial: Big-Fish-Little-Pond effect on academic self-concept. *Zeitschrift für Pädagogische Psychologie, 19*(3), 119–27.

McPherson, G., Davidson, J.W., & Faulkner, R. (2012). *Music in our lives. Rethinking musical ability, development and identity.* New York: Oxford University Press.

Mead, G.H. (1934). *Mind, self and society.* Chicago: University of Chicago Press.

Merker, B. (1999/2000). Synchronous chorusing and the origins of music. *Musicae Scientiae, 3*(Special Issue 1999–2000), 59–73.

Merriam, A.P. (1964). *The anthropology of music.* Evanston: Northwestern University Press.

Mischel, W., & Morf, C.C. (2003). The self as a psycho-social dynamic processing system: A meta-perspective on a century of the self in psychology. In: M.R. Leary & J.P. Tangney (Eds.) *Handbook of self and identity,* pp. 15–43. New York: Guilford Press.

Mlejnek, R. (2013). Physically experienced reactions and music: a questionnaire study of musicians and non-musicians. In: G. Luck & O. Brabant (Eds.) *Proceedings of the 3rd International Conference on Music & Emotion (ICME3),* Jyväskylä, Finland, June 11–15, 2013. Jyväskylä: University of Jyväskylä, Department of Music.

Neisser, U. (1993). *The perceived self: ecological and interpersonal sources of self knowledge.* New York, NY: Cambridge University Press.

Oyserman, D., Elmore, K., & Smith, G. (2012). Self, self-concept, and identity. In: M. R. Leary & J. P. Tangney (Eds.) *Handbook of self and identity,* 2nd edn, pp. 69–104. New York NY: Guilford Press.

Reynolds, J.W. (1992). *Music education and student self-concept: a review and synthesis of literature.* Tampa, FL: University of South Florida.

Ricoeur, P. (2004/2006). *Wege der Anerkennung.* Frankfurt a.M.: Suhrkamp.

Sameroff, A.J. (Ed.) (2009). *The transactional model of development: how children and contexts shape each other.* Washington, DC: American Psychological Association.

Schäfer, T., Sedlmeier, P., Städtler, C., & Huron, D. (2013). The psychological functions of music listening. *Frontiers in Psychology, 4,* 1–9.

Schmitt, M.C.J. (1979). *Development and validation of a measure of self-esteem of musical ability.* Ann Arbor: ProQuest Dissertations and Theses.

Searle, J.F. (1993). The problem of consciousness. *Social Research, 60*(1), 3–16.

Shavelson, R.J., Hubner, J.J., and Stanton, G.C. (1976). Self-concept: validation of construct interpretations. *Review of Educational Research, 46*(3), 407–41.

Spychiger, M. (2007). "Nein, ich bin ja unbegabt und liebe Musik". Ausführungen zu einer mehrdimensionalen Anlage des musikalischen Selbstkonzepts'. *Diskussion Musikpädagogik, 33,* 9–20.

Spychiger, M. (2008). Musikalisches Lernen als Ko-Konstruktion? Überlegungen zum Verhältnis individueller und sozialer Dimensionen musikbezogener Erfahrung und Lernprozesse. Einführung des Konstrukts der Koordination. *Diskussion Musikpädagogik, 40,* 4–12.

Spychiger, M. (2010). *Das musikalische Selbstkonzept. Konzeption des Konstrukts als mehrdimensionale Domäne und Entwicklung eines Messverfahrens.* Final report to the Swiss National Research Foundation. Frankfurt : University of Music and Performing Art, Department 2.

Spychiger, M., & Aktas, U. (2011). Primacanta:Jedem Kind seine Stimme. Eine Intervention in 3. und 4. Klassen. Erster Zwischenbericht über die wissenschaftliche Begleitung (nicht veröffentlicht), 1st report on "Primacanta", unpublished. Frankfurt : University of Music and Performing Arts.

Spychiger, M., Gruber, L., & Olbertz, F. (2009). Musical self-concept. Presentation of a multidimensional model and its empirical analyses. In: J. Louhivuori, T. Eerola, S. Saarikallio, T. Himberg, & P.-S. Eerola (Eds.) *Proceedings of the 7th Triennial Conference of European Society for the Cognitive Sciences of Music (ESCOM 2009) Jyväskylä, Finland.* pp. 505–7. Jyväskylä: University of Jyväskylä, Department of Music.

Vispoel, W.P. (2000). Music self-concept: instrumentation, structure, and theoretical linkages. In: R.G. Craven & H.W. Marsh (Eds.) *Self-concept theory, research and practice: Advances for the new millennium,* collected papers of the Inaugural Self-Concept Enhancement and Learning Facilitation (SELF) Research Centre International Conference, Sydney, Australia, October 5–6, 2000, pp. 100–7. Sydney: University of Western Sydney, SELF Research Centre.

Wylie, R.C. (1979). *The self-concept: theory and research on selected topics,* Vol. 2. Lincoln: University of Nebraska Press.

CHAPTER 16

DEFINING THE MUSICAL IDENTITY OF "NON-MUSICIANS"

NIKKI S. RICKARD AND TANCHYUAN CHIN

16.1 INTRODUCTION

IN the very first issue of the iconic music magazine *Rolling Stone*, editor Jann Wenner (1968) wrote that the content was "not just about the music, but about the things and attitudes that music embraces." A musical identity too, is not just about being a musician—it is determined by whether music helps define "who we are." Music preferences, and an individual's knowledge and passion about music can be highly distinctive and meaningful ways to define oneself—both internally and to others. Love of music can become a foundation of identity through a range of musical pursuits, many of which never involve picking up an instrument or singing. These non-performance music activities can contribute to the process of individuation, helping to define one's "uniqueness," and therefore warrant being included within any conceptualization of a "musical identity."

In this chapter, the utility of the traditional Western concept of "a musician" will be explored. Other forms of engaging with music are recognized, and tested with regard to their impact on the engager's "identity." The benefits of broadening the conceptualization of "musicianship" to embrace non-performance-based engagement with music will be considered, and evidence presented in support of distinct music identities—in addition to the performing or creating musician. This chapter concludes that rich musical identities exist in many non-musicians, and that an awareness of these other forms of musicianship will provide insight into research and applications in music psychology.

16.2 MUSICIANS: SKILLED PRODUCERS OF MUSIC

A musician has been broadly defined as someone who performs, conducts or composes music. Some level of music training is often assumed in "a musician," and some level of overt expertise or specialized skills, is also implied (Sloboda, 2005). Years of formal music training are often taken as the primary indicator of an individual's level of musicianship. Across a range of skills, it has been argued that it takes at least 10 years, or 10,000 hours of deliberate practice to become an expert (Ericsson, Krampe, & Tesch-Romer, 1993; Gladwell, 2008). This level of sustained practice often begins at a very young age, and its intensity limits time available for other activities, which would indeed limit the category of expert musician to a few specialized elite. A child may begin to see themselves as "a musician" around 8 years of age, when their musical ability becomes differentiated enough from other children for them to become aware of it (Harter, 1999). Music lessons are, however, not sufficient for this identity to emerge. Rather, engaged participation in music, both at school and at home, seems to be important (Borthwick & Davidson, 2002; Lamont, 2002). Identifying as "a musician" also impacts on non-musical aspects of identity, particularly one's social identity, which becomes a particularly significant developmental feature during adolescence (see Chapter 28, "Music in identity at adolescence across school transition"). For others, the term "musician" is reserved for those who demonstrate a certain level of creativity in their music-making or regard "musician" as part of their core self-concept. A social identity layer is included in the definition by others who reserve the term for one who has a reputation as a musician, or for whom music making is their profession. Popular views also often include a perception that musical talent runs in families; that musicians are "born not made."

This traditional conceptualization of musicianship is generally regarded now as inadequate for the breadth of musicianship observed, both cross-culturally, and across generations. Many non-Western cultures have no equivalent term for "musician," as all members of a society produce music in some form. Music is inherent in their social life, central to their group identity and cannot be extracted from it as an individual pursuit by any one "musician." The BaYaka pygmies of Central Africa have no direct term for "music," but their musical terms are broader than individuals producing music. For instance, "massana" refers to music making and cooperative musical play among children, while "eboka" refers to ritual dance and song (Lewis, 2013). Blacking (1973) described the Venda tribe in South Africa as "the musical people," as music is universal in their society—all members of the community participate musically and all contributions (including children's) are valued (Blacking, 1973). Messenger (1958, cited in Sloboda, Davidson, & Howe, 1994) described how he "searched in vain for the 'non-musical' person" amongst the Anang Ibibo of Nigeria and instead found that "everyone can dance and sing well." Musicians can also clearly be amateur, and many have become highly skilled with no formal music training. The proliferation of computer software for composing, producing, mixing, and distributing music has enabled a new generation of highly literate but untrained music producers (Cook, 1990; Durant, 1990; North & Hargreaves, 2009). Music aptitude or actual ability (e.g., Gordon, 1965, 1989; Seashore, 1919) may therefore more accurately reflect musical skill than does the traditional index of formal music training. Nonetheless, assessments of musicianship "quality" tend to be overlooked in research on musicianship (Elliott, 1995).

The more current understanding is that everyone is born with the capacity to be a skilled musician (Sloboda, 2005). There is no doubt that genetic predispositions may complement musicianship—long fingers make long stretches on the keyboard more accessible, and absolute pitch provides an advantage for singing in tune. Musicians also tend to be more emotionally sensitive and intuitive, open to aesthetics, introverted, aloof and self-sufficient than are non-musicians (Greenberg, Müllensiefen, Lamb, & Rentfrow, 2015; Kemp, 1996). Such personality attributes could promote emotional expressivity, and enable long hours of practice alone, which will improve musical performance skill. There is however, unlikely to be any "musician" gene (or even set of genes). The observation that musicianship "runs in the family" is explained just as well by nurture, with parental influence one of the key influences in development of musicianship (Davidson, Howe, Moore, & Sloboda, 1996; McPherson, 2006). North & Hargreaves (2008) argue that apparent musical precociousness is likely to be due to a favorable environment (home, school, and peers) that supports development and expression of musical behavior.

16.3 NON-MUSICIANS: NON-PRODUCERS OF MUSIC

Research on musicians routinely contrasts musicians with "non-musicians," but reflecting the lack of agreement in definition of a musician, the criteria for selection are inconsistent. Criteria for inclusion in the category of "musicians" vary on a number of dimensions, including years of training, regularity of practice, current experience, and professional/amateur status (Samson & Zatorre, 1991; Brandler & Rammsayer, 2003; Gaser & Schlaug, 2003; Margulis, 2008; see Fig. 16.1). For example, while in several studies, musicians are defined as current or recent graduates of music schools (e.g., Schlaug, Jancke, Huang, Staiger, & Steinmetz, 1995; Chartrand & Belin, 2006), others have limited this category to performers in professional orchestras (e.g., Lotze, Scheler, Tan, Braun, & Birbaumer, 2003).

Consequently, the "non-musician" category is similarly diverse, although it is never defined as one void of any music skills. The inclusion criteria for the "non-musician" category vary widely, from no formal music training, to several years of training, to training that has lapsed for a specific amount of time. For instance, individuals with prior experience of instrument training (Bonnel, Faïta, Peretz, & Besson, 2001) or music instruction of up to 10 years (Jones, Summerell, & Marshburn, 1987) have been included in this category. The "musician" and "non-musician" categories are clearly convenient, and in

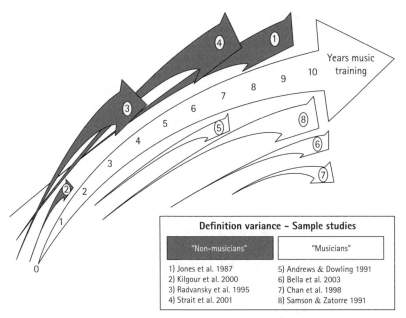

Definition variance – Sample studies

"Non-musicians"	"Musicians"
1) Jones et al. 1987	5) Andrews & Dowling 1991
2) Kilgour et al. 2000	6) Bella et al. 2003
3) Radvansky et al. 1995	7) Chan et al. 1998
4) Strait et al. 2001	8) Samson & Zatorre 1991

FIG. 16.1 Inconsistent operationalization of "musicians" (in open boxes) and "non-musician" (shaded boxes), with sample studies cited (scale is in years of music training).

certain contexts are useful; for instance, in neuroimaging or music education studies, it can be necessary to categorize participants on the basis of their music background. However, the looseness of these categories makes comparison across studies problematic. Moreover, the failure to acknowledge the multiple dimensions on which the definition is variously based risks inflating a particular characteristic, such as formal training, into a defining attribute (Margulis, 2008). In opposition to this trend, several studies have recruited participants with a range of music training (Jakobson, Cuddy, & Kilgour, 2003) or experience (Wallace, 1994; Johnson & Zatorre, 2005).

16.4 RECEPTIVE MUSICIANSHIP

The inconsistency in classifying musicianship on the basis of formal music training reflects the latent complexity of the construct. In his discussion of music expertise, Sloboda (2005) argues that there is both *productive* and *receptive* musical expertise, which is consistent with the Macquarie dictionary's definition of musicianship as the "skill and sensitivity in performing or *perception in appreciating* music" (Butler, 2009, p. 1101; our italics). Similarly, Elliott (1995, p. 42) defines music as a "multidimensional human phenomenon involving two interlocking forms of intentional human activity: music making and music listening." It is therefore remarkable that research on musical identity has focused so heavily on one form of activity (music-making), overlooking how an individual's musical identity might also be shaped by their participation in music reception (music listening).

Meaningful engagement with music can be observed in individuals listening analytically or interacting deeply with music pieces, attending concerts or music festivals, dancing, tapping or swaying to music, connecting in community choir or band performances, transcending the mundane during religious or trance rituals, or playing music games on handheld mobile devices and computers (Blacking, 1995; Veblen & Olsson, 2002; Becker, 2004; Chamorro-Premuzic & Furnham, 2007; Dillon, 2009; Gabrielsson, 2011; Lamont, 2011). Apart from personal pleasure and fulfilment, music plays a significant role in social interactions, facilitating expressions of emotion (Becker, 2001). Listening to preferred music can stimulate brain regions activated by pleasurable stimuli (Blood & Zatorre, 2001; Menon & Levitin, 2005) and induce flow in highly engaged listeners (Csikszentmihalyi, 2002). Further insight into how the highly engaged music listener differs from less engaged receivers of music, and from the highly trained and proficient performer, would therefore contribute significantly to the understanding of "musicianship."

16.5 MUSICIANSHIP OF LISTENING

The reception of music involves conscious attending to sounds, and processing of musical information to make sense of what is heard. This interpretation is shaped by personal beliefs and culture, so there are individual differences even at this fundamental level in how individuals perceive music (Elliott, 1995). Non-musicians, however, appear to make sense of music in a similar way as do trained musicians. They are able to efficiently discriminate, identify and predict key features and structures in music, categorize melodic sequences that are similar and different, apply segmentation rules to unfamiliar sequences, recall melodies on the basis of global features and identify intended emotions in a piece (Bigand, 2004; Bigand & Poulin-Charronnat, 2006; Deliege & El Ahmahdi, 1990; Krumhansl, 1995; Sloboda & Parker, 1985; Tillman, Bharucha, & Bigand, 2000).

This knowledge about music is acquired implicitly as a result of everyday exposure to music—through lullabies, play songs, and electronic media—independent of explicit music training (Bigand, 2003; Sloboda, 2005). Formal music training and performance can make this knowledge explicit, and can clearly focus and train listening skills (Sloboda, 2005). However, music training can also be quite an unreliable predictor of music listening ability, with a number of authors noting the poor relationship between years of music training and music competence (Day, 1981; Gjerdingen, 2003). For instance, there are many individuals who do not become musically competent, despite many years of music lessons, and others who become highly competent without having had formal music training. Influential self-taught musicians, for instance, include Frank Zappa, Edward Elgar, David Bowie, Jimi Hendrix, Django Reinhardt, and Arnold Schoenberg. In their review, Bigand & Poulin-Charronnat (2006) conclude that while trained musicians often perform better in tasks requiring explicit knowledge of music, the similarities in music processing ability between individuals who had received extensive conservatorium training and those considered "non-musicians" are greater than the differences. Furthermore, if sufficient time and effort is dedicated to listening, the music skills of non-trained musicians can become highly advanced (Finnas, 1989; Hedden, 1981). A strong musical identity as an expert listener could therefore clearly develop in engaged non-producers of music.

16.6 Musicianship of engagement

In addition to being a "sophisticated listener," non-musicians may identify themselves as musical in a number of other significant ways. Non-production forms of engaging with music include less observable, internal motivations—such as using music to regulate mood, forge group- or self-identity or belonging, and to facilitate relationships with family and peers (see De Nora, 1999). Again if sufficient time and effort underlies this engagement, these musical behaviors can become integrated into a non-musician's personal identity. DeNora (1999, p. 45) observes that music is used to facilitate recall of past experiences, which form the basis of one's self-identity; music is described as, "a technology for spinning the apparently 'continuous' tale of who one 'is.'" One of the most powerful illustrations of the role of music in one's identity can be seen in individuals with dementia, who have lost memory of many aspects of themselves (Baird & Samson, 2015). Regardless, music has quite a unique capacity to trigger strongly consolidated and often emotionally charged autobiographical memories in these individuals, and in this way, can represent one of the few remaining tangible elements of their self-identity. Music is often also referred to as a "mirror" in that it is used to bring aspects of one's own identity into sharper focus, but also to potentially view some of those aspects of the self in a modified way, as something more desirable (a "magic mirror," as described by DeNora, 1999). In this way, listening and identifying with music can offer a means of "trying out" different identities. As one's personal identity changes, so often does their engagement with certain styles of music.

Importantly, the limited attention to non-performance musical engagement in research is compounded by an absence of methodology suitable for identifying the "musical non-musician." Several formal measures have been developed that have begun to address this omission by more comprehensively assessing an individual's current and past musical experience, as well as their level of musical sophistication (Preisler, 1993; Müllensiefen, Gingras, Stewart, & Musil, 2012). The 141-item Music Experience Questionnaire (MEQ; Werner, Swope, & Heide, 2006) monitors how people use music in their lives, and the 40-item Music in Mood Regulation (MMR; Saarikallio, 2008) assesses how people use music to regulate their moods. The 32-item Music Use Questionnaire (MUSE; Chin & Rickard, 2012) was developed to more specifically capture the music engagement construct. This questionnaire collects information about an individual's music background, such as the years of training, frequency of music instrument playing and time spent listening to music. In addition, it assesses how individuals use music in their everyday lives (*such as for cognitive and emotional regulation, social connection, physical exercise and dance*). High scores on these factors reflect an individual identifying strongly with this type of music use, and can be considered a proxy for different "musical identities." Operationalization of musicianship via broader scope questionnaires, such as the MUSE should offer a more sensitive approach to exploring benefits of music use than the gross categorization of individuals as "musicians" or "non-musicians."

16.7 EMOTIONAL ENGAGEMENT WITH MUSIC

A capacity to respond emotionally to expectations and violations in the structure of music is acquired during childhood. Infants prefer consonant over dissonant music (Trainor, Tsang, & Cheung, 2002), and distinguish happy from sad music (Nawrot, 2003). The capacity to perceive and use the link between music structure and emotion is a key element of musical expertise (Sloboda, 2005). However, an individual's ability to recognize emotions in music is independent of music training (Juslin, 1997). One of the strongest internal motivations for pursuing long-term music activities in one's life is the experience of very strong emotions with music. Sloboda (2005) found that in people's recall of such events, these "peak" musical experiences were most likely to happen at home or with friends, and least likely to happen with teachers, or while performing. An individual's persistent music identity is therefore likely to be strongly shaped by emotional music experiences outside of formal training contexts.

Use of music for emotional purposes is one of the most commonly reported functions of music (Chamorro-Prezic & Furnham, 2007; Juslin & Sloboda, 2010). In particular, individuals routinely use everyday music to regulate their emotions. In an interview study involving 52 women between the ages of 18–78 years, DeNora (1999) found that music was used to "rev up" or "calm down," for "getting in" the mood for a particular event or for "getting out" of a bad mood. According to DeNora, the participants drew upon elaborate repertoires of music and displayed a sharp awareness of the use of music, despite not being accomplished musicians. These findings demonstrate that individuals are able to engage affectively with music, regardless of whether they had received formal music education or training. Saarikallio (2008, 2011) reported that people use music in a range of ways across the life span to manage their moods, including for diversion, discharge, solace, entertainment, and revival. For instance, older adults used music for "emotional work" to cope with identity changes associated with aging. She also demonstrated that strategies were used by individuals in a similar way regardless of music background, although musicians showed a greater awareness of using music for mood regulation than did non-musicians. Chin & Rickard (2012) found the strongest factor emerging in their study of individual styles of music use was for cognitive and emotion regulation purposes. This style of music engagement accounted for nearly, 20% of the variance in scores on the MUSE questionnaire. This was considerably more than that accounted for by the second highest loading factor, engaged production of music (the

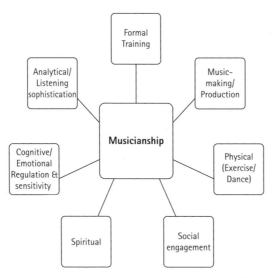

FIG. 16.2 Multidimensional conceptualization of musicianship, utilizing evidence from the literature.

Including data from *Music Perception*, 29(4) Chin, T.C., & Rickard, N.S. The Music USE (MUSE) Questionnaire: an instrument to measure engagement in music, pp. 429–46, 2012, University of California Press.

only performance-specific factor emerging from the data). Importantly, the two styles of engaging with music were not correlated, indicating one can identify as a user of music for emotional/cognitive regulation independently of the traditional "musician" identity.

While emotional engagement with music appears to be a dominant use, other potential music identities adopted by non-producers of music may include the social music user (e.g., the music "party animal"), the music exerciser (e.g., the jogger who is motivated by their portable music device), the dancer (e.g., any young aspirant in the popular television show, "So You Think You Can Dance?"), the intellectual music listener (e.g., the music critic), and the spiritual music user (e.g., someone who is energized by the evangelical choir). In an analysis of how individuals used music in everyday life, Chin & Rickard (2012) found, however, that these styles accounted for less variance (typically less than 10%) than "engaged performer of music" or "user of music for cognitive or emotional regulation" (see Fig. 16.2). This evidence therefore suggests that these two styles of music use are most often likely to emerge as part of an individual's musical identity.

16.8 UTILITY OF A BROADER CONCEPTUALIZATION OF "MUSICIANSHIP"

A dominant theme of psychological research on musicianship has been the investigation of neurological, cognitive, or socio-emotional benefits of music training. Musicians who begin their training from an early age (typically around 7 years) show evidence of cortical growth or enhanced connectivity, as well as more efficient functioning, in a range of brain areas. This includes observations of a larger corpus callosum, greater cerebellar volume, enlarged Heschl's gyrus, and changes in the primary motor cortex and Broca's area in musicians than in non-musicians (see Koelsch, Siebel, & Fritz, 2010; Merrett & Wilson, 2012, for reviews).

There is growing evidence that the brain may also be changed by non-performance music experiences. Neurological evidence demonstrates that listening to music can activate numerous brain regions, extending well beyond the auditory cortex. This activation involves a widespread bilateral network of frontal, temporal, parietal, and subcortical areas related to attention, semantic and music-syntactic processing, memory, and motor functions (Bhattacharya, Petsche, Feldmann, & Rescher, 2001; Janata, Birk, Van Horn, Leman, Tillman, & Bharucha, 2002; Koelsch, Kasper, Sammler, Schulze, Gunter, & Friederici, 2004; Popescu, Otsuka, & Ioannides, 2004). Emotional processing during music listening further recruits an interconnected network of subcortical and cortical brain regions, including prefrontal regions (e.g., orbitofrontal and ventral medial prefrontal cortex), temporal lobe regions (superior temporal gyrus), and limbic system and related structures (e.g., hippocampus, cingulate, nucleus accumbens, amygdala, and ventral striatum; Blood, Zatorre, Bermudez, & Evans, 1999; Blood & Zatorre, 2001; Brown, Martinez, & Parsons, 2004; Koelsch, Fritz, Schulze, Alsop, & Schlaug, 2005; Menon & Levitin, 2005; Koelsch, Fritz, von Cramon, Muller, & Friederici, 2006). These regions correspond to brain systems associated with reward and emotion, which partly accounts for the observation that music listening has become one of the most popular indoor leisure choices for many individuals (North, Hargreaves, & O'Neill, 2000; Rentfrow & Gosling, 2003). It may also explain why music listening can promote cognitive recovery and improve mood following stroke (Särkämö et al, 2008), and may imply some level of listening-related neuroplasticity. While learning a musical instrument has often been cited as a means of stimulating synaptic plasticity, there is good reason then to expect also that active listening and engagement with music would enrich one's auditory and emotional environment, and have the potential to promote neuroplasticity.

Musicians have been found to demonstrate superior performance when compared with non-musicians on a diverse range of cognitive tasks. The range of cognitive tests enhanced by music training for which reasonable evidence exists includes mathematics, literacy, spatial-temporal performance, general intelligence, and verbal memory (see Schellenberg, 2001, and Gill & Rickard, 2012 for reviews). There has been less investigation into the factors which mediate this superiority. Schellenberg (2004) notes that music training involves long periods of focused attention, reading, memorizing, and well-coordinated execution of extended musical passages, as well as daily practice and mastery of technical skills (Schellenberg, 2004). He speculates that this combination of experiences may account for the positive impact music training has on cognition, in particular, during childhood years, when brain development is highly plastic and sensitive to environmental enrichment (Huttenlocher, 2002). Researchers demonstrating benefits of music training on mathematical performance have also emphasized the importance of music listening and appreciation, in addition to performing, in their programs (Cheek & Smith, 1999; Gardiner, Fox, Knowles, & Jeffrey, 1996).Rickard, Vasquez, Murphy, Toukhsati, & Gill (2010) argued in fact that an improvement in listening skills (rather than instrumental proficiency) was likely to account for the verbal memory improvements they observed in primary school children following a year of enhanced music classes. As reviewed in the previous section, listening to music involves advanced auditory discrimination skills, which become refined as a result of extensive exposure to, and analysis of, complex music (Lerdahl & Jackendoff, 1983). Creativity may also be heightened as a result of music listening, as could attention, learning and memory (Judde & Rickard, 2010; Schellenberg, Nakata, Hunter, & Tamoto, 2007). This highlights the potential for at least some of the cognitive benefits observed in musicians to be also gained in non-producing "musicians."

Verbal memory for instance, is generally superior in musicians than non-musicians, an effect observed in those with extensive music training (at least Grade VIII Conservatory training; Kilgour, Jakobson, & Cuddy, 2000) to children with between 1 and 5 years classical music training; Ho, Cheung, & Chan, 2003). This effect has been attributed to refined temporal order processing skills (Jakobson, Cuddy, & Kilgour, 2003), which is also a skill that would be developed in advanced music listeners. Non-musicians who report extensive or highly engaging music listening styles could therefore also be expected to develop advanced verbal memory skills. In support, Chin & Rickard (2010) found that extensive listening to music predicted improved verbal learning and memory performance, even once music performance and intelligence were controlled. Music listening, in fact, predicted most indices of verbal learning and memory, and more so than did music training. In addition, individuals who reported using music in an emotional way (as measured by the Brief Music Experience Questionnaire) showed superior verbal learning and memory to other individuals.

A number of studies in which musicians demonstrate superior perception of emotional cues in auditory stimuli have also been reported. For example, individuals classified as musicians (at least 10 years of regular music training and/or with onset of music training prior to 8 years of age) show enhanced auditory brainstem responses to emotional cues in speech (Strait et al., 2009). Musically-trained adults (with on average 8 years musical training) also demonstrate more accurate prediction of happy, sad, fearful, and angry emotions in tone sequences that mimicked speech prosody (Thompson, Schellenberg, & Husain, 2004). In addition, these authors reported that children allocated to a year of music lessons (keyboard or singing) were more accurate at identifying emotional cues in speech than children who did not have the classes. Importantly, however, they found similar improvements in children receiving a year of drama lessons. In a separate investigation of emotion perception in a sample of Canadian undergraduates, Trimmer & Cuddy (2008) found that music training (as measured by an extensive music training survey) was not associated with emotion perception in speech. Instead, emotional intelligence significantly predicted emotion perception. It is highly plausible then that individuals highly engaged with music for emotional purposes are likely to have enhanced emotional capacity.

Identifying a broader range of musical identities may even help identify benefits of musicianship that are not observed in traditional musicians. In two recent studies (Chin & Rickard, 2013, 2014), non-performance related engagement with music was found to be more positively associated with a variety of aspects of mental health (depression and anxiety) and well-being (eudaimonic and hedonic) than was engaged production of music. Use of music for cognitive and emotional regulation purposes was positively associated with emotional, social, and psychological well-being—and negatively associated with depression and anxiety—via an adaptive emotion regulation strategy, reappraisal. In contrast, engaged productive use of music was *negatively* associated with well-being (but positively associated with depression and anxiety), via the often maladaptive emotion regulation strategy of suppression. These findings are the first to demonstrate that receptive engagement with music may be at times more beneficial for mental health and well-being than is production of music. Prediction of these indices from other musical identities (social connectors, dancers, and listeners) was further distinguished, providing validation of these distinct types of music engagement. Moreover, substantially more insight into the benefits of music use was enabled by distinguishing between these various types of musicianship (rather than grouping them collectively as "non-musicians"), and investigating them in their own right (rather than simply as controls).

16.9 CONCLUSIONS

In this chapter, the importance of acknowledging a wide variety of musical identities was explored. Highly trained musicians experience strong identification with the profession of music, and being musical shapes their lives, even at the most fundamental level of their brain anatomy. "Non-musicians" however, are rarely non-musical. Due to extensive exposure, most individuals are in the very least, sophisticated listeners of music. However, music can also engage listeners intensely in other ways, which can become central in defining "who we are." Individuals can become respected critical analysts of music, skilled users of music to manage their moods and thoughts, or socially outgoing "gig pigs." These musical identities are independent of music training and require no music production.

The utility of incorporating a more multidimensional conception of "musicianship" is validated empirically, with benefits of music training, music listening, and emotional engagement with music demonstrated across a range of neurobiological and cognitive studies. There is evidence that these effects might be mediated by neurological plasticity and a variety of cognitive skills, including auditory processing skill and emotional intelligence. Certain types of receptive musicianship appear to yield greater benefits than productive musicianship on some key mental health outcome measures. This highlights the importance of recognizing these other forms of musicianship, and potentially promoting identification with these forms of musical engagement. The inherent value in becoming an advanced listener of music, or in using music to manage one's own moods and thoughts, should be highly valued. This shift in perception of "musicianship" could also be acknowledged in educational and therapeutic settings. For instance, an alternative pathway for students who do not engage with instrumental performance could be to encourage a more extensive repertoire of analytical music listening and evaluation skills. In addition to improvisation, song-writing and music-making, the development of adaptive coping and emotion regulation training using personalized playlists could become a more frequently utilized goal of music therapy sessions. To summarize, the study of musicianship will benefit from broader recognition of the extensive ways people engage and identify with music. Extending on Jann Wenner, "musicianship" is *also* "about the things and attitudes that music embraces," and not just about producing music.

REFERENCES

Baird, A. & Samson, S. (2015). Music and dementia. In: E. Altenmüller, F. Boller, & S. Finger (Eds.), *Music, neurology, and neuroscience: history and modern perspectives* (Progress in Brain Research Series). London: Elsevier.

Becker, J. (2001). Anthropological perspectives on music and emotion. In: J. A. Sloboda & P. N. Juslin (Eds.) *Music and emotion: theory and research*, pp. 135–60. Oxford: Oxford University Press.

Becker, J.O. (2004). *Deep listeners: music, emotion, and trancing.* Bloomington: Indiana University Press.

Bella, S.D., Peretz, I., & Aronoff, N. (2003). Time course of melody recognition: a gating paradigm. *Perception and Psychophysics*, 65, 1019–28.

Bhattacharya, J., Petsche, H., Feldmann, U., & Rescher, B. (2001). EEG gamma-band phase synchronization between posterior and frontal cortex during mental rotation in humans. *Neuroscience Letters*, 311, 29–32.

Bigand, E. (2003). More about the musical expertise of musically untrained listeners. *Annals of the New York Academy of Sciences*, 999, 304–12.

Bigand, E. (2004). L'oreille musicale experte peut-elle se developper par l'ecoute passive de la musique? *Revue de Neuropsychologie*, 14, 191–221.

Bigand, E. & Poulin-Charronnat, B. (2006). Are we "experienced listeners"? A review of the musical capacities that do not depend on formal musical training. *Cognition*, 100, 100–30.

Blacking, J. (1973). *How musical is man?* Seattle, WA: University of Washington Press.

Blacking, J. (1995). *Music, culture and experience.* London: University of Chicago Press.

Blood, A.J. & Zatorre, R.J. (2001). Intensely pleasurable responses to music correlate with activity in brain regions implicated in reward and emotion. *Proceedings of the National Academy of Sciences of the United States of America*, 98, 11818–23.

Blood, A.J., Zatorre, R.J., Bermudez, P., & Evans, A.C. (1999). Emotional responses to pleasant and unpleasant music correlate with activity in paralimbic brain regions. *Nature Neuroscience*, 2, 382–7.

Bonnel, A.M., Faïta, F., Peretz, I., & Besson, M. (2001). Divided attention between lyrics and tunes of operatic songs: Evidence for independent processing. *Perception and Psychophysics*, 63, 1201–13.

Borthwick, S. & Davidson, S. (2002). Developing a child's identity as a musician: a family "script" perspective. In: R. MacDonald, D. Hargreaves, & D. Miell (Eds.) *Musical identities*, pp. 60–78. Oxford: Oxford University Press.

Brandler, S. & Rammsayer, T.H. (2003). Differences in mental abilities between musicians and non-musicians. *Psychology of Music*, 31, 123–38.

Brown, S., Martinez, M.J., & Parsons, L.M. (2004). Passive music listening spontaneously engages limbic and paralimbic systems. *NeuroReport*, 15, 2033–7.

Butler, S. (Ed.). (2009). *Macquarie dictionary*. Sydney: Macquarie Dictionary Publishers.

Chamorro-Premuzic, T. & Furnham, A. (2007). Personality and music: can traits explain how people use music in everyday life? *British Journal of Psychology*, 98, 175–85.

Chan, A.S., Ho, Y.C., & Cheung, M.C. (1998). Music training improves verbal memory. *Nature*, 396, 128.

Chartrand, J.P. & Belin, P. (2006). Superior voice timbre processing in musicians. *Neuroscience Letters*, 405, 154–67.

Cheek, J.M., & Smith, L.R. (1999). Music training and mathematics achievement. *Adolescence*, 34, 759–61.

Chin, T.C. & Rickard, N.S. (2010). Nonperformance, as well as performance, based music engagement predicts verbal recall. *Music Perception*, 27, 197–208.

Chin, T.C. & Rickard, N.S. (2012). The Music USE (MUSE) Questionnaire: an instrument to measure engagement in music. *Music Perception*, 29(4), 429–46.

Chin, T.C., & Rickard, N. S. (2013). Emotion regulation strategy mediates both positive and negative relationship between music uses and well-being. *Psychology of Music*, 42(5), 692–713.

Chin, T.C. & Rickard, N.S. (2014). Beyond positive and negative trait affect: flourishing through music engagement. *Psychology of Well-Being: Theory, Research and Practice*, 4, 25.

Cook, N. (1990). *Music, imagination, and culture*. Oxford: Oxford University Press.

Csikszentmihalyi, M. (2002). *Flow: the classic work on how to achieve happiness*. London: Rider.

Davidson, J., Howe, M., Moore, D., & Sloboda, J. (1996). The role of parental influences in the development of musical performance. *British Journal of Developmental Psychology*, 14(4), 399–412.

Day, R.S. (1981). Music ability and patterns of cognition. In: *Documentary Report of the Ann Arbor Symposium: National Symposium on the Applications of Psychology to the Teaching and Learning of Music*, pp. 270–84. Reston, VA: Music Educators National Conference.

Deliege, I. & El Ahmahdi, A. (1990). Mechanisms of cue extraction in musical groupings: a study of perception, on *Sequenz VI* for viola solo by Luciano Berio. *Psychology of Music*, 19, 18–44.

DeNora, T. (1999). Music as a technology of the self. *Poetics*, 27, 31–56.

Dillon, S. (2009). Examining meaningful engagement: musicology and virtual music making environments. In: E. Mackinlay, B. Bartleet, & K. Barney (Eds.) *Musical islands*, pp. 297–310. Newcastle upon Tyne: Cambridge Scholars Publishing.

Durant, A. (1990). A new day for music? Digital technology in contemporary music-making. In: P. Hayward (Ed.) *Culture, technology & creativity in the late twentieth century*, pp. 175–96. London: Arts Council and Libbey Press.

Elliott, D. (1995). *Music matters: a new philosophy of music education*. Oxford: Oxford University Press.

Ericsson , K.A., Krampe, R.T., & Tesch-Romer, C. (1993). The role of deliberate practice in the acquisition of expert performance. *Psychological Review*, 100(3), 363–406.

Finnas, L. (1989). How can musical preferences be modified? *Bulletin of the Council for Research in Music Education*, 102, 1–58.

Gabrielsson, A. (2011). *Strong experiences with music*. Oxford: Oxford University Press.

Gardiner, M.F., Fox, A., Knowles, F., & Jeffrey, D. (1996). Learning improved by arts training. *Nature*, 381, 284.

Gaser, C. & Schlaug, G. (2003). Brain structures differ between musicians and non-musicians. *Journal of Neuroscience*, 23, 9240–5.

Gill, A. & Rickard, N.S. (2012). Non-music benefits of school-based music training. In: N.S. Rickard & K. McFerran (Eds.) *Lifelong engagement in music: benefits for mental health and well-being*, pp. 57–72. New York, NY: Nova Publishers.

Gjerdingen, R. (2003). What to listen for in rock: a stylistic analysis. *Music Perception*, 20, 491–7.

Gladwell, M. (2008). *Outliers*. London: Little, Brown and Company.

Gordon, E.E. (1965). *Musical aptitude profile*. Chicago: GIA.

Gordon, E.E. (1989). *Advanced measures of music audiation*. Chicago: GIA.

Greenberg, D.M., Müllensiefen, D., Lamb, M.E., & Rentfrow, P.J. (2015). Personality predicts musical sophistication. *Journal of Research in Personality*, 58, 154–58.

Harter, S. (1999). *The construction of self: a developmental perspective*. New York: Guilford Press.

Hedden, S.K. (1981). Music listening skills and music listening preferences. *Bulletin of the Council for Research in Music Education*, 65, 16–26.

Ho, Y.C., Cheung, M.C., & Chan, A.S. (2003). Music training improves verbal but not visual memory: cross-sectional and longitudinal explorations in children. *Neuropsychology*, 17, 439–50.

Huttenlocher, P.R. (2002). *Neural plasticity: the effects of environment on the development of the cerebral cortex*. Cambridge, MA: Harvard University Press.

Jakobson, L.S., Cuddy, L.L., & Kilgour, A.R. (2003). Time-tagging: a key to musicians' superior memory. *Music Perception*, 20, 307–13.

Janata, P., Birk, J.L., Van Horn, J.D., Leman, M., Tillmann, B., & Bharucha, J.J. (2002). The cortical topography of tonal structures underlying Western music. *Science*, 298, 2167–70.

Johnson, J.A., & Zatorre, R.J. (2005). Attention to simultaneous unrelated auditory and visual events: behavioral and neural correlates. *Cerebral Cortex*, 15, 1609–20.

Jones, M.R., Summerell, L., & Marshburn, E. (1987). Recognizing melodies: a dynamic interpretation. *Quarterly Journal of Experimental Psychology*, 39, 89–121.

Judde, S. & Rickard, N.S. (2010). The effect of post-learning presentation of music on long-term word-list retention. *Neurobiology of Learning and Memory*, 94, 13–20.

Juslin, P.N. (1997). Emotional communication in music performance: a functionalist perspective and some data. *Music Perception*, 14, 383–418.

Juslin, P.N. & Sloboda, J.A. (2010). *Handbook of music and emotion*. Oxford: Oxford University Press.

Kemp, A. (1996). *The musical temperament*. Oxford: Oxford University Press.

Kilgour, A.R., Jakobson, L.S., & Cuddy, L.L. (2000). Music training and rate of presentation as mediators of text and song recall. *Memory & Cognition*, 28, 700–10.

Koelsch, S., Fritz, T., Schulze, K., Alsop, D., & Schlaug, G. (2005). Adults and children processing music: an fMRI study. *NeuroImage*, 25, 1068–76.

Koelsch, S., Fritz, T., von Cramon, D.Y., Muller, K., & Friederici, A.D. (2006). Investigating emotion with music: an fMRI study. *Human Brain Mapping*, 27, 239–50.

Koelsch, S., Kasper, E., Sammler, D., Schulze, K., Gunter, T., & Friederici, A.D. (2004). Music, language and meaning: brain signatures of semantic processing. *Nature Neuroscience*, 7, 302–7.

Koelsch, S., Siebel, W.A., & Fritz, T. (2010). Functional neuroimaging. In: P.N. Juslin & J.A. Sloboda (Eds.) *Handbook of music and emotion*, pp. 313–45. Oxford: Oxford University Press.

Krumhansl, C.L. (1995). Music psychology and music theory: problems and prospects. *Music Theory Spectrum*, 17, 53–90.

Lamont, A. (2002). Musical identities and the school environment. In: R. MacDonald, D. Hargreaves, & D. Miell (Eds.) *Musical identities*, pp. 41–59. Oxford: Oxford University Press.

Lamont, A. (2011). University students' strong experiences of music: pleasure, engagement, and meaning. *Musicae Scientiae*, 15, 229–49.

Lerdahl, F. & Jackendoff, R. (1983). *A generative theory of tonal music*. Cambridge, MA: MIT Press.

Lewis, J. (2013). A cross-cultural perspective on the significance of music and dance to culture and society. In: M. Arbib (Ed.) *Language, music and the brain: a mysterious relationship*, pp. 45–66. Cambridge, MA: MIT Press.

Lotze, M., Scheler, G., Tan, H.R., Braun, C., & Birbaumer, N. (2003). The musician's brain: functional imaging of amateurs and professionals during performance and imagery. *NeuroImage*, 20, 1817–29.

Margulis, E. (2008). Neuroscience, the food of musical culture? *Review of General Psychology*, 12, 159–69.

McPherson, G. (2006). *The child as a musician: a handbook of musical development*. New York: Oxford University Press.

Menon, V. & Levitin, D.J. (2005). The rewards of music listening: response and physiological connectivity of the mesolimbic system. *NeuroImage*, 28, 175–84.

Merrett, D.L & Wilson, S.J. (2012). Music and neural plasticity. In: N.S. Rickard & K. McFerran (Eds.) *Lifelong engagement in music: benefits for mental health and well-being*, pp. 119–160. New York: Nova Publishers.

Müllensiefen, D., Gingras, B., Stewart, L., & Musil, J.J. (2012). Goldsmiths Musical Sophistication Index (Gold-MSI) v1.0: Technical Report and Documentation Revision 0.3. [Online   http://www.gold.ac.uk/media/documents-by-section/departments/psychology/Gold-MSIv10_Documentation.pdf. [Accessed 17 February, 2016].

Nawrot, E.S. (2003). The perception of emotional expression in music: evidence from infants, children, and adults. *Psychology of Music*, 31, 75–92.

North, A.C. & Hargreaves, D.J. (2008). *The social and applied psychology of music*. Oxford: Oxford University Press.

North, A.C. & Hargreaves, D.J. (2009). The power of music. *Psychologist*, 22(12), 1012–15.

North, A.C., Hargreaves, D.J., & O'Neill, S.A. (2000). The importance of music to adolescents. *British Journal of Education Psychology*, 70, 255–72.

Popescu, M., Otsuka, A., & Ioannides, A. (2004). Dynamics of brain activity in motor and frontal cortical areas during music listening: a magnetoencephalographic study. *NeuroImage*, 21, 1622–38.

Preisler, A. (1993). The influence of spectral composition of complex tones and of musical experience on the perceptibility of virtual pitch. *Perception Psychophysics*, 54, 589–603.

Radvansky, G.A., Fleming, K.J., & Simmons, J.A. (1995). Timbre reliance in nonmusicians' and musicians' memory for melodies. *Music Perception*, 13, 127–40.

Rentfrow, P.J. & Gosling, S.D. (2003). The do re mi's of everyday life. The structure and personality correlates of music preferences. *Journal of Personality and Social Psychology*, 84, 1236–56.

Rickard, N.S., Vasquez, T., Murphy, F, Toukhsati, S.R., & Gill, A. (2010). Benefits of a classroom based instrumental music program on verbal memory of primary school children. *Australian Journal of Music Education*, 1, 36–47.

Samson, S., & Zatorre, R.J. (1991). Recognition memory for text and melody for songs after unilateral temporal lobe lesion: evidence for dual encoding. *Journal of Experimental psychology: Learning, Memory & Cognition*, 17, 793–804.

Saarikallio, S. (2008). Music in mood regulation: Initial scale development. *Musicae Scientiae*, 12, 291–309.

Saarikallio, S. (2011). Music as emotional self-regulation throughout adulthood. *Psychology of Music*, 39, 307–27.

Särkämö T., Tervaniemi, M., Laitinen, S., et al. (2008). Music listening enhances cognitive recovery and mood after middle cerebral artery stroke. *Brain*, 131, 866–76.

Schellenberg, E.G. (2001). Music and nonmusical abilities. *Annals of the New York Academy of Sciences*, 930, 355–71.

Schellenberg, E.G. (2004). Music lessons enhance IQ. *Psychological Science*, 15, 511–14.

Schellenberg, E.G., Nakata, T., Hunter, P.G., & tamoto, S. (2007). Exposure to music and cognitive performance: tests of children and adults. *Psychology of Music*, 35, 5–19.

Schlaug, G., Jancke, L., Huang, Y., Staiger, J.F., & Steinmetz, H. (1995). Increased corpus callosum size in musicians. *Neuropsychologia*, 33, 1047–55.

Seashore, C.E. (1919). *Seashore measures of musical talents*. New York, NY: Psychological Corporation.

Sloboda, J. A. (2005). *Exploring the musical mind*. New York, NY: Oxford University Press.

Sloboda, J.A., Davidson, J.W., & Howe, M.J.A. (1994). Is everyone musical? *The Psychologist*, 7(8), 349–54.

Sloboda, J.A. & Parker, D.H.H. (1985). Immediate recall of melodies. In: P. Howell, I. Cross, & R. West (Eds.) *Musical structure and cognition*, pp. 143–67. London: Academic Press.

Strait, D.L., Kraus, N., Skoe, E., & Ashley, R. (2009). Musical experience and neural efficiency: effects of training on subcortical processing of vocal expressions of emotion. *European Journal of Neuroscience*, 29, 661–8.

Thompson, W.F., Schellenberg, E.G., & Husain, G. (2004). Decoding speech prosody: do music lessons help? *Emotion*, 4, 46–64.

Tillman, B., Bharucha, J.J., & Bigand, E. (2000). Implicit learning of tonality: a self-organizing approach. *Psychological Review*, 107, 885–913.

Trainor, L.J., Tsang, C.D., & Cheung, V.H.W. (2002). Preference for consonance in two-month-old infants. *Music Perception*, 20, 185–92.

Trimmer, C.G. & Cuddy, L.L. (2008). Emotional intelligence, not music training, predicts recognition of emotional speech prosody. *Emotion*, 8, 838–49.

Veblen, K. & Olsson, B. (2002). Community music: toward an international overview. In: R. Colwell & C. Richardson (Eds.) *New handbook of music teaching and learning*, pp. 730–53. New York, NY: Oxford University Press.

Wallace, W.T. (1994). Memory for music: effect of melody on recall of text. *Journal of Experimental Psychology*, 20, 1471–85.

Wenner, J. (1968) *Rolling Stone*, 1.

Werner, P.D., Swope, A.J., & Heide, F.J. (2006). The music experience questionnaire: development and correlates. *Journal of Psychology*, 140, 329–45.

CHAPTER 17

THE SOCIAL PSYCHOLOGICAL UNDERPINNINGS OF MUSICAL IDENTITIES

A Study on how Personality Stereotypes are formed from Musical Cues

DAVID M. GREENBERG AND PETER J. RENTFROW

WHETHER wearing a t-shirt emblazoned with the name of a favorite band, blaring music loudly so that others can hear, or displaying a list of preferred bands on Facebook, music is often used in the service of self-expression. Presumably, this is because people believe that if you know something about the music they like, you can gain a glimpse of who they are. Once you know this about them, you can then decide to learn more about their preferences, values, or beliefs. If you find someone who likes the same style of music as you, then you'll probably get along with them; find someone who likes the same band as you, and you may have found a new best friend; and if you find someone who shares the same all-time favorite song as you, particularly if the song is rare and obscure, then you may have even found a soul-mate; but if you don't share the same preferences, you may choose to avoid them, concluding that the differences in musical preferences suggest that you are unlikely to see eye-to-eye on other matters, and thus not worth further time and effort. Even worse, if you find someone who absolutely despises your favorite music, then prepare for battle because you may have just met your archenemy. This begs the question, do our musical identities reveal about who we are and how do they shape our social lives?

Theory and research in music psychology has greatly informed our understanding of the psychological experiences associated with music listening. We know, for example, that music can "get under our skin" and affect the way we feel, from eliciting feelings of comfort, relaxation, and sadness, to inspiration, joy, and excitement. It can motivate us, help us to concentrate, and increase our understanding of others' thoughts and feelings. If the conditions are just right, music can evoke strong, intense, and peak experiences, drowning out the surrounding world, and absorbing the listener into the music so that the song and person are one. There is more to music than the periods of time when we are listening to it—music plays a role in our lives even when the play button is switched off.

Over the past decade, research in the field has begun to take a broader perspective by focussing on the social psychological aspects of musical experiences. Work in this area focusses less on the effects of music on mood or arousal, and instead examines the ways in which music relates to identity, social relations, and group processes. The research findings emerging in this area suggest that:

- Music is a prominent aspect of self-identity, especially for young people (e.g., North & Hargreaves, 1999; Rentfrow & Gosling, 2006; Rentfrow, McDonald, & Oldmeadow, 2009).
- The music people like is linked to their personalities, values, and beliefs (e.g., Delsing, ter Bogt, Engels, & Meeus, 2008; Rentfrow & Gosling, 2003; Zweigenhaft, 2008).
- Musical preferences can serve as a medium for establishing attraction and closeness in relationships (e.g., Selfhout, Branje, ter Bogt, & Meeus, 2009; Zillmann & Bhatia, 1989; Boer, Fischer, Strack, Bond, Lo, & Lam, 2011).

This chapter focuses on the social psychological aspects of music and presents data demonstrating the features that shape musical identities. First, we focus on the psychological underpinnings of musical identities—how does the music people listen to relate to self-identity and personality processes? Secondly, we consider the role music plays in interpersonal relationships—what is the interplay between musical identities and group processes? Next, we examine the impact of using music in the service of self-expression—what information is communicated about individuals through their musical preferences? Specifically, we present data that investigates the stereotypes linked to musical preferences, and how both auditory features of music and genre classifications impact associations between stereotypes and preferences. We conclude the chapter by considering directions for future research.

17.1 PSYCHOLOGICAL UNDERPINNINGS OF MUSICAL IDENTITIES

17.1.1 Self-identity

Listening to music can elicit feelings, beliefs, and personal qualities that we seek to embrace, it can remind us of who we once were and help us realize how far we have come, and it can inform and illuminate our future aspirations. According to DeNora

(2000), the reflexive process of remembering and constructing identities while listening to music can serve as a form of self-affirmation and insight. The associations that are made when listening to music may resonate with individuals because they bring to mind qualities they perceive in themselves or that they aspire to possess. According to research by Tarrant, North, & Hargreaves (2002), the social connotations that are evoked by music are a key factor in determining musical preferences. To the extent that individuals are attracted to a style of music, they align their personal self-image with the perceived characteristics associated with that music.

There is empirical evidence consistent with the view that music contributes to the development of identity. Indeed, results from several studies indicate that people believe their musical preferences represent who they are—their personalities, values, and lifestyles (North & Hargreaves, 1999; North, Hargreaves, & O'Neill, 2000; Rentfrow & Gosling, 2003). There is even evidence showing that individuals believe music reveals more about their identities than their preferences for clothing, films, books, or hobbies (Rentfrow & Gosling, 2003; Lonsdale & North, 2011). Results from these studies converge on the conclusion that individuals derive a sense of identity from the music they listen to, which in turn functions as a symbolic representation of the self.

In addition to facilitating self-exploration, music can also foster self-esteem and self-worth. Drawing on social identity theory, some studies have examined how affiliation with music-based social groups (e.g., punks, Goths, Emo, etc.) relates to self-esteem. Thus far, research in this area suggests that people assimilate the characteristics of their preferred music-based social group by endorsing the same values, wearing similar styles of clothing, and pursuing similar lifestyles. Furthermore, the degree to which individuals identify with a group with the same musical preferences increases in-group favoritism and out-group derogation (e.g., North & Hargreaves, 1999; Tarrant et al., 2002; Tekman & Hortaçsu, 2002). In this way, aligning one's identity with a particular musical style or artist can provide a sense of meaning, belonging, and act as a buffer against threats to the self.

Music can also satisfy a need to be different. Consider, for example, the record store clerks in Hornby's *High Fidelity,* who take pride in their knowledge and appreciation of obscure and unconventional styles of music. Their preferences place them in an elite group of music aficionados and at the same time make them distinct. Optimal distinctiveness theory provides a useful perspective for understanding how music could foster feelings of uniqueness (Brewer, 1991). According to this perspective, individuals have conflicting needs for similarity and uniqueness—too much similarity is insufficiently self-defining but too much uniqueness is isolating—so they strive to attain an optimal level of distinctiveness. Recent research indicates that music can be very effective for obtaining optimal distinctiveness. For example, work by Abrams (2009) revealed that people with preferences for musical styles that were moderately popular (and therefore optimally distinct) invested more resources and commitment to their musical identities than people who preferred musical styles that were either mainstream or highly obscure.

17.1.2 Personality

Given the prominent role music plays in self-identity, a reasonable question is whether there is a connection between the music people listen to and their personalities; after all, many researchers have argued that personality is the foundation for identity development (e.g., McCrae & Costa, 2008). Most of the research concerned with music and personality focuses on individual differences in preferences for music and how those preferences relate to various personality characteristics. Consistent with some of the research on self-identity and music, the assumption underlying research on personality and musical preferences is that people seek out styles of music that reinforce and reflect aspects of their personalities, attitudes, and self-views (Rentfrow & Gosling, 2003; Colley, 2008; Delsing et al., 2008; Zweigenhaft, 2008; Schäfer & Sedlmeier, 2009).

Because music is such a broad and multifaceted construct, much of the research concerned with musical preferences and personality has focussed on first identifying the structure of these preferences. Essentially, this research seeks to understand how preferences for particular styles of music group together in order to develop a framework for conceptualizing musical preferences and investigating their associations with personality. The most common approach for evaluating this is through factor analysis, which identifies groups of variables that share common variance. Several studies have examined the structure of preferences, and although the methods and styles of music assessed are not entirely the same, all the studies indicate that there is a structure underlying musical preferences (Rentfrow & Gosling, 2003; George, Stickle, Rachid, & Wopnford, 2007; Colley, 2008; Delsing et al., 2008; Schäfer & Sedlmeier, 2009; Rentfrow & McDonald, 2010; Rentfrow, Goldberg, & Levitin, 2011; Dunn, de Ruyter, & Bouwhuis, 2012; Rentfrow, Goldberg, Stillwell, Kosinksi, Gosling, & Levitin, 2012). For example, Rentfrow & Gosling (2003) examined individual differences in preferences for 14 broad music genres in three US samples and found four preference factors. A study of music preferences among Dutch adolescents assessed self-reported preferences for 11 music genres and also observed four factors (Delsing et al., 2008). An investigation of preferences for 11 music genres in a small sample of British university students revealed four factors for women and five for men (Colley, 2008). George et al. (2007) studied preferences for 30 music genres among Canadian adults and found nine music-preference factors. A study of preferences for 25 music genres among German young uncovered six music-preference factors (Schäfer & Sedlmeier, 2009). A large-scale study involving over 35,000 Internet users and over 100 musical genres revealed 10 preference factors (North, 2010).

Although the results from these studies are not identical, there are some consistent preference factors that emerge. In every sample, at least one factor emerged representing preferences for classical and jazz music; another factor representing preferences for rock music; and another factor representing preferences for rap and hip-hop music. In most of the studies a factor representing country or singer-songwriter music emerged, and another factor representing new age and electronic music. Based on all of this work, it seems reasonable to expect that preferences can be conceptualized in terms of at least five music-preference dimensions.

Indeed, recent work aimed at establishing a robust framework for conceptualizing musical preferences indicates that musical preferences within Western cultures can be represented in terms of five basic dimensions. More specifically, research based on multiple samples totaling over 250,000 participants and more than 250 pieces of music suggests that individual differences in musical preferences can be conceptualized in terms of five dimensions: Mellow, Unpretentious, Sophisticated, Intense, and Contemporary (MUSIC) (Rentfrow, et al., 2011, 2012; Bonneville-Roussy, Rentfrow, Xu, & Potter, 2013):

- Mellow comprises soft rock, R&B, and adult contemporary, and is characterized as romantic, relaxing, slow, and quiet.
- Unpretentious comprises country and folk, and characterized as uncomplicated, relaxing, unaggressive, and acoustic.
- Sophisticated comprises classical, opera, jazz, and world, and is characterized as inspiring, intelligent, complex, and dynamic.
- Intense comprises rock, punk, and heavy metal and is characterized as distorted, loud, aggressive, and not romantic, nor inspiring.
- Contemporary comprises rap, electronica, and pop, and is characterized as percussive, electric, energetic, and not sad.

The MUSIC model provides a useful framework for investigating associations between musical preferences and various psychological characteristics. For example, individuals with preferences for sophisticated musical styles, like classical, opera, and jazz, are high in openness, creativity, imagination, possess liberal values, value artistic expression, and score high on measures of verbal ability. People with preferences for intense styles of music, like heavy metal and punk, are high in openness, sensation seeking, impulsivity, and athletic ability. People with preferences for contemporary music, like pop, rap, and dance, are high in extraversion, value social recognition, endorse more gender stereotypes, have more permissive attitudes about sex, and consider themselves physically attractive (e.g., Rentfrow & Gosling, 2003; 2006; Delsing et al., 2008; Zweigenhaft, 2008; ter Bogt, Engels, Bogers, & Kloosterman, 2010; Rentfrow, Goldberg, & Zilca, 2011; Bonnevillie-Roussy et al., 2013).

Most of the research on the links between musical preferences and personality rely on adolescents and young adults, so less is known about the role music plays for middle-aged or older adults. Do preferences change with age? Do they reflect different stages in life? Recent research suggests that musical preferences change throughout the life span and that these changes correspond, in part, to developmental changes in personality (Bonnevillie-Roussy et al., 2013). Specifically, as people age, they become more agreeable and relaxed, and it appears that preferences for intense and aggressive music declines, while preferences for mellow and contemplative music increases.

17.2 MANIFESTATIONS OF MUSICAL IDENTITIES

The fact that musical identities have a psychological basis suggests that they could reveal valid information about individuals' self-identities, personalities, beliefs, and values. Indeed, consistent with research on music and self-identity, it seems reasonable to suppose that musical identities communicate information about the social groups people associate with. Research on individual differences in musical preferences and their links with personality also suggest that musical identities communicate information about such traits as sociability, friendliness, creativity, and stability. Therefore, publicly displaying musical preferences sends messages and social cues about peoples' self-views, personalities, and beliefs. Just because music has a psychological basis does not mean that observers can infer psychological information from musical preferences. Do people's musical identities influence how others perceive them?

Results from several studies suggest that there are normative beliefs, or stereotypes, about the social and psychological characteristics common to people who like certain styles of music (e.g., Zillmann & Bhatia, 1989; North & Hargreaves, 1999; Rentfrow & Gosling, 2007; Rentfrow, et al., 2009). For instance, in a study on music and attraction, men rated women with preferences for classical music as attractive and sophisticated, whereas women with preferences for heavy metal music were rated as rebellious and aggressive (Zillmann & Bhatia, 1989). Rentfrow and colleagues examined the content of stereotypes about fans of several different musical genres (Rentfrow & Gosling, 2007; Rentfrow et al., 2009). Results from their research revealed that people have very similar stereotypes about the psychological and social characteristics about fans of many different musical styles—especially about fans of classical, rap, and heavy metal music—and that the content of those stereotypes vary substantially. For example, fans of classical music were believed to be white, wealthy, hardworking, introverted, physically unattractive, intelligent, and artistic, whereas rap music fans are believed to be extraverted, relaxed, athletic, and to drink beer and smoke marijuana. When the content of these stereotypes were compared with the psychological characteristics of actual music fans, the results revealed that many of the stereotypes have some validity.

There is also evidence that people can form accurate impressions of individuals on the basis of their music preferences. Burroughs, Drews, and Hallman (1991) found that observers were able to form accurate impressions of targets based on their personal possessions (e.g., favorite clothing, favorite records). Rentfrow & Gosling (2006) focussed exclusively on music preferences and observed that judges were able to form accurate impressions of targets' personalities and values after only listening to targets' top-10 favorite songs. Although the focus of that research was not on the perceptual processes underlying music-based personality judgments, results suggested that judgments of targets were related both to attributes of the music (e.g., the amount of singing, emotional valence) and to the genre of the music.

These investigations clearly suggest that musical identities influence the ways in which individuals are perceived and, in some cases, it would appear as though these perceptions have some accuracy. What is less clear is how people translate information about musical preferences into a judgment about someone's psychological characteristics. In other words, are music-based impressions influenced mainly by the associations people have with a particular musical genre, or by specific psychological and sonic features in the music?

17.3 PERCEIVING MUSICAL IDENTITIES: DATA STUDY

Previous studies investigating the social connotations (i.e., stereotypes) of musical preferences have mainly examined associations of genre-based stereotypes, but genres are useful only if participants are aware of them. We conducted the present study to see if stereotypes of music fans can be assessed from excerpts of real music. In the Spring of 2011 and 2012, advertisements were posted on Amazon's Mechanical Turk (MTurk) inviting people to participate in a study on music perception in exchange for compensation; 41 judges from the United States with no formal music training agreed to participate. Of those who indicated, 14 (34%) were male and 27 (66%) were female, 33 (81%) were White Caucasian, three were Asian (7%), and five (12%) were of other ethnicities. The mean age was between 31 and 35 years of age[1] .

We presented participants with brief excerpts of actual music. We wanted to avoid popular musical pieces that participants may have heard before, so we selected pieces that were either not commercially released and obtained from Getty Images (GI), or those that were commercially released (CR) but had low sales figures (see Rentfrow et al., 2011, and Rentfrow et al. 2012, for details about the procedure used for selecting musical pieces). In total, there were 102 musical excerpts (representing 26 genres and subgenres) and each was approximately 15 seconds long. Every excerpt had been previously coded by judges on 57 musical attributes (e.g., sonic attributes such as instrumentation, tempo, and timbre, and psychological attributes such as depth, energy, warmth, and intensity) (see Rentfrow et al., 2011, 2012).

To reduce fatigue and order effects, each judge rated either a subset of 25 of the 50 excerpts from GI, or a subset of 26 of the 52 CR excerpts. Judges were informed that they would be presented with a variety of musical excerpts and asked to indicate the extent to which the terms presented to them were characteristic of the prototypical person who likes each excerpt. Specifically, after listening to each musical excerpt, judges were asked, "In general, people who like this music tend to be…". Judges then provided their rating for each of the listed items using a 9-point scale with endpoints at 1 (*extremely uncharacteristic*) and 9 (*extremely characteristic*).

---

[1] Judges were asked to indicate their age range (e.g., 21–25, 26–30, or 31–35), rather than their exact age.

Judges rated prototypes on similar attributes used in previous research on music stereotypes (see Rentfrow & Gosling, 2007). Specifically, personal qualities were measured using four items (artistic, athletic, intelligent, and physically attractive) from the Self-Attributes Questionnaire (SAQ; Pelham & Swann, 1989); three items related to political and religious orientation (politically conservative, politically liberal, and religious); one item measured social status (wealthy); and six items related to additional personal qualities (angry, happy, depressed, sophisticated, aggressive, and confident). Note that only a subsample of the attributes was rated for the CR clips. For all the excerpts, information on the perceptions of the Big Five personality traits of music fans was collected using items from the Ten-Item Personality Inventory (TIPI: Gosling, Rentfrow, & Swann, 2003).

To examine the agreement among judges for stereotypes associated with the musical excerpts, we calculated inter-judge agreement using intraclass correlations (ICC; Shrout and Fleiss, 1979), ICC (2, 1) among the judges. As shown in Table 17.1, agreement for all the stereotypes across both musical samples was generally high (*mean alpha* = 0.72; *mean ICC* = 0.65), and judges shared more agreement for stereotypes of personal qualities (*mean alpha* = 0.81; *mean ICC* = 0.75), than the Big Five personality traits (*mean alpha* = 0.60; *mean ICC* = 0.51).

Among the personal quality stereotypes of GI excerpts, judges shared the most agreement for sophisticated, angry, and aggressive stereotypes (*mean ICCs* = 0.86, 0.78, and 0.77, respectively) and least agreement for attractive, athletic, and confident stereotypes (*mean ICCs* = 0.23, 0.27, and 0.28, respectively). Among the Big Five personality stereotypes, judges shared the most agreement for Extraversion, Emotional Stability, and Agreeableness (*mean ICCs* = 0.65, 0.56, and 0.54, respectively) and least agreement for Openness and Conscientiousness (*mean ICCs* = 0.27 and 0.32, respectively). Among the personal quality stereotypes of the CR excerpts, judges shared the most agreement for sophisticated, politically conservative, and intelligent stereotypes (*mean ICCs* = 0.86, 0.86, and 0.83, respectively) and least agreement for happy and angry stereotypes (*mean ICCs* = 0.67 and 0.74, respectively). Among the Big Five personality stereotypes, judges shared the most agreement for Emotional Stability, Conscientiousness, and Openness (*mean ICCs* = 0.70, 0.62, and 0.58, respectively) and least agreement for Agreeableness and Extraversion (*mean ICCs* = 0.27 and 0.57, respectively).

We next sought to examine how these stereotypes are differentiated among musical preference dimensions as defined by the MUSIC Model. Table 17.2 reports correlations between musical stereotypes and MUSIC preference dimensions across each of the two musical samples. Specifically, using the song as the unit of analysis, we correlated the MUSIC factor loadings of each excerpt (see Rentfrow et al., 2011, 2012) with the mean stereotype ratings for each excerpt.

As can be seen in columns 1 and 2:

- People who prefer Mellow music are seen as politically conservative, religious, wealthy, agreeable, conscientious, and emotionally stable, but not athletic, angry, aggressive or extraverted.

Table 17.1 Agreement among judges for personality stereotypes derived from music

	Inter-judge agreement					
	GI Excerpts		CR Excerpts		All Excerpts	
	Alpha	*ICC*	*Alpha*	*ICC*	*Alpha*	*ICC*
PERSONAL *qualities*						
Conservative	0.76	0.71	0.87	0.86	0.81	0.78
Liberal	0.61	0.53	–	–	–	–
Intelligent	0.77	0.72	0.87	0.83	0.82	0.77
Religious	0.76	0.54	0.85	0.82	0.80	0.68
Attractive	0.51	0.23	–	–	–	–
Athletic	0.55	0.27	–	–	–	–
Artistic	0.72	0.68	–	–	–	–
Angry	0.86	0.78	0.79	0.74	0.83	0.76
Happy	0.69	0.61	0.72	0.67	0.70	0.64
Depressed	0.65	0.43	–	–	–	–
Sophisticated	0.89	0.86	0.89	0.86	0.89	0.86
Wealthy	0.81	0.70	0.84	0.81	0.83	0.75
Aggressive	0.83	0.77	–	–	–	–
Confident	0.42	0.28	–	–	–	–
Big Five						
Extraversion	0.70	0.65	0.64	0.57	0.67	0.61
Agreeableness	0.65	0.54	0.43	0.27	0.54	0.41
Conscientiousness	0.48	0.32	0.67	0.62	0.57	0.47
Emotional stability	0.68	0.56	0.75	0.70	0.72	0.63
Openness	0.39	0.27	0.65	0.58	0.52	0.43
Overall mean	0.65	0.53	0.75	0.69	0.72	0.65
Personal qualities mean	0.70	0.58	0.83	0.80	0.81	0.75
Big Five mean	0.58	0.47	0.63	0.55	0.60	0.51

Note. Agreement was computed using ICCs (2, 1). Cell entries are mean alphas and ICCs which were computed using Fisher's *r*-to-*z* transformation.

GI, Getty Images excerpts; CR, commercially released excerpts; *n* = 41.

Table 17.2 Correlations between the MUSIC model and personality stereotypes

	Mellow		Unpretentious		Sophisticated		Intense		Contemporary	
	GI	CR	GI	CR	GI	CR	GI	CR	GI	CR
PERSONAL qualities										
Conservative	0.31*	0.30*	0.59**	0.49**	0.38**	0.14	-0.61**	-0.38**	-0.28*	-0.61**
Liberal	-0.23	-0.71**	-	-0.20	-	0.56**	-	0.12	-	-
Intelligent	0.20	0.19	-0.44**	-0.39**	0.50**	0.60**	-0.06	-0.31*	-0.19	-0.37**
Religious	0.32*	0.21	0.62**	0.67**	0.35*	-0.07	-0.67**	-0.30*	-0.21	-0.43**
Attractive	-0.02	-	-0.01	-	0.03	-	0.00	-	0.12	-
Athletic	-0.49**	-	-0.19	-	-0.48**	-	0.41**	-	0.27	-
Artistic	0.11	-	-0.54**	-	0.52**	-	-0.02	-	-0.06	-
Angry	-0.52**	-0.27	-0.33*	-0.03	-0.60**	-0.37*	0.88**	0.42**	-0.07	0.38**
Happy	0.16	0.07	0.17	0.20	0.26	0.19	-0.53**	-0.25	0.15	-0.40**
Depressed	-0.08	-	-0.10	-	-0.47**	-	0.59**	-	-0.26	-
Sophisticated	0.28	0.19	-0.38**	-0.24	0.72**	0.57**	-0.36*	-0.40**	-0.08	-0.39**
Wealthy	0.39**	0.22	-0.31*	-0.24	0.65**	0.63**	-0.43**	-0.41**	-0.09	-0.44**
Aggressive	-0.64**	-	-0.28*	-	-0.55**	-	0.83**	-	0.00	-
Confident	-0.27	-	-0.17	-	0.22	-	-0.05	-	0.19	-

(continued)

Table 17.2 Continued

	Mellow		Unpretentious		Sophisticated		Intense		Contemporary	
Big Five										
Extraversion	-0.69**	-0.23	0.05	0.12	-0.42**	-0.29*	0.37**	0.26	0.26	0.15
Agreeableness	0.58**	0.25	0.36*	0.15	0.53**	0.14	-0.79**	-0.10	-0.06	-0.55**
Conscientiousness	0.41**	0.32*	0.26	-0.04	0.59**	0.46**	-0.63**	-0.38**	-0.25	-0.60**
Emotional Stability	0.46**	0.34*	0.21	0.11	0.65**	0.29	-0.79**	-0.29	0.00	0.68**
Openness	-0.19	-0.12	-0.66**	-0.45**	0.24	-0.04	0.29*	0.24	0.06	0.26

Note. Cell entries are correlations between the mean ratings of personality stereotypes and the MUSIC factor loadings.

GI, Getty Images excerpts; CR, commercially released excerpts; conservative = politically conservative; liberal = politically liberal; n = 50 for the GI sample, and n = 52 for the CR sample; * p < 0.05; ** p < 0.01.

- People who prefer Unpretentious music are seen as politically conservative, religious, and agreeable, but not politically liberal, artistic, angry, sophisticated, wealthy, or aggressive.
- People who prefer Sophisticated music are seen as politically conservative, intelligent, religious, artistic, sophisticated, agreeable, conscientious, and emotionally stable, but not athletic, angry, depressed, aggressive, or extraverted.
- People who prefer Intense music are seen as politically liberal, athletic, angry, depressed, aggressive, extraverted, and open, but not politically conservative, religious, happy, sophisticated, wealthy, agreeable, conscientious, or emotionally stable.
- Results for fans of Contemporary music were less consistent across the types of music, but it appears that such fans are seen as not politically conservative, intelligent, religious, sophisticated, wealthy, agreeable, or conscientious.

We next examined the extent to which musical stereotypes were driven by the genre or the attributes of a musical piece by running a series of multiple regressions. The results at the top of Table 17.3 showed that genres (26) accounted for significant proportions of variance for each of the musical stereotypes. When the attributes (57) were added to the regression models at step 2, the amount of variance increased significantly for four of the Big Five personality stereotypes (extraversion, agreeableness, contentiousness, and emotional stability; Δ Fs = 9.10, 3.91, 3.53, 3.30, respectively), and four of the seven personal quality stereotypes (angry, happy, sophisticated, wealthy; Δ Fs = 4.12, 4.44, 2.37, 3.47, respectively). We next examined whether genres account for significant variance over and above the attributes in another series of multiple regressions. The results shown at the bottom of Table 17.3 indicate that attributes accounted for significant proportions of variance for all the characteristics, and that when genres were added to the model the variance increased significantly for only one of the Big Five personality stereotypes (openness to experience, Δ F = 1.88), but increased significantly for five of the seven personal quality stereotypes (politically conservative, intelligent, religious, angry, happy, and sophisticated; Δ Fs = 1.81, 2.07, 1.23, 1.72, 1.72, 2.24, respectively). Taken together, the results indicate that both attributes and genres account for significant variance in determining stereotypes of music fans, but that attributes generally account for more variance than do genres.

The results provide strong evidence that people agree about the social connotations linked to auditory stimuli. Correlations between these stereotypes and the MUSIC model revealed that there are clear and transparent differences in the content of these stereotypes across musical preference dimensions. And results from hierarchical regressions indicate that musical attributes are better predictors of stereotypes than genres.

Table 17.3 Incremental changes in multiple correlations of personality stereotypes with genres and attributes as simultaneous predictors

| | Music stereotypes | | | | | | | | | | | |
| | Big five | | | | | Personal qualities | | | | | | |
	E	A	C	ES	O	Conservative	Intelligent	Religious	Angry	Happy	Sophisticated	Wealthy
Step 1: Genres	0.69	0.78	0.70	0.72	0.77	0.84	0.58	0.74	0.82	0.70	0.83	0.83
Step 2: Attributes	0.87	0.86	0.81	0.82	0.82	0.86	0.66	0.76	0.89	0.82	0.87	0.89
ΔF	90.10**	30.91**	30.54**	30.30**	10.85	10.00	10.22	0.48	40.12**	40.44**	20.37*	30.47**
Step 1: Attributes	0.81	0.78	0.70	0.72	0.67	0.75	0.48	0.50	0.83	0.69	0.78	0.79
Step 2: Genre	0.87	0.86	0.81	0.82	0.82	0.86	0.66	0.76	0.89	0.82	0.87	0.89
ΔF	10.13	10.51	10.19	10.27	10.88*	10.81*	0.96	20.07*	10.23*	10.72*	10.72*	20.24*

Note. Cell entries are multiple *R*s derived from stepwise regressions in which personality stereotypes from musical excerpts were regressed onto 26 genres and 57 musical attributes.

E, extraversion; A, agreeableness; C, conscientiousness; ES, emotional stability; O, openness to experience; *n* = 102.

*$p < 0.05$; **$p < 0.01$.

17.4 FUTURE DIRECTIONS: MUSICAL ENGAGEMENT

Researchers most often look to musical preferences as a construct to help inform theory and research on musical identity, justifiably so, since not only do anecdotal and empirical observations strongly suggest that people make inferences of others and themselves based on preferences, but this information is easily and quickly obtainable by researchers through survey methodologies. However, while musical preferences clearly form the face of musical identities, there are other important constructs that are more hidden beneath the surface, which may be linked to the content and formation of these identities. One such construct is musical engagement.

People vary greatly in the way that they engage with music in their everyday lives. In terms of frequency, some turn on the music every chance they get: from the song on their morning alarm clock, to the music they listen to while in transit, at work, on the computer, eating dinner, or preparing for bed. Here, music acts as a personal companion, accompanying the person for every step of their waking lives, while for others, music is listened to only on occasion: when a friend might be listening to it, or when it is playing in a television commercial or quietly in the background at a restaurant. Here, music acts as nothing much more than background noise, unintended to be listened to. In terms of degree, some connect profoundly with music—serving as a source of emotional comfort, hope, meaning, and spirituality. For others, music is more of a distraction from mundane tasks and something that simply helps to pass the time. In terms of style, some engage intellectually, following the movements of the melody lines and deconstructing the sonic elements in a song, while others engage more physically, dancing, moving their bodies, and feeling the musical vibrations from their toes to their fingertips. Some engage with the narrative in the music, connecting with the lyrics, storyline, and symbolism expressed therein, while others engage more socially, feeling connected to the musicians, and if at a live concert, with the audience members.

Although researchers in the field have begun to explore the individual differences (e.g., Chin & Rickard, 2012) and life-span development (e.g., Bonneville-Roussy et al., 2013) of musical engagement, not much, if any, is known about how these elements relate to musical identity. Accordingly, people may not only identify themselves only as a "metalhead" or a (jazz) "cat," but they may also identify themselves as a "deep" musical engager, or a "dancer," or "raver." It may be that a person who responds to music with more physical movement, for example, may seek out others who are dancers and physical engagers, rather than say, intellectual engagers. This information likely broadcasts aspects of a person's behavior and the environment that they spend time in (e.g., night clubs, salsa nights, tango lessons). Two dancers may appeal to each other, partly because they know that they are likely to enjoy similar types of musical activities. At least for those individuals that place considerable importance on music, *musical preferences may get you through the door, but your musical engagement will keep you there.* Do shared styles and degrees of musical engagement predict relationship success and satisfaction both interpersonally and even among larger group settings? How important is musical engagement in defining a person and a group's musical identity and what role does it play?

17.5 FUTURE DIRECTIONS: THE MUSICIAN'S IDENTITY

Arguably, those who engage most with music are the musicians themselves. This is particularly true for professional musicians. Yet the nature of musical identities for professional musicians remains largely unknown. Music has long been a source of self-expression for those who play, compose, and perform music—an expression of emotion, beliefs, values, personality, and life narratives. For those musicians whose "life is their music," the line which separates the person from the music they create is blurred. In a recent interview, the well-known jazz saxophonist J. D. Allen stated that, "There's no difference between me and my music … I've learned that and I accept it—that I am what I play" (see http://somethingelsereviews.com/2013/06/02/something-else-interview-jd-allen-preaching-the-word-through-music/).

Musicians at the highest level (those concerned with artistry) spend years finding and developing their own unique "voice" on their instrument. If successful in this endeavor, musical artists develop a specific tone and style that is unique to them and which audiences can identify them by. For example, the jazz fan can quickly identify the sound of a trumpet as belonging to Louis Armstrong, Miles Davis, or Chet Baker, when only hearing the first couple of notes of a record—even if they are hearing the record for the first time. Rather than having their musical identities being based on preferences for external musical stimuli (which is the case for those who are solely listeners), the musical identities of musicians are tied to their internal creative expression. What are the psychological processes and mechanisms involved when musicians develops their unique "voice" or style? What are the effects of this process on psychological functioning? Does it evoke self-discovery or can it lead to becoming a "tortured artist"?

17.6 FUTURE DIRECTIONS: INTERPERSONAL RELATIONSHIPS

The role of musical identities in the formation and development of interpersonal relationships remains a relatively unexplored area in the field. We know that based on both auditory and genre-based cues, people are able to make judgments of others with some degree of accuracy. We also know that we seek out others and respond more favorably to those who like the same music as we do. Clearly, musical preferences are a vital aspect of musical identities and play an important role in the early stages of the development of relationships. However, less is known about the role of music in the later stages of relationships. Not only is music likely to be present when people first meet, whether it's at a dinner party, pub, restaurant, or dance club, but it will likely be a prominent feature that accompanies people as the relationship develops. Will there be mixed tapes shared and what will be on them? How will the wedding song for the couple's first dance be selected? What role does music play for couples who engage deeply with music as compared to couples do not engage deeply? As is famously depicted by John Cusack in the movie *Say Anything*, what song will be playing if someone stands out in the front lawn with a stereo raised above their head in an attempt to win back their significant other?

17.7 Conclusions

Music plays a role in our lives even when the headphones are put down and the sound is turned off. The research explored in this chapter demonstrates the interplay between musical identities and various psychological and group processes. In particular, musical preferences clearly serve as a vehicle for self-expression, identity formation, self-esteem, and social judgments and stereotypes. The findings from the data reported in this chapter suggest that people form stereotypes from musical stimuli and agree about their content. These social connotations are clearly differentiated by individual differences in musical preferences. What is more, is that stereotypes appear to be derived more from the auditory cues in music than their genre classifications. We hope that this research draws attention to the notion that the sonic and psychological attributes in music should be taken into higher consideration when studying music-related psychological phenomena.

References

Abrams, D. (2009). Social identity on a national scale: Optimal distinctiveness and young people's self-expression through musical preference. *Group Processes and Intergroup Relations*, 12, 303–17.

Boer, D., Fischer, R., Strack, M., Bond, M.H., Lo, E., & Lam, J. (2011). How shared preferences in music create bonds between people values as the missing link. *Personality and Social Psychology Bulletin*, 37(9), 1159–71.

Bonneville-Roussy, A., Rentfrow, P.J., Xu, M.K., & Potter, J. (2013). Music through the ages: Trends in musical engagement and preferences from adolescence through middle adulthood. *Journal of Personality and Social Psychology*, 105(4), 703.

Burroughs, J.W., Drews, D.R., & Hallman, W.K. (1991). Predicting personality from personal possessions: a self-presentational analysis. *Journal of Social Behavior and Personality*, 6, 147–63.

Brewer, M.B. (1991). The social self: on being the same and different. *Personality and Social Psychology Bulletin*, 17, 475–81.

Chin, T. & Rickard, N.S. (2012). The music USE (MUSE) questionnaire: an instrument to measure engagement in music. *Music Perception*, 29(4), 429–46.

Colley, A. (2008). Young people's musical taste: relationship with gender and gender-related traits. *Journal of Applied Social Psychology*, 38, 2039–55.

Delsing, M.J.M.H, ter Bogt, T.F.M., Engels, R.C.M.E., & Meeus, W.H.J. (2008). Adolescents' music preferences and personality characteristics. *European Journal of Personality*, 22, 109–30.

DeNora, T. (2000). *Music in everyday life*. Cambridge: Cambridge University Press.

Dunn, P.G., de Ruyter, B., & Bouwhuis, D.G. (2012). Toward a better understanding of the relation between music preference, listening behavior, and personality. *Psychology of Music*, 40, 411–28.

George, D., Stickle, K., Rachid, F., & Wopnford, A. (2007). The association between types of music enjoyed and cognitive, behavioral, and personality factors of those who listen. *Psychomusicology*, 19, 32–56.

Gosling, S.D., Rentfrow, P.J., & Swann W.B. (2003). A very brief measure of the Big-Five personality domains. *Journal of Research in Personality*, 37, 504–28.

Lonsdale, A.J. & North, A.C. (2011). Why do we listen to music? A uses and gratifications analysis. *British Journal of Psychology*, 102(1), 108–34.

McCrae, R.R., & Costa, P.T., Jr. (2008). The five-factor theory of personality. In: O.P. John, R.W. Robins, & L.A. Pervin (Eds.) *Handbook of personality: theory and research*, 3rd edn, pp. 159–81. New York, NY: Guilford Press.

North, A.C. (2010). Individual differences in musical taste. *American Journal of Psychology*, 123, 199–208.

North, A.C. & Hargreaves, D.J. (1999). Music and adolescent identity. *Music Education Research*, 1, 75–92.

North, A.C., Hargreaves, D.J., & O'Neill, S.A. (2000). The importance of music to adolescents. *British Journal of Educational Psychology*, 70(2), 255–72.

Pelham, B.W. & Swann, W.B., Jr. (1989). From self-conceptions to self-worth: on the sources and structure of global self-esteem. *Journal of Personality and Social Psychology*, 57, 672–80.

Rentfrow, P.J., Goldberg, L.R., & Levitin, D.J. (2011). The structure of musical preferences: A five-factor model. *Journal of Personality and Social Psychology*, 100(6), 1139–57.

Rentfrow, P.J., Goldberg, L.R., Stillwell, D.J., Kosinski, M., Gosling, S.D., & Levitin, D.J. (2012). The song remains the same: a replication and extension of the MUSIC model. *Music Perception*, 30, 161–85.

Rentfrow, P.J., Goldberg, L.R., & Zilca, R. (2011). Listening, watching, and reading: the structure and correlates of entertainment preferences. *Journal of Personality*, 79(2), 223–58.

Rentfrow, P.J. & Gosling, S.D. (2003). The do re mi's of everyday life: the structure and personality correlates of music preferences. *Journal of Personality and Social Psychology*, 84, 1236–56.

Rentfrow, P.J. & Gosling, S.D. (2006). Message in a ballad: the role of music preferences in interpersonal perception. *Psychological Science*, 17, 236–42.

Rentfrow, P.J. & Gosling, S.D. (2007). The content and validity of music-genre stereotypes among college students. *Psychology of Music*, 35, 306–26.

Rentfrow, P.J. & McDonald, J.A. (2009). Music preferences and personality. In: P.N. Juslin & J. Sloboda (Eds.) *Handbook of music and emotion*, pp. 669–95. Oxford: Oxford University Press.

Rentfrow, P.J., McDonald, J.A., & Oldmeadow, J.A. (2009). You are what you listen to: young people's stereotypes about music fans. *Group Processes and Intergroup Relations*, 12, 329–44.

Schäfer, T., & Sedlmeier, P. (2009). From the functions of music to music preference. *Psychology of Music*, 37(3), 279–300.

Selfhout, M.H., Branje, S.J., ter Bogt, T.F., & Meeus, W.H. (2009). The role of music preferences in early adolescents' friendship formation and stability. *Journal of Adolescence*, 32(1), 95–107.

Shrout, P.E. & Fleiss, J.L. (1979). Intraclass correlations: uses in assessing rater reliability. *Psychological Bulletin*, 86, 420–8.

Tarrant, M., North, A.C., & Hargreaves, D.J. (2002). Youth identity and music. In R. MacDonald, D. Hargreaves, & D. Miell (Eds.), *Musical identities*, pp. 134–50. Oxford: Oxford University Press.

Tekman, H.G. & Hortaçsu, N. (2002). Music and social identity: stylistic identification as a response to musical style. *International Journal of Psychology*, 37(5), 277–85.

ter Bogt, T.F., Engels, R.C., Bogers, S., & Kloosterman, M. (2010). "Shake It Baby, Shake It": media preferences, sexual attitudes and gender stereotypes among adolescents. *Sex Roles*, 63(11–12), 844–59.

Zillmann, D. & Bhatia, A. (1989). Effects of associating with musical genres on heterosexual attraction. *Communication Research*, 16(2), 263–88.

Zweigenhaft, R.L. (2008). A do re mi encore: a closer look at the personality correlates of music preferences. *Journal of Individual Differences*, 29, 45–55.

CHAPTER 18

......

MUSICAL IDENTITY AND INDIVIDUAL DIFFERENCES IN EMPATHY

......

EMERY SCHUBERT

18.1 INTRODUCTION

......

SOME people are empathic, "people persons." They like company, and people like to be with them, making such individuals potentially important members of an in-group (Cialdini, Brown, Lewis, Luce, & Neuberg, 1997; Rae Westbury & Neumann, 2008). They are sensitive to what others are feeling and are likely to be helpful; in other words, "prosocial." In contrast, people low in empathy can find human company confusing and even stressful (Decety & Lamm, 2009; Fan et al., 2014). Non-empathizers can exhibit hostile, callous, or recalcitrant behavior, associated with psychopathy (Baron-Cohen, 2011; Brook & Kosson, 2013; Decety, Chen, Harenski, & Kiehl, 2013).

Recent research suggests that some people who are low empathizers, i.e., those who are poor at reading emotions in other people, are spared this deficit in music listening, being able to report emotion in music at levels statistically identical to normal empathizing listeners. What implications does this have for one's musical identity? After considering the structure and precursors of empathy, this chapter investigates what the role individual differences in empathy have in shaping musical identity. The apparently paradoxical finding that low empathizers can relate to emotion in music is reviewed and a model proposed to help disentangle the conundrum. The model, referred to as the "Common Coding Model of Prosocial Behavior Processing", is based on recent developments in cognitive neuroscience and on the idea that empathy utilizes mental circuits that share the processing of both actions and perceptions—so-called "common coding." I will argue that "contagion circuits" create psychological resonance between emotion action (experience) and emotion perception, which are also required for both social and musical engagement. I will conclude by proposing that individuals with low social empathy but without deficits in emotional contagion processing (such as individuals with autistic spectrum disorder) will develop a stronger, more idiosyncratic musical identity than people with normal levels of empathy who are more influenced by social norms.

18.2 THE STRUCTURE
OF EMPATHY: AFFECTIVE AND
COGNITIVE SYSTEMS

Like many psychological constructs, social empathy defies simple definition, despite its common usage and understanding (Decety & Lamm, 2006; Batson, 2009).[1] One simple definition is a psychological propensity to show appropriate caring for others (see also Table 1 in Decety & Lamm, 2006). From this definition, empathy is a propensity or trait, and not in itself an act or action. Thus, the act of showing caring may be referred to as compassion, and one may need to have empathy before they can show true, appropriate compassion. But one can have a trait of empathy without the compassionate act?

In recent times, there has been a boom in the literature on determining the structure of empathy, particularly since the rising interest in its neural correlates (e.g., see Decety & Jackson, 2004; Singer, Seymour, O'Doherty, Stephan, Dolan, & Frith, 2006; Bernhardt & Singer, 2012; Zaki & Ochsner, 2012). Current views on empathy indicate that it consists of two systems—affective and cognitive empathy (terminology adapted from Shamay-Tsoory, Aharon-Peretz, & Perry, 2009). The affective empathy system processes emotional aspects of empathy, such as automatically and involuntarily acquiring the emotion of another person with whom one is about to empathize, referred to as "emotional contagion." The cognitive empathy system processes the environmental context and other factors (such as knowing that a colleague is unhappy at work and after a long day, enters the room looking tense) and allows the empathizer to realize that the emotion registered by the affective empathy system is actually a simulation of the emotion that another individual is experiencing (putting one's self into their shoes, so to speak). Hence, the *cognitive* empathy system allows the correct "perspective" to be taken. This component is sometimes referred to as cognitive perspective taking, mind-reading, mentalizing, or Theory of Mind (ToM), each term treated as similes to varying degrees by different authors (Singer, 2006).

The Questionnaire of Cognitive and Affective Empathy (QCAE) is a psychometric instrument for measuring empathy, and builds on the idea that empathy consists of a cognitive and an affective system (Reniers, Corcoran, Drake, Shryane, & Völlm, 2011).

---

[1] As will be discussed later, empathy usually refers to social empathy and occurs when one human processes information about other beings in a certain way. It is usually defined as shorthand for "social" empathy. While the picture presented in this chapter is a bit more complex, the term "empathy" and "social empathy" are used interchangeably.

An item from the QCAE that exemplifies the cognitive empathy system is "I always try to consider the other fellow's feelings before I do something". That is, when the item is rated highly (strong agreement), it indicates that the individual is (or claims to be) able to simulate the action and state of another person, as required by cognitive perspective taking.[2] The affective system refers to the perceiver's own emotional experience that results from the observation and simulation. Having affective empathy leads to agreement with a statement from the QCAE, such as "I am happy when I am with a cheerful group and sad when the others are glum", showing that emotions of others are capable of infecting the perceiver (emotional contagion).

18.3 THE PRECURSORS OF EMPATHY: PERCEPTION, MIMICRY, EMOTIONAL CONTAGION, PERSPECTIVE TAKING, PROSOCIAL BEHAVIOR

According to Gonzalez-Liencres, Shamay-Tsoory, & Brüne (2013), empathy consists of two necessary precursors—mimicry and emotional contagion. Mimicry refers to the spontaneous, possibly imprecise copying of the actions presented by a source. It is a form of imitation (Jones, 2007), and there is evidence to suggest that the ability is innate, as shown by the imitation of adults by newborn infants, such as mouth opening, and tongue and lip protrusion (Meltzoff & Moore, 1977; Meltzoff & Decety, 2003).

Emotional contagion, as we have seen above, is considered by researchers to be a structural member of the affective empathy system. As a precursor to empathy it may be thought of as the embodiment of the emotion that is associated with the action that is being mimicked. Contagion, without emotion, can occur, too. For example, in observing someone yawning, the perceiver (the target) could attempt to imitate the head, jaw, and throat actions of the yawning person being observed (the source), and even the inhalation action, but without these coordinated actions actually becoming a "fully fledged," genuinely experienced yawn. It is when the actions are mimicked, *without consciously attending to the target*, that the yawn becomes "embodied" (Goldman & de Vignemont,

---

[2] There is considerably controversy about whether cognitive perspective taking is a kind of mental simulation of someone else's actions and emotions, or a theory of that person's mind held by the potential empathizer (ToM). This Simulation Theory versus Theory–Theory controversy need not concern the argument presented in this chapter, but interested readers are referred to Gallese & Goldman (1998), Pham & Taylor (1999), Adams (2001), Decety & Grèzes (2006), Gallese (2007), Oberman & Ramachandran (2007), Zahavi (2008), Jensen & Moran (2012), and Oatley (1999). In this chapter I aim to show that the two approaches are compatible, even though my argument does not hinge on this compatibility.

2009); *embodiment* distinguishes contagion from imitation. The yawn has spread from the source to the target via contagion. *Emotional* contagion refers to the embodiment by the target perceiver of the emotion associated with the perceived action. If one (a target) notices someone (a source) emitting the vocal sounds and body gestures of laughing because of a happy event, the automated action of laughing by the observer (target), and consequent sensation of happiness is an example of *emotional* contagion (Hatfield, Cacioppo, & Rapson, 1994; Laird et al., 1994; Hatfield, Rapson, & Le, 2009).

From both cognitive and neuroscientific perspectives, particularly since the work of Prinz (1997), the processes of mimicry and contagion are often explained under a broad umbrella of theories referred to as common coding, or common circuits. That is, parts of the mental processing of the *perception* of an action are identical to those used to *perform* the same action. An extreme example is when we observe an action and cannot help copying the action (mindless mimicry). However silly this may seem, this kind of uncontrolled copying may be a mechanism that helps with learning and internalizing the workings of the external world. It would be much harder for an infant to learn a language if he/she did not, at some point, mimic the sounds of the surrounding carers (Meltzoff & Decety, 2003; Preston & De Waal, 2002), and the earliest ontogenetic mimicry behaviors may even be a precursor to language development (Kuhl & Meltzoff, 1996; Zukow-Goldring, 2012). Thus, it could be that shared circuits for perception and for action are the norm and require inhibition and socialization through exposure to cultural norms (Preston & De Waal, 2002). Emotional contagion, then, is a special case of perception-action. The emotion perceived is acted out by the perceiver because it becomes an emotion felt—that is "acted out" internally (Preston & De Waal, 2002; Decety & Grèzes, 2006, Nummenmaa, Hirvonen, Parkkola, & Hietanen, 2008; Bernhardt & Singer, 2012). For this reason, and because of its significance for the issue of musical identity, I will refer to this special case of common coding as "contagion circuits."

Mimicry and contagion therefore appear in an ontological (as well as phylogenetic) sequence (for a more detailed discussion, see Singer, 2006). The third, and final, precursor to empathy is perspective taking or ToM, and appears at around the age of 3 or 4 years (Baron-Cohen, Leslie, & Frith, 1985; Clements & Perner, 1994), when the individual is able to act towards others in a non-ego driven way. The person doing the empathizing must do more than simply capture the perceived emotional state of the other. So by the third precursor to empathy, the perceiver must understand that it is another person who is having this contagiously captured experience, and therefore inhibit their own, contagiously received emotion, and replace it with an appropriate prosocial emotion, such as caring. This perspective taking motivates the prosocial action of the empathizer.

The cognitive empathy system integrates the contagiously captured emotion with the background situation and context of the perceived person/stimulus, and simulates the situation (e.g., identifying a distressed person). As Decety & Lamm (2009) suggest, the contagious emotion is then manipulated top down by the cognitive empathy system to help refine and understand the external situation. The bottom up perception–mimicry–emotional contagion paths and top-down perspective taking paths are illustrated in Fig. 18.1. The double arrows in the figure show that the perspective taking component is enacting a simulation via the upstream emotional contagion component, while tying these data with background and context information from the external environment and internal memory. The evaluation of the perspective taking leads to the prosocial behavior as its output. Thus, cognitive perspective taking is the hallmark of the cognitive empathy system.

The sequence of precursors can be conceptualized in terms of the distinction between the locus of the emotion at each processing stage (see top of Fig. 18.1). After perception (obviously external locus) the automatically felt emotion that is part of the affective empathy is an internal locus emotion (felt by the perceiver). The realization by the cognitive empathy system that the felt emotion can be used to simulate the emotion of the person being observed turns that emotion into an external locus, expressed emotion—"That is how the other person might be feeling ... what should I do now?" Once the contagious, "bottom-up" (Decety & Lamm, 2006) emotion and the appropriate, cognitive perspective taking, top-down processing and response have been completed,

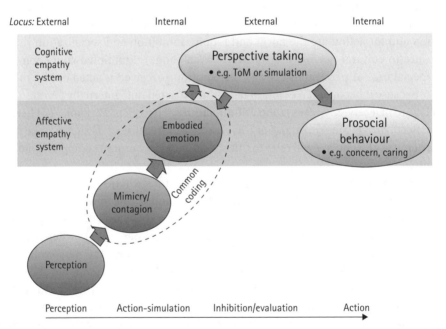

FIG. 18.1. A Common Coding Model of Prosocial Behavior Processing. Left-most three darker shaded ellipses denote bottom-up processing stages. The affective empathy system activates emotions. The Cognitive empathy system factors in matters such as context and background. Perspective taking is part of the cognitive empathy system and interrogates the incoming affective system output (hence double arrow). This may be viewed as theory of mind or as simulation. It also employs top down processing, meaning that it applies existing high level memories based on bottom up data, background information, context, and memory. Dashed ellipse denotes region of common coding or "contagion circuits."

("evaluation" in Fig. 18.1), the individual may then experience a new emotion, such as compassion, also an internal locus emotion, which then triggers a compassionate behavior. As will become evident, the distinction between emotion locus is also critical in recent studies of music perception.

18.4 EMPATHY AND MUSIC

18.4.1 Is it possible to have empathy for music?

From a literal, logical perspective, empathy refers to the capacity to show concern for living beings, whether real or imagined (fictional characters) (e.g., Hall & Bracken, 2011; Nomura & Akai, 2012). Cialdini and colleagues (Cialdini et al., 1997) demonstrated that empathic concern is strongly related to the feeling of oneness that one individual feels with another. More empathy is reported towards people who are socially close, such as close friends and family, compared to strangers and acquaintances. Non-human animals also fit into this scheme because, as demonstrated in a study by Paul (2000; see also Rae Westbury & Neumann, 2008), lower empathy scores are reported toward non-human animals than toward humans, in particular those animals who are phylogenetically distant from humans. However, empathy was higher toward non-human animals when the participant reported having a companion animal. That is, when the animal is socially closer and there is a consequent greater sense of oneness with the animal, empathy is more likely to be present toward that animal.

The implication of these findings is that the sense of oneness may be a more important aspect of empathy than if the source (e.g., a friend, a pet dog, a spider, a stranger, a robot—see Rosenthal-von der Pütten et al., 2013) of the empathy is a sentient being or not. People can report a sense of oneness with music (Pike, 1972). So, the idea that one can empathize with music (as distinct from what the music represents) is a subtle one. I will take a conservative approach to music-empathy and assert, for now, that one cannot empathize with musical emissions directly in a conventional sense. As Leman put it, "the musical audio stream is not an organism equipped with intentional capabilities" (Leman, 2008, p. 129). Within this more limited definition, it may be possible to empathize with that to which music makes reference, such as its political, spiritual, and social messages, or with the musicians making the music (Laurence, 2008). With regard to the musical signal, might some structural components of empathy discussed above have a relationship with it?

18.4.2 Transmission of emotion from music to listener

Evidence suggests that music can communicate emotion to the listener through the process of emotional contagion. This evidence is primarily demonstrated by the work of Juslin, with his early thesis of the Lens model and his later work identifying the mechanisms by which music communicates emotions. The Lens model provides a statistical explanation of how emotion is coded into musical features by the composer and performer, and then decoded by the listener (Gabrielsson & Juslin, 1996; Juslin, 1997, 2000; Juslin & Lindström, 2010). Juslin's model enables measurement of the success of transmission of emotion by asking the performer to play in a way that expresses a certain mood and then asking a listener what the mood was. Successful decoding of the mood by the listener indicates that the performer had coded the emotions into the performance appropriately. For example, a cluster of musical features organized a certain way by the composer and performer—such as slow tempo, expected melody, smooth rhythm—may encode an emotion of calmness. That cluster of musical features is then decoded by the listener ideally as calm, but in practice with some statistical noise (see also Schubert, Ferguson, Farrar, Taylor, & McPherson, 2013). While the Lens model traces the transmission of emotion via musical features, it is not directly claiming to explain the emotion presented to the listener (perceived by the listener) *and* the emotion that the listener feels as a result. It simply provides an explanation of the pathway of emotion from performance to perception.

18.4.3 Emotional contagion from music

Gabrielsson (2002) laid out the different kinds of relationships that were possible between felt and expressed emotions. Subsequent empirical work demonstrated that the relationships reported by listeners is quite often one of matching (felt emotion matched with expressed emotion; Evans & Schubert, 2008). Emotional contagion became an explicit process, or "mechanism," through which music could induce emotion in a listener through the work of Juslin published after the Lens model summarized above. Although the idea of emotional contagion from a music source has been identified by psychologists in the past (e.g., Clynes & Nettheim, 1982, p. 51; Juslin, 2001; Scherer & Zentner, 2001; Juslin & Laukka, 2003), Juslin and colleagues (Juslin & Västfjäll, 2008; Juslin & Lindström, 2010; Juslin, 2013) explicitly proposed direct listener acquisition of musically expressed emotion as a mechanism by which music communicates emotion. The emotions expressed by the music involuntarily and automatically become the felt emotion of the listener. Juslin & Västfjäll proposed that the contagion is a result of the mimicry of the music because of its resemblance to vocal delivery: "listeners' emotions to music sometimes reflect social, modular responses to the voice-like and emotion-specific acoustic patterns of the music" (Juslin & Västfjäll, 2008, p. 566). This could be why some people deal with loneliness by listening to music—the music has resemblance to the sound of the voice. Thus, generalized mental representations of vocal emotions can be activated by listening to non-vocal music and extracting its vocal resemblances.

Research in the last decade or so, particularly through the work of Gabrielsson & Juslin, has helped to conceptualize transmission of emotions by music through the process of contagion, which is also one of the components of the affective empathy system.

However, much less is known about which factors influence emotional contagion. In particular, how might individual differences modulate the susceptibility of the listener to capture the emotions transmitted by music? A logical place to seek an answer is to examine the social empathy of individuals and see how that relates to the identification of emotion in music.

18.5 INDIVIDUAL DIFFERENCES IN DETECTION OF EMOTIONAL CONTAGION AND MUSIC

18.5.1 High social empathizers detect emotion in music

Wöllner (2012) compared social empathy via the QCAE with the identification of expressiveness in music performance. Expressiveness in music data were collected through continuous ratings of expressiveness of a one minute extract from Vaughan Williams' first string quartet. The string quartet excerpt was rated for expressiveness in three conditions—the participant watched the video recording of the performance with the audio off, or with the audio on, and in the third condition, only the audio was rated for expressiveness without the video. Earlier, the string quartet players themselves made expressiveness ratings in each of the three conditions, and these ratings were used as the expected expressiveness level. That is, the string quartet mean rating was subtracted from each participant's score at each time sample to produce an expressiveness discrepancy data set.

The hypothesis was that high overall empathy scorers would make ratings that are commensurate with the quartet players' average rating, hence a negative correlation coefficient (high empathizers were expected to be associated with a small difference). In other words, empathizers should connect better with the musicians. From the perspective of the present chapter, it is of particular interest as to whether the empathy is related to the human cues and characteristics (hence, the two visual conditions), and whether empathizers "generalize" empathy to the musical emissions alone.

For the visual only condition, Wöllner reported a correlation coefficient of– 0.36, and even though it was not statistically significant ($p = 0.10$ with 22 participants for all conditions), the effect size was moderate (according to Cohen, 1992). When *affective* empathy was compared with the visual expressiveness discrepancy, a significant (negative) correlation was found, with a large effect size ($r = -0.69$). In brief, there were no significant correlations in the music-only condition for any of the empathy scales (overall, cognitive, and affective), but in the visual and the audio-visual conditions, overall and cognitive empathy were consistently significant with either medium or large effect sizes. The finding led Wöllner to conclude that empathy allows the observer to connect with the expressiveness communicated by the musician, and perhaps even derive greater pleasure in music than a low empathizing counterpart, concluding that "[s]ince music is the audible outcome of actions, empathic responses to a performer's movements may enhance the enjoyment of music" (p. 222). One's musical identity may therefore be modulated by empathy, particularly when music is part of a multimodal experience (not just audio emissions).

Consequently, another important point of the study is that human empathizing does not generalize to music listening alone. That is, the result could also reflect the preference by high empathizers to process emotional information using visual cues that were not available in the audio-only condition. Perhaps empathizers are susceptible to the emotions of other humans (emotional contagion), but this has no relationship with their proclivity to capture emotions from music. To test this idea several methodological approaches could be taken. For example, people who are low scoring on human empathy, particularly affective empathy, and possibly in emotional contagion (e.g., Doherty, 1997)—a component of the affective empathy system—could be recruited and tested to see if they also are susceptible to emotion in music.

In a study by Egermann & McAdams (2013) a similar result to Wöllner's study was obtained, but in terms of state empathy—that is, relatively short-term empathy generated by a particular situation or environment. When listeners were asked about whether they empathize with the musician whose music they were listening to, the response was found to modulate the degree to which there was a match between felt and expressed emotion rating of the music (felt and expressed emotion ratings were collected from different participants—a between-groups design). The greater the state of empathy toward the musician, the better the match between felt and expressed emotion ratings for the music. While Egermann & McAdams proposed a different model to the one discussed here, the results may be explained by the Common Coding model because social empathy (with the performer, composer, etc.) may be an indicator of the preparedness of contagion circuits for additional activation by the music. That is, if empathy for the musician is present, contagion circuits will already be activated by the social empathy "experience." However, it does not demonstrate that low *trait* empathizers *cannot* necessarily be affected by music through contagion. Activation of contagion circuits is necessary and sufficient for contagion. It is necessary but *not* sufficient for empathy. Still, Egermann & McAdams propose an interesting approach to investigating contagion in music and general empathy that warrants further research. Indeed, they present some interesting challenges to the present version of the Common Coding model because theirs proposes that empathy is an important part of the locus matching experience, whereas the present model predicts that preference is an important product of emotion locus matching (as will be discussed in Section 18.6, below; see also Schubert, 2013a), with high empathy being indicative of functioning contagion circuits, rather than the other way around (low empathy may or may not be due to deficits in contagion circuits). Contagion circuit functionality is more directly reflected by contagion experience, such as matching emotional locus during the perception of music.

18.5.2 Low social empathizers detect emotion in music

People with autistic spectrum disorder (ASD) have impaired social interaction and communication skills, but the condition is complex and not fully understood (Wing, Gould, & Gillberg, 2011). As Wing et al. explain,

> A person with an autism spectrum condition lacks empathy but may have sympathy in situations where they can perceive another's distress. When they do understand, they respond. Some of those of higher ability are very sad to read of the hardships of children in, for example, Africa, but are unable to understand the signs of emotional upset in their parents or siblings—which may be in response to the behaviour of the person with an autism spectrum condition.
>
> Wing et al., 2011, p. 789.

Thus, while the evidence for a deficit in the inability to resonate with the emotions of others—affective empathy—is not completely clear, there is considerable evidence that such individuals are poor at identifying what the other person is thinking—cognitive empathy. People with ASD may therefore experience normal levels of emotional contagion, even though overall empathy is lower compared with normal participants (Clark, Winkielman, & McIntosh, 2008; Dziobek et al., 2008; Jones, Happé, Gilbert, Burnett, & Viding, 2010). Several studies confirm that people with ASD, while finding it difficult to read emotions of others, are able to identify emotion in music (Heaton, Hermelin, & Pring, 1999; Molnar, Kondakor, Barta, Toth, & Weisz, 2001; Molnar-Szakacs Wang, Laugeson, Overy, Wu, and Piggot, 2009; Overy & Molnar-Szakacs, 2009; Caria, Venuti, & de Falco, 2011). In a study by Caria and colleagues (Caria et al., 2011), Asperger syndrome participants were compared with neurotypical participants in ratings of *a priori* happy, sad, and control music excerpts. Ratings were made along arousal and valence dimensions using a pictorial rating scale (Bradley & Lang, 1994). Happy excerpts were rated overall as being positive in valence, and sad excerpts were rated as overall low in valence regardless of the participant group in each case. In fact, Caria and colleagues observed the trend that the Aspergers group rated happy music as slightly higher in valence than the neurotypical participants, suggesting heightened sensitivity to the positive emotion cues presented in the happy pieces. At the very least, the evidence suggests that individuals who are relatively poor at identifying emotion in other people are spared of decrements in the identification of emotion in music. So is there something special about music, or is there some deficiency in social empathy processing, but one which has no influence upon the emotional contagion component of affective empathy?

Consistent with Caria et al.'s observations, a study by Fan, Chen, Chen, Decety, & Cheng (2014) indicated that ASD participants actually had increased sensitivity compared with neurotypical participants when observing images of someone in pain. They experienced emotional contagion and affective empathy, but poor social understanding or cognitive empathy. The authors concluded that the social deficits associated with ASD are multifaceted and that not all facets are impaired, and some may even be enhanced, relative to normal participants (see also Happé, 1999). The evidence, then, suggests that socially low empathizers may even find recluse and comfort in music, where emotion can be communicated, without having to deal with the complexities of the social world (Molnar-Szakacs et al., 2009).

18.5.3 Shared circuitry for social and music processing

The evidence presented in this chapter suggests that, despite numerous complexities, it is possible to explain how differential responses to music can be explained by individual differences in our empathy systems. The literature reviewed points to the following explanation. First, cognitive and affective empathy are dissociable (Dziobek et al., 2008), and individuals who have deficits in cognitive empathy can be spared a deficit in affective empathy. Furthermore, people with functional levels of affective empathy appear also to have the ability to relate to emotion in music. My assertion, therefore, is

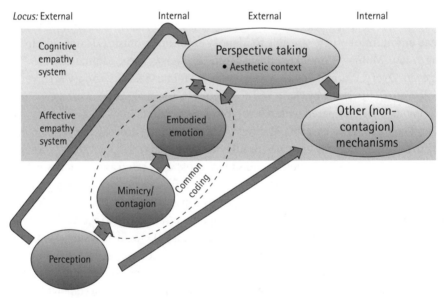

FIG. 18.2 A Common Coding model applied to music emotion processing. The affective empathy system is here apprehended by music perception. The cognitive empathy system detects that the source is music and so prosocial processing is not required. Emotional contagion is the focus of the figure, taking place in the common coding region (dashed ellipse), however, the additional arrows and the "Other" affective empathy system component remind us that emotional contagion is not the only mechanism through which emotion can be communicated (as per Juslin & Västfjäll, 2008; Juslin et al., 2010; Juslin, 2013). Other symbols and shapes are the same as for Fig. 18.1.

that affective empathy components are shared by both music and social stimulation. If my assertion is correct, it means that people are able to experience emotional contagion to a wide range of stimuli in a generalized way, and this lends support to the bottom up nature of the Common Coding Model of Prosocial Behavior Processing presented in Fig. 18.1. In the case of music, the only processing the *cognitive* empathy system needs to undertake is to identify that the stimulus causing the emotional contagion is the music. Two implications of the model are that:

- There is much less burden on the cognitive empathy system when processing music than when dealing with complex social interactions.
- The common coding perception-action emotional contagion component is shared by social and non-social (musical) sources—in other words, music apprehends the emotional contagion component of the affective empathy system.

A visual description of how this works is shown in Fig. 18.2. It should be noted, too, that the perspective taking component, in detecting an aesthetic context, activates a state of dissociation from pain circuits. This means that a wide range of emotional and other activation can be enjoyed (Schubert, 1996, 2009–2010, 2012, 2013b).

18.6 Implications for musical identity

The capacity for people with impairments in social processing, but good ability to identify emotion in music has important implications for musical identity. High empathizers may be well equipped to enjoy music that is socially desirable, while people with low capacity to process social situations, but with normal capacity to capture emotions through contagion, as appears to be the case for people with ASD, may find music a refuge from social activity, allowing such individuals to experience the pleasure of activating the common coding contagion circuits and so to develop a strong and eccentric musical identity unhindered by social desirability (Schubert Hargreaves, & North, 2014). In other words, because group identity shapes musical behavior (Hargreaves & North, 1999; Lamont, 2002), difficulties in interacting with groups due to social limitations must influence one's musical identity. For example, a study about musical preferences by Bhatara et al. found that adolescents with ASD reported a greater liking for classical music than normal developing individuals did. One of the explanations for this skewed preference was that the adolescents with ASD have a "lesser use of music as a mark of social affiliation and peer-group bonding" (Bhatara, Quintin, Fombonne, & Levitin, 2013, p. 100). The Common Coding Model of Prosocial Behavior Processing provides a compendious explanation of the behavior.

Because musical identity is a deeply personal and multifaceted aspect of the musical experience, it is important that theory building be used to help better understand how it comes about, changes and influences us. To date, the bulk of theory building in musical

identities finds its sources in social psychology, motivation, and music education literature (MacDonald, Hargreaves, & Miell, 2009). The current chapter presents a departure
from this trend by proposing a cognitive model that, although closely tied to social psychology, provides a cognitive explanation of one aspect of musical identity. We cannot,
of course, assert that all individual differences in musical identity can be attributed to
different levels of functioning of affective and cognitive empathy systems. The current
chapter, instead, proposes that people who have impaired levels of social processing
capacity will be open to a potentially diverse range of musical identities than their more
prosocially privileged counterparts. If affective empathy is intact in these individuals as
is the case in people with Asperger's syndrome (Dziobek et al., 2008; Harari, Shamay-
Tsoory, Ravid, & Levkovitz, 2010; Shamay-Tsoory, 2011; Volkmar, Klin, & McPartland,
2014), (emotional) contagion circuits can be activated when listening to music, which
both ignite and reinforce their identity (for example, by the feeling of oneness with a
style of music that they like). An interesting point along the range of social impairments
is the predicted acquisition of more extreme, passionate, and eccentric (e.g., non-popu-
lar) connections with music, partly as a refuge from complex social interactions, but
also as a reflection of an intact affective (as distinct from cognitive) empathy processing
system. Emotions can be enjoyed through contagion circuit activation, without worry-
ing about, or understanding, the pressures from others to maintain in-group values. In
some cases, matches in eccentric tastes with others may provide small steps for these
individuals in forming personal connections that are not available to a non-music loving, but also socially limited, individual. However, this is essentially speculation in need
of further research.

18.7 Conclusions and methodological considerations

Individual differences in empathy have a complex but potentially important relationship
with musical identity. In this chapter, I argued that individuals with deficits in their cognitive empathy system—namely, the reduced capacity to take the perspective of someone other than one's self—but with a normally functioning *affective* empathy system
have a stronger and more eccentric musical identity than neurotypical individuals. This
reflects behavioral data demonstrating that such individuals are not constrained by social
norms. The proposed Common Coding Model of Prosocial Behavior Processing leads
to the conclusion that as the cognitive empathizing system becomes poorer at processing socially relevant information, but stable levels of affective empathy functioning are
retained, one's musical identity will become a more important marker of who they are.
Therefore, non-social stimuli such as music become increasingly important to otherwise
normally functioning individuals who have impoverished capacity for social interaction.
This is a somewhat bold assertion which is perhaps an extreme interpretation of a limited

data set. However, the underlying intention is to present a theoretical stance that may help drive an understanding of findings and further research.

The common coding principle upon which the present model is based tells us that actions and emotions that are perceived are processed by the same mental circuits as the production of the same actions would. In the case of empathy, it is the perceived emotion that is seamlessly, automatically, and involuntarily converted into the emotional act, or felt emotion (internal locus). This perceived-felt equivalence then provides input to the perspective taking component, which uses the data to simulate the external locus emotion being perceived, and also adjusts the felt emotion presented by the emotional contagion, common coding circuits. The model used to develop the present argument is based on our current understanding of the structure and precursors of empathy, which will surely continue to change as new measurements and theoretical discoveries are made. While the present theory is a cognitive one, some of its inspiration comes from neuroscientific data and the idea of mirror neurons (Gallese & Goldman, 1998; Gallese, 2003, 2007; Gallese, Keysers, & Rizzolatti, 2004; Sevdalis & Keller, 2009, 2011).

It should be noted, too, that emotional contagion and the entire empathy system is not the only path through which emotions can be transmitted. Juslin proposes several others (Juslin & Västfjäll, 2008; Juslin, Liljeström, Västfjäll, D., & Lundqvist, 2010; Juslin, 2013), including those that require cognitive processing prior to emotional outputs, in contrast to the present model that only focuses on the case when emotion is generated virtually directly from perception (Zajonc, 1984).

Similarly, empathy is not the only system for generating prosocial behavior. Empathy focuses on social situations where caring and compassion are required, but some social situations may call for non-empathy related behaviors that are still prosocial, such as aggression to protect a vulnerable person (Johnson, Caron, Mikolajewski, Shirtcliff, Eckel, & Taylor, 2014). Furthermore, there are political and social norms that dictate what constitutes prosocial behavior. Factors such as psychopathy (which is sometimes conceptualized as the opposite of empathy) and group identity can explain apparently anti-social behavior such as victimization and cruelty (see, e.g., Baron-Cohen, 2011; White, 2014). Many social behavioral norms have elements that are culturally constructed (Cheon, Mathur, & Chiao, 2010).

These limitations should be considered when applying the Common Coding Model of Prosocial Behavior Processing proposed here. The limitations may lead to modifications of the model, such as relabeling the affective empathy and cognitive empathy systems without the term "empathy," hence making it more general. The important point is that of the apprehension of common coding contagion circuits by music perception. Furthermore, other social psychological and personality factors, apart from empathy related concepts, are known to influence one's musical identity (Hargreaves, MacDonald, & Miell, 2012). The present chapter focussed on the issue of empathy because it raises interesting questions and conundrums about how one who connects with music might not connect so well with people.

With these limitations in mind, some closing remarks are made regarding methodological issues. Future research should take into account the ability that an individual has to self-report both felt (internal locus) and perceived (external locus) emotions, both in response to music and in response to social settings. The matching of felt and expressed emotional loci reported by the participant provides evidence that emotional contagion has occurred (Schubert, 2013a). Even though this method appears to contradict the idea that contagion is an automated, involuntary process, such self-reporting is procedurally simple and inexpensive, and makes the (possibly justifiable) assumption that it raises a subconscious process to a level available to the introspection of the individual. The other critical variable that could help directly test the proposed model is the psychometric assessment of the various components of the model. For example, there exists an explicit self-report test for emotional contagion (Doherty, 1997), and the QCAE itself consists of subscales that can access different components of the affective and cognitive empathy systems.

Based on the Common Coding Model of Prosocial Behavior Processing, individual differences that lead to different musical identities can be narrowed down to two cognitive processes—one's vulnerability to emotional contagion and one's propensity to dissociate when listening to music (or engaging with any form of art). Dissociation here means the psychological capacity of the listener to "switch off" pain circuits, and therefore allow any activation caused by the music to be enjoyed. So, in addition to emotional contagion, the propensity of the individual to dissociate could be used as an indicator of how the cognitive empathy system processes musical and social information, for example by measuring Absorption proneness (Garrido & Schubert, 2011, 2013), but also through empathy measures that focus specifically on music (Kreutz, Mitchell, McDowall, & Schubert, 2008).

In the present context, the cognitive empathy system determines that the listener is in an aesthetic context and therefore triggers dissociation, explaining why activation of contagion circuits, when in an aesthetic (musically engaged) context, can be enjoyed, as reported in the study by Bhatara et al. (2013). The individual's trait-based potential to dissociate appears to be tied to their absorption proneness, but also with the ability to fantasize (Butler, 2006; Garrido & Schubert, 2011; Herbert, 2011). Fantasy proneness is a possible contender as a component of empathy (Davis, 1983; Niec & Russ, 2002; Nomura & Akai, 2012; Stotland, Matthews, Sherman, Hansson, & Richardson, 1978), and may be related to the ability of the perspective-taking component to simulate not just real but also imagined events. So, individual differences in fantasy and musical identity may be another potentially related area for further research.

Although empathy as a neuroscientifically and psychologically based phenomenon has received considerable research attention in recent years, this chapter has shown that it is only just beginning to be considered in relation to music. Aspects of empathy may in fact provide a key to understanding some highly powerful, individually varied experiences in music that could have important implications for understanding another path through which musical identity is formed. However, with such little work in the area, partly due to the complexity of the topic (e.g., that empathy itself is thought to consist of separable components, which can then be applied to music perception), much, further research awaits this fascinating topic.

References

Adams, F. (2001). Empathy, neural imaging and the theory versus simulation debate. *Mind & Language*, 16(4), 368–92.

Baron-Cohen, S. (2011). *Zero degrees of empathy: a new theory of human cruelty*. London: Penguin/Allen Lane.

Baron-Cohen, S., Leslie, A.M., & Frith, U. (1985). Does the autistic child have a "theory of mind"? *Cognition*, 21(1), 37–46.

Batson, C.D. (2009). These things called empathy: eight related but distinct phenomena. In: J. Decety & W. Ickes (Eds.) *The social neuroscience of empathy*, pp. 3–15. Cambridge: MIT Press.

Bernhardt, B.C. & Singer, T. (2012). The neural basis of empathy. *Annual Review of Neuroscience*, 35, 1–23.

Bhatara, A., Quintin, E.-M., Fombonne, E., & Levitin, D.J. (2013). Early sensitivity to sound and musical preferences and enjoyment in adolescents with autism spectrum disorders. *Psychomusicology: Music, Mind, and Brain*, 23(2), 100–8.

Bradley, M.M. & Lang, P.J. (1994). Measuring emotion: the self-assessment mannequin and the semantic differential. *Journal of Behavior Therapy and Experimental Psychiatry*, 25(1), 49–59.

Brook, M. & Kosson, D.S. (2013). Impaired cognitive empathy in criminal psychopathy: evidence from a laboratory measure of empathic accuracy. *Journal of Abnormal Psychology*, 122(1), 156–66.

Butler, L.D. (2006). Normative dissociation. *Psychiatric Clinics of North America*, 29(1), 45–62.

Caria, A., Venuti, P., & de Falco, S. (2011). Functional and dysfunctional brain circuits underlying emotional processing of music in autism spectrum disorders. *Cerebral Cortex*, 21(12), 2838–49.

Cheon, R.K., Mathur, V.A., & Chiao, J.Y. (2010). Empathy as cultural process: insights from the cultural neuroscience of empathy. *World Cultural Psychiatry Research Reviews*, 5, 32–42.

Cialdini, Brown, S.L., Lewis, B.P., Luce, C., & Neuberg, S.L.. (1997). Reinterpreting the empathy–altruism relationship: when one into one equals oneness. *Journal of Personality and Social Psychology*, 73(3), 481–94.

Clark, T.F., Winkielman, P., & McIntosh, D.N. (2008). Autism and the extraction of emotion from briefly presented facial expressions: stumbling at the first step of empathy. *Emotion*, 8(6), 803–9.

Clements, W.A. & Perner, J. (1994). Implicit understanding of belief. *Cognitive Development*, 9(4), 377–95.

Clynes, M. & Nettheim, N. (1982). The living quality of music: neurobiologic basis of communicating feeling. In: M. Clynes (Ed.) Music, mind, and brain: The neuropsychology of music, pp. 47–82. New York, NY: Plenum.

Cohen, J. (1992). A power primer. *Psychological Bulletin*, 112(1), 155–9.

Davis, M.H. (1983). Measuring individual differences in empathy: evidence for a multidimensional approach. *Journal of Personality and Social Psychology*, 44(1), 113–26.

Decety, J., Chen, C., Harenski, C., & Kiehl, K.A. (2013). An fMRI study of affective perspective taking in individuals with psychopathy: imagining another in pain does not evoke empathy. *Frontiers in Human Neuroscience*, 7(489), 1–12.

Decety, J. & Grèzes, J. (2006). The power of simulation: imagining one's own and others behavior. *Brain Research*, 1079(1), 4–14.

Decety, J., & Jackson, P.L. (2004). The functional architecture of human empathy. *Behavioral and Cognitive Neuroscience Reviews*, 3(2), 71–100.

Decety, J. & Lamm, C. (2006). Human empathy through the lens of social neuroscience. *Scientific World Journal*, 6, 1146–63.

Decety, J. & Lamm, C. (2009). Empathy versus personal distress: recent evidence from social neuroscience. In: J. Decety & W. Ickes (Eds.) *The social neuroscience of empathy*, pp. 199–213. Cambridge, MA: MIT Press.

Doherty, R.W. (1997). The emotional contagion scale: a measure of individual differences. *Journal of Nonverbal Behavior*, 21(2), 131–54.

Dziobek, I., Rogers, K., Fleck, S., et al. (2008). Dissociation of cognitive and emotional empathy in adults with Asperger syndrome using the Multifaceted Empathy Test (MET). *Journal of Autism and Developmental Disorders*, 38(3), 464–73.

Egermann, H. & McAdams, S. (2013). Empathy and emotional contagion as a link between recognized and felt emotions in music listening. *Music Perception*, 31(2), 139–56.

Evans, P. & Schubert, E. (2008). Relationships between expressed and felt emotions in music. *Musicae Scientiae*, 12(1), 75–99.

Fan, Y.-T., Chen, C., Chen, S.C., Decety, J., & Cheng, Y. (2014). Empathic arousal and social understanding in individuals with autism: evidence from fMRI and ERP measurements. *Social Cognitive and Affective Neuroscience*, 9(8), 1203–13.

Gabrielsson, A. (2002). Perceived emotion and felt emotion: same or different? *Musicae Scientiae*, 6(1, Special Issue), 123–48.

Gabrielsson, A. & Juslin, P.N. (1996). Emotional expression in music performance: Between the performer's intention and the listener's experience. *Psychology of Music*, 24(1), 68–91.

Gallese, V. (2003). The manifold nature of interpersonal relations: the quest for a common mechanism. *Philosophical Transactions of the Royal Society of London Series B: Biological Sciences*, 358(1431), 517–28.

Gallese, V. (2007). Before and below "theory of mind": embodied simulation and the neural correlates of social cognition. *Philosophical Transactions of the Royal Society of London B: Biological Sciences*, 362(1480), 659–69.

Gallese, V. & Goldman, A. (1998). Mirror neurons and the simulation theory of mind-reading. *Trends in Cognitive Sciences*, 2(12), 493–501.

Gallese, V., Keysers, C., & Rizzolatti, G. (2004). A unifying view of the basis of social cognition. *Trends in Cognitive Sciences*, 8(9), 396–403.

Garrido, S. & Schubert, E. (2011). Individual differences in the enjoyment of negative emotion in music: a literature review and experiment. *Music Perception*, 28(3), 279–95.

Garrido, S. & Schubert, E. (2013). Adaptive and maladaptive attraction to negative emotions in music. *Musicae Scientiae*, 17(2), 147–66.

Goldman, A. & de Vignemont, F. (2009). Is social cognition embodied? *Trends in Cognitive Sciences*, 13(4), 154–9.

Gonzalez-Liencres, C., Shamay-Tsoory, S.G., & Brüne, M. (2013). Towards a neuroscience of empathy: ontogeny, phylogeny, brain mechanisms, context and psychopathology. *Neuroscience & Biobehavioral Reviews*, 37, 1537–48.

Hall, A.E. & Bracken, C.C. (2011). "I really liked that movie": testing the relationship between trait empathy, transportation, perceived realism, and movie enjoyment. *Journal of Media Psychology: Theories, Methods, and Applications*, 23(2), 90–9.

Happé, F. (1999). Autism: cognitive deficit or cognitive style? *Trends in Cognitive Sciences*, 3(6), 216–22.

Harari, H., Shamay-Tsoory, S.G., Ravid, M., & Levkovitz, Y. (2010). Double dissociation between cognitive and affective empathy in borderline personality disorder. *Psychiatry Research*, 175(3), 277–9.

Hargreaves, D.J., MacDonald, R., & Miell, D. (2012). Musical identities mediate musical development. In: G.E. McPherson & G.F. Welch (Eds.) *The Oxford handbook of music education*, pp. 125–42. Oxford: Oxford University Press.

Hargreaves, D.J. & North, A.C. (1999). The functions of music in everyday life: redefining the social in music psychology. *Psychology of Music*, 27(1), 71–83.

Hatfield, E., Cacioppo, J.T., & Rapson, R.L. (1994). *Emotional contagion*. Cambridge: Cambridge University Press.

Hatfield, E., Rapson, R.L., & Le, Y.-C.L. (2009). Emotional contagion and empathy. In: J. Decety and W. Ickes (Eds.) *The social neuroscience of empathy*, pp. 19–30. Cambridge, MA: MIT Press.

Heaton, P., Hermelin, B., & Pring, L. (1999). Can children with autistic spectrum disorders perceive affect in music? An experimental investigation. *Psychological Medicine*, 29(6), 1405–10.

Herbert, R. (2011). *Everyday music listening: absorption, dissociation and trancing*. Farnham: Ashgate Publishing, Ltd.

Jensen, R.T. & Moran, D. (2012). Introduction: intersubjectivity and empathy. *Phenomenology and the Cognitive Sciences*, 11(2), 125–33.

Johnson, M.M, Caron, K.M., Mikolajewski, A.J., Shirtcliff, E.A., Eckel, L.A., & Taylor, J. (2014). Psychopathic traits, empathy, and aggression are differentially related to cortisol awakening response. *Journal of Psychopathology and Behavioral Assessment*, 36(3), 380–88.

Jones, S.S. (2007). Imitation in infancy the development of mimicry. *Psychological Science*, 18(7), 593–9.

Jones, A.P, Happé, F.G., Gilbert, F., Burnett, S., & Viding, E. (2010). Feeling, caring, knowing: different types of empathy deficit in boys with psychopathic tendencies and autism spectrum disorder. *Journal of Child Psychology and Psychiatry*, 51(11), 1188–97.

Juslin, P.N. (1997). Emotional communication in music performance: a functionalist perspective and some data. *Music Perception*, 14(4), 383–418.

Juslin, P.N. (2000). Cue utilization in communication of emotion in music performance: relating performance to perception. *Journal of Experimental Psychology: Human Perception & Performance*, 26(6), 1797–813.

Juslin, P.N. (2001). Communicating emotion in music performance: a review and a theoretical framework. In: P. N. Juslin & J. A. Sloboda (Eds.) *Music and emotion: theory and research* (Series in Affective Science), pp. 309–37. London: Oxford University Press.

Juslin, P.N. (2013). From everyday emotions to aesthetic emotions: towards a unified theory of musical emotions. *Physics of Life Reviews*, 10(3), 235–66.

Juslin, P.N. & Västfjäll, D. (2008). Emotional responses to music: the need to consider underlying mechanisms. *Behavioral and Brain Sciences*, 31(5), 559–75.

Juslin, P.N. & Laukka, P. (2003). Communication of emotions in vocal expression and music performance: different channels, same code? *Psychological Bulletin*, 129(5), 770–814.

Juslin, P.N. & Lindström, E. (2010). Musical expression of emotions: modelling listeners' judgements of composed and performed features. *Music Analysis*, 29, 334–64.

Juslin, P.N., Liljeström, S., Västfjäll, D., & Lundqvist, L.-O. (2010). How does music evoke emotions? Exploring the underlying mechanisms. In: P. N. Juslin & J. Sloboda (Eds.) *Handbook of music and emotion: theory, research, and applications*, 605–42. Oxford: Oxford University Press.

Kreutz, G., Mitchell, L.A., McDowall, J., & Schubert, E. (2008). Cognitive styles influence the perception of musical coherence. In: K. Miyazaki et al. (Eds.) *10th International Conference on Music Perception and Cognition* (Sapporo, Japan).

Kuhl, P.K. & Meltzoff, A.N. (1996). Infant vocalizations in response to speech: vocal imitation and developmental change. *Journal of the Acoustical Society of America*, 100 (401), 2425–38.

Laird, J.D., Alibozak, T., Davainis, D., et al. (1994). Individual differences in the effects of spontaneous mimicry on emotional contagion. *Motivation & Emotion*, 18(3), 231–47.

Lamont, A. (2002). Musical identities and the school environment. In: R.A.R. MacDonald, D.J. Hargreaves, & D. Miell (Eds.) *Musical identities*, pp. 41–59. Oxford: Oxford University Press.

Laurence, F. (2008). Music and empathy. In: O. Urbain (Ed.) *Music and conflict transformation harmonies and dissonances in geopolitics*, pp. 13–25. London: I. B Tauris & Co.

Leman, M. (2008). *Embodied music: cognition and mediation technology*. Cambridge, MA: MIT Press.

MacDonald, R.A.R., Hargreaves, D.J., & Miell, D. (2009). Musical identities. In: S. Hallam, I. Cross, & M. Thaut (Eds.) *The Oxford handbook of music psychology*, pp. 462–70. Oxford: Oxford University Press.

Meltzoff, A.N. & Decety, J. (2003). What imitation tells us about social cognition: a rapprochement between developmental psychology and cognitive neuroscience. *Philosophical Transactions of the Royal Society of London Series B: Biological Sciences*, 358(1431), 491–500.

Meltzoff, A.N. & Moore, M.K. (1977). Imitation of facial and manual gestures by human neonates. *Science*, 198(4312), 75–8.

Molnar, M., Kondakor, I., Barta, Z., Toth, E., & Weisz, J. (2001). Dimensional analysis of event-related potentials in animal experiments. *Pszichologia: Az MTA Pszichologiai Intezetenek Folyoirata*, 21(3), 227–48.

Molnar-Szakacs, I., Wang, M.J., Laugeson, E.A., Overy, K., Wu, W.-L., & Piggot, J. (2009). Autism, emotion recognition and the mirror neuron system: the case of music. *McGill Journal of Medicine*, 12(2), 87–98.

Niec, L.N. & Russ, S.W. (2002). Children's internal representations, empathy and fantasy play: a validity study of the SCORS-Q. *Psychological Assessment*, 14(3), 331–8.

Nomura, K. & Akai, S. (2012). Empathy with fictional stories: reconsideration of the fantasy scale of the interpersonal reactivity index. *Psychological Reports*, 110(1), 304–14.

Nummenmaa, L., Hirvonen, J., Parkkola, R., & Hietanen, J.K. (2008). Is emotional contagion special? An fMRI study on neural systems for affective and cognitive empathy. *NeuroImage*, 43(3), 571–80.

Oatley, K. (1999). Why fiction may be twice as true as fact: fiction as cognitive and emotional simulation. *Review of General Psychology*, 3(2), 101–17.

Oberman, L.M. & Ramachandran, V.S. (2007). The simulating social mind: the role of the mirror neuron system and simulation in the social and communicative deficits of autism spectrum disorders. *Psychological Bulletin*, 133(2), 310–27.

Overy, K. & Molnar-Szakacs, I. (2009). Being together in time: musical experience and the mirror neuron system. *Music Perception*, 26(5), 489–504.

Paul, E.S. (2000). Empathy with animals and with humans: are they linked? *Anthrozoos*, 13(4), 194–202.

Pham, L.B. & Taylor, S.E. (1999). From thought to action: effects of process-versus outcome-based mental simulations on performance. *Personality and Social Psychology Bulletin*, 25(2), 250–60.

Pike, A. (1972). A phenomenological analysis of emotional experience in music. *Journal of Research in Music Education*, 20, 262–8.

Preston, S.D. & De Waal, F. (2002). Empathy: its ultimate and proximate bases. *Behavioral and Brain Sciences*, 25(01), 1–20.

Prinz, W. (1997). Perception and action planning. *European Journal of Cognitive Psychology*, 9(2), 129–54.

Rae Westbury, H. & Neumann, D.L. (2008). Empathy-related responses to moving film stimuli depicting human and non-human animal targets in negative circumstances. *Biological Psychology*, 78(1), 66–74.

Reniers, R.L.E.P., Corcoran, R., Drake, R., Shryane, N.M., & Völlm, B.A. (2011). The QCAE: a questionnaire of cognitive and affective empathy. *Journal of Personality Assessment*, 93(1), 84–95.

Rosenthal-von der Pütten, A.M., Krämer, N.C., Hoffmann, L., Sobieraj, S., & Eimler, S.C. (2013). An experimental study on emotional reactions towards a robot. *International Journal of Social Robotics*, 5(1), 17–34.

Scherer, K.R. & Zentner, M.R. (2001). Emotional effects of music: production rules. In: P.N. Juslin & J.A. Sloboda (Eds.) *Music and emotion: theory and research* (Series in Affective Science), pp. 361–92. Oxford: Oxford University Press.

Schubert, E. (1996). Enjoyment of negative emotions in music: an associative network explanation. *Psychology of Music*, 24(1), 18–28.

Schubert, E. (2009–2010). The fundamental function of music. *Musicae Scientiae*, 13(2, Special Issue), 63–81.

Schubert, E. (2012). Spreading activation and dissociation: a cognitive mechanism for creative processing in music. In: D.J. Hargreaves, D.E. Miell, & R.A.R. MacDonald (Eds.) *Musical imaginations: multidisciplinary perspectives on creativity, performance, and perception*, pp. 124–40. Oxford: Oxford University Press.

Schubert, E. (2013a). Emotion felt by the listener and expressed by the music: literature review and theoretical perspectives. *Frontiers in Psychology*, 4, 837.

Schubert, E. (2013b). Loved music can make a listener feel negative emotions. *Musicae Scientiae*, 17(1), 11–26.

Schubert, E., Hargreaves, D.J., & North, A.C. (2014). A dynamically minimalist cognitive explanation of musical preference: is familiarity everything? *Frontiers in Psychology*, 5, 38.

Schubert, E., Ferguson, S., Farrar, N., Taylor, D., & McPherson, G.E. (2013). The six emotion-face clock as a tool for continuously rating discrete emotional responses to music. In: M. Aramaki, et al. (Eds.) *From sounds to music and emotions* (Lecture Notes in Computer Science), pp. 1–18. Berlin: Springer.

Sevdalis, V. & Keller, P.E. (2009). Self-recognition in the perception of actions performed in synchrony with music. *Annals of the New York Academy of Sciences*, 1169(1), 499–502.

Sevdalis, V. & Keller, P.E. (2011). Perceiving performer identity and intended expression intensity in point-light displays of dance. *Psychological Research*, 75(5), 423–34.

Shamay-Tsoory, S.G. (2011). The neural bases for empathy. *The Neuroscientist*, 17(10), 18–24.

Shamay-Tsoory, S.G, Aharon-Peretz, J., & Perry, D. (2009). Two systems for empathy: a double dissociation between emotional and cognitive empathy in inferior frontal gyrus versus ventromedial prefrontal lesions. *Brain*, 132(3), 617–27.

Singer, T. (2006). The neuronal basis and ontogeny of empathy and mind reading: review of literature and implications for future research. *Neuroscience & Biobehavioral Reviews*, 30(6), 855–63.

Singer, T., Seymour, B., O'Doherty, J.P., Stephan, K.E., Dolan, R.J., & Frith, C.D. (2006). Empathic neural responses are modulated by the perceived fairness of others. *Nature*, 439(7075), 466–9.

Stotland, E., Matthews, K.E., Sherman, S.E., Hansson, R.O., & Richardson, B.Z. (1978). *Empathy, fantasy and helping*. Beverley Hills, CA: Sage.

Volkmar, F.R., Klin, A., & McPartland, J.C. (2014). Asperger's syndrome: an overview. In: J.C. McPartland, A. Klin, & F.R. Volkmar (Eds.) *Asperger syndrome: assessing and treating high-functioning autism spectrum disorders*, 2nd edn, pp. 1–43. New York, NY: Guilford Publications.

White, B.A. (2014). Who cares when nobody is watching? Psychopathic traits and empathy in prosocial behaviors. *Personality and Individual Differences*, 56, 116–21.

Wing, L., Gould, J., & Gillberg, C. (2011). Autism spectrum disorders in the DSM-V: better or worse than the DSM-IV? *Research in Developmental Disabilities*, 32(2), 768–73.

Wöllner, C. (2012). Is empathy related to the perception of emotional expression in music? A multimodal time-series analysis. *Psychology of Aesthetics, Creativity, and the Arts*, 6(3), 214–23.

Zahavi, D. (2008). Simulation, projection and empathy. *Consciousness and Cognition*, 17(2), 514–22.

Zajonc, R.B. (1984). On the primacy of affect. *American Psychologist*, 39(2), 117–23.

Zaki, J. & Ochsner, K.N. (2012). The neuroscience of empathy: progress, pitfalls and promise. *Nature Neuroscience*, 15(5), 675–80.

Zukow-Goldring, P. (2012). Assisted imitation: first steps in the seed model of language development. *Language Sciences*, 34(5), 569–82.

Research for this chapter was supported by the Australian Research Council, FT120100053.

SECTION 5

··

MUSICAL INSTITUTIONS AND PRACTITIONERS

··

CHAPTER 19

....

IMPERSONATING THE MUSIC IN PERFORMANCE

....

JOHN RINK

19.1 REVELATIONS

....

IT seems appropriate to start by divulging my dual identities as pianist and musicologist, not least because these respectively inform the two halves of this chapter. First I describe a number of occasions when I found myself asking searching questions before or as I performed, or making discoveries that ended up preoccupying me long after the event; I then compare other musicians' experiences in the heat of the moment. From these, I conclude that "the music" one makes in performance not only emerges from but may constitute what one is as a performer—in other words, that one's *identity as a performer* may be shaped by one's sense of *identity with the music*. The musician's individuality may therefore be denied and realized at one and the same time in the act of performance.[1] The second half of the essay explores some writing on performance which, although problematic, nevertheless casts light on the "identity as"/"identity with" relationship despite appearances to the contrary. One of the chapter's main aims is to explore this sort of impersonation from the perspective of performers' own experiences and perceptions, rather than peering at it from the outside as in much of the literature on musical subjectivities.[2]

---

[1] At least three different meanings of "identity" are invoked here: (1) "Who or what a person or thing is; a distinct impression of a single person or thing presented to or perceived by others; a set of characteristics or a description that distinguishes a person or thing from others"; (2) "The quality or condition of being the same in substance, composition, nature, properties, or in particular qualities under consideration; absolute or essential sameness; oneness"; and (3) "The condition of being identified in feeling, interest, etc.; identification *with*." (*Oxford English Dictionary*, s.v. "identity," respectively definitions 1a, 2b and 6.)

[2] For example, see Auslander (2006), Cumming (2000), and select chapters in Auslander (2003) and Cook & Pettengill (2013). Davidson (2002) does write from the performer's perspective, although her focus is on "what makes a performer." Compare Doğantan-Dack (2008), Coessens, Crispin, & Douglas

19.2 CAUGHT IN THE ACT

Disconcerting questions have often entered my thoughts while waiting backstage before a public performance, among them: "Where is the music in my mind? What form does it have? How will I access it, and where will it come from?" Soul-searching along these lines is hardly advisable immediately before a solo recital or when playing a concerto with orchestra; yet such questions usefully remind us that for the musician—as indeed for the listener—"the music" is much more than the notes in the score, just as performance is not only a matter of reproducing a given composer's intentions. Fortunately, in all of my performances over the years, I have come unstuck only once: upon reaching a cadence in a challenging fugue by J. S. Bach in a lunchtime recital some 25 years ago, my memory suddenly failed and I was forced to limp to the next piece in the program. I later tried to determine why this embarrassing lapse had occurred, not least to ensure that it would never happen again. The answer was simple: I had not thoroughly assimilated the music. Although I could happily play it either with or without the score in rehearsal, my mental block in performance demonstrated that the music had not been properly internalized. This was a salutary lesson—one that led me to develop a technique to ward off the memory threats posed by performing in public. Now, several hours before going on stage, I play through the entire program in my mind away from the instrument, making certain that each and every note is felt and heard deep in my imagination, with mental reference to the score as required even though the score itself is kept well out of reach. What results is an all but physical enactment of the specific moves needed to bring the imagined sounds into reality, thereby paving the way for the public realization to follow.

This sort of visceral mental rehearsal requires enormous concentration if every detail of the music is to find its place in the unfolding narrative. But rehearsal along these lines also reaps rich rewards in terms of increased power of recall and intensity of focus during performance. I suspect it was because of this ingraining of the music's detail and trajectory that a different sort of experience began to characterize my music-making in public. One occasion stands out. I had been asked to play a nocturne in a performance "showcase" at the end of a 2-day conference on Chopin interpretation in 2004 at the Cité de la musique in Paris. Because of the demands of my university role, I arrived in Paris not only pianistically out of shape, but not having touched an instrument for over 2 years, so I reluctantly informed the organizers at the start of the conference that I would not perform after all. Just a few hours later, however, I found myself captivated by the

(2009), and Persson (1993), who observed over 20 years ago that, despite considerable scholarly attention to musical performance, "the literature has nevertheless remained conspicuously and surprisingly void of individual musicians' accounts of how they understand their own performance and how they develop an understanding of their chosen repertoire" (p. 36). This lacuna was the rationale behind a study day on musical performance, subjectivity, and experimentation at the University of York in June, 2014, focussing on how subjectivity is constituted through musical performance, how the performing self is embodied in performance, and "Who is the 'I' that performs?"

sound of a period piano that one of the presenters was using to play music examples. This Pleyel upright ("pianino") from 1855, which was of a type favored by Chopin and used throughout his adult life while teaching, so completely matched my conception of how Chopin "should" sound—at least as far as my own playing was concerned—that I organized a brief practice session the following day to try it myself. As soon as I put my hands on the instrument, I felt such an intimate connection with it that every stroke of the keys produced precisely the "sound of Chopin" that I had in my inner ear. Never before had my musical imagination been so completely engaged when playing Chopin. I vowed at once to perform in public that evening, and with only 10 minutes to warm up on a modern instrument later that afternoon, I played the nocturne from memory on the pianino before several hundred people, with the precise technical control that I might have achieved had I been in excellent performing shape from the start. Because it produces a comparatively quiet sound, the pianino had been turned so that its back faced the darkened auditorium. I was therefore looking straight at the audience, but in fact could see nothing but a black void because of the bright lights occluding my view. As the piece progressed, with each sound being anticipated in my inner ear, which in turn prompted the precise physical motions required to produce them on the instrument, I was increasingly immersed in the experiencing of the music to the point that I forgot I was playing in public. My world was that of the music, my perceptions of time and space utterly conforming to it. It was as if I had *become* the music.

Since then, I find that this state of immersion often occurs when I perform in public, to the point that I expect and crave it. I am by no means the only musician to have such experiences, which, it seems, are also common to listeners even though, for them, physical embodiment is inevitably more virtual than real.[3] Gabrielsson's extensive study (2011) of what he terms "strong experiences" with music provides manifold accounts of the deeply immersive qualities of performance. Based on his research, Gabrielsson concludes:

> When music takes over, the surrounding world disappears. Time stands still, all that counts is the music and me, here and now ... [W]hen it comes to strong experiences, there is often a form of "bonding" with the music. It is described in various terms: one lives the music, is embraced by the music, is embedded in the music, possessed by the music, one identifies oneself with the music, the music and oneself are on the same wavelength. Sometimes, it is described as a special understanding of the music, the music feels self-evident, it is already there and one knows how it is going to continue.
>
> Gabrielsson, 2011, p. 77.

The testimonies that follow here—all of which come from performers participating in Gabrielsson's study—not only highlight music's role as a "technology of the

---

[3] See Eitan & Granot (2006) for discussion of listeners' associations of changes in musical parameters with physical space and bodily motion.

self,"[4] but also point to the "identity as"/"identity with" relationship that I have proposed. They also confirm that my own experiences as described above are far from unique:

> *Testimony 1:* Everything around me didn't exist … I was so immersed in what I had done that I didn't hear anything else.
>
> Young woman on performing a bassoon solo with orchestral
accompaniment; Gabrielsson, 2011, p. 63.

> *Testimony 2:* Playing is tension. You work with your whole body when you play. Every note is from top to toe. It's enormous concentration … When I get to this sort of level, then I don't experience tension or anything. It's an enormously relaxed feeling, an enormous lightness. It feels physically light. You don't reflect on what you are playing any longer. You just play. In such moments you are there by yourself with the music! There isn't any audience, there are no fellow musicians there either. On an occasion like that it is just music.
>
> Young male musician in a rock band, from an edited interview;
Gabrielsson, 2011, p. 83.

> *Testimony 3:* [I] slipped into the trance-like semi-euphoric state I can sometimes find myself in during performances … [I]t disconnects all consciousness about motor activity and all irrelevant information. You simply concentrate on producing the music, not on what you should do to produce it; and you concentrate 100% without actually making an effort. This state, as a rule, ceases when you stop playing.
>
> Young man, on performing in an orchestral concert;
Gabrielsson, 2011, p. 224.

> *Testimony 4:* [Sometimes in performing] you get that deep concentration. The total involvement in the music, the "now" without anxiety or fear of the difficulties, when your hearing is sharpened, your enjoyment is increased, and above all when time ceases to exist, all that is there in a course of musical events. The closest you can get is to call it a state of trance, but keen and clear as crystal, without any thought of your own ego and your own life's circumstances, the focus is somewhere else, on a general human, or rather universal, plane.
>
> Middle-aged female instrumentalist on performing Wagner;
Gabrielsson, 2011, p. 225.

> *Testimony 5:* [S]ometimes during a concert there are certain moments when I might lose concentration. It's not that I don't have control of the course of the music, but still it is some sort of distraction, a feeling of being outside, a sort of vacuum. But

---

[4] DeNora's term (1999; cf. Foucault, 1988). Referring to the participants in one of her studies, DeNora wrote that music was "not used to 'express' some 'internal' feeling state. Indeed, that music is part of the reflexive constitution of that state; it is a resource for the identification work of 'knowing how one feels'—a building material of 'subjectivity.'" (1999, p. 45).

during virtually all of this work and in particular in certain passages, it felt as if time and space ceased to exist. There was only *music*.

> Middle-aged male conductor; Gabrielsson, 2011, p. 226.

Testimony 6: Suddenly there is a feeling of absolute concordance, between us as musicians but also in relation to the musical intention and our own creation. The form becomes clear as crystal, the interpretation, phrasing, agogics, dynamics, etc. are just perfect, down to the microsecond. The music immediately acquires a special meaning, content, function … You hardly know that you are playing—you simply "are" in the music. A state where you completely forget yourself, forget all everyday associations and find yourself in a flow of function with the universe.

> Middle-aged man on improvising with two other musicians;
> Gabrielsson, 2011, p. 236.

These testimonies invite comment. First, it is important to note that they reflect a range of performative contexts, not just solo piano performance, which not only dominates the literature, but might be expected to engender "strong experience" more than other forms of performance because of its comparatively solipsistic character. The fact that instrumentalists, conductors, rock musicians, and improvisers playing in ensembles have "strong experiences" like these suggests that the proposed "identity as"/"identity with" relationship might be more broadly relevant, whether or not "specific musical identities … exist in relation to particular instruments."[5] Secondly, although these testimonies are similar to those of the listeners represented in Gabrielsson's study, there is at least one significant difference, namely, the physical internalization that happens by definition on the part of performers and that listeners normally cannot literally experience (as previously noted). Thirdly, these "strong experiences," however widespread among performers and listeners, are not necessarily frequent; nevertheless, more typical performance conditions may have much in common with them or with the flow state to which they can be compared.[6] Finally, the six testimonies indicate that a paradoxical feature of finding oneself in performance can be losing oneself in the music: such actualization may involve "completely forgetting" who you are and simply "being," or being in, the music.[7]

The discussion thus far has begged an important question, namely, what do we mean when referring to "the music"? It is certainly not the case that this has one and only one universally understood meaning. What is of particular interest here is how performers conceptualize and experience "the music" that they are playing or singing, and one way of approaching this ontological as well as phenomenological issue is to consider which characteristics of "the music" might have elicited the sorts of reactions assembled above.

---

[5] This is proposed by MacDonald, Hargreaves, & Miell (2002, p.13).

[6] For discussion see Csikszentmihalyi ([1992] 2002).

[7] This does not mean that the performer necessarily "becomes" *the composer*, an elision encouraged by Erich Leinsdorf: "The musician should 'become' Brahms or Debussy or whoever is on his program" (1981, p. 42). For discussion see Cusick (1994, p. 89); see also the section below on Cone (1974).

Inferring from the manifold responses gathered in his research on both performers and listeners,[8] Gabrielsson points specifically to the roles of instrumental or vocal timbre, intonation, dynamics, rhythm, formal features, and mode and harmony, as well individual or multiple notes, chords, themes, phrases, and larger sections (including part/whole relations), along with text and "emotional expression" in general. All of this may be relevant, but what is missing is reference to the physical input and presence of the individual musicians who gave rise to the music in performance that, in turn, generated the particular responses. As Coessens et al. observe,

> Music is not only inscribed into a score; to be fully-experienced, it has to be performed, which entails its being inscribed into the body of the performer. In that sense, the relation between score and performance can be reconsidered as the relation between extended inscription and embodied inscription. Music, when fully realized in performance, is embodied, gesturally memorized, spatially present in its bodily inscription and "outed" in the particular performance. The embodied inscription is not materialized, but part of the experience of the performer …
>
> Coessens, Crispin, & Douglas, 2009, p. 151.

Doğantan-Dack similarly posits that:

> the sounds and sound-producing actions heard in and through a recording do not simply *refer* to the performer: they rather *constitute* the performer and her musicianship. The performer *qua* performer comes into being simultaneously with the sounds she makes; the kinaesthetic markers that are embedded in the sonorous qualities of musical sounds are essential for the identity of the performing musician. As Naomi Cumming has observed the performer's "identity as a musician cannot be known apart from the sounds she makes" …[9] Ontologically, performers, whether they are seen or not, are firmly connected to their performances.
>
> Doğantan-Dack, 2008, p. 299.

One explanation of how thought becomes embodied action and how the two in tandem form the basis of the musician's experience might be that "during a performance, musical structures and units are retrieved from memory according to the performer's conceptual interpretation, and are then prepared for production and transformed into appropriate movements" (Palmer, 1997, p. 116). But such an explanation—however enlightening—is divorced from how performances actually *feel* for the musicians taking part in them. Even if more or less "technical" description is required to understand how music is "inscribed into the body of the performer"

---

[8] Gabrielsson also included composers in his research, although they were very much in the minority. Approximately 81% of the accounts emanate from listeners and c. 19% from performers (see Gabrielsson, 2011, p. 397).

[9] See Cumming (2000, p. 26). Compare Cumming's comment (1997, p. 17) that "The music forms the listener's experience"—a phenomenon that certainly could be adapted to the performer's experience.

and how "kinaesthetic markers … are embedded in the sonorous qualities of musical sounds," my belief is that for some if not most performers, "the music" is both *heard* and *felt* above all else, although the hearing and feeling in question are not what is commonly understood by these terms. Although Dunsby for one warns that "how the performer feels" is an inadequate premise for the study and practice of music in performance,[10] he nevertheless insists that:

> musical "feeling" for the performer is an amalgam of emotion and intelligence, of response and control, of empathy and command, of the autonomic and proprioceptive (to use more technical physiological terms). To put this point at its simplest but also its most profound, and in a way that we can all somehow grasp, "feeling" is an amalgam of being and doing.
>
> Dunsby, 2002, p. 226.

Thus, "feeling" in the sense in which I am using it is not the same as simply experiencing emotions or physical sensations: instead, it has to do with what one is and what one does as a performer. It might be informally described as a "gut feeling," whereby the music's motion and trajectory are inscribed deep within (having developed both intuitively and through deliberate learning over time) and are then drawn upon in action, guiding what happens in the course of performance without necessarily being articulated explicitly or consciously within the mind of the performer before, during, or after the performance in question.[11] For example, one might "feel" the gravitational force (both progressive and recessive) as well as the hierarchical weight of a given dominant chord, a main theme, or any other musical element or group of elements, the role and significance of which may be profoundly understood, but in a manner defying conventional music-theoretical description. Equally, one might "feel" the ebb and flow of dynamics, of tempo, of motion of all kinds and trajectories. As we will see in the second half of the chapter, however, some authors' attempts to capture "feeling" of this kind verbally have not succeeded; conversely, such "feeling" may underlie their descriptions of music in performance despite apparent implications to the contrary.

Even if the ineffable quality of this sort of "feeling" makes it all but impossible to describe the experiencing of music on the part of performers (not to mention listeners),[12] the fact that music in performance is "felt" in this way seems indisputable. Consider, for example, the humming, groaning, and other inarticulate yet highly expressive

---

[10] Dunsby was referring here specifically to "the study and practice" of musical performance as represented in the volume of essays in which his chapter appeared, i.e. Rink (2002).

[11] Berry (1989, p. xi) refers to a "submerged level of consciousness" whereby the "details of performance" ideally fall "into place in a motivated stream of action and reaction shaped by exhaustive prior thought and conditioning experiment."

[12] See Throop (2003) for a useful summary of philosophical and anthropological writing on human experience, addressing in particular the difficulties inherent in "articulating experience."

vocalizations that emanate from some musicians when they are performing. These point to an internalized sound track which, however primitive it might seem in itself, bespeaks a deep-seated "identity with" the performed music, one having the potential to shape performative and listening experience alike.[13]

19.3 BEYOND WORDS

The inevitably partial, even misleading nature of verbal descriptions of musical experience serves as the point of departure for the following close readings of texts by three authors, each of whom casts light on the "identity as"/"identity with" relationship despite respective limitations. There is a further goal: re-evaluation of earlier writing about performance which might be too quickly dismissed at a time when the values underlying mid- to late 20th-century musicology are coming under fire from those in the field of performance studies. What we find is that the authors under investigation— Erwin Stein, Edward Cone, and Alfred Brendel—end up saying more than one might imagine about what I have called the "feeling" of music, almost despite the authorial identities they end up assuming. The first two case studies explore predominantly theoretical writing on performance, whereas the third reflects the work of a self-avowed "practical musician." The fact that these authors have been chosen rather than others is simply because of the resounding and unexpectedly complementary insights lurking beneath the surface. Needless to say, a wider casting of the net would be required were this discussion to be exhaustive.

19.3.1 The gist of performance

Stein's posthumous *Form and Performance* (1962) was a revelation when I first encountered it—but it was also a source of frustration. No doubt the author's extensive contact and collaboration with Schoenberg (not least as conductor in successive performances of *Pierrot lunaire*) motivated what Benjamin Britten[14] called "his insistence on the composer's actual notes, and on what lies behind them" (Stein, 1962, p. 8), as against "the over-excited and inaccurate bangings to which [Stein] was subjected" in performances of new music. Claiming that "*the details of performance have never systematically been investigated*" (Stein, 1962, p. 12; italics *sic*), Stein himself observes that "customary analyses" do not "help the performer" by simply identifying motives, themes, or "the course

---

[13] See Cook's discussion (2013, p. 317) of the "expressive croaking [that] seems to come from deep within [Alfred] Brendel's body" in the context of an open rehearsal in Cambridge conducted by the latter in 2011.

[14] Britten wrote the Foreword to Stein's book.

of a development or modulation" (Stein, 1962, p. 12). He therefore undertakes a study of the elements of musical sound and musical form, followed by consideration of structure, movement, and phrasing, in an attempt to shed light on the details and principles of performance for the sake of musicians themselves.

Stein declares that:

> the performer must have a crystal-clear conception of the music he is going to play, a conception which is necessarily in terms of sound. The better he understands the form, the clearer will be his conception. Form and sound must become identical in his mind. He ought to hear distinctly and vividly with his inner ear the exact shape of every passage, the extent of every *crescendo*, the accentuation of every phrase. It is not sufficient to rely on what he believes to be his knowledge of the music's emotional content. The purely emotional approach is bound to distort the proportions of the sound-forms.
>
> Stein, 1962, p. 19.

At the same time, Stein acknowledges that:

> The intelligent musician is supposed to feel instinctively at what rate, and how loud or soft, the notes are meant to follow each other. But the intelligent musician often goes wrong … The performer is tempted to supply in abundance what is most in demand [from listeners, i.e., music's physical sensation], to the neglect of the formal proportions which, anyhow, only comparatively few listeners are capable of appreciating. But worse, it is the performers themselves who, with rare exceptions, vaguely feel rather than precisely understand the relations of the notes.
>
> Stein, 1962, p. 19.

Thus,

> the performer's first task is to put the notes together so that they make sense. They must cohere. Every note must have its place and meaning in the context, and each shape must be clearly designed. The succession or coincidence of the notes must sound logical and inevitable, each note having its due duration, no longer and no shorter, no louder and no softer.
>
> Stein, 1962, p. 19.

All of this reflects what should be the performer's "paramount concern," namely, "to realize the character of the music," which is "the purpose for which the music was written" (Stein, 1962, p. 20).

These doctrinaire injunctions and the portrayal of performers as subservient to composers' intentions are out of step with the prevailing notion today of musical performance as a creative practice. On the other hand, Stein exclaims that "*the act of artistic creation consists in the shaping of the material*," and although in this context such shaping is avowedly that of the composer, he admits that "music must become sound to be real, and it is here that the performer comes in" (Stein, 1962, p. 17; italics *sic*). So creative input and "shaping" are part and parcel of the performer's work after all, even if Stein hardly admits it.

He nevertheless writes that "music gains shape while it continues, but the first impulse is decisive in setting the stage and pace of the subsequent events" (Stein, 1962, p. 71). Noting that this requires an understanding of the whole and of the relation of the music's constituent parts to that whole, Stein offers an intriguing observation:

> Every performer knows the high degree of concentration that he needs in order to have at the start and at a moment's notice a whole piece of music in a nutshell in his mind. He is embarking on a venture from which, once begun, there is no escape. While he performs, he is nothing but the music.
>
> Stein, 1962, p. 71.

This passage has been much discussed in the literature, generally in one of two ways. The first is epitomized by Cook's statement that Stein "clearly expressed a dualist [mind/body] conception when he referred to the need for the performer to have 'a whole piece of music in a nutshell in his mind'." Cook continues: "The page-to-stage approach [characteristic of performance-analytical writing] transforms such dualism into a means of disciplining the performing body, subjecting it to a mentalistic construal of the musical work" (Cook, 2013, p. 41). He also posits that, in Stein's book, as in much analysis-and-performance literature, this mind/body dualism "maps onto an equally reductive dualism between theory and practice, with the former in either case taking precedence over the latter ... It is implicit in Stein's formulation that first you get the piece into a nutshell in your mind, and then you perform it" (Cook, 2013, p. 42).

Although I concur with much of Cook's argument, I believe he misses the broader point of Stein's formulation. At least his take differs from my own, which is more akin to (though also different from) Doğantan-Dack's. Complaining about Cook's ostensible critique[15] of her conception of the second movement of Beethoven's *Pathétique* Sonata—namely, as a "concise image of progression from restraint to relative freedom"—Doğantan-Dack writes that such "mental representation[s]" of musical form function

> like a road map during performance, guiding the performer in her quest to create musical meaning. It is a way of representing the whole of the music to be performed to oneself before one plays the first note, as during a performance, there is no time to activate and play from a representation either of a Roman numeral analysis or of the levels of a Schenkerian one.
>
> Doğantan-Dack, 2008, p. 305.

Doğantan-Dack's point about limited attentional capacity while performing is undoubtedly true, and partly for that reason many performers do encapsulate the music

---

[15] See Cook (1999, pp. 13–15).

they are playing in terms of "concise images." However, I do not think this is what Stein was talking about. Perhaps his observation simply lends itself to multiple contradictory interpretations, but I confess that when I first discovered it many years ago, I felt I knew precisely what Stein meant. I believed then, as now, that he was writing about a "basic shape" in performance, a musically defined impulse, a gesture at the highest structural echelon,[16] a "gut feeling" about the course of the music that one is bringing forth. This potpourri of descriptions may seem imprecise or excessive, but there is no single or simple way of capturing what I am referring to any more than there is of putting a finger on the sort of "feeling" discussed above. Whether or not this "basic shape" has anything to do with the Schoenbergian *Grundgestalt*—and I have a hunch about this—the sort of gist I am referring to, which has no necessary relation to the concise images cited by Doğantan-Dack, may be likened to the top level of the generative performance structures once modelled by Clarke (1988).[17] The executive role of such a gist in shaping a performance can be gleaned from the types of self-talk that musicians engage in while performing. For example, "I'm rushing this section" (i.e., in relation to the whole), or "the climax will collapse unless I ramp up the volume" (i.e., to give it contextual weight and significance). Online decision-making is continually undertaken by performers with reference to higher-level representations of the music's course, representations which may not literally resemble Clarke's tree diagrams or those produced using conventional analytical techniques, but which may have much in common in terms of their underlying implications. Such depictions are likely to be of limited if any direct relevance to the act of performance not because, as Doğantan-Dack put it, "there is no time" to activate and play from Roman-numeral analyses of harmony or Schenkerian graphs, but because the higher-level representations under discussion here are *felt* in the sense I have been describing.

It is important to remember that Stein's injunctions did not spring solely from the practice of what Cook has called "theorist's analysis" (2013, pp. 33ff.): they would have reflected his experiences as a performer and with other performers. If nothing else, the passage quoted earlier reveals his awareness of what performers do by referring to "the high degree of concentration" required to conceive of a whole piece of music as a gist. There is an idealistic if not admonishing aspect to this, however. Stein is encouraging profound knowledge and concentration as a means of realizing the music *as composed*, versus more subjectively determined performances based on emotion and sensation. If one is to do more than "vaguely feel," as he wrote, assimilation of the music is required to the point that it inhabits one as a performer. All of the analytical discussion in Stein's book about elements of form, phrase structure, and so forth is intended to yield deep-seated understanding to the point that while performing one becomes "nothing but the

---

[16]   Elsewhere I have written: "While playing, the performer engages in a continual dialogue between the comprehensive architecture and the 'here-and-now,' between some sort of goal-directed impulse at the uppermost hierarchical level (the piece 'in a nutshell') and subsidiary motions extending down to the beat or sub-beat level, with different parts of the hierarchy activated at different points within the performance" (Rink, 1999, p. 218).

[17]   Compare the intensity curve in Rink (1999, p. 236), which could be understood along the lines of a "basic shape" of a given performance conception.

music." That need not result in the annihilation of identity that might be assumed from the composer-centric prose on offer, even if, paradoxically, performance does involve at least a partial surrender of identity. Stein thus puts his finger on an essential aspect of what performers are and what they do, despite his predominant characterization of their role as one of subservience rather than in terms of the enlightened, personal creativity that we now acknowledge and celebrate.

19.3.2 Persona in performance

Cone's *The Composer's Voice* (1974) is itself fascinating yet frustrating because of its composer-centric perspective, yet it too repays close reading and re-evaluation. Like Stein, Cone argues that "The good musician immerses himself so completely in the flow of the music that, for the duration of the performance, his own experience becomes identical with the course of the music." He continues:

> As an actual person, thinking about the composition, [the musician] can relate every passage to its past and to its future; he knows all that has happened, is happening, and will happen. But in his symbolic role he identifies himself with the musical persona, or with his own component of that persona, so completely that he lives through its experiences, as if for the first time. To be sure, his knowledge of the entire composition still functions, even on this symbolic level; that is what makes his performance unified and consistent. But at every point, his knowledge of past events becomes memory; knowledge of the future, foreboding. His synoptic overview of the entire composition is translated into an immediate experience of each event in its order of occurrence; this is what brings his performance to life.
>
> Cone, 1974, p. 127.

Not only are there parallels with Stein's claims about the performer "becoming" the music, but this passage recalls the six testimonies cited earlier in the essay. It also contains an intriguing reference to the performer's "symbolic role"—which I interpret to mean his or her *identity as* a performer—involving *identification with* the music (or, more precisely, with "the musical persona," discussed below). On the one hand, this alludes to the "as/with" relationship under consideration; it also confirms that Cone, who was an accomplished pianist as well as a composer and music theorist, understood at first hand the experience of performing.

This alone would give sufficient cause to probe beneath his sometimes dogmatic prose about what performers "must" do to fulfil their obligations to the composer and the musical work. By way of example, one of Cone's fundamental premises is that "every composition is an utterance depending on an act of impersonation which it is *the duty* of the performer or performers to make clear" (Cone, 1974, p. 5; my italics). Even this should not be taken at face value, not only because of the subjectivizing reference to impersonation—one of the main themes in Cone's passim discussions of performance— but also because of the elaboration that follows:

If, as I believe, Wilson Coker is correct in suggesting that "one can regard the musical work as an organism, a sort of spokesman who addresses listeners," then the performer, far from being an imperfect intermediary between composer and listener, ... is a living personification of that spokesman—of the mind that experiences the music; or, more clumsily but more precisely, of the mind whose experience the music is.

Cone, 1974, p. 5.

This reveals first of all that the performer is more than an intermediary: he or she "speaks for" and personifies the musical work while living out the mind experiencing the music, which is to say his or her own mind first and foremost. It also reminds us that music exists not in the abstract but in the form of performative experiences shaped by those responsible for the performances in question.

Cone expands on the role of the performer as well as his notion of "persona" in observations scattered throughout the book and eventually in a chapter on identification and "imaginative participation."[18] First, he states that the musical persona of each composition—roughly analogous to what Stein called "character"—is "uniquely created by and for that composition" and that it reflects, but is not identical to, the persona of the composer (Cone, 1974, p. 18). If performance is to be legitimate, he says, its aim should be the projection of the musical persona rather than "the self-indulgent display of [the performer's] own personality" (Cone, 1974, p. 46)—an attitude again recalling that of Stein. According to Cone, however, the *person* of the performer nevertheless invests the *persona* of the music with *personality*: as in "good acting," convincing performances depend on the "power of personality," provided the performer's "natural personality is converted into a vehicle for the projection of an artistic persona" (Cone, 1974, p. 138).

Cone argues that the "complete musical persona," which could never be captured in a single performance, "must be as multifarious as that of musical composition itself," whether "unitary, as in a piano solo," or "implied, as by a group of instruments"; it is to be "posited as an intelligence embracing and controlling all the elements of musical thought that comprise a work." These elements "subsist in its consciousness, which is in turn awakened by the performance (in actuality or in imagination) of the gestures that express them" (Cone, 1974, p. 109). The notion of "an intelligence," likewise that of persona more generally, provocatively implies that music is itself not only sentient but also capable of achieving integration and control of musical elements in performance. Equally noteworthy is the indication that these elements are expressed through "gestures."[19]

---

[18] See Monahan (2013) for an extended analysis of Cone's notion of "persona," including a perceptive comment about its variable relevance and/or comprehensibility to performers specializing in diverse repertoires (p. 323, n. 3).

[19] Although the gestures in question are "symbolic," Cone indicates (1974, p. 139) that the physical gestures of performers illustrate the musical design and stimulate awareness of their symbolic counterparts.

Despite Cone's silence on the subject, it is not music's own "intelligence" that achieves such integration and control: this is instead the province of those performers who give life to the music. Similarly, they themselves create the "gestures" that embody and project music's elements. Cone characterizes this sort of "identification" in terms of

> an active participation in the life of the music by following its progress, attentively and imaginatively, through the course of one's own thoughts, and by adapting the tempo and direction of one's own psychic energies to the tempo and direction of the music.
>
> Cone, 1974, p. 126.

As with Stein, we therefore find that Cone's politics are not quite as composer-oriented as they might appear: personal agency is revealed as an essential part of making music in performance, even if what results is "symbolic personification instead of true impersonation" (Cone, 1974, p. 126).[20]

Cone concludes by discussing "objective or impersonal performance" (which is "not to be confused with mechanical playing") and the role of analysis in deepening one's knowledge about the music being performed (Cone, 1974, p. 146). This is of particular relevance to our enquiry, given the need to determine how performers assimilate and potentially "become" the music they are performing.[21] Cone writes:

> the analytical approach ... characterizes an important stage in the comprehension of any work, ... but it is ideally neither the first nor the last stage. Some kind of personal contact with a piece must precede analysis; how else is one to know what, if anything, it contains that is of interest? Ideally, personal contact should follow analysis, for the aim of music is to provide intense experiences, not structures for contemplation. Analysis, then, should follow and grow out of one's intuitive grasp of a composition.
>
> Cone, 1974, pp. 146–7.

"Most satisfying of all," Cone says, is the "interpenetration of analysis and identification" that can characterize "one's response to music" (Cone, 1974, p. 147). He provides an example derived from his experience of performing a piece in which he sensed but did not fully apprehend an important long-range connection across two movements; this was revealed only on close analytical scrutiny, yielding what he terms "enriched participation" in the music (Cone, 1974, p. 146).

---

[20] See Maus (1988) and Monahan (2013, pp. 361–3) for discussion of agency in musical performance as well as listening.

[21] Cone himself refers to the experience of listening in a passage resonant with my observations about the experience of performing and with the testimonies quoted earlier: "When we listen to music, whether with words or not, we must follow it as if it were our own thought. We are bound to it—to its tempo, to its progression, to its dynamics. We can recall the past or foresee the future only as they are reflected in our awareness of each moment of the perpetually flowing present. And if that awareness is sufficiently acute, and our attention sufficiently constant, we can succeed in feeling that we have *become* the music, or that the music has become ourselves" (Cone, 1974, p. 156; italics *sic*).

It is worth noting Cone's three-fold emphasis on the intuitive (considered anathema in some literature on analysis and performance), on analysis for the sake of enhancing experience, and on the possibilities that it also yields to gain greater participation in, or immersion into, the life of the music that one is creating in performance. Here we find new ways to understand the performer's identification with that music, as well as the identity that might arise from it—a process that ideally involves "personal contact" and an "intuitive grasp," but also the kind of deeper probing that potentially underlies reflective music-making of all kinds.

19.3.3 The psychology of performance

Similar views about the value of analysis are expressed by Brendel in other contexts. Like Cone, he regards "true analysis" as "but a clarification and intensification of musical sensitivity, an additional push in the right direction as established by musical instinct." In other words, "analysis should be the outcome of an intimate familiarity with the piece rather than an input of established concepts" (1979/1989, p. 249). Elsewhere Brendel claims that analysis is "sometimes held to stand for a process of dissolving the whole into its component parts, while it ought in fact to guide us from specific details towards the whole" (1988, p. 88). This chimes not only with Cone's views, but also with Stein's allusions to a "gist" in performance. It also suggests that the performer's work should include analysis of a certain kind.

Brendel defines the task of the performer as two-fold: "to understand the intentions of the composer" and "to give each work the strongest possible effect." Noting that one often results from the other, he continues:

> To understand the composer's intentions means to translate them into one's own understanding. Music cannot "speak for itself." The notion that an interpreter can simply switch off his personal feelings and instead receive those of the composer "from above," as it were, belongs to the realm of fable. What the composer actually meant when he put pen to paper can only be unravelled with the help of one's own engaged emotions, one's own senses, one's own intellect, one's own refined ears. Such an attitude is as far removed from sterile "fidelity" as it is from transcription-mania. To force or to shun the "personal approach" is equally questionable; where this does not come of itself, any effort is in vain.
>
> Brendel, 1966, pp. 24–5.

This underscores an important point: "the composer's intentions" cannot be inferred without subjective judgement about what they might have constituted. One could go further by stating that any belief a performer or listener has that a given performance realizes "the composer's intentions" is not only untenable, but a fiction willingly entered into because it has the potential to justify and confirm individual responses as "right" even though they are inevitably those of the person in question.

Brendel elaborates on his references to engaged emotions, senses, intellect, and "refined ears" in an essay from 1970, where he insists that *"feeling* must remain the Alpha and Omega of a musician"—a point resonating with my comments earlier (1970, p. 38).[22] What this means is suggested in the very title: "Form and psychology in Beethoven's piano sonatas." By "psychology" it seems that Brendel has in mind something akin to what Stein called "character"[23] and Cone "persona." Brendel's statements on the subject are vague, however, among them his description (attributed to his teacher Edwin Fischer) of the Sonata Op. 26 as a "psychological composition" (Brendel, 1970, p. 47). Consider also the following:

> The later [Beethoven's] style, the more he tries to prevent psychological misunderstandings, [and] the more he confirms the psychological process by procedures of form and texture up to the point where they disclose each other mutually.
>
> Brendel, 1970, p. 47.

> [T]he psychological process establishes the form of the [first] movement [of Beethoven's Sonata Op. 54], but the form itself is also cast in such a way that one can deduce from it the psychological process.
>
> Brendel, 1970, p. 50.

Elsewhere he writes on similar lines:

> on the subject of musical time, a "psychological" tempo is to be distinguished from the metronomic one: an interpreter who follows the flow of the music as naturally as possible—and by "natural" I refer of course here to the nature of the music, not to that of the player—will always give the "psychological" listener the impression that he is "staying in tempo."
>
> Brendel, 1976, p. 37.

It is hard to know how listeners, tempo, compositions, and musical process alike could be understood as having "psychological" characteristics or a common type of "psychology." Recall, however, Cone's equally intriguing claim that the "musical persona" can be "posited as an intelligence" and as having "consciousness." As I previously commented, it is not music but performers who have "intelligence" and "consciousness," and whose control of musical elements is conveyed through real and virtual gestures. What Brendel seems to be driving at with his idiosyncratic term "psychology"[24] is that

---

[22] Brendel begins his essay by stating that "the remarks that follow are those of a practical musician" and that they "proceed from feeling and return to it" (1970, p. 38).

[23] The fact that Brendel equates the two is clear from his comment that "tracking down the character, the psychological processes of the music, ... demands talent" (1970, p. 44).

[24] I once queried this term in conversation with Brendel; he acknowledged its oddity while indicating that he had never encountered a suitable alternative, although he said he was open to suggestions.

For further discussion of the ascribing of psychological states to music and similar "psychodramatic assessments" see Maus (1988) and Monahan (2013).

performers and listeners bring music to life by attributing to that music not only char-acter but all manner of motivations, desires, frustrations, and other states and actions which together define the human condition. In other words, performers and listeners humanize music—*impersonate* music—by projecting themselves onto it and imagining themselves in it. That is not only why we make "the music" we are playing or listening to what we want it to be, but also why we have the potential to "become" the music as we interact with it.[25]

Brendel's "psychological tempo" is therefore one that reflects and captures the life of the music such that each and every element works together as if organically. "Psychological process" is the set of mutually related, motivated actions in which the "living music" engages over time; "psychological compositions" are those where every-thing seems to fit together and to achieve more than the sum of their parts; and "psy-chological listeners" and their performer counterparts are those with the ability to hear and to feel music in this way—as not only alive, but as having intelligence, conscious-ness, and all of the other human qualities that they themselves possess and project.

19.4 ON BEING AND BECOMING

I began by recounting my experiences as a performer and articulating some elusive questions prompted by them, notably "Where is the music in my mind?" Much of the essay has offered provisional answers to this question, first of all viewing it through the lens of other performers' experiences and then by undertaking close readings of rewarding if problematic texts. One of the goals has been to reorient the focus of theoretical discussion to reflect the perspectives and experiences of performers them-selves. In doing so, I suggested that "the music" in performance has the potential to define one as a performer—as I put it, that one's *identity as* a performer may be shaped by one's sense of *identity with* the music. The inquiry would need to go fur-ther if this conjecture was to be comprehensively verified across a range of perfor-mance conditions, idioms, and personal and cultural contexts. This would require additional ethnographic work along the lines of Gabrielsson's, as well as recourse to a wider body of theoretical literature to do with the construction and perception of identity, on the one hand, and with the ontology and phenomenology of music in performance, on the other. What I have provided is nevertheless an insider's per-spective on what lies behind the performer's thought, "feeling," and action. I have also pointed to a more profound understanding of performance than one might expect to find in seemingly doctrinaire, composer-focused writing from many dec-ades ago. For this reason, it might be propitious to revisit similar texts, while con-tinuing to sound out today's performers on their attitudes and actions. New insights would thereby accrue into "the music" in performance and how we project ourselves

---

[25] For discussion see Cumming (1997) and Auslander (2003, 2006).

onto it, eventually demonstrating more about its capacity to shape who we are and what we become as we and others experience it.

References

Auslander, P. (Ed.) (2003). *Performance. Critical concepts in literary and cultural studies*, vol. 4. London: Routledge.

Auslander, P. (2006). Musical personae. *The Drama Review*, 50(1), 10–19.

Berry, W. (1989). *Musical structure and performance*. New Haven, CT: Yale University Press.

Brendel, A. (1966). Notes on a complete recording of Beethoven's piano works. In: A. Brendel *Musical thoughts and afterthoughts*, pp. 13–25. London: Robson, 1976.

Brendel, A. 1970. Form and psychology in Beethoven's piano sonatas. In: A. Brendel *Musical thoughts and afterthoughts*, pp. 38–53. London: Robson, 1976.

Brendel, A. (1976). *Werktreue*: an afterthought. In: A. Brendel *Musical thoughts and afterthoughts*, pp. 26–37. London: Robson, 1976.

Brendel, A. (1979/1989). On Schnabel and interpretation. In: A. Brendel *Music sounded out*, pp. 225–50. London: Robson, 1990.

Brendel, A. (1988). Schubert's last sonatas. In: A. Brendel *Music sounded out*, pp. 72–141. London: Robson, 1990.

Clarke, E. (1988). Generative principles in music performance. In: J. Sloboda (Ed.) *Generative processes in music*, 1–26. Oxford: Clarendon.

Coessens, K., Crispin, D., & Douglas, A. (2009). *The artistic turn: a manifesto*. Ghent: Orpheus Instituut.

Cone, E.T. (1974). *The composer's voice*. Berkeley, CA: University of California Press.

Cook, N. (1999). Words about music, or analysis versus performance. In: N. Cook, P. Johnson, & H. Zender (Eds.) *Theory into practice: composition, performance and the listening experience*, pp. 9–52. Leuven: Leuven University Press.

Cook, N. (2013). *Beyond the score*. New York, NY: Oxford University Press.

Cook, N. & Pettengill, R. (Eds.) (2013). *Taking it to the bridge: music as performance*. Ann Arbor, MI: University of Michigan Press.

Csikszentmihalyi, M. ([1992] 2002). *Flow. The classic work on how to achieve happiness*. London: Rider.

Cumming, N. (1997). The subjectivities of "Erbarme Dich." *Music Analysis*, 16(1), 5–44.

Cumming, N. (2000). *The sonic self: musical subjectivity and signification*. Bloomington, IN: Indiana University Press.

Cusick, S. (1994). Gender and the cultural work of a classical music performance. *Repercussions*, 3(1), 77–110.

Davidson, J.W. (2002). The solo performer's identity. In: R.A.R. MacDonald, D.J. Hargreaves, & D. Miell (Eds.) *Musical identities*, pp. 97–113. Oxford: Oxford University Press.

DeNora, T. (1999). Music as a technology of the self. *Poetics*, 27, 31–56.

Doğantan-Dack, M. (2008). Recording the performer's voice. In: M. Doğantan-Dack (Ed.) *Recorded music: philosophical and critical reflections*, pp. 293–313. London: Middlesex University Press.

Dunsby, J. (2002). Performers on performance. In: J. Rink (Ed.) *Musical performance: a guide to understanding*, pp. 225–36. Cambridge: Cambridge University Press.

Eitan, Z. & Granot, R.Y. (2006). How music moves. musical parameters and listeners' images of motion. *Music Perception*, 23(3), 221–47.

Foucault, M. (1988). *Technologies of the self: a seminar with Michel Foucault*, ed. L. H. Martin, H. Gutman, & P. H. Hutton. Amherst, MA: University of Massachusetts Press.

Gabrielsson, A. (2011). *Strong experiences with music.* New York, NY: Oxford University Press.

Leinsdorf, E. (1981). *The composer's advocate: a radical orthodoxy for musicians.* New Haven, CT: Yale University Press.

MacDonald, R.A.R., Hargreaves, D.J., & Miell, D. (Eds.) (2002). *Musical identities.* Oxford: Oxford University Press.

Maus, F.E. (1988). Music as drama. *Music Theory Spectrum*, 10, 56–73.

Monahan, S. (2013). Action and agency revisited. *Journal of Music Theory*, 57(2), 321–71.

Palmer, C. (1997). Music performance. *Annual Review of Psychology*, 48, 115–38.

Persson, R.S. (1993). The subjectivity of musical performance: an exploratory music-psychological real world enquiry into the determinants and education of musical reality. PhD thesis, University of Huddersfield.

Rink, J. (1999). Translating musical meaning: the nineteenth-century performer as narrator. In: N. Cook and M. Everist (Eds.) *Rethinking music*, pp. 217–38. Oxford: Oxford University Press.

Rink, J. (Ed.) (2002). *Musical performance: a guide to understanding.* Cambridge: Cambridge University Press.

Stein, E. (1962). *Form and performance.* New York, NY: Knopf.

Throop, C.J. (2003). Articulating experience. *Anthropological Theory*, 3(2), 219–41.

CHAPTER 20

···

PERFORMANCE IDENTITY

···

JANE W. DAVIDSON

20.1 INTRODUCTION

IN 1808 a theatregoer, George Joseph Bell, annotated the play texts in Mrs Inchbald's *British Theatre*. He recorded commentaries on performances of the plays he attended, giving notes on how lines were delivered and how the performances were received. Remarks on the dramatic interpretations of the actress Mrs Sarah Siddons offer a starting point for the current chapter. Mrs Siddons' delivery of Lady Macbeth's famous Act 1, scene 5 speech "O never, Never shall sun that morrow see your face," led Bell to make the following notes:

> A long pause [after the first "never"], turned from him, her eye steadfast. Strong dwelling emphasis on [the second] "never," with deep downward inflection, "never shall sun that morrow see." Low, very slow sustained voice, her eye and her mind occupied steadfastly in the contemplation of her horrible purpose, pronunciation almost syllabic, note unvaried. Her self-collected solemn energy, her fixed posture, her determined eye and full deep voice of fixed resolve never should be forgot, cannot be conceived or described.
>
> Cited in McGillivray, 2014, p. 3, and attributed to H. Fleming
> Jenkin's transcription in: *Papers, literary, scientific, &c., by the late Fleeming Jenkin*, Vol. I. Eds. S. Colvin, and J. A. Ewing. London and New York: Longmans, Green, and Co., 1887, p. 54.

Bell's commentary offers a unique period snapshot, conjuring something of the power and impact of Mrs Siddons' vocally inflected gestures, the pitches, and rhythms employed, as well as her overall posture and gaze. It seems that it was these combined elements that moved Bell. Mrs Siddons had a distinctive, staged persona.

Cowgill & Poriss (2012) have drawn together essays that investigate the female opera singers of Mrs Siddons' epoch, exploring the ways in which the ego associated with the "prima donna" was constructed; that combination of stage persona, and public and private identities. The volume explores the artistic concerns relating to how singers performed musically and dramatically. In addition, bodily and visual aspects, such as clothing, posture, and physiognomy, are highlighted as subtle codes through which aspects of character are communicated. Further to this, cultural elements, such as career management, representation, and image manipulation in the press are all captured. Importantly, in an essay by Cowgill, the case of Angelica Catalani reveals the ambiguities of the lives these primae donnae led. For example, this particular singer developed a series of "attitudes with a shawl," which female audience members were to regard as the epitome of high society femininity, yet the press of the day indicated that these "attitudes" offered dangerous signs to men, highlighting sensual aspects of the body and provoking titillation. Through the example, Cowgill emphasizes how opera was a setting in which these primae donnae negotiated and performed their femininity, set within a social context of courtesans and social climbers (see Cowgill, 2012). While current social and cultural beliefs and practices do not lead to opera singers' gender being articulated in such ways today, these historical observations nonetheless reveal the potent impact of social-cultural context on identity.

The current chapter focuses on the topic of performer identity, exploring three contemporary categories of performer:

- Famous soloists in western classical music and popular music traditions.
- Music ensemble players from the two traditions.
- Amateurs taking part in community music activities.

This particular coverage intends to investigate the ways in which personal characteristics and social frameworks entwine with the music and context of performance nowadays. The chapter is situated in a social constructionist view that our selfhood emerges through the systems available to us in our social and cultural milieu, in relation to the roles we enact such as in our topic of specific concern, being a music performer (see Mead, 1934).

Identity in this context is not treated as a single construct, but a combination of elements developed in relation to others, and which is both multi-faceted and changing (Weber, 2000). In order to construct identity, it is argued that we draw upon verbal and non-verbal discourses that structure our social interactions (Gergen, 1994; Ekman, 2004). While much of the psychological research on self and identity relies heavily on verbal discourse to access knowledge and build information, non-verbal communication is also used to generate and detect cues which contribute to the self-constructs and perceptions we develop of those we observe or engage with in collaborative actions. The current chapter draws on contemporary data that emerged from verbal discourse, but also draws heavily on filmed and live performance and so refers to non-verbal analysis since this is also a primary means through which performance identity is mediated.

In the original edition of this book, the current author wrote a very different kind of chapter on the performer's identity in which she highlighted how her own training had channeled her towards developing a relationship with music that was based firmly in performance—a crucial part of making music was to present it to an audience. This was contrasted with a person who had a very different use for music—someone for whom public performance was neither wanted nor possible, given that he used to play music as a personal and reflective tool. Furthermore, he had a lack of confidence about presenting in public; in other words, he had not developed a performer identity in music (see Davidson, 2002 for more details). As this chapter will reveal, there are different types of performance identity. For the first part of the current exploration, it seems that understanding the professional soloist is a useful starting point, for they have often dedicated many years of their lives to their art. Given the historical perspective offered by Cowgill & Poriss (2012), the case studies in this chapter begin with solo singers, but as counterpoint to the prima donna, the singers are male. In context, perhaps singers are most affected by the cultural codes and ensuing social pressures that shape identity, as the presentation of their art is inextricably bound up with their bodies, with no musical instrument to mediate between the music and the audience.

20.2 THE STAR SOLO SINGER

20.2.1 Plácido Domingo

Plácido Domingo is matchless in terms of the numbers of operatic roles sung (147 at the time this book goes to press) and the longevity of his operatic career (still performing at 75 years of age, with a professional debut 55 years ago). Raised into a family of vocal performers, he has lived the majority of his life in the public eye. He has been complimented by many for numerous aspects of his professional artistry, and early in his career, the Swedish soprano Birgit Nilsson said of him:

> God must have been in excellent spirits the day He created Plácido who has everything needed for one of the greatest careers ever seen; an incredibly beautiful voice, great intelligence, an unbelievable musicality and acting ability, wonderful looks, a great heart, and he's a dear, dear colleague. He is almost the perfect linguist—but, alas, he has not yet learned how to say no in any language.
>
> *New York Times Magazine*, February 27 1972.[1]

The elements Nilsson highlights certainly contribute to Domingo's performance identity—appeal in terms of voice, body, mind, musicality, and acting ability. She gained some of these insights through her personal experience of working with him. Most of us only see him on stage, in the media, or read about him in biographies.

---

[1] http://www.encyclopedia.com/topic/Plácido_Domingo.aspx (accessed 1 September 2014).

He offers his audience a series of cultural signs against which we make our judgements of who he is and how he shares his identity with us. For those initiated in opera singing, the signs are clear when watching and listening to his performances. Those people outside of opera are most likely to recognize Domingo as an iconic figure whose performances of more popular vocal repertoire have introduced them to the operatic style.

While it is evident that Domingo has had a career-long strategy to keep in the public eye with TV appearances, gala concerts, etc. (Goodenough, 1997), he has also used his established position to fund raise through charity concerts. His causes have included the earthquake disaster in Mexico 1985, where he tragically lost four relatives. Through his association with José Carreras and Luciano Pavarotti, when they sang under the banner of the Three Tenors during the 1990s and early 2000s, the three superstars of opera raised huge sums for the José Carreras' International Leukaemia Foundation. This balance of career development and charity work is a formula used by many "star-status" performers (see Zurawicki, 2010). In Domingo's case, the altruism of the charity work cannot be denied, but if reference returns to the prima donnae of the nineteenth century, historical evidence reveals that acts of charity were used by singers to position themselves to soften popular images of their greed (Poriss, 2012). Such discussion reveals the complex tensions of identity that performers have to negotiate.

Of course the Three Tenors began with a good charitable intention, but those concerts also propelled all three men into worldwide mega-stardom through the huge interest their joint appearances generated. It also projected a totally different image of opera stars to the world. The three men were not only generous supporters of charity, but lovers of soccer, and sang at multiple soccer World Cups (Rome, 1990; Los Angeles, 1994, and Paris, 1998). This offered the world an image of machismo not readily recognized in the male opera singer (see Dauncey & Hare, 1999). They also introduced the soccer fan to an image of the male opera singer who can be passionate about popular culture activities, not just the elite art form of opera.

However, what of the act of performance per se? What of the identity Domingo presented on the concert platform? (This forum is selected over the operatic stage where it is clear that he is, at least in part, engaged in enacting a dramatic character.) To answer this question, let us begin by considering one of his concert performances. In 2008, The Royal Opera House Covent Garden held "The Gold and Silver Gala with Plácido Domingo and Friends."[2] Watching the entire evening, it is possible to see codified forms of behavior that comprise the current socialized norms of opera-styled performance. Some of these elements seem not far removed from aspects of the historical art of rhetoric, which demanded a particular stance for singing, the use of expansive arm gestures to command the audience's attention, and hand gestures matching emphasis of the words

[2] It was recorded by Opus Arte and is available as a DVD through Alexander Street Press, although it was accessed for this analysis through the University of Melbourne's website.

(Bizzell & Hurzburg, 2000). Indeed, writing on contemporary performance as a cultural rite, Frith (1996, p. 205) observes that

> performance is a form of rhetoric, a rhetoric of gestures in which [...] bodily movement and signs [...] dominate other forms of communicative signs.

Also, like in historical uses of rhetoric, the audience responds in a highly codified manner to the signals sent, for example, a flourishing arm gesture at the end of an aria resulting in an outburst of applause.

Of course, opera singers present all aspects of their art with stylistic coherence, and this is evident in the use of certain expressive musical devices—acceleration to the pitch climax, extension of held notes to create moments of tension, and the use of *messa di voce* to create contrasting dynamics (Potter, 1998). The voice itself is developed within a stylistic framework—singers are trained to sing with a specific type of even vibrato and change of register, the elements of the training comprising a recognizable operatic sound (Titze, 1994). Added to this, the unique timbral qualities of each voice mean that some sound thinner, finer, purer than others, and some richer, darker, and heavier. In opera, as Halliwell (2014) points out, the voice carries the signification of the words uttered and their role in the overall interpretive aspect of the performance and also possesses materiality not as a means of a form of communication through the use of text, but as a powerful and visceral communication. Barthes (1977) famously used the term "grain of the voice" to suggest the materiality that the voice comprises. Barthes, semiotic reference embraces much more than the timbre, also the voice's friction between music and text.

In the gala evening at The Royal Opera House, Domingo and his colleagues were performing in similar ways, yet was it possible to see his stardom shining above the others? Is his performance identity held in the combination of the elements Nilsson refers to, or are there other aspects that distinguish him from his colleagues, both male and female?

Observing the film, Domingo's performance displays all the qualities of the operatic artist familiar to us, delivering his "stage presence" including appropriate concert attire. He uses the postures and gestures his art form demands with fluency. The materiality of his voice is unique: timbrally velvety, yet simultaneously bright, able to articulate musical and textual effects with great emotional commitment, and with sufficient freedom in the vibrato to generate thrills in the listener. However, each voice in that performance gala has a unique quality, and the combined sum of the elements Domingo presents seems matched by his colleagues. Perhaps his "artistry" is no more or less than his colleagues? Repeated and detailed observations of the performances at the gala reveal three factors that distinguish Domingo from his colleagues. First, he offers a performance that is consistently fully absorbed, as if he is in a heightened state of being, alive and active within in every single musical and dramatic moment of the performance. No one else in the evening—neither man nor woman—projects such a state to the audience.

Secondly, although it is possible to see and hear the technique of his artistry in action (specific muscle engagement in the abdomen and throat), such is Domingo's attentional focus and engagement that it becomes evident that the audience is also drawn into his energized and engaged activity in a manner no other performer achieves. Thirdly, though the performance contains the expected postures and gestures of the operatic style, it also reveals a different kind of activity, actions that are more relaxed and "natural" looking. We see Domingo singing operatic arias with specific narratives and delivering certain emotional affect, and we are aware of Domingo interacting in the moment with the audience, the orchestra, his co-performers, and the conductor. He is not "rigid" and fixed in his postures—a style adopted by many of his other colleagues.

Insight into what Domingo's distinguishing factors may represent are found in Frith's discussion of performance. He comments: "acting performance involves gestures that are both false (they are only put on for the occasion) and true (they are appropriate to the emotions being described, expressed, or invoked)" (Frith, 1996, p. 198). He goes on to note that solo singers are always creating "a tension between an implied story (content: the singer in the song) and the real one (form: the singer on the stage)" (Frith, 1996, p. 209). Furthermore, he states that "stars must keep both their star personality and a song personality in play at once," (Frith, 1996, p. 212). Such a process of "double enactment" (Frith, 1996, p. 212) captures the processes observable in Domingo's performances.

In seminal research Abraham Maslow described the phenomenon of "peak experience," as unbidden, positive, and awe-inspiring. Triggers of such a state were reported to include love, sex, music, art, and creativity. Maslow regarded peak experience to be the pinnacle of human self-actualization (Maslow, 1970). Building on this concept, Csikszentmihalyi (1990) coined the term "flow" to describe a state of focussed absorption. He observed that flow occurs when a highly skilled person succeeds in the performance of a task of high challenge. Flow is characterized by focus on the activity to the exclusion of everything else. The energy and focus observed in Domingo's performances might well be described as flow. Indeed, Csikszentmihalyi describes nine dimensions of flow as including: a merging of action and awareness, sense of control, concentration, loss of self-consciousness, time transformation, unambiguous feedback, challenge-skill balance, clear goals, and self–reward. These descriptors are not only relevant to what we observe in Domingo's performances recorded in 2008, but perhaps encapsulate some of Nilsson's characterization of him as a man who cannot say no, in the sense that he loves and is inspired by what he does. Interestingly, Csikszentmihalyi (1996) describes people most likely to experience flow as those possessing low self-centeredness and who find intrinsic meaning in things. Given Domingo's love of music, his energy and a deep commitment to work, he may be someone particularly attuned to achieving flow. Csikszentmihalyi (1996) notes that the absorption experienced in flow makes for "excellence in life," and so it could be that these sorts of experiences play a crucial role in driving a continuing passion and engagement with performance.

20.2.2 Robbie Williams

In the tradition of popular performance, Williams co-writes some of his own material, performs pop standards, and has also collaborated with some top soloists. He is a leading international figure, having had a strong presence as a concert and recording artist for 20 years. Davidson (2006) undertook a detailed analysis of a concert given by Williams at Knebworth in 2003. In it, the song "She's the one" was featured. The song is highly repetitive, with simple harmonies and attractive lyrics, with the ideas of closeness, and the intermingling of self and other experiences of intimacy: Williams sings, "I was her. She was me. We were one. We were free."

How does Williams construct his identity or, indeed, the interaction of personal self and stage persona in the framework of this song? What are his codified behaviors? Intriguingly, Williams directs his performance to specific people in the audience (Kelly and her husband) and more broadly uses devices to embrace the whole audience. He asks Kelly her name and encourages the audience to join him by contributing their own supportive performance using movements and singing. Indeed, Williams is very active, and the thrust stage he uses has the appearance of a catwalk, enabling him to parade up and down, making it easy to elicit audience participation as he walks among them. His performance involves beating in time to the music, as if in "a groove." The audience also joins in this common pulse, waving their arms in the air in time.

In Williams' performance, a series of highly non-verbal codes are used: *emblematic* gestures (bows, salutes, blown kisses, peace signs); *illustrative* gestures (upward thrusting hand gestures highlighting the upward musical phrase, or arm-flapping movements demonstrating the action of flying); *adaptive* gestures (arm relaxing and flopping by his side); *display* gestures (posing with the microphone over the shoulder, or turning the back to the audience in a dramatic manner); and *regulator* gestures (raising arms and bringing them down in order to co-ordinate the band to commence the final verse together; see Ekman, 2004, for details.)

The skills show Williams to be working in and outside of the narrative of his song, adopting a multi-role identification as described by Frith (1996). If these skills are aligned with Domingo's stage work, common elements that might be labeled sub-identities are identifiable.

20.3 SUB-IDENTITIES
IN PERFORMANCE: WILLIAMS
AND DOMINGO COMPARED

20.3.1 The narrator

Both artists deliver the "story," animating the lyrics of their material with specific actions. We can see this specifically in the detailed analysis of Williams' song. In the final verse, for example, Williams adopts a downward-looking pose and keeps much stiller than in the rest of the song, communicating what is identified as a sense of intimacy and emotional intensity as he sings "We were one." These men are much more than effective narrators; they also "show off," as the focus of attention.

20.3.2 The show off

Both men use postures and gestures that might be labeled "showing off," that is, their practices draw attention to them as individuals, rather than them as narrators of the song. Domingo does this to a very limited degree, often through musical effects, rather than in lavish gestures. Williams, on the other hand, entwines within the narrative of the song, actions that are disconnected from the story, but that are strongly symbolic activities in their own right. For example, at one point he is observed throwing the microphone over his shoulder and spinning it like a revolver. The behavior makes a clear reference to other types of performance—the microphone movement a cleverly rehearsed trick, like a revolver spinning, reminiscent of a slick cowboy, or even James Bond. So, the bodily codes inform us that Williams is indeed a "showman." In other words, he is a larger than real-life character when on stage, playing the role of a powerful male star.

20.3.3 The manipulator

Whilst Domingo may apply the conventions of his art form, such as using an opening arm gesture or a musical rallentando to signal to the audience that the work is about to end, his "manipulation" seems to stop there. The audience itself is relatively passive, emitting outbursts of applause at the end of each performance item, and cheers as the final items are performed. Williams has an altogether more elaborate scheme. By focusing the story on two people in the audience, Williams sings the lyrics as if he were Kelly's husband and/or if he were a man for whom Kelly could indeed "be the one." The effect on Kelly is striking: she swoons at Williams and is flattered by his attention. Throughout, she is held and hugged by her husband who kisses her passionately at the song's end. The behavior all feeds a fantasy of desire: at the end of the song, Kelly's husband lifts her up, seeming to offer her to Williams. The layers of symbolism go on—it is perhaps no accident that Kelly's husband (are they actors planted in the audience?) bears a striking resemblance to Williams. So, every woman (Kelly) can have a Robbie Williams (Kelly's husband) just for herself.

The audience is complicit in the construction and delivery of Williams' manipulation. The audience sighs and cheers as Kelly is referenced during the song. The audience's pleasure involves participating in the performance—they know the song and sing along. The exchange of shared gestures and movements, such as swaying in time to the music, swirling and "flying" add to this sense of sharing. Indeed, the audience itself adopts a collective, group identity.

20.3.4 The coordinator

Both performers interact with their co-performers to coordinate musical entrances and exits. In Domingo's case, this principally involves a quick glance at the conductor, but Williams is much more obvious, leading a communal upper torso beat movement, which is found in audience movements. He coordinates the rhythmic union of performers and audience.

20.3.5 Intimate/private self

Between the two performers' staged movements and vocal gestures, *adaptive* intention is revealed (see Ekman, 2004). In Domingo's case, his postures look natural and relaxed. Some of the movements are self-referencing (scratching the head, rubbing the ear lobe, for example) and so self-reassuring. According to Ekman, on-lookers commonly use this type of signal to discover information about the core characteristics of an individual, or a particular state they are in. Williams' adaptive gestures include his arms "flopping" from side to side in familiar and comfortable movements, nothing being "presentational" about the movement. Since it is known that "kinematics specify dynamics" (movements specify their causes, Runeson and Frykholm, 1983), it is clear from these kinds of movements that within the performance we are given access to information about a more relaxed and intimate aspect of the singers' identities.

Together, these examples reveal common sub-identities that enmesh, enabling these performers to send strong messages to their audiences. From the analysis and discussion above, despite many elements shared between Williams and Domingo, a clear difference is that Williams, although very active and engaged, lacks the deep focused energy of Domingo. To some degree this could be the result of the stylistic demands of opera over pop music, although given that the other opera singers in his gala evening do not display such intensity, the type of "self-actualization" apparent in Domingo's work is highly distinctive.

20.4 CO-PERFORMERS

20.4.1 Classical chamber ensembles

Identity strongly depends on affiliation with social groups, and in ensemble music, this is certainly the case. Like all other forms of music making, the musical dynamics inevitably give the performers their focus, which in turn is projected to the audience through some of the means described for the soloist above. However, identity in small ensembles also depends on a number of additional factors. Research on string quartet cohesion (Young & Colman, 1979) revealed that trust and respect of individual boundaries is vital to securing group stability. An investigation of the group dynamics of a student string quartet revealed (Davidson & Good, 2002) that valuing of one another could be established through musical and social means. For example, one player was supported, with his sense of self as musician being expanded through the musical actions of his three co-performers.

As the weakest player in the student string guartet, the second violinist found difficulty in accurately tuning his part, which created inner thirds to harmonize with the first violinist. Yet, the rest of group adjusted themselves to a slightly slower tempo in order to give him more time to fine-tune his playing. The group supported him throughout, without explicitly telling him of their intention, and thus enabling him to gain confidence and expand his sense of self as a violinist through these sorts of supportive actions. More complexly, there were dynamics that privileged the male second violinist, making him a dominant identity within the group for social rather than musical reasons. The three other players were female, and better players than their male group member. Yet, when discussions about the musical decisions were made in rehearsal, it was the second violinist who was firm in his views, despite a lack of equivalent musicianship. This pattern had emerged, so it seems, with the females simply making their own arrangements in regard to the performance expression non-verbally, throughout the rehearsal, without the second violinist noticing. Furthermore, at a personal level, two of the females were extremely fond of the male violinist and went out of their way to bolster his performer identity. Ironically then, the second violinist's performativity of dominance and masculinity was highly influential on the ensemble as a whole.

Further differences of position and expressions of identity emerged in a study on flute and clarinet duos (Davidson, 2012). The investigation aimed to trace how players work to produce a coordinated duo from first sight-reading to an agreed collaborative performance. Data revealed a considerable amount of information on how two people with very different identities interact. The current chapter refers to only one of the duos studied, the two performers of interest being female professionals who were in mid-life, the clarinettist being approximately eight years older than the flautist. The study involved work on a short piece of music for flute and clarinet that was especially composed for the exercise, but the research revealed much more besides how the piece was learned.

The clarinettist revealed herself to be highly dynamic in both the verbal and physical articulation of her musical ideas. She was outgoing, active, and engaged with both rehearsal and performance processes. When the duo was observed rehearsing, it was clear that the clarinettist led the flautist and initiated the majority of suggestions about strategies for implementing specific effects, even how many times and in what way they should work on sections. The flautist was quiet, still, and not as forthcoming as the other player with ideas or conversation. In performance, their final work both looked and sounded somewhat unbalanced, with the clarity of musical ideas and bodily engagement and creativity of the clarinettist offset against the accurate, but stiffer performance of the flautist. These players were extremely close personally, and spoke freely about their personal and working relationship. It did not seem to affect them that they possessed such different musical and personal identities, including differences in musical style, stage presentation, and investment within the duo. For them, their ensemble seemed to work. Yet, to the on-looker, there was a great difference between them.

The influences of personality and performance style affect the identities of popular ensembles as well as classical ensembles.

20.4.2 Pop bands

The Corrs is an Irish band that combines rock with traditional Celtic Irish folk themes. The group consists of the Corr siblings Andrea, Sharon, Caroline, and Jim. The band's international success peaked from the mid-1990s to the mid-2000s. At the height of their popularity The Corrs offered a useful case study of how siblings worked together to develop a cohesive musical ensemble. Like the Bee Gees, Jacksons, and Osmonds before them, their strong musical upbringing gave them a shared history and sociocultural framework for their musical identities. Their data provide informative discussion material, for like other family bands, their roles within the group are often quite fluid, with different members taking leading or supporting parts according to the context (Kurosawa & Davidson, 2005).

In this close-knit band, flexibility and interchange are important. The three females sing solos, and all members play instruments: Andrea (tin whistle), Sharon (violin), Caroline (drum kit and bodhran), and Jim (guitars and keyboards). They were analyzed performing standard verse-chorus songs with different tempi and emotional content. The songs featured different family members in various musical roles. Despite the capacity to swap roles, it was Andrea who seemed to be the most effective at amplifying emotional expressions, presenting strong sub-identities of *show off* and *manipulator*. She also worked obviously as a *mediator*, working between family members to coordinate the musical whole. Unlike the soloists previously mentioned, however, Andrea does not reveal inner personal states on stage. Her sisters Sharon and Caroline, by contrast, highlighted their individual characteristics far more strongly when stepping into the role of vocal soloist. The change between them as an instrumentalist and/or solo singer was dramatic. In particular, Caroline used the highest percentage of *regulatory movements*, especially eye gaze. She was the least demonstrative of the sisters, and it was hypothesized that gaze was used by her as a means of concentrating support from her sisters.

The article discussing the performances of The Corrs posited that the differences between the female performers may have been the result of sibling order (see Kurosawa & Davidson, 2005). It is well documented that birth order impacts an individual's sense of self-identity, the younger sibling often being less independent and outgoing than the older (see Sulloway, 1997). Caroline is the youngest of the sisters and describes herself as the shyest member of the family, most in need of sibling support.

The current author followed the performance identity of a sibling ensemble in the 2014 TV series, The X-Factor Australia. Appearing in the first round, Brothers3 were "country boys" from Mudgee in rural New South Wales, aged 18, 17, and 16 years old at the time of broadcast. They sang in close harmony to self-accompaniment on guitar. They were immediately labeled "happy and joyful," dressed in chequered shirts, jeans, and work boots. Their rural background was quickly taken up in the media as their key identity. It was widely reported that the boys grew up with no regular electricity, television, or running water, and were home educated. Through the first TV episodes, this biographical detail seemed a match with the innocence of their beautiful harmonies. As members of the public commented:

> Their harmonies are amazing … soooo happy to see they got back in! BROTHERS 3 for the WIN!!!! You would think that Danni [Minogue and a judge and their mentor on the program] would recognize REAL talent when she heard it..... GOOOOO BOYS!!!!
>
> Kari Nichols[3]

The sibling associations were also made:

> There'll be nobody to replace the Bee Gees but these guys will have their own identity and if they are managed in a proper and right way they will be big and will have a place in the music industry in the future.
>
> Yourroyalcrankines[3]

The youngest brother spoke for the group, and took most of the lead vocals, closely followed by the eldest brother. The middle sibling seemed less comfortable in front of the growing studio and TV audiences, and was often left gawping, as the other two boys organized themselves around him in interviews. As the weeks went by, a collective sense of youth and fun was promoted. The performativity of country boys with considerable musical skill was coupled with youthful exuberance, and projected as a performance identity of honesty and sincerity that was both appealing and plausible.

As the TV show progressed, the farmer shirts were exchanged for dapper suits, unkempt curls were transformed into slick-back chic, and strawberry was transformed to peroxide blonde. The songs also changed, with the TV production team creating boy band choreographies and introducing their young artists to up-tempo pop songs.

The progression of Brothers3 through the rounds of the competition seems to offer a high-speed enactment of Ibarra's (1999) theory of provisional selves, where individuals work to develop strategies around their identity that will enable them to progress in a certain field. This can happen either when a single role model is adopted, or when characteristics from a number of different individuals are adopted. These provisional identities are endorsed or rejected through social contact. The changes brought to the siblings' performance by the TV production team were critiqued by the judges as misguided, and became the basis for much debate. The discussion focused on Brothers3 being at their

---

[3] https://www.youtube.com/watch?v=yF_ykOct7nY.

most "authentic" when performing acoustic numbers, dressed in their familiar boots and jeans. Perhaps the judgement was accurate: the boys seemed at their very best when the identities they projected through their performance materials related to their upbringing and context. Without question, the brothers were incredibly close in the music (literally in a three-part vocal sandwich, supported with the bass and rhythms of their guitar playing) and with one another (often in one another's space as they huddled together to share a microphone, or enthusiastically embraced one another after a performance).

It is important to ask whether the discrepancy between the decisions of the TV producers (the employers) and the judges (the employees) was based in real or fabricated differences. Observing the arc of decisions made about the competitors generally, it is not difficult to imagine that the producers and judges were directly manipulating the public. Ironically, as more information emerged about this family, it became increasingly apparent that the projected image of country folk living the good life was not the reality. In fact, all three boys were attending university, despite their tender years. All three had been performing on stage since toddlerhood, and despite the illusion of being fresh and new to the scene, their band had been formed since the youngest boy was only 11 years of age. In fact, the ensemble was highly experienced, having recorded several albums, as well as having won music awards. They were well-loved figures in their home region, and across the folk/country music scene more broadly. Finally, their mother worked in TV, film, and theatre, and had been a regular actor in a national TV show. She was not quite the country bumpkin portrayed on the TV trailers for The X-Factor.

Extensive discussion of musical events and techniques used to "produce" performer identities can be found in volumes such as Inglis (2006), though the vast majority of the work of this type is embedded in sociology and cultural theory, and concerns pop and rock performers. Music psychology enquiry has generally been slow to explore the profound impact cultural factors have in shaping social identity and role, let alone investigating how musical performers' identities are constructed and consumed. Bringing the discussion within the music psychology framework highlights the need for more culturally focused psychological enquiry.

Complex cultural production has featured strongly in the development of Plácido Domingo's career, and certainly played into the stardom of Robbie Williams, who began his mass popularity in a boy band, Take That. The music manager Nigel Martin-Smith selected boys through audition to create the band in 1989. The vision had been to create a teen-orientated band to embrace several segments of the music market. Martin-Smith constructed the band around Gary Barlow's lead vocals, so when the precocious Williams was selected at only 16 years of age, he was given backing vocals. Williams was kicked out of the band owing to bad behavior, but his subsequent emergence as a solo artist was played out as inter-group rivalry. Looking at the strength of Williams' own career, and also having seen video of Williams as a very young boy presenting polished song and dance routines that followed in tradition of his father's own career as a club entertainer, it is possible to hypothesize that Williams had the motivation, personality, and context in which to develop as a performer.

20.5 PERSONALITY, SELF-IDENTITY, AND THE MOTIVATION TO PERFORM

Groundbreaking work by Kemp (summarized in Kemp, 1996) began to explore the ways in which musicians' personality characteristics compare with other members of their society. Kemp's original work examined each type of musician in turn and noted that singers were the most extroverted, certainly fitting the insights gleaned in the case studies presented within this chapter.

String and woodwind players were identified as being the least outgoing of instrumentalists. Working within the Western European research context, Kemp found that, in general, musicians displayed characteristics associated with introversion—aloofness, being critical, individualistic, and introspective. Referring back to the examples of the duo studied (see Davidson, 2012), this would certainly seem to be the case for the flautist. The clarinettist was extremely open, and seeking collective experience; indeed, she clearly wanted to make the situation as comfortable and collaborative as possible. The clarinettist was no less expansive in her stage behaviors, offering highly energized performances. Indeed, parallels with Maslow's ideas on self-actualization (Maslow, 1970) would suggest that the clarinettist had a much stronger construct of self, related to her own potential for expression through music, than her flautist partner.

It is well reported that self-esteem affects how people perceive their own capacities, which in turn affects their personal desire to behave in certain ways (see Wilson, 2002). Self-esteem might feed explanations of the differences found in the roles adopted by all the performers explored in this chapter. Byng-Hall's (1995) script theory argues that we constantly negotiate scripts imposed on us by others and through this, find a way to develop and construct our own sense of self.

Motivating the self towards engagement in music has been investigated and is described in another chapter in the current volume (see this volume, McPherson & Evans, Chapter 12, "Processes of musical identity consolidation during adolescence"). Self-determination theory (Deci & Ryan, 2002) highlights that we perform at our best when our actions are self-regulated. Referring back to Plácido Domingo's story it is worth noting that he has always been highly engaged with music, and, likewise, Robbie Williams' musical upbringing shows that he also had a richly created musical self, balancing feelings of personal *competence*, along with a sense of *relatedness* to a social group, and *autonomy*. As McPherson and Evans (this volume) highlight, such engagement with music offers the ideal conditions for a positive musical identity formation. The cases presented in the current chapter all have strong musical identities. Their performer identities—those specific constructions of self and the skills involved in the activity of performance—have emerged perhaps in a parallel process, though as we saw from Davidson's (2002) chapter, not all musicians are performers.

Related to self-determination is the idea that the self has capacity for invention and re-invention. Weber (2000) demonstrates how individual choice and cultural context interact to provide a self that can both expand and contract according to personal, material, social, and spiritual concerns. According to William James' (1890) seminal model of the self, three principal components are said to interact: the *material self* (the body and the physical world), the *social self* (social relationships), and the *spiritual self* (religious or spiritual experience). Aspects of these components have already been covered in many aspects of the discussion. Weber's (2000) work builds on this framework, translating the material to the *body*, the social becomes the *persona* and the spiritual, the *spirit*. Weber argues that the contributing components of self are bound together in interplay of individual choices and cultural contexts, becoming the *created self*. In an auto-ethnographic piece, Faulkner (2013) explores his own musical identity and how it was shaped in terms of these three aspects. Importantly for the current chapter, Faulkner emphasizes the powerful spiritual nature of musical experience, reporting how music "levitated" him, both in his listening and his performing experiences, its power motivating him towards a lifelong commitment to making music and sharing with others. We do not have such well-articulated data on the experience of the spiritual self from other performers, so it is difficult to predict whether or not spiritual rewards are commonplace, though aspects of spirituality are seen to correspond with *flow*. Describing his long-term work with an Icelandic male community choir, Faulkner notes the powerful spiritual sharing between the male choristers. This type of experience was evidently a key aspect of why Faulkner and his choir wished to perform music. Faulkner writes at length about the men's identities and the strong way in which the music ensemble brings them a group identity they do not find in any other expression or aspect of their lives.

The current chapter has implicitly assumed that professional performers are those with the most clearly defined musical performance identities, developed either of their own volition or as the product of circumstance. A popular view of community music is that the performance aspect of music-making is often underplayed at the expense of capturing a developmental or therapeutic outcome. Research reveals, however, that performance and the development of a performance identity can be empowering and therapeutic in themselves.

20.6 THE SOUNDS OF SUCCESS

The work of music therapists and community musicians has explored ways in which musical interventions can assist in promoting physical and psychological wellbeing in a range of contexts. Examples encompass:

- Community music projects to celebrate intercultural differences, musical opportunities to vent anxiety and anger, or express grief and joy.
- Rhythmical musical exercises to regain functionality of motor coordination after injury.
- A music drop-in center in a mental health unit aiming to develop social capital as well as mood regulation (for an overview, see Pavlicevic & Ansdell, 2004).

These enterprises have been remarkably successful, with evaluations suggesting that music programs elicit immediate benefits that can subsequently lead to positive longer-term psychological and physical wellbeing (Ruud, 1997). It was with such a conception in mind that the current author began working in community music activity. To capture the nature of this work it is necessary for the authorial voice to speak, so I now present myself in this final narrative of the chapter.

For more than 20 years, I had amassed professional performance experience as an opera singer. Though not at all in the same sphere as Plácido Domingo, I have nonetheless "walked the boards," performing solo roles for opera companies, and giving recitals and performing in oratorios. This experience has combined with my scholarship to lead me to believe that I understand how I constructed my own performance identity. About a decade ago, I became interested in developing musical potentials for others and so worked on a series of community activities for people who had not formerly enjoyed musical opportunity, let alone performed on stage. The resulting work led me to create six community choirs whose typical membership have an average age of over 70 years, the participants including those living with dementia, as well as retirees from careers such as teaching, administrative, and manual work. Besides carefully structuring contexts to lead the participants in their musical experiences and developments, and offering activities to encourage social bonding, I have been struck by the eagerness of participants to perform. Indeed, the pilot project I ran was supposed to last only eight weeks and now, nine years on, it is still thriving, having shifted focus from being only a group for people to share in music, to a group that performs regularly across a range of community venues.

Here are some indicative quotes from interview data about motivations for performance (the quotes are taken from Davidson, 2011, p. 76):

> *Female*: My grandchildren thought it was brilliant that I was going to be performing in a concert. Of course I go and see them at swimming events and in school concerts, but when all the family came to see and hear me in a concert, now that was something special! I've never been one for the spotlight. Getting applause and being praised in public is important recognition. It gives you worth. I don't think I've ever had applause for anything else I do.

The sense of pride in the achievement of performance was startling. The activity had an incredibly positive impact on participants' self-worth and feelings of being valued by others.

> *Male*: Performing gives another side to my sense of who I am. I feel good at what I'm doing. I'm no trained musician, but I can do the job and other people tell me that.

In this example, an expanded sense of self is reported. In addition to specific comments about performance, the participants also spoke freely about the advantages that group music-making brought them: new social contact, a "spiritual" connection to others, a greater sense of who they were and what they could achieve—all self-expanding results. Additionally, another group motivation to perform was bound up with the desire to share the feelings and experiences of music with others. As one 89 year old woman commented:

> I have found such joy though this group. Performing is the icing on the cake. You can't just stand there and do it like in a rehearsal … Most of us really love performing to share the joy we feel about music and life.
>
> Personal communication, previously unpublished.

While these community performers may not possess the polished and projected performance personae of the professional soloists discussed in this chapter, their inclusion in the discussion reveals further layers to the construct "performance identity." Working with these people, I was able to offer them advice about how to use postures and gestures to clarify the signs they were trying to transmit to their audience. Without such instruction, there was a tendency for the performances to be intra-group focused, failing to have sufficient focus on the audience. Being with these groups, most importantly, I also understood how significant it was for them to use performance opportunity to express themselves in a public forum, expanding a sense of self and exploiting the spiritual feelings shared between group members.

20.7 THE FINAL WORD

This chapter has explored some of the factors that comprise the music performer's identity. The work has shown how an identity develops according to milieu. The examples studied herein have fitted with dominant cultural discourses on the performer and styles of performance: opera, pop, chamber music, and community music. Equally, there are performers who challenge dominant trends to develop new styles that transform ideas about what these identities might constitute. Indeed, much cultural history of popular music has explored this kind of material. For example, performances by the Sex Pistols were responded to with "utter shock, bemusement, admiration, perceptible distain and disinterest" in 1976 (Albiez, 2006, p. 96) and challenged and changed previous established notions of stage performance, by emphasizing sex, violence, insolence, and anarchy. Further to this, the case studies in this chapter have identified some of the interactive behaviors that generate performance communication, which feed into our understanding of the performer. It has also explored how temperament, motivation, and opportunity contribute to the development of the self and a performance identity.

The topic of music performance identity is multi-faceted and complex. The current chapter has inevitably been highly selective in the material discussed, but it has served to introduce the reader to a fascinating area of enquiry. It has also shown that the majority of research has been investigated from sociological and cultural study. The current chapter has attempted to represent some of those pieces of work, while also highlighting the useful types of enquiry the music psychologist can bring to understanding the identity of the music performer.

References

Albiez, S. (2006). Print the truth, not the legend. The Sex Pistols: Lesser Free Trade Hall, Manchester, June 4, 1976. In: Inglis, I. (Ed.) *Performance and popular music*, pp. 92–106. Aldershot: Ashgate.

Barthes, R. (1977). *Image—Music—Text*, transl. S. Heath. New York, NY: Fontana.

Bizzell, P. & Herzberg, B. (2000). *The rhetorical tradition: readings from classical times to the present*. New York, NY: Bedford/St Martin's.

Byng-Hall, J. (1995). *Rewriting family scripts*. London: Guildford.

Cowgill, R. (2012). "Attitudes with a Shawl": performance, femininity, and spectatorship at the Italian Opera in early nineteenth-century London. In: R. Cowgill and H. Poriss (Eds.) *The arts of the prima donna in the long nineteenth century*, pp. 217–51. Oxford: Oxford University Press.

Cowgill, R. & Poriss, H. (Eds.) (2012). *The arts of the prima donna in the long nineteenth century*. Oxford: Oxford University Press.

Csikszentmihalyi, M. (1990). *Flow*. New York, NY: Harper and Row.

Csikszentmihalyi, M. (1996). *Creativity: flow and the psychology of discovery and invention*. New York, NY: Harper Collins.

Dauncey, H. & Hare, G. (Eds.) (1999). *France and the 1998 World Cup: the national impact of a world sporting event*. Portland, OR: Frank Cass Publishers.

Davidson, J.W. (2002). The performer's identity. In: R.A.R. MacDonald, D.J. Hargreaves, and D. Miell (Eds.) *Musical identities*, pp. 97–116. Oxford: Oxford University Press.

Davidson J.W. (2006). "She's the One": multiple functions of body movement in a stage performance by Robbie Williams. In: A. Gritten and E.C. King (Eds.) *Music and gesture*, pp. 208–26. Aldershot: Ashgate.

Davidson, J.W. (2011). Musical participation: expectations, experiences and outcomes. In: J. W. Davidson and I. Deliege (Eds.) *Music and the mind*, pp. 65–87. Oxford: Oxford University Press.

Davidson, J.W. (2012). Bodily movement and facial actions in expressive musical performance by solo and duo instrumentalists: two distinctive case studies. *Psychology of Music*, 40(5), 595–633.

Davidson, J.W. & Good, J.M.M. (2002). Social and musical coordination between members of a string quartet: an exploratory study. *Psychology of Music*, 30, 186–201.

Deci, E. & Ryan, R. (Eds.) (2002). *Handbook of self-determination research*. Rochester, NY: University of Rochester Press.

Ekman, P. (2004). Emotional and conversational nonverbal signals. In: J. M. Lazzazabal and L. A. Perez Mirdana (Eds.) *Language, knowledge and representation*, pp. 39–50. Alphen aan den Rijn: Kluwer Academic Publishers.

Faulkner, R. (2013). *Icelandic men and me: sagas of singing, self and everyday life*. Farnham: Ashgate.

Frith, S. (1996). *Performance rites*. Oxford: Oxford University Press.

Gergen, K. (1994). *Towards transformation in social knowledge*, 2nd edn. London: Sage.

Goodnough, D. (1997). *Plácido Domingo: Opera Superstar* (Hispanic Biographies). Berkeley Heights, NJ: Enslow Publishers.

Halliwell, M. (2014). "Voices within the voice": conceiving voice in contemporary opera. *Musicology Australia* (Special Issue: Music Performance and Performativity), 36(2), 254–72.

Ibarra, H. (1999). Provisional selves: experimenting with image and identity in professional adaption. *Administrative Science Quarterly*, 44, 764–91.

Inglis, I. (Ed.) (2006). *Performance and popular music.* Aldershot: Ashgate.

Kemp, A.E. (1996). *The musical temperament.* Oxford: Oxford University Press.

Kurosawa, K. & Davidson, J.W. (2005). Nonverbal behaviours in popular music performance: a case study of The Corrs, *Musicae Scientiae,* 9, 111–36.

Maslow, A.H. (1970). *Motivation and personality,* 2nd edn. New York: Harper Collins.

Mead, G.H. (1934). *Mind, self and society.* Chicago: University of Chicago Press.

McGillivray, G. (2014). Listening for the voice of Sarah: Sarah Siddons' Lady Macbeth and the Eighteenth-Century Audience. Paper presented at Voice and Emotion, 1500–1800. Performance Collaboratory, University of Sydney, 29 September, 2014.

Pavlicevic, M., & Ansdell, G. (Eds.) (2004). *Community music therapy.* London: Jessica Kingsley.

Poriss, H. (2012). Prima donnas and the performance of altruism. In: R. Cowgill & H. Poriss (Eds.) *The arts of the prima donna in the long nineteenth century,* pp. 42–60. Oxford: Oxford University Press.

Potter, J. (1998). *Vocal authority: singing style and ideology.* Cambridge: Cambridge University Press.

Ruud, E. (1997). Music and the quality of life. *Nordic Journal of Music Therapy,* 6, 86–97.

Runeson, S. and Frykholm, G. (1983). Kinesmatic specification of dynamics as an informational basis for person-and-action perception: expectation, gender, recognition and deceptive intention. *Journal of Experimental Psychology: General,* 112(4), 585–615.

Sulloway, F.J. (1997). *Born to Tebel: birth order, family dynamics and creative lives.* New York, NY: Vintage Books.

Titze, I.R. (1994). *Principles of voice production.* New Jersey, NJ: Prentice Hall.

Weber, R. (2000). *The created self: reinventing body, persona and spirit.* New York, NY: W.W. Norton and Company.

Young, V.M. & Colman, A.M. (1979). Some psychological processes in string quartets. *Psychology of Music,* 7, 12–16.

James, W. (1890/1950). *The principles of psychology,* Volumes I and II. Reprinted by Dover Publications, 1950.

Wilson, G.D. (2002). *Psychology for performing artists,* 2nd end. London: Whurr.

Zurawicki, L. (2010). *Neuromarketing: exploring the brain of the consumer.* Berlin: Springer-Verlag.

CHAPTER 21

....

IMAGINING
IDENTIFICATIONS

How Musicians Align their Practices with Publics

....

BYRON DUECK

ACROSS a wide range of social groups, the transmission of musical traditions increasingly involves an orientation to imagined others. When young musicians learn to make music, they acquaint themselves with the practices of not only family members and local communities, but also distant and unknown musicians. They have been able to do so in part by engaging with performances, publications, and practices that circulate in mass-mediated form. In attuning their own doings to those of distant others, musicians both acknowledge and extend these networks of musical circulation. Their mutual attunement can be understood as an important component in contemporary processes of identity formation, and additionally as a kind of allegiance-building.

The orientation to imagined others is a longstanding aspect of education in so-called art musics, of course, but also the transmission of what are sometimes called traditional, vernacular, and folk musics. Accordingly, this chapter begins with a brief exploration of three contexts in which established practitioners help young people to learn genres performed by wider publics: jazz, Western classical music, and North American powwow. These vignettes lead into a discussion of what I will call musical publics or imaginaries, and their implications for identity construction and allegiance making. The material revisits theoretical ideas I have outlined elsewhere (see Dueck, 2007, 2013a,b); here, I am interested in connecting those arguments to the concept of identity, especially in light of some of the criticism that concept has recently encountered.

21.1 A JAZZ JAM SESSION

On a Sunday afternoon during the summer of 2009, two colleagues and I attended and recorded a jam session hosted at a pub in London's West End. The event was arranged by Dune Music, an organization that manages professional musicians and presents educational programs aimed at younger players. A trio of junior Dune-affiliated performers made up the house band at the session—a bassist, a drummer, and a saxophonist. Things started off somewhat uncertainly—the session typically opened and closed with performances by the house band, but the saxophonist's flight had been delayed, and the bassist and the drummer were forced to play a good part of the first set on their own. After a few very free improvisations, they asked one of the regulars at the session, a young pianist still in school, to sit in. He agreed, and together they performed McCoy Tyner's "Passion Dance," a harmonically static tune in a fast tempo that suited his playing style well. He sat in for the next, freely improvised, tune, too. The missing saxophonist arrived midway through that piece, unpacked his horn, and joined in. When they had finished, the pianist sat down with his father, who had brought him, and the band members turned to their own material, performing three original pieces.

The jam session per se started shortly afterward. The musicians who participated, younger players for the most part, included two university students who had come down from Leeds to hear a concert the night before and one or two musicians who were regulars at other Dune-sponsored events, including the aforementioned pianist and a young female guitarist. They performed a number of favorites, including "Stella by Starlight," "Blue Monk," "Have You Met Miss Jones," and "Softly as in a Morning Sunrise." For the final number of the jam, one of the members of the house band suggested they do a "rhythm changes" tune; that is, one built on the harmonic structure of George Gershwin's "I Got Rhythm." They decided on Thelonious Monk's well-known "Rhythm-a-ning," whose head (main melody) features some disorienting rhythmic twists and turns.[1] It was not during the head that accidents occurred, however, but rather the instrumental solos. One of the members of the house band counted off in a very fast tempo, and it was this, and a lack of close attention to the harmonic changes on the part of a few of the players, that led to the problems. Phrases spilled over the divisions in the form, and a number of musicians appeared to lose the count altogether at times.

At the end of the tune, as the jammers were walking off stage, the bassist in the house band reached out toward them, lightly tapping his hand on the piano. As if acknowledging that what he was about to say would not be particularly easy to hear, he said, "I don't want to be like this, but … ," and continuing when he had their attention, "If you feel like you're getting lost in the form, then stop playing and listen; don't just carry on playing …" Although several of the musicians who had participated in the final tune had gotten lost,

---

[1] Like "I Got Rhythm," "Rhythm-a-ning" has a 32-bar AABA form comprising four 8-bar segments, the third of which moves through a circle-of-fifths sequence.

he spoke directly to the young pianist who earlier that afternoon had played "Passion Dance":

> ... if you listen to myself and [the guitarist] ... and the drummer, the drummer ... will mark the form ... it's an eight-bar feel, or four bars ... And if you ... feel lost, or if it ... sounds ... really funny, there's nothing bad about stopping and just being like, "OK where am I" or even asking ... where the hell you are, you know.

He brought his remarks to a conclusion. "You're cool," he told the pianist, and added, to the other musicians, "But well done ... anyway. It was cool, apart from that." The audience applauded, and the house band went on to play a final number of their own.

This first vignette exemplifies some of the practices enabled by an orientation I have elsewhere (Dueck, 2013b) called "musical imagining," as well as some of the disciplinary work tied up with such a bearing. It shows how jazz players who have never met one another before—in this case, musicians from Leeds and London—are able to perform together without rehearsal or earlier agreement, in part because they have previously familiarized themselves with similar repertoires of circulating tunes, techniques, and styles (see Faulkner & Becker, 2009). It also demonstrates that these kinds of interactions are only possible to the extent to which musicians have developed ears, minds, and technical skills that allow them to perform competently with and for people they have never met. It further evidences the work required to develop this kind of attunement: it was common for more advanced Dune musicians to offer formative advice and criticism to younger ones at workshops and rehearsals, and there were enough of the latter at the jam session that it naturally, albeit momentarily, took on the character of one of these more educational gatherings, with one of the musicians making an explicitly pedagogical point. This highlights another aspect of the interaction: while some of the musicians had come to the jam without knowing anyone there, others were already intimates connected to one another by mentoring relationships. Thus, the session was a site where a number of ties were acknowledged or cultivated—connections to a broader jazz public on the one hand, and to known and knowable fellow musicians on the other. Put another way, the event fostered multiple overlapping identities—or, rather, identifications, the term I will tend to privilege in the discussions that follow.

21.2 A CLASSICAL MUSIC COMPETITION

For around a century, young Canadian musicians have participated in competitive arts festivals (Greene, 1923, 1932; Belyea, 1993). In my home province, Manitoba, singers, instrumentalists, dancers, and other participants take part in an array of regional festivals each year, singly and as members of ensembles. Such events were certainly an important part of my early musical life, and I regularly took part in them as a pianist and chorister in the 1970s and 1980s. As a pianist, I typically participated in several classes at each festival, categorized by playing level and musical style; for instance, "Piano Solo, Baroque, Grade 5."[2] Performances were evaluated by adjudicators, usually from outside the community, who marked competitors, commented on performances, and decided on winners in each category and overall. I remember long spring afternoons spent in cold churches, waiting to play, trying to keep my hands warm inside my mittens and praying not to suffer a memory lapse. I knew many of my fellow competitors well; several of us, including my sister, took piano and theory lessons from the same teacher.

My local festival (now called the Southeastern Manitoba Festival) benefited from the enthusiastic participation of people from the town of Steinbach and the surrounding area. Although the event welcomed all participants, it was patronized especially strongly by the descendants of Mennonite immigrants in the area. Large numbers of this Anabaptist sect came to western Canada from the Russian Empire beginning in the 1870s, settling in blocs. A significant portion of this population pursued education in music, with choral music cultivated in particular (see J. Dueck, 2008b). This engagement had benefits for collective musical worship in a community where many were religiously observant, but it had an outward orientation, too, being a way for Mennonites to negotiate a position vis-à-vis the surrounding Canadian society, as at once distinct from and valuable to it (see J. Dueck, 2008a,b).[3] Thus, my own musical training had an outlet in the immediate community: my parents encouraged me to accompany hymn singing and other music making in the church we attended. At the same time, this training oriented me to a larger world of music making: I took piano lessons, sat graded exams, and was encouraged to meet the standards and expectations of classical musicians and their audiences.

Like the jam session, the music festival and the forms of training that precede it evidence the kinds of work that go into calibrating musical minds and bodies toward those of unknown others. Young musicians practice, take lessons, and are evaluated by an adjudicator on how competently they meet the expectations of a wider musical public. Standards are widely enough agreed that a visiting stranger is competent to judge how well a community's children are doing.[4] Importantly, it is not

---

[2] There were also skills-focused classes, for instance, in sight-reading and quick study.

[3] In that broader social context, "Mennonite musicality" may harness a homology between the "Germanness" of Russian Mennonites and the "Germanness" of art music, with "German music" being something that "German people" do well. (Russian Mennonites traditionally spoke a Low German language at home and High German in church; the canon of Western art music, of course, has been dominated by the contributions of German-speaking composers.) Tellingly, oratorios and sacred works by Handel, Haydn, and Mendelssohn were popular in the community choral performances I heard in my youth (see J. Dueck, 2008b, p. 349).

[4] It is worth remarking on both the breadth of this public and its longstanding nature. The website for Associated Manitoba Arts Festivals (Associated Manitoba Arts Festivals, 2014) lists 29 festivals and claims 60,000 participants. Over a twentieth of the province's population, then, is annually involved in some way with its arts festivals. Greene's 1923 and 1932 accounts of music festivals in western Canada suggest that the popular pursuit of skill in the performance of Western art music has been part of musical life in the country for some time. Moreover, his remarks about the excellence of the music he heard evidence how, even before the widespread availability of recordings, broad publics of non-professional practice were coming into being around shared (and apparently comparable) engagement with circulating works, styles, and techniques .

only individuals who, by engaging with circulating works and styles, take up positions relative to publics of practice, but groups as well. The cultivation of art music in Mennonite communities has been a way to negotiate their place with respect to a broader national public.

Thus, participation in music festivals acknowledges and nurtures a wide range of relationships and identifications, committing competitors to the standards of a broader art-music public, preparing them for participation in the musical activities of their congregations, subjecting them to evaluation by adjudicators, and setting them in direct competition with intimates and strangers. Festival involvement is often encouraged by music teachers and agreed by parents, who pay the festival registration fees, drive children to the various events, and so on. In this way festival participation fosters a range of overlapping identifications, involving the domestic sphere, the local community, and international musical publics.

21.3 A POWWOW CLUB MEETING

During the same years that I was learning to play piano, Indigenous people from the province of Manitoba were increasingly engaging with powwow, a North American Aboriginal musical and choreographic form (see Whidden, 2007, pp. 113–19). Powwows are gatherings that feature several well-established men's and women's dance styles, each with associated choreography and regalia (see Fig. 21.1; for more on powwow see Browner, 2002; Ellis, Lassiter, & Dunham, 2005; Scales, 2012; Levine, 2013). The dancing is supported by the singing of drum groups, whose members sit and sometimes stand around large round drums placed skin-upward (see Fig. 21. 2). The contemporary powwow emerged among Indigenous groups of the North American Plains, drawing upon genres of dance and song that had been circulating since the nineteenth century (Levine, 2013). Powwows are public-facing, having emerged in a context where Native North American performers had already been part of touring Wild West shows for some time. As Victoria Levine (2013) notes, they range in size from "intimate, local gatherings of a few hundred people, to large arena shows with several thousand people from distant places."

Powwow and certain of its constituent elements have a close connection to some communities in Manitoba. Dakota people in the southwest of the province have held public powwows for over a century, while the jingle dress dance, one of three widely performed women's dances, may have originated just across the border in neighboring Ontario (Browner, 2002). All the same, powwow is new to many communities further north in the province. In some cases, it now complements older practices of singing, drumming, and dancing. In others—following centuries of contact, missionization, and colonial attempts to extinguish Indigenous cultures—it represents a return of drum song and related dance forms to communities that no longer practiced them (see Whidden, 2007).

FIG. 21.1 Jingle dress dancer. Sherry Starr and her daughter, Callie Starr, 6, participate in a kids'
powwow club at the Ma Mawi Wi Chi Itata Centre, Wednesday, December 12, 2012.

Trevor Hagan, Winnipeg Free Press.

So, for instance, Denise McLeod, an Indigenous woman who grew up in Manitoba
around the same time I did, told me that she was 16 years old when she saw her first powwow, at a convention center in Winnipeg.[5] She remembered being amazed by the dancing and wanting to try the same thing herself. She subsequently took up fancy shawl
dancing—one of the three main women's styles—and began to attend pow-wows. She
recalled that there had only been a few in the area to attend at the time—two or three in
Manitoba, some in neighboring Saskatchewan, and some in adjoining northern states.
She remembered how, as an enthusiastic young dancer, she had hitchhiked to one of the
latter, in North Dakota, at the age of seventeen.

Since that time, powwow has developed much more of a presence across the province, and new generations of Aboriginal people are being introduced to it in increasing
numbers. Some of the most important sites for learning powwow songs and dances have
been powwow clubs, many of which are sponsored by child and family service organizations or state schools. These have had particular prominence in the city of Winnipeg
(see Dueck, forthcoming). I visited one such club, run by Ray "Coco" Stevenson and

<hr>

[5] Denise McLeod is a pseudonym.

FIG. 21.2 Drum group.
"Brave Heart Drummers perform" from the article "Indiana University Bloomington hosts the Third Annual Traditional Powwow this weekend, October 26-27."

Photograph taken by John Teller, Brave Heart, Live at Priarie Island, Copyright © 2011 Bear Traks Media, LLC with permission from Bear Traks Media, LLC.

his wife Rhonda Stevenson, in the spring of 2013. There were about thirty-five people present, all told, including perhaps three children of pre-school age, five between the ages of 5 and 12, and ten between the ages of 13 and 17. There were a number of adults present, too. Some had come on their own to help supervise or sing, others had come with their children. Ray began the gathering with a few announcements about upcoming powwows: one was to be held at a school in the city in a few days' time, a second at a community college, and a third at one of the city's universities, this last celebrating the graduation of Aboriginal students. He also delivered a mild exhortation to some of the dancers, remarking that some of them had not danced as well as they might have at a recent powwow, having stopped in the middle of a song. He recommended that they listen to powwow music on the internet or on CD, and practice dancing all the way through songs from beginning to end.

Following the collective singing of a prayer song, "Miigwitch, Gitchi Manitou" (thank you, Great Spirit) to the accompaniment of the drum, the dancing began. The girls, who made up the great majority of young dancers present, practiced steps for three of the most common women's powwow dances: fancy shawl, jingle dress, and women's traditional. All of these are core powwow dances, each with its own movements and clothing style. Dancers perform simultaneously, but do not coordinate their steps with one another; the dances thus lend themselves to competitions in which a single winner can be designated from amongst many participants. It was evident that attendees were at various stages in the learning process: some were already familiar with the basic moves, while others were new to dancing. There were also opportunities for more general participation, not limited by gender or genre, the first an intertribal dance in which attendees could dance in whatever style they preferred, the second a round dance in a swinging rhythm, during which we held hands and moved through a series of complex winding patterns. The adults in attendance joined the children for these.

A few days later, I attended one of the powwows to which Ray had invited us, at a school in the eastern part of the city. Among the many dancers I recognized a few from the powwow club, now dressed in their regalia. The event drew together a large number of Aboriginal dancers and singers, but additionally non-Indigenous audience members, including children who attended the school and their parents.[6] Holding such events at schools is a relatively new phenomenon, and is related to initiatives, in Manitoba and other parts of Canada, to teach students more about Aboriginal history and culture.

As this account suggests, contemporary powwow instruction appears to cultivate similar kinds of "imagining" musical identifications to classical music and jazz. It prepares dancers and singers to take part in an international powwow scene, helping them to calibrate their dancing practices to what other, unknown participants are doing. Dancers learn and practice the steps of well-established dance styles and are corrected when they behave in ways that are out of line with what is expected. They are encouraged to practice dancing to powwow songs that circulate on recordings and the internet. And they deploy what they learn in new contexts, interacting with unfamiliar singers, dancers, and audiences. Even in the case of musical practices designated as traditional, then, there increasingly exist bearings toward broader publics of practice.[7] Certainly, the musical education of young people takes places in contexts of social intimacy, where instructors and fellow students often get to know one another well. However, the skills they acquire are not simply those they need to perform competently with intimates, but also ones that reflect what circulates in broader networks. Here again, learning of a musical practice involves the formation of a number of overlapping orientations or identifications.

---

[6] This event is discussed further in Dueck, forthcoming.

[7] In fact, as I suggest elsewhere (Dueck, 2013b), Aboriginal musical publicness is of very long standing in many parts of North America.

Like the music festival enthusiastically patronized by descendants of Russian Mennonites, powwow seems to acknowledge a sense of shared identity, on the one hand, and a minority relationship to a larger national public, on the other.[8] The relationship between Indigenous people and the national public has been considerably more troubled, however. As is well known, the federal government in Canada actively sought for decades to extinguish Aboriginal cultures, and economic and social advantages remain deeply divided along lines of race in that country. Indeed, the contemporary surge in powwow instruction can be understood in part as an attempt to reconnect to Indigenous traditions whose transmission was interrupted under colonialism.

21.4 ALLIANCES AND PUBLICS

Given the theme of this volume, and that this chapter is concerned in part with North American Aboriginal music, it is pertinent to address Beverley Diamond's call for studies of Indigenous music, and ethnomusicology more generally, to move away from a focus on identity and toward research into how music defines relationships (Diamond, 2007). In North America and elsewhere, studies of music and identity have often been allied to a politics of recognition—or what might be called an aesthetics of recognition—which calls upon majority populations to acknowledge the cultural and artistic differences of minorities.[9] However, as Diamond observes, the forms such recognition takes have often been limiting and reductive. It is not simply that majority groups, in embracing what they consider to be Indigenous musics, favor only a few from among a much wider range, but additionally that they (i.e., majority groups) tend to patronize only those practices that they themselves value. Those they find uninteresting—or that cannot be pressed into service of a task they regard as important—tend to get ignored.

The focus on relationships that Diamond proposes places the emphasis, not on what majority audiences are recognizing—which would only affirm the centrality

---

[8] That powwow is often felt to express a common identity is in no way to suggest that its component parts represent the diverse expressive practices of all North American Indigenous peoples. In fact, as I have suggested, many powwow practices originated in the center of the North American continent and have been transmitted to other areas. Practitioners of powwow, moreover, understand it to stand in complex relationships with their own histories and cultures. Powwow provides an opportunity to express Indigeneity to Aboriginal and non-Aboriginal audiences, and to launch a particular understanding of Aboriginality into the public sphere. However, this in no way means that Indigenous communities and practices are homogeneous.

[9] Charles Taylor popularized the concept of a "politics of recognition" in an essay of the same name (1994); see also Stokes (2010b). Diamond's critique draws upon the observations of Dunbar-Hall and Gibson (2004, pp. 24–6), who are in turn informed by van Toorn (1990) and Wark (2000).

of such audiences and their tastes, after all—but rather on the choices of Aboriginal musicians. In so doing, it highlights their agency in pursuing and cultivating relationships—with human intimates, the land and its other-than-human inhabitants, spiritual beings, Indigenous audiences, and national and international publics.[10] Diamond's intervention is productive in other ways, too. The term identity can suggest stasis or essence, while an emphasis on alignment and relating emphasizes practice and doing. Exploring whether or how majority groups are acknowledging minority differences can suggest that majorities are the ultimate arbiters of aesthetic, political, or social value, and obscure the wider range of connections that artists cultivate. A focus on relationships, in contrast, may enable more critical perspectives on the power dynamics of majority recognition while remaining sensitive to the wide range of relationships musicians pursue. An emphasis on acquaintanceship additionally resonates with ethnomusicological and anthropological interests in musical connections (see Diamond, 2007, pp. 2–3).

At the same time, a focus on allegiance does not obviate considerations of identity: as Diamond and John-Carlos Perea both suggest, relationships shape identities (Diamond, 2007, p. 2; Perea, 2012, p. 72). Indeed, a variant of the word identity, namely, identification, captures something of both identity and alliance—the relationality of "identifying as" and "identifying with," and the directedness and agency of "identifying an audience." In this spirit, this chapter explores musical identifications, placing the emphasis on the activity of identifying, and on relationships and social orientations.

21.5 WHAT IS A MUSICAL PUBLIC? A NETWORK OF CIRCULATING PERFORMANCES AND PUBLICATIONS

The identifications that are of particular concern in this chapter, and especially evident in the opening ethnographic episodes, are those that engender musical publics. These are several: the relationships between the musical performances and publications that together constitute spaces of musical circulation; those between performers and their mass-mediated publics; and those between mutually oriented musical practitioners.

Accordingly, this section and those that follow consider publics from three perspectives—as networks of circulation, as audiences of (intimate) strangers, and as

---

[10] Diamond suggests that extant and desired relationships are evidenced in musicians' choices of genre, mediating technologies, and language, as well as in their acts of citation and collaboration, assertions of ownership, and decisions about who is granted access to musical performances, pieces, and traditions.

social formations built around shared forms of embodied practice.[11] At the same time, this second half of the chapter acknowledges that a wide range of identifications are evident in the preceding ethnographic episodes, and not only ones that engender publics.

Musical publics can be understood in the first place as networks of circulating, mass-mediated performances and publications—sheet music, chord charts, records, cassettes, radio and television broadcasts, mp3s, YouTube videos, and so on. What makes these performances and publications into a public is that they are mutually referential, standing in dialogue with previously circulating ones while inviting future responses (Warner, 2002, p. 90). Certainly, they take up a wide range of relationships to one another—emulation, homage, parody, criticism, or rejection, for instance. What makes a public cohere as a formation is not that its components stand in agreement, however, but that they in some way acknowledge other elements in the same network.

The sites of learning and performance described above were very clearly connected to such webs of reflexive circulation. In all three ethnographic vignettes, performers drew upon mass-mediated texts or were directed to them by their mentors: the jazz musicians' session played familiar tunes ("Rhythm-a-ning," "Stella by Starlight"), the classical musicians performed published works by well-known composers, and the powwow dancers were directed to practice with the help of recordings and YouTube videos. Moreover, in all three contexts, young musicians were encouraged to pursue the kinds of standards to which circulating performances were held: the jazz musicians were told to attend closely to the musical form, the classical musicians were evaluated by a visiting adjudicator, and the powwow dancers were reminded to dance all the way until the end of a song.

21.5.1   Circulation and the "metaculture of modernity"

Greg Urban (2001) argues that networks of circulating publications are governed by a "metaculture of modernity," an ideology that especially values the mass dissemination of the new. Urban contrasts this metaculture with a "metaculture of tradition," which prefers the propinquitous (that is, socially intimate) replication of the old. Urban explains that the texts produced under a metaculture of modernity are never altogether new: they revisit the substance of previously circulating texts, often in indirect and abstract ways. This is because, while a metaculture of tradition values *replications* of what has gone before, a metaculture of modernity values *responses* to it (2001, p. 196). Indeed, cultures in which a metaculture of modernity operates often have amongst their ranks commentators and critics whose job consists in part of identifying the subtle, abstract ways in which the new responds to the old (2001, pp. 182–9).

---

[11] These aspects of publicness make up a much shorter list than those outlined in Warner's essay on "Publics and Counterpublics" (2002, pp. 65–124), a work that nevertheless deeply informs the writing here.

Urban's concept of the metaculture of modernity governing spheres of circulation also seems relevant to mass-mediated music and the discourses that surround it. Consider the complex ways in which Brahms's first symphony is "Beethoven's Tenth" or how the music of Oasis pays tribute to the Beatles, or even Heinrich Schenker's statement that important works of tonal music are "always the same, but not in the same way" (Jonas, 1975 [1955], p. xvi).

If Urban's theory is correct, the formation of musical identities in contexts of mass circulation involves acquiring an ideology that values innovation, and understands the role of a musician as one of bringing newness into the world (albeit a newness that responds to, and carries traces of, what has circulated before it).[12] This theory seems to ring true with respect to the contexts discussed earlier in this chapter, where certain manifestations of newness were clearly valued. The performances at the jam session layered new solos over old harmonic structures,[13] and at the beginning and end of the event, the members of the house band performed new works of their own. At the competitive music festivals I took part in, there was an expectation that the better musicians would offer new, personal interpretations of established works, while at powwows, dancers employ well-established dance steps, but find ways to perform these uniquely and personally. There are implications here for identity formation, most notably that many forms of musical pedagogy seek to foster a desire and ability to bring new things into being—to produce musicians who will contribute something unique to a particular network of circulation.

Is this too simple? If the sites of learning I discuss, all of which are oriented to the training of young musicians, impart an ideology of novelty, they seem equally or more concerned with teaching certain core practices. Very much in evidence is a more replicative kind of social transmission, focusing on passing on the central components of certain traditions. Indeed, all of the sites of musical learning I discussed earlier had close connections to domestic spaces—parents and children regularly attended powwow club meetings together, for instance. Domestic spaces, as Urban argues, are often ones where traditional, replicative forms of cultural transfer, including of language and taste, take place (for a fuller examination of the persistence of replication in contemporary music making; see Wilf, 2012).

Moreover, is the "new" that is valued in these contexts first and foremost a "new" in relation to a sphere of circulating performances? Here, powwow suggests some additional complications. Powwow dancers' regalia follows established patterns, but it is nevertheless often highly personalized. It sometimes incorporates symbols reflecting spiritual knowledge about the dancer received in the course of ceremony, for instance. Does "new" regalia always evidence a concern to contribute something distinctive to a circulatory network? Does it sometimes manifest a traditional orientation? Are there instances when perhaps both are true?

---

[12] As I discuss below, this newness responds to specific lineages of circulation, and, for this reason, varies from genre to genre and public to public.

[13] In the case of "Rhythm-a-ning," the layering of newnesses was somewhat more complex.

21.6 What is a Musical Public? An Intimate Orientation to Strangers

A second, and more common, understanding of "public" is as an audience of listeners, viewers, or readers. Lauren Berlant and others (Warner, 2002; Berlant, 2008; Stokes, 2010a) have recently enriched the understanding of such publics through explorations of their affective aspects. Berlant, writing of works aimed at a female audience in the United States, describes an "intimate public"—an audience authors address as though they already share a common fund of emotional experience (Berlant, 2008, p. 5). Berlant writes,

> participants in the intimate public *feel* as though it expresses what is common among them ... Their participation seems to confirm the sense that even before there was a market addressed to them, there existed a world of strangers who would be emotionally literate in each other's experience of power, intimacy, desire, and discontent.
>
> 2008, p. 5; Berlant's italics.

Berlant here not only identifies the affective nature of publicness, but asks whether the members of the public in fact share an identity before they are constituted as a group.

Much more broadly, Berlant and other recent theorists of publicness understand there to be many publics, rather than a single one. This plurality is engendered in part because the participants in publics presume their fellow members to have distinct kinds of commonalities—specific emotional competences or aesthetic preferences, for instance. Warner (2002) argues that, in a variety of ways, publicly circulating texts subtly identity the constituencies they address. Moreover, he argues that publics understand the discourses (linguistic, musical, filmic, and so on) they employ to stand in unequal relationships to one another, with some more prestigious and dominant and others less so.

Musical publics, like the formations discussed by Berlant and Warner, exist in the plural (this is not to say they are hermetic). Their multiplicity stems in part from the responsive character of networks of circulation, discussed earlier: performances and publications tend to acknowledge some precedents and lineages rather than others. For instance, powwow songs typically make use of very similar structural features, including an asymmetrical repetition form and a descending melodic contour.[14] They are much less likely to allude to a melody by Beethoven or employ the song structure

---

[14] I here use Levine & Nettl's (2011) term, "asymmetrical repetition form," which they propose as a replacement for "incomplete repetition form." The concept of tradition is important in powwow. Consequently, musical and choreographic forms have quite a bit of stability, and there seems to be less concern for innovation than in, for instance, jazz. This said, important regional and stylistic differences distinguish powwow songs from one another (Browner, 2002, pp. 66–87; 2009), and change does occur (Browner, 2009, pp. 138–9).

of "I Got Rhythm."[15] Indeed, Ray could encourage the young dancers at the pow-wow club to practice dancing to songs on recordings or the internet in the knowledge that they would be dancing to something very similar to what they would hear at a powwow.

The plurality of publicness also arises because performances, publications, venues, and gatherings seek to address audiences in ways they will find particularly resonant. This clearly has implications for identity, although, as Berlant seems to suggest, public cultures may simultaneously be identifying and nurturing commonalities amongst their participants. Denise McLeod's story, cited earlier, is a good example. Upon seeing a powwow for the first time as an Aboriginal teenager, McLeod was captivated, and decided to take up dancing herself. During the last several decades, powwow has spread across North America, including to Indigenous communities where drumming traditions had waned, or where dancing and singing styles were quite different from those of the North American Plains. It has been successful for a range of reasons, including because it has appealed to Aboriginal people who were separated from their traditions by colonialism. Thus, powwow singing and dancing identify commonalities among members of their expanding audience. However, these practices themselves foster common identifications, most obviously in the case of young people exposed to powwow from a young age at club meetings like those described earlier.

Here, again, the idea of relationality is important. Powwows and powwow clubs extend opportunities for affiliation with a continually expanding network of Indigenous performers: an Aboriginal musical public. Nor is this the only public for powwow practices, since in some parts of North America, powwows attract a substantial non-Indigenous audience. In this respect, they create opportunities to establish connections with a range of hearers and viewers, including spectators fascinated by the striking sonic and visual aspects of powwow, and members of settler society who are sympathetic to postcolonial revivals of Native American cultures. The sense that powwow is moving across some sort of boundary when it establishes relationships with audiences who are not North American Natives points, again, to the plurality of musical publics.

A final point might be made about publics-as-audiences, which is that they are distinguished by discrepancies of prestige and power. Just as dialects, accents, and speech registers are accorded different statuses, so too are musical idioms. Moreover, audiences are all too aware of these divergences, and of where the publics they belong to sit in the hierarchy. This has implications for both identification and allegiance. Warner writes, "The subordinate status of a [public] does not simply reflect identities formed elsewhere; participation in such a public is one of the ways by which its members' identities are formed and transformed" (2002, p. 121). To be a member of certain musical

---

[15] This is by no means outside the realm of possibility. It would, however, suggest that a broader set of precedents, and probably a broader public, was creatively being addressed.

publics, then, means allying oneself with stigmatized groups and idioms—or highly valued ones.[16]

21.7 WHAT IS A MUSICAL PUBLIC? EMBODIED ORIENTATIONS TO IMAGINED OTHERS

I have discussed two established understandings of musical publicness: on the one hand, as a network of mutually referential performances and publications, and on the other, as an "audience of intimates" understood by those who address it to share certain kinds of knowledge and experience (including in the aesthetic and affective realms). It is a third manifestation of publicness that is most evident in the ethnographic episodes at the beginning of this chapter, however: publics are formations that come into being as musicians bring their bodily and mental practices into line with those of unknown others. Jazz musicians prepare for future encounters by learning standards, internalizing melodic, rhythmic, and harmonic patterns, and getting acquainted with a range of popular idioms. Classical musicians learn works by respected composers, as well as nuances of expression and interpretation that classical audiences would consider appropriate in performances of these works. Young powwow singers and dancers learn songs, vocal techniques, and dance steps that allow them to participate in not only local powwows, but others across the continent. This third aspect of publicness is clearly linked to the other two, involving forms of discipline that enable musicians to address unknown audiences appropriately, and contribute competently to networks of mass-mediated, circulating performances. At the same time, it highlights aspects of the production of publicness that are not as evident in them.

In the first place, it highlights the democratic and everyday aspects of musical imaginaries. An embodied orientation to others is imparted in schools and at after-school clubs, and nurtured by families, neighborhoods, communities, and congregations. And while, in some cases, it involves learning highly specialized forms of literacy in formal contexts, in others it is transmitted aurally and informally. The acquisition of these "imagining" modes of sociability is significant precisely because it is so common.

Secondly, focusing on this aspect of publicness highlights how modes of imagining or stranger-oriented sociability develop in contexts of propinquity. Children often

---

[16] The Russian Mennonite engagement with art music comes to mind again. Certain Mennonite differences have been regarded as problematic by other Canadians, historically and in the present day: the cultivation of German languages, widespread conscientious objection during two world wars, and certain expressions of social conservatism, to name a few (not all people who identify as Russian Mennonites would recognize these as descriptions of themselves, it should be added). Whatever the nurturing of art music has done for Mennonite communities internally, it may also have been a way to build alliances and manage perceptions in the broader society. (This may also have been the case for Mennonites living in nineteenth- and twentieth-century Russia; see J. Dueck, 2008a.)

begin to learn the musical skills that articulate them to public cultures from a young age, in contexts where they are surrounded by family members and friends. This raises an interesting question. Urban suggests that such intimate sites are places where relatively "inertial" forms of cultural reproduction occur, places where children learn language, habitus, and taste (see Bourdieu, 1984; Urban, 2001). Do these replication-oriented contexts also lend themselves to the cultivation of ideologies of innovation, apparently characteristic of cultures of circulation (see Urban, 2001)?

Thirdly, that musical publicness is learned in contexts of intense, localized social reproduction suggests that these places are nodes where a wide range of affiliations are nurtured, and to both intimates and imagined others. Moreover, because not all of these affiliations are commensurable, they are places where negotiations over which ones should be prioritized are particularly in evidence. They are, in short, places that offer insights into how musicians navigate their placement relative to persons both distant and proximate.

The examples at the opening of this chapter demonstrate that the process of learning music is not only one of orienting body and mind to the practices of unknown others. It also often involves intensive engagement with co-present intimates. The bassist who criticized the younger musicians near the close of the London jam session was not simply explaining how members of the jazz public should comport themselves when they get lost in the form, but managing interactions at a particular gathering, and negotiating personal roles as an acquaintance of, and mentor to, some of the younger musicians present. His "I don't want to be like this, but ..." might be understood as an acknowledgment of the not-always-comfortable complexity of his obligations as a musician and pedagogue. Similarly, practicing in order to succeed at the music festivals of my youth was not only a matter of attuning myself to accepted ways of performing Western art music, but also acquiring skills that were valued by my family, community, and congregation. Participating in singing and dancing at a powwow club, meanwhile, sets children in a relationship with a broader, intertribal musical public even as it prepares them to participate in interactions with more localized communities. It additionally acknowledges other important relationships, for instance with the other-than-human participants addressed through prayer, song, and dance at rehearsals and powwows.

The instances of musical training considered at the opening of this chapter thus involve complex and overlapping connections; musicians are continually involved in various kinds of "face-work" (Goffman, 1967), managing relationships and roles relative to intimates, even as they attempt to create performances that are competently calibrated to broader circulatory networks (and sometimes more than one of these). To what degree are musical interactions oriented toward publics of strangers, and to what degree toward social intimates? Are musicians mainly cultivating relationships, pursuing allegiances, occupying roles, and forming identities in relation to known kin, friends, rivals, and enemies, or are they more occupied with imagined audiences and circulating works and performances? These queries are in no way simple: it could be that some musicians cultivate excellence (as it might be judged by a broader public) primarily to please or impress family members or friends.

Sites of musical acquisition also offer opportunities to think about the tensions between various ways of identifying. Musicians sometimes prioritize publics and sometimes intimates, occasionally exclusively. Contexts of Indigenous musical acquisition are especially indicative in this regard. As musicians gain familiarity with powwow, they learn that the music, dance, sacred observance, and the material culture related to them may be subject to special protocols. Some songs can only be sung by certain singers, for certain purposes, or in certain contexts, for instance (see Hoefnagels, 2002; Diamond, 2007; Dueck, 2013b). It is furthermore inappropriate for many ceremonial songs and practices to be recorded, broadcast, or sold. Thus, at public powwows in Manitoba, it is not uncommon for elders to ask for video cameras to be turned off at important moments.

There are controls on the circulation of music and dance in many societies, of course; copyright is one such set of limitations. Significant in the case of Aboriginal proscriptions is that they are often quite distinct from copyright and, when this is the case, do not benefit from its legal protections (see Harrison, 2002). Also significant, particularly from the perspective of this chapter, is that respecting restrictions on circulation may be a way of acknowledging the importance of intimate relationships with kin, community, sacred objects, and spiritual beings (see Diamond, 2007). Observing the restrictions on when, where, and by whom a song may be sung sets one in a proper relationship with its owner(s) and honors their relationship to the song. Avoiding the recording or broadcast of certain songs and dances demonstrates respect for the other-than-human persons who may be offended by the casual or improper treatment of their gifts.[17]

It is not only in North American Indigenous contexts that musicians must decide whether to prioritize certain relationships over others. Around twenty years ago, at a moment when many of my friends were reconciling the musical allegiances of their youth with their professional aspirations, a singer I knew who had grown up in a Mennonite community described to me how the expectations of that community had come into conflict with her broader musical development. As a young singer, she was regularly asked to contribute to worship services at her family church. The congregation expected, however, that she would present herself in a "humble" way and not draw too much attention to herself while performing—for instance by imbuing the singing with too much personal presence or dramatic force. She explained that this expectation interfered significantly with the mode of self-presentation she was encouraged to have as a performer of opera and art song, namely, the ability to communicate with an audience confidently and in an emotionally direct way. Her story suggested musical allegiances

---

[17] Among the allegiances that are important for many North American Indigenous peoples are relationships with the land and the "other-than-human persons" who inhabit it (Hallowell, 1955, 1992; Diamond, 2007). Songs and dances, in these communities, were traditionally often gifts from or forms of communication with spirits and ancestors.

divided between two groups—a congregation demanding a humble and emotionally neutral performance style, and an art-music audience expecting the self-assured projection of a certain emotional directness. It is important not to understand this as a conflict between "disciplining community" and "expressive freedom." Both the singer's church and the world of classical vocal performance made demands on her. Evident rather is a conflict between two different forms of musical regulation and two apparently incommensurable ideas regarding appropriate vocal performance. Evident, too, is that decisions about vocal style were decisions about social identification.

21.8 Conclusions

As indicated by the accounts presented here of learning and instruction in jazz, classical music, and powwow singing and dancing, the transmission of musical knowledge increasingly occurs in contexts that equip young learners to participate in not only close contexts of music making, but musical publics as well. Musical training and performance involve multiple, overlapping social orientations—to social intimates, as well as imagined others. Musical identities thus come into being in part as agents and communities prioritize certain relationships and limit others. Musical publicness invites a descriptive language that focuses on relationality: how musicians and their circulating performances respond to one another; how performers presume aesthetic, affective, and experiential intimacy with those they address; and how musicians train their bodies and minds to bring them into relationships with wider networks of mutually oriented performers. This focus on connections lends itself in turn to thinking about identity in particular ways: perhaps especially in terms of identification.

REFERENCES

Associated Manitoba Arts Festivals. (2014). Member festivals. Available at: http://www.amaf. mb.ca/member-festivals.html accessed 28 February, 2014.

Belyea, W.H. (1993). *Winnipeg music competition festival: 75th anniversary. 1919–1993: a historical perspective.* Held at the University of Manitoba Library.

Berlant, L. (2008). *The female complaint: the unfinished business of sentimentality in American culture.* Durham, NC: Duke University Press.

Bourdieu, P. (1984). *Distinction: a social critique of the judgement of taste*, transl. R. Nice. Cambridge, MA: Harvard University Press.

Browner, T. (2002). *Heartbeat of the people: music and dance of the northern pow-wow.* Urbana, IL: University of Illinois Press.

Browner, T. (2009). An acoustical geography of intertribal pow-wow songs. In: T. Browner (Ed.) *Music of the first nations: tradition and innovation in Native North America*, pp. 131–40. Urbana, IL: University of Illinois Press.

Diamond, B. (2007). Music of modern indigeneity: from identity to alliance studies, the John Blacking Distinguished Lecture for 2006, *European Meetings in Ethnomusicology*, 12, 169–90. [Draft of published article sent as personal communication by Diamond.]

Dueck, B. (2007). Public and intimate sociability in First Nations and Métis fiddling. *Ethnomusicology*, 51(1), 3–63.

Dueck, B. (2013a). "𝄽 𝄽 𝄽 𝄽": jazz endings, aesthetic discourse, and musical publics. *Black Music Research Journal*, 33(1), 91–115.

Dueck, B. (2013b). *Musical intimacies and Indigenous imaginaries: Aboriginal music and dance in public performance*. Oxford: Oxford University Press.

Dueck, B. (forthcoming) Expedient tradition? Indigenous drum song and dance in education and child welfare. In: V.L. Levine & D. Robinson (Eds.) *Music and modernity among First Peoples of North America*.

Dueck, J. (2008a). Empires, multiculturalisms, and borrowed heartsongs: what does it mean to sing Russian/Mennonite songs? Text of the Benjamin A. Botkin Folklife Lecture presented 21 May, 2008 at the American Folklife Center, Washington, D.C., sent as personal correspondence 27 February, 2014.

Dueck, J. (2008b). Mennonite choral music recordings of the West Coast Mennonite Chamber Choir (essay review). *Journal of American Folklore*, 121(481), 348–60.

Dunbar-Hall, P., & Gibson C. (2004). *Deadly sounds, deadly places: contemporary Aboriginal music in Australia*. Sydney: UNSW Press.

Ellis, C., Lassiter, L.E., & Dunham, G.H. (2005). *Powwow*. Lincoln, NE: University of Nebraska Press.

Faulkner, R.R., & Becker H.S. (2009). *"Do you know . . . ?": The jazz repertoire in action*. Chicago, IL: University of Chicago Press.

Finnegan, R. (2007 [1989]). *The hidden musicians: music-making in an English town*, new edn. Middletown, CN: Wesleyan University Press.

Goffman, E. (1967). *Interaction ritual: essays on face-to-face behavior*. Chicago, IL: Aldine.

Greene, H.P. (1923). A trip to the Canadian festivals. *Music & Letters*, 4(4), 356–70.

Greene, H.P. (1932). Another trip to the Canadian festivals. *Music & Letters*, 13(1), 19–30.

Hallowell, A.I. (1955). *Culture and experience*. Philadelphia, PA: Pennsylvania University Press.

Hallowell, A.I. (1992). *The Ojibwa of Berens River: ethnography into history*. Fort Worth, TX: Harcourt Bruce Jovanovich College.

Harrison, K. (2002). The Kwagiulth dancers: addressing intellectual property issues at Victoria's First People's Festival. *World of Music*, 44(1), 137–51.

Hoefnagels, A. (2002). Powwow songs: traveling songs and changing protocol. *World of Music*, 44(1), 127–36.

Jonas, O. (1979 [1955]). Preface to the Second German Edition. In: H. Schenker (Ed.) *Free composition (Der freie Satz): Volume III of new musical theories and fantasies*, transl. E. Oster. New York, NY: Longman.

Levine, V.L. (2013). Powwow. *Grove Music Online, Oxford Music Online*, Oxford University Press. Available at: http://www.oxfordmusiconline.com.libezproxy.open.ac.uk/subscriber/article/grove/music/A2252169 (accessed 1 March, 2014).

Levine, V.L., & Nettl, B. (2011). Strophic form and asymmetrical repetition in four American Indian songs. In: M. Tenzer & J. Roeder (Eds.) *Analytical and cross-cultural studies in world music*, pp. 288–315. Oxford: Oxford University Press.

Perea, J.-C. (2012). The unexpectedness of Jim Pepper. *MUSICultures*, 39(1), 7–82.

Scales, C.A. (2012). *Recording culture: powwow music and the Aboriginal recording industry on the Northern Plains*. Durham, NC: Duke University Press.

Stokes, M. (2010a). *The Republic of love: cultural intimacy in Turkish popular music*. Chicago, IL: University of Chicago Press.

Stokes, M. (2010b). Response to Rice. *Ethnomusicology*, 54(2), 339–41.

Taylor, C. (1994). The politics of recognition. In: A. Gutmann (Ed.) *Multiculturalism: examining the politics of recognition*, pp. 25–73. Princeton, NJ: Princeton University Press.

Urban, G. (2001). *Metaculture: how culture moves through the world*. Minneapolis MN: University of Minnesota Press.

van Toorn, P. (1990). Discourse/patron discourse: how minority texts command the attention of majority audiences. *Span*, 30, 102–15.

Wark, McK. (2000). Messenger beyond the middle class. *Australian*, 21 June, 43.

Warner, M. (2002). *Publics and counterpublics*. New York, NY: Zone Books.

Whidden, L. (2007). *Essential song: three decades of Northern Cree music*. Aboriginal Studies Series. Waterloo, ON: Wilfrid Laurier University Press.

Wilf, E. (2012). Rituals of creativity: tradition, modernity, and the "acoustic unconscious" in a U.S. collegiate jazz music program. *American Anthropologist*, 114(1), 32–44.

··

CHAPTER 22

PATTERNS OF SOCIOHISTORICAL INTERACTION BETWEEN MUSICAL IDENTITY AND TECHNOLOGY

··

ADAM LINSON

IN this chapter, I consider relationships between musical identity and technology from a sociohistorical perspective by tracing connections among music, technology, aesthetics, and social conditions, in a manner that aims to reveal their patterns of interaction, supported by historically contingent specific moments and lineages. In this respect, my approach grants that the historical moments presented here should be understood as rich, lived histories that can be analyzed and organized in various ways. The motivation for this analysis connects to a further aim of this chapter, which is to suggest that the perspectives of contemporary musicology and science and technology studies (STS) can be incorporated into a conception of social history that bears on our understanding of musical identity. The abstractions that facilitate this approach are not posed as reductions or supercessions of work in these fields, but instead serve to illuminate phenomena at the intersection of both that are not typically visible from either.

It will be useful to set the stage with some background. The field of STS has as its undertaking the consideration of science and technology in terms of history, sociology, and philosophy, or more generally, in terms of human sociality, primarily as it relates to practices and knowledge. I will not present a history of the field here, but instead point to Kuhn's (1970) widely known work that encompasses some of the core themes of STS. His study provided fundamental insights into the relation of science—previously regarded as a site of neutral objectivity—to historically contingent human practices, ontological commitments, and other socially-rooted phenomena that reveal certain limits of science's purported neutral objectivity.

While identity was arguably present "behind the scenes" in Kuhn's study (in its descriptions of personal and social relations), the topic of identity did not play a central role. The same can be said of works in STS that are more recent and narrower in scope, such as Pickering's (1984) account of a specific moment in the history of physics, which does not highlight identity per se. However, other perspectives within STS such as feminist theory have been more explicitly concerned with forms of social identity (for a recent overview of the intersection of STS and feminist scholarship, see Wajcman, 2009). For instance, a much different approach than that of Kuhn (1970) was introduced by Haraway (1985). Like Kuhn's, Haraway's study assumes a general perspective, while remaining grounded in specific historical evidence. Social identity is also considered from other perspectives in STS, not limited to feminist theory. For instance, Hecht's (2009) study of nuclear power in France analyses a specific historical moment, while examining issues of social identity in relation to French national identity and technopolitics. Her analysis explores phenomena such as divisions of labor, public–private distinctions, and other fundamental aspects of social identity.

Among the forms of social identity located by contemporary discourse, we also find musical identity. In the first edition of this volume, Hargreaves, Miell & MacDonald (2002) describe two types of musical identities—identities in music (IIM) and music in identities (MII). IIM "might be based on generic distinctions between broad categories of musical activity"—e.g., composers, performers, improvisors, teachers—"as well as on specific distinctions which cut across these categories, in particular, instruments and genres" (pp. 12–14). MII describes the relation of music to "other aspects of our personal identities, including gender identity; youth identity; national identity; and disability and identity" (p. 15). Although IIM and MII may be treated separately, it is also the case that these forms of musical identity interact (and interfere) with each other.

Although her study predates this terminology, a prime example of the interplay between IIM and MII can be found in Born's (1995) in-depth analysis of a specific moment in the history of the Institut de Recherche et Coordination Acoustique/ Musique (IRCAM). Among other facets of her study—which details the myriad interrelations among musical activities, aesthetic ideologies and institutional conditions, all of which are connected to formations of social hierarchy, divisions of labor, and other aspects of sociality (private-public distinctions, etc.)—she uncovers the interaction and interference between certain individuals' official institutional lives within IRCAM as IIM (e.g., aspiring "serious" composers), and their private lives outside of the institution as MII (e.g., fans of popular music).

With an emphasis on aesthetics, framed in relation to modernism and post-modernism, Born (1995) focussed primarily on the social relations both within a musical institution, and in its connections to the surrounding society. Her study is commendably inclusive in scope and, given the institution under analysis, considerations of science and technology play a large role. At the same time, we may draw a contrast with other studies (seemingly unrelated to music) that take science and technology as the focal point of investigations of sociality and identity (e.g., Hecht, 2009). This contrast is relevant here, in that, by drawing on multiple analytical perspectives, we may propose what is in essence a sociotechnological model that serves to reveal patterns of interaction between the specifically musical and the specifically technological, and to consider how these might relate to musical identity.

My approach to sketching this model requires a high degree of generality, in order to make the case that it can inform various histories of music, technology and identity. As a preliminary reference point, several examples of in-depth studies can be given that illustrate the basic relationships that I aim to take into account. For instance, Myles Jackson's (2006) study of "physicists, musicians and instrument makers in nineteenth-century Germany" frequently considers MII, primarily in relation to national identity but also professional and class identity. He notes that:

> physicists helped musical-instrument makers improve on the design of instruments by sharing their acoustical expertise, while these craftsman discussed the various designs and components of their instruments with natural scientists. Musicians turned to physicists for ways to quantify and standardize musical pitch and beat.
>
> Jackson, 2006, p. 2.

A much different consideration of music, science, technology and national identity is offered by Rehding (2003). As he describes, at the turn of the 20th century, "the adoption of the phonograph by what was then called 'comparative musicology' severely challenged the accepted musical paradigm," including entire systems of musical aesthetics that aspired to be scientifically descriptive and thereby, at the same time, prescriptive for practicing composers, according to more general aesthetic notions about nature and human activity (p. 177). He shows how this historically situated social configuration affected the perception of significant conceptual interrelationships, including those of Western and non-Western music; memory, transcription and recording; theorists, practitioners and "objects" of study—all of which are directly tied to aspects of national identity in his account.

Gordon's (2004) feminist analysis of Monteverdi appears on its surface to be a radically different approach from the latter two above-mentioned studies, and is not, in fact, even explicitly concerned with science and technology as such. Nevertheless, the following passage provides insight into how, in seventeenth-century Europe, science, technology and the aesthetics of musical composing, performing and listening were tied together and affected one another, in particular, in relation to gender identity:

> [New] instruments could make heard sounds that had previously been impossible. Just as the telescope expanded the visual universe, musical instruments expanded the sonic universe. What notes sounded like no longer necessarily revealed what existed below their surface or corresponded to anything else. Musical sound no longer necessarily revealed anything beyond itself. Composers presented new

ways of using voices, harmonies, and instruments that would eventually sever the link tying musical sounds to the represented emotions and the inner forces of the human body. This opened up a space filled with new musical conventions and which philosophers explained by separating the object that is sensed from the sensation. As musical practice slowly eroded existing theories, so too did the new reliance on sensory experience change the assumptions of natural philosophy. The changes in soundscape wrought by novel gestures eventually led to new ways of understanding the sensory effects of sound and to new representations and implications of women's voices.

Gordon, 2004, p. 192.

Text extract from Bonnie Gordon, Monteverdi's Unruly Women: the power of song in early modern Italy, p. 193, Copyright © 2005 Cambridge University Press, with permission from Cambridge University Press.

What Gordon is in part describing is a shift in ontology, or ontological commitments. Born (2005) offers a related view of the interrelationships among music, technology, and ontology (which I return to below) that describes a similar transformation brought about by 20th- and 21st- century developments pertaining to the category of a musical work (for a different perspective linking music, ontology, and "technicity," see Gallope, 2011).

22.1 Technology, technique, and aesthetics

Any casual mention of "technology" today almost inevitably suggests modern digital technology. However, with some additional context, we may acknowledge a more general sense of technology, one that would include, for instance, an ancient stone wheel. Technology, in both of these senses, shares an etymological root with "technique," which generally refers to a way of performing an activity. In the area of music, these senses of technology and the idea of technique are common themes. We speak of musical technologies in the first sense introduced above with the application of electronic and digital means to musical performance (and other music-related activities, such as recording, listening, etc.). In the second sense, we may think of the crafted acoustic technologies of bowed string instruments, valved horns, grand pianos, etc. We may also consider various performance *techniques*, especially those that allow for new sonic possibilities. These three notions, while in some respects distinct, are also closely interrelated. Understanding the relationships between them can provide insights into the conditions for the formation of musical identities.

Aside from a shared etymological root, it may not be immediately clear what musical instrument *technologies* of any kind have in common with instrumental performance *techniques*, such as those involving bodies, hands, embouchures, etc. The sociotechnological model presented below aims to bring to the fore interrelationships among musical instrument technologies, performance techniques, aesthetics, and social conditions, and suggests that this complex network forms part of the background against which varied senses of musical identity emerge. In doing so, it also connects older musical instrument technologies—bows, key and valve mechanisms, etc.—to more recent musical technologies, such as amplifiers, synthesizers, and digital musical instruments.

The notion of musical aesthetics under consideration here may be more appropriately understood as aesthetic ideology, a deliberately general term that encompasses a wide range of phenomena such as relations within a work of aesthetic production, within a field of art, among ideas that condition aesthetic production, consecration and reception, and so on. In other words, this general sense of aesthetics can be further subdivided in various ways, but is used here to refer to explicit and implicit normative social forces that directly affect the (re)production and reception of certain types of works and styles. Normative social forces include the personal consumption tastes of influential individuals ranging from monarchs and dictators to patrons and curators, and beyond personal consumption tastes, to positions that may be grounded in other ways, such as manifestos by artists and groups, and works of aesthetic criticism. (For a similar point about the multiple senses of "ideology," see Goehr, 2007, p. 78, n. 14; see also chapters 4–8 therein for a related historical analysis of socio-musical ideals and practices. For more general analyses of aesthetic ideology centered around literature, but extensible to music and other arts, see, e.g., Bourdieu, 1996; Eagleton, 1976; and for some analyses concerned with the relation between more localized historical conditions and their specific aesthetic ideologies, see, e.g., Guilbaut, 1983; Denning, 1996; Jameson, 2007.)

As indicated above, this chapter presents a general sketch that connects several historical examples, rather than a more detailed analysis of one particular case. This requires a degree of simplification in my exposition, including a limited set of examples and a relatively coarse-grained account of each one. However, my aim is to elaborate a model that can incorporate more fine-grained historical detail for the accounts given later, and also be applied to other historical moments not covered below.

The wide ranging set of examples I employ serves to reveal a fundamental continuity across various historical periods, including the present, regarding the patterns of sociohistorical interaction relevant to musical technologies. However, perhaps ironically, the continuity revealed is, in fact, constituted by a series of discontinuities or ruptures, in particular, of material agencies and ontological commitments that are continually being challenged and reworked. In this respect, the view presented here is consistent with Born's (2005) account of the ontological break in the understanding of the musical work, brought about by 20th- and 21st-century technological and social developments.

The wider historical focus I adopt aims to situate such breaks in a series of breaks throughout history, further underscoring that our ontological commitments have always been, and will always be, sociohistorically situated. This broader perspective thereby serves to highlight the future potential for further breaks in various forms of sociality, such as musical identities and conceptions of the musical work. We can already catch a glimpse of these potential futures in the latent tensions across and within presently predominant modes of practice and understanding. Following this logic, although we can identify a fundamental qualitative difference between the musical technologies of the past and present, my account serves to connect current musical technology to that of previous centuries, in relation to musical identity. (One could speculate that the model presented here may apply to prehistory as well.)

The remainder of this chapter is structured as follows: first, I give a brief, but sweeping history of bowed string instruments, based in part on Bachmann's (1969) historical account of the origins of bowing and bowed instruments, which serves as a preliminary scaffold for the proposed model. This initial sketch is further developed, in part by drawing on elements of Montagu's (2007) broader historical account of the origins of musical instruments. Then, to demonstrate the applicability of the model, I present a similarly potted history of the piano, connecting historical facts from several different accounts. The subsequent section covers mid-20th-century musical technologies from the same perspective, followed by a section on current musical technologies, both of which focus primarily on performance. The chapter concludes with thoughts on the future implications of the current situation in music technology with respect to musical identity and related socialities.

22.2 BOWED STRING INSTRUMENTS

In the Middle Ages, a segment of society advocated a musical aesthetic that was based in a high regard for the human voice and a (perhaps related) belief in the ideal of continuous sound. Although there is undoubtedly a complex source behind these ideals, here, we will limit ourselves to a consideration of their effect, as they drove the development of bow design and corresponding bowing practices. As this bowing technology and playing technique became more widely established, bowed string instruments gradually moved from the folk domain to the royal courts, where composers promoted new performance ideals and expectations. These ideals, in turn, placed further demands on instrumentalists and instrument-builders, as will be described in this section.

While string instruments in the lyre family date back to the ancient world, the medieval emergence of bowing will serve as an initial illustration of the sociotechnological model that I develop throughout this chapter. As Bachmann (1969) points out, the establishment of stringed instrument bowing:

> was perhaps a new application of techniques already widespread in folk music; conversely, some plectrum techniques, and the use of the friction stick to rub the strings, must also be considered as early forms of bowing. From such practices as these the bow may have evolved quite independently in different places.
>
> Bachmann, 1969, p. 137.

Although bowing opened up "new regions of musical expression" on popular existing instruments, the more widespread use of bowing did not take hold until a particular aesthetic issue, described below, was resolved.

Arab scholars in the Middle Ages viewed the continuous sound of the human voice as more pleasurable to listen to than other musical instruments found in that time period. However, the historical sources also imply that:

> the pleasure of listening to vocal music was by no means unalloyed, since the melodic line was constantly interrupted by pauses for breath. The remedy was clearly to design musical instruments which could join the notes together and provide a continuous melodic line. This demand was met by musical automata, to which many [medieval] Arabic sources refer, by the bagpipe, by the organ, and by the various types of bowed instrument.
>
> Bachmann, 1969, p. 137.

At first, new instrument technologies did not live up to the predominant aesthetic ideals of timbre and performance: "cultured [medieval] Arab musicians and theoreticians regarded bowed instruments with some disparagement because of their thin and rather unattractive tone" (p. 137). Probably as a result of this bias against a music that did not live up to ideals, "bowed instruments continued to be associated predominantly with folk music in this territory, and to begin with only rarely appeared in the context of court music."

A driving force in "the quest for new sonorities which would match contemporary ideals" was "the desire for an unbroken melodic line, which would bring instrumental music closer to vocal music" (p. 137). As the instrument, bow and playing techniques evolved to fulfil this goal, "playing became increasingly cantabile in character, so that, towards the end of the Middle Ages, musical instruments could frequently be substituted for the human voice" (pp. 137–8). With the emerging view that bowed string instruments could live up to the ideals of vocal music, the use of these instruments began to spread across Europe—not only to the folk musicians, but to the court musicians as well. This allowed court composers to imagine new forms of musical structure. For instance, along with the organ, "bowed instruments played a significant role in the making of European polyphony" (p. 138).

As the use of the bow in European court music became more widespread, the initial proliferation of bow shapes was gradually standardized into two types, partly driven by the demand for instrumental techniques called for by composers. New compositions required more refined articulations than was previously the case, thereby leading the primary trend in bow evolution away from bows designed for a closed fist playing style, "a grip which enabled the player to make a strong stroke and press harder on the strings, but which prevented a flexible wrist-action and any variation between one stroke and the next" (p. 139). This example already begins to indicate how social conditions, aesthetics, technology and technique mutually affect one another, and how a sensitivity to their deep-seated interconnections makes it difficult to draw clear distinctions among them.

Gradually, as the composers of Europe served their courtly patrons, more elaborate works were composed, for increasingly larger ensembles and productions. A turning point for composers' productions was reached in the early modern period, with a transition from private court audiences to widely accessible public spectacles (Montagu, 2007; Hobsbawm, 1962). Great concert halls were constructed with enough space for both the productions and the audience, to accommodate the composer's envisioned ensemble size, and to pack in enough members of the public to make possible the financing of such events.

This situation in turn brought about a new problem: acoustics. While there is no doubt that architectural design plays an important role for acoustics, once the halls were built, there was still another problem to consider. Faced by composers and producers alike, this other problem of acoustics concerned how to put together the right-sized ensemble—large enough to be heard in the far reaches of the building, but also with enough string players to balance out (e.g.) the horn players.

A pragmatic solution that emerged in this context was simply to make existing instruments louder. Louder instruments meant better projection in the halls, and ensemble sizes that were more easily balanced. Both of these aims could be achieved without productions becoming prohibitively expensive by the addition of more players. With string instruments, an obvious way to make them louder is to increase the string tension, and this is indeed what was done. Through this tightening of strings, from 1670 to 1870, "the pitch of each note name rose by about a minor third," with concert A going from 392 to 452 Hz. Later on, it was slightly lowered (the current standard is 440 Hz), because singers were overstraining their voices for the higher notes (Montagu, 2007, p. 117). As the string tension and pitch rose, however, it was not uncommon for the typically delicate wooden instruments to collapse. In response, string instruments in the violin and viol families were redesigned to have a longer neck, a stronger joint between the neck and body, a sturdier and heavier internal construction, and a thicker sound post.

To summarize this brief history thus far: an aesthetic ideal of the human voice and continuous sound contributed to developments in bow design and construction, as well as in playing techniques. In part, this led to the spread of bowed string instruments. Their proliferation, in turn, led to new musical imaginations and demands on performance technique, both by folk musicians and court composers. The latter had the social standing to expand ensemble size, and larger productions led to the construction of great performance halls. These halls in part led to a new social situation, with the expansion of the audience and the emergence of new public tastes. The financing of productions placed constraints on ensemble size, which led to instrument redesigns, and so forth.

Clearly, it is difficult to draw sharp boundaries among instrument technologies, performance techniques, musical aesthetics, and social conditions. A specialized history that considers only facts about the instruments, only facts about techniques, only facts about aesthetics, or only those about social conditions would, at best, lead to an impoverished understanding and, at worst, to an outright misunderstanding of these complex circumstances. With respect to musical identity, another example, offered by Dolan

(2013), will help illustrate the relation between the above-described circumstances, and both MII and IIM.

At the turn of the 19th century, a number of European nations in particular sought to differentiate their national character from one another vis-à-vis the arts, including music. Music also served a more direct role in national ideology, for instance:

> In the 1790s, the most opulent uses of instrumental forces in France were found in the spectacles, festivals, and commemorations designed to glorify the revolution. These events employed ensembles of massive proportions—with totals of upwards of 2,400 musicians—invented to fortify the spirit of the Republic. Noise and volume were essential to these events: two short-lived musical instruments were invented, or reinvented, for these spectacles—the *tuba curva* and the *buccin*—designed purely for volume to strengthen the bass in outdoor performances. Elements of these grand spectacles found their way onto the operatic stage.
>
> Dolan, 2013, pp. 231–2.
>
> Text extract from Emily I. Dolan, The Orchestral Revolution: Haydn and the technologies of timbre, pp. 231–2, Copyright © 2013 Cambridge University Press, with permission from Cambridge University Press.

In this sense, technology, technique, aesthetics, and social conditions are implicated in MII.

On the other hand, these circumstances also affected IIM. A number of more whimsical instruments were invented around that time that, as Dolan (2013) points out, Berlioz occasionally commented on. From Berlioz's point of view, "what was so harmful about many newly invented instruments was not their tone, but rather the kind of compositional engagement they allowed. An instrument was bad if it encouraged a separation between sound and composer or minimized the composer's role" (Dolan, 2013, p. 218). According to Berlioz, many newly invented instruments "eschew the composer and rely on the shallow reactions of the listener; [traditional instruments] reveal the composer's genius and imagination through his ability to manipulate any sound into music." Thus, in terms of IIM, "in Berlioz's world, great musical works demand that the performers efface themselves; they must suppress their individual identities in the service of the whole, and in honor of the genius of the composer" (Dolan, 2013, p. 215).

22.3 THE PIANO

Before moving on to electronic and digital musical instrument technologies, I will present another brief account of a similarly complex sociohistorical situation, namely, the one encompassing the piano. Continuing from the construction of expansive concert halls, we can note that the accompanying redesign of instruments was in part facilitated by the Industrial Revolution. Although the newly redesigned *string* instruments were still built in an older, more traditional manner, the related redesigning and fabrication of other instruments required new technologies. For instance, one of the ways to make woodwind instruments louder was to drill larger bore holes; however, this made it more difficult or even impossible to cover the holes with fingers alone. Given advances in industry, it became possible to design and manufacture metal key-and-pad mechanisms, the predecessors of those found on contemporary woodwinds. While brass instruments were already loud, they lacked the chromatic capabilities of many other instruments. Thus, new industries facilitated the design and manufacture of valve mechanisms for brass instruments, which co-evolved into contemporary valved brass instruments (Montagu, 2007, pp. 118–19).

The new instrument mechanisms brought about by the Industrial Revolution also included the 1821 introduction of the "double-escapement mechanism, the kind used in modern grand pianos, which facilitated greater speed in musical performance (because the hammers were made ready to repeat their movements more quickly after striking)" (Isacoff, 2011, p. 74). Such newly-attainable speed on the instrument led to new performance techniques, brought about by the interests of performers and composers alike. In turn, the new techniques allowed new musical styles to develop that incorporated faster playing.

Yet, from the perspective of physics alone, one could anticipate the necessary trade-off between playing faster and playing louder. This is significant, because some of the faster Romantic playing styles for solo piano were not well suited to the widely attended great halls, but rather to more intimate settings. As Jones (1998) points out, Chopin rarely played in large concert halls, because he was criticized for playing too quietly. He could make a better show of his technical dexterity at salons, "relatively private affairs where the nobility, literati, artists, musicians, and cognoscenti intermingled at will" (pp. 151–2). The salon culture had arisen in the new social circumstances surrounding class in industrialized societies, with respect to labor and leisure conditions and education (Hobsbawm, 1962). Here, as with the example of bowed string instruments, we can witness the complex interactions among social conditions, musical aesthetics, performance techniques, and instrument technologies, as well as between IIM and MII.

Romantic piano music, with its fast playing style and particular approach to flourishes, was disseminated via the sheet-music publishing industry and especially consumed by the new middle class (Hobsbawm, 1962, pp. 272–3). The power of the sheet music publishing industry in part related to patterns of social consumption, which also drove the mass production of pianos. At one point, pianos could be found even in the makeshift structures known as barrelhouses, among the African American laborer communities of the American South. The laborers, especially those in the lumber, turpentine and railroad industries, used such barrelhouses for their leisure activities, which typically included dancing (Silvester, 2009, p. 11).

Boogie-woogie was a piano style that developed largely in these barrelhouse environments. One characteristic of the style is the piano technique of strong, repetitive left-handed playing in the lower register of the instrument, which provided a basis for the dancing that went on; more generally, piano playing allows one to easily call out cues to the dancers (Silvester, 2009). The boogie-woogie style, however, due to the environment it was associated with, was at first "shunned by the respectable law-abiding and church-going element of black society, and it was not performed (even) in the highest-class bordellos and brothels of the larger towns and cities"; it was considered "music for the rough, uncultured, uneducated, and frequently illiterate workingman" (p. 19). Nevertheless, it eventually crystallized into a more widely known style, probably through the "cross-fertilisation of regional boogie-woogie styles [...] assisted by the newly laid railroads on which many itinerant pianists traveled" (p. 18). The railroad connected many regions of the South, which directly affected musical culture, as "the piano players worked clearly defined circuits" (p. 19).

From the sociohistorical conditions enveloping and emerging from the French and Industrial Revolutions—including political, economic, and other ideological and material developments—an ideology of individualism emerged that included the notions of the Romantic genius and revolutionary artist (Hobsbawm, 1962, pp. 261ff.). These notions would serve to reinforce musical identity, with the initial rise of "stars" (IIM) in the "powerful sheet-music publishing industry" and later in "radio, sound films, commercial recording and television," among them, pianists whose playing reflected the "stylistic contribution of African American idioms" (MII) (Priestley, 1998, p. 209).

The commercialization of musical styles through sheet music and sound recordings enabled music education in the early 20th century to incorporate the study of African American idioms, such as boogie-woogie and ragtime, alongside earlier music by European composers, such as that of Chopin, Liszt, and other Romantics, whether with sheet music or by ear, aided by recordings and broadcasts. The increased exposure to variety became the basis for new aesthetic possibilities. To take one example, pianist Art Tatum combined African American piano styles with "technical devices associated with the nineteenth-century [European] school of virtuosity—rapid scales in single notes and thirds, sweeping arpeggiated flourishes, hammering octaves" (Parakilas et al., 2002, p. 303). With respect to IIM in particular, Parakilas et al. note that Tatum's synthesis of styles can be viewed as the advent of "a new musical persona for the jazz pianist."

Even across longer historical periods, when considering, for example, the gap between Chopin and Tatum, we can see the relationships among musical performance techniques, instrument technologies, aesthetics, and social conditions. We can also note the possibility for the emergence of a certain conception of an identity in music (IIM), one associated with the advancement of a particular aesthetic, intelligible in relation to the narrower background of musical context, the wider background of social context, and that may also be associated with the use of particular instruments and techniques. Prior to the 20th century, it appears it was more common for composers to have this emergent type of identity, as with the example of Berlioz given above. However, eventually, in light of some of the historical developments described in this section, a similar form of musical identity became possible for individual performers as well, especially those who were also composers, improvisors, or both.

22.4 ELECTRONIC AND DIGITAL TECHNOLOGIES

The kinds of sociohistorical relationships described thus far do not cease as we move further into the 20th century and beyond. The Scientific and Industrial Revolutions, although obviously not primarily aimed at the development of mechanisms for musical instruments, nevertheless led to such developments through the new means they offered for realizing ideas. Moreover, they transformed the imaginative space of possibilities for such ideas to take shape, that is, they facilitated a shift in ontological commitments. A similar relationship between historical events and music technology can be located with respect to the Second World War, which drove the development of new technologies, including most of the components for modern amplification and audio synthesis.

Kittler (1999) notes that:

> when Karlheinz Stockhausen was mixing his first electronic composition, *Kontakte*, in the Cologne studio of the Westdeutscher Rundfunk between February 1958 and fall 1959, the pulse generator, indicating amplifier, band-pass filter, as well as the sine and square wave oscillators were made up of discarded U.S. Army equipment.
>
> (p. 97)

Similarly, as Kittler points out, it was wartime technology that made possible the music of Jimi Hendrix, Pink Floyd, and others, through the contribution of tube amplification for instruments such as the electric guitar, the advent of portable synthesizers, and even stereo recording, the latter of which could be deliberately manipulated in the studio to produce a variety of aesthetic effects.

Here, we find another interaction between IIM and MII, where, for instance, the roles of composers and studio operators, while seemingly identities in music, were significantly affected by other forms of social identity, such as class and race, which had specific relationships to musical sensibilities. As Born (1995) describes:

> by the 1950s tape recording technology and electronic wave generators became available to composers with access to radio stations or well-endowed university laboratories, so that access was limited in this period to those affiliated with large institutions, while less-credentialed composers had no such access.
>
> (p. 52)

A related example can be found in Meintjes' (2009) study of recording in apartheid and post-apartheid South Africa, in the following point summarized by Born (2010):

> In the apartheid era black musicians worked in a "white-controlled industry" personified in white sound engineers who knew very little about black musical styles.

Recording in this period was therefore the site of covert struggles over the control of musical gestures and sound qualities, struggles in which black musicians would try to wrest back control from the engineer at the mixing desk.

(p. 234)

Here, as well, we can witness the complex interactions among social conditions, musical aesthetics, performance techniques, and instrument technologies, and those between IIM and MII.

Continuing with the topic of electronic music technology, in a consideration of modular synthesizers, Pressing (1992) notes that, on one hand, given the combinatorial nature of interconnectable components, there is always room for innovation in setting up a synthesizer. On the other hand, however, different playing conditions are served by different modular configurations such that, in practice, some common standards for synthesizer set-up eventually emerged (p. 261). Ultimately, a synthesizer serves in a role analogous to any musical instrument, where aspects of musical identity may be partly based in the choice of instrument, and partly in the playing techniques and resulting sonorities. Thus, when Pressing refers to the "sonic goal" of synthesizer performance, he focusses on the musicians' intentions, rather than merely on the possibility space of modular construction (p. 254). He notes that, based on one's sonic goal, one may simply use learned techniques for achieving the desired outcome, or, depending on the nature of the goal and the performance context, one may find that "a more exploratory or trial-and-error approach is useful" (p. 254). This echoes the historically recurring quest to seek out new aesthetic possibilities among the interplay of timbres and techniques by exploiting, enhancing, augmenting, and otherwise reconfiguring and developing technologies for musical instruments.

In some cases, the seeking out of new aesthetic possibilities may relate to a transformation of relationships among ensemble performers, or, for instance, between performer and audience, performer and instrument designer, artist and artwork, and so on. Such transformations may stand in a clear relation to social conditions, while also functioning as an approach to incorporating new timbres, techniques and technologies. As Born (2011) notes, "in their autonomy, the socialities of performance and practice may be contrary to, and can become crucibles of transformation of or experimentation with, prevailing social relations" (p. 379). A case in point is collective free improvisation, which commonly enacts a non-hierarchical notion of musical relationships among performers (IIM). Addressing the past several decades of free improvisation, saxophonist Evan Parker (2014) speaks of the "co-evolution of instrument design and musical practice," while noting that "the clear development of personal vocabularies, styles or modes of operation by individual improvisers or by established groups led to a phase in the late 60s in which composers composed works around particular techniques and for specific performers" (pp. 2–3). As with the previous examples, this development involved performance techniques, musical aesthetics, and social conditions, and also directly involved newly available technologies.

Within the social conditions that facilitated these emergent forms of musical activity, Parker (2014) highlights some specific connections between technique, technology, and aesthetics:

> My own experiences with live electronics began with the very funky contact microphones and foot pedals that were available in the late 60s. Gradually the analogue equipment got better, such that it was feasible to bring portable battery powered cassette recorders to concerts. In fact the first "sampling" that I was involved in was in the duo with Paul Lytton, where we routinely used recordings of earlier sections of the same concert and then even recordings from other concerts. The tape recorder in playback mode would be sent spinning and swinging on a rope from left to right introducing strange Doppler effects and spatialisations on a very low budget.
>
> Parker, 2014, pp. 5–6.

In light of this multifaceted example and others given above, it becomes increasingly difficult to accept any more limited historical account that purports to pertain *only* to musical instrument technology. Such an account would fail to adequately address the complex interplay of mutually influential factors; it would be "reductive in the literal sense of the evasion of ineluctable complexity" (Born, 2011, p. 385). Although it may be tempting to limit our focus to relatively recent innovative applications of non-acoustic technologies for music-making—especially when considering music such as that of Stockhausen, Jimi Hendrix and Pink Floyd, or, more generally, synthesizer music, tape music, free improvisation and so forth—this always risks obscuring the complex interrelationships among social conditions, musical aesthetics, instrument technologies, and performance techniques that spans centuries, as portrayed throughout this chapter.

One way to conceptualize the commonalities across acoustic, electronic, and digital musical instruments is to take a functional view, subdividing an instrument into interface and sound-producing mechanism. It should be noted that a functional view may also serve to highlight at least one key difference between acoustic and non-acoustic instruments. Namely, it points to the fact that the physical separation of interface and sound-producing mechanism, common in electronic and digital instruments, is typically impossible in a traditional acoustic instrument, as is the case with (e.g.) a clarinet: "its reed, keys, and holes are at the same time both the gestural interface (where the performer interacts with the instrument) and the elements responsible for sound production" (Miranda & Wanderley, 2006, p. 4).

However, this general functional view also points to the fact that a collection of instrumental components, no matter how they are integrated, are typically used to achieve particular aesthetic aims through the use of specific techniques and technologies. It thus reveals commonalities across traditional historical performance modes that may currently include acoustic, electronic, and digital instruments, and contemporary forms of performance that may involve hybrid instruments or multiple players engaged in shaping the sound of a single instrumental voice. This latter scenario occurs in some cases of acoustic instruments that are electronically or digitally processed in real time, or in innovative live coding setups, where, for instance, an instrument's performer(s) and designer(s) interact in real time (see, e.g., Lee & Essl, 2013). Such novel configurations of performance and practice highlight the tensions inherent in current constructs of musical identity, and serve to reveal the sociohistorical contingency of the ontological commitments that underpin them.

22.5 CONCLUSIONS

Historically novel situations, such as multiple players behind a single instrumental voice, may lead to new socialities, including new conceptions of musical identity; once contextualized, it becomes clear that such situations exemplify, rather than break free of, longstanding historical relationships among technique, technology, aesthetics, and social conditions, as described throughout this chapter. Available technologies for instrument design lead to techniques that both drive and exploit these technologies, including bows, key and valve mechanisms, vacuum tubes and oscillators, and digital processors. Meanwhile, the same technologies are driven by contexts for dissemination and reception (including folk gatherings, courts, concert halls, salons, barrelhouses, broadcasting, and the consumer playback of recordings). In this context, a key link between IIM and MII can be found in the interrelated desires to produce and experience new musical sounds and structures, and new sociomusical and social configurations.

Technological changes, such as those that made possible the emergence of digital musical instruments, may provide new possibilities for music-making, but it is an open question as to how these possibilities are construed. In some cases, designers and performers may seek to repurpose available technologies, thereby opening up new areas for exploration. This may involve existing instruments, such as a historically stagnant piano design being transformed into a prepared piano; it may involve the transformation of sound-producing equipment, such as the use of turntables as a musical instrument; or it may involve instrument-building by the "hacking" of electronic devices (see, e.g., Collins, 2009). By understanding the driving forces behind innovative musical instrument technologies throughout history, and the ways in which these and related technologies have driven new forms of aesthetic production and reception, we can better equip ourselves to avoid being directed into passive consumerism and a narrow view of what is possible, as is conceivably entailed by the reification of currently prevailing ontologies. An uncritical historical approach not only limits our understanding of music technology, but also seriously threatens our ability to determine our own musical future.

The sociotechnological model presented in this chapter aims to resist reified conceptions of music, technology and identity. Such reified conceptions tend to suggest, on one hand, delusions of unlimited freedom to combine music and technology as though these were outside of history and not subject to social conditions. On the other hand, they dangerously suggest that our historically contingent inherited configuration of music, technology and identity is a static endpoint that confines us to the current state of affairs, and constrains our movements within a narrowly delimited space of possibilities. As this chapter has sought to demonstrate, the relationships among music, technology, and identity have always been fluid, dynamic and closely interrelated to other aspects of sociality. This perspective strongly suggests that the current configuration of these forces remains open to both gradual and radical transformation.

REFERENCES

Bachmann, W. (1969). *The origins of bowing and the development of bowed instruments up to the thirteenth century*. Oxford: Oxford University Press.

Born, G. (1995). *Rationalizing culture: IRCAM, Boulez, and the institutionalization of the musical avant-garde*. Berkeley, CA: University of California Press.

Born, G. (2005). On musical mediation: ontology, technology and creativity. *Twentieth-Century Music*, 2(1), 7–36.

Born, G. (2010). For a relational musicology: music and interdisciplinarity, beyond the practice turn: the 2007 Dent Medal Address. *Journal of the Royal Musical Association*, 135(2), 205–43.

Born, G. (2011). Music and the materialization of identities. *Journal of Material Culture*, 16(4), 376–88.

Bourdieu, P. (1996). *The rules of art: Genesis and structure of the literary field*. Stanford, CA: Stanford University Press.

Collins, N. (2009). *Handmade electronic music: the art of hardware hacking*. London: Routledge.

Denning, M. (1996). *The cultural front: the laboring of American culture in the twentieth century*. London: Verso.

Dolan, E. (2013). *The orchestral revolution: Haydn and the technologies of timbre*. Cambridge: Cambridge University Press.

Eagleton, T. (2006). *Criticism and ideology: a study in Marxist literary theory*. London: Verso.

Gallope, M. (2011). Technicity, consciousness, and musical objects. In: D. Clarke and E. Clarke (Eds.) *Music and consciousness: philosophical, psychological, and cultural perspectives*, pp. 47–64. Oxford: Oxford University Press.

Goehr, L. (2007). *The imaginary museum of musical works: an essay in the philosophy of music*, rev. edn. Oxford: Oxford University Press.

Gordon, B. (2004). *Monteverdi's unruly women: the power of song in early modern Italy*. Cambridge: Cambridge University Press.

Guilbaut, S. (1983). *How New York stole the idea of modern art: abstract expressionism, freedom, and the cold war*. Chicago, IL: University of Chicago Press.

Haraway, D.J. (1985). A manifesto for cyborgs: Science, technology, and socialist feminism in the 1980s. *Socialist Review*, 80, 65–108.

Hecht, G. (2009). *The radiance of France: nuclear power and national identity after World War II*. Cambridge, MA: MIT Press.

Hobsbawm, E. (1962). *History of civilization: the Age of Revolution. Europe 1789–1848*. New York: Random House.

Isacoff, S. (2011). *A natural history of the piano: the instrument, the music, the musicians–from Mozart to Modern Jazz, and everything in between*. New York: Random House.

Jackson, M. (2006). *Harmonious triads: physicists, musicians, and instrument makers in nineteenth-century Germany*. Cambridge, MA: MIT Press.

Jameson, F. (2007). *The modernist papers*. London: Verso.

Jones, J. B. (1998). Piano music for concert hall and salon c. 1830–1900. In: D. Rowland, (Ed.), *The Cambridge companion to the piano*, pp. 151–75. Cambridge: Cambridge University Press.

Kittler, F. (1999). *Gramophone, film, typewriter*. Stanford, CA: Stanford University Press.

Kuhn, T. (1970). *The structure of scientific revolutions*, 2nd edn. Chicago, IL: University of Chicago Press.

Lee, S., & Essl, G. (2013). Live coding the mobile music instrument. In: *Proceedings of NIME'13*, KAIST, Daejeon, Korea, pp. 493–8. Daejeon: KAIST.

MacDonald, R.A.R., Hargreaves, D.J., & Miell, D.E. (Eds.) (2002). *Musical identities*. Oxford: Oxford University Press.

Miranda, E., & Wanderley, M. (2006). *New digital musical instruments: control and interaction beyond the keyboard*. Middleton: A-R Editions.

Meintjes, L. (2009). The politics of the recording studio. In: N. Cook, E. Clarke, D. Leech-Wilkinson & J. Rink (Eds.) *The Cambridge companion to recorded music*, pp. 84–97. Cambridge: Cambridge University Press.

Montagu, J. (2007). *Origins and development of musical instruments*. Lanham: Scarecrow Press.

Parakilas, J. et al. (2001). *Piano roles: a new history of the piano*. New Haven, CT: Yale University Press.

Parker, E. (2014). Introduction. In: F. Schroeder (Ed.) *Soundweaving: writings on improvisation*, pp. 1–7. Cambridge: Cambridge Scholars Publishing.

Pickering, A. (1984). *Constructing quarks: a sociological history of particle physics*. Chicago, IL: University of Chicago Press.

Pressing, J. (1992). *Synthesizer performance and real-time techniques*. Middleton: A-R Editions.

Priestley, B. (1998). Ragtime, blues, jazz and popular music. In: D. Rowland (Ed.) *The Cambridge companion to the piano*, pp. 209–24. Cambridge: Cambridge University Press.

Rehding, A. (2003). *Hugo Riemann and the birth of modern musical thought*. Cambridge: Cambridge University Press.

Silvester, P. (2009). *The story of boogie-woogie: a left hand like God*. Lanham: Scarecrow Press.

Wajcman, J. (2010). Feminist theories of technology. *Cambridge Journal of Economics*, 34(1), 143–52.

CHAPTER 23

....

WHO AM I? THE PROCESS OF IDENTITY RENEGOTIATION FOR OPERA CHORISTERS FOLLOWING REDUNDANCY

....

JANE OAKLAND, RAYMOND MACDONALD,
AND PAUL FLOWERS

23.1 INTRODUCTION

....

IT is highly unlikely that professional musicians will experience a career trajectory without some form of crisis or disruption, which will inevitably affect self-perception both as a musician and a person. Much musical identity work is concerned with the way an identity develops through natural and expected points of progression such as starting music lessons (Sloboda & Howe, 1992) becoming a music student (Burland & Pitts, 2007) or entering the music profession (Burland & Davidson, 2004; Creech, Papageorgi, Duffy, et al., 2008). This chapter examines the implications for an identity in music for professional opera choristers who have been forced to revise their roles in the music profession as a result of a career crisis. Under discussion are the implications of a work-dependent identity in a music profession that is currently undergoing a momentous cultural and economic transition globally.

Smilde (2005) comments that a changing cultural climate and the use of technology can provide new ways of creating and consuming art. She also notes that audiences have changed, preferring shorter works in a variety of genres, and that the increasing heterogeneity of society has opened up new opportunities for creative work that crosses formerly well-established boundaries and thereby has the potential for gaining new audiences. It is now widely accepted that musicians who work in the classical music profession need to be more flexible in order to cope with decreasing performing opportunities, and to pursue a career which can incorporate many different roles, both musical and nonmusical (Rogers, 2002; Bennett, 2008b, 2009). Developing a positive and sustainable sense of self that is adaptable to a broad range of musical experiences is essential for career longevity. However, Bennett (2009, p. 312) notes that it is still common for musicians to define themselves according to their instrumental speciality, which as Hargreaves, Miell, & MacDonald (2002) point out, is central to our understanding of the concept of identities within music. The association between instrument and self can become so strong that if for any reason that identity is threatened, the question arises "who am I now?" without my cello or violin (Maitlis, 2009, p. 48). This association is even greater for singers whose instrument is physically embedded within the self. Consequently, any life events that prevent singers from communicating through their voices are likely to have a major impact on a sense of self.

Instrument specific identities also tend to be thought of as performance-based, but endorsing this type of identity can be challenging in a profession in which musicians increasingly rely on a portfolio of activities to make a living. Bennett (2009) suggests that students should be prepared to take a broader approach to musical self-definition so as to incorporate a variety of musical roles, and that a musical career should be evaluated on the basis of sustainability, rather than of successful performance. In a focus group study consisting of practicing musicians, Bennett (2008a) found that, although participants initially tended to self-define according to their intended role, as other roles were taken on they were more likely to use the broader definition of musician. An individual is then able to develop multiple identities under the umbrella of "being a musician", rather than constantly re-defining the self. This suggests that the narrow, instrument specific identity may be more of an aspiration, rather than a realistic perception of the modern profession. Bennett argues that because the manner in which a musician self-defines is critical to a successful career, re-defining the meaning of "being a musician," could greatly assist career sustainability. Music educators play a vital role in encouraging students to be resilient and adaptable in order to fit with their musical environment. Oakland, Macdonald, & Flowers (2014) draw attention to the physical and psychological impact of unrealistic career ideals and musical self-perception, and point to the need for all music professionals to be aware of the influence of identity in maintaining a musical career.

23.2 THE ARTISTIC IDENTITY

Bain (2005) examined the occupational identity of visual artists and noted the difficulties in self-labelling as an artist in a profession where there are no clear dividing lines between artist and non-artist, or amateur and professional. Interpreting the label of "opera singer" can be similarly ambiguous. Opera is still the main source of work for singers, but the opera singer label is often used by the wider public to describe any singer who has classical training. In addition, the criteria of what constitutes being an opera singer are also changing as many well-known artists now engage in what have become known as "cross-over" activities.

One of the problems in creative self-definition is the tension between a need to be both creative and commercially successful (Gotsi, Andriopoulos, Lewis, & Ingram, 2010). Friction arises when an artistic and a business identity are juxtaposed, causing a conflict of values and expectations (Hackley & Kover, 2007), such as the performing artist who spends more time working in an office. The concept of identity work treats identity as a process of forming and reforming of self through interactions with social settings (Watson, 2008). In other words, individuals have multiple aspects to their identity which vary in prominence according to time and circumstance (Watson, 2009; Ybema et al., 2009). In their study of creative designers, Gotsi et al. (2010) suggest that people accommodate identity friction by developing what they call a "meta-identity," in which the pragmatic and the idealist self are joined using a label of "practical artist." They suggest that if this meta-identity can be internalized, an individual is better able to accommodate any role ambiguity, rather than being constrained by it.

Mills (2004) addresses musical identity work by differentiating between a professional identity and a subjective identity. The former refers to what a person actually does in terms of employment, and is "what they present to the outside world" (Mills, 2004, p. 246), whereas the latter is what a person feels they are regardless of the amount of paid work. For some professions, such as doctors or lawyers, the professional and subjective identities are the same, but this is not necessarily the case for musicians. Mills gives the example of "performer teachers," who see themselves more as performing musicians even if the majority of their income comes from teaching. However, there are still a large number of musicians who work on full-time contracts with established orchestras and opera companies for whom a professional identity is their main source of self-definition. As artistic institutions are subjected to greater economic restraints, the likelihood of career disruption through job loss or stress is an increasing reality.

23.3 THE OPERA SINGER IDENTITY

In, 2005 there were five full-time opera choruses in Great Britain. To date, three of those companies have made singers redundant. Both The Royal Opera House and English National Opera made a substantial number of choristers redundant in 1998 and 2003 respectively, and in 2005 Scottish Opera made a complete chorus redundant. The scale of redundancies meant that it would be difficult for choristers to find other full-time work in the UK. If identity is the catalyst to success (Bennett, 2008a) then it is important to understand how identity work can help these singers and other musicians adapt to unexpected and undesired career disruption.

Opera singers occupy a unique place in the music profession because they are required to be versatile, all-round performing artists. In common with other musicians they are required to attain high levels of technical ability, but on a "human" instrument. In addition, modern opera production requires singers to engage in high levels of physical activity while on stage, to possess credible acting skills, and to be visually attractive.

The physical body is an important influence on a singer's perception of self, not only because it contains the vocal instrument, but the physicality of opera means that without a fit, healthy body a singer would not be able to carry out the work. Sandgren's (2009) study of performance anxiety amongst elite opera soloists found that many of her participants associated performance anxiety with physical and psychological variables, such as worry about illness and vocal functioning. She concluded that singers suffer a form of health anxiety in relation to their professional activity and are particularly concerned with health promotion techniques, such as attention to physical fitness and a protection from infections.

In a phenomenological study exploring the effects of redundancy on opera choristers, Oakland, MacDonald, & Flowers (2012) suggest that the opera singer identity has three main components: the relationship between self and voice, the influence of the theatrical environment where they live and work, and the status attached to the job title. The "opera singer identity" was considered to be a professional identity dependent on paid employment, but one that was underpinned by several sub-identities, such as being a performer, musician, or singer. Levels of engagement with these elements varied between the participants in the study, which in turn influenced their experiences of career disruption. Oakland, MacDonald, & Flowers (2012) also examined the process of re-defining the self after job loss. They found that the professional identity became fragmented and awareness of the various sub-identities was heightened. Successful transition involved minimizing or prioritizing these sub-identities in order to re-negotiate the self in a different social setting. For example, several singers came to realize the limitations of "just being an opera singer." Self-esteem was maintained by adopting an identity as a musician or a performer. Other singers rediscovered the act of singing as a means of self-expression, rather than a tool to maintain a professional identity.

Studying identity in this context provided a unique opportunity to examine the fragmentation of a complex musical identity in which interactions between the vocal self, performing self, musician self, and professional self are laid open. In the following section we present four case study examples taken from our recent work, which illustrate the individual nature of identity work undertaken by the singers in order to cope with a disrupted life. Making sense of a significant loss (as in that of a musical career) involves a need to maintain continuity with who you have been, while integrating the reality of the new world into a concept of who you might become (Neimeyer, 2002). We found that continuity of self was aspired to by revising the meanings and expectations assigned to a professional identity whereby certain elements of this identity were used as a basis for a self that was not dependent on full-time operatic employment.

23.4 THE SINGERS

Moira, Fiona, Andy, and Helen worked as opera choristers contracted to national (UK) companies until they were made redundant. They have been unable to find alternative full-time chorus work. In-depth semi-structured interviews were conducted with these singers to understand their personal experiences of career disruption. Data was analyzed using Interpretative Phenomenological Analysis (see Smith, Flowers, & Larkin, 2009). Each case study presented outlines the personal journey made by the singers as they negotiate and renegotiate their musician identities. We use the professional/ subjective identity concept of Mills (2004) as a framework for this discussion, but we replace the term "subjective identity" with "private identity." In this way, we account for the differences between a professional self that is presented to the world and dependent on external validation, and the private self, which places greater emphasis on self-validation. Attention is given to fragility of a professional identity and the strength of a private identity when coping with career crisis.

23.4.1 Moira

Moira came to opera singing later in life. She was 49 and had been a full-time chorister for 11 years with the same company. Previous employment included office work, singing in musicals, and straight acting. At the time of the interview she was working as a gardener, but considering a return to freelance opera work with the company that made her redundant. Moira's private identity as a performer was highly significant in the way she coped with career disruption:

> I have a huge sense of pride, when someone asks me what I do for a living and I say I'm an opera singer, it's immense and I don't want to let that go ... to tell someone you do that, I absolutely love it, you know, if you jump in a taxi and you're having a chat and he says "oh what do you do," "well I'm an opera singer." "Oh wow you're a singer, wow" it's great!

Moira enjoys public attention and gains much of her self-esteem from the perceptions of others to the label of opera singer. On being made redundant Moira enrolled on a gardening course. She likened the physicality of the work to the physical act of singing but also found a new outlet to reinforce her performer self and become the center of attention:

> ... I went into that course as an opera singer and I think I was accepted in the first week. The principal of the college found out that I had been an opera singer and he brought the local newspaper in and I have a photo of myself—the singing gardener or something like that.

At this stage in her transition, Moira still sees herself as an opera singer. She is able to transfer the values she associates with the title to a new environment. She feels that she fits with the gardening course because she is perceived by others as being different and special, and is still able to attract public recognition. She also experiments with an interim identity as a "singing gardener," which encompasses her creativity and the practical work in which she is engaged (see Gotsi et al., 2010). However, in the following extract she appears to be confused about her opera singer identity:

> *Interviewer*: So when you were not singing did you still view yourself as an opera singer?
> *Moira*: No never thought about it, didn't think about just seemed to go from my mind.
> *Interviewer*: So if someone asked you what you did in those times what did you say?
> *Moira*: I was doing country and gardening skills at college but then again I would say it's not only gardening it's fencing and slabbing 'cos again that would get a reaction. You see being a singer is attention seeking. I don't want to sit back and let someone else take center stage, I like sitting here chatting to you having centre stage.

Lack of paid operatic work makes it difficult for Moira to call herself an opera singer, but she still needs to be center stage. Moira now calls herself as a singer, not an opera singer because she felt it could still justify her craving for attention. Gardening, and the interview itself provided Moira with a stage in "real life," but this was only a temporary solution to Moira's transition. Because she felt she still had a voice she decided to reclaim her operatic identity by looking for part-time opera work. In this way, she could combine gardening with singing and, therefore, use the opera singer title legitimately:

> I do feel that if people ask me what I do for a living, although I'm not contracted full time I can still say I'm an opera singer and I'm not working in a baker's.

A sub-identity as a performer permeated the identity work that helped Moira through the trauma of redundancy, but it was the voice that informed her decision to return to professional singing. Moira's transition involved flirtations with different identities such as being a singer, rather than an opera singer, a gardener, and a combination of both, but she could not fully relinquish the opera singer label. In order to reclaim that identity she must renegotiate the terms on which it was based. Moira resolves these identity tensions when she considers that part time work is sufficient justification to use the title. What used to be a professional identity for Moira now forms a private identity in a portfolio career, but one that still needs the endorsement of some paid employment.

23.4.2 Fiona

Fiona was 50 at the time of the interview. She had worked as a full-time chorister for two national companies over a period of 25 years. After redundancy she moved away from her place of work to a small village, where she is now a teacher/performer. Fiona's journey was marked by a minor breakdown which she called her "light bulb" moment and which initiated a major evaluation of the limitations of her previous identity as an opera singer. Fiona's initial ambition was to be a music teacher and her vocal identity was influenced by a general perception that teachers were not good enough to be singers:

> My degree is in music education, not performing and I was always determined I was going to be a music teacher but on the education course there was this class thing that the education people weren't good, you're not really supposed to be any good as a singer.

When she got her first job as a full-time chorister she questioned whether she was worthy of it and after a move to a more prestigious company much of Fiona's self-esteem still relied on the status of the opera singer label and the reactions of others to the job title, rather than any subjective identities such as being a singer or performer:

> I think self-esteem wasn't great in other areas and this was something that felt quite good, nothing to do with the singing but the name of the job and the level of the job. I've just sort of always felt that being an opera singer is a kind of conversation stopper. "What do you do?" "Oohh that must be nice." I know I've taken some of my identity from being with a national opera company.

Like Moira, Fiona enjoyed the attention that being an opera singer brought in the wider community. Because Fiona was insecure about her singing abilities she found that she relied on a corporate identity, that of being a member of a prestigious company, for self-esteem and endorsement of her level of skills. However this form of external validation of self was not transferable to a new social setting. Without a professional organization to support her self-esteem, Fiona experienced difficulties when she tried to make a life in the wider community:

> When I first came here I didn't want anyone to know I was an opera singer, because I thought people would think it was a bit strange, I wanted to make friends and fit in.

Fiona had difficulty acknowledging her past self and felt that her opera singer identity may not be appropriate in her new environment. Although she wanted to hide what was previously a public self, she cannot deny the professional values that underpin her opera singer self. This is apparent in the way she makes clear divisions between herself as a professional singer and the amateur singers in her vicinity:

> Everybody's desperate for me to join the church choir and there's absolutely no way, if I was there I'd be wanting to fix their vowels and things. To actually sit in amongst them, it would affect my professional ear.

Fiona is moving between relinquishing a former identity, wanting to fit in to her new community, but not wanting to be placed in the same category as the amateur singers in her neighborhood. As the interview progressed so did Fiona's sense-making process and she began to realize that she had never had an identity of her own other than "someone who works with a national company:"

I'm beginning to get to the bottom of this now. I never developed any kind of identity of my own. I think I might have been able to transform myself into the person that was the opera singer, but that's an identity thing, it's not a professional thing because I could do the job standing on my head.

Fiona the opera singer is portrayed as a public version of the self, a self created to boost self-esteem. She now separates her professional identity from her professional abilities and the insecurity she talked about during her career is not apparent. Fiona also talked about the limitations of an identity that was formed principally on a job title and governed by institutional control. Re-evaluation of self has drawn greater awareness to the part played by singing in her life:

> Singing means energy, expression, not identity now, it was identity for years, it isn't identity now.

Singing now fulfils a different role in Fiona's life in which it is no longer dependent on external validation, so that she is able to separate singing from a professional identity. The act of singing now forms the foundation of a new sense of self which prioritizes artistic self-expression over what Fiona terms identity. Although the external validation of a professional title has been highly influential throughout Fiona's working life, it appears to have had a negative influence on her overall self-confidence as a singer and has denied access to other aspects of self. A traumatic experience enabled Fiona to rediscover the core elements of singing in her life without the need for the endorsement of a national organization.

23.4.3 Andy

Andy had been a chorister for 10 years with the same company. He studied trumpet before taking up singing and had already begun a musical portfolio career before embarking on a singing career. In the interview Andy used his over-arching self-perception as a musician as a means to disassociate himself from the professional title of opera singer. When Andy was asked what singing meant to him he immediately qualified his status as a musician:

> I think singing isn't the be all and end all for me. It's never been like that for me, I've always been a general musician, so maybe that's what singing means to me, it was a way of making a living, satisfying my musical desires. But it was never the sole focus of my music making. I've also done some music admin as well so I was also interested in that side of things. I worked for an orchestra for a couple of years doing orchestra management. I suppose at some time I must have said I was a singer but I don't think I ever said I was an opera singer 'cos I think I've been a musician longer than just a singer.

Andy makes clear divisions between being a singer, being an opera singer, and being a musician. He appears to disassociate to the greatest degree with the opera singer title, possibly because career disruption occurred in an operatic environment. He now favors the musician label as a better description of his broad musical abilities and emphasizes the limitations of just being a singer. Previously, Andy used singing as a tool to support his freelance career. He accepted a full-time chorus job because it was an easier way to earn a living than freelancing:

> I did look at it as a way to earning money without having to work so hard at finding my weeks' worth of jobs as a freelancer. It just seemed simpler, just to have one job to think about rather than trying to juggle everything, so it wasn't that I was mad keen on opera, I was mad keen on music.

Again, Andy distances himself from any connections to opera and minimizes the emotional importance of the job. However, later in the interview he talked about his love of singing and having to deal with losing a job he loved:

> I still don't do it, solo singing, ensemble singing. I just had to deal with those feelings of sadness or loss of having such a good job, going in and getting paid for what you love doing, singing.

It would appear that Andy has cut singing and opera out of his life as a way of coping with job loss. To replace this loss Andy prioritizes his musician identity and more specifically his experiences of choral conducting:

> I'd done six or seven years as a choral conductor before [name of opera company] so that's great 'cos I can impose my musical ideas on the choir—so yeh you've got your own musical persona but then in [name of company]you've got to understand that you've got to do what the director says and what the MD [musical director] says as well, so that can be a bit stifling but you accept they have a musical opinion and you have a musical opinion and just get on with it .

In this extract Andy reappraises his singing work by contrasting the autonomy he used to have in his music-making with the restrictions of conforming to the artistic vision of others. This loss of artistic control can be likened to the loss of control felt by redundancy and may be a reason he over-emphasizes the musical control he now has as a conductor:

> I'm more comfortable with performing now than I've ever been, more comfortable with myself than I've ever been. I choose the programme and I can drive it the way I want it, that's satisfying and I get to conduct the performance which I find very exciting, it's really good for me as a way of expressing myself, but I just find the conducting space a very comfortable place to be.

Andy unites his performer self and his real self when he talks about being comfortable. He appears to attribute this to his new identity as a conductor and the artistic freedom it gives, which would not have been possible as a full-time chorister.

Andy has embraced numerous musical identities during his career, although it is not clear if he was ever comfortable with his singing. He may have loved the physical process of singing and the ease with which it provided him with a living, but was reluctant to lay claim to a singing identity. A longer established musician identity has helped maintain self-esteem through job loss and provided a degree of continuity from where he can explore a new identity as a choral conductor.

23.4.4 Helen

Helen was 50 years old, and had worked for the same company for a period of 26 years. She had not known any other form of work and her identity as an opera singer with a prestigious company was firmly established. At the time of the interview, she had not fully dealt with the impact of what was an abrupt end to her singing career. She had been unable to sing physically for 2 years. Helen's sense of self as a singer was formed at an early age and she could not believe there would ever be a time when singing was not part of her life:

> I do think "gosh my life's changed enormously" and that part of my life. Sometimes I feel it's a relief that I don't have to practice every day and I don't have to worry about keeping up the standard of my voice but I'm aware that inside me—I still feel that that wonderful gift is still there and I'm not using it. I miss not using it.

Because Helen's voice still remains physically inside her it is a constant reminder of who she used to be. Helen experiences conflicting emotions between being grateful that she does not have to technically work at the voice, but sadness that her voice is not being used. Like Moira and Fiona, Helen enjoys the feeling of specialness attached to what she does, but Helen's specialness comes from being a singer and not an opera singer:

> If some-one asks you what's your job and you say "well actually I'm a singer," well call me shallow if you like but I get a great kick out of that because it was different and because I felt it was special. Whether they considered it to be special I don't know, I think a lot of people haven't a clue …

This extract highlights Helen's strong vocal identity that is not dependent on the perceptions of others or the job title but on her own perceptions of being different from the general public. Helen's most significant loss of status occurred when she felt no longer part of her professional musical community. She spent her final year working the same hours as her colleagues, but without full-time status:

> I was then classed as a part-time chorister and er that was the start of the loss of status if you like, it was the beginning of realising that I wasn't going to be the same person …

Helen now calls herself a chorister and, in contrast to her strong subjective identity as a singer, the extract above shows the fragility of a professional identity and its dependence on external validation, particularly from colleagues. Because of her change in work status Helen felt in a different class from colleagues with whom she had worked as an equal for more than 20 years. When she stopped working completely her self-perception as a singer was affected, as was any meaning she attached to being a singer:

> I never say I'm a singer—I don't think of myself as a singer any more, I don't think of myself as a professional singer anymore, in fact I don't count myself as a singer, whatever that means.

Helen's professional and private sense of self as a singer has been damaged. Without the validation of paid employment she can no longer portray herself as being a "special singer." Unlike the other singers Helen rarely uses the word "opera" in relation to her identity, which suggests that singing was perceived as a greater loss than the job title. Although Helen would like to return to some form of singing she is unable find a suitable outlet:

> I've got a lot of music in me, like I'm not at the stage where I feel I should be packing up. Even if it's obviously not full-time singing, but just being able to do some concerts and do justice to wonderful music that's been written. I know I've got it in me, I know that I've done it, and I don't know what's going to make me do it again. I don't know what is actually going to be that turning point.

Helen accepts that her previous self as a full-time singer is no longer possible, but ultimately wishes to find a place for her musical abilities in a future self. At present she is unsure as to how that integration can happen and unlike Fiona, has not yet found a turning point to facilitate the transition. Helen's professional and subjective identities as a singer were previously unified. Career crisis has damaged both these identities, such that Helen has little in reserve to form the basis of a new self. The intensity of the damage is reflected in Helen's inability to sing.

23.5 TRAUMA, TRANSITION, AND IDENTITY

Involuntary career transition is documented as one of the most stressful life events to affect individuals (Spera, Buhrfeind, & Pennebaker, 1994; Zikic & Klehe, 2006), which involves not only loss of income, but loss of self-esteem, loss of community and loss of identity (Jahoda, 1982). The singers' abilities to cope with this type of career-related trauma depended upon the degree to which they could re-evaluate previous identities and integrate elements of a past life into a future self. The case studies have shown how identities can be revised (Moira), reconstructed (Fiona), expanded (Andy) or con-tracted (Helen) in order to adapt (or not) to a changed social and professional environ-ment. Each individual adopted different strategies to cope with career transition. This is reflected in the theories of Schlossberg (1981), who argues that it is not the transition itself that is life changing, but an individual's perception of the transition. For exam-ple, transitions can be seen as positive life events, or what Moustakes (1990, p. 99) calls "Symbolic growth experiences," because "they create shifts in an individual's attitude to their sense of identity and the selfhood from which one grows." In contrast, if transitions are perceived as negative events, ill health and depression can be experienced (Fryer & Fagan, 2003; Waters, 2007).

Job loss is a traumatic experience for employees in all walks of life, but understand-ing the transitional experiences of opera singers primarily requires an understanding of the relationship between their professional singing and the embodied voice (Oakland et al., 2012). A commonality between all the participants was the need to re-evaluate the role of singing as an agent in the formation of self. All participants were able to sing physically, but because their vocal sense of self was wrapped up in the professional title of opera singer, their stories are those of repositioning a vocal identity away from the environment in which it was established and endorsed. Fiona reconstructed the self and was able to make greater connections between self and singing. Instead of depending on a prestigious company for her opera singer identity she found alternative means of self-validation, whereby she saw herself as a singer, rather than an opera singer. Andy coped by expanding the narrow specifications of opera singing and returned to a broader iden-tity as a musician, which could be endorsed by a variety of musical roles. Coping also involved disassociation with a singing identity by minimizing its importance in his life. Moira revised the way her opera singer identity was endorsed. Despite experimenting with transitional identities and the meta-identity of a singing gardener, the opera singer identity and the environment in which it was constructed remained a major source of self-validation. Helen was the only singer who admitted to a strong sense of self as a singer from an early age, which was so deeply embedded that job loss was not only loss of status but loss of her primary source of self-expression. Bennett (2009) advises on the need for continual expansion of identity to incorporate the multi-faceted nature of a musical career, but Helen has contracted her identity as a singer to the point where she is psychologically unable to sing. Helen's vocal identity appears to be more deeply embedded than the others and is perhaps not yet flexible enough to consider other areas of creative fulfilment.

In her work with injured musicians, Maitlis (2009) found that prior to injury the musicians all possessed powerful but restrictive identities in music which were vulner-able when exposed to external shock. Trauma experience provided the conditions that enabled the musicians in her study to gradually expand their self-understanding and grow through adversity. Similar observations were made by Oakland et al. (2012), in whose study only Helen was still traumatized by redundancy. Other singers proved to be more resourceful in seeking new opportunities for creative self-expression.

23.6 THE PLACE OF A PROFESSIONAL
IDENTITY IN MUSICAL SELF-VALIDATION

Work is a defining feature of contemporary society. It involves us in relations with others and gives us our sense of identity. Most introductory conversations include the question "What do you do?" Work is the way we define ourselves to others and the way we are judged by others. We proposed that the opera singer identity was a professional identity because it describes in specific terms the work of a singer. However, for the female singers it was more than a job description. The title brought self-esteem, status and a special place in society. Adopting the broader term of "musician" (Bennett, 2008a,b) was not an option for these singers because unlike Andy, the need for "specialness" was an integral part of who they were. Only Fiona had managed to retain her singing identity away from an operatic environment. Therefore, a self-definition based purely on work or corporate affiliations can be fragile if not underpinned by a private sense of self that is supported by, but not dependent on, external validation.

23.7 CONCLUSIONS

A professional identity appears crucial to the way we define ourselves to others, for personal self-esteem, status and recognition. However, the prospect of a job for life where an identity remains in place for as long as an individual wishes (Baruch, 2004) is likely to be a rare occurrence in many walks of life. It is therefore logical that the way we form and validate our professional identities must also change. For musicians, a sustainable identity in music is an essential element of career longevity, but the identity work involved in maintaining that identity may require a broader vision of what it means to work in music. Finding the balance between creative ideals and commercial viability is not only a challenge for individuals, but also for creative organizations. There is an increasing trend in many orchestras and opera houses to replace full-time positions with freelance musicians, which gives the company greater artistic and economic flexibility, but at the expense of job security for the musicians. Music conservatories are responding to this trend by emphasizing the need for students to prepare for a varied musical career that focusses on the musician as a multi-skilled, usually freelance worker whose work may not be exclusively performance based. Musicians need to fit with their musical environment if they are to strive for an identity in music that encourages personal growth, rather than constraint. Encouraging broad self-definition such as musician or vocal artist may help, but then questions should also be asked about the implications that being "a jack-of-all trades" has for musical excellence.

Much attention and research is devoted to helping student musicians prepare for what could be considered an exciting new working environment where loss of job security may be compensated for by a greater autonomy in the workplace and, therefore, over personal identity. However, this is often at the expense of neglecting the needs of older, more experienced musicians who may need to make significant changes to the way they perceive their roles in music. This chapter has shown identity work to be a crucial factor in the ability to adapt to changing work environment where the singers most able to cope with career transition were those able to internalize an identity based on personal goals and aspirations and move away from the fragility of an identity primarily based on external validation, such as public recognition and paid employment. Equally important is how do we help musicians cope with the question "Who am I?" when a career comes to an end? Unlike sport and dance there is little specialist help in place to support musicians through career transition. The usefulness of musical identity research depends on the degree to which it can make a practical difference in the lives of individuals. Taking part in this research was the first opportunity for all the participants to talk about and make sense of their experiences. Applied sport psychologists have an established role in the lives of professional athletes. The Association of Applied Sport Psychology provides information for athletes and coaches on a variety of issues, such as mental skills training, injury, and rehabilitation, retirement, and professional development. There are also a number of graduate programs in place to train registered sport psychologists. Hays (2002) comments on the similarities between athletes and performing artists and notes that sport psychologists may be in a strong position to transfer their knowledge to the performing arena, but adds a note of caution. When she interviewed a number of performing artists about expectations of psychological intervention, empathy, and experience of a specific performance domain were cited as essential qualities in a practitioner for trust and credibility to be established. Perhaps it is time to consider training applied music psychologists, who can make use of a growing bank of academic knowledge in order to help musicians cope with the rigors of professional life.

Negotiating musical identities is complex but of fundamental importance for professional musicians. Not only does identity work have crucial implications for employment opportunities, but it also has considerable impact upon the health and well-being of individuals whose professional life can be very precarious. It is of considerable importance that we continue research in this area in order to more fully uncover the complexities that underpin these crucial psychological processes.

References

Bain, A. (2005). Constructing an artist's identity. *Work, Employment and Society*, 19(1), 25–46.

Baruch, Y. (2004). Transforming careers: from linear to multi-directional career paths. *Career Development International*, 9(1), 58–73.

Bennett, D. (2008a). Identity as a catalyst for success. In: Hannan, M. (Ed.) *17th International Seminar of the Commission for the Education of the Professional Musician*, 15–18 July, 2008, pp. 1–4. Spilamberto: International Society for Music Education.

Bennett, D. (2008b). *Understanding the classical music profession. The past, the present and strategies for the future.* Aldergate: Ashforth.

Bennett, D. (2009). Academy and the real world: developing realistic notions of career in the performing arts. *Arts and Humanities in Higher Education*, 8, 309–27.

Burland, K., & Davidson, J.W. (2004). Tracing a musical life transition. In: J. Davidson (Ed.), *The music practitioner: research for the music performer, teacher and listener*, pp. 225–49. Aldershot: Ashgate.

Burland, K., & Pitts, S. (2007). Becoming a music student: investigating the skills and attitudes of students beginning a music degree. *Arts and Humanities in Higher Education*, 6, 289–308.

Creech, A., Papageorgi, I., Duffy, C., Morton, F., Haddon, E., Potter, J., & Welch, G. (2008). From music student to professional: the process of transition. *British Journal of Music Education*, 25(3), 315–31.

Fryer, D., & Fagan, R. (2003). Towards a critical community psychological perspective on unemployment and mental health research. *American Journal of Community Psychology*, 32, 89–96.

Gotsi, M., Andriopoulos, C., Lewis, M.W., & Ingram, A.E. (2010). Managing creatives: paradoxical approaches to identity regulation. *Human Relations*, 63(6), 781–805.

Hargreaves, D.J., Miell, D.E., & Macdonald, R.A.R. (2002). What are musical identities and why are they important. In: R.A.R. MacDonald, D. J. Hargreaves, & D. Miell (Eds.) *Musical identities*, pp. 1–16. Oxford: Oxford University Press.

Hackley, C., & Kover, A.J. (2007). The trouble with creatives: negotiating creative identity in advertising agencies. *International Journal of Advertising*, 26(1), 63–78.

Hays, K.F. (2002). The enhancement of performance excellence among performing artists. *Journal of Applied Sport Psychology*, 14(4), 299–312

Jahoda, M. (1982). *Employment and unemployment*. London: Cambridge University Press.

Maitlis, S. (2009). Who am I now? Sensemaking and identity in posttraumatic growth. In: L. Roberts & J. Dutton (Eds.) *Exploring positive identities and organizations: building a theoretical and research foundation*, pp. 47–76. New York: Psychology Press.

Moustakes, C. (1990). *Heuristic research: design, methodology and applications*. Thousand Oaks, CA: Sage Publications

Mills, J. (2004). Working in music: becoming a performer-teacher. *Music Education Research*, 6, 245–61.

Neimeyer, R.A. (2002). *Lessons of loss. Guide to coping*, 2nd. edn. New York, NY: Brunner Routledge.

Oakland, J., Macdonald, R.A., & Flowers, P. (2012). Re-defining "Me": exploring career transition and the experience of loss in the context of redundancy for professional opera choristers. *Musicae Scientiae*, 16, 135–47.

Oakland, J., Macdonald, R.A., & Flowers, P. (2013). Identity in crisis: the role of work in the formation and renegotiation of identity. *British Journal of Music Education*, 30(2), 261–76.

Oakland, J., Macdonald, R.A., & Flowers, P. (2014). Musical disembodiment: a phenomenological case study investigating the experiences of operatic career disruption due to physical incapacity. *Research Studies in Music Education*. published online 5 February, 2014 DOI: 10.1177/1321103X14521355.

Sandgren, M. (2009). Health anxiety instead of performance anxiety among opera singers. *Proceedings of the 7th Triennial Conference of European Society for the Cognitive Sciences of Music* (ESCOM, 2009) Jyväskylä, Finland.

Schlossberg, N. K. (1981). A model for analysing human adaptation to transition. *The Counselling Psychologist*, 9 (2), 2–17.

Sloboda, J.A., & Howe, M. J. (1992). Transitions in the early musical careers of able young musicians: Choosing instruments and teachers. *Journal of Research in Music Education*, 40(4), 283–294.

Smilde, R. (2005). "Lifelong Learning for Musicians." *Proceedings of the NASM Annual Meeting.* Boston, November, 20.

Smith, J. A., Flowers, P., & Larkin, M. (2009). *Interpretative phenomenological analysis: theory, method and research.* London: Sage.

Spera S.P., Buhrfeind, E.D., & Pennebaker, J.W. (1994). Expressive writing and coping with job loss. *Academy of Management Journal*, 37(3), 722–733.

Rogers, R. (2002). *Creating a land with music.* London: Youth Music.

Waters, L. (2007). Experiential differences between voluntary and involuntary job redundancy on depression, job search activity, affective employee outcomes and re-employment quality. *Journal of Occupational and Organizational Psychology*, 80, 279–299.

Watson, T.J. (2008). Managing identity: Identity work, personal predicaments and structural circumstances. *Organization* 15(1), 121–143.

Watson, T. (2009). Narrative, life story and manager identity: a case study in autobiographical identity work. *Human Relations*, 62(3), 425–52.

Ybema, S., Keenoy, T., Oswick, C., Beverungen, A., Ellis, N., & Sabelis, I. (2009). Articulating identities. *Human Relations*, 62(3), 299–322.

Zikic, J.,& Klehe, U. (2006). Job loss as a blessing in disguise: The role of career exploration and career planning in predicting reemployment quality. *Journal of Vocational Behaviour*, 69(3), 391–409.

CHAPTER 24

RE-AUTHORING THE SELF

Therapeutic Songwriting in Identity Work

FELICITY A. BAKER
AND RAYMOND MACDONALD

24.1 INTRODUCTION: WHAT IS THERAPEUTIC SONGWRITING?

Songs are ways that human beings explore emotions. They express who we are and how we feel, they bring us closer to others, they keep us company when we are alone. They articulate our beliefs and values. As the years pass, songs bear witness to our lives. They allow us to relieve the past, examine the present, and to voice our dreams of the future. Songs weave tales of our joys and sorrows, they reveal our innermost secrets, and they express our hopes and disappointments, our fears and triumphs. They are our musical diaries, our life-stories. They are the sounds of our personal development.

Bruscia, 1998, p. 9.
Text extract from Bruscia, K.E, *Defining Music Therapy*,
2nd edn © 1998 Barcelona Publishers with permission
from Barcelona Publishers.

THIS opening quotation not only highlights the universal importance of songs, but it also signals the inextricable relationship that songs have with identity. Every song written is an identity project for the composer and songwriting is therefore an excellent site to study the construction and negotiation of identities through music. As a songwriter develops musical and lyrical themes, sometimes alone, sometimes in collaboration, there is highly nuanced identity work taking place and this chapter explores these issues of identity and songwriting within clinical contexts. This context is important and there is a growing body of evidence to suggest that engagement in songwriting activities can have significant positive effects upon a range of psychological factors. The literature on songwriting with a specific focus on its therapeutic capacity to shape identities of those with complex health problems is reviewed. The chapter demonstrates how songwriting can be an important creative process where significant identity work is undertaken. It also highlights the relationship between creative activities such as songwriting and psychological processes that can have positive effects for those engaged in such activities. The chapter signals key identity issues involved in the process and points the way forward for future research this area.

Therapeutic songwriting is a music therapy intervention that aims to address emotional, communicative, cognitive, psychological, or social needs of an individual or group of individuals (Wigram & Baker, 2005; Baker, 2013c) and draws on the storytelling feature of songs. Therapists have drawn on songwriting methods with clinical groups across the lifespan including physical and intellectual disability, neurorehabilitation, mental health, trauma, oncology, palliative care, and aged care (Baker, Wigram, Stott, & McFerran, 2008). The process involves the creation, notation, and/or recording of lyrics and music within the context of a therapeutic relationship; a collaboration between a therapist and a songwriter or a group of songwriters[1] (Wigram & Baker, 2005). The therapeutic benefits of the process may extend beyond the song's creation as the song is repeatedly listened to, the song's significance and meaning is reflected on in further therapy sessions, or as the song is shared with or performed for others (Baker, 2013a,b).

In an international survey of songwriting practices (Baker, Wigram, Stott, & McFerran, 2008, 2009), clinicians ranked issues of self-identity as the most frequent reason for selecting songwriting as a method in their practice. More than 75% of clinicians choose songwriting as a means to:

- Externalize thoughts, fantasies, and emotions.
- Tell the participant's story.
- Develop a sense of self.
- Gain insight or clarify thoughts and feelings.

These are all integral to the formation, reformation, and maintenance of a healthy self-concept, a process of assimilation and accommodation (Hann, 1977).

---

[1] Several terms have been used in the literature to refer to the people creating the songs within the therapeutic context—participant, client, patient, resident, student, and child. In this chapter, we have chosen to refer to them as songwriters.

24.2 METHODS OF THERAPEUTIC SONGWRITING

Methods of therapeutic songwriting documented in the literature vary considerably according to the extent to which music and lyrical ideas and components are predetermined (y-axis, Fig. 24.1). At one end of the spectrum lie the approaches such as fill-in-the-blank, song parody and strategic songwriting, where the melodic line and musical accompaniment are drawn from a pre-existing song, and the lyrics are adapted or completely replaced to achieve a therapeutic outcome. The advantage of these approaches is that the therapist can draw on pre-existing songs whose genre and way of telling stories aligns with the musical preferences and identity of the songwriter. Rewriting words to songs within a person's preferred music collection may:

- Enable the therapist to gain rapport with the person.
- Acknowledge the person's musical identities thereby engaging him/her in the therapeutic songwriting process.
- Facilitate a collaborative process whereby music is the "glue" in the therapeutic relationship.

However, using preferred music does present a risk. People have special relationships with songs created by their admired artists. They may not appreciate these favorite songs being transformed. Similarly, if they hold personally meaningful associations with the songs (e.g., a song that reminds them of a deceased relative or favorite moment), then rewriting the words may change people's long-term relationship with the song.

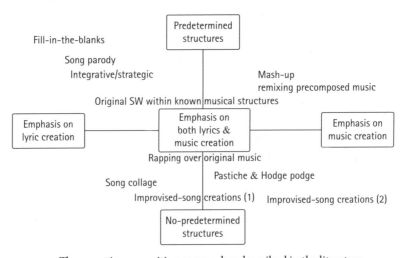

FIG. 24.1 Therapeutic songwriting approaches described in the literature.

Moving to the center of the continuum, mash-ups, song collages, pastiche, and writing original songs within known musical structures offers opportunities for songwriters to draw on musical elements of pre-existing songs and genres, but with more freedom to tailor the music and the lyrics to express their own identity. Tamplin (2006) uses the song collage technique with her adults with spinal cord injury or brain injury. Here, songwriters search songbooks and CD inserts, and select lyrics that reflect their feelings and experiences. Lyrics they identify with may have arisen from perusing songs by artists they admire and reflect their musical preferences and identity. From here, they assemble the lyrics together to form a collage of words but they may also contribute their own new lyrical material as well. This creates a collage of music and lyrics that combines musical preferences in a way that is completely their own and represents their musical identity as well as simultaneously telling their individual story. Baker, Dingle, & Gleadhill (2012) presented a group-composed song created by people in rehabilitation for substance use disorder that was a mash-up of reggae, gangsta rap and had incorporated lines from Kasey Chambers' "Am I not pretty enough" (2002), but rapped Chambers' lyrics, rather than singing them. At the other end of the spectrum, the creation of both music and lyrics are less predetermined. Rapping over self-composed music, as well as mixing and remixing rap music enables the songwriters to shape "their" sound, express their (musical) identity (Viega, 2013), and represent the sounds and stories of their communities (MacDonald & Viega, 2011).

Improvised songs facilitate a stream of consciousness where the songwriters musically and lyrically express issues and feelings as they move from the preconscious to conscious levels (Davies, 2005; Derrington, 2005). Here, the music and lyrics unfold in real time and in the moment. Identity issues are a key component within this process. Similar to psychodynamic free association, where the immediate and instantaneous thoughts have deeper significance, improvised songs can shed light on fundamental identity processes as they have links to important psychological processes for the songwriter. Moreover, improvisation has considerable utility in this context since it is a particularly accessible type of musical activity and can easily be viewed as real time composition (MacDonald & Wilson, in press). Improvisation also allows participants to develop a communicative relationship that can facilitate the therapeutic process (Pothoulaki, MacDonald, & Flowers, 2012). As a unique form of creativity that is social, creative, spontaneous, and accessible, improvisation activities not only have much to offer compositional strategies within therapeutic contexts, but they also involve important identity processes for participants (Wilson & MacDonald, 2012).

When considering the *x*-axis of Fig. 24.1, the same song methods can be understood according to whether the creation process emphasizes lyric creation, a balance of music and lyric creation processes, or a heavier emphasis on music creation processes. Detailed descriptions of these methods are presented in a book on therapeutic songwriting models and methods (Baker, 2015a).

24.3 MODELS OF THERAPEUTIC SONGWRITING

The theoretical orientation of the music therapist has a direct influence on the way song-writing methods unfold in practice, how the songwriting process is understood, and why songwriting is selected as a method in identity work. In recently undertaken research (Baker, 2015a), models of songwriting were categorized according to three broad areas. First, outcome-orientated songwriting focusses on songwriting models that focus on clear, predictable, and observable outcomes. Songwriting protocols are predetermined, operationally defined, and implemented according to behavioral, cognitive-behavioral, and neuroscience theories. For example, songwriting may focus on increasing aware-ness of distorted thinking and aims to restructure thinking about the self.

In experience-orientated thinking, songwriting is focussed on the process as it emerges in the moment. It focusses on meaning-making and identity building by explor-ing issues that may not be obvious at the outset. Within psychodynamic theory, songwrit-ing is used to connect people with their unconscious inner material through processes of free association. Songs express inner conflicts and the inner world of the songwriter through its use of symbols and metaphors. Humanistic songwriting approaches focus on authenticity, creativity, confidence building through a range of songwriting models such as insight-orientated songwriting, narrative songwriting, and strengths-based songwrit-ing (Baker, 2015a). More recently, songwriting has emerged as a practice within positive psychology orientations where there is a focus on finding meaning and purpose in life by creating songs about the self, and constructing or finding one's identity in the process.

The third group of models of songwriting are the most contemporary and have been classed as context-orientated models of songwriting. Here, songwriting is understood and practiced within feminist music therapy theory, community music therapy, and resource-orientated therapy. Feminist songwriting approaches focus on telling the songwriter's story as a form of empowerment and independence, and songs about their lives are considered in terms of their potential for sociopolitical transformation. Within community music therapy practices, songwriting models focus on health-musicing, cultivating musical communities, reducing the barriers to participation, and also pro-mote social justice. Similarly, resource-oriented songwriting approaches seek to draw out the resources within the songwriter and help them to build self-esteem, self-efficacy, but with an awareness of the songwriter within a social context.

24.4 THE THERAPIST'S ROLE, SONGWRITING, AND IDENTITY

There is scant literature that has specifically focussed on the role of the therapist in the process (Viega, 2013) or that even makes explicit the therapist's role (Roberts, 2008;

O'Grady, 2009). Taken collectively, and as elucidated by Baker in her ongoing research, the roles of the therapist are two-fold—the therapist's role in positively influencing identity, and the therapist's role in developing the lyrics and music.

Music therapist as facilitator is highlighted as one of the fundamental roles of a clinician when songs are created within the clinical setting. The therapists facilitate the generation and expansion of ideas through varied brainstorming techniques allowing the songwriters to speak freely, and without reservation about issues that are personally meaningful. Importantly, this process facilities a negotiation and development of music identities for the songwriters. The therapist is responsible for fostering a therapeutic environment that encourages the songwriters to tell their story; and share their identity through the medium of a song (Roberts, 2006; Baker, 2013c). The therapist's role is to create a therapeutic and creative space and where both conscious and unconscious processes can flow creatively.

The therapist's role is also to facilitate the lyric and music creation process by supporting songwriters' ideas and contributions, as well as offering suggestions, particularly for music. A key role for the therapist is to ensure the songwriters make the final decisions about the songs' content to safeguard ownership of the song (Davies, 2005; Baker, Kennelly, & Tamplin, 2005a).

24.5 ROLE OF LYRIC DEVELOPMENT IN IDENTITY WORK

Narrative approaches—journaling, poetry writing, lyric writing—allow people to explore their life stories whether these are stories of celebration, triumphs, uncertainty, crisis or loss (Pennebaker, Mayne, & Francis, 1997). Unexpected events such as being diagnosed with cancer, acquiring a permanent injury, being diagnosed with a mental illness, being subjected to physical, psychological, or sexual abuse, or the death of a loved one, throw people's lives into chaos. Such narrative disorganization occurs as "the world and the self as they were previously experienced, no longer exists" (Roos & Neimeyer, 2007, p. 91). In an effort to cope with such events, predictability and safety are threatened and they face an uncertain future (Neimeyer, 2000). To re-author one's own macro-narrative, focusing on meaning-making and developing an awareness of the implications of the new reality necessitates a revision and construction of self-identity (Neimeyer, 2000). Through telling stories at the micro-narrative level, people in crisis can gradually build a new identity that fits their changed circumstances. Lyric writing enables people to tell their stories (Baker et al., 2008). As people's lyrics tell and retell their stories, they begin to understand their stories and through a supportive therapeutic process, re-author these stories (Wallis, Burns, & Capdevila, 2011). In the right context these creative outputs become not only important markers of identity but a medium through which they process crises and construct a newer, richer, more complex, and healthier identity (Bruner, 1986).

Baker & MacDonald's (2013a,b) study of retirees and university students confirms the importance of lyric writing as an expression of identity and a meaningful opportunity to narrate their experiences—past and present. Day, Baker, & Darlington (2009a) and Rolvsjord (2005) studies songs of women who were victims of childhood abuse experienced emotional healing as they constructed their life histories, and communicated the long-term effects it had on them and who they were as people.

24.6 ROLE OF MUSIC IN THERAPEUTIC SONGWRITING

The therapeutic benefits of the music within the songwriting process are not yet well researched, although given broader knowledge of music, health and wellbeing (MacDonald, Kreutz, & Mitchell, 2012), there are many similarities and overlaps. For example, music in the songwriting process has a role in culture (Baker, 2013d). It contributes to social identity in a range of important ways, e.g., challenging and reinforcing social and political norms, and as a key component in religious rituals. Music serves to explore, express, and develop identity, while also communicating people's personal values and beliefs to the world, and providing possibilities for people to try out new ways of being, different personalities, and identities (Viega, 2013). Many of the chapters in this volume explore this issue in detail. Jane Davidson's chapter highlights how performers develop identities in music and how these identities are shaped by, and also projected through, numerous musical contexts. The chapters in this volume by Nicholas Cook (Chapter 38, "The clever boy from Croydon: music, identity, and race" and Tia DeNora (Chapter 3, "Music-ecology and everyday action: creating, changing and contesting identities"), also highlight the importance of music as a site for identity development.

Baker (2015b) reviews clinicians' perspectives of the importance of music in songwriting using modified grounded theory methods (Corbin & Strauss, 2008). Forty-five experienced music therapy researchers and clinicians who regularly use songwriting were interviewed about a range of issues related to songwriting as a therapeutic intervention, including what they perceived the role of music was in the process. Five main themes emerged from the data. First, music is important for *conveying meaning*. It assists in decoding the lyrical material. The music increased comprehension of the song's narrative, the meaning and significance of the lyrics (particularly if the lyrics were vague or ambiguous), and the feelings expressed. Music brought into focus, the emotional expression of the lyrics. In some circumstances, the music functioned to express the participants' inner worlds. The concreteness of the words communicates the story or issue and the music more fully expresses how the person feels about that issue, its degree of personal significance and ambivalence. Secondly, *music enhances the emotional dimensions of the lyrics*. It heightens the climax and resolution of lyrics, adding an emotional backing to them.

The study found that the *music stimulates connections with others*. When a therapy group join together and sing their song creation, feelings of intimacy, and mutual respect are experienced. Furthermore, as songwriters are typically admired for their talent, when songwriters share their songs with others, there is an opportunity to feel connected with those they share their songs with.

Music was important in *bolstering the therapeutic process and outcomes*. Music creation fosters experiences of achievement and self-esteem. Creating a finished product that society holds in high regard is important to the process. As a consequence, songwriters tend to be engaged and invested in the process. When songwriters experience blocks in the lyric writing, moving (at least temporarily) to the music creation process can unblock them. The music creation process also strengthens the ownership of and connection with the material and contributes to *identity building* (Baker & MacDonald, 2013a,b; Baker, 2015b).

It is important to note, however, that every songwriting process can be considered identity work even when the focus of the lyrics is not on the songwriter's personal story. A person creates lyrics and music, these elements are undoubtedly and extricably linked to fundamental aspects of the composers identity. Even songs about seemingly mundane topics, like the weather or food, will have personal resonances for the composer. These connections may be both conscious and unconscious, but the crucial point is that these personal resonances are key markers of identity for the composer.

24.7 EXAMPLES FROM THE LITERATURE

24.7.1 Striving for a non-sick identity

Whether in hospital for medical treatment or living with a mental illness, people who are "sick" experience an internal crisis about who they are as people. In particular, the issue of the *non-sick* versus *healthy self* becomes relevant. Hospitalized patients may be consumed by the illness disconnecting them from the *well self*, placing in jeopardy the effectiveness of the various treatments they may be receiving. In contrast, there is a social stigma associated with having a mental illness or a sexually transmitted disease that affect people's perceptions of the person with the illness as well as the person's own identity. These pervading sick identities are unhealthy and can lead to social isolation, deliberate or non-deliberate discrimination, depression, and anxiety.

By drawing on people's pre-existing musical identities, songwriting interventions can facilitate insight into the implications of the illness in the short and long-term and allow them to cathartically express their identity issues related to their illness.

Opportunities for personal growth via identity developments can then be created. These processes might include such issues as recognizing personal strengths and positive relationships.

For a sick child undergoing treatment for cancer, opportunities for expressing their personal and musical identities in creative and positive ways may be limited. By allowing children to create their own lyrics and melodies, songs emerge as reflections of their musical identities while simultaneously communicating an identity of being normal. Kennelly's (1999) case study of a young boy with cancer described how songwriting supported the boy's emerging positive sense of self, one of a fighter, someone who "doesn't quit" (lyrics from the boy's song, p. 232). The young boy commented as he approached discharge that he was a "different person now, a changed man" (p. 232) and that music therapy had contributed to his process. Ledger (2001) drew on song parody techniques in her work with a young adolescent with cancer. The young girl used the songwriting process to explore her identity as a "sick" child, but one that can still be strong despite her life circumstances now being different. By changing the words to a well-known song "I will survive" (Fekaris & Perren, 1978), the young girl explored her initial fear with a growing inner strength.

People with mental illness also present with challenges in overcoming a "sick" identity and coping with the illness. Several studies have reported benefits of songwriting as a means for people with mental illness to share their stories and struggles (e.g. Cordobés, 1997; McFerran, Baker, Patton, & Sawyer, 2006; Grocke, Bloch, & Castle, 2009; Vander Kooij, 2009; Baker et al., 2012). Cordobés (1997) suggests songwriting is a perfect medium for people to explore, appraise, problem-solve, and find meaning in their lives because it fits within a cognitive-conversational coping model. This model stipulates that both talking and writing are critical for insightful thinking and emotional response. Songwriting allows for an initial period of talking and reflection followed by organizing thinking and emotional responses further through the active construction of lyrics. In her analysis of song lyrics, Vander Kooij (2009) found that people with mental illness used the songwriting process to reflect on their journeys of illness and health as well as on their lost or restored identities. A lost identity was evident in the lyrics of "Who am I?:"

> Who am I?
> Am I so different?
> Why do the doctors keep giving me another name?
> I am lost like a pebble in the sand.
>
> Vander Kooij, 2009, p. 47.

Despite improvements in community education and awareness, people with mental illness still experience being misunderstood, disregarded, or persecuted. When they are continually dismissed as worthless, their sense of self and self-worth are at risk of collapse. Songwriting can be an opportunity to first acknowledge this self-perception, which is needed before one can build a new and healthy sense of self (Vander Kooij, 2009). One song explores feelings around this: "Who am I? I cannot say for everyone keeps running away, Who am I, that no one speaks, They giggle and laugh with their eyes they stare." (p. 49). Baker et al. (2012) provide lyrics for a song titled "Rehab rap" written by a group of people in rehabilitation for drug addiction. The song comprised lyrics that communicated the incompatibility of wanting to recover, but the "meds" they were prescribed were perceived as "fuckin with ma head" (p. 328). The music accompanying the group song was somewhat chaotic despite their intentions, and perhaps is indicative of their fractured identities.

24.7.2 Integrating a pre-injured with a post-injured self

Acquiring a sudden permanent disability following neurological injuries throws people into an existential crisis. The cognitive, communicative, psychosocial, and physical changes associated with acquiring a neurological impairment mark a sudden change in what may be possible in their future lives. They may no longer have the possibility to return to work, to play the same role in the family, to effectively communicate their thoughts and feelings, and to participate in life activities. Acquired disabilities challenge an individual's sense of meaning, sense of self, and basic human integrity (Hinkebein & Stucky, 2007, p. 393).

Perhaps the greatest challenge associated with integrating a pre-injured with a post-injured self through narrative processes is that people with neurological damage may present with significant cognitive challenges that negatively affect their short-term memory, abstract thinking, speed of information processing, and executive skills (Baker & Tamplin, 2006; Baker et al., 2005a). For example, each time a person attends a therapy session, they may be unable to recall the therapeutic discussions from the previous session due to limited short-term memory. So, in essence, there is a sense that they are beginning a new therapeutic process each time they attend therapy. Songwriting as a form of narrative (re)construction can adequately compensate for these cognitive barriers. For example, music functions as a mnemonic aid (Baker & Tamplin, 2006). Therefore, identity work explored through the songwriting process has a greater potential of being encoded in short-term memory and recalled during subsequent sessions.

A study of the song lyrics of people in active rehabilitation after sustaining traumatic brain injuries found that identity permeated through many of the songs created (Baker, Kennelly, & Tamplin, 2005b,c). Songs expressed memories (16.9% of lyrics) and reflections (11.5%) of past relationships and experiences (reflections on a pre-injured identity). Identity was explored through self-reflections such as "what makes them happy," "questioning life's meaning," and "concern of how they are perceived by others" (descriptions of a "present" self). The songwriting process contributed to building rich, complex identities while simultaneously allowing them to grieve and question.

24.8 SONG PRODUCTS, SHARING, PERFORMANCE, AND IDENTITY

Several research studies have outlined the therapeutic benefits associated with the sharing songs with and performing songs to an audience.[2] When performing a self-composed song, a performer is essentially presenting the self to others; a presentation of his/her identity to those who are present during the performance. Performing reinforces and validates internal changes within the songwriter and reminds them that they have moved through an important personal process (Baker, 2013b; Baker & Ballantyne, 2013; Day et al., 2009b; O'Grady, 2009).

Aasgaard (2002) followed the life of 19 songs composed by children with cancer, examining how, where, when, and by whom the songs were created, developed, performed, and used. Songs were created, shared, and performed in children's wards, the isolation room, hospital common room, home, school, or kindergarten, and involved family, hospital staff, visitors, school teachers, and classmates. Such events afforded children opportunities to express themselves, gain a sense of achievement, and engage in pleasure. Receiving positive praise from audiences enhances self-worth and, therefore, positively impacted self-identity.

Performing a self-composed song is an activity that opens up opportunities for songwriters to experience being "heard" by others (O'Brien, 2006; Day et al., 2009; MacDonald & Viega, 2011; Baker, 2013a,b). Songwriters feel validated when the song had clear impact and meaning for the audience (Baker, 2013b). When the songwriters perform their songs, audiences view the songwriters' identities through different lens (MacDonald, Hargreaves, & Miell, 2002; O'Grady, 2009; Soshensky, 2011; Baker, 2013b). Instead of perceiving their identities as people with complex health challenges, they recognize them as songwriters who are creative and musical (Baker, 2013b). Furthermore, the songwriters experience pride and ownership as they present a song worth sharing with an audience (Baker, 2013b). MacDonald et al. (2002) report a qualitative study exploring the social roots of personal identity; examining the detail of complex interactions between individuals involved in musical activities including composition and, in particular, the impact of such activities on their changing personal identities. A key finding of this study was that compositional activities can have significant positive benefits on issues relating to identity. The qualitative interviews highlighted the importance of these types of activities for developing positive music identities. For one participant, the analysis highlighted important changes in the difficulties experienced in interacting with others brought about by music. When his identity as "musician" became salient to them, rather than seeing him only as "disabled," people began to relate to him

---

[2] Here, performance may refer to the presentation of songs in a public context and may have been pre-planned or may refer to more private performances to one or more people selected by the songwriters (e.g., significant family members or friends).

directly, rather than ignoring and bypassing him. For the participants, their perceptions of the shift in people's assumptions and expectations following songwriting activities and music performance was striking. This study highlighted important and pervasive themes for understanding the powerful role which music (including compositional activities) can play in changing and enhancing identities.

While performing songs may have therapeutic benefits, songwriters may be vulnerable, as they share their identities and journeys towards building a new identity with an audience. Because of a lifetime of judgment and rejection by family and/or the broader community, people with complex health challenges may be afraid to re-experience rejection following the performance (Baker, 2013b). For example, women who have experience childhood abuse feared such judgment as they told the stories of their abuse and their struggle towards a new self (Day et al., 2009). However, facing these fears and challenging the songwriters to show themselves to the world can be a transformative experience in identity building (O'Brien, 2006; O'Grady, 2009a; MacDonald & Viega, 2011).

Song products contribute to the long-term development and maintenance of identity. Songs reinforce achievements made during their therapy process (Baker et al., 2005b; Grocke et al., 2009; Silverman, 2003), to reinforce positive feelings, or manage unwanted thoughts and feelings (Dalton & Krout, 2006; Mayers, 1995) and to remind participants of their inner strength and self-worth (Day et al., 2009a). When used in subsequent therapy sessions, transformational moments emerge as they "re-listen, re-experience, reflect, re-live, and recall the process of creating the song, and understand the song's significance in their own therapy process" and its impact on identity formation (Baker, 2013a, p. 46). At the same time, it has been suggested that over-listening can lead to excessive rumination (Baker, 2013a) Furthermore, songs that are created may be relevant at the time they were created but may not have been intended to represent "a fixed or unchanging story" (Baker, 2013a, p. 46).

24.9 SONGWRITING AND IDENTITY BEYOND THE CLINICAL CONTEXT

The paragraphs above situate songwriting and identities within a clinical context, however, this work has a number of important implications for songwriting outside of clinical situations. For example, songwriting is frequently constructed as an elite musical activity that can only be seriously undertaken by experienced and musically gifted individuals. However, the work outlined above highlights that songwriting can be an enjoyable, creative and rewarding activity that is universally accessible. This work therefore informs debates regarding the democratizing of musical communication. It provides evidence for the universal accessibility of musical activities and sheds lights upon important identity process at the heart of all songwriting activities not just therapeutic songwriting. Not only do identity processes lie at the heart of all songwriting activities, but the beneficial psychological effects of songwriting are discussed in sources beyond clinical and academic contexts. Many songwriters find the process of composing therapeutic as it help them process important aspects of their lives related to identity. Award winning Scottish singer songwriter R. M. Hubbert has discussed on a number of occasions how collaborative songwriting was, and remains, not only a central aspect of his artistic practice, but also an important therapeutic process for him, particularly during periods when he is experiencing personal problems. Therapeutic songwriting activities can be particularly effective as catalysts for identity development because of the high degree of mutual engagement necessary between participants, and because of the impact of being involved in highly valued activities on feelings of self-confidence and empowerment. Involvement in compositional activities can also have more general effects on the way in which people think about both themselves and their position within society. These two developments are related in that music can be thought of as not only facilitating specific changes in musical and psychological factors, but also as contributing to the identity projects in which individuals are engaged.

Our current and planned work in this area is further investigating the components of the songwriting process. For example, to what extent is the psychological construct of flow as defined by Csikszentmihalyi (1998) important within the songwriting process. Baker & MacDonald (2013a) report the songwriting experiences of 26 participants involved in a therapeutic songwriting project. Flow experiences of being fully immersed in the songwriting process, altered perception of time, and experiencing a balance between ability and effort were especially evident in participant description of their creative processes. Songwriting was viewed as an enjoyable means to explore the self, enhancing mood, and creating a satisfying artistic product. Flow experiences were evident in participants reporting of changes in perception of time. Time was perceived to have moved fast, participants sensed they "lost track of time," and were disappointed when their sessions came to an end. Other related areas for future research include investigating the content of the songs produced by participants at therapeutic songwriting sessions and relating the content to issues of identity discussed in interviews with the participants.

24.10 Conclusions

This chapter has highlighted the utility of songwriting as a therapeutic process. A number of different approaches were presented, comparing and contrasting the different types of creativity and artistic freedom within the various techniques. A particular emphasis was placed upon crucial identity processes implicated in all these activities. Central to this discussion is the assertion that creating new musical material involves important identity work for the composer irrespective of the context or of the type of material being developed. For example, generating new lyrics for an already existing song, a musical accompaniment for a poem or a completely new song including music and lyrics. Any artistic activity involves (consciously and/or unconsciously) the expression of ideas related to identity and this relationship between artistic expression and important identity work is harnessed during therapeutic songwriting with the aim of producing positive outcomes. The chapter also illustrated how this identity work can have positive effects by giving examples from the published literature. Illness always involves changes in identity and these changes can be extremely challenging, emotional, and debilitating. A number of examples highlighted how songwriting can have positive effects on these identity changes. The chapter also outlined how the related activities of sharing recorded material and performing self-written songs can have beneficial effects upon identity developments.

While there is still much to be learned about the process and outcomes of songwriting activities for therapeutic benefits there is growing evidence that it can facilitate a range of positive outcomes for the participants. Musical activities always involve more than just music (MacDonald, 2013). The inextricable link that music has to psychological and wider social and cultural variables means that our sense of self is implicated in most types of musical activities. Perhaps songwriting is the one musical activity that epitomizes most succinctly this relationship between identity and music. The stereotype of the heroic musical troubadour, strumming a guitar and revealing his soul has identities process at its core. Like most clichés, this image does reveal a wider truth—all songwriting projects are identity projects. Moreover, in the appropriate therapeutic context, this ubiquitous link can be utilized for positive outcomes.

References

Aasgaard, T. (2002). *Song creations by children with cancer: process and meaning.* Doctoral Dissertation, Aalborg University, Aalborg, Denmark.

Baker, F.A. (2013a). The ongoing life of participant-composed songs within and beyond the clinical setting. *Musicae Scientiae,* 17, 40–56.

Baker, F.A. (2013b). Front and center stage: participants performing songs created during music therapy. *Arts in Psychotherapy,* 40, 20–8.

Baker, F. (2013c). Therapeutic songwriting. In: K. Kirkwood (Ed.) *International dictionary of music therapy,* p. 31. London: Routledge.

Baker, F.A. (2013d). An investigation of the sociocultural factors impacting on the therapeutic songwriting process. *Nordic Journal of Music Therapy,* 23(2), 123–51.

Baker, F.A. (2015a). *Therapeutic songwriting: developments in theory, methods and practice.* London: Palgrave MacMillan.

Baker, F.A. (2015b). What about the music? Music therapists' perspectives of the role of music in the therapeutic songwriting process. *Psychology of Music,* 43(1), 122–39.

Baker, F.A., & Ballantyne, J. (2013). "You've got to accentuate the positive": group songwriting to promote a life of enjoyment, engagement, and meaning in aging Australians. *Nordic Journal of Music Therapy,* 22, 7–24.

Baker, F., Dingle, G., & Gleadhill, L. (2012). "Must be the ganja" (Eminem, 2009): Rap music in drug and alcohol rehabilitation. In: S. Hadley & G. Yancey (Eds.) *Therapeutic uses of rap music,* pp. 319–34. London: Routledge.

Baker, F., Kennelly, J., & Tamplin, J. (2005a). Song writing to explore identity change/sense of self/self concept following traumatic brain injury. In: F. Baker & T. Wigram (Eds.) *Song writing methods, techniques and clinical applications for music therapy clinicians, educators and students*, pp. 116–33. London: Jessica Kingsley Publishers.

Baker, F., Kennelly, J., & Tamplin, J. (2005b). Themes in songs written by clients with traumatic brain injury: differences across the lifespan. *Australian Journal of Music Therapy*, 16, 25–42.

Baker, F., Kennelly, J., & Tamplin, J. (2005c). Themes within songs written by people with traumatic brain injury: gender differences. *Journal of Music Therapy*, 42, 111–22.

Baker, F.A., & MacDonald, R.A.R. (2013a). Flow, identity, achievement, satisfaction and ownership during therapeutic songwriting experiences with university students and retirees *Musicae Scientiae*, 17, 129–44.

Baker, F.A., & MacDonald, R.A.R. (2013b). Students' and retirees' experiences of creating personally meaningful songs within a therapeutic context. *Arts and Health*, 35(1), 67–82.

Baker, F. & Tamplin, J. (2006). *Music therapy in neurorehabilitation: a clinician's manual.* London: Jessica Kingsley Publishers.

Baker, F., Wigram, T., Stott, D., & McFerran, K. (2008). Therapeutic songwriting in music therapy: Part 1. Who are the therapists, who are the clients, and why is songwriting used? *Nordic Journal of Music Therapy*, 17, 105–23.

Baker, F., Wigram, T., Stott, D., & McFerran, K. (2009). Therapeutic songwriting in music therapy: comparing the literature with practice across diverse populations. *Nordic Journal of Music Therapy*, 18, 32–56.

Bruner, J. (1986). *Actual minds, possible worlds.* Cambridge, MA: Harvard University Press.

Bruscia, K.E. (1998). *Defining music therapy*, 2nd edn. Gilsum, NH : Barcelona Publishers.

Chambers, K. (2002). *Not pretty enough. Barricades and brickwalls.* Burbank, CA: Warner Bros.

Corbin, J., & Strauss, A. (2008). *Basics of qualitative research*, 3rd edn. Los Angeles, CA: Sage.

Cordobés, T.K. (1997). Group songwriting as a method for developing group cohesion for HIV-seropositive adult patients with depression. *Journal of Music Therapy*, 34, 46–67.

Csikszentmihalyi, M. (1998). *Finding flow: the psychology of engagement with everyday life.* New York, NY: Basic Books

Dalton, T.A., & Krout, R.E. (2006). The grief song-writing process with bereaved adolescents: an integrated grief model and music therapy protocol. *Music Therapy Perspectives*, 24, 94–107.

Davies, E. (2005). You ask me why I'm singing: song-creating with children and parents in child and family psychiatry. In: F. Baker & T. Wigram (Eds.) *Song writing methods, techniques and clinical applications for music therapy clinicians, educators and students*, pp. 45–67. London: Jessica Kingsley.

Day, T., Baker, F., & Darlington, Y. (2009a). Participants' experiences of the song writing process and the on-going meaning of their song creations following completion of a music therapy program. *Nordic Journal of Music Therapy*, 18, 133–49.

Day, T., Baker, F., & Darlington, Y. (2009b). Beyond the therapy room: client experiences of 'going public' with song creations. *British Journal of Music Therapy*, 23, 19–26.

Derrington, P. (2005). Teenagers and songwriting: Supporting students in a mainstream secondary school. In: F. Baker & T. Wigram (Eds.) *Song writing methods, techniques and clinical applications for music therapy clinicians, educators and students*, pp. 71–85. London: Jessica Kingsley.

Fekaris, D., & Perren, F. (1978). I will survive [Gloria Gaynor]. On *I will survive: the anthology [compact disc]*. London: Polydor (1998).

Grocke, D., Bloch, S., & Castle, D. (2009). The effect of group music therapy on quality of life for participants living with a severe and enduring mental illness. *Journal of Music Therapy*, 46, 90–104.

Hann, N. (1977). *Coping and defending: processes of self-environment organization.* New York: Academic Press.

Hinkebein, J.H., & Stucky, R.C. (2007). Coping with traumatic brain injury: existential challenges and managing hope. In: E. Martz & H. Livneh (Eds.) *Coping with chronic illness and disability: theoretical, empirical, and clinical aspects,* pp. 389–409. New York: Springer.

Kennelly, J. (1999). Don't give us: providing music therapy to an adolescent boy in the bone marrow transplant unit. In: R.R. Pratt & D. Erdonmez Grocke (Eds.) *Music medicine 3,* pp. 228–35. Melbourne: University of Melbourne Press.

Ledger, A. (2001). Song parody for adolescents with cancer. *Australian Journal of Music Therapy,* 12, 21–7.

MacDonald, R. A. R. (2013). Music, health, and well-being: a review. *International Journal of Qualitative Studies on Health and Well-being,* 8, 10.3402/qhw.v8io.20635. http://doi.org/10.3402/qhw.v8io.20635.

MacDonald, R.A.R., Hargreaves, D.J., & Miell, D. (Eds.) (2002). *Musical identities.* New York: Oxford University Press.

MacDonald, R.A.R., Kreutz, G., & Mitchell, L.A. (Eds.) (2012). *Music, health and wellbeing.* Oxford: Oxford University Press.

MacDonald, S., & Viega, M. (2011). Hear our voices: a music therapy songwriting program and the message of the Little Saints through the medium of rap. In: S. Hadley & G. Yancey (Eds.) *Therapeutic uses of rap music,* pp. 153–71. London: Routledge.

MacDonald, R.A.R, & Wilson, G.B. in press. Billy Connolly, Daniel Barenboim, Willie Wonka, Jazz Bastards and the universality of improvisation. In: G. Lewis & B. Piekut (Eds.) *Oxford handbook of critical improvisation studies.* New York: Oxford University Press.

Mayers, K.S. (1995). Songwriting as a way to decrease anxiety and distress in traumatized children. *The Arts in Psychotherapy,* 22, 495–8.

McFerran, K., Baker, F., Patton, G.C., & Sawyer, S.M. (2006). A retrospective lyrical analysis of songs written by adolescent girls with disordered eating. *European Eating Disorder Review,* 14, 397–403.

Neimeyer, R.A. (2000). *Lessons of loss: a guide to coping.* Clayton South: Centre for Grief Education.

O'Brien, E. (2006). Opera therapy: creating and performing a new work with cancer patients and professional singers. *Nordic Journal of Music Therapy,* 15, 82–96.

O'Grady, L. (2009). The therapeutic potentials of creating and performing music with women in prison: a qualitative case study. Doctoral thesis, University of Melbourne.

Pennebaker, J.W., Mayne, T.J., & Francis, M.E. (1997). Linguistic predictors of adaptive bereavement. *Journal of Personality and Social Psychology,* 72, 863–71.

Pothoulaki, M., MacDonald, R.A.R., & Flowers, P. (2012). An interpretative phenomenological analysis of an improvisational music therapy program for cancer patients. *Journal of Music Therapy,* 49, 45–67.

Roberts, M. (2006). I want to play and sing my story: home-based songwriting for bereaved children and adolescents. *Australian Journal of Music Therapy,* 17, 18–34.

Roberts, M. (2008). A content analysis of song lyrics written by bereaved pre-adolescent (7–12 year old) children during individual music therapy. Master of Music, Dissertation, University of Melbourne.

Rolvsjord, R. (2005). Collaborations on songwriting with clients with mental health problems. In: F. Baker & T. Wigram (Eds.) *Song writing methods, techniques and clinical applications for music therapy clinicians, educators and students,* pp. 97–115. London: Jessica Kingsley.

Roos, S., & Neimeyer, R.A. (2007). Reauthoring the self: chronic sorrow and post traumatic stress following the onset of CID. In: E. Martz & H. Livneh (Eds.) *Coping with chronic illness and disability: theoretical, empirical, and clinical aspects*, pp. 89–106. New York: Springer.

Silverman, M.J. (2003). Contingency songwriting to reduce combativeness and non-cooperation in a client with schizophrenia: a case study. *The Arts in Psychotherapy*, 30, 25–33.

Soshensky, R. (2011). Everybody is a star: recording, performing, and community music therapy. *Music Therapy Perspectives*, 29, 23–30.

Tamplin, J. (2006). Song collage technique: a new approach to songwriting. *Nordic Journal of Music Therapy*, 15, 177–90.

Vander Kooij, C. (2009). Recovery themes in songs written by adults living with serious mental illnesses. *Canadian Journal of Music Therapy*, 15, 37–58.

Viega, M. (2012). *Loving me and my butterfly wings: a study of hip-hop songs written by adolescents in music therapy*. Doctoral Dissertation, Temple University, Philadelphia.

Wallis, J., Burns, J., & Capdevila, R. (2011). What is narrative therapy and what is it not? The usefulness of Q methodology to explore accounts of White and Epston's (1990) approach to narrative therapy. *Clinical Psychology and Psychotherapy*, 18, 486–97.

Wigram T. & Baker, F. (2005). Introduction: song writing as therapy. In: F. Baker & T. Wigram (Eds.) *Song writing methods, techniques and clinical applications for music therapy clinicians, educators and students*, pp. 1–23. London: Jessica Kingsley.

Wilson, G.B., & MacDonald, R.A.R. (2012). The sign of silence: negotiating musical identities in an improvising ensemble. *Psychology of Music*, 40, 558–73.

CHAPTER 25

STAYING ONE STEP AHEAD?

The Self-Identity of Japanese Concert Promoters

MARTIN CLOONAN

25.1 INTRODUCTION

THIS chapter is concerned with the self-identities of a key, but often ignored, group within the music industries—concert promoters. In particular, it seeks to broaden existing research in to concert promoters beyond its current Anglophone basis by examining the self-identities of Japanese promoters. Drawing on interviews conducted with concert promoters in Tokyo and Osaka during 2011, it argues that their promotional practices and ideologies illustrate the continuing importance of live music as a site of "the local" within popular music. It further suggests that live music practices serve to reinforce local identities in a global era. As Simon Frith (2010) has noted "Live music has to happen somewhere" and, as Brennan & Webster (2011) have shown, promoters play key roles in determining where there somewhere is and what happens to audiences when they get there. Promoters thus emerge as key figures in the live music experience and this chapter seeks to add to existing accounts of concert promotion both from within academia (Frith, 2007; Cloonan, 2012) and promoters themselves (Coupe, 2003; Chugg, 2011).

The chapter falls in to four parts. The first notes the growth of live music as an economic force and the growing academic interest in the area. The second part examines the role of promoters before the article goes on to situate the Japanese music industries in a global context. The fourth, and major, part of the article reports field work findings. It concludes with some thoughts about the continuing importance of the "local" in an era too often casually assumed to be one of globalization. In doing so it also seeks to shed light on the self-identities of a key group within the music industries.

25.2 THE RISE OF LIVE MUSIC

The decline of the economic value recording sector of the music industries has coincided with a surge in the value of live music. In the UK analysis by the songwriters' collecting agency PRS for Music found that in 2008 the value of live music in the UK exceeded that of recorded music for the first time in modern times, with the gap widening each year between, 2009 and, 2011 (Page & Carey, 2009, 2010, 2011; PRS for Music, 2012). Meanwhile Japan has witnessed a surge in live music events such as festivals (Schwartz, 2010b) and its market has been subject to investment by the world's leading concert promoter, Live Nation (Live Nation, 2012).

By 2011 when research for this chapter took place, it was possible to argue that the most important music company in the world was no longer a record company, but Live Nation Entertainment. This events company promotes a host of major concerts across the globe and owns the world's biggest ticket agency, Ticketmaster, as well as numerous venues. Importantly, the emergence of Live Nation as a global force arguably marks a new stage in the development of a live music industry, which has become increasingly transnational. While hitherto concert promotion has been largely national or regional, consumers of live popular music may now be getting used to multinational promoters in the same way that they came to take multinational record companies for granted.

Academic study of the live music sector has been slow to develop. However this is also changing in a period which, according to Holt (2010, p. 243) has witnessed "new economic centrality of live music." Perhaps the strongest manifestation of academic interest in the live music sector thus far has been the project undertaken by a team at the Universities of Edinburgh and Glasgow (of which I was a part) which sought to develop an analysis of the development of the live music sector in the UK from, 1950 to the present.[1] The world's first live music conference was held under the auspices of this project in spring, 2011 and resulted in a special edition of the journal *Arts Marketing* (1(2), 2011) and *Social Semiotics* (22(5), 2012).

While these developments are welcome, most research thus far has emerged from Anglophone areas. In addition there is still comparatively little research specifically on the activities and outlooks of concert promoters, especially outside the Anglophone world. It is with all this in mind that I sought to broaden existing analysis by examining promotional practices within the world's second largest music market—Japan.[2] This will be returned to in part three, but first it is necessary to look examine broader promotional practice.

---

[1] see www.gla.ac.uk/schools/cca/research/music/projectsandnetworks/livemusicproject/ and Frith, Brennan, Cloonan, & Webster (2013).

[2] Japan is the second largest market in the world for both live and recorded music. See, for example, Live Nation (2012) and Yasu (2013).

25.3 A BRIEF INTRODUCTION TO PROMOTIONAL PRACTICE

Concert promoters have been defined by Keith Negus (1992, p. 130) as the person or organization responsible for tasks such as "hiring venues, arranging stages, sorting out public address systems and lighting, employing caterers and security personnel, advertising the show and coordinating the sale of tickets." To this we can also add hiring the act, either via an agent or manager. So promoters can be seen as the individuals or organizations that book acts and venues, publicize shows, arrange the selling of tickets, produce the show, and, all being well, draw profits from these actions.

In reality, this rather simplistic model belies a myriad of different promotional practices and relationships within which promoters can be involved. Some promoters own the venues where they put shows on, others hire venues. Many do both. Promoters may work with other promoters to put on shows in cases where, for example, the other promoter has specialist local knowledge and/or can help the share the risk. Tickets are often sold via ticket agencies and/or book offices. Publicity for shows will vary, as will the amount of work involved in producing shows. Profits may or may not be made. Frith et al. (2013) posit three types of promoters—enthusiasts who put on music they love without necessarily seeking profits; state-funded, who use public money to stage events for the public good, which might not otherwise get funded, and commercial, who use live events to make a living.[3] While such typologies were not directly examined during this research, they form a backdrop to the discussion of Japanese promotional practice.

Meanwhile, whatever their exact involvement, promoters are at the heart of the business of live music. Importantly, promoters spend a great deal of time speculating about what *other* people will think about the shows they are planning—what they will be willing to pay, what they might think of the venue, the acts, and so on. In this sense, promoter's self-identities are wrapped up in other people's musical identities. They have to second guess what the public wants. This is not without its hazards and, in terms of their self-identities, previous research (Cloonan, 2012) has suggested that promoters of all sorts exhibit certain characteristics prime amongst which is a conception of themselves as risk takers selling a unique experience. While this can be overstated (not least by promoters themselves), the promotion of live music can be seen as an inherently risky business. Any promoter is only as good as their last show and, unlike record companies, they do not share in the spoils of the intellectual copyright of the artists they employ. Their geographical location is also likely to be more important than it may be for record labels and it was with such thoughts in mind that Japanese promotional practice was examined.

---

[3] For slight variations on this model see Brennan & Webster (2011) and Cloonan (2012).

25.4 LOCATING JAPAN

As noted above, Japan is the second largest music market in the world. In, 2011 the Japanese live music market was reported to be worth $US 1.5 billion annually (Schwartz, 2012) and the country had previously been described as being "the most valuable physical-music market in the world" (Schwartz, 2010a). This market remains a highly specialized one where historically domestic acts have tended to dominate (DeLauney, 1995, p. 206) and enjoy levels of success which is rarely transported to the outside world. Tales of Japanese "particularism" are legion, especially within literature from business studies[4] and form another backdrop to this research. Previous research has stressed factors such as the importance of lyrics to Japanese fans (DeLauney, 1995, pp. 220–2), Japanese business culture (Ford & Honeycutt, 1992, pp. 27–8), the relative importance of television for breaking international acts (Cogan & Cogan, 2007, p. 73) and the importance of tying music in to other products such as film and television in order to facilitate success (Asai, 2008, p. 481). The Japanese music market has also been one that has been to have sometimes bucked broader trends. For example, in the 1990s it was reported that the Japanese market for singles was growing at the same time that it was declining in the west (Asai, 2008, p. 205) and in 2013 it was reported that while in the US 34% of music sales were physical in Japan the figure was 80% (Yasu, 2103).

It has also long been noted that Japan's music market has become increasingly nationalistic in terms of its consumption of music and one characteristic of the country has been a constant ebbing and flowing of interest in western culture. Wade (2005, pp. 131–54) charts this in relation to music and cites an increasingly inward looking atmosphere in the contemporary era (ibid). One example of this has been the neo-nationalist movement within the country's contemporary music scene (Herd, 1989). In the 1990s it was noted that, having grown up in a country of some affluence, Japanese youth were becoming less deferential to the west (De Launey, 1995, p. 202). Its music market was dominated by domestic content, with the amount of western music consumed declining from the 1980s onward (De Launey, 1995, pp. 203–4), with the trend perhaps beginning in 1967 (De Launey, 1995, p. 206).

Local business practices are also apparent within music. Two examples—alcohol sales and gig times—serve to highlight how Japanese promotional practice blends global and national cultures and practices. In many western countries, takings from the sale of alcohol within venues form a key part of the gig economy and promoters, and/or venue owners will routinely assume a certain level of consumption. For example, the live music scene in Sydney has long been seen as being closely associated with alcohol consumption (Homan, 2000). However, this is not the case in Japan where alcohol consumption cannot be so routinely assumed. One result is the routine practice at Japanese gigs of

---

[4] See, for example, De Launey (1995), Ford & Honeycutt (1992), and Johnston & Selsky (2006). The latter attempt to explain this historically and suggest that paradox may be a useful analytical tool here.

concert attendees having to buy a drinks token on entry to venues. In 2011 the tokens generally cost around 500 Yen (approximately US $5) and all audience members were obliged to buy one. If alcohol consumption cannot be guaranteed, then this has implications for the economics of gigs which will be examined further below.

Gigs by international artists also tend to start and finish comparatively early. My fieldwork included attending shows in Tokyo and Osaka by Scottish band Belle and Sebastian. On both occasions they were on stage at 7 p.m., somewhat early by western standards. In Tokyo this was attributed to that fact that many gig goers will have to travel a long way across the city to get home, most public transport does not run all night and taxis are prohibitively expensive. Support bands are rare for international acts and as ticket prices tend to be expensive (in the region of US $75). Another example of "Japanese exceptionalism" is the system of Music House venues which is explored later.

Such examples are not meant to highlight Japanese exoticism, but to show how important local practices can shape the very experience of live music and the outlooks of those promoting it. Local regulations and customs obviously affect the climate for gigs and the savvy promoter needs to take this in to account. This will also be returned to below. Here is it suffice to re-iterate that live music must happen somewhere and things such as the culture, regulatory regime and business practices of that somewhere can have major impacts on promotional practice and the self-identities of those involved in it, to which I now turn.

25.4.1 Methodology

In February and March 2011 I visited Tokyo and Osaka to carry out field work. This was preceded by a visit to London to interview the UK office of Smash, one of Japan's leading concert promoters.[5] The research aimed to ascertain the attitudes of Japanese promoters and the extent to which they considered themselves to be acting in either local or global markets. I was keen to see the extent to which the self-identities adopted UK concert promoters (Cloonan, 2012) and which had been found elsewhere (Coupe, 2003; Chugg, 2011) were replicated in Japan. While the visit included only two cities, a number of promoters interviewed promoted across the country.

The prime methodology was that of face-to-face semi-structured interviews. A total of 10 promoters were interviewed face-to-face and another provided information by email (see Appendix 1). I interviewed a range of promoters including those who promoted both festivals and shows which attracting over 10,000 people, and those promoting in local clubs. I also had a number of informal conversations with Japanese music industries' personnel during my stay and was able to attend four gigs.[6] Questions

[5] Alongside numerous gigs in cities such as Tokyo and Osaka, Smash promotes Japan's largest music festival, Fuji Rock. See www.smash-jpn.com/index.php.
[6] These were Belle and Sebastian (Namba Hatch, Oaska, 3 March, 2011 and Studio Coast, Tokyo, 4 March), Japanese bands Merengue and Kicel (Liquid Room, Tokyo , 5 March) and a multi-band event (Lush , Tokyo, 6 March) promoted by Japonicus (see later).

focussed on promoters' self-perceptions and their view of the status and location of the Japanese live music market. Interviewees were generally from organizations whose main business was in promoting international, rather than Japanese, acts. Thus, they came from a commercial subsection of the overall live industry on Japan. One limitation of the research was my inability to speak Japanese, although previous research on the Japanese music sector has been undertaken under similar circumstances (Negus, 1999). In addition, I compensated to some extent by sending interviewees (all of whom spoke English) transcripts of the interviews for verification and further comments. While the interviews were semi-structured and the conversations ranged far and wide, all interviewees were asked similar questions and, as will now be shown, a number of key themes emerged.

25.5 Japanese promoters

It is possible to break down the respondents' responses in to two broad, overlapping, areas—those of concert promoting in general and those particularly germane to Japan. Both provide insights in to Japanese concert promoter's self-identities and will be dealt with in turn here.

25.5.1 General characteristics of promoting

Industrially promoters are located at the heart of facilitating the live music experience. It is they who have to deal with artists and/or their representatives (such as managers and agents), venues and audiences. Their daily routine involves thinking about where a gig will work, how much will be charged, how it will be marketed, how tickets will be sold and distributed, and how the show will actually be produced on the night. While over time these processes can become something of a routine, at all levels of the live music industry the promoter is the nexus for the live music event. They have unique oversight of the whole process of the gig from inception through to execution and afterwards. This centrality means that an understanding promoter's self-identities can provide key insights in to that part of the music industries that is increasingly economically dominant across the globe.

My research in to Japanese promoters' self-identities began via an exploration of what they though made a good promoter as I was keen to discover what qualities they valued in others. The range of responses received here revealed the ways in which promoters have to be adept at dealing with a range of third parties. Here, the importance is to see themselves as others might seem them and to develop relationships with artists, their representatives, and audiences. Naoki Shimizu, is the CEO of the Creativeman, one of

Japan's leading promotions companies.[7] He argued that what was needed was "an understanding of the average member of the audience and staying one step ahead of them" (Shimizu, interview, 2011). Importantly, he said that this had to be *one* step and no more. Audiences, he believed, had to be led gently to new experiences. Here, Shimizu cited festivals where he had been inspired to start the Summer Sonic festival—held simultaneously in Chiba (approximately 20 miles from Tokyo) and Osaka each year since 2000—after having himself visited numerous international festivals. His International PR/Marketing Manager, Onta Shiroh Kawaguchi (interviewed 2011), cited festivals themselves as an example of staying ahead of the audience as historically they were comparatively rare in Japan but had become very popular since the introduction of the Fuji Rock festival in 1997. Another innovation, claimed by in interview by both Smash and Creativeman, was being the first to put on gigs at which the audience stood up, rather than being seated.

> The theme of thinking about audience was also addressed by the London representatives of Smash, the other major promoter of international acts. Referring to its CEO, Masahiro Hidaka, Jason Mayall of Smash UK said that he had been successful because: (He has) always been: number one, take care of the audience … give them a decent venue, a good venue that's right for the band … so you don't rip them off … you give the best environment … So you're really taking care of the audience.
>
> Mayall, Interview, 2011.

Thus, again, promoters' sense of self was bound up in imaging how it might feel to be a member of the audience. Such considerations soon led on to consideration of artists, especially at festivals, where the construction of line-ups was held to be a key element of promotional practice. Shimizu (interview, 2011) was clear that this was the first thing he thought of for each year's Summer Sonic. This view was echoed by Mayuri Akama, DJ and owner of the Metamorphose festival who stated simply that "a strong line up is the most important" (interview, 2011). While this might appear to be a universal theme, there were local nuances such as the need to consider local audiences' tastes and the fact that, as Mayuri pointed out, it might take two or three years of negotiations before international acts became available for a festival. However, she also noted that it was getting increasingly hard to book bigger acts as the festival market had internationalized and there was now competition across the globe to attract the best acts that "everyone wants to book for their festival" (Mayuri, interview, 2011). As soon as one year's festival was finished, booking for the following year began. Such views were echoed by Shimizu who also noted the increasing internationalization of the festivals, where many of the bigger

---

[7] Creativeman promote gigs in Tokyo and other places as well as the annual Summer Sonic festival. See www.creativeman.co.jp/english.

acts are booked well in advance, had led to varying degrees of exclusivity. Thus, to act locally, promoters had to think globally.

In fact, in common with the rest of the live music market, the Japanese festival market has been subject to boom and slump. Thus, it was reported in the mid-2000s that they were booming, but might have peaked (McClure, 2006), that they were thriving in 2010 (Schwartz, 2010b), but struggling in 2011 (Schwartz, 2011), especially in the wake of the tsunami of 11 March 2011. Some recovery was reported in 2012, but with the caveat that spending at festivals might detract from spending on live music more broadly (Schwartz, 2012). However, it is clear that festivals remain a vital part of the Japanese live music ecology and further evidence of this was provided when Live Nation specifically cited trying to develop this market as one of its reasons for developing a partnership with Creativeman (Live Nation, 2012). Seemingly, no self-respecting promoter can now afford *not* to have a festival.

Englishman Daniel Robson promotes a range of club nights and gigs, including a series known as Bad Noise. He was also clear that, when constructing a bill, he began with the headliner and then constructed the rest of the bill around them (Robson, interview, 2011). But, once again, consideration of what worked as aesthetically and commercially could not be detached from considerations of others. As Mayall (interview, 2011) explained:

> … (promoters need) to take care of the audience, you need to put on a good line-up; sometimes that line-up is about putting on the names that draw people … what draws people to a festival is the names are very important … what makes your money, or what loses you money is how good your headliners are.

Once headliners were confirmed—and a certain audience level effectively guaranteed—promoters felt free to take more risks with acts that, while artistically may be of a high standard, may not necessarily be immediately appealing to a large audience. Mayall (interview, 2011) also believed that Smash's and its Fuji Rock festival had prospered: "because we have the reputation for breaking new ground, presenting new artists, and giving you the cream of the crop."

Others considered the artists. Here, promoters cited the importance of a good relationship with artists and/or their representatives as being an essential component of a good promoter. Thus, Koya Yasui of Smash West (Osaka) suggested that ideally, a promoter should love the artists they work with. The company's Tokyo representative, John Moylett (interview, 2011), argued that a promoter needed "a love of music and belief in the music you wish to promote. It is important to have the integrity and that belief, as often you will be offered an artist you know can make money but isn't for you."

Independent promoter and Pvine Record company employee, Koki Yahata, had a personal philosophy, whereby while he believed that he had to consider the needs of the artist first, "I try to find some sort of middle ground where I can satisfy both the artist and the audience in terms of, for instance, the turn out" (Yahata, interview, 2011). He emphasized the importance of thinking long term, so that a successful show increased the likelihood of both artist and audience returning. Choosing the right venue was important here as "It's important that people want to come back" (ibid).

Daniel Robson's Bad Noise nights sometimes involve putting on new bands with whom audiences may not be familiar. Here, the assessment of a successful night was one after which audience members would take the view that: "I had a good time last time I didn't know any of the bands, so next time I'll take a chance" (Robson, interview, 2011). Shugo Komiyama (interviewed 2011), owner of the Japonicus promotions company,[8] has also founded a Radical Music Network. His promotional activities focus on acts who have a social message. He was aware of attracting three different kinds of audiences to his (usually multiple line-up) shows—those who came for particular artists, those coming because it was a Japonicus show, and those coming out of curiosity. Overall, Japanese promoters saw that they had to balance the needs of artists and audiences. Their self-identity was clearly that of mediators trying to balance the needs of artists with the need to attract audiences.

The promoters' self-identity entailed other characteristics. Here, previous research in the UK (Cloonan, 2012) suggested that promoters self-identify as gamblers. This was replicated, and perhaps exacerbated, in Japan. Shimizu (interview, 2011) agreed that promotion was like gambling and suggested that it was particularly risky in Japan where promoters were generally less likely than some of their western counterparts to own their own venues. Shogo Komiyama, saw gambling as an inevitable part of the job—"If you don't take risks you cannot do anything" (interview, 2011). Smash's John Moylett (interview, 2011) noted that "It is a high risk business, It is very important to know the market and taste of the audience, as well as see the quality of the artist's live performance."

One aspect of gambling that recurred in interviews was that of challenging conventional practice, with some promoters clearly viewing themselves as people who did this. For Takeshi Sugisawa, Booking Manager at Tokyo's Liquid Room venue, gambling was something that could only take place once a venue had built a reputation. Thus, introducing new things had to be done incrementally and spotting emerging bands was deemed to be a key part of a booker's job. Daniel Robson explained that Bad Noise nights might use relatively down-market venues and charge less than the usual rate for admission. Often he did not sell tickets in advance, something that involved further gambling as "until you open the doors you've no idea whether anyone is going to show up" (Robson, interview, 2011). However, Koya Yasui of Smash West suggested that if a promoter failed in their gambles, then it was their own fault for misjudging the likelihood of success. Identifying oneself as a gambler did not mean identifying oneself being reckless.

Depending on what position a promoter occupies within the promotional world, self-identification as a gambler could also lead to certain sorts of business attitudes. Here, a crucial difference might be whether the motivation was love of the music or the need to make money. Mirroring Frith et al.'s (2013) distinction between commercial promoters and enthusiasts, Shogo Komiyama suggested that there are two types of promoters. The first consists of "pirates" whose prime interest is making money and building

---

[8] www.japonicus.com

empires—"If they have to kill, they will kill" (interview, 2011). The other sort, were those motivated by the music itself (and its potential for good)—"promoters like me and we call us the stupid guys" (interview, 2011). Importantly, the second category can be largely driven their own tastes, while the former constantly has to consider the tastes of *others*, as to put on gigs consisting of only acts one likes is to severely limit the market and thus money-making potential. It may even be the case that enthusiast promoters' self-identify is more aligned to the artists, while commercial promoters *have* to identify more with audiences.

The general economic climate also affected the extent—and type—of gambling that might take place. Within the record industry it is well-established that during economic recessions major record companies will tend to play safe by, for example, releasing compilations of previous hits, rather than new material. In live music the equivalent may be the practice of touring "classic" albums. In both cases, risk is minimized by the knowledge that a market already exists. Such playing safe was apparent within Japanese promotional practice with a common perception amongst interviewees that the global recession was taking its toll. Koki Yahata (interview, 2011) suggested that many promoters were playing safe and not taking the risks necessary to educate audiences. This affected not only Japanese acts, but also those wishing to tour the country as Moylett (interview, 2011) argued that: "The market is very soft for new up and coming artists to come and play club tours … for new artists it is very difficult to get interest unless they have huge success in their home countries." Daniel Robson (interview, 2011) argued that: "it's kind of a self-cannibalising industry at the moment. Because no one's really doing anything that is outright to support artists. It's all to support themselves." He believed that, in the wake of the global financial crisis, many in the live sector were playing it *extremely* safe and notions of safeness are explored further later.

One manifestation of this was that promoters were increasingly reluctant to promote shows by international acts outside of the main cities of Tokyo and Osaka. Several promoters referred to such acts now playing fewer cities and fewer shows. Yasui (interview, 2011) suggested that international bands now played a maximum of three cities, whereas they had previously played five or more. Yahata (interview, 2011) commented that: "Everything is like centred around Tokyo these days. So sometimes touring bands from the US or Europe only play the shows in Tokyo because it won't be really profitable at all by playing shows in Osaka and Nagoya." Yasui shared this view and attributed declining ticket sales to an over-supply of shows, thus reflecting the perennial concern about the amount of competition for consumers' leisure spending. However, it should be noted that there have also been criticisms of international acts who do not take the time to try and penetrate the Japanese market (De Launey, 1995, pp. 216 and 223; McClure, 2006).

Amongst my interviewees, Shogo Komiyama, of Japonicus Productions stood out. Of mixed Japanese and Argentinian heritage, following a successful business career, he has dedicated himself to provide alternative music events across Japan. This has included taking a number of Latin-American acts to Japan, such as Tudos Tus Meurtos and Manu

Chao. While Komiyama also identified with promotion being seen as a form of gambling, he also thought that it was less risky for him now that "I know how to do it." Thus, he minimized any losses and also did things like hiring the cheapest possible transport if he was promoting touring acts (interview, 2011). He was also particularly proud that he would try and arrange shows in any town in Japan to which he was invited as part of what he called a "revolution" "because we are doing something that nobody else is doing … We are swimming against the current" (interview, 2011). He explained that his Latino part meant that he had to show that music was about more than money (interview, 2011). Thus, altruism emerged as a key part of his self-identity.

Overall, the promoters believed that they needed to cultivate audiences, to try and lead them in to new areas, but minimize risks. These self-identifying characteristics of promoters replicated findings elsewhere (Coupe, 2003; Chugg, 2011; Cloonan, 2013). However, there were also areas of promotional practice that were particular to Japan, to which I now turn.

25.5.2 Promoting in Japan

Issues that arose in interview, which appeared particularly germane to Japan, can be divided in to two overlapping areas—those relating to business practices, and others relating to audiences.

The well-known success of Japanese electronics companies, such as Sony and Hitachi raises interesting questions about whether such models might provide a template for the country's promoters, encouraging them to enter the international market and challenge western promoters such as the US-based Live Nation and AEG.[9] Questions about this brought mixed views, with promoters such as Takeshi Sugisawa believing that this might happen, while Jonny Moylett and Koya Yasui being more skeptical. Robson (interview, 2011) summed up the latter view:

> I don't see it. I think the Japanese music industry in general is not very hungry for overseas success particularly … in general it's a huge market (and so does not see a need to export) … It doesn't feel it needs (to go international). It's got a language that nobody else speaks and it's got working practices that nobody else, literally nobody else, has used since the fifties … so I think a lot of Japanese companies freak out at the idea of working with companies that wouldn't understand their working practices. Definitely that's a big part of it. And the language barrier. And we're making enough money already so why bother you know? It's risky.

However, in reality international cooperation and expansion is already taking place. For example Creativeman provided production for U2's Japanese shows, promoted by Live Nation, in, 2011. This relationship was further cemented in, 2012 with the formation

---

[9] As noted earlier, Live Nation is the world's largest concert promoter. AEG is its nearest rival.

of Live Nation Japan as a joint venture between the two companies (Live Nation, 2012). Moreover, in addition to attracting inward investment from international promoters, Japanese promoters have made incursions into the international market, especially in southeast Asia. Mayuri Akama having her own club in Bali is just one example of this. In addition, Creativeman have considered promoting in other Asian cities, such as Shanghai and Taipei. Shimizu (interview, 2011) argued that this was the future—"My thinking now is not as Japan, but as Asia. Book in the big cities. That's my vision." He believed that the need was for a Japanese band to break in to a new territory to help enable this and suggested that dance—where language matters less—might be at the forefront of this. Koki Yahata also spoke of trying to work more in other Asian countries. However, it was also clear that the financial rewards of doing so must be worthwhile as Onta Kawaguchi warned that a combination bad exchange rates and low consumer spending power had made it too difficult for Creativeman to promote in China when domestic shows might prove to be much more lucrative. For him the answer was to attract Chinese visitors to Summer Sonic.

One obviously uniquely Japanese issue was the country's geographical location and its remoteness from the homes of Anglo-American music was referred to by a number of interviewees who noted that this meant that promoting international acts from Europe and the United States was necessarily expensive. It simply costs a lot of money to get most international acts to Japan. One common result was relatively high ticket prices for gigs. As Koya Yasui (interview, 2011) noted: "You know it's expensive for the travel cost so it's naturally the ticket price is high … so you can't do anything about it." In addition, Japan's reputation as an affluent nation means that some international acts see the potential to try and earn high fees when playing the country and some promoters commented that they believed acts they dealt with had raised their usual fees on being offered the chance to tour.

The question of fees was particularly felt in one key area of music promotion where Japan has shared broader international trends—the rise of festivals. While taking time to establish in Japan, festivals are now a key part of the Japanese live music industry's annual cycle. Onta Kawaguchi explained that for Creativeman it was initially important for their Summer Sonic festival to have a site which people from Tokyo could travel to and from in a day. This can be contrasted to Smash's Fuji Rock festival where camping had become a key part of the experience.

Takeshi Sugisawa was very aware that Japanese bands aspired to play major domestic festivals where they are guaranteed a large audience. For Koya Yasui the rise of festivals had been *the* major change in recent years to the extent that he could not imagine his company operating without a festival now. This was something of a turnaround, as Jason Mayall of Smash London said that at the time of the first Fuji Rock festival in, 1997, despite having bands such as Red Hot Chilli Peppers, Foo Fighters, The Prodigy, Green Day, and Rage Against the Machine

> the record companies in Japan, most of them said to their artists … don't do this, this is so risky, we don't have festivals in Japan, we don't have a culture of festivals, this

is wrong—don't put our artists on, we're possibly going to kill our artists' career in Japan. That has now completely swept around to the fact where festivals ... the record companies rely on them to an incredible degree now, to be either the launch pad, or the build-up to their band. In other words, now they say: let's get them on there, then next year we get them on *that* stage, and then *that* stage. And in six years they'll be headlining the main stage.

Mayall, interview, 2011, his emphasis.

The picture presented by interviewees was one where a somewhat conservative business culture had been successfully challenged by one or two promoters willing to take the risk that something that worked elsewhere could also work in Japan. Here, apparently considerable risks later bore fruit in the longer term and events which once seemed alien are now part of the Japanese live music calendar. James Smith from Smash UK explained that festivals had become particularly important in a context where, because of declining CD sales, labels had less money to invest in promotional budgets for new artists and increasingly used major festivals for promotional purposes. His colleague Koya Yasui agreed that for many new artists festivals were *the* most important promotional strategy,

Mayuri Akama of Metamorphose believed that the Japanese festival market was becoming saturated, lamenting that each year was harder, because of increased competition from other Japanese festivals and from the rise of different consumer goods. Koya Yahata also noted that many of the festivals now only Japanese artists and that it was getting harder and harder for international acts to tour successfully. Allied to this was a feeling amongst some interviewees that young Japanese fans were becomingly increasingly Japanese in their tastes, preferring domestic acts to international ones. As noted earlier such "nationalist" tastes are part of broader trends within Japan around new cultural nationalism and a lessening of interest in international music (Koizumi, 2002, p. 110).

Another key difference between Japanese and many western markets is the comparative strength of record labels, as witnessed by the strength of CD sales alluded to above. In addition, fans of English-speaking acts who do not speak English, do not visit English-language websites for information about artists. They are therefore more likely to be reliant of official channels such as record labels' sites or press sites on which the labels have influence. James Smith from Smash UK explained that.

I think, in a way, the difference between Japan and here (in the UK) is that the way the information about new music disseminates is ... here, now, people/kids don't rely on traditional channels like the record label scheduling records, doing a press campaign, magazines writing about it ... in Japan it's more dependent on: you put the label signing, agree with promoters, then get the press campaign launched, and getting previewed in the major magazines and kids reading the magazines and finding out—because they don't necessarily read the English-language blogs.

Smith, interview, 2011.

However, there were clearly limits to this and the general, worldwide, decline of CD sales had also had an impact (Marketline, 2013). Thus, Koya Yahata said that when deciding whether to promote an act, whereas 10 years ago he would simply have checked CD sales, he now tried to ascertain the general buzz around the act (mainly on the Internet). However, interviewees also felt that Japanese labels were still involved in an "old" business model, which had failed to take account of the digital revolution. Here, Yahata said that one benefit of this for artists was that some labels still offered tour support[10] to bands. However, Takeshi Sugisawa noted that labels were beginning to diversify and were looking to implement "360 degree" deals[11] with artists, which gave them income from every aspects of an artist's career.

One aspect on Japanese concerts involving international acts which may strike the outsider as usual is the lack of support acts. My visit included Belle and Sebastian shows in Tokyo and Osaka. Neither show involved a support act, something which Robson (interview, 2011) described as "totally normal." He lamented this and said that, ideally, Japanese bands should support touring international artists. He suggested that this need not involve extra costs for the promoters as "a lot of these bands would do it for free" (Robson, interview, 2011). His suspicion was that the reason for a lack of support acts for touring international acts this was that some labels helped financially to bring in international artists and were therefore reluctant to see another act (who may be from a different label) benefiting from supporting the act they had helped pay to bring in—"it's to do with that kind of it's mine mentality" (ibid). He argued that changing this would be "a major help" for local bands (ibid).

Another particularly Japanese phenomenon (or, more precisely, a Tokyo-dominant model) was that of Live Houses[12]—a range of venues that put on shows. The business practices of such venues has come under some scrutiny, especially in Tokyo where bands playing such venues generally have to a pay a fee to be on the bill. The venue itself will try and put on a very disparate bill in order to attract the widest possible range of customers. For audiences, the net effect may be that they go to see one band, then leave because they have no interest in the other bands on the bill.

Known as *noruma* the system is a variant of the ticket deal schemes that operate elsewhere (Cloonan, 2012). *Noruma* translates as "quota" (Hadfield, 2013). Generally, if bands don't sell a set number of tickets, they will be required to foot the bill themselves, to the tune of around 2000 yen ($US 20) per missing audience member. Bills of 30–40,000 yen were reported as being common (ibid). The result is that:

[10] The longstanding practice of tour support is a system whereby record companies subsidized their acts' participation in touring, in the belief that this would more than be repaid by increased record sales. The decline of record sales has severely diminished this practice.

[11] The idea of the "360-degree" deal is that the record company takes a proportion of the earnings of all an artist's income including merchandize and touring. This is in distinction to a more traditional model where record company income is limited to that generated by record sales.

[12] While the Live House phenomenon is most closely associated with Tokyo it exists in various forms across Japan. See japanmusicmarketing.com/livehouselist.htm for a list.

The path followed by many British bands, starting shambolic and then slowly honing themselves into a decent live act as they play more shows, is pretty much impossible ... unless you're well connected or have very, very, deep pockets. Instead bands practise furiously in the studio, emerging occasionally for the thrill of playing to a three-quarters-empty venue on a Wednesday evening.

ibid.

While such "pay-to-play" schemes are far from unknown elsewhere, its highly systematic use seems particular to Tokyo (ibid). However, the system is not without supporters who argue that it promotes diversity and that, without it, venues would be uneconomic and so close (Martin, 2011). Rather than being seen as a symptom of greedy promoters, *noruma* has been held to be a response to economic reality and to a system that lacks the sort of filters of quality provided by the press and radio elsewhere (ibid). It has also been noted that one result is that acoustic standards within Japanese venues are high (Martin, 2012).

However, some of the promoters interviewed resented a system that does not serve promoters' long-term interests, as it hampers the development of new talent. Robson (interview, 2011) explained that:

It's like going back in time forty, fifty years, sixty years even. It's like being stuck in the fifties. So it's basically pay to play until you get to ... a certa in level of quite a popular band it doesn't apply anymore. Small bands starting out, you have to guarantee like a certain number of tickets to get booked and ninety nine percent of the venues operate in this way. So you guarantee say twenty, roughly twenty tickets at around two thousand yen a ticket. That's a lot of money and most bands, most band members they don't want to sell the tickets to their friends you know ... Another problem is that the way the venues book the bands. The idea is to maximize turnover in a single night so nearly always five bands, nearly always starting ridiculously early while people are still stuck at work or whatever, maybe doors might open at six, six thirty, seven, and start half an hour later. And then those five bands will be as disparate as possible to ensure there's no customer crossover.

He lamented that the result was that people knew that they would end up paying a lot of money to see a friend's gig in an atmosphere that they would not enjoy. In addition, the bands who played were not necessarily the best, just those who were good at selling tickets and/or who could afford to pay to be on the bill.

So bands who have a good day job or rich parents, whatever, can play a lot of shows, and bands who don't have any money are fucked. But basically you really do end up watching a lot of rubbish bands. And there are so many good bands and they just can't, you know, progress. They can't play every night like they should do.

ibid.

Shugo Kamiyawa (interview, 2011) confirmed that bands having to sell tickets is normal and that "If they cannot sell that then they have to pay money to the venue. That's quite crazy. And I am against this you know." He thought that the average a band would have to pay to play a show would be around 30,000 yen. Smash UK's James Smith (interview, 2011) added that:

> For young bands, it's quite hard to get past those first stages—we're talking about domestic bands here, anyway—and the way bands here can go and play various shows, £50 ($ US80) and the support slots ... and at the early stage of their career it can be quite hard for Japanese bands to break through that point because there's this financial burden.

Robson noted that bands tended to be surprised when he told them that they did not have to pay to play as he generally operated on the basis of a split of the profits. He viewed change as necessary and was trying to play a part with his Bad Noise nights:

> The aim is ... to have somewhere that smaller bands can play. They don't have to pay us. We pay them and they can sort of rub shoulders with like-minded bands and grow their fan base. There's not very much of that happening but it's sort of slowly but surely other people are doing stuff like that.
>
> Robson, interview, 2011

As noted above, in Japan the role of alcohol at gigs varies considerably from the Anglo-USA model. In general, Japanese venues can expect to sell less alcohol than most European and American venues do. Because of the "relatively low alcohol consumption (by) ... young Japanese" (Martin, 2011). When this was added to an early evening start time for many gigs, this could result in a somewhat constrained atmosphere. As Robson (interview, 2011) explained:

> People aren't pissed and I think it makes a massive difference.... They haven't had a chance to get pissed because they've just got there and the fucking headliner's started already do you know what I mean? So you know, there's no force of habit even.

He noted that because bar revenues tended to be low such venues were much less likely to allow promoters to use their space for free because, unlike the UK, they could not be assured of making money from alcohol sales (Hadfield, 2013). He also believed that the reputation of the standard of the beer in many live venues also meant that large sales were unlikely. For the promoter all this added up to a situation where they had to pay high fees simply to rent a venue: "So that's one of the major challenges is putting on smaller shows especially, where the hell do you do it and how do you recoup that money?" (ibid). Thus, a combination of high fees for hiring venues and a lack of income from alcohol led to a somewhat different live music ecology to that of the Anglo-USA model. James Smith from Smash London explained that: "You don't have revenue from booze sales, basically, in Japan, so things are necessarily higher because people have to make up their costs" (Smith, interview, 2011). For promoters, the result was a music ecology within which the box office takes on added significance and income from alcohol sales less. It is simply harder to put on gigs in Tokyo than in other major cities, with the implication that promoters' identification with gambling is reinforced.

Meanwhile tales of Japanese business practices also recurred in the research, especially amongst those from outside the country. Smash London reported people tending to work longer for a company than they did in the UK, and also noted that wage differentials between the highest and lowest paid in a company tended to be smaller. They further noted that successful Japanese companies were built more like a family than customary employer-employee relationships in the west.

More broadly, certain conservatism was perceived. Robson (interview, 2011) commented that innovation was difficult as:

> You've got to really stick to your guns and you've got to make sure that in the end it works out well so that they see you were right ... Because you know business in Japan is all about trust and building relationships very slowly.

Shugo Komiyama commented that the "Japanese want to be always safe. It's it's a part of Japanese identity I would say ... They always double checking, they always you know ... Things take a lot of time here." Referring to the introduction of the Fuji Rock festival Jason Mayall of Smash UK commented of their staff that:

> In the original days, no one ... they were all against it; and even people within our office, you know, were against it. I'm not saying it was bad that they were against it, it was just that it was outside their remit, outside their comfort zone ... but they're all happy to follow. So once you've said "we're doing it, you're doing it, we're doing it," everyone does it. And they do an amazing job.
>
> Mayall, interview, 2011

Thus, overall within Japanese promotional practice it can be seen that traditional Japanese values and business cultures interacted with international trends in a number of ways. Japanese promoters work within local regulatory regimes and from a specific location with specific economic circumstances. While change was generally perceived as being incremental, it was also clear that promoters' self-identity was wrapped up in challenging convention and trying to stay a step ahead.

25.6 Conclusions

Perhaps not surprisingly, the interviews revealed that Japanese promoters face a number of both universal and local issues in their daily praxis. One of the key differences between live and recorded music is that whereas recorded music can be accessed from anywhere, live music has to take place in a location. It simply *matters* where a gig takes place. My research concerned promoters working in the approximately 15–20% of the market that it international acts. Their musings are therefore illustrative, rather than necessarily representative. Nevertheless, they reveal that such Japanese promoters deal on a daily basis with issues that are both local and international, and their self-identities are shaped by this. The savvy Japanese promoter working with international artists has to have an understanding of local audiences and of the protocols involved in bringing international artists to the country. They need to combine their own vision with perceptions of the views of others. They compete internationally for acts whose eventual performance will take place according to local rules, regulations, and business norms. Their self-identity mixes local pragmatism with international experience. Above all, they show that, for all its increasingly international nature, live music remains bound up in the local. Unless promoters appreciate this, they are unlikely to realize the self-actualization that many obviously seek. Staying one step ahead should not involve going one step beyond.

Acknowledgements

This chapter benefitted from funds provided by the Carnegie Trust for the Universities of Scotland and from internal funding from the University of Glasgow. I would like to thank both for their support. I would also like to thank all interviewees for their time and hospitality during the interviews. I remain in their debt. Special thanks are due to Ayano Onodera for her help and patience.

References

Asai, S. (2008). Firm organisation and marketing strategy in the Japanese music industry. *Popular Music*, 27(3), 473–85.

Brennan, M., & Webster, E. (2011). Why concert promoters matter. *Scottish Music Review*, 2(1), 1–25.

Chugg, M. (2011). *Hey you in the black T-shirt: the real story of the world's biggest acts.* Sydney: Pan Macmillan.

Cloonan, M. (2012). Selling the experience: the world-views of British concert promoters. *Creative Industries Journal*, 5(1–2), 151–70.

Cogan, B., & Cogan, G., (2007). Gender and authenticity in Japanese popular music: 1980–2000. *Popular Music and Society*, 29(1), 69–90.

Coupe, S. (2003). *The promoters.* Sydney: Hodder.

De Launey, G. (1995). Not so big in Japan. *Popular Music*, 14(2), 203–25.

Ford, J., & Honeycutt, E. (1992). Japanese national culture as a basis for understanding Japanese business practices. *Business Horizons*, 35(6), 27–34.

Frith, S. (2007). Live music matters. *Scottish Music Review*, 1(1), 1–17.

Frith, S. (2010). Analysing live music in the UK: findings one year into a three-year research project. *IASPM@Journal*, 1(1). Available at: www.iaspmjournal.net/index.php/IASPM_Journal/article/view/335/558 (accessed 26 February 2016).

Frith, S., Brennan, M., Cloonan, M., & Webster, E. (2013). *The history of live music in Britain, Volume 1, 1950–1967: from dance hall to the 100 club*. Farnham: Ashgate.

Hadfield, J. (2013). The pervasive curse of pay to play in Tokyo. Available at: http://livemusicexchange.org/blog/the-pervasive-curse-of-pay-to-play-in-tokyo-james-hadfield/ (accessed 29 November, 2013).

Herd, J.A. (1989). The neonationalist movement: origins of Japanese contemporary music. *Perspectives on Music*, 27(2), 118–63.

Holt, F. (2010). The economy of live music in the digital age. *European Journal of Cultural Studies*, 13(2), 243–61.

Homan, S. (2000). Losing the local: Sydney and the Oz Rock tradition. *Popular Music*, 19(1), 31–49.

Johnston, S., & Selsky, J. (2006). Duality and paradox: trust and duplicity in Japanese business practice. *Organization Studies*, 27, 183–205.

Koizumi, K. (2002). Popular music, gender and high school pupils in Japan: personal music in school and leisure sites. *Popular Music*, 21(1), 107–25.

Live Nation. (2012). Live Nation continues expansion in Asia through creation of joint venture with leading Japanese promoter Creativeman, press release, 23 February. Available at: www.prnewswire.com/news-releases/140130823.html (accessed 29 November, 2013).

McClure, S. (2006). Japan's festivals boom. *Billboard*, 7 August, 2006.

Marketline., (2013). *Music and video in Japan*. London: Marketline.

Martin, I., (2011). Cruel to be kind: does *noruma* work in bands' favor? *Japan Times*, 21 October, 2011.

Martin, I. (2012). The customer is always right, but that's what's wrong in Japan's live house scene. *Japan Times*, 30 August, 2012.

Negus, K., (1992). *Producing pop*. London: Arnold.

Negus, K. (1999). *Music genres and corporate cultures*. London: Routledge

Page, W., & Carey, C. (2009). *Adding up the music industry for 2008*. London: PRS for Music.

Page, W., & Carey, C. (2010). *Adding up the music industry for 2009*. London: PRS for Music.

Page, W., & Carey, C. (2011). *Adding up the music industry for 2010*. London: PRS for Music.

PRS for Music. (2012). *Adding up the music industry for 2011*. London: PRS for Music.

Schwartz, R., (2010a). Japan remains No.1 in physical music sales despite big drop. *Billboard*, 21 August, 2010.

Schwartz, R. (2010b). The rocking sun. *Billboard*, 21 August, 2010.

Schwartz, R. (2011). Japan recovers. *Billboard*, 20 August, 2011.

Schwartz, R. (2012). Rising sun shines of live shows. *Billboard*, 18 August, 2012.

Wade, B. (2005). *Music in Japan*. Oxford: Oxford University Press.

Yasu, M. (2013). CDs rule Japan's music market, thanks to girl groups and add-ons. *Blomberg Business Week*, 3 July, 2013.

Appendix one: List of Interviewees

Mayuri Akama, owner Metamorphose festival, Tokyo, 1 March, 2011.

Onta Shiroh Kawaguchi (International PR/Marketing) and Naoki Shimizu (CEO/President) Creativeman, Tokyo, 1 March, 2011.

Shogo Komiyama, owner, Japonicus Productions, Tokyo, 8 March, 2011.
Jason Mayall and James Smith, Smash UK, London, 18 February, 2011.
Johnny Moylett, Smash, 24 February, 2011 (via email).
Daniel Robson, independent promoter, Tokyo, 7 March, 2011.
Takeshi Sugisawa, Booking Manager, Liquid Room, Tokyo, 6 March, 2011.
Koki Yahata, Pvine Records and independent promoter, Tokyo, 2 March, 2011.
Koya Yasui, Smash West, Tokyo, 5 March, 2011.

SECTION 6

···

EDUCATION

···

CHAPTER 26

MUSICAL IDENTITY, LEARNING, AND TEACHING

SUSAN HALLAM

26.1 INTRODUCTION

THROUGHOUT our lives our identities change. They are constantly evolving as they are challenged and re-constructed based on the feedback that we receive from our interactions with others. This process is necessary to legitimize them (Schempp, Sparkes, & Templin, 1999). At any point in time, an individual may hold multiple identities depending on their current social context (Hallam, 2009). These may be complementary or contradictory. In extreme cases individuals can enact multiple identities (multiple personality disorder) each with its own characteristic moods, memories, and behavioral repertoire (Spanos, 1994). Clearly, the more closely different identities are related the greater the likelihood that the individual will be well adjusted (Beijaard, Meijer, & Verloop, 2004).

The concept of identity is relatively new. Historically, the term self-concept was used to refer to how individuals perceived and evaluated themselves in different areas of their lives. The self-system is made up of a number of self-images including those relating to self-esteem, self-efficacy, ideal selves, and possible selves, which are often context or situation specific and, which develop in interaction with our environment (Hallam, 2009). From a motivational perspective, possible selves are very important (Markus & Nurius, 1986). These are an individual's conceptions of future selves; selves that are ideal and hoped for as well as selves that are feared or dreaded. The possible selves that we hold can provide a conceptual scaffold from which we can develop, clearly important for providing a sense of direction in relation to education, particularly as our self-conceptions have a direct influence on our behavior (Stets & Burke, 2000).

This chapter will argue that:

- Musical identities related to learning and teaching, as other identities, constantly change and develop throughout the life span in response to cultural norms and the feedback received from interactions with others;
- That it is possible for music to be a central element of an individual's learning identity even though the descriptor "musician," as defined by the Oxford Dictionary as "a person who plays a musical instrument especially professionally," may not be appropriate to encapsulate that identity.

The chapter will consider the complex nature of musical identities in a wide range of educational contexts, formal and informal. It will examine the relationships between musical identities and a range of factors including perceived ability, understanding of music, the development of expertise, motivation, and cultural expectations. The relationships between musical and other identities will be explored and how musical identities change through the life span as individuals move between different learning and employment environments.

26.2 THE COMPLEXITY OF MUSICAL IDENTITIES

Music can play a range of roles in an individual's identities and behavior. It may contribute to a social identity through the kind of music that individuals prefer (North & Hargreaves, 2007), to an individual's moods and emotions (Juslin & Sloboda, 2010), or to their behavior as they experience music in the wider community in shops, restaurants, places of worship, and other public places (North & Hargreaves, 2009). The extent to which music is an important element of individuals' identities depends on its role in their lives. If they actively engage in making and creating music they may describe themselves as a "musician", perhaps also indicating whether their status is as a professional or amateur. This is usually dependent on the extent to which they make their living from music rather than their level of musical expertise. Others may not describe themselves as musicians, but music may still play a major role in their lives. Indeed, they may even earn their living from music, for instance in production, marketing, retail, journalism. The name that they give to their role may also include the word music. Whether an individual uses the descriptor "musician" does not necessarily provide an accurate assessment of their musical identity, particularly as it relates to learning and teaching.

When considering issues of musical identity we also need to be mindful of the ease of accessibility to music in the technological age. It is now possible for everyone to participate in making music should they wish to do so. Technology has increased the options for making, sharing, and learning music. Almost anyone can compose, arrange, record, and mix music. Children can make music electronically through their phones, a range of electronic games and learning software, and through avatars in the virtual world of Second Life. Open online communities can also be vehicles for developing identities (Partti & Karlsen, 2010). The increase in opportunities for engaging with music means that individuals can develop many musical identities and hold them simultaneously. A young person may learn to play the trombone and guitar at school, belong to a range of school musical groups, have formed a pop group outside school, and be an avid collector of rap music. Professional musicians who have a portfolio career may perceive themselves primarily to be performers, but with other less central identities as teacher, coach, or arranger. The evaluative elements of these various identities may differ, so they may see themselves as outstanding performers, but only adequate as a teacher. A key question is at what point do those who create or recreate music begin to describe themselves as musicians.

26.3 Musical identity and learning

There are many ways for musical identities to develop, in part, because learning is a natural process for human beings. We constantly learn in our everyday lives. Much of this learning occurs without conscious effort. For instance, when we repeatedly hear a piece of music we learn what it sounds like and, to some extent, remember it without having made a conscious effort to do so. In recent years, distinctions have been made between formal, informal, and non-formal learning. Formal learning is viewed as taking place within an educational establishment, has a predetermined curriculum and accredited assessment. Informal learning takes place within the home or work place, while non-formal learning may take place within an educational establishment, but in an informal context, for instance, a workshop, or seminar (OECD, 2010). In music, learning occurs formally (e.g., lessons, examinations), informally (e.g., practice of all kinds, listening, small untutored group work) and non-formally (e.g., workshops, large directed groups). Indeed, most individuals who participate in music making will at some time engage in activities which fall under each of these headings particularly as the range of opportunities for formal tuition now embraces many instruments, activities and genres. However, the balance between activities may vary, for instance, for non-classical musicians informal learning or self- or family-tuition is common, (Green, 2001; Coulson, 2010). Whatever, the specific nature of learning or the environment in which it is undertaken, the time spent in musical engagement is the most important predictor of the level of expertise attained (Coulson, 2010; Hallam, Rinta, Varvarigou, Creech, Papageogi, & Lani, 2012).

26.4 Identity, ability, and understanding

In Western cultures having an identity as a "musician" tends to be equated with making and creating music, usually through playing an instrument or singing. Lamont (2002), in the UK, showed that children did not classify themselves as musically active unless they were involved in instrumental lessons, even though they were participating in class school music, which involved listening, performing, and composing. Perceptions of having musical ability also seem to be related to being actively engaged in music making. Hallam & Prince (2003), in a qualitative study, explored the conceptions of musical ability of 395 individuals including musicians, non-music educators, adults in other occupations, students involved in extra-curricular activities, and some not involved in extra-curricular activity. By far the greatest number of responses (71%) indicated that musical ability was related to being able to play a musical instrument or sing. This was confirmed in a quantitative follow up study with 660 participants (Hallam, 2010). Being able to read music, play an instrument or sing, along with the skills to undertake these activities emerged as the strongest perceived indicators of musical ability. Similarly, perceptions of how musical understanding is developed are related to active engagement with making music. Understanding was perceived by 465 individuals with different levels of musical expertise as being able to recognize musical elements and create or recreate music. The development of musical understanding was overwhelmingly seen to take place through actively making or listening to music, the emphasis given to each of these varying depending on the extent to which the individual engaged with each (Hallam, 2009).

26.5 Musical identity, expertise, and motivation

Musical identities can develop in relation to many different genres and musical activities. Whatever the field of music, the level of expertise attained depends on involvement in a range of musical activities and the commitment of the individual to music. Hallam (2013a), in a quantitative study of 163 instrumental music students aged 7–17, explored, which motivational factors predicted three different future musical aspirations: always wanting to be involved in music; music being useful to a future career; and aspiring to be a musician. Enjoyment of musical activities, self-belief, and social support from family, friends, and teachers were the strongest predictors of music being useful in a future career; valuing music, enjoyment of performing, self-belief, and social support were the strongest predictors for always wanting to be involved in music; while valuing music, enjoyment, and practicing strategies best predicted aspirations to be a musician. Interestingly, support from others and self-belief were not strong predictors for those aspiring to be musicians.

A larger scale follow up study (Hallam, 2013b), which involved 3352 musicians across a wide range of levels of expertise (from beginner level to conservatoire entry standard) playing a wide range of instruments or singing used the same statements relating to aspirations. While there was some increase in positive responses to the aspirational statements as the young people reached higher levels of expertise, this was not as great as might have been expected. The three statements were also only moderately correlated with each other (from 0.38–0.54) indicating that different aspects of musical aspiration were being tapped by each statement. A factor analysis of statements relating to different elements of motivation revealed six factors. The first, "support and social affirmation" focussed on support from family, teachers, and positive feedback from others. The second factor "social life and enjoyment of musical activities" had high loadings on musical friendships, social activities, enjoying attending concerts, listening to music, and playing in musical groups. Factor 3 focussed on enjoying performing and playing in concerts and groups; Factor 4 was concerned with self-belief in relation to musical ability; Factor 5 enjoyment of playing, lessons, and practice, and Factor 6 disliking practice. Figs 26.1–26.6 show the relationships

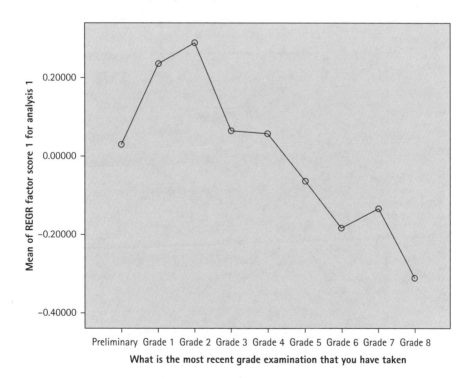

FIG. 26.1 Support and social affirmation by level of expertise.

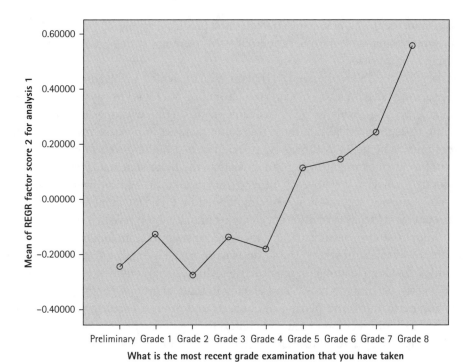

FIG. 26.2 Social life and enjoyment of musical activities by level of expertise.

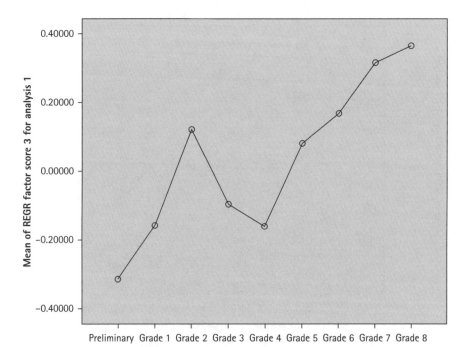

FIG. 26.3 Enjoyment of performing by level of expertise.

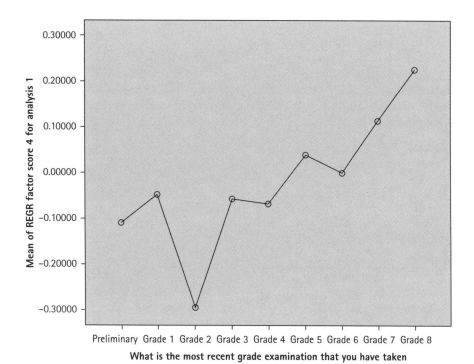

FIG. 26.4 Self-belief in musical ability by level of expertise.

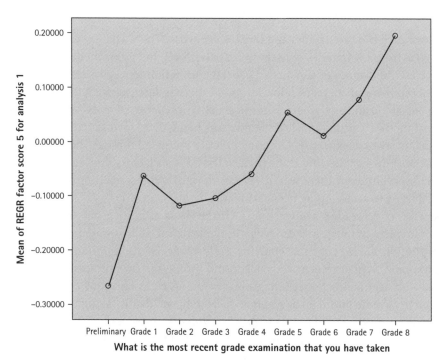

FIG. 26.5 Enjoyment of playing, lessons and practice by level of expertise.

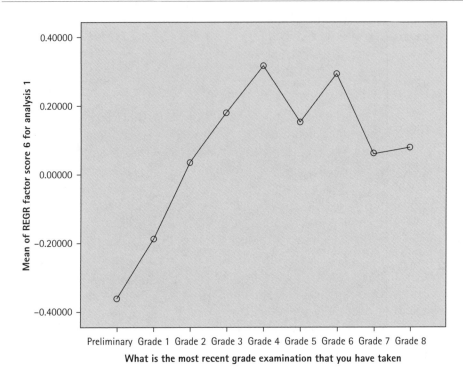

FIG. 26.6 Disliking practice by level of expertise.

between each of these factors and level of expertise. The x axis indicates the level of expertise from beginner to conservatoire entry level, the y axis the factor score. The perceived importance of support and social affirmation was at a relatively high level initially showing an increase at low levels of expertise, after, which it declined. In contrast, social life and enjoyment of musical activities increased as expertise developed suggesting that a strong musical identity was being developed as individuals gained increasing levels of expertise. Disliking practice increased through the lower levels of expertise showing a decline at the highest level. Other factors showed more complex trajectories, although there was always an upward trend suggesting that all made a contribution to a developing musical identity.

A series of regression analyses on the three facets of musical aspirations revealed that enjoyment of music and its role in individual's social lives were important across all aspirations. Self-belief and enjoying performance were important for long term commitment to involvement with music and wanting to be a professional musician. Those with aspirations to become professional musicians also showed greater liking for practice. These findings suggest that developing an identity as a musician depends on a range of motivational factors with subtle differences depending on specific aspirations. However, enjoyment of musical activities and having a musical social life were key for all.

26.6 Cultural expectations of musical identity

There are cultural expectations relating to musical identities which impact on individual identity development. One of the most significant of these is in relation to gender. Even in the Western world, where gender equality is enshrined in legislation and accepted by the majority, there continue to be gender differences in the instruments played by boys and girls with most "pop" instruments, electric guitar, drums, and large low pitched instruments being played by boys (Hallam, Rogers, & Creech, 2008). Some musical activities are perceived as more appropriate for males than females, and this continues into the music profession. There is some evidence from studies using self-completed rating scales that boys may need to have a greater love of music and enjoyment of musical participation to persevere with some musical activities (Hallam, 2013a), perhaps because they are more influenced by their friends in contrast to girls, for whom teachers and parents seem to be more important (Hallam, 2004).

26.7 Relationships between musical identities and other identities

Whether individuals decide to pursue a career in music, to continue with musical activities into adulthood as a hobby, or give up active engagement with music depends on the relationship of their musical identity with other identities and other demands in their lives. Lamont, Leighton, Underhill, & Hale (2009) identified that some primary school pupils who had received whole class instrumental or vocal lessons providing them with the experience of playing an instrument to stimulate later engagement with music had other priorities in their lives. While about a third wanted to continue with the instrument they had learned, about half wanted to learn a different instrument, and some indicated that they wanted to spend time on other activities, for instance, homework or sporting activities.

A useful conceptualization for considering the extent to which individuals commit to music is "serious leisure." This contrasts with casual and project-based leisure. Serious leisure is defined as "the systematic pursuit of an amateur, hobbyist, or volunteer core activity that is highly substantial, interesting, and fulfilling and where, in the typical case, participants find a career in acquiring and expressing a combination of its special skills, knowledge, and experience" (Stebbins, 1992, p. 3). Serious leisure is characterized by: the need to persevere at the activity; the availability of a leisure career; the need to put in effort to gain skill and knowledge; the realization of various special benefits; a unique ethos and social world; and an attractive personal and social identity. These characteristics reflect those needed to achieve high levels of expertise in music.

Amateur adult musicians frequently exemplify the concept of "serious leisure," spending much time in musical activities and exhibiting high levels of commitment with standards that may be equivalent to those of professionals (Gates, 1991). Music is a key element in their identity and they commit much time and energy to it (Pitts, 2005; Taylor, 2010). Love of music alongside the desire for challenge and an opportunity to develop new skills are key motivators and depend on the specific activity and opportunities to meet with like-minded others (Creech, Hallam, McQueen, & Varvarigou, 2013).

26.8 Rediscovering and changing musical identities

As people progress through their lives they may maintain musical activities begun in childhood, abandon them and then return to them at a later date, or learn to play an instrument that they had always wished to play (Taylor, 2011). As they make progress new musical identities are constructed by regenerating and reconstructing youthful musical selves as well as reinventing and empowering themselves as mature musical adults. Creech, Hallam, Varvarigou, Gaunt, McQueen & Pincas (2014) in a study of almost 400 older people found that for some music was a vehicle for redefining their identity as a musician or rediscovering a lost possible musical self. Through music-making, participants developed or, in some cases rekindled a strong musical identity, in some cases coming to identify themselves as "musicians." Older people, while they may struggle with the technical aspects of learning to play a musical instrument seem to enjoy the empowerment of connecting with two musical selves, one where they play an instrument and another where they listen to music (Taylor & Hallam, 2008).

Change in musical identity can come about through career change, for instance, leaving a non-musical career to become a music teacher. Typically, such change from amateur to professional status, while based on positive experiences of engagement with music, is brought about by changed circumstances unrelated to music, for instance, redundancy or altered family circumstances. The newly acquired identity as a professional musician leads to a desire to improve musical skills, which may involve increased practice, more involvement in group music making, a greater focus on critical analysis and in some cases the restarting of lessons (Taylor & Hallam, 2011).

26.9 Changes in identity during entry into the music profession

Entering and progressing through higher education music programs with the aim of pursuing a career in music is associated with the renegotiation of musical identities.

Juuti & Littleton (2010) interviewed ten classical solo piano students about their experiences of such change. Comparative dynamics between self and others were the key mediators of the students' re-negotiation of their musical identity. Identity was developed through comparative accounts of their own and others' performances in entrance tests and their early experiences of being in the academy. During this process the students were frequently self-deprecating and highly self-critical. Many students, on entering higher education, aspire to careers as performers or composers (Creech, Gaunt, & Hallam, 2009), but as they make comparisons with others their aspirations and identities can change (Miller & Baker, 2007).

A range of factors contribute towards the development of a music student's sense of professional self-concept including self-perception, self-interpretation, and self-evaluation (Long, 2013). The Plans and Aspirations of Young Musicians (PLAY) longitudinal study carried out at the Guildhall School of Music and Drama in London asked 301 music students (65% undergraduate, 35% postgraduate) to complete questionnaires. Twenty were also interviewed. The students were highly motivated and most wanted to perform professionally as soloists or chamber music musicians. Less than half wanted to be an instrumental music teacher and only about 10% a class music teacher. On entry to the conservatoire, there was a dip in self-esteem, self-efficacy, and motivation with an increase in anxiety compared with pre-entry, which was partially recovered during the second year of study. In the first year the students' main aspirations were to enjoy their work, earn enough money to live comfortably, and to perform professionally. By the second year these had changed little although fewer now agreed that they aspired to be a soloist. Career plans were partly determined by the instrument played and the genre that was studied. Undergraduate students generally aspired to becoming instrumental teachers and chamber musicians, perhaps reflecting a realistic appraisal of employment prospects and the likelihood of a portfolio career. Students seemed to become more realistic in their aspirations as they progressed through the conservatoire. In some cases this had a negative impact on motivation and self-perceptions. For instance, those aspiring to be teachers experienced difficulties in motivating themselves to practice, while those with high level performing aspirations were more likely to experience a loss of confidence (Creech et al, 2009; Long, Gaunt, Creech, & Hallam, 2010). The students' musical identities were constantly reformulated in response to comparisons made with the performance of their peers and feedback from teachers and others, which impacted on their motivation and self-belief.

26.10 THE IDENTITIES OF THOSE TEACHING MUSIC

Teaching music can take many forms from class music teaching to individual or group instrumental lessons in school, or at a teacher's home, or studio and can be at many different levels from beginner to postgraduate level. Typically, those teaching music in class, particularly at secondary level, will have received formal accredited training to do so. At primary level, teachers usually receive formal training, but this typically covers the whole curriculum and may not include training specific to music. In contrast, it is rare for formal training to be necessary to become an instrumental teacher. Musicians often begin teaching their instrument when they are still students themselves (Haddon, 2009) frequently because they are asked to do so by others (Taylor & Hallam, 2011). For some, positive musical experiences as a child or adult and/or a long-standing desire to teach are strong motivators as is inspiration from a previous teacher (Haddon, 2009). For instrumental teachers, there can be pragmatic reasons for pursuing a teaching career, for instance, the convenience of working from home or the need for a new job (Gibbs, 1993)

For those committed to a career teaching class music, positive and varied past musical experiences are critical factors in their motivation and identity construction (Dolloff, 2007). Jones and Parkes (2010), in a study of 143 students enrolled in music performance and music education programs at seven large US universities who completed an online questionnaire, found that one of the major reasons that students chose a career in teaching music was that this had become part of their identity distinct from their identity as a performer. Two main reasons for choosing a career in music education were given. Firstly, because it was part of their identity and they wanted to become role models or like one of their former teachers. Secondly, because they enjoyed music teaching and wanted to make music fun for their students. Of less importance was their perception of their ability as a music teacher or the usefulness of a music-teaching career.

In the UK, the Teacher Identities in Music Education (TIME) project (Hargreaves, Purves, Welch, & Marshall, 2007) focussed on the potential conflict between intending classroom teachers' identities as "musician" on the one hand, and as "teacher" on the other. Those students wishing to pursue a career in education tended to value skills, which emphasized the personal, social, and communicative aspects of the benefits of music, whereas the non-education students valued those deriving from the intrinsic value of music. Similarly, a qualitative study of music teachers in Sweden (Georgii-Hemming, 2006) found that they identified themselves as "teachers in music" not "musicians teaching music." They valued music as activity, a craft, and for the enjoyment that it could bring, rather than as a technical skill.

One of the tensions for those teaching music in the secondary school classroom is the extent to which their musical skills are too narrow to meet curriculum requirements. Currently, in the UK, most music teachers have been trained in the Western classical tradition. Very few tend to be from other backgrounds involving popular music or jazz (Hargreaves et al., 2007). As musical expertise tends to be acquired within particular genres and it is time consuming and challenging to learn how to play within a different genre (Sudnow, 1978), this can be problematic for teachers. For instance, the evaluation of the "Musical Futures" initiative, which promulgates new and imaginative ways of engaging young people, aged 11–19, in music activities, typically involving learning to play popular music by ear, found that some teachers found it difficult to adapt. Their skills were not always relevant and they found modelling and facilitating the work of students offering help, support, and guidance based on objectives that pupils set for themselves difficult (Hallam, Creech, and McQueen, 2011).

While the musical skills of some secondary school music teachers may not match the aspirations of all of their pupils, at primary level many trainees in the UK feel ill-equipped to teach music at all (Hallam, et al., 2009). Teacher training programs frequently include little specific training in teaching music, sometimes none at all, and the time is generally insufficient for them to develop the necessary musical skills unless they are already competent musicians. A variety of initiatives have been set up to try to enhance the skills of existing teachers. For instance, some primary school teachers were given the opportunity to work with the London Symphony Orchestra, which led to positive change in their identities and possible musical selves (Varvarigou, Creech & Hallam, 2012). Training by a primary music specialist has also been evaluated positively by teachers of children aged 5–7 years (Hallam, Creech & Varvarigou, 2011) and the Sing Up program provided materials and training for teachers (Welch, et al., 2011). However, providing funding for such training is typically not a priority for primary head teachers and to bring about major changes in the musical identities of classroom teachers would require initiatives being sustained over a substantial period of time.

There has been relatively little research on the identities and motivations of instrumental music teachers. Cathcart (2013) found that the 595 private piano teachers who participated in her research enjoyed their work and found it very rewarding, while Baker (2005) researching 28 mid-career peripatetic music teachers employed in local authority music services found that the teachers had positive self-perceptions, but experienced tedium in their work and had restricted occupational prospects. There were few opportunities for career advancement, pressures on managers of having to endorse policy, and demonstrate exemplary practice and a sense, for some, of being trapped in the job leading to frustration and lack of challenge.

26.11 CONCLUSIONS

Musical identities are not static and evolve throughout the life span in response to changing circumstances. While the term "musician" tends to be perceived as denoting someone who plays an instrument, frequently professionally, it can be used with a range of adjectives to denote other identities, which may relate to status (e.g., semi-professional, amateur, retired) or genre (e.g., classical, jazz, rock). Similarly, it may be elaborated in terms of the instrument played or the nature of the work undertaken.

Many individuals who would not describe themselves as musicians may still be employed within and crucial to the commercial music sector, for instance, critics, producers, engineers, presenters, DJs. Not using the term musician to describe themselves does not diminish their musical identity. Their commitment to music may equal or even exceed that of performers. Similarly, those who describe themselves as listeners may have an equally strong identity in terms of the kinds of music that they prefer and their motivation to engage with it by attending concerts, acquiring collections of recordings, and information about their favorite artistes.

There are a range of influences on the way in which musical identities develop, which can vary in their level of importance through the life span. These are set out in Fig. 26.7 and include love of music, opportunity, self-belief, musical preferences, friends, family, the educational environment including teachers, and the cultural environment.

From an educational perspective what is important is that individuals are given opportunities to engage with a wide variety of music to enable them to develop musical identities should they wish to do so. For some such opportunities may become "serious leisure" activities leading to the pursuit of high levels of expertise, which may lead to professional careers. For some of these, music may constitute such an integral part of their identity that it is almost an obsession (Kemp, 1996). Others may take musical activities seriously, but not wish to pursue music as a career and become amateur musicians with a lifelong love of and engagement with music. Others may wish to pursue other identities, which are unrelated to music per se, but may still enjoy listening to music and going to concerts. Others may have no interest in music. Those involved in music education need to accept that music will not be a key element in the identity of every individual in the same way that geography teachers would not expect everyone to describe themselves as a geographer, or a mathematics teacher expect everyone to describe themselves as a mathematician. In fact, in comparison with many school subjects music continues to be an important aspect of the identity of many people throughout the life span.

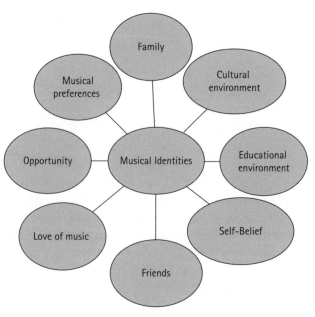

FIG. 26.7 Influences on musical identities.

For those who teach music, this is a challenging time. Music is easily available to everyone and individuals are able to develop a wide range of musical preferences. To be an effective teacher at a time when music is undergoing great technological change, and is becoming increasingly important in people's everyday lives, inevitably requires a far broader range of skills than was the case in the past. Role models are important in the development of possible selves, identity, and the aspirations of young people (Ibarra, 1999). Such models can be those who are viewed from afar, but are frequently in the immediate environment, e.g., teachers or mentors. Music teachers therefore have considerable responsibilities, which can have a major impact on students throughout their lives. They need to provide inspiration to young people, but also be aware of their limitations in relation to genres with which they are not familiar. This may mean that they have to draw on the expertise of others. More than ever before, musicians need to work together to ensure that every child has the opportunity to develop a positive musical identity, which is relevant to them.

To conclude, musical identities are many and varied and develop in response to individual learning opportunities, formal and informal. Identities change and develop in response to a wide range of environmental factors and the individual's assessment of them. This process leads to reconstruction of musical identities and can occur at any point in the life span.

REFERENCES

Baker, D. (2005). Peripatetic music teachers approaching mid-career: a cause for concern? *British Journal of Music Education*, 22(2), 141–54.

Beijaard, D., Meijer, P. C., & Verloop, N. (2004). Reconsidering research on teachers' professional identity. *Teaching and Teacher Education*, 20, 107–28.

Cathcart, S. (2013). *UK piano teaching in the 21st century: exploring common practices, expertise, values, attitudes and motivation to teach*. London: Institute of Education, University of London.

Coulson, S. (2010). Getting 'Capital' in the music world: musicians' learning experiences and working lives. *British Journal of Music Education*, 27(3), 255–70.

Creech, A., Gaunt, H., & Hallam, S. (2009). Plans and aspirations of young musicians: an investigation into aspirations and self-perceptions in the conservatoire. Paper presented at the conference on The Reflective Conservatoire. Guildhall School of Music & Drama, London, 28 February to 3 March, 2009.

Creech, A., Hallam, S., Varvarigou, M., Gaunt, H., McQueen, H. & Pincas, A. (2014). The role of musical possible selves in supporting well-being in later life. *Music Education Research*, 16(1) 32–49.

Creech, A., Hallam, S., McQueen, H., & Varvarigou, M. (2013). The power of music in the lives of older adults. *Research Studies in Music Education*, 35(1), 87–102.

Dolloff, L. (2007). "All the things we are": balancing our multiple identities in music teaching. *Action, Criticism, and Theory for Music Education*, 6(2), 1–21. Available at: http://act.maydaygroup.org/articles/Dolloff6_2.pdf (accessed 25 February 2016).

Gates J.T. (1991). Music participation: theory, research and policy, *Bulletin of the Council for Research in Music Education*, 109, 1–35, Summer.

Georgii-Hemming, E. (2006). Personal experiences an professional strategies, *Music Education Research*, 8(2), 217–36.

Gibbs, L. (1993). *Private lives: Report on the survey of private music teachers and their professional development and training.* London: Goldsmith's College, University of London.

Green, L. (2001). *How popular musicians learn: a way ahead for music education.* London & New York: Ashgate.

Haddon, E. (2009). Instrumental and vocal teaching: how do music students learn to teach? *British Journal of Music Education*, 26 (1), 57.

Hallam, S. (2004). Gender differences in the factors which predict musical attainment in school aged students. In: J. Tafuri (Ed.) *Research for Music Education, Proceedings of the 20th Seminar of the ISME Research Commission*, Las Palmas, Gran Canaria, 4–11 July, 2004, pp. 101–7.

Hallam, S. (2009). Motivation to learn. In: S. Hallam, I. Cross, & M, Thaut (Eds.) *Handbook of psychology of music*, pp. 285–94. Oxford: Oxford University Press.

Hallam, S. (2009). In what ways do we understand music. Key note presentation given at the Australian Society of Music Education XVII Conference Understanding Music 2009, 10–14 July, 2009, Launton, Tasmania.

Hallam, S. (2010). 21st century conceptions of musical ability. *Psychology of Music*, 38(3), 308–30.

Hallam, S. (2013a). What predicts level of expertise attained, quality of performance, and future musical aspirations in young instrumental players? *Psychology of Music*, 41(3), 265–89.

Hallam S. (2013b). *Musical talent: conceptualisation, identification and development.* Paper presented at the conference "Managing your talents," conservatorium van Amsterdam, 29–30 August, 2013, Amsterdam.

Hallam, S., Rogers, L., & Creech, A. (2008). Gender differences in musical instrument choice. *International Journal of Music Education*, 26(1), 7–19.

Hallam, S. Rinta, T. Varvarigou, M., Creech, A. Papageorgi, I., & Lani, J. (2012). The development of practising strategies in young people. *Psychology of Music*, 40(5), 652–80.

Hallam, S., & Prince, V. (2003). Conceptions of musical ability. *Research Studies in Music Education*, 20, 2–22.

Hallam, S., Creech, A. & McQueen, H. (2011). *Musical Futures: a case study investigation: Final Report October 2011.* London:Institute of Education, University of London

Hallam, S., Creech, A., & Varvarigou, A. (2011). *Evaluation of the EMI Music Sound Foundation Project rollout: Training Key Stage 1 Primary School Teachers (2010–2011).* London: Institute of Education, University of London

Hallam, S., Burnard, P., Robertson, A., Saleh, C., Davies, V., Rogers, L., et al. (2009). Trainee primary school teachers' perceptions of their effectiveness in teaching music. *Music Education Research*, 11(2), 221–40.

Kemp, A.E. (1996). *The musical temperament: psychology and personality of musicians.* Oxford: Oxford University Press.

Hargreaves, D.J., Purves, R.M., Welch, G.F., & Marshall, N.A. (2007). Developing identities and attitudes in musicians and classroom music teachers, *British Journal of Educational Psychology*, 77(3), 665–82.

Ibarra, H. (1999). Provisional selves: experimenting with image and identity in professional adaptation. *Administrative Science Quarterly*, 44, 764–92.

Jones, B.D., & Parkes, K.A. (2010). The motivation of undergraduate music students: The impact of identification and talent beliefs on choosing a career in music education. *Journal of Music Teacher Education*, 19(2), 41–56.

Juslin, P.N., & Sloboda, J.A. (2010). (Eds.) *Handbook of music and emotion*. Oxford: Oxford University Press.

Juuti, S. & Littleton, K. (2010). Musical identities in transition: solo-piano students' accounts of entering the academy. *Psychology of Music*, 38(4), 481–98.

Lamont, A. (2002). Musical identities and the school environment. In: R.A.R. MacDonald, D. J. Hargreaves, & D. E. Miell (Eds.) *Musical identities*, pp. 41–59. Oxford:Oxford University Press.

Lamont, A. , Leighton, G., Underhill, J., & Hale, R. (2009). The impact of whole-class instrumental tuition in primary schools: an evaluation of a wider opportunities initiative. Paper presented at the Research in Music Education conference. Exeter, University of Exeter, 14–18 April, 2009.

Long, M., Gaunt, H., Creech, A., & Hallam, S. (2010). Beyond the Conservatoire: a socio-cognitive perspective on the development of professional self-concept among advanced music students. In: *Proceedings from the Students' Ownership of Learning Symposium* at the Royal College of Music in Stockholm, 15–17 September, 2010.

Long, M. (2013). Conservatoire students' attitudes, self-efficacy and aspirations. In: M. Stakelum (Ed.) *Contemporary perspectives on teaching and learning*, pp. 29–44 Farnham: Ashgate

Markus, H., & Nurius, P. (1986). Possible selves. *American Psychologist*, 41(9), 954–69.

Miller, J. & Baker, B. (2007). Career orientation and pedagogical training: conservatoire undergraduates' insights. *British Journal of Music Education*, 24 (1), 5–19.

North, A.C., & Hargreaves, D.J. (2007). Lifestyle correlates of musical preference: 2. Media, leisure time and music. *Psychology of Music*, 35(2), 179–200.

North, A.C., & Hargreaves, D.J. (2009). *Music and consumer behaviour*. In: S. Hallam, I. Cross, & M. Thaut (Eds.) *Oxford handbook of music psychology*, pp. 481–90. Oxford: Oxford University Press.

OECD. (2010). Higher education and adult learning. Recognition of non-formal and informal learning. Available at: http://www.oecd.org/edu/skills-beyond-school/recognitionofnonformalandinformallearning-home.htm (accessed 12 June 2013).

Partti, H., & Karlsen, S. (2010). Reconceptualising musical learning: new media, identity and community in music education. *Music Education Research*, 12(4), 369–82.

Pitts, SE. (2005). *Valuing musical participation*. Ashgate, Aldershot.

Schempp, P.G., Sparkes, A.C., & Templin, T.J. (1999). Identity and induction: Establishing the self in the first year of teaching. In: R.P. Lipkos & T.M. Brinthaupt (Eds.) *The role of self in teacher development*, 142–64. Albany, NY: State University of New York Press.

Spanos, N.P. (1994). Multiple identity enactments and multiple personality disorder: a socio-cognitive perspective. *Psychological Bulletin*, 116(1), 143–65.

Stebbins, R.A. (1992). *Amateurs, professionals and serious leisure*. Montreal, QC: McGill-Queen's University Press.

Stets, J.E., & Burke, P.J. (2000). Identity theory and social identity theory, *Social Psychology Quarterly*, 63(3), 224–37.

Sudnow, D. (1978). *Ways of the hand: the organisation of improvised conduct*. London: Routledge and Kegan Paul.

Taylor, A. (2010). Participation in a master class: experiences of older amateur pianists. *Music Education Research*, 12(2), 199–218.

Taylor, A. (2011). Continuing, change and mature musical identity construction: using "Rivers of Musical Experience" to trace the musical lives of six mature-age keyboard players. *British Journal of Music Education*, 28(2), 195–212.

Taylor, A., & Hallam, S. (2008). Understanding what it means for older learners to learn basic musical skills on a keyboard instrument, *Music Education Research*, 10(2), 285–306.

Taylor, A., & Hallam, S. (2011). From leisure to work: amateur musicians taking up instrumental or vocal teaching as a second career, *Music Education Research*, 13(3), 307–26.

Varvarigou, M., Creech, A., & Hallam, S. (2012). Benefits of continuing professional development (CPD) programmes in music for KS2 (primary) teachers through the example of the London Symphony Orchestra (LSO) On Track programme. *Music Education Research*, 14(2), 149–69.

Welch, G.F., Himonides, E., Saunders, J., Papageorgi, I., Rinta, T., Preti, C., et al. (2011). Researching the first year of the national singing programme Sing Up in England, *Psychomusicology: Music, Mind and Brain*, 21(1–2), 83–97.

CHAPTER 27

IDENTITY FORMATION AND AGENCY IN THE DIVERSE MUSIC CLASSROOM

HEIDI WESTERLUND, HEIDI PARTTI,
AND SIDSEL KARLSEN

27.1 INTRODUCTION

IN our post-positivist and post-behavioralist times it is still rather uncommon to examine music education in schools from the perspective of students' identities. With its stubborn methods, school music has certainly been regarded primarily as an unnatural and artificial social context in terms of the development of musical identities. The recent increasing interest towards issues of musical identity in the school context can, at least to an extent, be explained by two related developments: firstly, a growing doubt of the belief in universal musical values and the shift towards contextuality, situationality, and deconstruction of power structures; and, secondly, a wider turn within learning theories where the focus has shifted from a simple transmission model of knowledge to wider recognitions of the significance of learning environments and the "relational network" (Fuller, 2007, p. 19) of people co-participating in the shared practices of social communities (Hakkarainen, 2013). According to the latter view, learning is, indeed, understood as an experience of identity, insofar as it changes our ability to engage in the world and hence potentially transforms our social positioning and self-understanding (e.g., Wenger, 1998). In other words, students' identity work in the music classroom takes place not only through the students' understandings of who they *are*, but also through questions of what they are able to *do*, and who they are *becoming*.

27.1.1 Who are the students?

The question of who our students are, what the society expects from them, and who they aspire themselves to become is one of great complexity. Interaction at the global level as a result of increasing immigration and new media has become a norm rather than an exception, having an impact also in schools (e.g., Banks & McGee Banks, 2010, p. v). Different forms of new media have heavily contributed in an eradication of, for example, geographical and cultural boundaries, and offer immense possibilities for music creation, collaboration, co-creation, recording, distribution, or promotion (Brown, 2012, p. 261). This highly mobile, unstable, ever-transforming and interconnected "runaway world" (Giddens, 1999/2003) is not only bound to influence us, but it also entails a constant requirement of learning necessary (intercultural) skills. As argued by Chapman (2012, p. 233), today's pivotal challenge is caused by "the scope of music education" being "far broader than it has ever been for music educators, while the actual cohorts of students are also becoming more multicultural". Moreover, if provisionality, contingency and multiple, parallel, intersectional, hybrid and cosmopolitan categories are now favored in general theorizations of identities over the previous assumption of sameness and continuity of a stable self (van Meijl, 2010, p. 65; Reay, 2010, p. 278), it seems clear that "musical culture" cannot simply be seen to create univocality and be treated as an unambiguous singular or homogeneous entity. Rather, as claimed by the sociologist Zygmunt Bauman (1999, p. xiv),

> "culture" is as much about inventing as it is about preserving; about discontinuity as much as about continuation; about novelty as much as about tradition; about routine as much as about pattern-breaking; about norm-following as much as about the transcendence of norm; about the unique as much as about the regular; about change as much as about monotony of reproduction; about the unexpected as much as about the predictable.

27.1.2 Music education, culture, and identity

Despite the diverse perspectives on identity, it has been symptomatic for music education research to examine issues of identity, music, culture, and indeed, the "culture of music education" (Bruner, 1996), chiefly within what has been called "a basic anthropological framework" (Jenkins, 2008, p. 116; see also, van Meijl, 2010) in which collective categories are linked to groups of people with assumed similarity even in terms of musical behaviors and expectations. This anthropological starting point has been repeated, for example, in theoretical accounts of so-called praxial philosophy of music education and its leading idea, according to which music in school must model real musical practices—praxes—by focusing on their authentic principles (see e.g., Elliott, 1995). It is argued in this chapter, that ethnically or geographically justified identity categories and related assumptions of shared musical values may be insufficient in explaining processes of identity construction in today's diverse music classrooms or when trying to uncover power issues related to schooling through music. Moreover, it is important to note that *learner identities* should not be conflated simply with identity categories such as race, ethnicity, or gender; rather, identity formation in school involves a multiplicity of social interactions with inclusion, exclusion, conflicts and solidarities, defences, and desires (Reay, 2010, p. 279).

27.1.3 Identity and agency—a matter of "reaching beyond"

This chapter makes an analytical distinction between the concepts of *identity* and *agency* to emphasize the interface between learner identities and other social identities in school and the democratic possibility for each student to act according to *identities as becoming*. The concepts of identity and agency are understood as overlapping, yet not synonymous. While identity here refers to individuals' understanding and reflexive construction of the various personal, social, and cultural aspects of the self or of groups of selves, the concept of agency refers to aspects related to one's perceived and actual ability to act in the world, and hence concerns matters such as self-esteem, experienced purpose of life, ego strength, and internal locus of control. In other words, agency here relates to

> a sense of responsibility for one's life course, the belief that one is in control of one's decisions and is responsible for their outcome, and the confidence that one will be able to overcome obstacles that impede one's progress along one's chosen life course.
>
> Schwartz et al., 2005, p. 207.

Agency hence enables and empowers one to "reach beyond" one's current identity or identities—the suggestions for who you are—and willfully act on something, even without a strong identification. Moreover, although musical identities in school can be explored also as the intrapsychic domain of an individual or self (e.g., Côté & Levine, 2002, p. 7), this chapter examines identity formation particularly on the collective and daily interactive level, as related to agency and as it might appear and has been studied within the contextual frames of localized music classrooms. These classrooms are, however, not only local, but also situated within increasingly multicultural and globalized realities. It is acknowledged that, for academic music education, it is as important to pay attention to the micro levels of identity formation within heterogeneous music class-rooms as to the macro levels of nation states and the global (see also Reay, 2010, p. 291). There may also be a crucial tension between the identification processes that students choose for themselves and those that are imposed on them by schooling as legitimate identities of becoming or by educators—identities that are often based on students' family background. As a theoretical lens to explore previous discourses and academic work on identities in music education in schools, the following three categories of collective identities by Castells (2010, p. xxvi) are utilized:

- *Legitimizing identities*: "introduced by the dominant institutions of society to extend and rationalize their domination *vis à vis* social actors" (p. 8) and thereby justifying the existing social order and also who students should become. In the context of music education, legitimizing identities will mainly refer to the taken-for-granted nationalistic or patriotic tendencies in music education in schools, but also, for instance, to the persistent universalizing, dominant, and hegemonic status of Western classical music in education beyond any particular local or student-related issues of identity.
- *Resistance identities*: "generated by those actors who are in positions/conditions devalued and/or stigmatized by the logic of domination" (p. 8), often looking to historical pasts for gathering the material necessary for the identity construction. In music education, this can be found particularly in the multicultural music education literature as ethical imperatives concerning people's right to be recognized and included in the school curriculum, and in discourses of popular music in education relating to student-centered pedagogy and assumed youth identity.
- *Project identities*: "aiming to change society by introducing new sets of values" (p. xxvi) and built for the purpose of redefining the actors' "position in society" (p. 8), which in music education often have been articulated through discussions on citizenship and the enhancement of new forms of democratic identities to further progressive social transformation.

The chapter constructs a lens of 'music classroom community identity' to serve as an educational pragmatic conceptual guideline for identity work that deals with the growing need of *vis-à-vis* solidarity and ethical values in music education.

27.2 Imagined communities and legitimizing identities: nationalism, patriotism and hegemonic Western classical music

27.2.1 Traditions of nationalism and patriotism in music education

According to Lehmann (2012, p. 641), "[m]usic education may be … primarily a national concern." Music in schools tends to be regulated by national laws, educational policy, and curriculum documents, and it is commonplace that institutional practices and teacher education systems form and sustain the "culture of music education" (see also, Bruner, 1996) at the national level. These institutional conditions tend to frame choices of musical activities and repertoires even when the national curriculum does not specify them (for an example in the Finnish context, see Kallio & Partti, 2013; Kallio, 2014). Moreover, as music is often used to express national identity in terms of creating and strengthening a sense of belonging both within a nation as well as to signify it to outsiders (Folkestad, 2002), this sense of belonging still seems to find its natural home in school music education (Veblen, 2013, p. 9).

According to the renowned thesis of Anderson (1983), nationalistic discourses in general can be seen as searching for "imagined communities" that were made possible by the decline of religion and a growing awareness of human diversity. Analytically, the sense of belonging, national cohesion, and unity may be understood to be manifested as either patriotism or nationalism, although the two are most often regarded on a continuum. In the writings in music education (see, e.g., Hebert and Kertz-Welzel, 2012; Kallio & Partti, 2013), patriotism refers to a form of constructive and "critical loyalty" (Staub, 1989; Schatz et al., 1999, p. 153) towards one's country, while nationalism may reflect beliefs of national superiority (Kosterman & Feshbach, 1989; Schatz et al., 1999) and hence entail an "out-group devaluation" (Ariely, 2012, p. 3). Recently, Hebert and Kertz-Welzel (2012, p. xiii) have noted that "while patriotism in ... music education might have been reasonable for emerging nations ... as a functional device for the establishment of their national identity"—such as recently in the legitimated Cambodian post-genocide context (see e.g., Kallio & Partti, 2013)—patriotism "still plays a significant role today when it may no longer be as necessary" (Hebert & Kertz-Welzel, 2012, p. xiii). Equally, "the idea of national identity" (O'Flynn, 2007, p. 36) still continues to hold its central place in music education, often through the national curricula—or textbooks—which are the public sites, or manifestos, for such identity formation (Benedict & Schmidt, 2012, p. 104). In music curricula, a national imagined community—which according to Hernández Castillo (2010) is more linked to a *historic memory* than to territory itself (p. 388)—"strive[s] to maintain repertoires which express national characteristics in one way or another, and which serve to stress the importance of national heritage to the rising generation" (Folkestad, 2002, p. 158). As Benedict and Schmidt (2012, p. 104) argue, the national curriculum typically functions as "a discursive tool in the actualization of political goals and ideological wants ... including the construction of 'we' and 'them'". Consequently, such inherently political collective identifications (see also, Jenkins, 2008, p. 131) can be set to contradict the modernist argument made by aesthetic music education, according to which music in schools ought to focus on music (education) "rather than on all of the societal issues that will always surround music education" (Reimer, 2009, p. 131).

27.2.2 Local music cultures and the troubling "objectivity" of Western classical music

The strong ties between music and national identities are to be found, however, not only in national curricula or in scholarly discussions on this phenomenon, but also in wider theorizations of music education in schools. According to Elliott's praxialism (1995), the starting point for music education practices should be in the acknowledgement of, and focus on students' " 'local' musical culture." For instance, according to Elliott, teaching in Finland ought to be comprised of "*both* Western classical practices *and* Finnish musical traditions" (Elliott, 1996, p. 12). Referring to Sparshott (1987), Elliott (1995, p. 86) claims that "people for whom the music of their own culture is all the music there is can live into that music as people of broader culture cannot". Interestingly, although Western classical music may appear as "foreign" and at the fringes of people's daily lives, it still seems to hold its self-evident position in schooling—advocated even by those scholars who argue for a more pluralistic approach. Furthermore, Western classical music is more often than not located theoretically at the other end of the dichotomy: it is perceived as more absolute than local, more universal instead of linked to specific groups and situations or identity; it is seen to involve objective judgments and thinking rather than experiences of social significance or entertainment (see e.g., Johnson, 2002, pp. 41–8). For some, Western culture is still the "highest moral resource, in a world that has come through to modernity" (Scruton, 2007, p. 85), and it is, indeed, the deepening cultural pluralism, which increases the social need to define ourselves by making cultural judgements and articulating allegiances instead of "inner constructions" and "inward meanings" (Johnson, 2002, pp. 41–3). According to Johnson (Johnson, 2002, pp. 43–4), what now seems to matter:

> is the activity of agreement and dispute, aligning oneself with certain positions and groups and differentiating oneself from others. Where music functions in this way, to define social space or membership in a certain group, it is analogous to the way a corporate logo or a national flag might function. What matters has less to do with the object's aesthetic quality and more to do with the complex signaling of identification and difference that the sign represents and accomplishes.

Consequently, music education that has intentionally aimed at pluralism, by for instance including popular music in school, steps into the battlefield of cultural capital in the society and may even be devalued through public criticism, as in Finland (see Väkevä & Westerlund, 2007) where most students attending out-of-school instrumental studies in the country's music schools study Western classical music and come from upper middle-class or upper-class families (Väkevä & Westerlund, 2007, p. 96). At the same time the resistance of classical musicians towards deepening pluralism is strategically given a minority voice and narrated from a hegemonic power stance of being culturally superior, historically the most significant, and therefore the music with the largest educative potential for future citizens. If learning is understood as an experience of identity, it needs to be asked why, if at all, classical music is a necessary part of the formation of identity in today's school context.

27.3 LEARNING THROUGH ONE'S (RESISTANCE) IDENTITY: YOUTH, POPULAR MUSIC, AND THE INTERSECTION OF GENDER AND ETHNICITY

While some identity categories, such as youth (Tarrant, North & Hargreaves, 2002; Lamont, Hargreaves, Marshall & Tarrant, 2003; Green, 2008; Saunders, 2010), gender (Green, 1996; Dibben, 2002; Björck, 2011), and to a certain degree ethnicity (Elliott, 1995; Volk, 1998; Sæther, 2008; Karlsen, 2013) have received much attention from a minority or resistance perspective in school music education, others, such as identity processes related to sexuality have until quite recently stayed in the margins of the music education literature (Abramo, 2011; Gould, 2012). Moreover, very few scholars have engaged in discussing music education practices from the perspective of multiple and multifaceted identities (Dyndahl & Ellefsen, 2009), in other words from the viewpoint of *intersectionality*. This section reviews studies mainly on how secondary school students, at least in some European countries, have been offered the opportunity to learn music through curricula and programs that aim to speak to their "resistance adolescent identities" by emphasizing popular or youth musics (Allsup, Westerlund, & Shieh, 2012) as the key content, as a response to earlier hegemonic pedagogies that emphasized Western classical musics. We will also look into how gender and ethnicity related identities may play out or be negotiated in music classrooms where such popular music pedagogy represents the main—if not the only—instructional approach.

27.3.1 The range and intensity of popular music identity work

Although identity work can be carried out in relation to practically any kind of music (DeNora, 2000), there is evidence from recent sociological research (Bennett et al., 2009) to suggest that the most intense negotiations in this respect are no longer between the "highbrow" culture of Western classical music and the perceived "lowbrow" culture of the popular music scene, but rather within the field of contemporary popular music itself, at least within European contexts. As such, popular music is, at least for the middle and younger generations, usually the preferred musical ingredient in identity work, and the medium through which they negotiate and express a wide range of identifications and disidentifications, the latter denoting ways in which they situate themselves both within and against the discourses surrounding them. As reminded by Tarrant et al. (2002, p. 135), there is a "consistent observation of research ... that involvement with (mainly popular) music is especially prominent during adolescence" and has great bearings on young people's identity formation. Furthermore, it is a well-known fact that adolescents' musical realities in and out of school may differ quite substantially from each other (see e.g., Lamont et al., 2003), and that what happens inside schools, musically speaking, may not at all, or only to a very little extent, correspond with the students' musical identities as developed and expressed outside the music classroom.

27.3.2 Nurturing popular music identities in school

Attempts to address and minimize this gap of musical worlds have been made both in curriculum work and through developing popular music pedagogies in music teacher education (see Westerlund, 2006). For instance, in the Norwegian music curriculum (Norwegian Directorate of Education and Training, 2006, p. 1) it is emphasized that "the musical background of pupils and the music and dance competence they acquire outside school should be used in the subject." Similarly, the Finnish curriculum (Finnish National Board of Education, 2004, p. 230) points out that the subject should provide "tools for the pupils to form their own musical identities." The idea that students' own musical interests and identities should form the basis for school-based instruction is also to be found in the popular music pedagogy articulated by Green (2008) in the UK, and in the subsequent work of implementing this pedagogy through organizations such as Musical Futures (s.a.). A main assumption of this important work, built on Green's previous research into popular musicians' learning practices (2002), is that "certain [popular] music learning practices are liable to arise naturally, or in other words, to come about instinctively or intuitively, without the intervention of a particular cultural or educational system, across a wide variety of social contexts" (Green, 2008, p. 41). Furthermore, Green argues that by investigating such learning practices and turning their most prominent features into educational principles (pp. 9–10), one can provide youngsters with a form of "authentic" music education that not only follows the inherent or organic learning practices of the respective styles, but which also originates from the students' own musical interests and aligns with their out-of-school musical identities. This view has been acknowledged, as well as criticized, among others by Väkevä (2012), who points out that the garage band practices studied and built on by Green, may not be relevant or applicable for most of the popular music practices that currently exist (or are about to be developed) in our globalized and digitalized world.

27.3.3 Popular music, gender, and ethnicity—facing the dangers of exclusion

Bringing popular music into the school context also allows for studies on how other aspects of students' identities are negotiated in and through such musics within a formal setting, and also on how these negotiations may allow or prevent access to roles and social positions within the musical world and thereby to learning experiences and outcomes. As noted by Green (1996, p. 51) already almost two decades ago, teachers may impose music learner identities on students, and in a popular music setting this may imply that they do "not see girls to be involved in performance on highly technological or electrical instruments ... most notably, drums and electric guitars." According to Björck (2011), this implicit style-association with various masculinities still holds true, and for girls and young women who want or are expected to play popular music in the classroom, it often involves complex negotiations of gender roles and femininity. Furthermore, popular music brings certain gender representations in the classroom, "including sexualized femininities" (ibid. p. 183), which can be problematic both for girls performing and playing in a school context as well as for the teachers facilitating such popular music practices.

As mentioned earlier, ethnic resistance identities have traditionally been acknowledged in music education by emphasizing people's right to have "their" musics recognized and included in the school curriculum, perhaps particularly in the North American discourse (see e.g., Elliott, 1995, pp. 211–12). However, even when popular musics are identified as one's "main musics of belonging," recognition and inclusion—or rather exclusion—may still happen along patterns of ethnicity. For example, Georgii-Hemming and Westvall (2012, p. 105) report that in the Swedish school context, certain kinds of "easy-to-play pop and rock songs" have become the prevalent content to such an extent that students identifying with musics that lie outside this norm face exclusion. Even students with a liking for other kinds of popular music, especially types that involve "the aid of computers" (p. 106), are disadvantaged, and this seems to especially affect boys with an immigrant background. Furthermore, from research on music education in immigrant-rich schools, it is evident that students often negotiate a certain popular music common denominator platform across various backgrounds (Sæther, 2008; Karlsen, 2012), but also that certain popular musics, such as rock and hip-hop, may be saturated with delineated meanings related to ethnicity (see Karlsen, 2014). Another related aspect is the complexity involved in handling the presence of the "homeland (popular) music" in the classroom, a process that may have very different outcomes, depending on the school and classroom climate and the students' perceived social position (see Karlsen, 2013).

As was argued at the beginning of this section, students' musical identity work will most likely be related to popular music, whether that music is present in their classrooms or not. However, the implementation and granting of the dominant position for popular music practices in the music classroom for the purpose of enabling students to learn through their resistance adolescent identities, often entails a reification of a certain type of identity "as more authentic or more emancipative than others" (Hernández Castillo, 2010, p. 389) and thus encourages new exclusions, as exemplified above.

27.4 Identities of becoming vis-à-vis relationships: The construction of "we" in the diverse music classroom

Given that any overarching collective identity, such as being French or American, Jewish or Christian, does not necessarily imply a relationship between the group members (Jenkins, 2008, p. 108), children and adolescents of today's societies may need other arenas for forming bonds of collectivity and hence for creating project identities (Castells, 2010) through which their positions in society can be negotiated and redefined. School is one evident place to start, as relationships certainly are central in classrooms where students spend most of their daytime. As such, classrooms form much of a child's or an adolescent's "local community" in which one learns, if anything, "who I am as a (music) learner." The peer group power dynamics effectively construct student identities as learners, and social agency in both positive and negative ways, as related to "what I am able to accomplish" and "what may not be within the range of my abilities." In this respect, music is no different from other school subjects. However, the collective aspects may be more central to the music subject than to some of the other subjects, since in music the group members cannot act musically—to "musick" (Small, 1998)—without considering the other members' musical actions. Otherwise, cacophony will follow. In schools where student diversity is widely represented and where, as Schmidt (2013, p. 25) has articulated, "us" and "them" are not anymore *geographically faraway categories*, teaching that does not aim to build a sense of collectivity among the students, but rather emphasizes the kind of:

> comparison that merely asserts value, categorizes, and creates hierarchy might not be only scholastically inept but also politically irresponsible [as it fails] to entice collaborative interaction and thus [also] to generate curiosity, criticism, and most significantly today, creative adaptability.

27.4.1 Ideas of collectivity and acts of collaboration within music education scholarship

Collaboration towards the collective identity of a classroom community may, however, be rarer amongst music education scholars than amongst practitioners. In the tradition of aesthetic music education, for example, the value of the subject in general education has been defined at the level of personal experience rather than "the horizontal relationships between person to person" (Reimer, 2009, p. 12). In his historical review, Jenkins (2008, p. 133) argues that while in social sciences in general, thinking in terms of community was put to the margins by the post-second world war intellectual climate, as well as by the postmodern celebration of difference, flux, and decentered polyvalence, now the idea of community has been revived, showing "signs of returning to a center-stage position that would have seemed unlikely twenty years ago." Similarly, the theorization of learning in general has moved towards collaborative and peer learning or "knowledge creation" and knowledge-creating agency by collectives, communities, and networks (Paavola & Hakkarainen, 2005, p. 541; Hakkarainen, 2013, p. 20). In music education, this shift is evident not yet so much in theories of musical learning (see, however, e.g., Gaunt & Westerlund, 2013), but particularly through the recent revival of so-called community music—referring at its widest to all kinds of musics of and in a community (Higgins, 2012, p. 3; see also, Veblen, 2013). In addition, some scholars paying attention to music-making as a rich, shared endeavor carrying great potential for exploration of collective identities can be found to be quite widespread in informing music education research. Small's (1998) work on *musicking* as a way of learning about and *exploring human relationships* already emphasizes the social power of music in vis-à-vis situations. Furthermore, scholars have investigated, for example, school performances as collective rituals that form not only the culture of the school, but also pupils' notion of who is allowed to perform (Nikkanen & Westerlund, 2009), as well as the collective identity and learning aspects of online music communities and their consequences for general music education (e.g., Partti & Karlsen, 2010; Partti & Westerlund, 2012; Waldron, 2011). Given the increasing diversity of schools, narratives that emphasize collaboration, and solidarity in classrooms are now appearing explicitly also in national curricular texts (see, e.g., Finnish National Board of Education, 2012) aiming to construct amongst educators, as earlier amongst cultural workers, "an image of the community-minded, active, engaged, participating, responsible, rather bustling citizen who is both immersed in and beyond culture" (Wetherell, 2007, p. 13).

27.4.2 The pluralist society and the increasing demands of constructing a "we"

Indeed, it is the increasing plurality of classrooms and the need to learn to live with this plurality (Bauman, 2011) that pushes also music education to reconsider how musical identification, learning, and community may relate to each other (see also UNESCO, s.a.). In general, scholars argue that people in a community may have weak or strong ties between each other, but it is through the concept of *community cohesion* that it is possible to form a "we," such as a collective identity in the social configurations of a music classroom; to create "comfort zones" and to find "unifying common ground, which will inspire assent across the board" within the diversity (Wetherell, 2007, p. 5). Since the concept of commonality and diversity are at the heart of community cohesion (p. 9) at the same time as the very policy of community cohesion "works against the gain of established identities" (p. 10), the vision for a classroom community may work as an educational tool in order to deal with the diversity of identities.

Consequently, instead of nursing legitimizing identities through nationalistic-patriotic and Western classical music, or resistance identities through building on limited popular music canons only, music education could foster collective, classroom-based project "identities of becoming" and thereby create fruitful learning environments for students from a rich variety of national, cultural, ethnic, linguistic, and geographical backgrounds. This might imply giving much attention to where to start building up a kind of collaboration that develops mutual respect and solidarity. Musically, this could mean, for instance, approaching the issue of repertoire from a global perspective by emphasizing "blended," "transcultural" or "world music" approaches (Chapman, 2012, p. 234), and including compositional collaborative projects and techniques in which students are allowed to bring the musical material they want to identify with for creating shared, hybrid artefacts, compositions, and collective "oeuvres" (Bruner, 1996).

The kind of community identity—of a shared "we"—created in music classrooms through such and similar approaches do not pre-exist and may not be formed simply through being together. It requires effort and willingness to become part of it, to share, and to develop it together with the others (Westerlund, 2002; Partti & Westerlund, 2013; Karlsen, 2014). Certainly it also requires the conscious planning and nurturing by a highly competent music teacher. As Boydston (1925, LW 2, p. 330) puts it, " 'we' and 'our' exist only when the consequences of combined action are perceived and become an object of desire and effort". Going once again back to Castells' (2010) three categories of identities, these kinds of processes may lead to the participants of the classroom community forming joint and possibly hybrid project identities in which the "we" relates to students' agency and to their increased ability to redefine their "position in society" (p. 8). This may take place through their experiences of learning musically and the practice of negotiation and navigation gained while relating and collaborating in pluralist classrooms and thus within a wide variety of musical resources belonging both in present and future society.

27.5 Conclusions

This chapter has argued that musical identities in the context of the school need to be examined from multiple perspectives, and that musical identity as an educational concept can be more misleading than useful if the complexity is ignored. Music education in multicultural societies and schools that balances the past and the future asks not simply what "ingredients" of identity students already possess, but rather what kind of ingredients for identity work and related choices should be provided along the pupils' educational journey for them to be able to develop agency and deal with plurality, change, and following uncertainty. The skill of navigating in rapidly changing settings and the ability to draw upon "different sets of expertise" (Jenkins et al., 2006, p. 22), collaborate in problem-solving, and extend the given frames for exercising one's agency (for example by breaking conventions) may therefore be crucial both for teachers and for pupils. As pointed out in the previous sections, some of the implications of these insights for music education might be for teachers to focus less on pre-established "canonic" material, whether that manifests itself in nationalist-patriotic, Western classical or popular music repertoire, and rather have the courage to explore genres and forms of music in which hybridity, transgression and open-endedness are significant characteristics. Moreover, allowing students to collaborate in *creating* such musical outputs by drawing on their various musical resources and frames of reference may also be one important approach. Unbeknown to the music teachers, their students might be quite skilled in such work already, for example through their participation in various music online communities (Partti & Karlsen, 2010; Partti & Westerlund, 2013). If so, this is a source of knowledge that the teachers can draw on when working on creating the "music classroom community identity."

In the kind of culture of music education created through such efforts, musical identifications can be seen as "temporary checkpoints" rather than permanent or tangible boundaries (see also, Jenkins, 2008, p. 127). We may hence hypothesize, as van Meijl (2010, p. 78) does, that a "disjunction between different cultural perspectives is becoming an inherent aspect of the lives of an increasing number of cosmopolitan citizens," and that the self may get its needed unity as this differentiation is becoming a natural part of people's lives. Ultimately, these questions are ones of what we understand the purpose of music in schools to be; to what degree the music curriculum is a vision of the future where the students will live rather than an effort to support the legitimate past; and what role music educators wish to play in their students' music-related work of identification, in the shaping and expanding of the past and future frames that circumscribe our subject.

REFERENCES

Allsup, R.E., Westerlund, H., & Shieh, E. (2012). Music learning and teaching during adolescence: ages 12–18. Youth culture and secondary education. In: G. McPherson & G. Welch (Eds.) *The Oxford handbook of music education*, vol. 1, pp. 460–75. Oxford: Oxford University Press.

Abramo, J. M. (2011). Queering informal pedagogy: sexuality and popular music in school. *Music Education Research*, 13(4), 465–77.

Anderson, B. (1983). *Imagined communities: reflection on the origin and spread of nationalism.* London: Verso.

Ariely, G. (2012). Globalization, immigration and national identity: How the level of globalization affects the relations between nationalism, constructive patriotism and attitudes toward immigrants? *Group Processes Intergroup Relations*, 15(4), 539–57.

Banks, J.A., & McGee Banks, C.A. (2010). Preface. In: J.A. Banks & C.A. McGee Banks (Eds.) *Multicultural education: issues and perspectives*, 7th edn, pp. v–viii. New York: Wiley.

Bauman, Z. (1999). *Culture as praxis.* London: Sage.

Bauman, Z. (2011). *Culture in a liquid modern world.* Cambridge, MA: Polity Press.

Benedict, C., & Schmidt, P. (2012). The National Curriculum as manifest destiny. In: C. Philpott & G. Spruce (Eds.) *Debates in music teaching*, pp. 102–17. London: Routledge.

Bennett, T., Savage, M., Silva, E., Warde, A., Gayo-Cal, M., & Wright, D. (2009). *Culture, class, distinction.* London & New York: Routledge.

Björck, C. (2011). *Claiming space: Discourses on gender, popular music, and social change.* (Doctoral dissertation). Gothenburg: University of Gothenburg.

Boydston, J.A. (1925). *The later works: 1925–1953. The collected works of John Dewey 1882–1953.* Carbondale, IL: Southern Illinois University Press.

Brown, A. (2012). Online musical cultures. In: A. Brown (Ed.). *Sound musicianship: Understanding the crafts of music,* pp. 251–63. Newcastle: Cambridge Scholars.

Bruner, J. (1996). *The culture of education.* Cambridge, MA: Harvard University Press.

Castells, M. (2010). *The power of identity.* 2nd edn. Singapore: Blackwell.

Chapman, J. (2012). Music education for a world of stylistic plurality and blending. In: A. Brown (Ed.). *Sound musicianship: Understanding the crafts of music,* pp. 228–40. Newcastle: Cambridge Scholars.

Côté, J.E., & Levine, C.G. (2002). *Identity formation, agency, and culture: A social-psychological synthesis.* New York, NY: Taylor & Francis Group.

DeNora, T. (2000). *Music in everyday life.* Cambridge: Cambridge University Press.

Dibben, N. (2002). Gender identity and music. In: R. MacDonald, D. J. Hargreaves, & D. Miell (Eds.) *Musical identities,* pp. 117–33. Oxford: Oxford University Press.

Dyndahl, P., & Ellefsen, L.W. (2009). Music didactics as a multifaceted field of cultural didactic studies. In: F. V. Nielsen, S.-E. Holgersen, & S.G. Nielsen (Eds.) *Nordic research in music education yearbook,* Vol. 11, pp. 9–32. Oslo: NMH-publikasjoner.

Elliott, D. (1995). *Music matters: A new philosophy of music education.* New York, NY: Oxford University Press.

Elliott, D. (1996). Music education in Finland: A new philosophical view. *Finnish Journal of Music Education,* 1(1), 6–20.

Finnish National Board of Education. (2004). *National core curriculum for basic education 2004: Music.* Available at: http://www.oph.fi/english/publications/2009/national_core_curricula_for_basic_education (accessed 10 August 2013).

Finnish National Board of Education. (2012). *Draft for national core curriculum for basic education 2014.* Available at: http://www.oph.fi/download/146131_Luonnos_perusopetuksen_opetussuunnitelman_perusteiksi_VALMIS_14_11_2012.pdf (accessed 10 August 2013).

Folkestad, G. (2002). National identity and music. In: R. MacDonald, D. J. Hargreaves, & D. Miell (Eds.) *Musical identities,* pp. 151–62. Oxford: Oxford University Press.

Fuller, A. (2007). Critiquing theories of learning and communities of practice. In: J. Hughes, N. Jewson, & L. Unwin (Eds.) *Communities of practice: critical perspectives,* pp. 17–29. New York, NY: Routledge.

Gaunt, H., & Westerlund, H. (2013). Prelude: the case for collaborative learning in higher music education. In: H. Gaunt & H. Westerlund (Eds.) *Collaborative learning in higher music education,* pp. 1–9. Farnham: Ashgate.

Georgii-Hemming, E., & Westvall, M. (2012). Music education: a personal matter? Examining the current discourses of music education in Sweden. In: S. Karlsen & L. Väkevä (Eds.) *Future prospects for music education: corroborating informal learning pedagogy,* pp. 97–114. Newcastle: Cambridge Scholars Publishing.

Giddens, A. (1999/2003). *Runaway world: how globalization is reshaping our lives.* New York, NY: Routledge.

Gould, E. (2012). Homosexual subject(ivitie)s in music (education): deconstructions of the disappeared. *Philosophy of Music Education Review,* 20(1), 45–62.

Green, L. (1996). The emergence of gender as an issue in music education. In: C. Plummeridge (Ed.) *Music education: trends and issues*, pp. 41–58. London: Institute of Education, University of London.

Green, L. (2002). *How popular musicians learn. A way ahead for music education*. Aldershot: Ashgate.

Green, L. (2008). *Music, informal learning and the school: a new classroom pedagogy*. London: Ashgate.

Hakkarainen, K. (2013). Mapping the research ground: expertise, collective creativity and shared knowledge practice. In: H. Gaunt & H. Westerlund (Eds.) *Collaborative learning in higher music education*, pp. 13–26. Farnham: Ashgate.

Hebert, D.G., & Kertz-Welzel, A. (2012). Introduction. In: D.G. Hebert & A. Kertz-Welzel (Eds.) *Patriotism and nationalism in music education*, pp. 1–20. Aldershot: Ashgate.

Hernández Castillo, A. (2010). Indigeneity as a field of power: Multiculturalism and indigenous identities in political struggles. In: M. Wetherell & C.T. Mohanty (Eds.) *The SAGE handbook of identities*, pp. 279–402. London: Sage.

Higgins, L. (2012). *Community Music in theory and practice*. Oxford: Oxford University Press.

Jenkins, H., Clinton, K., Purushotma, R., Robinson, A.J., & Weigel, M. (2006). *Confronting the challenges of participatory culture: Media education for the 21st century*. Available at: http://www.digitallearning.macfound.org/atf/cf/%7B7E45C7E0-A3E0-4B89-   AC9C-E807E1B0AE4E%7D/JENKINS_WHITE_PAPER.PDF (accessed 1 January 2009).

Jenkins, R. (2008). *Social identity*, 3rd edn. New York, NY: Routledge.

Johnson, J. (2002). *Who needs classical music? Cultural choice and musical value*. Oxford: Oxford University Press.

Kallio, A.A. (2014). Drawing a line in water: constructing the school censorship frame in Finnish secondary school popular music education. *International Journal of Music Education: Research*, 33(2), 195–209.

Kallio, A. A., & Partti, H. (2013). Music education for a nation: teaching patriotic ideas and ideals in global societies. *Action, Criticism, and Theory for Music Education*, 12(3), 5–30.

Karlsen, S. (2012). Multiple repertoires of ways of being and acting in music: immigrant students' musical agency as an impetus for democracy. *Music Education Research*, 14(2), 131–48.

Karlsen, S. (2013). Immigrant students and the 'homeland music': meanings, negotiations and implications. *Research Studies in Music Education*, 35(2), 158–74.

Karlsen, S. (2014). Exploring democracy: Nordic music teachers' approaches to the development of immigrant students' musical agency. *International Journal of Music Education: Research*, 32(4), 422–36.

Kosterman, R., & Feshbach, S. (1989). Toward a measure of patriotic and nationalistic attitudes. *Political Psychology*, 10, 257–74.

Lamont, A., Hargreaves, D., Marshall, N.A., & Tarrant, M. (2003). Young people's music in and out of schools. *British Journal of Music Education*, 20(3), 229–41.

Lehmann, A. (2012). Internationalizing music education. In: G.E. McPherson & G.F. Welch (Eds.) *The Oxford handbook of music education*, Vol. 2, pp. 641–3. Oxford: Oxford University Press.

van Meijl, T. (2010). Anthropological perspectives on identity: from sameness to difference. In: M. Wetherell & C.T. Mohanty (Eds.) *The SAGE Handbook of identities*, pp. 63–81. London: Sage.

Musical Futures. (n.d.). *Musical futures*. Available at: https://www.musicalfutures.org/ (accessed 5 August 2013).

Nikkanen, H., & Westerlund, H. (2009). Musiikkiesitys yhteisöllisen koulukulttuurin raken-tajana. Deweyn demokraattiset kasvatusperiaatteet perusopetuksen musiikkikasvatuksessa. *Musiikki*, 39(1), 27–41.

Norwegian Directorate of Education and Training. (2006). *Music subject curriculum*. Available at: http://www.udir.no/Stottemeny/English/Curriculum-in-English/_english/Curricula-in-English/ (accessed 10 August 2013).

O'Flynn, J. (2007). National identity and music in transition: issues of authenticity in a global setting. In: I. Biddle & V. Knights (Eds.) *Music, national identity and the politics of location: between the global and the local*, pp. 19–38. Farnham: Ashgate.

Paavola, S., & Hakkarainen, K. (2005). The knowledge creation metaphor—an emergent epis-temological approach to learning. *Science & Education*, 14, 535–57.

Partti, H., & Karlsen, S. (2010). Reconceptualising musical learning: New media, identity and community in music education. *Music Education Research*, 12(4), 369–82.

Partti, H., & Westerlund, H. (2012). Democratic musical learning: how the participatory revo-lution in new media challenges the culture of music education. In: A. Brown (Ed.) *Sound musicianship: Understanding the crafts of music*, pp. 300–12. Newcastle: Cambridge Scholars.

Partti, H., & Westerlund, H. (2013). Envisioning collaborative composing in music educa-tion: learning and negotiation of meaning in operabyyou.com. *British Journal of Music Education*, 30(2), 207–22.

Reay, D. (2010). Identity making in schools and classrooms. In: M. Wetherell & C. T. Mohanty (Eds.) *The SAGE handbook of identities*, pp. 277–94. London: Sage.

Reimer, B. (2009). *Seeking the significance of music education: Essays and reflections*. Lanham NY: MENC.

Saunders, J.A. (2010). Identity in music: Adolescents and the music classroom. *Action, Criticism, and Theory for Music Education*, 9(2), 70–8.

Schatz, R., Staub, E., & Lavine, H. (1999). On the varieties of national attachment: Blind versus constructive patriotism. *Political Psychology*, 20(1), 151–74.

Schmidt, P. (2013). A rabbi, an imam, and a priest walk into a bar…or, what can music educa-tion philosophy learn from comparative cosmopolitanism? *Philosophy of Music Education Review* 21(1), 23–40.

Schwartz, S.J., Côté, J.E., & Arnett, J.J. (2005). Identity and agency in emerging adulthood: Two developmental routes in the individualization process. *Youth Society* 37, 201–29.

Scruton, R. (2007). *Culture counts: Faith and feeling in a world besieged*. New York, NY: Brief Encounters.

Small, C. (1998). *Musicking: The meanings of performing and listening*. Middletown, CT: Wesleyan University Press.

Sparshott, F. (1987). Aesthetics of music: Limits and grounds. In: P. Alperson (Ed.) *What is music? An introduction to the philosophy of music*, pp. 33–100. New York, NY: Haven Publications.

Sæther, E. (2008). When minorities are the majority: Voices from a teacher/researcher project in a multicultural school in Sweden. *Research Studies in Music Education*, 30(1), 25–42.

Staub, E. (1989). *The roots of evil: the origins of genocide and other group violence*. New York, NY: Cambridge University Press.

Tarrant, M., North, A.C., & Hargreaves, D.J. (2002). Youth identity and music. In: R. MacDonald, D.J. Hargreaves, & D. Miell (Eds.) *Musical identities*, pp. 134–50. Oxford: Oxford University Press.

UNESCO. (n.d.). Learning to live together. Available at: http://en.unesco.org/themes/learning-live-together (accessed 1 August 2013).

Veblen, K. (2013). The tapestry: Introducing community music. In: K.K. Veblen, S.J. Messenger, M. Silverman, & D.J. Elliott (Eds.) *Community music today*, pp. 1–9. Lanham, NY: Rowman & Littlefield Education.

Väkevä, L. (2012). The world well lost, found: reality and authenticity in Green's "New Classroom Pedagogy." In: S. Karlsen & L. Väkevä (Eds.) *Future prospects for music education: corroborating informal learning pedagogy*, pp. 23–49. Newcastle: Cambridge Scholars Publishing.

Väkevä, L, & Westerlund, H. (2007). The "method" of democracy in music education. *Action, Criticism, and Theory for Music Education*, 6(4), 96–108.

Volk, T.M. (1998). *Music, education, and multiculturalism: Foundations and principles.* New York, NY: Oxford University Press.

Waldron, J. (2011). Locating narratives in postmodern spaces: a cyber ethnographic field study of informal music learning in online community. *Action, Criticism, and Theory for Music Education*, 10(2), 32–60.

Wenger, E. (1998). *Communities of practice: Learning, meaning, and identity.* Cambridge: Cambridge University Press.

Westerlund, H. (2002). *Bridging experience, action and culture in music education.* Studia Musica, 16. Helsinki: Sibelius Academy.

Westerlund, H. (2006). Garage rock bands: a future model for developing musical expertise? *International Journal of Music Education*, 24(2), 119–25.

Wetherell, M. (2007). Introduction. Community cohesion and identity dynamics: dilemmas and challenges. In: M. Wetherell, M. Laflèche, & R. Berkeley (Eds.) *Identity, ethnic diversity and community cohesion*, pp. 1–14. Los Angeles, CA: Sage.

CHAPTER 28

....

MUSIC IN IDENTITY IN ADOLESCENCE ACROSS SCHOOL TRANSITION

....

JENNIFER E. SYMONDS,
JONATHAN JAMES HARGREAVES,
AND MARION LONG

In the United Kingdom, the majority of children change schools during early adolescence (ages 10–14 years) just as they are managing the complex task of leaving childhood for a more adult role in society. In line with the national tradition of elementary education, before transition the schooling comes to the student: lessons all happen in the same classroom with the same teacher, often at the same desk or place around the table. There, teachers have more opportunity to become familiar with their students and children know each other well. From a child's viewpoint, the contrasts between this familiar setting and their new school can be keenly felt in the first year after transition: whether they are changing to a middle school (ages 8–10 to 12–14), a secondary school (ages 11–16/18) or a high school (ages 13–16/18).

Typically, these "transfer schools" are marked by an increase in the size of buildings and grounds, the number of students on roll, the number of teachers per student, work complexity, and focus on academic achievement (Symonds & Galton, 2014). There, children are responsible for managing their own equipment and moving between classrooms, encounter multiple teaching styles and experience lessons that are more goal-directed, structured around the subject for study, rather than the individual's involvement with it. In order to become a "successful" transfer student (academically and/or socially), children must employ greater self-management, fit into new social groups, and work out what type of student they will be, for example deviant or conformist (e.g., Measor & Woods, 1984).

At transition, several interesting things happen to children's identities. First, the move from the smaller, familiar feeder school to the larger, more impersonal transfer school means that, at least temporarily, their sense of self becomes diminished relative to its everyday environment. Typically, children feel more anonymous in the larger peer group (Simmons & Blyth, 1987) and lose their emotional connection with their teachers (de Wit, Karioja, & Rye 2011). However at the same time, more is required of the self as children struggle to redefine themselves and cope with increased personal responsibility. Here, transition acts as a prism, diffracting what children know about themselves as they encounter new self-related information (Noyes, 2006). This brings specific identity issues to the foreground, such as gender roles and sexuality in the larger, more advanced peer group (Symonds, Galton, & Hargreaves, 2014), academic selves in new classrooms (e.g., Gneiwotz, Eccles, & Noack, 2011) and coping resources, e.g., whether children are sufficiently well organized. In this sense transition also acts as a lens, focusing children on aspects of their identities that are most challenged by the move (Symonds, 2015).

Over the course of the journey into the transfer school, children will think, feel and act differently, and perhaps even look different, as evidenced by themselves and others around them. Their perceptions of their current and future identities will change, as will their outward projection of themselves within the school community. This chapter deals with these issues of personal and social identity construction within the context of music by synthesizing extant literature and presenting two case studies of how musical identity plays out at transition in individual lives. We begin by outlining our social developmental perspective on identity development in adolescence, which stems from Erikson's (1968) approach, and takes into account other more recent research (e.g., Côté & Levine, 2002; Eccles, 2009). We then focus more specifically on the central issue of musical identity at school transition, as defined by the factors common to three studies reviewed in this chapter: Sloboda (2001), Marshall & Hargreaves' (2007) *Humpback Bridge* study, and our own work, *Changing Key* (2011). Those earlier studies were influential for Changing Key, with their foci on changes within music education across school transition; however, the central thrust of our study was that identity development occurs across environments, both in and—perhaps even more crucially—out of, school and other educational contexts.

28.1 Identity in adolescence

The majority of children in the United Kingdom change schools at age 11/12 years, which is the average age that children begin puberty in developed nations (Coleman & Coleman, 2002). Here, sex hormones stimulate the development of reproductive organs, outward sexual characteristics and a growth spurt that occurs earlier for girls than for boys (Tanner, Whitehouse, Marubini, & Resele, 1976). This results in the body becoming visibly different and more differentiated in comparison to peers. Around the same time, although governed by a different developmental clock (Sisk & Forster, 2004), the mind grows more capable of generating abstract thought and metacognition (Vygotsky, 1931/ 1998), enabling 10–14-year-olds to reflect in more detail about their personal qualities and social roles. These changes coincide with a shift in people's expectations for how responsible children should be (Symonds, 2009) as they straddle the worlds of the child and the teenager (Measor & Woods, 1984).

This makes for a turning point in identity formation, where "development must move one way or another, marshalling resources of growth, recovery, and further differentiation" (Erikson, 1968, p. 16). Erikson referred to this stage as an identity crisis, although he meant a critical moment in human development, rather than an "impending catastrophe" (p. 16). In Erikson's perspective, adolescents build on identity elements formed in childhood such as preferences, desires, and perceived tendencies, which until this point are a dim reflection of the future self. They reassess their identity in the new social context of transition to adulthood, seeking a role, which will allow them to function with "unique excellence" (Erikson, 1968, p. 129). At this point, self-evaluation and career goals (or at least future selves) become inextricably linked, making for a shift in focus from *who I am now,* to *who I want to be.*

More recent philosophy specifies that early adolescents construct their identities by collating firsthand information about themselves into a second order abstraction. This firsthand information, such as their memories of playing the violin, is stored in a hypothetical neural network referred to as the self-concept or self-construct (Côté & Levine, 2002). The information in the self-concept is gathered and sorted often unconsciously, but can also be put together by the conscious, rational self, known as the ego (Côté & Levine, 2002). Not all of the self-concept is accessible at any one time and accordingly identity mutates according to which elements are brought forth within different contexts (Markus & Wurf, 1987). Commonly, identity entails two kinds of self-perceptions: a person's skills, characteristics and competencies, and their personal values and goals (Eccles, 2009). These elements are constructed in relation to the environment, so that when the environment changes at school transition, identity is reappraised and often reconstructed (Symonds, Long, & Hargreaves, 2011).

In line with Erikson's focus on career, the aspects of personal musical identity that help one form a career self, such as musical accomplishment and whether one is a musical person (e.g., Lamont, 2002) should become more salient at adolescence. Because adolescents also begin to emphasize peers and deprioritize families in their development, those aspects of musical identity that strengthen their ties to peer networks (Eccles, 2009) should also rise to the foreground. Having an investment in music becomes a symbol of social status, and can be used to denote peer group membership and belonging. Music is used to project identity, and transition to secondary school opens up new spaces in which such projections can resonate.

28.2 MUSICAL IDENTITY
AT SCHOOL TRANSITION

School transition alters many components of children's musical lives. In the context of learning they experience new music teachers, a new music curriculum, and different resources for learning music and musical extracurricular activities, and opportunities for school-based instrumental tuition. In the social realm their teachers and school peers provide new role models and companions for music. There are also musical influences outside of school, issuing from parents, siblings, local peers, and the neighborhood, such as church and other social activity groups, which can change as children enter a new phase in their educational careers. This chapter takes the perspective that school transition is a *life transition,* permeating these multiple contexts and altering children's musical identities in ways that transcend school experiences.

We conducted a literature review, which sought to establish how these changes in musical environment influence children's musical activity: for example, changes in how children gather and share music, listen to and discuss music, compose, practice, and perform music. We review how blockages to musical resources at transition can diminish children's musical activity, and how greater access to resources can stimulate it. Children's musical activity is also connected to their capability for conceptualizing and externalizing music, which alters for some as they become more independent across the transition, and more capable of metacognition. The critical point here is that changes in children's musical *activity* are directly connected to changes in their musical *identity,* as our review of an English national study and other relevant work clearly shows. This three-way interaction between musical environment, musical activity, and musical identity underpins our review, which first considers how musical identity changes at transition for most children (a thematic synthesis), and then how this occurred for two children whose musical careers diverged after transition.

28.3 Methods

28.3.1 Thematic review

Having performed a general survey of the literature regarding adolescence, music, and identity development, we narrowed our scope by searching several electronic databases including ERIC and Google Scholar for any publications that included the word *music* and at least one of the phrases *school transition* or *school transfer* in the title, abstract, or body of the manuscript. We also incorporated several publications on the Key Stage Two to Key Stage Three transition into the resulting list. Together, the documents were scrutinized for information relating to children's musical identity. This included any mention of perspectives on musical identity, psychological selves, emotions relating to music, or musical behavior. Three publications fulfilled these criteria (Table 28.1) including our recent study Changing Key. All were longitudinal, recording children's perspectives in the years immediately before and after transition.

We used our perspective that musical identity develops in multiple contexts at school transition to synthesize the findings into key domains of family, friendships, teachers, classroom music, extracurricular musical activities, instrumental music, and transition interventions. In each, we explored the types of musical environment present at school

Table 28.1 Studies of musical identity at school transition

Name	Schools	Data	Time scale
Sloboda (2001)	35 primary schools to 9 secondary schools.	636 children surveyed 3 times each. 44 children interviewed 2 times each.	Questionnaire in Year 6 (Spring), Year 7 (Autumn & Spring). Interviews in Year 6 (Spring) and Year 7 (Spring).
Marshall & Hargreaves (2007) *Humpback Bridge*	13 schools	68 children interviewed 2 times each.	Interviews in Year 6 (Summer) and Year 7 (Autumn).
Symonds, Long, & Hargreaves (2011) *Changing Key*	6 primary schools to 3 secondary schools.	25 children interviewed 4 times each.	Interviews in Year 6 (Summer) and Year 7 (Autumn, Spring, Summer).

transition, the musical activity undertaken by children and how these factors inter-played with children's musical identity development.

28.3.2 Case studies

We then illustrated how musical identity developed for two children in the Changing Key study. Changing Key was the student voice component of "Musical Bridges," a larger program of music at school transition research, convened by Adrian Chappell and funded by the Paul Hamlyn Foundation. Like this chapter, Changing Key took a holis-tic, multi-ecological approach to gathering data on musical identity development. That is, we considered that any changes in musical identity are negotiated and manifest in and across many environments. Accordingly, in our study we were keen to open up the notion of musical engagement to include, for example, listening, dancing, composing, performing, and talking in the playground or any other activity involving music.

Changing Key studied 24 children who transferred from primary to secondary school in 2009–2010. They were situated in three locations, chosen to represent one inner city community (Dagenham), one rural (Devon), and one somewhere in between (Bolton), spread around the UK. Within each of these locations, subjects were in the same school pyramid—two primary schools feeding into the same secondary school. We asked the primary teachers to select the participants, having requested that they had mixed musi-cal experience and enthusiasm, mixed ethnicity, and evenly mixed gender. The children were educated about the project and about their role as interviewees, in an active par-ticipation workshop, before the research commenced.

Data were collected over four school terms, spanning the final term of primary school, and the first year of secondary school. In each term, we conducted "Myself and music" interviews. Adolescents were asked to discuss their musical experiences and identity in the range of contexts described earlier. We repeated the interview questions across terms, only altering the tag lines to reflect the transition (e.g., "... now that you are in your second term at secondary school"). The two case studies in this chapter were selected from six children whose interview transcripts were analyzed and presented as personal narratives in the final Changing Key report (Symonds et al., 2011).

28.4 RESULTS

28.4.1 Thematic review

Table 28.2 displays those studies that reported data for each context of musical identity development at transition considered by this review. As the table demonstrates, Changing Key offered more information on relationships, whilst both Changing Key and the Humpback Bridge studied the schools' provision for music. In comparison, Sloboda (2001) focussed on learning an instrument.

28.4.2 Family

For the adolescents in Changing Key, families were something of a constant amidst the rapidly changing musical landscape at school transition. Parents continued to share their musical preferences with their children, transmitting information about specific forms including popular, ethnic, and religious music. Older siblings introduced

Table 28.2 Data on the contexts for musical identity development

	Study		
	Changing Key	Humpback Bridge	Sloboda (2001)
Context			
Family	Yes	–	–
Friendships	Yes	–	–
Teachers	Yes	–	–
Resources	Yes	Yes	Yes
Curriculum	Yes	Yes	–
Assessment	–	Yes	–
Extracurricular	Yes	Yes	–
Instrument	Yes	–	Yes

children to new music and listening technologies on both sides of the transition. Many children enjoyed listening to their parents and siblings' choices, and incorporated both styles and in some cases specific recordings into their musical preferences.

Before transition, mothers were heralded as especially important for ferrying children to music lessons and providing musical equipment. This facilitated children's musical activity and ability to perceive themselves as instrumentalists. At the same time, other children reported not learning an instrument because their parents could not afford lessons. These disparities were still present after transition, even when schools offered extracurricular instrumental lessons, as these still required parents to pay for an instrument so that children could practice at home.

28.4.3 Friendships

While at primary school, many children in Changing Key danced and sang with friends for an adult audience at home. These creative endeavors were stimulated by the children's sense of enjoyment and desire to emulate popular performers. However, a remarkable change in our data was that none of this activity was reported after transition, suggesting that as children's interests changed, their self-consciousness grew; perhaps they perceived dancing and performing to/for parents or other adults at home to be immature or embarrassing. Similarly in Sloboda's (2001) study, fewer children danced to music or sang after transition. At that point, the Changing Key children sang informally with friends when no adults were present, and one boy joined a rock band, which positioned his musical activity as being acceptable within adult worlds. This was similar to Sloboda's (2001) finding that one case study girl who gave up her instrument after transition said she would consider taking it up again, but only in the context of modern music performance.

In Changing Key, children also spent more time listening to music with friends after transition, as parents allowed them to play out later with friends. Transition spurred children to make new friends who, in many cases, introduced them to different musical forms including classical and hip hop. This burgeoning listening activity helped children justify their preferences in more detail by referring to specific musicians and styles, whereas at primary school many of their rationales had been vague, such as "I listen to my sister's music." Despite this widening of their experience, several children felt under more pressure to show a specific preference for 'new' music, as otherwise there would be a mismatch with the listening culture of their school peers. This finding resonates with thought from Zillmann & Gan (1997), that for musical identity development in adolescence, activity must be owned and directed by the peer group.

28.4.4 Teachers

Here, we focus on school music teachers as mentors and role models for music, rather than on the musical information they transmit. None of the reviewed studies reported children's perceptions about their primary school music teacher. In Changing Key, children were taught at primary school by music coordinators with specialist training, non-specialist classroom teachers, visiting music specialists and classroom assistants. As found in other studies, the non-specialist classroom teachers might have lacked confidence in teaching practical music (Henley, 2011), whilst the range of teacher types possibly arose from difficulty recruiting trained music coordinators at primary level (Lamont, Hargreaves, Marshall, & Tarrant, 2003).

After transition, the experiences of children in Changing Key were consolidated with the move to subject specialist music teachers, whom, according to Ofsted (2012), were likely to have a tertiary degree in music. Accordingly, many children described their new teachers as more knowledgeable, dedicated, and inspiring. Having these new role models strengthened some children's aspirations for a career in music, and had a positive impact on how children valued music in society. However in the second and third terms, some children's impressions of their new teachers soured after they were disciplined, and discovered that they did not enjoy learning music theory.

28.4.5 Resources

At the end of primary school, children have looked forward to better equipment for music at secondary school (Marshall & Hargreaves, 2007; Symonds et al., 2011), and to playing new instruments there, in order to gain skills and more adult experience (Lamont et al., 2003; Symonds et al., 2011). Children's hopes have been confirmed after transition, as discovered in Sloboda's (2001) study, in which children reported there being greater opportunity to do music in secondary schools. In Changing Key this increased opportunity fed their aspirations of becoming professional musicians. However some secondary schools prevented children from continuing with instruments from primary school, because they did not provide them. For example in the Humpback Bridge, children who enjoyed playing the glockenspiel at primary school could not use this as a criterion for evaluating their musical ability at secondary school (Marshall & Hargreaves, 2007). Similarly in Changing Key, Peter lost his ability to impress friends and classmates with his skill on the djembe (an African drum), which had a negative impact on his musical identity, as we explore in our first case study.

There is little information on changes in ICT provision in music across transition, however: we know from Ofsted (2012) that these resources are limited in many primary schools. This might relate to there being a lack of good quality, affordable equipment (Lamont et al., 2003) and appropriate training for primary school music teachers. In the Humpback Bridge, some children were introduced to IT in the first term, which helped them enjoy music more. However in Changing Key, children only reported using ICT in music in the third term, once the basics of theory and performance had been covered. This lag in using ICT for composing and performing is found in other research to frustrate children who desired a career in electronic music (Shehan Campbell, Connell, & Beegle, 2007).

28.4.6 Curriculum

In the majority of primary schools inspected by Ofsted (2012) and in Changing Key, there was little focus on practical music and more playing or singing along to songs and rhythms. In the Humpback Bridge, children were disillusioned, having little opportunity to play instruments other than percussion, being forced to sing hymns and traditional songs, and feeling bored by the way that music was taught. At primary school, children with more musical experience, for example those learning an instrument outside school, needed to be challenged more in class (Ofsted, 2012).

Despite some children's hopes for a more advanced musical curriculum after transition (Symonds et al., 2011), many schools in Changing Key and the Humpback Bridge, and those inspected by Ofsted (2012), started from scratch, i.e., taught the basics, to ensure an even spread of musical knowledge across different feeder students. This was embodied in the teaching unit *The Elements of Music*, which was used in many secondary schools (Ofsted, 2012). Starting from scratch in this way had a positive effect on the musical identities of less musically experienced children in Changing Key. There, a flurry of children began composing their own music at home for the first time after learning the basics. However, this activity was not reported in the second and third terms, as children became more pressured with homework and lost interest in composing. The opposite effect was reported by children with more musical knowledge, who were frustrated by returning to basics in the first term. Several schools responded by promoting these children to a student assistant position, which enhanced their perception of their musical ability. More advanced students enjoyed the freedom of composing their own pieces in the third term, when they were given more license to work at their own pace.

28.4.7 Assessment

Secondary school music teachers have typically assessed children with refined criteria for knowledge and mastery. However, at primary school, assessment was more often concerned with completing work (Ofsted, 2012). This shift in assessment practices has several potential consequences for children's musical identity, as suggested by Ofsted (2012). First, children might lose their enthusiasm for classroom music when being driven towards complicated assessment targets, rather than being free to enjoy learning for its intrinsic values (Ofsted, 2012). Secondly, children might feel less musically competent when their work is judged as poor quality in secondary school, whereas at primary school they only had to complete work in order to get a good grade (Ofsted, 2012).

In the Humpback Bridge, children were questioned about their musical experience by their new teachers, who did not seem to value non-academic experience such as belonging to community groups or listening to music. There, children felt judged by their teachers, and noticed that their teachers paid more attention to children with greater academic musical experience. A large majority of children felt powerless to contribute to how they were assessed, and this change in assessment practices appeared to affect how musical they perceived themselves to be.

28.4.8   Extracurricular activities

A survey of 83 primary schools found that nearly all had choirs and instrumental tuition, and roughly a third had orchestras (Ashworth, Atherley, & Chappell, 2011). Often, participation in choir and school concerts is compulsory (Lamont et al., 2003), which children in the Humpback Bridge recalled as a downside of primary school music, after they transferred. The focus on traditional extracurricular activities has persisted across transition, despite there being a wider range of non-traditional activities such as "junk band" (where instruments are made out of rubbish; Symonds et al., 2011) and vocal groups in the tradition of Glee clubs (Ofsted, 2012).

The dominant culture of traditional, selective activities at secondary school has had a significant impact on children's musical identities. In Changing Key, children who tried out for activities were usually more musically experienced, or had friends in those activities. When they passed auditions, children felt special and musically talented, which helped them perceive themselves as being musical. However, failure to get in damaged other children's musical aspirations and caused them to identify themselves as non musical.

It is surprising that schools do not offer more non-traditional activities, since children prefer those that match with their ambition for a career in modern music, e.g., in composing electronic music, or being in a rock band (Shehan Campbell et al., 2007). Before transition, children also looked forward to these activities because they were easier to get into (Symonds et al., 2011). Perhaps because few non-traditional activities are offered after transition, participation in musical extracurricular activities has plummeted to as low as 10% of all children in the first year of secondary school (Ofsted, 2012; Lamont et al., 2003).

28.4.9   Instrumental lessons

Sloboda (2001) focussed on children's participation in instrumental lessons across the transition. He found that of 684 children, 61% played a musical instrument at home or at school in primary school. Two girls in this cohort were tracked as case studies. They explained that they played an instrument because it was intrinsically enjoyable, provided a hobby and added to their sense of personal and social self-worth. Both presumed they would continue to play their instrument after transition. In fact, however, they stopped playing after transition, as did 45% of the larger group of children. When asked to explain why they gave up playing, they said that playing an instrument was boring, and prioritized homework and playing out with friends over practicing their instrument. They also felt under too much pressure emotionally and from parents to complete Grade exams and practice several hours a day, once in secondary school.

In contrast, in Changing Key, children were excited about taking up instruments for the first time at secondary school, when lessons were made available to them. However, these subsidized lessons were often oversubscribed, and children had to wait until Christmas to begin their instrument of choice. This delay in instrumental tuition encouraged one child to turn his interests to sports in order to sustain the self-esteem that he previously gained by playing music, whilst another child showed great self-management and determination by teaching herself the recorder at home until flute lessons became available in the second term.

The difference between the two studies, i.e., giving up vs. taking up an instrument, might relate to the types of children being studied. In Sloboda's (2001) study, the children receiving instrumental lessons presumably had some social privilege to begin with, as their parents could afford the monetary and time costs of the venture. There, perhaps children perceived learning an instrument as a hobby that could be discarded (Sloboda, 2001) whereas in Changing Key, instrumental lessons were a resource that was prized by children who could not afford the privilege beforehand.

28.4.10 Case studies

Our case studies of Amy and Peter (pseudonyms) from Changing Key illustrate some of the links between environment, activity, and identity observed in the thematic review. The case studies are underpinned by their answers to two general questions about music and identity. Simplistic though this may seem it provides a clear index of their trajectories over the year. Both students were classified as high achievers on leaving primary school, and both identified themselves as "a musical sort of person" there. However, their musical identities seemed to follow directly opposite courses across the transition: Amy's identity as a pianist strengthened and provided a basis for continuity, whilst Peter's enthusiasm for music waned and nearly expired during his first year at secondary school.

28.4.10.1 *Peter and the djembe: blocked resources*

In the first interview, Peter's confidence rode high: he was enthusiastic about music and focussed his attentions on the djembe, an African drum. The instrument is played as part of a troupe, in call and response structures with improvised breaks for soloists. This offered Peter a number of social opportunities: to lead the group, display improvisation and invention, execute complex rhythms, coordinate bodily movement, and perform to a ready-made, responsive audience (the troupe itself). In this manner, the resources for music provided at primary school facilitated Peter's perception of being a musical child. However, Peter was not allowed a djembe at home, even after having offered to save up for it himself and then only to play it in the shed or the garage. Peter's parents had told him this was to avoid upsetting his father who had migraines, although earlier his mother had offered to pay for djembe lessons, and said "we'll see" about the possibility of buying Peter a djembe. This was the first of several blockages that Peter described to us, regarding his musical development.

On arrival at secondary school, Peter was told that although there were djembes available, students only had access to them from Year 8 onwards. In order to overcome this, he and his friends asked about forming their own djembe group, Peter's application to join the "junk band" having been submitted too late. However, when the teacher eventually allowed them to start the group in the second term, Peter decided that actually he'd rather not join in. This rejection of musical resources coincided with Peter's uptake of other extracurricular activities including sport, where he gained self-confidence by displaying his prowess much like when playing djembe at primary school. Possibly, Peter's need for self-esteem was fulfilled by those other activities. Also Peter felt a disconnect with his music teacher and lessons, because of what might have been a learning disability, as he consistently reported struggling with mathematics and English, and likewise the theoretical and technical aspects of classroom music. Peter's reason for not joining the djembe troupe might simply have been that he didn't want anything more to do with classroom music, as it offered too many opportunities to feel incompetent.

Accordingly, over the course of Year 7, Peter became increasingly disaffected musically (see Table 28.3), his previously bullish confidence and musical activity almost

Table 28.3 Peter: musical identity statements

Peter	"Would you say you are a musical sort of person?"	"How much does music matter to you?"
Wave 1: Preparation (July (Y6))	Well people say ... I've got good taste in music. And I can really do stuff with it. Like a mixture of things. People say "can you do this?" And so I tried it out and I was actually really good at it. Like the way I got into acting and stuff ...	Well, it's quite an important thing in my life because if there wasn't music life wouldn't be fun. Because there wouldn't be...if there wasn't any music you couldn't sing together with your friends or stuff like that.
Wave 2: Encounter (October (Y7))	Well, I sort of haven't played a lot so my music [] sort of going down because loads of people are not up to my standard so they're all [gloomy] in my group.	Music is like I'm talented in music and everyone says so, even my parents and I'm just talented and playing different instruments. I'm a quick learner with instruments but when they say something I just go straightaway.
Wave 3: Adaptation (February (Y7))	No, because I've got more into other lessons that just music. So I'm like an all round type.	Well, it doesn't matter as much as when I was younger, because the school's just had a massive impact on me because I have lots of homework, I have to ... No, I don't have to worry about music as much because when I was in Year 6 I probably liked it so hard ... wanted to play it more. But as I got older I don't ... it sort of fades away.
Wave 4: Stabilization May (Y7)	Mm ... no.	Um not as much. ... Um, since I was in primary school.

drying up. He obtained popularity through deviancy, using music as a tool, for example by beatboxing in lessons in order to gain his classmates' attention. This uptake of a more deviant identity by boys after transition can be a bid to increase popularity in a new, unfamiliar peer group that values macho behavior (e.g., Measor & Woods, 1984). Music played several roles in creating Peter's masculinity, for example Peter's father listened to music when exercising in the gym, and played loud music to Peter when driving. This might have conveyed to Peter that male behavior is attached to strength and noise. At the same time, Peter identified his musical tastes as masculine by implication, saying that he didn't like "girly" solo artists, unlike his friend.

This attachment to macho behavior might have further dissuaded Peter from learning theoretical, abstract information in music lessons, as children attach this type of learning to non-active, feminine behavior (Whitehead, 2006). Accordingly, Peter was quick to befriend a fellow beatboxer, and the two mouthed music to each other outside of school, when in school the curriculum focussed on learning words and symbols. For Peter by the end of Year 7, music had become a symbol of school disengagement, rather than a means for personal and social accomplishment. This trajectory was reflected in Peter's ending comment that he was non-musical, the opposite of his description of being very musical at primary school.

28.4.10.2 *Amy's piano: an embedded identity*

In stark contrast to Peter, Amy was very well provided for by those around her, having access to many resources and supports in the forms of encouragement and discipline. Amy's parents, in particular her mother, played a very strong role in facilitating her piano playing, despite not being musicians themselves. They paid for her lessons, exams, and books; they bought her a piano and before that a keyboard; her mum drove her to her lessons (with music on in the car) and helped ensure she stuck to her regular practice regime. Amy also had a valuable resource in her young piano teacher, with whom she identified at a personal level and as a role model.

Amy said that she had reignited a previously extinguished flame in her family by taking up piano, and so she saw her identity as part of a transgenerational script. Her father wanted to play the drums as a little boy, but her grandparents could not afford a drum kit. Indeed, her first keyboard experience was after her father brought down his old electronic instrument from the attic. Amy said in her opening interview that she was "the first in her family to play an instrument and to carry on to Grade III." As torchbearer for the family tradition, she noted the new ground she had claimed, from sticking letter names on the keys of the keyboard to learning to read music: shifting from novice to learned status. Indeed, bridging the gap with earlier generations, she tried teaching her Nan, who learned how to read music although didn't carry through to play the piano.

Over the course of the study, Amy affirmed her identity as *a Pianist*. Having succeeded at Grade III, she was well in advance of many of her new classmates at secondary school. By the second term, her new classroom music teacher had appointed Amy and one other student as advisory friends to their peers, helping others with their work. Amy found the sheer volume of demand for her help quite stressful at times, and said "some people in my class are like 'She knows it all … she's like a piano player. It's not fair'". However, her identity as a pianist was strong enough for her not to be disturbed by this, and she valued the ability to play an instrument over being popular with her peers. In fact, following transition, this distinction from her peers was something she enjoyed. She noted that the school keyboard club was intended for people below her standard, and when she was appointed the first ever, and only, pianist in orchestra this was a great boost to her musical confidence.

Despite this initial increase in musical activity, Amy soon became overwhelmed by the academic stresses of the transfer school, where she was required to do a lot of homework. She overcame this by cutting down on extracurricular activities, including the school orchestra, and postponing her study for Grade IV, in favor of a more relaxed approach to the piano and life in general (see Table 28.2 Wave 3). For example she learned some Christmas songs from YouTube tutorials that she had been introduced to by a friend. In the third term after she had adjusted to the greater academic demands, Amy restarted formal piano study with the intention of one day becoming a piano teacher. Throughout the transition period, Amy showed remarkably efficient management of her emotional and personal needs in order to keep playing an instrument she enjoyed (see Table 28.4).

Table 28.4 Amy: musical identity statements

Amy	"Would you say you are a musical sort of person?"	"How much does music matter to you?"
Wave 1: preparation (July (Y6))	Yes. I think so… but I'm not one of those people that go to every musical and want to play music 24/7, but I do like music.	It matters a lot because when I play my piano, it's really fun and I'm used to it and it matters a lot. If I just gave that up I would have nothing to do in my spare time.
Wave 2: encounter (October (Y7))	Yeah. I'm really into music … because I play music out of school and in school and I just do everything really …	Music is a big part of my life really because if I didn't play the piano and I didn't listen to music I really would not know what to do … if they just cut out music that would be really cruel …
Wave 3: adaptation (February (Y7))	Yeah … at home, if there's music on in the background on my telly, and if it's like a Sunday and no-one's doing anything there's like the radio on then I'm always like dancing about the room and like singing along while I'm doing other things …	Well, it's quite a big thing in secondary school because if you don't like know any new music you're a bit weird.
Wave 4: stabilization (May (Y7))	Um, yeah. I would.	Um, it's quite important because if you didn't have music there wouldn't be a lot to do really.

28.5 CONCLUSIONS

Peter and Amy's distinct and contrasting—indeed opposed—music identity trajectories across transition both seem to be tied to the material and socio-cultural resources available. Amy had a piano to play, people to play it to/for, and, in her piano teacher, a model; Peter had neither a djembe nor any other instrument available after transition, and was told that in any case his father's migraines would not permit the noise. Extrapolating from these two local models and from the three thematic studies reviewed herein, these patterns might represent two groups of children, coming from musically advantaged and disadvantaged backgrounds. For both groups, secondary school presents new challenges to musical identity.

For children from advantaged, musically supportive backgrounds like Amy's, school transition creates a mixture of risk and protective factors for musical identity. For those who have had private instrumental tuition outside school or equivalent experiences, having to start from scratch in school music might be frustrating, leading to boredom and a loss of motivation. A further risk derives from being placed in a new social context: learning a classical instrument may be seen as uncool by peers, and transient; a hobby rather than a long-term pursuit in which identity is invested (Sloboda, 2001). In addition, as Amy found, the increased workload at secondary school is a threat to regular practice, so strategies for managing this conflict in order that the instrumental study, with its connotations for identity can be sustained, need to be in place. For children like Amy, transition imposes a decision to react towards or against their musical pursuits, and in so doing, to become more conscious of their musical identity. Alongside all these risks, musically experienced children have a certain social status over and above others: they have increased opportunity to be involved in selective musical extracurricular activities, and notice that they are more musically accomplished than their peers, which boosts their musical self-esteem.

For children from less privileged backgrounds, transition is a time of increased opportunity. At secondary school there are more, better musical resources, access to instrumental lessons, and school lessons education starting with the basics: suddenly for these children, there is a pathway to developing musical aspirations. However, they are still vulnerable to significant blockages. This group of children is more likely to struggle academically (Croll, 2002), and so as music lessons become more advanced, they may find their motivation drained. Also, not having the advantage of private lessons, they are less likely to be selected for musical extracurricular activities. Indeed, there is often some cost for instrumental lessons at schools, which may not be affordable to their parents.

In *Changing Key* we only studied schools in England, although patterns of musical identity development throughout the world are presumably dependent on resources, and people's access to them. The UK government's recommendation, made in response to Darren Henley's Review of Music Education (Henley, 2011), that children should be given the chance to learn a musical instrument for a year, or at least for a term, is surely a good thing. This provides a wonderful opportunity for those whose access to music lessons would otherwise be blocked. However, in terms of musical identity development, the *embeddedness* of musical pursuit within other areas of life seems to be what distinguishes children like Amy, whose backgrounds either serve to enable and support musical identity development, from those like Peter, whose development is stifled by a lack of resources.

It is not simply that Amy continued to play an instrument when Peter did not; rather the piano connected existing aspects of Amy's musical identity and experience, whereas for Peter, this fledgling network was quashed when the opportunity to play djembe was removed at transition. By providing equal musical opportunities to children from a range of backgrounds, schools can begin to address surface disparities in musical experience. Whether this promotes musicality may depend on how carefully schools develop *all* children's musical identities as a continual process, rather than simply increasing a certain type of resources after transition, as for some children, this offering will be made against the odds.

References

Ashworth, D., Atherley, M., & Chappell, A. (2011). *Sound tracks: Supporting young people's musical progression from primary to secondary school*: Paul Hamlyn Foundation. Available at: www.musicalbridges.org (accessed 25 February 2016).

Coleman, L., & Coleman, J. (2002). The measurement of puberty: a review. *Journal of Adolescence*, 25, 535–50.

Côté, J.E., & Levine, C.G. (2002). *Identity formation, agency and culture: a social psychological perspective*. Malwah, NJ: Lawrence Erlbaum Associates Inc.

Croll, P. (2002). Social deprivation, school-level achievement and special educational needs. *Educational Research*, 44(1), 43–53.

De Wit, D.J., Karioja, K., Rye, B.J., & Shain, M. (2011). Perceptions of declining classmate and teacher support following the transition to high school: Potential correlates of increasing student mental health difficulties. *Psychology in the Schools*, 48(6), 556–72.

Eccles, J. (2009). Who am I and what am I going to do with my life? Personal and collective identities as motivators of action. *Educational Psychologist*, 44(2), 78–89.

Erikson, E. (1968). *Identity, youth and crisis*. New York, NY: Norton.

Gniewosz, B., Eccles, J., & Noack, P. (2011). Secondary school transition and the use of different sources of information for the construction of the academic self-concept. *Social Development*, 21, 537–57.

Henley, D. (2011). *Music education in England*. Manchester: Department for Education.

Lamont, A. (2002). Musical identities and the school environment. In: R.A.R. MacDonald, D.J. Hargreaves, & D.E. Miell (Eds.) *Musical identities*, pp. 41–59. Oxford: Oxford University Press.

Lamont, A., Hargreaves, D.J., Marshall, N.A., & Tarrant, M. (2003). Young people's music in and out of school. *British Journal of Music Education*, 20(3), 229–41.

Markus, H., & Wurf, E. (1987). The dynamic self-concept: a social psychological perspective. *Annual Review of Psychology*, 38, 299–337.

Marshall, N.A., & Hargreaves, D. J. (2007). Crossing the humpback bridge: primary-secondary school transition in music education. *Music Education Research*, 9(1), 65–80.

Measor, L., & Woods, P. (1984). *Changing schools*. Milton Keynes: Open University Press.

Noyes, A. (2006). School transfer and the diffraction of learning trajectories. *Research Papers in Education*, 21(1), 43–62.

Ofsted. (2012). *Music in schools: sound partnerships*. London: Office for Standards in Education, Children's Services and Skills.

Shehan Campbell, P., Connell, C., & Beegle, A. (2007). Adolescents' expressed meanings of music in and out of school. *Journal of Research in Music Education*, 55(3), 220–36.

Simmons, R.G., & Blyth, D.A. (1987). *Moving into adolescence: the impact of pubertal change and school context*, Vol. 2. New Brunswick, NJ: Transaction Publishers.

Sisk, C.L., & Foster, D.L. (2004). The neural basis of puberty and adolescence. *Nature Neuroscience*, 7(10), 1040–7.

Sloboda, J. (2001). Emotion, functionality, and the everyday experience of music: where does music education fit? *Music Education Research*, 3(2), 243–54.

Symonds, J. (2009). Constructing stage-environment fit: early adolescents' psychological development and their attitudes to school in English middle and secondary school environments. Doctoral Thesis, Faculty of Education, University of Cambridge.

Symonds, J., & Galton, M. (2014). Moving to the next school at age 10–14 years: an international review of psychological development at school transition. *Review of Education*, 2(1), 1–27.

Symonds, J., Galton, M., & Hargreaves, L. (2014). Emerging gender differences in times of multiple transitions. In: I. Schoon & J. Eccles (Eds.) *Gender differences in aspirations and attainment*, pp. 101–22. London: Cambridge University Press.

Symonds, J. (2015). *Understanding transition: what happens to children and how to help them*. London: Routledge.

Symonds, J., Long, M., & Hargreaves, J. (2011). *Changing key: adolescents' views on their musical development across the primary to secondary school transition*. London: The Paul Hamlyn Foundation.

Tanner, J.M., Whitehouse, R.H., Marubini, E., & Resele, L.F. (1976). The adolescent growth spurt of boys and girls of the Harpenden Growth Study. *Annals of Human Biology*, 3(2), 109–29.

Vygotsky, L.S. (1931/1998). Development of thinking and formation of concepts in the adolescent. In: R.W. Reiber & A.S. Carton (Eds.) *The collected works of L. S. Vygotsky*, Vol. 5, pp. 29–82. Berlin: Springer.

Whitehead, J.M. (2006). Starting school—why girls are already ahead of boys. *Teacher Development*, 10(2), 249–70.

Zillmann, D., & Gan, S. (1997). Musical taste in adolescence. In: D.J. Hargreaves & A.C. North (Eds.) *The Social Psychology of Music*, pp. 161–87. New York, NY: Oxford University Press.

CHAPTER 29

....

CHILDREN'S ETHNIC IDENTITIES, CULTURAL DIVERSITY, AND MUSIC EDUCATION

....

BEATRIZ ILARI

29.1 INTRODUCTION

....

There is no more place of origin. Origin is existence. Don't tell me where I am from.
I am. I ain't. I'm just here.

Rosana & Zélia.

Text extract from Rosanna & Zélia, Postcard, Copyright © Peregrina Music,
with permission from Peregrina Music.

GLOBALIZATION, digital technologies, and new migration waves have transformed the
way most of us live. The rapid flow of information and the exchange of goods and ideas
coupled with the possibility of expanding geographical frontiers, both physically and
virtually, have brought about a myriad of ways of being in the world and interacting with
others. We are now able to wander through otherwise unchartered territories, and are
constantly confronted by experiences with individuals and groups of people whose lifestyles, practices, and belief systems differ considerably from our own. These increased
cultural and ethnic contacts have resulted in more awareness of differences among peoples, and brought cultural diversity to the forefront of social, political, and educational
debates (UNESCO, 2009).

Globalization and internationalization have certainly made the world more complex (Appadurai, 1993; Jensen, 2011), and have been viewed as both positive and negative forces, especially in their relationship to culture and identity (Huron, 2008; Räsänen, 2010; Jensen, Arnett & McKenzie, 2011). These two interrelated phenomena have also reinforced the notion that cultural diversity is a reality that needs to be better understood as it is directly related to ethnicity, language, religion, gender, and social class (Räsänen, 2010). Experiences with different cultures are eminently social as they are directly linked to the ongoing process of identity construction, or the ways we make sense of and position ourselves in relationship to others, based on both our similarities and differences (Reicher, Spears, & Haslam, 2010).

Likewise, music is typically experienced in a social realm, and is therefore related to the development and construction of identity. From a psychological perspective, music plays important social functions in regards to interpersonal relationships, mood, and self-identity (Hargreaves, Miell, & MacDonald, 2002). Musical identities relate primarily to self-identity, which is shaped in and through music. Yet they do not exist in a vacuum, but are a product of human experiences and interactions in cultural and social contexts. Hargreaves, Miell, & MacDonald (2002) further suggest that musical identities come in two main forms: identities in music (IIM) and music in identity (MII). While IIM relates to social and cultural roles of music (e.g., violinist, composer, DJ), MII refers to the ways in which music is used in the development and construction of other aspects of our identities.

IIM are many. The flamenco guitarist, the *puxador de samba* (i.e., the singer who leads the song in a samba ensemble), and the orchestra musician, for example, are all identities in music, which have been constructed over time and in association with specific groups and cultural practices. Speaking or thinking about one of these particular identities in music primes certain stereotypical associations that may or may not involve issues of ethnicity, race, culture, and gender (Ilari, 2010). How "ethnic" or "culturally diverse" they are depends, ultimately, on prior experiences and on the ways we position ourselves in relationship to them. The same can be said about MII, in its relationship to cultural diversity and ethnicity. Along with our personal histories, strong experiences—both positive and negative—with cultural groups and their musical practices, as well as identities in music, are likely to influence how we define ourselves.

Hence, there is little doubt that cultural diversity impacts the development and construction of social and musical identities across the lifespan, in a wide range of contexts, including educational settings. Apart from occasional presentations of multicultural repertoires to students, in what other ways does cultural diversity show itself in music teaching and learning settings? Who is the "other" in music education? How do children perceive issues of "otherness" as they explore different musical repertoires and interact with peers from different ethnic and cultural groups? And, finally, can music be used as a tool of social engineering in contexts where perceptions of ethnicity and culture have generated interpersonal conflict?

This chapter discusses the development and construction of social identity in childhood, through the lens of ethnicity and cultural diversity. Given the complexity of bicultural social development (Padilla, 2006), the main focus here is on the music education experiences of immigrant and ethnic minority groups, and on MII. The first section includes a brief review of select theories of social identity and ethnic identity development, and their connections with childhood musical experiences. The latter are based on the author's experience as a music educator and researcher. The second section brings forward a discussion on musical experiences of ethnic minority groups, immigrants, and refugees. Finally, the third section focuses on the relationship between music education, cultural diversity and identity construction. The promotion of cultural understanding and multiethnic integration is also considered in this closing section.

29.1 Theoretical framework: social identity

The concept of identity has undergone many changes across time, following different theoretical orientations, and according to standards from various disciplines (Hargreaves, Miell, & MacDonald, 2002). While there are many disagreements where theories are concerned, scholars seem to agree on the role of social experiences and institutions in shaping identities. As social and psychological constructions, identities are founded on perceived differences, as we define ourselves in relationship to the "other" (Clarke, 2008). That is, "who we are is partly defined in reference to who we are not" (Reichers, Spears, & Haslam, 2010, p. 47).

Social identity theory (SIT) is one of the main theories that have been applied to the study of social identity (Tajfel, 1978; Tajfel & Turner, 1979). This theory centers on the interplay between personal and social identities (Ellemers, 2010). According to SIT, humans belong to different social groups, such as national, ethnic, and cultural groups. Group membership is defined in terms of one's perception, evaluation, and identification with a particular collective of humans. In order to obtain a sense of positive self-worth from group membership, individuals perceive their own group (or the ingroup) as being different and somewhat better or superior than other groups (the outgroups). (Importantly, a lack or weak identification with a particular group does not necessarily generate ingroup favoritism (Bennett, 2011).) Over time, groups become internalized as part of one's self-concept (Bennett, 2011, p. 353).

Reichers, Spears, & Haslam (2010) argue that SIT is, above all, a theory of social change, given the context in which it emerged. Tajfel (1978), the author of SIT, was particularly concerned with the study of prejudice, stereotyping, and negative attitudes towards different groups. Unsurprisingly, this is also a concern of educators working in multicultural and multiethnic environments. Yet, it is important to stress that SIT was not formulated to explain developmental processes, even if some scholars (e.g., Nesdale, 1999, 2004) have attempted to connect them, as seen later on.

29.1.1 Social identity in childhood

The development and construction of social identity is an ongoing process that is influenced by the many contexts in which humans navigate in everyday life (Hargreaves, Miell, & MacDonald, 2002). A major influence in the lives of young children is the family, in the intimate, home environment. This is also true where musical participation is concerned (Campbell, 2011; Young & Ilari, 2012). As children develop and grow in culture, they begin to explore other contexts, which become equally important. Schooling is compulsory in most countries when children are 5 or 6, which coincides with the onset of middle childhood (Eccles, 1999). With formal schooling, a whole new world opens up in children's lives, not only in terms of academic contents, but also in respect to new social rules and interactions that have a profound impact on identity formation (Wortham, 2006). Likewise, engagement in extra-curricular activities such as sports programs and music classes, as well as participation in religious and cultural groups also impacts the development and construction of social identity in childhood and adolescence.

The development of social identity has been described as a complex process that requires exploration of four main areas or building blocks, namely:

- Awareness, as the child becomes aware of social categories.
- Identification, as the child identifies herself as a member of a particular category.
- Stability, as the child gradually develops stability of category membership for herself.
- Consistency, as the child realizes that there is some consistency of category membership in different contexts, for example, at home and in school (Garcia-Coll & Marks, 2009).

These building blocks can be seen in everyday musical experiences of children and youth, because music and musical practices are directly linked to a wide range of human groups that make up our social worlds (Turino, 2006). *Awareness* is exemplified by the child who shows a basic understanding that musical genres are related to specific social categories, yet without explicit knowledge of meanings associated with them. A Brazilian preschooler, for example, might learn quite early on that only girls dance in some local, traditional musical manifestations, like the *tambor de crioula* (Ilari, 2009b), but might not yet know that this particular genre is associated with the Afro-Brazilian experience. *Identification* occurs when a child identifies with specific repertoires and gains ownership of them. By doing so, she distinguishes between those who practice it and those who don't, or, "them" and "us." A classic example is when elementary grade students begin to describe children's nursery rhymes and tunes (e.g., the *itsy bitsy spider* and *twinkle twinkle little star*) that they used to love when they were younger as "too childish" or "babyish," and report preferences for more "adult" music, such as pop or rock tunes. *Stability and Consistency* are seen when the child repeatedly reiterates her identity as, for example, a pop music lover or orchestral player, and realizes that this identity does not change whether she is at home, at school, or hanging out at the mall with friends.

29.1.2   Ethnic identity in childhood

An important aspect of social identity that has received little attention from music education research is ethnic identity. There are many definitions of ethnic identity. Jensen (2011) suggests that ethnic identity refers to a person's sense of peoplehood based on one's ancestry and is associated with one's cultural values and traditions. It is an ascribed identity into which one is born, although ethnic groups themselves are fluid and dynamic, changing with historical and social events (p. 173).

Ethnic and cultural identities obviously intersect, as ethnicity is an important determinant of cultural identity. The latter can be understood as the adoption of beliefs and practices of one or more cultural communities, including in key areas of ideology, love, and work (Jensen, Arnett, & Mckenzie, 2011). A fundamental distinction in research on these two forms of identities is their foci. While studies on the construction of ethnic identity tend to focus predominantly on the perceptions and interactions of minority groups living among other ethnic and racial groups, studies on the formation of cultural identity normally center on a wide range of groups, including majority groups, who may or may not interact with other cultures (Jensen, Arnett, & Mackenzie, 2011).

How children understand and construct knowledge of one's ethnic membership is obviously associated with cultural socialization within and outside the home. Following a meticulous study of Mexican-American children, Bernal, Knight, Garza, Ocampo, & Cota, (1990) propose a three-stage model of development of ethnic identity in childhood, and that these are somewhat related to established stages of child development. In the early years, children learn ethnic labels by paying attention to concrete descriptions of appearance, physical characteristics, and behaviors. There is usually a lack of understanding of implicit meanings in ethnic labels, as well as a lack of preference or feelings associated with membership in specific groups. As children enter school, ethnic labels gain more complete meanings. That is, children begin to understand the constancy of their own ethnicity and some of the consequences of belonging to a particular ethnic group. In the late years of elementary school (i.e., roughly between ages 8 and 10 years), children become more proficient in identifying their ethnic membership, and show more ethnic constancy, knowledge of ethnic groups, and preferences. This three-stage model reinforces the notion that ethnic identity is "a work in progress" in middle-childhood (Garcia-Coll & Marks, 2009, p. 90), with social institutions such as schools playing a major role in the process. Interestingly, Bernal et al.'s (1990) model not only aligns with the building blocks of social identity described earlier, but is also linked to musical experiences, as seen in Table 29.1.

Based on SIT, Nesdale (1999, 2004) offers a different model of ethnic identity development, which could be viewed as complementary to Bernal et al.'s (1990) theorizing. For Nesdale (1999, 2004) ethnic and national identities develop in four phases. Phase

Table 29.1 Ethnic Identity Development Model proposed by Bernal et al. (1990) and children's musical experiences

Stage	Musical vignette
Early years	In São Paulo, a 3.5-year-old girl dances and sings to a children's musical video from Chile called "El soldado Trifaldon" (*Tikitiklip*). The video is based on images from muralist art painted by the group Unidade Muralista Luchador Ernesto Miranda. The girl is aware of the fact that the singer sings in some odd language, but does not question it. Much to her delight, she keeps asking her parents to replay the video, so that she can sing the refrain and move to it. Although the poem is "child-friendly", there are hidden political messages that the child does not capture.
Early school years (6–8 years)	In Los Angeles, a Mexican-American 6-year-old, who is taking part in a longitudinal research study, sings "Happy birthday". The child smiles frequently as she sings. The researcher also notes that to each verse, the child adds one full measure of "cha-cha-cha", and asks him about this compositional device. The child states: "That's how my family sings it because we are from Mexico. The Americans don't sing like this. They don't do the *cha-cha-cha*". Then, the child repeats the song, but without the "cha cha cha," to show the American version of it.
Late school years (8–10 years)	In Mexico City, a group of 9-year-olds from a distinguished conservatory is asked to listen to a recording of a Peruvian boy of the same age singing *a cappella* and notate what they hear. Song lyrics are about the boy's love for a "cholita" and the fear of not knowing what will happen in the future. After listening to the song a few times, the children are invited to share their notes with the class. Most notice that the Spanish language sounds different than what they are used to, and try to guess the country or region of origin. One boy states that the song is from somewhere in South America, because the singer uses a "wrong accent and is too romantic". When asked why does he think that it could not be a Mexican child singer, the child offers: "We, Mexican boys are tough people, 'somos hombres fuertes' [We are strong men!] South Americans are different. They are not as tough as we are!"

1 takes place when children are around ages 2–3, when ethnic, racial, and national cues are unimportant to them. Phase 2 begins around age 3, when the child becomes aware of ethnic and national labels, and begins to self-identify with the ingroup. According to Nesdale, this process may continue on until the child turns 10 or 11. In Phase 3, beginning at around age 4, children start to develop favoritism towards their ingroup, although there are usually no negative attributions towards outgroups. In Phase 4, which starts at about age 7, negative attributions towards outgroups and prejudice begin to emerge. Importantly, Nesdale cautions that not all children enter this phase. Entrance to this phase depends largely on:

- The child's level of identification with the ingroup.
- Attitudes of other ingroup members towards the outgroup.
- Whether the ingroup perceives the outgroup as a threat.

Table 29.2 Nesdale's ethnic identity development and children's musical experiences

Phase	Musical vignette
Phase 1	In Pasadena, an Asian-American toddler watches a musical video of DJ Lance (i.e., an African-American host) singing in an episode of TV show *Yo Gabba Gabba*. The child enjoys the show and does not make any comments regarding the singer's race, ethnicity, or skin color.
Phase 2	A few years later, the same Asian-American child who is now a preschooler, watches an old episode of *Yo Gabba Gabba* with her baby brother. She explains to him: "See? He is not Chinese like us."
Phase 3	In Rio de Janeiro, a kindergartner wearing a soccer jersey, sings the chorus of his soccer team's anthem in the playground. As he performs the tune, another kid runs across the playground displaying a jersey from a different team while singing a different anthem. He interrupts his singing and shouts: "Hey, you're not on my team!"
Phase 4	In Curitiba, a student teacher working in an expensive private school invites her students to learn an Afro-Brazilian dance called "jongo." Excited to show this traditional musical genre to her class, she notices that a fourth-grader is particularly upset. He refuses to join the class by stating that this is music of "poor black people," and that he is not there to learn this type of repertoire.

Once again, these phases of development are illustrated in Table 29.2 by musical vignettes that stem from the author's experience.

Taken together, these theories and models support the idea that the development and construction of social identity and its components is not only complex, but directly connected to experiences that children have at home, in schools, through the commercial world, and media, and in the community at large (see Young & Ilari, 2012).

Now that we have revised some theories of social and ethnic identity development, let's turn to the examination of cultural diversity in music education settings, and their relationships to identity construction and development.

29.2 CULTURAL DIVERSITY, ETHNIC IDENTITY, AND THE "OTHER" IN MUSIC EDUCATION

Cultural diversity presents itself in many different ways in music education settings. Schools and other educational spaces such as conservatories are "microcosms of society" in that these sites congregate members from different social, cultural, and professional groups (Räsänen, 2010). Multiple identities coexist in the music class as students often come from a wide range of social, cultural, ethnic, religious, and national backgrounds. Even if some still conceive of schools/educational spaces and their mandated curricula as being "neutral spaces," issues of race, ethnicity, and culture permeate them (Jo, 2009). Furthermore, conceptions of child, childhood, and development that inform educational discourses—including music education discourses—continue to be largely grounded in Eurocentric models and theories (see Fleer, Hedegaard, & Tudge, 2009).

Traditionally based on very specific views of repertoire, practices, and learners, music education is an invention of the West. Fortunately our definition of this field has broadened in the past few decades, so to include a wider range of experiences, repertoires, and practices (Schippers, 2009). While our definition of what counts as music education has expanded in the past few decades, our view of music learners continues to be somewhat "generalized," and based on some specific attributes of student identity such as age, grade, and musical ability. Apart from sparse attempts to examine learners' cultural and ethnic backgrounds or gender (e.g., Abril, 2002; Morrison, 1998), much music education research still tends to treat these important markers of student identity as independent variables. Fortunately, this situation is changing. In recent years, researchers have turned their attention to the experiences of "other" learners, including students from ethnic minority groups, immigrants, and refugees (Suárez-Orozco & Suárez-Orozco, 2001; Garcia-Coll & Marks, 2009; Ilari, 2009; Soto, 2011; Campbell, 2011; Marsh, 2012), as they navigate music classrooms.

29.2.1 Ethnic minority/majority students

Ethnic minority is a term used to designate an individual who self-identifies or is identified to an ethnic group that is marginalized by society due to social and cultural characteristics that are different or devalued by the dominant ethnic or cultural group (Nadal & Rivera, 2008).[1] The concept of ethnic minority can be broken down into two concepts: "ethnic group" and "minority." Ethnic groups normally include individuals who share common characteristics like country of origin, race, language, religion, beliefs, and values, which are transmitted to new generations and transformed over time (Nadal & Rivera, 2008). Ethnic groups are therefore heterogeneous, which makes their classification a difficult task. Minority is a term that is often used to designate social status assigned to particular groups in a society or culture. While majority groups usually hold the power in a given society, "minority groups are those that are negatively affected by an equal power distribution" (Nadal & Rivera, 2008). Minority groups can be based on different group characteristics such as gender, religion, race, sexual orientation, and ethnicity.

Many studies of ethnic minority group status have been conducted in countries with strong and recent histories of immigration and multiculturalism (e.g., Sweden), or

---

[1] In this chapter, ethnic minority is used as an inclusive term that encompasses people of all marginalized ethnicities, irrespective of their racial group (see Nadal & Rivera, 2008).

where ethnicity is an important constituent of everyday life (e.g., USA). While some ethnic minority groups may be related to recent or old migration waves (e.g., Mexicans in the USA or South East Asians in the UK), others refer to populations that gained minority status over time (e.g., the Aboriginal in Canada).

With regard to musical experiences, earlier studies have examined ethnic minority/ majority status and student listening preferences and attitudes. These studies suggest that children's decision-making processes are complex and likely to be influenced by a combination of factors including musical characteristics, visual and auditory cues, familiarity with the performer/style, and, of course, a combination of ethnicity and majority/minority status of child listeners themselves and performers (Morrison, 1998; McCrary, 2000; Abril, 2002). Some of these studies are also consistent with SIT, in that participating students tend to rate the music of their ingroups higher than the music of outgroups (Henninger, 1999; McCrary, 1993), and regardless of their own minority/ majority status. Unsurprisingly, ethnic minority/majority status is also known to affect student interactions in the music classroom (McCrary, 2000), with direct bearings on identity.

29.2.2   Immigrant and refugee students

Not all immigrants and refugees hold minority status. When they do, this is yet another important marker of their identities. Immigration is, above all, a major life decision that impacts the lives of individuals and families in multiple ways. Motivations to move to a new land are many, including socioeconomic reasons and/or fears of persecution due to ethnic, religious, or political reasons. In general, people who leave their countries on a voluntary basis are called immigrants, whereas those who are escaping freedom are often referred to as asylum seekers or refugees (Suárez-Orozco & Suárez-Orozco, 2001). These groups are far from being homogeneous as individual members may come from different social strata, have varied levels of education, and hold legal or illegal status in the new country (Suárez-Orozco & Suárez-Orozco, 2001).

The first months of immigration are particularly challenging for newly arrived students, who often feel isolated, inadequate, and disengaged (Howell, 2011). Furthermore, students who hold refugee statuses and who had limited access to formal schooling in their countries of origin, are often aware of how far behind they are in relationship to their peers, which directly impacts their sense of self-worth (Howell, 2011). Learning a new language along with new social and cultural rules is also challenging for many newcomers. Not to mention that some students come to a new land with psychological traumas and serious scars due to life circumstances in countries marked by war, poverty and other hardships that directly impact their lives (Marsh, 2012).

Thus, an important aspect of the immigrant and refugee experience refers to the ability to negotiate multiple identities. Immigrant and refugee students often struggle as they develop and construct their bilingual (or even multilingual), bicultural, and bimusical identities (Padilla, 2006; Soto, 2012). As Karlsen & Westerlund (2012) contend, "negotiating the self and one's deepest beliefs and values implies negotiating frames and possibilities for action in various cultural systems" (p. 232). As children navigate and express these identities in everyday life, they become proficient in code-switching, or the ability to shift between different cultural behaviors, languages, and even musical systems (Soto, 2012). Over time, children of immigrants and refugees may fully assimilate the new culture and construct identities around it, or may forge a composite identity that incorporates both their culture of origin and the new one (Suárez-Orozco & Suárez-Orozco, 2001).

Uses of music are directly linked to the construction and expression of these identities in everyday life (Folkestad, 2002). As an example, in an earlier project with Brazilian Dekasegi[2] children and adults residing in Japan (Ilari, 2009a), it became clear that the Dekasegi expressed their identities by using music in either emblematic or catalytic ways (see Folkestad, 2002), depending on the person or group they were interacting with (Ilari, 2009a). When interacting with Japanese peers, the function of music was often more emblematic, in that it reinforced locally held perceptions of Brazil and Brazilians. In these interactions, the Dekasegi expressed their identities by dancing, singing, or listening to songs that were representative of Brazil and some aspect of its culture (e.g., happy character, sensual moves, etc.), even if these were outdated or rather inaccurate. Conversely, when interacting with fellow Brazilians, the function of music was more catalytic, in that music was used to reinforce their "Brazilianess" and strengthen group cohesion (Ilari, 2009). In these situations, the Dekasegi reported listening, singing, and dancing to music that carried both personal and emotional connotations, such as familiar songs that marked different eras of their lives.

Importantly, while all children will be transformed by immigration, the "ethos of reception," or the opportunities and affordances, along with the attitudes and beliefs held by the members of the new country towards immigration and their group in particular, will determine the quality of their experience in the new homeland (Suárez-Orozco & Suárez-Orozco, 2001). These are seen in everyday experiences and interactions, in and out of schools, and pose a challenge to a wide range of fields, including music education.

29.3 CULTURAL DIVERSITY, ETHNIC IDENTITIES, AND MUSIC EDUCATION: POTENTIALS AND CHALLENGES

Globalization and internationalization have brought many challenges to education as a whole, as classrooms and learning environments are becoming increasingly diverse (Saether, 2010). In the case of music education, some pressing challenges include the

---

[2] Dekasegi, in Japanese means "to work away" from home. For a discussion refer to Daniel Touro Linger's book (1995), "No one home."

need for policies and attitudes to pedagogy, values, and teaching strategies that both celebrate and respect cultural diversity (Saether, 2010; Kelly-McHale, 2013). Given that the "integration through music education is neither simple nor evident" (Saether, 2010, p. 46), this is no simple task.

Following the rationale of MII, recent studies in music education show promising scenarios. They suggest that music might serve as a vehicle for self-expression, agency, and integration as children from ethnic minority groups, immigrants, and refugees navigate different communities of practice (Karlsen & Westerlund, 2010; Howell, 2011; Marsh, 2012). Creative projects, in music and related areas, have the potential to increase students' sense of connectedness to the school (Howell, 2011), which is also related to the "ethos of reception" discussed earlier (Suárez-Orozco & Suárez-Orozco, 2001). Furthermore, collective musical experiences may offer emotional safe spaces for students from immigrant, refugee, and ethnic minority groups to express themselves, as they synchronize their bodies and instruments with peers, giving room to self and group expression, and social cohesion (see Cross, 2005; Cross, Laurence, & Rabinowitch, 2012). This is consistent with Eisner's (2002) earlier suggestion that, "among all fields of study in our schools, the arts are at the forefront in the celebration of diversity, individuality, and surprise" (p. 235).

Aside from these promising scenarios, some challenges persist, including our general tendency to view the "other" with a certain degree of exoticism (Saether, 2010). As Saether (2010) argues, we often group culturally diverse musical practices into "theirs" and "ours" (in some ways consistent with SIT) instead of viewing cultural diversity in music education as a question of relationships between people. Furthermore, there is a strong tendency to adopt a pedagogical orientation of "learning about" instead of "learning from" (see Saether, 2010). While the former implies that we can easily understand the "other" and play down some internal differences between "them" and "us", the latter implies awareness that we cannot understand the "other", and need to be open-minded and conscious that learning is, above all, part of a relationship (Saether, 2010). As we enter the relationship and meet the "other", we may also lose our own sense of epistemological security (Saether, 2009).

When reflecting on cultural diversity in music education as a relationship, one needs to be aware of some deeply ingrained negative attitudes towards particular social, cultural, and ethnic groups, which, in turn, impact responses to musical repertoires and attitudes towards peers in the music classroom. Theories of social and ethnic identity development lead us to believe that positive attitudes towards different groups should be stressed from very early on in development and education. Hargreaves' (1982) *open-earedness* hypothesis is also consistent with this idea. Intervention studies, however, suggest a more complex scenario. While some studies found students to show more positive attitudes towards ethnic minority groups following short-term interventions (e.g., Edwards, 1994), others found a reduction of ethnic and cultural stereotypes, yet only in specific age groups (e.g., Sousa, Neto, & Mullet, 2005). In addition, some have argued that multicultural interventions may at times reinforce ethnic, racial, and cultural stereotypes (for a discussion see Ilari, Chen-Hafteck, & Crawford, 2013). Apart from curricula and teaching approaches (Abril, 2006), teachers' attitudes and knowledge, along with students' age and ethnic makeup are likely to influence music learning and ethnic stereotyping in the classroom. These, in turn, impact the perception and formation of musical identities, as discussed later on.

In spite of their relevance, discussions around cultural diversity and ethnicity have not been a priority of many music education programs, including teacher-training programs (Schippers & Campbell, 2012). The end result is that many teachers have difficulties when interacting with students from culturally diverse backgrounds, with some blaming it on language barriers. While language may, in fact, be a barrier, there are ways to circumvent it. Music is, after all, an alternative means for communication through sounds.

It is central for student teachers and teachers alike to learn more from the "other" (Saether, 2010). This includes learning about theoretical positions such as SIT and the models of ethnic identity development discussed earlier, as well as becoming familiar with current theorizing on musical identities (Hargreaves, Miell, & MacDonald, 2002), and actual musical experiences of immigrant, refugee, and ethnic minority students, in and out of classrooms. Such awareness is likely to impact the "ethos of reception" (Suárez-Orozco & Suárez-Orozco, 2001), which represents a step towards empowering the "other" in the classroom, and transforming the music classroom. That is, there is a clear need to adopt a sociocultural approach to music teaching and learning (Abril, 2006), and to include conversations about ethnic minorities, immigration, biculturalism, and bimusicality in music classrooms, as contentious as they may be.

29.4 CONCLUSIONS

> We see things not as they are, but as we are.
>
> (Anaïs Nin)

As the quote attributed to Anaïs Nin suggests, we perceive the world through our own lenses, or rather, our multiple perceptions of self and other. Experiences become internalized over time, as we develop and construct knowledge of people, culture, relationships, lifestyles, and values. As a form of knowing, music is one of many ways to experience the world and to delve into issues of otherness. Still, to relate to "the other" one needs to show a certain degree of openness, and, importantly, empathy. As a powerful form of social behavior, music is likely to be linked to empathy (Cross, Laurence, & Rabinowitch, 2012). That is, interactive musicking requires one to be sensitive to the inner states of others:

> Music seems to embody the attitudes and emotions of others, which provides us with a basis for engaging both reflexively and reflectively with the music and with the

inferred internal states of those with whom we are busy making music. Active participation in music-making helps make possible the alignment of our own emotional states with those of our collaborators, and may give rise to a sense of empathic community. Its effects might even outlive the activity itself; music may act as a scaffold that can help us to acquire the habit of empathizing.

Cross, Laurence, & Rabinowitch, 2012, p. 340.

Thus, as a social act, music has potential to generate empathy, which, in turn, may foster the development of positive interpersonal relationships.

Experiencing the music of the "other" can be joyful or hurtful, depending on their delineated meanings for individuals and groups across time. Thus, the question of music "of the 'other'" in the development and construction of identity, or MII, is a very challenging one, as it involves personal, social, historical, and moral issues. Furthermore, understanding the "other", in and through music, is no trivial task, yet a necessary one in the globalized world. Some have even argued that music education has a larger role in this conversation than traditionally envisioned: to foster cultural and cross-cultural understanding. Tenacious projects are attempting to bridge ethnic and cultural differences in regions of the world where these markers of identity have been the cause for hatred and armed conflict (for examples, see Urbain, 2008). Some examples include the West-Eastern Divan Orchestra led by Daniel Barenboim and the late Edward Said (Riiser, 2010), and the Youth Open Festival in Kumanovo, former Yugoslavia (Balandina, 2010), to name a few. While not without their own challenges and criticisms, such experiences further illustrate the importance of bridging different ethnic and cultural worlds through collective music making. Still, as with any social engineering experiment, only time will tell what their real outcomes are. In the meantime, teachers and practitioners alike can continue to work towards the integration of students from diverse ethnic and cultural backgrounds, through the creation of a learning environment that fosters openness to cultural diversity and willingness to "learn from the other". To do so, teachers and practitioners must construct musical experiences that enhance individual dispositions, while counteracting on inappropriate group norms (Nesdale, Griffith, Durking, & Maass, 2005). Such experiences, in turn, are likely to impact the everlasting process of identity development and construction in all those involved.

REFERENCES

Abril, C.R. (2002). Children's attitudes towards languages and perceptions of performers' social status in the context of songs. *International Journal of Music Education*, 39(1), 65–74.

Abril, C. (2006). Learning outcomes of two approaches to multicultural music education. *International Journal of Music Education*, 24, 30–42.

Appadurai, A. (1993). *Modernity at large: cultural dimensions of globalization*. Minneapolis, MN: University of Minnesota Press.

Balandina, A. (2010). Music and conflict transformation in the post-Yugoslav era: empowering youth to develop harmonic inter-ethnic relationships in Kumanovo, Macedonia. *International Journal of Community Music*, 3(2), 229–44.

Bennett, M. (2011). Children's social identities. *Infant & Child Development*, 20, 353–63.

Bernal, M., Knight, G.P., Garza, C.A., Ocampo, K.A., & Cota, M.K. (1990). The development of ethnic identity in Mexican-American children. *Hispanic Journal of Behavioral Sciences*, 12(1), 3–24.

Campbell, P.S. (2011). Musical enculturation: sociocultural influences and meanings of children's experiences in and through music. In: M.S. Barrett (Ed.) *A cultural psychology of music education*, pp. 61–81. New York, MY: Oxford University Press.

Clarke, S. (2008). Culture and identity. In: T. Bennett & J. Frow (Eds.) *SAGE handbook of cultural analysis*. Thousand Oaks, CA: Sage.

Cross, I. (2005). Music and meaning, ambiguity and evolution. In: D. Miell, R. MacDonald, & D.J. Hargreaves (Eds.). *Musical communication*, pp. 27–43. Oxford: Oxford University Press.

Cross, I., Laurence, F., & Rabinowitch, T. (2012). Empathy and creativity in group musical practices: Towards a concept of empathic creativity. In: G.E. McPherson & G. Welch (Eds.) *The Oxford handbook of music education*, pp. 337–53. Oxford: Oxford University Press.

Eccles, J. (1999). The development of children ages 6–14. *The Future Children*, 9(2), 30–44.

Edwards, K.L. (1994). North American Indian music instruction: influences upon attitudes, cultural perceptions, and achievement (Doctoral dissertation). *Dissertation Abstracts International*, 56.

Eisner, E. (2002). *The arts and the creation of mind*. New Haven, CT: Yale University Press.

Ellemers, N. (2010). Social identity theory. In: J.M. Levine & M.A. Hogg (Eds.) *Encyclopedia of group processes and intergroup relations*, pp. 797–801. London: Sage.

Fleer, M., Hedegaard, M., & Tudge, J. (2009). Constructing childhood: global-local policies and practices. In: M. Fleer, M. Hedegaard, & J. Tudge (Eds.) *World yearbook of education*, pp. 1–20. New York, NY: Routledge.

Folkestad, G. (2002). National identity and music. In: R. Macdonald, D. J. Hargreaves, & D. Miell (Eds.) *Musical identities*, pp. 151–62. Oxford: Oxford University Press.

Garcia-Coll, C., & Marks, A.K. (2009). *Immigrant stories: ethnicity and academics in middle-childhood*. Oxford: Oxford University Press.

Hargreaves, D.J. (1982). The development of aesthetic reaction to music. *Psychology of Music, Special Issue*, 51–4.

Hargreaves, D.J., Miell, D., & MacDonald, R. (2002). What are musical identities and why are they important? In: R. MacDonald, D.J. Hargreaves, & D. Miell (Eds.) *Musical identities*, pp. 1–20. Oxford: Oxford University Press.

Henninger, J.C. (1999). Ethnically diverse sixth graders' preferences for music of different cultures. *Texas Music Education Research*, 1, 37–42.

Howell, G. (2011). Do they know they are composing? Music making and understanding among newly arrived immigrant and refugee children. *International Journal of Community Music*, 4(1), 47–58.

Huron, D. (2008). Lost in music. *Nature*, 453, 456–7.

Ilari, B. (2009a). Tão longe, tão perto: Dekasseguis, música e construção da identidade na terra do sol nascente [So far, so close: Dekasegi, music, and identity construction in the land of the rising sun]. *Revista de Estudos Orientais*, 7(1), 37–48.

Ilari, B. (2009b). Music learning and the invisible: cultural appropriation, equity and identity of underprivileged Brazilian children and adolescents. In: E. Gould, J. Countryman, C. Morton, & L. S. Rose (Eds.) *Exploring social justice: how music education might matter*, pp. 121–39. Waterloo: Canadian Music Educators Association.

Ilari, B. (2010). Responses to foreign music as windows into social cognition: a preliminary study on ethnic and national stereotypes. Poster presentation at ICMPC11, August, 2010. University of Washington, Seattle.

Ilari, B., Chen-Hafteck, L., & Crawford, L. (2013). Singing and cultural understanding: A music education perspective. *International Journal of Music Education*, 31(2), 202–16.

Jensen, L.A. (2011). *Bridging cultural and developmental approaches to psychology*. Oxford: Oxford University Press.

Jensen, L.A., Arnett, J.J., & McKenzie, J. (2011). Globalization and cultural identity. In: S.J. Schwartz et al (Eds.) *Handbook of identity theory and research*, pp. 285–301. New York, NY: Springer.

Jo, J.O. (2009). Cross-cultural education. In: F. English (Ed.) *Online encyclopedia of educational leadership and administration*. Thousand Oaks: SAGE. Available at: http://sk.sagepub.com/reference/edleadership

Kelly-McHale, J. (2013). The influence of music teacher beliefs and practices on the expression of musical identity in an elementary general music classroom. *Journal of Research in Music Education*, 61(2), 195–216.

Linger, D.T (1995). *No one home: Brazilian selves remade in Japan*. Stanford: Stanford University Press.

Marsh, K. (2012). 'The beat will make you be courage': The role of a secondary music program in supporting young refugees and newly arrived immigrants in Australia. *Research Studies in Music Education*, 34(2), 93–111.

McCrary, J. (1993). Effect of listeners' and performers' race on music preferences. *Journal of Research in Music Education*, 41(3), 200–11.

McCrary, J. (2000). Ethnic majority/minority status: children's interactions and affective responses to music. *Journal of Research in Music Education*, 48(3), 249–61.

Morrison, S.J. (1998). A comparison of preference responses of White and African-American students to musical versus musical/visual stimuli. *Journal of Research in Music Education*, 46(2), 208–22.

Nadal, K.L., & Rivera, D.P. (2008). Ethnic minority. In: F.T.L. Leong (Ed.). *Encyclopedia of counseling online*. London: Sage. Available at: http://sk.sagepub.com/reference/counseling

Padilla, A. (2006). Bicultural social development. *Hispanic Journal of Behavioral Sciences*, 28(4), 467–97.

Nesdale, D. (1999). Social identity and ethnic prejudice in children. In: P. Martin & W. Noble (Eds.) *Psychology and society*, pp. 92–110. Brisbane: Australian Academic Press.

Nesdale, D. (2004). Developmental changes in children's ethnic preferences and social cognitions. *Journal of Applied Developmental Psychology*, 20(4), 501–19.

Nesdale, D., Griffith, J., Durkin, K., & Maass, A. (2005). Empathy, group norms, and children's ethnic attitudes. *Applied Developmental Psychology*, 26(6), 623–37.

Räsänen, R. (2010). Intercultural education and education for global responsibility in teacher education. *Finnish Journal of Music Education*, 13(1), 12–24.

Reichers, S., Spears, S., & Haslam, S.A. (2010). The social identity approach in social psychology. In: M. Wetherell & C.T. Mohanty (Eds.) *SAGE handbook of identities*, pp. 45–63. London: Sage.

Riiser, S. (2010). National identity and the West-Eastern Divan Orchestra. *Music & Arts in Action*, 2(2), 19–37.

Saether, E. (2010). Music education and the 'other'. *Finnish Journal of Music Education*, 13(1), 45–60.

Schippers, H. (2009). *Facing the music.* Oxford: Oxford University Press.

Schippers, H., & Campbell, P.S. (2012). Cultural diversity: beyond 'songs from every land'. In: G. McPherson & G. Welch (Eds.) *Oxford handbook of music education,* pp. 87–104. Oxford: Oxford University Press.

Sousa, M.R., Neto, F., & Mullet, E. (2005). Can music change ethnic attitudes among children? *Psychology of Music,* 33(3), 304–16.

Soto, A. (2012). *Bimusical identity of children in a Mexican American school.* Unpublished doctoral dissertation. Seattle, WA: University of Washington.

Suárez-Orozco, C., & Suárez-Orozco, M. (2001). *Children of immigration.* Harvard, MA: Harvard University Press.

Tajfel, H. (1978). *Differentiation between social groups: studies in the social psychology of intergroup relations.* London: Academic Press.

Tajfel, H., & Turner, J. (1979). An integrative theory of intergroup conflict. In: W.G. Austin & S. Worschel (Eds.) *The social psychology of intergroup relations,* pp. 33–47. Pacific Grove CA: Brooks/Cole Publishing.

Turino, T. (2006). *Music as social life: the politics of participation.* Champaign, IL: University of Illinois Press.

Urbain, O. (2008). *Music and conflict transformation: harmonies and dissonances in geopolitics.* London: I.B. Tauris and Co.

UNESCO. (2009). *World report: investigating in cultural diversity and intercultural dialogue.* Paris: UNESCO

Wortham, S. (2006). *Learning identity: the joint emergence of social identification and academic learning.* Cambridge: Cambridge University Press.

Young, S., & Ilari, B. (2012). Musical participation from birth to three: Towards a global perspective. In: G. McPherson & G. Welch (Eds.). *Oxford handbook of music education,* pp. 279–95. Oxford & New York: OUP.

CHAPTER 30

THE IDENTITIES OF SINGERS AND THEIR EDUCATIONAL ENVIRONMENTS

GRAHAM F. WELCH

30.1 INTRODUCTION: SINGER IDENTITY AS AN ADULT

OVER a decade ago, a music journalist visited me in central London. She worked for a leading English national broadsheet newspaper and had been in contact to follow up a public lecture that I had given on "The Misunderstanding of Music" (Welch, 2001). The central thesis of my lecture was that humankind is essentially musical, in that musical behavior is part of our basic neuropsychobiological design—a stance subsequently supported by a wide range of research literature, including from the neurosciences of music (cf. Patel, 2010; Schlaug, 2015; Snowdon, Zimmermann, & Altenmüller 2015). During the interview, the journalist mentioned that she could not sing. This surprised me as she had mentioned in passing that she was a pianist. So, I invited her to an adjacent lecture room to demonstrate her pianistic skills and also to explore her singing ability. It was evident from her ability vocally to copy simple pitch patterns that I played on the piano that she could sing, and sing "in tune." It transpired that what she had meant by her negative statement of her singer identity was not that she could not sing, but that she did not like the quality of her singing voice. Her singer identity was negative (despite her competent piano playing) because she had an internal image of what a singer should sound like and her actual perceived singing behavior could not match this self-generated ideal.

Similar mismatches between a perceived ideal and reality were reported by Knight (2010) in her doctoral research into adult "non-singers" in Newfoundland. Amongst her participants were case studies of nine long-standing self-identified non-singers, most of whom had not sung since childhood because of a traumatic early experience of singing, usually in school or a local community setting. Yet, when these same adults' singing ability was assessed empirically by Knight, all nine were much more competent than they believed. Detailed analyzes of the participants' biographies revealed a persistent belief that they did not have the ability to sing: "Non-singers are born that way—you come either able to sing or not. You can't change it." This seemed to be a self-belief that arose in childhood because of a particular negative experience, or was self-inferred by comparing their singing to that of others, or because they believed that they could not sing well enough for others to hear them. In each instance, a key component of their negative adult image was a sense of embarrassment about their singing and a feeling of general musical inadequacy. Such emotions are perhaps unsurprising given that a related survey of 197 Newfoundland adults revealed that singing is a particularly valued feature of cultural life in the family home (e.g., the "kitchen party"), at school and in the wider Newfoundland community (Knight, 2010). Being a "singer" was commonly understood as being able to "hold a tune" and be able to sing successfully in public. Written comments from the survey participants provided self-reports about their singing experiences and these typically fell into two main singer identity groupings:

> *Singers*: Singing Danny Boy for a group of my peers when I was 14 years old. Most of them had tears and commented that I had a beautiful voice for a beautiful song.
> In music in primary school sitting in a circle singing. I was next to my teacher and she leaned over and told me I was a good singer.
>
> Knight, 2010, p. 232.

> *Non-singers*: In Kindergarten, I was asked to sit and listen to the rest of the class. I continued to do so for 7 years.
> I was in grade one and Sister walked across each row and listened to us in a group. When she finished, she told several of us to pantomime [mime] during singing class. I ran home so excited to be one of the chosen few, until my mother told me what it meant. I was crushed! That was the first time I found out I couldn't sing.
>
> Knight, 2010, p. 239.

A recent Scottish study of adult "non-musicians" (Caldwell, 2014) echoed the personal narratives of the "non-singers" in Newfoundland (Knight, 2010). Caldwell reported the importance of musical memories in adulthood in relation to the shaping of their musical identity that changed over time in the light of experience. With hindsight, participants realized that their early musical experiences in social family events often had powerful impacts on subsequent musical identity into adolescence and adulthood.

> … my first recollection about music starts when I'm a wee boy [Yep] in the hoose [house], at parties [Mhmm] at aw-the-githirs [Scots for social gathering/party] … in ma [my] parents' hoose there wiz [was] nae [no] guitars or nae instruments, so people would jist [just] sing songs. [Mhmm] But that was the first, sort of, introduction to me, to music.
>
> Caldwell, 2014, pp. 143–4.

Qualitative data analyzes revealed that parental expectations were significant in generating a personal value towards music that could be lifelong, but not necessarily in creating a sense of musicianship, of being a "musician", even though it was possible to perceive oneself as "musical". Some of the adult participants in this study played instruments, but still considered themselves to be "non-musicians", e.g., "I'm musical, but not a musician" (Caldwell, 2014, p.127).

However, it was possible for negative self-identity concerning singing to be altered through successful individual experience as an adult. For example, when self-identified adult "non-singers" were enrolled by Knight to participate regularly in a program of specially designed singing classes, singing perceptions were altered:

> Thursday nights have to be the high point of the week. I love singing class. Never thought I'd say that. In fact, if anyone had told me last spring, I'd say that I'd seriously consider having them committed.
>
> Singing in public when you've always thought you couldn't must be more like undressing after you've had some mutilating surgery, like a mastectomy or an amputation. You know you won't measure up, you'll be a disappointment to yourself and your audience, and, worst of all, you fear you'll be the object of malicious humour. The miracle of singing classes is the discovery that I am not disfigured, that my voice can be a source of pleasure, and amazingly, the limb can re-grow.
>
> Knight, 2010, pp. 250–1.

Self-identity as a non- or incompetent singer appears to be culturally commonplace and longstanding, judging by references in literature, and as evidenced by two of my favorite quotes:

> I can't sing. As a singist I am not a success. I am saddest when I sing. So are those who hear me. They are sadder even than I am.
>
> Artemus Ward's Lecture
Oxford Dictionary of Quotations (1953, p. 560; original 1865).

> And an ill singer, my lord … An [sic] he had been a dog that should have howled thus, they would have hanged him …
>
> *Much Ado About Nothing.* Shakespeare, W. Act II,
Scene III: comment by Benedick on hearing Balthazar sing 'Sigh no
more, ladies' (believed to have been written around 1598).

However, despite such anecdotes, the empirical reality is somewhat more nuanced—as evidenced in my own research with children (e.g., Welch, Saunders, Papageorgi & Himonides, 2012; Welch et al., 2014), as well as in Knight's (2010) research with adults and also by Wise (2015), who has undertaken sustained research into the etiology of the term "tone deaf," particularly in adulthood. This particular label of apparent singing inability (disability) over the past century or more is an indication of the label user's conception of the singing "problem," but does not necessarily provide clarity as to its meaning. Other labels have surfaced over time, such as "note deafness", "tune deafness", being "tone dumb", a "monotone," "droner," "growler," "grunter," "poor pitch singer," "uncertain singer," and (for the Japanese) "*onchi*" or "tone idiot"—a label reportedly evidenced in public performance by some less-than-skilled karaoke singers (cf. Welch, 1979; Welch & Murao, 1994; see Wise, 2015, for an overview). My own label preference for those less skilled than others, based on several decades of researching children's singing, is "developing singer," not least because, for those of us involved in music education research, policy, and practice, this label is more optimistic in its implication that singing ability is open to improvement in appropriate circumstances. Nevertheless, an agreed and robust definition of what counts as competent versus incompetent singing (and what might be observed between such polar opposites) remains somewhat elusive, which may be why singer identity is prone to a bipartite, can/cannot, categorization.

The general public's bipartite view of singing is unlikely to have been helped by the outcomes of empirical studies that vary in their reports of the incidence of self-defined "tone-deafness" in its conventional interpretation as an inability to sing known melodies "in–tune" (while we should recognize that even professional singers are not "in-tune" in an absolute sense: Larrouy-Maestri, Magis, & Marsomme, 2014). Cuddy, Balkwill, Peretz, & Holden (2005) reported that approximately 17% of n = 2000 first year undergraduates defined themselves as "tone deaf," whereas a contemporary study of "poor pitch singing" in an undergraduate population found that the majority (59%) of n = 1105 questionnaire respondents answered that they could not imitate melodies by singing (Pfordresher & Brown, 2007). However, subsequent laboratory-based singing behavior experiments with a sample of the same participants found much smaller proportions of "poor pitch singing" of between 10–16% (Pfordresher & Brown, 2007). Just to add to the challenges of terminology and its assignment in pinning down the nature of singing competence, 43% of 197 adults identified themselves as "poor" or "non-singers" in Knight's (2010) Newfoundland questionnaire survey.

Furthermore, where individual assessment has been undertaken by researchers that allow a comparison between self-report and actual singing ability (such as by Cuddy et al., 2005; Pfordresher & Brown, 2007; Knight, 2010), there is a demonstrable and generally consistent trend for participants to underrate their singing competence. Why some adults should adopt a negative singing identity, despite actually being able to sing approximately in-tune when tested is not clear. Cumulative, published research evidence over many decades suggests that less than 5% of children aged 11 years are unable to sing a simple song recognizably "in-tune" (Welch, Sergeant & White, 1997; Welch, 2009). Similarly, reports of singing accuracy (the difference between the sung product and a target pitch or interval) suggest that around 85–90% of the general public can sing "in tune," although they may not be always consistent in their singing behaviors (Dalla Bella, Giguére, & Peretz, 2007; Dalla Bella & Berkowska, 2009—see Dalla Bella, 2015 for a review).

Consequently, it may be that adults' self-labelling of a singing deficit is on the basis of comparisons generated by a greater listening exposure over time through electronic media to those that they regard as highly skilled (and whose vocal products may have been tidied up by the recording industry prior to public distribution), allied to a lack of opportunity by such adults to continue to practice and develop their individual singing skills to the same degree as had happened previously in childhood. For example, in a landmark Canadian study (Dalla Bella et al., 2007), a member of the research team approached people in a public park, pretending that it was his birthday, and said that he had made a bet with friends that he could get 100 individuals each to sing the refrain of *Gens du pays* for him on this special occasion. When the results of the public participants' renditions were analyzed and compared with the same musical material sung by four professional singers, the data revealed that these "occasional singers" (a label created by the research team) were less accurate in producing pitch intervals (having an average deviation from the correct intervals of 0.6 semitones) compared with the professional singers (an average deviation of 0.3 semitones). However, the occasional singers typically sang faster than the professionals, a phenomenon linked to lower pitch accuracy. "Reducing performance tempo had a positive effect on the performance (i.e., increase pitch accuracy) in most of the cases" (Dalla Bella, 2015).

Perceiving oneself as "tone deaf" is often associated (unsurprisingly) with an inhibition towards singing, at least in public because of the perceived likelihood of an adverse social judgement being made about singing competency, and often allied to the adoption of coping strategies to avoid public situations where singing is expected (Knight, 2010). Relatedly, Wise & Sloboda (2008) found that the negative identity of self-labelled "tone deaf" singers was supported somewhat by empirical measures of their actual singing competence, i.e., "they are not imagining their difficulties" (Wise, in press). Nevertheless, the basis for such a belief is also strongly socially constructed, in that what counts as singing is a socio-cultural phenomenon, and it is singing in public that such self-identified individuals seek to avoid. They may sing to themselves in the privacy of their car or bathroom, while also desiring to ensure that they avoid any instance in which their perceived singing inability is made public.

In addition to the challenges evident in the singer identity discourse—the labels that are in vogue to denote an apparent lack of singing ability, allied to the public conventions of what such labels might imply—and the differences between a self-perception of singing disability in contrast to a general lack of validation, at least to the same degree by empirical study, there are also issues surrounding the contexts in which singer identity is shaped. For example, in terms of making sense of people's general propensity for self-attributions as part of their daily discourse, Bruner (1990, pp. 14–15) succinctly described its socio-cultural nature as follows:

> It is in terms of folk-psychological categories that we experience ourselves and others. It is through folk psychology that people anticipate and judge one another, draw conclusions about the worthwhileness of their lives and so on.

Kagan (2001, p. 188) offers a similar observation on human behavior:

> One of the unique products of human evolution is the automatic habit of imposing symbolic meaning on experience, especially the tendency to evaluate events and self with a good or bad gloss.

Consequently, in terms of a particular attribution in singer identity such as "tone deaf", this emerges within a social context, as does musical identity in general, whether this is identity in music (IIM)—defined by the individual's social and cultural roles in music, or music in identity (MII)—how music is used for developing other aspects of personal identity (Hargreaves, Miell, & MacDonald, 2002). One example of the latter is how some older children are reported to associate a national identity related to royalty, sport, and the military when they hear the National Anthem (Winstone & Witherspoon, 2015). It is not surprising, therefore, that adults commonly report on the formative experiences of childhood as essential features of their singer identity development (Welch, 2000; Ruismäki & Tereska, 2006; Whidden, 2009; Knight, 2010), and provide examples of being recipients of the power of social commentary in the family home (from parents and other relatives, such as siblings), in school (where the knowledge status of teachers adds weight to their positive or negative comments), and wider community where singing is evidenced (such as in the church or community play areas).

30.2 Potential changes in singer identity with countervailing experience

Perceived negative singer identity can be open to transformation into something more positive, as seen earlier in the quotations from the Newfoundland adults who had the opportunity to develop their singing in a group/1.1 setting despite their apparent disability. In another example, Numminen, Lonka, Rainio, & Ruismäki, (2015) report the results of an eighteen-month singing intervention with ten adults in Finland who had elected to participate on the basis of experiencing negative emotions in childhood about singing and, subsequently, "a non-singing life: most of the participants had not sung for years or even decades" (Numminen et al., 2015, p. 1667). Participants progressed from not being able to find a common starting note for a well-known children's song at the beginning of the program to being able to self-correct when making a pitch error against a melodic target. Some were even prepared to sing in public at the end of the program. Singing learning was structured through group and solo sessions, with the number of individual lessons being determined by the degree and nature of assessed singing need at the beginning of the program. Critical to the pedagogical approach was the desire to create an "emotionally safe context" (Numminen et al., 2015, p. 1671), not least because of the perceived need to address the emotional trauma around singing that had been reportedly experienced in many of the participants' childhoods.

Pedagogy that was sensitive to participants' "non-singer" identity was also reported as a core characteristic in the data from a systematic, seven-month case study of the rehearsal experiences of members of an adult "Can't Sing Choir" in London (Richards,

2002; Richards & Durrant, 2003). At the beginning, choir members were noticeably self-conscious, unsure of what to expect and somewhat fearful of exposing their singing inability to others. In addition to simple singing activities, opening with vocal warm up exercises and progressing to simple singing tasks and songs, each being modelled by the teacher, there were systematic opportunities provided each week for informal discussion between members and the choir director about vocal problems and anxieties. The director was observed to adopt a friendly, non-judgmental style in her singing pedagogy, with lots of physical gestures being added (such as for pitch direction) to support the vocal and auditory experiences with visual metaphor. Notwithstanding this approach, the researcher observed a continued mismatch between verbal (talk) and non-verbal (singing) behaviors, with the former being animated and positive, especially during break times, while the latter signaled a persistent wariness and lack of confidence during the actual singing activities.[1] Nevertheless, questionnaire responses at the end of the seven-month research period revealed an overwhelmingly optimistic reappraisal of participants' singing competency, with approximately two-thirds being more positive about their voice quality and their ability to know consciously if they were "singing in-tune or not". They reported experiencing a wider vocal pitch range, allied to a "better understanding of the voice and singing" (Richards, 2002, p. 63). Adjectives used to summarize their experiences of being in the "Can't Sing Choir" were exhilarating, uplifting, inspiring, fun, wonderful, joyful, encouraging, liberating, positive, energizing, relaxing, and enjoyable. Similarly, having had this experience, virtually all (97%) agreed that most adults can improve their singing voices with appropriate help and encouragement, a finding that echoed similar positive reports from an earlier Canadian study of "tone-deaf" university students (Mawhinney & Cuddy, 1984). The majority of students believed that they could improve their singing competency and address their perceived "tone-deafness" if provided with appropriate tuition.[2]

Other recent research into singer identity in a choral setting supports the view that singing is sensitive to social context, conductor behavior and also to physical organization of the singers (Bonshor, 2014). Identity can be impacted positively or negatively by the conductor's body language, which—in turn—can nurture (or not) a sense of collective expertise and confidence amongst choir members. Similarly, the physical configuration of the choir, of how closely the singers are placed in relation to each

---

[1] Singer anxiety is also evidenced in those with much greater skill levels, including professional singers. For example, a study of music performance anxiety (MPA) amongst 32 opera chorus singers working for Opera Australia revealed higher trait anxiety (a general tendency to be anxious) than in a normative sample (Kenny, Davis, & Oates, 2004).

[2] In another example of singing education with adults who have very poor competency, a study of a 7-week singing intervention with a group of so-called "congenitally amusic" adults led by a professional singing teacher revealed positive improvements in perception and production for several participants (Anderson, Himonides, Wise, Welch, & Stewart, 2012). According to Anderson et al, "congenital amusia is a developmental disorder that impacts negatively on the perception of music, which has been estimated to occur in about 4% of otherwise normal individuals" (2012, p. 345).

other, can create positive (or negative) feelings in amateur singers that influence their sense of individual as well as collective competency. In this particular study, amateur choral singer identity was perceived to be enhanced when singers were arranged in vocal sections (such as the sopranos being all together), rather than in a mixed voice configuration, as had been reported favorably by Daugherty (2003) for chamber choir placements.

The transformation of negative singer identity into something more positive suggests that adult singing ability and associated identity need not be fixed entities (cf. Dweck, 2013), but can be open to change, not least because cognitive development is shaped by social development, with dedicated neural networks being reported in the brain that represent self and others (Uddin, Iacobini, Lange, & Keenan, 2007; see Dweck, 2013 for a review). Similarly, although theoretically such singer identity transformation may be possible for children, i.e., from negative to positive, the evidence suggests that, for the majority (who go on to become the adult "occasional singers" reported earlier), this is not an appropriate conceptualization. It is more common in childhood for a generally positive singer identity to emerge until or unless there is some limiting experience to challenge such self-perception. It is only a minority of children who experience some form of emotional trauma about their singing, such that they will be reported subsequently as "singing disabled" adults (using whatever label that is current). As mentioned earlier, the available research data suggest that less than 5% of children aged 11 years sing "out-of-tune," a reduction from approximately one-third of 7-year-olds (Welch et al, 1997; Welch, 2009). The evidence suggests that, as children become more competent and confident in their singing abilities formed within social contexts, there are likely to be concomitant and reciprocal changes in their social selves, in their sense of being socially included, of being part of a community (Welch, Himonides, Saunders, Papageorgi, & Sarazin, 2014), which links to the emergence of a positive identity as a "singer" as defined by their social group. Where singing development is inhibited socially, it is more likely that children will experience a sense of otherness, of being an "outsider" compared with the majority of their peers and thus extend this identity into adult life in the absence of any countervailing experience.

> ... But it was a dread that you were going to have to go to music, singing I guess ... I really disliked it because it was an ordeal. You had to get in the back row and pretend you were singing while everybody else sang ... but you were not allowed to sing and you weren't allowed to turn it down. It was never "try a bit harder or half dozen of you girls come down a little earlier or stay after class"; there was no encouragement, none whatsoever ... There was no instruction. They worked with you to sing a song same as anybody. I guess practice makes perfect for those that could sing. But I never sing. You never hear me in the shower, accidentally, ever sing a note. Never in the car. Never even to myself.
>
> Carla, 43-year-old mother of three and one of five
> children who grew up in Newfoundland;
> Knight, 2010, p. 89.

30.3 THE EMERGENCE OF SINGER IDENTITY IN CHILDHOOD

The origins of singing identity begin early in life (cf. Welch, 2005). Initially, young children's earliest vocal products relate to their affective state (such as discomfort or distress, or eustress—the latter characterized by euphonic cooing, e.g., Papoušek, 1996a). Subsequently, the interfacing of infant neuro-psychobiological design and sonic experiences within the maternal culture shapes the infant's pre-linguistic vocalizations to create a form of parent-child/self-other communication that draws on the prosodic features of the mother tongue (such as pitch contours and basis harmonic intervals, thirds, fourths, fifths, octaves, as well as loudness, timbre, and rhythm) (e.g., Papousek, 1996b; Malloch, 1999—see Welch, 2005 for an overview). This form of "infant-directed speech" is complemented by "infant-directed singing," in which mothers sing to their infant more expressively, more slowly, and at a higher pitch level than when singing informally on their own (Trainor, Clark, Huntley, & Adams, 1997; Trehub et al., 1997). Communication is also reciprocal, in the sense of parents encouraging and responding to the infant's vocal products, while reinforcing and expanding these (Kirkpatrick, 1962; Trehub & Trainor, 1998; Tafuri, 2008). Knight (2010, p. 267) argues that such "'musical conversation' is singing *as* life [original emphasis], not merely singing in life."

Trehub & Gudmundsdottir (2015) report that mothers are "singing mentors" by revealing the ways that they intuitively use melodious talk and a limited repertoire of favorite songs to bring comfort and joy to their children. Maternal singing is a "caregiving tool" that is aimed primarily at emotional regulation, at least in the first year of life, with visual gestures forming an integral part of the behavior, and vocal repertoire shaped by the dominant culture. Infants respond in terms of levels of arousal, being sensitive to expressive variations in the maternal singing. Over time, the maternal "singing mentor" focus is reported to change from predominantly attention capture and emotional regulation towards more active singing games, including rudimentary vocal duets (Kirschner & Tomasello, 2010) and, subsequently, the playful singing of pre-schoolers that explores elements of the dominant musical culture and, which is often linked to language acquisition (Trehub & Gudmundsdottir, 2015). This maternal singer identity should be regarded as crucial in the infant's socio-musical development.

Whilst the acquisition of singing shows considerable individual variation, being related to home environment and community engagement (including the value placed on singing within the maternal culture), where encouraged, young children are likely to build a repertoire of known songs or fragments and to use elements of these in their own creative vocal play (cf. Barrett, 2006, 2009, 2011). For example, in an ongoing study, Wu is investigating musical activities in the family homes of members of the Chinese diaspora in London. Participants' mothers are keeping diaries, written and video, of their young children's musical behaviors, with emergent data being mapped onto a new developmental framework[3] to reveal how such behaviors, including singing, emerge, are repeated and develop. In one recent video clip, Lucy aged 4 was filmed by her mother singing a made-up song in the shower, drawing on music from a Disney CD that she had listened to previously in the family car.

> She sang a made-up song when having her shower. I asked her "What are you sing-ing?" She said "I am singing a Princess song made by myself." I asked her why there were some tongue-clicking sounds. She said that the Princess was knocking on the door. "She is going to visit me."
>
> Lucy's mother's diary entry 2, as reported by Wu, 2015.

At this stage in life it seems unlikely that the young child has a separate identity as a "singer," although there will be an awareness from exposure to adults and sib-lings, as well as the music performance media, of what "singers" do, such as danc-ing while vocalizing, a behavior that is often picked up and mimicked by the young child. Experience in community playgroups prior to nursery school, as well as in the home, nurtures the developing singer identity where the prime focus is on partici-pation, rather than accurate reproduction of song material. For the vast majority of young children, unless they are stopped in some way from expressing themselves through their recognizably sung products, their emerging singing identity is posi-tive, as evidenced within their imaginative play or in their growing awareness of the song repertoire of childhood (Barrett & Tafuri, 2012; see Barrett, Chapter 4, "From small stories: laying the foundations for narrative identities in and through music"). Anecdotally, over the past 3 years of new fatherhood, I have experienced how groups of mothers in voluntary community settings make regular time for collective song singing, with mothers (and sometimes fathers) sitting in a circle and each young child in turn being asked to choose a favorite song for everyone to sing, sometimes prompted by the mother, that is then performed enthusiastically by the collective group of parents and toddlers, often with actions.

As children get older and enter the school system, the focus tends to be more on the formal learning of songs in the classroom, while they will continue to experience infor-mal learning of other song repertoire outside, such as in the home and related contexts. These experiences are either virtual (as mediated by media), or direct through contact with another human, such as their peers, which may also be linked to shared listening to recorded or broadcast vocal music. The outcome is not just a sense of child singer iden-tity that is shaped by these two contexts of musical experiences (school/non-school), but of possible tension between the two. For example, as part of a national evaluation of

---

[3] The *Sounds of Intent in the Early Years* framework (Ockelford, 2015) is based on existing literature on young children's musical development, allied to newly collected empirical data, to provide a coherent developmental structure to map children's musical behavior hierarchically (simple to complex). It is based on an extended study that has mapped musical development in children and young people with complex needs (Ockelford & Welch, 2012).

the National Singing Programme (NSP) *Sing Up* in England, participant children were asked a series of questions concerning their identity as a singer. In design, this questionnaire drew on an earlier study (Joyce, 2005) that had investigated the possible symbiotic relationship between children's musical development and their experience of different musical environments (based on the socio-cultural stance taken by Welch, 2001). Joyce's findings, based on responses from 114 children aged 9 and 10 years, revealed a dichotomy between singing in the home and singing in school, in that 64% of children reported that they enjoyed singing at home, compared with 36% in school. Also, a quarter of the children reported that someone had told them that they could not sing, a finding that has echoes of the negative childhood experiences summarized earlier that carry over to singing identity in adulthood.

The contradiction in singer identity between singing in school and singing at home was reinforced by detailed analyzes of the large-scale *Sing Up* questionnaire data. Responses from 8124 participants aged 7 plus to 10 plus revealed that younger children were more positive about singing than older children. This is somewhat paradoxical, in that as children grew older and become more competent at singing (as measured comparatively for each individual in a separate strand of the *Sing Up* program evaluation, e.g., Welch et al., 2010), they tended to become more negative about singing in school. However, children in those schools that had participated in the *Sing Up* program and, by inference and researcher observation, had experienced a greater nurturing emphasis on the collective development of singing skills, were significantly more positive about singing in school than their non-*Sing Up* experienced peers. In these *Sing Up* cases, older children matched their younger peers' enthusiasm for school-based singing and tended to have sustained more positive singing identities.

Gender is also a factor, in that girls are often reported to be more competent at school-type song singing than boys, a common finding in studies of singing in primary (elementary) school settings (Welch, et al. 1997; Mang, 2006; Welch, 2009; Welch, 2015).[4] For example, detailed analyzes of the individual song singing behaviors of 11,388 participant children from across the first three years of the *Sing Up* program evaluation revealed that, overall, girls were approximately three years in advance of boys, a difference that held across all assessed age groups (5–12 years) (Welch et al., 2012). Nevertheless, both sexes demonstrated an improving trend of singing competency with age, and children in schools with experience of the *Sing Up* program at the time of assessment were rated as more competent than those without such experience (but with a similar gender bias being evidenced in favor of girls for both sets of children). Similarly, in earlier published studies of "out-of-tune" singing by children in Western cultures (a socially defined behavior that declines with increasing age), boys tend to outnumber girls, often by a ratio of 3 or 4:1 (Howard, Angus, & Welch, 1994; Welch, 1979).

---

[4] Note that such gender differences in singing competency are not evident for child singers that have undergone extensive training, such as those regularly rehearsing and performing a musically demanding repertoire as choristers in cathedrals alongside professional male singers (Owens & Welch, in press; Saunders et al, 2012; Welch, 2011).

Perceived singer identity in childhood is a psychoacoustic, socially constructed phenomenon. Gender is evidenced in the sung products of children, which are perceived as being feminine or masculine. Untrained young boys' singing can be mistaken as girls' up to around the age of eight years (Sergeant, Sjölander, & Welch, 2005). In contrast, trained girls' voices can be mistaken as trained boys' from around the age eight to fourteen years, depending on the musical piece being performed and the experience of the listener with this kind of repertoire (Howard, Szymanski, & Welch, 2002; Welch & Howard, 2002).

The shaping of children's sung products by the social contexts that they experience impacts on their emerging singing identity throughout childhood and into adolescence. The onset of puberty brings about changes in the underlying anatomical and physiological structures of the voice and, in turn, these impact on singing behaviors for both females and males (see overviews by McAllister & Sjölander, 2013; Welch, 2015). Boyhood singing behavior and consequently singer identity is particularly disrupted by the onset of puberty. For some, this creates a sense of loss as they enter their teens, and the products of their singing (and spoken) voice become unstable (Ashley & Mecke, 2013; Freer, 2015). Unfortunately, research and school inspection evidence suggests that the secondary school music curriculum and pedagogical practice, at least in England, is not always well suited to sustaining the singing identities of boys into adolescence and beyond (Ofsted, 2012; Ashley, 2013).

For some boys, the transition from primary to secondary schooling (or its equivalent in different countries) is reported also to mark a time when they reimagine themselves and the relative importance of singing in their lives (Freer, 2015). Factors that can support boys in continuing to explore and enjoy their singer identity include the teacher's personality, evidence of high levels of teacher musicianship such as reflected in the choice of the selected, appropriately challenging singing repertoire, and the social environment for singing. Where each of these three factors is perceived to be positive, then boys are more likely to continue to participate in choral singing (ibid).

By comparison, for girls, while puberty also brings about physical changes that can impact on singing identity (Gackle, 2014), these are more subtle, such as related to increased breathiness and short-term discomfort in the upper singing range. Consequently, because these changes are relatively minor, it is likely that girls may be unaware of such differences in their voices unless they have a regular performance schedule and are sensitized to small, perceived changes in their singing ability.

For some children in primary (elementary) school settings, there is an added challenge, as reported earlier, of inappropriate and adverse comments from teachers that can dissuade children from singing activities. Such comments significantly hinder their singing development and thus create a negative singer identity where previously the identity was more positive. In part, such experience may derive from a tendency for primary (elementary) teachers to feel less confident about leading music in their classes, often because they are reported to believe that they lack appropriate music subject knowledge and have limited faith in their own musicality (Mills, 1989; Hennessy, 2000; McCulloch, 2006; Stunell, 2007). Where teachers do not have a professional, research-based understanding of how singing develops and of how sing-ing might be fostered in children, possibly allied to their own personal adult negative singing self-concept, it is not surprising that they might seek to avoid having singing in the classroom curriculum. This would be reinforced if they also held a bipartite, "can"/"cannot" view of singing that is reflected in the musical competency expec-tations of themselves and others, including their pupils (Gifford, 1993; Abril, 2007; Grace, 2011).

Nevertheless, one strand of the *Sing Up* program was focused on developing compe-tency in singing pedagogy for teachers. A subsequent survey evaluation (Himonides, Saunders, Papageorgi, & Welch, 2011) of 1046 respondents nationally revealed that this program of in-service singing education was effective in bringing about positive changes in singer identity, both personally and professionally. Amongst the findings, respondents reported increased confidence in their ability to lead singing and in their own singing skills, as well as a greater awareness of how they could help all children to develop. Given that two-thirds of the respondents were aged 40 or over, represent-ing many years of collective teaching experience, but with over half having no formal qualification in music, the reported outcomes are commendable in suggesting that identity in singing can become more positive in terms of personal and professional self-efficacy.

30.4 SUMMARY AND CONCLUSIONS

As reported in the preceding narrative, singer identity has many different interrelated facets. These arise from an underlying interfacing of:

- The nature of the vocal instrument itself—its physical structure, and its psychologi-cal management, which change and develop over time as part of a normal matu-rational process, interfaced with experience, and in which singing behavior can have a close relationship with the other prime vocal function, namely that of speech (Patel, 2008; Thurman & Welch, 2000).
- A range of personal, musical, and socio-cultural contexts shape vocal behavior, including singing (see Fig. 30.1).

Different cultures and social groups place distinctive values on the act of singing. In some cultures (such as Afghanistan), the leading of singing is an expected role of particular families within the local community (Doubleday & Baily, 1995). This is in contrast to sub-Saharan communities in which singing and dance are customarily inter-woven as a common cultural activity (Blacking, 1973).

For infants, the definition of "singing" can be very fuzzy, in that some of their earli-est vocal products from the age of two months onwards can be construed by adults as "musical babbling" (Tafuri & Villa, 2002) and are the precursors of an emergent singing

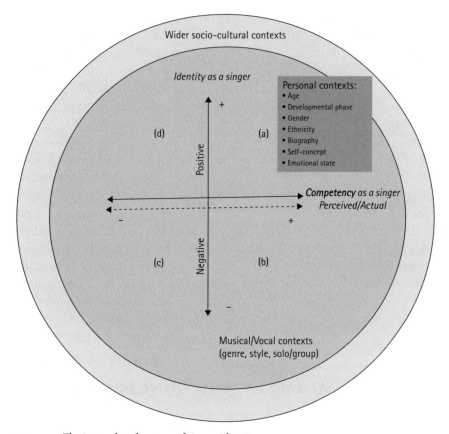

FIG. 30.1 The interrelated nature of singer identity.

identity. These kinds of utterance contain recognizable musical features, being closely related to the use by carers of symbiotic "infant-directed" vocal behaviors (speech and singing) (Trehub & Gudmundsdottir, 2015). As children enter toddlerhood, they explore and play with aspects of the song repertoire to which they have been exposed through interaction with adults in the home and in the wider community, as well as engaging with toys with musical features and music media.

Vocal products that are recognizable as "singing" (in a conventional sense) emerge from around the age of two years onwards. However, at times the boundaries between singing and speaking can still be blurred or ambiguous to the adult listener. Interaction with carers, especially the mother, is reported to be crucial in the development of a song repertoire (whether whole songs or fragments) by the time of entry to schooling, and singing competence, in the sense of being relatively tuneful, is reported to be closely related to the degree of exposure to maternal singing in the home (Ilari, 2005; Kirkpatrick, 1962). In turn, the rich experience of singing as a child is reported to be linked, subsequently, to the value and frequency of singing when the same child achieves adulthood and uses singing as part of their own childcare practice, a finding that implies that early singing exposure can cross generations (Mehr, 2014).

It is during childhood that singing identity comes more strongly into focus, in part because of the formalization of music in the school curriculum, but also because of increased access to popular music media in the home (for example, 57% of English children aged 3–4 years who go online are reported to listen to music, rising to 64% of children aged 5–7 years; Ofcom, 2014). It is also during this age phase that gender effects become more evident in singing, with girls growing up in Western-type cultures increasingly becoming more advanced in their singing competency than boys (Welch et al., 2012). In addition, gender becomes more prominent in children's sung products, with distinct acoustic features emerging that allow listeners (including the children themselves) to be able reliably to recognize the sex of a child singer (Sergeant et al., 2005). Furthermore, this is the age phase when the foundations for adult singer identity are laid, both in terms of competence and confidence. It is also an identity process that is challenged by the advent of physical voice change in puberty for males (and less so for females), which can provide a maturation-driven reason for some older children significantly to reduce their singing behavior. The possible emergence of a positive male singer identity in adolescence and beyond is not helped by conventional public discourse concerning voice change in males that refers to "voices breaking" (rather than the more neutral term "voice change," or the positive term "voice transformation").

Consequently, in adulthood, a variety of singer identities are evident within the population. This variety can be hypothesized as being biased towards four possible groupings. Each of these has their own singer *identity* predisposition along a continuum that embraces positive to negative and which interfaces with two other positive to negative continua that are related to singing *competency* (both self-perceived and actual). (The hypothesized spaces defined by the intersections of these continua are shown as (a)–(d) in Fig. 30.1, with the vertical continuum signaling singer identity and the two horizontal continua singing competence—perceived and actual). The characteristic biases of these four groupings are as follows:

- (a) Adults with positive self-identity as singers and who perceive themselves (and are perceived by others) as skilled (located in space (a) on Fig. 30.1).
- (b) Adults with a more negative self-identity who believe that they are not competent at singing, but who are actually more competent in reality, as assessed by independent judges (located in space (b), but likely to overlap with other groups).
- (c) Adults who have a negative self-identity as singers and whose singing competency is also poor (located in space (c)).
- (d) Adults who have a positive self-identity as singers, who believe themselves to be relatively competent, but who in reality are not (or not as good as they believe they are).

These four hypothesized groupings are also evidenced in different ways in the literature, although there are likely to be overlaps between them.

For those adults signaled by grouping (a), these can be seen on popular singing-based television shows that showcase adults who are sufficiently competent to perform on a public stage (such as in the TV program "The Voice"). Some of these participants report that they are already employed as part-time (occasionally, as full-time) singing entertainers; others are not so employed, but for each person, singing is a central part of their identity (cf. related to "music in identity," Hargreaves et al., 2002). Alongside these "amateur" singers are other adults who earn their living as "professional" singers within various parts of the music industry (such as in theatres, opera houses, concert halls, cathedrals and equivalent major churches, and on cruise ships), with opportunities for singing-based media engagements on television, radio and with the recording industry. It is also common for professional musicians, including singers, to include teaching as part of a portfolio career (Creech, 2014).

Those signaled in grouping (b) are more heterogeneous and represent attributes that are likely to overlap with groupings (a) and (d) to a certain extent. These adults are likely to be less confident about their singing, may avoid any kind of public context where they are expected to sing on their own (unless in a karaoke bar with friends), but some may be sufficiently encouraged by others to join workplace or community choirs, where they develop their singing competence as part of a larger ensemble and also gain enjoyment from the social aspects of singing (e.g., Bailey & Davidson, 2009; Clift & Hancox, 2010). Chorus America (2009), for example, reported that there were around 270,000 choirs in the USA, with 18.1% of households having one or more adults participating in chorus activities. The numbers of adults in choirs totaled 32.5 million. When children were added, participation increased to 22.9%, i.e., almost 1:4 of US households, numbering 42.6 million Americans (adults and children). Nevertheless, other members of grouping (b) would only ever sing at home, perhaps in the shower, with their young children, and/or in the car while listening to their favorite music. School teachers are likely to be widely represented in this broad grouping. These adults are "occasional singers," not always very accurate, nor consistent with their singing, and may be reluctant to sing in certain contexts outside those that are immediately familiar, such as family gatherings, or with peers attending sports events. The last of these socially located singing behaviors was evidenced in a study of football crowd singing by Professor David Howard, resulting in a "league table of English Premier League fans" singing [in which] Southampton topped the table [as the most tuneful] and Bolton came last [sounding the most "tone-deaf"]. (See the public discussion of the outcomes at http://news.bbc.co.uk/sport1/hi/sports_talk/1879433.stm.)

In contrast, those adults in grouping (c) are negative about their singing ability, demonstrate little if any singing competence, and may classify themselves as "non-singers". Several research studies have focused on this group in order to understand both the social reasons for their negative singing self-concept (e.g., Knight, 2010), but also to investigate from a neuro-psychobiological perspective the nature of the human process of singing and how this can be disrupted or deficient (for example, see the articles in the recent special issue on singing in the journal *Music Perception*, 2015, volume 2). A common finding reported from empirical studies with this grouping is the lifelong negative impact on singing identity of some emotional trauma associated with singing in childhood.

Finally, those adults in grouping (d) are likely to be less conscious about singing in public, for example, but are not very competent. Less is known from research about this group, but anecdote suggests that they exist, and it would appear that some television media exploit their existence to boost audience ratings by allowing expert panel members to provide negative commentary about less than competent live singing performance.

In summary, at any given moment, individual singer identity (Fig. 30.1) is closely related to age (biological and chronological), including the underlying development of the voice mechanism and its neurological management and monitoring (see Kleber & Zarate, 2014, for an overview of the neuroscience of singing), their biological sex, ethnicity, and also their emotional engagement with singing as a form of personal expression. In addition, social and cultural identities and roles (such as parenthood) exert influences, as well as the dominant forms of "singing" that exist in the locality.

There are a great number of musical genres and sub-genres in contemporary society, many of which embrace vocal performance. These include over 45 different musics enjoyed and practiced within the South Asian diaspora in the UK (Farrell, Bhowmick, & Welch, 2005); the 200+ folk musics in China exhibited across 56 different ethnic groups (Yang & Welch, 2014), the separate indigenous, African and Western music traditions of contemporary Brazil (Soares, 2006), as well as over 200 kinds of rock music listed on Wikipedia (Available at: http://en.wikipedia.org/wiki/List_of_rock_genres).

Singer identity is also shaped by the local, immediate social context, such as singing alone (whether to yourself as the audience, or in the presence of others), or in a collective setting (family, peer group, community, or school choir). Singing to yourself is likely to be perceived differently from singing on the concert stage in front of a paying audience. The former is private and personal, relaxed and usually unselfconscious, from infancy through to senescence. In contrast, public singing often involves a greater sense of "performance," of implied "correctness" against some perceived expectation of what counts as "appropriate" musical behavior, and offering a sense of "audience."

From an educational perspective, in which the prime imperative is usually to foster singing development by sustaining and extending current singing competency in some way, it becomes critical to understand how the forces reported above shape singer identity in childhood, adolescence, and adulthood, as well as for the precursors of singing identity in infancy. It may then be possible to provide a much richer and more effective singing pedagogy across the lifespan that is nuanced for age, gender, ethnicity, development age, and emotional engagement with singing and personal biography.

One example of the impact of an appropriate education intervention on singer identity is implied in a 19th century Boston, USA initiative to introduce vocal music into the schools' curriculum as a social and moral experiment. In May of the following year, the Mayor of Boston requested a report on progress. The schools' response was subsequently published by the Boston Music Gazette on Wednesday, July 25, 1838 as follows:

> … One thing has been made evident, that the musical ear is more common than has been generally supposed…Many who at the outset of the experiment believed

that they had neither ear nor voice, now sing with confidence and with considerable accuracy; and others who could hardly tell one sound from another, now sing the scale with ease ...

Birge (1937, p. 50).

Given the wealth of research evidence related to singing and singing-related behaviors across the lifespan that has emerged since the publication of this report, we should be ideally placed to ensure that the fostering of a positive singer identity is a realizable goal for everyone. This is not to say that everyone must sing (although it would be possible to articulate the wider physical, psychological, and social benefits of such a policy), but that an individual's decision to sing or not is based on a personal biography of successful singing engagement.

REFERENCES

Abril, C.R. (2007). I have a voice but I just can't sing: a narrative investigation of singing and social anxiety. *Music Education Research*, 9(1), 1–15.

Anderson, S., Himonides, E., Wise, K., Welch, G., & Stewart, L. (2012). Congenital amusia: is there potential for learning? A study of the effects of singing interventions on pitch production and perception of those with congenital amusia. *Annals of the New York Academy of Sciences*, 1252, 345–53.

Ashley, M. (2013). Broken voices or a broken curriculum? The impact of research on UK school choral practice with boys. *British Journal of Music Education*, 30(3), 311–27.

Ashley, M., & Mecke, A.-C. (2013). 'Boys are apt to change their voice at about fourteene yeeres of age': An historical background to the debate about longevity in boy treble singers. *Reviews of Research in Human Learning and Music*, 1: epub2013001.

Bailey, B.A.,& Davidson, J.W. (2009). Amateur group singing as a therapeutic instrument. *Nordic Journal of Music Therapy*, 12(1), 18–32.

Barrett, M.S. (2006). Inventing songs, inventing worlds: the 'genesis' of creative thought and activity in young children's lives. *International Journal of Early Years Education*, 14(3), 201–20.

Barrett, M.S. (2009). Sounding lives in and through music: a narrative inquiry of the 'everyday' musical engagement of a young child. *Journal of Early Childhood Research*, 7(2), 115–34.

Barrett, M.S. (2011). Musical narratives: a study of a young child's identity work in and through music-making. *Psychology of Music*, 39(4), 403–23.

Barrett, M.S., & Tafuri, J. (2012). Creative meaning-making in infants' and young children's musical cultures. In: G.E. McPherson & G.F. Welch (Eds.) *Oxford handbook of music education*, pp. 296–313. Oxford: Oxford University Press.

Birge, E.B. (1937). *History of public school music in the United States*. Bryn Mawr, PA: Oliver Ditson Company.

Blacking, J. (1973). *How musical is man?* Seattle: University of Washington Press

Bonshor, M.J. (2014). *Confidence and the choral singer: the effects of choir configuration, collaboration and communication*. Unpublished PhD Thesis, University of Sheffield.

Bruner, J. (1990). *Acts of meaning*. Cambridge, MA: Harvard University Press.

Caldwell, G.N. (2014). *Exploring the musical identities of adult-self-defined 'non-musicians': an interpretative phenomenological analysis (IPA)*. Unpublished PhD Thesis, Glasgow Caledonian University.

Chorus America. (2009). *How children, adults, and communities benefit from choruses*. Washington, DC: Chorus America.

Clift, S., & Hancox, G. (2010). The significance of choral singing for sustaining psychological wellbeing: findings from a survey of choristers in England, Australia and Germany, *Music Performance Research*, 3(1), 79–96.

Creech, A. (2014). Understanding professionalism: transitions and the contemporary professional musician. In: I. Papageorgi & G.F. Welch (Eds.) *Advanced musical performance: investigations in higher education learning*, pp. 349–63. Farnham, Surrey: Ashgate Publishing Ltd.

Cuddy, L.L., Balkwill, L.-L., Peretz, I., & Holden, R.R. (2005). Musical difficulties are rare. A study of "tone deafness" amongst university students. *New York: Annals of the New York Academy of Sciences*, 1060, 311–24.

Dalla Bella, S. (2015). Defining poor pitch singing: a problem of measurement and sensitivity. *Music Perception*, 32(3), 272–82.

Dalla Bella, S., & Berkowska, M. (2009). Singing proficiency in the majority: Normality and "phenotypes" of poor singing. *Annals of the New York Academy of Sciences*, 1169, 99–107.

Dalla Bella, S., Giguére, J.-F. & Peretz, I. (2007). Singing proficiency in the general population. *Journal of the Acoustical Society of America*, 121(2), 1182–9.

Daugherty, J. (2003). Choir spacing and formation: choral sound preferences in random, synergistic, and gender-specific chamber choir placements. *International Journal of Research in Choral Singing*, 1(1), 48–59.

Doubleday, V., & Baily, J. (1995). Patterns of musical development among children in Afghanistan. In: E.J. Fernea (Ed.) *Children in the Muslim Middle East*, pp. 431–44. Austin, TX: University of Texas Press.

Dweck, C. (2013). Social development. In: P.D. Zelazo (Ed.) *The Oxford handbook of developmental psychology, Vol 2: self and other*. Oxford: Oxford Handbooks Online. Available at: http://www.oxfordhandbooks.com/view/10.1093/oxfordhb/9780199958474.001.0001/oxfordhb-9780199958474-e-008?rskey=pn4rD5&result=4 (accessed 16 March 2016).

Farrell, G., Bhowmick, J., & Welch. G. (2005). South Asian music in Britain. In: H.-K. Um (Ed.) *Diasporas and interculturalism in Asian Performing Arts: translating traditions*, pp. 104–28. London: Routledge Curzon.

Freer, P.K. (2015). Perspectives of European boys about their voice change and school choral singing: developing the possible selves of adolescent male singers. *British Journal of Music Education*, 32(1), 87–106.

Gackle, L. (2014). Adolescent girls' singing development. In: G.F. Welch, D.M. Howard, & J. Nix. (Eds.) *Oxford handbook of singing*. New York, NY: Oxford University Press. Available at: http://www.oxfordhandbooks.com/view/10.1093/oxfordhb/9780199660773.001.0001/oxfordhb-9780199660773-e-22?rskey=Zbed6M&result=1 (accessed 16 March 2016).

Gifford, E. (1993). The musical training of primary teachers: Old problems, new insights and possible solutions. *British Journal of Music Education*, 10(1), 33–46.

Grace, A. (2011). *Singing teaching and generalist primary teachers*. Unpublished MA dissertation, Institute of Education, University of London.

Hargreaves, D.J., Miell, D., & MacDonald, R.A.R. (2002). What are musical identities and why are they important? In: R.A.R. MacDonald, D.J. Hargreaves, & D. Miell, (Eds.) *Musical identities*, pp. 1–20. Oxford: Oxford University Press.

Hennessy, S. (2000). Overcoming the red-feeling: the development of confidence to teach music in primary school amongst student teachers. *British Journal of Music Education*, 17(2), 183–96.

Himonides, E., Saunders, J., Papageorgi, I., & Welch, G.F. (2011). *Researching Sing Up's workforce development*. London: International Music Education Research Centre, Institute of Education, University of London.

Howard, D.M., Szymanski, J., & Welch, G.F. (2002). Listener's perception of English cathedral girl and boy choristers. *Music Perception*, 20(1), 35–49.

Howard, D.M., Angus, J.A., & Welch, G.F. (1994). Singing pitching accuracy from years 3 to 6 in a primary school. *Proceedings of the Institute of Acoustics*, 16(5), 223–30.

Ilari, B. (2005). On musical parenting of young children: beliefs and behaviors of mothers and infants. *Early Child Development and Care*, 175, 647–60.

Joyce, H. (2005). *The effects of sex, age and environment on attitudes to singing in Key Stage 2*. Unpublished Master's dissertation, Institute of Education, University of London.

Kagan, J. (2001). Biological constraint, cultural variety, and psychological structures. In: A. R. Damasio, A. Harrington, J. Kagan, B.S. McEwen, H. Moss, & R. Shaikh (Eds.) *Unity of knowledge: the convergence of natural and human science. Annals of the New York Academy of Sciences*, 935, 177–90. New York: New York Academy of Sciences.

Kenny, D.T., Davis, P., & Oates, J. (2004). Music performance anxiety and occupational stress amongst opera chorus artists and their relationship with state and trait anxiety and perfectionism. *Anxiety Disorders*, 18, 757–77.

Kirkpatrick, W. (1962). *Relationships between the singing ability of prekindergarten children and their home musical environment*. Unpublished Doctoral dissertation, University of Southern California.

Kirschner, S., & Tomasello, M. (2010). Joint music making promotes prosocial behavior in 4-year-old children. *Evolution and Human Behavior*, 31, 354–64.

Kleber, B.A., & Zarate, J.M. (2014). The neuroscience of singing. In: G.F. Welch, D.M. Howard, & J. Nix. (Eds.) *Oxford handbook of singing*. New York: Oxford University Press. DOI: 10.1093/oxfordhb/9780199660773.013.015.

Knight, S. (2010). *A study of adult 'non-singers' in Newfoundland*. Unpublished PhD thesis, Institute of Education, University of London.

Larrouy-Maestri, P., Magis, D., & Morsomme, D. (2014). The evaluation of vocal pitch accuracy: the case of operatic singing voices. *Music Perception*, 32(1), 1–10.

Malloch, S.N. (1999). Mothers and infants and communicative musicality. *Musicae Scientiae, Special Issue*, 29–57.

Mang, E. (2006). The effects of age, gender and language on children's singing competency. *British Journal of Music Education*, 23(2), 161–74.

Mawhinney, T.A., & Cuddy, L.L. (1984). *A factor analysis investigation of tone deafness*. Unpublished paper presented at MENC, Chicago.

Mehr, S.A. (2014). Music in the home. New evidence for an intergenerational link. *Journal of Research in Music Education*, 62(1), 78–88

McAllister, A., & Sjölander, P. (2013). Children's voice and voice disorders. *Seminars in Speech and Language*, 34(2), 71–9

McCulloch, L. (2006). "I don't know anything about music." An exploratory study of Primary teachers' knowledge about music in education. Unpublished PhD thesis, Northumbria University.

Mills, J. (1989). The generalist primary teacher of music: a problem of confidence. *British Journal of Music Education*, 6(2), 125–38.

Numminen, A., Lonka, K., Rainio, A.P., & Ruismäki. (2015). "Singing is no longer forbidden to me—it's like part of my human dignity has been restored." Adult non-singers learning to sing: An exploratory intervention study. *The European Journal of Social and Behavioural Sciences, XII.* Available at: http://dx.doi.org/10.15405/ejsbs.149.

Ockelford, A. (2015). *Sounds of intent in the early years.* Oxford: Soundabout.

Ockelford, A., & Welch, G. (2012) Mapping musical development in learners with the most complex needs: the *Sounds of Intent* project. In: G. McPherson & G. Welch (Eds.) *Oxford handbook of music education,* Vol. 2, pp. 11–30. Oxford: Oxford University Press.

Ofcom. (2014). *Children and parents: media use and attitudes report.* Available at: http://stakeholders.ofcom.org.uk/binaries/research/media-literacy/media-use-attitudes-14/Childrens_2014_Report.pdf 1 May 2015 (accessed 25 February 2016).

Ofsted [Office for Standards in Education, Children's Services and Skills]. (2012). *Music in schools: wider still, and wider.* Manchester: Ofsted.

Owens, M., & Welch, G.F. (in press). Choral pedagogy and the construction of identity: girls. In: F. Abrahams & P.D.Head (Eds.) *Oxford handbook of choral pedagogy.*

Papoušek, H. (1996a). Musicality in infancy research: biological and cultural origins of early musicality. In: I. Deliè & J. Sloboda (Eds.), *Musical beginnings,* pp. 88–112. Oxford: Oxford University Press.

Papousek, M. (1996b). Intuitive parenting: a hidden source of musical stimulation in infancy. In: I. Deliège and J. Sloboda (Eds.), *Musical beginnings,* pp. 88–112. Oxford: Oxford University Press.

Patel, A.D. (2008). *Music, language, and the brain.* New York, NY: Oxford University Press.

Patel, A.D. (2010). Music, biological evolution, and the brain. In: M. Bailar (Ed.) *Emerging disciplines,* pp. 91–144. Houston, TX: Rice University Press.

Pfordresher, P.Q., & Brown, S. (2007). Poor-pitch singing in the absence of "tone deafness". *Music Perception,* 25, 95–115.

Richards, H.M. (2002). *Offering an enjoyable choral experience to adult non-singers.* Unpublished Masters dissertation, University of Surrey Roehampton.

Richards, H., & Durrant, C. (2003). To sing or not to sing: a study on the development of 'non-singers' in choral activity. *Research Studies in Music Education,* 20(1), 78–89.

Ruismä H., & Tereska, T. (2006). Early childhood musical experiences: contributing to pre-service elementary teachers' self-concept in music and success in music education (during student age). *European Early Childhood Education Research Journal,* 14(1), 113–30.

Saunders, J., Papageorgi, I., Himonides, E., Vraka, M., Rinta, T., & Welch, G.F. (2012). *The Chorister Outreach Programme of the Choir Schools Association.* London: International Music Education Research Centre, Institute of Education, University of London.

Schlaug, G. (2015). Musicians and music making as a model for the study of brain plasticity. *Progress in Brain Research,* 217, 37–55.

Sergeant, D.C., Sjölander, P.J., & Welch, G.F. (2005). Listeners' identification of gender differences in children's singing. *Research Studies in Music Education,* 24, 28–39.

Snowdon, C.T., Zimmermann, E., & Altenmüller, E. (2015). Music evolution and neuroscience. *Progress in Brain Research,* 217, 17–34.

Soares, J. (2006). *Adolescents' engagement in computer-based composition in Brazil.* Unpublished PhD thesis, Institute of Education, University of London.

Stunell, G. (2007). *"Help, I'm worried about music!" Perceptions of generalist Primary teachers in the context of the National Curriculum for Music in England.* Unpublished PhD thesis, Institute of Education, University of London.

Tafuri, J. (2008). *Infant musicality*. Farnham: Ashgate.

Tafuri, J., & Villa, D. (2002). Musical elements in the vocalizations of infants aged 2 to 8 months. *British Journal of Music Education*, 19(1), 73–88.

Thurman, L., & Welch, G.F. (Eds.). (2000). *Bodymind and voice: foundations of voice education*, rev. edn. Iowa City, IO: National Center for Voice and Speech.

Trainor, L.J., Clark, E.D., Huntley, A., & Adams, B. (1997). The acoustic basis of preferences for infant-directed singing. *Infant Behavior and Development*, 20, 383–96.

Trehub, S.E., & Gudmundsdottir, H.R. (2015). Mothers as singing mentors for infants. In: G. F. Welch, D.M. Howard, & J. Nix. (Eds.) *Oxford handbook of singing*. New York: Oxford University Press. Available at: http://www.oxfordhandbooks.com/view/10.1093/oxfordhb/9780199660773.001.0001/oxfordhb-9780199660773-e-25?rskey=6LLLBj&result=1 (accessed 16 March 2016).

Trehub, S.E., & Trainor, L.J. (1998). Singing to infants: Lullabies and play songs. *Advances in Infancy Research*, 12, 43–77.

Trehub, S.E., Unyk, A.M., Kamenetsky, S.B., Hill, D.S., Trainor, L.J., Henderson, J.L., & Saraza, M. (1997). Mothers' and fathers' singing to infants. *Developmental Psychology*, 33, 500–7.

Uddin, L.Q., Iacobini, M., Lange, C., & Keenan, J. P. (2007). The self and social cognition: the role of cortical midline structures and mirror neurons. *Trends in Cognitive Sciences*, 11, 153–7.

Welch, G.F. (1979). Poor pitch singing: a review of the literature. *Psychology of Music*, 7(1), 50–8.

Welch, G.F. (2000). The ontogenesis of musical behaviour: a sociological perspective. *Research Studies in Music Education*, 14, 1–13.

Welch, G.F. (2001). *The misunderstanding of music*. London: Institute of Education,University of London.

Welch, G.F. (2005). Singing as communication. In: D. Miell, R. MacDonald, & D. Hargreaves (Eds.) *Musical communication*, pp. 239–59. New York, NY: Oxford University Press.

Welch, G.F. (2009). Evidence of the development of vocal pitch matching ability in children. *Japanese Journal of Music Education Research*, 39(1), 38–47.

Welch, G.F. (2011). Culture and gender in a cathedral music context: An activity theory exploration. In: M. Barrett (Ed.) *A cultural psychology of music education*, pp. 225–58. New York, NY: Oxford University Press.

Welch, G.F. (2015). Singing and vocal development. In: G. McPherson (Ed.) *The child as musician: a handbook of musical development*, 2nd edn, pp. 441–61. New York: Oxford University Press.

Welch, G.F., Himonides, E., Saunders, J., et al. (2010). *Researching the impact of the National Singing Programme 'Sing Up' in England: main findings from the first three years (2007-2010). Children's singing development, self-concept and sense of social inclusion*. London: International Music Education Research Centre, Institute of Education, University of London.

Welch, G.F., Himonides, E., Saunders, J., Papageorgi, I., & Sarazin, M. (2014). Singing and social inclusion. *Frontiers in Psychology*, 5, 803.

Welch, G.F. & Howard, D.M. (2002). Gendered voice in the cathedral choir. *Psychology of Music*, 30, 102–20.

Welch, G.F., & Murao, T. (Eds.). (1994). *Onchi and singing development*. London: David Fulton.

Welch, G.F., Saunders, J., Papageorgi, I., & Himonides, E. (2012). Sex, gender and singing development: Making a positive difference to boys' singing through a national programme in England. In: S. Harrison, G.F. Welch, & A. Adler (Eds.) *Perspectives on males and singing*, pp. 37–54. London: Springer.

Welch, G.F., Sergeant, D.C., & White, P. (1997). Age, sex and vocal task as factors in singing 'in-tune' during the first years of schooling. *Bulletin of the Council for Research in Music Education*, 133, 153–60.

Whidden, C. (2009). *The adult non-singer: connection, context and culture*. Unpublished PhD thesis, Department of Music, University of Calgary. [Available from ProQuest Dissertations and Theses. NR49638.]

Winstone, N., & Witherspoon, K. (2015). 'It's all about our great Queen': The British National Anthem and national identity in 8-10-year-old children. *Psychology of Music*, 44(2), 263–77

Wise, K. (2015). Defining and explaining singing difficulties in adults. In: G. Welch, D.M. Howard, & J. Nix (Eds.) *The Oxford handbook of singing*. New York, NY: Oxford University Press. DOI: 10.1093/oxfordhb/9780199660773.013.38

Wise, K.J., & Sloboda, J.A. (2008). Establishing an empirical profile of self-defined tone deafness: Perception, singing performance and self-assessment. *Musicae Scientiae*, 12, 3–26.

Wu, Y.-T. (2015). Musical environment and the development of young children of the Chinese diaspora in London. In: G. Lock & T. Selke (Eds.) *Proceedings, The Changing Face of Music and Art Education*, CFMAE-MERYC2015, Tallinn, 5–9 May, 2015.

Yang, Y., & Welch, G.F. (2014). Contemporary challenges in learning and teaching folk music in a higher education context: a case study of Hua'er music. *Music Education Research*, 16(2), 193–219.

CHAPTER 31

....

MUSIC GAMES AND MUSICAL IDENTITIES

....

GIANNA G. CASSIDY AND ANNA M. J. M. PAISLEY

31.1 INTRODUCTION

THIS chapter extends the study of identity in music and video games respectively, to their synergy in the music-game context, exploring how music-games are influencing both our understanding of socially defined parameters of musicality and our use of music to negotiate and express our personal and social identity. The digital revolution has created new opportunities to interact with music in everyday life, transforming what it means to be musical in the 21st century (Bloustien, Peters & Luckman, 2008). From downloading iPod playlists on the move, to becoming a Guitar Hero in our living room and real-time collaborative composition across geographically dispersed contexts, a new generation of music-makers are experiencing and expressing music through digital literacy. In particular, democratization of musical roles has increased opportunity and accessibility to participate in music for personal pleasure and education, and for others to enjoy, critique, and manipulate. Findings suggest 8–18-year-olds are spending six-and-a-half hours per day on average engaging with digital media, with music often central or background to this activity (see Roberts , Foehr, & Rideout, 2005). Such activity includes listening to and purchasing music, networking, and disseminating from home or virtual environments, and performing and composing with virtual instruments and online communities.

Music-games present one of the most pervasive new everyday modes of music interaction, and so potentially a new means of negotiating and expressing identity. However, the processes and practices of music-game participation, and the impact upon players' social, personal, and intellectual parameters, have been relatively neglected (see Cassidy & Paisley, 2013). In particular, there is a dearth of research addressing the role of music-game experience in personal and social identity, and in key themes and approaches of musical identity research. It is suggested that the study of identity should include reference to new technologies (Wood & Smith, 2004), with game technologies negating the necessity of the physical co-presence of others, creating new environments for identity exploration in virtual contexts (Cerulo, 1997). Furthermore, games facilitate the adoption of an avatar, allowing individuals to not only enter a virtual world, but to explore and create identities comprised of both self and game character, i.e., the virtual self (Murphy, 2004). In this way, music-games have altered the backdrop for the development of music-identities, expanding the array of generalized others and environments to draw upon in the process of identity construction (see Cerulo, 1997).

We present an overview of music-game literature, suggesting the study of musical identities should be approached with recourse to the impact of music-games upon music participation, and thus allow us to question what it means to be "musical" in the digital age. The chapter draws upon the conceptual distinction between identities in music (IIM) and music in identities (MII) to provide a useful tool to explore the link between music-games, the individual and the social situation (Hargreaves, Miell & MacDonald, 2002). Applying IIM to the music-game context calls for exploration of the relationship between music-game experience and, "those aspects of musical identities that are socially defined within given cultural roles and musical categories", deepening understanding of identities in music at the intersection of the "virtual" and the "real" (see Hargreaves, MacDonald & Miell, 2002, p. 2). Applying the concept MII to the music-game context calls for exploration of the relationship between music-game experience and "how we use music as a means or resource for developing other aspects of our individual identities", deepens understanding of music-game opportunities and outcomes for wider social and personal wellbeing (see Hargreaves, Miell & MacDonald, 2002 p. 2). The chapter concludes with a discussion of an in-depth interview study with players of Rock Band 3 Pro.

31.2 MUSIC GAMES

Video games are now a pervasive feature in everyday life, with music sales worth less than half of the UK's video Games market in 2013 (19.7% versus 41.4% of total entertainment sales, respectively), and video games worth a total US consumer spend of $21.53 billion in 2013 (see Entertainment Retailers Association, 2013; Entertainment Software Association, 2014). Perhaps surprisingly, the average "gamer" (game player) is 31 years old, plays socially with others and chooses action or strategy games, with more women aged 18 or older playing (36%) than boys age 18 or younger (17%) (see Entertainment Software Association, 2014). In over half a century, videogames have flourished from the first commercially successful arcade game such as "Pong" in 1972, the Atari 2600 home system in 1977, and the Massive Multiplayer Online Games (MMOG's) of the 1990s, to the integrative platforms of the 21st century such as Wii and Kinect, and current 8th generation consoles such as the Nintendo 3Ds, Playstation 4, and Xbox One (see Donovan, 2010). Music has been a fundamental and powerful channel of communication throughout this video-game history, long recognized by industry and consumer through formats such as puzzle games utilizing incremental tempos, driving games with player-selected music, and first person shooters with cinematic scores outselling box office soundtracks (see Collins, 2008a,b; Whalen 2004; Zehnder & Lipscomb, 2006). Music can enrich the game world aiding the creation and communication of context, semantic inference, navigation and feedback, and also to manipulate the nature of player performance and experience (see Cassidy & MacDonald, 2008, 2009, 2010; Whalen, 2004; Zehnder & Lipscomb, 2006).

Music-games, however, refer to a specific game genre in which music performance, appreciation and/or creation is integral to the gameplay mechanic itself (i.e., rules or methods designed for interaction with the game), and so the action of the player and their avatar within the game. With over 120 different games titles available (for time-line of music games see Miller, 2011), "rhythm action" games are the most popular genre and a pervasive feature in our everyday musical landscape, potentially influencing our musical behaviours and impacting our wider musical world (see Missingham, 2007; Schultz, 2008). The "rhythm-action" game (see Fig. 31.1) engages the player in rhythm-based action responses to generate music, through an interface, such as an instrument controller, microphone, dance-mat, or music creation software (as distinct from the alternative free form, generative or reactive music-game forms). The most popular titles include Samba de Amigo (employing bongos), Guitar Hero (employing guitar peripheries), and Rock Band (employing microphones and full rock band instruments and real-world instrument capabilities to plug in real electric guitar in Rock Band Pro; see Fig. 31.1), Dance Dance Revolution (employing a dance mat), DJ Hero and Beat Mania (employing turntables). Most titles have multi-play options (see Fig. 31.3), where the player can choose from playing alone or with one or more other "real-world" players, either collaboratively or competitively, to complete a musical goal such as the successful performance of a song or completion of an entire gig.

Rhythm-action games are extremely popular in everyday musical experience, with Guitar Hero becoming the fastest new video game franchise to reach $1 billion in retail sales, broken next by Rock Band the subsequent release from Harmonix (see Miller, 2011). Existing evidence indicates music-games are representative of the general game players profile discussed above, however, studies are biased toward the teenage market (see De Schutter, 2011). For example, Lenhart, Kahne, Middaugh, MacGill, Evans, & Vitak (2008) found a relatively equal gender split for music-game preference for teenagers, with 64% of girls and 58% of boys expressing preference for the genre over others. Roberts et al. (2005, 2010) found that on any given day 85% of 8–18-year-old Americans questioned ($n = 2032$) listened to music for an average of one and three quarter hours a day, while 83% had a video game console at home playing approximately 50 minutes per day on average, with 71% having played Guitar Hero or Rock Band (see Miller, 2012). In the UK, Missingham's (2007) Youth Music report found that over 51% of surveyed 13–18 year olds regularly played "Rhythm Action" music-games, inspiring potentially 2.5 million to take up a musical instrument, while 33% reported singing or paying a musical instrument. For adults, literature again suggests a relatively equal preference

FIG. 31.1 20-year-old girl playing Rock Band 3 Pro. N.B The figure Vocals and Keytar (left), with her avatar visible in the right hand picture illustrating both "reading mode" for vocals (indicated by blue line at top of picture) and "driving mode" for Keytar (indicated by fret board and colored buttons; refer to Fig. 31.2a,b).

for music-games, for example, Bilgihan, Cobanoglu, Nusair, Okumus, & Bujisic (2013) found no statistically significant difference between video gaming preferences of women and men, while evidence indicates music-games are a preferred genre of adult female gamers representative of a general female preference for games which facilitate social contact, motivation, and collaboration (see Bradley et al., 2010; Phan, Jardina & Hoyle, 2012; Vermeulen & Van Looy, 2014).

While music-games rarely aim to teach traditional musical skills directly, they increasingly employ peripherals that imitate real-world instruments, adapt notational systems, and require reference to musical critique and social reference (see Schultz, 2008). One of the most universal and engaging features of rhythm-action games is the mapping of musical time to physical space, where musical time can be understood and acted upon as a physical object (refer to Schultz, 2008). Interestingly, the quality of time appears in varying "axis" of orientation. For example, Rock Band Pro Vocal line (refer to top image in Fig. 31.1) employs a system similar to western notation resembling musical score, which Schultz (2008, p. 181) calls "reading mode", in which time passes left to right and relative pitch is arrange vertically with rising and falling lines to show pitch contour (see Fig. 31.2a). In contrast, "driving mode" used by Rock Band instruments (see Fig. 31.1 top image for "Keytar" example) requires the player to, as Schultz (2008, p. 182) put it, move "into the screen" in pursuit of the time arrow with notes approaching from the front presenting a "song as a space through which the player drives" (See Fig. 31.2b).

Rock Band in particular is receiving growing attention from researchers and educators, and is the first videogame to "let four player simultaneously jam online/in-person, together on guitar, bass, drum, and microphone peripherals" (see, Miller, 2012

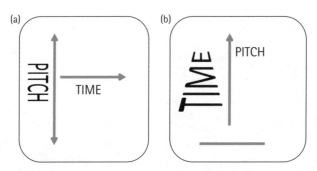

FIG. 31.2 (a) Diagram of "reading mode." (b) Diagram of "driving mode."

Adapted from Schultz (2008).

p. 77)— and as the successor to Guitar Hero, was informed by work at MIT to develop intuitive interfaces to increase accessibility of music technology to democratize exposure to the benefits of music participation (see Gower & McDowall, 2012; MacHover, 2008; Peppler, Downton, Lindsay & Hay, 2011). Alex Rigopulos (see Steinberg, 2011), Co-Founder and CEO Harmonix Music Systems, Inc., said:

> … we wondered: How might interactive media be used to tamper with the relationship between people and music? In particular, we were struck by the fact that the urge to *make* music is woven into every one of us. And yet very, very few of us are actually able to act on that innate desire … to endure the years of training and dedication that are the price of entry for musicianship. For most people, the path to having a joyful experience with a musical instrument is a prohibitively long one. This is the problem we set out to solve. In the beginning, we weren't making video games, we were making music creativity apps of various sorts, … for the first time I could see the potential of video games as a medium to amplify people's connection to music. And shortly thereafter, Harmonix started making games.
>
> Rigopulos, 2011 Foreword.
> Text extracts from Scott Steinberg, Music Games Rock: Rhythm
> Gaming's Greatest Hits Of All Time, Copyright © 2011 Scott
> Steinberg, with permission from Scott Steinberg.

Rock Band has sold over 35 million copies to date, and is described as "one of the most lucrative media franchises of the new millennium and a cornerstone gaming experience for millions of today's youth" (Peppler et al., 2011, p. 42). In Rock Band a player may choose to play guitar, bass, drums, keyboards, and or/vocals, or play with up to four others to make a classic rock band line up (see Fig. 31.3). The player(s) then chooses their avatar, repertoire of music, difficulty level of play (four levels from "easy" to "expert") etc., and are then encouraged or booed by a virtual audience depending on their performance of the chosen song. The game presents practice modes and tutorial guides; set list creation functions and ability to download new music, a "new music" personal preference song recommendation system; and the facility to share tracks via social networking and online communities.

Discussion in this chapter will focus upon the newest and most socially inclusive "Rhythm Action" game, the latest Rock Band incarnation, Rock Band 3 Pro (See Figs 31.1 and 31.3) with "pro instruments." For example, as well as the ability to hold 3 part vocal harmonies, plug in a real Stratocaster and 25-key MIDI keyboard, the "nearly real" peripheries include 102-button guitar simulating each possible chord combination (see Miller, 2011). With this new version, makers Harmonix (2010) aimed to close the gap between playing music-games and playing real instruments, asking, "Ever had someone ask you why you play plastic guitar instead of learning a real instrument? Now you can tell them you ARE learning a real instrument". Rock Band Pro contains over 2000 tracks spanning 5 decades, with over 5 million player accounts downloading over 7 million tracks from the Rock Band Store (Viacom, 2012). This has resulted in Rock Band digitally distributing over 100 million tracks from a music catalogue of over 900 artists, including from Otis Reading, David Bowie, the Ramones, and Ozzy Osbourne, to Foo Fighters and Lady Gaga who are were simultaneously promoting new records. The player may compete in their virtual band (in which they are the only real-world member) against other virtual bands or online competitors, or indeed may play with one or more other friends to form their own band of real-world players competing against a virtual band in the game through adoption of their own in-game avatars. The final section of this chapter will discuss an in depth-interview study with players of Rock Band 3, exploring themes of perceived musicality and role-playing.

FIG. 31.3 Rock Band 3 Pro being played by a group of four 20-year-old males, as observed from the eMotion Lab at Glasgow Caledonian University.

31.3 MUSIC GAMES AND IDENTITY

The appeal of Gaming is suggested to be in part the games' "ability to provide players with novel experiences that let them try on ideal aspects of themselves that might not find expression in everyday life" (Przybylski et al., 2012, p. 1). In this way, players can act congruently to their ideal self in ways they cannot explore in everyday life (see Klimmt, Hefner & Vorderer, 2009). Przybylski et al. (2012, p. 1) found that video games were most intrinsically motivating and had greatest influence on players' emotions, when players' in-game experience of themselves were most congruent with their ideal selves. Such congruence between actual and ideal self has in turn been linked to parameters of psychological wellbeing such as self-esteem and happiness. Drawing on self-determination theory, Ryan & Deci (2000) suggest that subjective wellbeing can be enhanced and perceived discrepancy between perceived actual and ideal self can be reduced, through interpersonal contexts which support the satisfaction of psychological needs such as autonomy and competence. Video games have been identified as such rich environments for exploration and expression of the self that promote the "trying-on" and adoption of new self-representations, experimenting with alternative skills, genders, roles, and ages among other identity parameters (e.g., Turkle, 1994; Kirsch, 2006; Olson, 2010). As Przybylski et al. (2012, p. 2) suggest, "video games provide a gamut of idealized attributes embodied in ready-made, idealized roles ... in highly immersive narratives" (p. 70).

At the intersection of "virtual" and "real", music-games present a unique relationship between the player, the game designer, the recorded music and artist, and the audience virtual and/or real. Miller (2012, p. 102) asserts that music-game players negotiate a complex relationship between musical and performance attributes, "paratexts" of the recording, the wider social and culture world of the performer, extra-musical association, and iconic representation of popular music and culture. Rhythm-action games such as Rock Band have been conceptualized as a "developing form of collaborative, participatory rock music performance", raising the question of what it means to be, "a live performer of a pre-recorded song"? (see Miller, 2009, 2012). Further, game mechanics, such as narrative, sound effects and cuing of feedback and control, reinforce player perception of agency, expression, and creativity. In this way, music-games challenge traditional distinctions between a sound and its source by presenting "the physical gestures of live musical performance with previously recorded sound" (Schafer 1969). Miller (2009, p. 424) refers to this phenomenon as "schizophonic performance"—music-game performance is a collaborative act of, "stitching musical sound and performing body back together."

Evidence indicates that music-games generate meaningful "real experience", in part because the games draw on players' pre-existing musical and cultural knowledge, and embodied understanding of musicianship and identity to put themselves in the shoes of the performer (Missingham, 2007; Miller, 2009; Prensky, 2009). Harmonix (2010), the makers of Rock Band, encourage players to adopt or project themselves into a rock star identity, presenting an immersive activity context full of cultural and social music cues, such as musical repertoire, archetypal rock star avatars, virtual audience, and other player characters to respond to player action, stylized instrumental controllers and physical performance guidance (Miller, 2012). In fact, the musical material used is approved by the real life artist before release in the game, reinforcing credibility of such interaction with the materials by the original artist themselves. Players can express their identity creating an imaginative self or actualizing a hidden self, addressing unexplored or unexpressed aspects of their identity through personalization of the environment such as avatar features, clothing, gender, and aesthetic scope of visual and auditory features, merging the players' role and identity with that of the avatar, etc. (see Marty & Consalvo, 2011).

"Avatar," a term derived from the Sanskrit for a bodily manifestation of an immortal being, can be conceived of as the "user's manifestation in the virtual universe" (Filiciak, 2003), or as "virtual constructs … controlled by human players […] function as a means of interacting with other characters" (Crawford, 2003, p. 8). In music-games, this adoption of an avatar facilitates exploration and creation of music and musical identities comprised of both self and game character i.e., the virtual self (Murphy, 2004). In Rock Band, for example, the avatar is the vehicle through which the player chooses their preferred song and instrument, their gender and aesthetics such as their outfit, and through which they act upon the game world. To apply Gee's (2003) tripartite approach to identity, "virtual-identity" refers to the avatar, which exists within the fictional musical world; real-world identity refers to the player's potentially numerous non-virtual musical identities; and "projective-identity" is the middle ground between the player's real-world musical identity and their avatar musical identity, or as Gee (2003, p. 56) describes:

> The kind of person I want to be, the kind of history I want her to have, the kind of person and history I am trying to build in and through her is what I mean by a projective identity. Since these aspirations are my desires for [the avatar], the projective identity is both mine and hers, and it is a space in which I can transcend both her limitations and my own … In this identity, the stress is on the interface between—the interactions between—the real-world person and the virtual character (p. 56).

Such a relationship between player and avatar is complex and may be thought of reciprocal through "ego-investing," by which players over time begin to share the motivations of the avatar, for example, the successful completion of the song at the virtual band's gig (Gee, 2003). Furthermore, music-games blur the boundaries between performer and listener, with players fluctuating between; performer and observer; collaborator and competitor; personal or avatar identity, observing real or virtual audience and feedback, etc … This "adopted" identity facilitates new pathways to experience novel and familiar music; the exploration and expansion of musical taste; understanding and listening skills; and greater appreciation of the relationship between a musician, their peers, audience, and instrument (see Miller, 2012).

31.4 EDUCATIONAL OPPORTUNITIES

Video games have the potential to create virtual environments that support learning, through the practice of constructing new identities and actions and the learner's realization of their capacity to do so. Gee (2003) states "deep learning" occurs when players bridge their real-world identities and new virtual identities and their values, while Wenger (1998, p. 215) suggests that learning transforms our identities: "Learning transforms who we are and what we can do, it is an experience of identity. It is not just an accumulation of skills and information, but a process of becoming—to become a certain person, conversely, to avoid becoming a certain person ... it is in that formation of an identity that learning can become a source of meaningfulness and of personal and social energy." The music-game literature to date has focussed on the potential educational opportunities of music-games to close the gap between informal and formal musical behavior. Indeed, Harmonix (2010) assert that they designed the game with learning intention: "Rock Band 3 empowers players to develop actual musical skills through the fun of Rock Band Pro gameplay."

Recent surveys of impact on musical behaviour indicate players are aware of music-games changing and extending their music appreciation and preference, improving perceived transferable skill and performance and notation negotiation (see Missingham, 2007; Miller, 2009, 2012). Most music-games encourage the mastery of semiotic domains related to real-world musical activities, and promote critical thinking and exploration and comparison of real-world identity and experience (see Schultz, 2008). In addition to accurate physical response to rhythmic cues through auditory and visual information, "... the players' physical response must be driven by a sufficiently robust conceptual response, a theory about the game's musical system" (Schultz, 2007, p. 188). In this way, as a player negotiates the game's musical system "they learn to process larger and more complicated musical units at one time, and to examine the relationship between performance in the game and in conventional musical circles" in the real-world (Schultz, 2008, p. 188).

Peppler et al. (2011) found that playing Rock Band can benefit the learning of fundamental mechanisms of music, supporting growing evidence of the importance of informal music practice to formal music learning, terming their findings the "Nirvana Effect." Peppler et al. (2011) suggest that learners make connections between virtual in-game experience of music participation and conventional music education practices. The authors found a close alignment between Rock Band notation and classical notation, suggesting that Rock Band's pre-recorded tracks and immediate feedback scaffold learning (Wiggins, 2009). Playing Rock Band positively correlated with learners' assessment levels in standard music abilities, with learners either employing their understanding of Rock Band as a tool to aid their reading and writing of conventional notation, or those who were more adept in conventional musical skill were more likely to persist with Rock Band participation.

Learners bring their music-game experience to the classroom, just as they bring their classroom experience to their wider musical world. The challenge is to better understand the nature of informal music-game participation, to harness this potential to support and enrich formal music engagement in the home, classroom, and third environment (see Gower & McDowall 2012; Hargreaves, Marshall & North 2003). Cassidy & Paisley (2012) investigated one learner's encounter with Rock Band 3 to; provide an in-depth account of the learner's experience with and views about music-games; addressing potential opportunities and outcomes for intellectual, personal, and social development. The authors assert that music-games have the potential to, "promote inclusive music participation; embody fundamental musical concepts in gameplay; and authenticate formal participation to help learners see the relevance of music curriculum to their own experiences and aspirations in the wider world" (p. 135). Music-game communities of learning may offer safe and self-directed learning space, more appropriated to the learning trajectory of individuals than formal music education (Wenger, 2006).

31.5 PERCEIVED AUTHENTICITY AND CREATIVITY

A contentious issue surrounding music-games is that of creativity and authenticity, with critics identifying an absence of authentic musical experience of creativity, originality, and authorship, in part due to a rigid constraint of musical input, limited interpretative freedom, and simplicity of instrument periphery (see Missingham, 2007; Miller, 2012). An apparent contradiction between game mechanics of music-games such as Rock Band and their "guiding musical aesthetic", mean that music-games require players to read from fixed notation with limited original input, while the popular music aesthetic would espouse originality and alternative expression. Frith (1996, pp. 124–5) observes,

> Rock performers are expected to revel in their own physicality … Rock acts conceal not the physical but the technological sources of their sounds; rock audiences remain uneasy about musical instruments that appear to require no effort to be played.
>
> By permission of Oxford University Press.

However, these viewpoints fail to capture the perceived experience and appeal of music-games for players. While the player may not be afforded control over subsequent sonic direction (excluding free play sections), neither does the player of sheet music or of work composed by another. Indeed, in the same way as describing piano playing as "hitting keys to make music," the assertion that the mechanical action alone represents the entire musical experience potential is lacking in consideration of the wider musical and extra-musical features of participation (Miller, 2012).

Each gameplay session creates a unique sound scape and experience, with changes in players' physical action and affective experiences, free play sections, and aesthetic changes, etc., creating a unique audio scape at each session (see Schultz, 2008; Miller, 2012). Miller (2012) asserts that music-games are designed to provide sensory evidence to the player to encourage the player to take responsibility for the sound being produced and become engaged in the experience and affiliated with the original artist and avatar. In this way, the engagement, energy and commitment to the music is quite real, even if we consider the resulting "performance" not to be. Miller's (2012) interviews with music-game players revealed one feature in particular perceived to be creative, that is, "role-playing." This includes either "jumping into" the culturally accepted artist in their time, as themselves in an alternative reality, or creating fantasy identities, projecting agency and exploring identity with a safe space. Others suggested that they were "channeling a creative force", that music-game play made them more creative listeners, or facilitated creative inspiration, which they then applied in the real world. Furthermore, players have freedom for creative behavior through the extended game contexts, such as creating mods and custom software hacks to insert new material into the games, online forums creating personalized tabs (see ScoreHero.com) and extending the song to real instrumentation practice.

31.6 ROCK BAND 3 INTERVIEW SESSIONS

Research asserts that motivational aspects of musical development and our self-perception influence the development of musical skill, and so the development of musical identities (McDonald, Hargreaves & Miell, 2009). In this way, it is important to explore the potential of music-games to foster positive self-perception with music, and provide motivation to engage in, support and enrich musical activity, and promote development of musicality and wider benefits of music activity. An exploratory investigation with Rock Band 3 (see Figs 31.1 and 31.3) was carried out to investigate individuals' reflection on their music-game experience and related identity (Willig, 2001; Braun & Clarke, 2006). This presents the first step in a wider EPSRC funded project (Principle Investigator Gianna Cassidy, co-investigator Anna Paisley, April 2011–April 2013) entitled "Music Games: Supporting New Opportunities in Music Education": a 24-month program of work investigating the nature of interaction with music-games and potential opportunities and outcomes for intellectual, social, and personal development.

Employing a sequential mixed-methods paradigm, learners of all ages, and experience ($n = 100$) were invited to take part in a 20-minute usability session with Rock Band 3, followed by a one-to-one semi-structured interview with the researcher (Creswell & Miller, 2000). Pre-test, details of musical background and video game experience were captured via a project-specific questionnaire built from pre-existing instruments (see Mitchell, MacDonald, Serpell, & Knussen, 2007). The session and interview took place in the "eMotion Lab" (see Fig. 31.3), a usability facility comprising a replica living room and observation room with two way mirror, where Rock Band peripherals were positioned across the seating area to encourage the participant to select the instrument of their choice. Participants were informed they were "free to explore" the game, request assistance from the researcher if needed, and terminate the study at any point upon request. Participants were recorded via discrete, in-built video cameras remotely controlled from the observation room, allowing the researcher to attend to non-verbal cues that may enhance the analyzes.

In accordance with the sequential design of the study, a nested sub-sample ($n = 18$, 12 males and 6 females, aged between 15 and 53 years old) of the overarching data corpus was selected as representative of the wider participant pool. An awareness of "personal reflexivity" was duly noted (Willig, 2001), and an inductive approach was employed as a means of foregoing any prior suppositions that may have contaminated any of the resultant findings. Accordingly, the overarching aim of this analytical approach was to explore each individual's personal reflections upon their participation in music-game activity, focussing upon the synergistic role of music and of games and the subsequent impact upon identity development. The approach took into account the context of music-game participation and the way in which this shaped subsequent talk, with language utilized being crucial to the understanding of one's experience with the game (Raskin, 2002). The epistemological stance adopted was thus akin to that of a social constructionist approach to identity, focusing upon the setting in which these interactions occurred and the construction or renegotiation of identity through verbal exchange and personal reflection (Gergen, 1985). Preliminary readings and semantic thematic analysis resulted in an initial set of recurrent themes subsumed under the superordinate theme of musical identities. Clustering and further latent thematic analysis was used to organize the themes identified at the semantic level, two of which are presented below.

31.6.1 Theme 1: perceived musicality

Discourse surrounding perceived musicality saturated the data items where the ostensible use of the music-game context as particular social milieu in which to explore one's identity in music was apparent. Indeed, talk surrounding the gameplay context appeared to provide a catalyst for musical identity exploration by allowing the individual to reflect upon their experience in such a way so as to reposition themselves in terms of their perceived "musicality", in relation to subjective personal and societal expectations. Participants appeared to approach the game utilizing their pre-existent identities in music to inform both their predicted performance outcomes and thus their decisions regarding instrument choice:

Extract 1

> *Mark*: Most of the time I went for "easy" 'cause em … I haven't really had any experience of playing the drums in real life … well not much … so I figured I'm going to do terrible at this so I'm just going to go the easiest so I picked "easy."

Extract 2

> *Rachel*: I was quite surprised from a musical point of view like my left hand was just as good as my right hand, if not better … at times … so that's quite pleasing … d'you [do you] know what I mean? … Because that level of coordination is … whatever, what you need … and I didn't imagine I had that.

In the extract above, we witness a distinct change in one's perceived musical ability as a direct result of their performance during the session. Rachel expressed a level of satisfaction with her performance relative to her prior suppositions, augmented by the recognition of the perceived musical skills required to play the game. Rachael reflects upon her musical ability in relation to the game, rather than simply their ability to play a game, utilizing their identity in music as a reference point throughout such talk. Further support for this particular notion stemmed from insight into the retrospective accounts of the processes involved in decisions made throughout the game, where one's prior musical training appeared to dictate choices such as peripheral selection and difficulty level.

Extract 3

> *I*: What made you go for the guitar [pro guitar] first?
> *Tony*: Oh well I'm a guitarist so my first instinct's just to go for what I know
> *I*: Mmm hmm [yes]
> *Tony*: Em … and I just probably went straight for the guitar [pro guitar peripheral] because thinking it's in the same layout, the frets and … the actual strings I thought it would be easier to play than the other one but … I obviously totally underestimated it and ended up being quite challenge.

In contrast the excerpt above, and indeed many of the extracts from those who reported some level of former musical training, often gave rise to incongruent feelings regarding performance, vindicated by Tony's espoused surprise at the "challenge" of the game. Quite often this bore a palpable need to renegotiate the participant's sense of self in relation to music, where talk appeared to be rooted in a desire to publically maintain a desirable musical identity as a result of their music-gameplay experience, as illustrated below.

Extract 4

> *John*: I'm feeling a wee [little] bit embarrassed by my lack of success … cause I'm a musician and I cannae [can't] do it (laughs).

Again, the extract above provides an example of the context of music-game participation being utilized as a vehicle for musical identity exploration and maintenance. Whilst John remarked feeling slightly "embarrassed" following the session, his performance appeared to do little to detract from his overall self-perception as a "musician." Rather he is keen to reinstate that label perhaps by way of reconciliation. Thus, it appeared that for those individuals that reported some level of "musician-ship", the music game context provided them with the opportunity to express this via choices made within the game and outward reflections upon their performance and to stake their position as musical, rather than allowing the game to lessen their perceived musical ability.

On the other hand, for those who encountered the game in the absence of prior musi-cal experience or knowledge, changes in their perceived musical ability were marked. Furthermore, such talk was underscored by the notion that the game itself may help foster a more positive identity with music, particularly for those with little prior expe-rience and, or, comparatively pessimistic viewpoints regarding their own musicality. Additional support emerged from the retrospective accounts of their initial experience with the game (prior to the session), which quite often contained explicit recourse to the process of gaining confidence in one's musical ability.

Extract 5

> *Michael*: I think em ... before Guitar Hero like em ... I wasn't like too interested in like learning to play the guitar ... after I started playing I started thinking "I'm actu-ally not too bad at this" so I actually got like em a full size guitar and started playing myself and ... actually learned em ... like a lot more than I would have ... if I didn't have like the ... motivation from playing Guitar Hero.

Extract 6

> *Pete*: I only knew about three chords on the guitar and then I played this and I thought ... guitar can't be that hard then (mimics playing guitar) ...well I was playing it on "easy" mode so ... but still I thought "oh guitar cannae [can't] be that hard"... and I kinda [kind of] went back to the guitar and I looked at it and I was kinda [kind of] like ... okay ... and then I sat down and I just started playing it again.

Indeed, across the data corpus an abundance of anecdotal accounts hailed music games as the chief motive for the participants' embarkation into further real-world musical participation. What surreptitiously permeated such utterances, were pro-nounced transformations in their perceived musical ability that appeared to ignite a need for wider musical engagement. What's more, inextricably linked to the change in the participants' subjective musicality, were notable shifts in their perception or defini-tion of musicality itself. That is, irrespective of any truths as to whether the game repre-sents an accurate reflection of real-world musical participation or not, the music game appeared to transcend conventional and socially defined parameters of music, as evi-denced by Pete's quotation in particular wherein he remarks that playing the "guitar cannae [can't] be that hard". This extract in particular provides a clear example of not only the games capacity to foster an increasingly more positive identity in music, but further, a more positive and accessible view of musicality overall.

Theme 31.6.2: role playing

The theme of "role playing" draws direct parallels with that of social constructionist views of identity: in line with an emphasis on the existence of multiple identities and the fluidity of one's identity across social contexts (Raskin, 2002), the music-game can be viewed here as a unique tool with which one could readily experiment with alternative identities.

Extract 7

> *Luke*: When you're playing a song you love … you're like "I'm playing a guitar solo!" …"I am, I am Lynyrd Skynyrd" … "I'm playing (mimics the sound of playing the guitar) … so yeah … that's what I like."

Extract 8

> *Robert*: It's quite good like … psychologically like … see when you're playing it … you like … 'cause you've got like the rest of the track playing … it kind of creates the illusion of like … playing in a band … but you're actually just sitting yourself (smiles).

Extract 9

> *Matthew*: It makes you feel like … part of the … music.

As demonstrated in the extracts above, it appears that the exploration of a *virtual self*, or a multitude of virtual selves, is accentuated via the adoption of a game character or avatar created by the individual. For this particular facet of the game provides the individual not only with the opportunity to create and act out a desirable identity in music, but to bring to the music-game context those aspects of one's own personal identity through the creation of that "virtual self." This particular feature of the game is further enhanced, as vindicated in Robert's quotation, by the real-time mechanics of the game wherein both audio and visual cues appear to intensify this process, with reference to the on-screen image of one's character within a virtual band and the simultaneous execution of the music in play. Indeed, sprinkled throughout subsequent talk were further instances of such "role play" where many of the individuals spoke not only of the ability to try on multiple, identities, but to adopt those of coveted others such as those of their favorite artists or bands and the definitive pleasure gained in doing so. Many participants vocalized a sense of almost being or becoming that individual, and quite often this process appeared to go beyond that of somewhat passively acting out a prescribed role within a band, where many individuals were keen to vocalize feelings of involvement in the musical performance, as a contributing band member, actively involved in the creation of music.

This seemingly high level of engagement routinely spawned further departure points for one's journey through their musical identity, where many individuals made reference to the illusionary feeling of being able to play a given instrument, irrespective of their actual musical ability. Indeed, a unique affordance of the game that seemed to temporarily blur the distinction between virtual and real world music participation, as well as break the boundaries of a socially defined definition of musicality, was noted where many of the individuals remarked not only upon a heightened sense of musical ability, but also of the capacity to adopt the persona of a known musician, and thus experience the inner feelings of that person in that space and time. What's more, it was often suggested that this particular avenue of identity exploration would otherwise be unavailable, particularly amongst those with little or no prior musical training and a somewhat negative self-perception of their musical aptitude.

Extract 10

> *Lucy*: it's like you're actually able to play all these songs … it took me ages to actually pick a song (laughs) because, 'cause it just makes you feel good that you're technically … playing those songs.

Such talk was also apparent for more advanced learners, who tended to highlight the ostensible gains from being able to try on a multitude of identities considered out-with their musical remit, from a desire to escape the boundaries imposed upon them by their prior identity in music. In the following excerpt Tony makes reference to the pleasure derived from being able to freely adopt a range of musical identities within the game context, foregoing the perceived shackles of his designated role in real-world musical participation.

Extract 11

> *Tony*: You can be a drummer for a couple of minutes which is quite good fun … which is cool … for a guitar player to do (laughs) … so you can basically … as a musician you can then … become the other guy in the band sort of thing, you can do what you want basically … em it's just good fun … em it appeals to a musician.

31.5 CONCLUSIONS

This chapter has explored the role of everyday music-game participation in both our understanding of socially defined parameters of musicality, and our use of music to negotiate and express our personal and social identity. We assert that music games, in presenting new paths to identity formation and communication with the self, can influence how we see ourselves and relate to the world around us, enabling players to meaningfully engage with concepts of music and musicianship, their musical identity and the wider musical world around them. Further, we argue that music-games bridge everyday formal and informal music practices, providing a safe space to negotiate and express our musical identity in supportive communities of practice. Such digital music participation inspires and enriches positive personal and social identity through fostering empowerment, motivation, reflection, and expression, while supporting authentic and inclusive everyday musical experience.

The complex interaction between player and game during music-game participation is a unique and powerful tool for identity development in music, in particular, fostering positive perceived musicality and the exploration of virtual and visceral identities through role-playing in a "safe-space". This self-directed, motivated, and engagement participation reveals high levels of player commitment and awareness of the positive benefits to musical identity and behaviour in the real world. The collective findings also emphasize the potential opportunities and outcomes provided by music-games and the positive effect on players, supporting the development of positive self-identity, and authenticating formal participation to the wider musical world of the learner. This includes inspiring greater interest in music; motivated engagement with formal and informal music participation; and increased opportunity for exposure to the wider benefits of music participation (see McDonald, Hargreaves, & Miell, 2009; Missingham, 2007; Peppler et al., 2011).

It appears that music-games help bridge the gulf between formal and informal musical activity by presenting a "third environment", which fosters embodied knowledge and transferable skill development: "… mastery of a myriad of related physical, personal, social and thinking skills, which may be translated to the musical domain" (Cassidy & Paisley, 2012, p. 135). Such findings support assertions of the importance of young people's emulation of recordings as a prime source of informal music learning and identity exploration, through peer driven listening and performing (Abril & Gault, 2008; Green, 2006). The collective work highlights important concepts for consideration of the role of music-games in what it means to be musical in the 21st century, bridging the virtual and visceral to blur boundaries of real and ideal self, player and avatar agency, conformity and creativity, performer and listener. It is suggested that further investigation is warranted, on a larger scale, across a wider sample, exploring the findings for a wider range of music-games and interactive technologies in specific goal-oriented contexts of use.

References

Abril, C.R, & Gault, B.M. (2008). The state of music in secondary schools: The principal's perspective. *Journal of Research in Music Education*, 56(1), 68–81.

Bilgihan, A., Cobanoglu, C., Nusair, K., Okumus, F., & Bujisic, M. (2013). A quantitative study exploring the difference between gaming genre preferences. *Computer Games Journal*, 2(1), 19–40.

Bloustien, G., Peters, M., & Luckman, S. (2008). *Sonic synergies: music, technology, community, identity*. Farnham: Ashgate.

Bradley, S.G, Sherry, J., Lachlan, K., Lucas, K., & Holmstrom, A. (2010). Orientations to video games among gender and age groups. *Simulation and Gaming*, 41(2), 238–59.

Braun, V., & Clarke, V. (2006). Using thematic analysis in psychology. *Qualitative Research in Psychology*, 3(2), 77–101.

Cassidy, G., & MacDonald, R.A.R. (2008). The role of music in videogames: the effects of self-selected and experimenter-selected music on driving game performance and experience. *10th International Conference on Music Perception and Cognition*, August 25–29, Sapporo, Japan.

Cassidy, G.G., & MacDonald, R.A.R. (2009). The effects of music choice on task performance: a study of the impact of self-selected and experimenter-selected music on driving game performance and experience (ESCOM Young Researcher of the Year Award). *Musicae Scientiae*, 13(2), 357–86.

Cassidy, G.G., & MacDonald, R.A.R. (2010). The effects of music on time perception and performance of a driving game. *Scandinavian Journal of Psychology*, 51(6), 455–64.

Cassidy, G.G., & Paisley, A.M. (2013). Music games: a case of their impact. *Research Studies in Music Education Journal*, 35(1), 119–38.

Cerulo, K.A. (1997). Identity construction: new issues, new directions. *Annual Review of Sociology*, 23, 385–409.

Collins, K. (2008a). *Game sound: an introduction to the history, theory and practice of video game music and sound design.* Cambridge, MA: MIT Press.

Collins, K. (Ed.) (2008b). *From Pac- Man to pop music: interactive audio in games and new media.* Aldershot: Ashgate.

Crawford, C. (2003). *Chris Crawford on game design*, New Riders Games Series. Harlow: New Riders.

Cresswell, J.W., & Miller, D.L. (2000). Determining validity in qualitative inquiry. *Theory into Practice*, 39(3), 124–30.

De Schutter, B. (2011). Never too old to play: the appeal of digital games to an older audience. *Games and Culture*, 6(2), 155–70.

Donovan, T. (2010). *Reply: The history of video games.* Hove:Yellow Ant Media Limited.

Entertainment Retailers Association. (2013). Booming digital services return entertainment retailing to growth. Available at: http://www.eraltd.org/news/era-news/booming-digital-services-return-entertainment-retailing-to-growth.aspx (accessed 27 February 2016).

Entertainment Software Association. (2014). *Sales, demographic and usage data: essential facts about the computer and video games industry.* Available at: http://www.theesa.com/facts/pdfs/esa_ef_2014.pdf (accessed 27 February 2016).

Filiciak, M. (2003) Hyperidentities: postmodern identity patterns in massively multiplayer online role-playing games. In:M.J.P. Wolf & B. Perron (Eds.) *The video game theory reader*, pp. 87–103. London: Routledge.

Frith, S. (1996). *Performing rites: on the value of popular music.* Cambridge, MA: Harvard University Press.

Gee, J.P. (2003). *What video games have to teach us about learning and literacy.* New York, NY: Palgrave Macmillan.

Gergen, K.J. (1985). The social constructionist movement in modern psychology. *American Psychologist*, 40(3), 266–75.

Gower, L., & McDowall, J. (2012). Interactive music video games and children's musical development, *British Journal of Music Education*, 1, 91–105.

Green, L. (2006). Popular music education in and for itself, and for 'other' music: Current research in the classroom. *International Journal of Music Education*, 24(2), 101–18.

Hargreaves, D.J., Marshall, N.A., & North, A.C. (2003). Music education in the twenty-first century: a psychological perspective. *British Journal of Music Education*, 20(2), 147–63.

Harmonix. (2010). Rock Band 3 features, set list and more! Available at: http://www.rockband.com/blog/rock-band-3-announcements (accessed 27 February 2016).

Hargreaves, D., Miell, D., & MacDonald, R.A.R. (2002). What are musical identities and why are they important? In: R.A.R. MacDonald, D. Hargreaves, & D. Miell (Eds.), *Musical identities*, pp. 1–20. Oxford: Oxford University Press.

Higgins, E.T. (1989). Self-discrepancy theory: what patterns of self beliefs cause people to suffer? In: L. Berkowitz (Ed.), *Advances in experimental social psychology*, Vol. 22, pp. 93–136. San Diego, CA: Academic Press.

Joy Tunes. (2013). Piano Dust Buster [Official website]. Available at: http://www.joytunes.com/piano/index.php (accessed 27 February 2016).

Kirsch, S.J. (2006). *Children, adolescents, and media violence*. Thousand Oaks, CA: Sage.

Klimmt, C., Hefner, H., & Vorderer, P. (2009). The video game experience as "true" identification: A theory of enjoyable alterations of players' self-perception. *Communication Theory*, 19, 351–73.

Lenhart, A., Kahne, J., Middaugh, E., MacGill, A., Evans, C., & Vitak, J. (2008). Report Part 1.2: basic gaming hardware and games played. Teens Video Games and Civics. Pew Research Internet Project. Numbers, Facts and Trends Shaping your World. Available at: http://www.pewinternet.org/2008/09/16/part-1-2-basic-gaming-hardware-and-games-played/ (accessed 27 February 2016) .

Marty, R., & Consalvo, M. (2011). Performing the looking-glass self: Avatar appearance and group identity in Second Life. *Popular Communication*, 9, 165–80.

MacDonald, R.A.R, Hargreaves, D.J., & Miell, D. (2009). Musical identities. In: S. Hallam, I, Cross, and M. Thau (Eds.) *The Oxford handbook of music psychology*. New York: Oxford University Press.

MacHover, T. (2008). Guitar Hero. *RSA Digital Journal*. Available at: http://www.thersa.org /fellowship/journal/archive/winter-2008/features/guitar-hero (accessed 27 February 2016).

Miller, K. (2012). *Playing along: digital games, YouTube, and virtual performance*. Oxford: Oxford University Press.

Miller, K. (2009). Schizophonic performance: Guitar Hero, Rock Band, and virtual virtuosity. *Journal of the Society for American Music*, 3(4), 395–429.

Miller, M. (2011). The past and future of Rock Band DLC. *GAMINFORMER*. Available at: http://www.gameinformer.com/b/features/archive/2011/05/04/the-past-and-future-of-rock-band-dlc.aspx?PostPageIndex=3 (accessed 27 February 2016).

Mitchell, L.A., MacDonald, R.A.R, Serpell, M.G., & Knussen, C. (2007). A survey investigation of the effects of music listening on chronic pain. *Psychology of Music*, 35(1), 39–59.

Missingham, A. (2007). *Why console-games are bigger than rock 'n' roll: What the music sector needs to know and how it can get a piece of the action. Report commissioned by Youth Music.* London: Youth Music.

Murphy, S.C. (2004). 'Live in your world, play in ours': the spaces of video game identity. *Journal of Visual Culture*, 3(2), 223–38.

Olson, C.K. (2010). Children's motivations for video game play in the context of normal development. *Review of General Psychology*, 14, 180–7.

Peppler, K., Downton, M., Lindsay, E., & Hay, K. (2011). The Nirvana effect: Tapping video games to mediate music learning and interest. *International Journal of Learning and Media*, 3(1), 41–59.

Phan, M.H., Jardina, J.R., & Hoyle, W.S. (2012). Video games: Males prefer violence while females prefer social. *Usability* News, 14(1).

Prensky, M. (2009). H. sapiens digital: From digital immigrants and digital natives to digital wisdom. *Journal of Online Education, Innovate*, 5(3).

Raskin, J.D. (2002). Constructivism in psychology: personal construct psychology, radical constructivism, and social constructionism. *American Communicational Journal*, 5(3).

Roberts, D.F., Foehr, U.G., & Rideout, V. (2005). *Generation M: media in the lives of 8-18 year-olds*. Menlo Park, CA: Henry J. Kaiser Family Foundation.

Roberts, D.F., Foehr, U.G., & Rideout, V. (2010). *Generation M2: Media in the Lives of 8-18 Year-Olds*. Menlo Park, CA: Henry J. Kaiser Family Foundation.

Roesner, D. (2011). The guitar hero's performance. *Contemporary Theatre Review*, 21(3), 276–85.

Ryan, R.M., & Deci, E.L. (2000). Self-determination theory and the facilitation of intrinsic motivation, social development, and wellbeing. *American Psychologist*, 55, 68–78.

Schultz,P. (2008). Music theory in music games. In: K. Collins (Ed.) *From Pac-Man to pop music: interactive audio in games and new media*, pp. 177–88. Aldershot: Ashgate.

Schafer, R.M. (1969). *The new soundscape. A handbook for the modern music teacher*. Don Mills, ON: BMI Canada Limited.

ScoreHero.com. Available at: http://www.scorehero.com.

Steinberg, S. (2011). *Music games rock: Rhythm gaming's greatest hits of all time*. Dix Hills:Power Play Publishing.

Turkle, S. (1994). Constructions and reconstructions of self in virtual reality: playing in the MUDs. *Mind, Culture, and Activity*, 3, 158–67.

Ubisoft. (2012). RockSmith: authentic guitar games [Official website]. Available at: http://rocksmith.ubi. com/rocksmith/en-gb/home/index.aspx (accessed 27 February 2016).

Viacom. (2012). Rock Band Music Catalog Surpasses 2,000 Sing Milestone with the Jimi Hendrix Experience's Classic Song 'Are You Experienced'. Available at: http://www.viacom. com/news/Pages/newstext.aspx?RID=1479151 (accessed 27 February 2016).

Vermeulen, L., & Van Looy, J. (2014). "I play so I am?" A gender study into stereotype perception and genre choice of digital game players. Paper presented at International Communication Association 2014 Conference, Seattle, WA.

Wenger, E. (2006). *Communities of practice: a brief introduction*. Available at: www.ewenger. com/theory (accessed 27 February 2016).

Whalen, Z. (2004). Play along—an approach to video game music. *Game Studies*, 4(1).

Wiggins, J. (2009). *Teaching for musical understanding*, 2nd edn. Rochester, MI: Center for Applied Research in Musical Understanding.

Willig, C. (2001). *Introducing qualitative research in psychology: adventures in theory and method*. Buckingham: Open University Press.

Wood, A.F., & Smith, M.J. (2004). *Online communication: linking technology, identity and culture*, 2nd edn. Mahwah, NJ: Lawrence Erlbaum Associates.

Zehnder, S., & Lipscomb, S.D. (2006). The role of music in video games. In: P. Vorderer & J. Bryant (Eds.), *Playing video games: motives, responses, and consequences*, pp. 241–58. Abingdon: Lawrence Erlbaum Associates.

SECTION 7

....

HEALTH AND WELL-BEING

....

CHAPTER 32

....

MUSIC, IDENTITY, AND HEALTH

....

EVEN RUUD

32.1 INTRODUCTION

MUSIC is linked to our construction of identity through the memory of musical experiences, as well as our ongoing identification with artists and works.[1] Music creates powerful emotional experiences, associations and memories which form the raw material for the narrative construction of identity. There are *four dimensions* or strategies of identity construction through music—our past and our future, and our inward reflection and outward relations. By recollecting our musical experiences, we create continuity and sameness, which are important qualities of the coherence of our identity. By projecting these sorts of subjectivities into the future—through our identification with certain musical figures, for example, or our adoption of certain subject positions within various discourses on musical values—we in turn stabilize, revise, and redirect our efforts to shape our identities in a rapidly changing world. By looking inward, through the cultivation of self-consciousness, we reflect upon and adjust our "selves" that lies at the core of our subjectivity. Finally, we perform our musical identities in our relations to other people and groups, within a particular culture and society.

If we accept an interpretative concept of "health" that transcends a strictly biomedical model and acknowledges that quality of life is part of how we experience our health from moment to moment, we in turn allow for the very promising possibility that music can act as a sort of *cultural immunogen* (Ruud, 2002, 2013)—that is, a self-technology that protects, promotes, and maintains our health and quality of life. A strong sense of identity derived from music can contribute specifically to the following four aspects of health: a *sense of vitality* (of being alive, of being empowered, of having internalized

---

[1] This article is based upon empirical work I did in the 1990s, first published in Norwegian in 1997, revised 2013. For publications in English, see Ruud, 1997a, 1998, 2010.

supporting self-objects), a *sense of agency* (of self-efficacy, of empowerment, of owner-ship of the "locus of control"), a *sense of belonging* (of participation, of a network, of social capital, of being recognized) and, not least, a *sense of coherence and meaning* (of strong emotional musical experiences, flow, transcendence). Our musical identity is, in fact, a prerequisite for the exercising of this self-caring technology—only via its engage-ment of our musical identity and musical preferences can music possibly begin to serve as a cultural immunogen and fulfil health functions. In what follows, I will discuss the relations among the prevalent notions of musical identity, health, and quality of life, beginning with the concept of music itself, in order to explore and, in some cases, clarify their profound interdependence.

32.2 A PRAGMATIC CONCEPT OF MUSIC

If we want to investigate any connections between music, identity, and health, we must first develop a broad and pragmatic concept of music, one based on the fundamental acknowledgment that music is not solely an aesthetic object, the only aim of which is to provide a kind of pleasure that transcends the everyday. Instead, we must recognize that music is very much intertwined with the everyday—it is something that gives pleas-ure, of course, but it also represents a means of relaxation and stress regulation, it is a social resource as well as an existential asset. This recognition seems to be in accordance with much recent research on people's everyday uses of music (DeNora, 2000; Bossius & Lilliestam, 2012).

There are many ways to conceptualize music—Philip Bohlman refers to them as the "metaphysical assumptions of music" (Bohlman, 1999). Ontologies of music—that is, what we fundamentally think music is or is not—are likewise constructed and articu-lated differently within the fields of music and health, respectively. In order to avoid an essentialist approach to music, whereby some given set of musical meanings is trans-ferred almost mechanically from the composer to the score, and in turn to the listener, we need a model of understanding that derives from the role of the listener in the actual construction of musical meaning. We need, in effect, a more processual conception of music that encompasses the influences of contextual, music-structural, and individual circumstances on the interpretation and experience of music.

Over the past decade or two, Christopher Small's concept of "musicking" (Small, 1998), as well as the concepts of "affordance" and "appropriation" (DeNora, 2000; Clarke, 2003, 2005), have gained wide acceptance in the literature. Small emphasizes that "music" must be understood as a practice and a process—as something we do—rather than as an object. This has profound implications for any understanding of the ways in which meanings are produced, while one is engaged with music, and it leads Small to nuance the catch-all noun "music" as the verb "musicking." This, in turn, seems uniquely suited to describing the use of music in health practice, as "health musicking" (Stige, 2012).

As the music sociologist Tia DeNora observes, in the company of researchers from both music psychology and cultural studies, music is present in a variety of social and personal contexts where mood is regulated, and attention is focussed (DeNora, 2000). It contributes to an emotional and cognitive context which is conducive to a feeling of well-being and a state of either alertness or repose, depending upon the demands of the given situation. Sociologically speaking, (health) musicking thus appears to be a way to regulate the relation between the person and the situation—between, that is, our psychological state and the demands that stem from our surroundings. This regulating role suggests, in turn, music's potential to act as a (cultural) immunogen (Ruud, 2013).

32.3 MUSIC AND IDENTITY

The sense of identity is above all else anchored in a sense of a self or a felt subjectivity. This sense of self or notion of individuality is in part the sense of experiencing the world from a unique location in space—that is, the location of the physical body (Harré & Gillett, 1994, p. 107). Identity is rooted in the particular discourse that one undertakes as one consciously monitors one's own activities, (musical) memories and fantasies. In the act of singling out life circumstances and memories of musical events, or through ongoing identifications, a musical identity may take form via stories we tell about ourselves. Via a narrative model such as this, we are able to ascertain that musical identity results from a particular discourse engaged in by the consciousness in the process of framing or contextualizing personal musical experiences.

The theoretical model behind the narrated identity, present in a variety of theoretical traditions, leads to a definition of identity as an "academic-metaphor-for-self-in-context" (Fitzgerald, 1993, p. 3). This definition will lead us to question which academic tradition or theoretical framework should, in fact, take part in the construction of identity. Psychology, for example, will emphasize the relational aspects of identity, as well as more basic bodily sensations or awareness—in other words, what I have placed in the "private space." If we extend this discourse on musical subjectivity to transpersonal psychology, we may even incorporate transcendental experiences, or aspects of meaning and values within our construction of ourselves. Anthropology and sociology bring a larger cultural and historical context into focus by emphasizing aspects of time and space in the construction of musical identity. Sociology also brings to the fore present social conditions affecting the construction of identity, heightening our awareness of the ways in which our embeddedness within different social and cultural fields can condition our sense of belongingness to a certain class, ethnic group, or gender.

What characterizes identity in our (post)modern cultural situation is, not least, reflexivity (Giddens, 1991). Identities do not come to us ready-made; they are created by a process that is never concluded. Identity comes about as we create the grid or model for who we want to be and where we want to belong. Within this grid or matrix, our private self and bodily sensibilities, our sense of history, our local and global attachments, our social relations, and our experience of personal agency are all important parameters.

Music cannot automatically depict identities, social formations, ideologies, or private value systems, but it can encode such dimensions. It is, however, our interpretative activity that brings forth these dimensions from music, often as we participate in a broader interpretative musical community. Music might be thought of as an object towards which we act in order to make more apparent our values and positioning in culture. It is all of our talk about music, which gives it its meaning; in other words—discourses about "authenticity," taste, style, genre, and "quality."

Activated by the emotional impact of music, our memories and identifications contribute to the foundation of a strong, coherent yet flexible musical identity in relation to the following "spaces," the summarizing of which will provide a context for our engagement with this contribution. The *private space*, first of all, encompasses our experiences of subjectivity via emotions or vitality affects activated by aesthetic experiences, our practice of early communicative musicality as a fundament to our developing self-consciousness, and our relational and empowerment experiences through music. The *social space* is where we actually perform our individual gender identities, ethnicities, social values, class relations, sense of authenticity, and so on. Our musical memories and identifications also contribute to our sense of belonging in *time and space* more generally, in terms of our efforts to ritualize the everyday, and otherwise cultivate a sense of history, nationality, regional identity, and global identity. Finally, music creates opportunities for entering a *transpersonal space*, one in which we transcend the everyday, enter a peak experience of some sort, and establish our existential values and sense of meaning in life (see also Ruud, 1998, 2013/1997). As we shall see later, these four spaces correspond to some extent to important dimensions of a concept of quality of life.

32.4 MUSICKING FOR HEALTH
AND LIFE QUALITY

There are many views about the nature of "health" in the literature (Blaxter, 2004). In general, they fall somewhere on a continuum between the strictly objectivist position, whereby health is seen as subject to empirical investigation, and the strictly interpretivist position, whereby health is seen as subject to interpretation (Duncan, 2007).

When actual people are asked about their own notions of health, however, it is often regarded pragmatically, as a relative phenomenon, and it is seen in relation to expectations about aging, the burden of illness and one's social situation. Described in general as an individual and personal phenomenon, health is at the end of a road that is different from person to person. What is more, notions of "good health" tend to encompass a sense of well-being, effective functioning, high spirits, feeling of empowerment, and a surplus of energy (Fugelli, 1998). Blaxter (2004) also refers to research that shows how one's view of one's health also depends on one's profession and social class.

From an interpretivist perspective, health is an experience, not a thing—in a sense, it is the same as the experience of well-being and meaning in life. Relatedly, a humanistic perspective upon health sees it as a resource or means of achieving the goals we have set for ourselves in our lives. In the interests of well-being, for example, health is a resource like education, work, and housing are resources. It is a reserve of energy, a force we can rely upon to resist illness or recover faster.

Such a notion of health does not allow it to be regarded as a fixed state. It is something in flux and it can be influenced. It is a product of the relation between the individual, his or her actions, and the environment (Medin & Alexandersson, 200, p. 70).

This interpretivist definition sees music as a way to *mobilize* oneself toward a better quality of life. Swedish philosopher Lennart Nordenfelt points to the fact that most "holistic" theories of health have been concerned with health as a feeling of well-being and even as a *capacity for action* (or, in the case of poor health, as a state of suffering or a lack of ability to act). In these cases, there is a strong conceptual connection between the state of well-being and the ability to act (Nordenfelt, 1991, p. 83).

As David Aldridge (1996) writes, health has a performative side, and "health behavior" is something we perform through the systematic influencing of our quality of life. Increasingly, we care as much about our cultural behaviors as we do about our eating and exercising habits—that is, how we spend our time in a general sense, managing our lives, align ourselves with certain values, other people or groups, and seek to derive meaning from things like music. "Good health" becomes a marker of a certain kind of constructive lifestyle—a means of showing others that we care about our bodies, but also our habits. Relatedly, Edvin Schei (2009) points to how "health" has to do with our ability to act as subjects, and cultivate integrity and self-respect in nurturing relations with other human beings. Health is a presupposition for subjectivity, a pre-intentional activity whereby we constitute ourselves as a "self", as stated by the Australian philosopher van Hooft (1997).

From an interpretivist perspective upon health, we may equate it with quality of life (for a discussion, see Ogden, 2000, chapter 14; see also Ruud, 1997b, 1998, 2001, chapter 4). Instead of comparing and contrasting the various concepts of quality of life that persist in the literature, I will turn to my own findings in my study of music and identity (Ruud, 1997a,b). As I worked out the four main categories I used to describe my concept of musical identity—personal space, social space, the space of time and place, and transpersonal space—I discovered that some of our narratives about musical experiences did not fall neatly within a single category alone, and some even touched all four. In that regard, I then realized that categories could be regrouped under another core category, *quality of life*. For example, life quality related to the state of our emotional life, our self-efficacy skills, our social relations and our experience of meaning in life (Ruud, 1998, 2001, 2011). Life quality, then, we could say has to do with musicking as a:

- *Provider of vitality*: that is, emotional stimulation, regulation, and expression.
- *Tool* for developing agency and empowerment.

- Resource in creating a sense of belonging.
- Means of achieving meaning and coherence in life (see Ruud, 1997b).

Our ability to regulate our emotions, to strengthen our agency and sense of belonging, as well as to achieve greater meaning in life, all through performing our musical identity, may potentially mean more resources put into own health promotion and thus increase our possibilities for action, as Nordenfelt identified as vital to our well-being.

32.5 VITALITY AND SELF-EXPRESSION

In my study on music and identity, I found that, from childhood forward, music contributed to an increased "awareness of feelings"—that is, the ability to experience, tolerate, and express emotional nuances of varying intensity and to develop precise concepts about those nuances. This awareness, in turn, contributed to a basic feeling of vitality and a confidence in one's ability to open oneself towards the world, other people, and oneself (Monsen, 1991). Vitality is a combination of spontaneity and reflexivity; as the Norwegian psychologist Jon Monsen notes, it derives from a certain reciprocity between how we feel and what we do with our feelings (Monsen, 1991, p. 150).

These sorts of emotional resources are an important part of health, in the sense that a strong and resistant "self" promotes health. This becomes particularly clear when one faces the alternative of not having these resources; one loses the ability to withstand one's own emotional experiences and begins to live in a way that does not activate any feelings at all. As is clear from clinical psychology, as one inhibits or represses one's feelings, one surrenders one's self-awareness in order to protect oneself against reality. In the end, one stops relating to a basic pre-verbal way of communicating and disrupts all of the information that is contained in a feeling. One becomes estranged from oneself. Energy becomes tied up in the body, resulting in lack of motor flexibility and possibly physiological failure. In some cases, this may even lead to a situation where one loses one's ability to indulge in new personal experiences at all (Monsen, 1991, p. 290).

In my study, I was struck by the human awareness of harmony, bodily relaxation, and basic psychological trust that all derived directly from repeated experiences with lullabies, children's melodies, and nursery rhymes throughout childhood. My informants easily brought forth memories of both these melodies and the situations in which they heard them, at the same time gaining access to or reproducing the concomitant feelings. I was especially aware of music's contribution to the child's sense of acceptance and validation in a host of meaningful situations.

Given that infant interaction can be seen as a series of events based upon musical parameters such as time, intensity and narrative, we can conclude that musical interaction via songs helps to establish a basic sense of intersubjectivity, through which the child may come from early on to make an impact upon the other (see Malloch & Trevarthen, 2009).

Emotional awareness was also present in song situations involving older children who could react to the words of the songs, interact verbally about them, and even seek conceptual clarification from an adult. These situations showed how song texts and longer musical narratives allowed for the experience of emotional tolerance and the development of the ability to contain complex and difficult emotions.

In adolescence, music often became an important source of authenticity, both personal and cultural—that is, a sense of having a "real" self, or a self that is felt as natural or "true", or a self that accords with how life is experienced in general. In some cases, the sense of authenticity also brought about a feeling of self-realization, not only in the sense of tapping into some sort of inner potential, but also through the exploitation of certain music, in the sense of aligning one's narrative of one's identity to a feeling of what life should be like.

32.6 AGENCY

Another important aspect of health relates to the ability to take responsibility for one's own life and actions—to the ability to make choices and follow plans set by oneself. With regard to health in particular, it has been observed that Western medical culture occasionally creates a feeling of disempowerment, of being asked to surrender oneself to treatment, often via an extended and sometimes unnecessary use of drugs. In the interests of encouraging people to practice more deliberate and strategic self-management of health, attention has been turned towards the individual and his or her sense of agency or responsibility for actions.

Within the notion of "agency," I include those aspects of human conduct which are related to achievement, competency, a feeling of mastery and empowerment. In the present context, of course, I am particularly interested in how music and one's musical behavior may come to influence this aspect of one's conduct.

As we know from the study of performance practice, music can be an important source of a sense of mastery and self-esteem. Many of my informants had experiences that made them look upon themselves as competent people who could enter a social space, take control of it and perform for others within in. The pleasure to be derived from skill with an instrument was clearly communicated. However, I also saw that certain performance situations, as well as occasions of excessive parental pressure or cultural collision, had led the informant to a state of ambivalence, the loss of self-confidence, and finally a sense of defeat.

A preoccupation with music, both listening to it and performing it, can in general contribute to the development of the child in every aspect—emotional, motor, social, and the growth of ego strength or self-esteem. The basic theory behind much developmentally orientated music therapy acknowledges that listening to music can help a child to master his or her sound environment and achieve new areas of competence. This is also true in relation to the sensory-motor skills involved in music-making and to some of the basic early social skills that are involved when music is shared between people. Engaging in music is not an isolated pursuit that is confined to a separate faculty of the mind often described as one's "musicality," but a complex behavior which involves perception, cognitive skills, motor performance, social-communicative skills, emotional, and bodily involvement and symbolic activity.

Music may then empower the child. It prepares one to master oneself and to take responsibility for one's own conduct. It provides a psychological and cultural platform from which to make decisions about personal matters. When one is successfully engaged with music, one feels like "somebody." One feels warranted to raise one's own voice.

Music is therefore an important source of basic social competency. To partake in a musical life through performing, going to concerts or buying CDs, is to partake in social life, to paraphrase Ruth Finnegan (1989). Through the formation of a personal musical taste, one enters into a dialogical relation with other people or groups in society. Through listening to and talking about music with other people, we learn about them—about how they experience music, of course, but also how they experience life in society in general. The Norwegian sociologist Ivar Frønes (1994) links this "basic social competency" to the ability to decenter oneself and adopt the perspective of another. One does this by identifying with certain artists or musical genres, but not others and in general positioning oneself within a broader cultural landscape. Through decoding the semiotics of music, we gain social resources and increase our basic social competency.

32.7 BELONGING

Our musical identity is not least shaped by our belongingness to a certain geographical space, to history, a certain culture, a community, a certain network, or group of people. Our belongingness, i.e. our relationships with other people will likewise always be an important factor in defining our state of health, which depends to a significant extent upon our "social capital"—that is, how well we are integrated with or at least connected to the community. According to Robert Putnam, many studies have established beyond reasonable doubt that social connectedness is one of the most decisive determinants of our wellbeing (Putnam, 2000, p. 326).

As should be clear by now, it is very important to approach health from a wider perspective than the biomedical complex of illnesses and hospitals. Social medicine has long tried to demonstrate the relevance of economic and societal factors, such as work, education, housing, nutrition, environment, self-respect, power, and belonging, to human health. Differences in states of health are never only a matter of poverty, of course, but they must be reconciled to the structural conditions of society, and specifically the given individual's degree of social cohesion and integration. We now realize that some of the greatest health problems afflicting Western societies derive from social isolation and existence outside the social network of neighbors, employment, and cultural activities. When people become physically ill or lose their jobs, they often shake free of their social bonds, which makes it more difficult to restore a sense of health. They find themselves in a "space between"—a limbo between illness and health, idleness and work, mental problems, and a sense of belonging and good relations with others.

Social capital, then, has to do with belonging and connectedness, with mutuality and trust between individuals, with shared activities in the local community, with influence and participation in local democracy, and with the general feeling of being included. Music groups are exactly these sorts of meeting places, where people can bond over a shared pursuit or performance. Although music groups vary with regard to how inclusive they are, they afford both tight communality, and looser bridgings and openings for social contact. Music in this way becomes a social resource or means of social capital (Procter, 2004). In a musical life that involves all kinds of grassroots activities, we can see how music as a social activity can accommodate community involvement. Outstanding examples of this would be the choir movement, brass bands, or school bands, rock groups, amateur orchestras, and so forth, the numbers of which, in fact, represent a large percentage of the population.

A sense of belonging can characterize both our relations with other people and larger groups or communities, as well as our sense of being "at home" in the world, historically, or geographically. Historical rootedness encompasses our contemporaneity as well. An identification with historical music allows us to participate in a larger historical narrative. Going to concerts or listening to contemporary music allows for a particularly vivid sense of the present. These different ways of being embedded in groups, subcultures and histories can be applied to situations of ethnicity or nationality as well (see Ruud 2013/1997).

Musical experiences can even mark important events in life, fixing them in the memory. Music in this way gives one a means of comparing one's sense of lived time with the public sense of time. Through memory work, one constructs coherence and continuity from a life that is regarded as a continuous trajectory with a beginning, a presence and an ending.

When one performs the story of who one is, the place one comes from seems especially important. Often, one uses music to symbolize or activate one's nationality, especially when abroad. In this contemporary global society, however, one is increasingly attached to regional and local, rather than national or global geography and culture. Regional musical movements carry powerful connotations of one's way of life.

32.8 Meaning and coherence

The Israeli medical sociologist Aaron Antonovsky has devoted significant time to understanding the connections between health and coping with life (Antonovsky, 1991). As the founder of what he calls "salutogenetic research," his overarching concern is with the ways in which one maintains health. In contrast to most medical researchers' preoccupation with "pathogenesis"—that is, why we become sick—Antonovsky focusses upon our general resources with which to resist disease. He concludes that when life is felt to be comprehensible (predictable), manageable (conceivable), and meaningful, people feel coherence and continuity in life, which in turn helps them resist disease.

When psychologist Erik Erikson described the last psychosocial stage in his epigenetic scheme, he emphasized the integration of the ego as the main developmental task (Erikson, 1968). Order and meaning became essential, acceptance of how life had to become what it had been. This identity work seemed to include the reconciliation of oneself with life's many choices, as well as the ability to distance oneself and reflect about one's own life.

In what follows, I will discuss only those aspects of involvement in music which seem most directly related to meaning. Among other things, of course, the construction of meaning in music encompasses both emotional and physical involvement in the practice.

When I reviewed the study responses I would ultimately include in the category of "transpersonal space," it became very clear that many individuals want to experience their lives and existence as part of something bigger. As we know from studies of strong musical experiences (Gabrielsson, 2011), as well the literature on BMGIM (Bruscia & Grocke 2002)[2], transpersonal or transcendental experiences are common to Western musical culture. Sometimes one's experiences with music can give one the feeling of something indefinite and indescribable—something beyond the limits of language. This experience, which in the field of aesthetics is described as the "sublime," may be linked to the feeling of being in touch with something greater than our everyday reality. This experience is often described in terms of being "outside of oneself" and one's time and place. Often, one also experiences strong feelings of energy and power that have a therapeutic quality or effect (Gabrielsson, 2011).

Transpersonal psychologists and researchers of psychosynthesis (Assagioli, 1998) study these experiences. Maslow, for example, refers to "peak experiences" and "acute experiences of identity" (Maslow, 1968, p. 103). It thus appears that the musical experience can add an existential dimension to our identity, which gives us the feeling that we are anchored in a reality outside ourselves. In this way, we may say that identity becomes rooted in a transpersonal space. For many people, this sense of a meaningful existence is anchored in the larger principles inscribed by certain religious values or the humanistic conceptions of "mankind", "nature," or "cosmos".

From the interviews about musical experiences conducted by British psychotherapist and musician Mary Butterton (2004), we see that many of her older informants used music as a metaphor when sorting out important themes in life. We also see that music has created a "home" for some, binding feelings and thoughts together with values to offer a sense of belonging, a means of connecting with the larger world. In the retrospective master narrative that becomes the core identity of a person, music offers an overall sense of coherence by pointing to the important themes and events of one's life.

Health philosopher van Hooft (1997) saw a mode of subjectivity, the integrative, in the efforts to create meaning in life. This integrative dimension seeks to link together events

---

[2] The Bonny Method of Guided Imagery and Music is a music psychotherapy method based upon listening to music.

and experiences with self-understanding by creating a bond between past, present and future in a coherent narrative about oneself that produces an identity (Schei, 2009).

In general, the emotional experience of music seems to help one both formulate and integrate memories using metaphors that gives a certain meaning to the personal narrative. Contained within the music-emotional memory is a sense of continuity and sameness in life. Sometimes a remembered piece of music even functions as a memory bank, a deposit box for a basic sense of self, an identity feeling or a strong positive feeling about life. This returns us to the starting point of this discussion—that is, how music can become a resource to strengthen one's resistance to illness or promote health. This aspect of musical identity seems to relate well to a conception of health, as we met earlier in Antonovsky's felt coherence and continuity in life with resistance towards disease.

32.9 CONCLUSIONS

Performing one's musical identity creates a free space, the musical asylums described by Tia DeNora (DeNora, 2013). Through our involvement in music, DeNora writes, we are enabled to achieve a state of ontological security, control and creativity, pleasure, validation of self, sense of fit, flow, comfort, ease, temporal fit. In listening to or performing and creating music, through strategies of "removal" and "refurnishing", we are gaining new strengths to cope with life, new resources to be invested in a shared life with others (DeNora, 2013).

The music we listen to or perform, as we have seen, has to be an integrated part of our musical and personal identity in order to perform such health functions. It is when the music resonates with our personal and social life, our values and belongings it can serve as a "cultural immunology".

The categories described in this chapter—vitality, agency, belonging, and meaning—were all drawn from my studies on music and identity. Seen in the context of my four parameters of identity—personal space, social space, the space of time and place, and the transpersonal space—we have located strong relations among music, identity, and health. If being involved in music generally strengthens one's sense of identity, and if the sense of having a strong and differentiated sense of identity is a resource for experiencing increased life quality, we have demonstrated how music can contribute to health in general.

REFERENCES

Antonovsky, A. (1991). *Hälsans mysterium* [Unraveling the mystery of health]. Köping: Natur och kultur.

Aldridge, D. (1996). *Music therapy research and practice in medicine. From out of the silence.* London: Jessica Kingsley Publishers.

Assagioli, R. (1988). *Lo sviluppo transpersonale.* Roma: Astrolabio.

Blaxter, M. (2004). *Health*. Cambridge, MA: Polity Press.

Bohlman, P. V. (1999). Ontologies of music. In: N. Cook and M. Everest (Eds.) *Rethinking music*, pp. 17–34. Oxford: Oxford University Press.

Bossius, T., and Lilliestam, L. (2012). *Musiken och jag* [Me and the music]. Göteborg: Bo Ejeby förlag.

Bruscia, K.E. & Grocke, D.E. (Eds.) (2002). *Guided imagery and music: The Bonny method and beyond*. Gilsum NH: Barcelona Publishers.

Butterton, M. (2004). *Music and meaning. Opening minds in the caring and healing professions*. Oxford: Radcliffe Medical Press.

Clarke, E.F. (2003). Music and psychology. In: H. Clayton, T. Herbert, & R. Middleton (Eds.) *The cultural study of music*, pp. 113–14. New York, NY: Routledge.

Clarke, E.F. (2005). *Ways of listening. An ecological approach to the perception of musical meaning*. Oxford: Oxford University Press.

DeNora, T. (2000). *Music in everyday life*. Cambridge: Cambridge University Press.

DeNora, T. (2013). *Music asylums: wellbeing through music in everyday life*. Farnham: Ashgate.

Duncan, P. (2007). *Critical perspectives on health*. New York, NY: Palgrave Macmillan.

Erikson, E.H. (1968). *Identity, youth and crisis*. New York, NY: W.W. Norton.

Finnegan, R. (1989). *The hidden musician. Music-making in an English town*. Cambridge: Cambridge University Press.

Fitzgerald, T.K. (1993). *Metaphors of identity. A culture–communication dialogue*. New York, NY: State University of New York Press.

Frønes, I. (1994). *De likeverdige. Om sosialisering og de jevnaldrendes betydning*. [The equivalents. On socialization and the significance of peers.] Oslo: Universitetsforlaget.

Fugelli, P. (1998). Fokehelse—folkets helse [Public health—the health of the people]. *Tidsskrift for Den norske lægeforening*, 118, 1421–5.

Gabrielsson, A. (2011). *Strong experiences with music. Music is much more than just music*. Oxford: Oxford University Press.

Giddens, A. (1991). *Modernity and self-identity. Self and society in the late Modern Age*. Cambridge, MA: Polity Press.

Harré, R. & Gillett, G. (1994). *The discursive mind*. London: Sage.

Levinas, E. (1969). *Totality and infinity: an essay on exteriority*. Pittsburgh, PA: Duquesne University Press.

Malloch, S. & Trevarthen, C. (Eds.) (2009). *Communicative musicality. Exploring the basis of human companionship*. Oxford: Oxford University Press.

Medin, J. & Alexanderson, K. (2000). *Begreppen hälsa och hälsofrämjande—en litteraturstudie*. [The concepts of health and health promotion–a study of literature.] Lund: Studentlitteratur.

Maslow, A.H. (1968). *Toward a psychology of being*, 2nd edn. New York, NY: Van Nostrand Reinhold Company.

Monsen, J. (1991). *Vitalitet, psykiske forstyrrelser og psykoterapi. Utdrag fra klinisk psykologi*. [Vitality, psychic disturbances and psychotherapy. Extracts from clinical psychology.] Oslo: Tano.

Nordenfelt, L. (1991). *Livskvalitet och hälsa. Teori och kritik*. [Quality of life and health. Theory and critique.] Falköping: Almquist & Wiksell Förlag.

Ogden, J. (2000). *Health psychology. A textbook*. Buckingham: Open University Press.

Putnam, R.D. (2000). *Bowling alone. The collapse and revival of American community*. New York, NY: Simon and Schuster.

Procter, S. (2004). Playing politics: community music therapy and the therapeutic redistribution of music capital for mental health. In: M. Pavlicevic & G. Ansdell (Eds.) *Community music therapy*, pp. 214–30. London: Jessica Kingsley Publishers.

Ruud, E. (1997a). Music and identity. *Nordic Journal of Music Therapy*, 6(1), 3–13.

Ruud, E. (1997b). Music and the quality of life. *Nordic Journal of Music Therapy*, 6(2), 86–97.

Ruud, E. (1998). *Music therapy. Improvisation, communication and culture*. Gilsum, NH: Barcelona Publishers.

Ruud, E. (2001). *Varme øyeblikk. Om musikk, helse og livskvalitet* [Hot moments. On music, health and life quality]. Oslo: UniPub.

Ruud, E. (2002). Music as a cultural immunogen—three narratives on the use of music as a technology of health. In: I. M. Hanken, S. Graabræk Nielsen, & M. Nerland (Eds.) *Research in and for higher music education. Festschrift for Harald Jørgensen*, pp. 109–20. Oslo: Norwegian Academy of Music Publications.

Ruud, E. (2010). *Music therapy. A perspective from the humanities*. Gilsum, NH: Barcelona Publishers.

Ruud, E. (2011). The new health musicians. In: R. MacDonald, G. Kreutz, & L. Mitchell (Eds.) *Handbook of music and well-being*, pp. 87–96. Oxford: Oxford University Press.

Ruud, E. (2013/1997). *Musikk og identitet* [Music and identity]. Oslo: Universitetsforlaget.

Ruud, E. (2013). Can music be a cultural immunogen? *International Journal of Qualitative Studies on Health and Well-Being*, 8, 17–28.

Schei, E. (2009). Helsebegrepet—selvet og cellen [The concept of health—the self and the cell]. In: E. Ruud (Ed.) *Musikk i psykisk helsearbeid med barn og unge* [Music in mental health work with children and adolescents], pp. 7–14. Oslo: Norges musikkhøgskole: Skriftserie fra Senter for musikk og helse. NMH-publications.

Small, C. (1998). *Musicking: the meanings of performing and listening*. Middletown, CT: Wesleyan University Press.

Stige, B. (2012). Health musicking. A perspective on music and health as action and performance. In: R. MacDonald, G. Kreutz, & L. Mitchell (Eds.) *Music, health, and wellbeing*, pp. 183–95. Oxford: Oxford University Press.

van Hooft, S. (1997). Health and subjectivity. *Health*, 23(1) 25–36.

CHAPTER 33

MUSICAL IDENTITY IN FOSTERING EMOTIONAL HEALTH

SUVI SAARIKALLIO

33.1 THE RELEVANCE OF EMOTIONS TO MUSICAL IDENTITY

EMOTIONS are among the most important aspects of human behavior promoting adaptive self-regulation, communication, and social behavior (e.g., Frijda, 1988; Damasio, 1995). Emotion-related competencies such as the ability to recognize and regulate emotions are known to be crucial for both intrapersonal and interpersonal health (e.g., Gross & John, 2013; Salovey, Bedell, Detweiler, & Mayer, 2000) and the concept of perceived emotional intelligence correlates with features like adaptive coping, perceptions of stressors as less threatening, lower levels of depression, and symptom reporting, and better interpersonal functioning (Salovey, Stroud, Woolery, & Epel, 2002). Emotions and emotional experiences are also at the core of musical experience, and over the last decade, the topic of emotion has rocketed into the forefront of music research, resulting in a handbook on the subject (Juslin & Sloboda, 2010). The realization of the emotional aspect being instrumental to the connection of music to health is by far not a new one. For instance, the idea of using music to advance emotional processing has been a core feature of various models of music therapy from its beginning (e.g., Trondalen & Bonde, 2012). However, recent years have further witnessed a vast growth of interest in the relevance of musical emotions to health and wellbeing also in the context of everyday life (e.g., McDonald, Kreutz, & Mitchell, 2012; Västfjäll, Julsin, & Hartig, 2012). New evidence regarding the health-relevance of musical emotions is actively emerging from both self-report studies (e.g., Miranda, Gaudreau, Debrosse, Morizot, Kirmayer, 2012) and physiological measures (e.g., Koelsch &

Stegemann, 2012; Kreutz, Quiroga Murcia, & Bongard, 2012) showing, for instance, that music-evoked emotions involve the very core of evolutionarily adaptive neuroaffective mechanisms (Koelsch, 2005).

Emotions and emotional health thus appear as concepts of utter importance for comprehensive understanding of musical behavior, including the concept of musical identity. Therefore, this chapter presents a framework for comprehending and investigating musical identity from the perspective of emotional health. Essential parts of recent knowledge on music, emotions, and mental health is compiled in order to present a set of psychological mechanisms of human emotional functioning that can be seen as the underlying routes for how and why emotions in particular play such a major role in connecting music to health both in daily life and in rehabilitation. The chapter raises a question of what kind of musical identity is supportive of emotional health, and suggests a set of features as its essential constituents. These features consist of emotion-related abilities of emotion recognition, emotion regulation, and positive emotion induction, as well as of attitudes related to self-reflectiveness, and self-control and agency. These key constituents of a musical identity that fosters emotional health are summarized in Fig. 33.1, and will be discussed in detail in the following pages.

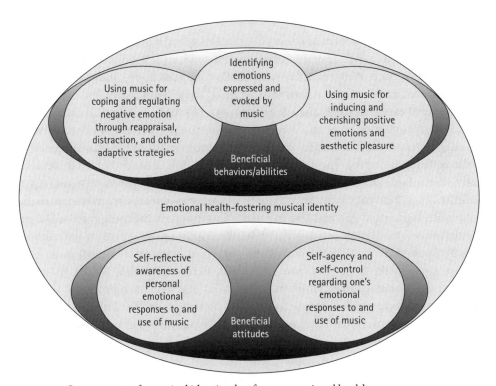

FIG. 33.1 Components of a musical identity that fosters emotional health.

33.2 EMOTION RECOGNITION

Among the most fundamental aspects of healthy emotional behavior is the ability to perceive and recognize emotional states in self and in others, a competence that is defined by concepts such as emotion labeling (Swinkels & Giuliano, 1995) or emotional clarity (Salovey, Mayer, Goldman, Turvey, & Palfai, 1995). A differentiation is made between the mere tendency to monitor emotions, which is related to negative outcomes, and the ability to identify and label emotions, which is related to positive outcomes (Swinkels & Giuliano, 1995), including empathy and prosocial behavior, adaptive coping strategies (Gohm, 2003), experience of positive emotions, high self-esteem, and greater satisfaction with social support (Swinkels & Giuliano, 1995), as well as lowered depression, social anxiety, physical symptom reporting, and cortisol release during repeated stress episodes (Salovey et al., 2002). Furthermore, it can be said that the more complex or higher order emotional skills, such as regulating emotions or using emotions in thought and behavior, are rooted in the basic skills of emotion perception and recognition (Salovey, Bedell, Detweiler, & Mayer, 1999).

33.3 EMOTION RECOGNITION IN MUSIC

Music undoubtedly is a form of conveying emotions, and a number of scholars have discussed music as a manifestation of emotional communication between individuals (Clayton, Sager & Will, 2004; Cross, 2008; Dissanayake, 2008). Indeed, people are highly capable in identifying at least the so-called "basic" emotions, not only through specific facial expressions (Ekman & Friesen, 1971; Ekman, 1982), vocal characteristics (Scherer, 1986), or body movement (Coulson, 2004; Wallbott, 1998), but also in musical expression (Gabrielsson & Lindström, 2001; Juslin & Laukka, 2003, 2004; Juslin & Timmers, 2010). The ability to perceive emotion in music begins to develop early, with infants already showing a preference for happy over sad expression (at 5–7 months of age; Nawrot, 2003), and children as young as 4 years correctly identifying happiness, sadness, anger, and fear in music (Cunningham & Sterling, 1988; Dolgin & Adelson, 1990). The general agreement between individuals regarding the connection between various musical features and perceived emotions is shown to be high (Juslin, 1997; Juslin & Laukka, 2004; Vieillard, Peretz, Gosselin, Khalfa, Gagnon, & Bouchard, 2008; Juslin & Timmers, 2010), but it has also been proposed that the ability to recognize musical emotions depends on factors such as musical expertise, personality, and emotional intelligence (Dibben, Coutinho, Vilar, & Estévez-Pérez, 2014).

33.4 CONNECTIONS OF MUSICAL EMOTION RECOGNITION TO BROADER EMOTIONAL HEALTH

Only a handful of studies have so far investigated whether the ability to recognize emotions in music correlates with general emotional abilities. Resnicow, Salovey, & Repp (2004) reported that better identification of musicians' intended expression of emotion (in three pieces of classical music by Bach, Bartok, & Perichetti) correlated with the emotional intelligence scores on the Mayer-Salovey-Caruso Emotional Intelligence Test (MSCEIT). Significant correlations were found for the overall score of the MSCEIT and two of its sub-scales—"Using emotions to facilitate thought," the general ability to generate a mood in the service of cognitive tasks, and "Perceiving emotions," the ability to recognize emotional information in faces and pictures. Emotion recognition ability in musical expression has also been shown to correlate with empathy (Saarikallio, Vuoskoski, & Luck, 2012; Wöllner, 2012). Wöllner (2012) reported that the accuracy of recognizing the intended emotion of music played by a string quartet correlated with participants' scores on the affective and overall empathy, not on the cognitive empathy (measured by the Questionnaire of Cognitive and Affective Empathy, QCAE; Reniers, Corcoran, Drake, Shryane, & Völlm, 2011). Meanwhile, Saarikallio and colleagues (2012), who used the Interpersonal Reactivity Index (IRI; Davis, 1980, 1983) for measuring empathy, reported that congruency of recognizing a particular intended emotion (tenderness) in music correlated with the cognitive component of empathy (perspective taking), while the affective component of empathy (empathic concern) correlated with a general bias for perceiving greater amounts of certain emotions (hope and fear) in the music.

Another line of studies has indeed particularly investigated the biases of music-related emotion perception as indicators of general emotional states or traits. For instance, negative mood (Vuoskoski & Eerola, 2011a) and clinical depression (Punkanen, Eerola, & Erkkilä, 2011) have been shown to correlate with a bias for perceiving higher amounts of negative, and lower amount of positive, emotion in music. Similar biases have also been found in relation to personality: Extraversion, Openness, and Agreeableness all correlate with higher ratings of perceived positive, and lower ratings of perceived negative, emotions in music, while Neuroticism relates to an opposite pattern (Liljeström, 2011; Vuoskoski & Eerola, 2011a). Furthermore, more intense emotional responses to music correlate with agreeableness (Ladinig & Schellenberg, 2012; Dibben et al., 2014), empathy (Vuoskoski & Eerola, 2012), and low emotional stability (Dibben et al, 2014). The biases in musical emotion perception appear trait-congruent, which gives rise to the idea of utilizing musical behavior in developing diagnostic measures for various emotion-related conditions.

Furthermore, the possibility for a transfer-effect of emotional abilities between musical and non-musical domains is preliminarily supported by recent evidence showing that emotional intelligence increases with years of musical training (Petrides, Niven & Mouskounti, 2006) and that musically-trained adults outperform musically untrained adults in recognizing various emotions in spoken sentences (Thompson, Schellenberg, & Husain, 2004). While other studies in this field have been correlational, Thompson and colleagues (2004) also conducted an intervention study with children, and found that 6-year-olds who received 1 year of musical training were better in identifying the difficult emotional expressions (anger and fear) in speech prosody than their peers in the control group (no training).

33.5 HOW DOES EMOTION RECOGNITION CONNECT MUSICAL IDENTITY TO EMOTIONAL HEALTH?

Evidence on the connections between the musical emotion recognition abilities and general emotional abilities is beginning to emerge. Nonetheless, the studies are few and they differ in their samples and types of stimuli, measures and procedures. Far more work is therefore needed for elaborate conclusions regarding these connections. The need for controlling relevant confounding factors such as general intelligence has also been stressed (Schellenberg & Mankarious, 2012). Moreover, to provide future research solid grounds it is important to discuss the theoretical propositions regarding the underlying psychological mechanisms that make emotion perception an important link between music and health. First, the obvious theoretical proposition is that the abilities of recognizing emotions in music may generalize to recognizing emotions also in self and in others. In addition, however, it would also be important to pay attention to a possible "mid-phase" of this transfer process, that is, the emotion labeling ability or emotional clarity regarding the emotions experienced to music. It has been established that the emotions perceived in music should theoretically be distinguished from emotions evoked by music (Gabrielsson, 2002). Thus, researchers dealing with the emotional competencies in music should also differentiate between these. The recognition of emotion expressed by music is an ability that essentially relates to emotional communication, resembling identification of emotional expression of other humans in their facial, postural, and vocal behavior, and may therefore mostly relate to competencies of emotional communication and interpersonal behavior. Meanwhile, emotion recognition regarding the emotions that music induces in self basically refers to identifying a true emotional reaction in oneself, and is therefore closer to the emotion recognition of everyday emotions in self. Indeed, while music-induced emotions might somewhat differ from everyday "utilitarian" emotions (Zentner & Scherer, 2008), emotional clarity regarding the felt emotions to music presents itself as a possibly highly relevant aspect particularly regarding the intrapsychic, self-reflective, and self-regulatory aspects of emotional health.

As regards the specific nature of emotion recognition in music, we can turn to Even Ruud's (1997) proposition about music being able to increase "awareness of feelings," i.e., the ability to experience various emotional nuances, express various degrees of intensity of emotions, and maintain precise concepts about feelings. This description also resembles what Nico Frijda and Louise Sundararajan (2007) write about refined emotions, emotional states that commonly occur both in daily life and in relation to aesthetic experiences, characterized by detachment, restraint, reflective awareness and elaboration of appraisal of the eliciting events. It could thus be argued that music-related emotion recognition holds potential for promoting emotional health particularly due to increased capability for self-reflective awareness regarding various emotional nuances, whether in musical expression, in aesthetic experiences evoked by music, or everyday emotional experiences. This self-reflective experience and understanding of emotion is also not far from the concepts of absorption and dissociation. Garrido & Schubert (2010, 2011) provide a literature review regarding these concepts and related individual differences, and note, for instance, that the ability to appropriately dissociate oneself from the affective content may partly explain the enjoyment of sad music. Finally, while music therapy work is beyond the scope of this chapter, it is relevant to note that the ability to use music as a symbolic (dissociated enough from self) reflection of personal emotional experiences also serves as the very basis for much of music therapy work related to emotional dysfunctions.

Taken together, we can posit that one of the essential areas of emotional health possibly promoted by musical behavior is the increased, or refined, ability of emotion perception and recognition, and a musical identity that would foster emotional health consists of an open and self-reflective stance towards the emotional nuances of music. Also, the connections and transfer-effects between the recognition of musically expressed, music-evoked, and everyday emotions and the role of individual differences regarding these connections appear as an important area for related research. Since the current base of empirical evidence basically consists of few correlational studies, far more research is needed to confirm whether every day musical behavior truly leads to improved emotion recognition in music and in general and what are the optimal circumstances for this to happen.

33.6 Regulation of negative emotion

The ability to successfully regulate emotions is a vital aspect of health that relates to the modification of the occurrence, duration, and intensity of affective states at the levels of subjective feelings, physiological reactions, and behavioral expressions (e.g., Gross, 1998; Larsen, 2000). This sub-chapter particularly focusses on the regulation of negative affect, while the induction of positive emotion is discussed in the next. Negative affect regulation closely relates to the concept of coping, with the main distinction of emotion regulation focusing on changes in the affective states per se while coping intrinsically also concerning the stressors and ways of managing them (e.g., Gross, 1998; Larsen, 2000). Current literature on coping (e.g., Skinner, Edge, Altman, & Sherwood, 2003) recognizes the distinction between dealing with a stressor and dealing with the elicited emotion (problem- vs. emotion-focussed coping), but many coping approaches (approach vs. avoidance, cognitive vs. behavioral) also fluently apply to emotion regulation, i.e., to how the emotion elicited is dealt with. The literature on coping and negative emotion regulation thus overlaps, with some scholars indeed considering coping primarily as a response to the negative emotions elicited by stressful life events (Salovey et al., 1999).

Whether one wants to discuss coping or emotion regulation, the ability to successfully cope with stressors and related negative emotions is a key aspect of health and wellbeing (Antonovsky, 1979; Collins, et al., 2003; Aldwin, 2007). Stress is an imbalance between demands and resources (Steptoe, 1997), and evokes a defense-arousal reaction characterized by emotions of fear and tension, increased levels of cortisol secretion, blood pressure, heart rate, and decreased heart rate variability (Berntson & Cacioppo, 2004; Pelletier, 2004; Lovallo, 2005). Short-term responses to stress support adaptation, but prolonged stress is detrimental to health (Berntson & Cacioppo, 2004; Brannon & Feist, 2010). Moreover, many disorders such as depression or hypertension centrally involve emotion dysregulation (e.g., Gross & John, 2013).

33.7 Music as regulation
of negative emotion

People actively engage in music in daily life to manage their negative emotion (e.g., Thayer, Newman & McClain, 1994; Saarikallio & Erkkilä, 2007; VanGoethem & Sloboda, 2011), and the power of music to influence emotions is demonstrated by both self-reports and physiology (Blood & Zatorre, 2001; Nater, Abbruzzese, Krebs, & Ehlert, 2006). Mounting psychological and physiological evidence exists about the efficacy of music in pain management (Bernatzky, Stickner, Perch, Wendtner, & Kullich, 2012; Mitchell, MacDonald, Knussen, & Serpell, 2007; Mitchell, ter Bogt, Raaijmakers, & Vollebergh, 2012) and stress reduction (Pelletier, 2004; Västfjäll, Juslin, & Hartig, 2012), showing, for example, that music listening relates to having no or less need for medical treatment for chronic pain (Mitchell, et al., 2007) and that musical behavior relates to lowered levels of cortisol (Koelsch, et al., 2011; Lindblad, Hogmark, & Theorell, 2007; Linnemann et al., 2015; Thoma et al., 2013). However, a range of studies also shows connections between musical behavior and various externalizing (disruptive) and internalizing (distress) symptoms (for review, see Miranda, et al, 2012). Current literature presents a somewhat inconsistent picture on whether music-related emotion regulation is adaptive and health-beneficial. McFerran, Garrido, & Saarikallio (2013) point out that participants themselves rarely describe negative consequences of their personal music use, while several correlational studies do indicate a relationship between music listening and ill-health, indicated by a range of psychosocial measures. Current evidence on the link between music and ill-health is almost solely correlational leaving it open whether it only is about the fact that music is actively called for in times of trouble, or whether it also is about music not functioning as effectively in emotion regulation as one would hope for. For instance, Thoma Scholz, Ehlert, & Nater (2012) found that musical emotion regulation (listening to music for reducing loneliness and aggression, and arousing and intensifying specific emotions) was related to lower psychological and physiological functioning, but it may well be that patterns of musical behavior were indicators, rather than causes of loneliness, aggression, and lowered psychological functioning.

33.8 THE RELEVANCE OF CHOOSING A REGULATORY STRATEGY

Part of the answer lies in looking at the musical emotion regulation from the more detailed perspective of specific emotion regulation strategies. General coping and emotion regulation literature has shown that efficacious emotion regulation strategies, such as distraction and positive reappraisal, buffer against stressors (Seiffge-Krenke, 1995) and relate negatively to undesirable outcomes, such as depression (Catanzaro, 2000; Oikawa, 2002; Gross & John, 2003; Garnefski Teerds, Kraaij, Legerstee, & Van den Kommer 2004), whereas inefficient emotion regulation strategies, such as venting, suppression, and rumination relate to various negative outcomes, such as depression (Salovey et al, 1999; Galaif, Sussman, Chou, & Wills, 2002; Gross & John, 2003; Garnefski et al., 2004), or use of alcohol, cigarettes, and marijuana (McCubbin Needle, & Wilson, 1985). Meanwhile, music researchers have begun to emphasize that music is not a single form of emotion regulation, but a tool or means for realizing a range of emotion regulation strategies (e.g., tension reduction, distraction, mental processing, or emotional release; Saarikallio & Erkkilä, 2007; Van Goethem & Sloboda, 2011) and coping strategies (e.g., problem-orientated, emotion-orientated, avoidant strategies; Miranda & Claes, 2009). It has been proposed, that the overall effect of music on psychopathology and health intrinsically depends on the type of musical behavior: adaptive patterns of musical behavior foster health and buffer against stressors while maladaptive patterns of musical behavior increase negative symptoms (Miranda et al., 2012). Thus, the efficacy and adaptiveness of musical coping or emotion regulation depends on the particular strategy employed. Indeed, preliminary evidence indicates that it is not the amount of music listening or even the personal relevance of music, but particularly the emotion-regulatory motivations for listening that seem to relate to psychological and physiological functioning (Thoma et al., 2012), and that certain musical emotion regulation strategies indeed are more effective than others in terms of dealing with sadness (Van den Toll & Edwards, 201) and combatting depression (Miranda & Claes, 2009).

33.9 NATURE OF HEATH-BENEFICIAL MUSICAL EMOTION REGULATION

Based on the evidence so far, the two music-related strategies that appear particularly beneficial regarding health are distraction and reappraisal. Both of these strategies are considered to be among the most advanced and effective ways of emotion regulation also in general emotion regulation literature: distraction refers to the use of pleasant activities to lighten moods (Salovey et al., 1999) and reappraisal refers to cognitive reinterpretation of the emotion-eliciting situation (Gross & John, 2003), and a strong body of research connects these strategies to positive psychological and physiological outcomes (Salovey et al., 1999; Gross & John, 2003). As regards music, it has been proposed that pleasant musical activities help to distance thoughts and feelings from personal burdens (distraction) and that music promotes mental reflection and regaining control over psychic processes (reappraisal) (e.g., Sloboda, 1992; Saarikallio & Erkkilä, 2007; Van den Toll & Edwards, 2011). Furthermore, Chin & Rickard (2013a,b, 2014) showed that engagement in music for cognitive and emotion regulation relates positively to well-being, negatively to depression, and functions efficiently in stress reduction, particularly in individuals who are high in habitual cognitive reappraisal. Similarly, Van den Toll & Edwards (2014) found that when people listen to sad music while feeling sad, they succeed in mood improvement particularly if the music simultaneously functions as a means for distraction and cognitive reappraisal. Mitchell and colleagues (2007) also showed that the success of music in pain management particularly relates to experiences of distraction and relaxation. The effectiveness of reappraisal and distraction may be based on their in-built capacity for mood repair—alteration of negative mood towards a positive one. It has been proposed that the regulation of negative moods generally divides into a tendency to focus on the negative emotion itself and a tendency to focus on something else, either some completely emotion-irrelevant material (as in distraction) or some positive aspects of the negative situation (as in reappraisal) (Rusting & DeHart, 2000). The relevance of using music for altering the experience towards positive emotion is further supported by results indicating that musical emotion regulation is effective without the presence of distraction or reappraisal if some other mechanism or behavior such as aesthetic pleasure (Van den Toll & Edwards, 2014) or dancing (Chin & Rickard, 2013b) leads to the positive emotional experience. In line with that, people also seem to like sad music particularly when they experience happiness due to it (Weth & Kickinger, 2013).

33.10 Nature of Maladaptive Musical Emotion Regulation

Evidence of possibly maladaptive music-related emotion regulation strategies also begins to emerge, and the most relevant candidates for such strategies include rumination, avoidant coping, and aggression ventilation. Rumination refers to repetitive and passive focus on negative emotions and other symptoms of distress (Joorman, 2005; Nolen-Hoeksma, Wisco, & Lyubomirsky, 2008), strongly relates to depression (Nolen-Hoeksma, 1991; Garnefski et al., 2004), and is also employed in relation to music listening (Garrido, 2009; Greenwood & Long, 2009). Miranda & Claes (2009) reported that recurrent avoidant/disengagement coping and emotion-oriented coping by music listening—strategies that can be considered reflective of ruminative tendencies—were related to higher depression. The key maladaptive feature of rumination includes overt focus on negative emotion instead of addressing the stressor or trying to improve mood. Interestingly, Garrido & Schubert (2015a,b) reported that individuals with high ruminative tendencies particularly benefitted from listening to happy music—their mood improved significantly more than other listeners—an atypical positive twist, listening to happy music, might thus be particularly beneficial to individuals who habitually ruminate.

Trapnell & Campbell (1999) further distinguish between the maladaptive type of rumination and an adaptive form of self-reflection they call reflectiveness. While both reappraisal and rumination involve self-reflection, the focus of mental processing essentially differs—rumination refers to passive, repetitive, and negative thoughts while reappraisal refers to finding new optimistic viewpoints or even solutions. Salovey and colleagues (1999, 2000) point out that ruminative people are constantly monitoring their feelings and get confused in their attempt to make sense of them, while the ability to identify and understand one's emotions would actually prevent rumination. This notion is not far from the concepts of emotional clarity, emotion labeling, awareness of feelings, and refined emotion discussed in the previous chapter—pointing to the relevance of the type of the self-reflective attention to emotion. That is, it may not necessarily be maladaptive to focus on or even intensify the current negative emotional state as long as the involvement involves reflectiveness instead of rumination, solution orientation instead of getting stuck in repetition, and focus on positive instead of negative aspects. Indeed, Miranda et al. (2012) note that shared engagement in listening to sad music with friends holds potential for encouraging both maladaptive co-rumination and adaptive experiences of increased social support and healthy socialization. Research conducted with healthy populations tends to emphasize the positive outcomes of listening to music that reflects one's negative mood, including notions about music being a valued friend (e.g., Sloboda, 1992), a means for solace (Saarikallio & Erkkilä, 2007) a form of emotional validation (Schwartz & Fouts, 2003), and a means for gaining increased insight of the affective state (Skånland, 2013). Instead, recent work with depressed individuals shows that instead of using music for successful processing of experiences these individuals are more inclined to use music to support repetitive thinking and rumination, actually leading to worsening of their social isolation and negative mood (Garrido & Schubert, 2015a,b; McFerran & Saarikallio, 2013).

The regulatory strategy of venting and releasing negative emotion may hold similar two-fold potential. In general, it has been proposed that emotional disclosure helps to restructure thoughts and feelings supporting adaptive functioning (Salovey et al., 1999, 2000), but anger ventilation is also shown to correlate with health risk behaviors and depression (Galaif et al., 2003; McCubbin et al., 1985). It has been proposed that music serves as a harmless form of discharging ager and helps in cathartic release of negative emotions (Sloboda, 1992; Saarikallio & Erkkilä, 2007; Schwartz & Fouts, 2003). However, a strong body of research also connects music listening, particularly the tendency for listening to "aggressive" and "rebellious" styles of music to a range of negative outcomes and behavioral problems (North & Hargreaves, 2012; Mulder et al., 2007). Furthermore, recent evidence shows that discharging negative emotions through music is actually negatively or not at all correlated with adaptive strategies of general emotion regulation such as mood repair, negative mood regulation, and cognitive reappraisal (Saarikallio, 2008).

33.11 Coping and emotion regulation as a part of musical identity

The personal ways of using music for coping and emotion regulation are an indisputable part of one's musical identity. These behavioral patterns further play a major role regarding one's emotional health. Emerging evidence points to favoring the use music for self-reflective, reappraising, and distractive forms of dealing with negative emotion, but various individual differences and causalities related to these connections are far from clear. Furthermore, while investigation of the emotion regulation strategies presents itself as an essential aspect of understanding the health-consequences of musical emotion regulation, other factors, such as the type of the stressor, are also likely to play a significant role. Indeed, music has been shown to be effective in stress regulation only during periods with generally low stress, while periods of more severe stress may require other regulatory behaviors (Linnemann, Ditzen, Strahler, Dörr & Nater, 2013). Individual features related to personality and general emotionality are also likely to play a role. For instance, people high in empathy seem to generally be more susceptible for musical emotion induction (Vuoskoski & Eerola, 2011b) and features such as stress reactivity (Thoma et al. 2012) and tendencies for absorption and dissociation (Garrido & Schubert, 2011, 2013) seem to moderate the connection between musical emotion regulation and health-outcomes. The greatly needed intervention research on the topic is also only beginning to emerge (Dingle & Fay, 2013; Van Goethem, 2010). Therefore, it must be concluded that we are only beginning to explore the complexity of this topic.

33.12 INDUCTION OF POSITIVE EMOTION

Positive emotions are fundamental for both psychological and physical aspects of well-being, having important consequences over and above negative emotions (Gable, Reis, Impett, & Asher, 2004). Positive emotions facilitate cognitive processing (Ashby, Isen, & Turken, 1999), broaden thought-action repertoires (Fredrickson, 2001), regulate and mitigate negative feelings and their ill-effects on self-control (Izard, 2002), and relate to decreased cortisol levels (Kemeny & Shestyuk, 2010). Indeed, the mere experience of positive instead of negative mood is related to improved coping and wellbeing (Pinto Kreipe, & McCoy, 1997; Fredrickson, 2000; Gohm, 2003). Fredrickson (2001) has postulated that positive emotions not only signal flourishing, but significantly produce it. They facilitate approach behavior, widen the array of thoughts and actions in momentary behavior, and facilitate coping and management of negative emotions, further fostering the development of enduring personal resources and increased resilience. Positive emotions are thus not significant, just as end states in themselves, but also as a means for achieving psychological growth and well-being over time.

33.13 MUSIC-INDUCED POSITIVE EMOTION

As regards music, the relevance of positive emotion is blatant. Enjoyment, mood improvement, and positive emotional experiences are central motivations for music listening (e.g., Roe, 1985; North, Hargreaves & Hargreaves, 2004), and hedonic motivation also dominates among performance motivations (Persson, 2001). As regards emotion-regulation, mood improvement is one of its most central goals (Saarikallio & Erkkilä, 2007), and the most typical regulatory strategies essentially involve positive emotion (entertainment, strong sensation, revival reported by Saarikallio, 2008; relaxation reported by Van Goethem & Sloboda, 2011). Furthermore, people do not only actively engage in music for the positive emotional experiences, but this endeavor also appears successful: positive emotions equally dominate in people's responses to music (Juslin & Zentner, 2002; Juslin & Laukka, 2004; Juslin, Liljeström, Västfjäll, Barradas, & Silva, 2008). Indeed, while Van Goethem and Sloboda (2011) listed calm/relaxed and happy/excited as the most typical emotions that music listening was used to create, the very same emotions also appear as the most typical felt emotional responses to music in daily life (e.g., happy, relaxed, and calm—the three most common emotions, reported by

Juslin & Laukka, 2004; calm/contentment and happiness/elation—the most common emotions reported by Juslin, et al, 2008). A variety of research has also evidenced the effect of music listening on physiological indicators of positive emotions, including activation of brain areas involved in reward (Blood & Zatorre, 2001; Evers & Suhr, 2000; Menon & Levitin, 2005) and frontal asymmetry of the alpha band power indicative of positive affect (Martinez, Nawrocki Pickens, Fox, & Schanberg, 1998; Field, Schmidt & Trainor 2001; Altenmueller, Schurmann, & Parlitz, 2002). Finally, while the most common emotional responses to music can be rounded to overall positive affect with varying levels of arousal, the more detailed nuances of the emotional experiences and affective rewards derived from music may somewhat differ from the everyday positive emotions, particularly in including a relatively high amount of the so called aesthetic emotions (Zentner & Scherer, 2008) such as experiences of beauty (Istók, Brattico, Jacobsen, Krohn, Müller, & Tervaniemi, 2009).

33.14 HOW DO POSITIVE EMOTIONS CONNECT MUSIC TO HEALTH?

While it has been thoroughly demonstrated that music can induce a range of positive emotions both in laboratory contexts and in everyday life, there is little research on how these positive music-related emotional experiences relate to health and wellbeing. It could naturally be argued that since the relevance of positive emotion to health and wellbeing is already shown in general emotion research there is no point in repeating these findings within music and emotion research. However, elaborate investigations would enlighten the role and specific applicability of music in health-promotion contexts. Also, the distinct nature of music as a form of aesthetic enjoyment is likely to enable music to afford somewhat different emotional gratifications than the everyday utilitarian positive emotions. Some of the recent findings on the topic should be mentioned. For instance, it has been shown that it actually is the positive emotions experienced to music that mediate the relationship between music and perceived stress (Helsing, 2012). Also, preliminary evidence indicates that the lowered experience (Rickard, Arjmand, & White, 2013), perception, and regulation (Saarikallio, et al., 2013) of positive emotion, not increased negative emotion, is the dominant deficit of emotional processing of music observed in depressed individuals in comparison to healthy controls. These findings point to the health-relevance of fostering the induction of positive, instead of only dampening the negative, emotion through musical engagement. Another line of findings indicates that the positive mood induced by music also is an intrinsic component in the effects of music on improved cognitive abilities both in laboratory settings (Thompson, et al., 2001) and in rehabilitation (Särkämö, et al. 2008), which is perfectly in line with the findings of general emotion research on the effect of positive emotion on cognition (e.g., Ashby et al., 1999).

33.15 The relevance of positive emotions to musical identity

The induction of positive emotion instead of managing negative emotion was long neglected in general emotion regulation, coping and health literature and became popular only after the rise of positive psychology and preventive medicine. As regards music, the role of positive emotions as a key feature between music and mental health cannot be emphasized enough, and similar neglect is simply not acceptable. Music intrinsically is a form of art and entertainment, a medium of pleasure, joy, enjoyment and happiness, and the research on the connections between music and emotional health should embrace this happiness-advancing quality as its core subject. Previous work has indeed proposed that pleasures of musical experiences may produce a sense of wellbeing, stability, wholeness, and purpose in life (Ruud, 1997), and future work should engage in elaborate explication of how the variety of positive emotional experiences of music relate to health. This is particularly important for understanding how a musical identity might foster emotional health in the context of everyday life. Some relevant aspects for future research might, for instance, include investigation of the particular nature of the musical versus non-musical positive emotional experiences, the self-reflective awareness and emotion recognition ability regarding these positive experiences, the tendency for absorption regarding the positive musical emotions, and the role that these positive experiences play in buffering stressors and mitigating the effects of negative emotions. Answers to these questions would elaborate our understanding about whether and why the use of music for inducing positive emotional experiences should be considered a major feature of musical identity.

33.16 Conclusions

What kind of musical identity is supportive of emotional health? This chapter has brought forward some features of emotion perception, regulation, and induction that are likely to be relevant for the construction of such identity. The exploration began with discussion of the ability of recognizing emotions that music expresses and also evokes. Not only may this ability transfer to general abilities of identifying emotions in self and in others, but it may also be the fundamental prerequisite for the adaptive use of music for emotion regulation and induction. In particular, while music abundantly—and negligently—affords intensification and enhancement of various emotional states, the health-implications of utilizing this power may vary, and the ability for self-reflective and dissociative stance—supported by emotion recognition capabilities—may hold a key for differentiating between health-beneficial and health-endangering emotional uses of music. This is particularly relevant for the negative, depressive, and aggressive moods that may endanger emotional health if passively prolonged and repeated, with no clarification, release, solution-orientation, active processing, and change towards the positive. However, the self-reflective, absorptive, emotion-identifying awareness may also be highly advantageous in relation to positive emotions, as it may foster experiences of refined and thorough enjoyment—savoring—of various beautiful shades and nuances imbedded in the positive emotional experiences, possibly allowing highly rewarding, enriching, and thought-broadening experiences that may be essential for the building of enduring resources for resilience, emotional stability, enjoyment, and satisfaction with life.

Moreover, the relevance of the self-reflective awareness may further extend to the meta-cognitive level regarding one's overall emotional engagement in music. McFerran & Saarikallio (2013) propose that vulnerable adolescents end up in repeating maladaptive patterns of musical engagement because they are unable to realize their own responsibility for allowing music to reinforce and fuel their negative emotions, ruminative tendencies and feelings of social isolation. Reflective awareness at the metacognitive level of observing and understanding the health-consequences of one's musical behavior can thus also be seen as an essential ability for fostering emotional balance and growth. This notion can further be expanded to discussion regarding the overall sense of self-control and self-agency regarding one's emotional engagement in music. In general, perceived control is known to be an important aspect of the coping process, as it increases the sense of agency and use of problem solving (Brannon & Feist, 2007). In relation to music, it has been proposed that the use of self-selected music brings autonomy and personalization to activities and facilitates emotional change (Sloboda & O'Neill, 2001). It has also been stated that music can be an important source of self-agency for adolescents (Gold, McFerran & Saarikallio, 2011), a resource of personal empowerment for the long-term ill (Batt-Rawden, et.al., 2005), and that the feeling of personal control may promote music-related pain management (Mitchell et.al., 2007). In addition, self-selected music is shown to be more effective than experimenter selected music in inducing pleasure (Blood & Zatorre, 2001), reducing pain (Bernatzky, et al., 2012; Mitchell, et al. 2007) and alleviating stress (Allen & Blascovich, 1994). These notions indicate that a health-fostering musical identity indeed should consist of a sense of agency and self-control regarding the various emotional effects that music so effortlessly seems to afford.

We can thus conclude that a musical identity that fosters emotional health essentially involves reflective awareness and sense of self-control regarding a set of complex emotional competencies related to recognition, induction and regulation of emotion in music. Furthermore, mastery of these emotional competencies may not be the optimal definition for a health-promoting musical identity—it may actually be the awareness of the possibility of music in nurturing and developing these abilities—and the willingness to learn, change, heal, and grow in relation to them. Finally, it needs to be acknowledged that the psychological processes and characteristics relevant for a health-promoting musical identity that have been brought forward in this chapter are only a propositional set of the underlying features and mechanisms and other aspects could also be included in a comprehensive theory. In particular, the studies reviewed here focus mainly on research conducted on music listening—research focussed on music production might stress different mechanisms, such as the relevance of emotional self-expression and the concept of flow in relation to the induction of positive and rewarding experiences. In addition, the processes discussed here are strongly rooted in theories and concepts of general emotion research, so a word of encouragement to pay more attention to the particular qualities of music as an aesthetic domain is given for future work. Nonetheless, the ideas proposed in this chapter provide future research a clarifying framework for considering and understanding musical identity from the perspective of the basic emotional competencies and processes that are known fundamental for sustaining, enhancing, and fostering mental health and wellbeing.

References

Aldwin, C.M. (2007). *Stress, coping, and development. An intergrative perspective.* New York, NY: Guilford Press.

Allen K. & Blascovich, J. (1994). Effects of music on cardiovascular reactivity among surgeons. *Journal of the American Medical Association,* 272, 882–4.

Altenmuller, E.K., Schurmann, V.K., & Parlitz, D. (2002). Hits to the left, flops to the right: Different emotions during listening to music are reflected in cortical lateralisation patterns. *Neuropsychologia,* 40, 2242–56.

Antonovsky, A. (1979). *Health, stress, and coping.* San Francisco, CA: Jossey-Bass Publishers.

Ashby, F.G., Isen, A.M., & Turken, A.U. (1999). A neuropsychological theory of positive affect and its influence on cognition. *Psychological Review,* 106, 529–50.

Batt-Rawden, K.B, DeNora, T, & Ruud, E. (2005). Music listening and empowerment in health promotion: A study of the role and significance of music in everyday life of the long-term ill. *Nordic Journal of Music Therapy,* 14 (2), 120–36.

Bernatzky, G., Stickner S., Perch, M, Wendtner, F., & Kullich, W. (2012). Music as non-pharmacological pain management in clinics. In: R. McDonald, G. Kreutz, & L. Mitchell (Eds.) *Music, health, and wellbeing,* pp. 257–75. Oxford: Oxford University Press.

Blood, A.J. & Zatorre, R.J. (2001). Intensely pleasurable responses to music correlate with activity in brain regions implicated in reward and emotion. *Proceedings of the National Academy of Sciences USA,* 98, 11818–23.

Brannon, L. & Feist, P. (2010). *Health psychology: an introduction to behaviour and health.* Belmont, CA: Wadsworth.

Catanzaro, S. (2000). Coping-related expectancies and dispositions as prospective predictors of coping responses and symptoms. *Journal of Personality,* 68(4), 757–89.

Chin, T.C. & Rickard, N.S. (2013a). Emotion regulation strategy mediates both positive and negative relationship between music uses and well-being. *Psychology of Music,* 42, 692–713.

Chin, T. & Rickard, N. (2014). Beyond positive and negative trait affect: Flourishing through music engagement. *Psychology of Well-being,* 4(25), doi:10.1186/s13612-014-0025-4.

Chin, T.C. & Rickard, N.S. (submitted). Relationships between music use, depression and anxiety are mediated by emotion regulation strategy. Manuscript submitted to a journal.

Clayton, M., Sager, R., & Will, U. (2004). In time with the music: the concept of entrainment and its significance for ethnomusicology. *European Seminar in Ethnomusicology CounterPoint,* 1, 1–45.

Collins, F.L., Sorocco, K.H., Haala, K.R., Miller, B.I., & Lovallo, W.R. (2003). Stress and health. In: L.M. Cohen, D.E. McChargue, & F.L. Collins (Eds.) *The health psychology handbook. Practical issues for the behavioral medicine specialist,* pp. 169–86. Thousand Oaks, CA: Sage.

Coulson, M. (2004). Attributing emotion to static body postures: recognition accuracy, confusions, and viewpoint dependence. *Journal of Nonverbal Behavior*, 28, 117–39.

Cross, I. (2008). Musicality and the human capacity for culture. *Musicae Scientiae*, Special Issue, 147–67.

Cunningham, J.G. & Sterling, R.S. (1988). Developmental change in the understanding of affective meaning in music. *Motivation and Emotion*, 12, 399–413.

Damasio, A.R. (1995). *Descartes' error: emotion, reason, and the human brain*. New York, NY: Picador: Avon Books.

Davis, M.H. (1980). A multidimensional approach to individual differences in empathy. *JSAS Catalog of Selected Documents in Psychology*, 10, 85.

Davis, M.H. (1983). Measuring individual differences in empathy: evidence for a multidimensional approach. *Journal of Personality and Social Psychology*, 44, 113–26.

Dibben, N., Coutinho, E., Vilar, J.A., & Estévez-Pérez, G. (2014). Perceiving emotion in music and speech prosody: do individual differences matter? The neurosciences and music – V Cognitive Stimulation and Rehabilitation, 29 May–1 June 2014, Dijon, France.

Dingle, G. & Fay, C. (2013). Tuned In: brief music emotion regulation intervention for young adults. Paper presented at *The 3rd International Conference on Music and Emotion*, Jyväskylä, June 11-15.

Dissanayake, E. (2008). If music is the food of love, what about survival and reproductive success? *Musicae Scientiae*, Special Issue: 169–95.

Dolgin, K.G. & Adelson, E.H. (1990). Age changes in the ability to interpret affect in sung and instrumentally presented melodies. *Psychology of Music*, 18: 87–98.

Ekman, P. (Ed.) (1982). *Emotion in the human face*, 2nd edn. Cambridge: Cambridge University Press.

Ekman, P. & Friesen, W.V. (1971). Constants across cultures in the face and emotion. *Journal of Personality and Social Psychology*, 17, 124–29.

Evers, S. & Suhr, B. (2000). Changes of the neurotransmitter serotonin but not of hormones during short time music perception. *European Archives of Psychiatry and Clinical Neuroscience*, 250, 144–7.

Feldman Barrett, L. & Gross, J.J. (2001). Emotional intelligence: a process model of emotion representation and regulation. In T.J. Mayne & G.A. Bonanno (Eds.) *Emotions: current issues and future directions*. New York: Guildford Press.

Field, T., Martinez, A., Nawrocki T., Pickens, J., Fox, N.A., & Schanberg, S. (1998). Music shifts frontal EEG in depressed adolescents. *Adolescence*, 33, 109–116.

Fredrickson, B.L. (2000). Cultivating positive emotions to optimize health and well-being. *Prevention & Treatment*, Vol. 3.

Fredrickson, B.L. (2001). The role of positive emotions in positive psychology: the broaden and build theory of positive emotions. *American Psychology*, 56 (3), 218–26.

Frijda, N.H. (1988). The laws of emotion. *American Psychologist*, 43(5), 349–58.

Frijda, N.H. & Sundararajan, L. (2007). Emotion refinement: a theory inspired by Chinese poetics. *Perspectives on Psychological Science*, 2, 227–241.

Gable, S.L., Reis, H.T., Impett, E.A., & Asher, E.R. (2004). What do you do when things go right? The intrapersonal and interpersonal benefits of sharing positive events. *Journal of Personality and Social Psychology*, 87(2), 228–45.

Gabrielsson, A. (2002). Emotion perceived and emotion felt: same or different? *Musicae Scientiae*, Special Issue 2001–2002, 123–47.

Gabrielsson, A. & Lindström, E. (2001). The influence of musical structure on emotional expression. In: P.N. Juslin & J.A. Sloboda (Eds.) *Music and emotion: theory and research*, pp. 223–48. New York, NY: Oxford University Press.

Galaif, E.R., Sussman, S., Chou, C., & Wills, T.A. (2003). Longitudinal relations among depression, stress, and coping in high risk youth, *Journal of Youth and Adolescence*, 32(4), 243–58.

Garnefski, N., Teerds, J., Kraaij, V., Legerstee, J., & Van den Kommer, T. (2004). Cognitive emotion regulation strategies and depressive symptoms: differences between males and females. *Personality and Individual Differences*, 36, 267–76.

Garrido, S. (2009). Rumination and sad music: a review of the literature and a future direction. *Proceedings of the Second International Conference on Music Communication Science*, 3–4 December 2009, Sydney, Australia.

Garrido S. & Schubert, E. (2010). Imagination, empathy, and dissociation in individual response to negative emotions in music. *Musica Humana*, 2, 53–78.

Garrido, S. & Schubert, E. (2011). Negative emotion in music: what is the attraction? A qualitative study. *Empirical Musicology Review*, 6(4), 214–30.

Garrido, S. & Schubert, E. (2013). Adaptive and maladaptive attraction to negative emotions in music. *Musicae Scientiae*, 17(2), 147–66.

Garrido, S. & Schubert, E. (2015a). Moody melodies: Do they cheer us up? A study of the effect of sad music on mood. *Psychology of Music,* 43(2), 244-61. doi:10.1177/0305735613501938.

Garrido, S.& Schubert, E. (2015b). Music and people with tendencies to depression. *Music Perception*, 32(4), 313-21. doi:10.1525/MP.2015.32.4.313.

Gohm, C.L. (2003). Mood regulation and emotional intelligence: individual differences. *Journal of Personality and Social Psychology*, 84(3), 594–607.

Greenwood, D.N. & Long, C.R. (2009). Mood specific media use and emotion regulation: patterns and individual differences. *Personality and Individual Differences*, 46, 616–21.

Gross, J.J. (1998). The emerging field of emotion regulation: an integrative review. *Review of General Psychology*, 2(3), 271–99.

Gross, J.J. & John, O.P. (2003). Individual differences in two emotion regulation processes: implications for affect, relationships, and well-being. *Journal of Personality and Social Psychology*, 85(2), 348–62.

Helsing, M. (2012). Everyday music listening: the importance of individual and situational factors for musical emotions and stress reduction. Doctoral dissertation, University of Gothenburg.

Istók, E., Brattico, E., Jacobsen, T., Krohn, K., Müller, M., & Tervaniemi, M. (2009). Aesthetic responses to music: A questionnaire study. *Musicae Scientiae*, 13(2), 183–206.

Izard, C.E. (2002). Translating emotion theory and research into preventive interventions. *Psychological Bulletin*, 128(5), 796–824.

Joorman, J. (2005). Inhibition, rumination and mood regulation in depression. In: R.W. Engle, G. Sedek, U. von Hecker, & D.N. McIntosh (Eds.) *Cognitive limitations in aging and psychopathology*. Cambridge: Cambridge University Press.

Juslin, P.N. (1997). Emotional communication in music performance: a functionalist perspective and some data. *Music Perception*, 14, 383–418.

Juslin, P.N. & Laukka, P. (2003). Communication of emotions in vocal expression and music performance: different channels, same code? *Psychological Bulletin*, 129, 770–814.

Juslin, P.N. & Laukka, P. (2004). Expression, perception, and induction of musical emotions: a review and a questionnaire study of everyday listening. *Journal of New Music Research*, 33(3), 217–38.

Juslin, P.N. & Timmers, R. (2010). Expression and communication of emotion in music. In: P.N. Juslin & J. Sloboda (Eds.) *Handbook of music and emotion: theory, research, applications*, New York: Oxford University Press.

Juslin, P. & Zentner, M. (2002). Current trends in the study of music and emotion *Musicae Scientiae,* Special Issue 2001–2002, 3–21.

Juslin, P.N., Liljeström, S., Västfjäll, D., Barradas, G., & Silva, A. (2008). An experience sampling study of emotional reactions to music: Listener, music, and situation. *Emotion,* 8, 668–83.

Juslin, P.N. & Sloboda, J. (Eds.) (2010). *Handbook of music and emotion: theory, research, applications.* New York, NY: Oxford University Press.

Kemeny, M.E. & Shestyuk, A. (2010). Emotions, the neuroendocrine and immune systems, and health. In: M. Lewis, J.M. Haviland-Jones, & L. Feldman Barrett (Eds.) *Handbook of emotions,* 3rd edn, pp. 661–75. New York, NY: Guilford Press.

Koelsch, S. (2005). Investigating emotion with music: neuroscientific approaches. *Annals of the New York Academy of Sciences,* 1060, 412–18.

Koelsch, S., Fuermetz, J., Sack, U., et al. (2011). Effects of music listening on cortisol levels and propofol consumption during spinal anaesthesia. *Frontiers in Auditory Cognitive Neuroscience,* 2(58), 1–9.

Koelsch, S. & Stegemann, T. (2012). The brain and positive biological effects in healthy and clinical populations. In: R. McDonald, G. Kreutz, & L. Mitchell (Eds.) *Music, health, and wellbeing,* pp. 436–56. Oxford: Oxford University Press.

Kreutz, G., Quiroga Mucia, C., & Bongard, S. (2012). Psychoneuroendoctrine research on music and health: an overview. In: R. McDonald, G. Kreutz, & L. Mitchell (Eds.) *Music, health, and wellbeing,* pp. 457–76. Oxford: Oxford University Press.

Ladinig, O. & Schellenberg, E.G. (2012). Liking unfamiliar music: effects of felt emotion and individual differences. *Psychology of Aesthetics, Creativity, and the Arts,* 6, 146–54.

Larsen, R.J. (2000). Toward a science of mood regulation. *Psychological Inquiry,* 11(3), 129–41.

Liljeström, S. (2011). Emotional reactions to music: prevalence and contributing factors. Dissertation, Uppsala University.

Lindblad, F., Hogmark, Å., & Theorell, T. (2007). Music intervention for 5th and 6th graders— effects on development and cortisol secretion. *Stress and Health,* 23, 9–14.

Linnemann, A., Ditzen, B., Strahler, J., Dörr, J., & Nater, U.M. (2013). Music as a means of stress reduction in daily life—an ambulatory assessment study among students. Paper presented at the 3rd International Conference on Music and Emotion, Jyväskylä, June 11–15.

Linnemann, A., Ditzen, B., Strahler, J., Doerr, J.M., & Nater, U.M. (2015). Music listening as a means of stress reduction in daily life. *Psychoneuroendocrinology,* 60, 82-90.

Lovallo, W.R. (2005). *Stress and health: biological and psychological interactions,* 2nd edn. Thousand Oaks, CA: Sage.

McCubbin, H.I., Needle, R.H., & Wilson, M. (1985). Adolescent health risk behaviors: family stress and adolescent coping as critical factors, *Family Relations,* 34(1), 51–63.

McDonald, R., Kreutz, G., & Mitchell, L. (Eds.) (2012). *Music, health, and wellbeing.* Oxford: Oxford University Press.

McFerran, K., Garrido, S., & Sarrikallio, S. (2013). A critical interpretive synthesis of the literature linking music and adolescent mental health. *Youth and Society.* Published online before print, December 2, 2013, doi: 10.1177 / 0044118X13501343.

McFerran K. & Saarikallio S. (2013). Depending on music to make me feel better: Who is responsible for the ways young people appropriate music for health benefits. *Arts in Psychotherapy,* 41(1), 89–97.

Menon, V. & Levitin, D. (2005). The rewards of music listening: response and physiological connectivity of mesolimbic system. *NeuroImage,* 228, 175–84.

Miranda, D., Gaudreau, P., Debrosse R., Morizot, J., & Kirmayer, L. J. (2012). Music listening and mental health: variations on internalizing psychopathology. In: R. McDonald, G. Kreutz, & L. Mitchell (Eds.) *Music, health, and wellbeing,* pp. 513–30. Oxford: Oxford University Press.

Mitchell, L.A., MacDonald, R.A.R., Knussen, K., & Serpell, M.G. (2007). A survey investigation of the effects of music on chronic pain. *Psychology of Music*, 35(1), 37–57.

Mulder, J., Ter Bogt, T., Raaijmakers, Q., & Vollebergh, W. (2007). Music taste groups and problem behavior. *Journal of Youth and Adolescence*, 36(3), 313–24.

Nater, U.M., Abbruzzese, E., Krebs, M., & Ehlert, U. (2006). Sex differences in emotional and psychophysiological responses to musical stimuli. *International Journal of Psychophysiology*, 62, 300–8.

Nawrot, E.S. (2003). The perception of emotional expression in music: evidence from infants, children, and adults. *Psychology of Music*, 31, 75–92.

Nolen-Hoeksema, S. (1991). Responses to depression and their effects on the duration of depressive episodes. *Journal of Abnormal Psychology*, 100(4), 569–82.

Nolen-Hoeksema, S., Wisco, B.E., & Lyubomirsky, S. (2008). Rethinking rumination. *Perspectives on Psychological Science*, 3(5), 400–24,

North, A.C. & Hargreaves, D.J. (2012). Pop music subcultures and wellbeing. In: McDonald R, Kreutz G, & Mitchell L, (Eds.) *Music, health and wellbeing*, pp. 502–12. Oxford: Oxford University Press..

North, A.C., Hargreaves, D.J., & Hargreaves, J.J. (2004). Uses of music in everyday life. *Music Perception*, 22(1), 41–77.

Oikawa, M. (2002). Distraction as an Intervention for depression: the distraction process. *Japanese Journal of Education Psychology*, 50(2), 185–92.

Pelletier, C.L. (2004). The effect of music on decreasing arousal due to stress: a meta-analysis. *Journal of Music Therapy*, 16(3), 192–214.

Persson, R.S. (2001). The subjective world of the performer. In: P.N. Juslin & J. Sloboda (Eds.) *Music and emotion: theory, and research*, pp. 275–90. Oxford: Oxford University Press.

Petrides, K.V., Niven, L., & Mouskounti, T. (2006). The trait emotional intelligence of ballet dancers and musicians. *Psicothema*, 18 suppl., 101–7.

Pinto, A., Kreipe, R.E., & McCoy, K.J.M. (1997). Impact of mood states on coping strategies in hospitalized adolescents. *Journal of Adolescent Health*, 20(2), 170.

Punkanen, M., Eerola, T., & Erkkilä, J. (2011). Biased emotional recognition in depression: Perception of emotions in music by depressed patients. *Journal of Affective Disorders*, 130(1–2), 118–26.

Reniers, R., Corcoran, R., Drake, R., Shryane, N.M., & Völlm, B.A. (2011). The QCAE: a questionnaire of cognitive and affective empathy. *Journal of Personality Assessment*, 93(1), 84–95.

Resnicow, J.E., Salovey, P., & Repp, B.H. (2004). Is recognition of emotion in musical performance an aspect of emotional intelligence? *Music Perception*, 22, 145–58.

Rickard, N., Arjmand, A., & White, E. (2013). Depressive deficits in the experience, but not regulation, of music-induced emotions. Paper presented at the 3rd International Conference on Music and Emotion, Jyväskylä, June 11–15.

Roe, K. (1985). Swedish youth and music: listening patterns and motivations. *Communication Research*, 12(3), 353–62.

Ruud, E. (1997). Music and the quality of life. *Nordic Journal of Music Therapy*, 6(2), 86–97.

Saarikallio, S. (2008). Music in mood regulation: initial scale development. *Musicae Scientiae*, 12 (2), 291–309.

Saarikallio, S. & Erkkilä, J. (2007). The role of music in adolescents' mood regulation. *Psychology of Music*, 35(1), 88–109.

Saarikallio, S., Vuoskoski, J., & Luck, G. (2012). Emotion perception in music is mediated by socio-emotional competence. In: E. Cambouropoulos, C. Tsougras, P. Mavromatis, & K. Pastiadis (Eds.) *Proceedings of the 12th International Conference on Music Perception and Cognition (ICMPC 2010)*, 23–28 August, Thessaloniki, Greece.

Salovey, P., Bedell, B.T., Detweiler, J.B., & Mayer, J.D. (1999). Coping intelligently. Emotional intelligence and the coping process. In: C.R. Snyder (Ed.) *Coping, the psychology of what works*. New York, NY: Oxford University Press.

Salovey, P., Bedell, B.T., Detweiler, J.B., & Mayer, J.D. (2000). Current directions in emotional intelligence research. In: M. Lewis & J.M. Haviland-Jones (Eds.) *Handbook of emotions*. New York: Guilford Press.

Salovey, P., Mayer, J.D., Goldman, S.L., Turvey, C., and Palfai, T.P. (1995). Emotional attention, clarity, and repair: exploring emotional intelligence using the trait meta-mood scale. In J.W. Pennebaker (Ed), *Emotion, disclosure, and health*, pp. 125–54. Washington, DC: American Psychological Association.

Salovey, P., Stroud, L.R., Woolery, A., & Epel, E.S. (2002). Perceived emotional intelligence, stress reactivity, and symptom reports: Further explorations using the trait meta-mood scale. *Psychology and Health*, 17(5), 611–27.

Schellenberg, E.G. & Mankarious, M. (2012). Music training and emotion comprehension in childhood. *Emotion*, 12(5), 887–91.

Scherer, K.R. (1986). Vocal affect expression: a review and a model for future research. *Psychological Bulletin*, 99, 143–65.

Schmidt, L.A. & Trainor, L.J. (2001). Frontal brain electrical activity (EEG) distinguishes valence and intensity of musical emotions. *Cognition & Emotion*, 15(4), 487–500.

Schwartz, K.D. & Fouts, G.T. (2003). Music preferences, personality style, and developmental issues of adolescents. *Journal of Youth and Adolescence*, 32(3), 205–13.

Seiffge-Krenke, I. (1995). Causal links between stressful events, coping style, and adolescent symptomatology. *Journal of Adolescence*, 23(6), 675–91.

Skånland, M. (2013). Everyday music listening and affect regulation: the role of MP3 players. *International Journal of Qualitative Studies on Health and Wellbeing*, 8, 20595.

Skinner, E.A., Edge, K., Altman, J., & Sherwood, H. (2003). Searching for the structure of coping: a review and critique of category systems for classifying ways of coping. *Psychological Bulletin*, 129, 216–69.

Sloboda, J.A. (1992). Empirical studies of emotional response to music. In: M.R. Jones & S. Holleran (Eds.) *Cognitive bases of musical communication*. Washington, DC: American Psychological Association.

Sloboda, J.A. & O'Neill, S.A. (2001). Emotions in everyday listening to music. In: P.N. Juslin & J.A. Sloboda (Eds.) *Music and emotion: theory and research*, pp. 415–29. Oxford: Oxford University Press.

Steptoe, A. (1997) Stress and disease. In: A. Baum, S. Newman, J. Weinman, & R.A.M.C. West (Eds.) *Cambridge handbook of psychology, health and medicine*, pp. 174–7. Cambridge: Cambridge University Press.

Swinkels, A. & Giuliano, Traci A. (1995). The measurement and conceptualization of mood awareness: monitoring and labeling one's mood states. *Personality and Social Psychology Bulletin*, 21(9), 934–49.

Thayer, R.E., Newman, J.R., & McClain, T.M. (1994). Self-regulation of mood: strategies for changing a bad mood, raising energy, and reducing tension. *Journal of Personality and Social Psychology*, 67(5), 910–25.

Thoma, MV., Scholz, U., Ehlert, U., & Nater, U.M. (2012). Listening to music and physiological and psychological functioning: the mediating role of emotion regulation and stress reactivity. *Psychology & Health*, 27(2), 227–41.

Thoma, M.V., La Marca, R., Brönnimann, R., Finkel, L., Ehlert, U., & Nater, U. M. (2013). The effect of music on the human stress response. *PlosOne*: http://dx.doi.org/10.1371/journal. pone.0070156.

Thompson, W.F., Schellenberg, E.G., & Husain, G. (2001). Arousal, mood, and the Mozart effect. *Psychological Science*, 12, 248–51.

Trapnell, P.D. & Campbell, J.D. (1999). Private self-consciousness and the five factor model of personality: distinguishing rumination from reflection. *Journal of Personality and Social Psychology*, 76(2), 284–304.

Trondalen, G. & Bonde, L.O. (2012). Music therapy: models and interventions. In: R. MacDonald, G. Kreutz, & L. Mitchell (Eds.) *Music, health and wellbeing*, pp. 40–61. Oxford: Oxford University Press.

Trimmer, C.G. & Cuddy, L.L. (2008). Emotional intelligence, not music training, predicts recognition of emotional speech prosody. *Emotion*, 8(6), 838–49.

Van den Tol, A.J. & Edwards, J. (2011). Exploring a rationale for choosing to listen to sad music when feeling sad. *Psychology of Music*, 23(1).

Van den Tol, A.J. & Edwards, J. (2014). Listening to sad music in adverse situations: How music selection strategies relate to self-regulatory goals, listening effects, and mood enhancement. *Psychology of Music*, 2014; Online first 29 January.

Van Goethem, A. & Sloboda, J. (2011). The functions of music for affect regulation. *Musicae Scientiae*, 15, 208–28.

Van Goethem, A. (2010). Affect regulation in everyday life: strategies, tactics, and the role of music. Unpublished dissertation, University of Keele.

Vieillard, S., Peretz, I., Gosselin, N., Khalfa, S., Gagnon, L., & Bouchard, B. (2008). Happy, sad, scary, and peaceful musical excerpts for research on emotions. *Cognition & Emotion*, 22, 720–52.

Västjfäll, D., Juslin, P. N., & Hartig, T. (2012). The role of everyday emotions. In: R. McDonald, G. Kreutz, & L. Mitchell (Eds.) *Music, health, and wellbeing*, pp. 405–23. Oxford: Oxford University Press.

Vuoskoski, J.K. & Eerola, T. (2011a). The role of mood and personality in the perception of emotions represented by music. *Cortex*, 47, 1099–106.

Vuoskoski, J.K. & Eerola, T. (2011b). Measuring music-induced emotion: a comparison of emotion models, personality biases, and intensity of experiences. *Musicae Scientiae*, 15, 159–73.

Vuoskoski, J.K. & Eerola, T. (2012). Can sad music really make you sad? Indirect measures of affective states induced by music and autobiographical memories. *Psychology of Aesthetics, Creativity, and the Arts*, 6, 204–13.

Wallbott, N. (1998). Bodily expression of emotion. *European Journal of Social Psychology*, 28, 879–96.

Weth, K. & Kickinger, M. (2013). Ambivalent emotions in music: we like sad music when it makes us happy. Paper presented at the 3rd International Conference on Music and Emotion, Jyväskylä, June 11–15.

Wöllner, C. (2012). Is empathy related to the perception of emotional expression in music? A multimodal time-series analysis. *Psychology of Aesthetics, Creativity, and the Arts*, 6(3), 214–23.

Zentner, M. & Scherer, K.R. (2008). Emotions evoked by the sound of music: characterization, classification, and measurement. *Emotion*, 8(4), 494–521.

CHAPTER 34

·····································

MUSIC-MAKING IN THERAPEUTIC CONTEXTS

Reframing Identity Following Disruptions to Health

·····································

WENDY L. MAGEE

34.1 INTRODUCTION

·····································

THIS chapter discusses music in therapeutic contexts with adults who have had disruptions to health, challenging their self-concepts and identity due to disability or disfigurement.

Unexpected disruptions to a person's health result in changes to every aspect of one's life. Chiefly, the physical effects of illness mean negotiating the environment with different physical abilities from before the illness, often along with pain and reduced mobility, and levels of independence. Many aspects of life that were once easily achievable and given little thought become laborious, energy-consuming, and challenging. Physical changes can include facial disfiguration, scarring from burns or other wounds, loss of limbs, or changes to mobility necessitating mobility aids. Physical or cognitive changes caused by disease processes or medication can affect communication skills, resulting in changes to expressive speech, receptive or expressive language, and most usually, the ability to engage in social communicative exchanges that were once so simple. Subtle cognitive changes can affect the person's ability to attend to a stimulus, and their skills in memory, planning and executive functioning, perception, or language.

The combination of some or even all of these factors usually means that temporary or permanent care may be required: moving away from support systems and into alien institutionalized environments. The emotional impact of institutional care typically results in anxiety, stress, fear, and confusion, and can cause depression and emotional withdrawal. Ill health can cause disruption to education or work, impacting upon one's capacity to maintain a career or educational trajectory, resulting in loss of income and risks financial hardship and a shift in socioeconomic status. Stigma is, unfortunately, closely linked with acquired ill health and disability, particularly when mental illness is involved. Those with intellectual disabilities and/or mental illness have been consistently found amongst the most socially excluded populations facing substantial health, housing, and employment disparities due to stigma (Ditchman et al., 2013).

34.2 MUSIC AND ITS ROLE IN HEALTH, WELL-BEING, AND IDENTITY

Artistic endeavors have been found to be particularly powerful for people encountering ill health and adversity. Engagement in music-making offers positive experiences that can empower an individual, laying the ground for agency, encompassing feelings of competency, achievement, and mastery (Ruud, 2009). Studies of people with chronic illness who engage in artistic occupations have found such occupations to enable reconnection with a "pre-illness" self, as well as offering opportunities to develop new skills, a sense of achievement and expertise, to be creative, and to promote hopes for the future (Reynolds, 2003; Magee & Davidson, 2004b; Magee, 2007; Burland & Magee, 2013).

Independence and autonomy are essential for maintaining a sense of preferred identity for people living with illness who are faced with increasing dependence and loss of control in everyday life. Interactive music-making challenges self-constructs involving dependency through the emergence of new and undiscovered skills, leading to a sense of "wholeness" of self. For the person living with disrupted health, music-making facilitates experiencing oneself as the agent for change. This is central to the process of music-making in therapeutic contexts. The therapist's goal is for music to increase sense of worth though enhancing feelings of mastery, agency and control, thereby challenging the sense of a "spoiled identity" (Charmaz, 1991).

The role of biography is important as disruptions to health profoundly impact on a sense of self in relation to previous representations of self and of one's function in social roles (Aujoulat, Marcolongo, Bonadiman, & Deccache, 2008). Goal achievement in the domains of physical abilities, social relations, and activity engagement contribute to how people assess their sense of self, contributing to identity reformation. Physical goals enable comparisons between previous abilities with current capabilities; social-relational goals monitor feelings of social isolation and the lack of social ties that are common in episodes of disrupted health; whilst activity goals can highlight a lack of involvement in previously enjoyed activities (Douglas, 2013).

Within the examples that follow, I discuss music-making in therapeutic contexts. Some examples offer illustrations of music therapy sessions, and others are not specifically therapy, but carry therapeutic value. Thus, I will refer to the music activity as "musicing," a term that has been discussed expansively by a number of authors (Small, 1998; DeNora, 2000). I aim to illustrate music as a cultural and social activity in which relationships are explored through the identities we adopt within the act of music-making and the musical relationships that develop. Musical relationships and social identities are in turn influenced by the social contexts in which the musical experience is taking place.

34.3 The role of musicing in shifting self-concepts in complex disability

A number of the studies I have conducted over more than 20 years have illustrated the role that musicing can play in assisting individuals living with chronic ill health to transcend physical boundaries experienced as a consequence of illness, and through the emotional response, experience shifts in identity. In the first study, "Singing my life, playing my self", I worked with a number of people living with complex disabilities stemming from advanced and chronic multiple sclerosis (MS; Magee, 1999a,b, 2002, 2007; Magee and Davidson, 2004a,b). These people were nearly all reliant on wheelchairs to get around, and their physical abilities were challenged to the extent that most of them were completely dependent on others for everyday activities, such as washing, dressing, eating, drinking, smoking, and carrying out any sort of activity that most of us take for granted. Several had difficulty speaking because the motor mechanisms involved in speech were also affected. Several had acquired visual impairments and one person had lost her sight entirely. Most battled with chronic fatigue that is a symptom of MS and some experienced pain through muscle spasms. Most, although not all, of the individuals lived in long-term nursing care due to the complexity of their needs stemming from disabilities. People came to individual music therapy sessions with different personal hopes and goals; some to find a place to "sing their special songs," some to explore musical identities such as by "playing in a band," others because of the sheer boredom of being on a day care unit or nursing home ward all day.

The sessions in the "Singing my life, playing my self" project revolved around live music-making and, if the person wished, reflecting on the music created. Early on, I established with each person a repertoire of favorite songs, which was quickly narrowed down to songs of particular personal meaning. Songs were usually played by me on piano, electric piano, or guitar: I sang the song and usually the person would join in singing, particularly during choruses that I would repeat, extend and extemporize upon so that the most familiar part of the song was extended. Song sheets were not provided as I have found that these can distract a person and take the focus away from the interpersonal experience of making music together. If the person was worried about missing the lyrics, I provided the lyrics through "chunking," or verbal prompts of lyrics just prior to their appearance in the song. Additionally, individuals were encouraged to explore a wide range of pitched and non-pitched percussion instruments, including non-Western frame drums and shakers, an alto metallophone and bass xylophone, woodblocks, standing drums (e.g., conga, tom tom, rotary drum), cymbals, wind chimes, temple bells, and lightweight wind instruments. The guitar, piano, electric piano, and an open stringed autoharp tuned to a tonal chord were also made available for exploration. Instrumental playing usually took the form of co-improvised music that started with exploring sounds, and moved into clinical improvisation, a method widely used in music therapy in which the client and therapist spontaneously generate musical dialogues in mutual partnership (Magee, 2002). Within these dialogues, the therapist pays particular attention to the emotional quality of the client's musical utterances, expressed through variations of elements such as tempo, articulation, dynamics, pitch range, and timbre along with harmony and melody, if the client's instrument allows for this.

34.3.1 The physical experience of musicing

Despite the person's motivation to engage in creative music-making, the first challenge was always trying to find instruments that could meet the person's physical difficulties. These included any combination of:

- Large uncontrolled ataxic movements making playing challenging and many instruments unsafe;
- Muscular weakness and difficulty with hand grasp;
- Limited range of motion;
- Problems with doing repetitive movements due to fatigue and muscle spasm;
- Sensory impairments such as pain and/or visual loss;
- Fine motor problems.

In short, engaging in instrumental playing confronted the person immediately with a physical task, something which most of the participants were challenged with from moment to moment in their everyday lives.

It had never occurred to me that music therapy could be a forum for testing physical boundaries, and yet this is what emerged in the findings of one of the studies (Magee, 1999a,b; Magee & Davidson, 2004b). Considering theories of identity in chronic illness, this might have been anticipated, as identity changes are enforced when the unity between the body and the self is undermined (Charmaz, 1995), and physical goals provide a means for defining self after disruptions to health (Douglas, 2013). Knowledge and interpretation of bodily sensations enhance self-awareness and coping with the emotional stress related to illness (Aujoulet et al., 2008). As improvising involved playing instruments, it was experienced as an intensely physical activity in which individuals tested their physical control, strength and stamina, negotiating this new task and environment with their physical abilities that were unpredictable much of the time. Despite this challenge, all the people involved in this study engaged fully in instrumental playing.

34.3.2 Biography in musicing

As a physical activity, whilst playing an improvisation, individuals engaged in a process of "physical monitoring," a strategy that related to the wider behavior of "illness monitoring" (Magee & Davidson, 2004b). Physical monitoring was noted when clients scrutinized their physical performance, noting subtle changes in different situations, at different times of the day, whilst engaged in different tasks, over periods of days, weeks, months, and years. In this way, they could check the extent of change in their physical performance, helping to increase self-knowledge and awareness. In turn, this increased an individual's sense of internal locus of control. Understanding one's body when dealing with ill health helps to increase self-awareness and coping with the emotional responses to illness (Aujoulet et al., 2008). Furthermore, mutual improvisation involves both leading and following as the parties involved engage in musical play. Thus, improvisation entails both "holding on" and "letting go," aspects of control that are helpful in enhancing insight into one's limits and resources, and facilitate exploration of the different types of self (Aujoulet et al., 2008).

As individuals engaged in physical monitoring, they reflected on their performance, making temporal comparisons to "yesterday," "last week," and "when I first came to music therapy." Taking the body as an object, appraising it, and comparing it with the self in different temporal and situational frameworks in this way has been described as the "dialectical self" (Charmaz, 1991). In so doing, the participants in this study compared their performance at different time points, encompassing feelings of ability, independence, skill, and ownership/creativity. These tended to be negatively or positively weighted around the pivotal concept of control. The more control one felt, the more able, independent, skilled, and greater ownership felt. The less control felt, then feelings of disability, dependence, being unskilled, and loss were expressed.

34.3.3 Performance validation in musicing

Early on in an individual's therapy, it seems that negotiating one's physical boundaries in this new environment is the primary experience. Moving beyond music as a purely physical experience can be difficult when the relationship with the therapist and musical partner is less developed and less trusting. Emotional engagement with the music seems to be secondary, with emotional expression being primarily focussed upon feelings of frustration and a sense of non-achievement. Being engrossed in the music at a purely physical level can make it difficult for the individual to engage with the music as a social activity and at a deeper emotional level. However, with time, the dynamic experience of improvisation provided an arena in which participants could play with different levels of control.

The dialect between "holding on" and "letting go" of control can aid individuals in understanding their limits alongside their resources (Aujoulet et al., 2008). In particular, the experience of relinquishing control can aid a person in exploring different types of self. We might think about this in terms of music-making and in particular, improvised music-making, where the musicians play with leading and following, initiating, imitating and developing. The experience of improvisation provides perfect opportunities for playing with "holding on" and "letting go" of control, thus enabling the player to experience alternative senses of self.

Through the activity of improvisation, where the mutual musical dialogue reflects the emotional qualities of the client's musical utterances, clients literally "sound out" their emotional selves. In doing so, the physical, social, and emotional experience of co-improvised music provides validation of their physical and emotional selves. In mutual music-making the client can feel supported in their attempts to physically interact with the environment. As a shared and mutual activity, my musical contributions to these improvisations framed the individual's physical and emotional self in the musicing, providing the "performance validation" that helps with reintegrating one's identity into a "new concept of wholeness" (Corbin & Strauss, 1987).

34.3.4 Case illustration of agency in therapeutic musicing

The following vignette illustrates this process. Guy was a 31-year-old man who, throughout his 20s, just as he was becoming independent and starting his professional life, had experienced increasingly bewildering symptoms that were finally diagnosed as multiple sclerosis. With a rapid deterioration in his physical and cognitive skills (insight, problem solving, executive functioning), he was first hospitalized due to medical complications, then later discharged to nursing home care. He never returned to his own home being unable to care for himself. When I met him, he was just 29, but fully dependent for all aspects of his daily life due to severe movement disorders. He relied on nursing staff to get him out of bed, wash, dress, eat, drink, and have a smoke. The possibility of an electric wheelchair was ruled out due to his cognitive problems, meaning that he would place himself and others at risk of harm. So he was dependent on others to push his wheelchair if he wanted to escape the ward environment and get out for a bit. His cognitive difficulties caused him many problems as with poor insight, impaired problem solving, and disinhibited behavior, he could not understand why his demands were not responded to more immediately, leaving him frustrated, angry, and often shouting at people around him. He was keen to come to music therapy as he had previously played in a band and wanted to engage in creative activity again. He shared his dream of being able to play in a band again.

However, his physical abilities overwhelmed his experience of improvising. Working with complex disability, it is the music therapist's skill to find instruments that people can access regardless of physical challenges.[1] However, it is also important to provide choice in the range of instruments available, and this can be challenging for someone with movement disorders. Each week we spent time exploring different instruments for him to try, using different positioning in an attempt to enable him to access the instruments and achieve an aesthetically satisfying sound. In his own words: "Well because I can play ... play ... *bash* the drum or something, but I can't really control my hands enough to get a proper rhythm". In a later session he became really frustrated, exclaiming "... but I *can't* play ... I shake like *that* (picking up a maraca and shaking with ataxic arm movements). It's not exactly music is it? To do *that*?" For some weeks, each time he came, he became fully engrossed in trying to play different instruments, but as he monitored his physical behaviors, he evaluated his performance and, due to the lack of control he experienced in the sounds created, evaluated his performance negatively. The outcome was to confirm and increase his "disabled" or "spoiled" identity where he expressed feeling little control, feeling unskilled and having a lack of achievement.

34.3.5 Development in the therapy process: agency and empowerment

We had been working together for 4 months when a breakthrough came for him. By this stage, our relationship had developed musically through the songs from his past that I played for him. As an active listener in the musicing he was transported to other stages of his life in which he was able to experience a past self, someone who could walk, lived independently, and had girlfriends. In this research, it emerged that songs of personal meaning held personal associations spanning an individual's life, including pre-illness stages (Magee & Davidson, 2004a; Magee, 2007). The associative and temporal properties of songs assisted with the biographical work that has been acknowledged as facilitating explorations of past, current and future selves (Magee, 2007). It felt highly significant when individuals spoke of hopes and dreams for the future in connection to their songs, as living with degenerative illness means facing an uncertain future. As Guy explained to me,

> All of my life bends around music. One piece in my head can symbolise somewhere I've been to. With the songs I'm singing parts of my life ... reliving a part of my life. What's in that song for me? ... I don't know ... I like the music. I've got memories to

---

[1] This was prior to the release of the iPad that would have met his needs by providing a number of touch sensitive apps with cool images and sampled sounds giving good quality realistic timbres. We did try some assistive devices linked to software that enabled him to play percussion sounds. However, he experienced the device as a totally disabling experience, a symbol of his disability that only served to reinforce a negative sense of self. So the device was dissatisfying for him and did not meet his aesthetic needs. The use of electronic music technologies to address issues of identity is discussed elsewhere (Burland & Magee, 2014).

it as well … I like to see what comes in the future with it as well. That music will never die for me.

Guy often visited his past self when we played and sung "his" songs, reminiscing of walking, living independently, dating girls, and hanging out with friends. The songs thus served as vehicles to transport him across his life. In this brief extract, he communicated that music helped project into the future and, in this way, his songs helped him maintain hope, in the face of what must have seemed a truly hopeless situation.

Our relationship in his therapy developed as our weekly meetings gave a continuity to his life. Given his increasingly challenging behavior towards others, he had few personal relationships and the relationships with staff were often strained. On this day, I collected him from his ward to take him to the therapy room. He was in a such a state of agitation that it was difficult to understand what he was saying—his voice was raised, he spoke so quickly that his words ran together, not helped by difficulties in speech articulation caused by the side effects of his disease progression. In essence, he was angry and upset that the carers had not got him out of bed, and washed and dressed him when he had asked. His cognitive difficulties prevented any insight into the difficulties of managing a ward full of people and responding to everyone's personal requests, and so his anger and agitation had built steadily over a period of several hours.

In the session, I managed to fix a frame drum upon his wheelchair tray and position this centrally to his body. This physical positioning gave him greater control of one arm that enabled him to "thump" the drum hard with a steady pulse. This contrasted with his usual tremor and uncontrolled sound. Instead, his musical sounds were loud, controlled, regular, and commanding. In response, the music I improvised at the piano was strong, sustained, and with a modal melody and tonality using open octaves in the lower registers of the piano. The music was powerful. However, several minutes in to the improvisation the drum slipped slightly, and in his attempt to secure it, his pulse faltered and became more rapid. In turn, my music moved from sustained chords that had previously been scaffolding his beating, and also became faster using shorter note values, moving register, and changing to shorter articulation. He sustained the faster pulse for a few more minutes, broken by him speaking, which was often the case.

He immediately and spontaneously offered "It sounded good! … I liked it—it was very good music … my beating the tambourine, and your counterpoint music, was very good. A music emblem for that. It seemed *saturnine*." I asked him to clarify what he meant by the word "saturnine." He told me:

It means somebody in charge of everything. Demanding you do things *his* way. You just don't do anything he doesn't want you to do. Well you were playing the bass bits on there—a very very aggressive bass. And me bashing the tambourine as well. That was aggressive … Aggressive music was coming out between the two of us.

Within this extract we can read how control was at the core of his experience in the music. His physical control of his playing freed him to engage to a greater degree in the emotional and social qualities of the musical exchange where I had reflected both the physical and emotional qualities of his playing. He had, literally, "sounded his self" with my contribution acting as a validation of his performance. I asked him what playing the music in this way had meant to him.

> I don't know—after talking about me not being cared for ... and that sort of thing ... it just proved that I can *do* it, you know, and we *did* it—it was pretty good music we did today. Proving I can play pretty good music as well. I wish we could write it up because it was just brilliant music!

Powerlessness is a distressing feeling of insecurity and a threat to one's personal and social identity, where one feels impoverished of internal resources for self-determination (Aujoulet et al., 2008). Control and mastery can be considered indicators of empowerment, particularly when these are expressed within the context of changed physical capabilities (Aujoulet et al., 2008). Guy's vignette illustrates how engaging in musicing can affirm positive self-concepts encompassing skill, achievements, and ownership in the face of loss and powerlessness caused by degenerative illness. His experience of this improvisation countered his experience earlier that day, when he felt an utter hopeless lack of agency in influencing events around him, and in the face of this had experienced unbearable frustration and anger. Music transported him to experience a past sense of self and helped him project to future selves, offering him as sense of control, mastery, empowerment, and hope.

34.4 COMMUNAL SINGING FOR PEOPLE LIVING WITH CHRONIC ILLNESS, THEIR FRIENDS AND CARERS

The people with whom I worked in this previous study lived with very complex needs that isolated them from the external world and the opportunity for experiencing new activities that might challenge existing self-concepts. Thus, it should be of little surprise that the experience of music therapy could transport them in the way described. However, research with individuals who have less severe disabilities and still live at home reflects similar findings. Between 2009 and 2011, I became involved with "Sing for Joy," a group of people who established a choir for people living with ill health of different etiologies, along with their friends and carers.[2] People have become involved in the choir for different reasons. Some bring a friend, partner, or carer, and others come independently. The repertoire sung by this choir spans around 60 years from 1940, and is led

---

[2] Sing for Joy was originally established in, 2001 for people living with Parkinson's disease, but now includes people living with any number of neurological and other diagnoses.

by a musical director and accompanied by a pianist, both of whom are noted jazz performers. A significant part of the choir session involves a vocal warm-up that offers the members a vocal work out for pitch variation and articulation, with particularly complex oral sounds. At least once a year, the choir performs as the main act at a public event that serves as a fundraiser and is an important part of the choir's experience (Temple, Grimes, Benton, & Magee, 2008).

Interested in why they felt so much "better" after singing, Sing for Joy contacted me to see if I could assist with providing evidence from health research to explain these improved feelings of well-being. Although a number of studies existed on therapeutic singing for Parkinson's disease (PD) and communal singing with other populations, there was little published evidence of the sort they were after at that time, which intersected communal singing and PD. Therefore, I suggested that they might consider generating some of their own evidence and offered to help them do this. We pursued a small study in which I became a member of the choir in order to gain a better understanding of the mechanisms of it, for the people involved to determine what it was they wanted to research, and to identify the most appropriate ways of doing this. In particular, the choir were interested in providing information for potential new members as well as for potential funders.

34.4.1 Sing for Joy: a user-led investigation of the effects of communal singing for people with Parkinson's disease

This study functioned more as a feasibility study to explore how the choir engaged with research and what types of data collection methods were manageable, aspects which are important for any research study. We needed to consider people's very differing motivation to be involved, the limited time available, and physical abilities that would affect the sorts of measures we used. Fifteen people chose to be involved, which was 75% of the choir. Some of the people who participated were carers or friends, and thus were not affected directly by the difficulties associated with disease as opposed to the experience of participants who were living with illness. We settled for the Visual Analogue Mood Scale (VAMS: Stern, 1997) as a way of capturing mood states immediately before and after the choir session, as this could be completed independently by all those wishing to be involved. Seven feelings were assessed: afraid, confused, sad, angry, energetic, tired, happy. We gathered a total of 154 completed sets of VAMS before and after choir sessions over a 14-week period, with each participant completing the questionnaire between 8 and 14 times (average 10.2 times). Although we hoped to supplement this quantitative data with qualitative data, time constraints did not allow for collecting, transcribing, and analyzing data. When we looked at changes in mood, we found that choir members responded differently before and after sessions of singing together. It was noted that choristers felt significantly more energetic ($p = 0.024$; mean change = 4.31) and less afraid

(p = 0.007; mean change = −4.28) after singing, and that feelings of sadness and happiness also moved in a positive direction, although they did not reach levels of significance.[3]

These findings are notable in the research that has since emerged with choirs or group music-making in therapeutic contexts with for people with neurological disorders. Elefant, Lotan, Baker, & Skeie (2012b) found that a music therapy group with people with PD that focussed on breathing, vocal, and singing exercises significantly enhanced facial expressions. This is an important finding as facial expressiveness is affected by the disease process in PD. As facial expressions are a central component in social relations with others, communicating not only mood, but responsiveness to others, loss of facial expressiveness can contribute to the growing social isolation faced by people with PD. However, another study by the same group using the same singing protocol found no significant changes for self-reported depressive symptoms in people living with PD who participated in group music therapy (Elefant, Baker, Lotan, Lagesen, & Skeie, 2012a). They felt that the functional focus of the group, which was to improve speech outcomes, may have affected depressive measures. In a choir for people with aphasia following stroke, Tamplin, Baker, Jones, Way, & Lee (2013) used a protocol that focussed on breathing and vocal exercises, and singing songs, with an identified social break, and also used the VAMS that Sing for Joy had used. They found that participants felt less tired after 12 weeks of singing in the choir, but that this was not sustained in a follow up at, 20 weeks when feelings of being tired increased. Most interestingly, this study also found that feelings of "afraid" increased between baseline and week 12, and were sustained to week 20. Although Elefant et al.'s (2012a,b) findings may support the benefit of coming together to sing in a relaxed and social environment for well-being, this cannot explain the findings by Tamplin et al. (2013)

34.4.2 Musicing and temporality, the body and identity

In discussing the findings of their research with the members of Sing for Joy, particularly the significant improvements in feeling less afraid and feeling more energetic, their reflections confirmed some of the ideas put forward in the health sociology models of identity. We measured mood outcomes for a number of pragmatic reasons in addition to the choir's decision that mood was an important outcome.

Considering the findings in the context of theories of identity, however, it seems that the improvements in well-being experienced by choir members can be linked with shifts in identity. Coping with uncertainty of chronic illness, its effects on the body over time and its impact on identity can be an experience filled with "terror" (Wiener & Dodd, 1993). Engaging in activities that lessen uncertainties relating to temporality, body and identity seem to better control feelings of terror and uncertainty (Wiener & Dodd, 1993). Engaging in communal singing offered the members of Sing for Joy an activity for connecting with others and feeling a sense of "belonging," aspects that help individuals

[3] Acknowledgement to Paul Seed for his role with the statistical analysis and Rita Monoori for her role in data collection in this research.

to feel in touch with something greater than everyday life and can transport people to being outside of themselves (Ruud, 1997). The experience of music is also associated with bodily reactions of feeling full of and energy and power (Ruud, 1997). Sing for Joy's weekly sessions offered activity that was physical, creative and, through the use of songs, carried associations from across participants' lives and thus related to temporality. All of these aspects—temporality, body and identity—can be understood to have improved feelings of control of terror and uncertainty associated with chronic illness. Living with fear limits how one is able to engage fully in life, affecting one's capability to how one feels about oneself, to social interactions and to mood in general.

34.5 MUSIC AND IDENTITY IN ACUTE ILLNESS AND REHABILITATION

In a more recent study, I interviewed people who had been in therapy following trauma or diagnoses of life-threatening illness that required periods of acute hospitalization, intensive treatment and rehabilitation (Magee, 2013). The nature of these types of inter-ruptions to health differ qualitatively from people who are diagnosed with chronic degenerative diseases such as those already discussed. Many medical conditions require surgical and treatment regimes with long periods of hospitalization, possibly with peri-ods of isolation for reasons of infection control. Traumatic events are sudden and life changing. The range of possible traumas are too numerous to list here, but in addition to the physical effects of the trauma, the person is left psychologically traumatized from the sudden shock of the event. The people I interviewed were several years post-diagnosis/ trauma and so were some way along in their journey of emotionally processing their trauma. I was particularly interested in their uses of electronic music technologies in their rehabilitation. However, each person discussed music therapy more generally and its impact on their life. For reasons of confidentiality, I have used people's participant reference numbers, rather than their names.

In the following extract, we read the experience of a man in his early 20s who was left quadriplegic following an accident. He discusses his slowly-acquired skills of using music software for composition that he has been working on in therapy. Previously, he had been an instrumentalist, a leisure activity that provided social opportunities. However, his physical abilities can no longer support this. We can read the painstaking effort of manipulating an assistive device to operate the mouse in his music therapy ses-sions, including reference to temporal aspects, such as "now," "what I used to do," and "years before my accident" and also how his precise knowledge of his body's capabilities directs how he engages with his environment.[4]

---

[4] Electronic music technologies enable people with profound physical impairments to achieve agency in music making when acoustic instruments are not responsive. See Magee (2013) for comprehensive examples.

In so many different aspects, physically using them now, it just helps me build strength. Just holding my arm in that position … I grew up on PCs and Mac … now even using my wrist in a different way instead of using my finger to push on the button. So it has me working that muscle differently than what I normally used to do, using a keyboard. My trunk control is limited and I sometimes have to move over to the side to get my finger to a certain point and then use my other hand to force … And sometimes, I even try to come back over without using my other support or I use my other arm to support. Mentally it just gives me—it brings me back to a place that I used to be before my accident, years before my accident when I was still in High School and I used to make music so that brings back a different kind of state of being and it forms different … I guess its different endorphins go off in my head it's kind of what happens. I definitely, I feel more at ease after a good session.

Participant #64.

In his reflections on his music therapy sessions, we can read how musicing provides the forum for him to engage in biographical work, exploring past and current selves, with particular focus on his body and physical self. Corbin & Strauss (1987) note that dimensions of biography include conceptions of the self; biographical time incorporating past, present, and future; and the body, the medium through which identity is formed. Could this reworking be achieved similarly with other activities? Possibly, however, it is his past identity as a musician that is the central component of this reflection. He tries to articulate the "different state of being" that his music therapy sessions trigger. We might wonder whether in his reworking of his self-concepts, some hope for the future is engendered as he gains a sense of sense of mastery-over-disability, thus developing a "future" self, which is seen as "more than one's body and the illness within it" (Charmaz, 1995 p. 671).

34.5.1 The impact of traumatically acquired disabilities on self-concepts

Living with disfigurement and disability acquired through a sudden traumatic event can be devastating. Difficulties related to negative self-perceptions and with social interaction are most frequently reported by people who are visibly different, including unfavorable self-perceptions (Rumsey & Harcourt, 2004). Although some individuals find ways of coping effectively, responses from others in social interactions can be full of uncertainties about how the person who is not disfigured should behave, including the desire to minimize embarrassment to him/herself and to the person with disfigurement (Rumsey & Harcourt, 2004). Self-doubt and low self-esteem can result from such social encounters. Social avoidance is one coping strategy, although ironically, greater social support is a factor influencing adjustment. Engaging in prior leisure interests and occupations might be more difficult due to social withdrawal or changes caused by ill health, affecting levels of independence and/or social issues. Hopes and dreams for the future can seem destroyed on many fronts, but none more so than developing new or maintaining existing intimate relationships. Negative perceptions and reactions of others can make it difficult for the person who has acquired a disability to maintain his or her identity, particularly if there is stigma and negativity associated with the condition (MacRae, 2011).

Maintaining hope for the future becomes a central therapeutic concern. The more meaning, hope and sense of direction an individual living with illness has, the more likely they are to be able to problem-solve/plan and become more actively involved in their own recovery (Buckley-Walker, Crowe, & Caputi, 2010). Hope in particular is important as it has been linked with agency (Lindström, Sjöström, & Lindberg, 2013) and involves being able to envisage a different future, one where the individual has survived current adversities. Theories of "possible selves" (Markus & Nurius, 1986) are applicable to maintaining hope during interruptions to health, where illness demands a changed way of being in the world. Concepts of "possible self" are based on past representations of the self, and although different to the current self, are connected to it (Markus & Nurius, 1986). Increased identification with one's "ideal self" reflects increased hopefulness in terms of recovery (Buckley-Walker et al., 2010). It seems that identifying to a greater degree with ideal images of "self" may increase hopefulness and improve the capacity to identify ways of meeting goals for a person with serious health difficulties. Improving one's capacity to meet goals increases agency and self-determination and this, in turn, can influence recovery (Buckley-Walker et al., 2010).

34.5.2 Musical identities for transition and building hope

As part of my most recent study, I met a man who was living with permanent disfiguring disabilities after a violent attack that left him for dead. He will be dependent on others for the rest of his life for all simple daily tasks, although, following a long period of rehabilitation had started to carve out a new life through education and hopes for a career. In his reflections on his music therapy that involved song-writing, and recording performances of his and others' songs, he describes how he questioned his existence in light of his new physical self and the hopelessness and uncertainties that surrounded him. He also discusses how music offered him hope.

> I was someone who questioning my own ability to function in the world, so therefore I felt like I wasn't functioning. I wasn't necessarily critical of my singing and ... it wasn't something that I was concerned with. I was more concerned with independence and the daily living and being home, whatever home was, because I was homeless at the time. So the initial song Moving On was ... it was just so spot on, you know. So now I'm in touch with my hope ... that's kind of what it was; got me in touch with some kind of promise of something. And I mean, it only served me that way because of the place that I was in at that time, which was just a lot of uncertainty. In those early times it really gave me a lot of hope, and maybe more hope than I realised at the

time, you know. But then I began to look forward to the music therapy and always was just excited about hearing my voice back.

Participant #68.

Homeless, hospitalized, and completely dependent, musicing provided him a sense of agency, control, and a means of experiencing alternative, possible selves. This was key in his rehabilitation—a way to understand that he could be something different from the damaged and disfigured person he had been left by the attack. Through the agency enabled by composing and singing he was able to perceive a future self.

It was a vehicle for me to ride in and see what was going on. And it really created some optimism about the future. (Music) sort of, animates it ... gives it a character, a personality, an identity you can identify. I was able to identify my desire to go on. Very helpful to hear it back. It gives life and it gives it an existence where it didn't have an actual existence before; It's something about hearing it in the song that, sort of, gave it life, gave it colour, gave it animation, you know, and then it became more of a reality. It's not just a song, it's like my only hope, you know? It wasn't like I was rejecting pessimism, it was just optimism, you know, it was there, you know, and it came out in these songs.

Participant #68.

Helplessness results in lesser feelings of control as the individual struggles to gain an external locus of control. The interface of control and action is the sense of agency. Agency means, in a general sense, the capacity to act (Lindström et al., 2013), to be the cause of events (Laukka, 2007) or be an agent within activity, having the ability to influence the events within that activity. People who are dependent upon others and have low control over their lives, for reasons that might include being in care, are at risk of becoming deprived of personal agency, something that is linked to having limited social interaction, and poor health and well-being (Laukka, 2007; Lindström et al., 2013). Agency is an important component within identity reconstitution as it relates to how a person feels about being able influence and change their lives, move away from a state of helplessness and, through making choices, hold a position of power and control over the outcomes of one's life. Mastery is intrinsically linked to control, being the sense where one feels an internal locus of control and that unfolding life events are self-directed (Bailey & Davidson, 2005).

And I set a tone for myself to the kind of songs that I was going to make, that it wasn't about love songs and try to delve into all this personal things. Because I had this feeling, that my story was about everybody, that my survival was about all of us, that it really spoke about what we could all be. What we still want to do, is go into a studio and actually produce these songs, because it feels like these songs are tangible evidence of that inspiration. I think it comes out in the songs, I think it comes out in my singing and the phrasing of the songs and it's all communication, you know. So it's more about communication and conveying certain feelings, you know, because not every feeling has words, you know, that get it across, you know, at that very moment.

Participant #68.

Singing afforded him the physical and emotional act of his music, with his music therapist providing the force for social interaction, and thus, performance validation. The act of song-writing in music therapy provided a forum for control and decision-making, determining the themes of his songs, giving him purpose and allowing him to use his personal experience for others.

34.6 Conclusions

The material presented in this chapter illustrates how the emotional responses to interruptions to health are neither static nor unidimensional. Responses to illness change over time and in response to situations as required. Thus, there are several interrelated factors that need to be kept in mind when working with people struggling to maintain or rework their identity due to periods of ill health and acquired disabilities. These include feelings of powerlessness; the struggle to gain control; the need for agency; and opportunities for experiencing mastery. For people living with chronic illness or disability, engaging in biographical work enables multiple reviews of one's life through imagery, which reworks the past, examines the present, and projects into the future. Biographical work means exploring past, current and future selves, and is an important part of reworking self-concepts, as the major dimensions of biography include conceptions of the self; biographical time incorporating past, present, and future; and the body, the medium through which identity is formed (Corbin & Strauss, 1987). Forums for social engagement are important for providing performance validation that reaffirms the individual's shifting sense of self.

Musicing within therapeutic contexts provides a creative medium that intersects the marriage of the physical, emotional and social selves. This happens within a supportive environment with performance validation offered by the therapist. It enables agency through exploring control, the ability to influence outcomes, and counter feelings of helplessness. Music is a temporal medium that enables the individual to journey through past, current and future selves. In this way, individuals can explore new and possible selves in order to maintain hope for a future and preferred self, and achieve reconstituted identity.

References

Aujoulat, I., Marcolongo, R., Bonadiman, L., & Deccache, A. (2008). Reconsidering patient empowerment in chronic illness: a critique of models of self-efficacy and bodily control. *Social Science & Medicine*, 66(5), 1228–39.

Bailey, B.A. & Davidson, J.W. (2005). Effects of group singing and performance for marginalized and middle-class singers. *Psychology of Music*, 33(3), 269–303.

Buckley-Walker, K., Crowe, T., & Caputi, P. (2010). Exploring identity within the recovery process of people with serious mental illnesses. *Psychiatric Rehabilitation Journal*, 33(3), 219–27.

Burland, K. & Magee, W.L. (2013). Music technology in therapy and its relevance to identity. In: W.L. Magee (Ed.) *Music technology in therapeutic and health settings*, pp. 327–48. London: Jessica Kingsley Publishers.

Burland, K. & Magee, W.L. (2014). Developing identities using music technology in therapeutic settings. *Psychology of Music*, 42(2), 177–89.

Charmaz, K. (1991). *Good days, bad days. The self in chronic illness and time*. New Brunswick, NJ: Rutgers University Press.

Charmaz, K. (1995). The body, identity, and self: adapting to impairment. *Sociological Quarterly*, 36 (4), 657–80.

Corbin, J. & Strauss, A. (1987). Accompaniments of chronic illness: changes in body, self, biography, and biographical time. In: J. Roth & P. Conrad (Eds.) *Research in the sociology of health care: a research annual. The experience and management of chronic illness*, Vol. 6, 249–81. London: JAI Press Inc.

DeNora, T. (2000). *Music in everyday life*. Cambridge: Cambridge University Press.

Ditchman, N., Werner, S., Kosyluk, K., Jones, N., Elg, B., & Corrigan, P.W. (2013). Stigma and intellectual disability: potential application of mental illness research. *Rehabilitation Psychology*, 58(2), 206–16.

Douglas, J.M. (2013). Conceptualizing self and maintaining social connection following severe traumatic brain injury. *Brain Injury*, 27(1), 60–74.

Elefant, C., Baker, F.A., Lotan, M., Lagesen, S.K., & Skeie, G.O. (2012a). The effect of group music therapy on mood, speech, and singing in individuals with Parkinson's disease—a feasibility study. *Journal of Music Therapy*, 49(3), 278–302.

Elefant, C., Lotan, M., Baker, F.A., & Skeie, G.O. (2012b). Effects of music therapy on facial expression of individuals with Parkinson's disease: a pilot study. *Musicae Scientiae*, 16(3), 392–400.

Laukka, P. (2007). Uses of music and psychological well-being among the elderly. *Journal of Happiness Studies*, 8(2), 215–41.

Lindström, M., Sjöström, S., & Lindberg, M. (2013). Stories of rediscovering agency: Home-based occupational therapy for people with severe psychiatric disability. *Qualitative Health Research*, 23(6), 728–40.

MacRae, H. (2011). Self and other: the importance of social interaction and social relationships in shaping the experience of early-stage Alzheimer's disease. *Journal of Aging Studies*, 25(4), 445–56.

Magee, W. (1999a). Music therapy in chronic degenerative illness: reflecting the dynamic sense of self. In: D. Aldridge (Ed.) *Music therapy in palliative care*, pp. 82–94. London: Jessica Kingsley Publishers.

Magee, W. (1999b). "Singing my life, playing my self". Music therapy in the treatment of chronic neurological illness. In: T. Wigram, & J. De Backer (Eds.) *Clinical applications of music therapy in developmental disability, pediatrics and neurology*, pp. 201–23. London: Jessica Kingsley Publishers.

Magee, W.L. (2002). Identity in clinical music therapy: shifting self-constructs through the therapeutic process. In: R. MacDonald, D.J. Hargreaves, & D. Miell (Eds.) *Musical identities*, pp. 179–97. Oxford: Oxford University Press.

Magee, W.L. (2007). A comparison between the use of songs and improvisation in music therapy with adults living with acquired and chronic illness. *Australian Journal of Music Therapy*,
18, 20–38

Magee, W.L. (Ed.) (2013). *Music technology in therapeutic and health settings*. London: Jessica
Kingsley.

Magee, W.L. & Davidson, J.W. (2004a). Singing in therapy: monitoring disease process in
chronic degenerative illness. *British Journal of Music Therapy*, 18(2), 65–77.

Magee, W.L. & Davidson, J.W. (2004b). Music therapy in multiple sclerosis: results of a systematic qualitative analysis. *Music Therapy Perspectives*, 22(1), 39–51.

Markus, H. & Nurius, P. (1986). Possible selves. *American Psychologist*, 41(9), 954–69.

Reynolds, F. (2003). Reclaiming a positive identity in chronic illness through artistic occupation. *Occupation, Participation and Health*, 23(3), 118–27.

Rumsey, N. & Harcourt, D. (2004). Body image and disfigurement: issues and interventions.
Body Image, 1(1), 83–97.

Ruud, E. (1997). Music and the quality of life. *Nordisk Tidskrift for Musikkterapi—Nordic
Journal of Music Therapy*, 6(2), 86–97.

Ruud, E. (2009). Music and identity. *Nordisk Tidskrift for Musikkterapi—Nordic Journal of
Music Therapy*, 6(1), 3–13.

Small, C. (1998). *Musicking: the meanings of performing and listening*. Middletown,
CT: Wesleyan University Press.

Stern, R.A. (1997). *Visual Analog Mood Scale: Professional manual*. Odessa, FL: Psychological
Assessment Resources, Inc.

Tamplin, J., Baker, F.A., Jones, B., Way, A., & Lee, S. (2013). "Stroke a chord": the effect of singing in a community choir on mood and social engagement for people living with aphasia
following a stroke. *Neurorehabilitation*, 32(4), 929–41.

Temple, N., Grimes, C., Benton, S., & Magee, W.L. (2008). Sing for Joy: making the best of
chronic and degenerative illnesses through voice work and becoming part of a new singing community. In: *Programme, Music and Health: Current Developments in Research and
Practice*, Sidney de Haan Research Centre for Arts and Health, Folkstone, September, 2008,
p. 28.

Wiener, C.L. & Dodd, M.J. (1993). Coping amid uncertainty: an illness trajectory perspective.
Scholarly Inquiry for Nursing Practice, 7(1), 17–31.

CHAPTER 35

IDENTITY AND MUSICAL DEVELOPMENT IN PEOPLE WITH SEVERE OR PROFOUND AND MULTIPLE LEARNING DIFFICULTIES

ADAM OCKELFORD AND JOHN VORHAUS

35.1 INTRODUCTION

WHAT can we learn about someone's identity from their capacity to engage with music? In this chapter we examine the relationship between identity and musical engagement on the part of children and young people with either severe learning difficulties (SLD) or profound and multiple learning difficulties (PMLD). We consider identity as it relates to a sense of self, we look at the concept of a "musical identity," and we draw some distinctions that are applied to six children engaging in a range of musical activities.

There are many terms in common parlance that purport to refer to the self, and an abundance of theories that seek to account for its existence. Philosophers, psychologists, neuroscientists, and cognitive scientists each have an array of rival candidates, and, beyond the most minimal claims, each is the subject of ongoing debate. No one, or almost no one,[1] doubts whether individual people exist. However, whether we should also allow that we possess or are even conscious of a self, and how this is related to our identity, remain keenly contested questions. These largely fall into three categories: there is a *phenomenological* question concerning what exactly we are aware of, or conscious of, or have experience of in relation to a self; there is an *epistemological* question of how we arrive at any knowledge of or about the self, whether that self is ours or somebody else's; and there is a *metaphysical* question about what there *is*, in the way of a self, and how the self is related to our experience.

---

[1] Perhaps there are solipsists who mean what they say, but that is a subject for another paper.

These questions are always difficult, but some aspects are especially problematic in the context of those with SLD and PMLD. This is because such people are unable to speak about these subjects for themselves. That is one reason for exploring their engagement with music, which may enable them both to communicate and to develop a musical identity in the absence of verbal language.

In a previous paper, Ockelford & Welch (2012) made reference to Gallagher's (2000) suggestion that philosophical conceptions of the self can be divided into two groups, according to whether they tend towards either a "minimal" or a "narrative" self. We will return to this distinction and draw attention to a number of questions that arise in relation to conceptions of the self, and how these are manifested in musical engagement. In section 2, we introduce the *Sounds of Intent* project, and in section 3 we show how the music-developmental framework that it sets out is related to various stages in the evolution of the sense of self, illustrating our argument with evidence from six case studies.

35.2 THE *SOUNDS OF INTENT* PROJECT

The *Sounds of Intent* project was set up in 2002 as a joint venture by the University of Roehampton and the Institute of Education, London. The aim was to map the musical development of children and young people with learning difficulties, an aspiration that has now been achieved following research over a number of years (see, for example, Ockelford, Welch, Zimmermann and Himonides, 2005; Welch, Ockelford, Carter, Zimmermann, & Himonides, 2009; Cheng, Ockelford, & Welch, 2010; Ockelford & Matawa, 2010; Ockelford, Welch, Jewell-Gore, Cheng, Vogaitzoglou, & Himonides, 2011). In the absence of pre-existing data or theories, the *Sounds of Intent* team adopted an empirical approach to exploring what musical development in young people with SLD or PMLD might mean. Working with a group of practitioners who were active in the field, principally music teachers and therapists, the research team developed shared interpretations of the different forms and levels of musical engagement that they observed among their pupils and clients. The children's responses, actions and interactions were encapsulated in short descriptions, such as those shown in Table 35.1.

Examples such as these showed that musical development could not be conceptualized in terms of a single dimension, since (for example) an individual's capacity for attending to sounds may well be greater than her or his ability to produce them. Therefore, at least two dimensions were required, and these were conceived as "listening and responding," for which the term "reactive" ("R") was used, and "causing, creating and controlling," for which the label "proactive" ("P") was adopted. In Table 35.1, observations 1, 2, 4, 7, 8, 10, 15, 18, 22, 23, 24, and 26 were considered to be entirely or predominantly "reactive" and 2, 5, 6, 13, 16, 17, and 23, "proactive." This left other observations (as in examples 3, 9, 11, 12, 14, 19, 20, 21, and 25), in which listening to sounds or making them occurred in the context of musical participation with others. It seemed that this form of activity merited the status of a distinct dimension, which was termed "interactive" ("I"). While the three dimensions are not entirely discrete, the crucial thing was

Table 35.1 Observations of musical engagement by children and young people with PMLD (after Ockelford et al., 2011).

#	Observation	R	P	I
1	A sits motionless in her chair. Her teacher approaches and plays a cymbal with a soft beater, gently at first, and then more loudly, in front of her and then near to each ear. A does not appear to react.	✓		
2	R is lying in the "Little Room" a small, resonant environment, with soundmakers suspended within easy reach, vocalizing in an almost constant drone. Occasionally a sudden movement of her right arm knocks her hand against a bell. Each time, she smiles and her vocalizing briefly turns into a laugh.	✓	✓	
3	M's music therapy session begins—as ever—with the "Hello" song. And as ever, he makes no discernible response.			✓
4	B startles and then smiles when someone drops a tray of cutlery in the dining room.	✓		
5	T brushes her left hand against the strings of guitar that someone is holding near to her. There is a pause and then she raises her hand and brushes the strings again, and then again.		✓	
6	Y usually makes a rasping sound as he breathes. He seems to be unaware of what he is doing, and the rasping persists, irrespective of external stimulation. His class teacher has tried to see whether Y can be made aware of his sounds by making them louder (using a microphone, amplifier, and speakers), but so far this approach has met with no response.		✓	
7	G's teacher notices that he often turns his head towards her when she sings to him, but she has never noticed him turn towards other sounds.	✓		
8	W giggles when people repeat patterns of syllables to her such as "ma ma ma ma ma," "da da da da da," or "ba ha ba ba ba."	✓		
9	J's short, sharp vocalizations are interpreted by his teachers and carers to mean that he wants someone to vocalize back.			✓
10	K gets very excited when she hears the regular beat on the school's drum machine.	✓		
11	U loves "call and response" games and joins in by making his own sounds.			✓
12	C copies simple patterns of vocalization—imitating the ups and downs of her speech and language therapist's voice.			✓

Table 35.1 Continued

#	Observation	R	P	I
13	S waves her hand more and more vigorously through an ultrasonic beam, creating an ever wider range of swirling sounds.		✓	
14	N often vocalizes in response to vocal sounds that are made close to him, although he does not seem to copy what he hears.			✓
15	Z loves the sound of the bell tree and, when it stops, she rocks in her chair' which staff interpret as a gesture for "more."	✓		
16	D has been able to make a wide range of vocal sounds since he started school, but recently he has begun to make more melodious vowel sounds, which he repeats in short sequences.		✓	
17	L hums distinct patterns of notes and repeats them. Her favorite pattern sounds rather like a playground chant, and her music teacher notices that she repeats it from one day to the next, though not always starting on the same note.		✓	
18	F cries whenever she hears the "goodbye" song. It only takes the first two or three notes to be played on the keyboard for her to experience a strong emotional reaction.	✓		
19	H enjoys copying simple rhythms on an untuned percussion instrument. Now he is started making his own rhythms up too, and he flaps his hands with delight when someone else copies what he is doing.			✓
20	E just laughs and laughs when people imitate her vocalizations.			✓
21	V vocalizes to get his therapist to make a sound—it does not matter what, he just seems to relish having a vocal response.			✓
22	I always gets excited in the middle of the "Slowly/Quickly" song, anticipating the sudden change of pace.	✓		
23	O scratches the tambourine, making a range of sounds. Whenever he plays near the rim and the bells jingle, he smiles.	✓	✓	
24	Q eye movements intensify when he hears the big band play.	✓		
25	X distinctly tries to copy high notes and low notes in vocal interaction sessions.			✓
26	P has learnt to associate his teacher's jangly bracelet, which she always wears, with her: for him, it seems to be an important part of her identity.	✓		

that the conceptualization was deemed by practitioners to be meaningful in terms of categorizing the types of musical engagement that they observed.

A number of attempts were made to place examples such as those shown in Table 35.1 along each of the three dimensions that had been identified:

- *Reactive* (in response to another).
- *Proactive* (initiating behavior without an obvious external prompt).
- *Interactive* (with another).

The location of the examples within a dimension was based on contingency, where each was identified as a necessary precursor or possible successor to another. For instance, it was clear that an awareness of sound (Example 2) must precede a differentiated response (Example 7), which in turn must precede the capacity to anticipate change (Example 22). This heuristic approach was necessary since the available evidence largely comprised observations of *different* children at various stages of development, rather than longitudinal data on the *same* children as they matured. Taking this exploratory tack was, however, deemed valid as a preliminary step, since it was believed that longitudinal studies of children with PMLD would be likely to last for several years at least. It was felt, though, that once an initial model had been developed, this could be used to inform longer-term empirical work.

Different configurations of the *Sounds of Intent* model were proposed and systematically trialed in the field. Practitioners offered feedback, which allowed the research team to refine the model, enabling it to capture a wider range of musical behaviors, and enhancing intra- and inter-domain consistency (Welch et al., 2009). Eventually, six levels of music-processing capacity emerged; see Table 35.2.

Table 35.2 The six levels of the *Sounds of Intent* framework (acronym "CIRCLE").

Level	Description	Core cognitive abilities
1	Confusion and chaos	None: no awareness of sound as a distinct perceptual entity
2	Awareness and intentionality	An emerging awareness of sound as a distinct perceptual entity and of the variety that is possible within the domain of sound
3	Relationships, repetition, regularity	A growing awareness of the possibility and significance of **relationships** between the basic aspects of sounds
4	Sounds forming clusters	An evolving perception of **groups** of sounds, and the relationships that may exist between them
5	Deeper structural links	A growing recognition of whole pieces, and of the **frameworks** of pitch and perceived time that lie behind them
6	Mature artistic expression	A developing awareness of the culturally determined "emotional syntax" of performance that articulates the "narrative metaphor" of pieces

Placing these six levels across the three domains of musical engagement that had been identified gave rise to 18 "level descriptors" of reactivity, proactivity, and interactivity. Visually, these were arranged as segments in circular form, which the practitioners on the *Sounds of Intent* team regarded as being an appropriate metaphor for children's development, ranging from the center, with its focus on self, outwards, to increasingly wider communities of others.

For ease of reference, levels were ranked from 1 to 6, each of which could be preceded with an "R," a "P," or an "I," to indicate, respectively, reactive, proactive, or interactive segments. Each was broken down into four more detailed "elements," as the examples in Table 35.3 show.

Table 35.3 Elements at levels 1–3 in the reactive, proactive, and interactive domains.

Level	R.1	R.2	R.3
REACTIVE DOMAIN			
Descriptor	encounters sounds	shows an emerging awareness of sound	responds to simple patterns in sound
Element A	is exposed to a rich variety of sounds	shows awareness (of a variety) of sounds	responds to the repetition of sounds
Element B	is exposed to a wide range of music	responds differently to sound qualities that differ (e.g. loud/ quiet), and/or change (e.g. getting louder)	responds to a regular beat
Element C	is exposed to music in different contexts	responds to sounds increasingly independently of context	responds to patterns of regular change
Element D	is exposed to sounds that are linked to other sensory input	responds to sounds that are linked to other sensory input	responds to sounds used to symbolize other things
Level	P.1	P.2	P.3
PROACTIVE DOMAIN			
Descriptor	makes sounds unknowingly	makes or controls sounds intentionally	makes simple patterns in sound intentionally
Element A	sounds made by life-processes are enhanced and/or involuntary movements are used to make sounds	makes sounds intentionally, through increasing variety of means and with greater range and control	intentionally makes simple patterns through repetition

(continued)

Table 35.3 Continued

Element B	sounds are made or controlled through co-active movements	expresses feelings through sound	intentionally makes a regular beat
Element C	activities to promote sound production occur in a range of contexts	produces sounds intentionally in a range of contexts	intentionally makes patterns through change; uses sound to symbolize other things
Element D	activities to promote sound production are multisensory in nature	produces sounds as part of multisensory activity	
Level	1.1	I.2	I.3
INTERACTIVE DOMAIN			
Descriptor	relates unwittingly through sound	interacts with others using sound	interacts imitating others' sounds or through recognizing self being imitated
Element A	co-workers stimulate interaction by prompting with sounds and responding to any sounds that are made	sounds made by another stimulate a response in sound	imitates the sounds made by another
Element B	co-workers model interaction through sound	sounds are made to stimulate a response in sound	shows awareness of own sounds being imitated
Element C	activity to promote interaction through sound occurs in a range of contexts	interactions occur increasingly independently of context	imitates simple patterns in sound made by another
Element D	some interaction is multisensory in nature	interaction through sound engages other senses too	recognizes own patterns in sound being imitated

35.3 RELATING THE *SOUNDS OF INTENT* FRAMEWORK TO A SENSE OF SELF

35.3.1 The *Sounds of Intent* framework

Although the *Sounds of Intent* project focussed on children's evolving capacities to engage with music, these cannot be separated from wider cognitive, emotional, and social development. Indeed, there is a substantial body of research indicating that music is

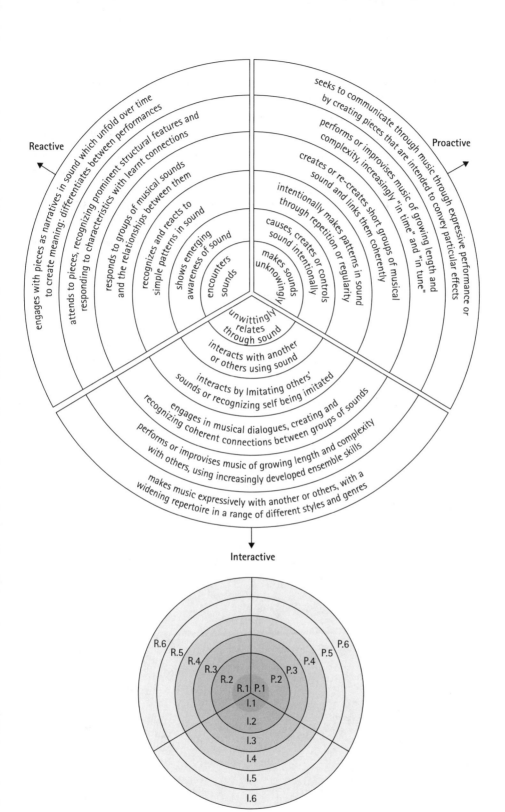

FIG. 35.1 The *Sounds of Intent* framework.

typically a key element in one's maturing sense of intrapersonal and interpersonal identity (MacDonald, Hargreaves, & Miell, 2002). Hence, it should be possible to relate conceptions of the self to the six *Sounds of Intent* levels of musical development. We will approach the issue first by setting out a theoretical connection between the *Sounds of Intent* framework (Fig. 35.1) and an evolving sense of self, before introducing Gallagher's notions of "minimal" and "narrative" selves, a number of philosophical questions that this distinction raises, and a series of case studies designed to illustrate the model that is proposed.

First, we consider how the *Sounds of Intent* levels relate more widely to early communication, since this will offer a broader context for what is proposed. Ockelford (2002) sets out a four-phase model of the development of expressive communication, which is reproduced in simplified form here, with the addition of a fifth stage, pertaining to pragmatics (see Table 35.4).

These five phases can be mapped onto the six *Sounds of Intent* levels as shown in Table 35.5 (cf. Ockelford, 2008, p. 132).

To consider how this composite developmental map may relate to an evolving self we can refer to Gallagher's distinction between the *minimal* self, considered as "a consciousness of oneself as an immediate subject of experience, unextended in time," and the *narrative* self, considered as "self-image that is constituted with a past and a future in the various stories that we and others tell about ourselves" (2000, p. 150). We can initially elaborate on this distinction as follows (see Table 35.6).

Table 35.6 offers an interpretation of Gallagher's "minimal" and "narrative" selves in terms of perception and cognition, perceived temporal status and symbolic representation. By drawing together the elements of Table 35.5 and Table 35.6 we might surmise that musical development and growing self-awareness can evolve together along the following lines (see Table 35.7).

Table 35.4 Model of the development of early communication (after Ockelford, 2002).

type and phase of expressive communication	vocal	gestural / visual (person-based)	gestural / visual (externally based)
non-intentional	cries in response to need	for example arches back in displeasure	looks at things
intentional	deliberately vocalizes to show need	for example extends arm to attract attention	points to things
symbolic	makes personal utterances: for example says "mmm" meaning "hairdrier"	makes personal signs: for example flaps hand for "yes"	points at pictures draws
formal	speaks (using words)	uses conventional signs	points at symbols or words writes
pragmatic	uses language (irrespective of domain) with appropriate contextual meaings		

Table 35.5 *Sounds of Intent* levels mapped onto the model of early expressive communication.

phase of expressive communication	*corresponding* Sounds of Intent *proactive levels*	*corresponding* Sounds of Intent *interactive levels*
non-intentional	P.1 makes sounds unknowingly	1.1 unwittingly relates through sound
intentional	P.2 causes, creates, or controls sound intentionally	1.2 interacts with another or other's using sound
symbolic	P.3 intentionally makes patterns in sound through repetition or regularity	1.3 interacts by imitating other's sounds or recognizing self being imitated
	P.4 creates or re-creates short groups of musical sounds and links them coherently	1.4 engages in musical dialogues, creating and recognizing coherent connections between groups of sounds
formal	P.5 performs or improvises music of growing length and complexity, increasingly "in time" and "in tune"	1.5 performs or improvises music of growing length and complexity with others, using increasingly developed ensemble skills
pragmatic	P.6 seeks to communicate through music through expressive performance or by creating pieces that are intended to convey particular effects	1.6 makes music expressively with another or others, with a widening repertoire in a range of different styles and genres

Table 35.6 Initial elaboration of Gallagher's "minimal" and "narrative" sense of self

Domain	Minimal self	Narrative self
Perceptual/cognitive processing	Pure sensation (perceptual) Phenomenally conscious	Interpretation of sensations (Cognitive) consciousness of self
Temporal status	Awareness of perceived present	Awareness of past, present, and future
Symbolic representation	No	Yes, can take the form of language

Table 35.7 Parallels between stages of musical development and an evolving sense of self (cf. Tables 35.2 and 35.5).

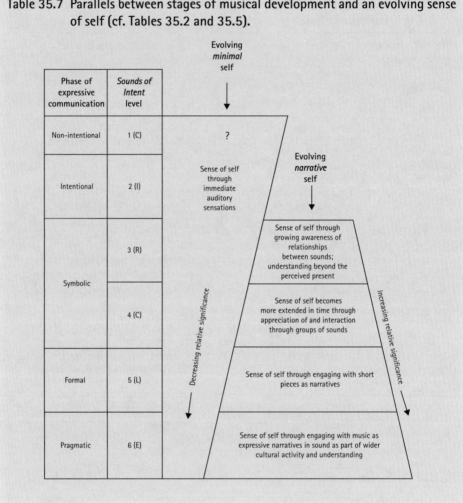

We can now elaborate on conceptions of the minimal and narrative self, while also exploring how the frameworks introduced in this section can be used to illustrate the relationship between musical engagement and self-development. In the sections that follow we introduce six case studies, each considered in relation to one of the six levels that together comprise the *Sounds of Intent* framework.

35.3.2 The "minimal" self: consciousness and self-consciousness

Gallagher (2000) conceives the minimal self phenomenologically:

> that is, in terms of how one experiences it, a consciousness of oneself as an immediate subject of experience, unextended in time ... Even if all of the unessential features

of self are stripped away, we still have an intuition that there is a basic, immediate, or primitive "something" that we are willing to call a self.

Gallagher, 2000, p. 15.
Reprinted from *Trends in Cognitive Science*, 4(1),
Gallagher, S., Philosophical conceptions of self:
implications for cognitive science, pp. 14– 21,
© 2000, with permission from Elsevier

The minimal self is characterized here in terms of phenomenal consciousness— consciousness of oneself as an immediate subject of experience. Bayne distinguishes between *phenomenal states* and *phenomenally conscious creatures*:

A phenomenal state is a state that there is something it is like to be in. Phenomenal states are individuated in terms of their phenomenal character—that is, in terms of what it is like to be in them. There is something it is like to hear a siren sound … to see a field of daffodils in spring … to smell freshly brewed coffee … A phenomenally conscious creature is a creature that there is something it is like to be. Phenomenally conscious creatures, and only phenomenally conscious creatures, have a phenomenal perspective.

Bayne, 2007, p. 1.
Text extract from Bayne, Conscious states and
conscious creatures: explanation in the scientific
study of consciousness, *Philosophical Perspective*, © 2007
John Wiley & Sons, Inc. with permission from John Wiley & Sons, Inc.

Creature consciousness is not identical with wakefulness. Dreamers can be phenomenally conscious without being awake, and it is conceivable that patients in a vegetative state could be awake without being phenomenally conscious (Bayne, 2007, p. 21). All the subjects of our case studies are in a state of wakefulness; our principal interest is the distinction between phenomenal states and phenomenally conscious creatures, between there being something it is like to hear a musical sound and something it is like to be a phenomenally conscious creature—someone who has a phenomenal perspective on their musical experience.

35.3.3 The *Sounds of Intent* framework: level 1

There is something it is like to be each one of the six children we discuss below; each child will experience their life in their own way, and most of the children will have a phenomenological awareness of music, certainly those at and above level 2. However, what about those at level 1? Level 1 includes "non-intentional" communication—"crying in response to a need," "making sounds unwittingly," and "unwittingly relating through sounds." Although these criteria include multiple possibilities, children functioning at this level may not experience their actions as making or responding to sound; they may not even be aware of the sounds that they are producing. It would be unwise to categorically assert that they are unaware of sound or of the sound that follows their cries. It is even possible that they could have some awareness that the sound they unwittingly produced is, in some way, related to something that they have done. Even were they to have some such awareness, this is at a considerable distance from being aware that they are responsible for the sounds that they can hear. Any such person is unlikely to have a sense of self, nor a sense of self characterized by engagement in music, nor, therefore, anything that we would recognize as a musical identity. Our first case study provides an illustration of some of these points.

35.3.3.1 *Case study 1: Joe*

Joe suffered perinatal brain injury, which profoundly affected his development. Today, aged 6, his *Sounds of Intent* assessment is as follows:

- *Reactive—level 1:*
  - Observation—Joe appears to pay no attention to the wide range of sounds to which he is exposed, and no responses can be observed.
  - Interpretation—his teacher takes this to mean that Joe does not process sound as a distinct or meaningful sensory experience.
- *Proactive—level 1:*
  - Observation—the only sounds Joe makes occur as a consequence of certain life-processes, such as breathing, for example.
  - Interpretation—Joe's teacher believes that he is unable to act with volition on his environment; he appears to have no sense of agency.
- *Interactive—level 1:*
  - Observation—attempts to interact with Joe through sound (for example, by physically supporting him to produce sounds in response to those that are created in his environment, or by responding to the sounds he makes through inhaling and exhaling) have no apparent effect.
  - Interpretation—this is interpreted as Joe having no sense of interagency involving himself and another person in the domain of sound.

This assessment suggests that Joe does not have even a minimal sense of self as defined by Gallagher, since he appears neither to have the capacity to process incoming sensory input (implying that he has no sensation of sound as it is generally understood) nor to be capable of acting with volition on his environment. It would also appear that he lacks any consciousness of a "self," or of himself as someone interacting with others, or of one and the same self enduring over time. It could be that there exists a more primitive sense of self than the "minimal" self or it may be that the concept of the "minimal" self needs to be extended, since recent neuro-scientific research has shown that patients who are unable to make voluntary "bedside" responses may, nonetheless, be able to communicate through the willful modulation of brain activity (Monti, et al., 2010). Since Joe's brain trauma occurred at birth, it seems unlikely that he would have acquired the necessary bank of sensory experiences required for the operation of the mechanism that is the subject of the protocol used by Monti et al. Nevertheless, it would be unwise categorically to assert that Joe has no sense of self unless and until this was the subject of a conclusive demonstration, although it is not immediately obvious what form any such demonstration would take.

35.3.4 The *Sounds of Intent* framework: level 2

Being a phenomenally conscious creature is related to having *self-conscious experience,* or, as Strawson puts it, "experiencing oneself specifically as *oneself*" (Strawson, 2011, p. xxi). Strawson proposes that we have experience of ourselves as a "*thing*" of some sort, and he characterizes this negatively by suggesting that:

> the alternative to experiencing oneself as a thing of one sort, in self-experience, would be to experience oneself as "merely" a property of something, in some manner, or as "merely" a process experienced as something that essentially involves the existence of an object or substance that is distinct from it and in which it can go on and occur.
>
> Strawson, 2011, p. xxi.

It may seem odd to refer to the self as a "thing," and some reject this notion; yet insofar as the self features in our experience, it is not as a state or a property or an event, or even as some sort of process. As Nozick writes, the self "has a particular character, that of an entity" (Nozick, 1989, p. 148). Perhaps the most important sense in which the self presents itself as a thing of some sort is related to how it presents itself as a *subject of experience.* We might think that each of us has a good basic understanding of what a subject of experience is just by virtue of being one and being self-conscious (Strawson, 2011, p. 63). That understanding does not require that we should be able to *articulate* what it is like, or what we understand by the notion. Strawson argues that the basic understanding is:

> available to young children, and it lies at the centre of ordinary human self-experience, and indeed of any self-experience at all, whether or not we can give it clear verbal expression. It's plausible that no sane self-conscious subject of experience can fail to have a good grasp of what a subject of experience is.
>
> Strawson, 2011, p. 64.

Someone operating at level 2 of the *Sounds of Intent* framework is capable of intentional expressive communication—for example "causing, creating or controlling sounds intentionally" and "interacting with others by using sounds." Is someone with these capabilities necessarily self-conscious or in possession of a good grasp of what a subject of experience is? It would appear not. It is plausible that some birds are capable of causing a sound intentionally and interacting with others using sounds, yet it is not plausible that these birds are conscious of themselves, nor that they understand that they are sub-jects of experience. The intentionality required by level 2 is exhibited by animals that lack self-consciousness. Equally some birds (and other animals) can produce sounds that can be interpreted as music to human ears (Ockelford, 2013a, pp. 141–3) and, con-ceivably, to theirs. Moreover, it would be dogmatic to assert that we cannot attribute the requisite intentionality to artificial intelligence, although whether we can also attribute self-consciousness to any such intelligence is a moot point.

Intentionality as exhibited in the communication of sounds is not sufficient for self-consciousness, not even if the sounds intentionally communicated are judged by us to be musical (Ockelford, 2013b, pp. 45–52). It follows that self-consciousness is not a necessary condition for the earliest stages of musical development; nor are the earliest stages of musical development sufficient for self-consciousness.

Self-conscious experience requires that one is aware of oneself as a subject of experience—one is both aware of sound, for example, and conscious that one is aware of sound. A bird may be aware of sound yet not conscious of being aware of this, while any human being with at least a minimal sense of self will have the requisite awareness. This is not yet to posit a musical identity, which implies some awareness of being musical, but it is to suggest how self-awareness is related to the presence of a minimal self, and our having a sense of that.

Our second case study—of Emily—illustrates someone who is developing a minimal sense of self.

35.3.4.1 *Case study 2: Emily*

Emily has cerebral palsy and PMLD. She is 12 years old. Her *Sounds of Intent* assessment is as follows.

- *Reactive—level 2:*
  - Observation—Emily responds to loud sounds (such as the clash of symbols or the bang of a drum near to her) with a smile, though quieter sounds appear to elicit no response.
  - Interpretation—Emily's music therapist takes this to mean that Emily can pro-cess certain stimuli in the auditory domain.
- *Proactive—level 2:*
  - Observation—in the "little room" (a specially constructed micro-environment in which she lies supine), Emily will reach up to the cowbell that is suspended from above and strike it with her hand to make it sound.
  - Interpretation—Emily's teacher interprets this is evidence of her having a sense of agency, with the necessary cognitive and motor capacities to produce or con-trol sounds intentionally.
- *Interactive—level 2:*
  - Observation—In the multisensory room, Emily will operate a switch to turn on lights and music, but only when prompted by her support worker sitting very close to her and singing "turn on the switch" in her ear.

- Interpretation—Emily's educational psychologist believes this shows that she has some notion of a sense of interagency that can exist between her and another person.

This assessment suggests that Emily has a minimal sense of self—pre-linguistic and non-conceptual—a sense that is reinforced through repeated perceptual experience. In the absence of verbal confirmation, the strongest evidence for this stems from her interactions in the multisensory room, where the singing of Emily's support worker is required to prompt her to turn the music on, which is arguably indicative of an early sense of self and other. There is, therefore, evidence that Emily is developing some (minimal) capacity to relate to another person and this, in turn, is likely to have a developmental impact on the sense that she has of herself.

35.4 THE NARRATIVE SELF: TIME, MEMORY, AND THE NARRATIVE OF OTHERS

Gallagher contrasts the minimal self with a narrative self. The narrative self is conceived as:

> a more or less coherent self (or self-image) that is constituted with a past and a future in the various stories that we and others tell about ourselves ... The narrative self is extended in time to include memories of the past and intentions toward the future.
>
> Gallagher, 2000, p. 15.
> Reprinted from *Trends in Cognitive Science*, 4(1), Gallagher, S.,
> Philosophical conceptions of self: implications for cognitive science,
> pp. 14– 21, © 2000, with permission from Elsevier.

The narrative self requires a sense of past and future, and this presupposes a sense of time. Clarke elucidates how music is related to temporality, experience, and consciousness:

> [M]usic models, moulds, and makes audible the flow of our inner, subjective life— the sense of our being-in-the-world ... these processes and their musical analogues are by definition *temporalities*. To be conscious is to know one's being from one moment to the next and to generate some apprehension of unity—an enduring self, an enduring world (whether "real" or illusory)—out of the experience. And while much in the everyday business of human doing furnishes such conditions for consciousness, the making of music might be argued as distinctive in these respects, since "musicking" captures in its very temporal essence the temporality that is essential to the knowing of being—i.e. consciousness.
>
> Clarke, 2011, p. 1.

35.4.1 The *Sounds of Intent* framework: level 3

It is a significant question how musical engagement offers evidence that a child has a sense not only of an "inner, subjective life," but also of an "enduring self"—of being the same subject of experience over time. To explore how engagement in music might provide evidence of a sense of a single, enduring self we would have to explore temporality in such cases as when someone is exposed to a single tone, in its various phases, or to a melody, when this is apprehended as more than an unsynthesized succession of notes (Clarke, 2011, p. 2). Within the *Sounds of Intent* framework we would most naturally be exploring people who are at level 3, who show a "growing awareness of the possibility and significance of relationships between the basic aspects of sounds." We would explore not only how any such awareness was evidence of a sense of a narrative self, but also how it might contribute to an emerging sense of musical identity, an identity characterized by some emerging responsiveness to sound experienced as music.

Consciousness of time and self is manifest not only in how people *listen* to music but also in how they *perform*. Montague writes:

> A performer who uses his or her body to produce sound through the medium of an instrument will need to know through physical gesture exactly "what comes next" and "what has just been;" and this knowledge, contained in the body, will rely on the experience of the melody as a serial temporal succession.
>
> Montague, 2011, p. 36.

Montague remarks that "it is of decisive importance that I play *in time*," and that when "I am playing, my body is playing *now*, in a focussed, committed engagement with time. One gesture follows another in necessary succession, and only when I finish, or stop suddenly, will this temporality end" (Montague, 2011, p. 36).

While practicing jazz, Sudnow recalls "playing one day and finding ... that I'd expressly aimed for the sounds of these next particular notes, that the sounds seemed to creep up into my fingers" (quoted in Montague, 2011, p. 36). Montague comments on how "Sudnow speaks of bodily knowledge, implying that his fingers are themselves agents. Such agency creates a particularly concentrated relationship with time as a series of events." Children learn to perform music in time, and to recognize that the music they are listening to is being played in time, and this is related to their being conscious of themselves as the same selves existing in time (cf. Husserl, 1905–1910/1964). Someone who can perform music in time and recognize that it is being played in time would probably be operating at (at least) levels 3 or 4 in the *Sounds of Intent* framework, showing awareness of the significance of relationships between sounds, and an evolving perception of groups of sounds and of the relationships between them. The emerging sense of a narrative self is therefore related to a growing understanding of how sounds are related to each other, whether at one moment in time, as when listening to a harmony, and over an extended period, as when following a melody or recognizing a rhythm or tempo.

Consciousness of time is related to memory. We can distinguish between episodic memory, semantic memory, and procedural memory. An example of episodic memory is remembering that my last piano lesson went well; remembering how to play the piano is an example of procedural memory; and remembering that my piano teacher is aged 52 is an example of semantic memory (Tulving, 1983). Gallagher emphasizes the relationship between the narrative self, time and *episodic memory* (Gallagher, 2000, p. 20):

> The importance of the proper functioning of episodic memory and time sense on the formation of the narrative self is indicated by the case of a young boy diagnosed with congenital damage to the right hemisphere and frontal cortex. He suffers from a profound episodic amnesia and because he lacks the ability to quantify the passage of time or to appreciate the meaning of temporal units, he is unable to formulate certain essential structures of narrative, namely, sequential structure and the demarcations of beginning and end.
>
> Gallagher, 2000, p. 20.
> Reprinted from *Trends in Cognitive Science*, 4(1), Gallagher, S.,
> Philosophical conceptions of self: implications for cognitive science,
> pp. 14– 21, © 2000, with permission from Elsevier

Engagement with music gives evidence of episodic memory, and this is related to the presence and development of a narrative self, as illustrated in our third case study.

35.4.1.1 *Case study 3: Matthew*

Matthew, eight, is blind and has severe learning difficulties. He communicates some everyday needs (such as "drink" and "more") using idiosyncratic sounds and gestures. He appears to understand a few key words when reinforced with on-body signing (for example, "toilet," and "swimming"), though his responses to these are not consistent, and it is often hard for his support workers to know whether he has taken the message on board. His *Sounds of Intent* assessment is as follows:

- *Reactive—level 3:*
  - Observation—Matthew gets very excited when he hears the drum being played, and is particularly responsive to a regular beat that starts quietly and get louder.
  - Interpretation—Matthew's music teacher at school takes this to mean that he can recognize simple musical structures that involve regularity and regular change over time.
- Proactive—level 3
  - Observation—Matthew can maintain a regular beat on a range of percussion instruments, and he particularly enjoys starting slowly and getting faster.
  - Interpretation—Matthew's music teacher interprets this as showing that he can produce simple musical structures that involve regularity and regular change over time.

- Interactive—level 3
    - Observation—Matthew enjoys engaging in simple musical dialogues with his music therapist—she taps a drum two or three times and he copies, and vice versa.
    - Interpretation—Matthew's music therapist believes that this shows he has a sense of reciprocal imitation. He is happy to be influenced by other people and shows this by copying what they do, and he also likes influencing what others do and understands that this occurs when they copy him.

This assessment suggests that, in addition to a "minimal" sense of self, shown by his responses to immediate auditory experiences, Matthew has an early form of "narrative" self, since he can process sensations over time and appreciate the simple patterns they can make, helping him to remember what has occurred previously and enabling him to anticipate what is coming next. Hence, he has a (non-conceptual) sense of personal location in time. Although Matthew's narrative self is pre-linguistic, he is aware at some level that sequences of sound can indicate mutual schemes of influence operating between himself and other people. He therefore gives evidence not only of being aware of his self enduring over time, but of relating to others and understanding that this is what he is doing.

35.4.2   The *Sounds of Intent* framework: level 4

Episodic memory brings us into contact with particular past events and episodes, such as my last piano lesson and the pleasure I took in playing a particular passage well. Sutton writes:

> Episodic memories are naturally expressed with a direct object: I remember arguing about Descartes yesterday, and I remember my feelings as we talked. Such personal memories can be generic or specific, and can be memories of more or less extended temporal periods. But the most characteristic feature of episodic remembering, arguably, is the way it brings us into contact with the particular past events which such memories are about and by which they are caused.
>
> Sutton, 2012.

This suggests, what Gallagher is elsewhere concerned to emphasize, that episodic memory is related to language, since to remember that I argued with Descartes yesterday, or that I had a piano lesson last week implies that I have the thought, "I argued with Descartes yesterday," or "I had a piano lesson last week," and to have thoughts such as these implies the capacity to use language. Certainly language is integral to Gallagher's conception of the narrative self:

Humans ... have language. And with language we begin to make our experience relatively coherent over extended time periods. We use words to tell stories, and in these stories we create what we call our selves. We extend our biological boundaries to encompass a life of meaningful experience.

Gallagher 2000, p. 19.

Reprinted from *Trends in Cognitive Science*, 4(1), Gallagher, S., Philosophical conceptions of self: implications for cognitive science, pp. 14–21, © 2000, with permission from Elsevier

Gallagher gives several examples of philosophers and psychologists for whom language is central to the sense of self. For Dennett, we cannot help but deploy our capacity to use language in creating our own stories, and Neisser includes a pivotal role for language and narrative play in developing our own self-concept (Gallagher, 2000, p. 19). However, a distinguishing feature of the children we are discussing here is a restricted or non-existent capacity to use language. What does a restricted capacity for language imply for the (sense of) development of a self, whether minimal or narrative, and what does engagement with music make possible even when language use and comprehension is (almost) entirely absent? Our fourth case study—Sandip—suggests that it is possible for someone to develop a narrative self even in the absence of a capacity to use and understand language.

35.4.2.1 *Case study 4: Sandip*

Sandip, 11, has severe learning disabilities, visual processing difficulties, and a diagnosis of autism. Although there is no evidence that he understands language, his reactions suggest that he knows what is going to happen next, and which activities have finished, by using a timetable employing "objects of reference" (Ockelford, 2002). He can make simple choices when presented with two objects of reference at the same time. His *Sounds of Intent* assessment is as follows.

- *Reactive—level 4:*
  - Observation—Sandip spends a good deal of time listening to excerpts from TV theme tunes. He will listen to the same fragments of music over and over again.
  - Interpretation—Sandip's parents (who are musicians) are of the view that their son's listening preferences indicate that he recognizes that music is constructed in distinct "chunks" (though that he is not yet engaging with pieces as extended narratives in sound).
- *Proactive—level 4:*
  - Observation—Sandip often sings or hums concatenations of musical motifs to himself from different pieces that he has heard.
  - Interpretation—Sandip's music teacher interprets this as evidence of his capacity to connect successive groups of notes coherently.

- *Interactive—level 4:*
  - Observation—Sandip revels in "call and response" activities in music, vocally copying and sometimes varying short phrases that are sung to him, and taking delight in offering ideas for others to copy, in either case systematically taking turns to listen and contribute.
  - Interpretation—Sandip's teacher takes this to mean that he can understand how musical dialogues can be created through imitating groups of sounds to form coherent chains.

This assessment suggests that, as well as a minimal sense of self, Sandip has acquired a significant (though presumably non-linguistic) form of narrative self, since he can understand how series of notes presented over time can form groups, and how these can be used to create more substantial sequences that he can formulate on his own or by participating with others. Through improvised musical exchanges, he can sense the effect of placing his own ideas in a shared domain, and having them picked up, repeated, and developed by others; and he is aware of his own capacity to imitate and vary the musical materials that other people offer—all within an extended temporal framework of turn-taking. Hence, Sandip is giving evidence of having an awareness of self that includes a developing sense of self-consciousness, a sense of a continuing self enduring over time, and a self that is able to interact with and respond to the non-linguistic communicative and other behaviors of his teacher and parents.

35.4.3   The *Sounds of Intent* framework: levels 5 and 6

Ricoeur conceives of the narrative self, not in the manner of Dennett, as an "abstract point at the intersection of various narratives," but as "something richer, more substantial and concrete." In particular, Ricoeur insists that "one's own self narrative is always entangled in the narrative of others" (Gallagher, 2000, p. 20). This is to make the point that the development of one's sense of self cannot be considered apart from a social context that includes interpersonal relations, a view frequently adopted in discussion about the concept of a person. Emphasizing the relational dimension of personhood Boddington & Podpadek (1991) argue that any definition will embody an element of social construction, and that normative considerations inevitably arise when communities make judgements about whether to accord human beings the status of persons. Boddington & Podpadek also note approvingly that in her discussion of personhood, Midgley (1985) emphasizes non-verbal communication, social interaction, and the "sensibility, social and emotional complexity of the kind which is expressed by the formation of deep, subtle and lasting relationships" (Midgley, 1985). Kitwood's view is similar, taking the concept of personhood as "a standing or status that is bestowed upon one human being, by others, in the context of relationship and social being;" hence, "personhood is not, at first, a property of the individual; rather it is provided, or guaranteed, by the presence of others" (Kitwood, cited in Baldwin & Capstick, 2007, p. 246).

The relational aspect of personhood is connected to the relational aspect of the narrative self, for the narrative sense of ourselves is sensitive to how others relate to us as people. Yet people with severe learning difficulties may be regarded by some as not having the status of persons, as if they were less than fully human (Margalit 1998). However, if severely disabled people are generally treated as somehow less than people, the likely consequence is withdrawal, inhibition, or a sense of rejection. If, on the other hand, they *are* accepted as people, and recognized as being fully human just like anyone else, this is liable to have a positive or re-enforcing impact on how they think of themselves in the eyes of others, and the confidence they have in themselves as people with whom it is worth interacting.

In our two final case studies we illustrate how a narrative self is revealed by engagement with music on the part of two children with varying linguistic, social, and interpersonal abilities.

35.4.3.1 *Case study 5: Mia*

Mia has moderate learning difficulties and autism spectrum condition. She is 17 years old. Her verbal communication, although limited to everyday topics, enables her to express her immediate needs, wishes, and views effectively. She is proud of her singing abilities, and likes to talk about her musical achievements with her friends and the adults in her life. Mia's *Sounds of Intent* assessment is as follows.

- *Reactive—level 5:*
  - Observation—Mia enjoys listening to music on her iPod, particularly pop music. She listens to pieces carefully all the way through and anticipates key structural features such as the choruses of songs.
  - Interpretation—Mia's music teacher takes this to mean that she recognizes pieces of music as entities comprising sequences of related groups of events that conform to given frameworks of pitch that unfold over time.
- *Proactive—level 5:*
  - Observation—Mia has taught herself to play the tunes of some of her favorite songs on the keyboard. Her playing is rather "wooden," but the elements appear in the correct order, and she enjoys singing along with her playing.
  - Interpretation—Mia's music teacher takes this as confirmation that she has a grasp of pieces of music as structural entities.
- Interactive—level 5
  - Observation—Mia provides the lead vocals in her school band. She and her classmates reproduce simple cover versions of well-known pop songs that faithfully follow the structure of the originals, though her capacity to perform with "authentic" expressivity is limited.
  - Interpretation—Mia's music teacher regards this group activity as being particularly significant, since it shows that she can attend to others' performances while performing herself, cognizant of their influence on her, and aware of her own influence on them.

This assessment suggests that Mia's engagement with music supports her evolving sense of narrative self in two ways, since she can recreate familiar pieces of music with others and is able to reflect on her capacity to perform with those around her. Hence, music provides her both with an immanent vehicle for perceiving herself in relation to abstract narratives in sound that unfold over time, as well as a means of relating to others socially, through acknowledged success in musical activity. This recognition is an important element in the construction of her intra- and interpersonal identity.

35.4.3.2 *Case study 6: Derek*

Derek is blind, has severe learning difficulties and autism spectrum condition. Thirty-four years old, he started to teach himself to play the piano when he was only two. Derek could perform competently before he could use verbal language in a comprehensible way, and today his grasp of music is still far more advanced than his capacity to engage in conversation. He is an acknowledged "musical savant": someone who has exceptional abilities in the context of global developmental delay. He spends a good deal of time engaging directly in musical activities, or planning them, or reflecting on performances in which he has played a part. Derek's abilities are internationally recognized, and he travels a good deal in the UK and abroad, giving concerts in a wide range of venues. He features regularly on television all over the world. He is aware of his fame, and, despite his verbal limitations, he relishes interacting with members of the public. Through numerous positive performing experiences in many different contexts, his social skills and self-esteem developed markedly through his twenties. When asked about his identity, he says: "I am Derek. I play the piano." Derek's *Sounds of Intent* assessment is as follows:

- *Reactive—level 6:*
  - Observation—Derek listens to a great deal of music, and can identify thousands of pieces, their performers and even, in some cases, particular performances. He is conversant with most well-known Western styles and genres.
  - Interpretation—Derek's mentor (the first author) takes this to mean that he recognizes the probabilistic patterns of sound in the domains of pitch and time that are the determinants of style, and the features of interpretation that mark out one performance from another.
- *Proactive—Level 6:*
  - Observation—Derek has a vast repertoire of pieces he can perform on request on the piano. He can improvise on the music with which he is familiar in any key and in a range of styles. He can deliberately evoke different moods in his playing.
  - Interpretation—Derek's mentor believes that this shows he understands the expressive capacity of music, and that he is able to use culturally learnt performance practices to communicate with audiences in predetermined ways.
- *Interactive—level 6:*
  - Observation—Derek enjoys performing with a range of other musicians, and is a particularly sensitive accompanist, picking up on the rubato, vibrato, and

dynamics used by singers, for example, and intuitively adapting his improvised accompaniments to support and enhance their expressive intentions as he
perceives them.

- Interpretation—Derek's mentor interprets this as evidence that Derek has learnt
  the "expressive grammars" of performance in different styles, and can incorporate them into his own playing in real time to create persuasive narratives
  in sound.

This assessment suggests that the evolution of Derek's sense of self—now so clearly
focussed—has been linked inextricably to his developing abilities and experiences as
a pianist. We can surmise that his narrative sense of self started to emerge when, as
a little boy, he recreated and improvised on the music he heard in his environment.
These early efforts would have given him a sense of auditory structures unfolding over
time: journeys in sound of his own making, where (unlike other areas of his life) he
was in control. Subsequently, in his teens, group improvisations and performances not
only enhanced his sense of self and other long before his linguistic abilities were up
to the task, but in adulthood, they have provided him with an avenue through which
he could sense the feelings of others, and offered him platforms to contribute to the
joint expression of emotion through sound. Through performing in countries across
Europe and the USA, and through the feedback he receives via the internet from audiences across the world in response to his television appearances, Derek's sense of self
has extended beyond local communities of interest to a wider cultural constituency.
The story of his life can be summarized as metaphorical narratives in sound becoming
narratives of self.

35.5 CONCLUSIONS

This chapter has included some introductory theory and six vignettes to illustrate how
engaging with music, at all levels, can promote a sense of self in children and young people with learning difficulties, and how such engagement can serve as a proxy indicator
of self-awareness and identity, particularly in those who are incapable of linguistic communication. Through reactive, proactive and interactive participation in musical activities one can hypothesize that a "narrative" sense of self evolves alongside a continuing
"minimal" sense of self as the capacity to engage with music develops.

Significant questions remain about the distinguishing features of the self and its development, as this applies to those who are non-linguistic but also musical, and to how
music can contribute to a sense of self when other human capacities, generally regarded
as elemental, are either absent or severely curtailed. Future research using brain imaging
and electroencephalography, used to gauge neurological responses to music, holds out
the prospect of being able to detect the existence of hitherto unidentified self-awareness
in those whose level of impairment does not permit a physical response.

REFERENCES

Baldwin, C. & Capstick, A. (Eds.) (2007). *Tom Kitwood on dementia: a reader and critical commentary*. Maidenhead: Open University Press.

Bayne, T. (2007). Conscious states and conscious creatures: explanation in the scientific study of consciousness. *Philosophical Perspectives, Philosophy of Mind*, 21, 1–22.

Boddington, P. & Podpadec, T. (1991). Who are the mentally handicapped? *Journal of Applied Philosophy*, 8(2), 177–90.

Clarke, D. (2011). Music, phenomenology, time consciousness: meditations after Husserl. In: D. Clarke & E. Clarke (Eds.) *Music and consciousness, philosophical psychological and cultural perspectives*, pp. 1–28. Oxford: Oxford University Press.

Cheng, E., Ockelford, A, & Welch, G. (2010). Researching and developing music provision in special schools in England for children and young people with complex needs. *Australian Journal of Music Education*, 2009(2), 27–48.

Gallagher, S. (2000). Philosophical conceptions of self: implications for cognitive science. *Trends in Cognitive Science*, 4(1), 14–21.

Husserl, E. (1905–1910/1964). *The phenomenology of internal time-consciousness*. The Hague: Martinus Nijhoff.

MacDonald, R., Hargreaves, D., & Miell, D. (Eds.) (2002) *Musical identities*. Oxford: Oxford University Press.

Margalit, A. (1998). *The decent society*. Cambridge, MA: Harvard University Press.

Midgley, M. (1985). Persons and non-persons. In: P. Singer (Ed.) *Defence of animals*, pp. 52–62. Oxford: Basil Blackwell.

Monti, M., Vanhaudenhuyse, A., Coleman, M., et al. (2010). Willful modulation of brain activity in disorders of consciousness. *New England Journal of Medicine*, 362(7), 579–89.

Montague, E. (2011). Phenomenology and the "hard problem" of consciousness and music. In: D. Clarke & E. Clarke (Eds.) *Music and consciousness: philosophical, pyschological and cultural perspectives*, pp. 29–46. Oxford: Oxford University Press.

Nozick, R. (1989). *The examined life: philosophical meditations*. New York, NY: Touchstone.

Ockelford, A. (2002). *Objects of reference: promoting early symbolic communication*. London: Royal National Institute of Blind People.

Ockelford, A. (2008). *Music for children and young people with complex needs*. Oxford: Oxford University Press.

Ockelford, A. (2013a). *Applied musicology: using zygonic theory to inform music education, therapy, and psychology research*. New York, NY: Oxford University Press.

Ockelford, A. (2013b). What makes music "music?" Theoretical explanations using zygonic theory. In: J.-L. Leroy (Ed.), *Actualités des universaux musicaux [Topicality of musical universals]*, pp. 123–148. Paris: Editions des Archives Contemporaines.

Ockelford, A. & Matawa, C. (2009). *Focus on music 2: exploring the musical interests and abilities of blind and partially-sighted children with retinopathy of prematurity*. London: Institute of Education.

Ockelford, A. & Welch, G. (2012). What can musical engagement in children with cognitive impairment tell us about their sense of self? In: S. O'Neill (Ed.) *Personhood and music learning: connecting perspectives and narratives*, Research to Practice Biennial Book Series, Vol. 5, pp.216–37. Waterloo, ON: Canadian Music Educators' Association.

Ockelford, A., Welch, G., Jewell-Gore, L., Cheng, E., Vogiatzoglou, A., & Himonides, E. (2011). *Sounds of Intent*, Phase 2: approaches to the quantification of music-developmental data pertaining to children with complex needs. *European Journal of Special Needs Education,* 26(2), 177–99.

Ockelford, A., Welch, G., Zimmermann, S., & Himonides, E. (2005). 'Sounds of intent': mapping, assessing and promoting the musical development of children with profound and multiple learning difficulties. *International Congress Series*, 1282, 898–902.

Strawson, G. (2011). *Selves*. Oxford: Clarendon Press.

Sutton, J. (2012). Memory. In: E. Zalata (Ed.) *The Stanford Encyclopedia of Philosophy.* http://plato.stanford.edu/archives/win2012/entries/memory/ (accessed October 8, 2016).

Tulving, E. (1983). *Elements of episodic memory*. Oxford: Oxford University Press.

Welch, G., Ockelford, A., Carter, F-C., Zimmermann, S.-A., & Himonides, E. (2009). "Sounds of Intent": mapping musical behaviour and development in children and young people with complex needs. *Psychology of Music*, 37(3), 348–70.

....

CHAPTER 36

"I WOULD DIE WITHOUT MY MUSIC"

Relying on Musical Identities to Cope with Difficult Times

....

KATRINA SKEWES MCFERRAN AND CHERRY HENSE

It is currently popular to adopt a naïve attitude when contemplating the relationship between music and adolescent identity. This trend is apparent both in the attitudes of teenagers themselves, and also the professionals contributing to the emergent interdisciplinary discourse on "Music, Health, and Wellbeing" (MacDonald, Kreutz, & Mitchell, 2012). Enthusiasm about the positive affordances of music has traditionally been tempered by psychodynamically informed scholars within the discipline of music therapy, who contend that music can provide a vehicle for the projection of both positive and negative aspects of the psyche (Hadley, 2003). However, this stance has been critiqued as pathologizing the relationship between individuals and their music (Purdon, 2006) and, as a result, some feminists have rejected the pairing of music and therapy (O'Grady, 2009). Public health funding bodies in Australia have been known to throw away applications that use the two words together, preferring to fund positively-framed community choir and garage band projects, rather than "therapists" who think that people need help to engage in health musicing (Batt-Rawden, Trythall, & DeNora, 2007; Ruud, 2010).

36.1 HEALTHY YOUNG PEOPLE
DESCRIBING MUSIC

....

Teenagers are seldom interested in acknowledging the darker sides of their relationship with music and regularly claim that their relationship with music is exclusively positive. Young people appear equally determined to communicate this positivity when being interviewed about their everyday engagement with music as their participation in music therapy. One of the first studies to formally illuminate this position was Suvi Saarikallio's interrogation of eight healthy Finnish teenagers (Saarikallio & Erkkila, 2007). Whilst the researchers constructed their theory in relation to mood regulation, a number of key ideas related to identity also emerged. The young Fins were able to clearly articulate the ways they used music to express themselves on a given day, including the ways that some songs were able to express a whole range of emotions depending on the mood they were in when listening. One way to interpret the informants' explanations of these multi-use songs is that they strongly identified with particular songs and it was their use of the song that varied according to the more changeable characteristic of mood. In other words, the song continued to represent their identity, even in different moods. All participants described how music helped—to improve mood, strengthen convictions, escape from their current situation, or clarify and reappraise their circumstances. This interpretation of the interviews is a persistent theme for Saarikallio, whose earlier conceptualization of the literature described emotions as central to adolescent uses of music, often in the service of identity formation, relationship building and agency (Laiho, 2004).

Marie Skanland (2011) adopts a similar position in her Norwegian research, although she is focussed on adult uses of mobile music. Affect regulation is once again a dominant theme in her data analysis, with participants also describing the way they maintained a sense of personal identity in public spaces. Here, music is used for establishing boundaries between self and others, providing a sense of personal control, and also being useful in negotiating busy urban spaces. Each adult participant in Skanland's study described how personally selected music was helpful in maintaining a sense of identity, despite the external challenges of negotiating their daily travels and experiences.

Similar themes have emerged in the analysis of interviews with teenagers who have participated in music therapy groups. McFerran's (2010) interpretation of interviews with 16 bereaved adolescents emphasized the positive value of fun and creativity that was experienced within groups. These young people described how they were able to express and release feelings of grief through participation in music therapy, and that the positive dimensions of the group were essential in order for them to grapple with the negative. They described how the musical conditions allowed for multiple aspects of their identity to be shared—both their bereaved selves and their fun-loving (healthy) selves. These statements are similar to those of the six grieving participants in McFerran's original doctoral research (McFerran & Grocke, 2000), who additionally emphasized the importance of freedom and control in providing the space they needed to express and process grief related feelings.

If grieving is accepted as a natural stage of life, rather than a pathological state,[1] then these investigations, and others like them, provide rich descriptions of the ways that relatively healthy young people use music for self-expression. Similarly to studies in the fields of American Humanism (i.e., Rogers, 1961; Maslow, 1968; May, 1981) or, more recently, in

---

[1] The grief and loss literature suggests this is the case, with the majority of bereaved people coping successfully with significant losses (Bonono, 2008)

positive psychology (Csikszentmihalyi, 2002; Seligman, 2011), there is a focus on what is associated with healthy behavior. This thinking is aligned with the positive frame of music, health, and well-being, but it neatly sidesteps the question of whether ill health produces different results. While this positive discourse generates better understanding of one end of the health continuum, there seems to be a collective avoidance of the reality that not all people engage music within a healthy context. When people struggle with mental illness, the ways they engage with music have been shown to differ.

36.2 UNHEALTHY YOUNG PEOPLE AND MUSIC

Music therapists are more often found working with people who have mental illness than those who are flourishing. Within a mental illness context, psychoanalysis continues to be a powerful theoretical influence and from this perspective, music is unlikely to provide the kind of neutral representation of identity suggested by the authors above. Within the *Encyclopaedia of adolescence*, the relationship between music and identity is described as "a way of experiencing something of the self as an external object: Music serves as a symbolic meta-structure, into which personal meanings can be placed" (Gold, Saarikallio, & McFerran, 2010, p. 1829). This definition locates music in a different relationship with identity—the self is projected on to music, rather than the music serving to fulfil the hedonistic desires of the self to be happy. This perspective suggests different understandings that may be more pertinent when considering the identity of young people struggling with mental illness.

In a study of the everyday uses of music by Australian adolescents with severe mental illness, Carmen Cheong-Clinch (2013) asked young people to describe their relationship with music. Once again, music was associated with being "happy and free" by the participants, but with some important distinctions. While the descriptions of younger teenagers were in accord with the happiness orientation presented in the health studies above, the older teenagers (who had potentially struggled with mental health issues for longer) described relationships between music and darker aspects of the psyche. For example, one young person described the ways that music would buy "3 minutes" of relief from the urge to self-harm, but that when the song ended, the desire to act returned. While these young people attempted to use music to regulate their mood in the same ways as Saarikallio's Finnish informants (Saarikallio & Erkkila, 2007), there were real limitations to how helpful music could be in achieving a desired state of being. Similar to Skanland's (2011) healthy adults, the majority of informants also relied on music to create personal space during difficult times. However, where the Norwegian adults were creating healthy boundaries that affirmed their own personal space, these young Australians were desperately trying to escape the reality of their difficult and painful personal context. While the same intentions were reported, the context of mental illness had a significant impact on how successfully music was appropriated in relation to identity. Isolation, rather than healthy boundaries, sometimes resulted.

Hege Beckmann (2013) tells a similar story about Norwegian adolescents with mental health problems. She presents the voices of three older teenagers who were each grappling with issues related to violence and aggression. Although Beckman constructs music as a resource for all of the young people, the descriptions reveal variable success in appropriating music for positive outcomes related to identity development. One young man describes how a particular lyric—"I will rip your face apart and feed it to the dogs"—motivated him to reconnect with his rage about an earlier betrayal by a girlfriend. He describes listening repeatedly to the song while thinking about battering her. Another of Beckmann's informants is a young woman experiencing depression in a violent relationship and she describes how listening to music influences her mood when she wakes up in the morning. When waking in a neutral state, she uses music to influence her mood in a positive direction, but when she is sad or depressed, listening to music makes the feeling worse.

These descriptions would not surprise therapy professionals working psychoanalytically. From an analytic music therapy perspective (Eschen, 2002), it is precisely these connections between pathology and music that inform the direction and content of therapy. Clients are actively encouraged to project repressed aspects of the psyche on to the music during shared improvisations so that the therapist can join them in processing the latent imagery. For example, one young girl described in the literature appropriates a hymn in therapy to connect with and process a relationship with a dead grandmother; another improvises a musical story with the therapist to symbolically act out the trauma of a long hospital stay (Purdon, 2002). Lillian Eyre (2007) describes how changes in identity are expressed musically in the analytic music therapy method, and works from the assumption that people present to therapy with the need for inner work, not seeking a forum for joyous expression of the idealized self.

36.3 RELATING TO THE YOUNG PERSON'S WHOLE IDENTITY

Rather than focussing purely on the positive potentials of music or rigidly assuming pathological reflections, we advocate a position that integrates both dimensions and allows for young people to have all aspects of their identity welcomed. This perspective aligns with contemporary understandings of recovery in mental health care that focus on an expanded sense of self, where illness is still acknowledged but no longer defines or limits the identity (Anthony, 1993; Davidson, Row, Tandora, O'Connell, & Lawless, 2009). Music affords opportunities for both pathology and positive growth, and while it is complex to allow for both of these concepts to be acknowledged in discussions of musical identity, it is also important that the attempt is made. In a recent study of young people attending a mental health service, we theorized one way in which this complexity could be conceptualized (Hense, McFerran & McGorry, 2014). Prior to music therapy, a range of different musical symptoms appeared to represent the ways in which each young person isolated their musical identity from the social world. Through a music therapy process, these young people described resolving their musical symptoms into more social forms of musical engagement. Music afforded positive growth of the identity because the symptoms did not have to be extinguished but could be expanded beyond an illness construction.

This complexity has also been embraced in a co-authored chapter written collaboratively by a young Australian woman and her music therapist (the primary author) as a reflection on the young woman's relationship with music (McFerran & Baird, 2013). At one level, this paper describes how music is "my best friend," as alluded to in the title of this chapter. However, it also illustrates how seeing music as a purely positive resource is both limiting and naïve within the lives of most young people with mental illness. Further descriptions by this young woman remind the reader that people with depression are inclined to ruminate on issues and events, rather than process them (Treynor, Gonzalez, & Nolen-Hoeksema, 2003). She describes how music affords rumination with recorded songs that repeat the same ideas in exactly the same ways with each listening. While healthy people describe changing their associations depending on their mood, this is precisely what people with depression struggle to do (Garrido & Schubert, 2011). Instead, they may be drawn more deeply into the very feeling they are trying to avoid through their music selections.

A similar tendency to rely on music as "a friend" is documented by Ivaldi & O'Neil (2008). Their investigation targeted teenagers identifying with musicians rather than songs, but they express similar concerns about the projection of desires onto an essentially inanimate object—the idol's popular image. Ivaldi & O'Neill show that it was not the music that drew the attention of their fans, but rather the perceived dedication of the artist and the popularity of their image. The authors draw on a range of studies to suggest that young people are increasingly identifying with far-away role models, rather than real-life persons who are actually known to them. The real (but flawed) adults available in the lives of adolescents can easily be rejected in preference for the seemingly perfect (but unattainable) adult projected on to the idol's popular image. Robert Epstein (2007) laments this disconnect between teenagers and their possible mentors in his critique of current conceptualizations of adolescence. He uses cross-cultural data to show that the stereotyping of all teens as "turbulent" serves to exaggerate naturally independent behaviors into problems and leads to a lack of faith in young people by the adults involved in their lives. As a result, teenagers do not turn to their co-located adults in times of crisis because they anticipate criticism and restriction, and are instead left to fend for themselves and rely on their peers or distant idols as substitutes.

Roger Levesque (2010) does not adopt such a critical perspective on the relationship between teenagers and their idols. He suggests that identifying with "parasocial" relationships can be helpful for forging identity during adolescence. However, once again, his notion relies on a foundation of good health. For those with existing mental illness, parasocial relationships with mentally unstable pop idols can be risky. This is illustrated in one study which shows that the rate of attempted suicides by Korean adolescents increases after the untimely death of a celebrity idol (Cheng et al., 2007). This corre-lation is only significant for young people who have made previous suicide attempts, further demonstrating how it is young people with suicidal inclinations that are likely to ideate their idol's attempts. What might be neutral or positive for some young people might be negative and dangerous for others.

Many of these findings seem to suggest that it is pre-recorded music and the pop industry that is to blame for any negative impacts on a young person's attempts to form a healthy identity. This was certainly the claim made by the Parent's Resource Centre in the 1980s when a number of parliamentary wives rallied to save their children from what they perceived to be overly sexualized and aggressive content of pop music at the time (Chastagner, 1999). The outcome of that battle was the introduction of "sexually explicit lyrics" stickers on CD covers, which Adrian North and David Hargreaves (2005) argue is the worst possible outcome because it promotes negative associations with particular types of music, creating a cycle of negativity. It is interesting to note that the response of musicians and the music industry at that time was to rely on the same argument as psy-choanalysts; claiming their music was not the issue, but rather it was the ways that young people interpreted meanings from their music that illustrated what was really going on in the minds of these (over) protected sons and daughters of the State (i.e., http://www. youtube.com/watch?v=KqxdYaDLZRQ). This point may be true, but not all music is so open to suggestion. DeNora (2000) proposes that music bears with it certain affor-dances—it is neither neutral, nor exact in terms of meaning, but some forms of music are more suggestive than others.

The recognition that certain music suggests particular possibilities (DeNora, 2011) helps to explain the findings of correlational studies where particular genres of music are associated with specific states of mental health. North & Hargreaves (2008) provide a review of the literature that confirms a connection between "problem music" and vulnerability to mental illness, and bring together the outcomes of various studies on this topic. However, what is not considered is the ways that researchers' assumptions about the nature of music actually influence their choice of designs and measures, and therefore the results they believe themselves to have found. In order to interrogate these assumptions more systematically, a critical synthesis was undertaken to identify what patterns could be found in the ways that the link between youth, depression, and music was examined (McFerran, Garrido, & Saarikallio, 2013).

Findings from this critical synthesis revealed a positive bias in the work of researchers orientated towards good health, with designs utilizing interviews revealing only positive health outcomes, whereas correlational and empirical studies exposed a more mixed picture. Even more interesting was the powerful influence exerted by the way that music was defined by different schools of researchers. In keeping with North's latest proposal (North & Hargreaves, 2012), if music was defined as a set of genres, then it was possible to link a particular genre with either mental health or mental illness. Dave Miranda's investigations alone have shown connections between French Rap and deviant behav-iors (Miranda & Claes, 2004) in one study, and how soul music (hip-hop, R&B) dimin-ishes the likelihood of depression in another (Miranda & Claes, 2008), but how metal music is related to higher depression levels for girls with friends who have similar mental health issues (Miranda & Claes, 2009). However, if music is defined as being either active or receptive, rather than being categorized by genre, the assumed influence of genre disappears completely. For example, active participation in writing rap songs can lead to improvements in mental health (Baker & Homan, 2007), whereas receptive listening to rap music can be linked to increases in aggression and inappropriate behavior (Doak, 2003). Therefore, it cannot be the inherent qualities of the musical genre that exerts the significant influence. As Ruud (2006) suggests, it is the combination of the music, the person and the situation that afford opportunities for identity construction.

In order to investigate the interaction of context, intentions, musical actions and consequences, McFerran conducted an interview study with 40 Australian teenagers (McFerran & Saarikallio, 2013). Beginning with students in mainstream schools, the interviewer asked young people to describe how they engaged with music to express themselves. Once the usual positive answers had been documented, the informants were asked to think of a time when their expectations of music had not been fulfilled—when they felt worse after or did not achieve the outcome they had been hoping for. After some initial resistance, most of the young people were able to identify such a time and describe it. They were then asked more detailed questions about the conditions in which that experience occurred, since the researchers were developing a theoretical understanding of what contexts and conditions lead to less positive experiences with music. After soliciting the responses of 22 relatively healthy young people, a somewhat consistent pattern began to emerge. At this point the context for interviews was varied (Strauss & Corbin, 1998, p. 210) and students in alternative school settings for young people with emotional and behavioral challenges were recruited, followed by young people receiving support for depression and anxiety. Despite the differences in mental health status, informants described a consistent tendency to depend on music to feel better when dealing with difficult times. Rather than being conscious of their own power in appropriating music in a chosen direction, young people often seemed to describe a blind faith in the power of the music and it's potential to help them.

36.4 MUSIC AS "MY BEST FRIEND"

A similar faith has been evidenced over a number of years in a class of several hundred university students who spend 2 hours a week in an elective subject called "Music and health." Amongst the many positive attributes ascribed to music is the frequent reference to music as "my best friend." Analysis of the online Discussion Board contributions revealed the following positive characteristics that were associated with the relationship.

- You never have to apologize (music is forgiving).
- There are no follow up questions (music just listens).
- You can change it to what you want it to be (music is flexible).

At first glance, this list reveals many positive qualities associated with American Humanism, or client-centered approaches to therapy. Key qualities of this approach include fostering understanding, offering acceptance, and facilitating improvements (Rogers, 1951). However, a less flattering interpretation is possible if the lens of narcissism is adopted (Raskin, Novacek, & Hogan, 1991). Narcissists fail to take other people's experiences into account and therefore do not see the need to apologize. They consider their view to be the correct one and have no desire for the other's perspective (unless it is in agreement with their own). Narcissists lack a stable personality (Bloch & Singh, 2001), usually thought to be the result of ambivalent parenting, where the primary caregiver's love is unpredictably available. Whichever psychological interpretation is adopted, there is also the simple view that most healthy people are looking for more in their relationships than an inanimate, repetitive object, no matter how aesthetically appealing he/she may be (surely?).

An interesting contrast is seen in the descriptions offered by seven men from different countries that had been fans of metal music during their adolescence (Hines & McFerran, 2013). A phenomenological analysis of their email interviews revealed that themes of power and emotion were an integral part of their decision to identify with metal music. However there were no assumptions about being an easy relationship, with one man describing how he had struggled to enjoy the genre at first, but persisted because of his belief that it was connected to his type of people. Other themes illustrated the importance of connecting to shared social values, learning about other issues, and making contact with others through metal music. Despite the bad reputation metal music has with links to suicide and depression (Stack, 1998), these men reveal themselves to be more capable of forming mature and loving relationships than the average, self-orientated university student.

36.4.1 An example

Music therapists regularly work in institutions with people who have mental illness. Subsequently, we have frequent experience of observing healthy and unhealthy dimensions in the ways that people appropriate the specific affordances of music. The following description conveys the ways that a music therapist might work with a young person to negotiate a healthier relationship with music. In this example, the young man has been admitted to an adolescent inpatient unit due to severe suicidal ideation and self-harming behavior in the form of cutting at his arms. His diagnosis is major depressive disorder and borderline personality disorder, characterized by feelings of hopelessness, emotional instability, and difficulties establishing and maintaining interpersonal relationships. This has resulted in him leaving school at a young age and having periods of homelessness. The character depicted in this story is typical of the kinds of young people who participate in music therapy sessions, and is based on interviews and experiences collected in a research project that has been approved by the University of Melbourne Ethics Committee (#1340308).

"Music is my best friend. Actually, more like a lover. Can you marry music?" Ryan says to me during one of his early music therapy sessions at the youth psychiatric inpatient unit in Melbourne. Having gradually lost all of his close relationships over the last few years, Ryan describes music as a surrogate friend. "Music's always there, it's helped me through good times and bad". In fact, music has become the "ideal friend" for Ryan. When people no longer meet his expectations, music seems to offer a stable and consistent partnership. However, the seeming perfection that music provides appears to have set the bar so high that no "person" could ever compare. Music never answers back in response to Ryan's uncontrollable outbursts of anger, and it is able to fluctuate quickly to meet his unstable moods between bursts of energy and enthusiasm to depression and despair.

Ryan insists that "music is helpful". He chooses to join the music therapy group and when asked to contribute a song to the group's chosen playlist theme of "music to get us going," he shares "My Immortal" by Evanessence (Lee, Moody, & Hodges, 2003). As he listens to the song, Ryan turns his back to the group, folds his arms and appears tearful. From that moment he seems hostile and rejects the song choices of the other group members. When we reflect together after the group, Ryan reports that his relationship with music is special, and it is frustrating to hear people select songs that do not match his preferences.

I suggest to Ryan that his rigid taste in music might be acting as a barrier to engaging with his peers, since he seems to privilege connecting with the music over connecting with others in the group. Although Ryan is challenged by this suggestion, he opens up and begins to describe how he sometimes uses music to invoke feelings of pain and hurt. This is the first time Ryan has shown agency in his music appropriation, and he seems torn between criticizing his friend (the music) and acknowledging that "his uses" of music do sometimes make him feel worse. Ryan bravely continues and describes how he uses "My Immortal" to heighten feelings of pain and hurt during self-harming behavior. However, he maintains that this is somehow helpful because it provides him with a sense of "achievement".

At his time of crisis on the inpatient unit, Ryan's musical identity is incestuously linked to his mental health problems and limited coping strategies. His mental illness is reflected in his belief that the greater the pain, the greater the achievement, and music is an important tool to get him there. However, he maintains a belief that music is helpful. In the absence of friends and family, and the midst of uncontrollable emotional swings, Ryan's actual commitment to music may be a sign of personal resilience and a potential strength, yet his use of music as a health resource appears to have significant limitations. An important part of my role as music therapist is recognizing Ryan's risky music uses and challenging him to reflect upon this.

Ryan also describes his past love of country music and guitar playing, both of which he ceased when his peers rejected this musical identity. Ryan had since pursued more socially approved "dance music" and taken up DJ-ing "to please other people". We negotiate what Ryan's chosen goals will be for the music therapy sessions with this in mind and he decides to reconnect with both the guitar and country music. I provide Ryan with access to a guitar for his personal use on the ward, and support him in developing his skills during our sessions.

In his individual music therapy sessions over the next four weeks, Ryan begins to play the guitar again, usually playing intense, loud and fast. In addition to exploring a range of existing country songs, he also chooses to write a song in that style. Initially the lyrics are about committing suicide, but this changes to being about "a special girl" in later sessions. As he develops the song, Ryan starts to ask about how he can learn to "play soft—you know, that country music style", and works hard on ways to cultivate this new way of playing. The reintroduction of guitar provides Ryan with a resource for developing a sense of achievement, as well as exploring other valued, yet limited aspects of his identity, such as calmness and gentleness.

As the individual sessions continue, Ryan reflects on the sense of achievement that he feels when playing guitar and I encourage him to trial this form of active music making when he feels distressed. This takes practice and patience, since Ryan's listening habits are deeply engrained. However, the recovery model of the mental health service encourages this kind of active engagement in living with mental illness and Ryan cultivates this new strategy as part of his overall treatment. He describes how engaging in music creation can temporarily distract his thoughts from self-harming and we recognize this as an important step. Ryan is pleased because this contributes to his discharge from the unit, and I am conscious that this is a significant expansion of his previously rigid and potentially dangerous music use.

Once in the community, however, Ryan again loses access to his guitar and his self-harming behavior returns. I connect with him again in a community-based mental health program and he expresses a desire for further support in developing his guitar and song-writing skills. I have access to a number of resources as part of the program and am able to loan him a guitar and collaborate with his case manager to establish a savings plan so that he can eventually purchase his own. Our sessions continue and we gradually develop an intentionally constructed playlist for Ryan to use in everyday situations where he may not have access to a guitar and needs to cope with self-harm thoughts. Ryan chooses mostly country music for this playlist, one artist in particular, and expresses pleasure at being able to confidently select music that he "actually likes", in what appears to be a self-affirming process. We also continue developing Ryan's guitar skills so he has access to a greater personal repertoire, and we begin writing another song in the style of "country."

Ryan's desire to reconnect with country music and develop varied styles of guitar playing appears to not only be an expansion of his musical relationship but a reconnection with a musical identity that had been suppressed for many years. The music therapy sessions provide a space in which this musical identity can be explored, extended and constructed.

36.5 CONCLUSIONS

Music therapists often work with the most vulnerable members of our society and have the opportunity to observe how music is related to health and well-being in a range of contexts. From this close proximity, it can be difficult to make assertions about the way music effects people because it is clearly particular to each individual. What is conspicuous is that mentally healthy and unhealthy people do not necessarily appropriate music for the expression of identity in the same ways. Within a therapeutic context, this difference can be explored and addressed within the therapeutic relationship. It is possible for the music therapist to negotiate what types of musical experiences might be most helpful, either for expressing unhealthy identity issues or for promoting more healthy engagement with identity. Beyond a therapeutic context, a more naïve attitude is dominant, and whilst this is likely a reflection of how healthy people experience music, a number of assumptions drive the academic discourse in dangerously predictable directions, as shown by our critical synthesis of the literature (McFerran, et al., 2013).

There is nothing simple about the relationship between teenage identity and music, particularly in the context of mental illness. Acknowledging this complexity requires caring adults to overcome simplistic assumptions about either positive or negative influences that music has on a person. Instead, our role should be to support adolescents in developing a critical consciousness about their use of music. Increased intentionality in selecting songs becomes of vital importance when a young person is most vulnerable. Sadly, this is also the time when they (and we) are most likely to rely on old habits and fall back on assumptions about what will help. Ruminative and unconscious uses of music abound during difficult times in young people's lives and the affordances of music can easily be used to reinforce depressive thinking and isolating behaviors. Music therapists, teachers, psychologists, and other adults have a critical function in encouraging young people to discriminate, without being judgmental about musical preferences. We need to suggest changes in musical strategies when it is necessary, based on our own critical and caring understandings. This does not mean removing music from young people's lives and certainly does not suggest that one type of music is more helpful than another. It means listening with young people, talking about how they are affected by music and spending the time that is required to move past assumptions about good and bad music. Young people with mental health problems are vulnerable to the power of music and deserve support. If not from you, then from who?

REFERENCES

Anthony, W.A. (1993). Recovery from mental illness: the guiding vision of the mental health service system in the 1990s. *Psychiatric Rehabilitation Journal*, 16(4), 11–23.

Baker, S. & Homan, S. (2007). Rap, recidivism and the creative self: a popular music programme for young offenders in detention. *Journal of Youth Studies*, 10(4), 459–76.

Batt-Rawden, K., Trythall, S., & DeNora, T. (2007). Health musicking as cultural inclusion. In: J. Edwards (Ed.), *Music: promoting health and creating community in healthcare contexts*, pp. 64–82. Newcastle: Cambridge Scholars Publishing.

Beckmann, H.B. (2013). Music, adolescents and health: narratives about how young people use music as a health resource in daily life. In L.O. Bonde, E. Ruud, M.S. Skanland, & G. Trondalen

(Eds.) *Musical life stories: Narratives on health musicking*, Vol. 6, pp. 95–116. Oslo: Norwegian Academy of Music.

Bloch,S. & Singh, B.S. (2001). *Foundations of clinical psychiatry.* Melbourne: Melbourne University Press.

Bonono, G.A. (2008). Grief, trauma and resilience. *Grief Matters: the Australian Journal of Grief and Bereavement,* 11(1), 11–17.

Chastagner, C. (1999). The parents' music resource center: from information to censorship. *Popular Music,* 18(2), 179–92.

Cheng, A.T., Hawton, K., Chen, T.H., et al. (2007). The influence of media coverage of a celebrity suicide on subsequent suicide attempts. *Journal of Clinical Psychiatry,* 68(6), 862–6.

Cheong-Clinch, C. (2013). *Musical diaries: an investigation of the everyday music engagement of young people with mental illness.* Doctoral Dissertation, University of Melbourne.

Csikszentmihalyi, M. (2002). *Flow: the classic work on how to achieve happiness.* London: Rider (Random House).

Davidson, L., Row, M., Tandora, J., O'Connell, M., & Lawless, M. (2009). *A practical guide to recovery-oriented practice: tools for transforming mental health care.* New York, NY: Oxford University Press.

DeNora, T. (2000). *Music in everyday life.* Cambridge: Cambridge University Press.

DeNora, T. (2011). *Music-in-action: selected essays in sonic ecology.* Farnham: Ashgate.

Doak, B. (2003). Relationships between adolescent psychiatric diagnoses, music preferences, and drug preferences. *Music Therapy Perspectives,* 21, 69–73.

Epstein, R. (2007). *The case against adolescence: Rediscovering the adult in every teen.* Fresno, CA: Quill Driver Books/ Word Dancer Press.

Eschen, J.T. (Ed.). (2002). *Analytical music therapy.* London: Jessica Kingsley Publishers.

Eyre, L. (2007). Changes in images, life events and music in Analytical Music Therapy: A reconstruction of Mary Priestley's case study of 'Curtis'. *Qualitative Inquiries in Music Therapy (A Monograph Series),* 3(1), 1–30.

Garrido, S. & Schubert, E. (2011). Negative emotion in music: What is the attraction? A qualitative study. *Empirical Musicology Review,* 6(4), 214–30.

Gold, C., Saarikallio, S., & McFerran, K.S. (2010). Music therapy. In: R.R. Levesque (Ed.), *Encyclopedia of adolescence.* New York, NY: Springer.

Hadley, S.(Ed.). (2003). *Psychodynamic music therapy: case studies.* Phoenixville, PA: Barcelona Publishers.

Hense, C., McFerran, K., & McGorry, P. (2014). Constructing a grounded theory of young people's recovery of musical identity in mental illness. *Arts in Psychotherapy,* 41, 594–603.

Hines, M. & McFerran, K.S. (2013). Metal made me who I am: seven adult men reflect on their engagement with metal music during adolescence. *International Journal of Community Music (Special Edition on Metal Music),* 7(2).

Ivaldi, A. & O'Neill, S.A. (2008). Adolescents' musical role models: whom do they admire and why? *Psychology of Music,* 36(4), 395–415.

Laiho, S. (2004). The psychological functions of music in adolescence. *Nordic Journal of Music Therapy,* 13(1), 47–63.

Lee, A., Moody, B., & Hodges, B. (2003). My immortal. In: D. Fortman (Ed.), *Fallen.* New York, NY: Wind-up Records.

Levesque, R.J.R. (2010). Idols and idolization. In: R.R. Levesque (Ed.), *Encyclopedia of adolescence,* pp. 1377–9. New York: Springer.

MacDonald, R., Kreutz, G., & Mitchell, L. (Eds.). (2012). *Music, health, and wellbeing.* New York, NY: Oxford University Press.

Maslow, A. (1968). *Toward a psychology of being.* New York, NY: John Wiley & Sons.

May, R. (1981). *Man's search for meaning.* London: W.W. Norton and Co.

McFerran, K.S. (2010). Tipping the scales: a substantive theory on the value of group music therapy for supporting grieving teenagers. *Qualitative Inquiries in Music Therapy,* 5, 2–49.

McFerran, K.S., & Baird, K. (2013). Is music really my best friend? Reflections of two maturing women on one's relationship with music. In: L.O. Bonde, E. Ruud, M. S. Skanland & G. Trondalen (Eds.) *Musical lifestories: narratives on health musicking,* Vol. 6, pp. 117–38. Oslo: Norwegian Academy of Music.

McFerran, K.S., Garrido, S., & Saarikallio, S. (2013). A critical interpretive synthesis of the literature linking music and adolescent depression. *Youth and Society, Online First,* 20(1), 103–21

McFerran, K.S. & Grocke, D. (2000). What does group music therapy offer to bereaved young people? A rounded approach to the grieving adolescent. *Grief Matters: the Australian Journal of Grief and Bereavement,* 3(3), 54–61.

McFerran, K.S. & Saarikallio, S. (2013). Depending on music to make me feel better: Who is responsible for the ways young people appropriate music for health benefits. *Arts in Psychotherapy,* 41(1), 89–97.

Miranda, D. & Claes, M. (2004). Rap music genres and deviant behaviors in French-Canadian adolescents. *Journal of Youth and Adolescence,* 33(2), 113–22.

Miranda, D. & Claes, M. (2008). Personality traits, music preferences and depression in adolescence. *International Journal of Adolescence and Youth,* 14(3), 277–98.

Miranda, D. & Claes, M. (2009). Music listening, coping, peer affiliation and depression in adolescence. *Psychology of Music,* 37(2), 215–33.

North, A.C. & Hargreaves, D.J. (2005). Brief report: labelling effects on the perceived deleterious consequences of pop music listening. *Journal of Adolescence,* 28, 433–40.

North, A.C. & Hargreaves, D.J. (2008). *The social and applied psychology of music.* New York, NY: Oxford University Press.

North, A.C. & Hargreaves, D.J. (2012). Pop music cultures and wellbeing. In: R. MacDonald, G. Kreutz, & L. Mitchell (Eds.) *Music, health and wellbeing,* pp. 502–12. Oxford: Oxford University Press.

O'Grady, L. (2009). *The therapeutic potentials of creating and performing music with women in prison: a qualitative case study.* Doctoral Dissertation, University of Melbourne.

Purdon, C. (2002). The role of music in analytical music therapy: music as a carrier of stories. In: J. Eschen (Ed.) *Analytical music therapy,* pp. 104–15. London: Jessica Kingsley Publishers.

Purdon, C. (2006). Feminist music therapy with abused teen girls. In: S. Hadley (Ed.), *Feminist perspectives in music therapy,* pp. 205–26. Gilsum, NH: Barcelona Publishers.

Raskin, R., Novacek, J., & Hogan, R. (1991). Narcissism, self-esteem, and defensive self-enhancement. *Journal of Personality,* 59(1), 19–38.

Rogers, C. (1951). *Client-centered therapy: its current practice, implications and theory.* London: Constable.

Rogers, C. (1961). *On becoming a person: a therapist's view of psychotherapy.* London: Constable.

Ruud, E. (2006). The role of music in the development of identity. *Music and human beings: Music and identity,* 1, 59–69.

Ruud, E. (2010). *Music therapy: A perspective from the humanities.* Gilsum, NH: Barcelona Publishers.

Saarikallio, S. & Erkkila, J. (2007). The role of music in adolescents' mood regulation. *Psychology of Music*, 35(1), 88–109.

Seligman, M. (2011). *Flourish: a visionary new understanding of happiness and well-being.* Sydney: Random House.

Skanland, M.S. (2011). Use of Mp3-players as a coping resource. *Music and Arts in Action*, 3(2), 15–33.

Stack, S. (1998). Heavy metal, religiosity, and suicide acceptability. *Suicide and Life-Threatening Behaviour*, 28(4), 388–94.

Strauss, A. & Corbin, J. (1998). *Basics of qualitative research: techniques and procedures for developing grounded theory*, 2nd edn. Thousand Oaks, CA: Sage.

Treynor, W., Gonzalez, R., & Nolen-Hoeksema, S. (2003). Rumination reconsidered: a psychometric analysis. *Cognitive Therapy and Research*, 27(3), 247–59.

CHAPTER 37

....

ON MUSICAL IDENTITIES, SOCIAL PHARMACOLOGY, AND INTERVENTION TIMING IN MUSIC THERAPY

....

JÖRG FACHNER, JAAKKO ERKKILÄ,
AND OLIVIER BRABANT

... when I was smarter, younger, cooler, braver, and on 150 mg of Effexor.

In "The medicated me" from C. Norris.
Text extract from Chris Norris, *The Medicated Me*, © 2011
Chris Norris, with permission from Chris Norris

In this chapter we discuss the issues of musical identities from the perspective of music therapy and social pharmacology. Social pharmacology focusses on the use of drugs as a social and cultural behavior. The aim of this approach is to understand and describe patterns of drug use and associated risk behaviors (Montagne 2004). However, in this chapter we are not interested in drug policy or the economic conditions of drug markets, nor do we need to discuss the harms and stigma of drug abuse. We want to discuss how drugs (in a wider sense, all psychotropic substances), will influence processes of musical identities in different contexts, especially in music therapy, while interacting with the performance or perception of music.

One of the key ideas of music therapy is that music symbolically represents mental content, such as emotions, images, metaphors, associations, and memories (Erkkilä, Ala-Ruona, Punkanen, & Fachner, 2012). Musical experiences in music therapy are typically spontaneous and authentic, and many agree that music has the ability to permeate defense mechanisms (e.g. Summer, 2002). Thus, musical experiences in music therapy often reflect a client's deeply personal qualities, including qualities caused by illness. Musical identity is therefore not separate from one's other identities or personal qualities in general. Musical identity is a vital source of data when getting to know a person and the various factors that affect that person, including the factors behind their pathology.

In music therapy, it is important to create a context that enables the client to be as open, authentic, spontaneous, and creative as possible. Winnicott (1968) likens this kind of ideal therapeutic context to children's play and calls it "potential space." In this space of play, fantasy and imagination occur and "everything" is possible. In terms of illness, one's innate creative competences can be used for finding solutions for recovery and for gaining insights into the mechanisms behind illness. Music as an abstract, emotional, and highly symbolic medium offers an ideal forum for fantasy and imagination, and is also therefore very useful for therapeutic work (Erkkilä et al., 2012).

Here, we see some parallel aspects to the use of recreational drugs. One of the reasons that musicians like to use recreational drugs, as described in Eric Clapton's statement below, is to stimulate creativity, facilitate associative and divergent thinking, and enhance emotions, memory retrieval, and intuition. In short, to alter normal conscious processing in order to create new perspectives on artistic material (Fachner, 2006). In this way, drugs act as a complement to music processing in order to expand the potential space of creativity. This process has also been utilized in a former version of Guided Imagery and Music where certain pieces of mainly classical and jazz music were conducted in a thematic therapeutic sequence. LSD was used to stimulate emotions, evoke peak experiences, elicit uncensored responses and associations, and to open a path to the inner world of the client's unconscious (Bonny & Pahnke, 1972). In this context, the specific drug action was utilized as a complement and as a catalyst of therapeutic endeavors. For these reasons, all factors that hide or color aspects of one's [musical] identity are important to take into account in music therapy. Illness, such as depression, affects identity and may make sad music more sad, fearful music more fearful, and joyful music less joyful (Punkanen, Eerola, & Erkkilä, 2011a,b). In this way, music can reveal much about the client's current state, albeit a provisional and illness-dependent state.

37.1 MUSICAL IDENTITIES IN A CONTINUUM OF DRUG EFFECTS

Medication, such as antidepressants, can also color the client's way of being, particularly from an emotional perspective. These drugs may dampen or they may balance, but they affect the client and therefore have an influence on one's identity. However, the issue is not whether medication is a good or bad component of the overall treatment. Rather, it is to understand its effect on one's identity, as well as on the therapeutic work. Drugs such as psychedelics may totally change our musical experience and open up new levels of consciousness, while antidepressants are meant to level and balance emotional activity. Typically, antidepressants will dampen intense emotional dynamics and sudden peak experiences connected to altered states of consciousness, lessening insights into one's unconscious. In short, we may ask, do antidepressants intrinsically hinder the occurrence of elements which are central to therapeutic

processes in music therapy? What kind of influence do they have on the musical identity of a person?

A possible answer might be found in the processing of music and emotion in the brain
and how musical identities, emotion, and drugs interact. Music and drugs are sometimes linked together in that each changes our emotions. The manifold use and misuse
of recreational drugs and alcohol in popular music culture has not been a sole indicator of this (Shapiro, 2003; Fachner, 2006; Van Havere, Vanderplasschen, Lammertyn,
Broekaert, & Bellis, 2011). Recent brain research shows that preferred, pleasing music is
processed in the same areas as recreational substances (Blood & Zatorre, 2001). This has
the effect of increasing cascades of dopaminergic interactions in cognition and reward
systems (Menon & Levitin, 2005; Salimpoor, Benovoy, Larcher, Dagher, & Zatorre,
2011) helping to distinguish where and when to place attention, including what in this
particular moment is of personal importance, and which current selection of perceptual and emotional content is consciously processed. What is processed specifically is, of
course, dependent upon the musical identity of a person, i.e. upon what in the music one
focusses on and what keeps or catches his or her attention accordingly.

37.2 MUSIC THERAPY REDUCES OR COMPLEMENTS MEDICATION

The similar brain activation of pleasure induced by drug action and listening to well-
loved music may indicate two directions that music therapy can take when considering
an accompanying use of prescribed medication: music therapy may reduce the need for
medication or music therapy may complement the effect of medication.

First, activating brain circuits inducing pleasure gives rise to the hope that the right
music therapy intervention stirring up the emotions of the individual client at the right
time, may *be a decrement, i.e. it reduces medication* prescribed for mental health issues, as
music can replace the drug's desired effects. For example, in a study with depressed clients comparing treatment with Indian "relaxation" music or hypnotics, the authors discussed that "the effects of music could be equivalent to 10 mg of Chlordiazepoxide or 7
mg of Diazepam" (Deshmukh, Sarvaiya, Seethalakshmi, & Nayak, 2009, p. 76). However,
when working with music in music therapy we are not simply replacing the medication
with music and prescribing certain music instead of pills, as we will discuss later.

Reductions of medication have been demonstrated in medicine employing music, for
example, as an adjunct to anesthetic medication (Spintge, 1991, 2012). For instance, sedatives are regularly administered before surgery to reduce a patient's anxiety. However,
sedatives often have negative side effects (drowsiness, respiratory depression, etc.),
and may interact with anesthetic agents, prolonging patient recovery and preventing
discharge. Therefore, increased attention is being paid to the introduction of music
to reduce medication during (Harikumar et al., 2006), and reducing anxiety before

(Bringman, Giesecke, Thörne, & Bringman, 2009) surgery. These few examples may indicate that there is hope that we can use music as a decrement of medication.

Additionally, studying the interaction of music and pharmacological substances may help to identify music (therapy) *as a complement to medication*. There is evidence that musicians use drugs to stimulate the creation of music (Boyd, 1992), or to perceive the music differently, i.e. the drug adds something to the creation and perception of music (Fachner, 2006). One prominent influence on time perception is that the passage of time seems to be perceived from an altered metric frame of reference (Fachner, 2011). How this is related to musical identities in a cultural context will be discussed later in this chapter.

The word "complementary" means "in addition to" or "allied to" and is seen as an addition to standard care. For example, research into treating chronic pain with music therapy indicates that "music therapy is an effective adjuvant intervention for patients suffering from chronic non-malignant pain, doubling the effects of pharmacological treatment" (Nickel, Hillecke, Argstatter, & Bolay, 2005, p. 287).

Our own research into the treatment of depression with music therapy indicates that a complementary interaction between improvisational music therapy and antidepressant medication may facilitate standard care (Erkkilä et al., 2011). Clients receiving music therapy and standard care showed significantly decreased depression and anxiety symptoms compared to those receiving only standard care. Later in this chapter, we will take a closer look at this research study and a selected case to exemplify how the interaction between music therapy, the client's musical identity, and antidepressant medication may work, in order to explore how music therapy reduces or complements medication.

37.3 PERFORMED IDENTITY, INDIVIDUAL TREATMENT, AND TIMING

Both a decrement (reduction) and a complement of medication are desirable from the stance of personalized medicine. Prescriptions are ideally based on the biopsychosocial identity of a particular person and not solely on a diagnostic classification. Personalized medicine hopes to address the right medication based on genotypes and biomarkers reflecting the client's biological condition (Holsboer, 2008), aiming to administer an individualized combination. While an antidepressant may be adequate for moderate or severe depression, it may not be the right choice for a first episode of mild depression. However, antidepressant prescriptions are on the rise (Lönnqvist, 2009) and once the proposed "chemical imbalances" are treated with antidepressants, they "may reduce sense of self and soul into dopamine, serotonin, neurons, milligrams" (Norris, 2011).

Furthermore, there is increasing knowledge surrounding the chronobiological component of drug action and the importance of determining the right time for drug administration (Smolensky & Peppa, 2007). Depressive clients may experience more (intense) symptoms in the morning than in the afternoon or evening; further, seasonal influences on depression are well documented (Peeters, Berkhof, Delespaul, Rottenberg, & Nicolson, 2006). EEG measures taken in the morning exhibit different patterns of lateralization than in the afternoon; moreover, summer days would differ from recordings in late autumn (Passynkova & Volf, 2001; Peterson & Harmon-Jones, 2009). According to Aldridge (1989), we are "patterned frequencies in a matrix of time" and music resonates with these patterns becoming our identity. Therefore, chronobiological perspectives on how deregulations of biological rhythms influence affect and emotion, how this relates to music (Tucek, 2006), and how this interacts with medication should be taken into account.

A healthy person's identity may fluctuate, but may display a coherent structure of responding to varying contexts, while a person experiencing a mental illness like depression may be restricted in his/her choices of cognitive and emotional response. We may hear this in the way that this person would improvise. Improvisation in music therapy can represent one's "free-floating" and healthy, or restricted and unhealthy musical identity; i.e. in the improvisation, we can sense the impulses, and hear the potentials and resources of the healthy person if not hindered by the disease (Gold, Rolvsjord, Aaro, Aarre, Tjemsland, & Stige, 2005; Nordoff & Robbins 2007). A free-floating, healthy identity might be understood as a flexible and dynamic use of musical opportunities while performing the self and creating music with a coherent and personal form of play. Instead, when under the influence of the disease, one can hear restrictions that somehow represent the unhealthy form of a musical identity (Aldridge 1989, 1996). However, when someone has lost his/her original healthy identity, one can hear when change is happening, or when it is the right time for the therapist to act. The influence of biological rhythms and seasonal change is a known issue in depression, thus we are interested in the role of chronobiological aspects. In other words, if we are not in the right mood or when drowsy or exhausted, we may not be able to improvise in a creative way in music (therapy) to show our real or appropriate identity. Although music therapy is adaptable to situations and individual circumstances, biological predispositions have an influence on our actual behavior.

37.4 PERFORMED IDENTITY I: CULTURE AND DRUG USE

Music and drugs may be linked, as we have already seen, and in this part of the chapter, we discuss the importance of an appropriate context, a demand and interest for the interaction, and a process to learn how to utilize this interaction for music-related purposes. Furthermore, we will explicate how preferences for musical styles and how a corresponding drug use preference may reflect a person's musical identity.

There are arguments against any psychotropic substance, including alcohol, in that they may temporarily open up capacities for relaxation or agitation, help to focus or un-focus attention, increase or decrease the distance to one's own emotions, among others. In short, psychotropic substances may show the individual what is possible if hurdles are overcome and point out what has not been recognized before (Fachner, 2010; Blätter, Fachner, & Winkelman, 2011). Baudelaire (1860) described the state experienced "under the influence" of drugs as being not much different from moments of bliss in which all seems to go well (without the pills). However, depending on the pharmacokinetic and dynamics of the substance and the habituation involved, the danger arises of finding oneself on a slippery slope towards a "medicated me" and a "false sense of well-being" (Norris, 2011). Nevertheless, drugs are tools that humans have developed or discovered for various purposes and, like all tools, they can be used or misused (Moore, 2008).

> To begin with, drink is very baffling and cunning. It's got a personality of its own. Part of the trap [of drugs and alcohol] is that they open the doors to unreleased channels or rooms you hadn't explored before or allowed to be open. A lot of my creative things came out first of all through marijuana. I started smoking when I was about eighteen or nineteen, and that would let out a whole string of humorous things as well as music. Then drink allowed me to be very self-piteous and opened up that whole kind of sorrowful musical side of myself. Unfortunately after that, the booze becomes more important than the doors it's opening, so that's the trap.
>
> Eric Clapton, cited in Boyd, 1992, p. 199.

37.4.1 Neuro-enhancers, creativity, and situational context

With the development of Prozac in the 1970s, antidepressants became "lifestyle agents, tools for unlocking potential and fine-tuning the self " (Norris, 2011). In recent years, so-called "neuro-enhancers" have become a means of boosting the brain's activity. Rolipram, donepezil, modafinil, or ritalin are used to promote focus and concentration, improve memory function and maintain wakefulness. Risk assessment of long-term use is in its infancy. Neuro-enhancers are utilized widely and one common observation is that, although some results indicate an additive effect to cognitive abilities (Turner, Robbins, Clark, Aron, Dowson, & Sahakian, 2003), proof has not been satisfactory shown (Moore, 2008).

However, users report their subjective effectiveness, i.e. they have experienced and are convinced that these drugs act as an enhancer. A similar observation—Weil (1998) refers to this as an "active placebo"—has been made with psychotropic drugs that do not have a context-independent, solid internal assessment, such as opiates. In other words, heroin will be the same independent of context, whereas drugs with a contextual bonding (cannabis, psychedelics, etc.) are related to situational and personal factors. Drug effects cannot be separated from the situation in which the drug is taken. The rituals that accompany use and addiction are important elements in continued use and show the important ritualistic aspect of use and dependence (Blätter, et al., 2011).

37.4.2 Lifestyle and identity

In his book entitled "Waiting for the man," Shapiro (2003) states that each popular music style in the last decades was also the expression of a certain lifestyle, to be seen in relation to the preferences of drug consumption of the artists and the scene around them coining this style. From a socio-pharmacological view, the preference of a subculture for a certain drug has always been a kind of mechanism to "turn on", i.e. to put them into certain physiological conditions to experience ordinary and extraordinary events, occurrences, and moods more intensely and from a different perspective.

How are these physiological conditions shared in music appreciation and how does this relate to musical identities? In drug cultures and drug therapies, it is a well-known practice that drug effects may be influenced by a combination of set pieces (physiological and psychological constitution), and setting (social and physical surroundings), and may be shaped with regard to the experience and interpretation of sensual stimulation by drugs and context (Zinberg, 1984; Weil, 1998;). The effect profile of certain drugs induces a temporarily similar socio-physiological effect on mood and cognition, such as the "contact high" as described by Weil (1998) or the "synch"-experience (Wolfe, 1989), and a corresponding preference for externally stimulating combinations. Jonnes (1999, p. 119 ff.) describes the emergence of a "lounge" setting of carpeting, dimmed blue light, armchairs, etc. in the Harlem Tea-Pads (tea rooms) and jazz clubs in New York in the 1930s, which is also common in the chill-out area of rave parties. Musicians and dancers using marihuana in New York in the 1930s preferred a setting as described in a newspaper article in 1936:

> While whites often buy reefers in Negro night clubs, planning to smoke them elsewhere, sometimes they manage to gain entrance to a mixed-colour party. The most talked of reefer parties—excluding those of Hollywood—take place in Harlem. Early in the morning, when night club singers, musicians and dancers are through work, they gather informally—these affairs apparently are never arranged—and have a few drinks.
>
> With their uncanny power for wheedling melody out of even the worst pianos, it isn't long before the crowd is humming, softly clapping hands or dancing in sensuous rhythms that have never been seen in nightclubs. There is little noise; windows are shut, keeping the smell of smoking weeds away from what might be curious nostrils.
>
> Nor there is any of the yelling, dashing about, playing of crude jokes or physical violence that often accompany alcoholic parties; under the influence of marihuana, one has a dread of these things.
>
> Anonymous, 1936, p. 8.

The question is whether such socio-pharmacological aspects of set and setting are to be considered a part of the drug culture, or rather as a socio-physiological, commonly shared and preferred sphere of regeneration, relaxation, and conversation at dance events; as a place where people sit down or lie down in relaxed positions in order to regenerate or reflect, to chat or just dream away. "Playing Jazz music, smoking cannabis and talking in jazz slang" can also be interpreted as a "way of life" characterized by specific identity postures and social performances of the artist's world, bohemians, the "night people" etc., concluded Curry (1968, p. 238) in his observations of jazz musicians and their audiences.

What becomes obvious in these lines is that there is a connection between a certain lifestyle, identity, time and place of listening to and creation of music. Personal history and lifestyle lead to an individual form of performed identity expressed in the preference of a certain music marking passages of personal experience (Aldridge, 1989). Thus, we may go so far as identifying a typology of drugs, and their influence on the creation of a certain sound and musical genre associated with that drug, indicating an interaction of drug effects and music appreciation (Shapiro, 2003; Fachner, 2010).

37.5 PERFORMED IDENTITY II: INDIVIDUALIZED TREATMENT AND MEDICATION USE IN MUSIC THERAPY

Now that we have presented a model of how the appreciation of music under drug reward influences may work when paired with a certain lifestyle and identity, we shall try to understand how the effect of antidepressants is experienced.

> Antidepressants didn't change me much at first. They brightened mornings, softened edges, padded landings, tilted my horizon by just one or two degrees … and keeping a whole mushy, messy part of life at a cool distance.
>
> Norris, 2011.

What happens in a therapeutic framework with clients habituated to antidepressant medication? In our study on individual music therapy for depression (Erkkilä et al., 2011), we found that about 70% of the participants ($n = 79$) were prescribed medication, typically different types of antidepressants. Compared to standard care only, in the music therapy group ($n = 29$) symptoms of depression and anxiety significantly decreased after 3 months of treatment, while global function increased (Erkkilä et al., 2011).

From the 22 out of 29 music therapy clients receiving antidepressant medication, nine decreased, nine maintained, and four increased the amount of medication taken after 3 months of music therapy. An increase or decrease was evidenced in the amount of the psychoactive ingredient as reported from the clients. For example, one client received 120 mg Duloxetine, a selective norepinephrine reuptake inhibitor (SNRI) prior to the study, but only 60 mg after music therapy. From those responding to music therapy, i.e. featuring a symptom decrease of more than 50 % on the Montgomery Åsberg Depression Rating Scale (MADRS), five showed a decrease, four maintained, and two clients increased medication after music therapy. Thus, about 60% of the 22 music therapy clients improved their depression status while keeping the same level or increasing their medication. The other 40% decreased their medication dosages.

This may indicate that music therapy was effective for those medicated, but also shows that it initiated a process by which medication was able to decrease. We are looking at a paradox of decrements and complements of medication following music therapy treatment. We may speculate that those participants maintaining a constant level of medication had not consulted their psychiatrist during treatment, but unfortunately we did not ask them systematically about this. Nevertheless, as clients were becoming highly emotionally engaged in therapy, several issues of suppressed anger and frustration and loss of will and power were identified, and turned into conscious processing (Fachner, Gold, Ala-Ruona, Punkanen, & Erkkilä, 2010: Erkkilä, Ala-Ruona, Punkanen, & Fachner, 2012). Although this is part of the therapy, it may well be that the emotions, memories and cognitive processes evoked during therapy frightened some, and increased medication was one way of coping with it.

Clients' views on the effect of antidepressants vary. Some said they help rid overwhelming negative emotions and anxiety, which is a relieving experience. However, others voiced complaints about the flattening of their emotions as a result of medication. For some, this was an unpleasant experience, whereas others felt that anything is better than the overwhelming hold of negative emotions. Some clients felt that antidepressants had an effect on their personality. Feelings of being a different person are typically experienced as unpleasant, and depression is a long, melancholic search for a lost identity and sense of self. The search takes a lot of energy, it causes withdrawal from activities that were part of the self, and anxiety becomes the leading emotional force hindering communication and work (Fachner et al., 2010).

Yet, there is convincing evidence that a combination of psychosocial support (such as psychotherapy) and medication is the best treatment, with psychotherapy acting as the initial treatment (Greenberg & Goldman, 2009). A striking example of the dominance of medication in depression treatment is a Finnish study (Honkonen, Aro, Isometsä, Virtanen, & Katila, 2007) that explored the treatments offered to people who were retired prematurely because of depression. The study revealed that 89% of the retired individuals during 1993 to 2004 never received any form of psychosocial treatment. Without a doubt, a better balance between the treatment choices could be achieved.

37.5.1 Antidepressants and musical identity—Maria's case

It is important to emphasize here that the issue is about a better balance, not that medication, such as antidepressants, is useless. In Maria's case, which will be introduced later in this chapter, an interesting finding was that the dosage of antidepressants was increased at the same time as the client's depressive symptoms decreased. In this case, we think that the decision to increase medication was right. Regardless, there is a need to increase psychosocial support, in particular psychotherapy-related treatments, and to focus on finding an effective interaction between chemical and psychosocial treatments.

This is important not only because of the better overall effect, but also because antidepressants are not harmless. Side effects such as sexual problems, insomnia, agitation, sedation, weight gain and loss, restlessness, and nervousness are typical for antidepressants (Brambilla, Hotopf, & Barbui, 2005). Although side effects, and even the overall effect of the antidepressants on the sense of the self, vary between individuals, it is easy to conclude that psychosocial help is needed not only for maximizing the effect of the treatment, but also for special support when facing possible intolerable side effects. Furthermore, a known problem of antidepressants is that it can take several weeks until the favorable effects take place and a better balance is achieved. However, during these weeks depressive disorders are also severe and thus weaken the patient's tolerance for additional side effects.

Previously (Erkkilä, et al., 2012; Fachner et al., 2010), through describing Maria's case, we have illustrated, from the angle of creativity and brain states, how music therapy improvisation can reflect healthy or unhealthy identities and lead to new insights. We also illustrate here how psychosocial treatment can vitally improve the client's condition, and how, in Maria's case, interaction between psychosocial treatment and medication (antidepressants) is exceptionally beneficial.

Maria started music therapy at the age of 30 as part of a music therapy research trial, which offered 20 twice-weekly hour-long music therapy sessions. She had been suffering from depression since the beginning of her studies at university, over 10 years ago. She could study and work in her family business only occasionally between severe depressive episodes. Her illness had postponed her graduation. She had received cognitive psychotherapy, but reported that it had not really worked out well for her. She liked music therapy because it was something more active, both from the client and the therapist's side, which she appreciated. Maria saw that her biggest problem was an inability to throw herself into situations and be spontaneous in social contexts. She also had difficulty expressing negative emotions, something she was aware of before the music therapy process. She had problems in separating herself from her family, which she had independently recognized earlier. She used medication (antidepressants) for depression before and during her music therapy process. She improved during music therapy from severe depression to no depression after 20 sessions, as seen in the MADRS (Montgomery & Åsberg, 1979). However, the dose of antidepressants was increased from 100 to 150 mg sertraline per day during the same period. One could assume that if the therapy works well, the dose of antidepressants can be reduced, which was the case with 40% of those clients who improved significantly in our study.

Perhaps the relationship between therapy and medication in a successful course of treatment does not always follow a positive correlation pattern. Maria, who evidently benefitted from the combination of music therapy and medication, was very active in music therapy, devoting much effort to her treatment. She quickly understood how freely improvising with the therapist was loaded with symbolic meaning, often connected to her own psychological history, personality, relations, and to aspects of her illness. In other words, to her healthy and unhealthy identities. Although Maria was rather avoidant at the beginning of the process, in particular regarding negative emotions, and not very energetic, this changed rapidly. Towards the end of the therapy process, she was working through painful experiences accompanied with strong (negative) emotions such as anger and fear. Maria also became more energetic and more frequently showed her humorous side. Not only was Maria hard-working in music therapy. When feeling better, she became more social and started to spend more time with her friends and relatives. Perhaps the most intense episode was a dramatic confrontation with her father, to whom she had never before been able to speak with about her real feelings, in particular, early disappointments and pent-up anger. In a way, she tested a new or repressed identity in real life, after first dealing with it in music therapy. At the same time when feeling better, she spent a lot of mental energy and was often confronted with negative emotions. Perhaps the increase of medication helped to balance this new dynamic lifestyle, where various exhausting situations and emotions now also existed. We can, perhaps, also conclude that sometimes medication (antidepressants) may equalize the effect of intense therapeutic progress, which can include burdening and overwhelming aspects.

From literature on depression we know that depression is typically related to problems in expressing and regulating negative emotions (Joormann & Gotlib, 2010), even including a tendency to turn negative emotions against the self (Blatt, 1998). This was evident in Maria's case, particularly at the beginning of music therapy. Depressed individuals have also been found to be avoidant towards stimuli which represent high energetic arousal because they suffer from a lack of energy (e.g., Beck & Brown, 1996). Maria often spoke about her life being in the tight grip of depression when she stayed at home with not enough energy to participate in many normal everyday activities, particularly if they included any kind of social activities.

Maria's way of expressing herself within free improvisation reflected her identity both as an individual with unique personal qualities, and as an individual suffering from depression. Needless to say, these two identities can be very different depending on the severity of illness. In an improvisation at the beginning of the process, the therapist assumed the role of a relative of Maria's who had been mean and dominating to her. Maria had just told the therapist how she often would have liked to speak to that person about how she felt in these situations, but she did not have enough courage (or energy) to do it. In improvisation, Maria stayed very cool and did not vary dramatically in her musical expression, though the therapist tried to play in a dominant and aggressive way. After the improvisation Maria said, "This is just how I am. I was totally incompetent to change my expression though I recognized your provocative expression." Symbolically, the improvisation offered a context to Maria for investigating aspects of her identity—this time, those aspects affected by her illness. At a later stage of the music therapy, Maria could easily recognize the overall mood of an improvisation and connect it to her current state of being in her illness. After a very "dark" solo improvisation by Maria, she said, "I did not plan to play this dark way, but it just happened." In the resulting discussion, Maria concluded that she was not totally healthy yet, and the darkness, in a way, reminds her of the possibility to become worse again. Maria's music therapy was very much based on investigating the "sick" identity, and on developing and training the "healthy" identity. Music therapy improvisation offers an excellent milieu for such a work.

How much of this identity development in therapy has been fostered or limited by medication, i.e., medication creating emotional borders that were helping her to develop a distance to the "depressive identity" and to focus on the healthy potentials, can only be speculated. However, she seemed to have the right medication at the right time to support music therapy (or vice versa). Conversely, the 40% of our clients that decreased their medication may have realized that it was time for a change and some of them expressed their wish to reduce medication.

37.6 PERFORMED IDENTITY III: CHRONOBIOLOGY OR WHY TIMING IS OF THE ESSENCE

There are two important lessons that can be learned from chronobiology (Smolensky & Lamberg, 2001; Palmer, 2002). The symptoms accompanying a disorder usually manifest in a cyclical way and the effects of a treatment vary depending on the moment of administration. This is not only true for somatic disorders, but also for psychological disorders, clinical depression being a very good example. Indeed, it is well known that people who suffer from depression experience their worst symptoms in the morning, with a gradual improvement as the day progresses. Eventually, in the evening, the mood of people with depression is almost identical to the mood of healthy individuals (Peeters et al., 2006). In addition to this circadian pattern, a seasonal effect has also been demonstrated, with mood being lowest in the autumn and winter, and highest in the summer. This difference applies to everybody, but it is much more pronounced among people suffering from depression, especially its seasonal form (Harmatz, Well, Overtree, Kawamura, Rosal, & Ockene, 2000).

Since chronotherapy has already proven to be very beneficial in biomedicine, it stands to reason that a similar approach could successfully be applied to music therapy. As we have seen, improvisational psychodynamic music therapy encourages clients to explore their thoughts, memories and emotions through musical expression. Therefore, applying the principles of chronotherapy to music therapy requires an understanding of the possible temporal fluctuations existing in mood states, music perception, and the perception of self.

We just mentioned the cyclical mood changes that characterize depression, however, the existence of a diurnal pattern in mood fluctuation is also present in healthy individuals. Indeed, mood researchers using the positive affect (PA)–negative affect (NA) paradigm to describe positive and negative moods have repeatedly shown the existence of a daily cycle for PA and the absence of such a cycle for NA (e.g., Clark, Watson, & Leeka, 1989; Murray, Allen, & Trinder, 2002; Hasler, Mehl, Bootzin, & Vazire, 2008). PA typically follows a bell-shaped curve, with low levels in the morning and in the evening, and a peak during the afternoon. There is strong evidence to suggest that this diurnal fluctuation is the result of endogenous rhythms as the PA cycle is only minimally affected by idiosyncratic habits and lifestyle factors (Watson, 2000). On the contrary, in the absence of external stressors, NA tends to remain constant and low throughout the day, thus displaying no specific circadian rhythmicity.

The case in favor of using a chronotherapeutic approach in music therapy becomes even stronger if we consider that our mood states noticeably influence the way we perceive emotions. Indeed, numerous studies have demonstrated that our current mood creates a bias in our perception and assessment of emotions. Furthermore, this perceptual bias seems to be mood-congruent, meaning that it leads to an amplification of emotions matching our current mood and/or a minimization of emotions having a different valence.

To give a few examples, Surguladze, Young, Senior, Brébion, Travis, & Phillips (2004) concluded that, compared with healthy volunteers, people with clinical depression were perceptually less sensitive to pictures of faces expressing happiness. In another experiment, when presented simultaneously with sad and neutral faces, people with depression tended to pay more attention to sad facial expressions (Gotlib, Krasnoperova, Yue, & Joormann, 2004).

Unsurprisingly, this phenomenon also applies to music perception. In a study investigating the role of mood and personality in the perception of emotions in music, Vuoskoski & Eerola (2011) found positive correlations between vigor (positive mood) and the ratings of happiness in the music, as well as between depression (negative mood) and the ratings of sadness. Punkanen, et al. (2011a) came to a similar conclusion in a study on emotional recognition and depression. They asked a group of participants with depression to rate the emotional content of musical excerpts and compared the scores to the ratings of healthy participants. The results indicated that participants with depression had a judgement bias towards negative emotions.

Brabant & Toiviainen (2014) used the same approach, but controlled for time by testing participants at two different times of day (09.00 and 16.00 hours). They discovered that sad and tender clips were rated higher in sadness and tenderness in the morning than in the afternoon. In other words, participants were more sensitive to musically expressed sadness and tenderness at 09.00 hours.

Interestingly enough, a bias similar to the one reported by Punkanen, et al. (2011a) has been observed by memory researchers. There appears to be a selective effect of emotions on memory, whereby people more easily retrieve memories when affective valence is matching their mood at the moment of retrieval. One of the recurrent findings is that people who currently feel happy recall more positive events and fewer negative events than people feeling sad (e.g., Madigan & Bollenbach, 1982; Bullington, 1990; Miranda & Kihlstrom, 2005). Obviously, the fact that our mood influences how we remember and perceive autobiographical elements has direct implications for our sense of self and our outlook on life.

To summarize the findings presented above, we know that some components of our mood states follow a predictable circadian rhythm, and that this is true for both healthy and depressed individuals. We also know that our current mood affects our perception of musically expressed emotions and the retrieval of autobiographical memories.

The logical conclusion is that the efficacy of music therapy could be increased even further by combining these elements and developing a chronotherapeutic approach. In this new approach, interventions could be adapted to the time of day and the season. Furthermore, sessions could be scheduled to take place at moments deemed optimal for the client's needs and the achievement of the therapeutic goals. In addition, knowledge of the time factor could help music therapists modulate their interpretation of the various events occurring in a session. Lastly, a better understanding of chronopharmacology, mood cyclicity, and music perception can only be beneficial towards a successful combination of medication and music therapy.

37.7 CONCLUSIONS

Discovering and unfolding the musical identity of the client is part of the music therapy process. Various factors affect highly sensitive music therapeutic expression and interaction. Medication is one of them. Considering how the effect of antidepressants in the context of music therapy is experienced, we discussed that a decrement and increment may be part of the therapeutic process, depending on the needs and the musical identity of the client.

There is a predictable rhythm behind the intensity of depressive symptoms, and this rhythm is both diurnal and seasonal. Furthermore, individuals' sensitivity to emotions fluctuates in a circadian manner, which affects not only music perception but also the sense of self through selective memory recollection. In other words, one's identity manifests differently—more melancholic, more positive—depending on the state of our chronobiological cycle at the moment of therapy. The effect of illness, which may take away part of our energy, and the effect of drugs, which may make us sleepy or cause insomnia, are additional factors that may also affect musical experiences and the therapeutic process.

Music and drugs seemed to be appreciated as a complement in several musical activities (Fachner, 2006) in (predominantly) popular music culture and identity (Manning, 2007). We have presented a model of how music appreciation may work alongside the positive stimuli and influence of drugs when embedded into a certain lifestyle and identity context. We discussed that this process needs an appropriate context, a demand and interest for the interaction, and a culture in which to learn how to utilize this complementary interaction for music-related purposes.

The reason music therapy may successfully replace medication is because it is able to substitute itself as both the drug effect and the placebo effect. These two elements are inherently present in the therapeutic response to any medication. Indeed, the overall treatment effect is always the result of the drug effect combined with psychosocial factors (Benedetti, 2009). The latter is directly connected to the placebo response, which could be defined as the activation of a person's innate ability to correct an imbalance and restore health. Music is able to trigger neurophysiological mechanisms similar to the ones activated by drugs (Salimpoor, Benovoy, Larcher, Dagher, & Zatorre, 2011). Furthermore, music therapy can obviously be a strong activator of the placebo response as defined above. This last aspect is not to be neglected since, in the case of antidepressants for example, the so-called "psychiatrist effect," which points on the interaction between drugs, psychiatrists, and clients has been shown to be at least as important as the drug effect in treatment outcome (McKay, Imel, & Wampold, 2006).

Drugs may increase or decrease the intensity of emotional moments and cognitive processes, although drug's pharmacokinetic effect varies according to the time-point of intake and the phase of biological rhythms. Music therapy acts on kairological principles of pivotal moments aiming for emotional and cognitive peak experiences to evoke change. Preferred music heard at the right time itself may act like a drug and induce trance, daydreaming, recharge, etc. (Herbert, 2011). The difference for music is that it has no known severe side effect and is less likely to become addictive. In light of the history of drugs, such as acting as different mind-enhancers, this quality of music shows its very potential, particularly since psychotherapy, especially music psychotherapy, emphasizes phenomena that are considered beneficial for therapeutic work, such as the creation of "potential space" and altered states of consciousness (Erkkilä et al., 2012). This has been successfully employed in addiction treatment where, for example, vibro/physio-acoustic relaxation-induction and creative work on recall of addictive states and motivation helped to overcome gambling (Erkkilä & Eerola, 2010). Exposure to slow pulsations and monochrome sound induces a relaxation response, shifting attention focus and altering consciousness (Fachner & Rittner, 2011; Lee et al., 2012). If music can enhance the mind and change the state of consciousness, it must have a huge potential to uncover one's real identity.

References

Aldridge, D. (1989). A phenomenological comparison of the organisation of music and the self. *Arts in Psychotherapy*, 16(2), 91–7.

Aldridge, D. (1996). *Music therapy and research in medicine—from out of the silence*. London: Jessica Kingsley.

Anonymous. (1936). Topics of the day—facts and fancies about marihuana. *The Literary Digest*, 24th October, 7–8.

Baudelaire, C. (1860). *Les paradis artificiels: opium et haschisch*. Paris: Poulet-Malassis et de Broise.

Beck, A.T., & Brown, G.K. (1996). *BDI-II, Beck depression inventory manual*, 2nd edn. San Antonio, TX: Harcourt.

Benedetti, F. (2009). *Placebo effects: understanding the mechanisms in health and disease*. Oxford: Oxford University Press.

Blatt, S.J. (1998). Contributions of psychoanalysis to the understanding and treatment of depression. *Journal of the American Psychoanalysis Association*, 46(3), 723–5.

Blätter, A.E., Fachner, J.C., & Winkelman, M. (2011). Addiction—dynamics and relations to altered states of consciousness. In: E. Cardenas & M. Winkelman (Eds.) *Altering consciousness: a multidisciplinary perspective*, Vol. 2, Biological and Psychological Perspectives, pp. 167–87. Santa Barbara, CA: Praeger.

Blood, A.J. & Zatorre, R.J. (2001). Intensely pleasurable responses to music correlate with activity in brain regions implicated in reward and emotion. *Proceedings of the National Academy of Sciences, USA*, 98(20), 11818–23.

Bonny, H.L. & Pahnke, W.N. (1972). The use of music in psychedelic (LSD) psychotherapy. *Journal of Music Therapy*, IX(Summer), 64–87.

Boyd, J. (1992). Musicians in tune—Seventy-five contempory musicians discuss the creative process. New York, NY: Fireside, a Simon & Schuster imprimateur.

Brabant, O. & Toiviainen, P. (2014). Diurnal changes in the perception of emotions in music: does the time of day matter? *Musicae Scientiae*, 18(3), 256–74.

Brambilla, P., Hotopf, A., & Barbui, C. (2005). Side-effect profile of fluoxetine in comparison with other SSRIs, tricyclic and newer antidepressants: a meta-analysis of clinical trial data. *Pharmacopsychiatry*, 38(2), 69–77.

Bringman, H., Giesecke, K., Thörne, A., & Bringman, S. (2009). Relaxing music as premedication before surgery: a randomised controlled trial. *Acta Anaesthesiologica Scandinavica*, 53(6), 759–64.

Bullington, J.C. (1990). Mood congruent memory: a replication of symmetrical effects for both positive and negative moods. *Journal of Social Behavior & Personality*, 5(4), 123–34.

Clark, L.A., Watson, D., & Leeka, J. (1989). Diurnal variation in the positive affects. *Motivation and Emotion*, 13(3), 205–34.

Curry, A. (1968). Drugs in rock and jazz music. *Clinical Toxicology*, 1(2), 235–44.

Deshmukh, A.D., Sarvaiya, A.A., Seethalakshmi, R., & Nayak, A.S. (2009). Effect of Indian classical music on quality of sleep in depressed patients: a randomized controlled trial. *Nordic Journal of Music Therapy*, 18(1), 70–8.

Erkkilä, J. & Eerola, T. (2010). Gambling addiction: Evaluation of a multimethod treatment programme including music therapy. In: D. Aldridge & J. Fachner (Eds.) *Music therapy and addictions*, pp. 140–55. London: Jessica Kingsley.

Erkkilä, J., Punkanen, M., Fachner, J., et al. (2011). Individual music therapy for depression: randomised controlled trial. *British Journal of Psychiatry*, 199(2), 132–9.

Erkkilä, J., Ala-Ruona, E., Punkanen, M., & Fachner, J. (2012). Perspectives on creativity in improvisational, psychodynamic music therapy. In: D. Hargreaves, D. Miell, & R. MacDonald (Eds.) *Musical imaginations: multidisciplinary perspectives on creativity, performance and perception*, pp. 414–28. Oxford: Oxford University Press.

Fachner, J. (2006). Music and drug induced altered states. In: D. Aldridge & J. Fachner (Eds.) *Music and altered states: consciousness, transcendence, therapy and addictions*, pp. 82–96. London: Jessica Kingsley.

Fachner, J. (2010). Music therapy, drugs and state-dependent recall. In: D. Aldridge & J. Fachner (Eds.) *Music therapy and addictions*, pp. 18–34. London: Jessica Kingsley.

Fachner, J. (2011). Drugs, altered states, and musical consciousness: reframing time and space. In: E. Clarke & D. Clarke (Eds.) *Music and consciousness*, pp. 263–80. Oxford: Oxford University Press.

Fachner, J., Gold, C., Ala-Ruona, E., Punkanen, M., & Erkkilä, J. (2010). Depression and music therapy treatment—clinical validity and reliability of EEG alpha asymmetry and frontal midline theta: three case studies. In: S.M. Demorest, S. J. Morrison & P.S. Campbell (Eds.) *Proceedings of the 11th International Conference on Music Perception and Cognition (CD-ROM)*, pp. 11–18. Seattle: University of Washington, School of Music.

Fachner, J. & Rittner, S. (2011). Ethno therapy, music and trance: an QEEG investigation into a sound-trance induction. In: D. Cvetkovic & I. Cosic (Eds.) *States of consciousness: experimental insights into meditation, waking, sleep and dreams*, pp. 233–54. Berlin: Springer.

Greenberg, R.P. & Goldman, E.D. (2009). Antidepressants, psychotherapy or their combination: weighing options for depression treatments. *Journal of Contemporary Psychotherapy*, 39, 83–91.

Gold, C., Rolvsjord, R., Aaro, L.E., Aarre, T., Tjemsland, L., & Stige, B. (2005). Resource-oriented music therapy for psychiatric patients with low therapy motivation: protocol for a randomised controlled trial [NCT00137189]. *BMC Psychiatry*, 5, 39.

Gotlib, I.H., Krasnoperova, E., Yue, D.N., & Joormann, J. (2004). Attentional biases for negative interpersonal stimuli in clinical depression. *Journal of Abnormal Psychology*, 113(1), 127–35.

Harikumar, R., Raj, M., Paul, A., et al. (2006). Listening to music decreases need for sedative medication during colonoscopy: a randomized, controlled trail. *Indian Journal of Gastroenterology*, 25(1), 3.

Harmatz, M.G., Well, A.D., Overtree, C.E., Kawamura, K.Y., Rosal, M., & Ockene, I.S. (2000). Seasonal variation of depression and other moods: a longitudinal approach. *Journal of Biological Rhythms*, 15(4), 344–50.

Hasler, B.P., Mehl, M.R., Bootzin, R.R., & Vazire, S. (2008). Preliminary evidence of diurnal rhythms in everyday behaviors associated with positive affect. *Journal of Research in Personality*, 42(6), 1537–46.

Herbert, R. (2011). Consciousness and everyday music listening: trancing, dissociation, and absorption. In: D. Clarke & E. Clarke (Eds.) *Music and consciousness*, pp. 295–308. Oxford: Oxford University Press.

Holsboer, F. (2008). How can we realize the promise of personalized antidepressant medicines? *Nature Reviews Neuroscience*, 9(8), 638–46.

Honkonen, T., Aro, T., Isometsä, E., Virtanen, M., & Katila, H. (2007). Quality of treatment and disability compensation in depression: comparison of 2 nationally representative samples with a 10-year interval in Finland. *Journal of Clinical Psychiatry*, 68(12), 1886–93.

Jonnes, J. (1999). *Hep-cats, narcs and pipe dreams*. Baltimore, MD: John Hopkins University Press.

Joormann, J. & Gotlib, I.H. (2010). Emotion regulation in depression: Relation to cognitive inhibition. *Cognitive Emotion*, 24(2), 281–98.

Lee, E.J., Bhattacharya, J., Sohn, C., & Verres, R. (2012). Monochord sounds and progressive muscle relaxation reduce anxiety and improve relaxation during chemotherapy: a pilot EEG study. *Complementary Therapies in Medicine*, 20(6), 409–16

Lönnqvist, J. (2009). *Stressi ja depressio* [Stress and depression]. Available at: http://www.terveyskirjasto.fi/terveyskirjasto/tk.plain?p_artikkeli=seh00020 (accessed May 1, 2016) (accessed 19 January 2009).

Madigan, R.J. & Bollenbach, A.K. (1982). Effects of induced mood on retrieval of personal episodic and semantic memories. *Psychological Reports*, 50(1), 147–57.

Manning, P. (2007). *Drugs and popular culture—drugs, media and identity in contempory society*. Cullompton: Willan Publishing.

McKay, K.M., Imel, Z.E., & Wampold, B.E. (2006). Psychiatrist effects in the psychopharmacological treatment of depression. *Journal of Affective Disorders*, 92(2–3), 287–90.

Menon, V. & Levitin, D.J. (2005). The rewards of music listening: response and physiological connectivity of the mesolimbic system. *NeuroImage*, 28(1), 175–84.

Miranda, R. & Kihlstrom, J. (2005). Mood congruence in childhood and recent autobiographical memory. *Cognition & Emotion*, 19(7), 981–98.

Montagne, M. (2004). Social pharmacology: integrating pharmaceutical and social science research on drug effects. *Drug Information Journal*, 38(4), 315–20.

Montgomery, S.A. & Åsberg, M. (1979). A new depression scale designed to be sensitive to change. *British Journal of Psychiatry*, 134, 382–9.

Moore, P. (2008). *Enhancing me: the hope and the hype of human enhancement*. Chichester: Wiley/Dana Centre.

Murray, G., Allen, N.B., & Trinder, J. (2002). Mood and the circadian system: investigation of a circadian component in positive affect. *Chronobiology International*, 19(6), 1151–69.

Nickel, A.K., Hillecke, T., Argstatter, H., & Bolay, H.V. (2005). Outcome research in music therapy: a step on the long road to an evidence-based treatment (randomized controlled trial). *Annals of the New York Academy of Sciences*, 1060, 283–93.

Nordoff, P. & Robbins, C. (2007). *Creative music therapy: a guide to fostering clinical musicianship*, 2nd edn. Gilsum, NH: Barcelona Publishers.

Norris, C. (2011). The medicated me. Available at: http://www.bychrisnorris.com/phenomena/the-medicated-me-2/ (accessed 17 October 2013).

Palmer, J.D. (2002). *The living clock: the orchestrator of biological rhythms*. Oxford: Oxford University Press.

Passynkova, N.R. & Volf, N.V. (2001). Seasonal affective disorder: spatial organization of EEG power and coherence in the depressive state and in light-induced and summer remission. *Psychiatry Research*, 108(3), 169–85.

Peeters, F., Berkhof, J., Delespaul, P., Rottenberg, J., & Nicolson, N.A. (2006). Diurnal mood variation in major depressive disorder. *Emotion*, 6(3), 383–91.

Peterson, C.K. & Harmon-Jones, E. (2009). Circadian and seasonal variability of resting frontal EEG asymmetry. *Biological Psychology*, 80(3), 315–20.

Punkanen, M., Eerola, T., & Erkkilä, J. (2011a). Biased emotional recognition in depression: Perception of emotions in music by depressed patients. *Journal of Affective Disorders*, 130(1–2), 118–26.

Punkanen, M., Eerola, T., & Erkkilä, J. (2011b). Biased emotional preferences in depression: decreased liking of angry and energetic music by depressed patients. *Music and Medicine*, 3(2), 114–20.

Salimpoor, V.N., Benovoy, M., Larcher, K., Dagher, A., & Zatorre, R.J. (2011). Anatomically distinct dopamine release during anticipation and experience of peak emotion to music. *Nature Neuroscience*, 14(2), 257–62.

Shapiro, H. (2003). *Waiting for the man—the story of drugs and popular music*, 2nd edn. London: Helter Skelter Publishing.

Smolensky, M., & Lamberg, L. (2001). *The body clock guide to better health: how to use your body's natural clock to fight illness and achieve maximum health*. New York, NY: Henry Holt and Company.

Smolensky, M. & Peppas, N. (2007). Chronobiology, drug delivery, and chronotherapeutics. *Advanced Drug Delivery Reviews*, 59(9-10), 828–51.

Spintge, R. (1991). Die therapeutisch-funktionalen Wirkungen von Musik aus medizinischer und neurphysiologischer Sicht: Musik als therapeutische Droge. In: H. Rösing (Ed.), *Musik als Droge? Zu Theorie und Praxis bewußtseinsverändernder Wirkungen von Musik*, Vol. 1, pp. 13–22. Mainz: Villa Musica.

Spintge, R. (2012). Clinical use of music in operating theaters. In: R. MacDonald, G. Kreutz & L. Mitchell (Eds.) *Music, health, and wellbeing*, pp. 277–86. Oxford: Oxford University Press.

Summer, L. (2002). Group music and imagery therapy: emergent receptive techniques in music therapy practice. In: K. Bruscia, D.E. Grocke, & E. Pickett (Eds.) *Guided imagery and music: the Bonny method and beyond*, pp. 297–306. Gilsum: Barcelona Publishers.

Surguladze, S.A., Young, A.W., Senior, C., Brébion, G., Travis, M.J., & Phillips, M. L. (2004). Recognition accuracy and response bias to happy and sad facial expressions in patients with major depression. *Neuropsychology*, 18(2), 212–18.

Tucek, G. (2006). Traditional oriental music therapy: a regulatory and relational approach. *Music Therapy Today* 7(3), 623–47.

Turner, D.C., Robbins, T.W., Clark, L., Aron, A.R., Dowson, J., & Sahakian, B.J. (2003). Cognitive enhancing effects of modafinil in healthy volunteers. *Psychopharmacology (Berlin)*, 165(3), 260–9.

Van Havere, T., Vanderplasschen, W., Lammertyn, J., Broekaert, E., & Bellis, M. (2011). Drug use and nightlife: more than just dance music. *Substance Abuse Treatment, Prevention, and Policy*, 6, 18.

Vuoskoski, J.K. & Eerola, T. (2011). The role of mood and personality in the perception of emotions represented by music. *Cortex*, 47(9), 1099–106.

Watson, D. (2000). *Mood and temperament*. New York, NY: Guilford Press.

Winnicott, D. (1968). Playing: its theoretical status in the clinical situation. *International Journal of Psychoanalysis*, 49, 591–9.

Wolfe, T. (1989). *The electric cool aid acid test*. New York, NY: Bantam Books.

Weil, A. (1998). *The natural mind*, 3rd edn. Boston, MA: Houghton Mifflin.

Zinberg, N.E. (1984). *Drug, set, and setting: the basis for controlled intoxicant use*. New Haven, CT: Yale University Press.

SECTION 8

··

CASE STUDIES

··

CHAPTER 38

....

THE IMAGINARY AFRICAN

Race, Identity, and Samuel Coleridge-Taylor

....

NICHOLAS COOK

I suppose you know his father is a negro. Hence his wonderful *freshness*.[1]

38.1 ONLY BLACK OUTSIDE

....

SOMETIME around 1893 a mainly female string orchestra was rehearsing at the Croydon Conservatoire of Music, under its regular conductor, Samuel Coleridge-Taylor (Fig. 38.1). Someone referred to him as black, a slightly impolite term (at that time British people of African ancestry generally referred to themselves as "colored"). As Coleridge-Taylor's first biographer, Berwick Sayers (1915, p. 71), tells the story, "one of the girls retorted indignantly, 'Please don't call Mr Coleridge-Taylor black; he is only black outside.'"

She had a point. Coleridge-Taylor's father was a medical student from Sierra Leone, but he left Britain in 1875, just before his son was born. The future composer was brought up in Croydon by his unmarried English mother, and at the age of fifteen entered the newly established Royal College of Music, where he studied composition with Charles Villiers Stanford and was seen as the outstanding figure in a cohort that included Gustav Holst and Ralph Vaughan Williams (Self, 1995, pp. 22, 52–3). Already in college he was reading Longfellow, and 1898—the year after he graduated—saw the first production of his cantata "Hiawatha's Wedding Feast," which rapidly became a sensation on both sides of the Atlantic, for a decade ousting *Messiah* from the top spot in the world of massed choral music. Coleridge-Taylor societies sprouted across North America, and if in the end the Coleridge-Taylor phenomenon proved short-lived, the principal reason was his

[1] August Jaeger, letter of 12 May 1898 to Herbert Brewer (Self, 1995: 63).

FIG. 38.1 Samuel Coleridge-Taylor, around 1899 (Sayers, 1915, facing p. 80).

sudden death in 1912: "We may call his death-sickness pneumonia", wrote the American civil rights activist and Pan-Africanist W. E. B. Du Bois (Sundquist, 1996, p. 583), "but we all know that it was sheer overwork."

Du Bois wrote about Coleridge-Taylor—indeed was personally acquainted with him—because, though brought up in an entirely white environment, Coleridge-Taylor became deeply involved in issues of music and race from his early twenties, not only musically, but also to some extent politically. As we will see, he and Du Bois met at the First Pan-African Conference, held at London in July 1900. Ostensibly, then, the composer started off white inside, as the girl at the Conservatoire implied, but reconstructed his identity as an adult: that makes him an obvious case study in the role that music can play in the transformation of identity. Of course, it wasn't as simple as that. The literature on Coleridge-Taylor's life—which is fairly extensive, but comes mainly from outside academic music studies—includes a novel by Charles Elford (2008, p. 11), near the beginning of which a violin teacher named Joseph Beckwith sees a small black boy playing marbles in the gutter, with a violin case next to him.

"Hello", said Beckwith as he put his hands in his pockets. He never put his hands in his pockets.

"Hello," said the boy without looking up.

"Do you speak English?"

He looked up. "I am English."

The story is true, or at least it is as Sayers (1915, pp. 5–6) tells it, except for one thing: it was in 1904, when boarding an American train and hearing comments about his color, that Coleridge-Taylor retorted, "I am an Englishman!" (Self, 1995, p. 159). At one level his English identity and black skin coexisted successfully: he was comfortably embedded in the professional and institutional structures of musical advancement almost from the moment he enrolled at the Royal College, and if his skin was black, that of his wife (Jessie Walmisley, herself a Royal College alumna) was white. He shared the ambition of practically all English composers at that time—to succeed in Germany. If, from 1897, he incorporated certain African materials in his compositions, then that might be seen as falling into established traditions of exotic representation, interpretable as a function of London's position as an imperial metropolis rather than as an investment of personal identity: Catherine Carr (2005, p. 246) writes that "Coleridge-Taylor's work is no different from those exotic (or 'oriental') works ... which experiment superficially with unusual 'foreign' techniques yet ultimately retain their western heritage and syntax". She mentions Rimsky-Korsakoff, Balakirev, and Holst as other examples.

That is obviously not the whole story. There were a few black people in Croydon (Green, 2001a, p. 153), but there is no evidence of any close acquaintances, and hence a lack of role models with whom Coleridge-Taylor could identify in this basic, because plainly and publicly visible, dimension of his selfhood: it is only as an adult, and an established composer, that he developed the extensive network of acquaintances with both resident and visiting West Africans and African Americans that leads Jeffrey Green (1990, p. 249) to suggest that it was among these acquaintances that "the composer had found his African soul." At the same time, because he was black outside, he was subject to the generally low-level and not necessarily malicious racism of the day. There are stories of a boy on a choir outing setting light to his curls to see if African hair would burn (J. Coleridge-Taylor, 1942–43, p. 18), of another student at the Royal College calling him a "nigger" (already in the 1890s a slur), and of a clergyman who asked Coleridge-Taylor if he really drank tea and ate bread-and-butter like other people (Sayers, 1915, pp. 27, 97). Boys routinely called out "Blackie" as he passed; just once, Sayers (1915, p. 262) says with evident approval, Coleridge-Taylor responded by thrashing the youth with his walking stick, though "the event affected him severely." Coleridge-Taylor's daughter Avril has a related story that must relate to when he was in his thirties: "There were lads in Croydon who sometimes laughed at him because of his dark skin, and what they said caused him great pain. When he saw them approaching along the street he held my hand more tightly, gripping it until it almost hurt" (A. Coleridge-Taylor, 1979, p. 96). Before that his future in-laws had raised vigorous objections to his marriage, on the grounds that "The negro ... necessarily belonged to a lower stage of development". Sayers (1915, p. 69) comments that we should not "blame them for notions which were common to the white race." Indeed such experiences are entirely in line with other accounts of black experience in London around 1900, even in professional circles. Theophilus Scholes, for example, speaks of white doctors elbowing a West Indian colleague out of the way and loudly asking, "What is he doing here?" (Fryer, 1984, p. 439). That racism is normal does not mean you get used to it, however, and it is hard not to look askance at Sayers's (1915, p. 26) claim that "In general the color-line was not a source of discomfort to the young composer."

While the effect of such abuse is to force a racial identity upon you and keep it permanently in the foreground, it is only from Coleridge-Taylor's early twenties that there is evidence of any overt identification with his African patrimony. Apparently referring to the period around 1897, Sayers (1915, p. 45) speaks of the "curious racial affinities" that Coleridge-Taylor felt for the work of Robert Browning, which he related to persistent rumors of the poet's creole ancestry. (Later he became an early adherent of the idea—which was widely circulated from the 1940s to the 1980s—that Beethoven was black [Sayers, 1915, p. 203; Broyles, 2011, pp. 267-91].) Less circumstantial is the evidence of the March 1897 issue of the *African Times*, which contains "A Liberian Patriotic Hymn" that Coleridge-Taylor wrote to celebrate the half-century since the establishment of the Republic of Liberia, one of a handful of self-governing African states (Green, 2011, p. 89). But the best documented and most important evidence is his involvement in the Pan-African Conference of 1900, which drew delegates from Africa, the West Indies, and America. According to Peter Fryer (1984, p. 282) the term had been coined only the previous year, meaning that the conference can be seen as one of the starting points for the Afrocentrism that constituted an important strand of the American Civil Rights Movement sixty years later.

Coleridge-Taylor provided music for the conference (Richards, 2001, pp. 239–40), but beyond that—as Green (2001c, p. 290) says—the nature of his contribution is not clear, although a short-lived Pan-African Association was established on whose executive committee Coleridge-Taylor served (Green, 2011, p. 96). The political tenor of the conference is indicated in an address "To the nations of the world" written by the conference's most famous delegate, Du Bois. "The problem of the twentieth century is the problem of the colour line," Du Bois proclaimed, and he followed this by calling for a comprehensive international program of education, enfranchisement, and decolonization (Sundquist, 1996, p. 626). Du Bois's influence can be traced through Coleridge-Taylor's life from then on, one of the last examples being a letter to the *Croydon Guardian* from 1912, prompted by a local debating group discussion of "The Negro Problem in North America" (Sayers, 1915, pp. 272–7). In it and a follow-up, Coleridge-Taylor cited Dumas as a mixed-race genius, and pointed out that "the coloured people of America ... did not go to that country of their own accord"—both points that Du Bois had made (Sundquist, 1996, pp. 157, 155). Coleridge-Taylor added, "Personally, I consider myself the equal of any white man who ever lived."

Geoffrey Self cites this statement in the course of an attempt to summarize Coleridge-Taylor's self-identity. "That Coleridge-Taylor was proud of his paternal descent is undoubted," he writes. "That he considered himself the equal of any man, we have on the authority of his own word. That he considered himself an Englishman, we have on the same authority" (Self, 1995, p. 60). Self then cites some of his compositions based on African themes, and concludes that Coleridge-Taylor's concern for "the plight of the black races may have brought about a crisis of identity, which may never have been finally resolved, for the pull of his English environment and his European creative tradition was too strong to be completely vanquished by his colored paternity." But perhaps there is a better way of thinking about this. Born & Hesmondhalgh (2000, p. 32) stress the importance of distinguishing "between individual self-identity and collective identity in relation to music," on the ground that multiple identities may coexist within the same individual. Turino (2008, p. 95) makes a similar point when he defines identity as "the *partial* selection of habits and attributes used to represent oneself to oneself and to others," adding that this "is relative to specific situations." Seen this way, Coleridge-Taylor might be seen as having access to a number of more or less stable collective identities, ranging from conductor of local musical groups such as the Croydon Conservatoire orchestra to distinguished English composer, and from victim of racial abuse to supporter of Pan-Africanism: in this way he situated himself within collectivities that ranged from the local to the national to the transnational, but like anyone else, his individual self-identity was more mobile, a performance of these divergent and sometimes contradictory identities that varied according to circumstance.

38.2 THE SOULS OF BLACK FOLK

Is it possible to throw light on this tangle of overlapping identities, both voluntary and enforced, by approaching the issue from the direction of the music? Just as there is evidence of Coleridge-Taylor's involvement in African and African American affairs from 1897, so there is a change in his compositional direction, with titles such as "Fantasiestücke" and Symphony in A, from 1895 to 1896, giving way to "Hiawathan Sketches" (1896) and "African Romances" (1897). The latter are songs written to texts by the poet and performer Paul Dunbar (1872–1906), apparently the first African American with whom Coleridge-Taylor developed a close relationship. In June 1897 he and Dunbar presented a joint performance at the Salle Erard that included Coleridge-Taylor's "Fantasiestücke" and "Hiawathan Sketches," with Dunbar reciting a selection of his poems, some of which were written in African American vernacular: Dunbar's father had been a slave in Kentucky. According to Avril, the encounter "made a profound effect on Coleridge-Taylor" (A. Coleridge-Taylor, 1979, p. 27). In this context we should remember what is often forgotten, that as a mixed-race composer Coleridge-Taylor's blackness was as precarious as his whiteness: perhaps the encounter with Dunbar opened up the possibility of seeing his English identity as a deficit. At all events, Avril continues that the encounter "deepened his pride in his origins and his concern for black people, and it inspired him with a feeling that there was a new philosophy concerning liberty to explore across the Atlantic." Indeed it has generally been seen as sparking off Coleridge-Taylor's engagement with African and African American issues more generally, but there are two points to be made about this. The first is that—as evidenced by the

"Liberian Patriotic Hymn"—this engagement almost certainly predated his first encounter with Dunbar, if only by a few months.[2] The second and more telling point is that even before this he had given musical expression to a concern for oppressed minorities.

Coleridge-Taylor first set the words of Henry Wadsworth Longfellow as early as 1893 (Green, 2011, p. 31). Evoking the dignity in suffering of the indigenous Americans, the decimation of whose tribes had been more or less completed by the 1890s, Longfellow's "Hiawatha" had an obvious resonance for Coleridge-Taylor. In Jack Sullivan's (1999, p. 59) words, "as a black man in a white musical establishment, he empathized with American Indians as outsiders, much as black Indians and Creoles celebrate what unites them at Mardi Gras". But the link Coleridge-Taylor forged between indigenous and African American is more direct than that. When Coleridge-Taylor composed his "Overture to the Song of Hiawatha," he incorporated "Nobody Knows the Trouble I See," a spiritual that was well known from the performances of the Fisk Jubilee Singers (of whom more shortly). In this way, via Longfellow, Coleridge-Taylor conflated the indigenous and African American, and through the further link to his own ethnicity created an image of the "African" that was perhaps as much symbolical as geographical. Paul Richards sees Coleridge-Taylor as a Pan-African—a self-defined member of an imagined supranational community—and draws a comparison with Paul Gilroy's (1993) "Black Atlantic" (Richards, 2001, p. 156), but one might argue that it is the abstract ideas of indigeneity and oppression that lie at the heart of his image. At all events, Richards (2001, p. 236) draws a telling contrast between Coleridge-Taylor's image of Africa and that of Edward Elgar, "the self-doubting praise singer of imperial adventure": while Elgar was writing his "Pomp and Circumstance Marches," Richards (2001, p. 238) observes, Coleridge-Taylor had "begun to express African—and by implication anti-imperialist—sympathies in his own compositions".

Coleridge-Taylor's involvement with Africa—however defined—is easy enough to trace in the titles, texts, and incorporation of ethnically marked musical materials within his compositions. His first-hand experience of African and African American music is more elusive. In London he would have had access to the commercialized black minstrel and coon songs that he condemned in 1904 as "the worst sort of rot" (McGinty, 2001, p. 211), while Self (1995, p. 58) suggests that Dunbar may have introduced him to some African songs.[3] More substantially, 1897 was the year when Frederick Loudin, who led one of the incarnations of the Fisk Jubilee Singers, returned to London after a world tour (Green, 2012, p. 14). From the 1870s the Jubilee Singers, an a cappella choir formed of students from the Nashville-based historically black university of that name, had toured in order to raise funds for the institution, and in doing so disseminated their repertory of spirituals on a national and eventually international basis. Loudin became a personal

---

[2]   Sayers (1915, p. 48) states that Dunbar and Coleridge-Taylor met in 1896, but that is wrong: Dunbar docked in Liverpool on 17 February 1897, going to Somerset before arriving in London some time before May (Green 2011, 40).

[3]   For an overview of African American musicians and dancers in Britain during the nineteenth and early twentieth centuries see Fryer 1984, pp. 440–4.

friend of Coleridge-Taylor's, also attending the 1900 Pan-African Conference and serving on the Pan-African Association's committee (Green, 2011, p. 96); there were Jubilee concerts in London during the late 1890s (Green, 2011, p. 97), and Sayers (1915, p. 259) confirms that Coleridge-Taylor attended them. It was through the Jubilee Singers, the composer wrote,[4] that "I first learned to appreciate the beautiful folk-music of my race."

Sayers says that "in particular it was the quality of the voices that impressed him", and goes on to explain that "the traditional reedy singing voice" had been replaced by "the purity of the tenor tones and the deep forward tones of the bass." The Jubilee Singers' repertory—much of it collected by the singers and their first music director, the white missionary George White—had from the beginning been transcribed into staff notation, and when he rehearsed the students White did so "with the same exactitude he brought to their official repertoire of cantatas and hymns and popular songs": he held his fiddle in hand so as to check the pitch and insisted on soft vocalization and blend (Ward, 2000, pp. 110, 114–15). This resonates with Samuel Floyd's (1995, p. 61) claims about the successive refinement of the Fisk Jubilee Singers. Floyd cites a description from 1878 that refers to their "most pleasing sweetness of tone," contrasts this with earlier descriptions of the singing of spirituals, and adds that this process of refinement "was to continue, generation after generation, until audiences would no longer hear spirituals even as the Jubilee Singers themselves had first sung them, let alone as they had been sung by the slaves." In short, the sound image evoked by Sayers had been disciplined by—or filtered through—staff notation. And the same might be said of the professional singers of the spiritual repertory whom Coleridge-Taylor heard, and performed with, in America—such as Harry Burleigh (1866–1949), who collected and arranged spirituals, but was also a product of the New York-based National Conservatory of Music of America (at that time directed by Antonín Dvořák) and a pioneer of African American art song. Recordings of Burleigh's singing, admittedly from a later stage of his career, exhibit a vocal style not unlike that, for example, of Paul Robeson.

If in this way Coleridge-Taylor encountered the spiritual tradition at one remove, his reception of it was also conditioned by the writings of Du Bois, with whom he kept up a personal relationship. Most important, he read Du Bois's most famous book, *The Souls of Black Folk*, shortly after its publication in 1903, and described it as "about the finest book I have ever read by a colored man, and one of the best by any author, white or black" (Sayers, 1915, pp. 149–50). The final chapter is devoted to the genre of spirituals that Du Bois terms "sorrow songs," and he interprets it as the repository of deep racial memory laid down in Africa. While the words change, Du Bois says, "the music is far more ancient," and he cites the example of a melody handed down in his own family: "two hundred years it has travelled down to us and we sing it to our children, knowing as little as our fathers what its words may mean, but knowing well the meaning of its music" (Sundquist, 1996, pp. 232–3). The idea of racial memory was more credible at the turn of the 20th century than it is now, and if Coleridge-Taylor was indeed in search of "his African soul"—Green's phrase—then he might logically have seen the

---

[4] Foreword to *Twenty-Four Negro Melodies*, reprinted in Tortolano 2002, p. 91.

spiritual as the place where it was to be found. At all events, during 1904 Coleridge-Taylor composed probably the most influential of his "African" works, the "Twenty-Four Negro Melodies," Op. 59, for solo piano, and they were published the following year by the Boston-based Oliver Ditson Company—which is itself significant: "As far as I am aware," writes Green (2007: 57), "no American had been able to convince a mainstream publisher to consider a volume of black music before 1905." The volume included a preface by Booker Washington, alongside the younger and more radical Du Bois the leading spokesman for the African American community. That demonstrates the elevated circles with which Coleridge-Taylor was linked even before his first visit to America: he sailed in October 1904, as Washington was writing the preface.

There was also a foreword by the composer, in which he developed the idea of the spiritual as folk song. In his preface Washington had written that "The Negro folk-song has for the Negro race the same value that the folk-song of any other people has for that people," and Du Bois's concept of racial memory is an appropriation for Pan-Africanism of the idea that had motivated the collection and arrangement of folk song during the nineteenth century more generally—what Johann Gottfried Herder called *Volksgeist*, the distillation through cultural products of national identity. This is the context within which Coleridge-Taylor positions himself when he writes: "What Brahms has done for the Hungarian folk-music, Dvořák for the Bohemian, and Grieg for the Norwegian, I have tried to do for these Negro Melodies." He also claims that, in contrast to the "monotony and shapelessness" of Indian, Chinese, and Japanese music,

> the music of Africa (I am not thinking of American Negro music, which may or may not have felt some white influence) … has all the elements of the European folk-song, and it is remarkable that no alterations have had to be made before treating the Melodies.

His parentheses imply that he sees the African melodies in his collection much as Du Bois described them: as musical fossils, unchanged survivals from a distant past, authentic repository of an ancient identity. There is an obvious problem here. Coleridge-Taylor's access to the melodies was in all cases through transcriptions. As I said in relation to the Fisk Jubilee Singers, the melodies had been filtered or reconstructed through the pitch and rhythmic categories of staff notation, and perhaps more important, Coleridge-Taylor received them in the context of performance practices conditioned by staff notation. This is where there is an obvious distinction between Coleridge-Taylor and American musicians such as Burleigh, whose work as an arranger and composer was grounded on first-hand experience of song collection in rural Georgia (Moon, 2004). In this respect, to borrow Du Bois's famous image of "the two worlds within and without the Veil" (Sunquist, 1996, p. 100), Coleridge-Taylor may be said to have never been really within the veil, and his arguably naïve approach to the transcriptions of African music from which he worked underlines this.

Two-thirds of the "Twenty-Four Negro Melodies" are African American, while others are West Indian or African; only one, "Oloba," is from West Africa, and in his foreword

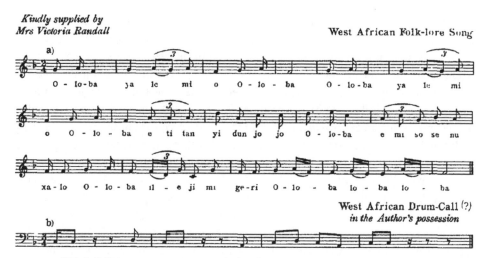

FIG. 38.2 "Oloba" ("Twenty-Four Negro Melodies," No. 7), transcriptions.

Coleridge-Taylor singles it out as "a highly original number." Normally, Coleridge-Taylor prefaces each of the arrangements, in which the melodies are elaborated into short, performable pieces for piano, with the transcription on which it is based, but in this case there are two (Fig. 38.2). The first is a Yoruba melody, with text, that he was given by a personal acquaintance from Sierra Leone. The second is a "West African Drum-Call (?) in the Author's possession": Coleridge-Taylor's form of words betrays a conception of the music as an artifact, rather than a trace of performance practice, and I know of no evidence that he was aware of the nature and variety of African drumming. Richards (2001, p. 246) interprets this transcription as invoking "the Yoruba 'hour-glass' tension drum," and makes the bold claim that "When played with suitable rhythmic flexibility, the drum-call and first statement of the theme are perhaps the closest the composer ever came to evoking the actual sound and texture of African music."[5]

At one level these materials are fully accommodated within the musical structures of the turn-of-the-century common practice style. Typically of the "Twenty-Four Negro Melodies," "Oloba" is structured around three variations of the complete theme; they are separated by statements of the drum call, which is used as a kind of fanfare, as if to command attention. Also typically, there is between the second and third variations a long episode freely based on motifs extracted from the theme, culminating in an extended version of the drum call. The piece ends with a coda that effectively prolongs the final tonic,

[5] Two commercial recordings of "Twenty-Four Negro Melodies" are currently available, by Frances Walker (Orion/Marquis 77471 83105 2 1), recorded in 1978, and by David Shaffer-Gottschalk (Albany/Troy 930/31), recorded in 2005. The sheet music may be downloaded from the IMSLP Petrucci Music Library http://imslp.org/wiki/24_Negro_Melodies,_Op.59_(Coleridge-Taylor,_Samuel)); this does not however include Washington's preface (accessible at http://www.press.jhu.edu/books/supplemental/booker_t/ch06_03_booker_t_washington_rediscovered.pdf) or Coleridge-Taylor's foreword (reprinted in Tortolano 2002, pp. 91–2).

combining melody and drum call in increasingly fragmentary forms. Coleridge-Taylor employs standard compositional techniques of variation and development, such as integrating thematic motifs within open-ended, harmonically directed textures; creates a different harmonic interpretation of the melody's opening three-note motif on almost every occasion of its appearance (the pitch classes remain the same, but the harmonic or tonal contexts change); and packages the variations into an A-B-A pattern that, in its modulating second section and return to the tonic for the third, carries a faint echo of sonata form.

But that kind of technical description misses everything that matters. One significant feature is the nature of the original melody. As shown in Fig. 38.2, it consists of four phrases each of four bars, largely made up of multiple variants, of differing lengths, of the opening G-A-F motif. The first two phrases consist of nothing but those three pitches; the third begins with a rise to D and adds the remaining notes of the F-major scale, while the fourth returns to the tessitura of the first two phrases, retaining C, D, and E, but now at the lower octave. With the exception of the third phrase, the theme is singularly undirected in nature: seen in terms of the common practice style, it comprises an irregularly spaced series of closing gestures. By contrast, the manner in which Coleridge-Taylor sets it is highly directed. After the initial variation in which the melody is camouflaged through the addition of upper and lower pedals, the second variation (bar 25) introduces a swaggering, Edwardian sound: the texture is now homophonic, with chromatic, often linear harmonies, and its sixteen bars are extended to culminate in an overblown tonic cadence (bar 44). The swagger returns during the long, freely composed episode (bar 65), now building into an even more overblown, *fortissimo* climax (bars 77–8). It returns once more in the third variation (bar 135), where the theme appears in triumphant augmentation; marked *largamente*, it is played in block chords, interspersed with extravagant rising arpeggios redolent of the hotel lounge or palm court.

Much of the piece consists of extended climax-building passages, with underlying dominant harmony, ascending linear motions, and dynamic build-ups creating a strong sense of forward motion. But what they lead to is often anti-climactic, out of proportion with what led up to it (as at bars 79 and 103). The effect is one of bathos. The same applies to the glaring mismatch between the rhetoric of Elgarian swagger and *largamente* on the one hand, and the harmonically undirected, noodling scraps of melodic material out of which most of the theme is made. Moreover, the overblown, perhaps intentionally tasteless nature of the music is quite out of kilter with the urbane geniality and light touch more characteristic of Coleridge-Taylor's music, for example the "The Bamboula" (another of the "Twenty-Four Negro Melodies"), or the orchestral piece that he made out of it ("The Bamboula," Op. 75). All this suggests that we might interpret "Oloba" as a critique, a parody or sending up of Elgar's Africa, in Richards's phrase the Africa of imperial adventure. Seen this way, the music constructs an identity through opposition—what Richards (2001, p. 236) would call an anti-imperial identity, that of "the collegial champion of indigenous peoples". Such an interpretation perhaps gains weight from the melody's provenance, suggesting that for Coleridge-Taylor it stood for the Africa of his father's people—an Africa, to be sure, that was hardly less fictive than Longfellow's America.

At all events, this symbolic encounter between Coleridge-Taylor and an imagined Africa results not in a seamless accommodation of the other within the structures of the self, as in "The Bamboula," but rather in what Floyd (1995, p. 271) calls a dialogue between self and other—a sign of which is the violence done to the tonal, textural, and generic dimensions of a common practice style that emerges as less easily defined, and more negotiable, than is often assumed. Born & Hesmondhalgh (2000, p. 42) invoke the literary critic and historian Colin McCabe's description of narrative as "a metalanguage which, in its transparency, denies its own discursivity and assumes the status of the 'real'". That description applies well to "The Bamboula." "Oloba", by contrast, is thoroughly opaque, presenting itself not as imagined African music, but rather as a critique of attitudes towards the African: the impact of the original melody emerges from the tensions and contradictions inherent in Coleridge-Taylor's score, rather than from any putative relationship to the actual sound and texture of African music. From this perspective one can at least begin to understand why, in his book about the impact of American culture on European music, Sullivan (1999, p. 35) describes "Twenty-Four Negro Melodies" as "an extraordinary example of multiculturalism, an Anglo-Negro hybrid unlike anything in modern culture."

The first two chapters of Sullivan's book focus respectively on the spiritual and on Longfellow, in each case emphasizing the importance not only of Coleridge-Taylor, but also of Dvořák, who died in the same year that Coleridge-Taylor wrote "Twenty-Four Negro Melodies." While Coleridge-Taylor said in his foreword to that work that he aimed to do for African music what Dvořák did for Bohemian music, the association with Dvořák goes back to his college days. Self calls Dvořák Coleridge-Taylor's mentor, even though they never met. A reviewer of Coleridge-Taylor's early Symphony in A Minor (1896) wrote that it "may be said to show the influence of Dvořák both with respect to the character of the themes and their development" (Snyder, 2013, p. ix), but it's not simply a matter of style and technique. In particular, their shared passion for Longfellow is revealing. In 1893 Dvořák told the *New York Herald* that he had been reading Longfellow for thirty years (Sullivan, 1999, p. 51), and in Sullivan's words, he wrote his Symphony "From the New World", composed the same year, "with a copy of Longfellow's poetry on his music stand and the soulful sounds of black folks, sung by his most gifted student, ringing in his ears". (The "gifted student" was Burleigh.) In short, Dvořák linked Longfellow and African America in precisely the same way that Coleridge-Taylor did, and was already bringing the spiritual tradition into dialogue with classical composition while Coleridge-Taylor was still at college.

But what *did* Dvořák do for Bohemian music? Sullivan (1999, p. 5) writes that, after his discovery that the American musical establishment had no interest in African American music, "Dvořák quickly resolved to do in America what he had already done in Europe: to mine a folk vernacular and convert it into art that would be both formal and accessible." That is true, but there is more to it. The assimilation of Dvořák into the mainstream of Western classical music, in effect as a more accessible and colorful version of Brahms, has had the effect of flattening out his achievement both musically and ideologically. Born & Hesmondhalgh (2000, p. 45) suggest that "because of its lack of denotation, and compared with the visual and literary arts, music hides the traces of its appropriations, hybridities, and representations, so that they come over time to be *naturalized and aestheticized*". Musical elements that begin as markers of national or ethnic groups are constantly being incorporated within a changing common practice style: that goes for the modal inflections, irregular phrase structures, and other aspects of stylized folk idiom found in Dvořák's music. The same applies in the ideological domain, where the naturalization and aestheticization to which Born & Hesmondhalgh refer is key to music's effect.

It was in the same year as Coleridge-Taylor met Dunbar that the Viennese music theorist Heinrich Schenker (who came from Galicia, on the northeast border of the Habsburg Empire) wrote that, because of his understanding of the "German logic of music," Smetana was able "to present Bohemian music in a perfection which will not be surpassed. Since then Dvořák has also succeeded ... His chamber music in particular, with all its Bohemian roots, is blessed with such outstanding German virtues that it justly seems to us most highly attractive" (McColl, 1996, p. 176). What might seem a purely musical form of politics acquires a broader significance when this quotation is juxtaposed with another, which dates from the year when Ditson published the "Twenty-Four Negro Melodies".: Guido Adler (who had moved from Prague to the Chair of Musicology at the University of Vienna) wrote that "as the motivic material is taken from the national stores, which the artists ... work up into classical structures, so may a higher states craft join the particularities of the peoples into a higher unity."[6] Seen this way, Dvořák's music symbolized and naturalized the hierarchical structure of the multinational empire. In America, however, its impact was quite different—though not so much because of the "New World" Symphony as because of what the composer said: "I am now satisfied," he told the *New York Herald* a few months before the symphony's first performance, "that the future music of this country must be founded upon what are called the negro melodies ... These are the folk songs of America" (Sullivan, 1999, pp. 1, 6). Two years later he proclaimed them "the most striking and appealing melodies that have yet been found on this side of the Atlantic." Sullivan (1999, pp. 8–12) describes the at times ugly controversies that ensued among critics and the chattering classes, which had hardly died down by the time Coleridge-Taylor arrived in America. He also points out the "uncanny resemblance," even down to the wording, between Dvořák's pronouncements and those of Du Bois in "The Souls of Black Folk," published just a few years later (Sullivan, 1999, p. 32).

38.3 ONE FOOT IN EACH REALITY

If Dvořák, perhaps unwittingly, made a powerful intervention in American racial politics, it might equally be said of Coleridge-Taylor's music that its symbolic meaning counts for less than the action it prompted. Richards (2001, p. 256) invokes Schenker's domain of musical logic when he writes that "African elements are perfectly at home in concert

[6] Notley 1999, p. 52. A more extended discussion may be found in Cook 2007, p. 12.

garb, forming a seamless garment with the European elements", but the more important point is that they were perfectly at home *in concert halls*, those canonical sites for the performance of white middle-class culture. Sayers (191, pp. 53–4) tells how, in 1898, the audience at a provincial English performance of Coleridge-Taylor's "Ballade in A Minor" knew that Coleridge-Taylor was "an Anglo-African," but assumed this meant he was "a white colonist." Sayers continues: "There was a general pause of astonishment at the entry of a short, swarthy, quick-moving ... young man, whose enormous head, with its long thick hair, broad nostrils, and flashing white teeth betrayed at once the race from which he came." Significantly, Sayers adds that the pause was followed by a "storm of applause" (he puts this down to the "sense of fair play ... characteristic of our race as a whole in its relations with the backward races"). If in this way, through his music, Coleridge-Taylor controverted expectations in England, he did so all the more in the "strange land of prejudice", as he once described racially segregated America (Self, 1995, p. 149).

There was obvious symbolic value in the fact that, at his first concert in Washington, Coleridge-Taylor conducted an orchestra drawn from America's most venerable military band, established by act of Congress in 1798: as a report in the *Georgia Baptist* said, "It was the first time that a man with African blood in his veins ever held a baton over the heads of the members of the great Marine Band" (Sayers, 1915, p. 162–3). It is equally significant that the soloists and chorus were also black, but what is perhaps most significant is the fact that, of the 2700 audience members (or 4000 according to the *Georgia Baptist*), at least one-third was white. Massed musical occasions such as this are performances of community, ritual acts in which everyone present is a participant; one might see them as playing the same community-forming role that music did in the early days of slavery, enabling slaves drawn from a wide variety of African ethnicities to develop a unified identity as Africans or African Americans (Jones, 2004, p. 255). Here, in Washington, community was being forged across the color line, constructing a liminal identity in which the normal divisions of turn-of-the-century American society were temporarily suspended. Coleridge-Taylor's host, and the chairman of the local Coleridge-Taylor Society, was Andrew Hilyer, who had been born a slave in Georgia and was the first African American to graduate from the University of Minnesota; four years after his visit, Hilyer told Coleridge-Taylor that "When we are going to have a Hiawatha concert here, for at least one month we seem, as it were, to be lifted above the clouds of American color-prejudice" (Sayers, 1915, p. 219). In short, music is a domain of social action the consequences of which go far beyond music. Indeed, Booker Washington made exactly that point, telling Coleridge-Taylor that "Hiawatha" "acts as a source of inspiration to us, not only musically, but in other lines of endeavor" (Self, 1995, p. 162).

Musical meaning is mediated by situated experience: you cannot read it directly from the text. Indeed Coleridge-Taylor is a prime illustration of this. To describe his music as orientalist, because on paper it resembles Rimsky-Korsakoff's, Balakirev's, or Holst's, is to interpret his appropriations of black music as "Africanisms" — in Lawrence Kramer's (1996, p. 201) words, "signs of blackness against which the subject of the dominant culture can seek to define itself as white." That is to over-simplify or misread a quite different play of identities. Coleridge-Taylor was not in the business of constructing a contrafactual whiteness in relation to a subordinate, exoticized other. On the other hand, neither was he engaged in the kind of self-exoticization illustrated by the slightly younger Kaikhosru Shapurji Sorabji, who made much of his father's Parsi ancestry and fabricated a story that his English mother was Spanish-Sicilian (Owen, 2006, p. 34): brought up in London by his mother and without significant knowledge of his father's culture, Sorabji—originally Leon Dudley Sorabji—seems to have had no interest in the real India, rather weaving Parsi and Tantric elements into a strictly imaginary orient. Depending on such things, the same notes may take on quite different meanings. It follows that the meaning of Coleridge-Taylor's music, and of all music, is not something deposited in the notes and laid down for all time, but rather something that emerges through interpretation and is embodied in the act of listening.

Concert reviews provide abundant evidence of how Coleridge-Taylor's music was heard by his contemporaries. However, the evidence is skewed. Despite Coleridge-Taylor's impact in the black community, the vast majority of American reviews of his music appeared in the white press. A rare exception, however, is Sylvester Russell, who wrote for newspapers oriented to the African American market and attended Coleridge-Taylor's 1904 concert in Philadelphia (which included settings of Dunbar's texts from the "African Romances"). Russell insisted that "the music, even those with African titles, had no African qualities" (McGinty, 2001, p. 216), and that is probably what most people would think today: the musical signifiers of place and ethnicity lie predominantly in sound production and performance practice, precisely the dimensions eliminated in Coleridge-Taylor's sources. Indeed, for us, the dissonance between Coleridge-Taylor's skin color and his music may have the effect of marking his music as white, so—for once—unmasking the assumed color neutrality of the Western "art" tradition. But that was simply not the experience of many contemporary critics on both sides of the Atlantic.

To these white critics the racial character of the music was self-evident, taken for granted: as they heard it, then, they were implicitly constructing relationships of self and other, and in this sense imposing a racially marked identity on the composer (who, according to Sayers [1915, p. 255], "hated the early criticisms which dealt equally with his skin and his music"). There is, perhaps, indirect evidence of racial hearing in certain epithets that were applied over and over again to Coleridge-Taylor's music, giving the impression of being some kind of code. August Jaeger's association of the composer's paternity and the "freshness" of his music is one example, and word duly crops up in reviews. References to the "savage" or "barbaric" quality of the music are ubiquitous and easily understood, though sometimes applied in contexts where there is to modern ears nothing remotely barbaric about it. Less predictable is the epithet "clever", which Elgar used twice in a letter to Jeager dated 17 April 1898 (Self, 1995, p. 62) and is equally pervasive. Again, Doris McGinty (2001, p. 208) notes that early American performances of "The Song of Hiawatha" constantly elicited terms such as "savage," "barbaric," "mysterious," and "weird," along with descriptions of it as "European, lacking the expected earmarks of an African heritage"—which implies a racialized expectation that, just because Coleridge-Taylor had African blood, he must compose in an "African" way, regardless of the particular subject or nature of the composition in question. That is also the implication of an obituary of Coleridge-Taylor that appeared in the *Henley and South Oxfordshire Standard*, according to which Massenet "was once glancing through a full score of one of Coleridge-Taylor's works, and without knowing the name of the composer he declared that he was certain the musician was of negro extraction, basing his belief on the character of the music" (Green, 2011, p. 208).

And the same might be said of the apparently innocuous praise for Coleridge-Taylor's orchestration that appeared in a *Staffordshire Sentinel* review from 1899: "we must look for an explanation in the African origin of the composer", the critic added (Green, 2011, p. 80). The apparent non-sequitur comes into focus when juxtaposed with a memorial tribute written by Sir Hubert Parry (at that time principal of the Royal College of Music) and published in *The Musical Times*. Having commented on Coleridge-Taylor's "strikingly unoccidental" appearance and explained the affinity between him and Dvořák in terms of "some racial analogy", Parry records that "like his half-brothers of primitive race he loved plenty of sound, plenty of colour, simple and definite rhythms, and above all things plenty of tune" (Tortolano, 2002, pp. 81–2). Parry also draws heavily on another racial stereotype that portrayed "women, the working class, and inferior races … as child-like and requiring the firm but benign hand of the white middle- and upper-class male" (Rattansi, 2007, p. 46). Rather than thirsting for intellectual analysis, Parry tells us, Coleridge-Taylor's "primitive nature delighted in stories. He himself said that he was mainly attracted to Longfellow's poem by the funny names in it". Parry concludes, "It was the very simplicity and unconsciousness of his character which caused the racial motives and impulses to be revealed so clearly".

Racism becomes fully articulate at the point when the intrinsically black nature of Coleridge-Taylor's music is coupled to his lack of an African upbringing. That is what *The Times* did in its obituary:

> In any of his work which one may take up it is obvious at once that it has certain features in its melody, style of treatment and use of orchestral color which distinguish it from the music of English composers. Yet he was born in London, all his early environment was English, and he was educated at the Royal College of Music.
>
> Green, 1990, p. 250.

The logic is clear. If the racial character of the music is not due to enculturation, then it must be due to what Sayers (1915, p. 15) euphemistically refers to as "the biological reason," in other words the scientific—or rather pseudo-scientific—theory that sought to define race through facial feature, texture of hair, or cranial measurement (and on which a paper by William Meyer, a medical student from Trinidad, featured during the second day of the Pan-African Conference; Fryer, 1984, p. 283). Such theories gave rise to what Ronald Radano & Philip Bohlman (2000, p. 7) call "the more extreme forms of racial prejudice," according to which, for example, "a music would 'sound Jewish' because its performer could not escape a race-specific predilection to a Jewish metaphysics of music."

Whether or not they subscribed to scientific racism, it is clear that many—probably most—of Coleridge-Taylor's white friends and colleagues thought in ways that would nowadays be seen as racist: they believed that "biological characteristics such as skin col-our, shape of nose, type of hair, and size of skull were associated with ingrained cultural and behavioural traits," in other words, that there are such things as distinct races and that they exist in a hierarchy (Rattansi, 2007, p. 13). Sayers, who was himself a friend and wrote his biography at Jessie's request (Sayers, 1915), provides a good illustration. On the one hand, as we have seen, he dismisses race as a cause of discomfort and seeks to excuse Jessie's relations; he notes the racial quality of Coleridge-Taylor's orchestration and his love of funny names, commenting of the latter that "A cursory study of the negro shows how true this is to his temperament." He even describes the composer's appearance in a way that is alarmingly suggestive of an ape ("short, rather undersized figure ... long, swinging arms, and short, rapid-striding legs;" Sayers, 1915, pp. 256, 260). On the other hand he condemns as "brutal nonsense" a publisher's description of the composer as "a damned nigger. He'll never do anything more," and cites Coleridge-Taylor as "a complete answer to all the biologists who generalize on the limitations of the negro genius" (Sayers, 1915, pp. 105, 280). What I said about the mobile performance of self-identity, of course, applies as much to Sayers as to Coleridge-Taylor, but the point is that while underlying racial patterns of thought may coexist with personal respect and even affection, they are always capable of being mobilized by pernicious ideologies—and remarkably quickly. That is Daniel Goldhagen's message in *Hitler's willing executioners* (1996).

For at least some of these critics, as for those who thought about Jews as Radano & Bohlman describe, personal identity was a reflection of a fixed racial identity: whatever you composed or played, whatever you said or did, you were inescapably black or Jewish. By contrast, what Tim Rice (2007, p. 24) calls a "constructivist" rather than "essentialist" concept of identity stresses its performative nature and therefore the self-determination involved in identity work. Rice (2007, p. 23) speaks of "authoring a self through music," and explains that this has two aspects: on the one hand "creating a sense of self-under-standing or self-worth," and on the other "creating a sense of belonging to preexisting social groups." Coleridge-Taylor illustrates both. His statement that he considered him-self the equal of any white man who ever lived speaks to a sense of self-worth gained through his extraordinary success as a composer and the position it earned him both within and beyond the social and institutional structures of English musicianship: as early as 1901, Jaeger—the same Jaeger who told Elgar what he could and could not com-pose—wrote in a letter to the critic Herbert Thompson that Coleridge-Taylor "is too big a celebrity now ever to come near me" (Self, 1995, p. 124). At the same time, Self's refer-ence to Dvořák being his mentor expresses Coleridge-Taylor's membership of the trans-national community of composers, to which his privileged position within cultured and political African American circles added a further dimension. These distinct spheres of Coleridge-Taylor's experience bear witness to the multiplicity of identity construction.

But that is the story of the Coleridge-Taylor who was only black outside: it does not bear upon the experience Du Bois famously characterized as "twoness ... two souls, two thoughts ... two warring ideals in one dark body" (Sundquist, 1996, p. 102). Coleridge-Taylor's dark body forced racial markedness on him, conditioned the availability of identities, as for all black residents of Victorian and Edwardian England, but at the same time, it afforded his construction of a Pan-African identity. If Richards is right about Coleridge-Taylor searching for "his African soul"—if he came to figure his whiteness as deficit—then the traces of that search may lie in his music. Earlier I suggested that Coleridge-Taylor may have thought of the sorrow song, the repository of African racial memory, as the place where he would find his new identity. But as Simon Frith (1996, p. 122) says, identity is "not something we reveal or discover," it is something we create, and so we might think of "Twenty-Four Negro Melodies" as a site where Coleridge-Taylor labored to construct a new social identity, that of the Pan-African—a member of another transnational community, which is to say a community more imagined than real. Sullivan (1999, p. 36) writes that "The *Negro Melodies* are richer and stranger precisely because their creator had one foot in each reality, his imagination set in the cotton field, his experience in the drawing room." That is Coleridge-Taylor's version of twoness.

Considered as a symbolic representation of black identity, "Twenty-Four Negro Melodies" falls far short of Floyd's (1980, p. 12) exacting, if vague, definition of "a work of *black* music" ("a *sonic temporal organism whose internal relationships express and communicate essentials of the Afro-American experience*"). Martin Stokes (1994, p. 5) writes that music and dance are not just "static symbolic objects which have to be understood in a context, but are themselves a patterned context within which other things happen." Stokes is talking about ritual, but what he says applies to music as performance more generally. I spoke of the negotiation of liminal identities that crossed the color line in American performances of Coleridge-Taylor's music. In England the massed choral performances of the "Hiawatha" trilogy at the turn of the century afforded their amateur participants a surrogate experience of indigeneity, the thrill of identification with an exotic other. Every year during most of the 1920s and 30s, in a last gasp of the Coleridge-Taylor story, there were two weeks of summer-time performances of "The Song of Hiawatha" at the Royal Albert Hall, at which soloists wore feathers, the chorus dressed up in Indian clothes, and everywhere there were children in war paint (Green, 2001b).

As for the composer, perhaps for him the conductor's podium was the only public place where he could be sure of transcending the politics of race. But then, there was an occasion, just a few months before Coleridge-Taylor's death, when Reginald Buckley tried to interest him in the idea of "a West African drama, with strong Imperial interest, and also with scope for native music, which he said laughingly would appeal to the 'savage' in him" (Sayers, 1915, p. 277). When Coleridge-Taylor conducted works such as "The Bamboula," we might speculate that some part of him was playing the role of the imaginary African, the denizen of a continent on which he never actually set foot.

ACKNOWLEDGEMENTS

This chapter is an output of "Musical encounters: Studies in relational musicology," a project funded through a British Academy Wolfson Research Professorship. Thanks to Ross Cole for his comments on a draft version.

REFERENCES

Born, G. & Hesmondhalgh, D. (2000). Introduction: on difference, representation, and appropriation in music. In: G. Born & D. Hesmondhalgh (Eds.) *Western music and its others: difference, representation, and appropriation in music*, pp. 1–58. Berkeley, CA: University of California Press.

Broyles, M. (2011). *Beethoven in America*. Bloomington, IN: Indiana University Press.

Carr, C. (2005). *The music of Samuel Coleridge-Taylor (1875–1912): a critical and analytical study*. PhD diss., Durham University. Available at Durham E-Theses Online: http://etheses.dur.ac.uk/2964/ (accessed 29 February 2016).

Coleridge-Taylor, A. (1979). *The heritage of Samuel Coleridge-Taylor*. London: Dennis Dobson.

Coleridge-Taylor, J. (1942–3). *A memory sketch or personal reminiscences of my husband. Genius and musician—S. Coleridge-Taylor 1875–1912*. Bognor Regis: John Crowther Ltd.

Cook, N. (2007). *The Schenker Project: culture, race, and music theory in fin-de-siècle Vienna*. New York, NY: Oxford University Press.

Elford, C. (2008). *Black Mahler: the Samuel Coleridge-Taylor story*. Guildford: Grosvenor House Publishing.

Floyd, S. (1980). Black American music and aesthetic communication. *Black Music Research Journal*, 1, 1–17.

Floyd, S. (1995). *The power of black music: interpreting its history from Africa to the United States*. New York, NY: Oxford University Press.

Frith, S. (1996). Music and identity. In: S. Hall & P. du Gay (Eds.) *Questions of cultural identity*, pp. 108–27. London: Sage.

Fryer, P. (1984). *Staying power: the history of Black people in Britain*. London: Pluto Press.

Gilroy, P. (1993). *The Black Atlantic: modernity and double consciousness*. Cambridge, MA: Harvard University Press.

Goldhagen, D. (1996). *Hitler's willing executioners: ordinary Germans and the Holocaust*. New York: Alfred Knopf.

Green, J. (1990). "The foremost musician of his race": Samuel Coleridge-Taylor of England, 1875–1912. *Black Music Research Journal*, 10, 233–52.

Green, J. (2001a). Samuel Coleridge-Taylor: the early years. *Black Music Research Journal*, 21, 133–57.

Green, J. (2001b). Requiem: *Hiawatha* in the 1920s and 1930s. *Black Music Research Journal*, 21, 283–8.

Green, J. (2001c). Future research. *Black Music Research Journal*, 21, 289–94.

Green, J. (2007). Spirituals to (nearly) Swing, 1873–1938. In: N.A. Wynn (Ed.) *Cross the water blues: African American music in Europe*, pp. 51–65. Jackson: University Press of Mississippi.

Green, J. (2011). *Samuel Coleridge-Taylor, a music life*. London: Pickering & Chatto.

Green, J. (2012). *Coleridge-Taylor: a centenary celebration*. London: History & Social Action Publications.

Jones, A. C. (2004). The foundational influence of spirituals in African-American culture: a psychological perspective. *Black Music Research Journal*, 24, 251–60.

Kramer, L. (1996). Powers of blackness: Africanist discourse in modern concert music. *Black Music Research Journal*, 16, 53–70.

McColl, S. (1996). *Music criticism in Vienna, 1896–1897: critically moving forms*. Oxford: Clarendon Press.

McGinty, D.E. (2001). "That you came so far to see us": Coleridge-Taylor in America. *Black Music Research Journal*, 21, 197–234.

Moon, B. (2004). Harry Burleigh as ethnomusicologist? Transcription, arranging, and "The Old Songs Hymnal." *Black Music Research Journal*, 24, 287–307.

Notley, M. (1999). Musical culture in Vienna at the turn of the twentieth century. In: B. Simms (Ed.). *Schoenberg, Berg, and Webern: a companion to the second Viennese school*, pp. 37–71. Westport, CT: Greenwood Press.

Owen, S.V. (2006). *Kaikhosru Shapurji Sorabji: an oral biography*. PhD diss, University of Southampton. Available at The Sorabji Archive: http://www.sorabji-archive.co.uk/books/owen-thesis.php.

Radano, R. & Bohlman, P.V. (2000). *Music and the racial imagination*. Chicago, IL: University of Chicago Press.

Rattansi, A. (2007). *Racism: a very short introduction*. Oxford: Oxford University Press.

Rice, T. (2007). Reflections on music and identity in Ethnomusicology. *Muzikologija/Musicology (Serbian Academy of Sciences and Arts)*, 7, 17–38.

Richards, P. (2001). A Pan-African composer? Coleridge-Taylor and Africa. *Black Music Research Journal*, 21, 235–60.

Sayers, W.C.B. (1915). *Samuel Taylor-Coleridge, musician: his life and letters*. London: Cassell.

Self, G. (1995). *The Hiawatha man: the life and work of Samuel Coleridge-Taylor*. Aldershot: Scolar Press.

Snyder, J.L. (2013). *Samuel Coleridge-Taylor: Symphony in A minor, opus 8. With the earlier finales and Idyll, opus 44*. Madison, WI: A-R Editions.

Stokes, M. (1994). Introduction: ethnicity, identity and music. In: M. Stokes (Ed.) *Ethnicity, identity and music: the musical construction of place*, pp. 1–27. Oxford: Berg.

Sullivan, J. (1999). *New World Symphonies: how American culture changed European Music*. New Haven, CT: Yale University Press.

Sundquist, E.J. (1996). *The Oxford W. E. B. Du Bois reader*. New York: Oxford University Press.

Tortolano, W. (2002). *Samuel Coleridge-Taylor: Anglo-Black composer, 1875–1912*, 2nd edn. Lanham, MD: Scarecrow Press.

Turino, T. (2008). *Music as social life: the politics of participation*. Chicago, IL: University of Chicago Press.

Ward, A. (2000). *Dark midnight when I rise: the story of the Jubilee Singers who introduced the world to the music of Black America*. New York, NY: Farrar, Straus and Giroux.

CHAPTER 39

THE IDENTITIES
OF SEVDA

From Graeco-Arabic Medicine to Music Therapy

NIGEL OSBORNE

SEVDA, sometimes referred to as *Sevdah, Sevdalinka,* or by its plural *Sevdalinke,* is a traditional music from Bosnia and Herzegovina which has related forms throughout the Balkan region, including Serbia, Macedonia, and Northern Greece. The music poses interesting, and in some ways key questions about culture and identity. On the one hand, Sevda is one of the most intercultural musical forms of Europe, a historical synthesis of many diverse social and cultural identities, embracing both Slav and Turkish social traditions, four religions, and a diversity of musical cultures ranging from the *Makams* (musical scales and melodic patterns) of the Near and Middle East to Slav folk music, Italian *bel canto* and Viennese romanticism. On the other hand, this diversity of identities is entirely integrated in a unique, characteristic, coherent musical and poetic language which expresses a collective cultural identity with profound implications for the "common life" of Bosnia and Herzegovina, for the region, and perhaps for Europe as a whole.

This chapter is organized in two halves. In the first half, I present a short overview of *Sevda* and a tentative musical "archeology" of its diverse identities through a small body of historical evidence and through discussion of musical examples. I also reflect on issues of social identity and the so-called ethnicities of Bosnia-Herzegovina, and review the effect of the conflicts of the 1990s on the Sevda tradition and implications for Bosnia's "common life" as a whole.

In the second half I consider the uses of the integrated identities and special characteristics of Sevda in education, reconciliation and therapeutic practice. I have based this on my own experiences of working with the music of Sevda with children who were the victims of the conflict, and with groups of young people in both an educational and therapeutic context. Although the chapter is, I hope, informed by respectable scholarship and science, it is essentially the personal view of a practicing creative and community musician.

39.1 THE IDENTITIES OF SEVDA

The origins of the term Sevda are as profoundly intercultural as the music itself. They are musical/aesthetic, but also psychological and biological. The underlying concept of Sevda derives from the Ancient Greek *melas* (μέλας), meaning "black," and *khole* (χολή), "bile" (the English "melancholy") one of the four Ancient Greek medical "humours." The idea was first introduced from Ancient Egyptian and Mesopotamian thought by Thales (640–546 BC) and adopted by Hippocrates (460–370 BC) (1931) as one of the four bodily liquids or temperaments responsible for human attributes and dispositions. The idea was transmitted to early Islamic medical theory and practice through the works of Al-Kindi (801–873 AD) and Avicenna (980–1037 AD). In the Canon of Medicine (Abu 'Ali al-Husayn Ibn Sina, 2012) Avicenna describes the black bile as "earthly, gross, thick, black and sour," tempering volatility in the blood. It is associated with suspicion, sorrowfulness, and terrifying impulse, and controls the body from 21.00 to 03.00 hours. As well as being the perceived "founder of modern medicine," Avicenna was an advocate of music therapy, prescribing music, for example, for the treatment of insomnia.

The "black bile" came to be described popularly as *Sawdah* (from *sawaad* meaning "black") in Arabic, or *Sevda* in Turkish (Janković, 2006), although in the Turkish tradition the word has cognates in Persian, and came to denote more specifically "love" or "lovesickness." From Turkey, the word spread through the Ottoman Empire to the Balkans (14–19th centuries) to describe a music of lost or unfulfilled love, pain, sorrow, regret, longing, and deep emotion. It also arrived with the Berbers and Arabs in Portugal (711–1249 AD) and is probably the origin of *Saudade*, the music of "the love that remains when someone has gone."

Little is known of the early development of Sevda in Bosnia and Herzegovina. It is likely that it arose in Bosnian urban centers in the years after the annexation to the Ottoman Empire in the mid-15th century. According to Ivan Lovrenović (2004), "this took place in a milieu of economically and materially better-off merchants and craftsmen … and *Sevda* can be perceived in the main as an expression of Muslim lifestyle and culture. This interpretation loses its force, however, when it becomes ethnically determined. In the construction of the integral social and cultural character of the larger towns and smaller urban settlements, other ethnic elements (Catholic-Croat, Orthodox-Serb, Sephardic-Jewish, Roma …) played an important role." Early Sevda was sung to the accompaniment of the *saz*, or *baglama*, a Turkish three-stringed lute in just "natural" intonation, and it is likely that many melodies followed the patterns of Turkish *Makam* scales, still to some extent audible in the Sevda tradition today. *Moj dilbere*, for example, a bitter-sweet song dating from Ottoman times about a pining lover

FIG. 39.1 My love … Where are you going? …

and the priceless treasures of attachment, has a resonance of the Turkish *Hicaz Makam* (Arabic *Hijaz Maqaam*), often associated in Sufi traditions with the pleasures and complications of love (Fig. 39.1).

Some older Sevda tunes also suggest the influence of more ancient Slav musical sources, for example, the repeated four-square rhythmic patterns and formulaic, descending cadential phrases of melodies like *Čudila, aman ja* (Fig. 39.2).

Bosnian Muslims were primarily of Slav and autochthonous Balkan origin, many of them converts from the oppressed Bosnian Church (Fine, 2007; Basić, 2009). Contemporary accounts indicate that some of their social behaviors, for example, in courtship (Cevdet Paşa, cited in Buturović, 2007)—of particular relevance to the culture of Sevda—differed from the expected Turkish-Islamic *mores*. The language they spoke on the street was the same Bosnian language as their neighbors, and the poetry of Sevda became a rich celebration of Slav language accented with colorful, poetic and

FIG. 39.2 She wondered, *aman*, Oh love. She wondered, *zeman*, Oh time …

FIG. 39.3 When I went to Bembaša, to the waters, I took a white lamb, a white lamb with me …
Original Sephardic text "El Dio alto con su gracia, mos mande muncha ganacia, non veamos mal
ni ansia, a nos y a todo Yisrael."

spiritually resonant words of Turkish and Arabic origin—like *akšam* (dusk, or evening
prayer), *bulbul* (nightingale), *kara-krzli* (black-red), or *rahmet* (peace, the love of God).

By the early 16th century significant numbers of Sephardic Jewish families fleeing
from the Inquisition had arrived in Bosnia. They lived, by all accounts, in a respectful
harmony with their neighbors and contributed, as the centuries passed, to the repertoire
of Sevda: several well-known tunes are anecdotally ascribed to the Sephardic tradition.
One of the best-loved "hymns" of Sarajevo *Kad ja podoh na Bembašu* (Fig. 39.3) has a
melody derived directly from the Sephardic song *El Dio alto con su gracia*. The Bosnian
text faithfully follows the *octosilabo* metrical structure of the original (Romero, 1988).

Movements of peoples back and forth through the centuries between Bosnia and
Dalmatia brought the *Ionian* melos of the music of the Adriatic coast, palpably evident
in many Sevda melodies (Lovrenović, 2004). *Ibrahim-bega svezana vode* begins with a
phrase that is reminiscent of *Puselik Makam*, or perhaps, more distantly, of the Arabic
Shad Araban; but from notated bar 4 it moves into a melos that is distinctly Dalmatian-
sounding (Fig. 39.4). The descent from the *Ionian* leading note to the third degree of
the scale at the end would be typical of an Adriatic fisherman's song (a melos echoed in
many Dalmatian popular songs, for example the well-known *Ćiribiribela Mare moje*).

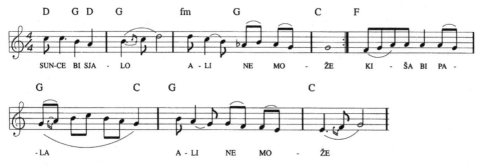

FIG. 39.4 The sun would shine, but cannot, the rain could fall, but would not; neither would wish,
from the deepest of misery.

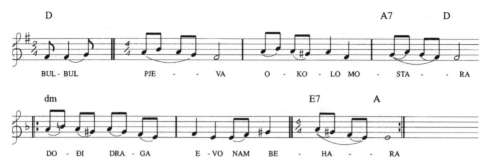

FIG. 39.5 A nightingale sings around Mostar, come my dear, the blossom is here …

There can of course be no conclusive historic proof for this influence, but if it is a coincidence, it is like finding a Palladian Venetian window in a traditional Turkish house.

The step-by-step erosion of Ottoman power and the arrival of the Austro-Hungarians after the Congress of Berlin (1878), brought a watershed for Sevda. The Austro-Hungarians established music schools, and western instruments became commonplace; the clarinet and violin, and later the accordion and guitar became the normal accompaniment for the form. With Western instruments came Western harmonic practices and Western equal temperament. No longer was the music to be accompanied exclusively by the delicate just intonation, melodic elaborations, and drones of the *saz*; it was harmonized with Central European functional progressions. Such standard harmonizations are notated for a number of musical examples in this chapter. *Bulbul pjeva okolo Mostara* begins with an almost Dalmatian feel, but then moves into a *Makam*-like section (Fig. 39.5). The Near Eastern *Hicaz*-like cadence is now normally harmonized by a distinctly Middle European secondary dominant progression (secondary dominant E major seventh to the dominant, A major).

The Austro-Hungarian period brought a more self-conscious "orientalism" to Sevda (Lovrenović). It was the result of an extraordinary collision of tradition, romanticism and modernism. In the late 1800s and early 1900s Sarajevo was catapulted into the avant-garde of European cities by an early integrated horse-drawn and electrical tram system (1883 and 1895, respectively), and an integrated water supply. At the same time the Austrians built the Vijećnica National Library constructing in an extravagant pseudo-Moorish "Arabian Nights" style which bore little relationship to the subtle aesthetics of Bosnian Islamic tradition, and printed tram tickets in Arabic script that few could read. It was in this atmosphere that Aleksa Šantić translated Heinrich Heine's orientalist poem *Der Asra* into Bosnian as *Kraj tanana šadrvana* and thus, strangely, a piece of western romantic exoticism—albeit, in Heine's case, self-critical—a fantasy of long-gone Sultans and fountains, became a classic song of contemporary Sevda (Fig. 39.6).

Šantić (1868–1924) was a Serb Orthodox Bosnian from Mostar, and made a significant contribution to the poetry of Sevda. He was a South Slav patriot who sought, among other things, to promote the unity of Slav Muslim and Christian communities. He steeped himself in the colorful Slav-Turkish language of Sevda, and produced some of its most

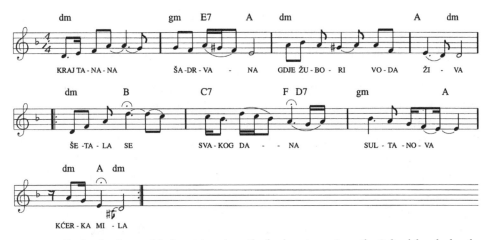

FIG. 39.6 By the slender marble fountain, where the fresh water springs, the Sultan's lovely daughter wandered every day… Heine's original poem "Täglich ging die wunderschöne Sultantochter auf und nieder, um die Abenzeit am Springbrunn, wo die weißen Wasser plätschem …"

outstanding literature, including the text of *Bulbul pjeva okolo Mostara*. The song *Što te nema* is written in the spirit of Šantić's own Heine translations; the traditional melody, and the usual manner of its interpretation, suggest an almost bel canto style. His most famous Sevda song is "Emina," the story of his own unrequited love for a beautiful Bosnian Muslim girl. Emina's great-granddaughter Alma Ferović, an opera singer and former fashion model, sang for me in my Sevda Opera "Differences in Demolition" (Fig. 39.7).

The next major impetus and change in Sevda was the period following the Second World War. The former Yugoslav Federal Constitution guaranteed equality of cultures within Yugoslavia, and Josip Broz Tito's cultural policies included national cohesion through sharing cultural knowledge. By 1968 there were 3,171,000 subscribers to 94 radio stations in Yugoslavia, with 143,000 hours of broadcasting annually of which music accounted for 60% of air time (Majstoiovic, 1972). I asked the distinguished actor Rade Šerbedžija, who was brought up in Lika in Croatia with little or no contact with

FIG. 39.7 Last night, as I returned from the warm Turkish baths, and crossed by the garden of the old Imam there in the garden, in the shade of the jasmine, stood Emina with a pitcher in her hand.

Bosnia, how he came to accumulate his encyclopaedic knowledge of Sevda and characteristic singing style. He replied "Well you know, when I was young my mother used to listen to the radio non-stop while she was working in the kitchen and around the house. She particularly enjoyed Sevda and would sing with the radio, and when the music on the radio stopped (laughs), she would carry on singing! I learnt Sevda from my mother." (Rade Šerbedžija, in conversation with the author, Rijeka, December 2010).

The communicative power of radio, and later television, fostered the careers of many Sevda singers of the period, outstanding Bosnian performers like Zaim Imamović (1920–1994) and Safet Isović (1936–2007) or the great Serbian interpreter of Sevda, Nada Mamula (1927–2001). To the list may be added names like Silvana Armenulić, Hanka Paldum, Omer Pobrić, Meho Puzić, Himzo Polovina, Zehra Deović, Beba Selimović, or Asim Brkan. By the late 1980s, Sevda had moved out of the bars and kafana's (coffee houses) into theatres, concert halls, and television studios. It had grown from being the music of the "common life" of Bosnia and Herzegovina into a music enjoyed and "owned" by a majority of Yugoslavs.

Both Sevda and the human values it represents became cultural victims of the conflicts of the 1990s in former Yugoslavia. The fate of Bosnia was decided at a meeting at Karađorđevo, Vojvodina, between Serbian President Slobodan Milošević and Croatian President Franjo Tuđman on 25th March 1991. The outcome was a Ribbentrop-Molotov style agreement to go to war and to divide Bosnia and Herzogovina between them along "ethnic" lines. The division would be implemented by an "ethnic cleansing" policy first hatched in the corridors of the Serbian Academy of Sciences in the mid-1980s and in some ways reflected publicly and politically in the SANU Memorandum of 1986. The implications for Bosnia were particularly grim. In 1981, 16.8% of marriages in Bosnia were of mixed religion (Bogoslavljević, 1992). In some cities, by the early 1990s, the proportion was as high as 40–50%. In 1992, and the eve of the war, Bosnian society enjoyed an almost entirely integrated common life. I remember sitting at a coffee shop on the Rondo in Mostar at that time and asking my friends mischievously who was Muslim, Serb Orthodox, or Catholic. I shall never forget the answer: "*Neznamo ... nema veze!*," "We don't know and we don't care!" At the outbreak of war, few people in Mostar believed the city could ever be divided along so-called "ethnic" lines.

The process of implementing the Karađorđevo agreement, and of breaking apart a society so closely integrated, was horrendously cruel beyond the imaginations of the Belgrade academicians. There is still debate about the number of people killed, but a figure of between 120,000 and 200,000 embraces the differing estimates. All people of Bosnia suffered—there were as many serious woundings as deaths, 2.2 million people driven out of their homes and up to 50,000 cases of rape, but the majority of victims were Bosniaks (Muslim or of secular Muslim heritage). It was a genocide, but for the perpetrators, many of whom were not Bosnian, it was also a cultural suicide—the wanton destruction of the "common life" identity of the Balkan heartland. The situation was compounded by weakness, apathy, misinformation and at times connivance among the international community. Sevda, as a prime cultural expression of the common life, came under pressure from all sides. It was scorned as "Islamic" by extreme Serbian and Croatian nationalists, and attempts were made to drive it out of both public and private spaces. At the same time a "reactive" nationalism grew for a time among political factions of the Bosniak community promoting an atmosphere in which Sevda came to be regarded, in some circles, as exclusively Bosniak.

The war, in its ambitions for power, money, division and *Lebensraum*, was an assault on the Bosnian common life and identity. The genetic make-up of Bosnia and Herzegovina is predominantly haplogroup I-P37, followed by E-M78, (Marjanović et al., 2005). Groups associated with autochthonous Balkan populations, spread more or less evenly among Bosnia's communities, and across Europe as far as Scandinavia and the British Isles. The different religious communities, Muslim, Serb Orthodox, and Catholic have cultivated some distinctive cultural practices (for example, in folk dance), but most Bosnians before the war lived their lives in the "common life" in between, the same common cultural area that the music and poetry of Sevda came to occupy. They shared the same genetic code, lived largely secular lives, dressed the same, enjoyed the same cuisine, went to the same schools, fell in love with one another and spoke the same language—Bosnian dialects of Serbo-Croat, in which minor linguistic differences were defined by region, rather than by community. I argue that it is misleading to speak of different "ethnicities" in Bosnia and Herzegovina; by most anthropological definitions it is a single, collective ethnicity (Peoples & Bailey, 2011). However, the growth of nationalism in the 19th century and the policies of the Federal Republic of Yugoslavia encouraged the construct of "nationalities" or "peoples"—Serb, Croat, and Muslim—an inconsistent terminology, which is why the predominantly secular "Muslim" population is now normally referred to as "Bosniak." At the end of the war, in the Dayton agreement of 1995, the objectives of ethnic cleansers and the interests of the international policymakers came together in the division of the country into the Federation, comprising a *de facto* division of Bosniak and Croat communities, and Republika Srpska, the Serb entity. From then onwards, Bosnia was to have three different school systems and three different languages.

As I have commented recently (Osborne, 2014), "the fact that ultra-nationalists and the international community conspired to create the illusion of difference and to generate a vocabulary of malapropisms (nation, race, ethnicity, people, entity, Serb, Croat, and Muslim ...) to support and justify the division, is one the great intellectual disasters of the era."

It is perhaps one of the few optimistic indications for Bosnia's future that the music of Sevda , the music of the "common life" and shared "ethnicity," somehow survived this attrition. Even at the height of the war, Croatian paramilitaries from Herzegovina were singing Sevda in their clubs around Zagreb (Slavko Goldstein, in conversation with the author, Zagreb, June 1996), and when I asked a friend whose brother was a high-ranking officer in the Serb forces what the soldiers and ex-soldiers were doing now the war was over, he replied "Some are still listening to Ceca ... but many are singing Sevda" (Goran Simić, in conversation with the author, Antwerp, December 1996; Ceca, Svetlana Ražnatović, is widow of the paramilitary leader Arkan, and a popular singer of *turbo-folk*, an "Asiatic" style of popular music associated at the time, paradoxically, with a brand of Serbian anti-Islamic nationalism).

The post-war period brought a modest revival of general interest in Sevda, both in Bosnia and Hezegovina, and in former Yugoslavia at large. An important role in this revival was played by groups such as The Mostar Sevdah Reunion. The mission of "reunion" in question was not only to bring the best musicians back together, but also to reunite those of different communities separated by the war. The group was founded in Mostar in 1998 by Dragi Šestić, and Mujo Šantić (accordion and clarinet) was an important early inspiration. Other band members include Mišo Petrović and Sandi Duraković (guitars), Nermin Alukić Ćerkez (voice and guitar), Marko Jakovljević (bass), Gabrijel Prusina (piano), Senad Trovac (drums), and Vanja Radoja (violin), musicians from all so-called "ethnic" identities of Bosnia and the region. The style ranges from traditional to popular, jazz and experimental influences, and guest performers have included two legendary Serbian Roma artists: the late Šaban Bajramović and the late Ljilijana Buttler.

A new generation has carried Sevda to new musical frontiers. Damir Imamović (born 1978), grandson of the celebrated Zaim Imamović, has developed a personal Sevda guitar technique that combines contemporary jazz influences with styles adapted directly from *Makam* and the techniques of the Near and Middle Eastern *oud:* a forerunner of the European lute (*al-ʿūd*). In a way, Imamović is propelling Sevda simultaneously deep into its past and prospectively into its future. An exceptional young singer, Amira Medunjanin, described by journalist Garth Cartwright as the "Bosnian Billie Holiday," has combined authentic traditional interpretations of Sevda of exceptional purity, in particular in her recordings with accordion player Merima Ključo, with influences from jazz, popular music and even flamenco. In her performances she often combines Sevda with songs from other former Yugoslav traditions, including Serbia, Croatia, Montenegro, and Macedonia. The plurality of the contemporary world of *Sevda* is sensitively captured in Robert Golden's film "Stories of Sevdah—the Balkan Blues" (Robert Golden Pictures, 2009).

39.2 FROM GRAECO-ARABIC MEDICINE TO MUSIC THERAPY

In the early 1990s I worked for organizations like Action for Bosnia and Scottish Action for Bosnia concerned with challenging an output of misinformation and disinformation about Bosnia and Herzegovina, and its identity, which was feeding both the war and Western attitudes to it. For example that the conflict was simply a "civil war," that it was fueled by "ancient ethnic hatreds," or that Bosnia was "an enclave of radical Islam in the middle of Europe." I also worked directly and politically to attempt to stop the war. This involved travelling to the besieged city of Sarajevo. But as the political process failed, I turned my attention to matters more familiar to me. I worked with artists in Sarajevo to support the cultural defence of the city: with the "Cellist of Sarajevo" Vedran Smailović, with Dževad Šabanagić, leader of the Sarajevo String Quartet, Faruk Sijarić Dean of the Music Academy, the Sarajevo (War) Philharmonic, young rock musicians, and with a number of writers and artists, like Goran Simić, Miki Trifunov,

Edo Numankadić, Nusret Pašić, and Mustafa Skopljak. Culture became a defensive weapon in Sarajevo, precisely because it expressed the common identity of people of different backgrounds trying to survive the medieval siege of a modern city. It offered self-respect to its citizens and the opportunity to resist primitive violence with meaningful human expression. Above all, it countered propagandists who attempted to portray Sarajevo as a hotbed of primitive radicalism with indisputable evidence that it was a sophisticated European city whose cultural icons were Beethoven, Anthony Gormley, Sevda, and U2. I documented some of these activities in a series of articles for *The Independent* newspaper at the time (Osborne, 1994a, b, 1995).

Most important of all, I was concerned about the plight of children in Sarajevo. At the time of my first visits (early in 1993) schools were closed, there was little food, water had to be carried from artesian wells through sniper fire, mortars fell at random on the city, and children were frequently subjected to traumatizing experiences of human carnage. I speculated that my background in community arts and therapeutic work with music (although I am not a clinically- qualified music therapist) might be of some use. From my artist friends, I discovered that there were plans to set up such an initiative, but as they put it, they were all "walking skeletons;" it would require outside energies and support. So we started a program of creative arts workshops for children together. Our objectives were simply to offer children distraction from the horrors around them and the chance to express themselves. It was only later that we were visited by representatives of the Ministry of Health who described our work as "therapeutic." Only much later did the scientific evidence come of the high levels of trauma among our children (Goldstein, Wampler, & Wise, 1997). The project in Sarajevo culminated in a number of large-scale events, including the first opera of the war *Evropa* in the National Theatre (during a ceasefire in 1995) and later *Alicja u zemlji čudesa* (Alice in Wonderland) in the Chamber Theatre.

In the meantime, I had begun work in Mostar, initially independently in 1994, and from 1995 in a collaboration with the charity "War Child." The work in Sarajevo was of necessity a series of "drops in the ocean," but after the Washington agreement of March 1994 brought a limited ceasefire to Mostar, it became possible to think of a project that would reach all children in the area, at least in East Mostar, a largely Bosniak enclave generated by ethnic cleansing and containing the most traumatized children. By late 1994, the EU had embarked upon a program for rebuilding schools, but there were few creative arts teachers left in East Mostar. So I approached the Minister of Education to give me permission to use the creative arts "hours" in the school timetable both to deliver the National Curriculum—an admirably liberal and ambitious program drawn up in Sarajevo at the worst point in the war—and to bring enlivening and therapeutic creative work to the children.

I set about recruiting a team of young people, many of whom were young demobilized and sometimes brutalized soldiers whose education had been interrupted by the war, and offered them a modest training in creative work with children. As hostilities ended, I began to bring groups of my Music in the Community students from Edinburgh University on placement as peer support for the team, who were by that time working regularly in schools throughout the Canton, reaching over 3000 children a week. In 1997, the Pavarotti Music Centre was built to house the schools outreach project, a Primary and Middle Music School, a recording studio, and a clinical Music Therapy Department—the first to be dedicated entirely to working with children with trauma. The outreach team and music therapists worked in tandem in a pyramid structure. The therapists focussed on a relatively small number of highly traumatized children, but mentored the large-scale operation of the outreach team at the base of the pyramid.

The work in Bosnia went on to embrace educational and development projects in Sarajevo, including the Sarajevo Experimental Schools project, a program that brings together schools from the divided "entities" of Sarajevo in creative activities, and social and creative development projects in locations such as Srebrenica. The University of Edinburgh has continued to be involved in summer camps, where the focus has slowly shifted from post-war trauma to more general concerns of special education development; the intervention as a whole has become a model for work with young victims of war in many parts of the world, including Kosovo, Chechnya, Israel and Palestine, Syria and Lebanon, East Africa, and South East Asia.

Sevda did not feature largely in our initial work with children, which was rather focussed on individual creativity, song writing and music theatre. The first time I worked with Sevda with children in Sarajevo was in the opera "Evropa," where it took on a largely symbolic role. The opera was "commissioned" by Ibrahim Spahić for the 1995 Sarajevo Winter Festival, and directed by Dino Mustafić. Goran Simić's libretto is set on an ocean liner called Europe, steered by Miss Europe, whose crown keeps falling down over her eyes. In the hold, there are rats, eating away at the ship's supplies and gnawing at the hull. On board is a crew of children who ask Miss Europe awkward questions, like "Where are we going?", "Are you aware that the rats will sink the ship?", or "Do the birds have a nationality?", and "Does the rain change its name when it falls on some river?". The children are particularly concerned about one of the passengers—*slijepi putnik*—a "blind traveler" who has been driven from his home. For the blind traveler, and for the children's dialogues with him I wrote music in Sevda style. The musical play of symbolisms was obvious, but it also represented an important enfolding of identities, one particularly significant for the citizens of Sarajevo. The blind traveler deep in the hull of Europe's ship represents a quality of common life embedded deeply in the European perception of its own identity. For the people of besieged Sarajevo, the betrayal of the common life was Europe's betrayal not only of them, but of itself. The opera was supported logistically by Britain's first wartime Ambassador to Bosnia, Robert Barnett; President Alija Izetbegović announced that it marked a "turning point in Bosnian-UK relations."

It was in Mostar and its surrounding village schools that I began to work with Sevda on a regular basis. Our schools program was based primarily on the voice. The young women and men of the team were comfortable with singing, and many played the guitar, an ideal instrument for accompanying songs in the classroom. The musical literacy requirements of the National Curriculum were easily met through the voice, supported by a small number of classroom percussion instruments. The core of the curriculum was song, and the enlightened authors in Sarajevo had made sure that they represented all cultures of Bosnia, as well as music of the world and the Western classical repertoire. I expanded this program through a series of projects: the Neretva River, the Mediterranean, and the Oceans of the World to include thousands of songs of contrasting emotional character from the world repertoire, mostly translated into Bosnian, but in the original languages where appropriate. In this educational/therapeutic process a further enfolding of identities took place. The citizens of pre-war Bosnia and former Yugoslavia had enjoyed considerable freedom to travel around the world, with a passport that guaranteed entry to nearly every country without a visa. After the conditions of siege and the "ghettoized" atmosphere of the post-war period, the music of the world became a way for the children to re-enter a larger mental and cultural space, and to reclaim a sense of world citizenship. I encouraged the team to create coherent emotional journeys in song through their lessons, with clear beginnings and endings to the experience, climaxes, and occasional surprises—a coherence and security of experience and emotional release traumatized children in particular relish.

Sevda songs were crafted into these journeys, and were met with overwhelming enthusiasm. In some of the village schools, for example, Blagaj, Gnojnice, Dračevice, Donja Drežnica, or Vrapčići, a predominantly Bosniak village, but with a significant number of Serb returnees, the children used to cheer almost triumphantly whenever we arrived at Sevda songs. Was this a defiant assertion of Bosniak identity, a celebration of the Bosnian common life, or simply the joy of singing songs they knew from home? Was it a justifiable refuge in Bosniak culture, such as fostered at times by political interest groups, or was it a respect for and a fond memory of better times? It would, of course, have been unethical to put these questions directly to children at the time. My own judgement, having worked with them and their families over many years, is that the answer is "all of these things." I hypothesize that the multi-layered and nested identities of the music of Sevda offer engagement at one or more levels simultaneously—perceived post-war "ethnicities" (Sevda as "Bosniak" or "Serb"—the Bosnian common life (Sevda as Bosnian), the ex-Yugoslav common life (Sevda as "Yugoslav"), European identity (Sevda as a synthesis of Balkan, Central European, and Adriatic forms), and the identity of Sevda as a synthesis of Near Eastern and European aesthetics and forms (Table 39.1).

At our summer camps, we now have children of all faith backgrounds from the whole of the Mostar region, including as far away as Međugorje, a major Centre for Bosnian Croatian culture and the Roman Catholic faith. At our daily singsongs we are never allowed to end the evening, at the clamorous insistence of all of the children, without exception, unless we sing together, at least once if not twice, the favorite Sevda song of the region *Čudna jada od Mostara grada*.

Our use of Sevda, both consciously and unconsciously, to foster a sense of identity and self-respect among our children segued naturally into therapeutic processes. When those whose identity and personal survival have been threatened are offered the opportunity to affirm and celebrate that identity, particularly through an agency as emotionally powerful as Sevda, a process of social and personal revaluation takes place, which

Table 39.1   The nested identities of Sevda

Bosnian identities	The identities of Sevda
Bosnia's Judaeo-Islamic-Christian heritage	Sevda as an integration of European, Near, and Middle Eastern aesthetics and forms
European identity	Sevda as an integration of Balkan, Central European, Adriatic, and migrant culture forms
The Yugoslav "common life" identity	Sevda as an expression of the Yugoslav common life
The Bosnian "common life" identity	Sevda as an expression of the Bosnian common life
Perceived post-war "ethnicities"	Sevda as an expression of subcultures, e.g., "Bosniak"

naturally impacts on a sense of self and self-belief. This may help activate other psycho-social processes, such as communication, self-expression, empathy, and trust that may, in turn, connect to the psychobiological thresholds of trauma.

I have written elsewhere about the uses of music in supporting children who are victims of war, including those with post-traumatic stress disorder (Osborne, 2009, 2012). These studies range from consideration of uses of music in relation to neurophysiological issues of trauma, such as dysregulation and regulation of the body, to discussion of psychobiological questions of "communicative musicality," and of an emerging social neuroscience of shared affective experience. As I have noted above, Sevda songs formed, in our work, part of a menu of carefully crafted emotional journeys for our children. I have described the experience of music as an "ocean of emotion," as an infinitely complex flow of autonomic responses, neurotransmission, and endocrine release. I have suggested that responses to music are not obliged to "land" on the islands of emotion defined by spoken language: the islands of love, hate, anger, or shame; rather that music flows safely through the straits and the caverns and the oceans in between. In this sense, I propose that the "sadness" of some Sevda songs is a safe sadness, and part of a necessary experience to help engage and balance the feelings of traumatized children, in a way not far from the intuitions of Graeco-Arabic medicine, an important ancestor of the philosophy of Sevda. There are, of course, many other emotional islands located in the neurophysiological ocean of Sevda—islands of joy, love, humor, optimism, and excitement. Excursions around these islands were all crafted into the children's musical and emotional journeys.

Sevda is a music that has synthesized different cultural identities, from its philosophical origins in Ancient Egypt, Ancient Greece and the Middle East, to its musical origins in Turkish *Makams*, old Slav folk music, the traditions of Bosnia's Islamic and Christian faith communities, the songs of Sephardic Jews, the melos of Dalmatia and the Venetian Adriatic, the music of the Roma, Italian *bel canto*, Austro-Hungarian harmony and Macedonian rhythms. Its rich genetic code has also made it resilient, thriving in good times, surviving in bad. For our work with children it has provided a deep resource of cultural, intellectual, emotional and physical stimulus. In synthesizing musical identities it has helped create a collective identity—for the Bosniak community, for the wider Bosnian "common life"—still not lost in spite of everything and perhaps in a way for Europe as a whole. In a period of European history overshadowed by islamophobia and a certain cultural-political autism, Sevda is a small, benign piece of the East fully integrated into the heart of Europe, a deeply moving, sorrowful, affectionate, and humane music Europeans may recognize as both "the other" and their own.

References

Abu 'Ali al-Husayn Ibn Sina. (2012). *Avicenna on the four humours*, Canon of Medicine. Chicago, IL: Kazi Publications.

Bašić, D. (2009). *The roots of the religious and national identity of the Bosnian-Herzrgovinan Muslims*. Seattle, WA: University of Washington.

Bogoslavljević, S. (1992). Bosna i hercegovina izmedju rata i mir. In: D.Janjić& P. Shoup, pp. 32–33. Belgrade: Dom Omladine.

Buturović, A. (2007). *Love and/or death, in women in the Ottoman Balkans: gender, culture and history*, Library of Ottoman Studies 15. London: I.B. Tauris.

Fine, J. (2007). *The Bosnian church, its place in state and society from the thirteenth to the fifteenth century*. London: Saqi Books.

Goldstein, R.D., Wampler, N.S., & Wise, P.H. (1997). War experiences and distress symptoms of Bosnian children. *Pediatrics*, 100(5), 873–8.

Hippocrates. (1931). *Volume IV: Nature of man*, part IV, WHS Loeb Classic Library, transl. W.H.S. Jones. Cambridge, MA: Harvard University Press.

Janković, I. (2006). *Geologija pesme*. Belgrade: Vreme.

Lovrenović, I. (2004). *Za Gradom Jabuka: 200 najljepših sevdalinki*. Sarajevo: Dani.

Marjanović, D., Fornarino, S., Montagna, S., et al. (2005) The peopling of modern Bosnia-Herzegovina: Y-chromosome haplogroups in the three main ethnic groups. *Annals of Human Genetics*, 69(6), 757–63.

Majstoiović, S. (1972), *Cultural policy in Yugoslavia*. Paris: UNESCO.

Osborne, N. (1994a) Playing at the very edge. *The Independent*, 2 April.

Osborne, N. (1994b). Towards the new Jerusalem *The Independent*, 30 July.

Osborne, N. (1995). Sarajevo: a resolution. *The Independent*, 9 January.

Osborne, N. (2009). Music for children in zones of conflict and post-conflict: a psychobiological approach. In: S. Malloch & C. Trevarthen (Eds.) *Communicative musicality*, pp. 331–56. Oxford: Oxford University Press.

Osborne, N. (2012). Neuroscience and "real world" practice: music as a therapeutic resource for children in zones of conflict., *Annals of the New York Academy of Sciences*, 1252, 69–76.

Osborne, N. (2014). The plenum brain in unbribable Bosnia and Herzegovina. In: D. Arsenijević (Ed.) *South East European integration perspectives*, p. 174. Baden-Baden: Nomos.

Peoples, J. & Bailey, G. (2011). *Humanity: an introduction to cultural anthropology*. Belmont, CA: Wadsworth.

Robert Golden Pictures. (2009). Available at: http://www.robertgoldenpictures.com/works-about-culture/ (accessed 1 March 2016).

Romero, E. (1988). *Coplas sefardíes: Primera selección, Córdoba*. Córdoba: El Almendro.

CHAPTER 40

....

MUSICAL IDENTITIES, RESILIENCE, AND WELLBEING

The Effects of Music on Displaced Children in Colombia

....

GLORIA P. ZAPATA RESTREPO
AND DAVID J. HARGREAVES

This chapter considers the implications of musical activities for children in the context of displacement and deprivation in Colombia, and also presents some of the key results of a recent doctoral study carried out by the first author on the effects of a specially-designed music program on the self-identities of some of these children. The chapter begins with a description of the consequences of violence and internal displacement for families and children in Colombia, and this leads on to a second section, which illustrates how hybridization and multiculturalism in music can provide a means of helping people from this background. The third section presents some theoretical approaches to the development of musical identities and considers how these might be used, with support from other family members, in achieving conflict transformation. The fourth section outlines the design, methods and some of the results of the doctoral study, and the fifth draws on these findings in formulating some general conclusions about the effects of music on children's socio-emotional and musical development in the Colombian context.

40.1 Symbolic implications of violence: the Colombian background

....

The origins of the current violence in Colombia are complex. Ibáñez (2009) points out that several factors are involved, including drug dealing, the weakness of the judicial system, the presence of guerrillas and paramilitaries in rural areas, poverty, and the inequity of the social system, as well as many years of armed conflict. Violence in Colombia has caused displacement of people from the countryside to the cities. Big cities like Bogotá therefore become the destination for the majority of those displaced. For most displaced families, arriving in the cities in impoverished conditions throws them into a "trap of poverty" from which they often cannot escape for several generations (Hernandez & Gutiérrez, 2008; Ibáñez, 2009; Nina, Álvarez, & Aguilar, 2009).

Beside the humanitarian crisis, the adverse effects of displacement on the individual are deep-seated and diverse. They include the eradication or rupture of the victims' social and cultural networks and their family and social lives, as well as the loss of their means of living: this makes displaced populations vulnerable to further disruptive influences. The impossibility of generating enough income, together with their arrival in a strange new city, restricts their access to social and public services. Forced displacement causes a severe decline in well-being, creating a residual population which is highly dependent on state aid, thus diminishing their resources still further, and restricting their strategies for risk mitigation (Ibáñez & Vélez, 2007).

Years of war in Colombia have had a powerful impact on the symbolic self-images built by displaced families. Barrero (2006) suggests that these self-images lead to some aspects of the conflict becoming personalized in the displaced families' opponents, thus creating a constant search for the guilty amongst the guerrilla groups, paramilitaries, and other armed groups. It is by eliminating these dynamics, which have been established over many years, that change can be achieved: this involves the construction of new social spaces from which people can recognize themselves and others.

> The political conflict is the result of an accumulating process of social tensions, highly idealized in a symbolic construct in which beliefs, customs, and values of the public and private life from the incorporation of political ideals, by their very nature hold a closed character . . . against their opponents.
>
> p. 28.

For displaced families and their children, probably the most serious consequences of political violence are the development of an absolute distrust of others, and the feeling of anger and powerlessness against the establishment. Psychological warfare seeks to produce a psychological impact on entire populations, so that barbaric actions are supported as "fair and necessary", making the civilian population direct or indirect participants in confrontation. This becomes evident in the games that children play: they incorporate behavioral patterns of force and violence, which they have absorbed into the solutions of their own conflicts. Political violence has been concretized and naturalized in children, as Martin-Baró (1992) points out: "war imposed forms of relationship based on fear, hostility, revenge, hatred and despair" (cited by Barrero (2006), p. 238). Through this process, people consciously or unconsciously incorporate some behavioral patterns mediated by the use of force to resolve the conflicts that they perceive. In this context, despair is one of the most dramatic consequences: because of their experience of physical violence and ideological bombardment, individuals and groups eventually fall into resignation and prostration, thus justifying violent actions against others. These circumstances make people's identities vulnerable not only in their attempts to live behind their pain, but also because of their ignoral by government institutions and society. In this respect we concur with Barrero's (2006) positive citation of García Marquez' (1967) views, expressed in his work *One Hundred Years of Solitude*:

> Maybe it's time to invent a memory machine similar to that of Jose Arcadio Buendia, when the plague of insomnia attacked Macondo and threatened to wipe out the memories, the identity of people and his own consciousness to sink into a kind of idiocy without a past. (. . .) Only that our machine would have to force feed it to dignity, respect, justice and truth, for there have been so many years of death, desolation and forgetting that a single individual is not enough to swing it, but needed from the collective memories to retrieve the meaning of human experience without resorting to any form of exclusion.

Children suffer the impact of war in several ways: they grow up in a country blighted with everyday instances of death and outrage. Displaced children have had different abrupt and significant losses. They have lost their vital spaces, the places in which they have constructed their particular forms of moving, of using time and, in general, of interacting with the environment. They have lost dear relatives, neighbors, and friends, as well as their belongings, clothes, documents, pets, and toys. Children who have been uprooted in this way internalize symbols, values, and particular means, thus adapting to the conflict and cultivating a disposition to participate in it. They become multipliers of a warlike culture, which proliferates the distorted image that weapons give them respect, security and that through weapons they can gain respect and identity; they provide the status and the protection that their families and the government have not offered (Bello & Ruiz, 2002).

Grajales (1999) points out that "the most devastating effect of the armed conflict on children living in areas of high confrontation is the creation of a pro-violence imaginary; children easily learn that guns are the 'reason', which they turn into violent forces, providing them recognition . . . even in acts of atrocity in which the enemy's body is mutilated . . . violence is exerted without limits or control" (p. 23). The impact of displacement in the lives of these children is not restricted to their responses to violent events and traumatic episodes: it is also seen in a serious deterioration in the quality of their lives and that of their families. Displaced children in the city lose their collective references, and their identities. In the past, they had been able to construct a sense of ownership in their relationship with the countryside or town in which they grew up: they could identify themselves as being part of a community, and to possess a sense of belonging. When these elements are lost, children have to learn how to survive amid the attractions of the typical consumer society in the big cities (ACNUR, 2003). Families that remain intact can survive in these new surroundings if they reassemble their identities within their new roles, and are able to meet the new demands placed upon them (Bello & Ruiz, 2002).

The confrontation between past and present cultural referents and the transformation of their roles and behaviors threaten the subjective realities of children because of the radical changes between past and present, which can result in "alternations" between the two (Berger & Luckman, 2008). This process involves several risks, but there are also factors which can protect them against those risks (Bello & Ruiz, 2002). One of the most important protection factors is resilience, and this demands socialization spaces, like games, music, and art, in which children can imagine and recreate positive social relationships with others: in these environments they can express their feelings, thereby transforming their social realities, and develop and flourish as equals within society.

40.2 COLOMBIAN CULTURAL HYBRIDIZATION AND MUSICAL IDENTITIES

Colombians mostly come from three main backgrounds: indigenous, blacks (Africans), and Spanish (Europeans) who have mixed over the last five centuries, producing hybridization, and a very rich cultural environment. Hybridization is a crucial component of Colombian musical culture, and can provide some resistance against the effects of deprivation: for García Canclini (2003), hybridization describes "socio-cultural processes in which discrete structures or practices that existed separately, combine to create new structures, objects and practices". In some ways, hybridization processes have provided underprivileged communities in Colombia (and in Latin America more widely) with some resources on which to draw in combatting the conditions of deprivation. These ancestral fusions could be said to have developed in order to give Colombians their imprint, their identity, and their strength. For many people, the wider family is one of the few milieux in which they feel welcome, and fully human, in the sense of feeling important to others; in this regard it gives them a sense of belonging.

Several studies propose, along with the mixture of cultures, that another significant feature of hybridization is the opportunity that it presents to reflect about what happens when different cultures encounter each other. This could be a useful intervention tool if displaced people are considered as "migrants". In Garcia Canclini´s words: "In exile, habits of life, expression or activity in the new environment inevitably occur in contrast to the remembrance of habits in another environment. Thus, both the new environment and the former are vivid, real and occur together in a counterpoint."

From this perspective, multiculturalism, and hybridization processes have clear advantages, and provide an opportunity for displaced people to think about their identities, and to develop other strategies to deal with their problems. As García Canclini suggests:

> A world in a growing movement of hybridization needs to be conceived not as a set of compact units, in homogeneity, but as radically different intersections, transitions and transactions . . .. When considering what is possible or what is not possible

to hybridize, we are considering what does unite us and what does separate us in this hyper-communicative life; the artistic approaches are crucial in this task if they can be both explicit, like the spoken language, and veiled, like arts; language and ambiguity.

In this sense, Colombia has a very rich musical environment due to its hybridization processes and its multicultural background. Its people dance, sing and enjoy music in a very natural way; it is an important part of their daily lives. This is central to the present topic, considering that displaced people come from diverse regions of the country, bringing with them their different musical traditions: their cultural backgrounds therefore constitute a very useful means by which they can cope with the tragedy of forced displacement. In her study of the musical practices in Chocó (the Colombian western Pacific coast), Ana María Arango (2008) proposes that: "Further than talking about a musical culture in the (Colombian) Pacific coast, we talk about a 'musical life,' which is permanently transformed and negotiated in communities of practice" (p. 162). The same is true for many regions and people in Colombia, from the North Coast to the south of the country (Miñana, 2008). People's daily lives are linked to several musical and dance practices; for Colombians, these are powerful means of self-expression.

40.3 Children's musical development, self-identity, and wellbeing

Several different theoretical perspectives were used to guide the investigation of the effects of music on the self-identities of displaced children in Colombia. Bronfenbrenner's (1979) ecological systems theory of children's development provides a framework for the study, enabling us to connect children's inner musical expressions, their family members, and their school environments, including the influence of parents and teachers within it. Bronfenbrenner distinguishes between four levels of system, ranging from the lowest, most specific level of social influence to the highest and most abstract. *Microsystems* refer to the immediate settings of children's lives in their families, in relation to peer groups, and schools, for example, and the links between these form *mesosystems*, in which different microsystems interact with one another (events at home might influence what children do at school, for example). *Exosystems* are the broader social settings which exert more indirect influences on children's behavior, such as community groups or parents' associations, and *macrosystems* exert the most indirect and abstract influences, such as government policies or social class-based institutions.

Miñana's (2008) views about musical learning and enculturation operate on the levels of meso- and exosystems: they are based on his work in Colombia with the musical practices of the *nasas*, an indigenous community in the south of the country. Miñana proposes that enculturation cannot be approached as a unidirectional process in which adults' culture is reproduced in children's learning: instead, he suggests that through inhabiting the world of adults and participating in their activities, children can build their own knowledge and experience. This musical learning is concerned not only with what parents can teach to the child, but also with the participation of the child in settings where music is performed, which is facilitated if the child has musicians in the family, among friends, or close neighbors. Miñana (2009) called this process "*learning among the legs of the elderly*", explaining it as follows:

> Learning to be a musician has to deal primarily with making music, something that is achieved by actively and creatively ("putting the ear among the legs of the elderly," as Don Virgilio Pabon says), participating in festivals and rituals, practising at home and in the field. But learning to be a musician is not only learning to be part of a band, but also learning to live in particular contexts by participating as a musician in *alumbranzas*, tours, festivals, dances, and stages . . . In other words what we have seen here, is not an intentional or functional mechanisms of a "society" or "culture" to reproduce or transmit a specific music, but agents of different ages (children, youth, adults) dealing to participate, to legitimize their participation in a band.
>
> p 227.

One of our main concerns here is to try to explain how the perspectives of music and conflict resolution, which in Bronfenbrenner's terms involves exosystems and probably also macrosystems, exert their influences at the level of the microsystem on children's self-identities. Researchers who have sought to explain how music might help people affected by war or conflict situations include Berg (2011), Osborne (2009), and Pavlicevic & Ansdell (2009). Osborne (2009) suggests that for these victims of circumstance, there are "psychosocial concerns involving identity, trust, self–belief, and creativity, and associated symptoms such as depersonalization, lack of trust, self-confidence, motivation, and anger, that are related to symptoms of trauma such as poor concentration, amnesia, avoidance, detachment and depression" (p. 350). Osborne found that in collective musical performances children created social identities for themselves, as well as developing trust in others by doing so, and that these provided the conditions for a sense of achievement and for enhanced self–esteem and self-belief, particularly in performances in a safe social/public space. Osborne (2009) suggests that "for traumatized children, it is perhaps even more significant that music may bring together our biological, psychological, and social lives in simultaneity, synergy and harmony in moments which are both aesthetically beautiful and humanly transforming" (p. 351).

Moving on to the level of microsystems, the doctoral study also draws on theories of the self-such as those of Harter (1999) and Dweck (1999). Harter's focus was on interpersonal relationships, in particular children's perceptions of the opinions of significant others, whereas Dweck (1999) was more interested in children's achievement motivation, and in particular their mastery motivation—the strength of their desire to exercise active control over their environment rather than passively to be controlled by it. Dweck proposed that these two contrasting types of motivation were related to corresponding "self-theories": "mastery-oriented" children tended to form "incremental" self-theories in which they saw their abilities as malleable and subject to change, whereas those with "helpless" motivational styles tended to form "fixed" self-theories in which abilities could not be changed. Furthermore, Dweck (2000) suggested that self-theories give rise to "mind sets", which are systems of assumptions, beliefs, and values that, once established, inform our goals, decisions, and the ways in which we view others and ourselves in our worlds.

O'Neill (2011) drew on Dweck's ideas in emphasizing the importance of a "growth mind set," which is "characterized by a passion for learning, the active seeking of challenges, a valuing of effort, and the resiliency necessary to persist in the face of obstacles or adversity" (p. 37)—she also suggested that "Resilient children who experience failure seem to bounce back faster and display the characteristics associated with mastery motivation and incremental self-theories—in other words, they display a growth mind set" (pp. 38–9). Resilience is a crucial concept in relation to self-theories and self-esteem: O'Neill (2011) sees it as associated with the growth mind set, which includes the ability to cope with the inevitable setbacks and problems that are experienced by young people at every level of ability, and which thereby serve to increase learning opportunities.

Furthermore, we could argue that self-identities are grounded in a *sense of belonging*, which Gratier & Apter-Danon (2009) have incorporated into the notion of *communicative musicality* (Malloch & Trevarthen, 2009): they refer to this as "a source of personal confidence—well-being—and a powerful motivating force generated in mothers' and infants' awareness of sharing a set of culturally derived expressive forms that are both predictable, and afford playful variation" (p. 305). Later they state that "belonging is implicit knowing that takes into account the cultural tones of every individual's ways of moving and meaning" (p. 311). These authors also suggest that mother-infant interactions are the origins of musical improvisation, which is thereby associated with the intersubjective experiences that give infants a sense of belonging and of being part of a community.

These theoretical perspectives give weight to our earlier views about the relevance of musical interactions and interpersonal experiences for the promotion of individual self-image and wellbeing, thereby providing the main impetus for the doctoral study, the main features and findings of which are briefly summarized in the next section.

40.4 THE DOCTORAL RESEARCH PROJECT: BRIEF SUMMARY AND KEY FINDINGS

The aim of the research project was to investigate the effects of music on the social and musical development of displaced 6–8-year-old children in Colombia: it adopted an ecological perspective and used a mixed methods strategy. The project comprised three studies: an experimental study, an interview study and a psychomusicological study. The experimental study was designed to evaluate the effects of a specially designed 18-week music program in which the children participated for two hours per week. It included a singing workshop, musical games, musical improvisation games, and musical improvisations. The children were randomly assigned either to an experimental group of 52 children who took part in the program each week, or to a control group of 52 children who did not: members of the control group followed an 18-week program of singing workshops. All of the members of both groups were pre-tested and post-tested on Harter´s (1999) *Perceived Competence Scale for Children* at the beginning and end of the 18 week period.

The interview study explored the musical preferences and experiences of seven of the participants in the experimental group, and interviews were also conducted with the parents of the seven children, and with six of their teachers. All three participant groups were asked questions about their specific musical likes and dislikes, about their enjoyment of different activities in music, and about their experiences of different forms of musical participation. The parents and teachers were also asked specific questions about their attitudes towards music for children, and also about the extent to which they perceived it to be an important activity for their children.

The psychomusicological study adopted a case study approach in order conduct indepth structural analyses of the musical improvisations of six of the experimental group children. It did so from the point of view of *zygonic theory* (see e.g., Ockelford, 2013) which enables musical structures to be broken down into their main constituent elements, and which looks for patterns of repetition, and repetition with variation, in these elements. It was used in this study to investigate patterns and regularities in the children's vocal improvisations: in other applications it can also be used to assess the precise similarities and differences between the musical structures produced by two or more members of performing groups, thereby providing an index of the mutual influence of one musician upon another.

We do not have space to present the details of all three studies here, and so will mainly focus on some of the findings from the experimental study. Harter's *Perceived Competence Scale for Children* gives rise to individual scores on each of 4 self-esteem scales, namely Social (having friends and getting on with other children), Physical appearance (feeling happy with your body and how you look), Behavioral (how you behave and how this affects your image with others), and Cognitive (how you are leading your life, and how happy you are with this). It is also possible to work out an aggregate score over all four scales, which represents an overall estimate of global self-esteem. Analyses of variance were carried out between the pre- and post-test scores of the two groups on each of the four scales separately, as well as on the aggregate scores, and the main finding to emerge was that there was a significant difference between the pre- and post-test means of the two groups on the aggregate measure of self-esteem, as well as a significant interaction between these two factors. This is shown in Fig. 40.1, which makes it clear that even though the pre-test scores of the experimental group were lower

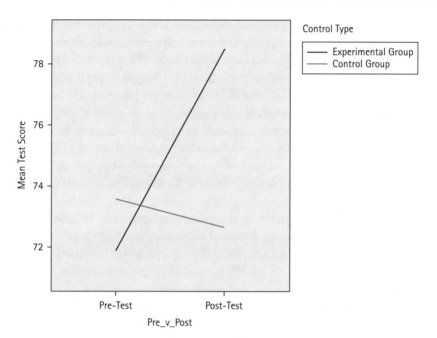

FIG. 40.1 Aggregate Harter test scores: interaction between mean pre- and post-test scores of experimental and control groups.

than those of the control group (71.9 and 73.6, respectively), the effect of the music program was to increase the scores of the experimental group between pre- and post-test (to 78.5), whereas those of the control group declined (to 72.7). When similar analyses were carried out for the four Harter Scale measures separately, it turned out that the results for the cognitive scale were significant and in the same direction as those of the aggregate measures; that those for the Physical scale were in the same direction as those for the aggregate measures, but that they just failed to reach statistical significance; and that those for the other two scales, Social and Behavioral, showed no significant main effects or interactions. This clearly indicates that the music program had some positive effects on the children`s socio-emotional development, and particularly on their self-esteem.

In interpreting these results it is important to observe the dilemma that some families face, in terms of their identities, when they suffer the "cultural loss" that occurs when they are forced to change the previously familiar activities which were natural for them; this influences their self-perceptions, not to mention the broader consequences of the cultural loss of ethnic languages and different life perspectives. It has been suggested that these families face a sort of "cultural sorrow" (e.g., Richman, 1998).

Bello & Ruiz (2002) point out that the personal and social identities of the displaced are disrupted by arriving in new places (generally large cities) with lifestyles different from their own. These losses and ruptures fragment their identities and challenge their value systems, leading them to re-construct their symbolic bases and their previously acquired knowledge. Nevertheless, some of them describe the ways in which they have used this positively by gathering friends and children almost every Saturday to dance and sing, which seems to show their resilience. As we suggested earlier, families that move with all their members can survive in the cities if they learn how to live in the new environment, and if they reassemble their identities in terms of their new roles and adapt to the new demands placed upon them (Bello & Ruiz, p. 2002). This was one of the themes which emerged from our interviews with parents in relation to questions about the influence of their roots, and the contexts from which they come.

Some of the children's interview responses also show some positive attitudes in that musical performance was associated with joy, as well as with anxiety. Joy was seen to come from performing for others, especially family and friends, and in gaining their recognition and support; anxiety, on the other hand, came from the challenge of performing, and wanting to do their best; although these children were just 6–8 years old, they were very aware of the audience expectations of the performances. We might conclude that musical activities can help not only the children, but also their families, to cope with the problems of displacement (as has also been suggested by authors such as Osborne, 2009; Pavlicevic & Ansdell, 2009; Berg, 2011). This indicates that shared family musical activities help them to cope with their daily struggles and also provide a kind of "oasis," a way of reminding them who they are and where they come from. Maintaining a view of their roots and identities is crucial, and is also a sign of resilience, whose importance was pointed out by O'Neill (2011), as we saw earlier. This perspective also shows how families can maintain their cultural musical traditions (for example, as revealed in the interview study, in vallenato and tambora music), which are deeply rooted in some of the families' musical identities.

40.5 Music, family, and cultural context: ecological influences on children's socio-emotional and musical development in Colombia

In this section our aim is to discuss the different aspects of this research project, and to offer some conclusions about the influence of the cultural environment on these children's musicality. We can see that the cultural and family environments play a key role in creating and nurturing their musicality: this could be seen in the ways that these children used their musical language as a means of expression in the psychomusicological case studies. Some of the subjects of these case studies had different origins—from the Caribbean Colombian musical tradition, from the context of marginalization in Bogotá, and from the Amazonian indigenous community. This background gave rise to musicalities with a diversity of conditions, materials, and possibilities, which enabled the children to use music in different ways to cope with marginalization. The differences between these children's approaches lead us to propose three different levels of uprooting—*partial, relative, and total uprooting*—in trying to explain the ways in which their musicality emerged from their conditions of marginalization.

The analysis of one of the cases in the psychomusicological study showed that vallenato and Colombian traditional music, as well as the family environment, could give children the materials and conditions to develop their musicality. In this case it was possible to propose that although some children come from internally displaced families, there is nevertheless some *continuity* between the music of the place of their origin, and their new musical environment in Bogotá. This is probably because many people in Bogotá are familiar with the vallenato and cantaoras' traditional music: when the families arrived in Bogotá, they could recognize their own musical roots. This child was therefore very confident and successful in using this repertoire to improvise and to communicate musically. We could see this as a case of *partial uprooting* because, although the children have been internally displaced, their musical materials can be used to communicate in the new environment, so that they can display resilience. This can fulfil the basic psychological need for *relatedness* (one of three such basic needs in Deci & Ryan's (2002) self-determination theory, along with *competence* and *autonomy*). In other words, it is a sense of belonging that enables these children to feel confident, and to be competent enough to be able to improvise musically.

Other children are in less favorable situations, living in Bogotá under harsh conditions of marginalization, and facing dysfunctional family situations, which may not include much interest in the children´s musical activities. This situation displays *ambiguous continuity* in that although the children are not dealing with an unfamiliar musical context, they are nevertheless dealing with family problems which may include abandonment, marginalization, and lack of opportunities. Although they may attempt to communicate through music, they lack the confidence to improvise, and to express ideas and emotions. We could say that their capacity to fulfil their need for competence, autonomy, and relatedness is diminished, along with their sense of belonging, as a result of the family situation. We could see these ambiguous conditions as representing what we might call *relative uprooting,* which makes it more difficult for them to display resilient behavior.

Finally, there are children whose musical background is very distant, and may be unknown to people outside their indigenous communities who, though identified as Colombians, speak a different language of their own. We could say that there is *total discontinuity* with their new musical environment in Bogotá, since they are not only speaking a different language, but also adapting themselves to a very unfamiliar and different musical culture. It is not that they do not possess musicality, but that their musical language is unknown to the people in their new environment, so that they are forced to adapt and change their ways of communicating with music.

These children have to try hard to be strategic in taking things on task by task. They do not know the elements of their new musical culture, and do not feel confident to express their feelings and ideas through music. They first have to make sense of this new symbolic world, introducing themselves to its sounds and its words, and these elements become tools which can be used in the deconstruction and reconstruction of their cognitive musical system. Their sense of belonging is severely diminished, which is associated with a decline in their level of autonomy, and their competence in improvising musically. We can describe this as a condition of *total uprooting*, which makes it much more difficult for them to cope with difficulties; their level of family support and encouragement is likely to influence their resilience.

It is important to bear this point in mind when considering not only the changes that internally displaced people must suffer, but also the nomadic life that many families have to face when they leave their original countries to migrate to a new one. In order to be successful in their new environment, they have to find ways to cope with their isolation, and to adapt themselves. The deconstruction and reconstruction of their cognitive musical systems described above can make them resilient because music is one of the main symbolic systems that they take with them when they migrate, and nobody can take this away from them. Indeed, this research project has shown that music is a symbolic tool that can help children in the process of adaptation to a new environment, giving them a means of communicating, expressing their feelings, and coping with difficulties. It represents not only a means of adapting to the new environment, but also a means for keeping their own roots and identities. In the process of hybridization, we propose that music can be a currency for cultural symbolic interchange that deserves further exploration in studies of cross-cultural migration.

40.6 CONCLUSIONS

Although we have not described them in detail in this chapter, the results of the interview study and the psychomusicological study in the doctoral research confirmed the importance of the family and school environments in children's musical development. The interview responses made it clear that socio-emotional development, and specifically children's self-identity, was affected by children's musical activities, and parents' attitudes were crucial in giving children confidence about their musicality. The interview study also showed that teachers' attitudes were directed more towards performance activities and presentations than they were to the children's musical knowledge and creativity.

The psychomusicological study provided a deeper view of children's musical development, showing how the cognitive components develop, and how the relationship between language and music builds their musicality: but also that it is important to recognize the wide variability and high level of complexity of children's musical development. In some ways the differences between the six individuals were the most striking feature of the psychomusicological case studies, which revealed that self-identity and self-concept are deeply related to musicality. The zygonic theory analysis of these children's musical improvisations was able to illustrate how the fulfilment of children's basic psychological needs for relatedness, competence, and autonomy influences the development of their musical languages, and therefore their musical development as a whole.

One final consideration concerns the relationship between musical activity and well-being (cf. MacDonald, Kreutz & Mitchell, 2012): it is important to emphasize that this is closely related to the aims of the doctoral project. This project showed how internally displaced children and their families use music to cope with their marginal situations in different ways: music became a tool for resilience and adaptation, as well as providing a means of communicating with others. In this sense music can improve children's well-being, allowing them not only to gather and share new songs, and to make them feel happier, but also to understand their new environments. There are many social and cultural factors that need to be investigated in trying to explain the role of musical identities in ameliorating the effects of violence and displacement: research in different places and on different age groups and cultures helps us to understand the nature of and differences in musical identities across the world.

REFERENCES

ACNUR. (2007). *Memorias de la Reunión*. Cartagena febrero 6. Available at: http://www.acnur.org (accessed 8 July 2007).

Arango, A.M. (2008). Espacios de educación musical en Quibdó (Choco-Colombia). *Revista Colombiana de Antropología*, 44(1), p. 157–89.

Barrero, E. (2006). *De Macondo a Mancuso. Conflicto, violencia política y guerra psicológica en Colombia. Una aproximación des de la psicología social*. Bogotá: Desde abajo ediciones.

Bello, M., Mantilla, L., Mosquera, C., & Camelo, E. (2000). *Relatos de la violencia impactos del desplazamiento forzado en la niñez y la juventud*. Bogotá: Universidad Nacional-Fundacion Educativa Amor.

Bello, M. & Ruiz, S. (2002). *Conflicto armado niñez y juventud una perspectiva psico-social*. Bogotá: Universidad Nacional de Colombia y Fundación Dos Mundos.

Berg, A. (2011). Emotions in motion: transforming conflict and music. In: I. Deliege and J. W. Davidson (Eds.) *Music and the mind: essays in honour of John Sloboda*, pp. 363–78. Oxford: Oxford University Press.

Berger, P. & Luckman, T. (2008) *La construcción social de la realidad*. Buenos Aires: Amorrurtu editores.

Borthwick, S. & Davidson, J. (2002). Developing a child´s identity as a musician: a "family script" perspective. In: R.A.R. MacDonald, D.J. Hargreaves & D.E. Miell (Eds.) *Musical identities*. Oxford: Oxford University Press.

Bronfenbrenner, U. (1979). *The ecology of human development*. Boston, MA: Harvard University Press. Spanish translation: (1987). *La ecología del desarrollo humano*. Barcelona: Editorial Paidós.

Deci, E.L. & Ryan, R.M. (Eds.) (2002). *The handbook of self-determination research*. Rochester: University of Rochester Press.

Dweck, C. (2000). *Self-theories: Their role in motivation, personality, and development*. Philadelphia, PA: Psychology Press.

Garcia Canclini, N. (2003). Noticias recientes sobre la hibridación. *Transcultural Music Review*, 7. http://www.sibetrans.com/trans/about-tran. Accessed 12/2014.

García Marquez, G. (1967). *Cien años de soledad*. New York, NY: Vintage-Random House.

Grajales, C. (1999). *El dolor oculto de la infancia*. Bogotá: Unicef Colombia.

Gratier, M. & Apter-Danon, G. (2009). The improvised musicality of belonging: Repetition and variation in mother–infant vocal interaction. In: S. Malloch & C. Trevarthen (Eds.) *Communicative musicality: exploring the basis of human companionship*, pp. 301–327. Oxford: Oxford University Press.

Hargreaves, D.J., Miell, D.E., & MacDonald, R.A.R. (2002). What are musical identities, and why are they important? In R.A.R. MacDonald, D.J. Hargreaves & D.E. Miell (Eds.) *Musical identities*. Oxford: Oxford University Press.

Hargreaves, D.J. (2012). Musical imagination: Perception and production, beauty and creativity. *Psychology of Music, 40*(5), 539–57.

Harter, S. (1999). *The construction of the self: a developmental perspective*. New York, NY: Guilford Press.

Hernandez, A.& Gutierrez, M. (2008). Familias desplazadas por la violencia asentadas en Bogotá: Nuevos moradores e intensas problematicas. In: M. Gutierrez (Ed.) *Las familias en Bogotá realidades y diversidad*, pp. 135–80. Bogotá: Pontificia Universidad Javeriana .

Ibañez, A.M. (2009). *El desplazamiento forzoso en Colombia: Un camino sin retorno hacia la pobreza*. Bogotá: Universidad de los Andes.

Ibañez, A.M., & Velez, C.E. (2007). Civil conflict and force migration: the micro determinants and welfare losses of displacement in Colombia. *World Development, 36*(4), 659–76.

MacDonald, R.A.R., Hargreaves, D.J., & Miell, D.E. (Eds.) (2002). *Musical identities*. Oxford: Oxford University Press.

MacDonald, R.A.R., Kreutz, G., & Mitchell, L. (Eds.) (2012). *Music, health and wellbeing*. Oxford: Oxford University Press.

Malloch, S.& Trevarthen, C. (Eds.) (2009). *Communicative musicality: exploring the basis of human companionship*. Oxford: Oxford University Press.

Martin-Baró, I. (1992). *Psicología social de la guerra trauma y terapia*. San Salvador: UCA Editores.

Miñana, C. (2008). Música y fiesta en la construcción del territorio nasa (Colombia). *Revista Colombiana de Antropología, 44*(1), pp. 123–56.

Nina, E., Álvarez, S., & Aguilar, A.I. (2008). Riesgo social, movilidad social y trampas de pobreza de las familias en Bogotá. In: M. Gutiérrez (Ed.) *Las familias en Bogotá realidades y diversidad*, pp. 79–116. Bogotá: Pontificia Universidad Javeriana.

North, A.C. & Hargreaves, D.J. (2008). *The social and applied psychology of music*. Oxford: Oxford University Press.

Ockelford, A. (2007). Exploring musical interaction between a teacher and pupil, and her evolving musicality, using a music-theoretical approach. *Research Studies in Music Education, 28*, 3–23.

O´Neill, S. (2011). Developing a young musician's growth mindset: the role of motivation, self-theories, and resilience. In: I. Deliege and J. W. Davidson (Eds.), *Music and the mind: essays in honour of John Sloboda*, pp. 31–46. Oxford: Oxford University Press.

Osborne, N. (2009). Music for children in zones of conflict and post-conflict: A psychobiological approach. In: S. Malloch & C. Trevarthen (Eds.) *Communicative musicality: exploring the basis of human companionship*, pp. 331–56. Oxford: Oxford University Press.

Pavlicevic, M. & Gary, A. (2009). Between communicative musicality and collaborative musicing: a perspective from community music therapy. In: S. Malloch & C. Trevarthen (Eds.) *Communicative musicality: exploring the basis of human companionship*, pp. 357–76. Oxford: Oxford University Press.

Richman, N. (1998). *In the midst of whirlwind: a manual for helping refugee children.* London: Trentham Books.

Sheldon, K.M. (2002). The self-concordance model of healthy goal striving: When personal goals correctly represent the person. In: Deci, Edward L. & Ryan, Richard M. (Eds.) *Handbook of self-determination research*, pp. 65–86. Suffolk: University of Rochester Press.

Sloboda, J. (1985). *The musical mind: the cognitive psychology of music.* Oxford: Oxford University Press.

Trevarthen, C. (2002). Origins of musical identity: evidence from infancy for musical social awareness. In: R.A.R. MacDonald, D.J. Hargreaves & D.E. Miell (Eds.) *Musical identities.* Oxford: Oxford University Press.

CHAPTER 41

···

MUSIC OF ENGLISHNESS

National Identity and the First Folk Revival

···

ROBERT COLLS AND KATIE PALMER HEATHMAN

41.1 AN IDEA OF ENGLAND

IN January 1907, in the middle of a performance of folksong and dance by Mary Neal's Espérance Guild, Edward Verrall Lucas, a writer and journalist, found himself watching through a veil of tears.[1] Later (1910: viii) he would reflect upon this as a profound moment in his life—that he had wept not only at the natural beauty of the songs ("these lovely, lovely airs"), but at "the thought of this lost England of ours:"

> … it was the thought of the loss of that spirit that perhaps formed part of my emotion. I do not know that the words had much to do with it; one did not hear them at all, except the refrains. But the idea of a sweet and simple England was intensely vivid, and possibly one was conscious, too, of the contrast between these songs and the singers themselves—the songs all lucid open-air gaiety, and the singers … members of a club for working girls in the north-western district of this grimy latter day London.

Lucas believed in an idea of England found in an idea of folksong. John Barr (1998, p. 15) says that Ralph Vaughan Williams, too, was enamored of an idea of folksong that was central to his music and his self-understanding. Williams admitted that if he could

---

[1] Clara Sophia Neal rejected her well-to-do background as the daughter of a Birmingham button manufacturer to do social work as "Sister Mary" with the West London Mission. She left the Mission along with Emmeline Pethick in order to found the Espérance Girls' Club, an experiment in living and working among those they were trying to help. Neal and her girls were instrumental in the revival of Morris dancing but, after a major quarrel with another revivalist, Cecil Sharp, over both the style of the dancing and its use in social work, her actual achievements have been eclipsed. See Judge (2006), "Neal, Mary Clara Sophia", *ODNB Online*.

not have found folksong in actual historical experience, he would have been obliged to imagine it theoretically (Vaughan Williams 1934, 1986, p. 15).[2]

Reaching its peak of activity in the years just before the outbreak of the First World War, the first folk revival (as it came to be known) was an attempt to track down, record, publicize, and otherwise celebrate what the revivalists saw as traditional English music and song. Folksong belonged to the people, they said, and now that it was in danger of being lost in the wake of agricultural depression and rural de-population, it had to be saved. It was in this light that the revivalists saw themselves as doing work of national importance. Mary Neal saw her Espérance Guild as part of a full "national revival" (Neal, 1910, pp. 1–2).

The first folksong collection in the modern sense was "Old English Songs," published by Rev. John Broadwood in 1847. These were songs of Sussex and Surrey, but other collectors followed, including his niece Lucy Broadwood and her compatriots Frank Kidson, Kate Lee, Sabine Baring-Gould, and most famously Cecil Sharp and Ralph Vaughan Williams. By the turn of the century, folksong had flowered into a serious campaign for national identity through musical identity.[3]

We are dealing, then, with an idea of "folksong" that was not shared by the people who sang the songs, but was invented by bands of energetic revivalists with bigger, purer ideas. Before them, it seems the songs had existed as an entirely ordinary and incidental part of the lives of the people. By contrast, Cecil Sharp, the revivalists' leading light, defined "folksong" theoretically as a unified body of work, formed in a process of national evolution, through a pure oral tradition. Folksong is the song *created* by the folk (Sharp, 1907, p. 3) he said; popularity had nothing to do with it. He also saw folksong as cast in the old church or Greek modes, making a point of stating the mode of many of his tunes or, in the case of those that were not sung to him modally, arguing that that was how they would have been sung in the original. His seven "Conclusions" regarding the nature of folksong are summarized partway through his *English Folk-Song. Some Conclusions* (1907)—folk songs are always anonymous; modal melodies are nearly always folk; tunes in the minor mode are

---

[2] Ralph Vaughan Williams was a composer and folksong collector who found his mature music through interaction with the songs. He also published several essays bringing together his ideas on "national" music, communal music-making, and socialism. He was President of the English Folk Dance and Song Society from 1932–58 (his death). See Vaughan Williams (1964) *R. V. W: A Biography of Ralph Vaughan Williams*. London: Oxford University Press.

[3] Lucy Broadwood, Rev. Sabine Baring-Gould and Frank Kidson had worked together in various combinations in the collection and publication of folk songs and tunes before the arrival of Cecil Sharp. Kate Lee was a professional singer who threw herself into the fieldwork of folksong collection, and eventually became the first secretary of the Folk Song Society in 1898: Bearman, C.J. (2008) "Lee, Catherine Anna," *ODNB Online*. It was Sharp who was the driving force. Building on the work of previous collectors and collecting over a thousand songs himself, he drove a fond obsession into a fully-fledged revival. Despite acrimonious fallings out with most other practitioners, it was Sharp's writings, particularly on the evolution of folksong, which shaped both the scholarly and practical development of the folk movement. See Heaney, M. (2008) Sharp, Cecil James, *ODNB Online*; and Fox Strangways & Karpeles, M. (1933, 1955) *Cecil Sharp*. London; Oxford University Press.

either compositions or folk airs that have been "corrupted;" five and seven time-measures generally prevail; folk melodies do not modulate; folk melodies often contain bars of irregular length; folk melodies are non-harmonic, "that is to say, they have been fashioned by those in whom the harmonic sense is undeveloped" (Sharp, 1907, p. 88).

This highly prescriptive and (some would say) insensitive intervention in the musical identity of working-class people is not to say that the songs lacked force, or beauty, or history, either to those who collected them, like Sharp, or to those who sang them, like his first auditioner the Somerset gardener John England. All Europe was falling under the idea of the Volk. Grieg was immensely popular in England in the 1890s. Holst wrote "A Somerset Rhapsody," and Butterworth "A Shropshire Rhapsody." Folksong and a corresponding notion of folk culture flickers through the works of the British literary and antiquarian elite all through the century. Thomas Hardy wrote of, and participated in, village music-making and, just as Robert Burns and Walter Scott had done for Scottish song before them, Mrs Gaskell, Emily Brontë, George Eliot, and William Wordsworth all demonstrated their knowledge of English working-class musical culture before the revivalists came to fan the "folk" embers in the Edwardian years.

All these authors recognized the phenomenon, but more solid evidence of the space that traditional song occupied in the lives of the poor is given by Michael Pickering (1987) in his examination of the singing of "The Husbandman and the Servantman" by Oxfordshire farm workers in the 1870s. While to Cecil Sharp and friends the appeal of folksong was undoubtedly in part due to its historicity—a sense of unchanging tradition harking back to the Elizabethans, Pickering on the other hand argues that we don't have to believe all that in order to see that for those who sang them, their songs held clear and immediate value (Pickering, 1987, pp. 44–5).

In other words, by the turn of the century the embers were still bright enough for the folk revivalists to stoke and, out of "archaic material" of uneven provenance and authenticity (Francmanis, 2002), in an era when the Industrial Revolution was beginning to be seen by intellectuals of all kinds as a terrible catastrophe, the folk revivalists presented folksong as a means of national redemption.[4] That they made this musical identity plausible only to themselves it is true; but it is not true that their collecting was useless or wrong. High handed and high minded (Collini, 1999, p. 110) they might have been, but it was on behalf of a rural people whose privations were greater than theirs and whose industrial struggles were no less real than those of the town. As late as 1910, rural laboring families in the south were periodically *starving* (Floud & McCloskey, 1981, pp. 161–2). People as poor as these had little more to offer than the rags they stood in. Yet still they believed that England belonged to them and, for all their faults, and there were a few, the revivalists offered their support.

---

[4] George Dangerfield famously characterized the era as *The Strange Death of Liberal England* in 1935. Robert Colls and Philip Dodd (1986, 2014) stress the more positive, transformative aspects in their (Eds.) *Englishness. Politics and Letters 1880-1920*. London; Croom Helm; London; Bloomsbury.

According to Sharp, folksong was "the product of a race" that reflected "feelings and tastes that are communal rather than personal" (1907, pp. 12, 15). In 1925, Stanley Baldwin spoke in praise of the building of Cecil Sharp House in London as a new national center. The project enjoyed his "entire sympathy," he said, for by it "we may know our national character" (Fox Strangways, 1925, p. 290). For Cecil Sharp, instead of the composer there was the folk, while for this Conservative Prime Minister at least, instead of class there was the nation. Baldwin thought "the widespread interest in the revival" was "one more proof that our class distinctions are really superficial in comparison with the underlying unity of feeling of our people." A year later this underlying unity of the people would be on display when Baldwin and his government faced a General Strike.

Appeals for national unity were not uncommon in the period. As well as rejecting German domination in music (as well as in other things), the idea of an English musical tradition served to reassure those who needed reassuring that the nation was united even when by any reckoning it wasn't (Dibble, 1998, p. 26). It is interesting to note that Baldwin, a Tory ironmaster from Staffordshire, and Ralph Vaughan Williams, a socialist intellectual from Surrey, both cast folksong and dance as classless or, more accurately, as able to transcend the divisions of class. Vaughan Williams (1934, p. 39) espoused an "ideal music which will be neither popular nor classical, highbrow nor lowbrow, but an art in which all can take part" and, as we have seen, Baldwin did the same.

Claims on folksong as the national music—or "the music of the people" as it was sometimes called—had to work with the fact that working-class people comprised the vast majority of the nation and in their search for the new Englishness the revivalists had to look beyond the cultural elite, usual guardians of national identity, and in the direction of the unofficial 85% who were not normally seen as cultured or, in the eyes of the folk revivalists, not normally seen as conscious (of their culture). Sharp (1907) put it like this: he went in search of those, he said, "least affected" by "extraneous educational influences" because "peasant music is genuine music" and "peasant speech is genuine language" (1907: 1, 33). This was a strange mission in a country that had no peasants, but if not real people, Sharp did expect a sort of composite wisdom instead; the voice of innumerable generations blended smooth and whole. Vaughan Williams (1934, p. 68) called this *soul*, and took his cue from it:

> The art of music above all the other arts is the expression of the soul of a nation, and by a nation I mean not necessarily aggregations of people, artificially divided from each other by political frontiers or economic barriers. What I mean is any community of people who are spiritually bound together by language, environment, history, and common ideals and, above all … continuity with the past.

In his newly established journal *Music & Letters*, Fox Strangways (1920, p. 79) wrote that Vaughan Williams' folk songs were "not set, like jewels, nor arranged, like flowers, but used, like common everyday things" for he wanted to free music from that snobbishness and "good taste" which he saw as "the stumbling block in the path of a 'Young English' national school of composers" (1902, pp. 27–8). Music was not "a mere sensation to be enjoyed by the epicure," he said, but something shared by the people in everyday life (1912: 40). So Vaughan Williams wove folk songs gracefully into his work and took that work to the outside world. His musical editorship of the *English Hymnal* brought together such combinations as the tune "Forest Green" for "O Little Town of Bethlehem" and "Kingsfold" for "I Heard the Voice of Jesus Say." Though at first an atheist and later a "cheerful agnostic," Vaughan Williams found in the Church of England's hymnody not only a source of inspiration, but a way of re-introducing the people to their native musical identity. He did this in other ways too, by writing for example pieces for wind band based on folk songs, "English Folk Song Suite" (1923), or "Sea Songs" (1923), or music for church organ, or cathedral choir, or army band, or by writing scores for films including the box office hits "49th Parallel" (1940) and "Scott of the Antarctic" (1948).

By celebrating the Tudor and Elizabethan composers (Tallis, Byrd, Gibbons, and Purcell), and by arranging their work to provide tunes for the *Hymnal* (Vaughan Williams, 1933, 1914), he also carved his name in a long English musical tradition. Most famous of these invocations was his "Fantasia on a Theme by Thomas Tallis" (1910)—"a temporal bridge between the Tudors and the modern Edwardians whose very orchestration creates the impression of a dialogue between the two ages, the divided string section calling and responding to each other across a great sea of history" (Young, 2010).

In his regard for "English music" as a "synthesis of what we now see as archetypical national elements" (Foreman, 1998: 3), and in his desire for a living tradition based on that, Vaughan Williams was in fact calling up his own musical career as "the man who set out deliberately...to turn himself into an English composer" (Kennedy, 1986, p. v). Asked what the folk revival meant for a young man like him, he (1934) invoked his own soul. He had been obliged to strip out foreign or superficial musical identities, he said, for:

> ... several of us found here in its simplest form the musical idiom which we unconsciously were cultivating in ourselves, [and] it gave a point to our imagination; far from fettering us, it freed us from foreign influences which weighed on us [...] The knowledge of our folk-songs did not so much discover for us something new, but uncovered for us something which had been hidden by foreign matter.

Existing in remote corners of the composer's psyche in the same way that the songs themselves existed in remote corners of the country, the idea of a hidden musical truth brought with it the notion of an unimpeachable authenticity. Where did one find it? Intellectuals failed to find it because they did not know where to look.[5] The people failed to find it because they did not want to look. Revivalists believed they had found it in the people, but looked inside themselves for confirmation. In their search for an authentic

---

[5] They failed "to distinguish between the instinctive music of the common people and the debased street music of the vulgar": Sharp, *Some Conclusions*, p. 33.

idea of England invested in a common people who hardly seemed to care anyway, and in their war with modernism, time and again we find the revivalists scanning not only the music, but their own sincerity (Sharp, 1907, p. 3).

41.2   BELIEVING IN THE PEOPLE

Cobbett and the early century radicals had always claimed that they wanted nothing new; that as freeborn Englishmen, England was their birth right. The late century folk revivalists took a similar stance. They believed England had once belonged to the people—in a common culture for sure, but also in common law and custom—and to want what was yours anyway was to want nothing new. Sharp re-invigorated the Folk Song Society along these lines after 1903 (Boyes, 1993, pp. 81–2), turning it from a tea party into a campaign.[6] As a Fabian socialist, he shared with key figures like Vaughan Williams and Mary Neal decidedly left of center political opinions aligned to decidedly left field cultural ones. Vaughan Williams' vision for the *English Hymnal*, for instance, was close to Conrad Noel's vision for his parish of Thaxted as a Christian socialist community. Rendered whole by their music and living in congregation, Noel told his poor parishioners not to pray for their souls, but to build the kingdom of God on earth—or in Essex at least (Noel, 1912).[7]

The folk revivalists hoped for the *re*-discovery of Englishness, not its discovery, still less its invention. They invented it just the same, starting with their treatment of English history.[8] Sharp claimed he had found pure survivals of English folksong in the American Appalachians. He reasoned that when he stood and heard Miss Lula McCoy of Chicopee County, Georgia, sing "Barbara Allen", he was listening to the song in its pure form just as it had been sung in 17th century England. In order to believe this, he had to also believe that the southern states of America had stood still for 300 years—a not unreasonable proposition in some people's eyes, but preposterous in point of fact (Campbell & Sharp, 1917, pp. iv–xx). Undaunted and unscholarly, Sharp advised young English composers that they would be better off studying music in American log cabins and nailed his 323 Appalachian tunes and 122 Appalachian songs to the door to prove it.

The cabin porch might have been where Sharp's music began, but it certainly was not where it was finished off. When Walter Johnson argued that even though folk music was the nation's "subliminal self" it had far more value "when the actors concerned belong[ed] to the educated class" he might have had Cecil Sharp in mind (Johnson, 1908, p. 12). Having tramped the counties in search of his songs, Sharp would come home to

---

[6] The English Folk-Song Society was founded in 1898 with 73 members and £24 in the bank. Elgar, Dvorak, and Grieg joined by invitation.

[7] Noel was a famous High Churchman, folk sympathizer, and communist.

[8] In 1893 the President of the Folklore Society had been subjected to brutal attack on his standards of scholarship by the constitutional historian F. W. Maitland (1893) The survival of archaic communities, *Law Quarterly Review*, 9, 211. Gomme's reputation did not recover, but the poor scholarship went on.

Church Row, Hampstead to set about restoring them to a fit state. Fit for what? We can be sure it was more North London than north Somerset, more concert hall than cottage door (Sharp, 1908–12):

> Our guiding principle has been, therefore, to alter those phrases only to which objection might be reasonably be made. No vocalist would sing words that are pointless, or ungrammatical. Nor could he even if he would sing accurately in dialect. Happily however, dialect is not an essential of the folk song … The words, therefore, of many of the songs in this collection have been altered. Gaps have been filled up, verses omitted, or softened, rhymes reconciled, redundant syllables pruned, bad grammar and dialect translated into King's English. On the other hand, archaic word and expressions have, of course, been retained.

Sharp believed in a theory of "corporate approbation" where although all European musical identity was founded on folk traditions, it only became *national* when stamped by corporate approbation and in England he saw himself as the corporate approbator-in-chief. There were other claimants, and they did not always agree. Neal & Sharp, for example, could hardly put a foot right when it came to dancing, while Baring-Gould and Sharp did not sing eye to eye when it came to interpreting the music of a people "possibly unused to continuous mental exertion" (and therefore not themselves consulted).[9]

There was an awful lot of musical false consciousness around and no shortage of theorists to correct it. Yet the theorists' encounters with a supposedly autochthonous people were odd, so odd that one wonders who was collecting what from whom (see Gammon, 1980, pp. 10, 65). George Sturt went in search of Surrey peasants as an "English breed unimpaired yet by culture" (Bourne, 1901, p. 9), but Sir Hubert Parry was driven more by the closet *ennui* of the rich than the closet unimpairment of the poor. In his inaugural address to the English Folk-Song Society, the head of the Royal College of Music and Oxford professor of Composition unwittingly launched a thousand terrible folk songs (see Boyes, 1993, p. 25):

> I think also we may legitimately reflect that in these late days when we are beginning to realize how little happiness money-profits can bring, and how much joy lies in the simple beauty of primitive thought, and the emotions which are common to all men alike, even to the sophisticated, it is a hopeful sign that a society like ours should be founded … *to comfort ourselves.*

Nor should we forget those who made a theory in order to reject a theory. Thomas Hardy, a man not unacquainted with either the *ennui* of the metropolitan rich or the tedium of the working lives of the rural poor, rejected the revival's belief in the people

---

[9] Burne, C.S. (1913) *The Handbook of Folklore*, London; Sidgwick and Jackson, 14; Sharp, C. J. (1902) *A Book of British Song. For Home and School*, London; John Murray. In Colls' copy of Sharp's book, a second anonymous approbator has written of a third, in pencil, in the margin, for "Strawberry Fair": "Baring Gould can't write in the old style. What he has put in is very poor & doesn't sing"; and of the song "Jordan," "words too big and ideas too far-fetched and not at all in the ancient spirit. I propose something like this …" (p. 59)

almost before it started. His *The Return of the Native* (1878), and *Tess of the D'Urbervilles* (1891) came down hard on the notion that outsiders could know the folk, let alone theorize on their behalf. As an alternative Hardy offered his own idea of the unbroken "primal unity" of the people—itself a theory, but given what he was dealing with, maybe a necessary one (see Barrell, 1982, p. 347).

The folk revivalists were not the first progressive intellectuals to find the people vulgar; in England, being middle class was virtually built upon the idea. Nineteenth-century Evangelicals had taken their war on popular culture into its very heartlands—the church, the pub, the wake, the races, the normal occasions of song and dance—and the folk revivalists' charge that left to their own devices the people did not measure up can be seen as a milder version of that. Then there were those public moralists who railed against markets and machines. It was said (Andrews, 1892, p. 253) that modern markets had destroyed the old street life ("There are still some cries in the Saturday market, but all … the music has gone out of them"), and Baring-Gould & Fleetwood Sheppard (1893, p. x) had no doubt that in a mechanical age "the yokel," if left to his own devices, was "as incapable of creating a beautiful melody as…of producing a piece of beautiful sculpture." Sharp (1909, p. 9) never doubted his own propensity to be right and the folk's propensity to be wrong. That he called himself a socialist hardly made up for his contempt for a popular taste he saw as "exterminating" his own ideals:

> In the village of today the polka, waltz, and quadrille are steadily displacing the old time country dances and jigs, just as the tawdry ballads and student street songs of the towns are no less severely exterminating the folk songs.

Some progressive intellectuals saw in the crowd the same sub-conscious quality that the folk theorists found in the folksong. Le Bon's path-breaking *The Crowd* saw "the popular mind" working subliminally and anonymously against liberal civilization (1896). Only the "thinnest crust," the "thinnest veneer," kept barbarism at bay (Mearns, 1883, p. 55; Downie, 1970, p. 60). Sharp's idea of folksong saw it as yet another subliminal, anonymous force (Sharp, 1907, p. 20). That Le Bon's urban crowd was degenerative, and Sharp's rural folk were regenerative, does not detract from what both men believed in common. The people needed tutelage.

41.3 TUTELAGE

Late 19th century liberal and left intellectuals believed that the Industrial Revolution had taken the people's land, cast them out, and buried their culture.[10] What did they

---

[10] The Hammonds made the classic case for expropriation and ejection, in this case from the commons: Hammond & Hammond (1911, 1978) *The Village Labourer*. London: Longmans, Green and Co.; Prentice Hall, 'For the commons are the patrimony of the poor. The commoner's child, however

mean by "culture"? In 1867 the word was used by Matthew Arnold to describe not how the people actually lived, but how people like him thought they *ought* to live. Lecturing in the Oxford Sheldonian on "Culture and its Enemies" (published in 1869 as the great national manifesto *Culture and Anarchy*), Arnold declared war on the lives of the people—a declaration which in itself was a continuation of that war on popular culture as waged by Evangelicals since the 1790s and on the Industrial Revolution as waged by senior British public moralists since the 1820s (Arnold was no Evangelical, but that is another matter). By the 1900s the anti-industrial idealism of Carlyle, Newman, Ruskin, Arnold, and Chesterton had aligned with left thinking on class struggle to find its way into a folk movement that, no different from the public moralists, preferred ideal over actual lives, but at the same time—and quite different from the moralists—had a sympathy for what it saw as the culture of the poor.[11] So the English people had had new identities thrust upon them before—by the political economists, by the social scientists, by the scientific socialists (Thompson, 1984; Goldman, 1986). No one before the folk revivalists had offered the people their own culture as both the subject and the object of their own salvation.[12]

Not that the revivalists made folk culture open to all. They shut out the middle classes by definition at the front door as they let themselves in at the back. Of the rich, they had nothing to say. Of the urban poor, they had nothing to say. Of women, even strong women like Mary Neal, Maud Karpeles, and Lucy Broadwood ("the one who held everything together"), they had too little to say (Gregory, 2010). Of the rural poor, they had too much to say. We have seen that they were more open to some musical features more than others: melody over words, modal over non-modal, solo over harmony, piano arrangement if possible.

It is not easy to account for the instincts of a people. Nor is it always sensible. When people actually wanted to sing, they just took what was to hand. They didn't seek Vaughan Williams' advice. They didn't ask Cecil Sharp's permission. They didn't invite Sir Hubert Parry to conduct the pub singalong. The Great War, as Paul Fussell (1977) has shown, was a literary war, but it was also a musical war and the boys turned to whatever was available: folk melodies, music hall ditties, national anthems, Sunday School hymns, silly songs, and what not. Cecil Sharp would have them singing for the love of Barbara Allen and no doubt they did, but more often than not the boys told the folks back home that when this lousy war is over it's a long way to Tipperary bonsoir old thing cheerio

needy, was born with a spoon in his mouth' (62). Maud Davies found the lack of gardens a prime cause of rural poverty: Davies, M. (1909) *Life in an English Village. An economic and historical survey of the parish of Corsley in Wiltshire*, London; T. Fisher Unwin, 286.

[11] In 1871 Edward Tylor widened the debate by extending the meaning of "culture" beyond the moralists to include all forms of human meaning, including ancient meanings as practiced by primitives abroad and dimly remembered by primitives at home: Tylor, E. (1871) *Primitive culture*, vol i. London; Murray. Tylor's primitives sound uncomfortably like the urban poor of his own day—"upset by a touch of distress, temptation, or violence" (p. 31).

[12] Robert Blatchford's (1893) best-selling tract *Merrie England* (London: Clarion) promised an English path to socialism, but once past the title page had hardly a word to say about England or being English.

chin chin Nap-poo toodle-oo Goodbye-eeee.[13] This was not folksong, it was the song of the folk and it fitted Tommy's old kit bag better than the officer's knapsack. "Barbara Allen" slid more easily alongside "A Shropshire Lad" than "Daddy Wouldn't Buy Me A Bow Wow." Vaughan Williams (1912, p. 41) had served at the front and understood more than most what the boys actually liked, and he did not give up on them:

> Have not we all about us forms of musical expression which we can take and purify and raise to the level of great art? For instance, the lilt of the chorus at a music-hall joining in a popular song, the children dancing to a barrel organ, the rousing fervour of a Salvation Army hymn, St Paul's and a great choir singing in one of its festivals, the Welshmen striking up one of their own hymns whenever they win a goal at the international football match, the cries of the street pedlars, the factory girls singing their sentimental songs? Have these nothing to say to us?

There was one great writer, England's best in fact, who was asking the self-same question, also trying to come to terms with the actual instincts and feelings of the English people at this time. Yet for all his Englishness ("my very vision"), and for all his sympathy with working-class people ("the only people who move me strongly"), and for all his understanding and all his originality and willingness to experiment ("he was like them ... only greater"), even D H Lawrence (1950, 1968, 1962; Goode, 1970, p. 106) came close to the folkist theory that something in the people's soul had been buried and until it was found the English would not know who they were. True, Lawrence was looking for what his agent Garnett called the "hard veracity" of working-class life (see Morrison, 2013). At the same time and as the entire world knows, he too was trying to find a lost idea of England.

41.4 Nationalists

If going to the people was new in England, it was certainly not new in other European countries struggling for identity and the independence that went with it (Mandler, 2006). It was not even new in the United Kingdom. While the English were happy with brass bands as an expression of the labor movement, and while they were well disposed to massed choirs as an expression of northern Nonconformity (Russell, 2004, p. 215), when it came to national identity, the mass of the English people had grown used to standing silent as state ceremonial (Stanford, Parry, Elgar, Sullivan) passed them by. At the same time as the English were squeezed to the national margins, it was a long time since anybody thought Irish, Scottish, or Welsh identities resided anywhere but in the hearts of the people, and there were Scottish ballads, Welsh *Eisteddfodau*, and

---

[13] Joan Littlewood's musical "Oh What a Lovely War!" (1963) sang the songs, and was taken to the screen by Richard Attenborough in 1969.

old and new Irish songs to prove it. At either end of the nationalist spectrum, Dublin Magistrates' Court had long proved a favorite place for singing Old Ireland's wrongs (Barclay, 2014), and Welsh scholars were not lacking in confidence when it came to identifying a modern Wales founded on its people (Rhys & Brynmor-Jones, 1906). The French had their "Marseillaise," the Russians their *narodnichestvo*, the Germans Wagner and the *volkisch* movement, the Norwegians Grieg, the Poles Chopin, the Italians Verdi, the Czechs Dvorak, and the Americans Dvorak *and* no end of 10 cent tunes—some of them 10 cent catchy folk tunes—which very soon would come to break upon English musical defenses and all those carefully arranged country songs and dances, which by the 1920s Sharp and his comrades had so assiduously built into the school curriculum. Violet Alford (1923, p. 88) called upon her countrymen and women to give up "sauntering with spiritless feet up and down a ball room to the syncopated beat of tuneless clamour," but by 1939 it was clear that American jazz and swing was flooding the plain. After the war the Ministry of Education was in favor of giving folk another go (Kennedy, 1949, p. 148), and in 1973 Sharp's old friend and collaborator Maud Karpeles reckoned that folk music was once again on the brink of being "the possession of every English man, woman and child" (Karpeles, 1973, p. 104), but it was all too late. Mass music had arrived, and not even a Cecil Sharp House in every parish could have stemmed it. By the 1930s, Sir Edward became the established voice of English music. "Elgar's music became associated with Englishness in a way that went beyond the fact that he was simply a composer in England" (Crump, 1986, p. 181; Gardiner, 1998, p. 389). By way of contrast, folk music was never really popular, even in state schools where, with the help of the BBC (the new curator of national music), it was a happy part of the curriculum. Apart from all the other kinds of music, some of it quite cheap, but extraordinarily potent, there were other claims on Englishness which were just too powerful (Joyce, 2013). The British state preached qualities of domination and disinterestedness, *not* communal feeling and native instinct. In the face of such a line, even though there was much middle-class sympathy for its softer, milder folksy qualities, most English people in the 1930s—especially progressive, intellectual, middle-class people—saw the first folk revival as eccentric. Elgar had been able to say that he alone was English folk music only because the idea was so weak.

It was different in Europe. A continent of new and would-be new nation-states had been built on folk identities—for every region a folk, and for every folk a musical identity (Augusteijn & Storm, 2012). Bretons march still. They work at *Intermarche* and *Monsieur Bricolage*, but at *pardons* and *defiles* they march in black and gold, in *coiffes* lace and *sabots*, with pipes and drums shoulder to shoulder swaying down narrow winding streets. Over a century ago this is how Bretons, the poorest people in France, straightened their backs to look their betters in the eye, and nobody condescended (Helias, 1978; Le Gall, 2013). Being Breton was seen as the product of a race. Anything can happen in a Breton landscape painted by modernists, *but not to individuals*. Faces are blanked or turned away. Bodies are lumpish or in costume. People move in herds. In much the same way that the English folk revivalists looked for meaning in anonymity, the Pont Aven School looked for meaning in body and landscape. Back at 27 Church Row Sharp toiled to let the people be heard, but Chesterton could judge still that this was a people who had not spoken yet.[14]

41.5 AFTERWORD: COMMERCIAL MUSICAL IDENTITIES

It is important to note that a completely different kind of people continued to be heard in the commercial song market—traditionally in the major chapbook publishing centers, but later in the concert rooms, music halls, and printed ephemera of the late 19th century town. In Newcastle upon Tyne for example, in 1910 miners, sailors, and keelmen had been key figures in song and rhyme for well over a hundred years. Bell's *Rhymes of Northern Bards* (1812) spoke of a rowdy world where it was not uncommon to end a rhyme with "Tommy cock'd, and Jenny spread" ("So here I leave them both in bed"), or to start one with a keelman "in blue bonnet a dimple in his chin" ("he sits in his haddock and claws his bare buttock"). In these songs colliers are forever turning up uninvited, and there is no shortage of young women who not only lose their modesty, but their bairns as well.[15] In this penny song market, there were no blanked faces and anonymous bodies: Cuddy Willy, Blind Willie, Cuckoo Jack, *Bob Cranky* most famously, but everyone his own man or woman, all on a spree. You'll not find any Sandgate Girls in Cecil Sharp. This one thought to marry a parson to hear her say her prayers (Bell, 1812, 1971, pp. 48–9):

> But I have married a keelman
> And he kicks me down the stairs.
> He's an ugly body, a bubbly body,
> An ill-fared ugly loon;
> And I have married a keelman,
> And my good days are done.

This so-called "Cranky" tradition (Colls, 1977) did not die with the first folk revival. It lasted well into the second half of the 20th century (Kelly, 1979; Duchene, 1963) and stands still, when it can still stand, in Newcastle's Bigg Market of a Friday night.

---

[14] "There are no folk in the whole world so helpless or so wise/There is hunger in our bellies, there is laughter in our eyes/You laugh at us and love us, both mugs and eyes are wet/Only you do not know us. For we have not spoken yet": Chesterton, G.K. (1907) The secret people, *The Neolith*, 1, 1–2. For Chesterton himself as a subliminal folk force in English politics, see Patrick Wright (2005), Last Orders, *The Guardian*, 9 April 2005. Tom Nairn (1977) looked to the folk movement to reinvigorate English national identity: *The break up of Britain*. London: New Left Books.

[15] Jenny and Tommy appear in Edward Chicken's (1778) *The Collier's Wedding*, 5th edtn., Newcastle; T. Saint. Cecil Sharp might have profited from Bell's warning, which came from Alexander Pope: "Whoever thinks a faultless piece to see / Thinks what ne'er was, nor is, nor e'er shall be". For the general flavor and context of these musical identities, see Robert Colls (1977), *The Collier's Rant, Song and Culture in the Industrial Village* London; Croom Helm.

The music keeps on coming. Cecil Sharp House still sees itself as a missionary organization, but frets about its failure to reach the people (Petridis, 2013). On the other side of folk, the best English bands (Fairport Convention, 1967; Steeleye Span, 1969; Oysterband, 1976; Jim Moray, 2001; Bellowhead, 2004) took their chances with rock and did not lose, influencing and in turn being influenced to take folk to greater and younger audiences than Cecil Sharp House ever dreamed of.[16]

In recent years, left wing writers and intellectuals have found much to hate in rural Englishness. They see it as fake, or reactionary, or racist, and are uncomfortable in the company of anything folksy or (as they see it) trying to be what it is not. Folk invention and adaptation never necessarily meant fake and, except for a few Edwardian and inter-war metros, rural life never meant folksy (Colls, 2002). The first folk revival found its second wind in Ewan MacColl and Peggy Seeger's *marxisant* folk club movement in the 1950s, and its third in a wider revival led by Dylan and Baez in the 1960s. The second revival was different from the first in that it moved from west to north and from peasants to miners, but still made the case for a people's England. The first edition of *New Left Review* (Bill Holdsworth, 1960; Julia Mitchell, 2014) drew attention to Folk's capacity "to become the bed-rock of a socialist people's culture." In the 1960s, from all corners south and mid-West the Americans came, including jazz and blues Americans, and Kentucky and Mississippi Americans, and Greenwich Village Americans, to lift English folk to new levels of excitement and reach. Not that the first folk revivalists ever went away. Some of their key ideas—particularly the idea of an authentic Englishness lost beneath high or commercial cultural forms—found new expression in new wave literary criticism (Leavis & Thompson, 1933, pp. 1–6), in local history (Hoskins, 1946, p. 28; 1957, p. 216), in social history (Thompson, 1963), in oral history (Ewart Evans, 1956), in people's history ("dig where you stand"; Samuel, 1994, p. 158), in theatre (MacColl, 1985, p. 254; Joan Littlewood, 1946), in painting (L S Lowry, 1919: see Rohde,1999, p. 86), in community studies (Peter Willmott & Michael Young, 1957, p. 187), and in pop music and London Olympic pageantry (Morra, 2014, p. 44, p. 188). Popular Front strategies after 1935 looked for national unity in aspects of folk Englishness (Bounds, 2009, p. 41), shared by Orwell (Colls, 2013, p. 159), while Ross McKibbin (1998, p. 139) saw "folk Marxism" at the heart of post-war industrial relations in Britain and Stefan Collini (1999, p. 214) saw the high moral authority vested in writers like Raymond Williams (1958) and Richard Hoggart (1957) stemming from the folkish qualities of their subjects. The first folk revival died, but never went away.

In 1991, in an important work, Patrick Joyce argued that the social historian's category of "experience" was not prior to language, but "actively constituted" by it (Joyce, 1991, p. 9).

---

[16] Needless to say, contemporary definitions of folk music are more permissive and our chapter reflects that. Contemporary "folk" is predicated more on a mixture of context, setting, arrangement, instrumentation and levels of informality than on any purity of origin or sound, although musical continuity still matters. Pop bands, such as Mumford & Sons or Fleet Foxes are often called "folky" because they use particular instruments.

It is equally true of music; folk music actively constituted, and does constitute, some part of being English. The English folk revivalists not only saved a musical identity, they helped it live another day.

References

Alford, V. (1923). *Peeps at English Folk dance*. London: A&C Black.

Andrews, W. (1892). *Bygone Leicestershire*. London; Simpkin, Marshall, Hamilton, Kent and Co.

Augusteijn, J., & Storm, E. (Eds.) (2012). *Region and State in 19c Europe. Nation-building, regional identities and separatism*. Basingstoke: Palgrave Macmillan.

Barclay, K. (2014). Singing performance and lower class masculinity in the Dublin Magistrates' Court 1820–50. *Journal of Social History*, Spring, 13–17.

Baring-Gould, S., Rev., & Fleetwood Sheppard, H., Rev. (1893). *Songs and ballads of the West. A collection made from the mouths of the people*. London: Methuen and Co.

Barr, J. (1998). The folk songs of Ralph Vaughan Williams. Six studies in English folksong. *Journal of the Ralph Vaughan Williams Society*, 13 October, 14–15.

Barrell, J. (1982). Geographies of Hardy's Wessex. *Journal of Historical Geography*, 8, 4.

Bearman, C.J. (2008). 'Lee, Catherine Anna', *ODNB Online*.

Bell, J. (Ed.) (1812, 1971). *Rhymes of Northern bards*. Newcastle upon Tyne: M. Angus; Frank Graham

Blatchford, R. (1893). *Merrie England*. London: Clarion.

Bounds, P. (2009). *Orwell and Marxism*. London: I.B. Tauris.

Bourne (Sturt),G. (1901). *The Bettesworth Book. Talks with a Surrey Peasant*. London: Duckworth.

Burne, C. S. (1913). *The handbook of folklore*. London: Sidgwick and Jackson.

Boyes, G. (1993). *The imagined village*. Manchester: Manchester University Press.

Campbell, O. & Sharp, C.J. (1917). *English folk songs from the Southern Appalachians*. New York, NY: G.P Putnam's Sons.

Chambers, J. (1962). In: H. T. Moore (Ed.) *Collected letters of D.H. Lawrence*, Vol. 1, p. 60. London: William Heinemann Ltd.

Chesterton, G.K. (1907). The secret people. *The Neolith*, 1, 1–2.

Chicken, E. (1778). *The collier's wedding*, 5th edn. Newcastle: T. Saint.

Collini, S. (1999). *English pasts*, Oxford: Oxford University Press.

Colls, R. (1977). *The collier's rant. Song and culture in the industrial village*. London: Croom Helm.

Colls, R., & Dodd, P. (Eds.) (1986), 2014. *Englishness. Politics and letters 1880–1920*, London: Croom Helm.

Colls, R. (2002). *Identity of England*. Oxford: Oxford University Press.

Colls, R. (2013). *George Orwell. English rebel*. Oxford: Oxford University Press.

Crump, J. (1986). The identity of English music: the reception of Elgar 1898–1935. In: R. Colls & P. Dodd (Eds.) *Englishness. Politics and letters 1880–1920*. London: Croom Helm.

Dangerfield, G. (1935). *The strange death of Liberal England*. New York: Harrison Smith and Robert Haas.

Davies, M. (1909). *Life in an English Village. An economic and historical survey of the parish of Corsley in Wiltshire*. London: T. Fisher Unwin.

Dibble, J. (1998). Parry, Stanford and Vaughan Williams: the creation of tradition. In: L. Foreman (Ed.) *Vaughan Williams in perspective: Studies of an English composer*, pp. 25–47. Colchester: Albion Press.

Downie, R.A. (1970). *Frazer and the Golden Bough*, London; Victor Gollancz.

Duchene, A. (1963). Geordie songs hit a rich seam of vitality. *The Guardian*, 22 November 1963.

Ewart Evans, G. (1956; 1975). *Ask the fellows who cut the hay.* London: Faber and Faber.

Floud, R. & McCloskey, D. (1981). *The economic history of Britain since 1700*, Vol. 2, *1860–1939*. Cambridge: Cambridge University Press.

Foreman, L. (1998). Restless explorations: articulating many visions. In: L. Foreman (Ed.) *Vaughan Williams in perspective: Studies of an English composer*, pp. 1–24. Colchester; Albion Press.

Fox Strangways, A.H. (1920). Ralph Vaughan Williams. *Music & Letters*, 1, April, 78–86.

Fox Strangways, A.H. (1925). Editorial note, *Music & Letters*, 6, October, 289–90.

Fox Strangways, A.H. & Karpeles, M. (1933, 1955). *Cecil Sharp.* London: Oxford University Press.

Francmanis, J. (2002). National music to national redeemer: the consolidation of a "Folk-Song" construct in Edwardian England. *Popular Music*, 21 January, 1–25.

Fussell, P. (1977). *The Great War and Modern Memory.* Oxford: Oxford University Press.

Gammon, V. (1980). Folk song collecting in Sussex and Surrey 1843–1914. *History Workshop Journal*, 10, 61–89.

Gardiner, J. (1998). The reception of Sir Edward Elgar 1918–34. *20c British History*, 9(3), 389.

Goldman, L. (1986). The Social Science Association 1851–86. *English Historical Review*, cl (cccxcviii) pp. 95–134.

Goode, J. (1970). D H Lawrence. In: B. Bergonzi (Ed.) *The twentieth century.* London: Sphere.

Gregory, E.D. (2010). *The late Victorian folksong revival.* Maryland, MD: Scarecrow.

Hammond, J.L. & Hammond B. (1911), 1978. *The village labourer.* London: Longmans, Green and Co.

Heaney, M. (2008). Sharp, Cecil James. *ODNB Online.* Available at: http://www.oxforddnb.com/view/article/36040 (accessed 3 March 2016).

Helias, P.J. (1978). *The horse of pride. Life in a Breton village*, New Haven, CT: Yale University.

Hoggart, R. (1957). *The uses of literacy.* London: Chatto & Windus.

Holdsworth, B. (1960). Songs of the People. *New Left Review*, 1, 48.

Hoskins, W.G. (1946). Leicestershire Yeoman Families. *Transactions of the Leicestershire Archaeological Society*, xxiii, part i.

Hoskins, W.G. (1957). *The Midland peasant. The economic and social history of a Leicestershire village.* London: Macmillan.

Johnson, W. (1908). *Folk memory, or the continuity of British archaeology.* New York, NY: Benjamin Blom.

Joyce, P. (1991). *Visions of the people. Industrial England and the question of class.* Cambridge: Cambridge University Press

Joyce, P. (2013). *The state of freedom. A social history of the British State since 1800.* Cambridge: Cambridge University Press.

Judge, R. (2006). Neal, Mary Clara Sophia. *ODNB Online.* Available at: http://www.oxforddnb.com/view/article/40485 (accessed 3 March 2016).

Karpeles, M. (1973). *An introduction to English folk song* London: Oxford University Press.

Kelly, R. (1979). Survival of the little waster. *The Observer*, 4 November 1979.

Kennedy, D. (1949). *England's dances. Folk dancing today and yesterday.* London: G. Bell and Sons.

Kennedy, M. (1986). Foreword. In : R. Vaughan Williams, *National Music*, pp.v–ix. Oxford, Oxford University Press.

Lawrence, D.H. (1950, 1978). *Selected letters.* Harmondsworth: Penguin.

Lawrence, D.H. (1915). Letter to Lady Asquith, 21 October 1915. In: W. Roberts & H.T. Moore (Eds.) *Phoenix II*, p. 264. London: Heinemann.

Le Bon, G. (1896). *The crowd. A study of the popular mind*. London: Macmillan.

Le Gall, M. (2013). *Les costumes bretons, entre tradition et reinvention*. Carhaix: L'Association du Kreizh Breizh.

Leavis, F.R. & Thompson, D. (1933). *Culture and environment. The training of cultural awareness*. London: Chatto & Windus.

Lucas, E.V. (1910). Introduction. In: Mary Neal (Ed.) *The Espérance Morris Book, Part I*. pp. vii–viii. London: Curwen and Sons.

MacColl, E. (1985). 'Theatre of Action'. In: R. Samuel, E. MacColl, & S. Cosgrove (Eds.) *Theatres of the left 188-1935, pp. 205–55*. London: Routledge Kegan Paul.

Maitland, F.W. (1893). The survival of archaic communities. *Law Quarterly Review*, 9, 211.

Mandler, P. (2006). *The English national character*. New Haven, CT: Yale University Press.

McKibbin, R. (1998). *Classes and cultures. England 1918–1951*. Oxford: Oxford University Press.

Mearns, A. (1883). *The bitter cry of outcast London*. London: James Clarke and Co.

Mitchell, J. (2014). 'Farewell to Cotia' The English Folk revival, the p elegy, and the nationalization of British coal 1947-70', *Twentieth Century British History*, 25(4), 585–601.

Morra, I. (2014). *Britishness, popular music and national identity. The making of modern Britain*. London: Routledge.

Morrison, B. (2013). Mother's boy. *The Guardian*, 25 May 2013.

Nairn, T. (1977). *The break up of Britain*. London: New Left Books.

Neal, M. (1910). Set to music. *Espérance Morris Book*, 1–2.

Noel, C. (1912). *Byways of belief*. London: Frank Palmer.

Petridis, A (2013). English heritage. *The Guardian*, 26 July 2013.

Pickering, M. (1987). The past as a source of aspiration: popular song and social change. In: M. Pickering & T. Green (Eds.) *Everyday culture: popular song and the vernacular milieu*, pp. 39–39. Milton Keynes: Open University Press.

Rhys, J. & Brynmor-Jones, D. (1906). *The Welsh people*. London: T. Fisher Unwin.

Rohde, S. (1999). *L S Lowry. A biography*. Salford: Salford Lowry Press.

Russell, D. (2004). *Looking North. Northern England and the national imagination*. Manchester: Manchester University Press.

Samuel, R. (1994). *Theatres of memory, 1, Past and present in contemporary culture*. London: Verso.

Sharp, C. J. (1902). *A book of British song. For home and school*. London: John Murray.

Sharp, C. J. (1907). *English Folk-song: Some conclusions*. London: Simpkin and Co.

Sharp, C. J. (1908-12: 1967). *English county folk songs*. London: Novello.

Sharp, C. J. (1909, 1934). *The country dance book*. London: Novello.

Thompson, E.P. (1963: 1968). *The making of the English working class*. London: Gollancz: Harmondsworth: Penguin.

Thompson, N.W. (1984). *The people's science*. Cambridge: Cambridge University Press.

Tylor, E. (1871). *Primitive culture*, Vol. 1. London: Murray.

Vaughan Williams, R. (1902). Good taste. The vocalist, May 1902. In: U. Vaughan Williams and I. Holst (Eds.) *Heirs and rebels: letters written to each other and occasional writings in music*, pp. 27–8. London: Oxford University Press.

Vaughan Williams, R. (1914). British music in the Tudor period. *The Music Student*, 7(2), 1914. In: D. Manning (Ed.). (2007). *Vaughan Williams on music*, pp. 47–50. Oxford: Oxford University Press.

Vaughan Williams, R. (1912). Who wants the English composer? *Royal College of Music Magazine*, 9/1, 1912, 11–15. In: D.Manning (Ed.). 2007. *Vaughan Williams on music*, pp. 39–42. Oxford: Oxford University Press.

Vaughan Williams, R. (1933). Elizabethan music and the modern world. *Monthly Musical Record*, 63/752, 1933. In: D.Manning (Ed.). 2007. *Vaughan Williams on music*, pp. 67–77. Oxford: Oxford University Press.

Vaughan Williams, R. (1934, 1986). National music. In: M. Kennedy (Ed.) *Ralph Vaughan Williams, national music and other essays*, pp. 1–82. Oxford: Oxford University Press.

Vaughan Williams, U. (1964). *R.V.W: a biography of Ralph Vaughan Williams*. London: Oxford University Press.

Williams , R. (1958). *Culture and society 1780–1950*. London: Chatto & Windus.

Willmott, P. &Young, M. (1957). *Family and kinship in East London*. Harmondsworth: Penguin.

Wright, P. (2005). Last orders. *The Guardian*, 9 April 2005.

Young, R. (2010). Cloud of knowing. *The Guardian*, 12th June 2010. Available at http://www.guardian.co.uk/culture/2010/jun/12/vaughan-williams-fantasia-theme-tallis (accessed 26 June 2013).

CHAPTER 42

....

SISTEMA SCOTLAND

Emerging Musical Identities in Big Noise, Raploch

....

KATHRYN JOURDAN WITH AN INTRODUCTION BY RICHARD HOLLOWAY

42.1 INTRODUCTION

....

THIS chapter explores the developing musical identities of members of Sistema Scotland's "Big Noise" community in Raploch, a housing estate lying in the shadow of Stirling Castle and the Wallace Monument. Established in the summer of 2008, this pilot scheme forms the first in what promises to become a network of Big Noise centers across Scotland—the second at Govanhill, Glasgow, having opened in April 2013, and the third at Torry, Aberdeen, starting in the spring of 2015. The chapter introduces the program in Raploch, where children are taught to play musical instruments within the context of an orchestra from the outset, with the aim of bringing about a transformation within the local community, and considers how this particular context for music-making contributes to conceptions of what it means to be a "musician," and shapes notions of "musical identities."

As the Big Noise program is introduced, themes are taken up from Elliott & Silverman (Chapter 2, "Identities and musics: Reclaiming personhood") in which the authors suggest that any discussion of the importance of music-making for individual or group identity must first grapple with the nature of personhood. Their notion of "praxial identity formation" brings an ethical basis to the conception of musical identity, through the notion of musical "praxes," in which music-making is conceptualized as ethical engagement. Elliott and Silverman (Chapter 2) write:

> Musics-as-social praxes provide powerful intersubjective contexts in which people of all ages and abilities can co-construct positively each other's musical-social-personal identities and narratives, and, more deeply, co-construct empathetically each

other as persons. In doing so, music makers and listeners acquire the musical means they need to build "a certain way of life"—a meaningful life of fellowship, happiness, healthfulness, joy, respect for others, an "ethic of care" for oneself and others, and many other dimensions of human flourishing that Aristotle summarized in the word *eudaimonia* (Elliott & Silverman, Chapter 2).

This chapter probes these intersubjective contexts and co-constructive processes further, in the setting of the Big Noise, Raploch, but goes deeper, behind the notion of personhood, to explore the basic ethical orientation which underlies our dealings with each other.

The chapter speaks in three different registers. The first voice is that of Richard Holloway, Chairman of the Board for Sistema Scotland and former Chair of the Scottish Arts Council, as he recalls the vision for and early beginnings of the Big Noise. The second is that of a founder staff member. Through her perspectives on her work at Big Noise, and on the development of her own musical identity, the chapter explores the effects upon the children and the wider community in Raploch of learning to make music together, considering how the forming of musical identities in Raploch may contribute to processes of generational change. The third voice is my own narrative and theoretically reflective voice, which begins by setting out the principles and practices of the Big Noise, and suggests what assumptions these practices make about the nature of music-making. I explore the perspectives of the Big Noise musician in the light of Elliott and Silverman's notion of musical "praxes," and strands of the thinking of both Christopher Small and French-Jewish philosopher Emmanuel Levinas are introduced as tools with which to explore the ethical parameters surrounding the development of musical identity amongst Big Noise community members. These form a lens through which to investigate emerging musical relationships, for instance the nurturing and hospitable musical practices of the Venezuelan musicians who played alongside the children of Raploch at their Big Concert in June 2012. The chapter concludes with a reflection upon the distinctive aspects of musical identity amongst those who come to work in the Big Noise, and, with the help of Levinas, suggestions as to how this fresh orientation may point towards transformational practices within the "classical" music profession in the future.

42.2 THE STORY BEGINS

16 August 2007 was a tense day in Edinburgh, where the Festival was pursuing its course. The population of the city had trebled in size, as always happens during these August weeks when the world descends upon our beautiful city, its grey sobriety made vibrant and vivid by the hundreds of artists, musicians, writers, TV crews, and visitors who crowd its ancient streets. The atmosphere was particularly expectant that year, because one of the most thrilling orchestras on earth was due to make its Edinburgh debut in the Usher Hall. The Simon Bolivar National Youth Orchestra of Venezuela was not only taking the world of classical music by storm, it was provoking interest among social reformers as a possible model for reaching out to young people whose communities have been marginalized and alienated by the industrial and social revolutions of recent decades.

I was preparing to meet the remarkable man who was responsible for the birth of the orchestra, because I wanted to enlist his help in doing something like it in Scotland. For Maestro Abreu, music has a transcendental power to change the lives and renew the hopes of poor children anywhere. This is the man who is responsible for the phenomenon that Sir Simon Rattle has described as the most important thing happening anywhere in classical music today. Half a million children have gone through it, and a quarter of a million children aged 2–25 are currently in the program, in a network of 125 youth orchestras, all in a country that did not get its first conservatoire until the 1920s.[1] What began with eleven young people in a back street garage in Caracas as an attempt to make the glories of classical music available to ordinary Venezuelans soon metamorphosed into one of the most effective and revolutionary programs of social transformation in our troubled and unequal world.

42.2.1 The vision

When I met the Maestro that afternoon in August two years ago I kissed his hands. For years I have been looking for something new to try here, for a way to turn around those damaged and despairing communities, which have become the victims of social and economic upheavals in Scotland over the past few decades. I knew that, since it took generations to destroy the spiritual and cultural fabric of these communities, it would take generations to restore it. Was there somehow a process of inward renewal that might overcome this damaging legacy and build new communities?

Shortly after I became Chair of the Scottish Arts Council in 2005 a journalist with the Guardian newspaper told me about El Sistema in Venezuela. (The Venezuelan program is now named Fundación Musical Simón Bolívar, but is still widely referred to as "El Sistema," part of its original title Fundación del Estado para el Sistema Nacional de las Orquestas Juveniles e Infantiles de Venezuela, FESNOJIV.) *She had been to see it for herself, and she said the quality of the music was extraordinary. I was interested too, but less in the music than in the change it seemed to be bringing to the lives of the children who played it, so I decided to go to Venezuela to investigate. What I saw in Venezuela had a profound and liberating effect on me, and I came back determined to replicate it in Scotland. What broke my heart was that I saw children playing again, playing with a joyous intensity that was transformative. Yes, playing. What we fail to realize in our*

---

[1] Accurate figures for participation in Venezuela's program are hard to find and those cited here are now out of date. In 2015 estimates put current participation at 700,000 young people within some 300 nucleos, but these are impossible to verify independently.

work-obsessed culture is that play is not only good for our spiritual and mental health; it has always been a vital element in our progress and development as a species.

This is where El Sistema comes in. It gets children playing again, playing arduously, and playing in orchestras from the very beginning. The two aspects of this revolution are intensity and immersion. It is this intense immersion in the orchestra and in the beauty of music that is the key to its revolutionary success in socializing children into disciplined, co-operative human beings, who discover pleasure in effort and joy in the exultation of music. That's what I saw in Venezuela and it is what I wanted for Scotland's children.

42.2.2 Starting work

We had created a board and registered ourselves as a charity—Sistema Scotland. We had raised enough money to hire a gifted young woman as director of the project; and we had found a community in Scotland that was regenerating itself after a difficult history, and was keen to let us try the experiment in their community. I wanted us to be El Sistema in Scotland. Above all, I wanted the blessing of the man of genius who had founded the system. All of that I got from Maestro Abreu, and more. He announced at a press conference on the afternoon of the concert that he would enter a covenant with us to help us deliver in Scotland what they were delivering in Venezuela; that they would share their wisdom with us; above all, they would invite us to become part of their family. All this we sealed that day, and a few months later we sent another delegation to Venezuela to sign the covenant. A few months after that we sent our newly hired team of musicians to Venezuela not only to gain some training in their approach, but to get the vibe, to be motivated by what they saw.

As "The Big Noise" we've been going for seven years in Raploch now. We are showing that the Venezuelan miracle can work in Scotland, a very different society with a very different culture. It works because children are children everywhere, and they know in their hearts how to play creatively, if given half a chance. That is the chance we are giving them. José Antonio Abreu has shown us how music can make beautiful the lives of the children who play it. We are thrilled because, through his genius, the children of Venezuela are teaching the children of Scotland how to play again.

42.2.3 The Big Noise: principles and pedagogy

The task of bringing something inspired by the Venezuelan Sistema model to Scotland's very different social and cultural setting involved board members, a management team, and musicians alike grappling with significant questions, recognizing that we must work creatively to re-envisage this model, to arrive at a program which would be effective in our Scottish context and be responsive to the needs of each different community we work alongside. Which elements of practice from Venezuela are central to the *Sistema* vision? Is there a *Sistema* methodology? Which is more important, social engagement or musical excellence? Is it even helpful to see these in terms of a polarity? How do we adapt leadership, teaching and learning styles to Scotland's educational and social setting, bearing in mind, for instance, progressive educational thinking and child protection practices in Britain? There emerged several basic elements drawn from Venezuelan practice which have come to structure Sistema Scotland's approach. The program should be:

4.2.3.1 *Immersive*

In order for the program to have a significant effect upon the community children must be able to take part in music-making for a significant number of hours each week. At present in the Big Noise, Raploch, children attend three or four sessions after school for a couple of hours or more each day during term time, and four days a week during holiday periods, in addition to the curriculum provision of musicianship lessons, one-to-one, and group instrumental teaching during the school day. The Big Noise is immersive too in its all-age provision. Baby Noise involves the youngest members of the community in music-making, who then move into the nursery classes, where Big Noise musicians lead several sessions each week. Curriculum and after-school music-making during the primary years leads on to after-school involvement at secondary level. An adult orchestra, "The Noise," provides adult members of the community with the opportunity to learn to play an instrument within the context of an orchestra, just as the young people do.

4.2.3.2 *Inclusive*

Big Noise is open to every child in Raploch. Those attending the three schools on the community campus receive curriculum sessions with Big Noise musicians from Nursery through to Primary 2 (6–7 year olds), choosing a stringed instrument to learn and joining the after-school classes by the end of their P2 year. Pupils who don't opt to play at this stage still take part in musicianship lessons in curriculum time, and are offered the opportunity again and again to learn an instrument, especially woodwind, brass, and percussion, which are introduced at P5 (9–10 year olds). Children who may need to take time out of full sessions, due to issues of challenging behavior, are always given another chance. Sistema Scotland staff are committed to making sure that every child is encouraged to participate, and go to extraordinary lengths to make this possible. Inclusive practice also means providing for children with all levels of additional support needs. In Raploch children from the Castleview School who are able, play in the mainstream ensembles using Figure notes, for instance, a specially adapted form of musical notation (see http://www.drakemusicscotland.org/figurenotes/). Children with more profound needs take part in curriculum sessions led by Big Noise musicians using various ingenious technologies to facilitate music-making.

The commitment to inclusivity is particularly significant in the light of Alexandra Lamont's research (Lamont, 1992) showing that primary school children have a tendency to identify themselves as "non-musicians" if they see others around them going out of curriculum lessons for instrumental instruction, but will think of themselves as "musicians" if there is no instrumental provision in the school, but the class participates together in general music lessons.[2] This effect increases as extra-curricular opportunities widen in secondary school. Big Noise's commitment to involve everyone in learning an instrument would seem significant in ensuring that most children grow up with a developing sense of themselves as a "musician," able to make music and therefore access the benefits this brings, especially its agential potential.

4.2.3.3 *Long term*

In order to bring about generational change it is imperative that Sistema Scotland establishes a permanent presence in the communities we work within, breaking out of models of fixed term funding and the "project" mentality, which soon moves on to another site and leaves behind only short-term benefits.

4.2.3.4 *Pedagogically pluralist*

No one particular methodology is predominant in the Big Noise, as in Venezuela's Sistema. Early year's musicianship and instrumental learning draw on, for instance, Colour Strings, Kodaly, Suzuki, Dalcroze, Paul Rolland. The musical director is responsible for a coherent approach to children's musical learning, which takes elements from all of these methods and ensures an effective pathway of progression.

4.2.3.5 *Musically excellent*

The Sistema Scotland team works on the basis that musical excellence and social transformation proceed hand in hand, that high aspirations and excellence in teaching and learning are key to change.

42.2.4 The vision of the Big Noise

Underpinning these approaches to teaching and learning at Big Noise are the convictions that:

- *Music-making is primarily a social activity* and that the orchestra is a healthy model in which to learn to build relationships, musical or otherwise, and to thrive as an individual within a community. Primary 1 (ages 5 and 6 years old) and Primary 2 (ages 6 and 7 years old) children learn how to behave as part of an orchestral section, learning basic technical skills in a group setting, hearing the collective sounds of the orchestra from the outset, and locating their own contribution as part of a larger whole, interdependent, complex and rich.

---

[2] The dichotomy between "musicians" and "non-musicians" in Lamont's study, however, has been criticized for "imposing a standard cultural identity" that the children [in the study] had not themselves internalized, and for an inappropriate emphasis on the learning of an instrument as an indicator of identity as a musician (Gracyck, 2004:3).

- *Music-making is agential;* that through participating in music-making together members of the community are empowered to bring about change in their own lives and to transform their community.

These tenets shape how we might approach notions of music-making and the developing of musical identities within the Big Noise. The vision is a communal one. The aim is gradual, long-term transformation of a community from a position of marginalization, from the perception of having no "voice" to become a beacon of good practice nationally and internationally in music-making and in community engagement. The emphasis is as much upon how people see themselves together as musicians, as upon how individuals develop their own sense of themselves. Musical identities emerge through relationships with others as music is experienced together.

42.3 DISCUSSION: RELATING
THROUGH MUSIC-MAKING

The building up of relationships, through music-making, which have the potential to bring about change within a community, resonates with Christopher Small's conception of "musicking" as "modelling ideal relationships" (Small, 1998):

> The act of musicking establishes in the place where it is happening a set of relationships, and it is in those relationships that the meaning of the act lies. (Small, 1998, p. 13)

More problematic for many in the music education research community is the Venezuelan Sistema commitment to the model of the orchestra as a vehicle for social change, alongside the prioritizing of the musical language of the Western European art music tradition through which the notion of the orchestra emerged (Baker, 2014). Small's notion of "musicking" emerges alongside his critique of the Western art music concert practices, which he interprets as preventing communication between the participants of a "music event," with the audience remaining "inert," practices which Small sees as dehumanizing. Yet Odendaal et al. suggest:

> In a more extensive sense, it should make no difference what musical–cultural genre is in question: there can be practices of musicking in any culture, and it is the task of general music educators to help people to participate in them. While Small builds his argument against dehumanizing musical practices on the empirical differences he finds between (certain) African or Afrodiasporic and European musical systems of agency, his more general argument seems to be that whatever music we are involved with, there is always a possibility to "do" it in a way that promotes ethical relationships between people immersed in community life. (Odendaal et al, 2014, p. 172)

The structures of the professional, classical music world may be seen by some as "oppressive" and "capitalist," and the working conditions of orchestral musicians as "authoritarian" and "infantalizing," (Baker, 2014, p. 115; Jourdan, 2015b), and there is little doubt that the practices of the profession are ripe for re-envisaging. Learning to play instrumental music in the context of the orchestra, however, is a mode of musicking in Scottish and British culture from which young people from Raploch have in the past been excluded. It is the possibility of helping them to " 'do' it in a way that promotes ethical relationships between people immersed in community life," which motivates the staff members of the Big Noise.

The provision of opportunities to learn to make music within the context of the orchestra provides members of the Raploch community with tools or "affordances" through which to create and inform their identities (Elliott and Silverman, Chapter 2). Elliott and Silverman ask, "can musics play a *positive* and unique role in the development and communication of various forms of identity?" This depends, they conclude, "on whether or not informal, non-formal, and/or formal music learning processes and contexts are *ethical* or not." The responsibility for ensuring *positive* and *ethical* musical identity formation rests on the shoulders of *ethical* music makers, teachers, and community musicians of all kinds. (Elliott and Silverman, Chapter 2). They propose a "praxial philosophy of musical identity," which ensures that "critically-reflective thinking-and-doing for the positive transformation of people's everyday lives and situations" is at the heart of the musician's teaching and learning of musical skills. It is not enough to be involved in teaching techniques of music-making, or information about music. These must be harnessed to a commitment to an "ethic of care," in pursuit of human flourishing—Aristotle's *eudaimonia*:

Providing that we conceptualize and engage with musics as musical *praxes*—a "move" that emphasizes the critically reflective and ethical dimensions of music making and listening—all forms of music making afford numerous means of pursuing *eudaimonia*. (Chapter 2)

So how do the musicians of the Big Noise engage in musical *praxes*, encouraging members of the Raploch community to develop positive and ethical musical identity formation? The next part of the chapter explores the perspectives of a founder team member of the Big Noise as she reflects on her own musical identity and those she sees developing amongst community members around her in Raploch.

42.4 A MUSICIAN'S PERSPECTIVE

Emma (a pseudonym) was one of the seven original string players employed by Sistema Scotland to set up the Big Noise in the community of Raploch. Emma's reflections on her own developing musical identity as she grew up making music give an insight into how she works to help the young people of the Big Noise develop their own musical identities together and into what kind of orientation musicians coming to work in the Big Noise must develop.

42.4.1 Music-making within a community

Emma's early experience, learning the violin at school from the age of seven, was from the outset of belonging to many different and often overlapping musical communities. She recalls:

> By the time I was a teenager I would say I was doing my own version of Sistema, where I was having violin lessons, piano lessons, I played percussion in a brass band, percussion in a concert band, violin in the local authority string orchestra, in the symphony orchestra, then also in the county youth orchestra. Then I played in my school orchestras and sang in my school choirs. Every day I was doing between two and four hours of music.

She remembers her first youth orchestra rehearsal when she was thirteen, the moment when she felt completely caught up with the shared experience of playing in an orchestra, when "suddenly it felt like the musical world opened." She highlights several facets of this experience. Firstly it involved "playing music to a high standard." Secondly she was playing alongside young people of varying ages and looked up to those of university age who might act as role models. Thirdly there was a plethora of different sorts of music-making going on:

> There were loads of people doing all sorts of different sorts of music, so the brass players were in a jazz band...

Fourthly she was being tutored by professional players who set exacting standards. Fifthly, the orchestra rehearsed in the local concert hall, a venue which she found inspiring and represented the pinnacle of music-making for her at the time. Finally she felt that music-making "was suddenly cool" and that at some deep level she "belonged."

42.4.2 Belonging

As she came to work alongside the children of Raploch at the Big Noise it was this feeling of belonging, of being at home, that she wanted to encourage in these young people. She recalled her own school days where as a teenager she had "the usual teenage insecurities" but that "when I went to orchestra everyone was doing the same thing and everyone was so welcoming." She describes the tell-tale signs that children feel they belong at the Big Noise:

You get more of a feeling of what Big Noise is about when it's the holidays. You have children who turn up an hour before their sessions are on, because they want to come and help out with the small kids or they just want to hang out there. Or if we're doing individual lessons in the afternoon they know they can pop in and see us.

The Big Noise has become a place to belong, to feel at home.

42.4.3 Learning together

Emma's own experience shapes how she values the relationships developing amongst the Big Noise children. She describes the quality of relationships she witnesses and the impact this has upon the way the young people learn together:

Every new piece we do, or new scale, they all want to get it. They're very driven but in a group way. They're very supportive of each other. My favourite thing is taking sectional rehearsals, because you are with between five and ten children and it's amazing the way they support and encourage each other. I can't believe how focused they can stay that late in the day—sometimes 5pm in the evening, the last thing.

The discipline of learning to play instrumental music together is fostering supportive relationships which enable group learning, where young people spur one another on to achieve. Emma comments, "I hope they're getting that real group satisfaction of knowing they can achieve something individually but also as a group." In the context of a sectional or full orchestral rehearsal the sound of the whole provides a sense of achievement every bit as motivating as individual successes and can spur the young people on to concentrate and persevere in a sustained manner, even when they might be tired.

42.4.4 Working hard, but being relaxed

There is little doubt that the children of the Big Noise, Raploch have had to work very hard. June 2012 saw them taking part in an outdoor, televised concert as part of the Cultural Olympiad, alongside the Simon Bolivar Orchestra from Venezuela, which required huge efforts in preparation. Regular side-by-side concerts with the BBC Scottish Symphony Orchestra involve learning demanding repertoire. The widening reputation of the Big Noise has led to a constant stream of visitors and invitations to take part in high-profile events, and the young players have become accustomed to having to perform in diverse circumstances and venues, whether to MSP's in the Holyrood Parliament building, to the Queen at Stirling Castle, in national brass competitions or in local care homes with elderly members of the Raploch community.

Emma described the atmosphere after the Big Concert of the summer of 2012:

> We'd worked so hard for it. Everyone was uplifted, relaxed and just happy. They knew it was an amazing experience but also I think these things have just become part of their lives. My feeling afterwards wasn't that it was a come-down or a flat period. They just seemed relaxed and happy. Sounds a bit boring, but … that's just what they do. At Big Noise they do Big Stuff!

The mountain-top experiences of June 2012 had been both treasured and taken simply as something to be expected when you play with the Big Noise. They had given the children confidence without leaving them deflated afterwards, part of their ongoing development together as young musicians.

Being "relaxed" is significant here; many of the children of the Big Noise experience significant levels of stress in their home lives and some are young carers living with responsibilities beyond their years. Providing an environment where young people can work hard, feel they belong while achieving beyond their expectations, and experience affirmation from musicians who have high aspirations for them, brings benefits in all sorts of areas of their lives. Here, musical identities are being formed within a supportive environment where learning occurs together and successes are shared, providing a healthy basis for young people's developing sense of themselves as musicians, avoiding some of the pressures of individual performance success experienced in other educational contexts.

42.4.5 Getting excited about music

Emma remembers vividly when she first felt inspired and motivated by music-making:

> The first time I thought music was totally amazing was my first rehearsal with my county youth orchestra when I was thirteen; it was on the stage at the [local concert venue] and we were playing Glazunov's *The Seasons*. I just thought it was beautiful, and as soon as we started to play it sounded good. I couldn't believe it. That was the moment when I got the most buzz out of playing. A really changing moment for me.

Emma was captured by the music itself, its beauty, its power to move and the excellence of the orchestra's playing together. This was a transformational moment for her, motivational and formative in terms of her future life choices. Emma explains how she endeavors to share her thrill of music-making with the young people in Raploch. How at certain moments, often catching her by surprise, she can inspire the children, or can see others doing so. These are precious times, unpredictable and fleeting, but with the potential to be transformational:

> I do tell them how I feel about music. I like to think that I'm getting them excited about music, and that they're feeling that excitement inside them. You can't do that

every day working at Big Noise. It's not that you pick your moments because I don't think you can, but when you have those opportunities with them you've got to make it happen … And you can tell the kids are getting really fired up about it. If I'm lit up by the music then they'll respond to that. And they do.

I asked Emma how she feels about the criticism from some quarters that Sistema is introducing Western European art music to communities instead of drawing out their own forms of music-making. She responded:

> Still, if you give the Big noise children an i-pod they're most likely to put on pop music—not always though, these days. I don't think they had pre-conceptions about the music when they were 7 years old, when they started. And now when they're 7-year-olds they see 12-year-olds playing it and they are inspired. They'll have their individual likes and dislikes with pieces. I hope that classical music is a starting point for them. We've done some improvisation with them. Some of them have been to the Tolbooth (in Stirling) to do Scottish traditional workshops. It's important to me not to get too hung up about it. I just think it's a waste of time worrying about it being classical music—they'll decide what they'll like and what they don't like. It works really well for us.

Emma's perspective is that "classical" musical education gives building blocks through which to learn techniques, practices and to develop aesthetic sensitivity, which can be transferred to other contexts, just as the wider social skills developed may be, to open up a whole world of music-making. Young people can use these basic musical skills to explore and take on other musical identities.

42.4.6 The responsibility of the Big Noise team

Emma explains how she sees the responsibility of the Big Noise staff towards the children in terms of their development in terms of musical learning and sense of themselves as musicians:

> You can't make the children have a belief in themselves. We have to set a really good example of ourselves but it's only by being positive with the children, by working them hard, by showing ourselves to be good musicians who care about music, that's our responsibility. I think then the children will come along with us, but they have to decide themselves, and we can only set up the situation.

Instead of focusing explicitly upon young people's sense of themselves, their self-esteem and confidence, Emma feels that Big Noise musicians create an environment where children can belong, work hard and be encouraged to enter more deeply into the richness of music-making through the guiding experience of older players, for whom music has already opened up whole worlds.

42.4.7 Transformational benefits

Emma reflects:

> I hope they're getting that real group satisfaction of knowing they can achieve something individually but also as a group. I hope that outside Big Noise they will be able to put that into other parts of their lives. The commitment and hard work and working with people will pay off. I think if you can really immerse yourself in music practice, if you can take that and use that in other places such as your school studies or your work when you're there, that it has such benefits.

She highlights the discipline of working hard at honing a skill, the ability to work alongside and in cooperation with others, and the commitment to persevere and to remain part of something which the children of Raploch are learning, skills which they can take with them into any other part of their lives. Developing identities as musicians spill over into a wider sense of self, preparing the young people for successful future life experiences, outcomes reported in the findings of the recent evaluation by Glasgow Centre for Population Health (GCPH, 2015).

Emma recognizes the wider benefits within the community of the Big Noise's introduction of music-making together. Individual families have already become caught up: "You see whole families now that are so committed." She explains that the wider community at Raploch is characterized by a caring ethos:

> Right from the beginning when you went into Raploch you could tell it was a very caring community where people care so deeply for their and other people's children and they know each other. It actually feels in some ways like a very old-fashioned community where if you need to find a specific child you can easily ask someone in the community, "Have you seen so-and-so's kids?" and they can often tell you where that child was or what house they were playing at, which number it was, and actually, that's the thing that people say is lacking in so many communities.

Emma believes that the Big Noise has given this capacity for care for one another within the community a new, agential aspect:

> What I feel has happened with Big Noise is that it's given them an opportunity to do something with that—they can develop themselves now with other skills. If they do really care about the community they can find other ways to get involved. Some of the adults are playing in the Noise—it's so brilliant to be able to be part of something if you've not been able to join in something for a long time, or felt the confidence to. It's so good that it's happening in this community where I think people care a lot but have maybe lacked the confidence to go outside of where they are.

The shared social and cultural capital experienced within the structures of the Big Noise have helped to open up possibilities for community members "to go outside of where they are:"

> The volunteer programme has been great because it has brought so many people from different backgrounds together, and I think it's good for everyone, wherever they are. You can't deny—Big Noise has opened out the world a lot to people from Raploch. If you bring three hundred people over from Venezuela ... that has to open the world up, whether you live here or whether you're a volunteer who's been actively involved getting the kids prepared. It can't not!

Volunteers from both within and outside the community facilitate the Big Noise program through support in every area of its functioning, and bring all kinds of life experience to their work and to the lives of the young people of Raploch. The Noise, the adult orchestra, is made up of parents, grandparents, volunteers (some of whom are retired professionals from outside the community) and teachers from the three Raploch schools. The diversity of backgrounds enables both a sharing of social capital and a levelling of social standing as everyone learns to play an instrument from scratch within the community of the orchestra.

42.4.8 A fresh community identity through music-making

Raploch is gaining a new and very different reputation from the one it has had in recent years, as it becomes known around Scotland, the UK and around the Sistema communities of the world for good practice and pioneering work. The partner organization in New Zealand has named its first symphony orchestra "Raploch," just as at the Big Noise the "Rinconada" name expresses the close links with Raploch's twin *nucleo* in Caracas, Venezuela. Emma sees that the community has achieved a huge amount for their children now to be taking their places alongside those normally seen as being in the "mainstream" of social life:

> People were already, before we came along, very proud of their children. But when everyone's talked down your community then it's difficult. Their children can achieve so much. I'm thinking about things like National Youth Orchestra of Scotland, where they sit amongst children from all over the country. They can really hold their own, and everyone is so proud of that.

Emma feels passionate about the achievements of the young people of the Raploch. What might be seen as an entitlement by those from more affluent backgrounds is hard-won in this community. It's not enough just to provide the same opportunities as others have. Emma highlights the need for interventions of affirmative action in disadvantaged communities in order to bring about social change.

42.4.9 Towards the future

Emma looks forward with hope to a future in Raploch where the community continues to be transformed through a broadening of horizons, a confident engagement with the wider world and where people have employment:

> I do think there is a lot of confidence in Raploch—about families, about people. They are very strong people who live there. They are proud of Big Noise and of it being there, of themselves and of their children. I think the parents know there's something very special going on. I would be delighted if many of these kids still lived in Raploch when they were older, but that more people work again and the regeneration flourishes. That would be brilliant. If they can keep that spirit that already exists. If they can always keep the character that was there. That is there already. But have broad horizons and more opportunities.

The vision of the Big Noise is not to take young people who show particular talent out of their community to thrive in a place of more opportunity, but rather to help people build on their community's strengths and transform life-trajectories of people within Raploch, allowing for the stability and commitment that Emma values so highly.

42.5 EXPLORING NEW PROFESSIONAL IDENTITIES

42.5.1 Widening of musical identities through skills training

The transformational benefits of Big Noise extend further. The musicians who come to work in Raploch benefit from a rich and varied on-going program of training. Emma reflects:

> It's been a total gift, being able to learn all those skills and being much more confident in those. It's been one of the best bits of musical training I've ever had, because you've learned so much—everyone's been each other's teachers, especially at the start. And going to Venezuela, to Finland, and to Auckland. You learn from other teachers. It's just the best thing ever!

The ethos of learning as a community is evident here amongst the staff too—Emma highly values the experience of observing others teaching to learn from their diverse methods and styles. As she represented the Big Noise around the world she found that she benefitted hugely from the shared experience of other practitioners.

Through the many-faceted nature of their jobs many discover areas of their own musical selves previously unrecognized or under-used:

> Trying to problem-solve—one thing that was great for me was that I didn't actually realise I had the skill, but I've written quite a lot of music for the children. The first piece I wrote came out of me trying to find how to sort out a technical music reading problem—trying to get the children who were struggling to read music. So I came up with a mixture of bowing exercise and reading. It had a crazy dance. It was just supposed to be a little exercise but it turned into a piece. That was great fun—I'd arranged music before, but if someone asked me "Can you compose?" I would have been "No way!" But I've done quite a bit of it now. I feel pleased about that. I've discovered something new.

Musicians at the Big Noise are engaged in exploring music-making in this rich context of relationship and community, becoming more accomplished and holistic in their range of skills, musical and otherwise. This stands in stark contrast to established practices within the orchestral profession, from which many Big Noise musicians are drawn. Here, a static conception of what it means to be a player traditionally allows for little personal or professional development within the context of the ensemble.

Emma recalls how her own development post-conservatoire led her into practice as a community musician where, through various free-lance and job opportunities, she could be more autonomous than as an orchestral player, developing her own projects, "Really exploring the things you were interested in." This helped her to discern her own vision for music-making:

> I'd thought of primary teaching, but I didn't like the idea of seeing kids for the year and then not seeing them ... All of a sudden I was thinking about what I wanted to do, what I really cared about in music. So then when the Big Noise job did come up I realised it was what I wanted to do and it fitted all the things that I cared about. I care so much about it. It's become more and more important to me.

42.5.2 Stability and long-term commitment

Stability and long-term commitment have become central tenets of Emma's vision for her own practice of music-making. She embraced the opportunity to develop permanent relationships with members of one particular community to whom she could be wholeheartedly committed into the future:

Doing music in a community setting but a community that you get to stay with and stick with and see people develop year on year—that's the main thing for me really. There are lots of bonuses in working for Big Noise but that's the main thing, actually working there for a long time.

42.5.3 Reorienting professional attitudes: hospitality

Emma has developed a sense of herself as a musician who is no longer constrained by some of the attitudes and practices tacitly passed on within the context of the conservatoire training:

> I wish sometimes that musicians would worry less about the usual musician things about always having to be the better than the next person, being embarrassed if you see yourself presented in such a way, or having to talk yourself up. I do feel that those things don't matter to me anymore. I feel really committed to what I do and it's really special to be in this situation with this community and these people and I just wish that more musicians could feel the same.

Emma identifies the ways in which professional identity is recast in a context where musical learning takes place in community, and where young musicians' sense of their own development goes hand in hand with that of the whole orchestral community.

This fresh conception of professional musical identity was witnessed in Raploch at midsummer in 2012. The players of the Simon Bolivar Orchestra demonstrated an extraordinary ability to reach out hospitably to their side-by-side Raploch juniors during the rehearsals and performances of the Big Concert, on 21st June 2012. As the Bolivar players leaned in towards the Scottish children, nurturing and affirming them in a physical and emotional commitment which required no language, they gently drew them into an encounter with the music's expression, and through their physical warmth and presence affirmed and taught them, encouraging risk-taking in learning, which brought undreamed-of achievements for the younger players as their vibrant sound supported and did not mask the musical "voice" of the young Scots.

42.5.4 It's a different way of doing it

Traditional benchmarks won't be found in Raploch, Emma suggests, with our commitment to inclusivity and learning in community. These are elements which conventionally, conservatoire-trained professional musicians may find hard to accept, finding the tension between achieving high musical standards and nurturing young people within their community setting difficult to negotiate:

> The way you learn to be a great musician—it still has to happen. I'm not saying that those things should go away. You have to go over the difficult bits again and again and

you're aspiring to get as close to perfect as you can. But if you go to Big Noise Raploch that's not the only thing you are going to see. I'm not saying there won't be good players in the end—of course there already are. But we work in large groups with varying individual standards. You're also working with a community who are relearning about long-term commitment and things like that. Everything you're doing is actually quite hard and it's not going to be perfect. That suits me fine because I do feel very strongly about it. But I think it's so difficult for many musicians to accept.

Emma believes that the Big Noise musicians must learn to look for quality in different ways, "And I don't think those things are in musicians' heads, or are encouraged." A fresh orientation is required of the Big Noise musicians as they work within the Raploch community.

The discipline of learning an instrument, of learning to play with others as part of a greater whole, of becoming excited about music, is still central to the children's experience of music-making, just as it always has been in the traditional conservatoire model. Yet at the Big Noise there is a richer context than merely achieving performing goals. Emma sees "success" as meaning that the children of Big Noise, Raploch feel they belong, are happy, thriving, working hard, becoming motivated to stretch themselves and to develop resilience, being part of everything, and that these things are achieved collectively, through music-making.

42.6 Discussion: music-making as ethical encounter

Emma's reflections give examples of ethical relating through music-making amongst the children of Raploch as they spur each other on to learn in groups, through the attentiveness of staff and volunteers as they nurture young people in their musical learning and expression, and in the inclusiveness with which opportunities for music-making are structured. Emma's perspectives suggest that music-making has become for the Raploch community a means of retooling people for engagement with the wider world, a mode of relating which enables members of the community to enter areas of life previously seen as inaccessible (such as the National Youth Orchestras of Scotland).

Just as Elliott and Silverman consider all forms of music-making to afford numerous means of pursuing *eudaimonia* (Chapter 2), Wayne Bowman writes of music and musical instruction as *practices*: "as rich ethical resources for exploring and developing potentials of character, identity, and selfhood" (Bowman, 2014, p. 6), "in and through which people wrestle with and seek to answer the vitally important educational question, What kind of person is it good to be?" (Bowman, 2014, p. 3). Developing a musical identity becomes a means of finding out what sort of people we want to be and to become. At the heart of who we are, and who we become, is the question of our orientation to others around us.

42.6.1 Music-making as encountering "infinity in the face of the Other"

Taking a step further back into philosophical reflection, the work of Emmanuel Levinas, French-Jewish philosopher of the twentieth century, points towards a radical ethical orientation which challenges conceptions of self and identity. Levinas' critique of Western philosophy forces us to recognize our "totalizing" tendency to make others the "same" as ourselves, to neutralize difference, to categorize in order to understand and to dominate. Levinas draws out a spectrum which stretches from Totality to Infinity in terms of our possible philosophical orientation towards "difference." For Levinas infinity is glimpsed in the face of the Other, the face which cannot be reduced to a set of features, nor to a category, but which overflows all our attempts to categorize and contain (Levinas, 1969, p. 194-7, 220), "the epiphany of the face" (Levinas, 1969, p. 51). (For a fuller discussion of the thinking of Levinas as a lens to explore ethical practice in music education, see Jourdan, 2012 and 2015).

Levinas sought to replace "ontology" with "ethics" as the first impulse in our thinking and in our lives together. Before all other ways of conceptualizing and understanding the world and our lives within it, our primary and enduring responsibility is to the Other, radically different from ourselves, in whose "infinity of the face" we recognize a profound, ethical call. The Other for Levinas denotes a spectrum from the person next to me to notions of "God" as infinitely different from me, never to be grasped in their entirety, impossible to categorize, understand and therefore dominate and control. The Other stands in a relation of teaching to us, bringing me "more than I contain." Receiving from the Other, being taught, is "to have the idea of infinity" (Levinas, 1969, p. 51). Levinas exhorts us to a radical openness and responsibility, an outward-reaching orientation which seeks the face of the Other, describing the act of teaching as "the presence of infinity breaking into the closed circle of totality" (Levinas, 1969, p. 171).

Music(s) and music-making may be seen in terms of "infinity" (following the thinking of philosopher of education Paul Standish, 2008, p. 64), which in Levinas' thought is opposed to the "totality," which limits and contains, an infinity into which Emma and her colleagues seek to draw the Raploch children, and into which the members of the Simon Bolivar Orchestra helped the children enter more deeply, as they played side-by-side. Music-making is a mode of encounter with the other, infinite in its possibilities. With Levinas' thinking as an ethical underpinning, music-making becomes a mode of practice available to a community of "looking into the face of the Other" and heeding the call to responsibility glimpsed in the face of each other. As we learn to make music together, handling parameters of sound and expression, we develop an aesthetic sensitivity which enables us to look, and to discern the face of the other (For a fuller discussion of how notions of aesthetic and praxial are brought together using philosophical tools from Levinas, see Jourdan, 2015).

42.6.2 Music-making as ethical impulse

Music is frequently and popularly conceived of as in some way functioning as a language, accessible to everyone everywhere. Levinas suggested that language is at its first impulse an ethical act, a reaching out to the other before any communication of meaning is intended. Using this lens to consider music-making, and particularly in the light of the holistic, relational practice of Small's "musicking," might we conceive of music-making as at its first impulse an ethical act, as a reaching out, breaking out of our own totalities of self in order to come into a hospitable encounter with others, in an orientation of asymmetric responsibility?

42.6.3 Music-making as agential

In developing Levinas' thinking in this way, to make music may be seen as firstly an intention to reach outside of ourselves to look into the face of the other. The children of Raploch experienced the "reaching out" to them of the Venezuelan musicians who visited in June 2012 and who played alongside them, leaning in towards them and drawing out the children's musical expression, beyond all their expectations, through their nurturing attentiveness. Levinas' infinite openness to the other, and the recognition of our ethical responsibility in the face of the other as the central practice in our lives together, points towards a conception of identity as empowering and agential, offering a way of approaching music-making in Raploch which resists totalizing practices of categorization, limitation, and marginalization.

42.7 REFLECTION

42.7.1 Musicking otherwise

Suggestive of what Lee Higgins, drawing on Levinas' pupil, Jacques Derrida, describes as community musicians' practice of "hospitality," "a togetherness of one face toward another" (Higgins, 2012, p. 16), the Venezuelans went further and demonstrated an asymmetrical, Levinasian taking-of-responsibility for the younger Other. These musicians revealed a wholly other way of being a musician. They looked into the faces of the Raploch children, heeded the ethical call they perceived there and took on a generous and hospitable responsibility for their nurture and flourishing, as they played together that week in June 2012.

What would the orchestral music profession look like if this sort of radical hospitality characterized practices of player and conductor, of composer and audience, where the initial impetus was to reach out to invite the listener to enter ever more deeply into the infinity of the music, and where looking into the face of the other, practices of facing, re-oriented rehearsals and transformed performance? (For a description of working as a professional player, with a conductor seen as taking on a Levinasian orientation, see Jourdan, 2013.)

These reflections take us to the heart of what it means to make music. Music-making becomes embedded in relationship, in keeping with Christopher Small's conception of musicing, but goes further. It becomes "musicking Otherwise" where, following Levinas, music-making's infinity is allowed to break through totalities which have constrained and alienated. Big Noise needs staff members who have hospitable musical identities which overflow the conventional outlook of the "classical" player, musicians who are committed to ways of making music which build relationship and take care of individuals in community, as the children and young people of the Big Noise develop technique and expressive ability, and as each community member explores their own developing sense of themselves as musicians.

References

Baker, G. (2014). *El Sistema: Orchestrating Venezuela's youth.* Oxford: Oxford University Press.

Bowman, W. (2014). The ethical significance of music-making. *Music Mark Magazine,* 3, 3–6.

Derrida, J. (2000). *On Hospitality.* Stanford, CA: Stanford University Press.

Glasgow Centre for Population Health, Education Scotland and Glasgow Caledonian University. 2015. *Evaluating Sistema Scotland—initial findings report.* Available at: http://www.gcph.co.uk/assets/0000/5096/Sistema_evaluation_June_2015.pdf

Gracyk, T. (2004). Does everyone have a musical identity? Reflections on musical identities. *Action, Criticism, and Theory for Music Education,* 3(1), (March 2004).

Higgins, L. (2012). *Community music: in theory and practice.* Oxford: Oxford University Press.

Jourdan, K. (2015a). *Through the lens of Levinas: An ethnographically-informed case study of pupils' practices of facing in music-making.* Unpublished doctoral dissertation, University of Cambridge.

Jourdan, K. (2015b). Book review: El Sistema: orchestrating Venezuela's youth, by Geoffrey Baker. *Scottish Journal of Performance,* 2 (2) (June 2015).

Jourdan, K. (2013). Musicking otherwise: ethical encounters in music-making. *National Association of Music Educators' Magazine,* Issue 1, 34–8.

Jourdan, K. (2012). Towards an ethical music education? Looking through the lens of Levinas. *Music Education Research,* 14(3), 381–99.

Lamont, A. (2002). Musical identities and the school environment. In:R.Macdonald, D., Hargreaves, & D.Miell (Eds.) *Musical identities,* pp. 41–59. Oxford: Oxford University Press.

Levinas, E. (1969). *Totality and infinity: an essay on exteriority,* transl. Alphonso Lingis. Pittsburgh PA: Duquesne University Press.

Small, C. (1998). *Musicking: The meanings and performing and listening.* Middletown, CT: Wesleyan University Press.

Standish, P. (2008). Levinas and the language of the curriculum. In: Egéa-Kuehne D. (Ed.) *Levinas and education: at the intersection of faith and reason,* Routledge international studies in the philosophy of education No. 18, pp. 56–66. New York, NY: Routledge.

CHAPTER 43

....

MUSICAL IDENTITIES IN AUSTRALIA AND SOUTH KOREA AND NEW IDENTITIES EMERGING THROUGH SOCIAL MEDIA AND DIGITAL TECHNOLOGY

....

MYUNG-SOOK AUH AND ROBERT WALKER

43.1 SIMILARITY AND DIVERSITY IN MUSICAL IDENTITIES IN AUSTRALIA AND SOUTH KOREA

....

THE choice of these two countries may at first appear unexpected. However, Australia and South Korea, at this point in the 21st century, share some surprising similarities, together with close links in trade, educational and research collaboration, as well as personal connections through Korean in-migration to Australia and the choice of Australian schools for many Korean teenagers. Geographically and ethnically Australia and South Korea are distinctly different yet they share important similarities. Today, both are very similar demographically in that most people are aged under 54 (Australia, 73.8%, cited in Australian Bureau of Statistics 2013; South Korea, 77%, cited in Index-OMundi, 2013).

Each has a similar educational provision from kindergarten to university fed by both public and private schools, although the OECD reports that a much higher proportion of young people currently attend university in Korea (72%) than in

Australia (37%). Each country has special music schools for nurturing the musically talented, and each has strong university music departments which focus on western classical music performance. Significant numbers of internationally acclaimed musicians who perform in the world's opera houses and symphony halls are produced by each country, as well as popular musicians who are both special to their country and yet attain international status. Each country is ruled by a vibrant democratic government where free speech, freedom of association are enshrined in law.

Both countries have long histories stretching back thousands of years, and both have been influenced by stronger powers from outside, and both have been colonized by a foreign power in recent times, Australia more extensively than Korea. However, major differences between the two lie in the status and role of indigenous inhabitants. In Korea, the original inhabitants have remained in control of the political, social, and cultural evolution of their country for several thousand years despite a strong and abiding influence from China and colonization by Japan from 1910 to 1945. The population of Korea is predominantly mono-cultural.

Australia was colonized by the British from 1788, from which time the Australian Aboriginal inhabitants have been subsumed into a new British-controlled political and socio-cultural system. The population increasingly comprised immigrants, initially from the United Kingdom, but more recently from across the world to form the complex multicultural society which characterizes Australia today. The Australian Aboriginal inhabitants lost their autonomy and their control over their land during this process. Nevertheless, Australian Aboriginal culture has survived in its music, dance, stories, and ceremonial, if not in its original political status.

Historically, a major influence in Korean life and culture has spread from China, especially through the teachings of Confucius. Chinese was the main language in Korea until King Sejong (1418–1442) invented a new language, *Hangul*, which became the official language in 1443. During the Japanese colonization the Japanese language and culture was imposed, attempting to eradicate several thousand years of Korean cultural evolution. Despite the destruction of major historical artefacts and buildings, the defeat of Japan by the Allies in 1945 ended that attempt at colonization. However, the Soviet Union having declared war on Japan at the end of World War Two resulted in Korea being divided with the North under Soviet control and the South under US control. A highly destructive war broke out in June, 1950, lasting until 1953, when a devastated Korea was permanently divided into two separate countries, each of which required significant rebuilding.

The North became a communist totalitarian state, while the South returned to its long historical traditions, developing into a democratic state, as well as retaining the impact and influence of 19th century western missionaries, which included western music. The Japanese developed a love of western classical music influenced by 19th century missionaries, as well as by German orchestral musicians fleeing Nazi Germany during the 1930s and 1940s. South Korea developed western musical practices in its educational system, and 30% of the population became Christian.

Australia has a long history of Aboriginal cultural development across the continent, and a recent history of colonization by the United Kingdom. The British colonization of Australia began in January, 1788, when the first migrants arrived from Britain. The Aboriginal inhabitants were gradually subdued and British political, social, and cultural norms established as the identity of Australia. For over one hundred years from this time on Australia was built as a country founded in British in-migration which, by the 1970s, had become multicultural.

Opportunities in music education in each country today are surprisingly similar, especially in regard to what music is valued at both secondary and tertiary levels. The secondary and tertiary education systems in both countries have a strong leaning towards western classical music, and in neither is there any acknowledgement in curriculum and qualifications offered nor in teacher training of any musical identities outside this tradition. In South Korea, as in Australia, there is a very strong tradition of private music lessons mostly in classical music performance. In both countries today the well-educated and affluent socio-economic groups in society identify with and support western classical music in education and in public symphony concerts and opera.

One major difference, however, lies in the socio-political and cultural role of historical music, which is specific to the unique culture of Korea. Korea has a long history of such music, whereas Australia adopted the musical identity of Great Britain, from the late 18th Century as a colony. The history of Korea can be traced back for several thousand years, during which time the special cultural life of Koreans was formed, with a strong influence of China and especially of Confucian philosophy. Despite external influences, Korea developed a specific identity in both music and language, especially over the last thousand years. There are long established traditions of both folk music, including *Pansori* (a folk drama performed by a single singer and drummer) and music for the royal courts of Korea involving large orchestras of percussion, strings, and wind instruments. The latter is due to the several thousand year-old history of royal courts where music, costume, and dance were important to royal ceremonial. This tradition remains at the heart of Korean identity and retains its position in ceremonial today at state events.

Australian history has also evolved over many thousands of years where Aborigines nurtured the land and travelled extensively over its vast distances. However, the British established a penal colony after landing at Botany Bay in 1788, and then proceeded to established colonies across the continent. Throughout the 19th and 20th centuries, Australia adopted British traditions of ceremonial and religious music exclusively as a British colony, with Aboriginal music and dance initially suppressed after colonization. Unlike in Korea, the music of the indigenous population in Australia has never supplanted that of the British traditions.

43.2 SOCIAL IDENTITY THEORY AND THE RESPECTIVE ROLES OF ENCULTURATION AND ACCULTURATION IN DEVELOPING IDENTITIES

Brown (2000, p. 768) explains that in part the origins of Social Identity Theory (SIT) began through the experiences of one of the originators who:

> drew much of his inspiration from his own personal experience of one of the last century's major social conflicts and was passionately concerned that social psychology should engage more closely with such societal problems as minority rights nationalism and racism.
>
> Tajfel, 1981, p. 160.

Since its inception, SIT has extended its application to include supporters of sports teams and more recently adherents to particular styles of music. It is clear, therefore, that SIT has many dimensions in its applications to real life, and some are far more crucial to the state of a nation or a group of nations than others. Supporting a particular sports team does not create serious socio-political tensions of a world-shattering nature. And neither does preferring one type of music to another. In which case, much of the research in SIT generally dealing with such matters as racism, socio-economic disadvantage, and political identities, is inapplicable to a study of group adherence to particular styles of music. However, within-group relations are important to individuals in the development of their sense of identity in relation to other group members and the group as a whole. Turner & Oakes (1986, p. 250) explain as follows:

> The group relations produced by social identity are psychologically creative in being the preconditions for the emergence of the social level of abstraction in the Categorization of self and others and the specific behavioural and normative content of social categories.

While it can be argued that individuals exist only within social groups, as Turner & Oakes (1986) do, and that their identity as such can only be defined within a particular social group. In the case of one musical identity described in this paper, for example the Australian Country and Western group, there exists a tacit understanding that individualism, as opposed to a mute surrender to group adherence, is a *sine quo non* characteristic of the hardy, outdoors, adherent of Australian Country Music. In which case, psychologically, both group and individualistic perceptions are equally important. An important point made by Turner & Oakes (1986, p. 239), citing Asch (1952) concerns the nature of individualism and the relationship between the individual and society:

> Individual minds are not individualistic in the ideological sense of being defined by some pre-social psychological dynamic but contain a "socially structured field"
>
> Asch, 1952, p. 253.

> society is in the individual as much as individuals are in society. Thus, the "nothing but" stance of individualism, that society contains nothing but individuals, is refuted and stood on its head by the argument that individuals are more than we had ever supposed, parts which can (psychologically) contain the whole.
>
> Asch 1952, p. 257.

In the case of individuals who identify with Australian Country Music, as explained below, there is a complex set of interactions relating to the individual and "society" or the social group. The individualism associated with this type of music is inextricably linked to a life-style—that of the Australian swagman, a transient laborer travelling alone looking for work, and the cattle drover, often working alone driving large numbers of cattle across hundreds of miles looking for grass to feed his cattle. Australian Country Music is full of songs and poems about such people, the most famous being "Waltzing Matilda". This type of individualism is psychologically *real* in the sense that such people as swagmen and drovers were only used to the individual life, historically, and to a great extent this is true today. There is little sense of the social group in such a life. Consequently, the fans of Australian Country Music, described below, are consciously adopting this notion of individualism, but vicariously in contemporary life as a means of identifying with the historical context of Australian life. The model for the Country Music fan is a clear sense of individualism against the elements (they had no house to come home to), but acted out within the social group of Country Music fans as a means of identification with the music and its connotations.

One mode of development of a specific musical identity is most obviously a product of enculturation. As one grows up in a specific cultural milieu, certain types and styles of music are common and favored by the social group within which one's family is active, or the social group to which an individual might belong through participation in musical activity such as a church choir, youth orchestra, or other musical organization. In these cases strong musical identities are formed, often from a young age, and these can be reinforced through time if both the family and social group remain committed to specific musical genres and styles.

However, the role of acculturation can be important, especially when the impact on young people, both pre-teens and teenagers, of the popular entertainment media is considered. As many commentators have pointed out, the entertainment media targets specific age and gender groups through music and associated advertising, which often includes attractive communications concerning life-styles, preferences, and empathetic messages. As Lewis (1992) points out, such communications can be seductive and helps to build allegiances between certain popular musicians and their music and individual pre-teens or teenage groups. Membership of a social group is important to both pre-teens and teenagers, and tends to enhance these allegiances because individual pre-teens and teenagers do not want to be seen as out of step with the group (Frith, 1996).

Turner, (1999), Turner & Reynolds, (2001), and Ellemers & Barreto, (2001) all favor a somewhat more complex conception of positive self-concept as a reflection of the ideologies and social values of the perceiver. Self-esteem is one relevant attribute contributing to a sense of identity, and in the case of identification with certain styles and genres of music this is clearly important. For example, identification in Australia with Country Music involves parading one's allegiance through adopting particular appropriate dress codes and modes of conversation using "Country Music" phrases. More importantly, such dress codes are not simply superficial adornment; they are necessary to the lifestyle of many in Australia who work on the huge sheep farms and cattle droving firms riding horses. Country Music in Australia is inextricably linked to people who live and work in the massive areas of grazing land in the outback and tablelands of New South Wales and Queensland. These people do not lack self-esteem, and are proud of their life-style and its contribution to Australian history through the poetry of writers such as Banjo Patterson and singers such as John Williamson. There is little or no sense of arrogance associated with lovers of Country Music.

43.3 Fandom and identity

Fandom has become a distinct identity structure in popular culture (Grossman, 1992; Connell & Gibson, 2003). Each fandom has one single identity and homogeneous fan members. Fandom is related to race, ethnic, gender, class distinctions, culture, and education. Fandom is an easy way to identify the fan members to the public; and using social media, this has become a part of daily life. The K-pop (Korean pop music) fandom members in Korea, for example, upload their imitations of K-pop performances or their reactions to the performers; then, other members comment on Twitter about them. Fandom promotes a group's favorite K-pop performers using Facebook and Twitter, and organizes instant concerts using *Flash Mob* approaches for attracting an instant audience for K-pop performances. Through the social media and the internet, K-pop fandoms are highly interactive with each other, and contribute to the success of specific K-pop performances. Some Asian fandom members find K-pop, with its new dances and songs, to be emancipating in that it signifies what they are looking for in their life-styles, and what they want to be identified with.

Identities formed through K-pop are not products of enculturation whereby the music of a family or social group is assimilated by younger members, but rather are a consequence of specific methods of building a sense of empathy and bonding between a particular popular music star and groups of young people. The rise of fandom provides examples of this type of identity building (Lewis, 1992; Whiteley, 2005). Steele & Brown (1995) argue that the basis of these types of musical identities are less to do with listening and more to do with ambience creation where the sounds of favored music played as background, especially in private bedrooms, act more like a security blanket. Connell & Gibson (2003) described such musical allegiances as more a product of fandom than of unbiased and reasoned critical analysis and judgement. However, Grossman (1992, p. 65) argues that:

the Fans' investment in certain practices and texts provides them with strategies which enable them to gain a certain amount of control over their affective life, which further enables them to invest in new forms of meaning, pleasure and identity in order to cope with new forms of pain, pessimism, frustration, alienation, terror, boredom.

As Middleton (1990, p. 9) argues, who the popular musician appears to be, and who they appear to be writing and performing for, are important components in forging musical identities. He goes on to cite the example of the Beatles who "epitomized the boy-next-door, man-in-the-street classlessness constructed, and this was one way in which the music's meaning was secured for the dominant social interest." However, Fowler (2008, p. 170) argues that the Beatles "sold themselves as working class heroes, a sobriquet which was belied by their luxurious and ostentatious lifestyles."

In both countries, identifying with western classical music is developed through family and associated social groups, particularly membership of a Catholic or Protestant church community and the socio-economic status of the family group. Membership of the specific empathetic socio-cultural group in Australia leads to identification with Australian Country and Western music and the cult of Elvis. On the other hand, identification of young Australians with Australian rock stars, such as INXS or Cold Play, would more likely be a product of acculturation and membership of relevant social groups. The same would apply to young South Koreans and their identification with K-pop groups such as Shinwha and stars such as Psy.

What is of particular interest concerning musical identities is how they operate within a society, what type of feelings, events, musical elements, and social contacts are generated, and how such identities fit into the complex socio-economic and socio-political structure of a society. It is highly unlikely that different group identification in music will cause any kind of serious disruption of the steady political state of a society through between-group hostility or bias. For example, it is unthinkable that those who identify with symphonic music would launch physical attacks on those who support jazz or Country Music, or vice versa. There is anecdotal evidence that those who favor symphonic music enjoy different life styles and different socio-economic circumstances from those enjoying Country Music. The interest, then, in describing and explaining different musical identities will be more focussed on life-styles, social and socio-economic factors, location of social groups, and various aesthetic attitudes, which delineate differences.

43.4 Musical identities in Australia

One of the most unique and well-defined musical identities in Australia is to be found in Australian Country Music. Although the source of Australian Country Music is obviously American, Australian Country Music performers argue strongly that their music is not simply a pale imitation of the American genre, but is a unique and wholly original form. Certainly, the overtly Australian content of most of the lyrics found in Australian Country Music would support this view.

43.4.1 The Tamworth Country Music Festival

The origins of Australian Country Music are to be found in attempts by some enthusiasts to support musicians who favored this genre. In January, 1968, a talent contest held in the northern New South Wales city of Tamworth, concerned exclusively with the genre of Country Music. By 1973 this had evolved into a major event: the Tamworth Country Music Festival. The population of Tamworth, now at around 55,000 people, welcomes in January each year at least the same number of visitors from across Australia and beyond, thus doubling the population for the weeks of Festival. Peel Street, in the main shopping center, is thronged with hundreds of buskers playing a variety of instruments ranging from the ubiquitous guitar to washboards, spoons, and other improvised instruments, with performer's ages ranging from under 10 to over 70 years.

Those many thousands who attend the annual Festival in Tamworth report strong identification with all aspects of the Festival, many attending year after year. These fans comprise whole families, often including several generations, who make the pilgrimage to Tamworth year after year to enjoy the company of other fans, to renew old acquaintances, to enjoy the atmosphere, the food, the camaraderie, to swap tales of long held affiliations with the Tamworth Festival, and mostly to enjoy the Country Music. Membership of the Country Music loving group is family based, where children are brought up as loving Country Music by virtue of their participation with their parents and grandparents in the annual Festival and at their homes, mostly in country towns, where Country Music is the preferred genre.

The enjoyment of the Festival includes camping, living in mobile caravans, hotels, hostels, local people's houses, and especially meeting old friends year after year, discussing the music, assessing new talent and bonding with like-minded people. Although musically based, the attractions are multi-faceted to include varied social interactions and cultural activities, suitable *country* clothing, manner of speaking, and the chance to see, meet, and enjoy the music of the heroes of Australian Country Music.

Comments in the local Tamworth newspaper, *The Northern Daily Leader* (Tamworth, 2013), indicate the level of excitement and commitment found among the fans during the 2013 Festival:

> A sea of buskers led by Adam Harvey and Beccy Cole strolled down Peel St yesterday in what was dubbed "probably the world's longest busk". There were dozens of guitars, and even some fiddles, parading down two blocks with a collective rendition of Slim Dusty's *Lights on the Hill*, to launch the 2014 country music festival theme.
>
> The heart and soul of Tamworth is this street and the buskers out there on the street.
>
> What I love about Tamworth is that [sic] gathering of like-minded Country Music people, fans and artists. Since I was young and coming up as a fan, it has never lost its magical feel to me. Some people love Disneyland, I love the Tamworth Country Music Festival.
>
> Troy Cassar-Daley.

43.4.2 The origins and Australian-ness of country music

Identity in Australian Country Music is most clearly understood through the idea of self-categorization (Turner & Oakes, 1986). Members regard themselves as Country Music fans in a country, Australia, which has no geographic connections with the original Country Music of the USA, and no obvious social or musical connections either. The typical Australian Country Music fan is brought up to regard themselves as such by family and social group influences and interactions. There is a sense that Country Music fans in Australia want to preserve their special status and their attraction to what is in effect an alien musical genre because of the remoteness of its home in the USA.

Identity is, then, a matter of self-categorization in the sense that the growth of and support for Country Music in Australia is rather like a cuckoo in the nest—there are no logical, social, socio-economic, or musical reasons why it should exist. To this extent, the Country Music Fan in Australia feels it important to assert their special identity, but historical origins exist in the lifestyle and activities of the old 19th century bushrangers.

Today, the typical cattle or sheep farmer still looks after his land on horseback, much like his American counter-part. Drovers, living mostly in the open air, still work the huge plains of the Australian outback driving thousands of cattle across huge areas looking for food in a country which has uneven rainfall. Such a life-style more naturally encourages the type of music where guitar accompaniment and singing songs suit the physical demands of work.

Bush poets, such as Banjo Paterson (1864–1941) who wrote "Waltzing Matilda" and "The Man from Snowy River," Henry Lawson (1867–1922) who wrote "Freedom on the Wallaby," and Dorothea Mackellar (1885–1968) famous for "My Country," feature strongly in the origins and heart-lands of Country music. The icons of Country music singing, such as John Williamson and Slim Dusty, rise above any narrow sectarianism or hostility to the singing style to become quintessentially Australian, acknowledged by all and with whom all Australians readily identify.

Such Country Classics as "Waltzing Matilda," regarded by many as Australia's unofficial national anthem, and "The pub with no beer," written by Dan Sheahan of Ingham, North Queensland, have become internationally famous. "True Blue" written and performed by John Williamson and containing typical Australian slang explains what it means to be truly Australian. To this extent, these examples transcend the narrowness of the label Country Music to become typically and solely Australian with which most, if not all, Australians would readily identify.

43.4.3 Religious and classical music traditions

An important musical identity found mostly, but not exclusively, in the major cities is that supporting the classical traditions of European history. This has strong origins in the England of the 19th century when many convicts were transported to Australia often for the most trivial offence, such as stealing a loaf of bread in times when large numbers of the population of the British Isles were starving. Along with the establishment of law and order came the cultural, especially the musical and religious, practices of England. Large cathedrals were built imitating English and European models, and choirs were instituted based on English models. Eventually, expert organists and choir trainers came over from England to take charge of the music in these new cathedrals. In Sydney, the huge Catholic Cathedral of St. Mary was begun in 1821, and St. Andrew's Anglican Cathedral was begun in 1837, with a large organ installed in 1866, and a choir and choir school established in 1885 on the English cathedral model. Similar buildings appeared in all major cities across Australia during the 19th century, and it is from these origins that the Australian cathedral choral traditions began.

The choir schools attached to cathedrals across Australia now have large music departments where the majority of students learn instruments and choral singing. At the same time, other organizations were establishing schools across Australia, including the Anglican, Catholic, and Presbyterian churches, all of whom opened many grammar schools in the large cities. These schools now form the basis of the large private school sector across Australia, many with large and very active music departments. It is from this school sector that a majority of those who identify more with classical music traditions emanate.

Music Conservatoriums were established in the major cities in the early years of the 20th century, and many musicians from England came to Australia to teach in them and to become directors of these institutions. Opera companies were established during the 20th century with experts from both the United Kingdom and Europe settling in Australia to direct and sing in performances. These beginnings of cathedral music, symphonic music, and opera were linked to the middle and upper classes of society where large sums of money were available to establish such practices. It is, therefore, the higher socio-economic sectors of Australian society who typically identify with these musical traditions.

43.4.4   The Elvis tradition

A smaller, but vibrant musical identity is to be found among the fans of Elvis Presley. Each year a special train travels from Sydney to the town of Parkes in central New South Wales to celebrate the birthday of Elvis Presley on January 8th. In Parkes, the annual Elvis Festival, begun in 1993, and is celebrated lasting over 5 days. The festival program features the Elvis Concerts in the club venues, an Elvis Gospel Church Service, a Street Parade, free *Elvis in the Park* entertainment, and various other novelty events such as the *Back to the Altar with Elvis—Renewal of Wedding Vows,* the *Trans Tank Miss Priscilla Dinner, Elvis Poet's Breakfast,* and other events form the backbone of the Festival. In 2012, over 18,000 people attended the Festival. Identification specifically with Elvis and his music is the focus. People dress in Elvis's clothes, adopt his postures, imitate his singing style and his gyrating hips, and spend the time celebrating their hero and his music.

43.5 MUSICAL IDENTITIES IN SOUTH KOREAN SINGING

Singing is very much part of every South Korean's daily life. The "Singing Rooms" are very popular in South Korea, where people go with friends, work colleagues, and family members, to sing songs with Karaoke style subtitles for lyrics in order to enjoy singing, have fun, and release stress.

In schools, choir competitions among individual classes are held as annual events, which build the momentum for singing and music. Many parents arrange private music lessons for their children either because they see potential musical talent in their children, or they believe that developing an artistic sense and musical skills will enhance general educational achievement.

Those students who plan to major in music at university take private music lessons from expert musicians. University entrance examinations for western classical music majors require evidence of performance ability. For example, for those intending to make singing their major, are required to perform one Italian Aria, one Lied, and a simple piano piece, plus sight singing. Similar requirements exist for instrumentalists and pianists. Most university professors in western classical music have higher degrees or advanced qualifications from music conservatoires or university schools of music in the US and Europe.

Those university graduates of western classical music intending to be performers go abroad for further study, often following the same path as their university professors. These musical practices build the audience for western classical music performances in concert halls and opera houses in Seoul and other major cities in South Korea, as well as producing internationally famous performers, ranging from opera singers, to conductors, pianists, and orchestral players.

43.5.1 Influence of religion

During the 19th century Korea became in part a Christian country as a result of visits from largely American and European missionaries. The result of this growth and development of Christianity by the 20th century was that around 60% of the populace were converted to Christianity, half of these being Catholic and the other half members of various protestant or non-conformist sects, with the remainder keeping to their traditional Buddhist faith. Along with Christianity came the singing of hymns and psalms and the insertion into Korean life of western music, especially the melodies and harmonies contained in hymns, which reflected the development of western classical music. Cathedrals and large churches were built across the country. Myeongdong Cathedral in Seoul is the most important cathedral center, where the Catholic Cardinal of South Korea is situated. In these Catholic cathedrals and churches large organs were installed and choirs were formed. The predominant influence from European church music became that from Italy and Germany, where many church musicians in South Korea were trained.

Typical of the music performed is that found at Myeongdong Cathedral where, for example, at Christmas a Bach Cantata would be performed complete with orchestra and full choir. The protestant and non-conformist churches also have extensive musical establishments across the country. Even local churches would have a choir and some instrumentalists performing at services. Most South Koreans attend one or other of the Christian churches regularly and regard their local church, or cathedral, as a major social center for meeting friends. It is in such contexts that musical identities are formed which are specific to South Korea because of the special sounds and structures of the Korean language—*Hangul*. The music sung by congregations tends to be culturally specific for the same reason. And when performing major works of the western European classical music tradition the texts are translated into Korean.

43.5.2 South Korean Identity

Korean traditional court music and folk music were revived during the preparations for the 1988 Seoul Olympics, as a means of presenting a distinct South Korean identity to the world. South Koreans, under heavy influence of the US in all aspects of life since the end of the Korean War, began to ask questions such as, "Who are we Koreans? What is our Korean national identity, which distinguishes us from non-Koreans?" These were important questions as the country prepared for the Seoul Olympics.

At this time Korean traditional musicians received overdue recognition from the South Korean government by being designated as *Human Treasures* for their performance expertise in various Korean traditional activities. From that time, school music curriculums in South Korea required teachers to teach Korean traditional music for 50% of the music classes. South Korean teachers were trained to teach Korean traditional music through teacher education programs and professional development programs.

This was a revolutionary change in school music education because before 1988 Korean traditional music was hardly taught and Korean people did not like the slow-tempo historical Korean court music. *Pansori*, the Korean traditional folk vocal music, was probably the most preferred musical genre by Korean people because of their exposure to *Pansori* through movies and the humor in the lyrics. Some western classical professional musicians began to attempt fusion of western classical music and Korean traditional court music. Also, *Chang-geuk* (Creative Korean traditional opera) was created by extending *Pansori* performance into an opera style performance. *Chang-geuk* is very similar to opera in that different characters are performed by different singers, and Korean traditional instrumental orchestras provided the accompaniment. *Changeuk* is performed on stage in concert halls. *Changeuk* was created to attract people to Korean traditional music, and is composed by Korean traditional music composers.

43.5.3 Korean popular music

After the Korean War ended in 1953, South Korea in all its political, educational, and social aspects was developed under the influence of the USA. Initially, popular music was solely from the USA, with large numbers of USA soldiers stationed in the country, exerting heavy influence over young Koreans. Lie (2012) explained the impact of the USA on Korean cultural life as follows:

> The US occupation and its aftermath brought popular American music: not only jazz and blues but also pop and rock via the US Armed Forces radio and television, US military camptown bars and dance halls, and movie theaters that largely showcased Hollywood films. The era of American cultural dominance—the 1950s and 1960s— affected an ever larger population.
>
> p. 343.

Despite the fact that many young South Koreans learned English and popular music identities were formed initially with American popular music, as Lie (2012) explains:

> South Korean popular music in the immediate post-Liberation decades was deeply influenced by contemporary Japanese popular music (p. 343) ... Just as South Koreans looking for something "new" or just good in popular music in the 1970s embraced someone like the Japanese folk singer Itsuwa Mayumi, they were slower to accept the alien sound of Western rock music.
>
> p. 346.

Korean popular music of the 1970s and 1980s contained lyrics with political messages and Confucian values, and it reflected South Korean society at that time, which often expressed people's anger with the then Military government. However, important differences between K-pop for the global audience and the older Korean popular music written for domestic audiences is that the former tries to avoid delicate expressions of emotions found in the latter, has more explicit expressions about sex, uses English, Japanese, and Chinese, as well as a mix of other languages, and uses extensive rapping often in the style of hip hop. Thus, K-pop is Korean music reflecting contemporary South Korea, which is transforming into a *globalized* country through the impact of one of the fastest broadband in the world, extensive use of the digital technology (e.g., tablets, smart phones, iPads), a large number of native English speaking teachers teaching and living in South Korea, and a migrant population from East Asia.

43.5.4 Korean Wave and K-pop

The Korean Wave or *Hallyu*, meaning the coming of South Korean popular culture, marked its beginning in Japan in 2002 through the Korean TV drama series *Winter*

Sonata. This was the perfect time and place for exporting Korean popular culture outside of South Korea, especially as South Korea and Japan jointly hosted the 2002 World Cup. Since then, K-pop became a success in Japan, Taiwan, and mainland China, and the Korean Wave spread with K-pop. The South Korean government, which traditionally had censored cultural products from Japan (due to Japan's colonization in 1910–1945) and other countries, promoted K-pop as a Korean cultural product, and even provided favorable financial arrangement for K-pop. However, the Korean-ness in K-pop was questioned by Lie (2012), who argued that K-pop is a type of Western pop music lacking traditional Korean music components and most of the music was composed by foreign musicians, not Koreans. Then, in July 2012, came the global phenomenon of Psy's "Gangnam Style," which has attracted literally hundreds of millions viewers on YouTube and generated many responses ranging from parodies to direct imitations by countries and institutions world-wide. Almost every country across the globe has produced a version of "Gangnam Style" on YouTube ranging from political parodies of presidential candidates in the USA to students from some of England's most exclusive and expensive private schools performing their own "Gangnam Style," to groups of teachers performing to their students, and others from South Africa to the North Pole.

43.5.5 K-pop explained

K-pop was born as a survival strategy of the South Korean music industry suffering from the downfall of the domestic market in 1997 due to rise of digital technology and the internet (e.g., free download of music from the internet) as well as the effects of the 1997 IMF financial crisis in South Korea. Sales of music CDs were minimal in the South Korean domestic market in mid-1990s, thus the music industry decided to target the large and potentially lucrative Asian market. K-pop was built on hip-hop and included rapping, while J-pop (Japanese popular music) is built on rock.

Success factors for K-pop have been investigated by several researchers (e.g., Lie, 2012; Limb, 2013; Shin, 2009). One important factor is the 5-year systematic training of potential K-pop performers using an approach called *Born Global*, which included *Talent Development* and *Talent Acquisition* (Limb, 2013). The South Korean entertainment groups hired foreign experts in popular music composition and choreography to train potential K-pop performers. When the K-pop hopefuls completed their training, the best performers were selected to make *Idol* groups who were promoted initially through the social media outlets of YouTube, Facebook, and iTunes.

This established them internationally and at the same time created a large fandom of young people who readily identified with their favorite K-pop performers. These were specially trained for the global market in order to appear natural and highly competent in the global context. The *Born Global* approach was the key to their success.

The effective use of digital technology (Lie, 2012; Limb, 2013) is important in the development of musical identities within K-pop. Without YouTube, which was created in 2005, K-pop would not have been distributed so quickly to the Asian and the global markets. K-pop has one dedicated YouTube channel for distribution of K-pop. Social Network Services (SNS) or social media, such as Facebook and Twitter, helped the audience to be active listeners and critiques of music, unlike passive listeners of the past. In this way, the word was spread about new K-pop stars and their songs instantly around the world. ITunes was used to distribute K-pop pieces free to the global audience through the internet. Digital technology, thus, changed the way that people purchased music; i.e., first listen, then purchase. The use of digital technology facilitated the promotion of K-pop globally and efficiently with minimal investment.

43.6 New Musical Identities Emerging Through Social Media and New Digital Technology

The emergence of new and more powerful digital technology over the last two decades has gradually changed the whole field of music perception and reception, especially in the popular music field. Communications and information about many of the musical activities described above have occurred through paper publications in newspapers, journals, magazines, and other localized print, or through radio, television, and more recently the internet. Now, however, with faster internet speeds, high definition televisions, mobile phones, tablets, and miniature laptops, the whole communication scene concerning music has been radically altered. Instead of local peer groups or localized interest groups generating identities through shared allegiances to certain types of music, the new technology has allowed individuals from anywhere in the world to become linked through interest, similar allegiances, and shared musical tastes.

The most important innovation enabling this startling and revolutionary development to grow and absorb practically all the older modes of communication are radically faster internet speeds now accessible in individual homes and by individuals in each house. South Korea leads the world in the number of individual homes with very fast broadband access (98% in 2010). Australia had only 60% with such access in 2010. In 2012, South Korea had one of the fastest broadband speeds in the world (80,000 kbps) compared with 34,500 kbps in Australia. Japan had the world's fastest broadband speed with 150,000 kbps (OECD, 2012).

Developments in high definition video transmission are now available through mobile phones with fast broadband access, enabling individuals to download music videos and send them to friends across the world. Musical identity is now a global phenomenon where individuals from any country can form musical identity groups with anyone, anywhere in the world. Moreover, musicians can now post their own compositions and performances on the internet for anyone to see and enjoy.

Examples of new types of musical identities being formed through the new technology enabling social media to communicate with anyone, anywhere in the world, are Psy from South Korea and Sia Furler from Australia. Psy's "Gangnam Style" video attracted 2043,535,814 viewers in 2012 (https://www.youtube.com/watch?v=9bZkp7q19fo). Sia Furler's latest album "1000 forms of fear" reached number one on the USA Billboard Charts in early July, 2014 elevating her to global status as a popular music star. Her video performance of *Chandelier* attracted 70,931, 929 viewers in May, 2014 (https://www.youtube.com/watch?v=2vjPBrBU-TM).

These huge numbers of viewers from across the world reflect the global context now within which young people search for their own particular type of music and performer, and who also put up their own musical performances on the internet for approval and exchange with others. It is impossible now to know who is forming identities with particular musical performances or artists. The record of millions of viewers to individual performances on YouTube indicate a quite different social context for forming musical identities to those described above where people meet physically, and communications occur through old media of print, radio, television, or membership of specialist groups of societies.

This is a new form of potent communication for young people and popular musicians involving anyone anywhere in the world. The new technology allows for hitherto unimagined forms of musical identification by individuals, with groups only involved through virtual communications across the globe. This new situation has shifted the focus from an initial attraction to a particular musical identity from within a social group, such as groups of pre-teens or teenagers meeting physically in school or other organizations, to the individual communication solely through iPhones, tablets, laptops, and other devices connected to the world wide web and able to download large digital files of music from anywhere in the world. The new social group is now the virtual meeting places of Facebook, Twitter, and a host of other social media.

However, it is not only popular music which has taken advantage of this new technology. Many individuals have posted their performance of western classical or popular music on the internet for anyone to see, comment on, and form friendships over. Large and prestigious organizations such as symphony orchestras and opera houses are now involved in the global means of communication in music. The Berlin Philharmonic Orchestra now has all its concerts in digital format on the web through live streaming. And similarly operas from the Metropolitan Opera in New York and Covent Garden Opera in London are available on the internet. Through minimal monthly subscription to these organizations one can access recent performances on one's own laptop, iPhone, tablet, or other digital device. Such developments, without doubt, herald a new dawn for musical identities to develop in ways which have not yet been studied or imagined.

References

Asch, S.E. (1952). *Social Psychology*. Englewood Cliffs, NJ: Prentice-Hall.

Brown, R. (2000). Social identity theory: past achievements, current problems and future challenges. *European Journal of Social Psychology*, 30, 745–78.

Cassar-Daley, T. (2011). Heartache for country star. *The Northern Daily Leader*, 20 January, 2011.

Connell, J., & Gibson, C. (2003). *Sound-tracks, popular music, identity and place.* London: Routledge.

Ellemers, N., & Barreto, M. (2001). The impact of relative group status: affective, perceptual and behavioural consequences. In: R. Brown & S. L. Gaertner. (Eds.) *Blackwell handbook of social psychology: intergroup processes* [Online]. Wiley-Blackwell, pp. 325–43. Available at: http://onlinelibrary.wiley.com/book/10.1002/9780470693421

Fowler, D. (2008). *Youth culture in modern Britain 1920–1970.* London: Palgrave.

Frith, S. (1996). *Performing rites.* Cambridge, MA: Harvard University Press.

Grossman, L. (1992). Is there a fan in the house? The affective sensibility of fandom. In: L. Lewis (Ed.) *The adoring audience: fan culture and pop media*, pp. 50–68. London: Routledge.

Index-OMundi Australia. (2013). Available at: http://www.indexmundi.com/australia/demographics_profile.html [Accessed 20 Sep 2013].

Index-OMundi Korea. (2013). Available at: http://www.indexmundi.com/south_korea/demographics_profile.html [Accessed 20 Sep 2013].

Lewis, L.A. (1992). *The adoring audience: fan culture and popular media.* London: Routledge.

Lie, J. (2012). What is the K in K-pop? South Korean popular music, the culture industry, and national identity. *Korea Observer*, 43(3), 339–63.

Limb, S.J. (2013). What makes K-Pop so successful? *Korean Business Review*, 17(2), 323–46.

Middleton, R. (1990). *Studying popular music.* Milton Keynes: Open University Press.

OECD. (2012). Available at: http://www.oecd.org/sti/broadbandandtelecom/oecdboradbandportal.htm (accessed October 8, 2016).

Shin, Hyunjoon. (2009). Have you ever seen the Rain? And who'll stop the Rain? The globalizing project of Korean pop (K-pop). *Inter-Asia Cultural Studies*, 10(4), 507–23.

Steele, J.R., & Brown, J.D. (1995). Adolescent room culture: studying media in the context of everyday life. *Journal of Youth and Adolescence*, 24(5), 551–75.

Tajfel, H. (1981). Social stereotypes and social groups. In: J. Turner, and H. Giles (Ed.) *Intergroup Behaviour*, pp. 144–67. Oxford: Blackwell.

Tamworth. (2013). Comments concerning the Country Music Festival in Tamworth, *Northern Daily Leader*, January, 11th 2013.

Turner, J., & Oakes, P. (1986). The significance of the social identity concept for social psychology with reference to individualism, interactionism and social influence. *British Journal of Social Psychology*, 25(3), 237–52.

Turner, J.C. (1999). Some current issues in research on social identity and self-categorization theories. In: Ellemers, N., Spears, R., and Doosje, B. (Eds) *Social identity*, pp. 6–34. Oxford: Blackwell.

Turner, J.C., & Reynolds, K.H. (2001). The social identity perspective in intergroup relations: theories, themes, and controversies. In: R. Brown & S.L. Gaertner (Eds.) *Blackwell handbook of social psychology: intergroup processes*, pp. 133–52. [Online] Hoboken: Wiley-Blackwell. Available at: http://onlinelibrary.wiley.com/book/10.1002/9780470693421.

Whiteley, S. (2005). *Too much too young: popular music, age, and gender.* London: Routledge.

CHAPTER 44

IDENTITY, MUSIC, AND FESTIVITY IN SOUTHERN TUNISIA

ALAN KARASS

FESTIVALS are an important part of public life in Tunisia. Most towns, no matter how small, manage to have an annual festival and in the capital, Tunis, there is at least one festival a month featuring music, theatre, poetry, film, comedy, or dance. Not only are they an important feature of social life, but festival performances also serve as opportunities for Tunisians to articulate their national, political, religious, and ethnic identities. Based on fieldwork conducted in Tunisia between 2008 and 2014, this chapter explores one festival in particular, the International Festival of the Sahara, or the "Douz Festival." It is the only Tunisian festival that simultaneously celebrates the culture of a town, its environs, and its early inhabitants, namely, the semi-nomadic Marazig people.

The International Festival of the Sahara is an annual event that takes place each year in Douz, a small town in southern Tunisia that is considered by many Tunisians to be the gateway to the Sahara Desert. The town is situated 125 km east of the Algerian border, 275 km west of the Libyan border, and 475 km south of the country's capitol, Tunis (see Fig. 44.1, page 807). Although historians have chronicled the history of Berber, Arab Bedouin, Roman, Arab Muslim, and French settlers in southern Tunisia (see Abun-Nasr, 1987; Perkins, 1986; Huskinson, 2000; Perkins, 2014), the residents of Douz have a strong affinity to the town's Bedouin heritage.

This exploration of the relationship between festivity and expressions of identity in southern Tunisia draws from two concepts pertaining to the construction of identity that can then be related to the Douz Festival. The first is based on Ali Jihad Racy's (1996) description of the "Bedouin ethos." He suggests that groups promulgate their connection to Bedouinism because it is equated throughout the Arab world with

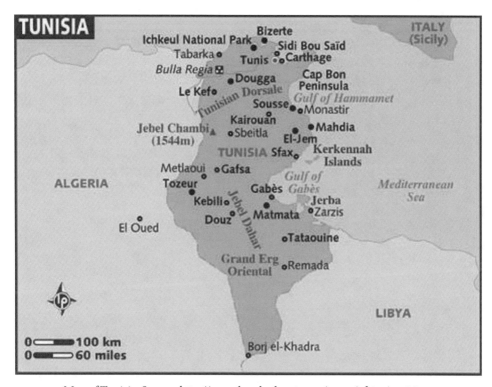

FIG. 44.1 Map of Tunisia. Source: http://www.lonelyplanet.com/maps/africa/tunisia

This map is reproduced with permission from Lonely Planet, Copyright © 2015 Lonely Planet, http://www.lonelyplanet.com/

the virtues of purity, honor, hospitality, chivalry, and bravery (Racy, 1996, p. 405). This implies that alignment with Bedouin identity in contemporary Douz, and its expression during the festival, is a way of describing oneself as pure, honest, and authentic—traits that my informants also equate with "being Marazig"—and one of the ways that both Marazig and the people "of Douz" distinguish themselves from their neighbors and other Tunisians. The second concept regarding identity is rooted in the ethnomusicological perspective of Timothy Rice, who explains that one of the primary roles of music is the performance of identity. He states "performance provides the opportunity for communities sharing an identity to see themselves in action" (2007, p. 35). While weddings serve this function to a degree, the Douz Festival is the only opportunity for all of the residents to do so. The Douz Festival is unique in the sense that it is open to every member of the community, whereas weddings are restricted to family, friends, and neighbors of the bride and groom. Drawing on Rice and Racy's theories, this chapter demonstrates that the Douz Festival is a public display of Bedouin identity for audience members, residents, and the performers themselves.

FIG. 44.2.   Zokra band at the 2009 Douz Festival (photograph by the author).

44.1 ALL THINGS DOUZ

The terms "Marazig," "of Douz," and "Bedouin" are used in this chapter to describe the people, practices, and objects associated with Douz. These adjectives convey the nuanced relationships with the town's history, legacy, and geography and are important to issues of identity.

"Marazig" refers to the ancestral ties that serve to identify residents of Douz. Most consider themselves to be descendants of Sidi Marzoug, Omar al Mahjoub, or Hamed el Ghouth, the first settlers of Douz. Although I met no family in Douz that could authoritatively document their ancestry back to them, individuals consider themselves to be Marazig because their parents and grandparents are from Douz. The idea that the family has lived in Douz as long as anyone can remember is considered ample evidence of Marazig-ness. The Marazig label is also used to convey the ideas that the community members have of themselves. It evokes an image of a tribe of Arab warriors who are deeply pious and attuned to the natural world. It also suggests an image of the Marazig as a confederation of nomadic Bedouin clans with their own distinctive stories, poetry, music, dances, and customs all rooted in a profound connection to the desert. While most contemporary Marazig lead sedentary lives in Douz and have abandoned many of the daily practices of Bedouin life, the Marazig image is a powerful one in Douz today. Not only are the terms "Marazig" or "*Marzougi*" used in this chapter as the residents of Douz use them, to denote all things related to their ethnic group, but also to convey the idea of the ancestral ideal of Marazig-ness that exists in Douz today.

The phrase "of Douz" includes all practices, objects, and people found in the town, whether Marazig or non-Marazig. My usage is identical to the phrases used in Douz "*min Douz*" (from, or in Douz) or "*Douzi*" (of Douz). The phrase suggests characteristics specific to the town and its people that transcend images of Marazig-ness. A very small percentage of the town's population is not Marazig. One informant suggested that less than 5% of the town's 27,000 permanent inhabitants are either Western Europeans that have retired or relocated to Douz, immigrants from sub-Saharan Africa, or the children of these immigrants.

Although the residents are no longer nomadic or even semi-nomadic, the Marazig and non-Marazig residents of Douz often invoke the image of the Bedouin, or more specifically *Sahrawi*—"of the desert and of the Sahara"—to describe local objects, practices, and people. For example, one young Marazig informant who is a self-taught *gas-biyah* (end-blown metal flute) player, described his daily ritual of driving to a secluded street near the desert to practice. He explained that despite the fact that he wears the newest fashions recently imported from France, drives a late-model Audi, and works in the livery business, he still identifies with his Marazig roots, and more specifically, being *Sahrawi*. Other informants described the spring holidays in the desert that many families enjoy. One stated that many people from Douz take several weeks each year to wander through the desert to reconnect with their roots and experience the serenity of the desert. I believe the citizens of Douz, mainly the Marazig, have a genuine sense of connection with the desert, but I suggest that there is more at work here. Racy, in his description of the "Bedouin ethos" suggests that Bedouinism and nomadism are equated throughout the Arab world with the virtues of purity, honor, hospitality, chivalry, and bravery (Racy, 1996, p. 405). Therefore, alignment with Bedouin and *Sahrawi* identities in contemporary Douz is a way of describing oneself as wholesome and virtuous. The expression of the Marazig's Bedouin heritage is a key component of the Douz Festival because residents consider the festival to be the highest profile public event for themselves as well as tourists.

44.2 THE DOUZ FESTIVAL

Founded in 1913 as the *Day of the Camel* while Tunisia was still a French colony, the Douz Festival is ostensibly the oldest of the country's 311 festivals. The early festivals, held before the start of World War I, were intended to bring together camel enthusiasts from among the French officers, residents of Douz, and nomadic groups from the region. It was a one-day event featuring camel races and competitions. Despite the fact that no festivals were held for decades during, between, and after the world wars, the residents consider the early festival to be the same event as the current one. The festival resumed in 1967 with a multi-day format that resembles the present event. Beginning in 1981, per the directive of President Habib Bourguiba, the festival adopted an international dimension by inviting participants from other Arab and African countries (Wasallati, 2003–2004, p. 33).

The contemporary festival takes place over four days in late December. The opening ceremonies begin at 09.00 hours on the first day. Hundreds of local residents and tourists gather along a 2-km stretch in the center of town. All vehicular traffic is diverted and everyday business is suspended as spectators gather to watch more than a dozen groups perform simultaneously. There are *zokra* (folk oboe) and drum bands, drum ensembles, folk dancers, rifle dancers, camel and horse drivers, jugglers, and a snake charmer. Performing groups, including folk bands and dance troupes, come from Tunisia, Morocco, Libya, Algeria, and Egypt, as well as from outside the Arab world. The groups slowly promenade up and down a short stretch of pavement, seemingly repeating the same pieces. This revolving showcase continues for about three hours and ends after dozens of dignitaries, including members of the Cultural Ministry, local government, and foreign delegates tour the venue and greet the performers.

During subsequent mornings, performing groups take turns entertaining onlookers in the *souq*, the central plaza surrounded by cafés and tourist-oriented shops in the heart of Douz. Two of Douz's major streets intersect in the *souq* and divide it into equal quadrants. During the festival, each quadrant is transformed into a performance space for at least one act, and sometimes two or three simultaneously. The groups rotate through the quadrants, each performing for approximately one hour.

After a long lunch break, daily activities resume at *Place H'nich*, a stadium at the edge of the Sahara Desert located 2 km from the center of town. Situated near the *Zone Touristique* adjacent to most of the town's hotels, *Place H'nich* also serves as Douz's gateway to the Sahara. It is the place where camel drivers and tourist groups begin and end their treks into the desert. A multitude of onlookers stand nearby, controlled by police officers trying to prevent them from wandering into the paths of the performers.

At *Place H'nich*, all of the performers who participated at the opening ceremonies offer short vignette performances interspersed with narration in French, English, and Arabic by a lively announcer. This is followed by performances demonstrating local wedding practices, folk dances, children's games, and traditional dances. The afternoon concludes with demonstrations of traditional hunting techniques, desert games, camel races, camel fights, and displays of horsemanship. The second and third days of afternoon performances at *Place H'nich* usually highlight camel and horse races and equestrian events.

Camel races are one of the featured events in the contemporary festival, as are several activities that are also part of local wedding traditions. During the festival, various components of traditional weddings are recreated, including music by *zokra* and drum bands, *nakh* (also called *nakhan*; the "hair dance" performed by young women), *jeffa* processions (the voyage of the bride to her new home in a decorated *howdah*, an elaborate carriage on a camel), and performances of *raqs mayazy* (the warrior's rifle dance).

For the residents of Douz, these performances are important markers of their Bedouin heritage.

44.3 Zokra bands

Another important element featured during the Douz Festival is the *zokra* band. Following the two-hour lunch break during the first day of the 2009 Douz Festival, performers and audience members gathered at *Place H'nich* for the festival's afternoon activities. After the announcer welcomed the audience, the performances began. Among the first set of acts to perform were the *zokra* bands. Each band consisted of one or two *zokra* players and three to five drummers. Usually three or four bands are in attendance. Each member of each band wore a full-length white tunic, a red or white waistcoat, white leather shoes, and a multi-colored hat—the customary *zokra* band costume. Each band's hat featured different colors and patterns that designate where they come from. Most years, *zokra* bands from the southern towns of Medinine, Matmata, Tatouine, and Zarzis perform during the festival. One at a time, the bands approached the center of the performance area in front of the crowd. They took turns promenading in front of the audience while playing folk songs and arrangements of pop songs. Band members often walk in a circle while performing; flashier bands and their members might spin in place, twirl their drums, or execute elaborate dance steps, kicks and jumps while playing. Audiences always cheer and applaud loudly for the *zokra* bands as they finish their performances, process out of the limelight and move to the perimeter of *Place H'nich*.

The *zokra* (also known as the *ghaita, raita, reta, or mizmar* in the Arab world, or *zurna* in Turkey and Eurasia) is a double-reed woodwind instrument, approximately 40 cm long and usually made of apricot wood (Nabti, 2010, p. 234). Each band has one or two *zokra* players and three or more percussionists playing large double-headed drums called *at-tbal, at-tablah*, or just *tamtam* (the generic Tunisian word for drum). Both heads are played alternately, using 40-cm long sticks, one in each hand. *Zokra* bands play folk, traditional, and popular songs. My musician-informants stated that, although each ensemble claims to have a special repertoire based on songs attributed to their hometown, most bands play the same music.

Throughout North Africa, the Middle East, Eurasia, and the Mediterranean, the *zokra* is associated with festivity, weddings, and mystical communities (see Farmer, 1936; Schuyler, 2000; Lundberg, 2010; Landau, 2012). Likewise in Tunisia and particularly in Douz, the *zokra* is an instrument that has become rich with meaning. One informant stated that the *zokra* is the musical symbol of wedding celebrations and that any wedding is incomplete without it. The instrument is also important to many Tunisians as a sign of the country's historical relationship to Turkey. Most of my musician-informants insist that the *zokra* was brought to Tunisia from Turkey during the Ottoman conquests of Tunisia in the sixteenth century. The desire to make a musical connection between

Tunisia and Turkey is not surprising. Tunisian musicians revere classical and popular Turkish music and perceive it as highly sophisticated. The *zokra* also features prominently as a symbol of Bedouin identity. There are many postcards, paintings, and murals, especially in Douz, that depict *zokra* bands with camels in the desert, highlighting the pride Tunisians express in their Bedouin heritage.

The *zokra* is often the principal melodic instrument in ceremonies for the Sufi orders. According to Nabti (2010), the *zokra* is essential to the rites of the Aïssâwa orders because they believe that it invokes the spirits and articulates, through music, important religious texts (Nabti, 2010, p. 237). Theodore Grame (1970) states that the *zokra* is part of the musical ensemble used by the Aïssâwa order in Jma al-Fna, the central market square in Marrakesh, to accompany snake charming (Grame, 1970, p. 83). Philip Schuyler (2000) describes the *zokra* [*ghaita*] as a central instrument for the Master Musicians of Jajouka, an ensemble from Jajouka, Morocco, a town well known for its music and mystical traditions. Schuyler states, "the spiritual and geographic center of Jajouka is the tomb of Sidi Hmed Shikh, who is credited by the villagers both with bringing Islam to the region and for providing them with their livelihood, music" (Schuyler, 2000, pp. 147–8). Some of my informants acknowledged the relationship between the *zokra* and Sufism, yet were reluctant to discuss it. I propose that the residents of Douz overlook the long and well-documented connection between the *zokra* and mysticism because it does not reflect the image they want to project of the Marazig and Douz. I suggest that instead they prefer to depict the Marazig as Bedouins who are strongly aligned with Sunni Islam. Thus, the *zokra* has become the symbol of Bedouin-ness and not the mystical heritage of the *Nefzaoua*, the name given to this region of southern Tunisia. The question then becomes why the Bedouin image is such a powerful one in the Arab world.

Racy's (1996) description of the "Bedouin ethos" answers this question. Racy suggests that nomadism is equated with the virtues of purity, honor, hospitality, chivalry, and bravery; these characteristics are perceived to decrease as a group becomes more sedentary and urbanized (Racy, 1996, p. 405). Despite the fact that many formerly nomadic groups throughout the Middle East have become sedentary, many writers have argued that the Bedouin ethos still influences many aspects of public life including, but not limited to ethnic identity, politics, and business practices (see Bates & Rassam, 1983; Barakat, 1993; Hickson & Pugh, 2001; Lacoste & Lacoste, 2004; Franz, 2011; Lalonde, 2013).

The promulgation of the Bedouin image of Douz and its residents does not only promote a sense of purity, sincerity, honor, and ethnic authenticity, but also differentiates the town and its people from others in the south, and Tunisia in general. It is both a proclamation of collective selfhood, and, as Longina Jakubowska points out, an identity that is distinct from that of the nation-state. Although Jakubowska's focus is on minority Bedouin communities within a Jewish state, I find that her assessment of the political dynamics of identity is applicable to the Bedouin ethos in Tunisia. Jakubowska states, "Bedouin maintenance of marginality and isolationism is a refusal to participate in the discourse of nationalism and an effective means of resistance against state hegemony over identity" (Jakubowska, 1992, pp. 85–6). During my visits to Douz, I witnessed both political and cultural resistance to engagement with the Tunisian national identity.

I was in Douz in December 2010 shortly after the self-immolation of Mohamed Bouazizi, a pivotal moment in Tunisia's history leading up to the Jasmine Revolution of January 2011. Each night, I would watch the national news on television with informants and their families. One informant was riveted to the television and mesmerized by the events unfolding. After the news each night he would say "it is amazing what is going on in Tunisia, but this does not happen here, Douz remains calm and unchanged." His view of the nation did not include Douz or its citizens. On one level he understood that these events were unfolding in his country, Tunisia. On another level he believed that Douz and its residents were removed from the conflicts, social problems, and political turmoil in the rest of Tunisia. During my fieldwork visits I found this to be generally true. Many informants suggested that Douz is different from the rest of the country, both culturally and politically. They explained that much of the country is influenced by trends and events in Europe, Egypt, and other Arab countries; however, Douz is not. One informant noted that Douz is distinct; its citizens embrace a lifestyle that reflects different values, Bedouin values.

Despite the efforts by Presidents Bourguiba (1957–1987) and Ben Ali (1987–2011) to create a unified Tunisia with a culturally homogenous population, there are a few communities that maintain a unique identity. The Minority Rights Group International cites the Berbers of southern Tunisia and the Jews of Djerba and Tunis as such populations ("Minority Rights Group International"); I argue that the Marazig of Douz fit this description as well. As Jakubowska describes, the steadfast adherence to the Bedouin ethos and image enables Bedouin communities to separate themselves from the politics, trends, and history of the rest of the region and the country and to create a distinct identity. This is very true of the Marazig in Douz. Based on fieldwork observations, many Tunisians in other parts of the country describe themselves as progressive Muslims with lifestyles similar to citizens of Western Europe and progressive Muslim countries such as Jordan, Morocco, and Turkey. The question remains as to why the residents of Douz present an image of themselves that is so deliberately different and separate from the national one.

Jakubowska offers one explanation, stating that Bedouin groups perceive identity differently. They understand it as "an internalized cultural construction embedded in the social system and manifested in the practices of everyday life" (Jakubowska, 1992, p. 85). In other words, Bedouin groups comprehend identity in terms of the distinctive daily acts that are associated with Bedouin-ness and their Bedouin ancestors. Their identity, based on these practices, supersedes their sense of connection to the nation-state. From this perspective the Bedouin ethos for the residents of Douz is strictly about local customs and morals despite an awareness of regional and national norms.

Another answer to the question of image may, in part, be tourism. Several informants have suggested that although the Douz lifestyle and its Bedouin identity are rooted in daily routines that go back many generations, residents recognize that the Bedouin traditions, customs, and lifestyle found in Douz (and represented at the festival) might be intriguing to visitors and therefore contribute to the tourism sector of the town's economy. However, the tourism infrastructure in Douz is limited and tourists have been reluctant to return since the revolution due to fears of political instability and violence.

Religion is also a vital component of life in Douz. Just as the Bedouin ethos is important to construction of identity in Douz, so are both the practice of a contemporary, conservative version of Sunni Islam and the rejection of Sufism and maraboutism. The residents of Douz suggest that Sunni Islam was the religion of their Bedouin ancestors. Many of my informants have clearly and repeatedly stated that the citizens of Douz unequivocally disapprove of Sufism and all forms of mysticism. They state that the veneration of anyone or anything other than *Allah* is *haram* (forbidden in Islam). Although some repertoires, practices, and instruments may have historical links to Sufism or maraboutism, they are accepted because they are part of the Marazig heritage and their connection to mysticism is ignored.

Many of my informants acknowledged that Sufi and maraboutic communities have existed in Douz and in the south for centuries; however, they believe the brotherhoods and their practices no longer have a place in Douz. Some of them mentioned that some practices do have mystical significance. One informant openly discussed the fact that the *zokra* has deep spiritual meaning to the Aïssâwa Sufis. Others talked about the ritual use of some *zokra* repertoire in neighboring towns. In these towns, such as Kebili and Tozeur, the residents do not identify with the region's historical connection to its Bedouin ancestors. The residents of Kebili and Tozeur perceive their towns as modern Tunisian ones, and for them the *zokra* is associated with the mystical rites that are still practiced locally, and is not equated with the Bedouin past. However, in Douz there is strong and persuasive town-wide public discourse, both oral and performative, which identifies with their Bedouin history and implies that the religion of Douz is mainstream Sunni Islam. Furthermore, it is not just any form of Sunni Islam; it is the interpretation of Islam that they imagine their Bedouin ancestors would have practiced. To the citizens of Douz, it is not merely the practice of Islam or the Bedouin ancestry that establishes citizenship and identity; the belief that they are practicing Islam in the same way as their Bedouin ancestors is critical.

Zokra band performances reaffirm for the whole community, and convey to the audience members as well, that the strong affiliation to and emphasis of Bedouin heritage is legitimate, authentic, deep-rooted, and encompassing of several important societal institutions, namely life-changing rituals and religion. The *zokra* and its repertoire are symbols of marriage celebrations, and marriages are the valued cultural institutions at which Bedouin-ness is reproduced. The prominence of *zokra* bands and representations of wedding festivities at the Douz Festival confirms that marriage and Bedouin identity are important to Marazig-ness.

44.4 NAKH

Like *zokra* bands, the *nakh* is a key marker of Bedouin-ness. It is also a feature of wedding celebrations and residents often understand it as a symbol of these celebrations.

Since it is an important practice for the Marazig, *nakh* is always performed at the Douz Festival.

After several opening acts at the afternoon session of the Douz Festival, there are more re-enactments of traditional wedding practices. One of those commonly performed is the *nakh*, the hair dance performed by young women. Between ten and twenty dancers dressed in Bedouin clothes sit in the center of the stage area waiting for the music to begin. Usually the music used for *nakh* at the festival is a recording that is broadcast over the public address system. Once the music begins, the dancers spin their heads and hair in a circular pattern in rhythm with the music, and they continue until the music stops. After the announcer invites the audience to thank the dancers with a round of applause at the end of their performance, they leave the stage and sit amongst the audience. If this were a real wedding, the *nakh* would be performed during one of the evening celebrations at a *salon de marriage* with family, friends, and neighbors watching. However, at the festival it is performed in middle of the afternoon at *Place H'nich* in front of residents and tourists.

Throughout the Arab world, women's hair is a complex religious, sexual, and political symbol (see Delany, 1994, p. 163). In Tunisia, like in many other parts of the Arab world, a woman's hair is highly treasured mark of beauty (see Abu-Lughod, 1999, p. 194). Many authors and ethnographies have demonstrated that women's hair is considered highly erotic and an object of sexual desire in the Middle East (Zuhur, 1992; Delany, 1994; El Guindi, 1999; Shirazi, 2001; Ciucci, 2008; Kahf, 2008; Zahedi, 2008). There seems not to be a sexualization of hair in Douz, which is in contrast to some other regions where the dance is performed. For the citizens of Douz, the dance evokes images of the Bedouin weddings celebrated in the desert by their grandparents.

I contend that the performance of the *nakh* at the festival is another symbol of Bedouin identity of Douz and its residents. The festival is an opportunity for community members, performers, and organizers to put acts on stage that they believe best represent Douz and its heritage. The town's residents thoroughly enjoy wedding celebrations, and the *nakh* is one of the wedding performances that are most memorable to them. Several informants mentioned that, in Douz, the *nakh* invokes the memories of the Marazig's Bedouin ancestry. One informant said that when he sees the *nakh* he can imagine what his great-grandparents' lives would have been like in the desert, including scenes of weddings in the desert, with traditional tents, bonfires, and banquets, and women doing the *nakh*. The public nature of the performances at *Place H'nich* reinforces my belief that the *nakh* does not have a blatantly sexual connotation in Douz. Given the visible presence of traditional Islamic modesty that prevails in Douz, the *nakh* would not be performed in public in front of an international audience if it was considered licentious. It appears, as my informants suggested, that the *nakh* is a public celebration of feminine beauty. Most of the time, women are expected to be veiled and modestly dressed when outside the home, in accordance with the local interpretation of Islam. However, it is the frame of festivity—both at weddings and the Douz Festival—that allows for the reversal of social norms and makes public displays of feminine beauty acceptable.

Additionally, the inclusion of the *nakh* at the festival confirms that weddings and the celebratory practices associated with them are important to the citizens of Douz. Weddings are central to family and social networks in town because they are opportunities to affirm friendships, family ties, and the importance of Islam to life in Douz.

44.5 JEFFA

Following the performance of *nakh* each year at the festival there is a representation of the *jeffa* processional. *Jeffa* is one of the last parts of the wedding celebration, usually held on the fourth and final day, and features the bride's ceremonial trip from her parent's house to her new home with her husband and his family. At the far edge of *Place H'nich*, a large crowd of women and girls gather alongside an elaborately decorated *howdah* (also referred to as a palanquin—a carriage that sits on top of a camel's back; see Fig. 44.3 below). All of the women and girls are outfitted in lavish Bedouin-style dresses and copious amounts of jewellery. A "festival bride" is guided into the *howdah* and the *jeffa* procession begins once she is ready and the music is played. A *zokra* band, or the recording of one, provides the music. As the procession traverses the *Place H'nich* "stage",

FIG. 44.3 Howdah at Place H'nich (photograph by the author).

the women ululate—a common sonic indicator of joy used by women throughout the Middle East. Once the procession arrives at the other side of *Place H'nich*, the women disperse and the music stops, representing the arrival of the bride at the groom's home.

The *jeffa* processional is another practice in Douz that reinforces the importance of weddings and the Bedouin ethos among the residents of Douz. In Tunis, as well as in towns in the south, automobiles decorated with white and pink ribbons are commonly used to transport the bride, groom, and the married couple from one destination to another during wedding celebrations. The citizens of Douz prefer to use a camel and *howdah*, obvious symbols of the Marazig's nomadic heritage.

Véronique Pardo's research on *jeffa* in the village of Douiret in southern Tunisia is very useful to understanding the wedding processional in Douz. Her work focuses on the relationship between the construction of the *howdah*, marriage rituals, and festivals (Pardo, 2006). The *howdah* is an important component of wedding celebrations in Douiret and is featured at the annual regional spring festival, the Festival of the *Ksour* (fortified village or fort) (Pardo, 2006, p. 4). Pardo explains that the decorations on, and construction of, the *howdah* are rich in symbols of masculinity, femininity, abundance, and fertility (Pardo, 2006, pp. 9–10, 19–21).

As part of the Festival of the *Ksour*, each village in the region prepares a performance for the event that represents its traditions. The citizens of Douiret always choose to perform a ritual re-enactment of the wedding procession including musicians and a camel with a *howdah* to represent their village (Pardo, 2006, p. 30). Pardo argues that the *howdah*, both at weddings and at the festival, represents the values of the society it presents, and the relationships that constitute it (Pardo, 2006, p. 36). The importance of the *howdah*, and the juxtaposition of symbols of masculinity and femininity embedded in it, suggests that the residents of Douiret consider marriage and male-female relationships to be central to the fabric of society in the village (Pardo, 2006, p. 36). Although this is also the case in Douz, more importantly it is seen as a marker of Bedouin heritage.

I argue that the use of the camel and *howdah* for nuptial transportation is yet another representation of the Bedouin ethos in Douz. The use of a camel instead of a decorated car is a clear evocation of a nomadic past that is unique to Douz. The camel is an important marker of Bedouin identity. The *howdah* itself completely conceals the bride from the sand and sun as well as from the glances of onlookers. Her protection from public gaze is an important component of the Islamic code of modesty as practiced in Douz and reinforces the value of the religion's code of personal conduct there. The *jeffa* processional at the festival therefore serves as a symbol of Bedouin and Islamic identity in Douz.

44.6 RAQS MAYAZY

During the 2010 opening ceremonies of the Douz Festival on the *Avenue 7 Novembre*, a folkloric dance troupe from Douz consisting of ten men dressed in traditional Bedouin clothing formed a circle and performed the *raqs mayazy*, the warrior's rifle dance. Two drummers, also in traditional dress, stood behind them. Each dancer held a mock rifle fashioned out of wood that was held approximately 10 cm from their bodies and was rhythmically twirled in time with the music. At the same time, the dance's footwork consisted of hopping on the left foot and kicking with the right, in alternation, and lunges at the end of every four-measure phrase. One informant explained that *raqs mayazy* is typically danced to a rhythm in 6/8 meter called *zigayli*:

FIG. 44.4 Zigayli rhythmic pattern.

A number of folk songs and dances use this rhythm. My informant added that the *zigayli* rhythm is frequently heard during festival performances because the image of the warrior is an important one at the festival. He stated that the only dance performed at the festival unique to Douz is *raqs mayazy*, and the only rhythm used for folk dance and music that is uniquely "of Douz" is *zigayli*.

Most young boys in Douz know the dance; many of my informants suggested that it is the quintessential symbol of Bedouin masculinity and bravery. One informant added that legend has it Bedouin warriors would perform the dance to demonstrate their physical prowess and readiness for battle. While visiting another informant, I asked about the dance. Instantly, he pulled out a plastic bucket from the garden and started drumming the *zigayli* pattern. Within seconds, his five year-old son ran in from the kitchen to offer his rendition of *raqs mayazy* that was, in my opinion, identical to the festival performance I had observed.

The dance appears in other contexts as well. During *araasa*, a social event held for a groom and his friends the morning before a wedding celebration, there are refreshments, a DJ, and dancing. Although much of the dancing is done freestyle, occasionally some of the guests will briefly transition into *raqs mayazy*. Since *araasa* is, in part, a pre-nuptial celebration of manliness, it is not surprising that some guests would use this opportunity to demonstrate their masculinity through the performance of this dance.

Raqs mayazy, and by association *zigayli*, are performative representations of the noble Bedouin warrior image that is told in the stories about Douz. Even within discourse about the dance, references to physical strength and courage reinforce this image.

In addition to the looking at the relationship between the Bedouin ethos, festivity, and identity in Douz, it is important to explore another way of looking at the role of the festival in Douz. Festival musical performances allow groups to witness themselves enact their own identities.

44.7 FESTIVITY AS A MIRROR OF IDENTITY

As Timothy Rice suggests, many authors have written about the theme of music and identity in the ethnomusicology literature. However, their articles "neither cite the general literature on identity nor one another" (2007, p. 17). In response to the lack of theoretical perspectives on music and identity, Rice identifies a number of theoretical points that, in his opinion, warrant further exploration in order to understand the connection between music and social identity. One of these is especially relevant in Douz, namely that "musical performance provides the opportunity for communities sharing an identity to see themselves in action" (2007, p. 35).

Music making in Douz occurs most commonly at weddings held throughout the year. However, only friends, family, and neighbors are invited. There are few public musical performances in Douz that are open to the entire community. Not only is the Douz Festival the only cultural event in Douz that is open to everyone, it is the only one in which all residents can also be participants. The following scene from festival activities at *Place H'nich* demonstrates this.

During the afternoon events at *Place H'nich*, Bedouin encampments surround the areas designated for performances. Black, three-sided Bedouin-style tents are erected and equipped with basic provisions such as pillows, cushions, blankets, food, and tea-making supplies. Herds of camels are tethered to the hitching posts beside the tents. Some families and visitors from the region sleep in this makeshift settlement during the festival while others just visit during the day. My informants, ranging in age from early twenties to late fifties, have suggested that this is a re-enactment of how their grandparents lived during most of the year and is an important visual marker of Bedouin-ness for both residents and tourists. It affirms the Bedouin heritage of the Marazig of Douz. Many people visit family and friends in the tents early in the afternoon, and stay during the start of the afternoon performances. It is for this reason that the Douz Festival is so important. It allows residents to be part of the performance by being actors "on stage" in the Bedouin encampment, and allows them to participate in the processionals that are part of the performances at *Place H'nich*.

There are at least three large processionals at *Place H'nich* during the festival, the opening procession and a re-enactment of a Bedouin wedding cortege on the first day, and the closing procession on the third day. Others are often planned as part of the festival's program. Although several *zokra* and drum bands are always hired to play at *Place H'nich* during the festival, some of the residents who are musicians also bring their instruments and participate in the processions. Others are able to slip through the police barrier separating the seats from the performance area in order to participate in the festivities by joining the processions or dancing. Still others participate in the festivities by wearing customary Bedouin attire (usually white, black, blue, or beige tunics and woollen cloaks), sitting on their camels or horses just outside the main gate of *Place H'nich*, and socializing with friends and family.

The festivities continue just outside of the main gate immediately after the scheduled performances at *Place H'nich* conclude in the late afternoon. As the crowd disperses, horsemen and *chameliers* (camel drivers) offer rides and photo opportunities for residents and tourists alike, for a nominal fee. Musicians play in the street. Vendors sell nuts and sweets. Participants from the afternoon's show mingle with attendees. Residents socialize with friends, family, and neighbors. The revelry continues until the *maghrib adhan* (evening call to prayer) is sounded.

Opportunities such as these at the Douz Festivals are vital to maintaining the social fabric of Douz because they are the only times when neighbors, friends, family, and colleagues gather publicly. Although weddings serve much the same function of bringing communities and kin together to renew relationships, attendance is restricted by invitation. The Douz Festival, in contrast, is an opportunity for everyone to gather publicly to display and celebrate their Marazig-ness, Bedouin heritage, and what it means to be "of Douz." Again, as Rice states, it is an opportunity for the community members to "see themselves in action" (2007, p. 35).

44.8 CONCLUSIONS

An important function of the Douz Festival—one that is not mentioned by residents, visitors, or researchers—is its role as a forum for the citizens to express their identity. Performances of music and dance at the festival frame and highlight what residents believe about themselves, and what they desire others to believe about them. It is an opportunity for residents to articulate through various performances what it means to be "of Douz" from their perspectives, and present these perspectives not only to themselves, but also to visitors. The festival is a public spectacle that reflects the symbols, beliefs, and values of the citizens.

The *zokra* bands, *nakh*, and *raqs mayazy* are understood as symbols of the Bedouin heritage of the Marazig and Douz. Although in North Africa the *zokra* and some of its repertoire is associated with Sufi brotherhoods, namely the Aïssâwa order, the residents of Douz embrace it as an emblem of their Bedouin ancestors. In other parts of North Africa, the *nakh* is understood as a sensual performance of femininity; in Douz it is seen as a celebration of innocent feminine beauty that would have been performed by their Bedouin ancestors. All three of these performances are used to reinforce the accounts of Douz and the Marazig that the residents tell about themselves.

Two theoretical concepts help explain the function of these performances of identity at the Douz Festival. Racy suggests that groups emphasize their connection to Bedouinism because it is equated throughout the Arab world with the virtues of purity, honor, hospitality, chivalry, and bravery (Racy, 1996, p. 405). This association with Bedouin identity in contemporary Douz, and its expression during the festival, is a way of describing oneself as pure, honest, and authentic—traits that the citizens of Douz also equate with "being Marazig"—and one of the ways that both Marazig and the people "of Douz" distinguish themselves from their neighbors and other Tunisians. Additionally, drawing from Rice's theory, performances at the Douz Festival are opportunities for the residents of Douz to "see themselves in action." Thus, festival performances serve as a public declaration, for citizens and visitors alike, that the people of Douz are honorable, kind, and brave Bedouins, strongly rooted in the practices and traditions of Sunni Islam.

References

Abu-Lughod, L. (1999). *Veiled sentiments: honor and poetry in a Bedouin society.* Berkeley, CA: University of California Press.

Abun-Nasr, J. (1987). *History of the Maghrib in the Islamic period.* Cambridge: Cambridge University Press.

Barakat, H. (1993). *The Arab World: society, culture, and state.* Berkeley, CA: University of California Press.

Bates, D., & Amal R.(1983). *Peoples and cultures of the Middle East.* Englewood Cliffs, NJ: Prentice-Hall.

Ciucci, A.M. (2008). *Poems of honor, voices of shame: the Aita and the Moroccan Shikhat.* New York, NY: City University of New York.

Delany, C. (1994). Untangling the meanings of hair in Turkish Society. *Anthropological Quarterly* 67 (4), 159–172.

El Guindi, F. (1999). *Veil: modesty, privacy and resistance.* Oxford: Berg.

Farmer, H.G. (1936). Turkish instruments of music in the seventeenth century. *Journal of the Royal Asiatic Society of Great Britain and Ireland* 1, 1–43.

Franz, K. (2011). The Bedouin in history or Bedouin history? *Nomadic Peoples*, 15(1), 11–53.

Grame, T. C. (1970). Music in the Jma al-Fna of Marrakesh. *Musical Quarterly*, 56(1), 74–87.

Hickson, D., & Derek P. (2001). *Management worldwide: distinctive styles amid globalization.* London: Penguin Books.

Huskinson, J. (2000). Essay one: looking for culture, identity and power. In: J. Huskinson (Ed.) *Experiencing Rome: culture, identity and power in the Roman Empire*, pp. 3–28. Abingdon: Routledge.

Jakubowska, L. (1992). Resisting "ethnicity:" the Israeli State and Bedouin identity. In: C. Nordstrom & J. Martin (Eds.) *The paths to domination, resistance, and terror*, pp. 85–105. Berkeley, CA: University of California Press.

Kahf, M. (2008). From Her Royal Body the Robe Was Removed: the blessings of the veil and the trauma of forced unveilings in the Middle East. In: J. Heath (Ed.) *The Veil: women writers on its history, lore, and politics*, pp. 27–43. Berkeley, CA: University of California Press.

Lacoste, C., & Lacoste, Y. (2004). *Maghreb, peuples et civilisations.* Paris: La Découverte.

Lalonde, J. F. (2013). Cultural determinants of Arab entrepreneurship: an ethnographic perspective. *Journal of Enterprising Communities*, 7(3), 213–32.

Landau, C. (2012). Disseminating music amongst Moroccans in Britain: exploring the value of archival sound recordings for a cultural heritage community in the diaspora. *Ethnomusicology Forum*, 21(2), 259–77.

Lundberg, D. (2010). Music as identity marker: individual vs. collective. *Migrações Journal*, 7, 29–43.

Nabti, M. (2010). *Les Aïssawa: Soufisme, musique et rituels de transe au Maroc.* Paris: L'Harmattan.

Pardo, V. (2006). Le palanquin nuptial à Douiret (sud-est tunisien): De la société à son image. *Journal des africanistes* 76(1), 43–58/1–37.

Perkins, K. (1986). *Tunisia: crossroads of the Islamic and European Worlds.* Boulder, CO: Westview Press.

Perkins, K. (2014). *A history of modern Tunisia.* New York, NY: Cambridge University Press.

Racy, A. J. (1996). Heroes, lovers, and poet-singers: the Bedouin ethos in the music of the Arab Near-East. *Journal of American Folklore*, 109(434), 404–24.

Rice, T. (2007). Reflections on music and identity in ethnomusicology. *Muzikologija/Musicology, Journal of the Serbian Academy of Sciences and Arts*, 7, 17–38.

Schuyler, P. (2000). Joujouka/Jajouka/Zahjoukah: Moroccan music and Euro-American imagination. In: Walter Armbrust (Ed.) *Mass mediations: new approaches to popular culture in the Middle East and beyond*, 146–60. Berkeley, CA: University of California Press.

Shirazi, F. (2001). *The veil unveiled: the hijab in modern culture*. Gainesville, FL: University of Florida Press.

Wasallati, W. (2003–2004). *Miharajain as-Asahara Adouali bi Douz bayna al-Muhafadha alla at-Turath wa Folkoratihi*. Tunis: Conservatoire de Tunis.

Zahedi, A. (2008). Concealing and revealing female hair: veiling dynamics in contemporary Iran. In: Jennifer Heath (Ed.) *The veil: women writers on its history, lore, and politics*, pp. 250–65. Berkeley, CA: University of California Press.

Zuhur, S. (1992). *Revealing reveiling: Islamist gender ideology in contemporary Egypt*. Albany, NY: State University of New York Press.

Author Index

Note: References to figures are indicated by *italics*. '*n*' indicates a footnote, with the number following '*n*' indicating the footnote number when there is more than one footnote on the page.

A

Aasgaard, T. 51, 446
Abbott, A. 184
Abbruzzese, E. 608
Abernethy, B. 184
Abramo, J.M. 499
Abrams, D. 248, 306
Abreu, J.A. 770, 771
Abril, C.R. 534, 535, 538, 555, 582
Abu 'Ali al-Husayn Ibn Sina 723
Abu-Lughod, L. 815
Abun-Nasr, J. 806
ACNUR 738
Adams, B. 551
Adams, F. 324*n*
Adams, G.R. 250, 257
Addessi, A.R. 204, 206, 207
Adelson, E.H. 604
Adler, D.R. 109, 115
Adler, G. 714
Agnello (thief in The Divine Comedy) 46,
    47, 48, 49
Aguilar, A.I. 737
Akai, S. 327, 336
Akama, M. 464, 465
Aktas, U. 280*n*
Al-Kindi 723
Ala-Ruona, E. 682, 690
Albiez, S. 380
Aldridge, D. 593, 686, 689
Aldwin, C.M. 608
Alexandersson, K. 593
Alfermann, D. 184
Alford, V. 761

Ali, B. 813
Alim, H.S. 146–7, 148, 149
Allen, J.D. 318
Allen, K. 616
Allen, N.B. 693
Allsup, R.E. 499
Almeida, A. *161*
Alperson, P. 273
Alsop, D. 296
Altenmueller, E.K. 614
Altenmüller, E. 543
Altman, J. 608
Álvarez, S. 737
Amanti, C. 84
Amighi, J.K. 237, 241, 242
Amir, D. 106
Anderson, B. 497
Anderson, S. 549*n*.2
Andrews, W. 758
Andriopoulos, C. 422
Angus, J.A. 553
Anonymous 688
Ansdell, G. 51, 53, 54, 167, 168, 378, 741, 745
Anthony, W.A. 671
Antonovsky, A. 597–8, 599, 608
Aporic 31
Appadurai, A. 528
Apter-Danon, G. 742
Arango, A.M. 740
Argstatter, H. 685
Ariely, G. 497
Aristotle 5, 33, 43, 775
Arjmand, A. 614
Arnett, J.J. 247, 528, 531

SUBJECT INDEX

Note: Tables and figures are indicated by an italic *t*, and *f*, following the page number. '*n*' indicates a footnote, with the number following '*n*' indicating the footnote number when there is more than one footnote on the page.